DATE DUE

			PRINTED IN U.S.A.

Literature Criticism from 1400 to 1800

Guide to Gale Literary Criticism Series

For criticism on	Consult these Gale series
Authors now living or who died after December 31, 1959	*CONTEMPORARY LITERARY CRITICISM (CLC)*
Authors who died between 1900 and 1959	*TWENTIETH-CENTURY LITERARY CRITICISM (TCLC)*
Authors who died between 1800 and 1899	*NINETEENTH-CENTURY LITERATURE CRITICISM (NCLC)*
Authors who died between 1400 and 1799	*LITERATURE CRITICISM FROM 1400 TO 1800 (LC)* *SHAKESPEAREAN CRITICISM (SC)*
Authors who died before 1400	*CLASSICAL AND MEDIEVAL LITERATURE CRITICISM (CMLC)*
Authors of books for children and young adults	*CHILDREN'S LITERATURE REVIEW (CLR)*
Dramatists	*DRAMA CRITICISM (DC)*
Poets	*POETRY CRITICISM (PC)*
Short story writers	*SHORT STORY CRITICISM (SSC)*
Black writers of the past two hundred years	*BLACK LITERATURE CRITICISM (BLC)*
Hispanic writers of the late nineteenth and twentieth centuries	*HISPANIC LITERATURE CRITICISM (HLC)*
Native North American writers and orators of the eighteenth, nineteenth, and twentieth centuries	*NATIVE NORTH AMERICAN LITERATURE (NNAL)*
Major authors from the Renaissance to the present	*WORLD LITERATURE CRITICISM, 1500 TO THE PRESENT (WLC)*

ISSN 0740-2880

Volume 45

Literature Criticism from 1400 to 1800

Critical Discussion of the Works
of Fifteenth-, Sixteenth-, Seventeenth-, and
Eighteenth-Century Novelists, Poets, Playwrights,
Philosophers, and Other Creative Writers

Jelena O. Krstović
Marie Lazzari
Editors

GALE

DETROIT · LONDON

STAFF

Jelena O. Krstović and Marie Lazzari, *Editors*
Suzanne Dewsbury, Ira Mark Milne, *Associate Editors*
Aarti Stephens, Janet Witalec, *Managing Editors*

Susan M. Trosky, *Permissions Manager*
Kimberly F. Smilay, *Permissions Specialist*
Steve Cusack, Kelly A. Quinn, *Permissions Associates*
Sandy Gore, *Permissions Assistant*

Victoria B. Cariappa, *Research Manager*
Tamara C. Nott, Tracie A. Richardson, Cheryl L. Warnock, *Research Associates*
Wendy Festerling, *Research Assistant*

Mary Beth Trimper, *Production Director*
Deborah Milliken, *Production Assistant*

Christine O'Bryan, *Desktop Publisher*
Randy Bassett, *Image Database Supervisor*
Mike Logusz, Robert Duncan, *Imaging Specialists*
Pamela A. Reed, *Imaging Coordinator*

This book is printed on acid-free paper that meets the minimum requirements of American National Standard for Information Sciences—Permanence Paper for Printed Library Materials, ANSI Z39.48-1984.

Library of Congress Catalog Card Number 94-29718
ISBN 0-7876-2414-4
ISSN 0740-2880
Printed in the United States of America

10 9 8 7 6 5 4 3 2 1

Contents

Preface vii

Acknowledgments xi

Preface

L *iterature Criticism from 1400 to 1800 (LC)* presents critical discussion of world authors of the fifteenth through eighteenth centuries. The literature of this period reflects a turbulent time of radical change that saw the rise of modern European drama, the birth of the novel and personal essay forms, the emergence of newspapers and periodicals, and major achievements in poetry and philosophy. Many of these historical forces continue to influence modern art and society. *LC,* therefore, provides valuable insight into the art, life, thought, and cultural transformations that took place during these centuries.

Scope of the Series

LC provides an introduction to the great poets, dramatists, novelists, essayists, and philosophers of the fifteenth through eighteenth centuries, and to the most significant interpretations of these authors' works. Because criticism of this literature spans nearly six hundred years, an overwhelming amount of scholarship confronts the student. *LC* organizes this material into volumes addressing specific historical and cultural topics, for example, "Literature of the Spanish Golden Age," or "Literature and the New World." Every attempt is made to reprint the most noteworthy, relevant, and educationally valuable essays available.

Readers should note that there is a separate Gale reference series devoted exclusively to Shakespearean studies. Although belonging properly to the period covered in *LC,* William Shakespeare has inspired such a tremendous and ever-growing corpus of secondary material that the editors have deemed it best to give his works extensive coverage in a separate series, *Shakespearean Criticism.*

Each author entry in *LC* presents a survey of critical response to a topic or an author's oeuvre. Early criticism is offered to indicate initial responses, later selections document any rise or decline in literary reputations, and retrospective analyses provide students with modern views. The size of each author entry is a relative reflection of the scope of criticism available in English. Every attempt has been made to identify and include the seminal essays on each author's work and to include recent commentary providing modern perspectives.

The need for *LC* among students and teachers of literature and history was suggested by the proven usefulness of Gale's *Contemporary Literary Criticism (CLC), Twentieth-Century Literary Criticism (TCLC),* and *Nineteenth-Century Literature Criticism (NCLC),* which excerpt criticism of works by nineteenth- and twentieth-century authors. There is no duplication of critical material in any of these literary criticism series. Major authors may appear more than once in one or more of the series because of the great quantity of critical material available and because of their relevance to a variety of thematic topics.

Thematic Approach

Beginning with Volume 12, the authors in each volume of *LC* are organized around such themes as specific literary or philosophical movements, writings surrounding important political and historical events, the philosophy and art associated with eras of cultural transformation, and the literature of specific social or ethnic groups. Each volume contains a topic entry providing a historical and literary overview, and several author entries which examine major representatives of the featured period.

Organization of the Book

Each entry consists of the following elements: author or thematic heading, introduction, list of principal works, annotated works of criticism (each preceded by a bibliographical citation), and a bibliography of further reading. Also, most author entries contain author portraits and other illustrations.

- The **Author Heading** consists of the author's name (the most commonly used form), followed by birth and death dates. (If an author wrote consistently under a pseudonym, the pseudonym is used in the author heading, with the real name given in parentheses on the first line of the biographical and critical introduction.) Also located here are any name variations under which an author wrote, including transliterated forms for authors whose native languages use nonroman alphabets. Uncertain birth or death dates are indicated by question marks. Topic entries are preceded by a **Thematic Heading,** which simply states the subject of the entry.

- The **Biographical and Critical Introduction** contains background information that concisely introduces the reader to the author or topic.

- Most *LC* author entries include **Portraits** of the author. Many entries also contain illustrations of materials pertinent to an author's career, including author holographs, title pages, letters, or representations of important people, places, and events in an author's life.

- The **List of Principal Works** is ordered chronologically, by date of first book publication, identifying the genre of each work. In the case of foreign authors whose works have been translated into English, the title and date (if available) of the first English-language edition are given in brackets following the foreign-language listing. Unless otherwise indicated, dramas are dated by first performance, not first publication.

- **Criticism** is arranged chronologically in each author entry to provide a useful perspective on changes in critical evaluation over time. For the purpose of easy identification, the critic's name and the date of first composition or publication of the critical work are given at the beginning of each piece of criticism. Unsigned criticism is preceded by the title of the source in which it appeared. All titles by the author featured in the critical entry are printed in boldface type. Publication information (such as publisher names and book prices) and some parenthetical numerical references (such as footnotes or page and line references to specific editions of works) have been occasionally deleted to provide smoother reading of the text. Footnotes that appear with previously published pieces of criticism are reprinted at the end of each essay or excerpt. In the case of excerpted criticism, only those footnotes that pertain to the excerpted text are included.

- Critical essays are prefaced by **Annotations** as an additional aid to students using *LC.* These explanatory notes provide information such as the importance of a work of criticism, the commentator's individual approach to literary criticism, and a brief summary of the reprinted essay. In some cases, these notes cross-reference the work of critics within the entry who agree or disagree with each other.

- A complete **Bibliographical Citation** of the original essay or book precedes each piece of criticism.

- An annotated bibliography of **Further Reading** appears at the end of each entry and suggests resources for additional study. In some cases, significant essays for which the editors could not obtain reprint rights are included here.

Cumulative Indexes

Each volume of *LC* includes a cumulative **Author Index** listing all the authors that have appeared in the following sources published by Gale: *Contemporary Literary Criticism, Twentieth-Century Literary Criticism, Nineteenth-Century Literature Criticism, Literature Criticism from 1400 to 1800,* and *Classical and Medieval Literature Criticism,* along with cross-references to the Gale series *Short Story Criticism, Poetry Criticism, Children's Literature Review, Authors in the News, Contemporary Authors, Contemporary Authors Autobiography Series, Contemporary Authors Bibliographical Series, Dictionary of Literary Biography, Concise Dictionary of Literary Biography, Something about the Author, Something about the Author Autobiography Series,* and *Yesterday's Authors of Books for Children.* Readers will welcome this cumulative author index as a useful tool for locating an author within the various series. The index, which includes authors' birth and death dates, is particularly valuable for those authors who are identified with a certain period but whose death dates cause them to be placed in another, or for those authors whose careers span two periods. For example, F. Scott Fitzgerald is found in *TCLC,* yet a writer often associated with him, Ernest Hemingway, is found in *CLC.*

Beginning with Volume 12, *LC* includes a cumulative **Topic Index** that lists all literary themes and topics treated in *LC, NCLC, TCLC,* and the *CLC* Yearbook. Each volume of *LC* also includes a cumulative **Nationality Index** in which authors' names are arranged alphabetically under their respective nationalities and followed by the numbers of the volumes in which they appear.

Each volume of *LC* also includes a cumulative **Title Index,** an alphabetical listing of all literary works discussed in the series. Each title listing includes the corresponding volume and page numbers where criticism may be located. Foreign-language titles that have been translated followed by the tiles of the translation—for example, *El ingenioso hidalgo Don Quixote de la Mancha (Don Quixote).* Page numbers following these translated titles refer to all pages on which any form of the titles, either foreign-language or translated, appear. Titles of novels, dramas, nonfiction books, and poetry, short story, or essay collections are printed in italics, while individual poems, short stories, and essays are printed in roman type within quotation marks.

A Note to the Reader

When writing papers, students who quote directly from any volume in the Literary Criticism Series may use the following general format to footnote reprinted criticism. The first example pertains to material drawn from periodicals, the second to material reprinted from books.

> T. S. Eliot, "John Donne," *The Nation and the Athenaeum,* 33 (9 June 1923), 321-32; excerpted and reprinted in *Literature Criticism from 1400 to 1800,* Vol. 10, ed. James E. Person, Jr. (Detroit: Gale Research, 1989), pp. 28-9.

> Clara G. Stillman, *Samuel Butler: A Mid-Victorian Modern* (Viking Press, 1932); excerpted and reprinted in *Twentieth-Century Literary Criticism,* Vol. 33, ed. Paula Kepos (Detroit: Gale Research, 1989), pp. 43-5.

Suggestions Are Welcome

Since the series began, features have been added to *LC* in response to various suggestions, including a nationality index, a Literary Criticism Series topic index, and thematic organization of entries.

Readers who wish to suggest new features, themes or authors to appear in future volumes, or who have other suggestions or comments are cordially invited to write to the editor (fax: 313 961-6599).

Acknowledgments

The editors wish to thank the copyright holders of the excerpted criticism included in this volume and the permissions managers of many book and magazine publishing companies for assisting us in securing reproduction rights. We are also grateful to the staffs of the Detroit Public Library, the Library of Congress, the University of Detroit Mercy Library, Wayne State University Purdy/Kresge Library Complex, and the University of Michigan Libraries for making their resources available to us. Following is a list of the copyright holders who have granted us permission to reproduce material in this volume of *LC*. Every effort has been made to trace copyright, but if omissions have been made, please let us know.

COPYRIGHTED EXCERPTS IN *LC,* VOLUME 45, WERE REPRODUCED FROM THE FOLLOWING PERIODICALS:

Archive for History of Exact Sciences, v. 24, 1981. © Springer-Verlag GmbH & Co. KG Berlin Heidelberg 1981. All rights reserved. Reproduced by permission.—*Archives Internationales D'Histoire Des Sciences*, v. 29, Juin-Décembre, 1979. © 1979 by Internat Academy for the History of Science. Reproduced by permission.—*Astronomy*, v. 18, December, 1990. Copyright © 1990 AstroMedia Corp. All rights reserved. Reproduced by permission of the Kalmbach Publishing Co. —*Isis*, v. 58, Spring, 1967; v. 76, March, 1985. Copyright © 1967, 1985 by the History of Science Society, Inc. Both reproduced by permission of the University of Chicago Press. v. 70, March, 1979 for "Tycho Brahe's German Treatise on the Comet of 1577: A Study in Science and Politics" by J. R. Christenson. Copyright © 1979 by the History of Science Society, Inc. Reproduced by permission of the University of Chicago Press and the author. —*Journal of the History of Ideas*, v. XLVI, July-September, 1985; v. LI, July-September, 1990; v. LIII, October-December, 1992. Copyright 1985, 1990, 1992 Journal of the History of Ideas, Inc. All reproduced by permission of The Johns Hopkins University Press. —*The Journal of Medieval and Renaissance Studies*, v. 21, Spring, 1991. Copyright © 1991 by Duke University Press, Durham, NC. Reproduced by permission. —*Proceedings of the American Philosophical Society*, v. 117, December, 1973. Copyright © 1973 by the American Philosophical Society. Reproduced by permission of the publisher. —*Renaissance Quarterly*, v.XXXVI, Winter, 1983.Reproduced by permission. —*Sixteenth Century Journal*, v. XIV, Fall, 1983; v. XXVI, 1995. Both reproduced by permission.—*Sky and Telescope*, v. 92, December, 1996. Reproduced by permission.

COPYRIGHTED EXCERPTS IN *LC,* VOLUME 45, WERE REPRODUCED FROM THE FOLLOWING BOOKS:

Biskup, Marian and Jerzy Dobrzycki. From *Copernicus: Scholar and Citizen*. Interpress Publishers, 1972. Reproduced by permission of the publisher and the authors.—Blumenberg, Hans. From *The Genesis of the Copernican World*. Translated by Robert M. Wallace. The MIT Press, 1987. Copyright © 1987 by The Massachusetts Institute of Technology. All rights reserved. Reproduced by permission of The MIT Press, Cambridge, MA.—de Santillana, Giorgio. From "Galileo in the Present" in *Homage to Galileo: Papers Presented at the Galileo Quadricentennial, University of Rochester, October 8 and 9, 1964*. Edited by Morton F. Kaplon. The M.I.T. Press, 1965. Copyright © 1965 by The Massachusetts Institute of Technology. All rights reserved. Reproduced by permission of The MIT Press, Cambridge, MA.—Drake, Stillman. From *Galileo Studies: Personality, Tradition, and Revolution*. The University of Michigan Press 1970. Copyright © by The University of Michigan 1970. All rights reserved. Reproduced by permission.—Einstein, Albert. From a foreword translated by Sonja Bargmann, in *Galileo Galilei: "Dialogue Concerning the Two Chief World Systems—Ptolemaic & Copernican."* By Galileo Galilei. Translated by Stillman Drake. University of California Press, 1953. Copyright , 1953, 1962, and 1967, by The Regents of the University of California. Reproduced by permission of the publisher. —Fantoli, Annibale. From "The Storm Breaks Loose: The Trial and Condemnation of Galileo" in *Galileo: For Copernicanism and for the Church*. Translated by George V. Coyne, S. J. Vatican Observatory Publications, 1994. © Copyright 1994 by the Vatican Observatory Foundation. Reproduced by permission. —Finocchiaro, Maurice A. From an introduction to *The Galileo Affair: A Documentary History*. Edited and translated by Maurice A. Finocchiaro. University of California Press, 1986. Copyright © 1986 by The Regents of the University of California. Reproduced by permission of the publisher.—Gingerich, Owen. From "'Crisis' versus 'Aesthetic' in the Copernican Revolution" in *Yesterday and Today: Proceedings of the Commemorative Conference Held in Washington in Honour of Nicolaus Copernicus*. Edited by Arthur Beer and K. Aa. Strand. Pergamon Press, 1975. Copyright © 1975 Pergamon Press Ltd. All rights reserved. Reproduced by permission of the author.—Gingerich, Owen. From *The Eye of Heaven: Ptolemy,*

PHOTOGRAPHS AND ILLUSTRATIONS APPEARING IN *LC*, VOLUME 45, WERE RECEIVED FROM THE FOLLOWING SOURCES:

Tycho Brahe

1546-1601

Danish astronomer and poet.

INTRODUCTION

An outstanding and influential sixteenth-century astronomer, Tycho Brahe is esteemed mostly for his comprehensive study of the visible planets and stars which announced the era of modern, scientific astronomy. An intermediate between the commanding figures of Nicolaus Copernicus and Johannes Kepler, Brahe devised a cosmological system that blends a degree of Copernican planetary mechanics with his own meticulous and exhaustive observations. Unwilling to abandon the centuries-old geocentric scheme as Copernicus had, Brahe nevertheless made significant advances in the technique of astronomical inquiry, and is credited with applying the scientific method of repeated experimentation and observation to the art of astronomy. In addition, his remarkable and detailed accounts of a new star (supernova) in the constellation of Cassiopeia, and of the comet of 1577 led some scholars to suggest that Brahe was among the first to offer incontrovertible evidence against the Church-sanctioned, Aristotelian belief in solid celestial spheres and a permanent, unchanging firmament.

Biographical Information

Brahe was born in December 1546 in Knudstrup, a town in the Scania region of southern Sweden (then controlled by Denmark), into a prosperous aristocratic Danish family. At an early age he was taken into the care of an uncle, who raised Brahe to adulthood and provided liberally for his education. In 1559 the youthful Brahe began the study of law at the University of Copenhagen, but soon discovered that his true interests lay in the field of astronomy. While pursuing his law studies, Brahe devoted his attention skyward and was introduced to the *Almagest* of Claudius Ptolemy, the dominant astronomical text since classical antiquity. In 1562, Brahe left Copenhagen for the University of Leipzig to further his education in astronomy. The following year, Brahe's observations of Jupiter and Saturn convinced him of the inaccuracy of the current, Copernican tables of planetary, solar, and stellar positions—a situation that Brahe spent the remainder of his life trying to rectify. In 1565, Brahe departed from Leipzig and continued his education in mathematics and astronomy at Wittenburg, Augsburg, and other eminent universities. By the early 1570s he had inherited funds from both his father and uncle, and

took to observing the nighttime skies in his native Scania. On November 11, 1572, Brahe witnessed one of the defining celestial events of his career, the light of a new star—produced by what modern astronomers call a supernova—in the constellation of Cassiopeia. His detailed account of this phenomenon—which had been perceived by others who, however, failed to record the event with the same comprehensive accuracy as Brahe—guaranteed him a rising reputation in the European scientific community.

Brahe's publication of *De nova stella* (1573) and continued astronomical work impressed King Frederick II of Denmark, who granted him the small Danish island-fief of Hven (now Ven) in 1576. With the continued support of Frederick II, Brahe undertook the construction of an observatory on Hven he would name Uranibourg. Drawing a small but thriving community of young mathematician-astronomers to Hven, Uranibourg provided Brahe with the means to accomplish his goal of cataloging the visible stars, and to more accurately update calculations of their positions, as well as those of the sun, moon, and known planets. Uranibourg was additionally the site of many discoveries, most importantly Brahe's observation of the comet of 1577, the impetus for his crowning astronomical treatise entitled *De mundi aetherei recentioribus phaenomenis liber secundus qui est de illustri stella caudata,* published in 1588. King Frederick II's death that same year and the subsequent decreases in Brahe's income over the next decade forced the astronomer from Hven in 1597. Scarching for patronage on the continent, he eventually settled in Prague under the support of Emperor Rudolf II in 1599. He died in Bohemia in 1601.

Major Works

The title of Brahe's earliest astronomical work of note, *De nova stella,* suggests its subject, the new star or supernova he witnessed in November of 1572. A decade and a half later, Brahe produced what scholars agree is his most significant work of astronomy, his *De mundi.* Ostensibly concerned with the comet of 1577, the work's eighth chapter, however, contains the astronomer's first detailed presentation of his theory of planetary cosmology, the Tychonic system, developed between the years 1583 and 1588. While Brahe believed that he had created a revolutionary cosmology, modern critics acknowledge that his system amounts to something of a compromise between the earth-centered Ptolemaic scheme of antiquity and the heliocentric system of Nicolaus Copernicus's *De revolutionibus* (1543). Believing that the Copernican system with its moving earth defied the laws of physics, Brahe devised a geocentric organization of the solar system. In the Tychonic system, the sun and moon are represented as orbiting the earth—as Ptolemy had shown them to do in his *Almagest,* and as most astronomers believed until the seventeenth century—while the remaining five planets then known (Mercury, Venus, Mars, Jupiter, and Saturn) are placed in ever-larger orbits around the sun, as Copernicus had theorized decades before. The remaining nine chapters of the *De mundi* are devoted to Brahe's observations on the size, composition, and behavior of comets—by far the most comprehensive and accurate treatment of the subject in the sixteenth century—as well as his observations of the work of previous and contemporary astronomers concerning these celestial objects. Brahe's other writings include his lengthy *Astronomiae instauratae progymnasmata* (1602) and *Astronomiae instauratae mechanica* (1598). The former includes Brahe's catalogue of 777 stars as well as his solar and lunar theories, the latter details the many innovative astronomical instruments he designed over the course of his career. Brahe's collected works, comprising his correspondence and poetry as well as his scientific writings, have been accumulated in the fifteen volumes of *Opera omnia Tychonis Brahe Dani* (1913-1929). Among many other writings—the majority of them previously unpublished or privately printed—this collection contains the representative poem *Urania Titani,* a verse epistle in the style of Ovid which is based on the love affair of Brahe's sister Sophie and her fiancé, Brahe's sometime colleague, Erik Lange.

Critical Reception

The overall assessment of Brahe's contribution to astronomy lies less in the details of his planetary system than in the scientific ideals and methods he pursued. Thus, scholars have been quick to point out that Brahe's earth-centered system does not represent a dramatically counterproductive step away from the Copernican heliocentric cosmology proposed more than four decades prior. Brahe, they have argued, by incorporating something of the Copernican scheme into his earth-centered system and supporting it with extensive observational data (as Copernicus had not) laid a great deal of the groundwork for a successful, inductive demonstration of the true nature of the solar system. Additionally, commentators have noted that Brahe's accumulated data of stellar and planetary motion, passed on to his student and assistant Johannes Kepler, offered the German mathematician the raw material he needed to develop his laws of planetary motion. Finally, Brahe's work on the new star of 1572 and comet of 1577 have generally been regarded as important evidence that presaged Galileo Galilei's dismantling of the traditional Aristotelian cosmology of solid celestial spheres in the early seventeenth century.

PRINCIPAL WORKS

De nova stella (astronomy) 1573
**De mundi aetherei recentioribus phaenomenis liber secundus qui est de illustri stella caudata ab elapso fere triente Nouembris anno MDLXXVII usque in finem Januarii sequentis conspecta* (astronomy) 1588
Epistolae astronomicae (letters) 1596
Astronomiae instauratae mechanica (astronomy) 1598
**Astronomiae instauratae progymnasmata* (astronomy) 1602
Opera omnia Tychonis Brahe Dani. 15 vols. (astronomy, poetry, and letters) 1913-1929

*These two works were parts of Brahe's proposed trilogy—the *Theatrum astronomicum.*

CRITICISM

J. L. E. Dreyer (essay date 1890)

SOURCE: "Tycho's Book on the Comet of 1577 and His System of the World," in *Tycho Brahe: A Picture*

of Scientific Life and Work in the Sixteenth Century,
Dover Publications, Inc., 1963, pp. 158-85.

[*In the following excerpt, originally published in 1890, Dreyer assesses Brahe's* De mundi—*a monograph on the comet of 1577, which contains Brahe's elaboration of his planetary system. Dreyer additionally comments on the state of astronomy in the sixteenth century and the overall significance of Brahe's theories.*]

The year 1588 is one of great importance in the life of Tycho Brahe, not only because his firm friend and benefactor died in that year, but also because he then published a volume containing some of the results of his work at Uraniborg, and embodying his views on the construction of the universe. The subject specially dealt with in this volume was the great comet of 1577, the most conspicuous of the seven comets observed in his time.

This comet was first noticed by Tycho on the 13th November 1577, but it had already been seen in Peru on the 1st, and in London on the 2nd November.[1] On the evening of the 13th, a little before sunset, Tycho was engaged at one of his fishponds, trying to catch some fish for supper, when he remarked a very brilliant star in the west, which he would have taken for Venus if he had not known that this planet was at that time west of the sun. Soon after sunset a splendid tail, 22° in length, revealed itself, and showed that a new comet had appeared. It was situated just above the head of Sagittarius, with the slightly curved tail pointing towards the horns of Capricornus, and it moved towards Pegasus, in which constellation it was last seen on the 26th January 1578. During the time it was visible Tycho observed it diligently, measuring with a radius and a sextant the distance of the head from various fixed stars, and occasionally also with a quadrant furnished with an azimuth circle (four feet in diameter), the altitude and azimuth of the comet. The sextant, which afterwards was placed in the large northern observing room at Uraniborg,[2] was constructed on the same principle as the one which Tycho had made at Augsburg in 1569, and was mounted on a convenient stand, which enabled the observer to place it in any plane he liked; the arms were about four feet long. The quadrant was about 32 inches in semi-diameter, and the arc was graduated both by the transversals nearly always employed by Tycho, and by the concentric circles on the plan proposed by Nunez; and on the back of the quadrant was a table, by means of which the readings of the latter could be converted into minutes without calculation.[3] When observing this comet, Tycho had not yet at his disposal as many instruments and observers as in after years, nor had he as yet perceived the necessity of accurate daily time determinations by observing altitudes of stars, but merely corrected his clocks by sunset.[4] The observations of this comet cannot therefore compare in accuracy with his

later ones, but still they were immeasurably superior to those made by other observers, and they demonstrated most decisively that the comet had no perceptible parallax, and was consequently very far above the "elementary sphere" to which the Aristotelean philosophy had consigned all comets as mere atmospherical phenomena. By showing that the star of 1572 was situated among the stars, Tycho had already dealt the Aristoteleans a heavy blow, as it was now clear that new bodies could appear in the æthereal regions. But still that star was not a comet, and Tycho, who had formerly believed in the atmospherical origin of comets, now took the opportunity of testing this matter, and found that the comet had no appreciable daily parallax. Though he was not the only observer who placed the comet beyond the moon, his observations were known by his contemporaries to be of very superior accuracy, and his authority was so great that this question was decided once for all.[5]

Before proceeding to pass in review the book which Tycho prepared on this comet, we shall shortly allude to the other comets observed at Hveen. On the 10th October 1580 Tycho found a comet in the constellation Pisces. It was observed at Hveen till the 25th November, and again after the perihelium passage on the morning of the 13th December. The observations are more numerous and better than those of the previous comet, and time determinations with a quadrant were made nearly every night, while there are very few quadrant observations of the comet. Moestlin had seen it already on the 2nd October, and both he and Hagecius observed it assiduously, but their observations are worthless compared with Tycho's.[6] The next comet was visible in May 1582, and was observed by Tycho on three nights only, the 12th, 17th, and 18th, after which date the strong twilight prevented further observations; but in Germany it was still seen on the 23rd, and in China it was seen for twenty days after the 20th May.[7] Of greater interest are the observations of the comet of 1585, which appeared at a time when Tycho's collection of instruments was complete, and when he was surrounded by a staff of assistants. The comet was first seen by Tycho on the 18th October after a week of cloudy weather, but at Cassel it had already been seen on the 8th (*st. v.*).[8] Tycho compares its appearance when it was first seen with the cluster (or nebula, as it was then called) Præsepe Cancri, without any tail. The observations are very numerous, and were made partly with a sextant, partly with the large armillæ at Stjerneborg, with which newly-acquired instrument the declinations of the comet and the difference of right ascension with various bright stars were observed at short intervals on every clear night up to the 12th November. The excellence of the observations and the care with which the instruments were treated are fully demonstrated by the most valuable memoir on this comet by C. A. F. Peters.[9] We have already mentioned that this comet gave rise to the correspondence between Tycho and the Landgrave and Rothmann. The next comet appeared in 1590, and was observed from the 23rd February to the 6th March inclusive, the declination with the armillæ, altitudes and azimuths with a quadrant, and distances with a sextant. The time determinations are numerous.[10] In July and August 1593 a comet appeared near the northern horizon. It was not observed at Hveen, but only by a former pupil of Tycho's, Christen Hansen, from Ribe in Jutland, who at that time was staying at Zerbst in Anhalt. He had only a radius with him, and his observations were therefore not better than those made by the generality of observers in those days.[11] The last comet observed at Hveen was that of 1596, which was first seen by Tycho at Copenhagen on the 14th July, south of the Great Bear. It was not properly observed till after his return home on the 17th, and then only on three nights. It was last seen on the 27th July.[12]

The star of 1572 and the comets observed at Hveen had cleared the way for the restoration of astronomy by helping to destroy old prejudices, and Tycho therefore resolved to write a great work on these recent phenomena which should embody all results of his observations in any way bearing on them. The first volume he devoted to the new star, but as the corrected star places which were necessary for the reduction of the observations of 1572-73 involved researches on the motion of the sun, on refraction, precession, &c., the volume gradually assumed greater proportions than was originally contemplated, and was never quite finished in Tycho's lifetime. On account of the wider scope of its contents he gave it the title *Astronomiæ Instauratæ Progymnasmata,* or Introduction to the New Astronomy, a title which marks the work as paving the way for the new planetary theory and tables which Tycho had hoped to prepare, but which it fell to Kepler's lot to work out in a very different manner from that contemplated by Tycho. The second volume was devoted to the comet of 1577, and as the subject did not lead to the introduction of extraneous matter, this volume was finished long before the first one. The third volume was in a similar manner to treat of the comets of 1580 and following years, but it was never published, nor even written, though a great deal of material about the comet of 1585 was put together and first published in 1845 with the observations of this comet.[13]

The two volumes about the new star and the comet of 1577 were printed in Tycho's own printing-office at Uraniborg, and after some delay caused by want of paper, the second volume was completed in 1588.[14] The title is *Tychonis Brahe Dani, De Mundi ætherei recentioribus phænomenis Liber secundus, qui est de illustri stella caudata ab elapso fere triente Nouembris anno MDLXXVII usque in finem Januarii sequentis conspecta. Vraniburgi cum Privilegio.* The book is in demy 4to, 465 pp., and the colophon is the vignette "Svspiciendo Despicio," with the words underneath "Uranibvrgi In Insula Hellesponti Danici Hvenna imprimebat Authoris Typographus Christophorus Weida. Anno Domini MDLXXXVIII."

The book is divided into ten chapters. The first contains most of the observations of the comet; the second deduces new positions for the twelve fixed stars from which the distance of the comet had been measured. Tycho mentions that while the comet was visible he had not yet any armillæ, and he therefore carefully placed a quadrant in the meridian, and thus determined the declination of the star, and by the time of transit (through the medium of the moon and the tabular place of the sun) also the right ascension. He does not give any particulars about the observations and method, but he goes through the computations of the latitude and longitude of each star from the right ascension, declination and the point of the ecliptic culminating with the star. In a note at the end of the chapter he gives improved star places from the later observations with better instruments and methods, and, as might be expected, these later results are really much better than those found in 1578.[15] In the third chapter the longitude and latitude of the comet for each day of observation are deduced from the observed distances from stars; but though he gives diagrams of all the triangles, and gives all the numerical data, the trigonometrical process is not shown. In the fourth chapter the right ascensions and declinations of the comet are computed from the longitudes and latitudes.[16] The fifth deals with the determination of the inclination and node of the apparent path of the comet with regard to the ecliptic, which Tycho found from two latitudes and the arc of the ecliptic between them; seven different combinations give results which only differ a few minutes *inter se.* The sixth chapter is a more lengthy one, and treats of the distance of the comet from the earth; and as this was of paramount importance as a test of the Aristotelean doctrine, he endeavours to determine the parallax in several different ways. First, he shows that the comet had moved in a great circle, and though not with a uniform velocity throughout, yet with a very gradually decreasing one; and if it had been a mere "meteor" in our atmosphere, it would have moved by fits and starts, and not in a great circle. The velocity never reached half that of the moon, the nearest celestial body. He next discusses two distance measures from ε Pegasi, made on the 23rd November, with an interval of three hours, and finds that if the comet had been at the same distance from the earth as the moon,[17] the parallax would have had the effect of making the second angular distance from the star equal to the first, even after allowing for the motion of the comet in the interval, while the second observed distance was 12′ smaller than the first one. At least the comet must have been at a distance six times as great as that of the moon, and all that can be concluded from the distance measures is that the comet was far beyond the moon, and at such a distance that its parallax could not be determined accurately. The same appears from comparisons between distance measures from stars made at Hveen and those made at Prague by Hagecius, which should differ six or seven minutes if the comet was as near as the moon, whereas they only differed one or two minutes. The observations of Cornelius Gemma at Louvain, when compared with those at Hveen, point in the same direction, but are much too inaccurate to build on. Again, Tycho takes two observations of altitude and azimuth; from the first he computes the declination, corrects this for the motion of the comet in the interval, and with this and the second azimuth computes the altitude for the time of the second observation. For a body as near as the moon there would be a considerable difference, while several examples show none. Finally, Tycho employs the method of Regiomontanus for finding the actual amount of parallax from two altitudes and azimuths, but several combinations gave the same result, that no parallax whatever could be detected in this way. Tycho was well aware that this was a bad method, and evidently only tried it as a duty.[18] (The comet of 1585 was chiefly observed with the large armillæ, and the want of parallax was demonstrated by comparing the right ascension and declination observed with an interval of some hours with the daily motion of the comet.[19]

In the seventh chapter the position of the comet's tail is examined. The increased attention which had been paid to comets during the sixteenth century had led to the discovery of the fact that their tails are turned away from the sun, and not only Peter Apianus, who is generally credited with the discovery, but also Fracastoro, and after them Gemma and Cardan, had pointed out this remarkable fact from observations of different comets. Tycho, who took nothing on trust, examined the matter, and computed from twelve observations of the direction of the tail of the comet of 1577 the position of the tail with regard to a great circle passing through the sun. He found that the direction of the tail never passed exactly through the sun, but seemed to pass much nearer to the planet Venus; he adds, that though the statement of Apianus was only approximately true, the opinion of Aristotle was far more erroneous, for according to him, the tails, as lighter than the head, should be turned straight away from the centre of the earth. The curvature he considers merely an illusion, caused by the head and the end of the tail being at different distances from the earth.

The eighth chapter is the most important in the whole book, as the consideration of the comet's orbit in space leads Tycho to explain his ideas about the construction of the universe. The "æthereal world," he says, is of wonderfully large extent; the greatest distance of the farthest planet, Saturn, is two hundred and thirty-five times as great as the semi-diameter of the "elementary world" as bordered by the orbit of the moon. The moon's distance he assumes equal to fifty-two times the semi-diameter of the earth, which latter he takes to be 860 German miles.[20] The distance of the sun he believes to be about twenty times that of the moon. In this vast space the comet has moved, and it therefore becomes necessary to explain shortly the system of the world, which he had worked out "four years ago," *i.e.,* in 1583.[21] The Ptolemean system was too complicated, and the new one which that great man Copernicus had proposed, following in the footsteps of Aristarchus of Samos, though there was nothing in it contrary to mathematical principles, was in opposition to those of physics, as the heavy and sluggish earth is unfit to move, and the system is even opposed to the authority of Scripture. The vast space which would have to be assumed between the orbit of Saturn and the fixed stars (to account for the want of annual parallax of these), was another difficulty in the Copernican system, and Tycho had therefore tried to find a hypothesis which was in accordance with mathematical and physical principles, and at the same time would not incur the censure of theologians. At last he had, "as if by inspiration," been led to the following idea on the planetary motions.

The earth is the centre of the universe, and the centre of the orbits of the sun and moon, as well as of the sphere of the fixed stars, which latter revolves round it in twenty-four hours, carrying all the planets with it. The sun is the centre of the orbits of the five planets, of which Mercury and Venus move in orbits whose radii are smaller than that of the solar orbit, while the orbits of Mars, Jupiter, and Saturn encircle the earth. This system accounts for the irregularities in the planetary motions which the ancients explained by epicycles and Copernicus by the annual motion of the earth, and it shows why the solar motion is mixed up in all the planetary theories.[22] The remaining inequalities, which formerly were explained by the excentric circle and the deferent, and by Copernicus by epicycles moving on excentric circles, could also, in the new hypothesis, be explained in a similar way. As the planets are not attached to any solid spheres, there is no absurdity in letting the orbits of Mars and the sun intersect each other, as the orbits are nothing real, but only geometrical representations.

This is all which Tycho considered it necessary to set forth about his system in the book on the comet, but he stated his intention of giving a fuller account of it on a future occasion, which never came. We shall finish our account of his labours connected with the comet of 1577 before we consider his system a little more closely.

The comet was by Tycho supposed to move round the sun in an orbit outside that of Venus, and in the direction opposite to that of the planets, the greatest elongation from the sun being 60°. He was unable to represent the observed places of the comet by a uniform motion in this orbit, and was obliged to assume an irregular motion, slowest when in inferior conjunction, increasing when the comet was first discovered, and afterwards again decreasing. Tycho remarks that an epicycle might be introduced to account for this, but as the inequality was only 5′, he did not deem it necessary to go so far in refining the theory of a transient body like a comet; and besides, it is probable that comets, which only last a short time, do not move with the same regularity as the planets do. He finds the inclination of the orbit to the ecliptic equal to 29° 15′, and shows how to compute the place of the comet for any given time by means of the table of its orbital motion with which he concludes the first part of the book. The ninth chapter is a very short one, and treats of the actual size of the comet; as the apparent diameter of the head on the 13th November was 7′, the diameter was 368 miles, or 3/14 of the diameter of the earth. Similarly he calculates the length of the tail, and finds it equal to 96 semi-diameters of the earth. This is on the assumption that the tail is really turned away from Venus, and though he adds that he had also found this to be the case with the comet of 1582, he suspects that some optical illusion must be the cause of this, as it would be more natural that the tail should be turned from the sun than from Venus. In a letter to Rothmann in 1589, he expresses the opinion that the tail is not a mere prolongation of the head, for in 1577 head and tail were of a different colour, and stars could be seen through the tail. He apparently thought that the tail was merely an effect of the light from the sun or Venus shining through the head, and referred to the opinion of Benedict of Venice that the illumination of the dark side of the moon was due to Venus, about which he, however, does not express any decided opinion.[23]

The only part of the tables of the comet's motion which requires notice is that relating to the horizontal parallax. This he makes out from his theory to have been nearly 20′ in the beginning of November, and then rapidly to have decreased; and, as an excuse for this considerable quantity not having been detected, he adds his belief that refraction would counteract the parallax near the horizon where the comet was observed.

The remainder of Tycho's book is devoted to a detailed examination of the writings and observations of other astronomers on the comet. This was the first comet which gave rise to a perfect deluge of pamphlets, in which the supposed significance of the terrible hairy star was set forth, and for more than a century afterwards every comet was followed by a flood of effusions from numberless scribblers. The astrological significance of the comet Tycho does not trouble himself about, though he takes the opportunity of stating that he does not consider astrology a delusive science, when it is kept within bounds and not abused by ignorant people. For the sun, moon, and fixed stars would have

suffced for dividing time and adorning the heavens, and the planets must have been created for some purpose, which is that of forecasting the future.[24] But he goes through the observations or speculations of eighteen of his contemporaries, taking first those who had acknowledged the comet to be beyond the lunar orbit (Wilhelm IV., Moestlin, Cornelius Gemma, and Helisæus Roeslin), and afterwards the great herd of those who believed it to move in the "elementary world." Among these there are no generally known names except those of Hagecius and Scultetus. A theory very like that of Tycho was proposed by Moestlin, who also let the comet move in a circle round the sun outside the orbit of Venus, and accounted for the irregular motion by a small circle of libration perpendicular to the plane of the orbit, along the diameter of which the comet moved to and fro. This idea was borrowed from Copernicus, whose lead Moestlin also followed with regard to the motion of the earth.

That the great Danish astronomer did not become convinced of the truth of the Copernican system, but, on the contrary, set up a system of his own founded on the immovability of the earth, may appear strange to many who are unacquainted with the state of astronomy in the sixteenth century, and it may to them appear to show that he cannot have been such a great reformer of astronomical science, as is generally supposed. But it is not necessary to concoct an apology for Tycho; we shall only endeavour to give an intelligible and correct picture of the state of science at that time with regard to the construction of the universe.

That Copernicus had precursors among the ancients who taught that the earth was in motion, is well known, and he was well aware of this fact himself. But none of those precursors had done more than throw out their ideas for the consideration of philosophers; they had not drawn the scientific conclusions from those ideas, and had not worked them into a complete system by which the complicated motions of the planets could be accounted for and made subject to calculation. Neither had this been done by the philosophers who made the earth the centre of the universe, and let it be surrounded by numerous solid crystal spheres to which the heavenly bodies were attached. All this was only philosophical speculation, and was not founded on accurate observations; but the only two great astronomers of antiquity, Hipparchus and Ptolemy, have handed down to posterity a complete astronomical system, by which the intricate celestial motions could be explained and the positions of the planets calculated. But this "Ptolemean system," in which a planet moved on an epicycle, whose centre moved on another circle (the deferent), with a velocity which was uniform with regard to the centre of a third circle, the equant,[25] was only a most ingenious mathematical representation of the phenomena—a working hypothesis; it did not pretend to give a physically true description of the actual state of things in the universe.[26] No doubt there were many smaller minds to which this did not become clear, but both by the great mathematician who completed it, and by astronomers of succeeding ages the Ptolemean system was merely considered a mathematical means of computing the positions of the planets.

When astronomy towards the end of the fifteenth century again began to be cultivated in Europe, the inconvenience of the extremely complicated system became felt, and soon the great astronomer of Frauenburg conceived how a different system might be devised on the basis of the earth's motion round the sun. But Copernicus did a great deal more than merely suggest that the earth went round the sun. He worked out the idea into a perfect system, and developed the geometrical theory for each planet so as to make it possible to construct new tables for their motion. And though he had but few and poor instruments, and did not observe systematically, he took from 1497 to 1529 occasional observations in order to get materials for finding the variations of the elements of the orbits since the time of Ptolemy. He was therefore able to produce a complete new system of astronomy, the first since the days of the Alexandrian school, and the first of all which gave the means of determining the relative distances of the planets. And it was in this way that he showed himself as the great master, and was valued as such by Tycho Brahe, who was better able than any one else to appreciate Copernicus, since his own activity left no part of astronomy untouched. But unfortunately the edifice which Copernicus had constructed was not very far from being as artificial and unnatural as that of Ptolemy. The expedient of letting the earth move in a circular orbit round the sun could explain those irregularities in the planetary motions (stations and retrogradations) of which the synodic revolution was the period (the second inequalities, as the ancients had called them), because they were caused by the observer being carried round by the moving earth. But this could not account for the variable distance and velocity (the first inequality) of which the orbital revolution was the period, and of which Kepler gave the explanation when he found that the planets move in ellipses, and detected the law which regulates the velocities in these. Until Kepler had discovered the laws which bear his name, there was no way of accounting for these variations, except by having recourse to the same epicycles and excentrics which Ptolemy had used so literally; and the planetary theory of Copernicus was therefore nothing but an adaptation of the Ptolemean system to the heliocentric idea.[27] And the motions were not referred to the real place of the sun, but to the middle sun, *i.e.,* to the centre of the earth's orbit, while the orbit of Mercury required a combination of seven circles, Venus of five, the earth of three, the moon of four, and each of the three outer planets of five circles; and even with this complicated machinery the new system did not represent the actual motions in the

heavens any better than the Ptolemean did. Copernicus himself said that he would be as delighted as Pythagoras was when he had discovered his theorem, if he could make his planetary theory agree with the observed positions of the planets within 10′.[28] But the accuracy was very far indeed from reaching even that limit.[29] Doubtless the Prutenic tables were better than the Alphonsine ones, but that was simply because Copernicus had been able to apply empiric corrections to the elements of the orbits, and because Reinhold did his work better than the numerous computers at Toledo had done theirs. The Copernican system as set forth by Copernicus, therefore, did not advance astronomy in the least; it merely showed that it was possible to calculate the motions of the planets without having the origin of co-ordinates in the centre of the earth. But of proofs of the physical truth of his system Copernicus had given none, and could give none; and though there can hardly be any doubt that he himself believed in the reality of the earth's motion, it is extremely difficult to say of most of his so-called followers whether they had any faith in that motion, or merely preferred it for geometrical reasons.[30]

It is always difficult to avoid judging the ideas of former ages by our own, instead of viewing them in their connection with those which went before them and from which they were developed. The physical objections to the earth's motion, which to us seem so easy to refute, were in the sixteenth century most serious difficulties, and the merits of Galileo in conceiving the principles of elementary mechanics and fixing them by experiments must not be underrated. Neither should the advantage be forgotten which the seventeenth century had over the sixteenth from the invention of the telescope, which revealed the shape of the planets, the satellites of Jupiter, and the phases of Venus, and thus placed the planets on an equal footing with the earth, to which the unassisted vision could never have seen any similarity in them.

Tycho Brahe evidently was not content with a mere geometrical representation of the planetary system, but wanted to know how the universe was actually constructed. He felt the "physical absurdity" of letting the earth move, but, on the other hand, the clearness of mind which made him so determined an opponent of the scholastic philosophy enabled him to see how unfounded some of the objections to the earth's motion were. In a letter to Rothmann in 1587 Tycho remarks that the apparent absurdity is not so great as that of the Ptolemean idea of letting a point move on one circle with a velocity which is uniform with regard to the centre of another circle. He adds that the objections which Buchanan had made to the revolution of the earth in his poem on the sphere are futile, since the sea and the air would revolve with the earth without any violent commotion being caused in them.[31] But all the same he thought that a stone falling from a high tower ought to fall very far from the foot of the tower if the earth really turned on its axis. This remark is made in another letter to Rothmann in 1589, in which he made several objections to the annual motion of the earth.[32] The immense space between Saturn and the fixed stars would be wasted. And if the annual parallax of a star of the third magnitude was as great as one minute, such a star, which he believes to have an angular diameter of one minute, would be as large as the annual orbit of the earth. And how big would the brightest stars have to be, which he believes to have diameters of two or three minutes? And how enormously large would they be if the annual parallax was still smaller?[33] It was also very difficult to conceive the so-called "third motion" of the earth, which Copernicus (so needlessly) had introduced to account for the immovable direction of the earth's axis.

Tycho alludes in several places to the difficulty of reconciling the motion of the earth with certain passages of Scripture.[34] He was far from being the only one who believed this difficulty to be a very serious one against accepting the new doctrine. The Roman Church had not yet taken any official notice of the Copernican system, but in Protestant countries the tendency of the age was decidedly against the adoption of so stupendous a change in cosmological ideas. Nobody cared to study anything but theology, and theology meant a petrified dogmatism which would not allow the smallest iota in the Bible to be taken in anything but a strictly literal sense. Luther had in his usual pithy manner declared what he thought of Copernicus,[35] and even Melanchthon, who was better able to take a dispassionate view of the matter, had declared that the authority of Scripture was against accepting the theory of the earth's motion.[36] This may have had some weight with Tycho, at least it might at first have made him indisposed openly to advocate the Copernican system, as the most narrow-minded intolerance was rampant in Denmark (as in most other countries), notwithstanding the king's more liberal disposition. But the king did not wish to be considered unorthodox, and had yielded to the importunity of his brother-in-law, the Elector of Saxony, by dismissing the distinguished theologian Niels Hemmingsen from his professorship at the University, as suspected of leaning to Calvinism. It would certainly not have been prudent for the highly-salaried and highly-envied pensioner of the king, to declare himself an open adherent of a system of the world which was supposed not to be orthodox.

How far this consideration influenced Tycho it is not easy to decide, but the supposed physical difficulties of the Copernican system and a disinclination to adopt a mere geometrical representation, in the reality of which he could not believe, led him to attempt the planning of a system which possessed the advantages of the Copernican system without its supposed defects. In a letter to Rothmann in 1589[37] Tycho states that he was induced to give up the Ptolemean system by finding from morning and evening observations of Mars at opposition (between November 1582 and April 1583) that this planet was nearer to the earth than the sun was, while according to the Ptolemean system the orbit of the sun intervened between that of Mars and the earth. To the modern reader who knows that the horizontal parallax of Mars can at most reach about 23″, a quantity which Tycho's instruments could not possibly measure, this looks a surprising statement, particularly when it is remembered that Tycho, like his predecessors, assumed the solar parallax equal to 3′. This mystery was believed to have been solved by Kepler, who states that he examined the observations of 1582-83, and found little or no parallax from them; but, to his surprise, he found among Tycho's manuscripts one written by one of his disciples, in which the observed places were compared with the orbit of Mars according to the planetary theory and numerical data of Copernicus, and a most laborious calculation of triangles ended in the result that the parallax of Mars was greater than that of the sun. Kepler suggests that Tycho meant his pupil to calculate the parallax from the observations, but that the pupil, by a misunderstanding, worked out the distance of Mars from the diameters of the excentrics and epicycles of Copernicus.[38] The subject of the parallax of Mars is alluded to by Tycho in a letter to Brucæus, written in 1584. Here he does not hint at having already constructed a new system himself, but merely tries to disprove that of Copernicus, and among his arguments is, that, according to Copernicus, Mars should in 1582 have been at a distance equal to two-thirds of that of the sun, and consequently have had a greater parallax, whereas he found by very frequent and most exquisite observations that Mars had a far smaller parallax, and therefore was much farther from us than the sun.[39] In other words, Tycho could not find any parallax of Mars from his observations, but somehow he afterwards imagined that he had found Mars to be nearer the earth at opposition than the sun was, and this decided him to reject the Ptolemean system. He adds in his letter to Rothmann, that the comets when in opposition did not move in a retrograde direction like the planets, for which reason he had to reject the Copernican system also. It did not strike him that comets might move in orbits greatly differing from those of the planets. Having rejected the two existing systems, there was nothing to do but to design a new one.

The Tychonic system could explain the apparent motions of the planets (including their various latitudes), and it might have been completed in detail by being furnished with excentrics and epicycles like its rival. Copernicus had referred the planetary motions, not to the sun, but to the centre of the earth's orbit, from which the excentricities were counted, and through which the lines of nodes passed, so that the earth still seemed to hold an exceptional position. The Copernican system, so long as it was not purged of the artificial appendage of epicycles by the laws of Kepler, was not very much simpler than the Tychonic, and, mathematically speaking, the only difference between them was, that the one placed the origin of co-ordinates in the sun (or rather in the centre of the earth's orbit), the other in the earth.[40] Tycho's early death prevented the further development of the theory of the planets by his system, which he intended to do in a work to be called *Theatrum astronomicum.* He only gives a sketch of the theory of Saturn in the first volume of his book, in which the planet moves in a small epicycle in retrograde direction, making two revolutions while the centre of the small epicycle moves once round the circumference of a larger one in the same direction in which the centre of the latter moves along the orbit of Saturn.[41]

The Tychonic system did not retard the adoption of the Copernican one, but acted as a stepping-stone to the latter from the Ptolemean. By his destruction of the solid spheres of the ancients and by the thorough discomfiture of the scholastics caused by this and other results of his observations of comets, he helped the Copernican principle onward far more effectually than he could have done by merely acquiescing in the imperfectly formed system, which the results of his own observations were to mould into the beautiful and simple system which is the foundation of modern astronomy.

The book on the comet of 1577 was ready from the press in 1588, and though not regularly published as yet, copies were sent to friends and correspondents whenever an opportunity offered.[42] Thus Tycho's pupil, Gellius Sascerides, who in the summer of 1588 started on a journey to Germany, Switzerland, and Italy, brought copies to Rothmann and Maestlin, to whom he was also the bearer of letters.[43] The Landgrave did not receive a copy, but studied Rothmann's copy with great interest, and thought that it must have been meant for himself, until Rothmann suggested that it was only part of an unfinished work, and that he would get one later on, which of course he did as soon as Tycho heard of this incident. In the following year, while he was at the fair of Frankfurt, Gellius received another copy of the book, which he was to bring to Bologna to Magini, and this he forwarded from Padua in 1590, together with a letter in which he gave an account of the unfinished first volume of Tycho's work.[44] A copy was sent to Tycho's old friend Scultetus, who let Monavius of Breslau partake of his joy over it. To Thomas Savelle of Oxford, a younger brother of the celebrated founder of the two Savillian professorships, who was then travelling on the Continent, Tycho sent two copies of the book, together with a letter in which he, among other things, asked him to remind Daniel Rogers about the copyright which he had promised to procure Tycho for his books in England.[45] To Caspar Peucer, who had already heard of the book from Rantzov, Tycho sent a copy, and added a very long letter in which he entered fully into his reasons for rejecting

the Copernican system, and discussed some passages of Scripture which had been made use of to prove the solidity of the celestial spheres. In this letter he also gives an interesting sketch of the plan of the great work to which the three volumes on the new star and comets were to be introductory. It was to consist of seven books; the first was to describe his instruments, the second the trigonometrical formulæ required in astronomy, the third the new positions of fixed stars from his observations, the fourth was to deal with the theories of the sun and moon, the fifth and sixth with the theories of the planets, the seventh with the latitudes of the planets.[46] With the exception of the first chapter (which he made into a separate book), the contents of this projected work (or at least the outlines of them) were afterwards incorporated in Tycho's first volume of **Progymnasmata.**

When Rothmann had received the book he wrote to Tycho to thank him for it, and remarked that the new system of the world seemed to be the same as one which the Landgrave a few years previously had got his instrument-maker to represent by a planetarium.[47] Tycho, who had kept his system a deep secret until the book was ready, was at first unable to understand from whom the Landgrave could have got a description of it,[48] but he soon after received from a correspondent in Germany a recently published book which solved the riddle. The title of the book was *Nicolai Raymari Ursi Dithmarsi Fundamentum astronomicum,* printed at Strassburg in 1588. The author, Nicolai Reymers Bär, was a native of Ditmarschen, in the west of Holstein, and a son of very poor parents. He is even said to have earned his bread as a swineherd, but possessing great natural abilities, he rapidly acquired considerable knowledge both in science and in classics. In 1580 he published a Latin Grammar, and in 1583, at Leipzig, a *Geodaesia Ranzoviana,* dedicated to his patron, Heinrich Rantzov, Governor of Holstein.[49] Having for some time worked as a surveyor, he seems to have entered the service of a Danish nobleman, Erik Lange of Engelholm, in Jutland, who was a devoted student of alchemy. Lange went on a visit to Tycho in September 1584, and brought Reymers with him, but this probably somewhat uncouth self-taught man seems to have been treated with but scant civility at Uraniborg. After having spent a winter as tutor in Pomerania, Reymers went to Cassel in the spring of 1586, where he informed the Landgrave that he had the previous winter, while living on the outskirts of Pomerania, designed a system of the world. This was exactly like Tycho's, except that it admitted the rotation of the earth. The Landgrave was so pleased with the idea, that he got Bürgi to make a model of the new system; but though he had been well received at Cassel, Reymers was not long in favour there, as he fell out with Rothmann, to whom he abused Tycho. Rothmann mentioned this in a letter to Tycho in September 1586,[50] but did not mention Reymers' system, which first became known in 1588 by the above-mentioned book.[51] This contains some chapters on trigonometry and some on astronomy, and in the last chapter the new system is explained and illustrated by a large diagram on about twice as large a scale as that in Tycho's book. The only important difference is, that the orbit of Mars does not intersect that of the sun, but lies quite outside it.

Tycho was apparently very proud of his system, and (as in the case of Wittich) he immediately jumped to the conclusion that Reymers Bär had robbed him of his glory.[52] He wrote at once to Rothmann (in February 1589) that Reymers must have seen a drawing of the new system during his stay at Uraniborg in 1584, and as a proof of this he refers to the orbit of Mars, which in a drawing made before that time, by a mistake, had been made to surround the solar orbit instead of intersecting it. This cancelled drawing had got in among a number of maps in a portfolio, where Reymers must have seen it, as he copied the erroneous orbit of Mars in the diagram of his book. He therefore expressed his concurrence in the not very flattering expression which Rothmann had applied to Reymers Bär in a former letter.[53]

It must, however, be said that this accusation of plagiarism is founded on very slight evidence, and the verdict of posterity can only be "not proved." In his writings Reymers has shown himself an able mathematician, and there is no reason whatever why he should not independently have arrived at a conclusion similar to the idea which Tycho conceived on the planetary motions. We shall afterwards see what a curious end this affair got, and how Tycho and Rothmann may have regretted that they had not let the *bear* alone.

Notes

[1] According to Tycho, it had been seen by mariners on the 9th. In a copy of *Cometæ anno humanitatis* 1577 *a* 10 VIIII*bris . . . adparentis descriptio,* by Bart. Scultetus (Gorlicii, 1578), which I picked up at Copenhagen some years ago, and which now belongs to the Royal Observatory, Edinburgh, there is written in a neat hand the following on the last blank page:—"Ego Londini in Anglia cometam hoc libro descriptum, et 2 die Nouembris visum, tertio obseruare coepi ut potui radio nautico necdum sesquipedali, ita ut triangulum faceret cometa cum stellis subnotatis, caudæ arcu comprehendente gradus 6m.30 et amplius." [Then follow distance measures on November 3, 9, 13, 15, 24, and 25, but without indication of time.] "Tanto lumine corruscabat hic cometes primo meo aspectu idque per nubes obuersantes, ut antequam integram ejus formam vidissem, Lunam esse suspicarer, quam tamen eo tum loci et temporis lucere non potuisse statim, idque in tanto maiore admiratione, colligebam."

[2] Figured in *De Mundi Æth. Rec. Phenom.,* p. 460, and *Astr. Inst. Mech.,* fol. D. 6 *verso.*

[3] The quadrant is figured in *De Mundi Æth. Rec. Phen.,* p. 463, and *Mech.,* fol. A. 2.

[4] The orbit of the comet of 1577 was computed from Tycho's sextant observations by F. Woldstedt, "De Gradu Præcisionis Positionum Cometæ Anni 1577 a celeberrimo T. B. . . . determinatarum et de fide elementorum orbitæ," &c. Helsingfors, 1844, 15 pp. 4to.

[5] Except that Scipione Chiaramonte and an obscure Scotchman, Craig, vainly endeavoured to deduce the very opposite result from Tycho's observations, but they were easily reduced *in absurdum.*

[6] The orbit was determined by Schjellerup from a complete discussion of Tycho's sextant observations (*Det kgl. danske Videnskabernes Selskabs Skrifter, math. Afdeling,* 5te Række, 4de Bind, 1854).

[7] The orbit is very uncertain. D'Arrest, *Astr. Nachr.,* xxxviii. p. 35.

[8] Tycho returned home from Copenhagen on October 18th. Elias Olsen Morsing had seen it on the 10th, as he wrote in the meteorological diary, *"Stellam ignotam vidi."* See also Introduction to the Observations.

[9] *Astr. Nachr.,* vol. xxix. The observations had been published by Schumacher in 1845 (*Observationes cometæ anni* 1585 *Uraniburgi habitæ a Tychone Brahe.* Altona, 4to).

[10] Orbit computed by Hind, *Astr. Nachr.,* xxv. p. 111.

[11] Orbit by Lacaille, in Pingré's *Cométographie,* i. p. 560.

[12] Orbits by Hind and Valz, *Astr. Nachr.,* xxiii. pp. 229 and 383; the observations are published ibid., p. 371 *et seq.* Pingré gives the results of most of the observations of the seven comets from a copy of them which is still preserved at the Paris Observatory. A complete edition of all the observations was published in 1867 at Copenhagen, under the supervision of D'Arrest, *Tychonis Brahe Dani Observationes Septem Cometarum. nunc primum edidit F. R. Friis.* 4to.

[13] The third volume is alluded to in several places in Tycho's writings, *e.g. Progym.,* i. pp. 513 and 714; *Epist.,* pp. 12, 20, 104, &c.

[14] In the above-mentioned letter to Below, Tycho wrote in December 1587 that he should soon be in want of paper for a book which was being printed in his office, and had applied to the managers of two paper-mills in Mecklenburg without getting an answer. He therefore asked Below to write to the managers of these mills, and to ask some friend at the Duke's court to intercede for him; that he would willingly pay for the paper,

which might be sent through his friend Brucæus at Rostock. Below wrote at once (28th December 1587) to Duke Ulrich, and asked him to do Tycho this favour, "der löblichen Kunst der Astronomie zur Beförderung" (Lisch, *l. c.,* p. 6). To avoid a repetition of this inconvenience the paper-mill at Hveen was built a few years later.

[15] In the above-mentioned paper Woldstedt compares the two sets of positions with modern star places (Åbo or Pond with proper motions from Bessel's Bradley or Åbo). The means of the errors of Tycho's places, irrespective of sign, are in longitude and latitude, for the older positions, 4′.8 and 1′.1, for the later ones, 1′.4 and 1′.5. About the methods by which these positions were found, see Chapter XII.

[16] By the method of Al Battani, which employs the point of the equator having the same longitude as the comet. Delambre, *Astr. du Moyen Age,* p. 21.

[17] Which he, with Copernicus, assumes = 52 semi-diameters of the earth.

[18] See his remarks about the method, *De mundi œth. rec. phen.,* p. 156, and in a letter to Hagecius (who had found a parallax of five degrees by the method), *T. B. et doct. vir. Epist.,* p. 60. Delambre sets forth the method with his usual prolixity in *Hist. de l'Astr. du Moyen Age,* p. 341; *Astr. Moderne,* i. p. 212 *et seq.*

[19] *Epist. Astron.,* pp. 16-17.

[20] The value for the earth's semi-diameter was probably taken from Fernels well-known *Cosmotheoria,* Paris, 1528. We shall see in the next chapter what ideas Tycho had formed as to the distance of the outer planets and the fixed stars (*Progym.,* i. p. 465 *et seq.*).

[21] The book was written in 1587, as appears from several allusions to time in it.

[22] This alludes to the circumstance, which had appeared so strange to the ancients, that the period of the motion of each upper planet in its epicycle was precisely equal to the synodical period of the planet, while in the case of the two inferior planets the period in the deferent in the Ptolemean system was equal to the sun's period of revolution.

[23] *Epist. astron.,* p. 142.

[24] *De mundi œth. rec. phen.,* p. 287. . . .

[25] The earth, the centre of the deferent, and the centre of the equant were in a straight line and equidistant; only in the case of Mercury the centre of the equant was midway between the earth and the centre of the deferent.

[26] Perhaps we may illustrate this by an example from modern science. When the deflection of a magnetic needle in the neighbourhood of an electric current was first discovered, some difficulty was felt in giving a rule for the direction in which either pole of a needle is deflected by a current, whatever their relative positions may be, until Ampère suggested that if we imagine a human figure lying in the current facing the needle, so that the current comes in at his feet and out at his head, then the deflection of the north-seeking pole will be to his left. Nobody ever suspected Ampère of believing that there really was a little man lying in the current, but to many people in the Middle Ages the epicycles were doubtless really existing.

[27] The chief claim of the system of Copernicus to be considered simpler than the Ptolemean was that it dispensed with the equant (which really violated the principle of uniform motion, so much thought of), and let the motion on the deferent be uniform with regard to its centre.

[28] *Rhetici Ephemerides novæ,* 1550, p. 6.

[29] Möbius has shown that the use of the mean place of the sun (*i.e.,* the centre of the earth's orbit) instead of the true place might, in the Copernican theory of Mars, lead to errors of 2°. See a note in Apelt's *Die Reformation der Sternkunde,* Jena, 1852, p. 261.

[30] The contemporaries of Copernicus were not aware that the introduction to his book, in which the system is spoken of as a mere hypothesis, was written without the knowledge of the author by Osiander of Nürnberg.

[31] *Epist. astron.,* p. 74.

[32] Ibid., p. 167.

[33] Tycho had in vain tried to find an annual parallax of the pole star and other stars. Letter to Kepler, December 1599, *Kepleri Opera Omnia,* viii. p. 717.

[34] *Epist.,* p. 148. He says here that Moses must have known astronomy, since he calls the moon the lesser light, though sun and moon are apparently of equal size. Therefore the prophets must also be assumed to have known more about astronomy than other people of their time did.

[35] "Der Narr will die ganze Kunst Astronomiä umkehren! Aber wie die heilige Schrift anzeigt, so hiess Josua die Sonne still stehen und nicht das Erdreich."—*Luther's Tischreden,* p. 2260.

[36] Melanchthon's *Initia doctrinæ physicæ,* in the chapter "Quis est motus mundi."

[37] *Epist. astr.,* p. 148; see also ibid., p. 42, and letter to Peucer of 1588, Weistritz, i. p. 243.

[38] Kepler, *De motibus stellœ Martis,* ch. xi., *Opera omnia,* iii. p. 219; see also p. 474. In his *Progymnasmata,* i. p. 414, Tycho says that the outer planets have scarcely perceptible parallaxes, but that he had found by an exquisite instrument that Mars at opposition was nearer than the sun. On p. 661 he alludes to it again.

[39] *T. Brahei et doct. vir. Epistolœ,* p. 76.

[40] Might Tycho have got the idea of his system by reading the remark of Copernicus (*De revol.,* iii. 15) when talking about the earth's orbit: "Estque prorsus eadem demonstratio, si terra quiesceret atque Sol in circumcurrente moveretur, ut apud Ptolemæum et alios"? According to Prowe (*Nic. Coppernicus,* Bd. i. Part 2, p. 509), this is one of the sentences struck out in the original MS., but reinserted by the editor of the first edition.

[41] *Progymn.,* i. p. 477, where he also alludes to the "Commentariolus" of Copernicus. . . .

[42] The book was not for sale till 1603. There are three copies in the Royal Library at Copenhagen with the original title-page of 1588.

[43] About Maestlin see *Kepleri Opera,* i. p. 190.

[44] *Carteggio inedito di Ticone Brahe, G. Keplero, &c.,* con G. A. Magini. Ed. Ant. Favaro, Bologna, 1886, p. 193.

[45] A Collection of letters illustrative of the progress of science in England. Edited by J. O. Halliwell. London, 1841, p. 32. Tycho also sent Savelle four copies of his portrait engraved at Amsterdam (by Geyn, 1586), and inquired whether there were any good poets in England who would write an epigram on this portrait or in praise of his works. He added that Rogers might also show his friendship by helping him in this matter.

[46] Weistritz, i. pp. 239-264, reprinted from Resen's *Inscriptiones Hafnienses.*

[47] *Epist. astron.,* pp. 128, 129.

[48] So Tycho says in his reply to Rothmann (*Epist.,* p. 149), but before Rothmann's letter was written Tycho had in his letter to Peucer (dated 13th September 1588) mentioned that a German mathematician had two years previously heard of the system "per quendam meum fugitivum ministrum" (Weistritz, i. p. 255), and this he also mentions in the letter to Rothmann.

[49] Kästner, *Geschichte der Mathematik,* i. p. 669; *Kepleri Opera* ed. Frisch, i. p. 218.

[50] *Epist. astron.,* p. 33, where Rothmann (who thought that Reymers had been employed in Tycho's printing-office) calls him a dirty blackguard ("plura scriberem, præsertim de impuro illo nebulone"), which expression Tycho now found very suitable (ibid., p. 149).

[51] For accounts of this book see Kästner, i. p. 631; Delambre, *Astron. moderne,* i. p. 287; and Rudolf Wolf's *Astronomische Mittheilungen,* No. lxviii.

[52] Already in 1589 or 1590 Duncan Liddel lectured at Rostock on the Tychonic system, calling it by this name. A report afterwards reached Tycho to the effect that Liddel privately took the credit of the new system to himself, and that he later on did so openly at Helmstadt (see letter from Cramer, a clergyman of Rostock, to Holger Rosenkrands, in *Epistolœ ad J. Kepplerum,* ed. Hanschius, p. 114 *et seq.*). It appears, however, that Liddel indignantly denied the charge, though he claimed to have deduced the system himself, and to owe Tycho nothing except the incitation to speculate on the matter, for which reason he had mentioned the system as the "Tychonic" (*Kepleri Opera omnia,* i. pp. 227, 228).

[53] *Epist. astr.,* pp. 149, 150.

Robert S. Ball (essay date 1895)

SOURCE: "Tycho Brahe," in *Great Astronomers,* Isbister and Company, Ltd., 1895, pp. 44-66.

[*In the following essay, Ball recounts the life of Brahe, noting his character, technical innovations, and impact on the field of astronomy.*]

The most picturesque figure in the history of astronomy is undoubtedly that of the famous old Danish astronomer whose name stands at the head of this chapter. Tycho Brahe was alike notable for his astronomical genius and for the extraordinary vehemence of a character which was by no means perfect. His romantic career as a philosopher, and his taste for splendour as a Danish noble, his ardent friendships and his furious quarrels, make him an ideal subject for a biographer, while the magnificent astronomical work which he accomplished has given him imperishable fame.

The history of Tycho Brahe has been admirably told by Dr. Dreyer, the accomplished astronomer who now directs the observatory at Armagh, though himself a countryman of Tycho. Every student of the career of the great Dane must necessarily look on Dr. Dreyer's work as the chief authority on the subject. Tycho sprang from an illustrious stock. His family had flourished for centuries, both in Sweden and in Denmark, where his descendants are to be met with at the present day. The astronomer's father was a privy councillor, and having filled important positions in the Danish government, he was ultimately promoted to be governor of Helsingborg Castle, where he spent the last years of his life. His illustrious son Tycho was born in 1546, and was the second child and eldest boy in a family of ten.

It appears that Otto, the father of Tycho, had a brother named George, who was childless. George, however, desired to adopt a boy on whom he could lavish his affection and to whom he could bequeath his wealth. A somewhat singular arrangement was accordingly entered into by the brothers at the time when Otto was married. It was agreed that the first son who might be born to Otto should be forthwith handed over by the parents to George to be reared and adopted by him. In due time little Tycho appeared, and was immediately claimed by George in pursuance of the compact. But it was not unnatural that the parental instinct, which had been dormant when the agreement was made, should here interpose. Tycho's father and mother recoded from the bargain, and refused to part with their son. George thought he was badly treated. However, he took no violent steps until a year later, when a brother was born to Tycho. The uncle then felt no scruple in asserting what he believed to be his rights by the simple process of stealing the first-born nephew, which the original bargain had promised him. After a little time it would seem that the parents acquiesced in the loss, and thus it was in Uncle George's home that the future astronomer passed his childhood.

When we read that Tycho was no more than thirteen years old at the time he entered the University of Copenhagen, it might be at first supposed that even in his boyish years he must have exhibited some of those remarkable talents with which he was afterwards to astonish the world. Such an inference should not, however, be drawn. The fact is that in those days it was customary for students to enter the universities at a much earlier age than is now the case. Not, indeed, that the boys of thirteen knew more then than the boys of thirteen know now. But the education imparted in the universities at that time was of a much more rudimentary kind than that which we understand by university education at present. In illustration of this Dr. Dreyer tells us how, in the University of Wittenberg, one of the professors, in his opening address, was accustomed to point out that even the processes of multiplication and division in arithmetic might be learned by any student who possessed the necessary diligence.

It was the wish and the intention of his uncle that Tycho's education should be specially directed to those branches of rhetoric and philosophy which were then supposed to be a necessary preparation for the career of a statesman. Tycho, however, speedily made it plain to his teachers that though he was an ardent student, yet the things which interested him were the movements of the heavenly bodies and not the subtleties of metaphysics.

On the 21st October, 1560, an eclipse of the sun occurred, which was partially visible at Copenhagen. Tycho, boy though he was, took the utmost interest in this event. His ardour and astonishment in connection with the circumstance were chiefly excited by the fact that the time of the occurrence of the phenomenon could be predicted with so much accuracy. Urged by his desire to understand the matter thoroughly, Tycho sought to procure some book which might explain what he so greatly wanted to know. In those days books of any kind were but few and scarce, and scientific books were especially unattainable. It so happened, however, that a Latin version of Ptolemy's astronomical works had appeared a few years before the eclipse took place, and Tycho managed to buy a copy of this book, which was then the chief authority on celestial matters. Young as the boy astronomer was, he studied hard, although perhaps not always successfully, to understand Ptolemy, and to this day his copy of the great work, copiously annotated and marked by the schoolboy hand, is preserved as one of the chief treasures in the library of the University at Prague.

After Tycho had studied for about three years at the University of Copenhagen, his uncle thought it would be better to send him, as was usual in those days, to complete his education by a course of study in some foreign university. The uncle cherished the hope that in this way the attention of the young astronomer might be withdrawn from the study of the stars and directed in what appeared to him a more useful way. Indeed, to the wise heads of those days, the pursuit of natural science seemed so much waste of good time which might otherwise be devoted to logic or rhetoric or some other branch of study more in vogue at that time. To assist in this attempt to wean Tycho from his scientific tastes, his uncle chose as a tutor to accompany him an intelligent and upright young man named Vedel, who was four years senior to his pupil, and accordingly, in 1562, we find the pair taking up their abode at the University of Leipzig.

The tutor, however, soon found that he had undertaken a most hopeless task. He could not succeed in imbuing Tycho with the slightest taste for the study of the law or the other branches of knowledge which were then thought so desirable. The stars, and nothing but the stars, engrossed the attention of his pupil. We are told that all the money he could obtain was spent secretly in buying astronomical books and instruments. He learned the name of the stars from a little globe, which he kept hidden from Vedel, and only ventured to use during the latter's absence. No little friction was at first caused by all this, but in after years a fast and enduring friendship grew up between Tycho and his tutor, each of whom learned to respect and to love the other.

Before Tycho was seventeen he had commenced the difficult task of calculating the movements of the planets and the places which they occupied on the sky from time to time. He was not a little surprised to find that the actual positions of the planets differed very widely from those which were assigned to them by calculations from the best existing works of astronomers. With the insight of genius he saw that the only true method of investigating the movements of the heavenly bodies would be to carry on a protracted series of measurements of their places. This, which now seems to us so obvious, was then an entirely new doctrine. Tycho at once commenced regular observations in such fashion as he could. His first instrument was, indeed, a very primitive one, consisting of a simple pair of compasses, which he used in this way. He placed his eye at the hinge, and then opened the legs of the compass so that one leg pointed to one star and the other leg to the other star. The compass was then brought down to a divided circle, by which means the number of degrees in the apparent angular distance of the two stars was determined.

His next advance in instrumental equipment was to provide himself with the contrivance known as the "cross-staff," with which he used to observe the stars whenever opportunity offered. It must, of course, be remembered that in those days there were no telescopes. In the absence of optical aid, such as lenses afford the modern observers, astronomers had to rely on mechanical appliances alone to measure the places of the stars. . . .

. . . [The] cross-staff is a very primitive contrivance, but when handled by one so skilful as Tycho it afforded results of considerable accuracy. . . .

To employ this little instrument Tycho had to evade the vigilance of his conscientious tutor, who felt it his duty to interdict all such occupations as being a frivolous waste of time. It was when Vedel was asleep that Tycho managed to escape with his cross-staff and measure the places of the heavenly bodies. Even at this early age Tycho used to conduct his observations on those thoroughly sound principles which lie at the foundation of all accurate modern astronomy. Recognising the inevitable errors of workmanship in his little instrument, he ascertained their amount and allowed for their influence on the results which he deduced. This principle, employed by the boy with his cross-staff in 1564, is employed at the present day by the Astronomer Royal at Greenwich with the most superb instruments that the skill of modern opticians has been able to construct.

After the death of his uncle, when Tycho was nineteen years of age, it appears that the young philosopher was no longer interfered with in so far as the line which his studies were to take was concerned. Always of a somewhat restless temperament, we now find that he shifted his abode to the University of Rostock, where he speedily made himself notable in connection with an eclipse

of the moon on 28th October, 1566. Like every other astronomer of those days, Tycho had always associated astronomy with astrology. He considered that the phenomena of the heavenly bodies always had some significance in connection with human affairs. Tycho was also a poet, and in the united capacity of poet, astrologer, and astronomer, he posted up some verses in the college at Rostock announcing that the lunar eclipse was a prognostication of the death of the great Turkish Sultan, whose mighty deeds at that time filled men's minds. Presently news did arrive of the death of the Sultan, and Tycho was accordingly triumphant; but a little later it appeared that the decease had taken place *before* the eclipse, a circumstance which caused many a laugh at Tycho's expense.

Tycho being of a somewhat turbulent disposition, it appears that, while at the University of Rostock, he had a serious quarrel with another Danish nobleman. We are not told for certain what was the cause of the dispute. It does not, however, seem to have had any more romantic origin than a difference of opinion as to which of them knew the more mathematics. They fought, as perhaps it was becoming for two astronomers to fight, under the canopy of heaven in utter darkness, at the dead of night, and the duel was honourably terminated when a slice was taken off Tycho's nose by the insinuating sword of his antagonist. For the repair of this injury the ingenuity of the great instrument-maker was here again useful, and he made a substitute for his nose "with a composition of gold and silver." The imitation was so good that it is declared to have been quite equal to the original. Dr. Lodge, however, pointedly observes that it does not appear whether this remark was made by a friend or an enemy.

The next few years Tycho spent in various places ardently pursuing somewhat varied branches of scientific study. At one time we hear of him assisting an astronomical alderman, in the ancient city of Augsburg, to erect a tremendous wooden machine—a quadrant of 19-feet radius—to be used in observing the heavens. At another time we learn that the King of Denmark had recognised the talents of his illustrious subject, and promised to confer on him a pleasant sinecure in the shape of a canonry, which would assist him with the means for indulging his scientific pursuits. Again we are told that Tycho is pursuing experiments in chemistry with the greatest energy, nor is this so incompatible as might at first be thought with his devotion to astronomy. In those early days of knowledge the different sciences seemed bound together by mysterious bonds. Alchemists and astrologers taught that the several planets were correlated in some mysterious manner with the several metals. It was, therefore, hardly surprising that Tycho should have included a study of the properties of the metals in the programme of his astronomical work.

An event, however, occurred in 1572 which stimulated Tycho's astronomical labours, and started him on his life's work. On the 11th of November in that year, he was returning home to supper after a day's work in his laboratory, when he happened to lift his face to the sky, and there he beheld a brilliant new star. It was in the constellation of Cassiopeia, and occupied a position in which there had certainly been no bright star visible when his attention had last been directed to that part of the heavens. Such a phenomenon was so startling that he found it hard to trust the evidence of his senses. He thought he must be the subject of some hallucination. He therefore called to the servants who were accompanying him, and asked them whether they, too, could see a brilliant object in the direction in which he pointed. They certainly could, and thus he became convinced that this marvellous object was no mere creation of the fancy, but a veritable celestial body—a new star of surpassing splendour which had suddenly burst forth. In these days of careful scrutiny of the heavens, we are accustomed to the occasional outbreak of new stars. It is not, however, believed that any new star which has ever appeared has displayed the same phenomenal brilliance as was exhibited by the star of 1572.

This object has a value in astronomy far greater than might at first appear. It is true, in one sense, that Tycho discovered the new star, but it is equally true, in a different sense, that it was the new star which discovered Tycho. Had it not been for this opportune apparition, it is quite possible that Tycho might have found a career in some direction less beneficial to science than that which he ultimately pursued.

When he reached his home on this memorable evening, Tycho immediately applied his great quadrant to the measurement of the place of the new star. His observations were specially directed to the determination of the distance of the object. He rightly conjectured that if it were very much nearer to us than the stars in its vicinity, the distance of the brilliant body might be determined in a short time by the apparent changes in its distance from the surrounding points. It was speedily demonstrated that the new star could not be as near as the moon, by the simple fact that its apparent place, as compared with the stars in its neighbourhood, was not appreciably altered when it was observed below the pole, and again above the pole at an interval of twelve hours. Such observations were possible, inasmuch as the star was bright enough to be seen in full daylight. Tycho thus showed conclusively that the body was so remote that the diameter of the earth bore an insignificant ratio to the star's distance. His success in this respect is the more noteworthy when we find that many other observers, who studied the same object, came to the erroneous conclusion that the new star was quite as near as the moon, or even much nearer. In fact, it may be said, that with regard to this object

Tycho discovered everything which could possibly have been discovered in the days before telescopes were invented. He not only proved that the star's distance was too great for measurement, but he showed that it had no proper motion on the heavens. He recorded the successive changes in its brightness from week to week, as well as the fluctuations in hue with which the alterations in lustre were accompanied.

It seems, nowadays, strange to find that such thoroughly scientific observations of the new star as those which Tycho made, possessed, even in the eyes of the great astronomer himself, a profound astrological significance. We learn from Dr. Dreyer that, in Tycho's opinion, "the star was at first like Venus and Jupiter, and its effects will therefore, first, be pleasant; but as it then became like Mars, there will next come a period of wars, seditions, captivity, and death of princes, and destruction of cities, together with dryness and fiery meteors in the air, pestilence, and venomous snakes. Lastly, the star became like Saturn, and thus will finally come a time of want, death, imprisonment, and all kinds of sad things!" Ideas of this kind were, however, universally entertained. It seemed, indeed, obvious to learned men of that period that such an apparition must forebode startling events. One of the chief theories then held was, that just as the Star of Bethlehem announced the first coming of Christ, so the second coming, and the end of the world, was heralded by the new star of 1572.

The researches of Tycho on this object were the occasion of his first appearance as an author. The publication of his book was, however, for some time delayed by the urgent remonstrances of his friends, who thought it was entirely beneath the dignity of a nobleman to condescend to write a book. Happily, Tycho determined to brave the opinion of his order; the book appeared, and was the first of a series of great astronomical productions from the same pen.

The fame of the noble Dane being now widespread, the King of Denmark entreated him to return to his native country, and to deliver a course of lectures on astronomy in the University of Copenhagen. With some reluctance he consented, and his introductory oration has been preserved. He dwells, in fervent language, upon the beauty and the interest of the celestial phenomena. He points out the imperative necessity of continuous and systematic observation of the heavenly bodies in order to extend our knowledge. He appeals to the practical utility of the science, for what civilised nation could exist without having the means of measuring time? He sets forth how the study of these beautiful objects "exalts the mind from earthly and trivial things to heavenly ones;" and then he winds up by assuring them that "a special use of astronomy is that it enables us to draw conclusions from the movements in the celestial regions as to human fate."

An interesting event, which occurred in 1572, distracted Tycho's attention from astronomical matters. He fell in love. The young girl on whom his affections were set appears to have sprung from humble origin. Here again his august family friends sought to dissuade him from a match they thought unsuitable for a nobleman. But Tycho never gave way in anything. It is suggested that he did not seek a wife among the high-born dames of his own rank from the dread that the demands of a fashionable lady would make too great an inroad on the time that he wished to devote to science. At all events, Tycho's union seems to have been a happy one, and he had a large family of childen; none of whom, however, inherited their father's talents.

Tycho had many scientific friends in Germany, among whom his work was held in high esteem. The treatment that he there met with seemed to him so much more encouraging than that which he received in Denmark that he formed the notion of emigrating to Basle and making it his permanent abode. A whisper of this intention was conveyed to the large-hearted King of Denmark, Frederick II. He wisely realised how great would be the fame which would accrue to his realm if he could induce Tycho to remain within Danish territory and carry on there the great work of his life. A resolution to make a splendid proposal to Tycho was immediately formed. A noble youth was forthwith despatched as a messenger, and ordered to travel day and night until he reached Tycho, whom he was to summon to the king. The astronomer was in bed on the morning of 11th February, 1576, when the message was delivered. Tycho, of course, set off at once, and had an audience of the king at Copenhagen. The astronomer explained that what he wanted was the means to pursue his studies unmolested, whereupon the king offered him the Island of Hven, in the Sound near Elsinore. There he would enjoy all the seclusion that he could desire. The king further promised that he would provide the funds necessary for building a house and for founding the greatest observatory that had ever yet been reared for the study of the heavens. After due deliberation and consultation with his friends, Tycho accepted the king's offer. He was forthwith granted a pension, and a deed was drawn up formally assigning the Island of Hven to his use all the days of his life.

The foundation of the famous castle of Uraniborg was laid on 30th August, 1576. The ceremony was a formal and imposing one, in accordance with Tycho's ideas of splendour. A party of scientific friends had assembled, and the time had been chosen so that the heavenly bodies were auspiciously placed. Libations of costly wines were poured forth, and the stone was placed with due solemnity. . . .

One of the most remarkable instruments that has ever been employed in studying the heavens was the mural quadrant which Tycho erected in one of the apartments of Uraniborg. By its means the altitudes of the celestial bodies could be observed with much greater accuracy than had been previously attainable. . . .

A few years later, when the fame of the observatory at Hven became more widely spread, a number of young men flocked to Tycho to study under his direction. He therefore built another observatory for their use in which the instruments were placed in subterranean rooms of which only the roofs appeared above the ground. There was a wonderful poetical inscription over the entrance to this underground observatory, expressing the astonishment of Urania at finding, even in the interior of the earth, a cavern devoted to the study of the heavens. Tycho was indeed always fond of versifying, and he lost no opportunity of indulging this taste whenever an occasion presented itself.

Around the walls of the subterranean observatory were the pictures of eight astronomers, each with a suitable inscription—one of these of course represented Tycho himself, and beneath were written words to the effect that posterity should judge of his work. The eighth picture depicted an astronomer who has not yet come into existence. Tychonides was his name, and the inscription expresses the modest hope that when he does appear he will be worthy of his great predecessor. The vast expenses incurred in the erection and the maintenance of this strange establishment were defrayed by a succession of grants from the royal purse.

For twenty years Tycho laboured hard at Uraniborg in the pursuit of science. His work mainly consisted in the determination of the places of the moon, the planets, and the stars on the celestial sphere. The extraordinary pains taken by Tycho to have his observations as accurate as his instruments would permit, have justly entitled him to the admiration of all succeeding astronomers. His island home provided the means of recreation as well as a place for work. He was surrounded by his family, troops of friends were not wanting, and a pet dwarf seems to have been an inmate of his curious residence. By way of change from his astronomical labours he used frequently to work with his students in his chemical laboratory. It is not indeed known what particular problems in chemistry occupied his attention. We are told, however, that he engaged largely in the production of medicines, and as these appear to have been dispensed gratuitously there was no lack of patients.

Tycho's imperious and grasping character frequently brought him into difficulties, which seem to have increased with his advancing years. He had ill-treated one of his tenants on Hven, and an adverse decision by the courts seems to have greatly exasperated the astronomer. Serious changes also took place in his relations to the court at Copenhagen. When the young king was crowned in 1596, he reversed the policy of his predecessor with reference to Hven. The liberal allowances to Tycho were one after another withdrawn, and finally even his pension was stopped. Tycho accordingly abandoned Hven in a tumult of rage and mortification. A few years later we find him in Bohemia a prematurely aged man, and he died on the 24th October, 1601.

Victor E. Thoren (essay date 1967)

SOURCE: "An Early Instance of Deductive Discovery: Tycho Brahe's Lunar Theory," in *Isis,* Vol. 58, Pt. 1, No. 191, Spring, 1967, pp. 19-36.

[*In the following excerpt, Thoren probes the gradual, deductive creation of Brahe's theory of the moon.*]

Of all the projects undertaken by Tycho Brahe in his *redintegration* of astronomy, his researches on the lunar theory proved far the most fruitful for him. As a result of his perseverance in the study of the moon's motion, he succeeded in adding four new inequalities to the theory that was already the most complicated of the orbital representations, thereby reducing its discrepancies by a factor of about five. It is with Tycho's discovery of two of these inequalities—the inequalities in latitude—that this paper is concerned.

When Tycho began his researches on the lunar theory in the early 1580's, the existing model of the moon's motion in latitude was about two thousand years old: conceived sometime during the century between Anaxagoras and Eudoxus, it had required no subsequent modification.[1] Its basic task was to reconcile Anaxagoras' explanation of eclipses with the fact that eclipses did not occur at every new and full moon. To that end, the moon had been supposed—from the time of Eudoxus, and probably earlier—to travel in a path somewhat inclined to the ecliptic . . ., whereby it could generally pass through syzygy (when it is most nearly in line with the sun, at new or full moon) either above or below the ecliptic and thus not lead to an eclipse. From about the same era, the necessity for a further assumption had also been apparent. The exceptional occasions on which the moon actually did encounter either the sun or the earth's shadow were known to occur at all times of the year, rather than at the same two seasons (longitudes) year after year: it was therefore recognized that the oblique plane in which the moon moved could not be regarded as maintaining a fixed orientation, but that its intersections with the ecliptic (the nodes) had to shift slowly through the years. Reasonably accurate values for the rate of this shift and the angle between the two orbit planes were readily obtained, and by the time of Hipparchus the results were fairly well stabilized. Generations of succeeding Greek and Arabic astronomers adopted values of about 1½° per month for the regression of the nodes,

and 5° for the inclination of the moon's orbit. As classical astronomy gained a foothold in the Latin West, the traditional theory of latitude passed unobtrusively into European literature.[2] There it remained intact until Tycho's day; for, although Copernicus altered significantly the Ptolemaic model of the moon's motion in longitude, he in no respect challenged the ancient account of the moon's motion in latitude.

Like most components of the lunar theory, the theory of latitude was designed and used primarily for the prediction of eclipses. For that purpose it was quite adequate, as its longevity might indicate. Unlike the theory of longitude, however, it had never been seriously tested against appearances outside of syzygy,[3] probably because it was inextricably associated with the theory of parallaxes, which was known to be untrustworthy.[4] In point of fact, the latitudes predicted by the accepted theory were almost perpetually erroneous, differing from actuality by an amount varying with the distance of the moon from the node, and the distance of the node from quadrature.[5] And since the discrepancies exceeded ¼° on occasion, they were nominally susceptible to detection among the observational uncertainties of traditional astronomy.[6] From a practical standpoint, however, they were not detectable because of the shortcomings of the Ptolemaic account of the moon's parallaxes. Departures of 12′-18′ could easily be obscured by faulty parallax corrections, and, of course, anomalous results could be explained away in the same terms. It was therefore only with the invention by Copernicus of a more reasonable model of the moon's radius vectors[7] that the ancient theory of latitude was rendered liable to trial and correction.

Although Copernicus' work was a virtual prerequisite to an improved theory of latitudes, it by no means assured accomplishment of the task. In the first place, there was no way of knowing that the theory even needed rectification: quite to the contrary, it had given no cause for complaint through its long existence. In the second place, even if the theory were known to or assumed to require improvement, there was no way of knowing that the new theory of parallaxes was sufficient to the task. That it was better than the old one was apparent to everyone, because of the patent absurdity of Ptolemy's model; but the extent of the improvement remained to be established.[8] It was from this standpoint that Tycho conducted his "trial" of the theory of latitude—as an incidental aspect of his work with lunar parallaxes.

Tycho struggled intermittently with the moon's parallaxes for many years. They were the subject of virtually all his early lunar computations during the 1580's, yet remained as the last feature to be generalized into his final theory in 1600. No small part of his difficulty arose from his refusal to abandon the traditional means of deducing parallaxes. One of Tycho's more important contributions to astronomical science was his establishment of the *direct* determination of parallax as a valid observational enterprise. Yet he never applied to the moon the methods that he demonstrated so convincingly on the new star of 1572 and the comet of 1577. As one might expect, he had good reason not to. The direct method depended not only on errorless low-altitude refraction corrections, but also on a correct assessment of the moon's motion in longitude[9]—a desideratum that Tycho knew to be unobtainable. The Ptolemaic and Copernican theories frequently differed by over ½° in predicting the longitude of the moon, and it was common knowledge that the moon was rarely to be found in the place assigned to it by either theory. Tycho, in fact, had already given up the traditional practice of using the moon as intermediary in determining star positions, for the very reason that its theoretical velocities could not be depended upon.[10] The alternative to this so-called "direct" method of getting the moon's parallax was to operate through the theory of latitudes, which was doubtless regarded as nearly perfect, and which, at any rate, was far better than either of the available theories of longitude. On this scheme, the moon's parallax was simply the difference between the observed latitude (corrected for refraction) and its true latitude as computed from theory.[11] Obviously, a theory that did not give true latitude would be a severe handicap in such a venture. Before Tycho could proceed to a consistent account of the moon's parallaxes and, hence, of its radius vectors, he had to discover and rectify the inadequacies in the existing theory of latitudes.

With all due respect to the magnitude of the problem facing Tycho, it is fair to say that the protraction of his struggle with it was due to Tycho himself. Tycho, of course, was never prone to analyze data in the manner rendered notorious by Kepler; but in the first five years of his work on the lunar theory he did virtually no paper work at all. Of the 150-odd sets of data accumulated from 1582 to 1587,[12] very few were ever reduced to ecliptic coordinates, and fewer still were compared with predictions computed from theory. Thus it would be misleading to describe Tycho as concerning himself with *any* aspect of theory in his early work. One can only say that the handful of calculations performed in that era dealt generally with the moon's parallax. Few as they were, they provided potentially interesting results, but none of them ever came to anything. On at least three occasions he deduced parallaxes well in excess of the Copernican values (and must have recognized the fact, although he did not compare them explicitly), but merely recorded them in the log without comment.[13] Working the opposite way on a fourth occasion, he applied a (Copernican) parallax correction to an observed latitude and obtained a true latitude of 5°14½', which he then unhesitatingly attributed to observational error, since it exceeded the theoretical maximum of 5°.[14] Only in the data of 9 January 1587, five years into his program of lunar observations, did

Tycho encounter a situation in which he recognized clearly that he was unable to reconcile theory and observation. An extended discussion of the problem led nowhere, but an appended passage reveals the source of his difficulty.

> Note: I later found that a sensible error is concealed in the maximum latitude of the moon, which I discovered to be a fourth of a degree larger than the Ptolemaic value; if this is applied here, everything will agree much better.[15]

Tycho's first discovery pertaining to the theory of latitude (or, for that matter, to any aspect of the lunar theory), then, was that the inclination of the moon's orbit ought to be taken as 5° 15' rather than the traditional 5°. It is dated unambiguously by four lunar observations made in August 1587. Regarding the circumstances of the discovery, little need be said beyond the fact that Tycho undertook the observations expecting to find a discrepancy of some type, and that his suspicion appears to have been aroused rather fortuitously as a result of his reconsideration of a conflict between two sightings of the comet of 1577.[16] The discovery itself was straightforward. The data consisted of two pairs of observations separated by an interval of two weeks, the first pair taken at low altitude with the moon near its northern limit and the second pair taken at high altitude with the moon near its southern limit.[17] The four observations yielded a consistent variance of nearly 15' from what astronomical theory indicated. Since the discrepancies were about the same at both low and high altitudes, the possibility that they were due to faulty corrections for either parallax or refraction was more or less eliminated, leaving the theory of latitude as the culprit. And since the observations had all been made near the limits, it was clear that the amount by which the inclination required correction was very nearly the 15' that was unaccounted for in each case. Tycho's conclusion—published the following year (1588) as a sort of footnote buried in his lengthy treatise on the comet of 1577—was also entirely routine:

> But that such a sensible difference between the Ptolemaic maximum latitude and our own should have to be admitted, I do not claim to be due to the fact that the observations of Ptolemy cannot be trusted. For to an astronomer of his attainment, it was a trivial matter to investigate this when the moon was near maximum latitude and about the beginning of Cancer, and in the meridian. For she then very nearly attained the zenith at his location, and therefore suffered neither parallax nor refraction. Nor should anyone suspect that there is any doubt about our determination, for I have checked the correctness of it several times and have always found a quarter of a degree lacking in the Ptolemaic value. I have made many trials of this, especially in this year 1587 when the latitude of the moon reached

maximum near the beginning of Cancer and Capricorn, and have carefully guarded against the pitfalls of parallax and refraction. Wherefore it seems more reasonable that the maximum latitude of the moon has indeed changed from the time of Ptolemy just as the path of the sun now inclines a little differently to the equator than in his era.[18]

It would be unreasonable to quarrel with Tycho's assessment of the situation. All of the explicit decisions from which it derived were not only logical, but correct. The problem *did* lie in the theory of latitudes. Ptolemy's determination of 5° *was* unquestionable. His own result of 5¼° *was* accurate. But Tycho's conclusion demanded an additional premise—one which he used implicitly without facing the problem of whether or not it was warranted. Tycho's deduction of a secular change in the inclination of the moon's orbit proceeded not only from the recognized difference between Ptolemy's result and his, but from the tacit assumption that the inclination was stable in the short term. It did not occur to him that the difference could also be accounted for by supposing the inclination to vary during each synodic month—from 5° when the moon was at syzygy, to 5¼° when it was in quadrature.

That Tycho should have jumped to the conclusion that he had discovered a secular increase in the inclination of the lunar orbit is by no means remarkable. There was ample precedent for such shifts in orbital elements, and little reason for him to suspect that he had isolated a special case of any kind. Not only was his initial discovery based on no less than four observations, but he had also reduced the data of at least one previous observation and obtained a latitude (5°6′) "which agree[d] with calculation."[19] Finally, it will be remembered that the new inclination made "everything agree much better" when used in a recalculation of the observation (9 January 1587) which had provided his first challenging results.[20] Thus, to repeat, it is not remarkable that Tycho should have failed to recognize the fact that this determination rested solely on observations made in quadrature. What is remarkable is that when he did notice it a year later, he made no effort whatever to ascertain that his results were independent of the special conditions of his determination.

Tycho's announcement of the change in the moon's orbital inclination was so well buried in his volume on the comet of 1577 that one is amazed to find it received any notice at all. In fact, however, it provoked comments by two of Tycho's correspondents. The remarks of Christopher Rothmann, astronomer to the Landgrave of Hesse, are more interesting in another context, and will be mentioned later. It was the reaction of Tycho's old friend, Professor (of Medicine) Brucaeus, that drove him into a corner. Brucaeus professed to be

astonished at what you teach about the maximum latitude of the moon being greater than the Ptolemaic value by 15′, since both the extent and the timing *(magnitudo et calculus)* of eclipses would have to correspond to this latitude. Besides, Regiomontanus, Copernicus, Wernerus, and other distinguished astronomers who were no doubt diligent observers of her latitudes retained the Ptolemaic value.[21]

Not content with this, he went on to express his admiration for the unparalleled circumstances surrounding Ptolemy's determination, before dropping the subject abruptly.

Tycho was not one to ignore a challenge like this. Relative to Brucaeus' objections, he was on very solid ground. He had no trouble refuting the implication that the success of eclipse computations constituted a priori evidence that the alteration was unwarranted.[22] And he rejected outright Brucaeus' appeal to authority.

> The authority of Regiomontanus, Copernicus, Wernerus, and others (whoever they are) on this subject does not impress me, since the reformation of astronomy should proceed not by the authority of men, but from precise observations and deductions from them.[23]

But during the course of his lengthy rejoinder, Tycho admitted that his determination might be deficient in another respect. The first hint came in his opening lines, where he delayed his argument long enough to reassert his original findings in a rather injured tone.

> You should know therefore, that I did not establish the maximum latitude of the moon 15′ greater than the Ptolemaic value either capriciously or without numerous and exact observations. And that the situation really is so, especially near the quadratures, I have been taught by the sky itself through many precise trials, although some showed a minute or two greater and others a little less. And if it should turn out to be an inequality (which I do not rule out), I shall find that out shortly.[24]

Further on in his letter, Tycho became even more explicit about the limitations of his determination. One could scarcely ask for a more complete clarification of his qualification "especially near the quadratures" than Tycho's admission "that I am uncertain whether the latitude of the moon behaves in the same way around new and full moon as it does in the quadratures where I particularly noticed this divergency."[25] He also found occasion to reiterate his conjecture that the inclination might be variable. Brucaeus, with his praise of Ptolemy's observing conditions, had rather rudely implied that he regarded the two determinations as fundamentally incompatible, and that he preferred Ptolemy's, either forgetting or ignoring the fact that Tycho had gone on record in his notice as being every bit as impressed with Ptolemy's results as Brucaeus himself was. After recalling his correspondent's attention to his explicit attribution of the difference to a secular variation, and disclaiming having ever interpreted it as being due to an inaccurate determination by Ptolemy, Tycho went on to say that, in fact,

> I did not even state whether it was equally great in all elongations. For some observations near full moon, which very nearly agree with the Ptolemaic latitude, contradict, so that I suspect some inequality to lurk here; nevertheless, I wish to pronounce nothing definite on this before, as I said, I shall have examined everything more fully.[26]

Little more than a year after his examination of the moon's maximum latitude, then, Tycho is found recognizing clearly the special character of his observations, and expressing a most commendable open-mindedness concerning the interpretation of them. How old this attitude was is impossible to say. It does not seem to be straining his words, "I did not even state whether it was equally great in all elongations," to infer a hint that his published notice had been a studied equivocation.[27] At any rate, his reference to conflicting full-moon observations suggests a certain amount of thought on the subject, rather than spontaneous speculation. Tycho's notebooks, however, provide no basis for taking either possibility seriously. In the interval between the August 1587 determination and the November 1588 letter to Brucaeus, Tycho made two full-moon observations—both of them eclipse observations, with the moon at minimum rather than maximum latitude. The remaining alternative, and prima facie the most reasonable one, is that Tycho's second thoughts arose virtually in the composition of his letter to Brucaeus, and that he simply researched the matter briefly from observations already in stock. Even it, however, involves difficulties. Unless Tycho made some observations that did not get into his logbooks (which he intended to publish eventually), his contradicting "observations near the full moon" could have referred to no more than three, none of which is accompanied by any suggestive computations.[28] But then, one must admit that abundance of supporting data had not been a characteristic of his earlier findings either.

Regardless of the source of Tycho's speculations, one would expect to see evidence of attempts to check them. Moreover, if he was at all excited about the prospect—and one would think that the possibility of discovering the first new lunar inequality in 1,400 years would excite him—there should have been some urgency in the matter. Nevertheless, three weeks after he wrote to Brucaeus, Tycho neglected a rare opportunity to observe the full moon at the southern limit: moreover, he continued to neglect opportunities for observing at opposition, in any latitude whatever, for the next six years. Only twice[29] during that period did he happen to catch the moon in syzygy, and both times it was far from the limit. Obviously then, Tycho's avowed intention of dispatching his investigations of the moon's latitude in syzygy must be understood, at the most, as a plan to research prior observations, and at the least, as a simple means of getting Brucaeus off his back. In this paper, it will be maintained that whatever Tycho's motive in writing as he did, and regardless of whether he ever reopened his former investigations, it was another six and one-half years before he discovered the variability of the moon's orbital inclination.

Since the dating of Tycho's discovery of the variability of the moon's maximum latitude is absolutely crucial to the ultimate argument of this paper, it will be necessary to offer some justification for dismissing Tycho's extraordinary remarks. Let it be said first of all that Tycho's behavior in other contexts of discovery is quite opposed to the presumption that he was able to satisfy himself in the present case from old observations alone. Regardless of their logically equivalent status, Tycho appears to have preferred "live" data to stored data: his other discoveries in the lunar theory are all readily linked to definite confirmatory observations, even though it often entailed waiting a considerable period of time for just the right conjunction of circumstances.[30] From that standpoint, then, his failure to follow through with observations of the full moon in the months after writing to Brucaeus makes it seem rather unlikely that he gave the matter any further thought. At any rate, when Brucaeus responded some four months later with a brief, vague rebuttal of Tycho's argument, Tycho lost his patience and inquired rather pointedly of Brucaeus just what it would take to convince him, why he was again bringing to a boil cabbage already cooked to the point of being unpalatable, and why he did not give up and accept what had been so surely demonstrated.[31] A second indication that Tycho's speculations came to naught is found in another phase of his work. When the book on the comet of 1577 left the press in the middle of 1588, Tycho immediately undertook the printing of his researches on the new star of 1572. By early 1589, part of the volume had been printed, and by February 1590, the first seven chapters had been essentially completed.[32] It seems reasonable to assume, then, that when Tycho wrote to Brucaeus in November of 1588, the sixth of those seven chapters would not have been printed. In that sixth chapter Tycho had occasion to discuss the moon's parallaxes, providing in the process six examples of the calculation of parallax. Since he deduced them in his usual manner—through the theory of latitudes—the following rider was necessary:

> It is to be noted, indeed, that we have in all cases treated the true latitude of the moon not according to the usual account, which assumes a maximum deviation from the eliptic of exactly 5°, but rather

according to our findings, which render it a quarter of a degree higher. . . . [33]

The most direct way of ascertaining the status of Tycho's theory of latitude is, of course, to find a tabular latitude (for some place other than quadrature) given in Tycho's log. Such an entity exists—in connection with one of the two full-moon observations (23 August 1591) recorded by Tycho in the six years following his letter to Brucaeus. For the date in question, Tycho applied a Copernican parallax correction of 59' 20" to the raw latitude of 4°30'34" to obtain an observed latitude of about 3°31'. From the Alphonsine argument of latitude, however, he computed a theoretical latitude of 3°40'; from the Copernican Tables he got almost 3°44'. Obviously the 9' and 13' discrepancies derived from Tycho's using his "corrected" value for the inclination, instead of the accepted 5°. But in spite of Tycho's supposed familiarity with difficulties in full-moon latitudes, it was not obvious to him. Although he quite definitely realized that something was wrong, the best excuse he could offer was that ". . . either the parallax of the moon ought to be greater, or all of it [the parallax] does not belong to the latitude, although the moon was in the nonagesimal."[34]

With his theory of parallaxes already formulated and printed (in Chapter 6 of his book on the new star of 1572), and his mind made up (one way or the other) on the theory of latitude, Tycho had no further occasion to concern himself with either parallaxes or latitude until special circumstances dictated it. In 1595 such circumstances arose, as the moon's orbit began to shift into an orientation particularly favorable to the determination of its inclination. . . .

On 11 February 1595 Tycho undertook the first of what eventually amounted to a considerable number of observations designed to produce a more precise determination of the inclination. After one sighting he was forced by cloud cover to abbreviate the evening's work, but Tycho felt that he had made a

> moderately good observation for limiting the maximum latitude of the moon. For it should be near the limits of maximum northern latitude in Cancer almost at 28°; while the northern limit should be in 5° of Leo, so that the distance from the limit would be about 7°, which can alter the latitude only 2⅔' from maximum.[35]

Quantitatively the passage is worthless,[36] but Tycho's statement of the purpose of the observation merits comment. Note that Tycho's expressed goal was to limit the "maximum latitude of the moon." In the short discussion that follows the quoted passage there is no mention of, say, finding the maximum latitude of the moon at such and such an elongation—no mention of the fact that the moon was only 30° from opposition. Tycho expected simply that "the maximum departure

of the moon from the ecliptic [could] be found"[37] by the procedure he outlined. What clearer indication could there be that Tycho still conceived of the inclination as fixed, and had in mind nothing more than checking the results of his August 1587 observations to determine the value right down to the minute. Most likely he had adopted 5¼° provisionally through the intervening years, intending to decide under optimum conditions whether it was actually a minute or two more or less, as his scatter (reported to Brucaeus) rendered quite possible. One can only say that a reduction of his first night's data would have provided him with more scatter than he would have dreamed possible: only his policy of averaging *pairs* of sightings (clouds had limited him to one) stood between his previous results of 5¼° and a finding of less than 5°4'. As things worked out, it was another five months to the observation that finally provoked Tycho to a serious reconsideration of his presumptions regarding the moon's orbital inclination.

With the lunar orbit oriented so that its northern limit was in Cancer, its southern limit was, of course, in Capricorn. And just as the one situation conduced to determination of the orbital inclination, the other facilitated examination of the theories of parallax and refraction, for the moon could then be observed in the nonagesimal at an altitude 5° below the lowest point of the ecliptic. On 9 July 1595 Tycho decided to take advantage of the opportunity to submit his tables of refraction and parallax to the acid test.[38] The undertaking was something less than a rousing success, for Tycho found a discrepancy of 5'. In fact he was fortunate to come that close, for his tabular latitude can be shown beyond doubt to have derived from an inclination of 5¼°, despite the fact that the moon was within 20° of opposition.[39] At the time he was not prepared to place the blame for the discrepancy; but neither was he prepared to overlook it, so he noted: "Differ. 5', but to be examined again."[40]

Apparently Tycho did reexamine the offending observation. No direct record of his procedure has survived. It would be interesting to know how he managed, in an observation designed explicitly to test parallax and refraction, to wind up attributing the discrepancy to the theory of latitude. But however he did it, there can be no doubt that sometime in the following two months he broke the whole problem wide open, discovering not only the one inequality in latitude, but a second also. The evidence is found in an observation, of 11 September 1595, taken to provide data for a calculation headed "Examination of the node from the meridian altitude." Tycho's first step was to obtain the true latitude—not from theory as he virtually always did, but from observation, by transforming his sighted equatorial coordinates and applying Copernican parallax corrections.[41] With the true latitude he was then in a position to deduce the argument of latitude, which turned out to be 39¼° "taking the angle of maximum latitude for this place [!] to be 5°7'."[42] Finally, a comparison of the longitude of the node with the Copernican value showed a difference of 35', a result which agreed at least qualitatively with trials of two past observations. Tycho therefore felt justified in concluding:

> Whence it becomes clear that the nodes are changed unequally because of the small circle, and by the greatest difference in aspects of 60° and 120°, just as it [the small circle] changes the maximum latitude in syzygy and quadrature.[43]

Tycho's note leaves little doubt about the novelty of his findings in regard to the oscillation of the nodes, but the reference to the variation in the inclination is less clear. That Tycho is speaking of it as a firmly established phenomenon seems certain yet vaguely incompatible with the proposition that he had been totally ignorant of it only two months earlier. Further, it might appear unlikely that Tycho should have discovered a second inequality almost, as it were, in the same dip of the pen as the first. It is easy to show, however, that the two inequalities are related in a way that actually converts this indubitable dating of the second discovery into strong corroboration of the dating of the first.

Until the summer of 1595 Tycho's conception of the moon's motion in latitude was the traditional one. . . . His discovery in 1587 had affected this conception only to the extent of indicating that the tilt of the moon's orbital plane was no longer 5°, as it had been in Ptolemy's day, but 5¼°. . . . In his review of the discrepant calculation of 9 July, however, Tycho was forced to reconsider his interpretation, and ultimately to conclude: that the moon's maximum latitude actually varied throughout the synodic month; that the critical difference between his and Ptolemy's determinations had been not the epoch of the observation, but the phase of the moon. . . .

Tycho could not have worked with his new model very long before noticing that the model itself implies a further phenomenon. As the pole of the lunar orbit moves around its circle, the line determined by it and the pole of the solar orbit oscillates back and forth. . . . As it oscillates, the nodes, being 90° from the limits, will naturally oscillate in the same manner. Hence the model that Tycho adopted to explain the one inequality implied a second! Such an implication might have been ignored, or deplored and eliminated, depending on one's attitude toward models;[44] but it could scarcely have been overlooked—particularly since Copernicus had actually used the same type of arrangement to connect and account for the changing obliquity of the ecliptic and the supposed oscillation of the equinoxes.[45] There is independent evidence that Tycho did not ignore it. The commentary attending the calculations

of 11 September leaves no doubt that Tycho's "Examination of the node" was confirmatory rather than exploratory. Tycho had already checked his suspicions with calculations on two stocked observations, the former of which is in his log, clearly identified as a calculation performed at a subsequent date (*adscriptis*), and headed "For examination of the node from observation."[46] The computation is similar to the one performed on the data of 11 September,[47] and is similarly summarized: "Compare with others especially in aspects of 60° and 120° and you will see a change of the node."[48] Accordingly, after obtaining the same results from a live observation on 11 September, Tycho was satisfied. Note, again, his reference to the "small circle" in the very passage declaring his confirmation of the nodal inequality.

> Whence it becomes clear that the nodes are changed unequally because of the small circle, and by the greatest difference in aspects of 60° and 120°, just as it [the small circle] changes the maximum latitude in syzygy and quadrature.

Surely Tycho's statement provides not only proof that he had already seized on the association between the two inequalities, but also a strong suggestion that he regarded the second as a derivative of the first. Tycho's final published (1602) exposition of the theory gives the same impression. Both the argument and the coefficient of the nodal inequality are trigonometrically derived directly from the geometrical representation of the inequality in maximum latitude, Tycho's only comment being that the relationship "follows both from observation and the doctrine of triangles."[49]

What has been a rather involved argument can now be summarized as follows. Sometime between 9 July and 11 September 1595, Tycho carried out his threat to reexamine the offending parallax observation. As a result, he decided that his earlier speculation to Brucaeus regarding the possible variability of the moon's maximum latitude had to be taken seriously. After formulating a hypothesis to account for the variability, Tycho noticed that the model for his new inequality entailed, in turn, a second inequality. It was then a simple matter to test a number of observations and confirm, finally, on 11 September, the implications of his model. The evidence for believing that Tycho had discovered both aspects of the perturbations in latitude by the latter date is of the most direct kind. In a computation of that date, Tycho reckoned the "maximum latitude at this place to be 5°7'," and then deduced a 35' displacement of the node. The evidence for the other premise required to complete the temporal bracket—that Tycho was still unaware of either inequality as of 9 July 1595—is less overwhelming, but still strong. The tabular latitude used in the parallax calculation of that date agrees perfectly with the value consequent on a fixed inclination of 5¼° and exceeds by nearly 13′ the latitude attributable to a variable inclination for that elongation. A previous computation (23 August 1591) provides the same type of result, and no others offer contradictory evidence. In addition, an observation made earlier in 1595 (11 February) suggests strongly that Tycho expected to be able to make a definitive determination of the moon's orbital inclination at a time when the moon was well outside of quadrature. Finally, the geometrical connection between the two inequalities renders an essentially simultaneous discovery highly probable, and the existence of the nodal inequality was confirmed only on 11 September 1595.

Tycho's discovery of the nodal inequality, then, was a true deductive discovery.[50] It did not originate along the lines of Delambre's conjecture that "Tycho, pour la reconnaître, a pu chercher quelle était la longitude, quand la latitude se trouvait nulle.'[51] Far from being a generalization induced from the phenomena, Tycho's concept of the nodal inequality sprang full-blown from theory, as a complete prediction of the existence of a previously unnoticed phenomenon, needing nothing but observational confirmation. Fortunately, Tycho was willing to seek the necessary confirmation: it is doubtful that he had any precedent for doing so. Only several generations later did such deductions come to constitute an acknowledged source of scientific progress, and even then they were rare and awe-inspiring. Flamsteed's instinctive distrust of Newton's armchair lunar theory indicates how alien such results were even a century after Tycho. Tycho's interest in the physical reality of astronomical models was probably primarily responsible for his pursuit of the implication of his model, but it is interesting that, just as with the inclination, Tycho had a preliminary skirmish with the nodes long before he actually fought his decisive battle with them.

It was mentioned earlier that Brucaeus' was not the only comment on Tycho's announcement of the change in the moon's orbital inclination. Christopher Rothmann, astronomer to the Landgrave of Hesse and a regular correspondent of Tycho's, also found occasion to refer to Tycho's finding: "In the third chapter you make mention of the maximum latitude of the moon, which I also found almost the same as you." He then proceeded to volunteer, just as briefly, news of some related findings of his own.

> But the ascending node departs from the Tables more than 4°, as I found by distances and a globe [i.e., graphically]. Nor do I believe that calculation will produce a lesser difference, although I would gladly have examined it if I had been able to spare the time.[52]

Naturally, Tycho was happy to receive corroboration of his results from Rothmann, and even cited

Rothmann's approval in his letter to Brucaeus. But Rothmann's reply seems to have been as ambiguous to Tycho as it appears in translation. Being in some doubt as to whether Rothmann might be subtly staking out a claim to independent discovery, Tycho responded in an equally ambiguous manner ("And that the maximum latitude of the moon was found almost the same by you as what I proclaim in chapter 3, is agreeable to me"[53]), and issued a veiled challenge to produce the pertinent observations. Regarding the asserted displacement of the node, however, he had no doubts at all. For Tycho, the idea was inconceivable, and he made no effort to conceal his skepticism. He had, he said, observed a large number of eclipses over many years, and, although the theory frequently was not completely satisfactory as far as the timings were concerned, its predicted magnitudes had never deviated by anything near the amount that such a displacement of the node would entail. If during an eclipse the moon were 4° from the node instead of at the node, it would actually have a latitude of 21′ instead of being in the ecliptic; which, as Tycho pointed out, amounts to a difference of two-thirds of its angular diameter. It therefore seemed probable that the difficulties with eclipse computations were due to some still unresolved aspect of the synodic motion, but that the nodes were, indeed, "almost perpetually where the Alphonsine and Copernican tables (which disagree mildly in this) put them."[54]

There is no need to belabor either the soundness of Tycho's argument or the critical premise on which it rested. Tycho had much more fruitful ways to spend his time than in formulating and entertaining such Berkeleyan hypotheses as "Perhaps the nodes regress uniformly only with respect to those places where they can be readily observed: perhaps between syzygies— or even, *ecliptic* syzygies—they perform all sorts of strange gyrations." Similarly, it could only be misleading to try to make anything at all out of the "almost" permanent agreement of the nodes with the theory. The truth is that Tycho had no reasonable way of ascertaining the position of the node except by lunar eclipses.[55] If he had happened to observe the moon at the node and in an octant, he could have found a discrepancy of several minutes, but, whether to attribute it to refraction or parallax or simply a bad observation would not have been at all obvious—which is just another way of pointing up the role of the model in his eventual discovery. Perhaps it was the uncertainties mentioned that also kept Tycho from choosing between the mildly disagreeing constants supplied by the Alphonsine and Prussian Tables; until at least late 1592, he solved this problem by averaging the two.[56]

Thus Tycho succeeded—by cold logic and vigorous application of the quantitative relationships of the current theory—in silencing Rothmann, just as he was in the process of doing with Brucaeus. Did Tycho remember these incidents when he later discovered the perturbations in latitude? And how about Rothmann, who was still alive in 1598 when Tycho published his findings on the oscillation of the node? What must he have thought of Tycho for (apparently) arguing against it sufficiently to discourage him from pursuing the idea, and then developing it himself, particularly since Tycho was by then energetically persecuting Nicolai Reymers for alleged plagiarism? Such questions cannot be answered, and serve only as reminders that the history of astronomy is also the history of astronomers. Whatever the reasons, the fact that Tycho declined these unwitting gambits is unimportant. What was important was that when the phenomena spoke six years later, Tycho listened.

Notes

[1] All succeeding modifications in the theory of longitude, of course, had repercussions in the theory of latitude. In the present context, however, the theory of latitude will be regarded as distinct from rather than inclusive of the theory of longitude.

[2] The theory of the moon's latitudes was one of the few aspects of planetary theory presented in Sacrobosco.

[3] According to Ptolemy, Hipparchus tested the theory of longitude in quadrature and found it wanting. When Ptolemy succeeded in generalizing the discrepancies in quadrature, he, in turn, proceeded to examine the octants.

[4] In accounting for the second inequality in longitude, Ptolemy introduced a great variation in the distances of the moon, as given by the model. Since the moon's angular diameter did not vary by anything near the two-to-one ratio implied by the theory, it was clear that Ptolemy's representation of the radius vectors, and, hence, the parallaxes, was inaccurate.

[5] The ancient representation of the latitude was effectively $b = 5° \sin \beta$; the modern is essentially $b = 5°9' \sin \beta + 9' \sin (\beta - 2\phi)$, where β is the distance of the moon from the node and ϕ the distance of the node from the *sun*. The difference between the two is

$$\Delta b = 9' [\sin \beta (1 + \cos 2\phi) - \cos \beta \sin 2\phi]$$

$$= 9' [2 \sin \beta \cos^2 \phi - 2 \cos \beta \sin \phi \cos \phi]$$

Let $\vartheta = \phi - 90°$ = distance of the node from *quadrature;* then $\Delta b = 18' \sin \vartheta \cos (\beta + \vartheta)$.

[6] Astronomical accuracy before Tycho's time is generally regarded as having been about 10'.

[7] Victor Roberts has found that the same happy device was available to the Muslim world from the 14th century. See "The Solar and Lunar Theory of Ibn ash-Shātir, a Pre-Copernican Copernican Model," *Isis,* 1957, *48:* 428-432.

[8] Copernicus' limits, $52^p17'$ to $68^p21'$, still spanned about twice the actual range of the moon's distances.

[9] Tycho could probably have obtained a reasonably accurate result, however, if he had taken care to optimize rather than maximize his baseline. By observing about 2 hours from each horizon, for example, he could have utilized effectively all of his baseline (about $\frac{7}{8}$ of it), while at the same time reducing the effect of the error in his mean hourly motion of the moon by $\frac{1}{3}$, and avoiding the introduction of errors due to low-altitude refraction corrections.

[10] Tycho followed Bernard Walther in using Venus instead of the moon. See J. L. E. Dreyer, *Tycho Brahe* (Edinburgh, 1890), pp. 348-350.

[11] Of course, the observed latitude had to be taken at the nonagesimal, where the parallax in longitude was null, but Tycho always followed this practice in observing the moon.

[12] The complete works of Tycho were edited by J. L. E. Dreyer (*Tychonis Brahe Dani Opera Omnia,* Copenhagen: Libraria Glydendaliana, 1913-1929) in 15 volumes, of which numbers X-XIII contain the observations, grouped for each planet within each year. Future citations will be abbreviated to XI, 370.

[13] In a notable series of observations covering 24-26 Oct. 1586, Tycho obtained 7 raw latitudes exceeding the theoretical values by amounts ranging from 58' up to 75' (XI, 31-32).

[14] X, 379; Tycho was so far from taking the result seriously that he did not even bother to reduce the observations made the following night, which would have confirmed it.

[15] XI, 146.

[16] Further detail can be found in my dissertation "Tycho Brahe on the Lunar Theory" (Indiana University, 1965), pp. 26-31.

[17] XI, 157, 162-163.

[18] *De mundi ætherei recentioribus phœnomenie* (1588) (IV, 42-43).

[19] 5 Apr. 1587 (XI, 155).

[20] The August observations were all made near quadrature, as was that of 5 Apr. 1587, which Tycho used to check his results. The observation of 9 Jan. 1587, however, was made in the 3rd octant, so the agreement with theory can have been no more than "much better," using the new inclination.

[21] Sept. 1588 (VII, 143).

[22] "Nor can observations of eclipses detract anything perceptible from my assertion, for if the maximum latitude were established at 15′ greater than what is currently and traditionally accepted, the difference around those areas (near the nodes) where eclipses can occur would introduce nothing that could be noticed. In fact, at a distance of 12° from the node, within (approximately) which all lunar eclipses must occur, the difference between the Ptolemaic latitude and ours rises to only 3′, which can cause only one digit of obscuration in the moon, which is scarcely perceptible anyway because the outline of the shadow of the earth is not sharply demarcated. Nor have the times of eclipses hitherto been noted precisely so that anyone would be able to challenge this discovery of ours . . ." (VII, 151).

[23] VII, 152.

[24] ". . . et si quae alia subest, uti non negavero, inequalitas, eam penitius enodabo" (VII, 151).

[25] "Accedit et hoc, quod incertus sim, an latitudo Lunae eodem modo se habeat juxta novilunia et plenilunia quemadmodum prope quadraturas, ubi hanc divagationem potissimum animadverti" (VII, 152).

[26] ". . . Quae an in omni ad Solem dispositione aeque magna esse possit, necdum tuto affirmarim. Reclamitant etenim nonnullae circa plenilunia observationes, quae Ptolemaicae divagationi quam proxime accedunt, ut ob id inequalitatem aliquam hic latere suspicer, de qua tamen nihil certi pronunciare volo, antequam plenius, uti dixi, rem omnem expendero" (VII, 153).

[27] It is not at all difficult to imagine circumstances under which Tycho might have issued an announcement expressing something less than his complete current apprehension of the subject. Suppose, for instance, that he did indeed have doubts about the value of the inclination at syzygy. He could not have checked it during the August observations; he would have had to wait until the full moon occurred at maximum latitude, i.e., until the sun had moved from the node into the limits—roughly 3 months at 30° per month. And if, in the meantime, his book had approached completion, it is quite possible that neither delaying his book further nor deferring his announcement to his next publication would have appealed to him. It would therefore have been simple prudence to phrase his notice in such a way as to secure what priority he could, without placing further credit in jeopardy.

[28] 8 Sept. 1584 (X, 305); 25 Dec. 1585 (X, 377); and 23 Jan. 1586 (XI, 30). Of course, Tycho could have used any of several full-moon observations in which the latitude was not maximum, but such an operation would have been unique in Tycho's work on the subject.

[29] 23 Aug. 1591 and 17 Nov. 1594.

[30] Tycho's handling of the variation (the 3rd inequality in the theory of longitude) is a case in point. After discovering the phenomenon in 1594, Tycho could easily have dispatched the investigation by using relevant material from his 13-year accumulation of observations, yet he chose instead to allow it to drag out some 3 months while he waited for the moon to cycle through the (apparently) appropriate positions.

[31] "Cum igitur haec sint satis evidenter a me demonstrata et scrupulose numerata, ut nulla restat contradicendi justa occasio . . . cur, quaeso, ea nunc denua in dubium vocas, et cramben semel coctam ad fastidium recoquis?" (VII, 171-172).

[32] VII, 165, 225, 274.

[33] II, 413.

[34] "Sed haec possunt repeti, nam parallaxeis ☽ aut maiores justis sunt, aut non totae debentur latitudini ☽, quod ☽ 90 gradum transierat" (XII, 126).

[35] "Est autem mediocriter bona observation pro latitudine ☽ maxima limitanda" (XII, 378).

[36] It is regrettable that Tycho happened to state the true latitude in such an oblique way. Had he stated it directly instead of maximum minus 2⅔′, the issue would be settled. Had he even stated precisely (to minutes and seconds, as he often did) the figure he did provide, instead of rounding it off—and very crudely, at that—the issue might be resolved. As it turns out, however, the fixed inclination would allow the moon to drop about 2′22″ through 7°, while the variable (about 5°4′, in this case) would allow only 2′14″. The prospect of choosing between two values differing by 8″ could never be attractive for the purpose at hand; but neither value can possibly be reconciled with 2⅔′, which implies an inclination of nearly 6°.

[37] ". . . poterit singula invicem trutinando erui hinc ☽ maxima ab Ecliptica evagatio" (XII, 378).

[38] "Observatur ☽ circa Tropicum Hybernum in 90 & Meridiano pro parallaxi & refractione, quin etiam pro

Longitudine, quando ☌ cum ☉ mediae vincina esset" (XII, 392).

[39] Tycho lists (XII, 392) the true latitude as 4°57′, which, with an inclination of 5¼°, implies an argument of latitude of 270 ± 19½′, Tycho's later tables show a mean argument of 246°, and extrapolation from an argument of latitude listed for 6 May 1595 (XII, 392) also gives about 246°. The first two inequalities would have added about 5°, to bring the true argument to 251°, and good agreement with 270 – 19½°. In fact, however, the moon was only 19° from opposition, so that Tycho should have been expecting an inclination of about 5°1½′ (5° + 15′ sin² α) if he knew of its variability. To get the listed 4°57′, from such a low inclination, Tycho would have to have used an argument of latitude of about 261°. A deviation of such magnitude from the 251° already established is inconceivable.

[40] "Differ. 5′, sed denuo examinandum" (XII, 393).

[41] XII, 394. Parallax corrections were necessary for both longitude and latitude, since the observation was made in the meridian rather than in the nonagesimal.

[42] Note Tycho's matter-of-fact reference to the varying inclination: "Resp. Distantia a ☊ 0 39¼ posito angulo maximae latitudinus hoc loco 5ᵍ 7‴" (XII, 394).

[43] "Unde palam fiet nodos inaequaliter mutari ratione parvi circelli & differentia maxima in ✳ & △ , quemadmodum in ☍ & □ mutat maximam latitudinem" (XII, 394). Of course, *aspectus sextillis* and *aspectus trigonus* do not really convey the situation accurately, but Tycho had no alternative to taking refuge in astrological terminology. Since the octants had never before been critical points in the lunar theory, no shortcut reference to them had ever been needed. Tycho, it is true, had understood the effects of the third inequality for the better part of a year, but could still describe its maximum points only as "four places which are intermediate." With the discovery of a second context in which these intermediate places figured, Tycho soon coined the very natural term "octants." See my unpublished dissertation, "Tycho Brahe on the Lunar Theory," p. 166.

[44] Tycho could, for instance, have used a second circle to convert the circular motion into rectilinear motion, as Copernicus had done for his libration of Mercury. *De revolutionibus,* V, 25.

[45] *Ibid.,* III, 3.

[46] "Conferatur cum anno 92 die 12 Feb. Item anno 95 die 17 Feb" (XII, 394). The calculation to which Tycho refers is actually that of *anno 91 die 22.* The permutation is not an editorial misprint, for it is in Tycho's original logs; but it is surely a mistake, for the moon was in quadrature on the stated day.

[47] For this calculation, also, Tycho assumes a varying inclination. From an observed (and corrected) latitude of 56′, he deduces an argument of latitude of 10°21′, without any comment whatsoever, although the two show that he was taking the inclination to be about 5°12′ (XII, 124).

[48] "Confer cum aliis praecipuis in ✳ et △ et videbis mutationem ☊ . . ." (XII, 124).

[49] II, 122. Dreyer saw no reason to regard this association as anything but purely formal. Having caught the two most significant bits of evidence on Tycho's discoveries of the perturbations in latitude, and having no reason to check further, he naturally assumed that the two had been discovered independently: "sed jam anno sequenti (ut ex epistula ad BRUCAEUM Rostochium missa apparet) novam inaequalitatem lunarem hanc esse intellexit." " . . . et mense Septembri anni 1595 retrogradationem nodorum non aequabilem esse, sed ita variare invenit, . . ." (I, liv).

[50] Although Tycho's discovery issued from so-called "mathematical astronomy" rather than "physical astronomy," it was still purely deductive. It seems doubtful, actually, whether any meaningful distinction can be sustained between a "mathematical" and a "physical" theory. To Newton's Cartesian contemporaries, for instance, the theory of gravitation was physically incomprehensible, and therefore the ultimate in a mathematical theory. At any rate, Tycho's model for the variation of the inclination accounted for a (very limited) set of appearances in almost exactly the same way that the Young-Fresnel wave theory accounted for known optical phenomena in the early 19th century. Tycho's discovery of the modal inequality thus parallels very nicely the Fresnel-Poisson prediction regarding the spot in the shadow of a circular disk.

[51] J. B. B. Delambre, *Histoire de L'Astronomie Moderne* (Paris: Courcier, 1817), Vol. 1, p. 168.

[52] "In tertio Capite facis mentionem Maximae Latitudinis Lunae, quam & ipse tecum candem fere inveni: sed Caput Draconis abest plus quatuor Gradibus, ut per distantias & Globum reperi, nec a Tabulis arbitror calculum minorem differentiam productorum, quod facile examinarem si tempus mihi non deesset" (VI, 155).

[53] VI, 170-171.

[54] " . . . quo Tabulae Alphonsinae & Copernianae (quae permodicum in his discrepant) eas reponunt, quamproxime permanentibus" (VI, 171).

55 In any other circumstances his finding depended on an accurate observed latitude (and, thus, an accurate parallax correction from theory) and a correct value for the orbital inclination. In lunar eclipses, the latitude was much less of a problem, and an error in the assumed inclination was much less damaging.

56 XI, 263; XII, 203, 209.

J. R. Christianson (essay date 1979)

SOURCE: "Tycho Brahe's German Treatise on the Comet of 1577: A Study in Science and Politics," in *Isis,* Vol. 70, No. 251, March, 1979, pp. 110-40.

[In the following excerpt, Christianson details the political, religious, and cosmological implications of Brahe's publication of his vernacular treatise on the comet of 1577.]

I

Tycho Brahe was born into a family with strong political traditions. His father was governor of Aalborg castle and fief, then of the key stronghold of Helsingborg on the Sound, and he ended his days as a Councillor of the Realm. Both of Tycho's grandfathers, all four of his great-grandfathers, and many of his more distant ancestors had also been members of this sovereign Council (*Rigsråd*) which elected kings, declared wars, made peace, and in short functioned as the core of an aristocratic oligarchical regime for much of the fifteenth and sixteenth centuries.[1] In Tycho's own day, two of his brothers and one of his brothers-in-law sat in the Council, and both of these brothers also sat in Regency Councils.[2] Tycho's great-great-grandfather and his great-uncle had both been Lord Marshal (*Rigsmarsk*), and another great-uncle, as well as one of Tycho's brothers, was Statholder of Skåne.[3] On his mother's side Tycho descended from the house of Vasa, and he was thus a kinsman to the monarchs of Sweden and Poland in his own day.[4] Many of his kinsmen, including his favorite uncle, had been in the Danish diplomatic service.[5] His foster mother, then his mother, served as *maitresse de la cour* to Queen Sophie.[6] Finally, the great Danish statesman and virtual ruler of the realm in Tycho's youth, Peter Oxe, was a brother of Tycho's foster mother.[7]

In his younger days, however, Tycho revealed a decided reluctance to become involved in politics. As a young lad in Leipzig, he developed a distaste for the study of law and even took to ridiculing juridical pedantry in Latin verse.[8] This was not the attitude that made a diplomat or a governor of great fiefs. Later on, when his university education was finished, he did put in the term of service at court which was all but obligatory for a member of his family returning from studies abroad, but when King Frederick II, late in the year 1575, asked him to state his own requirements in terms of fiefs and honors, this bewildering young courtier simply failed to reply.[9] To close friends Tycho confessed that he was planning to emigrate in order to avoid just such obligations and to devote himself wholly to astronomy and various arcane studies. "I did not want to take possession of any of the castles our benevolent king so graciously offered me," he wrote to one intimate friend in Copenhagen, " . . . I am displeased with society here, customary forms and the whole rubbish. . . . Among people of my own class . . . I waste much time."[10] To Petrus Severinus, who had just become the king's physician in ordinary, he wrote of the perils of courtly life: "For the court accepts one and all with flattery and benevolence, but sends them away unsatisfied and against their will."[11]

Tycho's devotion to astronomy and related disciplines seemed eccentric and even harmful to one of his social standing. Great aristocrats might dabble in such matters or even display considerable erudition, but they seldom turned down fiefs and honors because of their studies. When Tycho did so, it had apparently caused the king, Peter Oxe, and some of Tycho's uncles and other kinsmen to speculate concerning a suitable employment for his gifts. In 1568 he had been promised the next vacant canonry of Roskilde cathedral, a sinecure suitable to the dignity of a nobleman.[12] Peter Oxe had encouraged him to publish a manuscript he had written on the new star of 1572, either under his own name or an anagram.[13] In 1574 friends like Charles de Danzay and Johannes Pratensis, and finally even King Frederick himself, requested that Tycho gratify the wishes of aristocratic students at the University of Copenhagen by lecturing on the mathematical disciplines. This was the background for an oration which he delivered in the presence of the French legate and the entire university community in early September of 1574.[14]

II

The French legate, Charles de Danzay, was a Protestant who enjoyed a great deal of popularity at the Danish court, where he had been accredited for over twenty years. In earlier days Danzay had wielded considerable influence in the direction of peace in the Baltic region, working at the same time to keep Denmark from becoming too friendly toward England to the jeopardy of Franco-Scottish relations. He played a large part in mediating the Peace of Stettin in 1570.[15] Two years later, however, it had been his painful duty to inform the Danish court of the murder of Admiral Coligny "and others" on the night of St. Bartholomew. From that time, Franco-Danish relations deteriorated ever so gradually.[16] Danzay's privy dispatches were sometimes critical of the "excessive liberties" of the Danish aristocracy, and he was particularly wary of Peter Oxe, who had been in the service of the Duchess of Lorraine before coming home to Denmark in 1566.[17] This charming and sophisticated diplomat had quickly become a confidant of the young Tycho Brahe, who had returned home from several years of foreign study at the end of 1571.[18]

Tycho's lectures of 1574-1575 did raise some ticklish problems of decorum. He held no university degrees, and in any case it would not have been appropriate for him as a nobleman to ascend the cathedra of an ordinary university lecture hall. A request, however, not from ordinary academicians but from noblemen studying at the university, advocated in addition by the king himself, elevated the whole matter from an academic plane to the appropriate aristocratic social level where Tycho's lectures were perfectly acceptable. The oration was delivered before an audience of doctors, professors, students, and distinguished guests, including the French legate.

Tycho's oration traced the origins of astronomy, the noblest of all disciplines, from geometry and arithmetic, descending in a genealogy of wisdom from Seth to Abraham, the Egyptians, Timocharus and Hipparchus, Ptolemy, Albetegnius, Alfonso the Wise, and Copernicus. From astronomy, Tycho progressed to astrology and made it the principal subject, but the spirit which permeated the oration was that of humanism, and its major theme was the dignity of man. Tycho spoke with erudition and with poetic power, merging the ideals of Pico and Ficino with Melanchthon's concept of the rational free will. He described the macrocosm in detail as a human environment charged with Paracelsian energy, where "There is no herb so insignificant, no mineral nor metal, no object, no animalcule so vile that it is not endowed with some special and particular virtue."[19] Perhaps Ramus also made his contribution to Tycho's thought, as when the young orator drew a distinction between the realm of natural philosophy and that of God's "arcane council of which no creature is participant."[20] Most striking of all, however, was the pervasive Copernican spirit of Tycho's characterization of astronomy.[21]

This Copernicanism set the tone for the series of lectures which followed during the winter semester of 1574-1575. Since others lectured regularly on spherical astronomy, Tycho limited his lectures to planetary theory, explaining the method of calculating planetary motions from the Prutenic tables and describing the theory according to which these tables had been computed, but departing from Copernican cosmology by referring everything to an immobile earth.[22] He lectured in this manner on the fixed stars, the sun, and the moon, but broke off before dealing with the planets. Caspar Peucer had lectured on Copernicus in a similar vein at Wittenberg in 1559, and his lectures had suddenly appeared in print in three different editions during the years 1568-1573.[23] Tycho would not accept the approach of Peucer, whom he criticized along with Dasipodius for mixing Copernicus and Ptolemy together. Tycho himself held exclusively to the mathematical models of Copernicus, though he transposed them to fit a geostatic assumption. Thus, in the words of Kristian P. Moesgaard, it is evident that "Copernicus and Copernican astronomy was introduced in Denmark in a thorough and competent way by an expert."[24]

III

The mere fact that Tycho's oration was delivered in the French legation may have reflected to the honor of Charles de Danzay and the monarch he represented. In the actual content of the oration, however, there was nothing specifically political in the modern sense, though the careful sixteenth-century auditor may have been able to detect political overtones in Tycho's long description of planetary virtues and their effects upon the microcosm, or in similar passages.

At a dinner following the talk, as Tycho stood by, Danzay remarked lightly to Professor Niels Hemmingsen that Tycho had not only attacked the other faculties for their disbelief in astrology but had gone so far as to do the same to the theologians. For his own part Danzay thought that astrological predictions were a hindrance to the Evangelical teaching. Tycho said he replied that astrology was not a threat if it held to its proper sphere and did not get involved in politics.[25] Throughout this whole conversation there seem to be undertones that only these two friends were able to appreciate fully. Danzay certainly knew full well, for example, that part of Tycho's oration was a loosely veiled critique of Hemmingsen's writing on astrology. One can only guess at the implications of Tycho's reply.

Niels Hemmingsen, the senior professor of theology at the University of Copenhagen, was Denmark's brightest theological light in those years. Like virtually all of his colleagues, he was a disciple of Philipp Melanchthon and had spent the crucial part of his student days in Wittenberg. The Philippists shared Melanchthon's humanist orientation and also his tolerance and his irenic striving for religious harmony. Their theology included a symbolical interpretation of the Eucharist which caused other Lutherans to suspect them of crypto-Calvinism, but this was coupled with a strong emphasis upon free will which contradicted the doctrine of predestination. Like Melanchthon, they associated free will with reason and consequently became strong advocates of education. Hemmingsen had been the foremost spokesman of Danish Philippism for a good twenty years.[26] In the present context, however, it is significant that he did differ with Melanchthon on at least one point: whereas Melanchthon had conceived of man as a microcosm and had been a dedicated believer in astrological influences, Luther had scoffed at this, and a good many of Melanchthon's own disciples, including Hemmingsen, also rejected astrology.[27] Tycho's attack upon Hemmingsen's disparagement of astrology should not be allowed to obscure the fact that they both stood in the same theological camp. Tycho was also a Philippist, though of course a layman, and he shared Melanchthon's belief in astrological influences. Following Tycho's oration, Hemmingsen had replied to Danzay's remarks by saying that he would tolerate Tycho's belief in astrology on two conditions: if complete freedom of action were left to God and free will to men. Tycho was more than willing to concede them both.[28]

IV

When Tycho delivered his oration, Philippism had reigned supreme in the Danish church for almost a generation, humane and mild, while the thunder of German theological controversy rumbled in the distance. In the spring of 1575, as Tycho was concluding his lectures on Copernican astronomy, that controversy cast a mighty bolt against Niels Hemmingsen. It came from Saxony.

Elector Augustus of Saxony, a brother-in-law of King Frederick II, had spent a part of the summer of 1572 in Copenhagen and elsewhere in Denmark helping to celebrate the Danish king's wedding. Of course he had brought his Saxon theologians along, and they had passed much of the time with their Danish colleagues. Elector Augustus was a man who took great pride in his role as protector of the holy places of Lutheranism. Apparently he was not aware that crypto-Calvinism was rife all around him. Early in 1574, however, he discovered it with a vengeance and cast all of his leading theologians into prison, including Melanchthon's son-in-law, Caspar Peucer, who was a friend of Tycho even though they were not always in complete agreement. The next spring a Danish scholar, Master Jørgen Dybvad, came into Denmark from Saxony with a personal letter from the Elector to King Frederick. Crypto-Calvinism had been discovered in Saxony; the culprits had defended themselves by pleading the precedent of Denmark; this evil must be purged. Elector Augustus was particularly aware of Hemmingsen's recent work, *Syntagma institutionum christianarum,* which had appeared simultaneously with an anonymous work of the same tenor in Saxony, thus giving away the "plot" which had been hatched in Denmark during the summer of 1572.[29]

It was true that this work of Hemmingsen's had presented a thoroughly Calvinist interpretation of the Eucharist, though without actually mentioning Calvin. This had already caused no little embarrassment to the Danish crown. The missive from Saxony, and Jørgen Dybvad's oral elaborations, brought action. Early on the morning of June 15, 1575, all endowed professors of the University of Copenhagen, all pastors of Copenhagen churches, and the bishop of Roskilde were summoned in a body to the Castle of Copenhagen to answer the Elector's charges. They met before a commission of three great lords: Peter Oxe, Chancellor Niels Kaas, and Councillor Jørgen Rosenkrantz. Hemmingsen defended what he described as the unity of the Danish church against attacks from abroad. German theologians are manifold, he said, and they all leap like cooks to please the palate of their lord. If we hearken to them all, we shall have utter confusion in Denmark, instead of unity of belief and religious practice. This was an argument of no little weight, given the political instincts of his inquisitors. Rosenkrantz remained harsh in his queries, but Peter Oxe concluded the hearing with the words, spoken to Hemmingsen, "No misfortune will come over you for my sake."[30]

Within a few months, however, the great statesman Peter Oxe was dead. Hemmingsen now moved under a cloud. Most Danish theologians stood by him, and Tycho's close friend Anders Sørensen Vedel translated one of Hemmingsen's vernacular works into Latin to demonstrate abroad that it was harmless to orthodoxy.[31] But Hemmingsen's enemies were relentless. On the recommendation of Elector Augustus, Jørgen Dybvad was appointed extraordinary professor of theology in Copenhagen. In April of 1576 Saxon pressures upon the Danish crown forced Hemmingsen to sign a formal retraction of his offensive views in *Syntagma institutionum christianarum.*[32] All Danish theologians were forbidden to dispute concerning the Eucharist. In May of 1576 Danish censorship was tightened, while a conference assembled in Germany to define a common Lutheran confession and especially to differentiate Lutheran belief from Calvinism. Elector Augustus twice sent the resulting confessional statement, the Torgau Book, to King Frederick, requesting that the Danish theologians debate it, but the king refused, saying that he would not disrupt the unimpeachably Lutheran consensus that prevailed within his kingdoms since Hemmingsen's retraction. Dano-Saxon relations cooled markedly as a result of this royal attitude, but the pressures upon Hemmingsen did not diminish.[33] He was a much embattled man in the spring of 1577, when he seems to have turned to Tycho Brahe for support.

On May 18, 1577, Hemmingsen proposed in the Consistory of the University of Copenhagen that Tycho Brahe be elected rector of the university for the forthcoming twelvemonth.[34] This office was normally held by a professor, elected annually by his colleagues in rotation among the four faculties. The rector was the actual administrative and ceremonial leader of the academic community, ultimately responsible to the chancellor of the university, who was always the Royal Chancellor.[35] Tycho's lectures on astronomy two years earlier might have served to establish an identity with the university and to clothe this extraordinary election with some semblance of logic, but his astronomical eloquence was hardly sufficient motivation. In the spring of 1577 Hemmingsen craved strong support, not only within the inner sancta of government, in order to dampen the king's reaction to pressures from Saxony, but also within the university itself, where only a resolute rector could curb the pernicious energy of Jørgen Dybvad. As a nobleman, Tycho Brahe radiated an authority no middle-class professor could deny; yet he declined the nomination, pleading that he was too busy with his building on the isle of Hven.[36] Once again, he seemed to draw back from political involvement.

V

Tycho had withdrawn even more dramatically during the year 1575. In the midst of his lectures on Copernican astronomy, coming into a considerable inheritance, he had simply departed Denmark on an extended tour of the Continent.[37] He had earlier spent some eight years abroad, residing in Leipzig, Rostock, Wittenberg, Basel, and Augsburg, and he now visited old acquaintances in many of these places. More important politically, however, were the new contacts he established, which were all with states that opposed the policy of confessional polarization advocated by Saxony.

Tycho went first to Cassel and spent a week at the court of William IV, Landgrave of Hesse-Cassel, who shared a fascination with astronomy and related arts. A close personal rapport developed which was renewed in later years.[38] In Venice, Tycho found admittance to the learned gatherings and "academies" that flourished among the patricians of the republic and the scholars from nearby Padua, and he participated in many an erudite discourse. There is no evidence that he helped to introduce the Copernican philosophy to these circles, but he did establish contacts that were maintained for many years.[39] Finally, in Regensburg, Tycho attended the coronation as King of the Romans of the future Emperor Rudolf II. Once again he penetrated into the inner circles, and he established a particularly close contact with the court physician, Thaddeus Hagecius, who presented him a manuscript of Copernicus' *Commentariolus*.[40]

It was Basel, however, that caught Tycho's fancy more than any other place, and his reasons bespoke a striving for peace, wisdom, and universal harmony. Tycho spoke of the city's favorable location for a "student interested in learned subjects, or for one who loves Apollonian tranquility and the Muses," a bridge between creeds and cultures, "near to Italy, France and Germany."[41] This striving preyed upon his mind when he returned home to Denmark toward the end of 1575.

VI

Tycho has left a dramatic letter, written three days after the event, which tells how his future plans were suddenly changed by a summons from King Frederick II which reached him at Knutstorp manor on February 11, 1576. He hastened to the royal hunting lodge of Ibstrup and was shown into the privy chamber, where he conversed with the king in private. The Landgrave of Hesse-Cassel had written and admonished King Frederick not to overlook the talents of this young nobleman, and the king had heard indirectly that Tycho was planning to emigrate. All of this, and Tycho's reluctance to accept a royal command, had been on the king's mind recently, when he had been residing at the castle of Elsinore, "'and when I looked out through a window, I spied the little isle of Hven. . . .'"[42] One of Tycho's uncles had once mentioned that the isle appealed to Tycho. The king now offered it to him in lifetime fee. Tycho was profoundly moved by this proposal, originating, as he felt, with the king himself. He deliberated for seven days, and he consulted in secret with his two French friends Danzay and Pratensis; then he accepted.[43]

The king immediately granted him 500 dalers per annum from the Sound Dues collected in Elsinore, a sum that seems to have been equal to around three quarters of the annual income from Tycho's patrimony.[44] Three months later, Tycho was granted the isle of Hven in fee, quit and free of all dues and services to the crown, for the duration of his lifetime.[45] On the same day he was granted an additional 400 dalers to begin construction of a suitable residence on the isle.[46] In August of 1577 he was granted another fief with extensive tracts of forest, apparently in order to fire the brick kilns, and later the alchemical furnaces, of Hven.[47] In 1578 he was granted a minor fief in Skåne and a larger one in Norway to augment his income, and in 1579 he received his canonry in the chapter of Roskilde.[48] These endowments finally enticed Tycho Brahe into royal service and drew him directly into the realm of politics.

VII

Perhaps the royal appetite had been whetted by a short treatise in humanist format which Tycho had published, with Peter Oxe's encouragement, just three years before he entered the royal Danish service. The treatise dealt with the new star, or supernova, of 1572. One brief section had attempted to analyze the astrological effects of the star. Tycho's conclusions had been ones with rather direct political implications: he had predicted that the star would induce great and unusual effects, originating in northern regions such as Russia, Livonia, Finland, Sweden, or Norway, bringing serious tumults, spreading throughout Europe, followed by "a new condition in kingdoms, different from the earlier, and likewise a different order of religious conditions and laws."[49] Yet the forecast was cryptic and unclear. It did not attempt to determine when the effects would occur, and it concluded with the remark that Tycho also knew of a "truer and more secret" astrology which he was not willing to divulge in writing.[50] In short, this treatise might be enticing to a believer in astrology, but it could not be of much use to practical statesmen like Peter Oxe and King Frederick II in planning future policies.

VIII

The obligations that fell upon Tycho's shoulders, in return for the lavish royal patronage that followed the year 1576, seem surprisingly light. He served as a sort of royal consultant on astronomical and astrological matters, compiled a horoscope upon the birth of each royal son, replied to royal inquiries like the one in 1578 concerning rumors that another new star had appeared, and he apparently supplied the royal family with an almanac or prognostication in manuscript annually.[51] He also fabricated and repaired instruments for the crown, worked on various cartographic and iconographic projects, and supplied Queen Sophie with alchemical equipment.[52] On one occasion Tycho, upon the request of King Frederick, had one of his disciples write a book on weather prognostication.[53] In later years Tycho entertained princely and royal guests to Denmark with tours of the isle of Hven,[54] where he maintained a sort of royal academy and advanced institute.[55] He served as a versatile royal consultant on many matters in the realm of empirical natural philosophy, but he was still free to devote much time to his own research.

In times of cosmic crisis, however, his counsel was quickly summoned, which happened within a year after Tycho became a vassal of the Danish king. The event which gave Tycho the first opportunity to offer his particular kind of counsel to his liege lord was the birth of a royal son and heir, the future King Christian IV, on April 12, 1577. This birth had been predicted the year before by a mermaid who appeared out of the sea and foresaw a glorious future under the coming prince.[56] Tycho Brahe was called upon to be more specific. On July 1, 1577, he presented a detailed horoscope, in Latin with a German summary, which naturally concentrated on the mature years of the prince.[57] Its political implications were manifold, but they all applied to a period some thirty to fifty years in the future. The horoscope did not provide guidelines to royal policy in the immediate future any more than did the earlier treatise on the new star of 1572.

The second cosmic event of 1577 occurred around the time of Martinmas, when a great comet appeared in the constellation Capricorn. It was seen in Danish court circles as an omen of awful significance. For Tycho its most immediate effect was to call forth a dangerous rival among Danish astrologers. This time the rival was no mermaid from the briny deep but a professor from the king's own University of Copenhagen, none other than Jørgen Dybvad.

IX

Jørgen Dybvad had been at Sorø Abbey on St. Martin's day, November 11, 1577. On the evening of that day, he had first seen the great comet in the skies. He later applied 'Ali ibn Ridwan's method and calculated that the comet had arisen the previous evening at the time of the new moon but had been hidden at first by dark weather and rain.[58]

There were others at Sorø Abbey on that feast of St. Martin in 1577. One of them was King Frederick II;[59] another was Abbot Ivar Bertelsen; still another may have been the king's physician, Petrus Severinus. The sources do not tell whether these men discussed the comet on the evening it appeared, but such a dramatic and ominous event could hardly have failed to be among the topics of conversation around the abbot's table that evening.

Ivar Bertelsen, the abbot of Sorø, knew something about astronomy. He had once been a man of restless and choleric temper like Dybvad, plagued by visions of righteousness and doom. Violent changes in fortune had buffeted him since student days as Melanchthon's disciple in Wittenberg, and for three years he had been a ragged prisoner, incarcerated in the very abbey of which he was now the Lutheran abbot. He spent his latter days as a great royal favorite, married to a young noblewoman, with a flock of sons and daughters who were destined for distinguished careers.[60]

In 1561, as a young professor of rhetoric in Copenhagen, Bertelsen had published a pamphlet which predicted the apocalypse in phrases of poetic fury, describing how the Lord had let the winds and weather and the very fires of the firmament preach over Denmark to show His wrath.[61] This same apocalyptic theme was taken up by Dybvad in analyzing the effects of the comet of Martinmas, 1577.

Within five weeks of the first sighting, Dybvad had produced a pamphlet on the comet. The fact that it was written in the vernacular and dedicated to King Frederick is enough to establish that it had political as well as scientific aims. In the dedication Dybvad asserted that the "terrible great comet" was one of manifold signs which revealed that "the day of the Lord, according to His promise, is at hand." Besides the comet, he cited a profusion of prophetic, chronological, and astral evidence, including the new star of 1572, which he accepted as a celestial phenomenon. He then proceeded to list almost fifty previous sightings of comets over the course of more than two thousand years as evidence for the assertion that comets are always followed by great changes in politics and weather. Finally, he asserted that the comet of 1577 would bring a cold, snow-laden winter, followed by a hot, dry summer, with tempests, crop failure, and "gruesome treachery in affairs of religion."[62] Dybvad expected these effects to be felt in many lands:

> Hungary may well fear highly of the Turk. Hispania will feel a hard rod. Cologne on the Rhine will not be left out. Saxony, Thüringen, Hesse, Steiermark, the Brandenburg lands, Augsburg, Kostnitz, Cleve, Berg, Ghent, Mecklenburg, Lithuania, must make ready for the effects of this comet, and especially for pestilence. Poland dare not be proud, for it must also drink of the cup, and it appears in particular, that the Muscovite or the Tartar will bring a sour visitation upon them. . . . Denmark, uplift thine eyes, shake off the sleep . . . look about thee, and mark, that this comet does also threaten thee with pestilence and dear times. . . . The Muscovite, Sweden, Walachia, Westphalia, Trent, Hamburg, Bremen, Salzburg, Calabria, Portugal, Alexandria, and many other realms and lands will also receive something of this comet's effects.[63]

Dybvad predicted that "Great Lords" in particular would be affected by the comet, though it threatened not only mankind, but also "birds, fishes, and beasts of the field." He asserted at last that it was "greatly necessary, that we seriously turn unto the LORD," and he concluded his treatise with a prayer for mercy and for divine protection over Denmark and the Danish royal family.[64]

X

Martinmas had been overcast on the isle of Hven. Two days later, on the afternoon of November 13, 1577, in clear weather, Tycho Brahe had been out by his fish ponds catching fish for the evening meal. As the sun went down, sometime before five o'clock, Tycho noticed a bright star in the western sky over Sjælland. He knew it could not be Venus, because Venus was a morning star at that time, and it was too bright to be Saturn. Tycho watched as the dusk turned to darkness. The star held its position, and a long ruddy tail gradually grew visible, stretching in the opposite direction from the point of sunset. This was a comet, the first Tycho had ever seen.[65] He was about thirty-one years old at the time.

Tycho went immediately to his new manor house of Uraniborg. He took forth some folio sheets of paper, folded them into a little notebook in quarto format, took forth his radius, later also his quadrants, and began to record his observations of the comet. The next day he wrote to Petrus Severinus, asking him to arrange affairs with the king so that he could observe without being disturbed. Of course

he knew that the king would be anxious to hear his counsel concerning the comet, but he wanted to study the phenomenon carefully before venturing a prognosis. He also asked Severinus to send him any observations he might have taken of the comet.[66]

For the next two and a half months, whenever the sky was clear, Tycho observed the comet and entered his observations in the little notebook, which has survived,[67] though a bit tattered by weather and use. On the night of November 13 Tycho sketched the comet. . . .

As the observations began to fill the little notebook, Tycho began to ponder their significance. Aristotle had taught, nearly two thousand years earlier, that comets occurred in the upper atmosphere, like lightning and meteors.[68] Tycho studied the parallax of the comet, however, and concluded that it was located far beyond those regions and even beyond the moon, in the celestial regions which Aristotle had described as the realm of eternal, unchanging circular motion, where nothing new could ever occur. In the back of his little notebook Tycho made two rough sketches illustrating the parallax of the comet. . . . They show the comet to be about one third of the way from earth to the stars.

Tycho was not particularly disturbed to discover that this comet violated Aristotle's teaching. In the first place, he was skeptical of Aristotle's sharp distinction between the celestial and terrestrial regions and was apparently more inclined to accept the teaching of Paracelsus—that the whole universe was a living, dynamic cosmos, subject to growth and diminution in due time.[69] What is more, Tycho had already observed one earlier creation in the upper heavens and had accepted it as such: the new star of 1572. Consequently the problem as he saw it was, not to explain the celestial location of the comet, but to discover precisely where it fit in among the other bodies of the celestial spheres.

Tycho had observed, among other things, that the tail of the comet always pointed away from the sun. He explained this by assuming that the comet rotated around the sun. In the back of his little notebook he made two rough sketches illustrating this arrangement in terms of the laws of perspective, showing the real and apparent locations of the comet's tail as observed from earth.

Tycho now turned to the question of the comet's location with respect to the other celestial bodies. His heliocentric orbit for the comet indicates that he still favored the theories of Copernicus. He assumed that the planets also rotated around the sun, and his next step was to determine the location of the comet among them. He made two more rough sketches . . . , the first showing the orbits of Mercury and Venus around the sun, with the orbit of the comet outside that of Venus.

This sketch also reveals that Tycho was still referring everything to an immobile earth, as he had done in his lectures of 1574-1575.

Gradually, Tycho was coming to grips with the comet in the sky. Now he must bring its cosmic message down to earth. Early in the year 1578 Tycho wrote a brief vernacular manuscript on the comet, a work with immediate political implications. In that brief manuscript Tycho launched an attack upon the astrological conclusions of Jørgen Dybvad, though he refrained from mentioning him by name.

XI

Tycho and his rival represented two different social strata: compared with Tycho's aristocracy, Dybvad was of prosperous yeoman stock, but he was a man of intense ambition. His political instincts were sound. In those early years they led him to curry the favor of those who wielded power. In the face of great majesty, such as that of the comet of 1577, his solution was to cower and pray, but in other circumstances he used other methods, dedicating a prolific flow of writings to influential courtiers and learned noblemen, and ingratiating himself at court with his reports from Saxony.[70]

These tactics had their reward. Early in 1578 a rather inert professor in Copenhagen was exiled to the chapter of Lund, and Dybvad was appointed to the chair of mathematics thus vacated. He was also granted a monopoly on the publication of almanacs. The other professors conceived these changes as infringements upon their liberties and stubbornly resisted, but by the summer of 1578 they had been broken to the royal will.[71] Dybvad, immune to the lack of cordiality among his colleagues, soundly entrenched in the royal favor and his tenured professorship of mathematics, began to cast ever more covetous eyes upon Professor Niels Hemmingsen's prestigious chair of theology.

Here was a dangerous rival for Tycho as well as for Hemmingsen. Dybvad had won the ear of the king, no less than Tycho had done. This fact went far to obviate Tycho's decided advantages of birth, wealth, social status, and kinship within the ruling oligarchy. So did the fact that their rivalry was caught up in a web of social, political, and intellectual issues, so that each of them acted, half unwittingly, as the spokesman for forces more powerful than himself. Tycho stood on the side of Hemmingsen and the Philippist tradition in the Danish church; in politics, he was closely allied to the great magnates who were the heirs of Peter Oxe; in foreign affairs, his ties were with the opponents of confessional militance.[72] Dybvad, on the other hand, had been the very herald of the Saxon attack upon Hemmingsen; he was a royalist, certainly not a magnate, and he stood among those who worked for closer ties with more orthodox Lutherans.

Dybvad was a first-rate scholar. His writings on astronomy, meteorology, and mathematics revealed a tendency toward new, radically anti-Aristotelian patterns of thought.[73] He was the first Dane to publish a commentary on Copernicus,[74] and he was quite willing to accept the new star of 1572 as evidence of celestial mutability.[75] Observational astronomy, however, was not his strong point, and there is no evidence that he observed the comet of 1577 systematically. His astrology merged the Ptolemaic tradition with a strong sixteenth-century tradition of historical chronology, establishing a temporal cosmic scheme with overtones of apocalyptic violence, reminiscent of the Reformation era. Dybvad was a Hebrew scholar, but he does not seem to have used the caballa to interpret celestial events, and his denial of Democritus appears to derive from an aloofness toward the Pythagorean tradition in general.[76] The arena for their rivalry was not the consistory of the university, for Tycho had rejected the office of rector which would have brought him into academic politics. It seems rather to have been the royal court itself.

XII

The ways in which late-sixteenth-century philosophers and astrologers related celestial occurrences to contemporary politics have been the subject of much scholarship in recent years. Frances Yates' work on the French monarchy is intriguing in the light of Tycho's French ties,[77] though she refrained from investigating the Danish connections in her book on the Rosicrucian movement.[78] French, Howell, and Yates have probed some of the celestial dimensions of Elizabethan politics.[79] Evans has established a new context for the later years of Tycho's life with his book on the court of Emperor Rudolf II.[80] This literature, supplemented by Hellman's classic study of treatises on the comet of 1577,[81] establishes a general framework for the consideration of Tycho's brief vernacular manuscript on the comet of 1577.

This manuscript was discovered in two copies among the Tychonic papers in Vienna and was first published in 1922.[82] A number of factors indicate that this treatise may have been Tycho's report to the Danish crown. The clear implication of Tycho's letter to Severinus is that he will present a confidential analysis of the comet to the king in due time. This manuscript is the only known contemporary account of that comet from Tycho's hand. The language is German, which Tycho also used in other manuscripts written expressly for the crown.[83] The form is a close parallel to Tycho's royal horoscopes. The manuscript exists in a revised and finished version, but it was never printed.[84] All of this is circumstantial evidence, but the chains of circumstance seem firmly linked.

Its contents are interesting from a cosmological as well as a political point of view. Tycho began the manuscript with a summary description of the cosmos, and he went on to establish the location, appearance, and effects of the comet within that framework. In the very first sentence he parenthetically rejected Aristotle's four elements in favor of three. As the manuscript progressed, its consistently anti-Aristotelian tone became more evident and it simultaneously began to infuse the geostatic world picture with new concepts derived from Paracelsus. The basic idea of three elements, rather than four, is a sign of this process. It became most explicit in Tycho's review of the historiography of cometary theory. He began with the Pythagoreans, showed how they were refuted by Aristotle, then used the evidence of the heavens themselves (in the form of the new star of 1572) to refute Aristotle, before concluding with the modern view of Paracelsus. Tycho presented this Paracelsian view as one that was consistent with Pythagorean thought and not inconsistent with the evidence of the new star. Later on in the manuscript he adopted the Paracelsian terminology of "pseudoplanet" to describe the comet. Tycho was also careful to give a precise description of color changes in the comet and its tail, which he may have seen as the signatures of some powerful cosmic alchemy. He did reject the more specifically mystical or spiritual aspects of Paracelsus, however, such as the existence of the Superior Penates, by applying a distinction which he may have derived from Ramus, between those things which can be known through the study of nature and those which cannot and therefore fall into the realm of theology. This was a crucial step: it allowed Tycho to strip away the Hermetic mysticism from Paracelsus' dynamic conception of the heavens and to merge it with the astronomical tradition of mathematical analysis. This freed Tycho of Aristotle and gave him a new, dynamic cosmological framework for his investigations.

Tycho dealt at length with physical questions such as the diameter and mass of the comet, its actual distance from earth, the length and physical nature of its tail. He derived its spatial location from its parallax. His ideas developed rapidly under the stimulus of these investigations, which seem to have been carried out during the early months of 1578. In the manuscript Tycho referred to "this year of '78," and he noted that he lost sight of the comet on January 26 of that year. Owen Gingerich has recently discovered a series of diagrams in Tycho's hand, derived from work done in January and February of 1578 and revealing that the comet of 1577 stimulated Tycho to work out various new models of Copernican planetary theory accommodated to an immobile earth.[85] These diagrams are closely related to the rougher sketches reproduced above, and to Tycho's vernacular manuscript on the comet.

With this in mind, it is interesting to notice the slight shifts in emphasis through successive versions of Tycho's draft manuscript on the comet. They indicate a progressively clearer commitment to the concept of Copernican theory accommodated to geocentricity.[86]

I.[87]

Therefore, I conclude that it was in the sphere of Venus, if one wants to follow the usual distribution of the celestial orbs. But if one prefers to accept as valid the opinion of various ancient philosophers and of Copernicus in our own time, that Mercury *is next to* the sun, and Venus around Mercury, both with the sun at the approximate center of their orbs, which reasoning is not entirely out of harmony with truth, even if the sun [several variant expressions struck in the MS] is not put to rest in the center of the universe as the hypotheses of Copernicus would have it.

II.[88]

Therefore, I conclude that it was in the sphere of Venus, if one wants to follow the usual distribution of the celestial orbs. According to the opinion of various ancient philosophers and of Copernicus in our own time, they hold that Mercury comes after the sun, and Venus around Mercury, both with the sun at the approximate center of their orbs. . . .

III.[89]

Therefore, I conclude that it was in the sphere of Venus, *but if one does not* want to follow the usual distribution of the celestial orbs but would rather accept as valid the opinion of various ancient philosophers and of Copernicus in our own time, that Mercury *has its orb around the sun,* and Venus around Mercury, with the sun at the approximate center of their orbs, which reasoning is not entirely out of harmony with truth, even if the sun is not put to rest in the center of the universe as with the hypotheses of Copernicus. . . .

While Tycho Brahe was thus pondering the shape of the universe and groping his way toward a new understanding of it, his royal patron must have been waiting impatiently. King Frederick believed in astrology, as Tycho did. He knew that this great comet was an omen of awful significance. He wanted to know its true astrological meaning in detail, so he could plan his spiritual affairs as well as the foreign and domestic policies of his realm.

The last half of Tycho's manuscript came to bear upon astrological analysis. He began by confuting those astrologers (like Dybvad) who associated the significance of comets with regular and predictable celestial events, because comets, as "new and supernatural" creations of God, actually worked in opposition to such "natural courses of the heavens." Then Tycho summarized the comet's effects. Like Dybvad and others, he predicted warfare, pestilence, and extremes of heat and cold; he also laid a particular emphasis upon changes in religion. His words were moderate, but their implications were startling. To a king raised on tales of the bloodshed and rebellion of the Reformation era, Tycho spoke of a forthcoming "great alteration and turmoil in the spiritual matters of religion, which will be something more than has hitherto been experienced." At the same time, he emphatically denied that the comet of 1577 or any other celestial sign presaged the apocalypse. Tycho thus threw down a direct challenge to the Dybvads and Bertelsens among Danish astronomers. In another brief, furious passage, he chastized "pseudoprophets . . . who have mounted too high in their arrogance, and have not wandered in divine wisdom," and he concluded that they "will be punished."

Tycho associated his prophecy of the new religion with such potent harbingers as the new star of 1572 and the great planetary conjunction in the beginning of Aries more than with the comet of 1577, the effects of which he saw as subsidiary to the greater cosmic events. He predicted that the alteration "may even bode more for the better of Christendom than for the worse," for it was possible that "the eternal Sabbath of all Creation is at hand" and would commence sometime during the forthcoming decade. Just what Tycho meant by this is difficult to say, but he was undoubtedly able to elaborate at length in confidential conversation. He may have had the astrologers' ominous year of 1588 in mind.[90] There are implications of cabalist influence and overtones of the "religion of the world." An urge for universal peace was certainly part of the expectation. There may also have been some association with a political schema of correspondences between terrestrial states and celestial bodies, such as that which associated "solar" effects with France, or "saturnine" with Spain. In any case, it was apparent that the apocalyptic violence of the Reformation era, still evident in Dybvad's treatise on the comet, was giving way in Tycho's mind to a more irenic and pacific millenarianism, with its roots in Philippism but charged with tremendous arcane significance as well.

There is no evidence that Tycho agreed with his many contemporaries who advocated magical solutions to political or cosmic problems.[91] Tycho's response was that of a politically mature aristocrat, tempered by the cool rationality of Melanchthon. What Tycho urged was a rational exercise of the free will, leading to action which could moderate or control the predictable effects of the comet and other cosmic events. This was a response different from the labyrinthine operations of the Magus, and equally different from Dybvad's solution of anguished prayers for deliverance from divine wrath.

This consideration led Tycho to treat the comet's effects in a clearly political manner, so that they could be mitigated by appropriate policies. He did not sound a doomsday roll call of places and plagues, but rather he indicated three specific areas that would be affected by the comet. To the east of Denmark the comet would bring warfare and bloodshed to the Muscovites and Tartars in the years around 1579-1580, possibly even bringing the downfall of the tyrannical Ivan the Terrible by 1583. To the south it would cause trouble for the Spaniards, especially in the Netherlands and in the realm of religion, beginning "this year of '78," reaching a head in 1579-1580 and lasting till 1583. During these same years the comet would threaten Emperor Rudolf II and cause great disunity within the Holy Roman Empire, while Spanish machinations would pose a serious threat to the Saxon Circle, where King Frederick II had some of his best allies and where he himself was Duke of Holstein. These evil effects would finally be counteracted by some person arising under the sign of Libra: dignified, harmonious, rational, just, diplomatic, peace-loving, conciliatory, charming, tolerant, impartial, persuasive, honorable. Here was a prediction which could be translated directly into policy: oppose Spain in the Saxon Circle, aid the Dutch rebels, be prepared to benefit from disorder in Muscovy, but strive withal for harmony and peace.

XIII

The aim of this paper has been to probe the political, religious, and cosmological background of a single treatise by Tycho Brahe, written at a crucial time in his intellectual development. I have tried to show that his cosmological framework was not essentially Aristotelian but Paracelsian, though in a rationalized version developed by Tycho under the influence of thinkers like Severinus, Melanchthon, Niels Hemmingsen, and Ramus. This matter has really only been touched upon and needs further investigation. Tycho's method at this stage, as the text to follow will make quite clear, was a radical empiricism based upon mathematical analysis. His belief in astrology was genuine, though it was of a special kind, tempered by the Philippist theology with its strong emphasis upon rationality and freedom of the will. Finally, we have seen how Tycho used Copernican concepts, accommodated to a stable earth, during this period when he was groping his way toward a more satisfying planetary theory.

Besides these internal considerations, there has been an external dimension to the investigation. I have tried to place this treatise of Tycho Brahe in the context of Danish affairs as well as in a broader European intellectual and political framework. I have tried to demonstrate an affinity between Tycho Brahe, Philippism, and the foreign policy of peace based on alignment with the *politique* powers. Tycho Brahe was not an isolated figure, some tempest-torn Prospero on his isle of Hven, nor were his occasional references to plots and covert pressures the sign of paranoia. He was intimately involved in the affairs of his day, and those affairs were frequently complex and hard fought. Perhaps it would not be an overstatement to say that the party with which he was allied stood strong for the next two decades in Denmark, but when its power diminished, he fell. It will take more research, however, to verify such a statement. In any case, Tycho's work does take on new significance when seen in its social and political milieu as well as its specifically Danish intellectual context.[92]

Notes

[1] Tycho's father was Otte Brahe; see Povl Engelstoft and Svend Dahl, eds., *Dansk biografisk leksikon* (hereafter cited as *DBL*), Vol. III (Copenhagen: Schultz, 1934), pp. 574-575. His grandfathers were Tyge Brahe and Claus Bille; see *DBL,* Vol. III, pp. 23-26, 583. His great-grandfathers were Axel Brahe (d. 1487), Jørgen Rud (*DBL,* Vol. XX [1941], pp. 286-287), Steen Basse Bille (*DBL,* Vol. III, pp. 50-51), and Jens Holgersen Ulfstand (*DBL,* Vol. XXIV [1943], pp. 496-497). On the Brahe family, see Albert Fabritius, "Brahe," *Danmarks adels aarbog* (hereafter cited *DAA*) (Copenhagen: Schultz, 1950), Pt. 2, pp. 3-32.

[2] Axel Brahe (d. 1616; *DBL,* Vol. III, pp. 564-565), Steen Brahe (*DBL,* Vol. III, pp. 580-582), and Christen Skeel (*DAA,* 1943, Pt. 2, pp. 99-100).

[3] Claus Rønnow (*DAA,* 1913, p. 484); Eskild Gøye, married to Sidsel Brahe (*DBL,* Vol. VII [1936], pp. 132-133); Axel Brahe (d. 1551; *DBL,* Vol. III, pp. 563-564); and Axel Brahe (d. 1616).

[4] Claus Bille was a second cousin of King Gustavus Vasa through his maternal grandmother, Birgitta Kristiernsdotter (Vasa), a sister of the king's grandfather.

[5] Steen Bille; see *DBL,* Vol. III, pp. 51-52. See also Emil Marquard, *Danske gesandter og gesandtskabspersonale indtil 1914* (Copenhagen: Munksgaard, 1952).

[6] Inger Oxe was *dronningens hofmesterinde* 1572-1584; see *DAA,* 1907, p. 343. Beate Bille was *dronningens hofmesterinde* 1584-1592; see *DAA,* 1950, Pt. 2, p. 13. Danish noblewomen of the 16th century did not relinquish their maiden name upon marriage.

[7] On Peter Oxe, see *DBL,* Vol. XVII (1939), pp. 547-562.

[8] Wilhelm Norlind, *Tycho Brahe. En levnadsteckning med nya bidrag belysande hans liv och verk* (Lund: Gleerup, 1970), p. 17.

[9] I. L. E. Dreyer, Ioannes Ræder and Eiler Nyström, eds., *Tychonis Brahe Dani Opera Omnia* (hereafter cited as *TBDOO*), Vol. VII (Copenhagen: Gyldendal, 1924), p. 26.

[10] *Ibid.,* Vol. VII, p. 25.

[11] *Ibid.,* Vol. VII, p. 39.

[12] *Ibid.,* Vol. XIV (1928), pp. 3-4.

[13] J. L. E. Dreyer, *Tycho Brahe. A Picture of Scientific Life and Work in the Sixteenth Century* (Edinburgh: Adam & Charles Black, 1890; reprinted New York: Dover, 1963), p. 43.

[14] Frances A. Yates has probed the relationships between French politics and intellectual life during this era in various works, including *The French Academies of the Sixteenth Century* (London: The Warburg Institute, 1947; reprinted Nendeln, Liechtenstein: Kraus, 1968); and *Giordano Bruno and the Hermetic Tradition* (New York: Vintage, 1969). At the University of Copenhagen there was no festive auditorium at that time; see William Norvin, *Københavns universitet i reformationens og orthodoxiens tidsalder,* Vol. I (Copenhagen: Gyldendal, 1937), pp. 243-245.

[15] L. Laursen, *Danmark-Norges traktater 1523-1750,* Vol. II (Copenhagen: Gad, 1912), pp. 213-260. See also Holger Rørdam, "Return bello Svetico gestarum (1563-70) series et narratio succincta, autore Mag. Andrea Severini Velleio," *Monumenta Historiae Daniae. Historiske kildeskrifter,* Vol. II (Copenhagen: Gad, 1875), pp. 163-198. Holger Rørdam, "Charles de Danzay, fransk resident ved det danske hof," *Historiske samlinger og studier,* Vol. II (Copenhagen: Gad, 1898), pp. 269-283.

[16] Rørdam, "Danzay," pp. 284, 319-324.

[17] *Ibid.,* pp. 281, 289. C. F. Bricka, *Indberetninger fra Charles de Dançay til det franske hof om forholdene i Norden 1567-1573* (Copenhagen: Reitzel, 1901), contains Danzay's dispatches; see pp. 12 and 15-18. On Peter Oxe, see Poul Colding, *Studier i Danmarks politiske historie i slutningen af Christian III.s og begyndelsen af Frederik II.s tid* (Copenhagen: Busck, 1939); see also Poul Colding, "Danmark-Lothringen 1565-66 og Peder Oxes hjemkomst," *Historisk tidsskrift,* 1944, 10th Ser., *6:* 637-659.

[18] Rørdam, "Danzay," pp. 293-297. Their earliest correspondence still extant is from 1576; see *TBDOO,* Vol. VII, p. 34, *passim.* Danzay was in Poland from the autumn of 1573 till August 1574, playing an important role in the Polish adventure of Henry of Anjou; see Rørdam, "Danzay," pp. 284-287.

[19] *TBDOO,* Vol. I (1913), p. 154, translation by Jeremiah Reedy. The oration, given on pp. 143-173, is treated at length in J.-S. Bailly, *Histoire de l'astronomie moderne depuis la fondation de l'ecole d'Alexandrie jusqu'à l'epoque de M.D.CC.XXX.,* Vol. I (Paris: Frères de Bure, 1779), pp. 429-442. See also Dreyer, *Tycho,* pp. 73-78, and Norlind, *Tycho,* pp. 53-63.

[20] *TBDOO*, Vol. I, p. 154, translation by Jeremiah Reedy. On Ramism in Denmark, see William Norvin, "Petrus Ramus og Danmark," *Lychnos*, 1943, 97-110.

[21] *TBDOO*, Vol. I, pp. 147-150 *et passim*. Kristian Peder Moesgaard, "Copernican Influence on Tycho Brahe," in Jerzy Dobrzycki, ed., *The Reception of Copernicus' Heliocentric Theory* (Dordrecht, Holland/Boston: D. Reidel, 1972), pp. 31-33.

[22] *TBDOO*, Vol. I, pp. 172-173. On the tradition of geostatic Copernicanism, see J. R. Christianson, "Copernicus and the Lutherans," *Sixteenth Century Journal*, 1973, *4, 2:* 1-10; Robert S. Westman, "The Wittenberg Interpretation of the Copernican Theory," in Owen Gingerich, ed., *The Nature of Scientific Discovery* (Washington, D.C.: Smithsonian Institution Press, 1975), pp. 393-429 and discussion, pp. 430-457; and Robert S. Westman, "The Melanchthon Circle, Rheticus, and the Wittenberg Interpretation of the Copernican Theory," *Isis*, 1975, *66:* 165-193.

[23] Ernst Zinner, *Entstehung und Ausbreitung der coppernicanischen Lehre* (Sitzungsberichte der Physikalisch-medizinischen Societät zu Erlangen, LXXIV) (Erlangen: Mencke, 1943), p. 273, see also p. 294. Reinhold's approach was also in this spirit; see Alexandre Birkenmajer, "Le commentaire inedit d'Erasme Reinhold sur le *De revolutionibus* de Nicolas Copernic," *La science au seizième siècle* (Paris: Hermann, 1960), pp. 168-178.

[24] Moesgaard, "Copernican Influence," p. 32.

[25] *TBDOO*, Vol. I, p. 172.

[26] Bjørn Kornerup, *Den danske kirkes historie*, Vol. IV (Copenhagen: Gyldendal, 1959), pp. 69-73, 138-141 *et passim*.

[27] Karl Hartfelder, *Philipp Melanchthon als Preceptor Germaniae* (Berlin: Hofmann, 1899; reprinted Nieuwkoop: De Graaf, 1964), pp. 190-197. On Niels Hemmingsen, see Oluf Friis, *Den danske litteraturs historie*, Vol. I (Copenhagen: Hirschsprung, 1945), pp. 353-356.

[28] *TBDOO*, Vol. I, p. 172.

[29] Holger Fr. Rørdam, *Kjøbenhavns universitets historie fra 1537 til 1621*, Vol. II (Copenhagen: Bianco Luno, 1872), pp. 123-139. Kornerup, *Den danske kirkes historie*, Vol. IV, pp. 131-147, is essentially dependent upon Rørdam.

[30] Holger Fr. Rørdam, "Bidrag til de filippistiske bevægelsers og til D. Niels Hemmingsens historie," *Kirkehistoriske samlinger*, 1867-68, *6:* 297-300.

[31] C. F. Wegener, *Historiske efterretninger om Anders Sørensen Vedel* [Copenhagen, 1851], pp. 75-78. It was also during these years that a great many of Hemmingsen's works were translated into English: see Lauritz Nielsen, *Dansk bibliografi 1551-1600* (Copenhagen: Gyldendal, 1933; hereafter cited as *LN*), Nos. 810, 814, 839, 868, 869, 893-897, 928, and 929; for Latin editions printed in London see Nos. 809, 813, 819, 848, and 849.

[32] Rørdam, *Universitets historie*, Vol. II, pp. 141-151. On Dybvad, see *DBL*, Vol. VI (1935), pp. 151-153; Holger Fr. Rørdam, "Efterretninger om Jørgen og Christoffer Dybvad," *Danske magazin*, 1873, 4th Ser., *2:* 107-108; and Kristian Peder Moesgaard, "How Copernicanism took Root in Denmark and Norway," in Dobrzycki, ed., *Reception*, pp. 117-119.

[33] Rørdam, *Universitets historie*, Vol. II, pp. 152-160.

[34] *TBDOO*, Vol. XIV, p. 6. See also Rørdam, *Universitets historie*, Vol. II, pp. 170-175.

[35] Niels Kaas, who was chancellor in 1573-1594, was a former pupil of Hemmingsen and had resided for four of his student years in Hemmingsen's household; see Rørdam, *Universitets historie*, Vol. II, pp. 373-396.

[36] *TBDOO*, Vol. VII, pp. 45-46.

[37] Tycho's father died in 1571, leaving an extensive estate. See his manuscript cadaster in Rigsarkivet, Copenhagen—Privatarkiv: Otte Tygesen Brahe (d. 1571), "Otte Brahes Jordebog, 17. april 1570." Of this estate I estimate that Tycho inherited something over 100 copyhold farms comprising one half of Knutstorp manor minus his mother's widow's portion, worth roughly 650 dalers per annum. See also J. R. Christianson, "Tycho Brahe and Patronage of Science 1576-1597," *American Philosophical Society, Year Book 1972* (Philadelphia: American Philosophical Society, 1973), pp. 572-573.

[38] See their correspondence in *TBDOO*, Vol. VI (1919), pp. 31-54, *et passim*.

[39] Norlind, *Tycho*, pp. 66-68, also discusses Tycho's later connections with G. F. Sagredo. On Tycho's contacts with G. A. Magini, either directly or through Tengnagel, Gellius, and Kepler, see Antonio Favaro, *Carteggio inedito di Ticone Brahe, Giovanni Keplero e de altri celebri astronomi e matematici dei secoli XVI. e XVII. con Giovanni Antonio Magini tratto dall' Archivio Malvezzi de' Medici in Bologna* (Bologna: Zanichelli, 1886).

[40] *TBDOO*, Vol. VII, p. 37. Norlind, *Tycho*, p. 343.

[41] *TBDOO*, Vol. VII, p. 25.

[42] *Ibid.,* Vol. VII, p. 27.

[43] *Ibid.,* Vol. VII, p. 28. Pratensis was born in Denmark, but his father, Philippe du Pre, had come into Denmark in 1514 with King Christian II's bride, Isabella of Habsburg, a sister of Emperor Charles V. Pratensis spent his student years abroad and held his medical degree from a French university. See Rørdam, *Universitets historie,* Vol. II, pp. 598-607.

[44] *TBDOO,* Vol. XIV, pp. 4-5; see also pp. 19-20, 23, and 102.

[45] *Ibid.,* Vol. XIV, p. 5; see also pp. 7, 15-19, 26-27, 41-43, 49, 51-52, 98-105, 125-128, 184-189, and 245.

[46] *Ibid.,* Vol. XIV, pp. 5-6.

[47] Kullan; see *ibid.,* Vol. XIV, pp. 6-7, 12-14, 21-29, 49-50, and J. R. Christianson, "Addenda to Tychonis Brahe Opera Omnia tomus XIV," *Centaurus,* 1972, *16:* 231-235, 241-242.

[48] Farms in Skåne, see *TBDOO,* Vol. XIV, pp. 8-9; see also Kullan. Nordfjord in Norway, see *TBDOO,* Vol. XIV, pp. 7-11, 14-17, 19, 32, 34-38, 48-49, 54, 62-63, 67, 97-98, 130, 139, and Christianson, "Addenda," p. 243. Chapel of the Magi, see *TBDOO,* Vol. XIV, pp. 3-4, 12-14, 24-25, 35-36, 55-60, 63-66, 68-71, 91 *et seq.,* 106, and Christianson, "Addenda," pp. 240-241.

[49] *TBDOO,* Vol. I, pp. 30-34. There is also a facsimile edition edited by F. R. Friis, *Tychonis Brahe Dani die XXIV Octobris A.D. MDCI Defuncti Operum Primitias De Nova Stella* (Copenhagen: Ioergensen, 1901); see sig. [D2v]-E3. In the year 1632 this prophecy was widely associated with King Gustavus Adolphus.

[50] *TBDOO,* Vol. I, p. 34.

[51] *Ibid.,* Vol. XIV, pp. 9 and 37-39.

[52] *Ibid.,* Vol. XIV, pp. 28, 30-31, 48, and 61-62.

[53] J. R. Christianson, "Tycho Brahe's Cosmology from the *Astrologia* of 1591," *Isis,* 1968, *59:* 313.

[54] These included King James VI of Scotland in 1590; Duke Heinrich Julius of Braunschweig-Wolfenbüttel in 1590 (both married daughters of King Frederick II); Queen Sophie of Denmark and her parents, Duke Ulrich of Mecklenburg-Güstrow and Duchess Elizabeth, in 1586; and King Christian IV of Denmark in 1592; see Dreyer, *Tycho,* pp. 138-139, 202-205 and 214-217. There were also innumerable foreign diplomats among Tycho's visitors to Hven; see Harald Ilsøe, "Gesandtskaber som kulturformidlende faktor. Forbindelser mellem Danmark og England-Skotland o. 1580-1607," *Historisk tidsskrift,* 1962, 11th Ser. *6:* 574-600.

See also Tycho's meteorological journal, which also records many visitors to Hven, in *TBDOO,* Vol. IX, pp. 39-146.

[55] Norlind, *Tycho,* pp. 93-94, 101-103, and 168-170.

[56] Troels-Lund, "Christian den fjerdes fødsel og daab," *Historiske fortællinger. Tider og tanker,* Vol. I (Copenhagen: Gyldendal, 1910), pp. 10-13 and 113-119.

[57] *TBDOO,* Vol. I, pp. 179-208. The German version, which was the one actually intended to be read by the parents, is omitted from all three of Tycho's royal horoscopes in *TBDOO;* see also Vol. I, pp. 209-280. The importance of the German section is emphasized in the manuscript horoscope for Prince Hans, where it is the only section in Tycho's own autograph (the Latin section was delegated to an amanuensis); see Dreyer, *Tycho,* p. 153, and MS, Det kongelige bibliotek, *Gammel kongelig samling 1823, 4°.*

[58] Jørgen Christoffersen Dybvad, *En nyttig Vnderuissning Om den COMET, som dette Aar 1577. in Nouembrj først haffuer ladet sig see* (Copenhagen: Laurentz Benedicht, 1578), sig. D-[D^v]. For the 1577 edition of this work, see *LN* No. 553 (the 1578 edition is *LN* No. 554). See also C. Doris Hellman, *The Comet of 1577: Its Place in the History of Astronomy* (New York: Columbia University, 1944), pp. 350-352.

[59] Dybvad, *Vnderuissning,* sig. D.

[60] *DBL,* Vol. II (1933), pp. 548-549. Ivar Bertelsen may have been Tycho's teacher of rhetoric; see J. R. Christianson, "Tycho Brahe at the University of Copenhagen, 1559-1562," *Isis,* 1967, *58:* 200.

[61] Ivar Bertelsen, *Formaning til en Christelig och alffuorlig Poenitentze* (Copenhagen: Laurentz Benedicht, 1561). *LN* No. 395.

[62] Following the introduction to King Frederick II, Dybvad's first chapter treats what a pious Christian should learn from "this gruesome comet" and runs sig. [Aii-ij^v]-C of *Vnderuissning;* the second chapter treats previous comets and runs sig. [C^v]-D; the third chapter contains Dybvad's analysis of the comet of 1577 and runs sig. D-[Diiij].

[63] Dybvad, *Vnderuissning,* sig. [Dij^v]-Diij.

[64] *Ibid.,* sig. [Diij^v]-[Diiij].

[65] *TBDOO,* Vol. IV (1922), p. 5.

[66] *Ibid.,* Vol. VII, p. 47.

[67] The manuscript is now in the Royal Library (Det kongelige bibliotek), Copenhagen, Denmark, bound with other manuscripts of Tycho Brahe's cometary ob-

servations and catalogued as *Gammel kongelig samling 1826, 4°*. Fols. 32v, 33r, 33v, 34r, 35r, 35v, and 36r are omitted from the printed version of the manuscript, *TBDOO*. Vol. XIII (1926), pp. 289-304. In the manuscript, they follow the text with which *TBDOO* concludes page 304 (fol. 33ᵛ and 34ʳ are blank). Victor E. Thoren's perceptive remarks were a great help to me in the interpretation of these sketches.

[68] Tycho summarizes this view in *TBDOO,* Vol. IV (1922), p. 382.

[69] *Ibid.,* Vol. IV, pp. 382-383. Tycho's relationship to Paracelsus was certainly not one of slavish dependence, but he did speak in laudatory terms of Paracelsus on various occasions, see, e.g., *ibid.,* Vol. VI, p. 224, or Vol. VII, pp. 169-171. Karin Figala's analysis of Tycho's approach to alchemy revealed it to be thoroughly Paracelsian; see "Tycho Brahes Elixier," *Veröffentlichungen des Forschungsinstituts des Deutschen Museums für die Geschichte der Naturwissenschaften und der Technik,* Reihe C. Quellentexte und Übersetzungen, 1972, *13:* 139-176. See also Sten Lindroth, *Paracelsismen i Sverige till 1600-talets mitt* (Uppsala: Almqvist & Wiksell, 1943), pp. 68-69 *et passim.* J. L. E. Dreyer has pointed to the Paracelsian character of Tycho's famous "hieroglyphs' of astronomy and alchemy, bearing the legends "Svspiciendo Despicio" and "Despiciendo Svspicio," which he displayed over the portals of Uraniborg and on the title page and colophon of his published works; see *TBDOO,* Vol. I, p. xi, Vol. VI, pp. 144-146, Vol. V, pp. 3 and 162. In celestial matters, Paracelsus may have been the stimulus to Tycho's rejection of the Aristotelian sphere of fire below the moon, though Tycho remained ambivalent toward Paracelsus' transposition of that element into the celestial regions; see the lengthy discussion in his letter to Christopher Rothmann, some twelve years later (Feb. 21, 1589), in *TBDOO,* Vol. VI, pp. 166-181. Tycho also recognized that Paracelsian cosmology was consistent with the evidence of the new star of 1572 and the comet of 1577, whereas Aristotle's view was not. Pratensis was a Paracelsian, and Petrus Severinus was one of the most famous interpreters of Paracelsus in that generation; both were close to Tycho in the 1570s.

[70] For his dedications, see particularly *LN* Nos. 532, 544-546, and 552.

[71] Rørdam, "Dybvad," pp. 109-110.

[72] Besides Tycho's ties with Hesse-Cassel, Venice, and the court of Emperor Rudolf II, he later had many contacts with England and Scotland; see Ilsøe, "Gesandtskaber." Likewise, Tycho's Dutch connections at a later date were numerous, but the most significant fact at this time is that at least three of his four brothers had served in armor to defend the Dutch cause; two

of them won their spurs of the Count of Schwarzburg-Rudolstadt, a brother-in-law of the Prince of Orange; and Steen Brahe was one of those who accompanied William the Silent on his first invasion of the Low Countries in 1568.

[73] Dybvad's mathematical, scientific, and theological theses, treatises, orations, and editions are listed in *LN* Nos. 479, 532-552, 678, and 987.

[74] Moesgaard, "How Copernicanism took Root," pp. 117-119.

[75] Dybvad, *Vnderuissning,* sig. [Biiij].

[76] *Ibid.,* sig. Bij.

[77] See n. 14 above. The manuscript of seventeen discourses from the Palace Academy of Henry III is now in the Royal Library in Copenhagen, according to Yates, *French Academies,* p. 107, n. 3, though she does not explain how it got there. I have not examined this manuscript.

[78] Frances A. Yates, *The Rosicrucian Enlightenment* (London/Boston: Routledge & Kegan Paul, 1972), pp. 34-35, discusses a purported meeting of princes at Lüneberg on July 17, 1586, including representatives of Navarre, Denmark, and England, with the object of forming a Protestant league of defense against the Catholic League in France. Yates notes that some scholars have associated this league or "Confederatio Militiae Evangelicae" with the origin of the Rosicrucian movement, and she states that this would be in accord with her own interpretation, but she pursues the particular matter no further. According to V. Mollerup, *Danmarks riges historie,* Vol. III, Part 2 (Copenhagen: Det nordiske forlag, 1906), p. 226, this meeting was called by King Frederick II. More central to Yates' interpretation is the role of Elizabeth, daughter of King James I of England and Anne of Denmark. Yates describes the "magical" atmosphere of Elizabeth's garden and castle in Heidelberg as "an outpost of Jacobean England, a citadel of advanced seventeenth century culture" (p. 14). Elizabeth was a granddaughter of King Frederick II of Denmark, and her mother, Anne of Denmark, maintained a rather brilliant court in England. H. D. Schepelern, *Museum Wormianum* (Odense: Wormianum, 1971), pp. 314-315, goes so far as to trace the aesthetic interests of Elizabeth's brother, King Charles I, to their mother, and he shows that similar interests were strong among the Danish descendants of King Frederick II, frequently merging with religious and arcane interests. Most striking in the present context of Rosicrucian influences is Schepelern's description, pp. 315-323 and English summary, pp. 382-383, of the tremendous labor of King Christian IV (Elizabeth's uncle) at Frederiks-

borg, where he tore down his father's great castle and rebuilt it as an immense Rosicrucian emblem in the very years when Elizabeth was living in Heidelberg.

[79] Peter J. French, *John Dee. The World of an Elizabethan Magus* (London: Routledge & Kegan Paul, 1972). Roger Howell, *Sir Philip Sidney. The Shepherd Knight* (Boston: Little, Brown, 1968). Yates, *Astraea* and *Giordano Bruno.* Thomas Keith, *Religion and the Decline of Magic* (New York: Scribner's, 1971), pp. 312-314, treats the role of astrology, but only in rather trivial matters and not in the realm of policy; his view of the clash between religion and astrology, pp. 358-370, reveals a picture in England which was quite different from that in Denmark.

[80] R. J. W. Evans, *Rudolf II and His World. A Study in Intellectual History 1576-1612* (Oxford: Clarendon Press, 1973). For a clearer sketch of the role of Tycho at the imperial court, however, see Norlind, *Tycho,* pp. 265-266 and 300-320, German summary pp. 438-441.

[81] Hellman, *Comet of 1577.*

[82] *TBDOO,* Vol. IV, pp. 379-396.

[83] This is not apparent from *TBDOO;* see n. 57 above. None of Tycho's almanacs or annual prognostications are known to be extant. On P. J. Flemløse's *Astrologia,* which Tycho had him write in response to a request from King Frederick, see Christianson, *"Astrologia,"* p. 213.

[84] Note that the diagram mentioned in the text on p. 386 is not found in either extant copy of the manuscript. If my argument is correct, it would have been in a royal presentation copy, now lost. For Dreyer's notes on this manuscript, see *TBDOO,* Vol. IV, pp. 511-512. See also Norlind, *Tycho,* pp. 127-129, and Hellman, *Comet of 1577,* pp. 122-136.

[85] Owen Gingerich, "The Astronomy and Cosmology of Copernicus," in G. Contopoulos and G. Contopoulos, eds., *Highlights of Astronomy* (Boston: Reidel, 1974), pp. 67-85. See also Owen Gingerich, "Copernicus and Tycho," *Scientific American,* Dec. 1973, *224* (6):86-11. These diagrams are in a copy of the first edition of Nicolaus Copernicus, *De revolutionibus orbium coelestium* (Nürnberg, 1543). Gingerich and Robert S. Westman have recently located two other first-edition copies of Copernicus containing annotations by Tycho. They are preparing a detailed analysis of the Tychonic materials in all three copies for future publication in *Centaurus.*

[86] Tycho specifically cites Copernicus, not Albumasur, whom Hartner saw as his inspiration; see Willy

Hartner, "Tycho Brahe et Albumasar," *La science au seizième siècle,* pp. 135-150. See also Moesgaard, "Copernican Influence," and Wilhelm Norlind, "Tycho Brahes Världssystem. Hur det tillkom och utformades," *Cassiopeia,* 1944, 55-75. By a similar process, Maestlin's studies of the comet of 1577 made him a Copernican; see Robert S. Westman, "The Comet and the Cosmos: Kepler, Mästlin and the Copernican Hypothesis," in Dobrzycki, ed., *Reception,* pp. 7-30. Bruno's Hermetic Copernicanism, on the other hand, is quite another thing as described by Yates, *Giordano Bruno,* pp. 235-247 *et passim.*

[87] Die Österreichische Nationalbibliothek, MS *Codex Vindobonensis 10.689*[32], ". . . HieZuischen hab ich durch meine obseruation den locum Cometæ gefunden Darumb achte ich das er sseij in Spera Veneris gestanden So man die gemeine Austeilung orbium Celestium nachfolgen Will. Wan Man aber Nach meinung etliche alten Philosopham Vnd Zu Vnssere Zeiten des Copernicj Vur gutt Anstehe das der ♀ Necht der Sonne vnd die Venus Rundtt vmb den Mercurio Circa Centrum Solis ire orbes haben quæ ratio non admodum absona est Veritatj etiamsi Sol prexet Copernicj habent Hypoteses non statuantur quessere in Centro Vniuersj. So Volgtt hie aus das diesser Comet sseij generiet Zuischen den Orbe ☾ vnd den Vorgenante Orbe Veneris Welchen Sie vmb die Sonne designirt. . . ."

[88] Die Österreichische Nationalbibliothek, MS *Codex Vindobonensis 10.689*[33], previous to final rewriting.

[89] Die Österreichische Nationalbibliothek, MS *Codex Vindobonensis 10.689*[33], after rewriting. See *TBDOO,* Vol. IV, p. 388.

[90] Garrett Mattingly, *The Armada* (Boston: Houghton Mifflin, 1959), pp. 172-86. In his later, major works, Tycho used the word *instauratio* to describe what he was attempting to achieve in the field of astronomy. *Cf.* Charles Webster, *The Great Instauration: Science, Medicine and Reform 1626-1660* (London: Duckworth, 1975), who argues that *instauratio* to 17th-century British puritans expressed a conviction that Christian civilization was approaching its final age, characterized by the revival of learning. Webster links his *instauratio* to the thought of Bacon, but much of it is similar to Tycho's thought in 1577; this emphasizes the urgency of investigating Bacon's connections with Tycho, which to my knowledge have never been studied in detail.

[91] E.g., John Dee, Giordano Bruno, and Emperor Rudolf II; see Yates, *Giordano Bruno,* French, *John Dee,* and Evans, *Rudolf.*

[92] A number of Scandinavian scholars have anticipated various aspects of this approach. Oskar Garstein, *Cort Aslakssøn* (Oslo: Lutherstiftelsen, 1953), pp. 51-67 *et passim,* investigated the relationship between science

and religion in Tycho's thought. Vello Helk, *Laurentius Nicolai Norvegus S.J.* (Copenhagen: Gad, 1966), probing the Counter Reformation in Scandinavia, has touched upon Tycho and his circle in several surprising contexts, see esp. pp. 287-289 and 345. Kristian Peder Moesgaard has written on Tycho and the tradition of Copernicanism in Denmark, and William Norvin on Ramism. Oluf Friis summarized Tycho's influence upon a whole era of Danish intellectual life. Troels-Lund, "Peder Oxe," *Historiske fortællinger. Tider og tanker,* 1911, *2:* 327-329, and after him, Erik Arup, *Danmarks historie,* Vol. II (Copenhagen: Hagerup, 1932), pp. 620-622 and 645-647, pointed to the affiliation between Tycho and such political figures as Peter Oxe and Niels Kaas; *cf.* Svend Cedergreen Bech, *Danmarks historie,* Vol. VI (Copenhagen: Politiken, 1963), pp. 458-472 and 496-497. Harald Ilsøe has written a splendid article on the cultural dimensions of diplomacy in Tycho's day. Wilhelm Norlind devoted a lifetime to Tychonic research and besides his monumental biography of Tycho, wrote an article on the origin of the Tychonic system, "Tycho Brahes världssystem. Hur det tillkom och utformades," *Cassiopeia,* 1944, 55-75. H. D. Schepelern did much to illuminate the transition to a new generation of Danish scientists in the years following Tycho's demise.

Victor E. Thoren (essay date 1979)

SOURCE: "The Comet of 1577 and Tycho Brahe's System of the World," in *Archives internationales d'histoire des sciences,* Vol. 29, No. 104, June-December, 1979, pp. 53-67.

[In the following excerpt, Thoren explores the development of Brahe's cosmological system after his observance of the comet of 1577 until his publication of De mundi *in 1588.]*

Although Tycho's system of the world has traditionally been associated with the comet of 1577, the connection between them has been treated by most commentators as essentially circumstantial: the two have been discussed in the same chapter because Tycho published his accounts of them in the same book, his *De mundi aetherei recentioribus phaenomenis* of 1588. Only rarely has even the logical relationship between the two—the fact that they represent parallel challenges to the cosmological assumptions of Aristotle and Copernicus—been pointed out. And the historical links between the two have never been satisfactorily explained. Not surprisingly, this problem stems in large part from the fact that neither of the two separate stories, themselves, has ever been fully elucidated. It is to the task of rectifying these deficiencies that the following study of Tycho's cosmological struggles is devoted.

Insofar as there is an identifiable beginning to Tycho's occupation with the world order, it lies in his research on the New Star of 1572. Already in the publication announcing his findings on it, he argued explicitly that the New Star contradicted the Aristotelian view of the cosmos, and suggested implicitly that comets might well do the same[1]. The comet of 1577 represented Tycho's first chance to test this hunch, and the results were every bit as interesting as Tycho had thought they might be. Moreover, since the comet was as bright as Venus and attended by a tail 22° long, it attracted so much attention as to seem almost made to order for Tycho's purposes. Of course, it guaranteed an audience for everyone else's opinion, too; and Tycho's experience with the literature on the New Star gave him a very good idea as to how close-minded and muddle-headed those opinions would be, and how difficult it would be to prevail against them among a public who tended to share these intellectual handicaps[2]. Accordingly, he seems to have conceived from the beginning a book considerably more ambitious than his ineffective work on the New Star[3], one that would stand out from its competitors in rigor, in detail, in sheer weight, if nothing else. So while he was still observing the comet he initiated observations of the sun (at winter solstice) which would provide him (after analogous ones at summer solstice)[4] with his own value for the obliquity of the ecliptic for computations involving the comet. And as soon as the comet disappeared, he began a notebook of star observations[5] so that he could determine his own co-ordinates for the various reference stars, instead of accepting the catalogue values of Copernicus. Not long thereafter he embarked on the exhaustive analysis of his observations which would comprise the first five and a half chapters of *De mundi.*

Of course, all of this took time—time which the King would begrudge, even if Tycho did not; for Tycho well knew that the King expected to have to react in some way to whatever astrological significance Tycho judged the comet to have. Since Frederick did not read Latin, anyway, Tycho composed a short tract in German for the court[6], summarizing the traditional cosmological view of comets, describing technically the impressive one everybody had recently seen, sketching the implications of its celestial path for Aristotelian theory, and discussing in a general way its probable terrestrial influence. While the details of this report are not generally significant in themselves, comparison between them and the ones published by Tycho in *De mundi* provides interesting clues regarding the development of Tycho's ideas on the comet.

The result which dwarfed all the others in significance, of course, was that the comet was indisputably *above* the moon. How far above, Tycho was not prepared to specify. But he was certain that the horizontal parallax could not have exceeded 15′, so that the comet had to be at least 230 earth radii away[7]. Since the lower bound of the moon's sphere (and hence the upper bound of terrestrial bodies) was 52 e.r., there was no room for doubt that the comet was a celestial body, contrary to the teaching of Aristotle. This finding and a number of lesser ones combined to lead Tycho to a conclusion which was almost as important as that regarding the distance of the comet. First of all, the comet had, throughout its brief existence, moved in the direction in which the planets normally move: viz., in the direction opposite to that followed nightly by the rotation of the vault of stars. This movement had for the first week carried the comet out in front of the sun very swiftly; but thereafter the elongation had crept slowly (for two weeks) up to 59° 55′, and then begun to diminish again[8]. During all this time the comet had progressively faded, suggesting that it was moving away from the earth. These data virtually cried out for an orbit circling the sun, and that is how Tycho accounted for them already in his report to King Frederick early in 1578[9].

Although these two conclusions may also be regarded as the principal themes of *De mundi,* it is remarkable how differently each was treated in the longer work. The argument for the contra-Aristotelian location of the comet Tycho presented in a detail which was unprecedented in the history of astronomy. Starting from observed distances between the comet and various reference stars[10] whose co-ordinates he re-determined himself[11], Tycho painstakingly determined successive positions for virtually every one of the thirty non-cloudy nights of the comet's duration[12]. He then rationalized these positions into a trajectory which he defined in both ecliptic and equatorial co-ordinates, by determining its intersection with and inclination to both the ecliptic and the equator. If his results are irrelevant in the present context, his methods are not. For, by making—and reporting—seven trials of each element[13], rather than the single determination which any of his predecessors would have offered, Tycho inaugurated the modern scientific practice of using redundant data and admitting scatter in his results.

By the time Tycho marshalled these elaborately derived data into geometrical proof that the comet at no time displayed any parallax, and therefore "ran its course high above the sphere of the moon in the Aether itself"[14], he was five and a half chapters along in his book. If he planned to say anything at all about his belief that the comet's spatial path circumvolved the sun, it is not obvious where he anticipated doing so. For, after establishing the supra-lunary position of the comet, he moved on to consider the physical description of the comet itself. In his German tract, Tycho had been very brief on this subject, merely mentioning that the comet's tail followed the general rule of being directed away from the sun, and using his estimate of the comet's distance to convert the angular dimensions of the head and tail to linear dimensions[15]. But what he eventually published as chapter VII of *De Mundi* is a 25-page day-by-day instantiation of the contention that,

contrary to the findings of Apian, Gemma, Fracastoro, and Cardan that comets' tails always oppose the sun, the tail of this comet was directed away from Venus[16]. Similarly, his discussion of the sizes of the head and tail involves numbers that are noticeably different[17] from these in the German tract. For these and other reasons, it is rather doubtful that Tycho wrote up this material during the winter of 1578/9, when he says he composed everything discussed so far[18]. Most likely, these findings date from sometime in the early 1580's, when Tycho resumed his work by adding a section to chapter VI (on parallax), utilizing data received from Hayek in the Fall of 1580[19]; wrote anew or recomputed most of chapter VII, using solar positions from his own theory which only became available at about the same time[20]; and added the short discussion on the size of the comet which was going to be an appendix to chapter VII[21]. At this stage, the book was done, except for the task of reviewing critically all of the other publications on the comet. These reviews were supposed to comprise chapter VIII. But they may well not have existed in any complete form even when Tycho started printing the book in 1586.

If *De Mundi* had been completed as planned, it would have been an eminently forgettable book—however much one might still wish to insist on the necessity of some such monograph to drive home the contradiction of Aristotelian cosmology embodied in the comet. Sometime during the printing, however, Tycho added the chapter depicting and describing his system of the world. Historians have unanimously recognized it as "the most important in the whole book"[22], both in personal significance to Tycho and historical impact on his successors. In spite of its importance, however, or perhaps *because* of it, no one has ever thought to investigate the logical or historical relationship of this chapter to the rest of the book[23]. As we shall see when we return to this question later, answers to it are an important part of the story of Tycho's path to his world system.

In view of the fact that the Tychonic system is nothing but the rather trivial-looking inversion of the Copernican system . . . , it is rather startling to contemplate the fact that it bears Tycho's name, and that even he dated his conception of it to about 1583[24], some forty years after the publication of *De revolutionibus.* Actually, however, recent scholarship has shown that he was not the only one, and probably not even the first one, to grope toward what we now call the Tychonic system. Right from the publication of *De revolutionibus,* various mathematicians seem to have recognized, with varying degrees of clarity, that Copernican astronomy was by no means inextricably tied to Copernican cosmology. For many of them, no doubt, the theory was something in the nature of a black box, whose internal machinations they neither understood nor cared to understand as long as its predictions were better than the ones gener-

Postage stamp showing Brahe's observatory, Uraniborg; the star he discovered in 1572; and his quadrant, a tool used for measuring the altitude of stars.

ated by the Ptolemaic theory[25]. Others were so thoroughly imbued with the traditional Ptolemaic cosmology that the best they could do was recognize that the old numbers associated with that cosmology might very profitably be re-established from the technical researches of Copernicus[26]. But already in the first generation after Copernicus, Erasmus Reinhold and Gemma Frisius made statements which suggest that they understood fully the geometrical possibility of utilizing Copernican models for a geostatic cosmology[27]. And Tycho had conceived the project in a fairly definite form by the time he gave his lectures on astronomy at the University of Copenhagen in the Fall of 1574[28]. Unfortunately, however, he seems initially to have chosen the less felicitous of the two possible ways of conceiving the project. Thus, instead of regarding the Copernican system as essentially correct, and just looking for a way to eliminate its unsatisfactory feature, the motion of the earth; Tycho tended to regard the Ptolemaic system as basically correct, and sought for a way to remove its objectionable feature, the equant. The latter task was no more difficult than the former. The Copernican mechanism for representing orbital irregularities . . . could simply be substituted for the Ptolemaic equivalent. . . . Presumably,

therefore, in his lectures of 1574, "expounding the motions of the planets according to the models and parameters of Copernicus, but reducing everything to the stability of the earth", so as to avoid "both the mathematical absurdity of Ptolemy and the physical absurdity of Copernicus", Tycho was working with a [new] generalized planetary mechanism. . . . [29]

At this time he probably still conceived of the larger picture of the universe in completely Ptolemaic terms; i.e., as a collection of more or less independent sets of spheres . . . [30]. Sometime in the next three years, however, he took the fundamental step toward the Tychonic System—putting planets in orbits around the sun. The evidence is a bit ambiguous because both Tycho's statement of the proposition and his commitment to it were very limited. The context was his report to the King that the great comet probably moved in the sphere of Venus. While reminding the King where the sphere of Venus was located, he mentioned briefly for the sake of completeness that some people not implausibly imagined that Mercury and Venus circle the sun[31]. Given the statement itself, however, and the fact that Tycho immediately rebutted the proposition that the earth would also have to be moving in such a scheme, it is difficult not to take his citation seriously; particularly since he is known to have picked up on his travels in 1575 a book which depicted precisely that (Capellan) arrangement of the inferior planets[32]. All that really appears to be debatable is the question of whether he had yet invisioned the possibility that the idea could be applied to the superior planets, as well[33]. And to this, the answer seems clearly negative. Historical statements by Tycho consistently point to a period in 1583/4 as the date of origin of his system[74]. If these references can have any meaning at all, they must surely apply to the instant at which the beauty of inverting the entire Copernican scheme first flashed across his mind. For, as it turned out, catching a glimpse of the inversion was only half of Tycho's struggle toward the Tychonic System.

Although it is difficult to resurrect the ontology encapsulated in medieval and renaissance references to the celestial spheres, there can be no doubt that, in the second half of the 16th century, at least, intellectuals in general and Tycho Brahe in particular believed that something real existed in the heavens to carry the planets through their appointed rounds[34]. The objections raised by such people as Maestlin, Magini, Craig, and Praetorius to the notion that two such spheres might be conceived to intersect[35] could be cited as strong suggestions of Tycho's reaction to the proposition, if they were necessary. In fact, however, Tycho confessed that he initially "could not bring myself to allow this ridiculous penetration of the orbs, so that for some time, this, my own discovery, was suspect to me"[36]. What was at stake, for all of them, was the fact that the Tychonic System required an intersection of the orbits of Mars and the sun. The fact that the orbits of Mercury and Venus would have to intersect the sun's in exactly the same way seems to have escaped everyone. But, whatever the illogicalities involved, the one required intersection was enough to ensure that it would take more than the flash of insight which inspired the system, to make Tycho a believer in the system. It is this additional input which ties Tycho's system to his work on the comet of 1577.

Sometime after he did the bulk of his own write-up on the comet, Tycho wrote a final chapter describing and criticizing the findings of other commentators on it. Having seen his earlier findings on the New Star overwhelmed by a flood of ill-founded proclamation, he wanted this time to distinguish his conclusions by exposing the incompetence of those who differed with him. Of course, pragmatic polemics demanded that he also publicize the opinions of those who agreed with him. And among these was Michael Maestlin, whose careful and perceptive discussion of the New Star had induced Tycho to search eagerly for his remarks on the comet[37]. Maestlin's approach to the comet was very

similar to what Tycho's had been, but included a plotting of daily *distances* of the comet, as well as its various angular co-ordinates. While composing his generally laudatory, but hair-splittingly critical discussion of Maestlin's results, Tycho noticed that these distances ran from 155 earth radii—three times the distances of the moon—upward past the sun to 1495 earth radii[38]: right through the Ptolemaic spheres of Venus and Mercury. If the comet had really behaved thus, there could be no solid spheres—and therefore no reason why the orbit of Mars could not intersect the orbit of the sun. When similar computations yielded similar results (173 to 1733 earth radii)[39] from his own data, all that stood in the way of the Tychonic system was the vexed question of parallax.

Just how vulnerable the Copernican System was on the subject of parallax is generally overlooked. Of course, the fact that stellar parallax could not be detected is notorious, even if the enormity of explaining it away by expanding the stellar sphere appropriately and successively for ten generations is not generally noted. But there was another kind of parallax that looked as if it should be even more accessible, planetary parallax. It stemmed from the fact that everyone until Kepler accepted a parallax value of 3′ for the sun[40]. Obviously, such a value implied an even larger figure for the inferior planets. But since they were inferior both on the Ptolemaic and Copernican schemes, the project of checking their parallax closely was not an exciting one. For Mars, however, the incentive was considerable; for while Ptolemy made it a truly superior planet—one that was always above the sun—Copernicus placed it "below" the sun at opposition, at a distance that should have given it a parallax of about 4½′. It is hard to imagine a more obvious test situation, and Tycho looked into it during the winter of 1582-3[41], at the first opposition to occur after the large instruments began to issue from his shop. Not surprisingly, in view of the fact that he was measuring a quantity which never exceeds ½′, he did not find the requisite parallax. As he duly reported in a letter to Brucaeus in the spring of 1584[42], therefore, it was clear that the Copernican System was disproved.

Exactly what the status of the Tychonic system was at this time has been the subject of much discussion, beginning with Tycho himself. In several letters written well after the fact, he alludes vaguely (and variously) to the period 1583-4 as the time of origin of his system. Unfortunately, however, any determination of the parallax of Mars which ruled out the Copernican system, also ruled out its inverse, the Tychonic system. So if the Copernican system was untenable when Tycho wrote to Brucaeus, so was the Tychonic. Norlind sought to resolve the problem by accepting Tycho's statements that he had the system by the Fall of 1584, and assuming that Tycho must somehow have reversed his finding on the parallax issue in the interim[43]. But while

Tycho obviously had to find a way to reverse his parallax determination sooner or later, there are three reasons for doubting that he did it mid-1584: the system of the world published by the nemesis of Tycho's later life, Nicolas Reymers Ursus, a diagram drawn for some computations made after the Spring of 1585, and the chronology of his write-up of the last chapters of *De Mundi.*

In the Fall of 1584, as the story was later told by an outraged Tycho to anyone who would listen[44], an ambitious but unscrupulous mathematician turned up at Uraniborg in the company of Tycho's old friend and eventual brother-in-law, Eric Lange. Whether because he seemed just a bit too clever, or a bit too presumptuous, Tycho became sufficiently distrustful of him first to exclude him from his conversation with the other guests, and then to search and expel him from Hven when he caught him snooping around in the library. Although Reymers and Tycho kept the same intellectual company[45], and were almost bound to meet at some time or other, their paths crossed only that once. How expensive the encounter had been for Tycho, he did not find out until late 1588, after he had completed *De Mundi* and sent copies of it, containing his system of the world, to his friends. First from an acquaintance of Ranzov's and then from Rothmann, he learned that Reymers, in a book published that same year[46], had printed the same system . . . almost.

It is unnecessary here to go into Tycho's reaction to the situation and the way in which he subsequently compounded whatever loss he actually suffered, by attempting frantically in later years to punish Reymers for plagiarism. What is important is the almost irrational intensity of Tycho's conviction that he had been plagiarized. For, while Reymers' system bore a general resemblance to Tycho's, it was different in two respects. The first was in utilizing a rotating earth to account for the diurnal motion. This was a matter of taste, as much as anything else. Tycho did not believe that the earth was rotating, but would admit privately, at least, that such a phenomenon was conceivable[47]. The second was an orbit for Mars that totally enclosed— did not intersect—the orbit of the sun. This was impossible. As Tycho told several correspondents in the next couple of years, publishing such a scheme was a confession of incompetence, because it simply could not reproduce the gross synodic phenomena of Mars, its stations and retro-gradations[48]. Yet, in virtually the same dip of the pen, Tycho was accusing Reymers of having stolen the scheme from him—but, of course, from a diagram that had been mis-drawn.

But was the drawing found by Reymers a defective one, in the sense Tycho was implying? If so, if Tycho really had his system by that time, one would surely expect any diagram of the theory of Mars subsequently drawn by him to be drawn according to the system.

Yet, as Jones and Moesgaard have both noted, . . . [it was not so drawn. Instead he used one labeled] "Inversion of the Copernican Hypothesis". . . .[49] Much more curiously, he had not yet made plans to publish his new system—the scientific result which he undoubtedly regarded as the most important of his career—in *De Mundi.*

To take first things first, it is necessary to recall briefly the role of Maestlin's orbit for the comet, in the dissolution of the spheres. While the chapter in which the discussion of Maestlin appears could obviously have been written, altered, and re-written any number of times, the fact is that all the signs point to a very late composition. The discussion of the Landgrave's observations which begins the chapter was written from information which only became available to Tycho after mid-1586[50]. And there are subsequent references to the Landgrave in the critiques not only of Maestlin, but of several other observers in the hundred-odd pages following Maestlin[51]. When this lengthy chapter was being written, it was intended as the eighth and last chapter of *De Mundi.* There is actually extant a printed title-quarto for the book whose table of contents describes eight chapters in some detail without saying anything about either the table of distances or Tycho's system[52]. In fact, the printing had probably advanced past chapter II, before Tycho made the decision to insert his world system; for an extended *additio authoris* appended to that chapter, claiming that all "excepting only the last chapter" had been written "nine years ago" is contradicted by an equally explicit statement in connection with Tycho's system, to the effect that it had been thought out four years ago[53].

The simplest way of reconciling all this evidence—the denial of parallax to Brucaeus in 1584, the diagram Tycho admits that Reymers found a few months later, the diagram accompanying Tycho's computations for Mars in 1585, and the lateness of the decision to publish the system of which he was so manifestly proud— is to assume that Tycho only reconciled himself to his system at a very late date. The later one supposes it to have happened, the more of these problems one solves.

Presumably, Tycho actually did first "see" his system in the period around 1583 to which he subsequently refers its origin on several occasions—including one written *before*[54] he knew he had to protect his priority from Reymers. Unfortunately, at the very time he glimpsed the system, he saw that it was impossible! How many hours he must have stared at the geometry looking for a means of escape. For if he was not prepared to go so far as Copernicans did to retain the aesthetic sense of unity and simplicity which in the 16th century constituted the sole grounds for taking the motion of the earth seriously, neither was he willing to abandon what he had labored so long to achieve. At the same time, however, the intersection was so offensive that Tycho could not even bring himself to depict it—certainly not after the failure to find parallax for Mars had confirmed his instincts. Until he resolved that question, therefore, he had drawn the diagram published by Reymers—the one seen by Reymers in the Fall of 1584.

The difference, of course, was that Tycho knew enough not to publish the system in that form. In fact, it could not even be used "internally" on Hven for any serious purpose: hence the inverted Copernican diagram for Mars in 1585. Sometime after mid-1586, with the printing of **De Mundi** already in progress, Tycho finally sat down to compose (no doubt from extensive notes for much of the material) what would turn out to be the last half of the book. In the process of treating Maestlin, he seized on the plot of distances printed well into the tract, which he had either not noticed, or, more likely, not attached any special significance to, at his first reading, because he had not yet reached his inversion in 1579[55]. Seven years later, however, the pieces would have fallen into place quickly. By mid-January, 1587, they had. Letters written at that time to Rothman and the Landgrave contain Tycho's first references to his disbelief in the existence of planetary spheres, and his belief that Mars showed more parallax than the sun[56]. Any residual qualms over this latter reversal of opinion were resolved a month later, when he conducted a final quick trial for parallaxes of Mars. If the results are not exemplary of Tycho's best work[57], they must be explained away in *any* account, and are at least as understandable as the product of excitement and relative haste in 1587, as they can be on any other assumption. Even before this last trial, Tycho must have made up his mind to include the System in his book on the comet, not only because he would have regarded it as too noteworthy to omit, but because his path to it had been intimately associated with his deliberations on the comet for nine years[58].

In marked contrast to the misfortune which would attend the decision to make a similar insertion into the **Progymnasmata** a few years later, the consequences of publishing the Tychonic System in **De Mundi** were uniformly happy. In fact, it is very doubtful that the system would now be called "Tychonic" if Tycho had been just a bit faster in getting his book printed[59], or a bit slower in developing his thoughts, or a bit more cautious about altering his manuscript. Even as it was, the priority question was a ticklish one[60]. Because Tycho had been depicting the system in 1584 in the form in which Reymers published it, he could be morally certain that Reymers had, indeed, plagiarized it. But he apparently did not feel that he could be entirely candid about the situation. If a complete explanation might assure the branding of Reymers as a plagiarist (something that Tycho never actually managed to do[61]), it would be a very risky business, requiring not only an extensive exposition of the crucial technical difference

between the two schemes, but an elaborate explanation as to how Tycho himself had happened to be using the untenable one in 1584. If all of his argumentation proved unpersuasive, Tycho's confession would not only have been in vain, but might actually leave Reymers with some kind of priority. Fortunately, Tycho himself tended to refer the genesis of his system to the time when he first saw how all the planetary theories could be put together in the inverted Copernican scheme, rather than the time when he finally succeeded in rationalizing the intersection of Mars orbit that was required by the scheme. Even in his publication of the system, therefore, he had mentioned discovering it "four years ago". Thus, when he learned of Reymers' pretensions, it was only natural that he would refer his discovery back to the parallax investigations of 1582-3, and patch the remaining hole by claiming that Reymers had found a faulty diagram. In the midst of such considerations, it can scarcely be remarkable that he never got around to relating the interaction between his thoughts on the comet of 1577 and the evolution of his system of the world.

Notes

[1] Brahe; Vol. I, pp. 27-8: hereafter cited in the form I; 27-8.

[2] Tycho's concern is demonstrated by the fact that he later issued a second publication on the New Star, *Astronomiae Instauratae Progymnasmata,* which contained 300 pages of review and rebuttal of the writings of his comtemporaries: III; 5-299.

[3] For an independent judgment on the lack of impact of Tycho's first publication, see Hellman (1963, 1964).

[4] X; 52-3, 55, 59.

[5] X; 69.

[6] This pamphlet, printed in IV; 381-96, was only discovered during the collection of materials for Tycho's *Opera Omnia.* Its true rationale, not understood by either Dreyer or Norlind, has recently been explained by Christianson (1978).

[7] IV; 387.

[8] See IV; 177-9 for an idealized daily tabulation of the comet's elongations.

[9] IV; 388. Actually, the passage is so vague that Tycho's conception is far from clear. But a contemporary drawing disregarded by Dreyer displays his intention unambiguously. See the drawing in Christianson (1978), p. 125, and variant readings of the cited passage on p. 129.

[10] IV; 11-20. These observations do not generally agree with the raw measurements found in XIII; 288-303, because of corrections Tycho had to make for the optical parallaxes of his cross-staff and sextant (see Thoren (1973)).

[11] IV; 21-32.

[12] IV; 38-69.

[13] IV; 70-78.

[14] IV; 83.

[15] IV; 386, 9.

[16] IV; 135-54 (original pagination, 158-184). The orientation from Venus arose from Tycho's faulty inclination: see Delambre (1821;222). Tycho later came to believe that the phenomenon was some kind of illusion or special effect of perspective (IV; 175: VI; 171).

[17] IV; 171-2.

[18] IV; 34.

[19] IV; 107-134. For the post-1580 dating, see VII; 59. The work was probably done before late 1583, when Tycho discovered that the 55° 53′ latitude he had been using for Hven was too low because of atmospheric refraction (IV; 108, 127, 131-2).

[20] VII; 160.

[21] IV; 497. See further discussion below.

[22] Dreyer (1890): 167.

[23] Dreyer *(ibid.)*, for example, assumed that the entire book was written in 1587.

[24] IV; 155-6; V; 115: VI; 179: VII; 199: VIII; 205.

[25] Insofar as its predictions were better, however, they were by virtue of improved (up-dated) constants rather than inherently superior theories. See Price (1959), Gingerich (1975), and Neugebauer (1968).

[26] Caspar Peucer seems actually to have performed this "translation" sometime well before 1568, when Conrad Dasypodius published the results without knowing who their author was: Gingerich (1973; 59-60). Praetorius fully subscribed to the same goals: Westman (1975: 293ff.).

[27] Reinhold may well have actually conceived the scheme before he died in 1553: see analyses of his manuscript commentary on *De Revolutionibus* by Jones (1965; 292-3) and Gingerich (1973; 51, 58-9).

[28] I; 172-3.

[29] *Ibid.* See further discussion below, and Tycho's diagram on V; 284.

[30] For further details, see Hartner (1964) and Goldstein (1967).

[31] IV; 388. See also Tycho's drawings of the orbit in his manuscript, as per reference at end of note 9, above.

[32] Westman (1975; 322-4).

[33] Tycho's travels in 1575 carried him to Saalfeld, where he was given access to Erasmus Reinhold's papers (III; 213), and might thus have seen a diagram or description of Reinhold's thoughts (see note 27, above).

[34] Donahue (1975).

[35] IV; 474-6: VIII; 206: Westman (1975; 299-301).

[36] VII; 130. Swerdlow (1973; 471-8) has argued plausibly that Copernicus arrived at the same intellectual dilemma, and (lacking the "evidence" found by Tycho) chose to put the earth in motion. For more argument on the subject, see *Archives Internationale d'Histoire des Sciences:* 1975; 82-92 and 1976; 108-58. Tycho certainly thought Copernicus subscribed to literal spheres (III; 173).

[37] IV; 207-38: VII; 48, 50, 52.

[38] *Observatio & demonstratio cometae aetherei, qui anno* 1577. *et* 1578. *constitutio in sphaera veneris, apparuit, . . .* (1578), 52-3.

[39] IV; 177-9. On the distances to the various Ptolemaic spheres, see note 30, above.

[40] For a review of the origin of the 3′ value, see Henderson (1975).

[41] X; 174-8, 243-9, 283-8. Tycho would conduct other tests later (see below), and even look at Venus because of its partially supra-solar orbit in Copernican system (XI; 195-8).

[42] VII; 80.

[43] While all commentators have followed *Dreyer* (179) in noting the statement to Brucaeus, Norlind (1944) was the first to try to build any substantial case on it.

[44] VI; 179: VII; 135, 149, 200, 321, 387: VIII; 47.

[45] Reymers had been patronized by Ranzov since 1580, travelled with Lange in 1584, appeared at Cassel in 1586, later met (and impressed very favorably) Hayek

and Kepler at Prague, and even won appointment as imperial mathematician to Rudolph II.

[46] VII; 135, 385: VI; 157. On Reymers, see Jones (1964; 108 ff.).

[47] VII; 80: VIII; 45-6. Tycho's principal disciple, Longomontanus, would later adopt what has come to be called the semi-Tychonic system, involving a rotating earth.

[48] VII; 149, 200-1, 388: VIII; 47.

[49] See Jones (1964; 35-6) and Moesgaard (1973; 47), and V; 284. On 286, 7, Tycho refers to it as his "novam Hypothesin".

[50] VI; 48 ff.: IV; 182.

[51] There are four references to the Landgrave's observations in the critique of Maestlin, and half a dozen scattered in the subsequent discussion—a considerable amount of interpolating to do for no obvious reason if the write-up of the Landgrave was simply inserted at the front of a completed chapter. In addition, it is worth noting that Tycho devoted observing time during 1587 to the reference stars used by Maestlin and Hayek (XI; 224-5, 30) so that he could show how erroneous their Copernican co-ordinates were (IV; 217-8, 264).

[52] IV; 491, 7. Tycho says on IV; 174, that his table of distances was derived after chapter VII, on the tail of the comet, was written.

[53] IV; 34, 155-6.

[54] IV; 155-6. Note the rationale already given above for conducting the parallax test—to adjudicate between Ptolemy and Copernicus. In fact, such a test makes little sense for the Tychonic System until the *intersection* of Mars' orbit can be tolerated.

[55] Tycho first received a copy of Maestlin in 1579: VII; 50, 52.

[56] VI; 88, 70.

[57] XI; 181-7. See similar attempts for Venus on 195-8. Actually, given the astronomy (refraction) and trigonometry of the situation, it would not seem to have been at all difficult to expand a relatively minor observational uncertainty into the requisite parallax—especially if one were looking for it as eagerly as Tycho surely was in 1587. Kepler's explanation (*Dreyer;* 179) of the parallax as a mix-up between Tycho and one of his calculators on observations of the opposition of 1582-3 is deficient in two respects. First, the calculations could have been done anytime *after* the event;

and second, publication of the *Opera Omnia* showed that the anomalous calculation was done by Tycho, himself: X; 283-6.

[58] In September 1588, after *De Mundi* was out and Tycho was just beginning to get feedback on it, he wrote a lengthy letter to Caspar Peucer, in which he provided the most nearly complete account of the genesis of his system that is available (VII; 129-30). Allowing for a bit of poetic license on the timing of his parallax *computations,* it outlines the one just given *in extenso*. First the parallax test on Mars to decide between the accounts of Ptolemy and Copernicus (lines 8-26). According to Tycho, exhaustive trials showed a *greater* parallax for Mars, and thus tended to favor the Copernican model. Although he refers these tests to the opposition of 1582-3, he is candid enough to mention that he confirmed the preference of the phenomena for Copernicus by a special trial on Venus, around the 24th of February, 1587! So if his chronology is not perfectly consistent with the evidence available, it at least shows signs that Tycho was uncertain about the parallax issue right up to 1587 (26-34). Given the tendency of the appearances to deny Ptolemy, and the manifest absurdity of imagining the earth to move, there was nothing else to do but to find some alternative hypothesis. At first it seemed impossible, but finally it came to him (34-40). And yet, his inspiration had one flaw in it—that the orb of Mars had to intersect the orb of the sun in two places. Because he still subscribed to the notion that there were real orbs in the sky, his system remained suspect to him for some time (6-13). Only when he had examined the motions and parallaxes of comets did he realize that they ruled out the existence of those orbs (13-21).

[59] Thus, the problem of obtaining paper for the book which figures prominently in his correspondence in 1587-8 and ultimately induced him to construct his own paper mill on Hven, turned out to be a blessing in disguise.

[60] In more ways than one! By Tycho's own testimony (IV; 159: VII; 130), his system absolutely depended on the destruction of the solid spheres, which, in turn, rested on the distances derived by Tycho from his orbit for the comet of 1577. Both internal evidence and Tycho's own testimony show that those distances were obtained after Tycho saw Maestlin's scheme (see footnotes 19, 52, 55), and after he had written up his own analysis of the comet's path. We therefore have the spectacle of Tycho borrowing Maestlin's spatial conception of the orbit, without giving any credit to him, but then prosecuting Reymers relentlessly for borrowing his (admittedly more significant) system of the world. Delambre and Westman have both suggested that Tycho borrowed from Maestlin, but for different reasons. Delambre (1821; 223) thought the similarity of Tycho's and Maestlin's inclinations (29° 13' and 28° 58') and

nodes (8ˢ 21°) was "un hasard assez remarquable", because he did not note that the results were standard—that Schultz got an inclination of 29° 36′ (IV; 296), and that he, Roselin, and Hayek got 8ˢ 21° for the node (IV; 251, 266). Westman (1972; 25) saw the heliocentric orbit as too similar for coincidence. But several drawings by Tycho on his manuscript observations (Christiansón [1978; 124-5]) show that he reached this conception long before he saw Maestlin's treatise.

[61] Both *Dreyer* (185) and Norlind (114) considered the case unproved. Jones (1964; 113 ff.) examined the pertinent facts and assertions in detail, and concluded that there could not be a reasonable doubt of his guilt.

Bibliography

Brahe, Tycho, *Tychonis Brahe Opera Omnia,* ed. J. L. E. Dreyer, 15 vols., Hauniae, 1913-1929.

Christianson, John R., "Tycho Brahe's German Treatise on the Comet of 1577: A Study in Science and Politics", *Isis;* vol. 70 (1979), pp. 110-140.

Delambre, J.-B. J., *Histoire de l'astronomie moderne* (Vol. I); Paris, 1821.

Donahue, William H., "The Solid Planetary Spheres in Post-Copernican Natural Philosophy", in Westman (1975), pp. 244-275.

Dreyer, J. L. E., *Tycho Brahe: A Picture of Scientific Life and Work in the Sixteenth Century.* Edinburgh, 1890, 1963.

Gingerich, Owen, "The Role of Erasmus Reinhold and the Prutenic Tables in the Dissemination of Copernican Theory", *Studia Copernicana,* vol. 6 (1973), pp. 43-62.

———, "'Crisis' versus Aesthetic in the Copernican Revolution", *Vistas in Astronomy,* vol. 17 (1975), pp. 85-93.

Goldstein, Bernard R., "The Arabic Version of Ptolemy's Planetary Hypotheses", *Transactions of the American Philosophical Society,* Vol. 57 (1967), pp. 1-55.

Hartner, Willy, "Tycho Brahe et Albumasar", in *La science au seizieme siecle* (Paris, 1960), pp. 137-50.
Hellman, C. D., "Was Tycho Brahe as Influential as He Thought?", *British Journal for the History of Science,* Vol. I (1963), pp. 295-324.

———, "The Gradual Abandonment of the Aristotelian Universe", in *Mélanges Alexandre Koyre* (Paris, 1964), pp. 283-93.

Henderson, Janice, "Erasmus Reinhold's Determination of the Distance of the Sun from the Earth", in Westman (1975), pp. 108-129.

Jones, Christine, *The Geoheliocentric Planetary System: Its Development and Influence in the Late Sixteenth and Seventeenth Centuries.* Cambridge University Doctoral Dissertation, 1964.

(Jones) Schofield, Christine, "The Geoheliocentric Mathematical Hypothesis in Sixteenth-Century Planetary Theory", *The British Journal for the History of Science;* vol. 2 (1965), pp. 290-6.

Moesgaard, K. P., "Copernican Influence on Tycho Brahe", *Studia Copernicana,* V (1972). [Published also as *The Reception of Copernicus' Heliocentric Theory:* ed. Jerzy Dobrzycki, (1973)], pp. 31-55.

Neugebauer, Otto, "On the Planetary Theory of Copernicus", *Vistas in Astronomy,* vol. 10 (1968), pp. 89-103.

Norlind, Wilhelm, *Tycho Brahe: En Levnadsteckning.* Lund, 1970.

———, "Tycho Brahes Världssystem: Hur det tillkom och utformades", *Cassiopeia* (1944), pp. 55-75.

Price, Derek J. De S., "Contra-Copernicus: A critical re-estimation of the mathematical planetary theory of Ptolemy, Copernicus, and Kepler", in *Critical Problems in the History of Science* (Marshall Clagett, ed)., 1959, pp. 197-218.

Swerdlow, Noel, "The Derivation and First Draft of Copernicus' Planetary Theory: A Translation of the Commentariolus with Commentary", *Proceedings of the American Philosophical Society,* Vol. 117 (1973), pp. 423-512.

Thoren, V. E., "New Light on Tycho's instruments", *Journal for the History of Astronomy,* IV (1973), pp. 25-45.

Westman, Robert S., "The Comet and the Cosmos: Kepler, Mästlin, and the Copernican Hypothesis" [Published also as *The Reception of Copernicus' Heliocentric Theory,* ed. Jerzy Dobrzycki, (1973), pp. 7-30].

———, *The Copernican Achievement,* 1975.

Edward Rosen (essay date 1981)

SOURCE: "In Defense of Tycho Brahe," in *Archive for History of Exact Sciences,* Vol. 24, 1981, pp. 257-65.

[*In the following essay, Rosen argues that Brahe was not the annotator of the Prague copy of Nicolaus*

Copernicus's De revolutionibus, *as some have contended.*]

Nicholas Copernicus' On the Revolutions of the Heavenly Spheres, *in Six Books (Basel Edition) with Annotations Written by the Hand of Tycho Brahe*[1] was published in facsimile (Prague, 1971), as volume XVI, Editio cimelia Bohemica (cited hereafter as "Cimelia"). On Cimelia's title page an unidentified hand wrote: "Property of the Imperial College of the Society of Jesus in Prague, in the year 1642."[2] The same hand added, just below: "From the Library and Scrutiny of Tycho."[3] On the flyleaf preceding the title page a different hand pointed out: "Observe: There are present marginal notes written by Tycho Brahe's own hand."[4] At the top of this flyleaf a third hand wrote some entries, which were ignored by Cimelia, although they throw valuable light on the history of this copy and will be considered later on.

In a brochure accompanying the facsimile, Cimelia conceded that the Jesuit attribution of its marginal notes to Brahe was "not entirely free of possible doubt."[5] Nevertheless, it came down on the affirmative side, maintaining that

> Tycho Brahe is really the author of these notes . . . [W]e have the possibility of judging the handwriting . . . [E]ssentially it is like the writing in well-known and undoubted relics of Tycho's manuscripts.[6]

But Cimelia did not document this asserted essential similarity by presenting samples of the handwriting of Tycho and the annotator side by side. Yet this very presentation had already been made (inadvertently) by *Astronomy in Czechoslovakia from its Early Beginning to Present Times,*[7] pages 90 and 91. Page 90 shows Cimelia, folio 75r, with notes in all four margins. Page 91 shows page 268 of the copy of an edition of Ptolemy (Basel, 1551), which was bought by Brahe in Copenhagen for two dollars on 30 November 1560,[8] with his notes in the left margin. One need not be an expert paleographer to see at a glance that Tycho's handwriting is "essentially" different from the handwriting in Cimelia. Yet this difference was not recognized by *Astronomy in Czechoslovakia,* which attributed to Tycho the annotations in Cimelia.

Cimelia also claimed that the

> extensive commentary by Tycho Brahe makes it possible to judge in detail how Brahe's relation toward Copernicus' views was formed.[9]

To test Cimelia's claim, let us look at the obliquity of the ecliptic. Copernicus says that "in our time it is found not greater than 23° 28½'".[10] In Cimelia, folio 65v, this value is repeated in the left margin by the annotator, who accepts a steady decrease in the obliquity of the ecliptic from 23° 52' in the time of Aristarchus to 23° 28' in his own time: "At this time [it is] 23° 28' 0"." Brahe, however, states that "Now, after the passage of several years with the aid of many instruments and by the use of great care, I have found this to be 23° 31½'."[11] Evidently, Brahe is not the annotator.

Looking back at previous students of this subject, Cimelia declared:

> Absolutely no one of the relatively numerous experts in historical science and bibliography who have written about this book has raised the slightest objection to the authenticity of Brahe's commentary.[12]

Thus, the Jesuit ascription in 1642 of the annotations in Cimelia to Brahe was accepted by the historian of the Prague University library, Joseph Adolph Hanslik.[13] In commemorating the tercentenary of Brahe's death, Studnička exclaimed: "A Copernicus annotated by a Brahe will not be found again."[14] This prediction was quoted with approval by Bořivoj Prusík, who remarked that from the annotations

> one sees what position Brahe took with regard to particular views of Copernicus . . . How closely Brahe studied Copernicus' work and wanted to study it further is shown by the large amount of blank paper which is bound into the volume.[15]

Agreement with the previous writers was expressed by Richard Kukula, director of the Prague University library from 1897 to 1918,[16] Wilhelm Prandtl,[17] Flora Kleinschnitzová,[18] and Emma Urbánková.[19] This long string of those who accepted the Jesuit ascription ignored the well-informed judgment of the distinguished biographer of Brahe and editor of his correspondence and cometary observations, Frederik Reinholdt Friis, who said about Cimelia:

> This copy is completely provided on nearly every page with added notes and corrections, but these could not be additions by the astronomer [Brahe], as has been assumed heretofore.[20]

Cimelia's claim that its annotations are Brahe's collapses because their handwriting and contents are not his, as was recognized by an outstanding authority on Tycho.

Shortly after the publication of Cimelia, annotations written by the same hand and conveying similar content were discovered by Owen Gingerich in the Vatican Library's Ottoboniano Latino #1902, a copy of the first edition (Nuremberg, 1543) of Copernicus' *Revolutions.*[21] Although this is a printed book, it was grouped by the Vatican Library with the manuscripts on account of its numerous marginal notes and supplementary handwritten sheets. Accepting Cimelia's claims at face value, Gingerich hailed Ottoboniano Latino #1902 as "probably the most important Tycho manuscript in existence."[22]

Like Cimelia, Ottoboniano Latino #1902 has extra sheets bound in with its printed pages. But unlike Cimelia's extra sheets, which remained blank, Ottoboniano Latino #1902's thirty supplementary sheets were written on.[23] The first two, dated 27 January 1578, contain diagrams of the cosmos according to Copernicus,[24] with the earth treated as a planet revolving around the sun, which is stationary at the center of the universe. Later on, however, the annotator devised a "Theory of the Three Outer Planets Adjusted to a Stationary Earth," and proclaimed that "This new system of hypotheses was discovered by me on 13 February 1578."[25] In those two and a half weeks the annotator shifted from a Copernican to a non-Copernican stance, from the earth as a planet in motion to a motionless earth.

Believing that Ottoboniano Latino #1902 is "Tycho's personal copy" of Copernicus' *Revolutions,* Gingerich maintained that "Tycho's notes show how he evolved his non-Copernican model."[26] Acknowledging that there is a chronological difficulty here, since Brahe "did not establish the Tychonic system until around 1583, five years after he drew these diagrams," Gingerich added: "I can only suppose that these five years were an important time of maturing"[27] from 1578 to 1583.

In the Tychonic system, Brahe had the three outer planets (Saturn, Jupiter, Mars) orbit the sun,[28] whereas they orbit the earth in Ottoboniano Latino #1902's diagram, drawn on 17 February 1578.[29] Ten years later, in 1588, Brahe first published the Tychonic system,[30] which provoked a spate of correspondence, including a letter in which he looked back over his intellectual development from his acquiescing youth until he rejected the contemporary competing cosmologies. At that time he asked himself what

> if the sun were established as the center of the five planets, and nevertheless revolved once a year around the earth, at rest in the center of the universe.[31]

Thus, from the very beginning of his independent swing away from the prevailing conventional wisdom, Brahe centered all five planets on the sun. From this Copernican conception Brahe never deviated throughout the rest of his life. He first adopted this view some five years after Ottoboniano Latino #1902's annotator had centered the three outer planets on the earth. Those five years were not "an important time of maturing" for Brahe, as Gingerich supposed. Instead, those five years measured the lag between the modification of Copernicus' cosmology in one direction by Ottoboniano Latino #1902's annotator and Brahe's somewhat later divergence in another direction.

As late as January 1578 Ottoboniano Latino #1902's annotator still adhered to Copernicus' stationary sun and moving earth. But early in September 1574, in a lecture delivered to the University of Copenhagen, Brahe upbraided Copernicus for upholding certain doctrines

> contrary to physical principles, for example, that the sun is at rest in the center of the universe, and that the earth, the elements associated with it, and the moon, move around the sun.[32]

Speaking again on the following day, Tycho explained that he would expound planetary theory succinctly

> in accordance with Copernicus' thinking and tables, but referring everything to the stationary earth, which Copernicus had imagined to be moving.[33]

Resting on faith in the Bible and physical (better called "metaphysical") principles, Brahe's earth remained stationary throughout his life. His allegiance never swerved, as did the annotator's in 1578, between 27 January and 13 February, in Ottoboniano Latino #1902. Before abandoning Copernicanism, the annotator had written at the top of the right margin of folio 10r in Cimelia:

> The evidence of the planets in particular conforms exactly to the earth's mobility, and in this way it is confirmed that Copernicus' hypotheses were assumed correctly (*vere*).[34]

The annotator's astronomical views, like his handwriting, differed from Brahe's. Yet with regard to the contention by Horský, the editor of Cimelia, that its annotator was Brahe, Robert S. Westman, limiting the possible alternative annotators to four astronomers, stated:

> On the basis of a handwriting comparison, which I have undertaken, between works and letters of the above mentioned writers and DR Prague [= Cimelia], there can be no doubt that Horský's identification is correct.[35]

There can, however, be the gravest doubt. For, to establish that the Cimelia annotator was Brahe, what is gained by showing that the annotator was not one of four other men? Perhaps he was a fifth.

In fact, in a personal letter dated 31 July 1980, Gingerich identified the annotator of Ottoboniano and Cimelia as Paul Wittich without furnishing any evidence. In 1582-1584 Wittich gave private instruction to Duncan Liddel (1561-1613), who later became the "first in Germany to teach the theories of the heavenly motions according to the hypothesis of Ptolemy and Copernicus at the same time."[36] In the winter semester of 1579 Liddel, a Scot from Aberdeen, had enrolled in the University of Frankfurt on the Oder,[37] where his fellow-countryman John Craig was then teaching. The "first principles" of Copernicanism were imparted by Craig to Liddel, who "learned more completely from Wittich . . . about Copernicus' innovative hypotheses."[38]

Liddel interleaved his copy of the second edition of Copernicus' *Revolutions,* which is preserved in the Aberdeen University Library.[39] A facsimile of the interleaf facing folio 9v in Liddel's copy may be conveniently compared with a facsimile of folio 9v in Wittich's Ottoboniano copy.[40] In the left margin Wittich had tabulated the planets' periodic motions, and his table was repeated by Liddel, with only two variants. First, as regards the earth, in the column for the years, Wittich had miswritten 365, which he struck out and transferred to the column for the days, while leaving only a smudge in the column for the years. Wittich had evidently made this scribal correction before the arrival of Liddel, who has 0 in the years column for the earth. A second telltale sign of Liddel's dependence on Wittich concerns the moon, where Wittich had 0 27 19 18, and Liddel interchanged the last two columns: 0 27 18 19.

The rectification of a bad blunder committed by Copernicus concerning Venus' sidereal period throws further light on the time when Wittich wrote his annotations. Liddel left undisturbed not only *Venus nonimestris* in Copernicus' famous diagram of the cosmos, but also Copernicus' *Venus nono mense reducitur* (Venus returns in nine months)[41] three lines above the diagram. After Liddel's departure, however, Wittich changed *nono* to *octavo,* and *nonimestris* to *octimestris,* since his marginal table gave only 224 (plus a fraction) days for Venus' sidereal period. By the same token, since his table showed 87 (plus more than 1/2) days for Mercury, he altered Copernicus' text by adding *et octo* (and eight) to *octuaginta* (eighty). These alterations were made by Wittich after the departure of Liddel, whose copy does not show them. Evidently Wittich continued to annotate his copy of Copernicus after Liddel had left.

No clue to Wittich's identity has been found either in his copy of the first edition of Copernicus' *Revolutions* (Ottoboniano Latino #1902) or in his copy of the second edition (Cimelia). Nevertheless, the handwriting in these two copies can be compared with an authenticated sample of Wittich's handwriting.

Wittich was one of Brahe's assistants while the comet of 1580 was visible. During Brahe's absence from his observatory, the observations of 21, 22, and 26 October 1580 were recorded by Wittich, who remained at the observatory. This handwriting was certified as his by a fellow-townsman.

> These pages marked with the letters ABCDE, I recognize to have been written by the hand of Paul Wittich, of blessed memory, which is very well known to me,

and I so testify with this handwritten note which I left at Prague with the magnificent and most noble lord Tycho Brahe on 23 October 1600.
> Jacob Monaw
> with my own hand[42]

A small specimen of these cometary observations in Wittich's handwriting was reproduced in Brahe's complete works.[43] The words *Occasus, aquila,* and *Informis* as written by Wittich, when compared with the same words written by Brahe, show marked differences.[44] On the other hand, Wittich's *occasus* in the cometary observations matches *occasus* in Cimelia, folio 10r, right margin, 2↑. This comparison of handwritings eliminates Brahe, and establishes Wittich, as the annotator of Cimelia, and therefore also of Ottoboniano Latino #1902. Hence we may discard Westman's conclusion:

> We now have dramatic evidence from the manuscript notes bound into the back of DR Vatican [= Ottoboniano Latino #1902], that the first step toward his [Brahe's] final system was initially formulated, on paper at least, on 17 February 1578.[45]

Brahe himself, however, related that

> finally almost against hope[46] I realized by what arrangement the order of the heavenly revolutions comes to be disposed most appropriately.[47]

Brahe dated this realization in 1583, without any first step or initial formulation in 1578.

Although Brahe was not the annotator of Cimelia, he was its owner. But he was not its "original owner", an erroneous inference drawn from *Ex Bibliotheca . . . Tichoniana,* the inscription on its title page, by Cimelia[48] and Westman.[49] Its original owner was Wittich, who died on 5 January 1586.[50] More than a decade later, on 24 March 1598, Brahe sent an inquiry to a favorite pupil:

> A few days ago my very dear friend Jacob Monaw of Wrocław wrote to me that at the end of last year [1597] you came to Wrocław. . . . In the same letter Monaw reported that he arranged to have you introduced to the sister of Wittich, of blessed memory, where you examined all his books. I therefore ask you to inform me about them, what they were and of what sort, especially the manuscripts, and whether she wants to sell them and at what price.[51]

Nearly two years later Monaw (1546-1603) wrote to Brahe on 14 March 1600:

> As far as Wittich's books are concerned, I want you to know that at the time when your letter was delivered here, Paul Wittich's sister, already advanced in age, celebrated her second marriage, of which the result was that the newlywed died after sixty

days. She left one son as her heir, for whom legitimate guardians have not yet been appointed. When this is taken care of, I shall see whether anything can be done with them.[52]

A little more than seven months later, on 23 October 1600 Monaw deposited with Brahe in Prague his attestation that the cometary observations made two decades earlier were in Wittich's handwriting.[53] It was on this occasion in 1600 that Monaw delivered to Brahe Wittich's copy of the second edition of Copernicus' *Revolutions,* our Cimelia. How Wittich's copy of the first edition of Copernicus' *Revolutions* was seized by the invading Swedes and subsequently became Ottoboniano Latino #1902 has not yet been completely unraveled.

The top of the flyleaf preceding Cimelia's title page carries an inscription arranged in two columns. The left-hand column concerns a male's professional career, and the right-hand column his marital career:

At the beginning of the month of March in both	[15]66 in October I married my first wife
1568 to the senate, Rahvitz	[15]90 in the month of October she died
1588 to the magistracy[54]	[15]93 in the month of October I married my second wife

This unknown individual may be a guardian of Wittich's nephew. If so, he wrote these entries shortly after his second marriage in October 1593, while Wittich's library was under the control of the nephew's guardians.

In any case, Wittich's copy of the second edition of Copernicus' *Revolutions* was taken to Brahe in Prague by Monaw in 1600. It had already been heavily annotated by Wittich, its original owner, before it reached Brahe, its second owner, who was not its annotator, and who had acquired it only a year before he died on 24 October 1601.

Notes

[1] *Nicolai Copernici De revolutionibus orbium coelestium libri sex (editio Basileensis) cum commentariis manu scriptis Tychonis Brahe,* ed. Zdeněk Horský.

[2] *Collegii Caesarei Societatis Jesu Pragae Anno 1642.*

[3] *Ex Bibliotheca et Recognitione Tichoniana.*

[4] *NB Insunt notae marginales manu Tychonis Brahe propria inscriptae.*

[5] Cimelia, 12/22-23.

[6] *Ibid.,* 12/11↑-6↑.

[7] *Astronomie v Československu od dob nejstarších do dneška* (Prague, 1952).

[8] Zincograph in František Josef Studnička, *Prager Tychoniana* (Prague, 1901), 38.

[9] Cimelia, 11/last 3 lines.

[10] *Nicolas Copernicus On the Revolutions,* translation and commentary by Edward Rosen (Baltimore, 1978), 122/30.

[11] *Tychonis Brahe Dani opera omnia* (Copenhagen, 1913-1929; cited hereafter as "TB"), II, 18/8-9.

[12] Cimelia, 12/14↑-12↑.

[13] J. A. Hanslik, *Geschichte und Beschreibung der Prager Universitätsbibliothek* (Prague, 1851), 274; *Zusätze,* ed. I. J. Hanuš (Prague, 1863), 9.

[14] Studnička, *Prager Tychoniana,* 43.

[15] B. Prusík, "Tychoniana der Prager k. k. Universitäts-Bibliothek," *Mittheilungen des österreichischen Vereines für Bibliothekswesen,* 5 (1901), 199/#VI. Cimelia (15/10↑-9↑) counts "21 blank folios in front of the actual work and another 71 folios after it."

[16] R. Kukula, "Die Tychoniana der Prager K. K. Universitäts-Bibliothek," *Zeitschrift für Bücherfreunde,* 10 (1906-1907), 24/10↑-7↑.

[17] W. Prandtl, "Die Bibliothek des Tycho Brahe," *Philobiblon, Zeitschrift für Bücherliebhaber,* 5 (1932), 323/#14; reprinted, Vienna, 1933, 11/#14.

[18] F. Kleinschnitzová, "Ex bibliotheca Tychoniana Collegii Soc. Jesu Pragae ad S. Clementem," *Nordisk Tidskrift för Bok- och Biblioteksväsen,* 20 (1933), 86/#11.

[19] E. Urbánková, *Rukopisy a vzacné tisky pražské Universitní knihovny* (Prague, 1957), 72/8-11.

[20] F. R. Friis, "Tyge Brahe's Haandskrifter i Wien og Prag," *Danske Samlinger,* 4 (1868-1869), 267/7-10.

[21] Paul Oskar Kristeller, *Iter Italicum,* II (London/Leiden, 1967), 419/#1902; not #1901, as in O. Gingerich, "The Astronomy and Cosmology of Copernicus," International Astronomical Union, *Highlights of Astronomy,* 3 (1974), 83 (cited hereafter as "Highlights").

[22] Highlights, 81/18-19; Gingerich, "Copernicus and Tycho," *Scientific American,* 229 (December 1973), 99/14↑-13↑ (cited hereafter as "C and T").

[23] C and T, 99/34-35; Highlights, 80/4↑-3↑.

[24] C and T, 99/37-44; Highlights, 81-82.

[25] Fascimile in C and T, 90, and in Robert S. Westman, ed., *The Copernican Achievement* (Berkeley/London, 1975), 312, Figure 6 (cited hereafter as "Achievement").

[26] C and T, 87/3-4.

[27] C and T, 101/11-16; Highlights, 82/22-24.

[28] Marie Boas & A. Rupert Hall, "Tycho Brahe's System of the World," *Occasional Notes of the Royal Astronomical Society,* 3 (1959), 259/5-10, translating a part of Chapter VIII of Brahe's *De mundi aetherei recentioribus phaenomenis liber secundus, qui est de illustri stella caudata anno 1577 . . . conspecta* (Uraniborg, 1588).

[29] Four days after the annotator's shift to a non-Copernican stance on 13 February 1578; not "two days later," as in C and T, 99/7 , nor "three days later," as in Highlights. 82/7; facsimiles in C and T, 100, and Highlights, 83, Fig. 6.

[30] TB, IV, 155-170.

[31] TB, VII, 129/40-42.

[32] TB, I, 149/30-32.

[33] TB, I, 172/37-39.

[34] Achievement's attempt (317/7↑-4↑) at a translation omits the crucial word *vere*.

[35] *Ibid.,* 342/6↑-4↑. Achievement was reviewed in the *Polish Review,* 21 (1976), 225-235.

[36] Duncan Liddel, *Ars medica* (Hamburg, 1607-1608, 1617, 1628), letter of 1 May 1607 from Johannes Caselius to John Craig (?-1620).

[37] *Aeltere Universitäts-Matrikeln,* I, Universität Frankfurt a. O., ed. Ernst Friedlaender (Leipzig, 1887; reprint, Osnabrück, 1965; Publicationen aus den k. Preussischen Staatsarchiven, 32, 277/#75.

[38] Liddel, *Ars medica,* Caselius to Craig.

[39] William P. D. Wightman, *Science and the Renaissance* (Edinburgh/New York, 1962), II, 66-67/#172.

[40] Achievement, 318, Fig. 7, and 320, Fig. 8.

[41] Copernicus, *Revolutions,* tr. Rosen, 21-22.

[42] TB, XIII, 316, n. 1; English paraphrase by J. L. E. Dreyer, "On Tycho Brahe's Manual of Trigonometry," *Observatory,* 39 (1916), 129-130. On 29 October 1580, when Wittich was leaving the observatory, Brahe presented him with a copy of Peter Apian's *Astronomicum caesareum* (Ingolstadt, 1540), now in the Regenstein Library, University of Chicago. A photocopy of the title page showing the presentation was kindly supplied by Professor Martin J. Hardeman, Roosevelt University.

[43] TB, XIII, 317, upper left corner.

[44] TB, XIII, 308, 319.

[45] Achievement, 345/6↑-3↑.

[46] On the basis of an incorrect reading (TB, I, xli/2: *ex inspirato,* as against *ex insperato,* TB, IV, 156/29-30), Dreyer mistranslated "by inspiration" (*Tycho Brahe,* Edinburgh, 1890; reprinted, New York, 1963, 168/9; *History of the Planetary Systems from Thales to Kepler,* Cambridge, 1906; reprinted, New York, 1953, 363/12-13).

[47] TB, IV, 156/29-30.

[48] P. 12/27.

[49] Achievement, 341/17.

[50] Rudolf Wolf, "Beiträge zur Geschichte der Astronomie. 3. Paul Wittich aus Breslau," *Vierteljahrsschrift der astronomischen Gesellschaft,* 17 (1882), 129/12↑, citing an unpublished manuscript *Silesia togata* by Nicholas Henel of Hennefeld (1584-1656). A microfilm of Henel's discussion of Wittich was kindly provided by the library of the University of Wroclav. On fol. 415v, in giving the year of Wittich's death, Henel wrote 6 over a previous 5, faintly suggesting a 7 to Wolf's informant, who also misread the day 5 as 9. Wolf's misdating (9 January 1587) was repeated in *Dictionary oe Scientific Biography,* XIV (New York, 1976), 470/5↑.

[51] TB, VIII, 34/4-16.

[52] TB, VIII, 266/1-6.

[53] See the text at n. 42, above.

[54] Reading *capitaneatum,* as in Ludwik Antoni Birkenmajer, *Mikolaj Kopernik* (Cracow, 1900), 476/4↑.

Edward Rosen (essay date 1986)

SOURCE: "Brahe's Publication of His Hypothesis" and "Brahe's Discovery of Ursus's Plagiarism," in *Three Imperial Mathematicians: Kepler Trapped between Tycho Brahe and Ursus,* Abaris Books, Inc., 1986, pp. 17-44.

[*In the following excerpt, Rosen describes the publication, and the possible plagiarizing, of Brahe's celestial system in 1588.*]

I. Brahe's Publication of His Hypothesis

Tycho Brahe (1546-1601) was one of the greatest observational astronomers of all time. Some people think he was the greatest. But his innovation and skill in observing were not ends in themselves. Their ultimate purpose was to reveal the hidden structure of the universe. This secret had not been revealed, he felt, by the cosmologies he had learned as a student. Conscious of their defects, he devised his own hypothesis, the Tychonic system.

Two major celestial events shaped his thinking: the new star of 1572 and the brilliant comet of 1577. Around these spectacular heavenly displays he planned a comprehensive work in three volumes. Of these, the earliest to be published was the second: ***Recent Phenomena in the Celestial World, Book II, about the brilliant comet*** (stella caudata) *which was seen from about the end of the* [first] *third of November in the year 1577 to the end of January in the following* [year]. In the place of Brahe's exceedingly long title, a short title is preferable for easy reference. Since Brahe often called this work his "comet" book, ***Stella caudata*** (The Star with a Tail) will serve as the short title here.

The printing of ***Stella caudata,*** as originally planned in eight chapters, began in 1587. But something happened that made Brahe change his plan. He increased the number of chapters to ten, with Chapter X of the published version corresponding to what had been the eighth and final chapter of the original version. In its place Chapter VIII of the published version set forth Brahe's hypothesis. This is on the face of it an intrusion in ***Stella caudata.*** It is not smoothly linked with what precedes and follows it. ***Stella caudata*** was printed on Brahe's own press in his own observatory, Uraniburg, on the island of Hven in the Danish Sound. Why did he suddenly interrupt the printing process and recast ***Stella caudata*** so that its Chaper VIII hastily presented in a brief and general form the hypothesis he had intended to publish much later in full detail? As he recalled the situation a decade later,

> Having devised the system of hypotheses long before, I would not have inserted it in my book on the comet of the year [15]77 had I not been afraid of such plagiarists, to whom it had become known in my establishment.[1]

When the printing of ***Stella caudata*** was finished, Brahe sent copies in May 1588 to some friends, including Heinrich Rantzau (1526-1599), the royal governor of Holstein in the kingdom of Denmark. In western Hol-

stein Rantzau had participated in the conquest of Dithmarschen, of which he wrote an account under the pseudonym Cilicius Cimber (Basel, 1570).[2] But his military and administrative activities were overshadowed by his devotion to culture. His library became famous, and he won renown as a patron of learning. Recognizing the importance of Brahe's hypothesis, Rantzau asked the author for additional copies, and Brahe sent him five.[3] Excerpting Chapter VIII, Rantzau transmitted it to a number of astronomers. Two of them reacted by raising questions about Brahe's hypothesis in their replies to Rantzau, who continued to serve as a message center by relaying their doubts to Brahe. One of these critics was well known to him, the other not at all. The familiar figure, Caspar Peucer (1525-1602), had been a professor under whom Brahe had studied more than two decades earlier at the University of Wittenberg, in 1566. After receiving an excerpt of his former professor's reply to Rantzau, on 13 September 1588 Brahe wrote to Peucer:

> In response to the request of my dear friend, the most noble Heinrich Rantzau, I sent him several copies of my work on ***Recent Phenomena in the Celestial World, Book II.*** I understand that he excerpted the exposition of the hypothesis which is found there in Chapter VIII,[4] and sent it to you and other scholars in Germany.[5]

Later on in this very long letter to Peucer, Brahe referred to the other German astronomer who had replied to Rantzau and whose name he had not previously known:

> A certain other astronomer, unknown to me, likewise had a certain other doubt about this arrangement in my hypothesis. He too wrote about it to the most noble lord Heinrich Rantzau, pointing out that the hypotheses had been imparted to him two years earlier by a certain runaway employee of mine.[6]

On the same day on which Brahe wrote to Peucer, he enclosed a copy of his Peucer letter in a communication to Rantzau. In it he referred to the doubts about his hypothesis raised by "that other astronomer, of uncommon ability as it appears, George Rullenhagen (although his name had not previously been known to me)."[7] Brahe's unfamiliarity with George Rollenhagen (1542-1609) is apparent in his misspelling of the surname as Rullenhagen four times in this letter of 13 September 1588 to Rantzau.

Unfortunately we do not have Rollenhagen's letter, written well before 13 September 1588, in which he told Rantzau that Brahe's hypothesis had been communicated to him two years earlier, in 1586. Nor do we have Rantzau's letter promptly transmitting this news to Brahe, who was astounded, since none of his employees had ever run away. Nobody had left his tight little island of Hven without his knowledge or permission. Worst of all, he had not been aware that on 31 July 1588 Nicholas Reimers Ursus of Dithmarschen (1551-1600) had published in Strasbourg his *Foundation of Astronomy,* claiming as his own a slightly modified form of Brahe's hypothesis.[8]

II. Brahe's Discovery of Ursus's Plagiarism

In September 1566 Brahe was forced to flee from Wittenberg because of the plague raging there. He betook himself instead to the University of Rostock, where he became friendly with the professor of astronomy, Henry van den Brock (Brucaeus, 1530-1593). After leaving Rostock, where Brahe lost a piece of his nose in a duel, he corresponded with Brock. On 4 November 1588 he sent Brock a copy of his 13 September 1588 letter to Peucer:

> I am sending you a copy of the letter I recently wrote to the most illustrious and most learned Caspar Peucer, in which I thought I had to reply to certain doubts of his. (He communicated them to the most noble Heinrich Rantzau, who had sent him the straightforward exposition of the hypothesis excerpted from my book [**Stella caudata**]. I am also providing a copy of Peucer's remarks, together with the indecisive opinion of a certain other astronomer on the same subject.)[1]

This "certain other astronomer" is Brahe's Rullenhagen (Rollenhagen), who had already informed Rantzau (and thereby Brahe, too) about his conversation in 1586 concerning the cosmic hypotheses. As regards his letter of 4 November 1588, Brahe told Brock:

> When you have finished reading this letter, or even if you want to, have taken the trouble to have it copied, please send it back to me, since I want to keep this copy, and I don't have the facilities now to have it transcribed again.[2]

One of the reasons why Brahe wanted his letter returned was that it expressed his grievance about

> a certain excessively arrogant individual, whom I deem unworthy of being named here and who also, wherever he was or is, makes known what he is by shamelessly claiming for himself my invention of these hypotheses, and asserting this claim in a published book [*Foundation of Astronomy*], printed this year in Strasbourg. He may know whether he swiped this innovation together with the other things which he secretly copied in my establishment while he was serving the most noble man Eric Lange, in whose retinue he was present for several days, or by what method he otherwise removed that arrangement from here [Uraniburg]. My students pointed out that lying at that time among the discarded papers was something similar, which had been drawn less than

accurately. How crookedly and craftily he acted here is certainly proved satisfactorily by the other things which he copied here without my knowledge. I recovered a part of them written with his own hand. Yet I do not find that hypothesis among those sheets. But he could have hidden it elsewhere or memorized it, when perhaps the opportunity for copying it was not available. The students in my establishment know that I devised this hypothesis and showed it to them several years ago. Indeed, although that book [**Stella caudata**] on the comet of the year [15]77 carries the imprint of this year [15]88, nevertheless all those who are with me know that it was printed on my press in the year [15]87, pains being taken to date it one year later to make it more acceptable on account of its recency. In this book, as you and I are not unaware on the basis of what has already been said, the same hypothesis is explained in general terms. But he who recently claimed it for himself makes it extraordinarily clear that he does not understand it properly, let alone that he is its author, by depicting and imagining Mars's sphere totally surrounding the sun's.[3]

In his *Foundation of Astronomy,* fol. 41, Ursus drew Mars's orbit completely enclosing the sun's, while fol. 38r/#5 he talked about

> Mars, the reddish planet, closest to the sun, located between the sun and Jupiter. These three planets [Saturn, Jupiter, Mars] encircle not only the sun, located almost at the center [of the universe], but also the earthly globe, which is sometimes closer to Mars, at other times farther away from it. When these planets are closest to the earth, they are said to be in perigee, but when they are farthest from it, they are said to be in apogee. The other two [Venus, Mercury], which follow in order, do not encircle the earth but the sun, just as the other three [Saturn, Jupiter, Mars] encircle the sun, which is located in the center of the universe.

Brahe often emphasized, as he did here in his letter to Brock, that Ursus deviated from the Tychonic system by depicting Mars's orbit surrounding the sun's, without intersecting it. This absence of intersection was Brahe's main weapon in his attack on Ursus for plagiarism. Had Brahe also been concerned to prove his plagiarist's incompetence, he could have pointed out that at fol. 38r/#5 Ursus described the sun as "located almost at the center" (*in medio fere positum*) and "located in the center of the universe" (*in medio omnium situm*). These expressions echoed Copernicus, whose sun was central on the universal scale and nearly central on the planetary scale.[4] On the larger scale Copernicus's sun was stationary; on the smaller scale, it might or might not have a tiny correctional movement. On neither scale did it perform the annual revolution. This was performed, according to Ursus, by the sun far from the center of the universe (fol. 38r/XII, 1; fol. 41), while his sun also occupied that center (fol. 38r/5). Copernicus's "sun stationary in the middle of the world" was an error, according to Ursus's poem below the

Diagram of the System of Nature (fol. 41/ right/2).
As regards Mars's orbit completely surrounding the
sun's, in his letter of 4 November 1588 to Brock, Brahe
contended that his plagiarist

> could have learned that this is impossible even from
> a merely superficial glance at Copernicus all by
> himself. And how, I ask, will he ever establish new
> hypotheses corresponding to the heavenly revolutions,
> since he has not mastered the precise observations
> of many years so as to elicit adroitly from them the
> defect in the hypotheses adopted heretofore, and the
> remedy capable of repairing that defect? Without
> these aids, bragging about a new discovery is pitiful
> and thoroughly ludicrous. For he lacks the means
> by which to prove from the phenomena why the
> earlier views must be abandoned and revised in this
> way, and how to establish by manifold observations
> that this innovation conforms more closely to the
> heavenly phenomena. These shortcomings, however,
> create a lack of confidence in them on the part of
> anybody, unless he fails to understand the subject.[5]

After listening to this vehement tirade against the plagiarist, Brock tried to clam his former pupil down by
belittling the Dithmarschian in his response to Brahe
on 23 March 1589:

> The fact that the man from Dithmarschen swiped
> your hypothesis is no reason for you to be greatly
> aroused. For since he lacks the observations by
> which the hypothesis is confirmed and the theory of
> the motions is constructed, he has gained nothing
> by adorning himself with the plumage of others,
> nor will he convince intelligent people that the
> innovation is his. Press forward with the work which
> you have begun, and prosecute your undertaking in
> the right spirit. This is the road to immortal glory.[6]

Meanwhile, on 21 December 1588, Brahe wrote to
Rantzau about Ursus, who had deliberately adopted
this Latin surname meaning "bear":

> In some letters which you sent me recently, you
> mentioned a certain Dithmarschian, who is like a bear
> in name and in fact. At the same time you transmitted
> an extract from a letter by the most renowned and
> most learned George Rollenhagen, together with that
> insolent plagiarist's book [*Foundation of Astronomy*,
> a copy of] which I had obtained previously elsewhere.[7]

In a letter written two months later, on 21 February
1589, Brahe said: "Ursus of Dithmarschen's book . . .
had been sent to me . . . [in April 1588] by the very
learned George Rollenhagen."[8] In his letter of 21 December 1588 to Rantzau, Brahe continued:

> Both you and Rollenhagen correctly suspect that
> the rearrangement of the hypotheses, which the
> Dithmarschian shamelessly attributed to himself,

was swiped from me. That in fact is the case. True,
he never worked for me or was part of my household,
as you perhaps believe.[9]

In a letter to Rantzau, Rollenhagen had described Ursus as a former employee of Brahe.[10] In this letter of
21 December 1588, however, Brahe told Rantzau that
Ursus had never been an employee of his, but had
worked for a friend of his:

> Nevertheless four years ago the Dithmarschian was
> here [in Uraniburg] for about fourteen days with
> the most noble and most learned man Eric Lange of
> Engelsholm, who is well known to you, and for
> whom he was then working. While I was having a
> jolly good time with my close friend Eric and certain
> other nobles who were here with him, that crook
> secretly copied very many of the things I had
> researched with much labor and care. He sketched
> the design and arrangement of all the instruments
> which were then in service. He removed many other
> things which he could examine, nevertheless
> pretending he was doing none of these things, indeed
> he did not care for them but despised them. After I
> had smelled a whiff of his cunning, however, I
> arranged for someone else to recover a large part of
> what he had stolen, and I still have it. I see now
> that he sketched more than I recovered or even
> committed it to memory. For this rearrangement of
> the hypotheses never occurred to anybody before
> me, as far as I know. But from what I recently
> wrote to Peucer you will have an adequate under-
> standing of how this discovery came about.[11]

In his letter to Rantzau of 13 September 1588 Brahe
had enclosed a copy of his letter of the same date to
Peucer in which he explained in full detail why he
rejected the old cosmic hypotheses and devised his
own.[12] In his letter to Rantzau of 21 December 1588
Brahe continued his account of what happened in
Uraniburg in 1584:

> On the other hand, the Dithmarschian's theft of this
> hypothesis from me at that time is quite clearly deduced
> by me from the following considerations. My friend
> Eric wanted me to account for the planets' varying
> appearances and retrograde motions. I gave him the
> explanation according to the ancient Ptolemaic as well
> as the Copernican thinking by drawing it on the table.
> I also added that the same results could be achieved
> by a certain other assumption, and I exposed certain
> absurdities in those earlier views. Eric (with his
> thoroughly open mind and thirst for knowledge) asked
> me to show him this arrangement, too. He noticed that
> I was reluctant to do so while that Dithmarschian
> servant of his was standing around and watching (for
> I had previously indicated to him that from the fellow's
> habits and appearance I had surmised what type he
> was). Sending him outside to do something else, Eric
> obtained from me what he wanted. I sketched for him
> my hypotheses, too, drawn in a general and brief
> manner, but I erased them right away.

But that Dithmarschian sensed that something secret was being discussed, as he was somewhat nosy. For that reason he investigated pretty carefully whether he could find something of this sort and take it away futively. Thus among my papers lying on a window sill he came across a certain sketch of this arrangement of the heavenly motions which, however, through some negligence or other was drawn in such a way that Mars's sphere completely enveloped the sun's. This, being incorrect, was discarded and set aside as unsuitable and out of line. Yet he grabbed it as the true and correct sketch. Later on, either he drew it secretly or committed it to memory. Now, lying insolently, he advertises it as his own invention. He has pretended that he thought it out three years ago in a certain corner of the kingdom of Poland (where undoubtedly he never was). Without any shame he dedicates it to the most illustrious prince, the Landgrave, as though it were his own discovery.[13]

In his *Foundation of Astronomy* Ursus dedicated his Diagram of the System of Nature (fol. 41) to the Landgrave of Hesse, William IV (1532-1592). At fol. 37r/ 5-23 he introduced

> my new, not untrue, and natural hypotheses of the motions of the planets or heavenly bodies. I thought them out about three years ago in a certain remote corner of the very extensive kingdom of Poland. Afterwards I offered them to the most illustrious prince of Hesse,

whose technician constructed a bronze instrument to exhibit them mechanically. This instrument was lauded by Ursus as

> previously unheard of, absolutely unknown in all [previous] ages, and about to be disclosed to inspection by the whole world, to facilitate the observation and computation of all the motions of the heavenly bodies or movable components in the cosmic structure.

In his letter to Rantzau of 21 December 1588 Brahe continued his onslaught against Ursus:

> So vast is the disreputable impertinence of this man or rather bear. He copies the style of the erroneous drawing which he finds here and reproduces the same size [of Mars's orbit in comparison with the sun's] (for the sketch he saw here was erroneous, drawn on a whole unfolded sheet). He himself thereby sufficiently exposes his theft, and with indications that are not unclear he proclaims that he does not really understand the very things he brags about, much less that he originated and discovered them. In like manner very many of the other things, indeed the most important and nearly everything which he advertises in that book as his own, even though not all of it was derived from me, were nevertheless taken from other mathematicians, either with their

knowledge or without it. Consequently, he does almost nothing else in that entire book than adorn himself with the feathers of others by attributing to himself with excessive arrogance the discoveries and results of others, and by promising what he never learned or can provide. But that despoiler is not worth my writing more about him, and perhaps this is too much. Nevertheless I could not refrain from pointing out to you how it happened that he got hold of my hypotheses and published them right away. Thus not only you but also Rollenhagen may know for a fact that his display of this hypothesis is pure theft. Indeed you are right in asserting that even though Ursus swiped my results, basically he still did not understand everything. This is clear from that mistaken drawing he presents, where he disgracefully does not know the size of Mars's sphere in relation to the sun's.

Rollenhagen also forthrightly and sagely points out that I should list what was removed from me by a runaway employee and taken away, so that it may be rightfully restored to the true inventor. For I understand he immediately recognized in Ursus's book that the innovation which he advertises as his own came from me, since he had previously written to you that this hypothesis had been communicated to him two years earlier by a runaway employee of mine. Yet I cannot quite infer from this whether he knows this Ursus, perhaps supposing that he once worked for me or is thinking of someone else who slipped away secretly from my establishment here. I therefore ask you, as soon as you have an opportunity to write to Rollenhagen, kindly to find out who that runaway employee of mine was and what his name was. Rollenhagen writes that he obtained the design of this hypothesis by way of this employee. For I would like to know whether he was Ursus or someone else. In fact, I know that none of my students who worked for me up to now in matters of astronomy left here secretly without my knowledge or permission. Nor can I quite figure out who that runaway was, mentioned by Rollenhagen more than once. Therefore if Rollenhagen identifies him for me, he will do me a very great favor.

I see that this Rollenhagen is not only a well-informed man, very impressive in his sound judgment, but also irreproachable, honest, and favorably disposed toward the researches of others. Accordingly, when the opportunity occurs, I shall not hesitate to initiate a friendly correspondence with him. But if he makes the first move, that in itself will provide a satisfactory opportunity.

This letter, however, is longer than I intended. Yours will be the task of honestly interpreting this waste of time, caused by a just complaint.

If you receive a letter from Dr. Peucer addressed to me, I ask you not to find it any trouble to send it here right away. Farewell, most noble and most distinguished sir. Do not fail to serve scholarly pursuits, as you do, and in this way gain imperishable fame. Once more, live and be well in complete happiness and for a very long time.

Written in Uraniburg, 21 December 1588[14]

Abbreviations

Dreyer: J. L. E. Dreyer, *Tycho Brahe* (Edinburgh, 1890; reprint, New York, 1963)

F: *Joannis Kepleri astronomi opera omnia,* ed. Christian Frisch, 8 vols (Frankfurt a.M. / Erlangen, 1858-1871); reprint, Hildesheim, I (1971), II (1977)

GW: Johannes Kepler, *Gesammelte Werke* (Munich, 1937-)

NCCW: *Nicholas Copernicus Complete Works,* I (New York/London, 1972); II, *Revolutions,* translated by Edward Rosen, with commentary (Baltimore, 1978); III, Minor Works (1985)

TB: *Tychonis Brahe Dani opera omnia,* 15 vols (Copenhagen, 1913-1929)

UFA: Ursus, *Fundamentum astronomicum* (Strasbourg, 1588)

Notes for "Brahe's Publication of His Hypothesis"

[1] TB *8:*47/11-13; GW *13:*200/125-128; F *1:*219/9↑-7↑. The time when Brahe wrote Chapter VIII of *Stella caudata,* as published, was grossly misunderstood by Pierre Duhem (1861-1916). In his famous essay "Sozein ta phainomena" (*Annales de philosophie chrétienne, 1908, 156:*566; reprinted in book form, Paris: Vrin, 1983), Duhem stated: "c'est en 1578 que Tycho Brahé rédigea les huit premiers chapitres de son ouvrage sur la comète de 1577." This serious blunder was made even worse by the English mistranslation: "the first eight chapters were completed by 1578"; P. Duhem, *To Save the Phenomena,* tr. E. Doland and C. Maschler (University of Chicago Press, 1969), p. 96.

[2] A heroic poem in Latin verse about the *History of the Ditmarschen War, Waged in 1559,* completed by the poet laureate Hieronymus (H)Osius on 1 January 1560, was published in Simon Schard, *Rerum germanicarum scriptores varii,* ed. Hieronymus Thomae (Giessen, 1673), III, 46-65. For recent views of the Ditmarschen War, see Nis Rudolf Nissen in Alfred Kamphausen, N.R. Nissen, and Erich Wohlenberg, *Ditmarschen: Geschichte und Bild einer Landschaft* (Heide in Holstein, 1968), pp. 61-62, and Gottfried Ernst Hoffman, in *Geschichte Schleswig-Holsteins* (begun by Volquart Pauls), V, 1 (Neumünster, 1972), pp. 17-26. Under his own name Rantzau wrote about the preservation of health (Leipzig, 1576; 5 editions in all); interpretation of dreams (Rostock, 1591); patrons of astrology (Antwerp, 1580; Leipzig, 1581, 1584, 1585); *Horoscopographia* (Strasbourg, 1585; Wittenberg, 1588; Schleswig, 1591); *Ranzovianum calendarium* (Hamburg, 1590; Leipzig, 1592); *Diarium* (Wittenberg, 1593, 1598; Hamburg, 1594, 1596; Leipzig, 1596); *Tractatus astrologicus* (Frankfurt, 1593, 1600, 1602, 1615, 1625, 1633; Wittenberg, 1594; Hamburg, 1594). *Directiones* was a posthumous work (Frankfurt, 1611, 1624, 1627). Brahe's *Astronomiae instauratae mechanica* (Wandsbek, 1598) was printed on his own press while he was a guest in a castle owned by Rantzau, who helped to obtain Brahe's appointment as Imperial Mathematician of the Holy Roman Empire after Brahe had left Denmark. A useful lecture on Rantzau was published by P. Hasse in *Zeitschrift der Gesellschaft für Schleswig-Holstein-Lauenburgische Geschichte,* 1878, *8:*329-348; for additional discussion of Rantzau in this periodical, see the Index to volumes 1-20 (Kiel, 1899), p. 157/left/9-7↑; Index to volumes 21-30 (Kiel, 1904), p. 152/left/2-14; and the Index to volumes 51-60 (Neumünster, 1938), p. 182/left/3↑-right/8.

[3] TB *7:*127/9-10.

[4] *De mundi aetherei recentioribus phaenomenis liber secundus qui est de illustri stella caudata* (Uraniburg, 1588), VIII; TB *4:*156/34-157/41, with diagram at *4:*158; summary and diagram in Dreyer, pp. 167-169; diagram in *Vistas in Astronomy,* 1975, *17:*xxxiii, fig. 25; partial translation in Marie Boas (Hall) and A. Rupert Hall, "Tycho Brahe's System of the World," *Occasional Notes of the Royal Astronomical Society,* 1959, *3:*257-263.

[5] TB *7:*131/14-20.

[6] TB *7:*135/38-42.

[7] TB *7:*125/20-22. Rollenhagen became better known for his satirical poem *Froschmeuseler* (Battle of the Frogs and Mice), which he dedicated to Rantzau on 21 March 1595 (ed. Magdeburg, 1608, sig. A 2v-3v, 3v-6v).

[8] Ursus, *Fundamentum astronomicum* (Strasbourg, 1588; cited hereafter as UFA), fol. 41: Diagram of the System of Nature, representing the hypotheses of the motions of the heavenly bodies.

Notes for "Brahe's Discovery of Ursus's Plagiarism"

[1] TB *7:*148/22-28.

[2] TB *7:*148/33-35.

[3] TB *7:*149/8-30.

[4] NCCW, I, fol. 9r/17 -16 : *circa ipsum esse centrum mundi;* fol. 10r/2: *In medio . . . omnium resident.*

[5] TB *7:*149/30-41.

[6] TB *7:*167/1-7.

[7] TB *7:*387/16-19.

[8] TB *6:*179/20-23.

[9] TB *7:*387/19-23.

[10] See Ch. i at n. 6.

[11] TB *7:*387/23-38.

[12] TB *7:*126/5-9; 127/26-131/8.

[13] TB *7:*387/388/21.

[14] TB *7:*388/21-389/31.

William J. McPeak (essay date 1990)

SOURCE: "Tycho Brahe Lights Up the Universe," in *Astronomy,* Vol. 18, No. 12, December, 1990, pp. 28-35.

[*In the following essay, McPeak investigates Brahe's scientific accomplishments at Uraniborg and Stjerneborg, detailing the wide variety of astronomical equipment he designed for his two island observatories.*]

Tycho Brahe is a forgotten man. When we think of great astronomers of the past, Nicholas Copernicus, Johannes Kepler, and Galileo Galilei come to mind quickly. But what about the Dane, Tycho Brahe? Most amateur astronomers have a hard time naming his greatest accomplishments.

Despite this, Tycho was one of the all-time greats in science. He was the first full-time astronomer, founding the great observatories Uraniborg and Stjerneborg and providing them with equipment that for its time was on the cutting-edge of technology—sextants, armillary spheres, and quadrants. Tycho was the first to apply what we think of as modern systematic and qualitative observation to astronomy. He provided the first logical basis for determining relative cosmic distances and disproved ancient, primitive conceptions of comets and celestial space. And he laid the groundwork for the triumph of the Copernican revolution because he meticulously plotted solar, lunar, and planetary motions.

Born To Be an Astronomer?

The eldest of eleven children of Otto Brahe, Tycho was born on December 14, 1546, at the family seat of Knudstrup in Scania. His youth was relatively comfortable. Under a family agreement, his childless uncle Jörgen acquired the responsibility for educating young Tycho. By the time he was a teenager, Tycho was sent by his uncle to the University of Copenhagen and to Leipzig to study for a career in statesmanship.

The sudden death of his uncle in 1565 gave Tycho the freedom to pursue his own education. The most painful event at school didn't involve books, however. On December 29, 1566, Tycho sought to resolve a disagreement with another Danish nobleman by duel. The two fought with swords, and Tycho lost part of the bridge of his nose. He subsequently patched the wound with a waxy form inlaid with gold and silver. Thereafter, he carried a box of salve, frequently applying the medication to his sore nose.

Classical studies and a solar eclipse in 1560 turned Tycho's attention toward the stars. In his school days, Tycho became acutely aware of the need for accurate observations with instruments superior to the current tools used by astronomers. Naked-eye instruments, little changed from ancient times, were used as positional plotting tools. The most common instruments were a graduated arc limb with partial or full circumference and a radial ruler (alidade) with a sight at each end. The quadrant (90° arc) and the early sextant (60° arc) used by both mariners and astronomers were based on the earlier two-armed compass. These tools were used to measure angular dimensions in the sky or altitudes of celestial objects.

Other tools were somewhat more sophisticated. These included rings and armillary spheres. An armillary sphere was a globe-shaped device that provided a three-dimensional representation of the heavens as a celestial sphere, with Earth at the center. By including lines representing the celestial equator, the ecliptic, and the latitude and longitude, an astronomer could use an armillary sphere to study stars and planets relative to celestial space rather than the Earthly horizon.

These instruments served 16th-century astronomers well, but Tycho wanted to improve them. He wasn't satisfied with being a mere participant; he wanted to innovate. Tycho realized that he could gain more accuracy in his instruments by making them bigger. He set about building large versions of his instruments during the next stage of his life. He realized two key qualities for building large instruments: Graduated angular scales had to be made accurately enough to subdivide degrees into arcminutes. He also realized the need to correct for parallax and atmospheric refraction.

In 1568 Tycho built a quadrant with a radius of 14 cubits (21 feet) at Augsburg. The quadrant was so heavy that it required twenty men to set up. The quadrant pivoted at the intersection of its two arms by means of a massive beam placed vertically in a cubical wooden frame. This made it possible to sight along the arm and move the limb, which was graduated to ten-arcsecond intervals, to indicate degrees of altitude. This instrument was used in the open until 1574, when it was destroyed in a storm.

Having gained valuable experience with equipment construction and use, Tycho returned to Denmark late in 1570. On the night of November 11, 1572, his life was dramatically changed. That evening he went outside to watch the sky over Heridsvad Abbey, and he saw a star as bright as Venus in the constellation Cassiopeia. By coincidence he had just finished building a 60° sextant of walnut about five and a half feet long in the arms. This time Tycho made the eyepiece with a vertical slit for aligning the star precisely with the top of the object sight and positioned it with a hand crank. The workmanship of this fine sextant allowed him to plot the position of his new star accurately.

The new star was what we know today as a supernova. Tycho measured its angular distance from the stars of Cassiopeia in order to plot the supernova's celestial latitude and longitude. He noted as time passed that the supernova's coordinates did not change relative to the stars. Tycho published an account of the new star in late 1573, and the star finally faded from naked-eye visibility in March 1574. Tycho's supernova allowed him to accomplish two big breakthroughs: he showed that the heavens were changeable (which Aristotle had denied), and he concluded that the new star was as distant as the ordinary stars, because it had no detectable parallax.

Think I'll Build a Castle

Discovering the new star changed Tycho's attitude about astronomy. He now saw himself as completely devoted to the subject. Probably thinking of the repercussions of the astronomer's reclusive life he would now pursue—not the thing for a noble lady—he married a commoner named Christine. She eventually bore him eight children.

Tycho's fame caused by the supernova discovery resulted in an acquaintance with the king of Denmark. In February 1576, the king told Tycho that he could forget courtly duties and accept a life of isolation more suitable for his astronomical pursuits. Tycho moved to the little island of Hven, situated in the sound between Elsinore and Landskrona, in Scania. Funds would be forthcoming to build a great house, and the king let Tycho know that the island and its inhabitants were Tycho's for life. At that time Hven was sparsely populated by tenant farmers. Consisting of a bare 2,000 acres, it was the perfect spot to erect a monument to stargazing. Tycho decided to build a great observatory and call it Uraniborg, Castle of the Heavens.

Uraniborg was no medieval castle of thick gray walls, but a mixture of Renaissance styles. Tycho was already making observations from unfinished quarters in December 1576, although the structure was not completed until 1580. Made of red brick with sandstone ornamention, the central residence measured 49 feet square and was 37 feet high. An octagonal pavilion was topped by an onion dome with clocks and a gilt weather vane in the shape of Pegasus.

The north and south ends of Uraniborg housed two observation turrets 18 feet in diameter and 18 feet in height. Platforms were located at the top. The roofs were cone-shaped, comprised of hinged triangular sections of wood that could be folded back for observing any part of the sky. At the outer end of each of these were two small observation towers on single pillars, sporting the same sort of roof and connected by galleries and catwalks to the platform levels of the large parent turrets.

Gardens and orchards spread out 248 feet on all sides of Uraniborg and were enclosed by earthen walls 18 feet high and 16 feet thick at the base. Within the pavilion was an octagonal room with a ceiling clock and a wind indicator connected to the weather vane outside—a means of anticipating possible wind problems for the instruments. Below this, above the second-story rooms, were eight small rooms or garrets for student astronomers.

The ground floor comprised two large guest rooms, a family sitting room, and a study. The south observatory turret had a ground-floor library for study and a basement chemical laboratory. The northern observatory housed the kitchen at the ground level and a well in the basement, which provided pumped water to the floors above. Tycho's collection of instruments, often reworked at extra cost until made correctly, began to fill Uraniborg.

The observatory's library housed a great celestial globe five feet in diameter and covered in brass plates that Tycho had commissioned on his trip to Augsburg in 1570. On this globe, Tycho had his own goldsmith, Hans Crol, engrave celestial, equatorial, and zodiacal circles graduated in minutes and the positions of several hundred stars.

Uraniborg's study contained one of Tycho's most important instruments, a mural quadrant. The mural quadrant was a meridian instrument—that is, it was fixed in place on the south wall to await stars or the Sun ascending across its position, as seen through a square window cut in the wall. The graduations were marked off to ten-arcsecond intervals. For the convenience of low- or high-angle observing, two large sights could slide along the arc and were aligned with a star along a brass cylinder inserted outside the window.

Tycho was proud of this instrument and considered it an original idea. A few such quadrants had existed before Tycho's, but Tycho's was far superior. He used it as a means of showcasing Uraniborg. The observer sighted a star for altitude and called it out to the recorder. For transits across the meridian, the observer also sighted through the left slit, calling out the start of the observation to a third observer who marked the time on interregulated minute and second clocks. After the star crossed the meridian and appeared in the right slit, its position and transit time were noted as well.

The instrumentation on the rooftop observatory turrets was an impressive collection that included equatorial armillaries, four quadrants with graduated azimuth rings for altitude and azimuth positioning of stars and time determination, and a two-observer double brass and iron arc.

One Just Isn't Enough

By 1584 Uraniborg felt cramped. So Tycho constructed a second observatory on a small rise about a hundred feet south of the perimeter of Uraniborg. This was called Stjerneborg, or Castle of the Stars. This facility was comprised of a wooden enclosure 57 feet square housing five observing rooms and a central study with a brass mechanical statue of the god Mercury rotating at the top.

Stjerneborg's study and its three contiguous circular rooms were essentially subterranean crypts designed to protect observing instruments from wind. The crypts were supplied with circular ramps for descending and ascending along the exterior of the instruments employed at Stjerneborg. The largest of these observation rooms was built with a dome and capital like Uraniborg's. The dome was made of triangular wood segments that could be removed as necessary. This crypt housed Tycho's largest instrument, a great equatorial armillary composed of a huge, revolving iron declination ring nine feet across fitted with two sights and strutted for stability to a tubular steel axis with a brass objective cylinder sight at its center.

The other two subterranean rooms were supplied with ground-level, special-beamed, doubled skylight roofs equipped with circumferential wheels. The left room held a ten-foot diameter quadrant. The right room held a 12-foot diameter steel quadrant. These instruments joined the mural quadrant as principal tools for star transits and for determining solar orbital motion from altitude and declination observations.

Uraniborg was not only a working observatory; it was an astronomy school. Tycho felt that observing assignments given to many observers and then averaged together would provide the most reliable data. This was required for all of the stellar, lunar, solar, and planetary observations made at both of the observatories.

Employing this impressive array of instrumentation for nearly twenty years, Tycho trained observers and computers. He filled the meteorological diary and his data ledgers with plots showing solar, lunar, stellar, and planetary data. Tycho's solar observations allowed him to calculate a table of refraction corrections for each degree of altitude. From the lunar data—distances from fixed stars, altitudes, and declinations—Tycho discovered anomalies in lunar orbital motion. But lacking the gravitational theory that Isaac Newton would develop one hundred years later, Tycho could not completely account for them.

One outstanding area of neglect in Tycho's time was creating a star catalog. The basic job done by Hipparchus was then more than 1,600 years old. Using a mean value for the right ascension of Alpha Arietis as a base star, Tycho determined the positions of the nine brightest stars and twelve others close to the zodiacal circle. Between the years 1578 and 1591, he used these data to determine the right ascensions of all other prominent naked-eye stars, 777 in all.

In addition to the supernova of 1572, Tycho and his assistants carefully observed positions and parallaxes of comets that appeared in 1577, 1580, 1585, 1590, 1593, and 1596. The comet of 1577 provided Tycho with his first solid physical data since the supernova to suggest serious flaws in the ancient model of the cosmos. In tracking this comet (particularly with the one-observer sextant), Tycho saw no appreciable diurnal parallax. This meant the comet cut a path through the heavens that lay beyond the Moon and must, in fact, travel through the orbits of the planets. The other cometary data reinforced his important findings and helped to define a new cosmos.

Tycho's study of cometary trajectories proved that the Aristotelian theory of crystalline planetary orbital spheres was impossible. And he demonstrated that comets move in celestial space and are not products of earth's atmosphere. The importance of this is incalculable. It thrust astronomy forward as a modern conception for the first time. Prior to that it had roots deeply planted in unscientific thought. In one series of arguments Tycho succeeded in liberating fundamental ideas about the universe that would echo throughout future astronomy and set the stage for the eventual success of the Copernican revolution. (Ironically, Galileo still believed that comets were part of Earth's atmosphere, while Kepler could not shake off solid, geometrically arranged celestial spheres. Both were contemporaries of Tycho.) Change was a slow process, however—elder astronomers continued to try to explain away any physical data contrary to ancient conceptions.

Unfortunately Tycho did not oversee Hven carefully, being distracted by his intense astronomical work. He put off duties such as repairing buildings and treated some of his tenants with a snobbish arrogance. Consequently, though King Frederick II overlooked complaints, Tycho's brash and stubborn behavior came home to roost after the king's death in 1588. Royal cutbacks came with the new king, Christian I, and Tycho's pride over the importance of his work and resentment of criticism kept him from making apologies and compromises. This deterioration of relations precipitated Tycho's departure from Hven and his native land. He had made an insignificant island into the showpiece of Renaissance science. But Tycho had also grown tired of his isolation and wished for greater opportunities.

In 1597 Tycho packed up his family and all but the four largest instruments and made his way to Rostock with the intention of becoming Imperial mathematician for Emperor Rudolf II in Prague. The bulk of instruments and books was stored at Magdeburg, while the remaining instruments at Hven were shipped to Lübeck and then forwarded to Hamburg for shipment down the Elbe. Meanwhile, Tycho took up residence in the imperial castle Benatky, where he planned to recreate a Uraniborg-style observatory and laboratory. But instead Tycho drifted back to Prague. Desperately in need of a colleague, Tycho discovered the man who would fall heir to his legacy, Johannes Kepler. The two were not strangers. Kepler had already published his first book in 1596 on the Copernican system and was known by Tycho.

Tycho had always shown an affection for Kepler and he now expressed enthusiasm for Kepler's assistance. Kepler came to Prague in January 1600, but his right to the wealth of lunar and planetary observations, which no one was more qualified to examine and decipher, was in doubt until he was treated as an equal. Kepler grew eager for full access to Tycho's life's work, for Tycho was showing signs of approaching old age, which might complicate timely research.

Barely a year later Tycho died, suffering a stroke at the dinner table on October 13, 1601. With his family and close associates at his bedside, Tycho lingered for ten days before succumbing. Tycho had entrusted to Kepler his life's observations and asked him to complete a logical planetary theory. Of course Kepler went on to great success, determining the laws of orbital motion. Tycho's influence resonated not only in Kepler but throughout the lives and thoughts of all astronomers to come. And what of Uraniborg and Stjerneborg? Hven changed hands in 1602, 1616, and in 1645. A new dwelling called Kongsgaarden was erected from Uraniborg bricks. In 1671 the foundation of Uraniborg was still visible, though Stjerneborg was but a hollow in the ground.

During the 19th century, antiquarians unearthed the Uraniborg laboratory and the three crypts at Stjerneborg. Simple markers indicate the location of Uraniborg to-day. One would hardly think that 400 years ago on that deserted spot lay the world's first scientific observatory and one of the great centers of free thought for humanity. Because he established the foundation of modern astronomy, it's difficult not to feel the contributions of the lord of Hven, Tycho Brahe.

Victor E. Thoren (essay date 1990)

SOURCE: "The Tychonic System of the World," in *The Lord of Uraniborg: A Biography of Tycho Brahe,* Cambridge University Press, 1990, pp. 236-64.

[*In the following excerpt, Thoren examines the evolution of Brahe's planetary system and the slow publication of the astronomer's* De mundi. *Thoren concludes that the observations in Brahe's monograph were insufficient in themselves to overthrow the Aristotelian cosmology of solid celestial spheres, though they were necessary to set this process into motion.*]

At the time [Paul] Wittich came to Hven [in 1580], Tycho had probably not thought about planetary theory or cosmology since his deliberations on the comet [of 1577]. The same may have been true of Wittich, whose contemplations on the subject had occurred, oddly enough, at almost exactly the same time. But although Tycho's had been almost incidental thoughts, provoked only by his consideration of the comet, Wittich's had been self-conscious, explicit explorations of the various models and combinations thereof available for planetary theorizing.

In a series of twenty-six drawings only recently found, recognized, and published by Gingerich,[15] Wittich had permuted the Copernican planetary mechanisms—both the double-epicycle . . . and double-hypocycle . . . forms of the *Commentariolus* and the epicycle-eccentric combination of *De revolutionibus*—through various orientations to produce an abundance of options that must have left Tycho astonished by both the power of the methods and the ingenuity of Wittich. As a conclusion of his efforts, he obtained a "Theory of the Three Superior [Planets] adapted to the Immobility of the Earth."[16] . . . [The] theory used a Ptolemaic epicycle . . . for the synodic phenomena and then accounted for the anomalistic realities of the planet's orbit by making the center of the orbit . . . ride on a double hypocycle . . . around the stationary earth.

What probably did not seem as exciting at the time but proved most significant in the long run was a final diagram that was strictly not part of the series at all, in which Wittich had abandoned any consideration of the anomalistic theme of the rest of the diagrams and simply sketched a synodic schematic . . . of the entire planetary system.[17] The similarity to Tycho's conception is striking, but so is the difference: Wittich arbitrarily used epicycles for the superior planets that were not only mutually equal in absolute size but also equal to the size of the sun's orbit around the earth.

If Tycho was as blunt on this occasion as he showed himself to be on most others involving scientific issues, he must have lost no time in telling Wittich that his diagram was wrong. For although Wittich certainly had the right to establish an arbitrary size for any epicycle, he then had a corresponding obligation to make each deferent "fit" its epicycle astronomically. In particular, as Saturn's (Copernican) orbit is roughly ten times the size of the earth's, its deferent has to be about ten times the size of its epicycle in order to account for the phenomenon of Saturn's retrograde arc. Tycho would have sympathized with Wittich's instinct for placing (and, therefore, sizing) the deferents so that each successive "orb" was as close to its inside neighbor as it could be without interfering with the operation of either assemblage.

Everyone since Ptolemy had followed this tradition,[18] and every astronomer of Tycho's era was thoroughly familiar with the picture that derived from it. The sphere of Mercury began just outside the sphere of the moon, about 64 earth radii away, according to the best astronomical information. When astronomers placed an appropriately eccentric deferent so that an appropriately sized epicycle carried Mercury just down to 64 e.r. at perigee of the epicycle and perigee of the eccentric, the same machinery carried Mercury at apogee of the epicycle and apogee of the eccentric to 167 e.r.[19] Similar computations for Venus extended its sphere from 167 to 1,160 e.r., and those for the sun took its sphere out to 1,260 e.r. For Mars, the epicycle (corresponding to the earth's orbit) and deferent had to be in the ratio of approximately 100 to 152. For a simple circular deferent, this would have entailed a mean distance for Mars of $1,260 + 2,423$ earth radii and a maximum distance of $1,260 + 2(2,423)$ e.r.[20] A more complicated adjustment for the eccentricity of Mars's orbit pushed its maximum distance out to 9,200 e.r. Jupiter's orbit occupied the space out to 14,400, and Saturn's extended out to about 20,000.

If these numbers seem arbitrary, they were only partly arbitrary. As Tycho probably reminded Wittich, one could specify only one item at a time: either the size of the epicycle, or the size of the deferent, but not both. If Wittich had not simply lost track of this basic astronomical fact, he would have defended himself by saying that he was simply schematizing the system and had not drawn the eccentrics to scale. They may even have discussed the implications of "opening up" the heavens to allow the space between the spheres that would be demanded by the proper scale. By using the Capellan arrangement for the inferior planets, both Tycho and Wittich had, in fact, already introduced some wasted space in the heavens, although Wittich had

forgotten or refused to show it in his diagram. But whatever the degree of intent behind the shortcomings of Wittich's diagram, making all the epicycles the same size was a thought-provoking idea.

By inverting this isolated part of Copernicus's logic, Wittich unwittingly took the penultimate step toward the system that bears Tycho's name. All that remained to be done was to convert the epicycle-deferent mechanism of the three outer planets to their equivalent eccentrics. This step would add circles the sizes of the (appropriate) respective deferents, but centered on the sun, to the circles for Mercury and Venus already drawn around the sun. But it was a step that neither Wittich nor any of the other people who may have contemplated his diagrams during his travels was ever able to take. Even for Tycho it took at least a couple of years, and reconsideration in another context, to arrive at the Tychonic system of the world.

On 18 October 1580, the theoretical contemplations of Tycho and Wittich were disturbed by the appearance of a comet.[21] Halfway through the observations of the comet, Wittich told Tycho that he had to go home for a few weeks to collect an inheritance from a rich uncle.[22] Never one to pass up an opportunity to send mail with a traveler, Tycho composed a quick note to Hayek apologizing for his delay in responding to two earlier letters from Hayek and bringing him up to date on developments at Uraniborg. Then Tycho broached the matter that had been lying between them ever since he had received Hayek's book on the comet of 1577— that Hayek had determined the comet to be sublunary. Whether because he had not yet analyzed Hayek's argument in detail or whether he was just being diplomatic, Tycho attributed the differences between their findings to shortcomings in Hayek's instruments and contented himself with asserting that he could "prove by many observations and computations that neither [the last large comet nor the small one currently visible] existed in the elementary region but [that they] traced out their motions far above the moon in the ethereal abode."[23]

It would be interesting to know whether Tycho was able to exercise similar restraint in his dealings with Wittich. The appearance of the comet must have strained the relationship in two respects, first by subjecting Wittich to the unfamiliar and uncongenial labors of handling observational instruments and computing data and then by raising an issue that emphasized the differences in their philosophical orientation. Wittich's interests were clearly much more abstract than Tycho's; indeed, it is not clear that he should be regarded as an astronomer at all. With the exception of Wittich's planetary model juggling, his sole known foray into astronomical work before coming to Hven was some consultation with Hayek and Schultz that enabled the two of them independently to obtain, using a well-publicized method of Regiomontanus,[24] a large parallax for the comet of 1577.

Tycho had probably not yet developed his great contempt for this method. But his unshakable conviction that there had been no sensible parallax for the comet of 1577, the null determination that he reached for the comet of 1580 about a week before Wittich left Hven,[25] and Tycho's confident allusion to having changed Wittich's mind on the subject of comets[26] all add up to the certainty that Wittich discussed the issue with Tycho at some length, whether or not he wanted to. At the same time, it seems almost certain that the restless Wittich was destined to move on no matter how Tycho behaved. The only contemporary statement about his peripatetic life-style is a later letter by Andraeus Dudith stating that Wittich left the *landgrave*'s circle after a short stay in 1584 because he did not like the *landgrave*.[27]

After Wittich's departure, Tycho and [his assistant Peter Jacobsen] Flemløse continued to observe the comet in the early morning sky until it disappeared into the sun in mid-December. Having mentioned to Hayek that he hoped to find leisure during the winter to finish his discussion of the comet of 1577, Tycho probably spent at least some time on it. This may well have been the period during which he analyzed Hayek's and Schultz's misuse of Regiomontanus's method and added to his own Chapter VI the demonstration that the method could show a null parallax if used properly.[28] When he wrote to Schultz the following fall, at any rate, Tycho was able to catalogue his old friend's transgressions very specifically if also very diplomatically. But because that letter contains almost the same reference to the need for finding leisure to finish his manuscript that Tycho had made to Hayek a year earlier, it is clear that Tycho had not progressed very far in the meantime.[29]

Sometime during the next three or four winters. Tycho composed the next chapter, describing the comet itself.[30] In the German tract Tycho had sent to the king in 1578, this description had been very brief, merely mentioning that the comet's tail followed the general rule of being directed away from the sun and converting the apparent sizes of the head and tail to true sizes.[31] What was eventually published as Chapter VII of *De mundi* is a twenty-five-page day-by-day instantiation of Tycho's contention that contrary to the findings of Apian, Gemma, Fracastoro, and Cardan that comets' tails always oppose the sun, the tail of this comet was directed away from Venus.[32] Similarly, the discussion of the sizes of the comet's head and tail which was going to be an appendix to Chapter VII, involves numbers that are noticeably different[33] from those in Tycho's report to the king.

At this stage the book was finished, except for the task of reviewing critically all of the other publications on the comet (adding material that was destined to constitute Chapter VIII). Tycho started the printing of the book and even printed a title-quarto for it, whose table of contents describes in some detail the eight chapters.[34] If the book had been completed as planned, it would have been an eminently forgettable one, however much one might still wish to insist on the necessity of a monograph that would drive home the contradiction of Aristotelian cosmology embodied in the comet. Sometime during the printing, however, Tycho added the chapter on his world system that has subsequently commanded virtually all the attention given to the book. Tycho would certainly have agreed with the unanimous assessment of this chapter as "the most important [one] in the whole book."[35] As Lagrange later said about Newton's work, it is given to only one person to discover the system of the world. Tycho thought he had done it. The question naturally arises, then, why was he so late in making plans to publish it? The answer appears to begin with Tycho's investigation of the parallax of Mars in the winter of 1582-3.

Exactly when Tycho first encountered the proposition that the earth was moving, he does not say. Lecture syllabi from Wittenberg suggest that he was probably introduced to the technical achievements of Copernicus without being told of the great mathematician's cosmological speculations.[36] But it is hard to believe that his innocence could have survived the period he spent with Schultz when he was seventeen. By the early 1580s, therefore, Tycho had presumably been aware of the issue for close to twenty years and clearly understood that Copernicus truly believed ("his" preface notwithstanding) that the earth was moving. Whether Tycho himself was ever able to take the proposition seriously, however, is doubtful. His few references to the motion of the earth all characterize it as physically absurd. And through a career in which he developed instruments whose accuracy rose higher and higher above any standard previously achieved, he never documented any attempt to detect the stellar parallax that alone could verify the annual motion of the earth.

There was, however, another kind of parallax that looked as if it should be more accessible: planetary parallax. Given the actual (modern) values of these parallaxes—about 25″ maximum for Mars—Tycho was not going to find any real evidence on the issue. But because he had adopted Ptolemy's ancient 3′ parallax for the sun, he thought he would be dealing with detectable quantities. At the very same time that this unworthy stepchild was working mischief with Tycho's solar theory and table of refractions, therefore, it would also do its best to cause him to misinterpret evidence on what was the much more significant scientific question of the system of the world.

A value of 3′ for the sun implied an even larger figure for the inferior planets, if they were truly inferior in the Ptolemaic sense. But as Tycho had already decided that they moved in Capellan orbits (which were indistinguishable from Copernican orbits), there was no cosmological distinction to be inferred from their parallaxes. For Mars, however, the situations were quite different. According to the Ptolemaic conception, what happened when Mars went through opposition (to the sun) was that the planet moved (counterclockwise) through perigee of its epicycle . . . , producing both retrograde motion and Mars's nearest approach to the stationary earth. At that time, according to the Ptolemaic cosmology, Mars's distance was just a bit greater than the sun's maximum distance, for the scheme was based on the assumption that Mars's entire "orb" was situated above (i.e., outside) the sun's.

According to Copernicus's interpretation of Ptolemy's epicycles, the retrograde motion and closest approach of Mars were caused by the fact that the earth, in its orbital movement, was overtaking its slower-moving outer neighbor. Without reference to something outside the system, it was impossible to distinguish between these two views on the basis of motion alone. However, if one assumed, after Copernicus, that Mars's epicycle was actually the orbit of the earth, then the astronomically determined ratio of Mars's orbit (to its epicycle) implied that Mars, around opposition, was considerably closer to the earth than the sun was.

On the basis of a 3′ solar parallax, Tycho could expect Mars to show 4½. It was so obvious a test situation that Tycho probably did not give much thought to the fact that even on the Ptolemaic scheme Mars should show nearly 3′ of parallax. During the winter of 1582-3, at the first opposition to occur after the large instruments began to issue from his shop, Tycho looked for parallax. When he failed to find an amount that should have been very easily detectable, he concluded that the Copernican hypothesis was untenable. Given Tycho's opinion about the motion of the earth, one would expect this apparently nullifying result to have been very gratifying. But by the time Tycho reported his result in a letter to Brucaeus in the spring of 1584,[37] he may well have developed reasons for having a curious ambivalence about the result.

Because the Tychonic system is nothing but [a] rather trivial-looking inversion of the Copernican system . . ., it is rather startling to see the numerous attestations by Tycho that he discovered or invented it sometime around 1583.[38] Although it is tempting to take refuge in the fact that most of Tycho's professional contemporaries lived and died without seeing their way to the inversion, to account for its decade-long gestation period in Tycho there are two more satisfying explanations available more or less directly from Tycho himself. The first is that Tycho stated explicitly that he did not derive his system merely by inverting Copernicus's.[39] He was undoubtedly an enthusiastic admirer of Copernicus. But his admiration was for the geometry (and perhaps the astronomical data processing) of Copernicus's planetary theory, not for his cosmology (or his observational prowess). Once he had done his thinking about cosmology and found himself unable to believe that the earth could be moving, he had little incentive to think about cosmology at all. Having once consciously adopted the geocentric worldview, he subsequently did all of his technical thinking within that framework.

Thus, although Tycho was capable of entertaining individual Copernican theories for the planets, when he was thinking technically, the framework within which he viewed them was a Ptolemaic one. This situation rendered it unlikely that Tycho would ever contemplate the Copernican cosmology as a whole long enough to see that it could be stood on one ear and converted instantly into a geostatic system. Although he certainly recognized that Copernicus's revolution of the earth provided a geometrical equivalent to Ptolemy's epicycles, even that knowledge seems to have been at a formal, academic level, for Tycho made too many references—even in his mature years—to "proving" the rectitude of his system for the equivalence to have been second nature.[40] But somehow and sometime, presumably during his contemplation of Mars's parallax, and sometime before the fall of 1584, Tycho struck on the conversion, inversion, or whatever means he used that produced his system. Unfortunately, however, getting a glimpse of the system was only half the battle. When he actually set out the scheme in detail, with the proper ratios of planetary orbits to the sun's orbit, he found that his new system required that the orbit of Mars intersect the orbit of the sun.

Although it is difficult to resurrect the ontology encapsulated in medieval and Renaissance references to the celestial spheres, there can be no doubt that in the second half of the sixteenth century at least, intellectuals in general and Tycho Brahe in particular believed that something real existed in the heavens to carry the planets through their appointed rounds.[41] The objections raised by such well-known contemporaries as Mästlin, Magini, and Praetorius[42] to the notion that two such spheres might be conceived to intersect could be cited as strong suggestions of Tycho's reaction to the proposition, if there were no other evidence. In fact, however, Tycho himself confessed that he initially "could not bring myself to allow this ridiculous penetration of the orbs, so that for some time, this, my own discovery, was suspect to me."[43]

What was at stake, for all of them, was the fact that the Tychonic system required an intersection of the orbits of Mars and the sun. The fact that the orbits of Mercury and Venus would have to intersect the sun's in exactly the same way seems to have escaped everyone. But whatever the illogicalities involved, the one required intersection was enough to ensure that it would take more than the flash of insight that inspired the system to make Tycho a believer in it. How many hours he must have stared at the relationships between the geometry and the astronomy, looking for a means of escape.

For if Tycho was not prepared to go so far as Copernicans did to retain the aesthetic sense of unity and simplicity that in the sixteenth century constituted the sole grounds for taking seriously the motion of the earth, neither was he willing to abandon what he had labored so long to achieve. One can well imagine, therefore, that the only way Tycho could cope with those intersections at the time would simply have been to refuse to acknowledge them—to draw the system with the orbit of Mars arbitrarily enlarged so as to encompass the orbit of the sun completely[44]—and then hope for some kind of inspiration that would solve the technical problem of accounting for Mars's stations and retrogradations. Complicating the whole issue was the problem of Mars's (null-) parallax, for any determination that ruled out the Copernican system also ruled out its inverse, the Tychonic system.

Exactly how long Tycho's system languished in this status is a matter of dispute. It has generally been assumed that Tycho had resolved his difficulties by the fall of 1584, when a mathematician by the name of Nicolai Reymers Ursus turned up at Uraniborg in the company of Tycho's friend Erik Lange. Ursus came from very deprived circumstances and is supposed even to have worked for a time as a swineherd while educating himself. By the time he arrived at Hven, however, he had published a Latin grammar (1580) and a work on surveying (1583), both dedicated to Heinrich Rantzov.[45] Later he was to work for a while at Cassel with the *landgrave* of Hesse and eventually go to Prague where he favorably impressed Hayek and even won appointment as imperial mathematician to Rudolph II (in which post he was succeeded by Tycho and Kepler).

Ursus should have been a prime candidate for employment at Hven, and indeed Tycho said that he paid Ursus for service of some kind. Things went well enough in the first week that Ursus composed a poem to Tycho thanking him for wining and dining and even giving money to a penniless scholar.[46] But Ursus seems already to have begun to rub Tycho the wrong way. Whether because he seemed just a bit too clever, a bit too ambitious, or a bit too presumptuous, Tycho became sufficiently distrustful of him, first, to exclude him from discussions of his system with Lange and the other guests and then to search and expel him from Hven when he learned that he had been snooping in the library. But his precautions were in vain. Four years later Ursus published Tycho's system—almost.

What is probably more important than the details of Tycho's reaction to the situation is the intensity of his conviction that he had been plagiarized. For although Ursus's system bore a general resemblance to Tycho's, it differed in two respects. The first was in using a rotating earth to account for the diurnal motion. This was a matter of taste as much as anything else. Tycho did not believe that the earth was rotating but admitted privately that such a phenomenon was conceivable.[47] The second difference was Ursus's orbit for Mars, which totally enclosed—did not intersect—the orbit of the sun. This was impossible. As Tycho told several correspondents in the next few years, publishing such a scheme was a confession of incompetence, because it simply could not reproduce the gross synodic phenomena of Mars, its stations and retrogradations.[48] Yet in virtually the same dip of the pen, Tycho accused Ursus of having stolen the scheme from him, but, of course, from a diagram that had been misdrawn.

In fact, however, there are several reasons for doubting that the drawing Ursus found was defective, at least in the sense implied by Tycho. What Tycho had on his hands was a defective system—one that could not even be used "internally" on Hven for any serious purpose. A few months later, when Tycho computed some positions for Mars in the spring of 1585, the only diagram he could draw for it . . . he labeled "Inversion of the Copernican Hypothesis."[49]

More curiously, as we have seen, Tycho had not yet made any plans to publish his system. In late 1585, he printed at Hven the astrological calendar that appeared under Elias Olsen's name and appended to it a brief discussion of the comet of 1585, which would have offered as plausible a context for announcing Tycho's system as his discussion of the comet of 1577 did. Shortly thereafter, he printed a title-quarto for what was to be an eight-chapter book on the comet of 1577, which included no mention at all of either Tycho's system or a table of distances that was eventually included.[50] What other conclusion can there be but that as of, say, the fall of 1586 Tycho's system was still in a form that he—as opposed to Ursus—knew was unpublishable?

In the summer of 1586, after entering into correspondence with the *landgrave* as a result of the comet of 1585, Tycho received Wilhelm's observations of the comet of 1577.[51] The opportunity to use these independent observations, made with instruments that were probably superior to those that Tycho had used in 1577, to make a new determination of parallax may well have been the spark that ignited Tycho's final drive to get his book finished. Because the results corroborated the supralunary findings that Tycho had obtained from his own data, Tycho eagerly placed them at the beginning of his chapter of critiques and went on from there.

Although the rest of the chapter could obviously have been written, altered, and rewritten any number of times, the fact remains that for several years this unfinished chapter had been the sole barrier to publishing the book. So, even though Tycho had surely looked over the literature on the comet as it came into him in 1578 and 1579 and had probably noted significant points and even made marginal comments or extensive notes for the day when he would eventually compose his critiques, it seems very unlikely that he actually had them written. The fact that references to the *landgrave*'s observations appear in the critiques of several other commentators and in particular in that of Michael Mästlin, argues in the same direction.

Although Mästlin is best known to history as the teacher of Johannes Kepler, he was a prominent astronomer in his own right. The fact that he had produced one of the few competent treatments of the new star had induced Tycho to search eagerly for his findings on the comet,[52] and when Tycho finally obtained them in 1579, he was not disappointed. Indeed, he must have been gratified to see how closely Mästlin's printed results agreed with his own. But in addition to the various angular coordinates Tycho had provided for his orbit, Mästlin had computed and plotted the comet's daily distances.[53] These distances ran from 155 earth radii (about three times the distance of the moon) upward past the sun (situated at about 1,150 earth radii) and out to 1,495 earth radii. Perhaps they should have meant as much to Tycho—to say nothing of Mästlin—when he first saw them, as they did later.

Indeed, the implication that the comet had gone right through what Tycho and everyone else regarded as the Ptolemaic spheres of Mercury and Venus, and thus that those spheres could not be the solid objects everyone seems to have thought them to be, was worthy of publication in and of itself. Presumably Tycho had either not noticed this table on first reading or, more likely, had not attached any special significance to it, because he had not yet formulated the system that made it an issue for him. Seven years later, however, the pieces appear to have fallen into place quickly, probably because Tycho was also just reading a manuscript by Christoph Rothmann that asserted (without any reference to numbers) that "the very motion of the comets is the strongest argument that the planetary spheres cannot be solid bodies."[54] Mästlin's figures seemed to provide exactly the demonstration needed for Rothmann's theory. If both were correct, if the comet had really moved in this fashion, there could be no solid spheres—and therefore no reason that the orbit of Mars could not intersect the orbit of the sun. When similar computations from his own data yielded similar distances (173 to 1,733 earth radii), Tycho registered, in letters written in mid-January 1587, his first doubts concerning the existence of solid spheres.[55] All that now stood between him and his system was a reevaluation of the question of parallax.

With the dissolution of the planetary spheres, the $4\frac{1}{2}'$ of parallax that earlier had been so threatening to Tycho's conception of things were now indispensable to it. Not surprisingly, Tycho's view of the results of earlier trials for parallax underwent a similarly rapid and profound transformation. Perhaps he made at this time the confused calculations that so mystified Kepler and various later commentators.[56] But Tycho may also have simply rationalized slightly different values for one or more of the uncertainties in the calculation (refraction, the position of a reference star, or the proper motion of the planet) to raise his parallax to $4\frac{1}{2}'$ from whatever he first thought he detected.

Already in his letters of mid-January 1587, conveying the first statements of his disbelief in the existence of solid spheres, Tycho expressed his conviction that Mars, in opposition, showed more parallax than the sun did. Any residual qualms he may have had about this startling reversal of opinion were resolved a month later, with "live" but obviously none-too-tidy parallax checks on both Venus and Mars.[57] If this remarkable achievement is not exemplary of Tycho's best work, the fact that he thought he found something, sometime, must be explained away in any account of his discovery and is at least as comprehensible (if not defensible) as the product of excitement and haste in 1587 as it can be for any other circumstances.

To literally his dying day, Tycho regarded his system of the world as the most significant achievement of his career. Clearly, then, there could scarcely be any question about publishing it, particularly as he happened to have at that very moment a book going through his own press, dealing with a subject closely related to his discovery. Quickly, therefore, Tycho wrote up an exposition of his system . . . and labeled it Chapter VIII. Then, for no other apparent reason than to avoid having a nine-chapter book, he added what had previously been an appendix to Chapter VII, dealing with the sizes and distances of the head and tail of the comet, to his new table of distances of the comet and called that material Chapter IX. All that then remained was to finish writing the extremely lengthy final chapter, now labeled X, and print up a new title-quarto describing ten chapters instead of eight.[58] Even with some problems in obtaining the quantities of paper he needed, the printing was completed by the beginning of 1588,[59] under the title *De mundi aetherei recentioribus phaenomenis. . . .* or Concerning the more recent phenomena of the ethereal world.

In marked contrast with the misfortune that was to attend Tycho's decision to make a similar insertion into the *Progymnasmata* a few years later, the consequences of publishing the Tychonic system in *De mundi* were uniformly happy. In fact, it is doubtful that the system would now be called Tychonic if Tycho had been just a bit faster in getting his book printed,[60] or a bit slower in developing his thoughts, or a bit more cautious about altering his manuscript. Even as it was, the priority question was a ticklish one.[61]

Only a month or so after Tycho began to circulate *De mundi,* one of the several people to whom Rantzov sent the seven copies that Tycho gave to him reported that someone had shown him the same system a couple of years earlier. The correspondent, a rather prominent German astrologer named Rollenhagen, could not remember the name of his informant, for when Tycho alluded to the problem in September 1588, he was able to refer to the culprit only as "some run-away servant of mine."[62] But by the time Rothmann wrote saying that the *landgrave* had already had his instrument maker construct a model of that system a few years earlier,[63] Tycho had the solution to the problem in his hands: It was a book bearing the pompous title *Fundamentum astronomicum,* published in 1588 by the person Tycho had ejected from Hven four years earlier, Nicolai Reymers Ursus.

Because what Ursus published was the form of the system that Tycho had been using at Hven in 1584, Tycho could be morally certain that Ursus had indeed plagiarized it. But the only way a charge of intellectual theft could make sense was for Tycho to admit that he himself had been using through 1584 the nonintersecting (i.e., Ursus's) form of the system. And because in that form, the system could not account for the stations and retrogradations of Mars, such a claim would have to be accompanied by an elaborate explanation, indeed, if it were to be any more than a confession of his own incompetence. Whatever Tycho said about his conversion from one form to the other might even have revealed the role of Mästlin's table of distances in the conversion.

It cannot be surprising, then, that Tycho should have been unwilling to risk this approach. He did, however, have two circumstances in his favor. One was the technical untenability of the nonintersecting system—the fact that it failed to represent the gross synodic phenomena of Mars and still involved intersections of spheres (Mercury's and Venus's with the sun).[64] The second was the fact that Tycho himself had tended—even before he knew that he had to defend his priority—to refer the genesis of his system not to the stage at which he finally decided that the celestial spheres were not a problem but to the time when he first saw how all of the planetary theories could be put together in an inverted Copernican scheme. Thus in his publication of the system, he mentioned having discovered it "four years ago."[65] So when Tycho poured out his tale of woe in letters to Brucaeus, Rantzov, Rothmann, and Hayek, he was at least able to point, with some plausibility, to the parallax investigations of 1583 and thus antedate Ursus's claim of having conceived the system in Pomerania during the winter of 1585-6.[66] All

that remained was to patch the final hole by claiming that Ursus had found a faulty diagram.

Although Tycho's pride in his system may seem inordinate from a modern perspective, it is important to realize that in its day it represented the best of both worlds. Until the advent of the telescope, at the very earliest, the available evidence did not render belief in the mobility of the earth even plausible, let alone convincing. It is not necessary to deny either that the specter of a moving earth may have been the crucial incentive to a new physics of motion or that the traumatic seventeenth-century battle with the Roman Catholic church may have had the life-and-death implications for early modern science that its practitioners saw in the struggle. It is reasonable to insist, however, that neither of these issues had much to do with the progress of astronomy, at least during the generation or two after Tycho. The geometry of the Copernican system, on the other hand, represented a significant astronomical advance. By extricating it from the controversial, and perhaps even unrespectable, company of Copernicus's moving earth, Tycho provided an important technical service to his discipline and almost surely also hastened acceptance of the motion of the earth.

Between the excitement induced by his discovery and the haste involved in keeping the manuscript flowing to his printer, Tycho produced a description of his discovery that was considerably less than perfect in both organization and composition. His exposition of the system itself was so sketchy that at least one reader (Rollenhagen) envisioned actual collisions between Mars and the sun.[67] Tycho's discussion of the intersections was sufficiently detailed to remove any excuse for mistaking the nature of the problem in this way, but the method he adopted for dealing with the intersections was completely inadequate. All Tycho said was that the intersections were not a problem, because he could prove (and would in a later work) that there were no solid spheres.[68] How Tycho can have expected such an unsupported assertion to have resolved, for any appreciable fraction of his readers, a difficulty that he himself had found sufficiently fundamental to dictate an a priori rejection of the system, is hard to imagine.

Tycho's readers were indoctrinated in a physical and metaphysical worldview in which comets were terrestrial bodies. Only for those who had been convinced by the first seven chapters of *De mundi* that the comet of 1577 was actually celestial would Tycho's claim that it had penetrated the sphere of Venus not be a definitional impossibility. And even for those few, the rest of the "proof" would have to come from one or two delicate observations of one comet, and an intricate chain of trigonometric calculations.

Apparently, Tycho decided that his argument was premature at best, and that however convinced he might be (by the beauty of his system, if nothing else) that the celestial machinery that everyone else seems to have taken for granted could not exist, he would at least require an induction from several comets to establish reasonable proof. The result was that he left his crucial table of distances buried in the other new chapter, some twenty pages behind the presentation of his system,[69] and provided so little connecting commentary in either place that even historians, let alone his contemporaries, were unable to perceive its role in the development of his system.

Whatever purpose Tycho envisioned for his final chapter, he must have accomplished it. Longer than the preceding nine chapters combined, it consisted of point-by-point analyses of the results of eight authors, and concise but reasoned dismissals of the efforts of eleven others.[70] The most positive aspect of the enormous amount of work that went into these critiques appeared in the first discussion, devoted to the observations of the *landgrave* of Hesse.

Although the *landgrave* had hired an astronomer after Tycho's departure in 1575, he no longer enjoyed his services when the comet appeared. When Tycho inquired in 1586 about his conclusions concerning the comet, therefore, the *landgrave* could send only a few observations he had made himself and say that if the comet of 1577 was anything like that of 1585, it would show too little parallax to be anywhere near the moon. Tycho converted those observations into a minor treatise.[71] He printed the observations, reduced them to usable data, and utilized them to conduct first a thorough investigation for parallax and then a concerted attack on the most frequently used method of finding parallax, the one developed by Regiomontanus a century earlier.[72]

The motivation for this attack was Tycho's conviction that the method was worthless from beginning to end but was so well known and ill used as to be responsible for most of the parallax that had been found for the comet.[73] The method consisted of noting two positions of the comet, and the time interval between the observations.[74] It included no provision for taking into account the comet's intrinsic motion during the interval. For the comet of 1577 this motion had been eight to ten minutes per hour during the first ten days, when most people conducted their checks for parallax. If uncompensated, it alone could produce "parallaxes" of several degrees from a long trial near the horizon and place the comet at a corresponding fraction of the moon's distance from the earth. Scarcely less palatable to Tycho was the dependence on clocks: An error of a few seconds in the timing of the interval could likewise produce a parallax of some degrees.[75]

In short, this method was a textbook example of Tycho's pet peeve: esoteric mathematical techniques with no practical felicity.[76] Of course, Tycho knew well the status that Regiomontanus enjoyed. Rather than alienate readers by seeming to denigrate him, or leave any room at all for the feeling that he disliked the method merely because it produced results that conflicted with his view of the comet's distance, Tycho decided to show that the method could work, provided—as he hastened to point out—that one used very good observations, such as the *landgrave*'s.[77] Tycho then proceeded to give seven examples, spaced from the beginning to the end of the *landgrave*'s observations, in which the method showed no parallax.[78]

From the *landgrave,* Tycho moved to Mästlin and then to two other writers, who had likewise found the comet to be above the moon.[79] Their success, however, did not earn them immunity from Tycho's criticism of their instruments, data (e.g., Copernicus's star positions), computational errors, and the like. Neither did friendship, as Tycho began his attack on the mass of writers who had found sublunarity, by reviewing the efforts of his confidant Hayek and his old mentor Schultz. (Quoting what he took to be an ancient aphorism, Tycho said, "Friend of Plato, friend of Socrates, but more a friend of truth.")[80]

If Tycho's criticism was uncompromising, it at least was fairly gentle and thoroughly constructive. Although he felt obliged to point out that Hayek had committed three sins (observed with a cross staff, used existing star coordinates, and done his calculations on a small globe),[81] he was careful to praise his earlier results on the new star and to go through his work carefully enough to show that one of the grosser errors arose from a mix-up over his reference star.[82] After detailed critiques of two more parallax findings,[83] Tycho turned to more general criticisms of eleven writers whose efforts did not deserve anything more. He then concluded with a summary providing the first public description of any of his instruments.[84]

Although **De mundi** was a book characterized more by the perspiration than the inspiration that went into it, it was nevertheless a project that Tycho perceived as necessary to get the job done. Tycho did not expect **De mundi** to establish the celestial nature of comets, much less to overthrow the Aristotelian worldview. Fortunately, it did achieve the former task, so that Tycho's failure to complete a second work treating all the subsequent comets he observed at Hven cost nothing.[85] On the other hand, not even the fact that Tycho eventually published a similarly ponderous volume on the new star was enough to overthrow the Aristotelian cosmology. Only Galileo would achieve that, after Tycho's death. And he would do it with a completeness that would surely have left Tycho with doubts about the wisdom of having set the process in motion in the first place.

Notes

...[15] O. Gingerich, "Copernicus and Tycho," *Scientific American* 229 (1973). The diagrams are dated 22 January and 13 February 1578. At the time this article was written, Gingerich thought the diagrams were in Tycho's hand. For the correction of this assumption, see Gingerich and Westman, *The Wittich Connection*, pp. 5-9 and 23-6.

[16] Gingerich, "Copernicus and Tycho," p. 90.

[17] Ibid., 100.

[18] The Islamic tradition attributing the original idea to Ptolemy was not verified until Bernard R. Goldstein, "The Arabic Version of Ptolemy's Planetary Hypotheses," *Transactions of the American Philosophical Society* 57 (1967), recognized the discussion in an Arabic text of Ptolemy's *Planetary Hypotheses*.

[19] The numbers used here are Willy Hartner's, "Mediaeval Views on Cosmic Dimensions," *Mélanges Alexandre Koyre* (Paris: Hermann, 1964) from the Islamic tradition. For the sixteenth-century use of similar numbers, see Westman, "Three Responses," p. 302; and Tycho ([in *Tychonis Brahe Dani Opera Omnia*, edited by J. L. E. Dreyer, 15 vols., Copenhagen Libraria Gyldendaliana, 1913-29] II, 417).

[20] In Figure A.4.2 of Appendix 4, the minimum distance, 1,260, must equal $R-r$, and r must be to R as 100 is to 152. So, $R-R$ (100/152) = 1,260 = 52/152 R; thus $R = 3,683$, $r = 2,423$.

[21] XIII, 305-33.

[22] VII, 63.

[23] VII, 59.

[24] IV, 448-56. See also C. D. Hellman, *The Comet of 1577: Its Place in the History of Astronomy* (New York: 1944), p 204.

[25] XIII, 319.

[26] IV, 455-6.

[27] Gingerich and Westman, *The Wittich Connection*, p. 17. Dudith was a Catholic bishop who left the church in 1567 to marry a Polish noblewoman. In 1589 he reported that (the deceased) Paul Wittich had obtained a copy of Copernicus's "Commentariolus" from his uncle, Balthasar Sartorius, who presumably got it from Rheticus. This was apparently the pipeline through which Tycho got his copy from Hayek in 1575. . . . Jerzy Dobrzycki and Lech Szczucki "On the Transmissions of Copernicus's Commentariolus in the Sixteenth Century," *Journal for the History of Astronomy* 20 (1989): 25-7.

[28] IV, 123-34.

[29] VII, 61.

[30] IV, 107-34. The computations were made with the constants of Tycho's new solar theory, which became available in 1580 (VII, 60).

[31] IV, 386, 389.

[32] IV, 135-54 (original pagination, 158-84). The orientation from Venus arose from Tycho's faulty inclination: see J.-B. J. Delambre, *Histoire de l'astronomie moderne* (Paris, 1821), p. 222. Tycho later came to believe that the phenomenon was some kind of illusion or special effect of perspective (IV, 175; VI, 171).

[33] IV, 171-2, 497.

[34] IV, 491, 497. Tycho says in IV, 174, that his table of distances was derived after Chapter VII, on the tail of the comet, was written.

[35] Dreyer, [*Tycho Brahe: A Picture of Scientific Life and Work in the Sixteenth Century*, edited by J. L. E. Dreyer, Edinburgh: Adam & Charles black, 1890; 2nd ed., New York: Dover, 1963] 167.

[36] See O. Gingerich, "From Copernicus to Kepler: Heliocentrism As Model and As Reality," *Proceedings of the American Philosophical Society* 117 (1973):516-20, for evidence "that Copernicus was well known and esteemed as a mathematician and astronomer" but that his heliocentric theory was generally ignored.

[37] VII, 80. Tycho's trials for parallax are on X, 174-8, 243-9, 283-8.

[38] IV, 155-6; V, 115; VI, 179; VII, 199; VIII, 205.

[39] VI, 178.

[40] See VI, 178-9, 236, 239, and VII, 130, 230, 294-5 for the most extended of such statements. They start by implying an equivalence between the systems and recognizing that the distinction between them rests on disproving the motion of the earth but then come around to testing astronomically instead of physically for the motion of the earth—the failure of comets in opposition to display any motion reflecting the earth's. In III, 175, Tycho speaks of testing the planets at their stations to see whether they show any parallax to indicate that the earth is moving! Derek Price, "Contra-Copernicus: A Critical Re-estimation of the Mathematical Planetary Theory of Ptolemy, Copernicus, and Kepler," in Marshall Clagett, ed., *Critical Prob-*

lems in the History of Science (Madison: University of Wisconsin Press, 1959), pp. 212-13, pointed out that Copernicus was guilty of the same kind of lapse, and Robert S. Westman likewise for Mästlin, "The Comet and the Cosmos: Kepler, Mästlin, and the Copernican Hypothesis," in Jerzy Dobrzycki, ed., *The Reception of Copernicus' Heliocentric Theory* (Dordrecht, Netherlands: Nÿhoff, 1973), p. 24.

[41] See William H. Donohue, "The Solid Planetary Spheres in Post-Copernican Natural Philosophy," *Westman* (1975); and Eric Aiton, "Celestial Spheres and Circles," *History of Science* 19 (1981): 75-113.

[42] IV, 474-6; VIII, 206; Westman, "Three Responses," 299-301.

[43] VII, 130. Noel Swerdlow, "The Derivation and First Draft of Copernicus' Planetary Theory: A Translation of the Commentariolus with Commentary," *Proceedings of the American Philosophical Society* 117 (1973): 471-8 argued that Copernicus arrived at the same intellectual dilemma and (lacking the "evidence" found by Tycho) chose to put the earth in motion. For more argument on the subject, see *Archives Internationale d'Histoire des Sciences* (1975): 82-92, and (1976): 108-58. Tycho certainly thought Copernicus subscribed to literal spheres (III, 173).

[44] Indeed, this is exactly what *Gassendi* ([*Tychonis Brahei Vita, Accessit Nicolai Copernici, Georgii Peurbachii et Joannis Regiomontani Vita*, by Pierre Gassendi, Paris, 1654; cited from Swedish edition, *Tycho Brahe: Mannen och Verket*, Efter Gassendi översatt med Kommentar av Wilhelm Norlind, Lund, Sweden: C. W. K. Gleerup, 1951] 78) says Tycho did.

[45] *Dreyer,* 184.

[46] VIII, 204.

[47] VII, 80: VIII, 45-6. Tycho's principal disciple, Longomontanus, later adopted what has come to be called the semi-Tychonic system involving a rotating earth.

[48] VII, 149, 200-1, 388: VIII, 47.

[49] X, 284. C. Jones, "The Geoheliocentric Planetary System: Its Development and Influence in the Late Sixteenth and Seventeenth Centuries" (Ph.D. diss., Cambridge University, 1964), pp. 35-6; and K. P. Moesgaard "Copernican Influence on Tycho Brahe," in Dobrzycki, "The Reception of Copernicus," pp. 311-55, both commented on this apparently anomalous diagram.

[50] IV, 496-7.

[51] IV, 207-38.

[52] *Observatio & demonstratio cometae aetherei, qui anno 1577 et 1578. Constitutio in sphaera veneris, apparuit, . . .* (1578), pp. 52-3. Hayek did not like Mästlin's conclusions and attacked them in letters to Tycho. When Tycho finally received the letters (they had gone astray), he replied to Hayek that he did not defend Mästlin out of friendship, because he did not even know him, but if he had to name the foremost astronomer in Germany, Mästlin would be one of his two choices. VII, 205-6, 48, 50, 52.

[53] IV, 177-9. Tycho later praised Mästlin's discussion by telling Hayek that "no one has produced so erudite and ingenious a work, and no one has provided anything so agreeable and probable." VII, 20. In his analysis of Mästlin's tract, Tycho said that the chart of distances was not perfect but that Mästlin was the only one in Germany to have come up with it: IV, 209.

[54] Edward Rosen, "The Dissolution of the Celestial Spheres," *Journal of the History of Ideas* 45 (1985): 28-9. In his return letter to Rothmann, Tycho said he was wonderfully pleased with the treatise: VI, 85.

[55] VI, 88, 70.

[56] What is involved is an apparently circular computation (X, 283-6) that first assumes parallax and then derives it. Kepler's explanation (*Dreyer,* 179) of the parallax as a mix-up between Tycho and one of his calculators on observations of the opposition of 1582-3 is deficient in two respects. First, the calculations could have been done anytime after the event, and second, publication of the *Opera omnia* showed that the anomalous calculation was done by Tycho himself.

[57] XI, 181-7, 195-8.

[58] In September 1588, after *De mundi* was out and Tycho was just beginning to hear responses to it, he wrote a lengthy letter to Caspar Peucer, in which he provided the most complete account of the genesis of his system that is available (VII, 129-30). Allowing for a bit of poetic license on the timing of his parallax computations, it outlines the one just given *in extenso.* First, the parallax test on Mars to decide between the accounts of Ptolemy and Copernicus (lines 8-26): According to Tycho, exhaustive trials showed a greater parallax for Mars and thus tended to favor the Copernican model. Although he referred these tests to the opposition of 1582-3, he was candid enough to mention that he confirmed the fit of the phenomena with Copernicus's numbers by a special trial on Venus, around 24 February 1587. So if his chronology were not perfectly consistent with the available evidence, it at least showed that Tycho was uncertain about the parallax issue right up to 1587 (lines 26-34). Given the tendency of the appearances to deny Ptolemy, Tycho continued, and the manifest absurdity of imagining the

earth to move, there was nothing else to do but to find an alternative hypothesis. At first it seemed impossible, but finally it came to him (lines 34-40). And yet his inspiration had one flaw in it, that the orb of Mars had to intersect the orb of the sun in two places. Because he still subscribed to the notion that there were real orbs in the sky, his system remained suspect to him for some time (lines 6-13). Only when he had examined the motions and parallaxes of comets did he realize that they ruled out the existence of those orbs (lines 13-21).

[59] The earliest inscribed copy is dated 20 March 88 (*Norlind,* [*Tycho Brahe: En Levnadsteckning,* med nya bidrag belysande hans liv och verk Wilhelm Norlind, Lund, Sweden: C. W. K. Gleerup, 1970]122), but a correspondent of Kepler related having visited Hven on 6 January 1588 and seeing the book completely printed (G. W. [*Johannes Kepler Gesammelte Werke,* edited by Walter Van Dyck, Max Caspar, and Franz Hammer, Munich: C. H. Beck, 1939-], XIII, 101-2).

[60] Thus the problem of obtaining paper for the book, which figures prominently in Tycho's correspondence in 1586-7 and ultimately induced him to construct his own paper mill on Hven, turned out to be a blessing in disguise.

[61] In more ways than one. By Tycho's own testimony (IV, 159; VII, 130), his system depended on the destruction of the solid spheres, which in turn, rested on the distances derived by Tycho from his orbit for the comet of 1577. Both internal evidence and Tycho's own testimony show that those distances were obtained after Tycho saw Mästlin's scheme and after he had written his own analysis of the comet's path. We therefore have the spectacle of Tycho's borrowing Mästlin's spatial conception of the orbit, without giving any credit to him, but then attacking Ursus for borrowing his (admittedly more significant) system of the world. Both Delambre and Westman suggested that Tycho borrowed from Mästlin, but for different reasons. Delambre, *Histoire de l'astronomie moderne,* p. 223, thought the similarity of Tycho's and Mästlin's inclinations (29°13′ and 28°58′) and nodes (8ˢ21°) was "un hasard assez remarquable," because he did not note that the results were standard— that Schultz got an inclination of 29°36′ (IV, 296) and that he, Roeslin, and Hayek all got 8ˢ21° for the node (IV, 251, 266). Westman, "The Comet and the Cosmos," p. 25, saw the heliocentric orbit as too similar for coincidence, although it, likewise, was surely written into the German tract and presented to King Frederick long before Tycho saw Mästlin's treatise.

[62] VII, 135, 387-9.

[63] VI, 157.

[64] VII, 149, 200, 338, and VIII, 47.

[65] IV, 155.

[66] Nicolai Raymari Ursi Dithmarsi, *Fundamentum Astronomicum* (1597), p. 37.

[67] VII, 125.

[68] IV, 159.

[69] IV, 155-6, 177-9.

[70] IV, 180-377.

[71] IV, 182-207.

[72] "De cometae magnitudine longitudineque ac de loco ejus vero problemata XVI." Although written after the comet of 1472, it was not printed until 1531 (and thereafter).

[73] IV, 83, 129, 206, 440; VII, 107-8.

[74] IV, 194.

[75] IV, 441. Even for the new star, for which proper motion was not a problem, Tycho frowned on the method because of the difficulty of getting accurate timings (III, 202).

[76] III, 184; IV, 441.

[77] IV, 195.

[78] IV, 195-206. In fact, all the parallaxes were negative rather than null. But Tycho was not one to concern himself with philosophical technicalities and did not even bother to mention the difference of refractions uniformly responsible for the anomaly.

[79] IV, 207-58. The other writers were Cornelius Gemma and Helisaeus Roeslin. See descriptions of all writings on the comet in Hellman, *The Comet of 1577.*

[80] As Tycho said (IV, 336): "Amicus Plato, Amicus Socrates, sed magis Amica Veritas." Henry Guerlac, "Amicus Plato and Other Friends," *Journal of the History of Ideas,* 39 (1978): 627-33, showed that this passage was in Luther and that variants of it were used throughout the seventeenth century.

[81] IV, 263.

[82] IV, 265.

[83] IV, 337-55 (Andreas Nolthius and Nicolaus Wincklerus).

[84] IV, 368-77.

[85] See III, 26; V, 23; VII, 131, for examples. *Norlind* (142) described the order of printing projected for the volume, which was to concern comets observed in 1580, 1582, 1585, 1590, and 1593.

Peter Zeeberg (essay date 1994)

SOURCE: "Alchemy, Astrology, and Ovid—A Love Poem by Tycho Brahe," in *Acta Conventus Neo-Latini: Proceedings of the Eighth International Congress of Neo-Latin Studies,* edited by Rhoda Schnur, *et al.,* Medieval & Renaissance Texts & Studies, No. 120, 1994, pp. 997-1007.

[*In the following essay, Zeeberg studies Brahe's Latin poem* Urania Titani *as a work that blends mythic astrology, the pseudoscience of alchemy, and the literary influence of Ovid.*]

The famous Danish astronomer Tycho Brahe (1546-1601) was a scientist and a nobleman.[1] In the society of the day that was not a suitable combination. Indeed he was forced to make a choice between his allegiance to science and his allegiance to his class and its norms and ideals. When, at an early age, he decided to devote his life to astronomy and chemistry, he went so far as to make actual plans for emigration to some great city in central Europe where he would feel the ties to his background less.

That this did not happen was due to the Danish government. Someone must have seen Tycho's greatness, and they decided to invest enough money in him to reconcile science with nobility. He was offered the island of Hven (in the Sound between Zeeland and Scania) as a fief for life, the money to build a palace designed for his purpose, plus an annual grant to run a scientific academy in a style becoming to a nobleman. This was in 1576. Tycho accepted the offer, and for the next twenty years Hven was the center of the Danish Renaissance. Not only was it a scientific institution on an international level. The place had a sophisticated, international style, which was not found elsewhere in Denmark. Apart from some letters this sophistication is most clearly recognized in Tycho's Latin poetry—and that is what I want to illustrate here through one of the finest examples: the Ovidian Heroid *Urania Titani.*[2]

"Urania's letter to Titan" pretends to be a letter from Tycho's sister Sophie (or Sophia) to her fiancé Erik Lange. Therefore I have to begin with a few words about her.[3] Sophie Brahe is quite famous in Denmark, both because she was one of the first learned ladies in Denmark, and because of her romantic love story. (It is the sort that you write novels about. And indeed there have been.) Although she was thirteen years younger than Tycho,[4] they were very close. Especially after she became a widow, at the age of twenty-nine, she spent much time with him at Hven. By that time it seems she was already well versed in both chemistry and astrology. According to Tycho he helped her to a certain degree, but when he refrained, believing that the topics were too difficult for a woman, she bought books and learned it all by herself. And then of course he had to surrender. Indeed he seems to have had a high opinion of her abilities, because we know that he intended to print one of her letters in the second volume of his *Astronomical letters* (which in the event never appeared). The letter has not been preserved, but we have his very eloquent introduction to it, which testifies both to his feelings for her and to his willingness to accept her as a woman scientist.[5] At Hven she must have met Erik Lange. He too was a nobleman, but his science was alchemy, goldmaking. Alchemy, as you will know, does not produce gold, in fact, it does quite the opposite. And very soon he had to leave Denmark in order to escape from his creditors. Sophie waited in vain for years. But finally she joined him, and in 1602 they were married, and lived together in Northern Germany in extreme poverty. In a famous letter she describes how she never even had one decent pair of stockings to wear, and some friends had to get Erik's clothes back from the pawnbroker for their wedding.[6] We do not know when Erik died, but at some time Sophie returned to Denmark, where she lived for many years in Elsinore, and died forty-five years after Tycho, at the age of eighty-seven.

All this is background. *Urania Titani,* as I said, is an Ovidian Heroid. It was written in 1594, in the period when Erik had gone to Germany and Sophie was waiting for him back in Scania. It is a letter of precisely 600 verses, exhorting Erik, or Titan, to return to her, Urania. The names are the ones they used at Hven. Sophie was the earthly muse of astronomy. Erik was the sun (we shall see why in a moment). Tycho himself was called Apollo.[7] From the beginning it is obvious that this is an erotic poem. Titan has left Urania in favor of alchemy. Alchemy therefore is her rival. In a very Ovidian way it is described how alchemy steals him from her by molesting the beautiful body which was meant for her to hug and hold, etc. Titan really is in love with his alchemy, just as she is in love with him. And to stress that point, we are given a whole series of parallels between Urania's longing for Titan and Titan's alchemy:

> Ars vana et linquens vacuatas ære crumenas,
> Quam propter vacuo linquor et ipsa thoro.
>
> (11-12)

Your science is empty [or vain], and it leaves your purse empty too. I too have been left, and my bed is empty because of your science.

Urania suffers for her love, just as Titan suffers because of his alchemy. When she complains about his desperate toiling night and day to make alchemy friendly towards his wishes, she has just, a few lines before, said that alchemy is jealous of *her* wishes, and that:

> Quam propter sine sole dies, sine sidere
>   noctes
> Orba traho, quod abes, Solque Jubarque
>   meum.
>
> (13-14)

Because of that I live alone through days without sun and nights without stars, because you are gone, my sun.

Titan, of course, is a name for the sun. And that is all the more interesting as the sun has an alchemical meaning too. In the system of analogies which, according to the science of the time, tied all parts of the universe together, the sun is analogous to gold.[8] Therefore not only their sufferings but also their aims are analogous. Urania's longing for the sun is analogous to Titan's longing for gold. And, we may conclude, equally impossible! But Urania does not reach that conclusion. It is hinted, at, but not made explicit.

Then follows a description of her anxiety (43-102). She goes through all the things that can go wrong, and all the dangers she can think of. This passage is closely modeled on the first of Ovid's *Heroides*, the letter from Penelope to Ulysses. For example, Tycho shows his Ovidian spirit by making Titan's alchemy into a complete Trojan war. Urania, of course, is the faithful Penelope awaiting her far-roaming Ulysses, Titan. This means that Urania is not only faithful but trusting. She trusts that he will return some time—as of course he will, being a Ulysses—and that he has some good reason for staying away now. The listing of these reasons, or dangers, ends like this:

> Quid multis? cum scire nequit, cur lentior absis
>   Mens mea per caussas irrequieta volat.
> Tempora si memores, bene quæ memoramus
>   amantes,
>   Nostra querela suam non venit ante diem;
> Nam mihi discedens tremulo es sic ore locutus,
>   Pallentes lachrymis cum maduere genæ:
> Sol prius auriferi non tanget velleris astrum,
>   Quam tibi me reducem Scania vestra ferat.
> Coelicus is Titan vellus bis terve revisit
>   Phryxæum, at Titan Terree noster abes.
>
> (101-10)

In short: because I do not know your reasons for staying away my mind wanders from cause to cause. But if you cast your mind back to the times that we lovers remember so well, you will see that I do not complain too soon. Remember what you said at your departure, your lips all trembling, your cheeks all wet with tears: "The sun won't reach the sign of the golden fleece before you have me back in Scania!" But now the Titan of the sky has been twice—even three times—at the Phrixean fleece—while you, the Titan of the earth, still stay away.

He has not kept his promise to return before the sun reached the sign of Aries, i.e., before the vernal equinox.

This too is Ovid, not the first of the *Heroides,* but the second. The second, Phyllis to Demophoon, is not the letter of a trustful wife, rather the half-mad howling of a woman realizing that she has been left forever by a deceitful man. The whole passage is a rewriting of a passage from there. Or rather, Tycho has taken two passages, which in Ovid are separated by two distichs, and switched them around, leaving out the distichs in the middle, in which Phyllis says that she has kept up her hope for a long time, because we are slow in believing when belief hurts, and that she has been lying to herself.[9]

Has Tycho left out these lines because they would not fit in—or, on the contrary, to emphasize them? I believe we are supposed to know our Ovid, and to observe that the words are missing. I see this as a hint at the doubt which lurks under the surface of Urania's trustfulness. But the passage has more to it. Titan has promised to return before "the other sun" reaches the golden fleece. That too has an alchemical undertone. The twelve signs of the zodiac were used as symbols for the different steps through which the "great work" of alchemy should be performed—so that the beginning of a new year (at Aries) would signify the successful completion of the work. The same was also true of the myth about Jason's quest for the golden fleece. This, of course, once more gives the parallel between his aims and hers. Titan's returning to Scania and Titan's making gold are both covered by the image of the sun reaching the sign of Aries. But there is a bit more to it.

Urania says that the sun of the sky has already been at the golden fleece, while Titan is still far away. That is ambiguous. On the surface, he is far from *her,* but it might just as well mean *far from the golden fleece,* i.e., from making gold—and that is the course Urania now takes. She tries to convince him that alchemy could just as well be performed at her place, in her garden in Scania, where she has an alchemical laboratory: "You are not Jason," she says, "and I am not Medea—but if you want a Colchis it is here."[10] This claim she now sets out to prove scientifically, so to speak. She starts by expounding one of the central alchemical texts, the so called "Emerald Tablet," "Tabula Smaragdina."[11] This text gives some typically opaque prescriptions on how to produce the philosophers' stone (at least that is how it would be read in this period). Urania's expounding is done in rather an offhand manner:

> Sol pater (ut referunt) Lunaque mater erit.
> Sis igitur Titan pater et sim Femina Lunæ
> Persimilis Mater; sexus et ordo juvant.
>   (166-68)[12]

The sun, so they say, shall be its father, the moon its mother. You, Titan, are the father, and I, being a woman and very similar to the moon, can be the mother—sex and position help.

Similarly the stone is said first to rise towards heaven and then to return to earth. This, says Urania, corresponds to her being "the earthly Urania."[13] Rather unconvincing really. And later on:

> Ventus et hunc utero fertur portasse, vel isto
>   Forte etiam possit qui meliora mihi est.
>   (173-74)[14]

They say that the wind has born it in its womb—and perhaps I have a womb which can bear something even better.

The problem of why she should be called "the wind" is simply left unexplained.

A "normal" explanation of these passages would be that it all has to do with the separation of the spirit from matter. The material you are working with has to be separated into a volatile part (the spirit or "the philosophical mercury"—that must be "the wind") and a fixed part (the body or "sulphur"). This spirit has to "rise towards heaven," and then to descend to earth. The two are to be united again in a new form, spirit and body in one—the philosophers' stone. The stone is the offspring of "the chemical marriage" between the two.[15] This is obviously what Tycho is thinking of. A chemical wedding is what it is all about. And the distinction between mercury and sulphur matches the two personalities quite well. Titan (whose horoscope, as it turns up later, is ruled by Mercury) is restless, hard to catch (volatile, so to speak)—as opposed to the stability of Urania.[16]

Urania then proceeds to the actual chemical processes (179-222). Here again the connection between the production of the philosophers' stone and the production of a child is stressed. The two processes are supposed to be analogous. But Urania is not fettered by the distinction between analogy and identity. She just examines all the points at which the stone can be likened to a child, and concludes that if Titan wants to practice alchemy, he might just as well come back to Denmark, to make a child with her in her garden! The whole passage must be meant as a parody of alchemy, and a witty one, in my opinion. It clearly makes fun of the alchemical tendency to excessive mystification. In reality the fifty verses of alchemy amount to very little.

Love is alchemy, therefore Titan ought to come home to make love. Also, I think, the confusion of analogy with identity might be a hint at a tendency which Tycho disliked in some of his colleagues. At least that is a topic which was discussed quite a lot by the scientists of this period.[17]

At the same time the passage characterizes Urania. If the hope of Titan's returning is rather feeble, she must create a hope. And she does it by all available means. She may not even believe in the argumentation herself, at bottom. But she does it as an act of will. It therefore appears quite natural that doubt and hesitation crop up immediately after her rejoicing over the good prospects (223ff.). Of course he must not think that she is trying to force him. He can take the time he needs. She trusts in him. "Only, others are suspicious of my trust." And now her doubt shows itself as a second voice, the voice of "the others," which rings in her head. They say that she has been deceived by his eloquence. And as if to signal her wavering, Tycho has put one line from the second of Ovid's *Heroides* into her attempt to answer the attack. "I have not been deceived," she says:

> At non mellifluis, quorum tibi copia, verbis,[18]
>   Quod decepta, queror; si qua ea culpa, mea
>   est;
> Sponte tuis cessi votis, te sponte probavi,
>   Ut Chalybem magnes attrahit, ipsa sequor.
> Inter tot genere illustres, quos Dania nutrit,
>   Solus es, ex imo qui mihi corde places.
>   (237-42)

I do not complain that I have been deceived by all your sweet words. If anyone is to blame it is me. I have followed your wishes of my own free will. I love you of my own free will. I am attracted to you as steel is attracted to a magnet. Among all the noblemen that Denmark has produced, you are the only one I like sincerely.

Here Tycho shows his sister's pride—and her evasiveness. Faced with her lover's possible infidelity, she answers that *she* has not been deceived. She will not tolerate being called naive or credulous. The obvious answer would have been to deny his infidelity, but in this way she manages to evade that question altogether.

But the question is not going to be evaded. As an afterthought she claims that Titan's eloquence is not fictitious at all, as it was given him by nature. It is in his horoscope. It is doubtful whether that is a relevant point at all. Why should he not be able to misuse a gift from nature? Another evasion—and at the same time an attempt to move the discussion to a field where she feels at home, namely astrology:

> Hanc [facundiam] tibi Mercurius Veneri
>   sociatus in ortu,
> Ædibus e propriis largus habere dedit;

Nec mirum, Superum Præconi quod Venus
   adstans
   Blanda tibi et pariter verba diserta parit;
Quin simul his Phoebus Geminorum iungitur
   astro,
   Noster et hinc Geminus forte oriundus amor.
Sed levis est Stilbon, levis est Cytheræa,
   Gemelli
   Sunt duplices, constans quid queat inde
   sequi?

                 (251-58)

This [i.e., eloquence] was given you abundantly by Mercury, united with Venus at the ascendant and in his own domicile. It is no wonder that the spokesman of the gods, standing close to Venus, makes your words both sweet and eloquent. And at the same time Phoebus joins the two in the sign of Gemini. Perhaps this is the basis for our mutual love. But Stilbon [Mercury] is fickle, Cytherea is fickle, the twins are two-faced— what constancy can come from this?

Thus Urania's attempt to get away from the question of Titan's infidelity backfires. His horoscope shows precisely what she did not want to talk about: fickleness, infidelity.

Now she is in dire straits, and her desperation is obvious when she resorts to the impossible wish that Titan's infidelity may at least be a problem to his other girls rather than herself (265-66)! Now the imagined words of "the others" are malicious:

Te procul ex oculis quæ distas, scilicet, unam
   Absens, tamque diu, tamque remotus amet?
Quid faciat, quæso, longinquis deses in oris,
   Qui, Paris alter ut est, nil nisi amare potest?
Crede peregrino captivus amore tenetur,
   Quænam illa Urania est forsan et unde rogat.

                 (269-74)

Do you really think he still loves you, now that he has been so far from you for so long? What do you think he is doing, on distant shores with nothing to do, he who like another Paris, can do nothing else but make love. You can be sure that he is being held captive by the love of someone else. He may even be asking himself who that Urania is, and where she comes from.

I need hardly say that here again was a line from the second of the *Heroides:*[19]

Sic aiunt; surdæ at frustra mihi talia narrant,
   Et surdam et cæcam me facit Arctus Amor.

                 (275-76)

That is what they say, but they preach to deaf ears. My love stands firm, and makes me deaf and blind.

Her love makes her deaf and blind. That really is sadly appropriate!

For a long time astrology seems like a maze where she keeps moving further in, the more she tries to get out. In an attempt to remedy the threatening position of the virgin, she refers to her own horoscope where the virgin is positively placed—only to realize, of course, that a virgin is not the proper figure to involve in her love life (291-94). When at last she manages to find some details indicating that they will get married after all (329-62), she just sticks to them, discarding, or rather forgetting, all the negative signs—both deaf and blind!

We are by now about halfway through the poem. She has dealt with her rival, alchemy, and counter-attacked with the help of astrology, but has accomplished neither part very convincingly. The following passages concerned with family and friends we shall go into in less detail. In these passages we find several references to *Heroides* I. Urania is comforted by the thought of her son, whose horoscope is very promising. But suddenly she hears a rumor that a common friend of hers, Titan's, and Apollo's (i.e., Tycho's) has died. This brings back her sorrow. She tries not to write about it, but it reminds her of how isolated she and Titan have become. Even her brothers are very hostile towards her affair with Titan. Only Tycho, the eldest brother, is left. He has always supported her, and always will— and that is consonant with all the fine qualities and virtues that can be deduced from his horoscope. Thus, through a neat play of allusions Tycho declares his solidarity with his sister by making her praise him! At the very end all her fears reappear with great force.

Attamen haud credam, quod sint tam Numina
   sæva
   Nuper ut incepta spe spoliare velint.
Id saltem vereor, ne, dum lentissimus absis,
   Quod mea sit reduci forma probata minus.

                 (567-70)

I really cannot believe that the gods would be so cruel as to deprive me of my recently acquired hope. I only fear that I will be less attractive to you when you return. . . .

This idea of her getting old is the last reference to the first of Ovid's *Heroides.*[20] But she fears more than that:

Anxietas me multa premit, nec deserit
   unquam,
   Hæc quoque dum scribo, durior, ecce! redit.
Nam modo qui fuerat de morte incertus amici
   Rumor, en hunc nimium littera missa probat.

                 (575-78)

Anxiety of many kinds haunts, and never leaves me. Even while I write it comes back in even harsher form. For what was earlier an uncertain rumor of the death of a friend, is now shown to be true by a letter.

Urania is shaken. She now reveals that she has had premonitions about it long ago, but, as she says:

Attamen haud potui cito persentiscere, rumor
   Quod nimium verus (proh dolor) iste foret.
                                        (587-88)

I really could not comprehend so soon that the rumor spoke so very true.

Here the Latin wording definitively recalls not Ovid, but Tycho himself, twenty verses ago when Urania said that she could not believe that the gods would deprive her of her hope. Now that she sees, in another connection, that hope can be frustrated, the wording ("attamen haud . . .") refers back to her own hope! And as if that was not enough, the ominous second poem of the *Heroides* is in the next distich:

Nempe ægre quæ grata minus sunt, credimus,
   at quæ
Sunt accepta satis, mox meruere fidem.
                                        (589-90)[21]

Only unwillingly do we believe what is less welcome, but what is pleasing will soon gain credence.

Not only is this the sentiment of Ovid's second Heroid. These are the words that were so demonstratively left out earlier! Urania's self-deception has come to the surface in a case closely analogous to her hopes about Titan. But still, of course, she does not have to draw conclusions from that analogy. She is as close to giving up as she can be, but she does not. A few lines later the poem ends with the wish that Titan will "live well, so that he can return safe and sound."[22]

The last verses of all provide the date: The letter is written "while the sun on its way back catches the two fishes."[23] That is one month before the vernal equinox, which earlier in the poem was used with its alchemical meaning. Therefore, one could say, the date either signifies that we are in the last phase of the great alchemical work—and that means hope—or it is a reference to Titan's three times broken vow to return before the vernal equinox—and that would mean despair. The end balances. Urania has kept hope living, against all odds, perhaps against all reason.

Through these three languages, so to speak, the language of alchemy, of astrology and of imitation, Tycho

has managed to produce a shrewd psychological description of his sister. Here we have a woman who shows great strength, as an act of will, although at heart she is weak and frightened, a woman whose love conquers everything, even her own sense of reality. The element of self-deception may not seem very flattering, but there is an extra side to it. It appears from the manuscript in which the text is preserved[24] that the poem was meant to be signed by Sophie herself and sent to Erik Lange as a real letter. Titan himself was the primary reader of the poem. Therefore the hints that Urania is deceiving herself when she believes that Titan will return some day, are in fact meant as a challenge to Erik. Indirectly he is accused of infidelity. To refute the accusation, he will have to come home. In that way the poem not only shows the high standard of the products from Tycho Brahe's milieu. It also shows the sophistication of the milieu itself, a milieu where a poem like this could form part of the social intercourse.

Notes

[1] A new standard biography of Tycho Brahe has recently appeared: Victor E. Thoren, *The Lord of Uraniborg* (Cambridge, 1990). This deals in much greater detail than earlier biographies with the problems involved in Tycho's noble status. Other biographies are: J. L. E. Dreyer, *Tycho Brahe, a Picture of Scientific Life and Work in the Sixteenth Century* (Edinburgh, 1890; repr., New York, 1963), and Wilhelm Norlind, *Tycho Brahe, En levnadsteckning med nya bidrag belysande hans liv och verk* (Lund, 1970), (in Swedish). Tycho's complete works have been published in fifteen volumes: *Opera Omnia Tychonis Brahe Dani*, ed. J. L. E. Dreyer, Hans Ræder and Eiler Nystrøm (Copenhagen, 1913-29; repr., Amsterdam: Swets & Zeitlinger, 1972).

[2] *Opera Omnia*, 9:193-207. See: Peter Zeeberg, "Kemi og kærlighed: naturvidenskab i Tycho Brahes latindigtning," in *Litteratur og lærdom. Dansk-svenske nylatindage april 1985*, ed. Marianne Alenius and Peter Zeeberg. Renæssancestudier, vol. 1 (Copenhagen: Museum Tusculanum Press, 1987), 149-61; Karsten Friis-Jensen and Minna Skafte Jensen in *Dansk litteraturhistorie*, vol. 2 (Copenhagen: Gyldendal, 1984), 404-12; Oluf Friis, *Den danske Litteraturs Historie* (Copenhagen, 1937), 448-50. A new edition with translation, commentary and introduction in Danish by me is forthcoming. Other treatments of Tycho Brahe's Latin poetry are: Peter Zeeberg, "Amor pa Hven, Tycho Brahes digt til Erik Lange," in *Renæssancen—Dansk, Europæisk, Globalt*, ed. Minna Skafte Jensen and Marianne Pade. Renæssancestudier, vol. 2 (Copenhagen: Museum Tusculanum Press, 1988), 161-81; Peter Zeeburg, "Adel og Lærdom hos Tycho Brahe," in *Latin og nationalsprog i Norden efter reformationen*, ed. M. Alenius, B. Bergh, I. Boserup, K. Friis-Jensen, and M. Skafte Jensen. Renæssancestudier, vol. 5 (Copenhagen, 1991), 21-31.

[3] The only existing biography of Sophie Brahe is: F. R. Friis, *Sofie Brahe Ottesdatter. En biografisk Skildring* (Copenhagen, 1905).

[4] There is some confusion as to the year of her birth. Tycho's first biographer, Gassendi (1655), says that she was ten years younger than him, which would make it 1556, and that is what everybody has believed since then. But Tycho himself refers to her being fourteen years old in 1573 (*Opera Omnia,* 1:131). I have preferred the latter, especially as it seems to be in accordance with the astrological information in *Urania Titani.*

[5] *Opera Omnia,* 9:324-26.

[6] Letter to Margrete Brahe, 23 August 1602: *Danske Magazin* 3 (1747): 28ff. and 43ff.

[7] "Apollo" is found only in *Urania Titani,* but "Urania" and "Titan" are found also in Tycho's correspondence.

[8] Tycho Brahe himself has given a good description of this system in a letter to Christopher Rothmann (17 August 1588): *Opera Omnia* 6:144ff. For introductions to alchemy, with bibliographies see: Wayne Shumaker, *The Occult Sciences in the Renaissance. A Study in Intellectual Patterns* (Berkeley/Los Angeles/London, 1972), and Charles Nicholl, *The Chemical Theatre* (London, 1980).

[9] Ov. *Her.* II, 9-12: "Spes quoque lenta fuit. Tarde quae credita laedunt / credimus. Invita nunc et amante nocent. / Saepe fui mendax pro te mihi, saepe putavi / alba procellosos vela referre notos." Lines 95-100 in *Urania Titani* imitate Ov. *Her.* II, 13-16; lines 103-4 imitate *Her.* II, 7-8; and lines 107-10 imitate *Her.* II, 3-6.

[10] Lines 111-16: "Non puto, quod ratibus secteris Iasonis aurum / Aut furtum lanæ versicoloris ames. / Nec Medæa fui, nec ero, nil fraudibus utor, / Colchida si cupias, hic quoque Colchis erit. / Pergula læta mihi est, pulcher quam circuit hortus, / Vix cui par dabitur, Colchida utrumque vocem."

[11] On this see: Julius Ruska, *Tabula Smaragdina. Ein Beitrag zur Geschichte der hermetischen Literatur.* Heidelberger Akten der von-Portheim-stiftung 16. Arbeiten aus dem Institut für Geschichte der Naturwissenschaft, vol. 4 (Heidelberg, 1926), with critical edition.

[12] *Tabula Smaragdina,* 4: "Pater ejus est Sol, mater ejus Luna. . . ."

[13] "Scandit is in coelos, iterum terrena revisit; / Sic terrena etiam dicor ego Urania" (lines 169-70). Cf.

Tabula smaragdina, 8: "Ascendit a terra in coelum, iterumque descendit in terram, et recipit vim superiorum et inferiorum."

[14] *Tabula Smaragdina,* 4: " . . . portavit illud ventus in ventre suo; nutrix ejus terra est."

[15] For a good description of these ideas, see Nicholl, 29ff.

[16] This does not fit exactly, though, as normally mercury is feminine and sulphur masculine. But the opposite can be found: see Maurice P. Crosland, *Historical Studies in the Language of Chemistry* (London, 1962), 18, note 51.

[17] Brian Vickers, "Analogy versus identity: the rejection of occult symbolism, 1580-1680," in *Occult and Scientific Mentalities in the Renaissance,* ed. Brian Vickers (Cambridge: Cambridge University Press, 1984), 95-163.

[18] Ov. *Her.* II, 49: "Credidimus blandis, quorum tibi copia verbis."

[19] Ov. *Her.* II, 106: "Ei mihi, si, quae sim Phyllis et unde rogas."

[20] Ov. *Her.* I, 115-16: "Certe ego, quae fueram te discedente puella, / protinus ut venias, facta videbor anus."

[21] Ov. *Her.* II, 9-10: "Spes quoque lenta fuit. Tarde quae credita laedunt / credimus. . . ."

[22] Lines 603-4: "Quod superest, bene vive diu; ut salvusque revisas / Uraniam; o Titan semper amate, vale!"

[23] Lines 605-8: "Hæc in Erichsholmi perarata est litera Castro, / Cum geminos Pisces Sol redeundo capit. / Di cito dent gemini hic pisces capiamus Amantes, / Tuque redux Titan et tua ego Urania."

[24] The National Library in Vienna: Cod. Lat. 10686[12]. In the manuscript the first four verses, which contain the name of the addressee, appear after the rest of the text with the heading: "Superscriptio Epistolæ huius, ubi composita et ab Urania obsignata fuerit, hæc erit."

E. C. Krupp (essay date 1996)

SOURCE: "Observing the Occasion," in *Sky and Telescope,* Vol. 92, No. 6, December, 1996, pp. 68-69.

[*In the following essay, Krupp evaluates the legacy of Brahe's astronomical observations.*]

Once you get past a sesquicentennial—the felicitously fabricated designation for a 150th anniversary—half-century acknowledgments are awkward and contrived commemorations. Masquerading as milestones, they are missing that zero in the tens place that tells you we really have something to celebrate. Ordinarily, then, I would have let this month's 450th anniversary of the birth of that great Dane Tycho Brahe—on December 14th—pass without cake and candle. But I was too young in 1946 to appreciate the quadricentennial, and I suspect that the quincentennial in 2046 may be observed without me. If I'm still around, I'll be 102 and grateful to carpe any diem at all. So, seizing the half century, I have decided to salute Tycho now.

I am not the only one mindful of Tycho's midcentenary. A little over a year ago, two scholars in the Czech Republic—Alena Hadravova and Petr Hadrava—announced their intention to honor him with a translation into Czech of Tycho's treatise on his innovative instruments, ***Astronomiae instauratae mechanica.*** Tycho spent the last two years of his life in Prague, now the capital of the Czech Republic, and is entombed there in Tyn Church.

Tycho has been called the greatest observational astronomer who lived before the invention of the telescope, and his instruments are what qualify him for the title. He established Uraniborg, Europe's first national observatory, on the Baltic island of Hven in 1576 with support from Frederick II, the Danish king. He left his astronomical headquarters 21 years later, however, when Frederick's successor put Tycho on waivers. This kind of thing still seems to go on at national observatories.

Despite the reversal of royal fortunes, December's sky is committed to high-level acclaim for Tycho by lifting aloft Cassiopeia, the Queen. Tycho's careful surveillance of the 1572 supernova in that constellation helped solidify the value of accurate observation and precise measurement.

Cassiopeia is near the top of the sky during the early evening hours this month. . . . It's where the meridian—the blue vertical line that splits the map in half—crosses the Milky Way, a little north of the zenith at the chart's center. Cassiopeia presides overhead more or less as she did on November 11, 1572, when Tycho spotted her stars hosting the supernova that became known as Tycho's Star. He later wrote he was "contemplating, as usual, the celestial vault," territory he knew as well as his own neighborhood, when he saw "with inexpressible astonishment, near the zenith, in Cassiopeia, a radiant star of extraordinary magnitude."

Tycho didn't realize he was witnessing the explosive, catastrophic finale of a star. He actually thought the *stella nova,* or new star, had condensed out of the cloudy vapors of the Milky Way. For two weeks the supernova was brighter than any other star in the sky. Changing color as it gradually faded, it completely disappeared by spring 1574. Although the true protocols of stellar evolution eluded him, Tycho understood the enormous significance of the new star. Never mind its initial brightness—the star's mere presence was enough to astonish Tycho. It contradicted Aristotle's authoritative judgment that stars populate a pure, unchanging kingdom.

Tycho was not the first person to notice the supernova, but he observed it more carefully than anyone else. He not only chronicled its unprecedented performance but also confirmed its exemption from the daily parallax that displaces the Moon with respect to the more distant stars. It could not be a planet vagrantly adrift from the ecliptic, nor could it be a comet dashing through the sky. Aristotle's conviction that comets are atmospheric phenomena also prevailed in the 16th century, but when Tycho failed to detect any daily parallax in the position of the comet of 1577, he argued that comets also introduce change into the celestial zone. So careful measurement, rather than ancient authority, revealed nature. No wonder Tycho was astonished.

Dedicated to the "renovation" of technical astronomy—according to Victor E. Thoren, his most recent biographer—Tycho "created almost single handedly the empirical ethic on which modern astronomy is founded." He believed that the price of accurate knowledge is greater precision, so he engineered instruments accurate to one arcminute. These were four times better than those he had used to observe the comet and supernova and 10 to 15 times better than those of most of his predecessors.

Tycho's observing regimen reflected an appreciation of observational error. Rather than rely upon a single measurement, he performed up to seven determinations of fundamental data, reported them all, and let the uncertainty scatter in an honest display of the limits of his procedure and apparatus. The quality and integrity of Tycho's observations eventually permitted Johannes Kepler to formulate accurately his three laws of planetary motion as well as a representation of the solar system's dynamics. These, in turn, let Isaac Newton explain everything with gravity.

In a duel with a rival over competing assertions of personal mathematical preeminence, Tycho lost the bridge of his nose. The unhappy slice forced him to don a gold-and-silver alloy prosthetic, making him a genuinely hard-nosed scientist and not a melancholy Dane. Romantics often criticize hard-nosed analysis as an attempt to overpower nature with intellect. They also may regard scientific observation as too disengaged to appreciate intuitive understanding. For Tycho, however, indulging in untestable romantic allegations and idiosyncratic thought was like cutting off your nose to spite your face.

Tycho's disciplined approach to the acquisition and understanding of knowledge is encapsulated in the famous illustration of the mural quadrant he installed in Uraniborg. Although a portrait of Tycho dominates the painting nested in the curve of the quadrant, the background tells the real story of science. A mountain profile with the Sun lodged in a horizon notch fills the top register and illustrates nature, which not only runs the show but is the show. The sky is doing its usual work, unencumbered by human activity. Below that we see the upper level of Uraniborg. Its balustraded terraces support astronomical instruments representing observation and accurate measurement of the natural world. On the next floor down, staff members gather at tables. Accompanied by Tycho's five-foot celestial globe, they analyze data, the next step after acquisition. Finally, in the basement we see Tycho's alchemical laboratory. Although today we regard alchemy as an occult enterprise, in Tycho's time it was regarded as respectable inquiry. In the mural, alchemy provides a reference to experimentation.

Tycho's belief in the coherence of nature and the unity of the cosmos persuaded him that accurate, detailed knowledge of nature could harmonize human affairs with natural law through the rhythms of the heavens. His vision of cosmic order was reflected in the layout of Uraniborg. With corners aligned to the cardinal directions, it belonged to an archaic tradition that brought the cosmos down to Earth in symbolic architecture. The astronomy, geometry, and symmetry of its garden, towers, turrets, and spires proclaim the principles of celestial harmony and congruence Tycho judged could be teased from nature through observation.

If Tycho were still with us, he would see in this anniversary of his birth 450 circuits of the Sun around the Earth, not 450 orbits of the Earth around the Sun. The world system he devised put the planets in solar orbits but centered the path of the Sun on a stationary Earth. He thought this picture was the best interpretation of the data, but the system capitulated to Keplerian motion and universal gravitation.

It is now hard to find any celestial acknowledgments of four and a half centuries of Tychonic legacy. Tycho's supernova is long gone, and no one knows when, if ever, the comet of 1577 will come back. But the statue of Tycho installed near the ruins of his observatory lifts his face to the zenith. He observes Cassiopeia every time she sails by, and he probably caught Comet Hyakutake in the corner of his eye.

FURTHER READING

Biography

Crowther, J. G. "Tycho Brahe," in *Six Great Astronomers,* pp. 21-49. London: Hamish Hamilton, 1961.
   Biographical sketch of Brahe that emphasizes his "establishment of the modern outlook in practical astronomy."

Dreyer, J. L. E. "Tycho Brahe and his Contemporaries." In *A History of Astronomy from Thales to Kepler,* pp. 345-71. Cambridge: Dover Publications, Inc., 1953.
   Survey of Brahe's life, thought, and influence preceded by an evaluation of his immediate predecessors and his contemporary European astronomers.

Criticism

Dreyer, J. L. E. "On Tycho Brahe's Manual of Trigonometry." *The Observatory* XXXIX, No. 498 (March 1916): 127-31.
   Notes the contents, date, and origin of Brahe's *Triangulorum planorum et sphaericorum Praxis arithmetica,* a work of practical trigonometry not printed until the early twentieth century publication of Brahe's *Opera omnia.*

——. "On Tycho Brahe's Catalogue of Stars." *The Observatory* XL, No. 514 (June 1917): 229-33.
   Assesses the accuracy of Brahe's sixteenth-century star catalogue.

Gingerich, Owen. "Copernicus and Tycho." *Scientific American* 229, No. 6 (December 1973): 87-90, 95-101.
   Attempts to vindicate Brahe's earth-centered planetary system as historically forward-looking, based on what are believed to be Brahe's notes found in a copy of Copernicus's *De revolutionibus.*

——. "Astronomical Scrapbook: Dreyer and Tycho's World System." *Sky and Telescope* 64, No. 2 (August 1982): 138-40.
   Investigates the question of why Brahe rejected the ancient Ptolemaic cosmological system, tracing this decision to his observations of Mars in 1583 rather than to his sighting of the comet of 1577.

Gingerich, Owen and Robert S. Westman. "A Reattribution of the Tychonic Annotations in Copies of Copernicus's *De revolutionibus.*" *Journal for the History of Astronomy* 12, No. 33 (February 1981): 53-54.
   Corrects the erroneous attribution of Brahe as annotator of Vatican edition of Copernicus's *De revolutionibus,* arguing that these notes are instead the work of the itinerant sixteenth-century mathematician Paul Wittich.

——. "The Libraries of Tycho and Wittich." *Transactions of the American Philosophical Society* 78, No. 7 (1988): 5-26. .

Further discussion of the relationship between Brahe and Wittich and the latter's annotations of Copernicus's *De revolutionibus.*

Hellman, C. Doris. "Was Tycho Brahe as Influential as He Thought?" *The British Journal for the History of Science* I, No. 4 (December 1963): 295-324.

Offers a critical history of Brahe's work in astronomy. Hellman emphasizes the enduring importance of his emphasis on accurate observation and considerable influence in the late sixteenth-century and beyond.

Margolis, Howard. "Tycho's System and Galileo's *Dialogue.*" *Studies in the History and Philosophy of Science* 22, No. 2 (June 1991): 259-75.

Studies Galileo's apparent failure to address the Tychonic planetary system by name in his *Dialogues.*

Moran, Bruce T. "German Prince-Practitioners: Aspects in the Development of Courtly Science, Technology, and Procedures in the Renaissance." *Technology and Culture* 22, No. 2 (April 1981): 253-74.

Mentions Brahe within a survey of German mathematics and astronomy in the fifteenth and sixteenth centuries.

Rosen, Edward. "Render Not Unto Tycho That Which Is Not Tycho." *Sky and Telescope* 61, No. 6 (June 1981): 476-77.

Comments on the improper attribution of Brahe as the annotator of the Vatican edition of Copernicus's *De revolutionibus.*

———. "Tycho Brahe and Erasmus Reinhold." *Archives internationales d'histoire des sciences* 32, No. 108 (1982): 3-8.

Argues the indebtedness of Brahe to astronomer Erasmus Reinhold for certain aspects of the Tychonic cosmological system.

———. "The Dissolution of the Solid Celestial Spheres." *Journal of the History of Ideas* XLVI, No. 1 (January-March 1985): 13-31.

Contends that, "Unless a better qualified competitor is put forward, [Christopher] Rothmann, rather than Brahe, is to be credited with dissolving the solid celestial spheres" first posited by Aristotle.

Thoren, Victor E. "Tycho Brahe as the Dean of a Renaissance Research Institute." In *Religion, Science, and Worldview: Essays in Honor of Richard S. Westfall,* edited by Margaret J. Osler and Paul Lawrence Farber, pp. 275-95. Cambridge: Cambridge University Press, 1985.

Explores Brahe's role as an instructor and as scientific administrator of the astronomical observatories he created on the Danish island-fief of Hven.

Nicolaus Copernicus

1473-1543

(Also Kopernik) Polish astronomer and mathematician.

INTRODUCTION

Copernicus is one of the extraordinary thinkers credited with inaugurating the Scientific Revolution in the sixteenth century with the publication of his *De revolutionibus orbitum coelestium* (*On the Revolutions of the Heavenly Bodies,* 1543). The revolution in science represents one of the greatest developments in the Western intellectual tradition. Thinkers such as Copernicus, the French philosopher Rene Descartes (1596-1650) and the British mathematician Sir Isaac Newton (1642-1727) departed radically from classical thought and from the ecclesiastical institutions of the Middle Ages. These thinkers brought about a change in the way people think and perceive both themselves and their place in the universe.

Biographical Information

Copernicus was born into a well-to-do family in 1473. Copernicus's father, a copper merchant, died when Copernicus was ten, and Copernicus was taken in by an uncle. In 1491, Copernicus entered the University of Krakow where he studied mathematics and painting. In 1496, he went to Italy for ten years where he studied medicine at Padua and obtained a doctor's degree in canon law at Ferrara. In 1500, in the midst of his studies, Copernicus experienced two events that helped to shape the rest of his life: he attended a conference in Rome dealing with calendar reform and in November of that year witnessed a lunar eclipse. Copernicus continued his medical and legal studies, but also pursued his interest in astronomy, being exposed to the Pythagorean doctrines of cosmology taught in Italy. He developed a dissatisfaction with the Ptolemaic system and conceived the idea of a solar system with the sun at the center. In 1505, Copernicus returned to his native Poland, where he worked as physician to his uncle in his uncle's palace in Heilsberg. In 1512, when Copernicus's uncle died, Copernicus moved to Frauenberg where he belonged to the chapter or regular staff of the cathedral of Frauenberg. While serving in this capacity, Copernicus also developed a system of reform for the currency of the Prussian provinces of Poland (presented as *De monetae cudendae ratione,* 1526, and published in 1816) and began to make astronomical observations to test his belief in a heliocentric world system.

Copernicus was reluctant to make his ideas public because of their controversial nature. He did allow a summary of the *Commentariolus* (1530) to circulate among scholars. Johann Albrecht Widmanstadt presented Copernicus' views in lectures at Rome with the current pope, Pope Clement VII, expressing no disapproval. Cardinal Schönberg made a formal request for publication of Copernicus's views. Copernicus published the treatise *On the Revolutions of the Heavenly Bodies* in 1540. That same year, George Joachim Rheticus, a follower of Copernicus, published another brief account of Copernicus' views in his *Narratio prima.* The task of overseeing the publication of Copernicus's book was undertaken by a Lutheran minister named Andreas Osiander. Osiander seems to have felt obliged to present Copernicus's material in a way that would not offend Church officials (Martin Luther, the founder of Lutheranism, firmly opposed Copernicus's new theory). Osiander wrote and appended a preface to *On the Revolutions of the Heavenly Bodies* stating that the heliocentric theory was being presented as a concept to allow for better calculations of planetary positions. The unsigned preface gave the impression that Copernicus himself was undercutting his own theory. In 1542, Copernicus suffered a stroke and paralysis, and continued to decline until his death on May 24, 1543. Tradition relates that the first copy of Copernicus's book *On the Revolutions of the Heavenly Bodies* reached him on his death-bed, but in face he may never have seen his most important work published. In 1609 German astronomer Johannes Kepler (1571-1630) discovered that Osiander was the author of the preface to the first edition of Copernicus's *On the Revolutions of the Heavenly Bodies*.

Major Works

On the Revolution of the Heavenly Bodies sets forth Copernicus's heliocentric theory of the solar system, with the sun as the center of a number of plaentary orbits including that of the Earth. Long before Copernicus, Aristarchus of Samos, a Greek astronomer living around 270 BC, had proposed that the sun was the center of things, but his theory was displaced by the teachings of Claudius Ptolemy (c.90-168 AD). Ptolemy proposed that the Earth was the center of the universe. In this system, all the planets, including the Sun and Moon (which were classified as planets) were attached to concentric spheres surrounding and rotating around the Earth.Their motion was governed by the Prime Mover or Just Cause, God. Motions of the planets that presented problems for this geocentric and spherical model were accounted for by means of epicycles (or cycles within cycles). Ptolemy's model of the universe remained dominant for over a thousand years. By Copernicus's time, the tables of planetary positions had become very complex but still did not offer accurate predictions of the positions of the planets over long periods of time. Copernicus realized that tables of planetary positions could be calculated more accurately by working from the assumption that the Sun, not the Earth, was the center of the world system and that the planets, including the Earth, moved around the sun. Copernicus was not an especially good astronomical observer. It is said that he never saw the planet Mercury, and he made an incorrect assumption about planetary orbits, believing that they were perfectly circular. Because of this, he found it necessary to use Ptolemy's cumbersome concept of epicycles (smaller orbits centered on the larger ones) to reduce the discrepancy between his predicted orbits and those he observed. It wasn't until Johannes Kepler that the elliptical nature of planetary orbits was understood. According to critic Harold P. Nebelsick, Copernicus's system was able to describe the "main movements of the planets with greater simplicity and harmony" than the Ptolemaic system could, and it was able to provide "a more accurate measurement of the distance of planetary orbits" from one orbit to another.The heliocen-

tric model developed by Copernicus could explain the astronomical phenomenon known as retrograde ("backwards") motion better than Ptolemy's geocentric model. The fact that most of the planets appear to change direction periodically is more readily explained by the fact that their orbits are outside that of the Earth. The heliocentric model also explained the absence of such "backward" motion in the planet Venus, whose orbit is inside that of the Earth and therefore smaller.

Critical Reception

The earliest reaction to *On the Revolution of the Heavenly Bodies* was subdued. Only a limited number of books were printed. Books—and in particular scientific texts with numerous illustrations—were expensive and consequently had limited circulation. The book did achieve a number of converts, but only a few highly advanced mathematicians and astronomers could fully understand it. Copernicus himself dedicated the book to mathematicians and did not seem to think that his findings would appeal to a general readership. A later generation of astronomers building on Copernican theories, including Tycho Brahe (1546-1601) and Johannes Kepler, continued to demonstrate that humankind was still learning about what had previously been thought to be a "fixed firmamant' of stars and planets, and Copernicus has grown in regard as a significant and revolutionary thinker for his times.

PRINCIPAL WORKS

Monetae cudendae ratio [*On Minting Money*] (essay) 1528
De revolutionibus orbitum coelestium [*On the Revolutions of the Heavenly Bodies*] (essay) 1543

CRITICISM

Robert Small (essay date 1804)

SOURCE: "Of the Copernican System" in *An Account of the Astronomical Discoveries of Kepler,* The University of Wisconsin Press, 1963, pp. 81-92.

[*In the following excerpt from an essay originally written in 1804, Small discusses how Copernicus came to his conclusions regarding heliocentrism and the diurnal rotation of the earth.*]

Though the imperfections of the Ptolemaic system were not immediately perceived, especially during the confusion which attended the decline and destruction of the Roman empire, their effects did not fail, in process of time, to become fully evident. In the ninth century, on the revival of science in the east, under the encouragement of the caliphs, surnamed Abassides, Ptolemy's astronomical tables were found to deviate so widely from the actual situations of the celestial bodies, as to be no longer useful in calculations: and it became necessary for the Saracen astronomers at Bagdat to form tables entirely new. The Saracens carried their astronomical knowledge with them into Spain; and, in the thirteenth century again, the new tables were found unfit to represent the celestial motions; and, to supply their place, the tables, called Alphonsine, were constructed, by the direction of Alphonso the 10th, king of Castile. The errors even of the Alphonsine tables became, in the fifteenth century, equally sensible with the former. But though it was hence evident, that the revolutions of the celestial bodies were not precisely what the excentric circles and epicycles of the ancients represented, such was the veneration of astronomers for Hipparchus and Ptolemy, from whom they derived all that was valuable in their science; and, indeed, so great was the merit of subjecting motions, so intricate as the apparent celestial revolutions, to any settled rules; that no suspicions concerning the principles of the theory appear to have been entertained. All that was proposed even by eminent astronomers, such as Purbach and Muller, surnamed Regiomontanus, was only to correct the theory by more accurate observations: and none of the amendments, which they introduced, was inconsistent with its principles. It was the celebrated Copernicus, a native of Thorn in Polish Prussia, who first called in question the principles themselves, and to whom the exclusive honour belongs, of substituting for the Ptolemaic a new and more beautiful system, representing the celestial motions with much more simplicity, and, after its principles were fully understood, with incomparably greater accuracy.

It does not appear that Copernicus originally meditated such a total revolt from the authority of Ptolemy, as that to which, in the course of forming his theory, he was eventually led. Though equally sensible with others of the deviation of the Ptolemaic tables from the actual state of the heavens, the chief cause of his dissatisfaction with Ptolemy's theory related to his explications of the first planetary inequalities, and was his departure in these explications from the principle of uniform motion in perfect circles, which all astronomers considered as sacred and inviolable. When Hipparchus introduced an excentric orbit into the solar theory, no trespass against this principle was committed; because the sun was supposed to move uniformly round its centre: but when Ptolemy extended the application of excentrics to the planetary orbits, and supposed every epicycle to move uniformly round a point, not in the centre of the deferent, the principle was undeniably abandoned: for the uniformity attained was in a foreign orbit, called an equant; and there was a real and evident inequality in its own. It was this part of the theory of Ptolemy which, Copernicus tells us, he chiefly disapproved; and, as he found the explication of the first inequality, by means of an excentric with an equant, irreconcileable with his favourite principle, he seems to have had at first no higher purpose in view, than to substitute an explication of a different kind, and more consonant to that principle.

The theory which he proposed to substitute, for explaining the first inequalities in a manner more consistent with the principle of uniformity, was the ancient concentric one: and it was in restoring this from its neglected state, that the distinguishing and essential part of his system, in which he ventured to depart, not only from the authority of Ptolemy, but from all the established opinions of mankind, seems first to have presented itself to his thoughts. When both inequalities were represented by means of concentric circles with epicycles, the necessary multiplicity of epicycles confounded the imagination; and the chief recommendation of the excentric theory, and even the original cause of framing it, was the banishing several of the epicycles by which the imagination had been perplexed. The same desire therefore of simplicity, which led Ptolemy to substitute an excentric orbit, in the explication of the first inequality, for the concentric with its epicycle, seems to have had equal influence, in suggesting to Copernicus a like substitution for the epicycles used in the explication of the second. He discovered in the annual orbit of the sun, or earth, an universal epicycle, which explained the second inequalities more advantageously than all the various separate ones with which the planetary orbits had been encumbered: and in fact the solar orbit had been already employed in this explication, at least in some degree; for while the ancients formed the argument of the equation of the second inequality, by taking the difference between the places of the sun and the planet (47), they were actually converting the sun's orbit into an epicycle. These seem to have been the motives by which Copernicus was led to conceive the bold design of attributing motion to the earth; and, by the application which he made of her annual orbit, he found the simplicity which he sought; not like Ptolemy, at the expence of the sacred principle of uniformity, but in some sense perfectly consistent with it. This attachment indeed to the doctrines of uniform circular motion, which made him reject the excentric of Ptolemy, was merely a prejudice connected with the imperfect state of physical knowledge; for the motions of the planets are in reality neither circular, nor uniform: but, in the present instance, it produced the happiest and most important effects, and proved the introduction of all that is true and valuable in astronomy.

When the design was thus conceived of ascribing motion to the earth, and displacing her from the centre of the planetary system, Copernicus found that, bold as it was, it was not destitute of support from many powerful arguments, and even from several striking astronomical phenomena. In particular, he found that an acknowledgment of its propriety was made, however undesignedly, in the whole theory of the epicycles, which, by the annual orbit of the earth, he proposed to abolish. The ratio of the semi-diameter of the epicycle of Mars, to the semi-diameter of his orbit, exceeded that of 6 to 10; and, in the theory of Venus it was still greater; for it exceeded that of 7 to 10; and therefore, when the distance of the former planet from the earth varied from 4 to 16, and of the latter from 3 to 17, it was undeniably absurd to consider the earth as the centre of their motions: and the absurdity was the same, though not so evident, of supposing the earth to be the centre of the motions of the other planets. Copernicus found also that the Ptolemaic arrangement of the inferior planets had not always been generally received; for Plato, and his followers, placed them beyond the sun; and he saw that the reasons for inverting this order, and including their orbits between those of the sun and moon, were unsatisfactory and inconclusive. The distance of the sun from the earth, Ptolemy reckoned at 1160 of the earth's semi-diameters, and that of the moon in apogee, at 64. The interjacent space between these two orbits he filled up, first, with the epicycle of Mercury of 177 in diameter, and next with that of Venus of 910; thus bringing Mercury's epicycle almost in contact with the lunar orbit, and the epicycle of Venus almost in contact with the solar orbit: and the principal reason which he assigns for crowding them in these positions, is the improbability of supposing a space so vast to have been left wholly empty; forgetting that, by this very arrangement, he had allotted, to the single epicycle of Venus, a space more than four times, or according to a more probable deduction, more than six times as extensive in breadth, as the space allotted to the earth, the moon, and Mercury, all together. The other reason alleged for this arrangement, viz. the propriety of the sun's holding the middle station, between the planets whose digressions permitted them to come into opposition with him, and those whose digressions were more limited, was both false and frivolous: for the moon's digressions were unlimited, though her orbit was arranged on the same side of the sun with those of Venus and Mercury. No reason also appeared from this arrangement, why the digressions of Venus and Mercury should be limited, why their revolutions should be so intimately connected with those of the sun, or why any one of all the planets, the superior ones not excepted, should be placed nearer to the earth than any other. On these accounts Copernicus could not fail to consider the theory of the inferior planets, attributed to the ancient Egyptians, and held by several Latin astronomers, and particularly by Martianus Capella in the fifth century, as much more worthy of attention than the Ptolemaic, and as giving a much more consistent explication of their phenomena. In this, the sun was the centre about

which Venus and Mercury performed their revolutions: and, as the earth was not included within their orbits, it was impossible that they should be seen from the earth, to make any greater digressions from the sun than the limits of these orbits would allow: and the reason was also manifest, both of the relative positions assigned them with respect to the sun, and of the intimate connection of their apparent annual circuit round the earth with the apparent solar revolution. This theory Copernicus applied to the superior planets, and found the application attended with like success; for, though their oppositions shewed that the earth was included within their orbits, their near approaches to the earth in their oppositions, and the vast distances to which they removed in their conjunctions, made it impossible that the earth could be the centre of their motions. This variation of distance was especially remarkable in the planet Mars; who, in oppositions, appears equal in size to Jupiter, but towards his conjunctions no larger than a star of the second or third magnitude; and afforded an unquestionable proof that none of the superior orbits approaches so near the earth. It was from this extension of the Egyptian theory concerning the inferior planets to the superior, and making the sun the centre of all the planetary orbits, that the transition seems to have been more immediately made to the doctrine of the motion, or revolution, of the earth, like any other planet, round the sun. For, as the variations of distance shewed the earth to be nearest to the orbits of Mars and Venus, and as she was evidently within the former, and without the latter, no reason appeared why she should not partake of the revolutions round the sun, in which so many other bodies, and some of them thought to be of greater magnitude, on both sides of her, were supposed to be involved: nay, on the contrary, strong probability appeared that she did partake in those revolutions; for, on this principle, all the varieties of the distances of the planets, and all the circumstances of their second inequalities were at once and easily explained: and they could not be explained otherwise, without the improbable supposition of the annual revolution of the whole planetary orbits, round her centre. The only celestial body, which could not be subjected to the general law of describing an orbit round the sun as a centre, was the moon: for, though her oppositions, like those of Mars, proved that the earth was included within her orbit, her parallaxes shewed her distances to be much less than the least distance of Venus; and the variations of her distance were so inconsiderable as not to require, or even to admit, of any other centre of her motions than the earth. In the interjacent space, therefore, between the orbits of Mars and Venus, and where the former system made the sun to move, Copernicus placed the orbit of the moon with the earth in its centre; and supposed both together, like some great planet, to revolve round the sun, in the precise time of an apparent solar revolution. The sun was now considered as the only immoveable body in the system: for Copernicus was not influenced by the objection of his apparent progress through the zodiac; being convinced, from innumerable examples, how unavoidably we ascribe to surrounding objects all the real motions of which we are not sensible: and, by the immoveable position of the sun in the centre, and the continual revolutions of the earth and planets round it, at different distances, and in different times, not only were the second inequalities explained in general, without the embarrassment of epicycles, but the causes also of the different times of the revolutions in these imaginary epicycles, and of their different magnitudes, became fully evident. In particular, the cause became evident, why both the direct and retrograde arches of Jupiter were greater, and required longer time than those of Saturn, and less than those of Mars; and the like arches of Venus greater than those of Mercury: and why those vicissitudes returned more frequently in Saturn than in Jupiter and Mars; and more frequently in Mercury than in Mars and Venus. It is true that no reciprocations of this kind had been observed in any of the fixed stars: but this Copernicus boldly, though justly ascribed to their immense distance, in comparison with which the diameter of the whole terrestrial orbit, though bearing a sensible ratio to the distance even of the remotest planet, entirely vanished. When he had thus ascribed a periodical revolution to the earth, the transition was more easy to the doctrine of her diurnal rotation, by which his theory was completed; for, if it was improbable that the sun, carrying along with him the whole planetary orbits, should revolve annually round the earth; it was much more improbable that all these, together with the immense sphere of the fixed stars, should revolve round her every 24 hours, with a rapidity incomparably greater, and almost indeed inconceivable.

There were also some ancient authorities which seemed to encourage Copernicus in the opinions he was thus led to conceive, or at least tended to introduce them to the world with less appearance of absolute innovation. He first found, as he tells us, in Cicero's writings, a tradition, transmitted by Theophrastus, of the opinion of Nicetas of Syracuse, which made the sun, the moon, and the whole starry heavens immoveable, and ascribed their constant apparent diurnal revolutions to the sole rotation of the earth on an axis. Next, he found in Plutarch, not only a similar tradition, that the same doctrine of the diurnal rotation of the earth was asserted by Heraclides of Pontus, and Zephantus the Pythagorean; but also, what he thought had a reference to her annual revolution, and that this was said by Philolaus of Crotona, another disciple of Pythagoras, to be performed about the central fire, or sun. We have also seen the favourable opinion which he entertained, and the more extensive use which he made, of what is called the ancient Egyptian system; where Venus and Mercury are considered as *satellites* to the sun: and this opinion could not fail to be confirmed, when he saw that Ptolemy, though not in words, had in effect

adopted it, by making the mean place of the sun the centre of both their epicycles; and that the framers of the Alphonsine tables had, at least with respect to Venus, expressly adopted it, by considering the solar orbit not only as her equant, but even as the deferent of her epicycle. But the reasons which were decisive with Copernicus, and far outweighed all authorities, in the formation of his system, were certainly the satisfactory explication which it gave of all the circumstances of the second inequalities, and the symmetry and proportion, which he calls admirable, of all its parts. It was not a mere assemblage, like the Ptolemaic, of unconnected parts in arbitrary positions: but, as the ratio of his general epicycle to every particular orbit was given, the ratios were also given of the orbits to one another; and the position of every one was determinate, and not arbitrarily assumed.

In the Copernican system, the sun is placed in the centre of the universe, and Copernicus expresses a peculiar satisfaction at contemplating him in this situation, the most commodious for diffusing light and heat to the whole celestial bodies: for he supposed that the fixed stars, equally with the planets, derived their splendour from him. The planets perform round him their periodical revolutions, in the following order determined by the ratio of every orbit to that of the earth; Mercury, Venus, the Earth attended by her satellite the moon, Mars, Jupiter, and Saturn; and after these may now be added the planet discovered by Herschel. The earth, instead of continuing to be the centre of the motions of the sun and planets, is degraded to become herself a planet, and is the centre only of the motions of the moon. It has been since discovered, that Jupiter has four moons, and Saturn five, which they carry along with them, as our moon is carried along by the earth, in accomplishing their revolutions about the sun. To the five moons, *or satellites,* of Saturn, Herschel has also discovered that two more ought to be added, and that his own planet is accompanied by two. Beyond these, and at an immense distance, is placed the sphere of the fixed stars; and its diurnal revolution, together with that of all the moveable celestial bodies referred to it, is considered in this system merely as apparent, and produced by the diurnal rotation of the terrestrial globe.

Notwithstanding the simplicity and symmetry of this system, and all the advantages by which it was recommended, Copernicus was so much aware of the objections that would be made to it, and the prejudices which it would have to encounter, that he was deterred from publishing it to the world, and forbore, for thirty years, to communicate it, except to some confidential friends. Many of the astronomical phenomena, by which it is supported, were then undiscovered: the rotation, for example, of other celestial bodies on their axes, had not been observed: none of the changes had been seen, in the phases especially of Venus and Mercury, which this system rendered necessary: the principle of gravitation and its important consequences were almost wholly unknown: and, till the aberration of the fixed stars was discovered, it seemed altogether incredible, that the translation of the earth, in her annual revolution, from one extremity of her immense orbit to another, should produce no change on the apparent magnitudes, or the relative positions, of the fixed stars. It was not, therefore, till near the close of life, nor even then without the importunities of his friends, particularly of Schomberg cardinal of Capua, and Gisius bishop of Culm, that his consent to the publication was obtained: and, when the first edition of his work was completed, under the inspection of the eminent George Joachim Rheticus, at Nurenberg, on the 24th of May, 1543, the illustrious author, a few days after receiving a copy, died in his 72d year at Frawenberg.

Marian Biskup and Jerzy Dobrzycki (essay date 1972)

SOURCE: "Copernicus the Economist" and *"De Revolutionibus"* in *Copernicus: Scholar and Citizen,* Interpress Publishers, 1972, pp. 83-115.

[*In the essays below, Biskup and Dobrzycki discuss first Copernicus's work as an economic advisor to the Prussian Estates and then the development of the ideas and text of his* De Revolutionibus.]

Copernicus the Economist

Copernicus was for many years in Warmia engrossed in economic matters and monetary questions. He introduced many new and stimulating ideas into economics, some of them much ahead of his time, and hence did not always meet with understanding. But it is worth looking closer at his practical measures and theoretical writings in this field for it forms a separate and important chapter in his life.

Among the economic problems which were examined by Copernicus that of the Prussian coinage occupies pride of place.

This problem first attracted his attention in 1510. Working in the administration and becoming acquainted with the realities of everyday life provided him with valuable experience which, with the help of source materials from Warmian archives, later (after 1517) made it possible for him to carry out an expert analysis of the monetary situation in Royal Prussia.

At the beginning of the 16th century, Royal Prussia went through a monetary crisis brought about by depreciation. The coins struck since 1457 by the Gdansk and Torun mints with royal permission, and by Elblag without such permission (the basic unit was the shilling) had

a steadily diminishing silver content. Apart from the local and Crown coins, there were also several other kinds of money minted in foreign countries and cities in western Europe. These coins, together with Royal Prussian shillings, were constantly driven out by coins from the Prussia of the Teutonic Order where shillings and *grosze* of ever poorer quality were struck in the mint belonging to the Grand Masters. Better money disappeared from the market, for it was taken out of the country or melted down by local goldsmiths and silversmiths. All this caused considerable losses, especially among the knights, peasants and merchants, in all deals in which money was used. It had also an adverse effect on the value of rents paid by the peasantry to the administrators of the Chapter's estates in Warmia. That is why the knights and representatives of the higher clergy became advocates of the monetary reform in Royal Prussia and of pegging the Prussian currency to the Polish one in order to simplify the system of conversion for everyday purposes. Doubtless, such a reform must have had supporters among the middle merchants in the big Prussian cities. On the other hand, the town councils, that is to say the representatives of the patricians of Gdansk, Elblag and Torun, although they did not reject the proposals for a monetary reform, yet strove to keep their minting rights and the attendant income. From the very first they discouraged the bolder projects for reforming the monetary system in Prussia.

The Estates of Royal Prussia had been concerning themselves with this matter ever since the beginning of the 16th century. The situation became more acute after 1511, when the Teutonic Order began to mint silver coins of a still lower value. The Royal Prussian Estates protested against such a procedure (1516). It was probably then that Copernicus took up the matter, either at the initiative of Bishop Luzjanski or the Chapter. In any case, in the middle of August 1517, during his stay at Olsztyn, he wrote the first outline of a monetary treatise, entitled **Meditata.** This outline contained most of the later ideas for reform which Copernicus elaborated in further studies.

In 1519, the Prussian Estates formally requested Copernicus to give his opinion in the matter of monetary reform. During that year, when still in Olsztyn, Copernicus translated (with minor amendments) his first study in Latin, into German which language was easier to understand for, at least, the burghers of the Third Estate. The treatise was to be discussed at the assembly in Torun at the close of 1519, but the outbreak of the war postponed the whole matter for more than two years.

It was only after the truce between Poland and the Teutonic Knights had been concluded that the question of monetary reform was put on the agenda of the assembly in Grudzadz, in the later half of March 1522. At the motion of Maciej Drzewicki, Bishop of Włocławek and envoy of King Sigismund I, the assembly was to discuss the introduction of a uniform Crown currency which would be legal tender also in Royal Prussia. Copernicus, as mentioned before, was present at the convention as the envoy of the Warmian Chapter. He was then asked to read his treatise on the monetary system.

In this treatise, entitled ***Modus cudendi monetam*** (***On the Method of Minting Money***), Copernicus, mathematician and astronomer, first analysed conditions in Prussia, and then proceeded to use the scientific method of observation of Nature in dealing with socio-economic phenomena. He treated money exclusively as an economic factor, and he saw the source of its value only in its silver or gold content; in this, he was a follower of the so-called metallistic or substantional theory. He also formulated an important economic law called the law of bad money, according to which good money is driven out of circulation by bad money and is taken away either for reminting or for commercial purposes (this law was later attributed to Sir Thomas Gresham and is now called Gresham's law). In order to remedy this evil, he proposed to withdraw inferior currency and introduce a uniform silver coin of high intrinsic value, struck in one mint only in Royal Prussia, with the stamp and in its name, and that the very minting of money should not bring any profit. These views were in harmony with progressive economic theories in the age of the Renaissance and represented a definite break with the opinions prevalent in both Prussias. They were in line with the interests of the rural population of the poorer town dwellers as well as of landowners. The then modern stipulation that the striking of the new money should be centralized and the large Prussian towns deprived of profit from minting rights was certain to arouse protests.

Copernicus, prompted by Bishop Drzewicki's demands that uniform royal money should be introduced on the entire territory of the Polish Kingdom, added in Grudziadz one more important and vital stipulation at the close of the treatise: he suggested that the value of the new Royal Prussian money should be the same as that of the money minted in Cracow by striking three Prussian shillings equal in value to one Polish *grosz*. In this way, without depriving Royal Prussia of the right to her own money, an important step would have been taken towards a more efficient circulation of the royal and Prussian currencies, which in turn would facilitate financial transactions and become a factor in the integration of the Polish Crown and Royal Prussia. This then was also a contribution on Copernicus' part to an even closer bringing together of the Prussian lands with the Polish Kingdom. After the secularization of the Prussia of the Teutonic Order (1525) and the emergence of the vassal Duchy of Prussia, ruled by Duke Albrecht, the money question in both parts of Prussia required regulating. The reform which King Sigismund I requested was based on the ***Treatise on Minting Money,*** drawn

up and presented, in 1526, to the Estates of Royal Prussia by Justus Ludwik Decius, adviser and personal secretary to the King. The draft reform provided for the minting of a new coinage, of higher quality, which would, however, continue to be a source of income to the ruler. Decius did not provide for the withdrawal from circulation of the old coins of low value, for he supposed erroneously that it would be automatically driven out by the new currency. He proposed that the coinage in the Crown territories, in Prussia and Lithuania should be made uniform in respect of weight and metallic composition, with the provision that there should be one mint in Prussia, to be set up in Torun.

These assumptions, which differed considerably from Copernicus' projects and were not so far reaching, were discussed by the assembly of Prussian Estates in summer 1526, during King Sigismund I's visit to Gdansk. On July 17th, the King proclaimed a new ordinance (i.e. statute) for Royal Prussia, in which the monetary reform was announced (there were to be *grosze,* shillings and *denarii*), which would lead to the currency's being unified with that in the Polish Kingdom; the reform was also to be introduced in the Duchy of Prussia. The King's decision caused an animated discussion among the Estates and a number of reservations regarding Decius' treatise.

It is very probable that Copernicus was also invited to attend the debates in Gdansk, or he may have been there in the company of Bishop Maurycy Ferber. In any case, the letter (in Latin) from the Royal Prussian Estates to Decius, written in Gdansk, and dated July 18th, 1526, bears all the marks of his style and views. The letter contains a critique of Decius' project: once again, the effect of the "law of bad money" is recalled, which will drive out of circulation the new, better royal money. Copernicus, whom we may take to have been the author of the letter, did not agree to the minting of money being a source of income to the king. But he accepted the proposal of one monetary system for the Crown lands, Prussia and Lithuania. He considered that coins of the same alloy and value should circulate freely throughout the territory of the Commonwealth of Poland, although the shilling was to remain the basic monetary unit in Royal Prussia because of its long-standing tradition. Next, Copernicus suggested that the monetary unit of the Duchy of Prussia (i.e. *grosz*) should have the image of King Sigismund with his name and title in Latin on the rim, while the shillings of Royal Prussia should bear the crest of the Polish Kingdom and the royal title on the rim, the reverse having the crest of Prussia.

While criticizing some of the provisions of Decius' project, Copernicus called on him to take part in the discussions on carrying out the monetary reform in Prussia in connection with the opening of the Torun mint, as intended by the King.

Eventually, the proposal for a new uniform currency for Royal Prussia and the Duchy of Prussia was to be put on the agenda of the assembly of Prussian Estates and Duke Albrecht's envoys on May 8th, 1528, at Malbork. At the end of March, Bishop Ferber, who appreciated the importance of this matter, summoned Dr Nicolaus to Lidzbark in order to discuss with him the attitude which should be adopted towards the monetary question. There seems to be no doubt that Copernicus prepared a third version of his treatise on money precisely for this meeting, in which he made use of the results of the discussions and arguments against Decius' ideas. At the beginning of April, in Lidzbark, this version, entitled *Monetae cudendae ratio (On Minting Money)*, was probably amended finally after the talks with Bishop Ferber. On April 7th, the Bishop summoned the Chapter and requested it to send Copernicus to the assembly at Malbork, where he would assist the Bishop with his experienced counsel. Canon Feliks Reich, who also attended the discussions on monetary questions and possibly expected to take part in the Malbork sessions, wanted to become acquainted with Copernicus' treatise. Not everything was clear to him in the new version of the reform. In his letter of April 19th, Copernicus elucidated some of its principles. He also emphasized the need of voting the reform and introducing it as soon as possible, which would also be of advantage to the "King, Our Lord", who would receive the planned tax from the Estates in a new and better money.

Monetae cudendae ratio, the most extensive and also the most mature version of Copernicus' monetary treatise, written again in Latin (spring 1528), contained all the fruit of the several years of discussions at the forum of the Prussian Estates and of the polemics with Decius. Dr Nicolaus reiterated in it most of his ideas including the thesis of good money being driven out by bad, and substantiated them with an extensive exposition of the history of Prussia from the end of the 14th century. The part about the dire effects of the debasement of money has a truly dramatic ring. Copernicus appealed warmly to the rulers of the Prussian lands who "look on with indifference and permit their sweetest Motherland, towards which their duties, after love of God, are the greatest, and for the sake of which they should sacrifice even their life, to decline painfully through their everyday lazy negligence". The rulers ought not to seek profits from minting money, and after new good money is introduced, the old debased money should be withdrawn. Though Copernicus agreed to the establishment of two Prussian mints, one for Royal Prussia, the other for the Duchy of Prussia, coins issuing from both mints were to bear the crest of the Polish king. Prussian money, which enjoyed royal protection, should be on equal footing with Crown money.

As envoy of the Warmian Chapter, Copernicus attended the debates of the General Diet of Royal Prus-

sia, held in Malbork some time after May 9th, 1528, at which envoys of Albrecht, Duke of Prussia, were also present. On May 14th, he was elected member of the special working commission, made up of representatives of Royal Prussia and the Duchy of Prussia; among them were minters from Gdansk and Elblag. The commission discussed, above all, the ways and means of withdrawing the old coins, and the form and size of the new Prussian *grosz,* to be introduced by order of the King. It is not known whether Dr Nicolaus acquinted the commission with the contents of the final version of his treatise on money. Perhaps the differences in opinion between the other members of the commission (especially the envoys of the large Prussian towns) held him back; perhaps also his reticence was due to the absence of Decius, his main opponent, whose ideas were beginning to win over a majority of the representatives of the Estates.

Anyway, his treatise was made available to the envoys of Duke Albrecht, whose chancellery received a copy, made by Canon Feliks Reich also for the benefit of the Warmian Chapter. He it was who represented Bishop Ferber at the General Diet of Royal Prussia in the second half of July 1528, in Torun, attended also by Decius. Reich took part in the deliberation of the Estates on the draft monetary reform in Prussia, tabled by him, and on July 22nd, at the request of the meeting, he summed up the proposals put forward so far; it is possible that he presented also some of the principles contained in the final version of the Copernican treatise.

The next day, the Estates voted into effect the principles of the monetary reform, i.e. the ordinance of the Torun mint which was to serve both Royal Prussia and Ducal Prussia. This then—initially—amounted to the fulfilment of one of Copernicus' main stipulations. The new Prussian money was to circulate freely throughout the territory of the Polish Crown and was to be standardized with its currency, which constituted another success for Copernicus' ideas.

But his other proposals were never realized. First of all, minting continued to be considered a source of profit for the king. Neither were all the types of old coins withdrawn from circulation, apart from those struck prior to 1521. Also the proposal to maintain the shilling as the basic monetary unit in Prussia was rejected, and the Polish *grosz* introduced instead, which turned out later to be no bad thing as it made for closer ties between the monetary systems of Prussia and the Crown. But as early as in 1530, King Sigismund permitted Gdansk, Elblag and Duke Albrecht to open their own mints (the latter in Königsberg). The coins were struck in accordance with the Polish standards but the names of the towns were marked on them.

The reform of the Prussian coinage, adopted in 1528, realized, if only in part, some of the ideas advanced by Copernicus. In a modified form, it introduced order into the financial relations in Prussia and bound it even closer to the Polish Crown.

The enforcement of the reform, to be sure, ran into difficulties. The Torun mint issued an insufficient amount of the new Prussian coins, so that the old inferior ones continued in circulation. This became the subject of the deliberations at the assembly held in Elblag during February 1529, and most probably attended by Copernicus and Bishop Ferber. The assembly adopted a resolution on the withdrawal of old Prussian *denarii*.

Copernicus also took part in the convention of Prussian Estates held between October 28th and 31st 1530, in Elblag, to which he was delegated by Bishop Ferber, who was already ill, as the most experienced representative of the Chapter. The Elblag convention, attended by Decius and Albrecht's envoys, was to discuss the vital question of the relation of the gold coins, then in circulation, to the new silver Prussian coins. During the session of October 30th, Dr Nicolaus took the floor in the controversial matter of the value of the gold coin. Copernicus said that it was impossible to establish the value of the gold coin for it was not known how many additives the alloy had. It would be better, therefore, to consider how many coins could be minted from one *grzywna* (an ancient monetary unit containing 3,688 grams of silver) of pure silver or gold. Thus the problem was put on the level of scientific analysis instead of improvized calculations, and the envoys of the large towns refused to take part in the discussion. Copernicus was also for maintaining the old value of the gold coins, a proposal which ran counter to the demands of Duke Albrecht's envoys. Eventually, the whole matter was shelved.

After 1530, Copernicus did not attend any more assemblies which concerned themselves with the detailed procedures to be adopted to secure full implementation of the Prussian monetary reform.

Copernicus turned once more to economic matters in 1531, when inspecting the estates of the Warmian Chapter in the region of Olsztyn; he drew up what was called the **"Olsztyn Bread Tariff"** (*Ratio panaria Allensteinensis*) which was to be enforced in all the towns of Warmia. This time it was a matter concerning trade and prices. In the Tariff, Copernicus examined the ratio between the price of grain and that of bread, taking the view that the price of bread should be equal to that of the grain used for its baking; the costs of other ingredients in the bread and the baker's fee ought to be contained in the value of the by-products left over from milling (as bran). The price of bread should therefore be dependent on the material costs of its

production. In this Copernicus followed the mediaeval principle of what was called a "just price," a principle fitting the condition of small scale commodity production. It protected the consumer against excessive exploitation on the part of bread producers. So in this case, too, Dr Nicolaus had in mind the good of society at large.

The achievements of Copernicus the economist are considerable. Through his exact and innovatory definition of the essence and function of money and his original proposal for monetary reform, he secured for himself a permanent place in the history of European, progressive economic thinking, showing in this domain, too, the unusually wide scope of his mind. His research methods led him not only to the description and cognition of the essence of the subject investigated but also to establishing the relationship between various phenomena and to a comprehensive examination of the problem in its purely economic aspects, irrespective of religious or legal motives.

De Revolutionibus

Astronomy was Copernicus' greatest passion. He conducted studies and research even during the 1520-1521 war and the destruction of his Frombork home. We know that when writing the **Commentariolus** he had already in mind a larger work in which he intended to present a new astronomical theory. At the time, he made use of data taken from other sources, and only in determining the length of the year did he refer to his own observations. The writing of another, more extensive work demanded the making of many new observations.

The number of astronomical observations now known to have been made by Copernicus is not very big. This is because, on the one hand, we know only about those observations which have been used and noted in the book; and on the other, because, it must be said that not many observations were really needed for a reform in astronomy. Those that we know about had a purposefully selected subject and served, in conjunction with analogous observations made in antiquity, to determine the fundamental parametres of the new theory, and their purposefulness was confirmed in the form of new and important (though not bearing on the very essence of Copernican astronomy) determinations.

Purposefulness and the systematic conduct of his observations distinguish Copernicus as an observer, while the observations themselves are neither particularly accurate nor new as concerns the methods with which they were carried out. The measuring instruments, made by the astronomer himself, were a replica of the classical instruments of ancient astronomers, described by Ptolemy in the *Almagest*. The only original instrument he used was the one he made during his first stay in

Olsztyn, around 1517, preserved in part to this day on the wall of the arcaded gallery in Olsztyn castle. In this instrument, the beam of sunlight reflected from a horizontal mirror fell on a chart or table on the wall, the grid of which made it possible to calculate the time separating the moment of observation from the equinox.

It was no accident that the Olsztyn table, which was probably used more for demonstration purposes than accurate measurements, was constructed at a time when Copernicus was intent on investigations into the apparent movement of the Sun and the theory of precession. It was precisely in 1516 that Copernicus found himself among a group of experts who were invited by the Lateran Council, then taking place in Rome, to send their opinions on the ways and means of reforming the Julian calendar. The invitation was transmitted by Bernard Sculteti, Dean of the Warmian Chapter, who was in Rome at the time. This shows that Copernicus was already well-known as a competent astronomer, at least to a close circle of specialists, in spite of his living so far away from the European centres of learning.

Copernicus' opinion in the matter of the reform of the calendar has not been preserved; we know its substance only indirectly from a reference to it by the author in the introduction to *De Revolutionibus.* Copernicus said that amendments could be introduced into the calendar only after more accurate study of the movements of Sun and Moon. It is from this introduction or dedication to Pope Paul III that we learn that he had begun these more accurate studies, connected with the reform of the calendar, at the time of the Lateran Council. It was in the years 1515-1516 that he conducted his observations of the positions of the Sun. These observations he later used in *De Revolutionibus,* which he was soon to begin the long and arduous labour of writing.

Scientific contacts with Cracow were maintained throughout. In 1524, Bernard Wapowski, who had befriended Copernicus during his student days in Cracow, sent him a book by Johannes Werner, a mathematician and astronomer from Nuremberg who had lately died, which contained a treatise entitled *De Motu Octavae Sphaerae (On the Movement of the Eighth Sphere).* In it were discussed various questions connected with precession, which in geocentric astronomy was explained as the movement of the "eighth" sphere of fixed stars, moved by appropriate outer supra-stellar spheres. Werner needed three such outer spheres for his theory. Copernicus wrote to Wapowski on June 3rd, 1524, a letter containing an extensive negative review of Werner's book. He did not reveal in this letter his own theory of precession the details of which he was now working out for his *De Revolutionibus,* but simply criticized Werner's methods of investigation. He was particularly critical of his loose treatment of the observations of ancient astronomers and their negative assessment which ran counter to Copernicus' own opinion, for he considered their observations to be the basis for new studies.

In the twenties, and more precisely sometime around 1523, Copernicus' investigations led him to a new discovery. This resulted from the observation of planets in opposition, that is at the moment when they are at a point on the celestial sphere opposite to the Sun. Three observations of a planet in three oppositions allow for the determination of its orbit, among other things, for the determination of the direction taken in space by the line of apsides, i.e. the line joining a planet's aphelion and perihelion. The comparison of the data obtained from his own observations with those of the ancient astronomers, as expounded in Ptolemy's *Almagest,* led him to the assertion that the notion about the immobility of the position of planetary orbits in space, prevalent since antiquity, was wrong. For it appeared that the lines of apsides had changed their position when compared with the position given 1300 years before by Ptolemy. This discovery by Copernicus, which was later eclipsed by his great heliocentric theory, has nevertheless remained for science ever since, although the figures for the velocity of the motion of the lines of apsides required considerable corrections.

The discovery of the mobility of planetary apsides led Copernicus to the introduction of certain changes in the geometrical models of planetary orbits as compared with those in the *Commentariolus.* The difference lay in that the system of two circles was, for each planet, replaced by an eccentric circle. From the mathematical point of view, the new model was exactly equivalent to the old one, but it simplified the presentation of the motion of the lines of apsides.

De Revolutionibus was ready in manuscript from around 1530 (the latest observation entered in it is dated March 12th, 1529). But Copernicus did not intend to publish it, as he said himself, for he was afraid of the ridicule on the part of those "who are dull of wit and flit amidst the true scholars like drones among bees". When in 1535, Bernard Wapowski paid a visit to the astronomer at Frombork, he obtained only his consent to publish an astronomical almanac calculated with the use of tables drawn up in accordance with the new theory. This project, however, was not carried out because of Bernard Wapowski's death in the same year.

Copernicus' unwillingness to publicize the results of his inquiries did not prevent the information about them spreading slowly throughout Europe. In 1533, Copernicus' ideas on the motion of the Earth were discussed at the papal court; three years later, Cardinal Nicholas Schonberg wrote from Rome to Copernicus, encouraging him to make his discoveries known. But of really decisive influence was the visit in 1539 of a young mathematician, Georg Joachim von Lauchen, known as Rheticus, a professor at Wittenberg University. He undertook the journey to Poland especially in order to learn about the work of Copernicus, about which news had already reached the Wittenberg group of scholars headed by Philip Melanchthon. The latter was soon to reject the heliocentric theory as absurd. Rheticus, however, became an enthusiast for Copernican astronomy. The first result of this visit was that Copernicus resumed work on the manuscript of *De Revolutionibus.* He now had at his disposal books presented to him by Rheticus, including the original Greek text of the *Almagest,* free of the many errors and distortions of the Latin edition, and Regiomontanus' *Trigonometry.* This made possible the introduction of certain additions to the chapter dealing with spherical trigonometry. Also the layout of the whole book was altered. Rheticus' enthusiasm and the encouragement of those close to him, particularly by, as he described him in *De Revolutionibus,* "my great friend Tiedeman Giese, Bishop of Chelmno" converted the astronomer to the idea of having the book published.

The first exposition of the new theory in print came in 1540, during Rheticus' stay in Warmia. Having studied Copernicus' manuscript, Rheticus compiled an extensive summary, published in Gdansk as *The First Narration about Nicolaus Copernicus' Book on Revolutions.* This *Narratio prima* is valuable especially for the parts in which the author presents the facts and opinions known to him from his direct contacts with Copernicus. Particularly important is the list of motives which apparently led Copernicus to recognize the facts of the Earth's motion. In the first place he mentions precession. Only later come the premises concerning the place of the Sun in the planetary system and the preservation of the principle of the uniform circular motion. The closing arguments are certainly the outcome of a discovery already made earlier. They speak of the teleological value of the theory of the Earth's motion and about the harmony of the world revealed by them.

The First Narration was in the form of a letter to Johannes Schoner, a Nuremberg astronomer, and publisher of scientific books. Probably the plans for the publication of the new theory were discussed earlier in Nuremberg, during Rheticus' visit there.

On leaving Frombork in the autumn of 1541, Rheticus took with him the manuscript of *De Revolutionibus.* The work was to be printed in Nuremberg. But before that, as a permanent resident of Wittenberg, he published the trigonometry which was contained in the closing chapters of Book One. It is composed of plane and spherical trigonometry and a seven-figure table of the sinus function, compounded by Rheticus, which

here took the place of the five-figure table of Copernicus.

Copernicus' trigonometry, like the slightly earlier works by Regiomontanus and Werner, was based on formulae used by ancient (Ptolemy) and Arab (Jabir ibn Aflah) scholars. The introduction of the secant function, new in European science, was Copernicus' own achievement. It is not mentioned in the printed Trigonometry, but he calculated the table for this function and noted it in one of the books in his library.

The printing of *De Revolutionibus* began in Nuremberg in the first half of 1542. The manuscript which the printer Johannes Petreius received from Rheticus was not entirely ready for print. More important in its effects, as it turned out, was the fact that the publication was entrusted to the publisher and theologian, Andreas Osiander. He had for some time been interested in the publication of *De Revolutionibus* and wrote to Copernicus and Rheticus suggesting to the author that in order to "quieten the peripatetics and theologians whose protests you fear" he should present his new theory as a hypothesis convenient for calculations, not as a description of the world corresponding to reality. Copernicus rejected those suggestions and explicitly presented his view in the dedicating letter written for *De Revolutionibus* in June 1542. This did not alter Osiander's attitude, who introduced changes in the book in accordance with the conventional view on the veracity of scientific theories. The anonymous preface, which he added, *To the Reader About the Assumptions of this Work* reduced the contents of the book to the level of hypothesis " . . . for it is clear that this science completely ignores and simply does not know the causes of the apparent inequalities of movements. . . . So let no one expect from astronomy anything certain in relation to hypotheses, for it cannot produce anything certain in this respect." Moreover, the title of the book was distorted. Instead of simply *On Revolutions* or *Six Books on Revolutions* the longer title was introduced, *De Revolutionibus orbium coelestium (On the Revolutions of Heavenly Bodies).* Finally, Copernicus' preface to Book One was removed, an eulogy of the astronomical sciences which "treat . . . of the causes of all the phenomena in the sky, and finally explain the whole system of the universe".

Nicolai Copernici Torunensi De Revolutionibus orbium coelestium, Libri VI appeared in March 1543, shortly before the death of its author. The Nuremberg edition opens with the anonymous preface by Osiander and the letter by Cardinal Schonberg of 1536. Then comes the Letter of Dedication to Pope Paul III. In this letter Copernicus returns to the reasons which prompted him to entertain the idea that the Earth moved:

"That is why I wish Your Holiness to know that, in turning my thoughts to another principle for calculating the motions of the spheres of the universe, I was prompted by nothing other than the observation that in their studies of them the mathematicians are not in agreement with one another. Above all, they have so many doubts as to the motion of the Sun and the Moon that they are unable even to determine and calculate the constant magnitude of the tropical year. Next, when determining the motions both of those two and of the other five planets they do not use the same assumptions and premises ... . They adopted . . . a great many assumptions which are obviously inconsistent with the fundamental principles of uniformity of motion. Neither did they discover or they failed to deduce the most important thing, namely, the system of the universe and the established order of its parts . . ."

Here we have the most important motives which made Copernicus undertake a reconstruction of astronomy: "determination of the tropical year" which required a correct theory of precession, mentioned already by Rheticus in the *Narratio prima;* inconsistency with the fundamental principles of the uniformity of motion, mentioned in the first place in the **Commentariolus;** lastly, the "system of the universe and the established order of its parts," an argument which probably resulted from the later rationalization of the process of discovery. Further on in the Letter Copernicus refers to the precursory statements by ancient writers: "I have taken the trouble to read anew all the works of the philosophers accessible to me in order to find out whether any of them did not by chance express an opinion on the motion of the spheres of the universe differing from the hypotheses accepted by the professors of mathematical sciences. And I did find, first in Cicero's, a remark that Niketas thought that the Earth moved. Then in Plutarch I found a few more names of people of the same opinion . . . : the Pythagorean Phylolaos thinks that (the Earth) revolves round the fire along an inclined circle as do the Sun and the Moon. Heracleides of Pontus and the Pythagorean Ekphantos though they believe that the Earth does move, think that it is a rotary, not translatory motion . . . My interest having thus been aroused, I too began to ponder about the movements of the Earth". Here also, it is easy to find the elements of the later reasoning. In the closing paragraph of the Letter, the author anticipates objections of theological nature concerning the inconsistency of the new theory with the teachings of Holy Scripture: "It is possible that there will be such who like to drivel and in spite of complete ignorance of mathematics arrogate to themselves the right to express their opinions about them referring to some place in the Holy Scripture, wrongly and fallaciously explained to suit their intentions, and who dare to denounce and persecute this theory of mine. However I care not for such people . . .".

The opening chapters of Book One discuss the foundations of astronomy according to the Ptolemaic mod-

el. While rejecting Ptolemy's arguments about the Earth's being stationary, Copernicus considers natural (in the Aristotelian sense) the revolution of the Earth together with its surrounding atmosphere, and not requiring any external cause. He also modifies the philosophical concept of gravity, identified with gravitation towards the centre of the world, by describing it as a natural tendency of parts to concentrate into the form of a sphere, a tendency "existing also in the Sun, Moon and other shining planets." This essential modification of the Aristotelean laws of physic shows that in Copernicus' research methods the prime role was played by purely astronomical speculations, and that it is on results of these that the interpretation of the philosophy of nature depended.

Later on in the general part the author declares that the position of the Sun in the centre of the universe "is taught to us by the law of the order in which these bodies (planets) follow one another and by the harmony of the whole universe". This law of order is one of the most important arguments against the Ptolemaic system in which each planet was studied separately from the rest of the system. This argument is developed in the famous tenth chapter containing a description of the solar system, in which an "admirable order of the world and an established harmonious connection between the motion and the magnitude of the spheres, which cannot be discovered in any other way" is found to exist. The descriptive part of the book closes with a short exposition of the triple motion of the Earth. The rest of Book One is taken up with an exposition of plane and spherical trigonometry, printed earlier in a separate edition of 1542.

In Book Two Copernicus explains spherical astronomy. It closes with a catalogue of over 1,000 stars, patterned after Ptolemy. The sphere of fixed stars constituted a system to which Copernicus relates the phenomena connected with the apparent motion of the Sun, which he describes in Book Three. The first part of this book is devoted to a detailed exposition of the new theory of precession.

The discovery of the true cause of precession phenomena in the movement of the Earth's axis is among the most important elements of the new astronomy. The theory of this "third motion of the Earth," carefully documented mathematically, is based on more than 1800 years of observations, which made it possible to establish with great accuracy the velocity of precession motion. The observations used by Copernicus led him, on the other hand, to erroneously consider as real a periodic insignificant disturbance in that motion.

Copernicus presented the Earth's orbit in the same way as he had done in the **Commentariolus** i.e. using an eccentric circle (the centre of the circle did not therefore correspond to the Sun). An additional construction was needed to present the discovered changes in the eccentricity of the Earth's orbit.

Book Four contains the theory of the Moon's motion and methods for calculating solar and lunar eclipses. In developing his arguments against the Ptolemaic theory of the Moon, Copernicus expounds his own theory which corresponds to that in *Commentariolus,* but here it is extensively documented with the use of both old and new (i.e. his own) observations.

The last two books are devoted to the planets. In Book Five Copernicus studies the motion of the planets in the plane of the ecliptic, excluding, like his predecessors, the analysis of the latitudinal motion of the planets, which follows from the various inclinations of the planetary orbits in relation to the plane of the ecliptic. This analysis takes up the sixth and last book.

His own solution to the theory of the motion of the planets the author has prefaced with a short survey of the Ptolemaic theory, in which he criticizes, as he did in discussing the Moon, the use of the equant. The next chapter deals with phenomena observed in the motion of the planets as a result of the motion of the Earth. Heliocentric astronomy explains the loops described on the celestial sphere by the planets without recourse to the epicycle, used by Ptolemy, but by attributing them to the changing position of the observer, carried by the Earth in its movement round the Sun. Still requiring explanation, however, were the deviations from the uniform motion, caused by what is in fact the uneven motion of a planet on an elliptical orbit. We have already mentioned that the earlier solution to this problem given in the *Commentariolus,* which consisted of a circle concentric with the centre of the universe and of two epicycles, was replaced by an eccentric circle with only one small epicycle. These two equivalent geometrical constructions replace the real orbit of the planet just as well as did the Ptolemaic model with the equant. The equivalence of these two solutions was confirmed by Copernicus himself when he chose the new model (eccentric circle with epicycle) because he wanted to determine the changing planetary eccentricities without having recourse to additional constructions. The particular planets are discussed in the order of their diminishing distance from the Sun, i.e. beginning with Saturn and ending with Mercury. Using ancient observations together with his own, Copernicus was able to determine the dimensions and position of orbits, noting at the same time the mobility of the lines of the apsides.

The explanation of the motion of the lower planets, Venus and Mercury, required certain modifications. The relic from geocentric astronomy, which was preserved in *De Revolutionibus* in the determination of planetary orbits not in relation to the Sun but to the centre of the

Earth's orbit (which lay outside the Sun), introduced certain disturbances in the motion of those planets, dependent on the position of the Earth at a given moment and most noticeable in the motion of Venus, the planet nearest to the Earth.

Mercury's orbit required special treatment. Because of the considerable eccentricity of this orbit and the impossibility of observing the planet except during the short periods when its angular distance from the Sun was greatest, the schema used by Copernicus yielded satisfactory results only for the moments close to the greatest elongation of Mercury. Similarly imprecise was the theory of Mercury's motion in geocentric astronomy. Unlike in the case of the other planets Copernicus worked out his theory of Mercury without the use of any observations of his own, which he could not carry out, as he himself says, because of the "Vistula vapours" obscuring the view. He had to make do with those recorded by the Nuremberg astronomer Bernard Walther. The comparison of ancient with new observations made it possible for Copernicus to establish the motion of Mercury's perihelion which amounts to one degree in 63 years, "if that motion is uniform."

The theory of the latitudinal motion of the planets in width, which comprises Book Six, bears the visible traces of geocentric astronomy in the form of periodic oscillations of the planetary orbits in the rhythm of the Earth's annual motion. Here, the true innovation consisted in the introduction by Copernicus of the inclination to the plane of the ecliptic of entire planetary orbits instead of, as in Ptolemy, the changing inclination of the epicycles. Apart from that, the exposition of the problem is modelled strictly on the *Almagest.*

The exhaustive presentation of all the astronomical questions of the day, the documented process of transition from information supplied by observation to theory, led to the universal recognition of Copernicus, the author of *De Revolutionibus,* as an innovator in astronomy even before leading scholars at the turn of the 16th century realized the significance and implications of the fundamental discoveries made by the Frombork astronomer.

Authors' Note.

Twenty-five years since the publication of our essay, research on the science of the Renaissance has enormously enriched our understanding of what happened on the way to the "scientific revolution" of the seventeenth-century. In particular, the in-depth studies of Copernicus's mathematical astronomy have evaluated the astronomer's mathematical tools and the problems that he had to cope with or that he tried to cope with. We also may add here an unknown case of Copernicus's error in his geometric argument against Johann Werner's astronomical work of 1524 (cf. ch. 7 in *Co-*

pernicus: Scholar and Citizen, Interpress Publishers, 1972). Yet, the recent Copernican literature itself is not free from errors distorting the overall picture of the astronomer's work. To name but one glaring example, there is the unfounded critique of the "postulates" in Copernicus's *Commentariolus* (cf. ch. 4 in *Copernicus: Scholar and Citizen*), presenting them as an orderless, logically-unrelated sequence. This has missed the obvious historical context of Copernicus's presentation, addressed to his contemporaries. It is enough to read the new "postulates" side by side with the corresponding opening chapters of a standard textbook of Ptolemaic astronomy (such as the "Epitome" by Peurbach and Regiomontanus). In short, there is a large number of valuable books on Copernicus and on the history of astronomy in general, but these books should always be read with an open mind.

Owen Gingerich (essay date 1973)

SOURCE: "From Copernicus to Kepler: Heliocentrism as Model and as Reality" in *Proceedings of the American Philosophical Society,* Vol. 117, No. 6, December, 1973, pp. 513-22.

[In the following essay, Gingerich discusses controversies in the early publishing history of De revolutionibus.*]*

Near the close of Book One of the autograph manuscript of his great work, Copernicus writes:

> And if we should admit that the course of the sun and moon could be demonstrated even if the earth is fixed, then with respect to the other wandering bodies there is less agreement. It is credible that, for these and similar causes (and not because of the reason of motion, which Aristotle mentions and rejects), Philolaus was aware of the mobility of the earth, and some even say that Aristarchus of Samos was of the same opinion. But since things were such that they could not be comprehended except by a sharp intellect and continuing diligence, Plato says that generally very few philosophers in that time understood the reason for the sidereal motion.[1]

Before a copy of Copernicus's manuscript was sent to the printer, the work was somewhat reorganized and in the process this passage was struck out. The original first and second books were merged into a single section, and the deleted material was rewritten into the preface to Pope Paul III. Apparently by that time Copernicus had access to the 1531 Greek edition of Plutarch,[2] and so he chose to use a direct quotation in Greek, which reads in translation:

> Some think that the earth is at rest, but Philolaus the Pythagorean says that it moves around the fire with an obliquely circular motion, like the sun and

moon. Herakleides of Pontus and Ekphantus the Pythagorean do not give the earth any movement of locomotion, but rather a limited movement of rising and setting around its center, like a wheel.[3]

In this way the name of Aristarchus, often called the "Copernicus of Antiquity," was eliminated from the printed edition of *De revolutionibus.* An anniversary such as this, when Copernicus is everywhere apotheosized, inevitably breeds detractors. Among their complaints is the large measure of glory attributed to Copernicus and the silence that attends the speculative suggestions of Aristarchus.

I do not intend to give a judgment here, but rather, I shall first answer with the platitude that nothing succeeds like success. Surely a critical factor is that Copernicus's system has been universally adopted, and that of Aristarchus was not. This, then, leads us to the fascinating study of the reception, the near rejection, and the ultimate acceptance of the heliocentric system. By this I do not mean the dramatic story of Galileo and the Inquisition, but a pattern of events that unfolded and reached their denouement before Galileo wrote his *Dialogo* in 1632.

Two of the key figures in the dessemination of the Copernican doctrine were professors of mathematics at the Lutheran University of Wittenberg. About the senior member of the pair, Erasmus Reinhold, few personal facts are known. In 1531 his name is inscribed in the Dean's Book of the University of Wittenberg along with other students, and in 1536, at age twenty-five, he became professor of higher mathematics, that is, of astronomy. On two occasions he served as dean, and he later became rector of the University of Wittenberg. In 1553, at the peak of his astronomical career, he died of the plague, being only forty-one years old.[4]

In the same year that Reinhold became professor of higher mathematics, Georg Joachim Rheticus received the chair of lower mathematics at age twenty-two. Apart from the fact that they both served together for a few years on the Wittenberg faculty, and both played fundamental although different roles in making Copernicus famous, their subsequent lives have little in common. Unlike Reinhold, who became an establishment figure at Wittenberg, Rheticus became a scholastic itinerant, his interest in Copernicus quickly fading. Nevertheless, his part in getting Copernicus's work published was memorable, and rather similar to Halley's role with respect to Newton's *Principia.*

In 1539 the young Rheticus journeyed to Frauenburg (now the town of Frombork) in remote Polish Prussia to gain first-hand knowledge concerning the astronomical innovations suggested by Copernicus. Although Rheticus came from the hotbed of Lutheranism, the Catholic Copernicus received him with courage and cordiality. Swept along by the enthusiasm of his young disciple, Copernicus allowed Rheticus to publish a first-printed report about the heliocentric system. In a particularly beautiful passage, Rheticus wrote:

> With regard to the apparent motions of the sun and moon, it is perhaps possible to deny what is said about the motion of the earth. . . . But if anyone desires to look either to the principal end of astronomy and the order and harmony of the system of the spheres or to ease and elegance and a complete explanation of the causes of the phenomena, by no other hypotheses will he demonstrate more neatly and correctly the apparent motions of the remaining planets. For all these phenomena appear to be linked most nobly together, as by a golden chain; and each of the planets, by its position and order and very inequality of its motion, bears witness that the earth moves and that we who dwell upon the globe of the earth, instead of accepting its changes of position, believe that the planets wander in all sorts of motions of their own.[5]

His use of the word "hypotheses" is particularly interesting. This reappears on a subsequent page where Rheticus wrote:

> But my teacher had long been aware that in their own right the observations in a certain way required hypotheses which would overturn the ideas concerning the order of the motions and spheres that had hitherto been discussed and promulgated and that were commonly accepted and believed to be true; moreover, the required hypotheses would contradict our senses.

Both of these passages use the word "hypotheses" in a somewhat different sense from our modern meaning of the word. Rheticus, in common with most other sixteenth-century astronomical writers, uses "hypothesis" to mean an arbitrary geometrical device by which the observed celestial motions can be explained. Included within this set of geometrical devices was the grand hypothesis of them all, the heliocentric concept itself. The ultimate nature of the hypotheses, that is to say, whether they were hypothetical models or something real, became a fundamental issue in deciding on the relevance of the heliocentric idea.

As a preface to the next stage in our examination of "hypotheses" in Copernican astronomy, we must note that Rheticus not only gained permission to publish the *Narratio prima,* but he also persuaded Copernicus to allow publication of the *magnum opus* itself. Consequently, Rheticus obtained a copy of the manuscript, and upon returning to Germany he arranged for the publication of the book in Nuremberg by Johann Petreius, one of the leading scientific publishers of northern Europe. Rheticus temporarily resumed his teaching duties at Wittenberg but then moved to a professorship at Leipzig. Because he was still too far away to oversee the printing, the job fell to a Lutheran theologian, Andreas Osiander, who had previously worked as an editor for Petreius.

When Rheticus received his copies of the printed volume in the spring of 1543, he was annoyed to discover that an anonymous introduction on the nature of hypotheses had been added to the work. On two copies—one in the private collection of Mr. Harrison Horblit in Connecticut and the other preserved in the Uppsala University Library—Rheticus crossed out Osiander's unsigned introduction, in each case with a red pencil or crayon.

Osiander's introduction contains statements that seem quite innocent today, and which must have struck most sixteenth-century readers as eminently reasonable. I cannot believe that his anonymity in the matter stemmed from any malicious mischievousness, but rather simply from a Lutheran reluctance to be associated with a book dedicated to the Pope. He wrote:

> Since the novelty of the hypotheses of this work has already been widely reported, I have no doubt that some learned men have taken serious offense because the book declares that the earth moves; these men undoubtedly believe that the long established liberal arts should not be thrown into confusion. But if they examine the matter closely, they will find that the author of this work has done nothing blameworthy. For it is the duty of an astronomer to record celestial motions through careful observation. Then, turning to the causes of these motions he must conceive and devise hypotheses about them, since he cannot in any way attain to the true cause. . . . The present author has performed both these duties excellently. For these hypotheses need not be true nor even probable; if they provide a calculus consistent with the observations, that alone is sufficient. . . . Now when there are offered for the same motion different hypotheses, the astronomer will accept the one which is the easiest to grasp. The philosopher will perhaps rather seek the semblance of the truth. But neither of them will understand or state anything certain, unless it has been divinely revealed to him. . . . So far as hypotheses are concerned, let no one expect anything certain from astronomy, which cannot furnish it, lest he accept as the truth ideas conceived for another purpose, and depart from this study a greater fool than when he entered it. Farewell.[6]

In addition to striking out the introduction, in both copies Rheticus deleted the last two words of the printed title, *De revolutionibus orbium coelestium.* There is an old tradition, further attested to by copies at Yale University and at the Jagiellonian University in Cracow, that Osiander assisted the printer in changing the title from "Concerning the Revolutions" to *Concerning the Revolutions of the Heavenly Spheres.* It is difficult to see precisely what Rheticus thought was offensive about the additional words except that, like the introduction, the expression "heavenly spheres" perhaps suggests the idea of model building.

Rheticus's role as midwife in the publication of *De revolutionibus* guarantees his enduring fame. But after his return to Wittenberg, the torch was in effect passed to Erasmus Reinhold. Reinhold himself remains a rather ambiguous figure. In 1551, he published his *Prutenicae tabulae* in the first of several editions. These were a handy and much expanded form of the Copernican tables in *De revolutionibus.* This widely used reference work became a principal avenue for making Copernicus's name known. In the work Reinhold wrote:

> All posterity will gratefully remember the name of Copernicus, by whose labor and study the doctrine of celestial motions was again restored from its near collapse. Under the light kindled in him by a beneficent God, he found and explained much which from antiquity till now was either unknown or veiled in darkness.[7]

Though Reinhold's name was closely linked with Copernicus and Copernicanism through these handy tables, his printed writings show a notable lack of commitment with respect to the heliocentric astronomy. For example, his *Prutenic Tables* are carefully framed so that they are essentially independent of the mobility of the earth.

A number of authors have argued that Reinhold's own philosophical position was very close to that of Osiander.[8] He has left scattered clues throughout his writings, and a few hints in a single long manuscript preserved in Berlin. Although we seem to have less material extant from Reinhold than from Copernicus himself, I was able, by a happy piece of serendipity, to find and identify his personal copy of *De revolutionibus,* now preserved in the Crawford Library of the Royal Observatory in Edinburgh. At the bottom of its title page he wrote in Latin "The axiom of astronomy: celestial motion is circular and uniform or made up of circular and uniform parts." Clearly, what Reinhold saw as important in Copernicus's work was not the heliocentric cosmology, but some of the small technical details—minor hypotheses that were not part of the major cosmological revolution. In particular, he appreciated that Copernicus, in seeking to reform astronomy, had adopted a mechanism to eliminate the so-called equant of Ptolemaic astronomy, thereby returning the description of celestial motion to a pure combination of circles. Reinhold's *Prutenic Tables* are strictly based on this technical scheme, as I have demonstrated by a modern recomputation.

I should now like to describe some new material that shows the influence of this attitude on the teaching of astronomy at Reinhold's university twenty-five years after the publication of *De revolutionibus.* Two years ago, when the Smithsonian Institution enabled me to spend part of a sabbatical year in England, I made a systematic search of the manuscript astronomical tables in the Cambridge colleges. In the course of this investigation, I came upon a manuscript that proved to be a set of notes for the astronomy lectures at the University of Wittenberg in the late 1560's, roughly two decades after the death of Reinhold. Because no comparable material has ever been described in the literature, I should like to present some details, especially to show in what connection Copernicus's name came up in the lectures.

At that time, the introductory astronomy course was based on the late medieval text of John of Hollywood, better known as Sacrobosco. Sacrobosco's *Sphere* was a very low-level treatment of spherical astronomy that scarcely mentioned planetary motion or the sophistication of the Ptolemaic theory. A new feature of the teaching at Wittenberg, however, was the recent availability of cheap printed textbooks. It almost seemed as if each astronomy teacher had printed, or was organizing his notes for the printing of, a new commentary on Sacrobosco.

The manuscript is No. 387 in the Gonville and Caius College Library; it contains about 200 leaves, written in two different hands.[9] The first three quires of eight leaves each appear to have been written by Laurentius Rankghe of Colburg in 1564,[10] and constitute a Latin commentary on Sacrobosco's *Sphere.* The commentary goes up to the definitions of circles including the zodiac, and then stops in midstream. Rankghe's writing ends on the first page of the fourth quire, thus suggesting that the entire volume with its vellum binding was bound together originally as a blank notebook.

The rest of the manuscript has apparently been written by Johannes Balduinus between May 27, 1566, and sometime in 1570. All the dates given are consecutive, and sometimes record weekly progress through the astronomy lectures. Balduinus became dean in the autumn of 1569 and, therefore, he may have been taking an official record of the lectures.[11] This could perhaps account for the fact that elementary material is covered repeatedly. He begins by recording the "Erotemata in Questiones Sphaerae" (which might be roughly translated "questions on the questions of the sphere") of Sebastian Theodoricus Winshemius. Theodoricus was professor of mathematics at Wittenberg at that time, and his textbook on this subject was printed at least seven times in Wittenberg beginning in 1564.[12] The manuscript notes approximately parallel the printed textbook. Of particular interest are the references to Copernicus, who is first mentioned in both the manuscript and the printed text in connection with the size of the earth.[13] A little later, in a discussion of precession found in the notes but not in the printed textbook, Copernicus is cited for his numerical values, along with Reinhold's *Prutenic Tables*.[14] A few pages later Copernicus's name appears again in a discussion of the moon.[15]

Both the manuscript and textbook then move on to the question "does the earth move?" The discussion proceeds through the standard arguments of the preceding centuries, and there is no hint that Copernicus had proposed the mobility of the earth.

The next group of notes in the manuscript probably comes from lectures given in the 1567 winter term by Bartholomew Schönborn, a medical doctor who published some small astronomical works during that decade.[16] The material follows in part the Wittenberg astronomer Casper Peucer's *Elementa doctrinae de circulis coelestibus*.[17] Needless to say this book does not espouse heliocentrism, but it does give Copernicus, as well as Reinhold, a certain prominence in the chronological section that opens the book. In the manuscript Copernicus is mentioned along with Regiomontanus and Apianus for his trigonometric tables.[18] The manuscript notes then turn to a second book by Peucer, a *De dimensione terrae*, where another reference to Copernicus's trigonometric tables occurs.[19] The section ends with calculations and a poem for the eclipse of April 8, 1567, by Sebastian Theodoricus.

In May, Schönborn lectured on still another work of Peucer, *Novae questiones sphaerae*, another of the seemingly endless commentaries on Sacrobosco, but one not actually printed until 1573. Here we find a more interesting and more technical citation of Copernicus, in connection with the motion of the solar apogee. The words "Etsi aut Copernici hypothesis ut absurdas" jump out from the page, the reference turns out to be a technical point on the motion of the apogee, and not on the mobility of the earth itself.[20] However, a few pages later, the numerical information for Mars is quoted with a book and chapter reference to *De revolutionibus*. Several pages later, after a section of rough calculations, Copernicus's name appears again, in a discussion on the measurement of star positions. The same topic reappears in more detail again with Copernicus's name, in the next section, in which yet another commentary on the sphere becomes the subject of the lectures.[21] This time the book is apparently *Epitome doctrinae de primo motu* of Vitorin Strigel,[22] a former student of Caspar Peucer who was at that time professor of theology at Leipzig and just about to be silenced because of suspected Calvinism. Once more Copernicus's sine table is mentioned, and a few pages later his value of the obliquity of ecliptic is contrasted with that of Ptolemy. But when the notes discuss the possible mobility of the earth, once more the standard rebuttals appear, and Copernicus is nowhere in sight.

The concluding, and largest single section of the manuscript, deals with a slightly different work, Caspar Peucer's *Hypotheses astronomicae*. It is not clear to me whether these lectures were given by Sebastian Theodoricus, or by Peucer himself. Peucer, the son-in-law of the Lutheran theologian Melanchthon, held considerable authority in the University at that time, although in 1576 he lost out in a faculty power struggle and was jailed, ostensibly for theological errors. In any event, the first part of the lectures mostly parallels a work called *Hypotyposes orbium coelestium*, published anonymously in Strasbourg in 1568, but republished in 1571 (that is, a year or two after the date of the lectures) under the title *Hypotyposes astronomicae* with Caspar Peucer as author. At the beginning Peucer declared that the Strasbourg edition had been pirated from him. His preface to this rare printed text is an extraordinary commentary on the state of the Copernican hypothesis as taught in Wittenberg. Peucer complains of the "offensive absurdity so alien to the truth, of the Copernican theories."[23] The proper solution, he contends, is the Ptolemaic model made consistent with recent observations. This is implied in the full title of his book, which in English reads "Astronomical Hypotheses or the Theory of the Planets, from Ptolemy and other old doctrines, accommodated to the observations of Nicholas Copernicus and the canon of motion based on them."

Interestingly enough, the manuscript notes themselves are not so specific in their rejection of Copernican cosmology, but nonetheless this topic is given the treatment of silence. The manuscript contains numerous numerical comparisons between the tables of Johann Schöner, and Reinhold's *Prutentic Tables*, but entirely divorced from any questions of the earth's motion. Finally the manuscript ends with a horoscope and calculations for the eclipse of August 15, 1570, these apparently being the ultimate product of an astronomical education at Wittenberg on the eve of the first centenary of Copernicus's birth.

The document shows clearly that Copernicus was well known and esteemed as a mathematician and astronomer. Nevertheless, at that great academic center—the home of the *Prutenic Tables* and the spot from which Rheticus had gone to Poland to encourage the publication of *De revolutionibus*—the students were fully protected from possible confusion by Copernicus's absurd cosmology. These lecture notes show vividly the remarkable silence that seemed almost everywhere to shroud the Copernican system in the sixteenth century.

In fact, this is not news to any attentive reader of the astronomical literature between 1550 and 1600. Thus, Copernicus's name appears often in print, but his heliocentric system is virtually never discussed. A nice example, worth noting only because it is comparatively early, 1556, is the *Tractatus Brevis et utilis, de Erigendis Figuris Coeli* of Johannes Garcaeus. Primarily an astrological work, it cites Copernicus ten times and uses his numbers to get celestial positions of the planets. Another, more interesting, example is Michael Maestlin's *Epitome astronomiae,* first printed in 1582 and then issued six more times, the last in 1624. In this textbook Maestlin mentioned the name of Copernicus several times, but never once did he breathe a hint of the heliocentric cosmology.

In spite of the silence accorded the Copernican system in printed works and in academic lectures, I am convinced that Copernicus's arguments were rather widely known. Arthur Koestler, in his *Sleepwalkers,* has called *De revolutionibus* "the book that nobody read" and "all-time worst seller." In fact, my examination of over 100 copies of the first edition of the book has convinced me that the contrary is the case. Sixteenth-century astronomers read with pen in hand, and their tracks persuade me that the book had a fair readership. So far I have found locations for approximately 180 copies of the original 1543 edition of the book. It is difficult to estimate the rate of attribution, but the original edition must have totaled at least 400 copies, a substantial number for a Renaissance science book. Nevertheless, by 1566 a second edition of a comparable size had become economically feasible. It would seem then, that anyone seriously interested in astronomy would not have had much difficulty in encountering Copernicus's ideas.

This then leads us back to the theme of this paper—from model to reality. I can well imagine that the majority of sixteenth-century readers found Copernicus's ideas profoundly unsettling. As long as people could view the heliocentric idea as just another geometrical hypothesis for saving the phenomena, there was no need to get particularly upset. One could always hope for another alternative, such as the geocentric model later developed by Tycho Brahe. The matter is very nicely put around 1555 in a letter from Gemma Frisius that was published in several editions of Stadius's *Ephemerides.* In one of the rather few printed references in that century to the heliocentric hypothesis, Gemma allowed that the Copernican system gave a better understanding of planetary distances as well as certain features of retrograde motion. He added, however, that those who objected to the ephemerides because of the underlying hypothesis understood neither causes nor the use of hypotheses. "For these are not posited by the authors as if this must exist this way and no other." He further remarks: "Nay, even if someone wished to refer to the sky those motions that Copernicus assigns to the earth, he could do so and according to the very canons of calculation."[24]

This position is even more clearly confirmed by the censorship imposed by the Inquisition when *De revolutionibus* was placed on the *Index* "until corrected," and by the dozen corrections issued in 1620. For example, the title of chapter 11 was changed from "On the demonstration of the triple motion of the earth" to "On the hypothesis of the triple motion of the earth and its demonstration." Most of the other corrections have a similar nature.

Nowadays this Osianderian view of hypotheses strikes a sympathetic chord. Hypothetical model building is once more a familiar procedure not only for astronomers and physicists, but for biologists and sociologists. To this extent our world view finds kinship with the astronomers of the late 1500's. Thus the "progress" from model to realism in the sixteenth century and the profound philosophical revolution of the early seventeenth century concerning the knowability of physical reality now takes on a bitter-sweet poignancy.

How did the view of heliocentrism change from a mere model to physical reality? Two men played the leading roles in the transformation of the prevailing opinions: Johannes Kepler, who found that the aesthetic arrangement of the Copernican system led to a coherent mathematical description of the motions, and Galileo Galilei, whose telescopic observations helped convince people that the Copernican system was not so absurd after all.

Kepler's own account of becoming a Copernican appears in the introduction to his *Mysterium cosmographicum,* where he mentions hearing about Copernicus in Michael Maestlin's astronomy lectures at Tübingen; Kepler was so delighted that he began to collect all the advantages that Copernicus had over Ptolemy, and he initiated a quest for the mathematical relationships between the number, the dimensions, and the motions of the planets. "At last on a quite trifling occasion I came near the truth," he wrote. "I believe Divine Providence intervened so that by chance I found what I could never obtain by my own efforts. I believe this all the more because I have constantly prayed to God that I might succeed if what Copernicus had said was true."[25]

What Kepler found was that the spacing of the planets could be closely approximated by an appropriately arranged nesting of the five regular polyhedra between spheres for the six planets of the Copernican system. Quixotic or chimeral as Kepler's polyhedra may appear today, we must remember that the *Mysterium cosmographicum* was essentially the first Copernican treatise of any significance since *De revolutionibus* itself. Without a sun-centered universe, the entire rationale of his book would have collapsed.

Furthermore, Kepler recognized that, although in the Copernican system the sun was near the center, it played no physical role. Kepler argued that the sun's centrality was crucial, for the sun itself must provide the driving force to keep the planets in motion, and he set out for the first time to show this connection mathematically.

Kepler knew that the more distant a planet was from the sun, the longer its period—indeed, this was one of the most important regularities of the heliocentric system, already noted by Copernicus, who wrote:

> In this arrangement, therefore, we discover a marvelous symmetry of the universe, and an established harmonious linkage between the motion of the spheres and their size, such as can be found in no other way.[26]

Undoubtedly Kepler himself had been inspired by this passage in *De revolutionibus.* And it is fascinating to notice that at least one of Kepler's contemporaries recognized this connection. Johannes Broscius, professor at Cracow, underscored those lines in his own copy of Copernicus's book, and in the margin wrote in Latin:

> Was perhaps this underlined part what Kepler afterwards deduced in his *Mysterium cosmographicum?* It seems by the brevity that something more is involved. See also Kepler in his *Commentary on the Motion of Mars.*[27]

For Kepler, there was an essential physical difference between a geocentric and a heliocentric universe; only in the latter case would the sun provide the central motive power for the planetary system. Hence, Kepler believed firmly in the reality of the Copernican system. Armed with this conviction, he realized that, if the orbit had a physical reality, the same orbit must yield latitudes as well as longitudes. This may be obvious today but, in Kepler's age, this was a novel idea that became a fundamental tool for his attack on the problem of Mars and an important link in the chain that led to the discovery of the elliptical orbit of Mars. Thus, for Kepler's work, belief in the heliocentric system really mattered, and made a vital difference in his approach to the subject.

In 1609, when Kepler published the results of his researches on Mars and his *Astronomia nova,* he placed on the back of the title page an indignant notice revealing in print for the first time that Osiander was the author of the anonymous preface to Copernicus's book. He wrote, "It is a most absurd fiction, I admit, that the phenomena of nature can be demonstrated by false causes. But this fiction is not in Copernicus . . . as evidence, I offer this work."

Accompanying Kepler's bold proclamation was a second remarkable paragraph. Petrus Ramus, professor of philosophy and rhetoric in Paris during the middle of the sixteenth century, had offered his chair to anyone who could produce an "astronomy without hypotheses," and Kepler declared that if Ramus were still alive he would have claimed the reward. Clearly Kepler believed that his recourse to physics had freed astronomy from the arbitrary geometrical devices that were still present in the work of Copernicus. Fundamental to Kepler's "astronomy without hypotheses" was the concept that one special physical object, the sun, was physically and mathematically linked to planetary motions. In essence this is the central power of the Copernican idea of the essential stepping stone to Newton's law of gravitation. It is, of course, in this context that Copernicus, rather than Aristarchus, is being celebrated in 1973.

Notes

[1] Translated from the transcription given in *Nikolaus Kopernicus Gesamtausgabe* 2 (F. Zeller and C. Zeller, eds., Munich, 1949): p. 30. I wish to thank Miss Joanne Phillips for preparing an initial translation.

[2] . . . The location of the copy Copernicus used is unknown, although his copy of 1516 Strasbourg Latin edition is preserved in Uppsala. I have compared the Copernicus text against the British Museum copy of the Basel edition, 524, g. 18, where it is cataloged under "Suppositious Works." In spite of a few minor differences, it seems likely that Copernicus used the Basel edition for his quotation.

[3] N. Copernicus, *Revolutions of the Heavenly Spheres,* in: *Great Books of the Western World* 16 (Chicago, 1952): p. 508.

[4] See my "Reinhold" in a forthcoming volume of the *Dictionary of Scientific Biography*; also see Karl Heinz Burmeister, Georg Joachim Rheticus (3 v., Wiesbaden, 1967-1968).

[5] Translations of the *Narratio prima* slightly modified from E. Rosen, *Three Copernican Treatises* (New York, 1971), pp. 165 and 192.

[6] The greatly abridged text printed here is based on the translation of E. Rosen, *op. cit.*, pp. 24 25.

[7] E. Reinhold, *Prutenicae tabulae* (Tübingen, 1551), part 1, f. 35 in section 21, "Praeceptum. De Calculo adparentis magnitudinis tropici anni ad datum tempus." This quotation was inserted as an advertisement in the second edition of Copernicus, *De revolutionibus* (Basel, 1566).

[8] O. Gingerich, "The Role of Erasmus Reinhold and the Prutenic Tables in the Dissemination of the Copernican Theory," *Studia Copernicana* 6 (Wroclaw, 1973), pp. 43-62; this article cites previous authors including P. Duhem, L. A. Birkenmajer, E. Zinner, and Á. Birkenmajer.

[9] See M. R. James, *A Descriptive Catalogue of the Manuscripts in the Library of Gonville and Caius College* (Cambridge, 1907-1908). Under 387, p. 447, in line 3 read "Vuinshemii" in place of "Avinstemii" and in lines 9 and 10, read "Peueeri" in place of "Pruerii."

[10] I have not been able to locate Rankghe in the student lists in *Album Academiae Vitebergensis ab A. Ch. MDII Usque ad A. MDCII 2* (Halle, 1894), but since there is no name index I could have overlooked him.

[11] Balduinus's handwriting in this manuscript agrees with the more formal specimen in the Wittenberg Dean's Book, which is now preserved at the Archives of the Martin Luther University in Halle. In 1574 Balduinus published *Vorhersage für 1574* (Wittenberg), Zinner 2664, but I have found no other trace of him.

[12] Sebastian Theodoricus Winshemius, *Novae questiones spherae, hoc est, de circulis coelestis, primo mobile, in gratiam studiosae iuuentutis scriptae* (Wittenberg, 1564, 1567, 1570, 1578, 1583, 1591, 1605). Theodoricus served as dean at Wittenberg in the spring of 1568.

[13] MS. section 4, f. 2r. The printed text reads on p. 90: "Terra maior est centies sexagies sexies. Est enim proportio Diametrorum secundum Ptolemaeum, quintupla sesquialtera, que est 11 ad 2. Secundum Copernicum vero quintupla superpartiens novem vicesimas, quae est 5 inteq. & 27 scrup ad unum."

[14] MS. section 4, f. 64; also f. 7r. On f. 7v, "vide Reinholdum in tabulis Prutenicis."

[15] *Ibid.*, f. 8v.

[16] Schönborn authored *Computus astronomicus* (Wittenberg, 1567, 1579) and Oratio de studiis astronomices astronomices (Wittenberg, 1564). He was dean at Wittenberg in 1564.

[17] Caspar Peucer, *Elementa doctrinae de circulis coelestibus* (Wittenberg, 1551, 1553, 1558, 1563, 1569, 1576, 1587); *De dimensione Terrae* (Wittenberg, 1550, 1554, 1579); *Novae questione sphaerae* (Wittenberg, 1573).

[18] MS. section 6, f. 3v.

[19] MS. section 7, f. 10v.

[20] MS. section 9, f. 9v; also f. 9r.

[21] MS. section 11, f. 16r; also section 10, f. 5r.

[22] Victorin Strigelius, *Epitome doctrinae de primo motu, aliguot demonstrationibus illustrata* (Leipzig, 1564; Wittenberg, 1565). MS. section 11, f. 22r; f. 24v.

[23] Caspar Peucer, *Hypotyposes astronomicae, seu theoriae planetarium. Ex Ptolemaei et aliorum veterum doctrina ad observationes Nicolai Copernici & canones motuum ab eo conditos accomodatae* (Wittenberg, 1571).

[24] In Johannes Stadius, *Ephemerides novae* (Cologne, 1556, 1559, 1560, 1570). Translation by Joanne Phillips.

[25] Johannes Kepler, *Mysterium cosmographicum* (Tübingen, 1596), p. 6; translated by Owen Gingerich in "Kepler," *Dictionary of Scientific Biography* 7 (New York, 1973): pp. 289-312.

[26] Nicholas Copernicus *Complete Works II On the Revolutions*, Edward Rosen, translator (London-Warsaw-Cracow, 1973), Book 1, chap. 10.

[27] "An etiam haec subindicat quam postea Keplerus deduxit in Mysterio Cosmographico. Videtur hic quiddam ista brevitate involvere. Videatur et Keplerus in Commentariis de Motibus Martis." Broscius's copy of the 1566 edition is preserved at the Observatory in Cracow. I wish to thank Professor E. Rybka for arranging for me to see and photograph this book. My transcription differs slightly from the one given by L. Birkenmajer, Mikolaj Kopernik (Cracow, 1900), p. 657.

Owen Gingerich (essay date 1975)

SOURCE: "'Crisis' versus Aesthetic in the Copernican Revolution" in *Yesterday and Today: Proceedings of the Commemorative Conference Held in Washington in Honour of Nicolaus Copernicus*, Vistas in Astronomy, Vol. 17, 1975, pp. 85-93.

[In the following essay, Gingerich argues against the notion that there was an astronomical crisis in astronomy before Copernicus published his theories.]

In a chapter in *The Structure of Scientific Revolutions* entitled "Crisis and the Emergence of Scientific Theories", Thomas Kuhn states: "If awareness of anomaly plays a role in the emergence of phenomena, it should surprise no one that a similar but more profound awareness is prerequisite to all acceptable changes of theory. On this point historical evidence is, I think, unequivocal. The state of Ptolemaic astronomy was a scandal before Copernicus' announcement."[1] A paragraph later he elaborates:

> For some time astronomers had every reason to suppose that these attempts would be as successful as those that had led to Ptolemy's system. Given a

particular discrepancy, astronomers were invariably able to eliminate it by making some particular adjustment in Ptolemy's system of compounded circles. But as time went on, a man looking at the net result of the normal research effort of many astronomers could observe that astronomy's complexity was increasing far more rapidly than its accuracy and that a discrepancy corrected in one place was likely to show up in another.

The existence of an astronomical crisis facing Copernicus in the early 1500s is presupposed by one author after another; perhaps it is most vividly expressed by de Vaucouleurs, who writes:

> The Ptolemaic system was finally overthrown as a result of the complexity which arose when an ever-increasing number of superimposed circles had to be postulated in order to represent the ever-multiplying inequalities in the planetary motions revealed by observational progress.[2]

Nevertheless, my own researches have convinced me that this supposed crisis in astronomy is very elusive and hard to find, at least in the places where we are normally told to look. As a simple but powerful example of what I have in mind, let me cite the work of two leading ephemeris-makers of the sixteenth century, Johannes Stoeffler and Johannes Stadius.

Stoeffler was born in 1452. When late in life he became professor of mathematics at Tübingen, he already enjoyed a virtual monopoly with the ephemerides prepared by himself and Jacob Pflaum; these had continued through 1531 those of Regiomontanus. At Tübingen he extended his calculations to 1551, and these were published there posthumously in 1531.[3]

At about the same time that Stoeffler died (1530), Johannes Stadius was born (1527). In the 1560s Stadius taught mathematics at Louvain, and later he worked in Paris. Stadius was the first computer to adopt the Copernican parameters for a major ephemeris.[4] His own tables were, in effect, the successors to Stoeffler's, and their users included Tycho Brahe.

In this modern age of refined planetary theory and of electronic computers, it has become possible to calculate with fair precision where the planets really were in the sixteenth century, and hence I have been able to graph the errors in the planetary positions predicted by Stoeffler and by Stadius. These error patterns are as distinctive as fingerprints and reflect the characteristics of the underlying tables. That is, the error patterns for Stoeffler are different from those of Stadius, but the error patterns of Stadius closely resemble those of Maestlin, Magini, Origanus, and others who followed the Copernican parameters. . . .[5]

The first result of this comparison is the fact that the errors reach approximately the same magnitude before and after Copernicus. In the Regiomontanus and Stoeffler ephemerides, the error in longitude for Mars is sometimes as large as 5°, as Kepler complained in the Preface to his Rudolphine Tables.[6] And in Tycho's observation books, we can see occasional examples where the older scheme based on the Alfonsine Tables yielded better predictions than could be obtained from the Copernican Prutenic Tables. Now if the scandalous crisis of Ptolemaic astronomy was its failure to predict planetary positions accurately, Urania was left with nearly as much of a crisis on her hands after Copernicus.

Many simple historical accounts of the Copernican revolution emphasize not the accuracy but the simplicity of the new system, generally in contrast to the horrendous complex scheme of epicycles-upon-epicycles supposedly perpetrated by pre-Copernican astronomers. This tale reaches its most bizarre heights in a recent Encyclopœdia Britannica,[7] where the article on astronomy states that by the time of Alfonso in the thirteenth century, forty to sixty epicycles were required for each planet! More typically, we find what Robert Palter has called the "80-34 syndrome"—the claim that the simpler Copernican system required only thirty-four circles in contrast to the eighty supposedly needed by Ptolemy.[8] The Copernican count derives from the closing statement of his *Commentariolus:* "Altogether, therefore, thirty-four circles suffice to explain the entire structure of the universe and the entire ballet of the planets."[9] By the time Copernicus had refined his theory for his more mature *De revolutionibus,* he had rearranged the longitude mechanism, thereby using six fewer circles, but he had added an elaborate precession-trepidation device as well as a more complicated latitude scheme for the inner planets. Even Copernicus would have had difficulty in establishing an unambiguous final count.[10] A comparison between the Copernican and the classical Ptolemaic system is more precise if we limit the count of circles to the longitude mechanisms for the (Sun), Moon, and planets: Copernicus requires 18, Ptolemy 15.[11] Thus, the Copernican system is slightly more complicated than the original Ptolemaic system.

The 80-34 myth claims that the original simplicity of the Ptolemaic system was lost over the course of the ensuing centuries. "Theory patching was the order of the day", writes one recent author. The eighty circles presumably resulted from the piling of one epicycle on another, reminiscent of the lines

> Great fleas have little fleas
>   upon their backs to bite 'em,
> And little fleas have lesser fleas,
>   and so ad infinitum.

Astronomers have been fond of this view, because of the parallel between epicycles-on-epicycles and an analysis by Fourier series.[12] Nevertheless, this contrast between the simplicity of the Copernican system and the complexity of the detailed Ptolemaic mechanisms proves to be entirely fictitious.

Consider Stoeffler once more, the successor of Regiomontanus and the most successful ephemeris-maker of his day. If improvements were available in a patched-up scheme of epicycles-on-epicycles, surely Stoeffler would have used them. Two extensive sets of calculations allowed me to investigate this possibility.

First, I recomputed the thirteenth-century Alfonsine Tables, showing that they are based on a pure Ptolemaic theory, that is, with an eccentric, equant and single epicycle for the superior planets. The parameters were almost all identical to those originally adopted by Ptolemy, but the precessional motion had been augmented by trepidation, an improvement irrelevant to the discussion of epicycles-on-epicycles. Second, I used the Alfonsine Tables to generate a daily ephemeris for three centuries;[13] these positions agreed so closely with those published by Stoeffler that I am forced to conclude he used the unembellished Ptolemaic system, as transmitted through the Alfonsine Tables. . . . [14]

Thus, this second result of investigating the ephemerides indicates that only a simple, classical Ptolemaic scheme was used for the prediction of planetary positions in 1500. I am convinced that the complex, highly embroidered Ptolemaic system with all the added circles is a latter-day myth. To support my view, there are at least two more good arguments, although I can mention them only in passing. First, the most sophisticated understanding of the Ptolemaic system in the fifteenth century is reflected in the tract against Cremonensis,[15] in which Regiomontanus picks faults with an anonymous Medieval work, the Theorica Planetarum. One receives the impression here that in 1464 astronomers were once again just able to comprehend Ptolemy, but scarcely able to improve on his work. Second, the astonishing, almost complete absence of recorded observations before 1450 again suggests that pre-Copernican astronomers had little basis for adding those mythical epicycles-on-epicycles. I simply cannot believe Kuhn's statement that "as time went on, a man looking at the net result of the normal research effort of many astronomers could observe that astronomy's complexity was increasing far more rapidly than its accuracy and that a discrepancy corrected in one place was likely to show up in another".

I am willing to grant that Copernicus' cosmology represents, in a certain profound sense, a simplification, but I refuse to concede that the Ptolemaic theory had by the beginning of the sixteenth century reached a complex, patched-up state nearing collapse. In terms of the detailed mechanism for any particular planet, it would have been very difficult for Copernicus' contemporaries to distinguish between the two schemes on the basis of complexity.

Where, then, is the astronomical crisis that Copernicus faced? Kuhn goes on to say:

> By the early sixteenth century an increasing number of Europe's best astronomers were recognizing that the astronomical paradigm was failing in application to its own traditional problems. That recognition was prerequisite to Copernicus' rejection of the Ptolemaic paradigm and his search for a new one. His famous preface still provides one of the classic descriptions of a crisis state.[16]

This preface is the last extant piece of Copernican prose, written just before the publication of his book. A polemical passage, it attempts to justify his radical departure from traditional cosmology and to protect his work from future detractors. If one believes astronomy was at the point of crisis, then it is perhaps possible to read it as a classic description of a crisis state.

On the other hand, I believe that an alternative reading is preferable. After criticizing the alternative system of homocentric spheres, and indirectly, Ptolemy's equant, Copernicus says:

> Nor have they been able thereby to discern or deduce the principal thing—namely the design of the universe and the fixed symmetry of its parts. With them it is as though one were to gather various hands, feet, head and other members, each part excellently drawn, but not related to a single body, and since they in no way match each other, the result would be monster rather than man.[17]

This "fixed symmetry of its parts" refers to the fact that, unlike in the Ptolemaic scheme, the relative sizes of the planetary orbits in the Copernican system are fixed with respect to each other and can no longer be independently scaled in size. This is certainly one of the most striking unifications brought about by the Copernican system—what I would call a profound simplification. Clearly, this interlinking makes the unified man, and in contrast the individual pieces of Ptolemy's arrangement become a monster.

What has struck Copernicus is a new cosmological vision, a grand aesthetic view of the structure of the Universe. If this is a response to a crisis, the crisis had existed since A.D. 150. Kuhn has written that the astronomical tradition Copernicus inherited "had finally created a monster", but the cosmological monster had been created by Ptolemy himself.

In this view, there is no particular astronomical reason why the heliocentric cosmology could not have been defended centuries earlier, and it is in fact shocking that Copernicus, with the accumulated experience of fourteen more centuries, did not come up with a substantial advance in predictive technique over the well-honed mechanisms of Ptolemy. The debased positivism that has so thoroughly penetrated our philosophical framework urges us to look to data as the foundation of a scientific theory, but Copernicus' radical cosmology came forth not from new observations but from insight. It was, like Einstein's revolution four centuries later, motivated by the passionate search for symmetries and an aesthetic structure of the universe. Only afterward the facts, and even the crisis, are marshalled in support of the new world view.[18]

But why, if all this is true, did a Copernicus come in the sixteenth century, and not in the fourteenth or even the tenth century? Were the astronomical questions in Krakow in 1492 particularly conducive to challenging the old order? I have no doubt but that the growing problems of precession, trepidation, and the motion of the eighth sphere acted as a spur to Copernicus' thinking about astronomy. His attack on this problem demonstrates his unusual level of technical ability, which had certainly been rare in the Middle Ages. Copernicus' examination of precession may have led him to consider a moving Earth.[19] Nevertheless, the heliocentric system is scarcely a necessary consequence of the observation of precession.

No, I believe that it was something outside astronomy in the European intellectual climate in the sixteenth century that set the stage for the introduction of a new paradigm; as Professor Benjamin Nelson put it in an earlier paper in this symposium—it had something to do with "societies, communities, and communications". In his words, the flowering of new world views must be considered within the context of complex sociocultural structures. The sixteenth century was manifestly an age of change. While Copernicus was a student at Krakow, Columbus set sail across an unknown ocean. The new explorations made Ptolemy's time-honored geography obsolete. Discoveries of classical authors brought in a new humanism with fresh Neoplatonic ideals. Even the traditional authority of the Church was to crumble before the challenge of Luther and the reformers.

A powerful catalyst for these changes was the explosive proliferation of printing.[20] As a student in Krakow, Copernicus could secure and annotate his own printed set of Alfonsine Tables as well as Regiomontanus' Ephemerides. Later, probably in Italy, he obtained Regiomontanus' Epitome of Ptolemy's Almagest; the close paraphrases of many of its passages in the *De revolutionibus* show the formative role this book played in his researches. Still later, the first full printed Almagest of 1515 provided another useful source

of data.[21] Ultimately, it was the printed edition of his *De revolutionibus* that prevented his ideas from falling into oblivion.

In many ways, the world was ready for an innovative view of the cosmos. Copernicus, with both the intellect and the leisure to fashion a new cosmology, arrived on the scene at the very moment when the increased flow of information could both bring him the raw materials for his theory and rapidly disseminate his own ideas. An imaginative thinker striving to uncover fresh harmonies in the universe, he also achieved the technical proficiency to command respect for his mathematics and his planetary tables. One can easily argue that Copernicus was not the equal of Ptolemy or of Kepler in mathematics, although for his day he stood well above his contemporaries. Yet as a sensitive visionary who precipitated a scientific revolution, Copernicus stands as a cosmological genius with few equals. In celebrating his birth, we celebrate the man who, perhaps unwittingly, is the founder of modern science.

Notes

[1] Thomas S. Kuhn, *The Structure of Scientific Revolutions*, pp. 67-68, Chicago, 1962.

[2] Gérard de Vaucouleurs, *Discovery of the Universe*, pp. 32-33, London, 1957.

[3] See Note A. . . .

[4] See Note B. . . .

[5] See Note C. . . .

[6] See Note D. . . .

[7] See Note E. . . .

[8] Robert Palter, "An approach to the history of early astronomy", *History and Philosophy of Science,* 1, 93-133 (1970). Palter traces the 80-34 myth back as far as Arthur Berry's *A Short History of Astronomy* (London, 1898).

[9] Edward Rosen, "Nicholas Copernicus, a biography", in his *Three Copernican Treatises*, 3rd ed., p. 90 (New York, 1971).

[10] According to Ernst Zinner, *Entstehung und Ausbreitung der Copernicanischen Lehre*, pp. 186-7 (Erlangen, 1943), Copernicus should have included precession, the regression of the lunar nodes, and the change of solar distance in his count in the Commentariolus, thus getting a total of thirty-eight circles. Arthur Koestler in *The Sleepwalkers*, pp. 572-3 (London, 1959), attempted to count the circles in *De rev-*

olutionibus, but he overlooked the fact that Copernicus had by then replaced the longitude mechanisms by an eccentric, thereby listing at least six unnecessary circles; on the other hand, he could have claimed that the motion of the apsidal lines for Mercury and the superior planets each required a circle.

[11] Copernicus replaced the Ptolemaic mechanism for varying the site of Mercury's orbit with a couple, and he also accounted for the apsidal motion of the Earth's orbit with two circles. If the apsidal motions for Mercury and the superior planets are counted, then Copernicus required twenty-two circles for the motions in longitude.

[12] A recent letter to *Physics Today* (24, p. 11) remarked that 400 years ago the Physical Review might have been full of such papers as "A ten epicycle fit to the orbit of Mars", and a review article on radio galaxies in *The Astronomical Journal*, 77, p. 541, 1972, summarized with "The question is, 'Are we drawing too many epicycles?'"

[13] E. Poulle and O. Gingerich, "Les positions des planètes au moyen âge: Application du calcul electronique aux tables Alphonsines", *Comptes Rendus de l'Académie des Inscriptions et Belles Lettres*, pp. 531-48, 1968.

[14] Recently, I found in the *Badische Landesbibliothek* in Karlsruhe what I believe to be Stoeffler's personal manuscript copy of these tables, which he may have used in calculating his ephemerides. It is *Codex Ettenheim-Münster* 33, 93r-198r. I wish to thank the director, Dr. Kurt Hannemann, for showing me this manuscript. See Karl Preisendanz, *Die Handschriften des Klosters Ettenheim-Münster, IX in Die Handschriften der Badischen Landesbibliothek* in Karlsruhe, Wiesbaden, 1932.

[15] Johannes Regiomontanus, *Disputationes contra Cremonensia deliramenta*, Nuremberg, 1474 or 1475. According to Ernst Zinner, *Leben und Wirken des Joh. Müller von Königsberg*, 2nd ed., p. 335 (Osnabrück, 1968), Regiomontanus wrote the tract in August 1464.

[16] Kuhn, op. cit., p. 69.

[17] N. Copernicus, *De revolutionibus orbium coelestium*, f. iii(v), Nuremberg 1543. Edward Rosen suggests for "certam symmetriam" the term "true symmetry". I believe that "fixed" conveys a slightly better nuance in this context.

[18] See Gerald Holton, "Einstein, Michelson, and the 'Crucial Experiment'", *Isis*, 62, 133-97 (1969).

[19] J. R. Ravetz, in *Astronomy and Cosmology in the Achievement of Nicolaus Copernicus* (Wroclaw, 1965),

argues that studies of precession may have led to the Copernican cosmology. L. Birkenmajer, in *Mikolaj Kopernik* (Krakow, 1900), suggested that the deficiencies in the Ptolemaic lunar model may have started Copernicus on the road to the heliocentric system. Important as these may have been in the development of Copernicus' technical proficiency, there is no convincing argument that these studies would have led to a Sun-centered cosmology.

[20] See Owen Gingerich, "Copernicus and the impact of printing" on pp. 201-20 of this volume. See also E. L. Eisenstein, "The advent of printing and the problem of the Renasissance", *Past and Present*, no. 45, pp. 19-89 (1972).

[21] A detailed discussion of Copernicus' use of these books is found in L. Birkenmajer, *Mikolaj Kopernik* (Krakow, 1900). A useful list of books owned by, or available to, Copernicus is found in L. Jarzabowski's *Biblioteka Mikolaja Kopernika* (Torun, 1971). An earlier list, of the Copernican books now found in Sweden, is E. Barwiski, L. Birkenmajer, and Jos. Sprawozdanie z Poszukiwa w Szwecyi, pp. 94-119 (Krakow, 1914).

Additional Notes

NOTE A. In 1474 in Nuremberg, Regiomontanus printed his own ephemerides for 1475 through 1506, and these were reissued by various printers, including Ratdolt in Venice. Stoeffler and Pflaum issued their ephemerides in Ulm in 1499 for the years 1499 to 1531, with the title *Almanach nova plurimis annis venturis inservientia*, and these were repeatedly reissued by Liechtenstein in Venice. I have not yet ascertained if they recalculated the overlapping period from 1499 to 1506. Stoeffler's 1531 edition in Tübingen, with the title *Ephemeridum opus*, was edited by the successor to his professorial chair, Phillip Imsser; these tables were also promptly reprinted by Liechtenstein in Venice.

Edward Sherburne gives a charming account of the death of Stoeffler in the biographical appendix to his *The Sphere of Marcus Manilius* (London, 1675), p. 46:

> His death, or the occasion thereof at least, was very remarkable (if the Story be True). Having found by calculation, that upon a certain Day his life was like to be endangered by some ruinous accident, and the day being come, to divert his thoughts from the apprehension of the danger threatening him, he invites some Friends of his into his Study, where, after discourse, enticing into some dispute, he, to decide the controversie reaches for a Book, but the Shelf on which it stood being loose came down with all the Books upon him, and with its fall so bruised him, that he died soon after of the hurt,

Voss. in Addend. ad Scient. Mathemat. But the whole Story of his Death, of which some make Calvisius the Author, is false by the Testimony of Jo. Rudolphus Camerarius Genitur. 69. Centur. 2. who had it from Andraas Ruttellius his Auditour; for he died of the Plague at Blabira Feb. 16. 1531 in the 78th year of his Age, happening (according to Calculation if you will believe it) from the Direction of ____ to ____ .

NOTE B. Copernicus' own almanac was never printed and is now lost (see Edward Rosen, "Nicholas Copernicus, a biography", in his *Three Copernican Treatises,* pp. 374-5, 3rd ed., New York, 1971). Rheticus published an ephemeris for a single year, 1551, based on the tables in *De revolutionibus*. E. Reinhold published an ephemeris for 1550 and 1551, using his *Copernican-based Tabulae Prutenicae* (Tübingen, 1551); subsequent workers generally adopted Reinhold's tables as their avenue to the Copernican parameters. Stadius' *Ephemerides novae* (Cologne, 1556) included predictions for 1554-70, and later editions carried the tables through 1600. A posthumous edition went to 1606, but the additional years were probably appended by the publisher from the Alfonsine-based ephemerides of Leovitius. Stadius published his own planetary tables, *Tabulae Bergenses aequabilis et apparentis motus orbium coelestium* (Cologne, 1560), but these were essentially a plagiarism of the *Tabulae Prutenicae*. Lynn Thorndike (*A History of Magic and Experimental Science,* vol. 5, pp. 303-4, New York, 1941) quotes Tycho Brahe's estimate of Stadius as having been "more facile than accurate", an opinion apparently shared by Maestlin and Magini, who eventually produced major alternative ephemerides of their own.

NOTE C. The ephemerides used for the figures are Johannes Stoeffler op. cit.; Cyprian Leowitz, *Ephemeridum novum atque insigne opus ab anno 1556 usque in 1606 accuratissime supputatum,* Augsburg, 1557; Johannes Stadius, *Ephemerides novae et epactae ab anno 1554 ad annum 1600,* Cologne, 1570; Michael Maestlin, *Ephemerides novae ex tabulis Prutenices anno 1577 ad annum 1590 supputatae,* Tübingen, 1580; G. A. Magini, *Ephemerides coelestium motuum secundum Copernici observationes supputatae,* Venice, 1582. The comparisons were made against the computed longitudes in Bryant Tuckerman, *Planetary, Lunar, and Solar Positions A.D. 2 to A.D. 1649, Memoirs of the American Philosophical Society,* vol. 59, Philadelphia, 1964. Both figures were prepared by Barbara L. Welther.

Additional error graphs from sixteenth- and seventeenth-century ephemerides can be found in Owen Gingerich, "The Theory of Mercury from Antiquity to Kepler", *Actes du XII Congrès International d'Histoire des Sciences,* vol. IIIA, pp. 57-64, 1971, and "Kepler's

place in astronomy", *Vistas in Astronomy,* vol. 18, ed. A. and P. Beer, pp. 261-78, 1974.

NOTE D. "Johannes Kepler: Preface to the Rudolphine Tables", translated by Owen Gingerich and William Walderman, *Quarterly Journal of the Royal Astronomical Society,* 13, pp. 360-73, 1972; see especially p. 367.

Tycho frequently compared his own observations to the predictions from the Alfonsine and Copernican tables, usually to the advantage of Copernicus. A particularly favourable comparison occurred at the time of the great conjunction of Jupiter and Saturn in 1583 . . . , although by 20 August, 1584, Tycho's comparison for Jupiter showed the two schemes equally in error, and by 21 December, 1586, the Alfonsine calculation was decidedly better, especially in latitude. Frequently, the Copernican latitudes proved inferior, even when the longitude excelled—for example, for Saturn on January 24, 1595. Tycho compared lunar positions in December 1594, and toward the end of the month the Alfonsine-based Leovitius ephemeris was superior. The most conspicuous Copernican errors found by Tycho occurred during the August opposition of Mars in 1593, exceeding 5°; this configuration repeated in 1625 when Kepler noted the large errors during the particularly close approach of Mars. Tycho's investigations are published in J. L. E. Dreyer (ed.), *Tychonis Brahe Dani Opera Omnia,* 10-13, Copenhagen, 1923-6.

NOTE E. "Astronomy. I. History of astronomy. B. Mediaeval astronomy", Encyclopædia Britannica, vol. 2, p. 645, Chicago, 1969:

> King Alfonso X of Castile kept a number of scholars occupied for ten years constructing tables (the Alphonsine tables, *c.* 1270) for predicting positions of the planetary bodies. By this time each planet had been provided with from 40 to 60 epicycles to represent after a fashion its complex movement among the stars. Amazed at the difficulty of the project, Alfonso is credited with the remark that had he been present at the Creation he might have given excellent advice. After surviving for more than a millennium, the Ptolemaic system had failed; its geometrical clockwork had become unbelievably cumbersome and without satisfactory improvements in its effectiveness.

John Norris (essay date 1981)

SOURCE: "Copernicus: Science versus Theology" in *The Tradition of Polish Ideals: Essays in History and Literature,* Orbis Books (London) Ltd., 1981, pp. 132-49.

[In the following essay, Norris discusses the reception of Copernicus's astronomical findings by the Catholic

and Protestant churches during the sixteenth century.],

This paper is about a Polish citizen and about a revolution which he made. Unlike most Poles, he didn't know he was going to make a revolution, and he probably didn't intend it. He wrote a great and abstruse work, **De Revolutionibus orbium coelestium,** which hardly any of his contemporaries could read, let alone understand. It was intended to correct astronomical measurements; instead it revolutionized man's ideas about the universe and his place in it. We have never been quite comfortable in it since.

This paper is like Johann Kepler's ellipse—that is, it has two foci: the accomplishments of Copernicus and the question of the apparent conflict of science and theology. It is this way because, although the first depends very much on the second, they are not co-terminous. The apparent conflict between science and theology appeared only in the ninety years following Copernicus' death.

In order to make clear the significance of Copernicus' work, it is necessary first to look briefly at the universe as it appeared to astronomers after the Copernican Revolution, then at the universe of the ancients, and then at the Copernical Revolution itself—in which was embodied the apparent clash of science and theology.

The universe, by the beginning of the eighteenth century, was accepted as being infinite, with the mathematical probability of the duplication of our world and system somewhere else in the heavens. The universe had no centre and no limits. And it had no cosy, special man-centred purpose about it. Our particular small part of this universe was regarded as centring on the sun. Planets, among them the Earth, revolved around the sun in rounded elliptical orbits with the sun in one focus of the ellipse. These planets moved, according to the principle of inertia, having been set in their curved pattern in much the same way as a projectile; and they remained in that curved pattern for the same reason that a projectile remains in its trajectory—a balance of the centrifugal force flinging the planet into orbit, and the centripetal force of the sun's gravity holding it in orbit. The orbits of the planets are not entirely harmonious or regular, nor is their speed, since they are acted on by the gravity of other planets when they come close to one another. This fact enabled astronomers to predict the existence of the two most distant planets—Neptune and Pluto—years before they actually discovered them. But generally the speed of the orbits around the sun is regulated according to the distance of the planet in its orbit from the sun. A line drawn from the sun to the planet moving in its orbit will describe equal areas in equal times. Hence the planets move fastest when close to the sun, and slowest when farthest away

from it. The Earth, which is closest to the sun in January, moves fastest then, and slowest in summer. The relative speeds of the planets are harmonized according to the formula that the ratio of the squares of the periods of the orbits of any two planets is equal to the ratio of the cubes of their mean distances from the sun.

The Earth revolves clockwise in its orbit about the sun in 365 days, 5 hours, 48 minutes and 46 seconds, and rotates once in a little less than 24 hours, a rotation that is gradually getting slower due to tidal friction and other physical pressures. The axis of the Earth, which is inclined at an angle of 23 and one-half degrees to the perpendicular of the plane of the Earth's orbit, has a slight wobble in it which describes a circle of 23 and one-half degrees from its centre, a wobble which completes this circle every 26,000 years, or thereabouts, resulting in an apparent movement of the position of the north celestial pole—providing the Earth with five successive pole stars in the process. This movement is due to the pull of the gravity of the moon. In antiquity, it was called the precession of the equinoxes.

The moon revolves around the Earth once every 27 and one-third days on average, but because its rotation in the face of the sun is slightly slower, it completes a cycle of its phases only in 29 and one-half days (on average). It also wanders north and south of the plane of the Earth's orbit, a fact which ensures that eclipses do not happen regularly but only a few times a year.

As can be seen, the post-Copernican universe is rather a colourless place. It could be thoroughly measured and conceptualized, long before it was proven experimentally in 1957 when the first sputnik demonstrated physically that Copernicus, Kepler and Newton had been right. The idea of a limitless universe has a profound and negative effect on the way we view our place in things. In effect it has no active part in our lives. With the possible exception of some devoted professional astronomers, we do not feel ourselves to be at one with the spiral nebulae moving and multiplying in the heavens at incredible speeds; we do not depend on this universe as our ancestors did on theirs to help determine our ideas about physics and chemistry, mechanics and medicine, economics and sociology, theology, prophecy and eschatology. Even the word 'heavens' is now inapplicable, for in antiquity and medieval times it was defined as the celestial abode of immortal beings, the habitation of God and His angels, and of beatified spirits. Copernicus did not intend to create this sort of universe, though he was responsible for its conception.

Keep now this universe in mind, while we go back more than two thousand years to the world of our ancestors and predecessors; and we will, as they did, look up to the heavens on a clear summer evening and endeavour to relate the panorama of the heavens to our life here below. It is not difficult. The great canopy appears to rotate across the sky from the eastern to the western horizon, circling on the pole star, visible in our latitude about 50 degrees above the northern horizon. It is not hard to imagine, as the ancients imagined, that this amazing sight has a personal importance for us. We can see that the stars have a fixed position with relation to Earth, set in a canopy that rotates regularly above us. In the daytime, we can notice that the sun moves daily westward across the skies, north and south from vernal equinox to vernal equinox, and, if we observe very closely and take careful notes, slowly eastward, circling the heavens once a year.

Very early, men began to conceptualize all this—to make a picture out of their observations and calculations to help their memories and demonstrate a logical relationship between the observations. Like all good conceptual schemes, that created by the Greeks two thousand years ago in the two-sphere universe was logical in explaining the known facts, and it was psychologically satisfying in that it gave a convenient and easily acceptable picture which could be fitted into people's impressions of things as they are—into their cosmologies, which are ideas of the universe as an ordered whole. This scheme lasted for two thousand years, and Copernicus had to work from it and was able to change it very little. This is because it was satisfactory for most purposes, and because men work from what they know to what they do not know, not from total ignorance to total knowledge. Copernicus changed a vital part of this scheme, but only a part; and he learned enormously from the past and from this particular scheme. That is what Newton meant when he said that he had seen farther than most men because he stood on the shoulders of giants. Copernicus, too, stood on the shoulders of giants—the men who had conceptualized the heavens.

The two-sphere universe was made up of a fixed sphere, the Earth, centrally located in a huge rotating sphere marked with the stars, outside of which there was nothing. The planets—Moon, Mercury, Venus, Sun, Mars, Jupiter and Saturn moved in between the two spheres on orbits centred on the Earth. These planets, unlike the stars, wandered. The phases of the moon did not correspond with its revolutions around the Earth; the planets appeared to retrogress or backtrack in their paths, at which time they appeared brightest; and the two inner planets—Mercury and Venus—appeared to be tied very closely to the sun. This description does not explain the real problem of the planets which is one not of describing how they move, but of measuring their movement exactly so as to be able to predict and track them. It was this problem, of measurement

not description, which Copernicus set himself to solve. In the course of it he profoundly changed the description.

This distinction may be best illustrated by the two great schools of astronomy in antiquity: the homocentric school associated with the Hellenic philosophers Eudoxus and Aristotle in the fourth century B.C., and the mathematical school associated with the Hellenistic astronomer Ptolemy in the second century A.D. The homocentric system, especially as developed by Aristotle, went far beyond astronomy. It depended on a conceptual system of interlocking spheres, the outer driving the inner, but rotating in different planes. These spheres, which were supposed to be made up of a crystalline ethereal substance, apparently incorruptible, carried the various planets around with them, and their effect was to make the planets follow a figure-eight path, which was supposed to account for the retrograde motion. It took no account of the variations in distances of the heavenly bodies from the Earth, nor of eclipses. It was enormously influential because it was supported by Aristotle, the most influential of the ancients. But it was accepted also because Aristotle went much further than his predecessors had done in explaining the universe. The elements of the Earth—earth, water, air and fire—he also arranged in concentric circles which, however, were disturbed by the movement of the moon which mixed them up. Indeed, change, degeneration and corruption were natural to the Earth, as immutability and perfection were peculiar to the heavens. The Earth stood still and changed; the heavens moved, yet were unchangeable. Motion in the heavens, which was natural, was always circular; motion on Earth was in a straight line, and always required a mover, except in the case of natural motion, which was to the centre of the Earth. It followed that there could be no movement of the Earth, since all objects moved naturally towards its centre. This separation of terrestial and celestial physics proved to be one of the greatest stumbling blocks in the way of adopting the Copernican system. Space, according to Aristotle, was filled because nature abhorred a vacuum; hence it was possible to have movers in space— one homocentric circle moving another. The universe must be a closed one, because otherwise it would have no centre at which the Earth could concentrate. In any case, in an infinite universe, the known uniqueness of the Earth would vanish.

The scheme was coherent with observation, but not logical so far as measurement went. It was to be integrated in detail into Christian theology in the Middle Ages, creating a universe with religious as well as physical purpose. Hell was at the centre of the corruptible Earth, and all corruptible matter gravitated there; God's throne was beyond the stellar sphere; each planetary sphere was pushed by an angel. Distance and unchangeableness made heaven a logical place for the mysterious gods. Astrologers, too, found this mysterious distance convenient for giving the essential air of mystery to their trade. Astrology was a pseudo-science and disapproved of by the Church; but the Church's demand for accurate astronomical tables provided the largest impetus for astrological exploration in the fifteen hundred years between Ptolemy and Copernicus. However, the Aristotelian system had almost nothing to do with mathematics.

Mathematical explanations were developed in the system of Ptolemy, in his great work the Almagest (Mathematike Syntaxis) about 150 A.D. Ptolemy was not interested in a qualitative description of the universe, but rather in a mathematical measurement and explanation of the motions. He developed geometric explanations of the irregularities of the planets. First, the epicycle—this was a circle in which a planet revolved about a point that was attached to a main orbit called a deferent. Depending on the size and speed of the epicycle and the deferent, the retrogression of planets could be accounted for by this means. Second, minor epicycles were used to account for small quantitative differences between theory and observations. Ptolemy had five major epicycles—Copernicus got rid of them, but had to keep the minor ones. The epicycle caused the planet to go through its orbit in large loops. Third, eccentrics: these were centres of orbits which themselves revolved about another centre, giving somewhat the same effect as the crankshaft of a car. Fourth, equants: these were used to explain the fact that the summer season—between 21 March and 23 September—is six days longer than the winter season—from 23 September to 21 March.

Ptolemy said that the rate of revolution of the sun in its ecliptic, or path through the heavens, was uniform, not with respect to its own centre, but with respect to an equant point displaced from that centre. Copernicus disapproved of this because it was messy and unsymmetrical. He got rid of the equant from his system. All sorts of combinations of these devices could be used to explain the geometry of the universe. Ptolemy's successors over nearly 1500 years kept adding to the scheme to account for inaccuracies, until there were about eighty epicycles. It was partly to clean up Ptolemy and make him mathematically more accurate that Copernicus undertook his great work. Meanwhile Ptolemy gave no clear conceptual picture of the universe, and Aristotle gave no mathematical scheme to support the idea of homocentric spheres.

Astronomers took their mathematics from Ptolemy, cosmologists their scheme from Aristotle, and the disharmony was ignored. Only after the thirteenth century was the disharmony much discussed, and in the process the defects of each became clear. The Ptolemaic scheme was logical, the Aristotelian scheme was satisfying, and though alternative schemes were put forward by the ancients—including a moving Earth suggested by Aristarchus—and though the scholastic philosophers from the thirteenth century on increasingly criticized Aristotle, the systems were still more coherent than the unsupported bright ideas brought forward as alternatives.

Indeed, the Church provided, during the later Middle Ages, the intellectual matrix within which modern science was born. The central interest of the Middle Ages was theological rather than scientific, and science was supposed to explain the 'mysterious ways' in which God moved in the natural universe 'His wonders to perform'. The Aristotelian scheme provided the framework after the thirteenth century for this explanation.

The centuries of scholasticism were the centuries in which the tradition of ancient science and philosophy was reconstituted, assimilated and vigorously tested for adequacy. The new scientific theories of the sixteenth and seventeenth centuries emerged largely from the debate and examination to which all phenomena were subjected by the medieval philosophers. They had an unbounded faith in the capacity of human reason to solve the problems of science, and modern science has inherited this. More important, they had a disciplined way of going about their enquiries and recording the results. If you wish to judge the superiority of the scholastics in this regard, just compare the scientific results of working from a subtle and many-sided philosophy such as the Christian in the fifteenth and sixteenth centuries, with those of working from the simplistic and superficial philosopies of China and India in the same period. The one produced modern science; the other retarded scientific development until the twentieth century.

Copernicus stood on the shoulders of giants, but most of those shoulders were clothed in the uniform of the medieval Church. This is worth remembering, because in Copernicus' own lifetime most of the great work of the medieval Church, including the beginnings of modern science, was called in question by the Renaissance thinkers, and the degree to which Copernicus is supposed to have shared these criticisms depends on the identification of his principal inspiration. If his opposition to existing astronomy may be seen to arise out of a strong theoretical antipathy to scholasticism, his inspiration concerning the movement of the Earth can be traced to purely geometric origins. Renaissance humanism, as well as being childishly anti-scholastic and anti-scientific, inspired, too, in its neo-Platonic aspects, a non-theological, other-wordly idea of the universe, depending on the mystic magic of geometry and the worship of the sun as the source of all vital principles.

Copernicus, following his teacher at Bologna, Domenico Maria de Novara, complained in his preface to *De*

Revolutionibus that the homocentric astronomers had been unable to establish a system that agreed with the phenomena; while the Ptolemaic astronomers had been unable to deduce 'the shape of the Universe and the unchangeable symmetry of its parts'. But undoubtedly the most famous piece of evidence for regarding Copernicus as inspired by a dogmatic neo-Platonic sun-worship is his justification for placing the sun at the centre of the Universe, written in Chapter 10, Book I of *De Revolutionibus.*

> In the middle of all sits the Sun enthroned. In this most beautiful temple could we place this Luminary in any better position from which he can illuminate the whole at once? He is rightly called the Lamp, the Mind, the Ruler, of the Universe; Hermes Trismegistus names him the Visible God; Sophocles' Electra calls him the All-Seeing. So the Sun sits as upon a royal throne ruling his children the planets which circle around him.

Thomas Kuhn also suggests that since no fundamental new astronomical discovery occurred during Copernicus' lifetime to persuade him of the necessity of change, the inspiration for the revolution must be sought in 'the larger intellectual milieu inhabited by astronomy's practitioners'.[1] It was on this ground that historians have suggested that Copernicus was a neo-Platonic crackpot, a sun-worshipper, suffering from spheromania.

On the other hand, if we examine the text of Copernicus' preface to *De Revolutionibus,* which may have been begun while he was still a student at Cracow, and if, in particular, we look at the practical problems facing Copernicus and all other astronomers of his time, then the inspiration for his great idea appears to be a purely practical one—the need to make Ptolemaic astronomy more accurate for calendar, astrological and other computational purposes.

The improvement in classical learning had now made it clear that the inadequacies of Ptolemy were not simply due to bad translation; and geographic exploration, having discredited Ptolemy's geography, by analogy cast doubt on his astronomy as well. Most eloquent of all, the Julian Calendar was ten days out of harmony with sidereal time and, as Copernicus had pointed out when asked to reform it in 1514 by Pope Leo X, this required first that the precise movements of the sun and moon be ascertained. As soon as one addressed oneself to this problem, it was necessary to consider the problem of the 'precession of the equinoxes' (due, we now know, to the wobble in the Earth's axis, operating over 26,000 years) and the shift in the stellar longitudes that results from it. Recently it has been suggested, on good evidence, that Copernicus came to his idea of a moving Earth by the successive stages of endeavouring to correct the Calendar, and explain the precession of the equinoxes; and that he came on it not latter than 1497, while he was still a young student at the Jagiellonian University.[2] Certainly it is the problem of the precession of the equinoxes which underlay his opening complaint to Pope Paul that 'the mathematicians are so unsure of the movements of the Sun and Moon that they cannot even explain or observe the constant length of the seasonal year'.

In fact, these two interpretations of Copernicus—as neo-Platonic mathematical fanatic, and as practical astronomer endeavouring to reform the Calendar—can be reconciled. He was both. In his early years at Cracow, interested in the reform of the Calendar and the key problem of the equinoxes, and not being in touch with the latest intellectual currents—not even possessing a copy of Ptolemy's *Almagest* before 1497—he was necessarily the practical astronomer. It was in Cracow, almost certainly, that he decided to try to solve the problem of the precession of the equinoxes by moving the Earth in the scheme. He was certainly not at this time a fanatical neo-Platonic opponent of scholastic learning—indeed he never became one, endeavouring to preserve as much as possible of the old Aristotelian universe. We should emphasize this. Copernicus was never at any time in conscious conflict with Aristotelianism or the Church. Later, when he went to Italy, he was caught up in the neo-Platonic intellectual tide, and developed the argument of mathematical disharmony against the Ptolemaic and Aristotelian astronomers. He also developed here the astronomical and mathematical skill without which his central idea would have remained just a guess. It is important to remember that what made the revolution was that Copernicus was a very competent astronomer, who rejected for professional reasons a long-accepted scientific tradition. His neo-Platonic bias, especially in favour of pure geometric circles, coupled with his technical proficiency, would lead him all the more quickly to challenging Ptolemy, as he makes clear in the preface to Paul III. This I believe to be the true sequence of inspiration for the ideas of the moving Earth and the heliocentric universe.

What did Copernicus actually say in his great book? We can only give a brief and non-mathematical summary here. He began by explaining that well-known phenomena such as the daily turning of the heavens, the seasonal travel of the sun through the ecliptic, and the precession of the equinoxes can be accounted for by reference to corresponding motions which he attributed to the Earth—specifically the daily rotation of the Earth on its axis, its yearly revolution around the sun, and its wobble on its own axis every 26 000 years. Secondly, by means of a skilfully-chosen combination of epicycles, the relative sizes of which were determined from selected observations, he was able to give a representation of the moon's motion from night to night without assuming, as Ptolemy had done, variations in the moon's distance from the Earth and its apparent size out of all proportion to what observation reveals. But Copernicus made no improvement on Ptolemy's calculations. The most important part of *De Revolutionibus* is contained in Book V, which discusses the planets. Copernicus shows that according to his hypothesis, the characteristic apparent motions of the planets including retrogression and the closeness of Mercury and Venus to the sun can be accounted for as optical effects resulting from the revolution of the observer moving on the Earth around the sun. This eliminated Ptolemy's five major epicycles. The minor epicycles were still retained to account for minor fluctuations in the rates of planetary motion. Copernicus also found that it was possible, by observing a planet from two points on the Earth's orbit, to determine the relative distances of the planet and Earth from the sun.

The significance of his work can now be judged. Copernicus, we can see, retained most of the Aristotelian universe (including especially the perfect circular orbits for the planets and the innate naturalness of the Earth's circular motion). He even had to introduce a superfluous third motion (which he also used to explain the precession of the equinoxes), a motion of the Earth's axis around 23 and one-half degrees to account for the Earth being simultaneously fixed in a sphere and keeping the slant of its axis always parallel to a line drawn through the centre of the sun. His planetary mathematical system, which he intended to be an improvement on Ptolemy, does not work and is, if anything, worse than Ptolemy's inaccuracy. But qualitatively he did what he did not intend: he challenged the Aristotelian system. He gave a better conceptual description, accounting better for retrograde motion and the closeness of Mercury and Venus to the sun than Aristotle had done. And his scheme did unite the system of the planets harmoniously. According to Copernicus:

> . . . the orders and magnitudes of all the stars and spheres . . . became so bound together that nothing in any part thereof could be moved from its place without producing confusion of all parts and the universe as a whole.

But the real significance of Copernicus' work lies in the future, in the reactions that other people were forced to make to it. He had recognized the need for technical change; he had directed attention to the motion of the Earth; and he had given sufficient mathematical evidence to back up this idea so that never again could astronomers ignore its implications. They had to argue for or against it, test it, investigate it. And the more they did, the more they discovered of the supporting evidence that Copernicus had not discovered, the more they contributed to the Copernican Revolution. Only gradually, however, did the full implications become apparent: that Earth's motion implied a fixed heaven

of stars, and required that this should be an enormous distance away in order that the motions of the Earth should not give the impression of movement or irregularity in the stars; that the concentric Aristotelian spheres were lost; that the distinction between terrestial corruption and celestial purity was gone beyond hope of recall. The growing bitterness of opposition to Copernicus' ideas by the beginning of the seventeenth century is largely due to the fact that the system was succeeding.

It was at this point, in the ninety years following Copernicus' death in 1543, that the apparent clash between science and theology emerged. The first theological attack against Copernicanism, like the first lay attacks, concentrated on the absurdity of the idea of the Earth moving. Martin Luther called Copernicus a fool for forgetting that Joshua had commanded the sun and the moon (not the Earth) to stand still. Melanchthon and Calvin similarly regarded him as being ridiculous to place his ideas in competition with the truth of Holy Scripture. But by 1600 Protestants were labelling Copernicus as an atheist and an infidel, and increasingly the Catholics were inclined to view his influence as heretical.

Copernicus' proposal raised important questions for Christian cosmology, morality and theology. If the Earth was merely one of the six planets, how were the stories of the Fall and Salvation to be preserved? More especially, if there were other bodies essentially like the Earth, God's goodness would command that they be peopled too; but how could these people be descendants of Adam and Eve, and how could they have inherited Original Sin, the element which explains man's otherwise inexplicable trial on this imperfect Earth? How could beings on other worlds know of the Saviour who gave them the possibility of Salvation? If the Earth is a part of the infinite heavens, what becomes of the division between terrestial corruption and celestial perfection, of God's abode in a perfect heaven, and of man's intermediate position between the devils and the angels? As knowledge supporting Copernicanism grew, the time approached when Christians would have to change their cosmology.

For the Protestants, the reasons for resistance were obvious. They had just undertaken a religious revolution, partly on behalf of re-emphasizing the supremacy of Scriptural truth above all other doctrines and practices of the Church. To them this work of a canon of the Church of Rome could be regarded as yet another attempt by that Church to undercut Scripture. Reinhold, Osiander and Rheticus, all from Protestant districts, and all associates of Copernicus, found it necessary to modify their support for Copernicanism by saying that the astronomical calculations were simply mathematical abstractions and not representations of reality.

But the increasing opposition of the Catholic Church is harder to account for. Before 1600, as during the Middle Ages, there had been wide latitude for scientific speculation. Oresme and Nicholas Cusanus—the latter a cardinal—had propounded new cosmologies and had not worried about conflicts with Scripture; the reformed calendar, decreed by Pope Gregory XIII in 1582, had been based on Copernicus' calculations. But in the conditions of the conflict with the Protestants in the sixteenth century, Catholic doctrine was tightened up, scriptural references were more exactly observed, and heresies more harshly dealt with. In the circumstances, the authorities probably exaggerated the dangers of the crisis, and showed an unfortunate tendency to nail their colours to the mast in circumstances where it was clear that they would have to climb up and unnail them shortly. The case of Giordano Bruno illustrates this alarm. He was an alchemist and astrologer, often called the last magician and the first scientist. He found Copernicus' ideas useful in his neo-Platonic vision of the universe. He was executed in 1600 for heresies concerning the Trinity. But the Church almost certainly associated Copernicanism with Bruno. Good Catholics, including Cardinal Bellarmine who was to lead the condemnation of Galileo's Copernicanism in 1616, could see the clash coming and hoped to avoid it, especially as new evidence was being discovered yearly in support of the Copernican system.

In any case Copernicanism and the Church were on a collision course before 1616. In his contention with Bellarmine in 1615 and 1616, Galileo endeavoured to convert the Church to Copernicanism, and Bellarmine endeavoured to save it from the consequences of Galileo's outspoken discrediting of the Church's cosmology, and Galileo from the consequences of his outspokenness. Since 1609 Galileo had been using a telescope to contribute new qualitative data—new descriptive data—to support Copernicanism, and to persuade the Church to admit that Copernicanism represented reality rather than merely a convenient mathematical hypothesis. In the telescope the shape of the stars was different (refined from blobs to points of light), stars appeared and disappeared, the Milky Way was seen to be a vast collection of millions of stars. Suddenly, the infinity of worlds declared by Nicholas Cusanus and Giordano Bruno appeared to be a probability. The surface of the moon seemed to be not much different from that of the Earth. Spots appeared on the face of the sun; Jupiter had moons revolving around it. There was now less and less reason for the distinction between a corruptible changing Earth and a pure immutable heaven.

But in 1616 Galileo found that this sort of evidence did not do him any good, because it could not provide direct proof of the Copernican theses. The Ptolemaic universe contained enough space in which to include the distant stars, now that these were reduced in size by the telescope; the moons of Jupiter didn't prove that the Earth acted in the same way; and the imperfections in the movements of the planets could be explained by epicycles. Indeed, the Danish astronomer Tycho Brahe had already developed a modified Earth-centered pattern of the universe using Copernicus' mathematics and improving on them, and producing in the process a more accurate system. Hence it was that Galileo was defeated in disputation by Bellarmine. He was right, but he could not prove it, and that is almost as bad as being wrong. He was not required to recant his beliefs, but merely made a private undertaking not to publish them. But because the undertaking was private and equivocal he, later, under a new pope, thought he was free to publish his *Dialogues Concerning the Two Chief Systems of the World*. In 1633 he was once more condemned by the Church. This time he was placed under house arrest and the Copernican theses were unequivocally condemned as descriptions of reality. Not until 1752 was this sentence reversed; not until 1822 were Copernican books permitted by the Church to be published.

The Church, as Galileo warned, had put itself in an impossible position, just at a time when the last proofs of the Copernican system were about to be established. Tycho Brahe by 1604, for all his conservatism, had already made enough new observations to discredit the idea of the immutability of the heavens; Kepler by 1630 has established the elliptical orbits of the planets, the equal areas in equal times law, and the equality of ratios between the squares of the periods of orbits and the cubes of the mean distances of planets from the sun. The final integration of the mechanical universe came in the fifty years after Galileo's second condemnation, in which astronomy and celestial mechanics went far beyond anything envisaged by Copernicus. The idea of the infinite universe was revived from the ancients and applied to the new framework; Descartes revived the Aristotelian idea of the full universe in the corpuscular theory to account for the motions of planets, and in the doctrine of inertia went part-way to explaining the force of orbits; magnetism was used to explain gravity and the pull of the sun; the theory of the pendulum was employed to explain the ellipse; and finally Sir Isaac Newton in 1687 set out a full, integrated, mathematically proven system of celestial mechanics accounting for the motions and the balance of forces that explain the motions of the planets.

Copernicus' work now stood justified and integrated in a complete world system which had totally replaced the Aristotelian and Ptolemaic ones. He had not set out to do this. Nor had he dreamed that his discoveries would alienate the Church. He had merely endeavoured to correct the Ptolemaic mathematics. But the conceptual device that he adopted to do this, exchanging the roles of the Earth and the sun, made a vital change in the conceptual framework of the universe, and in the cosmologies tied to it. More important, perhaps, it forced an adjustment in all aspects of the two systems. We can now appreciate that Copernicus created a framework in which each set of answers in science brought forth a new set of questions. Copernicanism, as Newton left it, has now itself been successfully challenged, but we have become used to this repeated challenging and steady acceleration in the growth of scientific knowledge. This was not the case in the Age of Copernicus, but he helped to make it so. As Lord Acton wrote: 'Copernicus erected an invincible power that set forever the mark of progress upon the time that was to come'.

Notes

[1] Thomas Kuhn, The Copernican Revolution (New York, 1959), p. 132.

[2] Jerome R. Ravetz, 'The Origins of the Copernican Revolution', Scientific American, 215, No. 4 (October 1966), pp. 88-98.

Edward Rosen (essay date 1983)

SOURCE: "The Exposure of the Fraudulent Address to the Reader in Copernicus' *Revolutions*" in *Sixteenth Century Journal,* Vol. XIV, No. 3, Fall, 1983, pp. 283-91.

[*In the following article, Rosen discusses the reasons for and outcome of Andreas Osiander'inserting an anonymous preface into the first publication of Copernicus's* De revolutionibus.],

In opposition to the immemorial belief that the earth is stationary, Nicholas Copernicus' *De revolutionibus orbium coelestium* (Nuremborg, 1543)[1] proclaimed that the earth is a planet in motion. On its title page this epoch-making work announced the names of its author and publisher. But it gave no hint that between author Copernicus (1473-1543) in distant Frombork (Frauenburg) and the printing process in publisher Johannes Petreius' shop in Nuremberg, two successive editors had intervened. The first was Copernicus' only disciple, George Joachim Rheticus (1514-1574), unswervingly loyal to his master both before and after the publication of the *Revolutions.* But Rheticus could not remain as editor until the typesetting of all six Books of the *Revolutions* was completed. For as the newly appointed professor of astronomy at the University of Leipzig, which was then being reorganized by Joachim Camerarius, Sr. (1500-1574), a vigorous humanist receptive to fresh ideas, Rheticus had to leave Nuremberg. His departure for Leipzig in October 1542[2] left the *Revolutions* without an editor. This vacancy was filled by Petreius with Andreas Osiander (1498-1552), an uncompromising theologian, whose doctrinal writings he had published,[3] but whom he chose to succeed Rheticus as editor of the *Revolutions* because Osiander's hobby was the mathematical sciences.

When Copernicus said that the earth moves, he meant what he said. Rheticus agreed, but Osiander did not. Without informing Petreius, Osiander placed on the verso of the title page his own Address to the Reader (Ad lectorem de hypothesibus huius operis), the authorship of which he deliberately concealed. Osiander's unsigned Address insisted that the *Revolutions'* "hypotheses need not be true nor even probable; if they provide a calculus consistent with the observations, that alone is sufficient."[4] As a result the ordinary reader, who had no idea about this covert operation in the Nuremberg printing shop, saw a book whose principal thesis throughout was controverted by this introductory Address.

When the printing of the *Revolutions* was finished, Address and all, in mid-March 1543, complimentary copies were sent to Rheticus in Leipzig. What he beheld enraged him. He sent two copies to Copernicus' closest friend, together with an indignant letter (which has not been preserved). His annoyance was shared by his correspondent, Tiedemann Giese (1480-1550). As former editor of the *Revolutions,* Rheticus on his own might have protested to Nuremberg against his successor's Address. Instead, he elicited from Giese a grave complaint to Nuremberg against the maltreatment of the book in which Copernicus called Giese "a man who loves me dearly . . . a close student of sacred letters as well as of all good literature."[5] The complaint of Giese, the Roman Catholic bishop of Chelmno (Culm), would carry greater weight in Nuremberg since the *Revolutions'* dedication was directed to the reigning pope, and its covering letter came from a cardinal, who "with the utmost earnestness" entreated Copernicus "to communicate this discovery of yours to scholars."[6] Giese, however, was aware that Rheticus was more familiar with the Nuremberg situation than he himself was. Hence on July 26, 1543, he informed Rheticus:

> I have written to the city council of Nuremberg, indicating what I thought had to be done in order to restore faith in the author [Copernicus]. I am sending you the letter together with a copy of it, to enable you to decide how the affair should be managed on the basis of what has been started. For I see nobody better equipped or more eager than you to take this matter up with that city council.[7]

Keeping the copy for his own files, Rheticus forwarded the bishop's complaint to the city council, which in turn relayed it to Petreius. His reply was just as sharp as the bishop's complaint. On August 29, 1543, the city council decided to soften the publisher's acerbities and inform the bishop that "no punishment can be inflicted on Petreius in this matter on the basis of his answer"[8] (which has not survived). Petreius' contention that the Address "had been turned over to him with the rest of the treatise,"[9] without any differentiation of authorship, was revealed to the city councillors, whose proceedings were confidential. In addition, Osiander admitted to a personal friend that he had added this Address "as his own idea."[10] Thus, the true story was learned by a handful of insiders, while the outside world knew nothing about it.

When Rheticus undertook to edit the **Revolutions** in Nuremberg, he had to go on leave from his post as professor of astronomy at the University of Wittenberg. His replacement was his classmate, Jerome Schreiber of Nuremberg, who had entered the University of Wittenberg with him in the summer semester of 1531.[11] Schreiber had previously attended the Upper School in Nuremberg,[12] where his mathematics teacher was Johann Schöner (1477-1547). In 1541 Schöner dedicated to Schreiber his edition of three mathematical treatises published by Petreius in Nuremberg.[13] But in Wittenberg Schreiber lived as a house guest of Philip Melanchthon (1497-1560), Martin Luther's principal lieutenant. Thus, early in April 1543, shortly after the printing of the **Revolutions** in Nuremberg was completed, Melanchthon wrote to Osiander in Nuremberg, saying that he and Schreiber in Wittenberg had both read Osiander's letter.[14] On April 17, accompanied by Schreiber and escorted by two armed knights, Melanchthon left Wittenberg to help introduce the Protestant Reformation along the lower Rhine.[15] The reformers entered Bonn on May 4. But Schreiber, who was suffering from a painful ailment, sought relief in the hydrotherapeutic baths in Aachen, 45 miles to the west. Writing to him on May 14, Melanchthon addressed him as Hieronymo Schreiber Noribergensi,[16] his birthplace, not his residence. Melanchthon's subsequent letters of June 11, July 3, and July 21 were all addressed to Hieronymo Schreiber Noribergensi[17] in Aachen. Toward the end of July Melanchthon left Bonn, and on August 15 returned to Wittenberg,[18] where Schreiber reentered his household. On September 17 he was described by Melanchthon as a house guest,[19] who was eager to travel since his health had improved.

His opportunity came two weeks later, when he left for Italy accompanying Valerius Cordus, the author of the first official pharmacopeia. On October 1 Melanchthon gave Schreiber two letters of recommendation. One was addressed to Luca Gaurico,[20] who had edited a translation of Ptolemy's *Syntaxis* into Latin (Venice, 1528). The other was directed to a senator of Nuremberg, of patrician family, Jerome Baumgartner (1498-1565).[21] For Schreiber planned to visit his mother in Nuremberg and renew old friendships there on his way to Italy. Thus, early in October Schreiber called on Petreius, who presented him with a copy of the **Revolutions**.[22] The lower right-hand corner of the title page reads: "D. Hieronymo Schr/ [ei] ber petreius dd 1543" (Given to Jerome Schreiber by Petreius in 1543), the month and day being left unspecified.[23] Was it on this unspecified day and month in 1543 that Petreius told Schreiber about Osiander's interpolation of the Address to the Reader? Or did Schreiber hear the story from Baumgartner, who had been the secretary to the city council of Nuremberg on August 29, 1543, when the council decided how to answer Giese's complaint against Petreius?[24] Whether from Petreius or Baumgartner or both, Schreiber learned the truth. Over the Address to the Reader in Petreius' presentation copy, with his own hand Schreiber wrote ANDREAS OSIANDER in capital letters.

Leaving this copy with his other books in his mother's house in Nuremberg, Schreiber set out on horseback for Italy with Cordus. Unlucky Cordus! He was kicked by a horse and on account of the injury died a lingering death in Rome on September 25, 1544. Deeply affected by this tragic loss of so gifted a man at the early age of 29, on December 1, 1544, in Padua Schreiber addressed *De morbo et obitu Valerii Cordi epistola*[25] to their erstwhile traveling companion, Wolfgang Meurer (1513-1585). From Padua Schreiber extended his trip to France, where he himself died in Paris in 1547 in his early thirties. Six years later Caspar Peucer (1525-1602), Melanchthon's son-in-law, in his *Commentary on the Principal Types of Divination* mentioned that "a certain friend of mine having died in Paris, I remember, when the autopsy was performed, a big stone was cut out of his liver."[26] Besides publishing this report in 1553, Peucer also told his friend, Dr. Johann Ken(n)tmann (1518-1574), a little more about the autopsy of Schreiber, whose name he did not refrain from disclosing in a private conversation.[27] Schreiber's liver stones had been tormenting the poor man for years. While enduring this suffering, little did he realize that one day he would be immortalized in the annals of science because he wrote Osiander's name over the Address to the Reader in the copy of Copernicus' **Revolutions** which Petreius presented to him.

After Schreiber's death in Paris in 1547, his library in Nuremberg was sold to a local book dealer named Kepner.[28] Another branch of the family, calling itself Kepler, produced the great astronomer Johannes Kepler (1571-1630). When he went off to study that subject at the University of Tübingen, he had the astronomical component of Schreiber's library. At Tübingen Kepler pored over the Copernican astronomy with Michael Maestlin (1550-1631). During their discussion of a critical passage in the **Revolutions,** Maestlin wrote in Kepler's copy the second note in the right margin of fol. 96r. Maestlin's handwriting is known from the numerous annotations in his personal copy of the **Revolutions,** which is now in the municipal library of Schaffhausen, Switzerland. At fol. 96r (**Revolutions,** III, 25, end) Copernicus promises to return to the undecided question where the center of his universe is located.[29] The relevant marginal note in Kepler's copy indicates that the uncertainty in III, 25 reappears in the latter treatment. At fol. 142v/12 Kepler may have inserted tamen interlinearly between *differentia* and *insensibili,* in agreement with the emendation in Maestlin's copy. These entries show that Kepler had the Petreius-Schreiber copy of the *Revolutions* in Tübingen, before he left on March 13, 1594, to become a teacher in Graz.[30]

On October 3, 1595, Kepler wrote from Graz to Maestlin in Tübingen that at a crucial passage in the *Revolutions,* V, 4, "either my copy is . . . defective or I am blind."[31] Had Kepler owned a second copy, by comparing the two he could easily have discovered whether the defect was in his eye or in his copy. But he did not refer to the possibility of such a comparison. Hence on October 3, 1595, he had only one copy of the *Revolutions*—the Petreius-Schreiber copy, which he had taken with him from Tübingen to Graz.

On February 27, 1596, Maestlin sent Kepler the appendix which he was adding to his former pupil's Mysterium cosmographicum,[32] then being printed in Tübingen under Maestlin's editorship. Disagreeing to some extent with Maestlin, in his reply of March 1596 Kepler argued: "Unless my fallible memory of these things deceives me (for I lack Copernicus), Copernicus assumes. . . . "[33] This lack of a copy of Copernicus has been misinterpreted to mean that Kepler still had no copy of the printed *Revolutions* as late as March 1596.[34] But at that time Kepler was in Stuttgart, trying to persuade the duke to have a model built to illustrate the cosmos envisaged in the *Mysterium cosmographicum.* In Stuttgart Kepler lacked Copernicus temporarily only because he had left his Petreius-Schreiber copy behind in Graz.

In addition to the Petreius-Schreiber copy of the *Revolutions,* Kepler also owned Schreiber's copy of an *Ephemerides.* For when his astronomical friend David Fabricius (1564-1617), who initiated the study of variable stars, asked him about the solar eclipse at sunrise on April 6, 1540, Kepler replied that he had no precise information: "I own the *Ephemerides* which belonged to the Nuremberger Schreiber, who was in Wittenberg on that day. Alongside April 6 he notes that the morning was cloudy."[35] Schreiber's notes in the Ephemerides could be compared with the handwritten capital letters ANDREAS OSIANDER over the Address to the Reader in the Petreius-Schreiber copy of the *Revolutions,* and with the names of the planets VENERIS MERCURII handwritten on slips pasted over misprints on fol. 194v, 195r. These slips also contained handwritten lower-case headings over twelve tabular columns, which could be compared with some marginal notes (e.g., fol. 72v, 192v, 193r) in the Petreius-Schreiber *Revolutions* and in the Schreiber *Ephemerides.* By these two sets of comparisons Kepler could have satisfied himself that Osiander's name over the Address to the Reader on the verso of the title page was in Schreiber's handwriting.

On the flyleaf preceding the title page in the Petreius-Schreiber copy of the *Revolutions,* with his own hand Kepler wrote out a translation of a dialog into Latin, which he signed with his initials, followed by *vertit*[36] ("translated") and the date, December 22, 1598. The original was a dialog that had been composed in Greek half a century earlier by Joachim Camerarius, Sr.,[37] who, as was indicated above, had been instrumental in bringing Rheticus to the University of Leipzig. When Rheticus received complimentary copies of the *Revolutions* from the publisher in the spring of 1543, he gave one to Camerarius, who wrote this dialog saluting the *Revolutions* as new, everything in it being beautiful, and predicting immortal fame for its author among scholars. To what extent does Camerarius' unstinted praise of Copernicus and the *Revolutions* explain why Rheticus left Wittenberg, whose shapers of opinion were sorely vexed by his promotion of Copernicus,[38] the supposedly anti-Biblical earth-mover?

When Styria, of which Graz was the capital, was recatholicized, Kepler had to leave. Fortunately for the development of mankind's understanding of the physical universe, Kepler was able to join the staff of that outstanding observer of the heavens, Tycho Brahe (1546-1601). Embroiled in a savage priority dispute with the imperial mathematician, Nicholas Reimers Ursus (1551-1600), Brahe imposed on Kepler the task of composing a *Defense of Tycho against Ursus*, who had published a treatise On *Astronomical Hypotheses* (Prague, 1597). At sig. C 1r-v Ursus reprinted the *Revolutions*' Address to the Reader. Being astute enough to recognize that this Address had not been written by Copernicus himself, Ursus attributed it to an extremely learned, but unidentified author. Answering Ursus point by point, Kepler responded:

> After stating his position, Ursus fortifies it with a ludicrous authority. Why would I be impressed by an author whose identity is not known? Hence, while adding an authority to his own authority, Ursus asserts that this author is extremely learned. I shall help Ursus out of his difficulty. The author of that Address, in case you do not know, is Andreas Osiander.[39]

In his quarrel with Brahe Ursus lost his position as imperial mathematician and died on August 15, 1600. As imperial mathematician, he was succeeded by Brahe, who soon died on October 24, 1601, to be succeeded by Kepler. At that time Kepler's Defense of Tycho against Ursus was not quite finished. Fabricius wrote to Kepler about it: "I hear that you have also refuted the absurdities of Reimers Ursus' hypotheses.

I ask you to publish [your refutation] at the earliest possible time, as you promised Tycho."[40] Kepler replied: "I have written against Ursus. But I am not satisfied. I must first look at Proclus and Averroes on the history of hypotheses. I shall publish [this material] some time, when that can be done with less ill-will than now. After all, Ursus was my predecessor"[41] as imperial mathematician. Kepler never did the further research he felt was necessary to finish his *Defense,* which remained unpublished among his papers until rescued from oblivion in the mid-nineteenth century.[42] But he repeated his exposure of Osiander as the hidden author of the Address to the Reader on the verso of the title page of his *Astronomia nova* (Heidelberg, 1609).[43] This book attracted attention everywhere because it revealed for the first time in human history that the orbit of a planet is elliptical. What place could have been more prominent for the exposure of Osiander than the verso of the title page? Yet Giambattista Riccioli (1598-1671), the extremely learned writer of the *Almagestum novum* (Bologna, 1651), who cited Kepler's *Astronomia nova* at I, 2, 290/IV/9, could still refer to the "nameless author, who placed the Address to the Reader in the front matter of Copernicus' work" (I, 2, 294/left/29up-27 up). Even more astounding is the great French historian of astronomy, J.B.J. Delambre (1749-1822), who devoted 80 pages (390-469) of his Histoire de l'astronomie moderne, I,[44] to analyzing Kepler's Astronomia nova, but still regarded Copernicus as the author of the Address to the Reader.[45]

Notes

[1] *Nicholas Copernicus Complete Works,* II, English translation and commentary by Edward Rosen (Baltimore: Johns Hopkins University Press, 1978). Cited hereafter as "NCCW, II."

[2] By that time Books I-IV had been printed, so that his successor edited Books V-VI. NCCW, II: 414-415.

[3] Joseph C. Shipman, "Johannes Petreius, Nuremberg Publisher of Scientific Works, 1524-1550," in *Homage to a Bookman: Essays on Manuscripts, Books and Printing Written for Hans P. Kraus* (Berlin: Mann, 1967), pp. 155, 157, 160-161.

[4] Edward Rosen, *Three Copernican Treatises*, 3. ed. (New York: Farrar, Strauss, & Giroux, 1971), p. 25/1-3. Cited hereafter as "TCT."

[5] NCCW, II: 3/32-34.

[6] NCCW, II: xvii/14-15.

[7] NCCW, II: 339/27-31.

[8] NCCW, II: 340/9-10. According to *Georgii Joachimi Rhetici Narratio Prima* (Wrocław: Polish Academy of Sciences Press, 1982, *Studia Copernicana*, XX), p. 218, n. 8, the city council of Nuremberg decided to send to Giese Petreius' reply, and to attach a letter specifying its intention to proceed against Petreius (" . . . décide d'adresser à Giese la réponse de Petreius et de joindre une lettre précisant son intention de poursuivre Petreius"). The *Narratio Prima*'s editors' cited source is M. Biskup, *Regesta Copernicana* (Wroclaw: Polish Academy of Sciences Press, 1973, *Studia Copernicana*, VIII), #506. This says that the city council decided to send Petreius' answer, and "also decided to enclose a letter that it would not take steps against Petreius." Regesta correctly stated that the city council would not take steps against Petreius. In this respect *Narratio Prima*'s editors failed to follow their source. But they did follow it where it erred in saying that the city council decided to enclose a letter of its own in Petreius' answer. For, *Regesta*'s source is the memorandum of the city council's secretary. He was instructed, in sending Petreius' answer, "daneben schreyben: man koenn dem petreyo derhalb nach gestallt seiner antwurt nichtz ufflegen" (Ludwik Antoni Birkenmajer, Mikolaj Kopernik, [Cracow, 1900], p. 403). In the secretary's memorandum, "daneben schreyben" means "write on Petreius' answer," so that no second letter was enclosed or joined; "nichtz ufflegen" means "no action to be taken" against Petreius.

[9] NCCW, II: 340/24.

[10] NCCW, II: 340/28.

[11] *Album academiae Vitebergensis,* I (Leipzig, 1841), 146/right/2, 20.

[12] Hugo Steiger, *Das Melanchthongymnasium in Nürnberg 1526-1926* (Munich/Berlin: Oldenbourg, 1926), p. 31/16up.

[13] Shipman (n. 3), p. 160.

[14] *Corpus reformatorum*, V (Halle, 1838), col. 82, #2674/1-2.

[15] *Ibid.*, p. viii.

[16] *Ibid.*, #2704, col. 110.

[17] *Ibid.*, #2714, 2721, 2729, col. 119, 138, 146.

[18] *Ibid.*, pp. viii-ix.

[19] *Ibid.*, col. 177, #2757/1-3.

[20] *Ibid.*, #2765, col. 185-186.

[21] *Ibid.*, #2764, col. 184-185; Melchior Adam, Vitae, 3 ed. (Frankfurt am Main, 1705), Jurisconsults, pp. 78-79. Baumgartner served as secretary of the City

Council of Nuremberg when it dealt with Giese's complaint against Petreius. The surname of Schreiber (the German word for "scribe") was sometimes written *scriba* in Latin documents. This use of *scriba* has been misunderstood to mean scribe or secretary of Nuremberg, an office never held by Schreiber, whose baptismal name, Jerome, was also Baumgartner's. Schreiber by error was elevated to the rank of Senator of Nuremberg; Ludwik Antoni Birkenmajer, *Stromata Copernicana* (Cracow: Polska Akademia Umiejtnosci, 1924), p. 362, n. 1, with a question mark, that was dropped in the index (p. 397). The index was followed by Jeremi Wasiutynski, *Kopernik twórca nowego nieba* (Warsaw: Przeworski, 1938), a prize-winning monograph that made Schreiber a patrician and a member of the Nuremberg Senate (p. 476/12up, p. 511/18). By the same token the Leipzig facsimile edition of the Petreius-Schreiber copy of the *Revolutions* (see n. 22) made Schreiber "a Nuremberg alderman" and "the Nuremberg senator" (p. vi/5up, p. vii/15).

22 The Petreius-Schreiber copy is now in the library of the Univesity of Leipzig. A facsimile edition (Leipzig, 1965) was distributed by Edition Leipzig in the socialist countries, and elsewhere by Johnson Reprint Corp., New York/London.

23 L. A. Birkenmajer, M. Kopernik, the first scholarly work to call attention to the Petreius-Schreiber copy, misdated the presentation (p. 649/10-11) right after the printing of the *Revolutions* was finished (Dr. Erna Hilfstein read this material for me). According to Dr. Martha List, "Marginalien zum Handexemplar Keplers von Copernicus: *De revolutionibus orbium coelestium (Nürnberg,* 1543)," in *Science and History, Studies in Honor of Edward Rosen* (Studia Copernicana, XVI, Wrocław: Polish Academy of Sciences Press, 1978), p. 449/3-5, "the presentation of the book by Petreius probably occurred in those days of May 1543 when Schreiber was in Nuremberg." But in May 1543 Schreiber was taking the cure in Aachen.

24 NCCW, II: 340.

25 Although Schreiber's brief *Letter about the Illness and Death of Valerius Cordus* was printed twice (Strasbourg, 1560, 1563), it has survived essentially because it was reprinted in Conrad Gesner's *Opera botanica* (Nuremberg, 1757), pp. 15-17.

26 Caspar Peucer, *Commentarius de praecipuis divinationum generibus,* rev. ed. (Zerbst, 1591), fol. 320r/12-15.

27 Johann Kentmann, *Calculorum quae in corpore et membris hominum innascuntur genera XII* (Zürich, 1565), fol. 22r, dated April 21, 1564, in Conrad Gesner, *De omni rerum fossilium genere* (Zürich, 1565-1566).

28 List (n. 23), pp. 451/18-452/4.

29 NCCW, II: 169/36-47.

30 *Joannis Kepleri astronomi opera omnia,* ed. Christian Frisch (Frankfurt am Main and Erlangen, 1858-1871; reprint, I-II, Hildesheim: Gerstenberg, 1971-1977), VIII: 677/19. Cited hereafter as "F."

31 *Johannes Kepler, Gesammelte Werke* (Munich: Beck, 1937-), XIII: 45/455 456. Cited hereafter as "GW."

32 Translated by A. M. Duncan, with an introduction and commentary by E. J. Aiton, and a preface by I. B. Cohen (New York: Abaris, 1981).

33 GW, XIII: 72/1-2.

34 List (n. 23), p. 450/10-14.

35 GW, XV: 279/1551-1553.

36 L. A. Brikenmajer missed the meaning of *vertit* since he called the dialog a work by Kepler (M. Kopernik, p. 651/22; read by Dr. Erna Hilfstein). What Kepler did was later correctly described as a translation by Ernst Zinner, *Die Entstehung und Ausbreitung der coppernicanischen Lehre* (Erlangen: Mencke, 1943), p. 452/25-26. Nevertheless, the scholar who first translated the dialog into German ascribed it to Kepler; Gerhard Harig, "Kepler und das Vorwort von Osiander zu dem Hauptwerk von Kopernikus," *NTM: Zeitschrift für Geschichte der Wissenschaften Technik und Medizin,* I, pt. 2 (1960), 13-26, here 18-19; Plate I, p. 15: facsimile of the Leipzig copy's Address to the Reader; Plate 2, p. 16: facsimile of the Leipzig copy's title page. The facsimile edition (p. vi/13-15) attributed the dialog to Kepler. It was even made the partial subject of an analysis of Kepler's style as a Latin poet; Friedrich Seck, "Johannes Kepler als Dichter," *Internationales Kepler-Symposium Weil der Stadt 1971* (Hildesheim: Gerstenberg, 1973), p. 441/1-8, pp. 447-448; List (n. 23), p. 450/14-18.

37 Professor Owen Gingerich of Harvard University and Smithsonian Astrophysical Observatory, together with Professor Jerzy Dobrzycki of the Institute for the History of Science, Warsaw, found a privately owned copy of the first edition of the *Revolutions,* which bears the Greek dialog on both sides of its flyleaf in Camerarius' handwriting.

38 *Luther's Works,* 54, *Table Talk,* ed. and trans. Theodore G. Tappert (Philadelphia: Fortress, 1967), No. 4638, pp. 358-359; *Corpus reformatorum,* IV, 679.

39 F, I: 245/17-21.

40 GW, XIV: 281/22-24.

[41] GW, XIV: 334/641-643.

[42] F, I: 215-276.

[43] GW, III: 6/32-37.

[44] Paris, 1821, reprint, New York/London, 1969.

[45] P. 85/last 3 lines; p. 139/3up-140/11up.

Harold P. Nebelsick (essay date 1985)

SOURCE: "Copernican Cosmology" in *Circles of God: Theology and Science from the Greeks to Copernicus*, Scottish Academic Press, 1985, pp. 200-57.

[*In the following chapter, Nebelsick discusses in detail Copernicus's contributions to astronomical research, including his theory of heliocentrism and his revision of the work of Ptolemy and other ancient astronomers.*]

The Development of "Heliocentricity"

When and where Copernicus first began to think seriously about his "heliocentric" system is as difficult to ascertain as are his motives for developing it.[57] By the end of the fifteenth century Cracow had gained a reputation as a good place to study mathematics and astronomy. Hard times had fallen on the universities of Prague and Vienna with the result that a good number of peripatetic students and other interested persons brought their books and astronomical instruments to the city. Copernicus went up to the University of Cracow in 1491 to begin his study of mathematics. It was there, as far as we know, that his acquaintance with astronomy began. Birkenmajer, who is an unabashed apologete for Copernicus' originality, reports that the two theories of cosmology taught at Cracow at the time were Aristotle's theory of homocentric spheres and the Ptolemaic system. Both were geocentric but whereas the Aristotelian system consisted of a nest of fifty-five concentric spheres which turned and influenced one another in order to explain the apparent irregularity of planetary motion, Ptolemy used a whole series of eccentrics, circular orbits, epicycles, and equants to "save the appearances".[58]

However, according to Ernst Zinner's fascinating *Entstehung und Ausbreitung der Coppernicanischen Lehre (The Establishment and Propagation of the Copernican Doctrine)*, astronomy at Cracow when Copernicus was a student there between 1491-93,[59] as everywhere in Europe at the time, was under the influence of the combined teachings of the Viennese professor Georg Peurbach (1423-61) and his student and colleague Regiomontanus (Johann Müller) (1436-76). Zinner shows that at Cracow, the Professor of Astronomy, Albert Blarer von Brudzewo (1446-95), interpreted Peurbach's planetary theory and noted in particular the sun's influence upon the movement of the planets, especially as it affected the angle of their retrograde motion.[60]

Peurbach had published his *Theoricae novae planetarum (Planetary Theory)* in Nuremberg in 1472 or 1473. The book was destined to go through fifty-six editions and by the time Copernicus took up mathematics and astronomy at Cracow, it had replaced Sacrobosco's *De Sphaera* as the basic textbook in astronomy throughout Europe. The publication dealt with the sun, the moon, the seven planets and their characteristic phenomena. It explained the theory of altitude, gave a description of the solid celestial spheres, illustrated them by way of Ptolemaic planetary models, and interpreted the motion of the eighth sphere. Most importantly, Peurbach adjusted Ptolemy's astronomy according to the mathematical notations of the Alfonsine Tables.

This in itself would have assured Peurbach a place in history as a major contributor to astronomical theory. The work was of especial importance at the time because it showed the limitations of the Ptolemaic system. Peurbach's second work, *Tabulae Eclipsum (Ecliptic Tables)*, is even more astounding than the first for demonstrating the author's ability to combine theory and mathematics and coordinate these with observation. In the book, which Peurbach probably wrote in 1459 but which was not published until 1514, he rearranged the Alfonsine Tables so as to be able to use their notations to designate the times of the occurrences and the duration of the eclipses of the sun and the moon with comparative accuracy. Also, as in his better known *Planetary Theory*, so in the *Ecliptic Tables* Peurbach adjusted the Ptolemaic notations according to the more exact measurements given by Arab astronomers. Here he followed the Toledan Tables in particular. The result was a series of notations which, because they were much more exact than those of Ptolemy, served to call the *Almagest* into question. In addition when Peurbach, like Ptolemy, coordinated theory with notation and observation, he laid foundations for astronomy as an experimental science. Peurbach climaxed his efforts by producing, along with Regiomontanus, the *Epitome of the Almagest* which both simplified the *Almagest* and supplied it with corrected notations. Very importantly as it turned out, the authors pointed out Ptolemy's erroneous calculation of the distance of the moon from the earth at different points in its orbit.

Thus if Zinner is correct, which seems likely, Peurbach and Regiomontanus had a direct relationship to the study of astronomy at Cracow and at least an indirect influence on Copernicus. That influence was to continue when in 1496, without having completed a degree at Cracow, Copernicus went up to the University of Bologna ostensibly to study law but, as Birken-majer says, "for the purpose of pushing on with his studies in astronomy".[61] He took with him a copy of the edition of the Alfonsine Tables by Regiomontanus which he had purchased in Cracow about 1493.[62]

In 1492, just four years before Copernicus enrolled, the University of Bologna was the site of the well-publicised dispute between Marsilio Ficino and Alexander Achillini (1463-1512).[63] Ficino, it will be recalled, was the translator of the *Corpus Hermeticum* and of Plato's *Dialogues.* He was the head of the Platonic Academy of Florence which had been founded by Cosimo de Medici as well. As far as astronomy was concerned, Ficino, in good Hermetic fashion, was the champion of heliocentric speculations. In his Hermetically inspired *De Sole (The Sun)* printed in Florence in 1493, the year following the debate, and the year Copernicus went up to Bologna, Ficino published his claim that the sun was the heart of the world.[64] He likened it to a king occupying the central position toward which the planets moved and before which they paraded.[65] The sun was the pilot of the heavens and the criterion of divinity for the heavenly bodies. All the bodies turned to it for their direction.[66]

The impact of the meeting between Ficino and Achillini is evident from Achillini's answer to Ficino's challenge. In 1498 Achillini published his *De Orbibus (On the Orbits of the Planets)*[67] in order to re-emphasise and re-establish the Aristotelian-Ptolemaic cosmology largely on the basis of Averroës' explanation of Aristotle's *De Caelo.* In particular, and as if to answer Ficino directly, Achillini claimed that it was quite illegitimate to set the sun in the middle or to compare the *heavenly* sphere with the *earthly* one.[68] The idea of heliocentricity, then, rather than being "newly discovered" or even "rediscovered" by Copernicus, was public property and a matter of discussion both before and during Copernicus' years in Italy. The idea was propounded and attacked from philosophical, cultic, and astronomical points of view. The singular importance of the sun had been suggested by the writings of the astronomers Peurbach and Regiomontanus and these in turn set the stage for astronomy from Cracow to Bologna and even Ferrara where Copernicus pursued his academic efforts.

Whether or not Neopythagorean-Hermetic speculation had any influence on Regiomontanus' thoughts with regard to the control of the sun over the movement of the planets cannot be documented. We do know, however, that he had doubts about the limitations of the reigning Aristotelian-Ptolemaic cosmology and, in a letter to Giovanni Bianchini (d. 1466), he expressed his desire for a new system to be worked out on the basis of observation. In that both Domenico Maria Novara (1454-1504), who was Professor of Astrology at Bologna during the time Copernicus was a student

there, and Pellegrino Prisciano (b. c.1450), who became Professor of Astrology at Ferrara where Copernicus took his degree in law in 1503, claimed to be students of Regiomontanus, Copernicus was in the stream of the most advanced cosmological speculation of the time.[69]

Whether or not Copernicus knew Prisciano is not documented although there has been a good deal of conjecture as to the reason why he took his degree at Ferrara rather than at Bologna.[70] There is, however, documented evidence that Francesco Patrizzi (1529-97), who in the Preface to his 1597 edition of the *Hermetica,* recommended to Pope Gregory XIV (1535-91) that the Hermetic teachings replace those of Aristotle in the Church, taught the *Hermetica* along with the philosophy of Plato in Ferrara from 1597 onward. At Bologna, Copernicus studied mathematics and astronomy with Novara and he evidently became more of a colleague to him than a student. A. C. Crombie's statement that it was Novara, "a leading Platonist", who taught Copernicus "the desire to conceive of the constitution of the universe in terms of simple mathematical relationships",[71] seems borne out by the record. On March 9, 1497, shortly after he had purchased a copy of Peurbach and Regiomontanus' *Epitome of the Almagest,* Copernicus and Novara together made the first of the relatively few astronomical observations which Copernicus recorded.[72]

The purchase of the book is important because it was in the *Epitome of the Almagest* that Peurbach and Regiomontanus had noted the large discrepancy in respect to the distance of the moon from the earth between the full moon and the first quarter. As a result Ptolemy had provided the moon with a disproportionally large epicycle in relation to the size of its eccentric deferent. In checking out the distances by observation, Novara and Copernicus noted that the earth-moon distance was, at the two phases, all but invariant. They confirmed thereby that Peurbach and Regiomontanus were right and that Ptolemy was wrong.[73] This, along with his knowledge of the heliocentric hypothesis argued for by people like Ficino, whose apology for the heliocentric system was well enough known so that Copernicus would no doubt have been familiar with it, may well have caused him to question the Ptolemaic system as a whole.

Ptolemy's miscalculation of the moon's distance, which Copernicus notes in his *De Revolutionibus,* and even Copernicus' acceptance of the corrections which Peurbach and Regiomontanus made of Ptolemy on the basis of the Alfonsine Tables, did not bring him to admit doubt with regard to Ptolemy's observational notations in general.[74] Although Crombie seems correct in stating that Copernicus took the data for his own system not from Ptolemy's *Almagest* but from Peurbach and Regiomontanus' *Epitome of the Almagest* as well as from Gerard of Cremona's (c.1114-87) Latin translation of the Almagest,[75] Copernicus never once mentioned any inaccuracy in Ptolemy's mathematical notations as a reason for wanting to alter the system. On the contrary, as we shall see, he had nothing but compliments for Ptolemy's measurements and he preserved as much of Ptolemy's system as was possible.

More surprising is the fact that even heliocentricity was not Copernicus' concern. In fact, precisely speaking, his system was not heliocentric. Rather, it was centred on the supposed centre of the earth's orbit, a mathematical point which Copernicus set adjacent to the sun.[76] With this in mind we can understand, perhaps, the reason that in the dedication to Pope Paul III, with which Copernicus prefaced the *De Revolutionibus,* he placed much more emphasis upon the movement of the earth than upon the necessity of centring the planets on the sun.[77]

One could argue, of course, that Copernicus was more worried about the movement of the earth than about the position of the sun because the idea of a moving earth was antithetical to the major concepts of Aristotelian physics and astronomy.[78] Copernicus had no trouble, however, setting Aristotle aside in this respect. He readily admitted that he knew of the idea of the moving earth from the history of astronomy and he knew that history from the early Pythagoreans to Ptolemy with admirable thoroughness. Philolaus had attempted to show that the earth, along with the sun and moon, orbited a central fire. Heraclides, whom Copernicus referred to as "Pontus", and Ekphantus depicted the earth as rotating on its axis "like a wheel" but without orbital motion ("movement of locomotion").[79]

The history of astronomy also revealed to Copernicus that the heliocentric idea had precedent. Since he knew his history and stressed that he knew it, it does not surprise us to learn that in the first manuscript of the *De Revolutionibus,* he mentions the third-century B.C. heliocentric theory of Aristarchus of Samos. It is somewhat disappointing, however, to note that he deleted any reference to Aristarchus in the copy that went to the publishers. Although Copernicus admitted in the published version of the *De Revolutionibus* that he had found in the writings of Plutarch "others" who were of the opinion that the earth moved,[80] he expunged from the record the fact that the main "other" (whom Plutarch had in fact mentioned at some length) was Aristarchus whose heliocentric system was exactly that which he represented in the diagram he drew to symbolise his own system. The sun was placed in the centre and was surrounded by the perfectly circular and heliocentric orbits of the seven planets. The moon was set in orbit around the earth and the whole was surrounded by the immobile sphere of the fixed stars. Copernicus' own system in which the planets moved on epicycles attached to deferents, which were themselves eccentrics, was much more complicated, of course.

The passage in the original manuscript of the *De Revolutionibus* which is struck through with black ink so that it was not reproduced in the copy delivered to the printer reads:

> Although we acknowledge that the course of the sun and moon might also be demonstrated on the supposition of the earth being immovable, this agrees less with the other planets. It is likely that for these other reasons Philolaus perceived the mobility of the earth, which also some say was the opinion of Aristarchus of Samos, though not moved by that reasoning which Aristotle mentions and refutes.[81]

It is tempting to think that Plutarch's reference to Aristarchus in his dialogue, *The Face on the Moon,* may have given Copernicus pause. In the dialogue Lucius had been accused of turning the world upside down for saying the moon was a solid body. Asked to elucidate his views, he began by saying:

> Oh, sir, just don't bring suit against us for impiety as Cleanthes thought that the Greeks ought to lay an action for impiety against Aristarchus the Samian on the ground that he was disturbing the hearth of the universe because he sought to save [the] phenomena by assuming that the heaven is at rest while the earth is revolving along the ecliptic and at the same time is rotating about its own axis.[82]

However, in that Copernicus seemed much less concerned, nor need he at the time have been concerned, about being accused of impiety than of being taken to task by the Aristotelians, he, or whoever was responsible for deleting the reference to Aristarchus, may simply have wanted Copernicus to be known as the author of heliocentrism.[83]

Whatever the reason for the deletion, the passage, along with Copernicus' **"Ode to the Sun"** and the circumstantial evidence from his studies in Italy, would seem to leave little doubt that he was well aware of a good measure of speculation about a sun-centred system with its concomitant earth movements from both the history of astronomy and from Renaissance literature.

Heavenly Harmony

Although the Copernican system is renowned for having placed the sun in the centre of the universe, the exact position of the sun was really of secondary importance. Copernicus' prime concern was another. His main interest was to fashion a system which would reflect the exact agreement between circularity and regularity of motion which was the *sine qua non* of Greek astronomy and was basic to their theology and rationality as grounded upon the thought of the Pythagoreans, Plato and Aristotle. In Copernicus' own time this demand for the unity and harmony of the heavens had been re-emphasised by Aristotelian Thomism, Neoplatonism, and Hermeticism. It was celebrated by Dante, accentuated by Cusa, and lauded by Ficino who, in order to express it, had placed the sun in the centre of his Hermetically inspired astronomical system. It was because Copernicus found that Ptolemy's circles did not reflect the unity and harmony of the heavens in terms of perfect circularity and regularity of motion that he found the system wanting and set out to replace it.

Thus, Copernicus' primary objection to the Ptolemaic cosmology was neither the inaccuracy of its mathematics nor any error with regard to its notations of the planetary positions. Rather, to repeat, Copernicus took exception to the system because of its lack of harmony. Although he had been aware of the inaccuracy of Ptolemy's notations since his student days, in the **Commentariolus** (the full title of which Rosen appropriately translates as "Nicholas Copernicus' Sketch of His Hypothesis for the Heavenly Motions"), he boldly stated that the theories of Ptolemy were consistent with the numerical data. He pointed out, however, that the system lacked symmetry and that this was the reason for his desire to propose his own hypothesis.

> Yet the planetary theories of Ptolemy and most other astronomers, although consistent with the numerical data, seemed likewise to present no small difficulty. For these theories were not adequate unless certain equants were also conceived; it then appeared that a planet moved with uniform velocity neither on its deferent nor about the centre of its epicycle. Hence a system of this sort seemed neither sufficiently absolute nor sufficiently pleasing to the mind.

> Having become aware of these defects, I often considered whether there could perhaps be found a more reasonable arrangement of circles, from which every apparent inequality would be derived and in which everything would move uniformly about its *proper centre*, as the rule of absolute motion requires.[84]

In order to re-establish the absoluteness of circularity which was, for Copernicus, essential to his aesthetic judgement of harmony, i.e., that which was "pleasing to the mind", he set out on his quest for "a more reasonable arrangement of circles" which would both explain the "apparent inequalities" of planetary motion and be a system "in which every thing would move uniformly about its proper centre, as the rule of absolute motion requires". Rheticus captured the intention of his "teacher", Copernicus, in his *Narratio Prima*:

> My teacher saw that only on this theory could all the circles in the universe be satisfactorily made to

revolve uniformly and regularly about their own centres, and not about other centres—an essential property of circular motion.[85]

The rule of absolute motion required of Copernicus that he eliminate Ptolemy's equant, the device which, as indicated in our discussion of Ptolemy, was a mathematical point off centre from the geometric centre of a planet's deferent. Ptolemy had used the equant to explain the difference between the centre of regular motion and the geometric centre of the planet's orbit. For Copernicus, however, such a device was against everything he had learned about the harmony of celestial motion and geometry. It was a direct affront to the idea of harmony stressed by the ancient Pythagoreans through Plato and Aristotle to the Renaissance Hermeticists alike. All believed that the heavens reflected the pattern of divine perfection.

Saving the Circles

Having eliminated the equants in order to follow the demand that everything "move uniformly about its proper centre as the rule of absolute motion requires",[86] Copernicus, as he explained in the **Commentariolus,** adopted the pattern of explication Euclid had used in his *Elements of Geometry*. He first set out the seven basic axioms or assumptions on which his system was to be based and then explained them. The assumptions were:

(1) The heavenly bodies do not have a single common centre of motion.

(2) The earth is not at the centre of the universe but only at the centre of the orbit of the moon and of terrestrial gravity.

(3) The sun is the centre of the planetary system and also the centre of the universe.

(4) The earth's distance from the sun is minute compared to the distance to the fixed stars.

(5) The apparent diurnal revolution of the firmament is due to the daily rotation of the earth on its own axis.

(6) The apparent annual rotation of the sun is explained by the fact that the earth, like the other planets, orbits around the sun.

(7) The apparent irregular movements of the planets, their stopping (stations) and moving backward (retrogressions) are due to the planets and the earth orbiting the sun in different periods of time.[87]

Thereafter, as Koyré explains with admirable brevity, Copernicus, in just seven short chapters, set forth the sequence of the celestial spheres, dealt with the earth's triple motion, explained the advantage of referring all motions to the fixed stars, described the mechanism of planetary motion and gave the data for the dimensions of the epicycles and circles.[88] The scheme, of course, was no more than the description of the Aristarchian heliocentric system with the addition of Ptolemy's epicycles so that, as the first axiom prescribed, the heavenly bodies did not have a single centre of motion but each deferent and epicycle had its own centre. Copernicus knew that the multiplicity of centres already represented a compromise when compared to Aristotle's system of homocentric spheres but the compromise was necessary in order to bring the system into closer compliance with observation.

> Callippus and Eudoxus, who endeavoured to solve the problem by the use of concentric spheres, were unable to account for all the planetary movements; they had to explain not merely the apparent revolutions of the planets but also the fact that these bodies appear to us sometimes to mount higher in the heavens, sometimes to descend; and this fact is incompatible with the principle of concentricity. Therefore it seemed better to employ eccentrics and epicycles, a system which most scholars finally accepted.[89]

The Copernican innovation, then, was to impose Ptolemy upon Aristarchus.[90] He explained his position by first stating that no one should suppose that he had "gratuitously asserted, with the Pythagoreans, the motion of the earth". He then described the circles and epicycles of the moon and the planets. Thereafter he gave notice that he had reserved mathematics (which he took largely directly from Ptolemy) for the larger work (*De Revolutionibus*) and closed the writing with a paragraph in which he enumerated the circles (deferents and epicycles) which were necessary for his system.[91]

> Then Mercury runs on seven circles in all; Venus on five; the earth on three, and round it the moon on four; finally, Mars, Jupiter, and Saturn on five each. Altogether, therefore, thirty-four circles suffice to explain the entire structure of the universe and the entire ballet of the planets.[92]

One of the best summary descriptions of the system as it was later worked out in the *De Revolutionibus* is given by Rheticus:

> My teacher dispenses with equants for the other planets as well [as also in the case of the moon], by assigning to each of the three superior planets only one epicycle and eccentric; each of these moves uniformly about its own centre, while the planet revolves on the epicycle in equal periods with the eccentric. To Venus and Mercury, however, he assigns an eccentric on an eccentric. . . . These phenomena, besides being ascribed to the planets, can be explained, as my teacher shows, by a regular motion of the spherical earth; that is, by having the sun occupy the centre of the universe, while the earth revolves instead of the sun on the eccentric.[93]

We now know, of course, that Copernicus was extremely generous with himself as far as his count of the circles necessary for his system was concerned. In actuality, if Koestler has counted correctly, Copernicus' system demanded forty-eight different circular movements, eight more than the forty which Peurbach had advanced for the Ptolemaic system. Zinner has counted thirty-eight circles and Koyré at least forty-one.[94] After enumerating the circles Koyré, like Koestler, went on to explain that, from the point of view of the number of circles or spheres involved (Copernicus does not differentiate between them) the system, as seen from a general point of view, was more complicated than that of Ptolemy.[95] It would seem that of all the astronomers who bothered to count, only Kepler, who by the way was extremely *pro-Copernican*, estimated that the number of actual circular movements in the Copernican system was less (ten less) than in the Ptolemaic one.[96]

All things considered, the general consensus is that the Copernican system demanded at least as many circles as the Ptolemaic plan, if not more. From our point of view, Copernicus may have achieved an aesthetic advantage in following Aristarchus and in placing the planets, including the earth, in orbit around the sun. Aesthetics, however, is a matter of choice. If simplicity in terms of numbers has any validity, Copernicus made no gain at all over Ptolemy.

Copernicus' own basic explanation of the circles of the planets around the sun in the *De Revolutionibus* is confusing simply because he referred only to their major orbits at their deferents.

> Thus the orbital circle of Mercury will be enclosed within the orbital circle of Venus—which would have to be more than twice as large—and will find adequate room for itself within that amplitude. Therefore if anyone should take this as an occasion to refer Saturn, Jupiter, and Mars also to this same centre, provided he understands the magnitude of those orbital circles to be such as to comprehend and encircle the Earth remaining within them, he would not be in error, as the table of ratios of their movements makes clear. For it is manifest that the planets are always nearer the Earth at the time of their evening rising, i.e., when they are opposite to the Sun and the Earth is in the middle between them and the Sun. But they are farthest away from the Earth at the time of their evening setting, i.e., when they are occulted in the neighbourhood of the Sun, namely, when we have the sun between them and the Earth. All that shows clearly enough that their centre is more directly related to the Sun and is the same as that to which Venus and Mercury refer their revolutions.[97]

Thus, Copernicus followed the lead of Aristarchus who had improved on Heraclides' partial heliocentric system in which only Venus and Mercury circled the sun by developing the first complete "heliocentric" system of which we are aware. Copernicus, in turn, improved on Aristarchus by adding Ptolemy's epicycles and eccentrics. Although the result was at least as complicated as the Ptolemaic system, it did have two definite advantages. The first was that Copernicus displayed the main movements of the planets with greater simplicity and harmony than Ptolemy. The second was that the Copernican system allowed for a more accurate measurement of the distance of planetary orbits from one another than the Ptolemaic one.[98] When, however, Copernicus added the epicycles there were at least as many circles involved. Even more serious, because Copernicus refused to use equants—the feature of the Ptolemaic theory which robbed it of its unity and harmony—his system was actually less accurate, i.e., it described the actual movements of the planetary system with less precision than the Ptolemaic plan. To make matters worse, Copernicus attempted to compensate for eliminating the equants by reintroducing Ptolemy's eccentrics. This both caused the planets to wobble in their orbits and made the orbit of Mars, for instance, less circular than that which Ptolemy had described.[99]

Kuhn's explanation is that in the Ptolemaic system, where regular motion was centred on an equant, the movement of the heavenly bodies, if calculated from the exact geometric centre of their orbits, would move against their orbits at different rates and "wobble". However, if in the Copernican system motion were likewise calculated from the orbital centres, the eccentrics which Copernicus used would cause the epicycles and hence the planets which were supposedly attached to them to wobble in their orbits as well. It would seem, therefore, that Kuhn is quite right when he says, "It is hard to imagine how Copernicus might have considered this aspect of Ptolemaic astronomy monstrous."[100]

Although it is difficult to believe, the facts would seem to indicate that, although Copernicus eliminated the equant which explained irregular motion because he found motion of that kind quite unacceptable, he reintroduced that same irregular motion with the adoption of the eccentrics although in his explanation of his system he did not admit having done so. Hence, instead of improving upon Ptolemy, his system displayed the same kind of irregularity that he found objectionable in the Ptolemaic plan, and on the basis of which he decided to reform the system in the first place. To make matters worse, the orbit of Mars actually bulged more at the quadrants of periodic time in the Copernican system than they did in the Ptolemaic[101]—an illustration of the inaccuracy which resulted from Copernicus' attempt to press the heavens into a geometry which would reflect the harmony of circularity and regularity of motion. Thus, in his attempt to achieve harmony, Copernicus not only sacrificed accuracy but, in the end, he lost out on the harmony as well.

Much as Copernicus advocated *saving the appearances*, therefore, there is little doubt that his primary interest was in *saving the circles*. The fact that he reintroduced the eccentrics in what appears to be an attempt to eliminate a number of epicycles in his original scheme (an eccentric deferent plus one epicycle would equal the variation of motion of a circular deferent and two epicycles) meant that he had not lost sight of the criterion of simplicity nor had he given up his attempt to represent reality as closely as his "circles" would allow. He apparently considered the eccentrics a lesser evil than multiple epicycles. However, in adopting them in the system as worked out in the *De Revolutionibus* he lost the aesthetic advantage, which according to both the *Commentariolus* and the preface to the *De Revolutionibus* had been the impetus for the whole effort.

As described in the *Commentariolus* the system was "concentrobiepicyclic", i.e., a system of concentric deferents each with two or more epicycles attached in tandem to their perimeters.[102] The planets rode on the perimeter of the outer edge of an outer epicycle, the inner centre of which was carried along on the edge of the first epicycle. The centre of the first epicycle in turn was carried around by the edge of the deferent whose centre was coincident with the centre of the universe.[103] In the *De Revolutionibus,* however, the system became "eccentrepicyclic". The outer epicycle was eliminated and in order to compensate for the movement it would have imparted to the planet, the centre of the deferent was moved off the centre of the universe so that the deferent became an eccentric in relationship to the centre of the planet's movement. Thus, whereas in the first system Copernicus attempted to maintain the concentricity of all motions around their own centres, in his more developed system he was concerned only for the uniformity of the motion of the planet around the centre of its orbit which was coincident with the centre of the universe even if the motion of individual deferents was eccentric to that centre. To repeat, although Copernicus objected to the Ptolemaic system because "it appeared that a planet moved with uniform velocity neither on its deferent nor about the centre of its epicycle" and conceived his own theory so that "everything would move uniformly about its own proper centre", he lost the "aesthetic advantage" which was the *raison d'être* of the whole effort by reinserting the eccentrics.[104]

It was just because Ptolemy realised that eccentrics did not allow for uniform motion around the proper centres of the circle involved that he invented the equant, that mathematical point off centre from the proper centre of the circle from which uniform motion was to be observed. Copernicus eliminated the equant but reinstated the eccentric which was as responsible for the non-uniformity of motion in his system as it was in the Ptolemaic one. He then developed his system of circles in accordance with the data of the corrected but still inaccurate Alfonsine Tables and made observations which assured him that the heavenly movements fit his geometric patterns. Hence, in contrast to Einstein who, as T. F. Torrance has pointed out, insisted that "science is an attempt to make the chaotic diversity of sense-experience correspond to a logically uniform system of thought"[105], for Copernicus the "logically uniform system of thought" predetermined his "sense experience" or at least his geometric representation of it.

In modern epistemology we have become aware that all our observations of reality are "theory laden", i.e., we see things with our minds. Thus, we look for things we believe to be there and within "acceptable" parameters are able to "see" the things we look for. In this event, it should not surprise us that Copernicus was convinced that his doctrine, which described the movements of the planets on paper, was a proper representation of the heavenly movements. However, in view of the fact that he knew that the Alfonsine Tables, on the basis of which he calculated his measurements, were inaccurate and that he must have been aware that the eccentrics of his system ruined its symmetry, we may now understand better the reason why he was reluctant to release his work for publication. Although he finally offered it as an orderly account of the world which has "a wonderful commensurability" and "a sure bond of harmony for the movement and magnitude of the orbital circles such as cannot be found in any other way",[106] there can be little question that he must have remained dissatisfied with the system until the last.

We judge Copernicus too harshly if we think of him as a modern astronomer. He was, rather, the last of the Pythagoreans and was less concerned about the "wobble" of the planets, exact measurements, and the relationship between geometry and observation, than he was about the inter-harmony of the geometry of circles by which the heavens must at all costs be represented. Holding on to as much of Aristotle as possible, Copernicus adjusted his divinely given circles to observation only as far as the circularity and uniformity of the system would allow.[107] Thus, in one sense, Copernicus was even more conservative than Ptolemy. In line with the Renaissance reemphasis on unity and harmony, he wished to reinstitute the harmony of geometry and motion along with the concentricity of the main orbits of the planets which Ptolemy, in the light of observation, had long since discarded.

To repeat, although Copernicus effectively turned the Ptolemaic world inside out and made minor changes in Ptolemy's description of the motion of the moon, by and large he had no quarrel with Ptolemy's observations or measurements. In his *Letter against Werner*[108] he praised Ptolemy, saying that "since Ptolemy based his tables on fresh observations of his own, it is incredible that the tables should contain any sensible error or any departure from the observations that would make the tables inconsistent with the principles on which they rest".[109] He went on to castigate anyone who, in trying to determine the motion of the celestial spheres, would disregard the observation of the ancient astronomers.

> We must follow in their footsteps and hold fast to their observations, bequeathed to us like an inheritance. And if anyone on the contrary thinks that the ancients are untrustworthy in this regard, surely the gates of this art are closed to him. Lying before the entrance, he will dream the dreams of the disordered about the motion of the eighth sphere and will receive his deserts for supposing that he must support his own hallucination by defaming the ancients.[110]

In his *Narratio Prima*, Rheticus would seem to agree completely with his "teacher". After asserting that Copernicus fully intended to imitate Ptolemy, he also assured his readers that Ptolemy could well be followed.[111]

> For Ptolemy's tireless diligence in calculating, his almost superhuman accuracy in observing, his truly divine procedure in examining and investigating all the motions and appearances, and finally his completely consistent method of statement and proof cannot be sufficiently admired and praised by anyone to whom Urania is gracious.[112]

In sum, Copernicus set out his system with the same purpose as that of the Pythagoreans, Plato, and Aristotle, "to show how the uniformity of motions can be saved in a systematic way".[113] His system of circles was not a result of observations, of which he made comparatively few. Rather it was the result of a genial geometrical arrangement which followed Ptolemy as far as possible, but which attempted to rearrange the system in order to harmonise the movements of the heavens so that "the first principles of the regularity of motion" could be saved.[114]

The Relationship of Theory to Reality

Devoted as Copernicus was to developing a system which would reinstate the classical concept of harmony and "save the circles", he clearly had no intention of abstracting his geometry from the actual motions of the heavens as such. He was, in fact, deeply critical of schemes which did not "fully correspond to the phenomena".[115] Osiander, on the other hand, who saw the *De Revolutionibus* through the press, was of quite the opposite opinion. For him, as he expressed it in the anonymous preface with which he supplied Copernicus' work, "It is not necessary that these hypotheses be true, or even probable but it is enough if they provide a calculus which fits the observations".[116] The comparison of Copernicus, who was supported by Rheticus, with Osiander, whose ideas of the relationship between theory and reality can be traced back to Aristotle, presents us with a classic contrast in the way theory and reality are thought to be related.

Although there was a fundamental disagreement between Osiander and Copernicus as far as their understanding of the relationship between theory and reality is concerned, there can be no doubt that Osiander added the "Preface" to the *De Revolutionibus* as a gesture of good will. As he explained in letters to both Copernicus and Rheticus, letters which we know about by way of Kepler, his intent was "to appease the Peripatetics [Aristotelians] and theologians whose contradictions you fear".[117]

From the correspondence we can deduce that, for Osiander, truth was a matter of revelation as articulated in the articles of faith. Scientific theory, on the other hand, was simply a symbolic representation of reality. According to Kepler, Osiander in his letter to Copernicus dated April 20, 1541 treated Ptolemy's theory of eccentrics and epicycles as "hypothesis" in exactly the same way he was to treat Copernicus' theory in the "Preface" to the *De Revolutionibus.*

> With regard to hypotheses, I have always thought that, rather than being articles of faith [*articulos fidei*], they are only the basis of calculation, so that it makes no difference if they are false provided they present the phenomena exactly.[118]

Again, according to Kepler, Osiander wrote Rheticus on the same day and repeated the same message in slightly different words:

> The Peripatetics [Aristotelians] and theologians will easily be appeased if they are told that a variety of hypotheses are able to explain the same apparent motions and that those which have been published are really certain but that they calculate most appropriately the apparent composite motions.[119]

Thus it is obvious that Osiander's policy of appeasement was not only motivated by expediency, but coincided with his own judgement of "scientific" hypotheses in general whether they were those of Ptolemy or those of Copernicus. In Aristotelian terms both Ptolemy and Copernicus were, according to Osiander, "mathematicians" rather than "physical astronomers". Aristotle differentiated between the physical astronomer and the mathematician on the basis of the relationships between the lines and figures they used to reflect re-

ality and reality itself.[120] For Aristotle, whereas the physical astronomer attempts to represent reality with his drawings and schemes, the mathematician is not concerned with these concepts *qua* boundaries of natural bodies. Rather, "he [the mathematician] abstracts them from physical conditions; for they are capable of being considered in the mind in separation from the motions of the bodies to which they pertain".[121] Further, a point of considerable importance for Aristotle as for Osiander, was that "such abstraction does not affect the validity of the reasoning or lead to any false conclusions".[122] According to Osiander, Copernicus was doing mathematics as indeed he was. Copernicus, however, attempted to use mathematics as the language of physics.

Rheticus, who knew Aristotle's distinction between the mathematician and the physicist, also knew of the place and importance of hypotheses.[123] He was aware that "the results to which the observations and the evidence of heaven itself lead us again and again must be accepted".[124] In other words, theory must be corrected by observation. He also recognised, however, that hypotheses were not simple abstractions from the reality observed.

> Propositions assumed without proof, if once they are perceived to be in agreement with the phenomena, cannot be established without some method and reflection; and the procedure for apprehending them is hard to explain, since in general, of first principles, there naturally is either no cause or one difficult to set forth.[125]

Thus, as Torrance points out, the formulation of scientific theory is indeed troublesome.

> It may take very intricate and complicated processes of thought to arrive at it, but the elemental forms reached will be minimal and basic and will have the effect of illuminating a great variety of otherwise incomprehensible facts, and will thus represent a vast simplification of our knowledge over a wide area.[126]

According to Rheticus, Copernicus conceived his hypothesis *in relation to* but not *from* the data which were later used to verify them. Their appropriateness depended on their ability to conform to the truth of past observations, on the one hand, and to serve as the basis for astronomical predictions, on the other.[127] Such hypotheses, then, although they were not simply abstracted from the observational data, were tested by ascertaining their conformity with observations both past and future. So far so good, but like all hypothetical constructs, whether valid or invalid, the Copernican hypotheses tended to force the data into their own prescription. Copernicus intended his system to be "realistic", so realistic, in fact that, as we have pointed out, according to Rheticus' explanation in his *Narratio Prima* "the hypothesis of my teacher agrees so well with the phenomena that they can be mutually interchanged, like a good definition and the thing defined".[128]

Rheticus then went on to contrast Copernicus' "realistic theory" with Averroës' whose judgement of Ptolemy followed Aristotle's definition of a "mathematician". Accordingly, for Averroës, "The Ptolemaic astronomy is nothing so far as existence is concerned; but it is convenient for computing the non-existent."[129] Rheticus, of course, was of a quite contrary opinion. He was, however, far too astute to think that the Copernican system would be readily accepted. He thought it too sophisticated for the "untutored". It was to be expected that the ones whom the Greeks called "'those who do not know theory, music, philosophy and geometry'" would object to Copernicus' system; and he advised that their shouting should "be ignored".[130] The fact that Copernicus himself asked Pope Paul III to disregard objections to his theory which might come from those who were "ignorant of mathematics" indicates that he too was aware that objections would most likely be raised to his system.[131] There is little doubt, however, that he considered the theory to be "true". He was convinced that its geometry reflected the regularity and circularity of the heavens. He was also certain that his mathematics, which was based upon Ptolemy or, to be more precise, which was based upon the Ptolemaic notations as corrected by Peurbach and Regiomontanus, reflected reality closely enough at least for his system of circles to be accepted as accurate.

Copernicus, after all, was primarily a mathematician. Thus, rather than depend on observations of his own, Copernicus, as Taliaferro has indicated, simply used Ptolemy's values [as corrected] and transposed them according to his own scheme. To take the case of the outer planets, the movement of the epicycles which centre on the deferent in Ptolemy's system corresponds to the revolutions of the planets about the sun in his own. The radius of the deferent then corresponds to the planet's mean distance from the sun. Also, with regard to the periodic time and radius, the orbit of the epicycle's centre on the deferent about the earth in Ptolemy's system was exactly that of the planet about the sun in Copernicus' scheme (if the zodiacal anomalies are ignored, which they were). In other words, Copernicus combined the epicycle and the eccentric with reference to the mean sun so that they were exactly equivalent to Ptolemy's eccentric and equant with respect to the earth.[132]

Copernicus, to his own satisfaction or at least according to his intention, summed up the whole history of astronomy and re-established the Pythagorean demand for harmony between geometry and motion which Ptolemy had broken with his equants. It was a truly magnificent feat of mathematical genius. Unfortunately, because the eccentrics had to be maintained for the sake of simplicity, the planetary orbits remained irregular.[133] In the case of Mars at least, that irregularity was compounded by the fact that the orbit bulged more at the quadrants of its periodic time than it did in the Ptolemaic model.[134]

The Copernican Non-Revolution

To repeat, Copernicus sacrificed accuracy for the sake of desired elegance, an elegance that could not be substantiated either by observation or by the mathematics involved. The demand for that elegance, it would seem, was elicited by a deep sense of the "rightness" of the Neoplatonic-Neopythagorean understanding of unity and harmony along with the Hermetically inspired placement of the sun in the middle of the world from where it could express its primacy over the earth and the other planets and indeed over the whole cosmos as then understood. The scheme, in other words, was brought about in the first instance not on the basis of observational or mathematical data but through re-interpreting the symbols and numbers by which the universe was represented.[135] Since, however, in Copernican heliocentricity, genial as we know the system to have been, the symbolisation had to follow the demand of harmony both in terms of the coincidence of the centres of circularity and regular motion and in terms of a coincidence between theory and actuality, success was ruled out simply because the heavenly "circles" were not really circular. Therefore, any scheme which was based on circularity was ipso facto bound to fail both in terms of the inner harmony of the system and in terms of the accuracy of its representation. Thus, elegant as it attempted to be or really because it attempted to reflect an elegance to which the heavens did not conform, the system was "scientifically" untenable. As Kuhn puts it, it was simply too inaccurate to work.[136]

Little wonder, then, that the system had scant appeal. Copernicus' arguments had no appeal to laypersons who, even if they understood them, "were unwilling to substitute minor celestial harmonies for major terrestrial discord".[137] In this sense, though, without excusing the mendacity of the whole episode, we can understand Cardinal Bellarmine, who in 1616 upbraided Galileo for having accepted the Copernican position as truth. Bellarmine represented the mediaeval Church's Aristotelian understanding in respect to the centrality and immobility of the earth. He noted that the Copernican system disagreed with biblical evidence,[138] and since it was without proof, he could quite properly insist that Galileo teach the heliocentric theory as an hypothesis only and not as fact.[139]

More importantly, as far as science is concerned, Copernicus' argument "did not necessarily appeal to astronomers".[140] A prime example was Tycho Brahe who, along with Hipparchus and Ptolemy, must be reckoned as one of the most persistent and accurate of astronomical observers of all time. Tycho's notations were to become the basis for Kepler's discovery of the elliptical orbits of the planets, a discovery which eventually saved the heliocentric system. He refused, however, to adopt the Copernican principle of an orbiting earth as a *sine qua non* of the system simply because at the time there was no way of determining any parallactic motion in the observation of the fixed stars as the earth supposedly changed positions in its relations to them.

It was not until 1838, some three centuries after the publication of the **De Revolutionibus,** that telescopes became accurate enough to observe any change of angle between the earth and the fixed stars as the earth moved from one extreme of its orbit to the other.[141] Hence Tycho found himself in the same position as those who had rejected Aristarchus' heliocentric theory some seventeen hundred years previously and who had argued that the non-existence of an observable "parallactic motion" implied that the universe is many, many times larger than it was thought to be. Interestingly enough, the argument which Copernicus put forward to explain the enormous distance necessary between the earth's orbit and the fixed stars, i.e., the size of the universe, so that the parallax need not have been observable, came right out of Aristarchus; and it was as unconvincing in the sixteenth century A.D. as it was in the third century B.C.[142]

Copernicus explained the immensity of the heavens in relation to the earth by saying, "In the judgement of sense perception the earth is to the heavens as a point to a body and as a finite to an infinite magnitude".[143] Since "points", "finite", and "infinite" are of no measurable quantity, the statement meant nothing except that the distance to the fixed stars was very great indeed and that one should not expect to measure any differentiation in angle in observing them, no matter where the earth was located in its orbit beneath them. Copernicus attempted to elucidate the immensity with another proposition which, although illustrative, was convincing only if one believed his theory in the first place. He explained that the magnitude of the world was such that, great as the distance is between the sun and the earth or between the sun and any other planetary sphere, "this distance as compared with the sphere of the fixed stars, is imperceptible".[144]

The actual distance from the earth of the celestial sphere which was needed for the Copernican system was more than 1,500,000 earth radii. When this figure is compared to the 20,110 earth radii that had been given by Alfargani and was the then currently accepted measurement, it is not difficult to understand the scepticism with which astronomers greeted the Copernican theory. The Copernican system demanded that the universe be more than seventy-five times as large as even the most generous estimates of the time.[145] Even among astronomers, then, the Copernican system, like the original heliocentric theory of Aristarchus, seemed "too hare-brained" to be taken seriously, as Koyré has put it.[146]

As a possible alternative Tycho Brahe, who was the best astronomer of the day and whose notations in the hands of Kepler saved the Copernican system from the fate of joining that of Aristarchus on the junk heap of brilliant but useless theories, adopted an expanded partial heliocentric theory of the type first proposed by Heraclides of Pontus. Whereas Heraclides, it will be remembered, had Mercury and Venus orbiting the sun and the sun with the two planets orbiting the earth, Tycho put all the planets except the moon in circular orbits around the sun. He then put the sun trailing the planets in orbit about the stationary earth and at a great enough distance so that the orbit even of the outermost Saturn would not intercept that of the moon. The system had all the advantages of the Copernican system without the tremendous disadvantages—physical, practical, and theological—of the moving earth.[147]

In the end, then, even the best astronomers found the Copernican theory unconvincing. In addition, of course, as we have indicated, the Copernican harmonies did not really satisfy the two primary criteria of a valid scientific theory, *simplicity* and *accuracy*. Rheticus, like Copernicus himself, saw the system as being simpler than that of Ptolemy. Hence, he quoted the Greek physician Galen's version of "Ockham's razor", "'Nature does nothing without purpose'".[148] He went on to ask, "Should we not attribute to God, the Creator of nature, that skill which we observe in the common makers of clocks? For they carefully avoid inserting in the mechanism any superfluous wheel."[149] As we have seen, however, so far as the number of circles was concerned, the Copernican system offered no obvious advantage over the Ptolemaic one.

Kuhn puts the matter well, saying that the Copernican arguments "could and did appeal primarily to that limited and perhaps irrational subgroup of mathematical astronomers whose Neoplatonic ear for mathematical harmonies could not be obstructed by page after page of complex mathematics leading finally to numerical predictions scarcely better than those they had known before".[150] Zinner makes the same point. After indicating that the Alphonsine Tables, which Peurbach and Regiomontus used in their summary of the Ptolemaic system and on which Copernicus had depended, were not known to be inaccurate by astronomers in general including Copernicus, he asks, "Why should they [the astronomers] change their views in order to describe the heavenly processes less adequately than heretofore?"[151]

Thus, although the Copernican theory was judged to be wrong according to science and common sense, it appealed to those whose scientific imagination and common sense had been distorted to believe that which by all counts was irrational. In time, however, some of the "facts" which these distorted minds perceived were proven to be true. Eventually the seven basic axioms which Copernicus set out in his **Commentariolus** all proved to be more or less valid in respect of the planets, except the first: "The heavenly bodies do not have a single common centre of motion", by which Copernicus justified his use of epicycles.[152] Strictly speaking the statement is true even for Kepler's system of eliptical orbits since eliptical orbits do not have a centre as such, but have dual foci. However, Copernicus' point was that the epicycles which centred on the circumference of the deferents had different centres from the deferents themselves. The deferents were roughly centred on the sun. I say "roughly centred on the sun" because as Copernicus finally developed the system in the **De Revolutionibus,** the only way he could achieve the semblance of the *circular harmony* he desired was to locate the common centre of the deferents of the planets on a point which marked the supposed centre of the earth's orbit. This was located somewhat off the side of the sun itself. Hence in a literal sense, Copernicus' third axiom: "The sun is the centre of the planetary system and also the centre of the universe", was negated.

The above investigation of the evidence would seem to suggest that the question of whether or not and to what extent Copernicus was swayed by the Neoplatonic-Neopythagorean-Hermetic literature of his day to revive Aristarchan heliocentricity and put the sun in the centre of the world, must finally be given a somewhat ambiguous answer. There is no doubt that he was aware of the Hermetic literature which celebrated the centrality of the sun and there is no reason to believe that either his mathematics or his observation would necessarily have persuaded him to adopt the heliocentric model of the universe. At the same time he never succumbed to Hermeticism as such. Copernicus' own ode to the sun in which he repeated the well-known Hermetic epithets in reference to it—"the lantern", "the mind", "the pilot of the world", "the visible god", "resting on a kingly throne" from where it "governs the stars which wheel around"—sound as if he, like Ficino, could well have placed the sun in the middle of the world for religious and philosophical reasons rather than for astronomical ones. As we have seen, for Ficino, the sun in the centre of the world was "the universal generator", "nourisher", and "mover", "the very signification of God".[153]

Nevertheless, in contrast to Rheticus, without whose assistance the Copernican "nocturnal study"[154] would probably never have seen the light of the sun, and in contrast to Kepler without whom the theory would probably have been forgotten, Copernicus gave no evidence of being a Hermeticist. Although his imagi-nation and his search for harmony, like that of his teacher Novara at Bologna, may very well have been stimulated by Neoplatonic, Neopythagorean Hermetic conceptualities, his arrangements of the planets and his explanation of their relationships were purely mathematical. Thus, while there is evidence for Koyré's statement, referred to above, that Copernicus adored the sun and for his contention that Copernicus' geometrising of nature was probably inspired by Nicolas of Cusa,[155] it is also true, as Butterfield has pointed out, that Copernicus was extremely conservative. Butterfield, it seems, is quite wrong in applauding the Copernican system for its evident simplicity. He is quite right, however, in showing that Copernicus went back to Aristotle.[156] Copernicus as a true Renaissance person thus combined the interest in unity and harmony with the search for truth in antiquity. Although it is not known why he adopted the heliocentric model, once having adopted it he bent his astronomy to fit it and refused to give it up in spite of the fact that he must have realised its inadequacies. If so his reason for adopting the heliocentric system was beyond reason. It lay within the realm of presupposition, the presupposition of the elegance of heliocentricity and circularity to which his reason was persuaded to comply.

The Collapse of Circularity

So far as Aristotle was concerned, the heavenly bodies were "simple" rather than complex. They were also "spherical". The "natural movement" of "simple" as well as spherical bodies was "circular" in contradistinction to "rectilinear". Thus following Aristotle, Copernicus wrote that the movement of a "simple" (heavenly) body was "none other than circular which remains entirely in itself as though at rest".[157] It was because Copernicus presupposed that the heavenly orbits were necessarily circular that he saw a "wonderful commensurability" and a "sure bond of harmony" between the movement of the planets and the magnitude of the orbital circles".[158] Copernicus was so convinced of the "commensurability" between the form of the heavenly spheres, the regularity of their motion and the pattern of their orbits, that he held to the supposed heavenly harmonies in spite of the fact that even his own system was inharmonious. This "commensurability" had been espoused by astronomers from the early Pythagoreans to Ptolemy. In the late Middle Ages and the Renaissance it was re-emphasised in Hermeticism and Aristotelian-inspired Thomistic theology. Dante, Nicholas of Cusa, and Copernicus followed in train. The fact that Copernicus' presuppositions both prevented him from taking the inharmonious relationships of his system seriously and compelled him to see commensurability where none existed prevented him also from discovering the irregularity of planetary motion. This in turn prevented him from bringing about the "Copernican revolution" for which he is given credit.[159]

Diagram depicting Copernican theory regarding the Earth's position relative to the sun.

We usually think of the Copernican system as being heliocentric because he said it was. As we have seen, however, Copernicus responded to the classical and Renaissance insistence on regularity and harmony with a system of geometrical elegance so uncompromisingly that, in spite of what he had to say about the sun in the centre of the world ("in the centre of all rests the sun"), he did not actually put it at the centre.[160] Rather, he centred his universe on a point which represented the "centre" of the earth's orbit. To complicate the matter still further, the mathematics involved demanded that the point, which represented the centre of the earth's orbit and on which the orbits of the other planets were centred as well, rotate in a circle of its own around a second mathematical point.[161] Finally the second mathematical point orbited in a circle round the sun.[162]

It may be somewhat ironic to realise that Copernicus' rotating mathematical point on which he centred the orbits of the planets resembled nothing so much as Ptolemy's rotating equant of the orbit of Mercury to which Copernicus had made vehement objection. Thus,

Copernicus replaced Ptolemy's multiple equants with a single orbiting equant of his own. It was this "equant" which he supposed was the very centre of his system, the centre of both geometry and motion. The fact that this equant rotated around another mathematical point which in turn rotated around the sun so complicated things that one would have thought the complexity would have made him call the whole system into question.[163] However, the rotating point that allowed his system to follow a concentricity of pattern in approximate harmony with the regularity of motion apparently persuaded him to overlook even the strict demands of the harmony he desired his system to display. Since, according to his own measurements, the central rotating point moved in perfect circularity and with regular motion, the all-important circularity, but it alone, was maintained and this was apparently quite enough to allow him to think of his system as a valid representation of the universe.

We now know that Copernicus' "central equant" was not the centre of either geometry or regular motion.

However, the fact that Copernicus thought it was inspired him to develop his system and to hold on to it after he had developed it. Even though his conception of the universe was false and in spite of the fact that by and large it was rejected in his own time, it reflected reality well enough to be fruitful. When Kepler squashed the circles of Copernicus' primary deferents (the circles which described the orbits of the planets about the sun and that of the moon about the earth) into ellipses, the heliocentric system proved to be correct. To express it more accurately, the helio-focused system of Kepler replaced the "equantocentric system" of Copernicus. Nevertheless, by distorting history, we credit Copernicus for having developed heliocentricity.

By placing the planets in elliptical orbits around the sun with the sun as the main focus of the ellipses, Kepler did away with the system of multiple circles presupposed by Copernicus' first axiom, "The heavenly bodies do not have a simple common centre of motion". He retained the sense of the other six: (2) the earth is a planet and the (approximate) centre of the moon's orbit; (3) the sun is the "centre" or at least the central focus of the planetary system; (4) the universe is immense compared to the earth-sun distance; (5) the daily apparent revolution of the stars is due to the rotation of the earth on its axis; (6) the apparent annual rotation of the sun [through the ecliptic] is due to the earth's rotation about the sun; and (7) the apparent irregular movements of the planets are due to the different planets and the earth orbiting the sun with individual periodicities.

In general these were nothing more nor less than the axioms which undergirded the heliocentric system of Aristarchus of Samos. Copernicus' rediscovery of them, even though for the sake of accuracy he compromised their simplicity with his first axiom (that announcing the epicycles), brought them back to consciousness and allowed them to become the basis for further experimentation and eventually to become the foundation of modern astronomy.

In the end, then, we cannot agree with Rosen who said that Galileo and Kepler "preserved the solid underpinnings of the **Revolutions,** discarded its extraneous trimmings and added the new wings which completed the structure of Copernican cosmology".[164] It would be more accurate to say that Kepler discarded the heart of Copernicanism (his harmony between uniform motion and circularity), trimmed the system back to its Aristarchan foundation, squashed Aristarchus' circles into ellipses, and founded the first workable heliocentric or actually "heliofocused" universe.

The Use of Hypothesis

The Copernican theory represents an excellent example of what Einstein was talking about when he referred to physical concepts as being "free creations" of the human mind.[165] Such hypotheses may or may not later prove useful in the development of science but their original inception is the result of what Michael Polanyi referred to as a "heuristic leap".[166] Hypotheses arise in a leap of faith based upon a conviction that may or may not have its impetus in the hitherto observed data of science. They result in a theory that, more often than not, is not verifiable under circumstances contemporary with it. If the theory is worthwhile it will be fruitful in generating the kind of interest and experiments that will prove its worth. In the process of proof, those aspects of the theory which reflect reality, e.g., in Copernicus' case the centrality of the sun and the movements of the planets about it, will be retained but other aspects of the theory itself may be either forgotten or changed quite beyond recognition. However, in that the original theory was the impetus on which the evidence for "the proof" was based, its inadequacies will often be ignored and the whole theory will be mistakenly remembered as having been *true.*

Comparison with Kepler may help elucidate this matter. Kepler, of course, was even less of an observational astronomer than Copernicus. He, however, was adamant in basing his calculations on the observations of Tycho Brahe, who night after night for some twenty years had noted the positions of the stars from his observatory, Uraniburg. When, in 1599, Tycho was invited by Emperor Rudolph II in Prague to become his court astronomer, he took his notations with him. A year later Tycho invited Kepler to join him, and when Tycho died in 1601 Kepler was appointed Imperial Mathematician. He eventually gained access to Tycho's extremely accurate observational data.

Try as he might to follow his own Neopythagorean-Hermetic presuppositions and force the rotations of the planets into circular orbits, Kepler found that the orbit of Mars which, as we have seen in the Copernican system, bulged appreciably at the quadrants of its periodic time, resisted his subtlest mathematical manipulations. It deviated from the circular by a mere eight minutes of an arc (equal to just one-fourth of the diameter of the moon as seen at its mean distance from the earth) but it deviated. In contrast to Copernicus, however, Kepler, who believed in harmony at least as much as Copernicus, was not wedded to the Aristotelian circles. Therefore, rather than continuing to "save the appearances" by creating another epicycle for Mars or by increasing the eccentricity of the deferent which would simply have extended the Copernican universe of circles on circles, he allowed the heavenly patterns to break free from the confinement imposed upon them by the presupposed circles and followed the data of observation. By showing that the notations which defined the orbit of Mars described a simple ellipse, he revolutionised astronomy.

The process of discovery was extremely painstaking. In 1604, just three years after Tycho's death and after trying hundreds of possible geometric configurations, Kepler made his discovery and accounted for it in the first of his three laws of planetary motion: Mars followed an ellipse rather than a circle and the sun was not located at midpoint in the orbit but was situated slightly nearer one end than the other.[167] The fact that the original term "ellipse" (Greek elleipsis) comes from the verb elleipein meaning "to fall short", "to be imperfect", or "to be defective", may help us understand why, from the early Pythagoreans to Copernicus, such a figure for heavenly motion was considered monstrous. To be so persuaded was to shut one's eyes to the possibility of such an abrogation of heavenly perfection, and the only alternative was to ignore observational deviations from the circular and treat those irregularities as apparent rather than real.

In his second law defining the velocity of the planets, Kepler showed that the regular motion of the planets was calculated not in relation to the linear movement of the planet but in relation to the area enclosed by its orbit.[168] Rather than have each planet describing equal arcs in equal times (the kind of motion which could supposedly be calculated from Ptolemy's equants, for instance, and according to which Copernicus had defined "regular motion"), Kepler demonstrated that an imaginary line (a vector) drawn from any particular planet to the sun would sweep over equal areas in equal times. This meant that the nearer the planet was to the sun in its elliptical orbit, the greater was its velocity. The concept of uniform or regular motion in the Greek and Copernican sense was seen to be no more than a geometrical construct that had no basis in reality. The Greeks and, following them, Copernicus had maintained this "regular motion" in spite of contradictory observational evidence because it was part and parcel of the theological and philosophical conceptuality which attempted to project the simplicity and rationality "of God" upon the movement of the heavens.

Kepler's third law, which is ancillary to the interest of our present discussion, compared the periodicities of the planets and their distances from the sun. The ratio of the squares of the orbital periods of any particular planet was defined as equal to the cube of the mean distance of the planet from the sun.

Thus, Kepler saved the "heliocentric" theory by destroying the Copernican demand for circles and the harmony of pattern and motion on which it was based. In doing so, however, he established a kind of harmony of which the ancient astronomers and Copernicus could only dream. This harmony was not of geometry and motion as designated by preconceived patterns but a harmony which, when translated into mathematics, showed nature to have an order of its own. That order could be penetrated only by ignoring preconceived theological and philosophical misconceptions and by moving below the then obvious aspects of phenomena on the strength of subtle clues given by the phenomena themselves. Ironically enough, Kepler's search for harmony came from the same Renaissance-Neopythagorean-Hermetic influences with which Copernicus, too, was familiar. Kepler, who allowed his sense of harmony to be reformed by observation, followed his mathematics and revolutionised astronomy. Copernicus, whose ideas of harmony circumscribed his data, was fated to continue to propagate the ancient, erroneous Aristotelian-Ptolemaic system of complicated circles.[169]

Thus, to repeat, Kepler, whose Neopythagorean-Hermetic ideas demanded that the sun be the centre, proved that the sun-centred system of Copernicus was "true" by destroying its basic tenet, the concentricity of the geometry of planetary motion and the regular motion of the planets in terms of which "harmony" was defined. Only when Kepler showed that the god-like circles were ellipses, i.e., that the orbits of the planets were "defective", was the "Copernican system" saved. In Greek terms, the actual orbits of the planets "fell short" of circularity and perfection. They had two foci rather than one. That would have been monstrous indeed to Copernicus' Renaissance mind.

To state the matter somewhat differently for the sake of emphasis, Copernicus' primary concept was that the heavenly bodies followed perfect circles. Actually, however, the planetary orbits were "defective", i.e., ellipses. Secondly, Copernicus objected to the Ptolemaic system because Ptolemy used "equants" to explain the non-coincidence of the centres of the geometry of the heavenly bodies and the regularity of their motion. Since there is no coincidence of the centre of motion and the centre of the geometry of ellipses, Kepler saved the Copernican system by showing that, in this instance, Ptolemy was right and Copernicus was wrong. Thirdly, Copernicus centred both the geometry of the planetary orbits and the regularity of planetary movements on a mathematical point which he calculated to be the centre of the earth's motion, a point which itself orbited a second point. This second point (which we have termed the Copernican "universal equant") in turn orbited the sun. However, Kepler showed that planetary motion had no single centre and that each planetary orbit had two foci. One of the foci of each elliptical orbit of each planet was located near the centre of the sun, while the other was located outside the sun between the sun and the planet. Whereas Copernicus had, for all intents and purposes, avoided the sun in the geometry of his system, Kepler showed that it occupied the position of the main focus of the ellipse. Thus Kepler "proved" what the Hermeticists had proclaimed for over a thousand years, that the sun was the pilot of the heavens, the commander of the planets which guided them according to its power!

Kepler showed every sign of being a Neopythagorean Hermeticist. Like the Pythagoreans and Plato, he even listened for the melody of the spheres.[170] Copernicus too gave indications of having been well acquainted with the mystical world-view of Hermeticism. However, once he conceived the model of his system of ellipses, Kepler's work, like that of Copernicus, was a pure and ingenious mathematical achievement. Kepler proved Copernicus right by showing where he was wrong. His own model which enabled him to reflect reality by means of geometry and mathematics enabled him to abandon the "divine circles" as so much theological and philosophical mythology which had imprisoned both Copernicus and his science within its prescription. So powerful was Copernicus' trust in the prescription which had united theology, philosophy, and science from the ancient Pythagoreans onward, that the only possible alternative he was enabled to fathom was one that perfected, rather than abandoned, circularity of geometry and regularity of motion. Since, however, the system was based upon false premises, the more perfect the system became with regard to its own inner logic, the less descriptive it was of the reality it sought to represent. Hence, the more true it was in its own terms, the more false it became in terms of reality.

In a strict sense, then, when we compare Kepler with Copernicus, we should speak of Kepler's "heliofocused series of ellipses" which he based on Copernicus' distorted attempt to combine the heliocentric system of Aristarchus with the eccentrics and epicycles of Ptolemy. Aristarchus, Ptolemy, and Copernicus were able to see the world only so far as their theologies allowed God's "perfect circles", whether dictated by ancient Pythagorean mysticism or by Aristotelian physics, to be incorporated into their systems. Aristotelian astronomy itself pivoted upon Pythagorean mystical concepts of the world. These became a part of the theology of Thomas Aquinas. The mystical ideas were resuscitated by the Neoplatonists and Hermeticists of the Renaissance and were a powerful force in shaping the Renaissance mind. In the case of astronomy the Renaissance mind, whatever else it achieved, was so misshapen by a 2000-year-old "theological" perversion— the belief that the circles of God represented the quintessence of divinity—that it prevented the heavenly movements to be seen for what they were. The "circles" so defined beauty, harmony and, indeed, all rationality and reality that, until Kepler allowed the heavens to force his mind to conform to their inherent pattern, even observational data was skewed according to the perception of circularity.

Eventually, then, the heavens that "declare the glory of God" (Ps. 19:1) were seen to declare it in terms of creation and not of divinity. The form of the heavenly movements was elleipsis, exactly that form which Greek and the renewal of Greek thought in the Renaissance could not allow because elleipsis meant imperfection. Hence Kepler's discovery underscored the realisation that Christian astronomers insisted upon from the beginning, namely that the heavens were not of godly stuff but of earthly reality with a contingent, rational order of their own. With that the heavenly movements shed the halo of harmony defined in terms of circularity and regularity, and astronomy became science which understood those movements in appropriate terms.

The Copernican theory, then, magnificent as it was as a demonstration of single-mindedness and mathematical genius, is a prime example of how the same theological dedication that may inspire us to turn our eyes to the heavens to discover the wonderful works of God may also prevent us from seeing those works as they are. It shows, too, as Kuhn has pointed out, that sometimes at least revolution in science comes about by default rather than by design.[171] Theories which may be fictitious in origin and largely fallacious in content may prove later to be fruitful if a number of their basic tenets are true. . . .

Notes

[57] Jaki's statement is made on the basis of Birkenmajer's evidence that Copernicus had questions about the Ptolemaic system as early as Cracow. "By the time Copernicus arrived in Italy, his commitment to the heliocentric system seems to have been firmly established." Jaki, *Science and Creation*, p. 259, stands in contradiction to Rosen's statement made on the basis of a reference to Copernicus' discussion in 1508 as to "the swift course of the moon, and its brother's [the sun] alternating movements" that "Copernicus had not yet glimpsed the geokinetic cosmos in 1508", some fifteen years after he first went to Italy. Rosen, *Copernican Treatises*, p. 339.

[58] Birkenmajer, "Copernic", pp. 120f.

[59] The dates are taken from Zinner, *Coppernicanischen Lehre*, p. 150; cf. *ibid.*, p. 156. Birkenmajer and Rosen record his going up to the University of Cracow in 1491 but do not record his length of stay. Birkenmajer, "Copernic", p. 114. Rosen, *Copernican Treatises*, p. 315. Rosen says he did not stay the full four years, *ibid.*, p. 316. Koestler records 1591-94 as the dates at Cracow. Koestler, *Sleepwalkers*, p. 221.

[60] Cf. Zinner, *Coppernicanischen Lehre*, "Die Studien des Coppernicus in Krakau", pp. 143-156. Cf. Poggendorf Encyclopaedia, Old Series (Leipzig: Barth, 1863-1904), II, 587; *Dictionary of Scientific Biography*, 15 vols. (New York: Scribners, 1975), XI, 348-352. Both Zinner and Koyré note that Brudzewo had written a commentary on Peurbach's *Planetary Theory*. Koyré,

Astronomical Revolution, p. 21. Zinner, *Coppernicanischen Lehre*, p. 150. Zinner dates the commentary 1482.

[61] Birkenmajer, "Copernic", p. 114.

[62] Ibid., p. 114, n. 2.

[63] Zinner, *Coppernicanischen Lehre*, pp. 159f.

[64] Marsilio Ficino, *Liber de Sole, Opera Omnia*, 2 vols. in 4 (Torino: Bottega d'Erasmo, 1959, photocopy of the Basel edition of 1576), cap. VI.

[65] *Ibid.*, cap. VII.

[66] *Ibid.*, cap. XIII.

[67] Alexander Achillini, *De orbibus*, cited by Zinner, *Coppernicanischen Lehre*, p. 160.

[68] Zinner, *Coppernicanischen Lehre*, p. 160.

[69] Ibid., p. 161. Rather than going directly from Bologna to Ferrara between 1501-03, Copernicus studied medicine at the University of Padua. Unfortunately, as Zinner reports, nothing is known about his study in Padua. Ibid., p. 165.

[70] Cf. Scott, *Hermetica*, I, pp. 36ff. Koestler's speculation that Copernicus took his degree at Ferrara rather than Bologna to escape the financial burdens of the attendant graduation festivities seems somewhat unconvincing. Cf. Koestler, *Sleepwalkers*, p. 130.

[71] A. C. Crombie, *Augustine to Galileo*, Vol. II (London: Heinemann, 1979), p. 174.

[72] Birkenmajer, "Copernic", p. 126. Birkenmajer also records, however, that the copy has been lost. Rosen states but does not document that Copernicus "may not have possessed his own copy of the *Epitome*". Rosen, *Copernican Treatises*, p. 324. Copernicus records just twenty-seven observations in his *De Revolutionibus*. Birkenmajer, however, gives evidence that he made more than sixty in all, "Copernic", p. 131. Cf. Dreyer, History of Astronomy, p. 307.

[73] Birkenmajer, "Copernic", pp. 124-126. Birkenmajer tells us that Copernicus purchased the book in the second half of 1496 or the first part of 1497.

[74] Copernicus, *Revolutions*, Book I. 10, p. 523.

[75] Crombie, *Augustine to Galileo*, p. 174.

[76] Cf. the diagrams in Kuhn, *Copernican Revolution*, p. 170, and Koyré, *Astronomical Revolution*, pp. 60f.

[77] Hence, Rosen is quite right in calling the system "geokinetic" and "heliostatic". Rosen, *Copernican Treatises*, p. 339.

[78] Cf. [Nebelsick, *Circles of God*, pp. 25ff., 35ff., 74ff.]

[79] Cf. [Nebelsick, *Circles of God*, p. 32f.]

[80] Copernicus, *Revolutions*, Preface, p. 508.

[81] Dreyer, *History of Astronomy*, pp. 314f.

[82] Plutarch, *De Facie Quae in Orbe Lunae*, 6.923 A. Cf. Thomas L. Heath, Greek Astronomy (New York: AMS Press, 1969), p. 169.

[83] Copernicus records respect for the "partial heliocentric system" which he knew by way of Martinus Capella, the fifth-century encyclopedist, who apparently had reported on the system of Heraclides of Pontus, saying that "Venus and Mercury circle around the sun as a centre". Copernicus, *Revolutions*, Book I. 10, p. 523.

[84] Copernicus, *Commentariolus*, pp. 57ff.

[85] Rheticus, *Narratio Prima*, p. 137.

[86] Copernicus, *Commentariolus*, pp. 57f.

[87] Ibid., pp. 58f. Cf. Rosen, *Copernican Treatises*, p. 345.

[88] Koyré, *Astronomical Revolution*, p. 27.

[89] Copernicus, *Commentariolus*, p. 57.

[90] Koyré indicates that in his . . . *Hypothesis of the Planets, Ptolemy* already attempted to harmonise the Platonic and Ptolemaic systems by adopting real spheres and placing them inside one another. *Astronomical Revolution*, p. 82, n. 43.

[91] Copernicus, *Commentariolus*, p. 59.

[92] *Ibid.*, p. 90.

[93] Rheticus, *Narratio Prima*, p. 135. The explanation is of the system of the *De Revolutionibus* rather than of the *Commentariolus*. . . .

[94] Koestler, *Sleepwalkers*, p. 192; p. 572, fn. 9 where Koestler enumerates the circles. Koestler's reference to Peurbach is from Peurbach's *Epitomae* on the authority of Koyré, cf. ibid., p. 573, fn. 11. For the discussion of "sphere" vs. "circles", cf. Rosen, *Copernican Treatises*, pp. 18-21. For Zinner's count, cf. Zinner, *Coppernicanischen Lehre*, pp. 186f. For Koyré's, cf. Koyré, *Astronomical Revolution*, p. 89, n. 59; p. 27.

95 Koyré, *Astronomical Revolution*, p. 49. Tycho Brahe was the first to deny that the putative spheres existed. Cf. Rosen, *Copernican Treatises*, p. 289.

96 Noted by Koyré, *Astronomical Revolution*, p. 49.

97 Copernicus, *Revolutions*, Book I. 10, pp. 524f.

98 Kuhn, *Copernican Revolution*, p. 71.

99 Taliaferro, "Appendix B", *Almagest*, p. 476.

100 Kuhn, *Copernican Revolution*, p. 71.

101 Ibid., Taliaferro, "Appendix B", *Almagest*, p. 476.

102 Rosen, *Copernican Treatises*, p. 390. . . .

103 *Ibid.*

104 Copernicus, *Commentariolus*, pp. 57f.

105 Einstein, *Out of My Later Years*, p. 98. Cf. Torrance, Theological Science, pp. 110f. for an illuminating elucidation of the scientific method in general as well as its relationship to theology, and also the chapter, "Theology and General Scientific Method", pp. 116-131.

106 Copernicus, *Revolutions*, Book I. 10, p. 528.

107 Kuhn, *Copernican Revolution*, p. 154. There is thus a certain validity in Koestler's statement that "Copernicus was the last of the Aristotelians among the great men of science", cf. *Sleepwalkers*, p. 199. James Nebelsick has argued that Copernicus belongs to the pre-scientific era rather than that of modern science. "Is Copernicus the Last Member of the Old Era in Astronomy or the First Member of a New Era?", unpublished paper prepared for the Department of Philosophy and the History of Science, Cambridge University, November, 1979.

108 Nicholas Copernicus, *Letter Against Werner* in *Three Copernican Treatises*, trans. Edward Rosen (New York: Octogaon, 1971), pp. 94-106. The letter, written in 1522 and referred to above, is a reply to a request from Bernard Wapowski to comment on Johann Werner's astronomical treatise, *De motu octavae sphaerae tractatus primus (On the Motion of the Eighth Sphere)* in which Werner had called into question certain of Ptolemy's observations with regard to the positions of the fixed stars.

109 Copernicus, *Letter Against Werner*, p. 97. This in spite of the fact that Copernicus depends upon the correction of Ptolemy's notations made by Peurbach and Regiomontanus from the *Alfonsine Tables*.

110 *Ibid.*, p. 99.

111 Rheticus, *Narratio Prima*, p. 109.

112 *Ibid.*, p. 131.

113 Copernicus, *Commentariolus*, p. 59.

114 Copernicus, *Revolutions*, Preface, p. 507. Birkenmajer's evidence indicates that Copernicus made over sixty observations as against the twenty-seven which he records in the *De Revolutionibus*. Though the instruments Copernicus used were not particularly accurate, the observations apparently served only to support his illegitimate system of circles; hence, they do less to save Copernicus as a modern type of scientist than to condemn him. Had he been prone to believe his eyes rather than his predetermined theory, the observations might have persuaded him that his system of circles did not reflect reality. Cf. also Birkenmajer's rather chauvinistic attempt to ensure that Copernicus was Polish rather than German which imposes a nineteenth- and twentieth-century concept of nationality on a fifteenth-century situation when belonging to a Volk and one's political allegiance in central Europe were far from being coincidental. Birkenmajer, "Copernic", p. 131, fn. 1. For other discussions of Copernicus' nationality, cf. Zinner, Coppernicanischen Lehre, pp. 141f. and 158; Koestler, Sleepwalkers, pp. 125, 129; Koyré, Astronomical Revolution, pp. 18-20; Rosen, Copernican Treatises, pp. 313-318.

115 Copernicus, *Revolutions*, Preface, p. 507.

116 Osiander, "To the Reader", *Revolutions*, p. 505.

117 Kepler, *Apologia Tychonis*, p. 246.

118 *Ibid.*

119 *Ibid.*

120 Cf. [Nebelsick, *Circles of God*, pp. 25ff. for Aristotle's astronomical concepts.]

121 Aristotle, *Physics*, II. ii. 193b.

122 *Ibid.*

123 Rheticus, *Narratio Prima*, p. 140.

124 Ibid.

125 The citation is from the first Greek edition of the *Syntaxis (Almagest)* printed in Basel, 1538 which Rheticus presented to Copernicus. Cf. Rosen, *Three Copernican Treatises*, p. 141, n. 127. Hence, as Einstein explains, "The connection of the elementary concepts of everyday thinking with complexes of sense experiences can only be comprehended intuitively". Einstein, *Out of My Later Years*, p. 62.

[126] Torrance, *Theological Science*, p. 117.

[127] Rheticus, *Narratio Prima*, pp. 142f.

[128] *Ibid.*, p. 186. Since Rheticus wrote the *Narratio Prima* in 1540, three years before the publication of *De Revolutionibus*, he apparently hoped to protect Copernicus by referring to him not by name but as "my teacher" throughout the manuscript. Though Rheticus was steeped in Neopythagorean Hermeticism, he was primarily a mathematician who felt that Copernicus served both his own Neoplatonic-pantheistic God and mathematics by his system. Hence it is not surprising that he could also outline the basic scientific procedure from the formation of hypotheses which, when verified by observation, constituted the principles of a system that became the basis of prediction. Koestler argues that after helping to persuade Copernicus to publish his *De Revolutionibus* and spending a year and a half copying, editing, and correcting some of the calculations of the manuscript and seeing it to the press, Rheticus said no more about the system or "his teacher" because he took umbrage at not being mentioned in the Preface. Rheticus was most generous in commending Tiedemann Giese, Bishop of Kulm, for his part in persuading Copernicus to allow the manuscript to be published. *Ibid.*, pp. 192ff. He was fully aware of the necessity of ecclesiastical loyalties and seemed much more interested in the theory than his own pride. Koestler's interpretation of Rheticus' pique seems far-fetched.

Zinner's evidence is that in later years Rheticus had nothing but praise for Copernicus and fully intended to continue his work. Indeed, though Rheticus may well have had personal problems which made him *persona non grata* in a number of contexts, the fact that after working on projects of trigonometry and planning works on geometry, knowledge of the stars, the eclipses, comparison of the planetary movements and a table of sines and, apparently after some wandering, he erected an obelisk forty-five feet high in Cracow to "prove" the Copernican theory, indicates full well his continuing interest in his "teacher". He intended to prove the theory on the basis of "the Egyptian use" of the obelisk for, as he said, "no device is better than the obelisk; armillaries, Jacob's staffs, astrolobes and quadrants are human inventions, the obelisk, however, erected on God's advice, surpasses all of them"—cited by Zinner, *Coppernicanischen Lehre*, p. 261. There is no record of Rheticus having used the obelisk. The last writing known from Rheticus (but for whom Copernicus' theory may well have died with its author) was a prophecy written in 1572 after the death of the Polish King Sigismund in which he foretold the succession of the next seven kings. Rheticus died in Kaschau, Hungary, December 4, 1574. Ibid., p. 262. Cf. Koestler, *Sleepwalkers*, pp.

172-174, 187-190 for more information on this extraordinarily talented and unusual man.

[129] Rheticus, *Narratio Prima*, pp. 194f. quoting Averroës, *Commentary on Aristotle's Metaphysics*, Book xii, summa ii, caput iv. no. 45. . . .

[130] *Ibid.*, p. 195 quoting Aulus Gellius, *Noctes Atticae*, i.9.8. Cf. above, pp. 205f.

[131] Copernicus, "Dedication," *Revolutions*, p. 509.

[132] Taliaferro, "Appendix B," *Almagest*, p. 474.

[133] Kuhn, *Copernican Revolution*, p. 71.

[134] Taliaferro, "Appendix B", *Almagest*, p. 476.

[135] *Ibid.*, p. 470. To follow Taliaferro, the system is an illustration of a revolution in astronomical theory which depended less on accurate observation than "on the reinterpretation of the symbols represented by the appearances and of the numbers immediately symbolising these symbols". Ibid.

[136] Kuhn, *Copernican Revolution*, p. 181.

[137] *Ibid.*

[138] Cf. [Nebelsick, *Circles of God*, p. 204.]

[139] The equating of theological doctrine with the teachings of science and the questionability of ecclesiastical control of science and opinion, to say nothing of the impropriety of the evidence on which Galileo was convicted in 1633, are all of course to be condemned out of hand. The accusations of 1633 after Galileo's telescopic discoveries became well known and after Kepler had promulgated his laws of planetary motion are of quite a different and reprehensible category from Bellarmine's formal objections to the Copernican theory in 1616. To make matters worse, the evidence would seem to indicate that Galileo was convicted on the basis of a document, possibly "planted" in the record, which allegedly prohibited him from teaching the Copernican system at all. Cf. Crombie, *Augustine to Galileo*, II, 218f. . . .

[140] Kuhn, *Copernican Revolution*, p. 181.

[141] *Ibid.*, pp. 163f.

[142] Cf. [Nebelsick, *Circles of God*, pp. 34f.]

[143] Copernicus, *Revolutions*, Book I. 6, p. 516.

[144] *Ibid.*, Book I. 10, p. 526.

[145] Kuhn, *Copernican Revolution*, p. 160.

LITERATURE CRITICISM FROM 1400 TO 1800, Vol. 45

[146] Koyré, *Astronomical Revolution*, p. 16.

[147] Kuhn, *Copernican Revolution*, pp. 200-226.

[148] Rheticus, *Narratio Prima*, p. 137 quoting Galen, De usu partium X. 14.

[149] Rheticus, *Narratio Prima*, p. 137.

[150] Kuhn, *Copernican Revolution*, p. 181.

[151] Zinner, *Coppernicanischen Lehre*, p. 187.

[152] The moon, of course, continues to orbit the earth even in Kepler's system.

[153] Ficino, *Liber de Sole*, I. 966.

[154] Copernicus' own description of his work, *Revolutions*, Preface, pp. 508f.

[155] Koyré, *Astronomical Revolutions*, pp. 66, 58.

[156] Butterfield, *Origins of Modern Science*, "The Conservatism of Copernicus," pp. 17-36.

[157] Copernicus, *Revolutions*, Book I. 9, p. 520. Aristotle, *On the Heavens*, I, ii. 268b-269b.

[158] Copernicus, *Revolutions*, Book I. 10, p. 528. Cf. Koyré, *Astronomical Revolution*, p. 58.

[159] Jaki's commendation of Copernicus' conservatism so as to shield him from the effects of Renaissance Neoplatonism and paganism would seem to overlook the fact that it was Aristotelian paganistic tendency to identify God with the heavens that prevented Copernicus from really being scientific. Cf. Jaki, *Science and Creation*, pp. 259f.

[160] Copernicus, *Revolutions*, Book I. 10, p. 526.

[161] Hence, as Koyré points out, the earth's sphere is eccentric with regard to the sun, *Astronomical Revolution*, p. 59.

[162] Kuhn, *Copernican Revolution*, p. 170.

[163] In order to "save his circles", Copernicus was forced to fashion the centre of his system with utter disregard for the concentricity of geometry and regular motion for which he designed the system in the first place. His rejection of Ptolemy's equant forced him to centre his system upon a "revolving equant", as I have shown. Koyré explains, "The centre of the terrestrial sphere certainly revolves about the Sun, it is placed on a small epicycle whose deferent has the Sun for centre, but its motion is so slow—the epicycle makes one revolution in 3434 years and the deferent in 53,000 years—that,

for practical purposes, it does not enter into the calculations." Koyré, *Astronomical Revolutions*, p. 59.

[164] Rosen, *Copernican Treatises*, p. 408.

[165] Albert Einstein and Leopold Infeld, *The Evolution of Physics* (Cambridge: University Press, 1938), p. 33. It is only in a restricted and formal sense that we can agree with Edward Grant that the Copernican theory represents the "function and rôle" of a proper scientific hypothesis. Edward Grant, "Late Medieval Thought, Copernicus, and the Scientific Revolution", *Journal of the History of Ideas* (April-June 1962), Vol. XXIII, no. 2, p. 197. Though it is quite true, as Grant claims, that Copernicus insisted on the correlation of a scientific hypothesis and reality as Averroës, Jean Buridan (d. c.1358), and Nicole Oresme (c.1320-82) did not, that very correlation was already current with Peurbach, Regiomontanus, and most likely with Novara from whom Copernicus learned his astronomy. *Ibid.*, pp. 205-215. Also, Grant does not seem to be sufficiently aware of the positivistic nature of the theory-reality correlation which in Copernicus caused him to hold on to circularity in spite of the evidence against it and which in Newton, whom Grant cites with approval, led to the absolutisation of space and time, and the equating of the space-time continuum with God's sensorium. *Ibid.*, p. 219. Cf. Isaac Newton, *Opticks* (New York: Dover, 1952, based on the Fourth Edition, London, 1730), 3.1, qu. 31 and "The General Scholium", *Principia* (Berkeley: University of California, 1946, revision of the Andrew Motte translation of 1729).

[166] For Polyani's discussion of a heuristic act in modifying knowledge frameworks, cf. Michael Polanyi, *Personal Knowledge* (Chicago: University of Chicago, 1958), p. 106; also pp. 124-131 and p. 382.

[167] C. F. von Weizsäcker has rightly argued that the truly revolutionary discovery in modern astronomy was not the Copernican system but Kepler's first law. Weizsäcker, *Relevance of Science*, p. 101.

[168] Kuhn shows that Kepler's second law, which interestingly enough was built upon his Neoplatonic-Hermetic intuition that the planets were guided by the rays of the sun, was not quite accurate but was a good enough approximation for the time. Kuhn, *Copernican Revolution*, pp. 214f.

[169] For Kuhn's discussion of Kepler, cf. *ibid.*, pp. 209-219. For Koestler's perhaps over-complimentary evaluation, cf. *Sleepwalkers*, pp. 379-422.

[170] Cf. [Nebelsick, *Circles of God*, pp. 13, 15, and 23.]

[171] Cf. Thomas S. Kuhn, *The Structure of Scientific Revolutions*, 2nd ed. (Chicago: University of Chicago,

1970), esp. Chap. VI, "Anomaly and the Emergence of Scientific Discoveries", pp. 52-65. Kuhn's thesis seems to me to be most helpful in understanding the development of science. However, like others, I have some hesitation in endorsing what appears to be his lack of emphasis on continuity in scientific discovery, his over-emphasis on the difference between "revelationary science" and "ordinary science", and his making science somewhat over-dependent on sociological factors. Cf. also Kuhn's reply to his critics in "Postscript 1969", *ibid.*, pp. 174-210.

Bernard Vinaty (essay date 1987)

SOURCE: "Galileo and Copernicus" in *Galileo Galilei: Toward a Resolution of 350 Years of Debate—1633-1983,* Duquesne University Press, 1987, pp. 3-43.

[*In the following article, Vinaty discusses the relevance of Copernicus's research to the development of Galilean cosmology.*]

In the course of the second day of the "Dialogue Concerning the Two Principal World Systems, the Ptolemaic and Copernican," Gianfrancesco Sagredo, Venetian patrician and one of the three persons taking part in the dialogue, recounts:

> Certain events had but recently befallen me, when I began to hear this new opinion [Copernican] talked about. Being still very young and having just finished my course of philosophy, which I subsequently neglected in order to devote myself to other occupations, there chanced to come into these parts someone from over the mountains, from Rostock—and I believe his name was Christian Wursteisen—a follower of the Copernican opinion, who gave two or three lectures on this subject in an academy, having many present in his audience, rather on account of the novelty of the subject, I think, than for any other reason. I did not attend, however, having convinced myself that such an opinion could only be a solemn oddity. Later, having questioned some of those who had been present, I found that they all made fun of it, except one, who told me that the matter was not at all absurd. Because I considered this man to be very intelligent and extremely circumspect, I was sorry I had not been there. Accordingly, from that moment, whenever I met anyone who upheld the Copernican opinion, I began to ask him if he had always thought thus; and however many I questioned, I did not find one who did not tell me that he had for a long time been of the contrary opinion, but had gone over to the new viewpoint, moved by the force of the reasons that rendered it persuasive. Then, having examined them one by one, to see to what extent they grasped the reasons for the counterarguments, I found them all very ready to expound them, so that I could not truthfully say that it was from ignorance or vanity

or, because they wanted to show themselves clever, so to speak, that they had adopted this opinion.[1]

The one member of the audience who had heard the exposition of Christopher Wursteisen[2] without finding anything to make fun of was Galileo himself. And inasmuch as Sagredo was his pupil in the Studium at Padua in 1597, it is probable that Galileo's first attraction to Copernicanism dates back to about 1595. Galileo had been named lector (lecturer) in mathematics in that city by the Senate of the Venetian Republic, effective September 26, 1592. Under this title he was obliged to give lectures in the disciplines of the traditional *quadrivium*: geometry, arithmetic, harmony, and astronomy.[3]

Galileo's Adoption of the Copernican Theory

We possess several copies of Galileo's teaching of the elements of cosmography—today, the rudiments of physical geography. In conformity with tradition, this teaching consisted of a commentary on the *Traité de la Sphère* of Sacrobosco.[4] After having demonstrated the elements and properties of the circle, the author of the *Traité*, and its commentators, described in Ptolemaic terms the principal circles having a cosmological function (horizon, equator, zodiac, and ecliptic) leading up to the explanation of the inequalities of days and seasons. The *Traité* concluded with the explanation of eclipses by the relative motions of the moon and the sun.[5] Strangely, Galileo makes no mention of Copernicus in his commentary. Two reasons may account for this. The copy that served for the official edition of Galileo's works, the *Edizione Nazionale delle Opere di Galileo Galilei* by Antonio Favaro and Isidoro Del Lungo,[6] dates from 1602, but represents the corrected version of a text that goes back to 1593, when Galileo had not yet gone over to the side of Copernican astronomy. Another reason seems more pertinent: apart from the elementary course on cosmography, the syllabuses foresaw an advanced course on planetary astronomy, in which the professor commented on Ptolemy's *Almagest*.[7] No note of this course has survived. Nothing could have prevented Galileo from introducing into the corrected text to his *Traité de la Sphère*, if not under the title of a retractation, at least as a supplement, some indications on the doctrines of Copernicus. If he did not do this, it is probably because the new Copernican astronomy changed nothing of the traditional framework of cosmography, and it played a role of the first rank in the explanation of the apparent irregularities of planetary motions (stations and retrogradations).[8]

The statement by Sagredo is of interest in raising the question, How did one become a Copernican fifty years after the death of Copernicus?[9] Two letters of Galileo, representing his first two explicit professions of Copernicanism, help us to answer this question.

The first, dated May 30, 1597, is addressed to Jacopo Mazzoni (1548-1598), a former colleague of Galileo at the Pisa Studium. Galileo congratulates him on the appearance of his work *De comparatione Aristotelis et Platonis* (Padua, 1597) and replies to an objection lodged against Copernicus by the author:

> To speak the truth, although as to the other conclusions I remain assured, on the question of the first point I remain confused and cautious, because I see Your Excellency attacking with such frank resolve the opinion of the Pythagoreans and Copernicus on the movement and location of the earth. Because I hold the latter to be much more probable than the opinion of Aristotle and Ptolemy, this causes me to open my ears wide as to the reasoning you have invoked.[10]

In the second letter, dated August 4, 1597, Galileo thanks Johannes Kepler for having sent him a copy of his work *Prodromus dissertationum cosmographicarum continens mysterium cosmographicum* ("Forerunner of cosmographic dissertations, containing the cosmographic mystery") (Tübingen, 1596). In his letter we read:

> I promise you I will read your book attentively in serenity of spirit, because in it I am sure to find very beautiful things. Truly, I will do it all the more willingly because for many years I have accepted the doctrine of Copernicus, and because starting with these principles I have discovered the causes of many natural effects that remain inexplicable by current theories. I have composed many studies in favor of this [opinion] and against the contrary doctrines, which I have not hitherto ventured to publish, frightened by the fate of our Master, Copernicus himself, who, if he has gained immortal renown in some quarters, has become a laughing-stock and has been banned in others—so great, in fact, is the number of blockheads. If those who think like you were more numerous, I would certainly have the courage to publish my reflections; but because this is not the case, I prefer in such circumstances to wait.[11]

The Copernican Projection

The letter to Mazzoni raises the question, Was it, then, necessary to be a Platonist in order to become a Copernican? The letter to Kepler allows a glimpse not so much of a program, properly speaking, as, more probably, a projection of Copernican research activities. Of what did this projection consist?

Furthermore we are going to be involved in the animated history of relationships with Kepler, which cannot be passed over in silence when one is examining the relationships of Galileo with the thought of Copernicus.

Alexandre Koyré has maintained that Platonic thought constituted the conceptual intermediary that led to acceptance of Copernicanism. This thesis has recently been subjected to a number of critical reevaluations. Galileo did not know Greek, and of Plato he knew only those doctrines that the Florentine Academy had integrated into general learning.[12] It could be that reading Mazzoni's work had helped to fix in his mind the memory of several cosmological conjectures, in particular the "admirable speculation" of the Timaeus concerning the formation of the solar system, to which he referred thirty years later in the first day of the "Dialogue."[13] But all in all, the "divine" Archimedes exercised a more profound and wider influence on Galileo's thought than did Plato.

In fact, with what did Galileo's mind concern itself during these years? Essentially with mechanics, which he soon began to refashion. Until the Reinassance, mechanics occupied a subordinate and subsidiary position among the university disciplines; it was only the practical and empirical science of machines or engines, by its very nature foreign to rational science, the Greek *episteme*. Now Galileo had just composed "The Mechanics"[14] and a treatise *De motu*, which he carried about with him all his life, adding touches of improvement in the course of several successive editions, up to the point of discussing and commenting on the definitive version in the last of his major works, "Discourse and Mathematical Demonstrations concerning Two New Sciences Dealing with Mechanics and Local Motion."[15] In "The Mechanics" he elaborated a general theory of simple machines (the balance, the lever, the windlass and pulleys, the screw), starting from the Archimedean model of the lever. To explain the action of a weight he introduced the notion of "static moment"—that is to say, the product of a weight and the distance that separates it from the point at which it exerts a turning effect. In *De motu* he undertook a revision of the Aristotelian distinction between natural movements and constrained or violent movements. Observing that not all movement communicated to a body is necessarily a movement imposed on it, inasmuch as it is not contrary to its nature, he inserted, as a third term, neutral movements, which are neither natural nor constrained, and which prefigure inertial movements, about which he began to gain a clear idea after 1602. It is hardly an exaggeration to say that at the moment when he first turned to Copernicanism, Galileo was already working toward the construction of a rational mechanics that would allow the application of geometry to physical phenomena.

In the light of the above data, are we in a position to understand what in fact were the "natural effects" that Galileo claimed to explain in taking Copernican astronomy as a premise? Interpreters suspect that out of rivalry with Kepler, Galileo had exaggerated in speaking of "numerous studies over a period of many years."

Stillman Drake dates to ca. 1595 Galileo's conversion to Copernican astronomy.[16] Interpreters agree in recognizing in Galileo's words an allusion to the explanation of ocean tides and the trade winds by combining the first two movements attributed to the earth by Copernicus—the annual revolution around the sun and the diurnal rotation about the axis of the poles. The first idea as to this explanation thus goes back to a time twenty years before the "Discourse on the Ebb and Flow of the Sea" (1616).

I dispute even less the supposition that in a notebook of the Servite, Fra' Paolo Sarpi, the celebrated theologian of the Venetian Republic and historian of the Council of Trent, friend of Galileo, there has been found a summary of the new explanation.[17] But I propose to complement it by another more general consideration. Research in mechanics led Galileo, progressively but rapidly, to undertake a revision of Aristotelian physics. He had begun by attacking the division of material elements into light and heavy, a division that Aristotle had to some extent "axiomatized." Galileo showed that all the effects attributed to levity were, in fact, due to relative differences in gravity—that is, to differences in "specific weights." In a word, Galileo extended Archimedean hydrostatics to aerostatics.

From that time on, Galileo asserted that a volume of air has weight in the air mass in which it resides, in the same way that a volume of water continues to have weight in the mass of water in which it is in equilibrium. This gave Galileo a way to refute the Aristotelian doctrine according to which gravity was a tendency of heavy bodies to occupy the "natural" place proper to them, just as levity brought light bodies to their proper place.

We are here touching on a central theme of Galilean thought, which served as a link between the new mechanics and Copernican astronomy: reflection on the fall of bodies, a "cosmological" phenomenon, if indeed it was one. Galileo came to ask himself, What information concerning the real constitution of the world can we gain from an attentive observation of the fall of bodies, always under the condition that reasoning is carried out after replacing the debatable Aristotelian premises by geometric theorems? At the same time as he posed this problem, Kepler posed to himself the same question, but in speculative terms that I willingly call Platonist, and even Kantian: How should most of the world be constructed that we can observe the effects due to gravity, such as they manifest themselves?

Undoubtedly Galileo (1564-1642) and Johannes Kepler (1571-1630) were the two greatest artisans of the Copernican revolution in their generation, much more so than Descartes, who in this matter occupies only a modest place.[18] However, almost everything set

Galileo and Kepler in opposition. The contrast in the respective unfoldings of their thought was so great that their relationships via their correspondence very soon turned into misunderstanding and were broken off, to be resumed much later. In their mutual misunderstanding, doctrinal reasons had less weight than personal quarrels.[19]

The cosmological importance of gravity did not escape Copernicus, but he had hardly fathomed its exact significance:

> For myself, at least, I consider that gravity is nothing more than a natural appetition; by this means the divine Providence of the Architect of the world gives to [its] parts [the ability] to find themselves in their unity and integrality, gathering together in the form of a globe. And one can believe that this tendency belongs equally to the sun, to the moon, and to the other wandering stars, so that thanks to its efficacity, they remain in that sphericity in which they appear, even though in their divers ways they effect their circuits.[20]

Copernicus thus remained faithful to the traditional doctrine concerning gravity. His only revolutionary innovation, but a decisive one, was that of assigning to each star its own particular center of gravity, instead of considering that the earth was the center of gravity of the whole stellar world.

Whereas Kepler sought to make gravity conceivable in a world system, Galileo applied himself to rendering the fall of heavy bodies observable. For Kepler the world—one did not as yet speak of the universe, except in the works of Giordano Bruno (1548-1600)—was animated by forces: the forces that caused the moon to circle the earth, for example, was opposed to the force that tended to bring them together and merge them into a single body by virtue of their affinity.[21] Kepler was the first to speak of gravity in terms of a mutual attraction between two bodies linked by a certain material affinity. In 1609, in his introduction to the "New Astronomy according to Causes; or Celestial Physics," he wrote: "It is not the stone that [in its fall] goes in search of the earth, it is the earth that attracts the stone."[22]

The falling stone does not tend toward the center of the earth, like a voyager seeking the terminus of his voyage, but the stone and the earth meet at their center of gravity, and if the stone had the same mass as the earth, their meeting would be at the midpoint of their initial distance of separation.[23] But Keplerian gravity had nothing to do with the gravitation of the stars, and we are still far from Newton's universal gravitation. In Kepler's eyes, a pulsive force emanated from the sun and set the planets in motion in their orbits; the sun communicated this same pulsive force to other planets so that these in turn, in a derivative and secondary fashion, caused their satellites to orbit—the term "satellite" was created by Kepler himself.[24] According to Kepler gravity and solar force act with an intensity inversely proportional to distance, as in the case of magnetic force, with which latter the gravitational and solar forces have many analogies of nature, whereas light is attenuated proportionally to the square of the distance from the luminous source.

By a kind of allergy, Galileo altogether rejected Kepler's thinking. In the influences and affinities of which Kepler spoke, Galileo believed that he could recognize the occult properties of Aristotelian "nature." He was later to write in the "Dialogue":

> Among all the great men who have philosophized on such an admirable effect of nature [the tides produced by the double movement of the earth], Kepler surprises me more than the others, and I am astonished that he, a free and perspicacious spirit, who had within his grasp the movements attributed to the earth [by Copernicus], subsequently lent his ear and his assent to supremacies over the waters and to occult properties, as well as to other infantilities.[25]

Strangely, the Galilean universe is deprived of forces, as if the very idea of force had to be exorcised. Galileo analyzes movements, and for him physical explanation consists in showing that one physical movement results from another. To the essentially dynamic thought of Kepler there is opposed the essentially kinematic thought of Galileo. And in this sense, the Galilean mechanism is much more radical.

During the years of Padua (1592-1610), Galileo arrived at three important results concerning the fall of heavy bodies:

1. Contrary to the teaching of Aristotle, bodies do not fall with a speed proportional to their mass. If Galileo had not yet arrived at the actual formulation, "*in vacuo* all bodies fall with the same speed," it is because he thought that the theoretically possible vacuum was physically impossible. In effect, Galileo remained a partisan of the "abhorrence of a vacuum," which he moreover interpreted, in a mechanistic sense, as the resistance of different materials to deprivation of their cohesion. He did not see in what way this resistance/cohesion could be overcome. In any case, abstracting from the resistance of the medium (air or water, for example), and from aerostatic or hydrostatic up-thrusts, bodies fall with the same speed, independently of their masses. Galileo had arrived at this result as early as the first years of his teaching in Pisa (1589-1592).

2. To sensible perception, the fall of bodies has always appeared to be the most natural movement that there is, the archetype of natural movements; and this is an accelerated motion. The Aristotelians in general considered that after the phase of initial acceleration by discontinuous increments of the initial speed, a body then continued its fall with a high but constant speed. Galileo established that the fall of heavy bodies is a naturally accelerated motion and that by "naturally accelerated" there should be understood "continuously and uniformly accelerated."[26] As early as 1602 Galileo had demonstrated the continuous character of acceleration during fall. From 1604 Galileo was in possession of a law of uniformly accelerated motion, but it was incorrect, because at that time he considered that the speed of the body was proportional to the distance traversed from the commencement of the fall. Although after 1604 he knew that distances traversed in the fall are proportional to the square of the time elapsed, it is probably only in 1615 that he arrived at the exact law of the proportionality of the speed, at a given instant, to the time elapsed since the beginning of the fall.

3. Finally if the fall of bodies is natural movement par excellence, the uplifting of bodies is the archetype of violent movements, and the contrariety of these two species of movement is illustrated by their reversibility. In fact, a perfectly elastic body rebounds to the same height as that from which it has fallen. Starting from this conclusion, Galileo conceived the existence of a perfectly neutral movement, neither natural nor violent, in the course of which a body moves without losing or gaining height—that is, a horizontal movement that one can imagine on a surface polished so as to eliminate friction and to allow abstraction from it. With an ingenuity truly of genius, Galileo applied himself to studying the oscillations of the pendulum, which clearly represent the reversibility of descents and re-ascents, and also to the study of rolling motions along inclined planes, which amount to prolonged and retarded falls. By a bold transition to the limit, considering planes of progressively reduced inclination, he deduced that if a body rolling down one inclined plane climbs to the same height up another inclined plane of the same slope, then uniform motion—that is, with no acceleration—should be prolonged indefinitely on a horizontal plane. In this way Galileo discovered the formulation that we today call the principle of inertia.

The laws of uniform motion, exemplified in inertial motion, and the laws of uniformly accelerated motion, exemplified in the fall of bodies, were expounded in their definitive form in the "Discourses and Demonstrations" of 1638. They are one of Galileo's principal claims to glory. But what bearing did they have on what is conveniently called the "Copernican revolution"? On a number of occasions Galileo returned to the consideration that the geometric notion of a horizontal plane is physically realized on the earth's surface, which is a spherical surface.[27] Let us say that, for Galileo, the surface of the sea, abstracting from tides and waves, is something more than a simple local reference frame for defining horizontality. It is physically that surface on which inertial movements are verified. This view, which the best authorities were to regard as a gross mistake,[28] is not however without importance, because it induced Galileo to consider that the orbital movements of the stars are endowed with perenniality, because they are truly inertial. In their case gravity does not have any effect, because they follow a course at a fixed distance from a determinate center. Today we find it difficult to understand the Galilean conception of an inertial circular motion, because we are accustomed to consider velocities "vectorially." For us a velocity has a magnitude and a direction, and a uniform velocity can only be a velocity with a constant magnitude and an invariant direction; that is why we do not recognize any movement as inertial, apart from uniform rectilinear motion. Neither Galileo nor Descartes mastered the consideration of the direction of a velocity. It is only with Christian Huygens and Isaac Newton that this consideration is arrived at.

During the years 1600-1610 it was Kepler who most closely approached the goal being pursued. In effect, the second law of planetary motion formulated in the New Astronomy (*Astronomia Nova*) states that the radius joining an orbiting body to the sun covers equal areas in equal times. The law of areas to a certain extent integrated the direction and magnitude of velocity in the analysis of orbital displacements. But above all, starting with the consideration that the planet Mars has a greater velocity at perihelion (passage through the orbital point closest to the sun) and a lesser velocity at aphelion (passage through the orbital point farthest from the sun), Kepler concluded that planetary orbits could not be circular. After much hesitation, he assigned them the elliptical form, propounding in the New Astronomy the first law of planetary motion: "The planets traverse orbits that are ellipses, of which one of the foci is occupied by the sun." Inasmuch as the variations in velocity of a particular planet are minimal, the eccentricities of its orbital ellipses are minute.

The circular inertia postulated by Galileo rendered the elliptical nature of planetary orbits unacceptable to him; and in fact, he never accepted the law established by Kepler. Furthermore, he always took it that the acceleration due to gravity is constant at any distance from the center of the earth. Consequently neither Galileo, nor even Kepler, ever made a distinction between the mass and the weight of a body. As to the question of the nature of gravity, this was a problem of little interest for Galileo, who was ready to admit that it lay outside the range of our judgment:

> SIMPLICIUS: The cause of this effect (the fall of bodies) is very well understood and everybody knows that it is due to gravity.

> SALVIATI: You are mistaken, Signor Simplicius; you ought to say that everyone knows that it is

called gravity. But for my part, I do not ask of you the name but the essence of the thing, about which you know no more than you know about the essence that causes the stars to follow their orbits, apart from the name assigned to it, rendered familiar and current by the frequent experience of that which we see a thousand times every day. But it is not that we really understand what is the principle or virtue that moves the stone down better than that which raises it up, once it has left the hand of the thrower, nor that we understand it better than that which causes the moon to orbit, except, as I have said, the name we have assigned to it as the most singularly appropriate appellation, as also whenever we give to the principle of projectile motion the general term *virtus impressa*, to planetary motion the name "intelligence," "assistant," "informant," and to an infinity of other movements we attribute "nature" as cause.[29]

Despite all their differences, Galileo and Kepler were at least in agreement as to a project essential to the Copernican revolution: to construct a universal physics—that is, equally celestial and terrestrial, on the basis of a rational mechanics with laws valid from one end of the universe to the other. Thus the ancient division into celestial and sublunary worlds was abolished, and the planetary group could be organized into a true solar system, the existence of which had been foreseen and affirmed by Copernicus.

The Copernican Program

Though a genius at mechanics, in astronomy Galileo was certainly not of the same stature as Kepler, the greatest astronomer of his generation. But at the very moment when Galileo had returned to his research on the acceleration of falling bodies, he invented the telescope, which cast him willy-nilly into astronomy.[30] Henceforward, to the end of his life, mechanical research and astronomical observation were to alternate in an incessant interchange. In the end there came the publication of his two major works, the "Dialogue" (1632) and the "Discourses and Demonstrations" (1638), which followed each other in the reverse order of priority in their programing. It happened several times that Galileo, on the point of announcing an important proposition in mechanics, had to delay the communication because in the interim he found himself engaged in a polemic arising from an unexpected astronomical discovery, often, in fact, his own.

The moment had come for Galileo to pursue the astronomy of Copernicus in the open sky. Galileo constructed his first telescope in July 1609. In the first quarter of 1610, he gave himself up to astronomical observations with a fervor bordering on frenzy. As early as the autumn of 1609 he had observed the lunar mountains at length; on January 7 he discovered the three first satellites of Jupiter; on the 13th he discovered a fourth. In July, he discovered the strange appearance of Saturn, which he considered as being formed of three distinct bodies.[31] In September, when he finally left Padua to go to Florence, he observed the phases of Venus.

Guest of his friend Filippo Salviati in the villa "Le Selve," on the outskirts of Florence, he began the systematic observation of sunspots from January 1611 onward. In the spring, he compiled the tables of movements of the four satellites of Jupiter, and spent a long time bringing them to perfection. Stillman Drake, who has explored the textual notes of Galileo kept in the National Library of Florence, noticed that he had the good luck to observe, for the first time in history, the planet Neptune in December 1612, before its occultation by Jupiter in January 1613. Because it has a very long period of revolution—165 years—it was not identified as the eight planet of the solar system until 234 years later—and Galileo thought he had observed a fixed star of feeble luminosity![32]

As a result of these astronomical discoveries, what had the Copernican cause gained? It is customarily emphasized that from then onward, more and more analogies were drawn in support of the Copernican point of view. Apart from the dismantling of the ancient and medieval dogma of the unalterability of the heavens, a number of phenomena, hitherto apparent singularities, found corresponding entities within the solar system. The earth was not alone in being accompanied by a satellite; Venus showed phases similar to those of the moon; the surface of the latter did not have a mirror-like polish, and the reliefs of "selenography" were altogether similar to those of the terrestrial geography.

The phases of Venus were particularly interesting. If the moon presents different aspects spread over a number of phases, it is because it revolves around the earth at the same time as it reflects the light of the sun. If Venus, viewed from the earth, presents similar phases, this can only be because it revolves around the sun while reflecting its light:

> The apparent diameter of Venus is at present about five times greater than it was at its first appearance at the vesper hour. From this marvelous experience I draw the sensible and certain demonstration of two great questions hitherto cast in doubt by the greatest intellects of the world.
>
> The first is that all the planets are by nature dark (the same thing applying to Mercury and Venus).
>
> The second is that of necessity Venus orbits the sun, as does Mercury and all the other planets, something that was firmly believed by the Pythagoreans, Copernicus, Kepler, and myself, but

which had not been proved by the senses, as is now the case with Venus and with Mercury.[33]

Scholars have, mistakenly, neglected a line of thought that accompanied Galileo up to the writing of the "Dialogue" and that, alongside his reflection on the movement of a falling body under gravity, constitutes a second directive theme of his Copernican research. Very soon attacked on the allegedly fallacious nature of the image in the telescope, Galileo never conceded the slightest doubt as to its objectivity. He explained the matter in a letter to Piero Dini, dated May 21, 1611.[34] He advanced the principle that in every place reached by the light excited or reflected by a body, it is possible to obtain an image of that body. An excellent practician and theoretician of perspective, which he had learned in the school of Guidobaldo del Monte and had applied in the design of fortifications, he had understood that every optical image reduces to a geometric construct obtained by projection. Thus it is not by recourse to a sensation, at least virtual, that illusions of visions are remedied, but by reasoning in accord with the laws of geometrical optics:

> That these gentlemen could entertain the doubt that there is illusion in the telescope seems to me a truly astonishing thing: because I know that they will not contradict me on the point that the detection of illusions and errors due to an instrument or to any other device rests with the competence of the one who is proficient in the art on which the instrument depends.[35]

An exceptional observer, Galileo knew from the outset how to draw the maximum results from a relatively rudimentary instrument. Recently received, in April 1611, into the Lincean Academy, founded in 1603 by his friend Prince Federico de Cesi, there had been no lack of occasions to praise the virtuosity of his telescope. But his gifts, unique rather than rare, were to be the root of unpleasant polemics. Martin Horky, pupil of the Bolognese astronomer Giovanni Antonio Magini, had taken part in a session of celestial observations in which Galileo had sought to demonstrate his discoveries before representatives of the University of Bologna. But they saw nothing, and the setback had been a bitter one. A correspondent of Kepler's, Horky, wrote to him: [*Perspicillium*] *in inferioribus facit mirabilia; in coelo fallit* (in terrestrial observations the telescope works marvels; in the heavens it fails).[36]

To hold to this diagnosis would have been to bring to trial the particularly significant Galilean project of utilizing the telescope to observe celestial appearances, particularly the appearances of the planets. Galileo knew that he could not resign himself to this without abandoning the hope of basing Copernican astronomy on "sensible experiences," because only the telescope permitted the determination of stellar diameters and parallaxes with some accuracy:

SAGREDO: How, then, has this matter been hidden from Copernicus and manifest to you?

SALVIATI: These things cannot be understood unless by the sense of sight, which nature has not accorded to all with sufficient perfection for them to be able to discern such differences. I would even say that it is the organ of sight itself that is the cause of its own hindrance. But after it had pleased God to grant to human intelligence, in our day, an invention so marvelous that it can perfect our sight, multiplying it 4, 6, 10, 20, 30, and 40 times, innumerable objects that had been invisible to us because of their distance or because of their smallness, have become visible to us by means of the telescope. . . .

SAGREDO: Oh, Nicholas Copernicus, what would have been your satisfaction in seeing such clear experiences confirm this part of your system![37]

And, further on, Sagredo adds: "The error of these [the adversaries of Copernican astronomy] consists in being extremely mistaken in taking the apparent diameter of the fixed stars."[38]

Galileo had built the first telescopes by assembling a converging lens (the objective) and a divergent lens (the eye-lens), so that the eye-lens was located between one of its own faces and the focal point of its other face. He did not yet have a micrometric screw, but he put a wire grid on the objective so as to obtain a division into squares of the 30-fold enlarged image. He does not seem to have published anything on findings on the refraction of light rays obtained several years previously by Kepler—perhaps he was not even aware of them—expounded by Kepler in the "Compliments to Witelo, in which is Treated the Optical Part of Astronomy."[39] The ambassador of the grand duke of Tuscany in Prague, Giuliano de'Medici, applied himself to restoring relations between Galileo and Kepler. Through his intercession, Kepler obtained a telescope from Galileo's workshop.[40] He set to work to perfect it and develop the theory. He replaced the divergent eye-lens with a converging lens, which worked in the same way as in the microscope; thus he obtained better enlargement of the image. He immediately published his "Dioptric, or Demonstration of the Vision and Images Obtained by the Telescope."[41]

The most Copernican aspect of Galileo's reflections on the nature and properties of telescopic images concerns the formation of an image in the conditions of immensity proper to astronomy. Scholars have often neglected to mention that to the two premises of his system—the negation of the centrality of the earth and the affirmation of its mobility—Galileo added a third: the immensity of the sphere of fixed stars. Copernicus had deduced that, if the earth orbits the sun in the course of an annual revolution, then the so-

called fixed stars are not absolutely fixed, but should appear to us as subject to an annual displacement in the sky detectable by a parallax—that is, by the angular separation of the two positions of the same star determined when the earth is at perihelion and aphelion. The extreme distance of the stars rendered their annual parallaxes practically indeterminable.[42] To Galileo belongs the merit of having methodically shown that it is precisely the conditions of immensity that render imperceptible the effects that are the consequences of Copernican astronomy. Galileo returns several times to this argument in the third day of the "Dialogue."

With the invention of the telescope, Galileo's Copernican project was transformed into a program that took into account writing as well as research. At the moment of negotiating his return from Padua to Florence, he entered into negotiations with Belisario Vinta, secretary of state to the Grand Duke Cosimo II. During the preceding year, in January 1610, he had published in Venice the "Starry Message,"[43] in which he announced to the world his first astronomical discoveries and in which he dedicated the four satellites of Jupiter to the glory of the Medici dynasty. In Prague a copy had been sent to Kepler by the ambassador Giuliano de'Medici, perhaps without Galileo's knowledge. Ever an enthusiast and incomparably magnanimous, Kepler wrote in April his "Conversation with the Starry Messenger," which was printed in August.[44] In it he confirmed the existence of the Medici stars and the other Galilean discoveries.

In May of the same year, Galileo addressed to Vinta a letter in which he traced out a detailed and articulate program of his current undertakings:

I am determined in every way, seeing how the days pass by, to nail down the future that remains to me and to apply myself with all my strength to bring to a conclusion the fruits of the wearyings of all my past studies, from which I can hope to gain some renown. . . . The works that I have to bring to a conclusion are principally:

—two books *de systemate seu constitutione universi*, an immense concept, full of philosophy, astronomy, and geometry;

—three books de motu locali, an entirely new science, for up to now nobody else, ancient or modern, has discovered a single one of the many wonderful characteristics whose presence I have demonstrated in both natural and violent movements, so that I can reasonably call it a "new science" discovered by myself from its very foundation.[45]

One can here recognize the two principal works of Galileo, the "Dialogue," and the "Discourses and Demonstrations." The negotiations ended in July with his nomination as "First Mathematician and Philosopher of the Grand Duke of Tuscany," coupled with the appreciable dispensation from any necessity to teach. In the spring of the following year, Galileo went to Rome, where he stayed from the end of March to the beginning of June. There he met the Jesuit professors of the Roman College, who confirmed the truth of his discoveries by their observations at the specola (observatory) of the college. He was admitted to the Lincean Academy and feted there. The Academy decided to publish at its own expense the work he was in course of writing, "Description and Demonstration on the Subject of Sunspots."[46]

The Censure of Copernican Astronomy

From the end of 1612 events developed rapidly. Florence was rife with rumor, and anyone who knows the Florentines is aware that they have sharp tongues. Sacred eloquence had to involve itself in all this. From the pulpit of the monastery of St. Mark, the Dominican Niccolò Lorini took issue vigorously against "Ipernic" and the "diabolical sect of mathematicians," in November 1613.

A year later, on December 2, 1614, another Dominican, Tomasso Caccini, returned to the attack during an Advent sermon delivered in the monastery church of New St. Mary's. Before explaining the tenth chapter of the Book of Joshua, which relates how the latter stopped the sun on the plain of Gibeon until complete victory of the Israelite forces, Fr. Caccini cried out in the course of a moving peroration: "Men of Galilee [Galileo], why do you stand here looking up at the sky?"[47] Did he count on winning over to his side those who laughed? But are we not in the full tide of the baroque? At that time one did not hold back from any effect or any abuse of figurative meaning.[48]

Uneasy at the turn of events in these attacks, Galileo wrote to his friend and close confidant, the Benedictine Benedetto Castelli, who was also his collaborator in the observations of the phases of Venus and the sunspots, a letter on the interpretation of the holy scriptures in matters of natural philosophy. This was the first of three letters on the same subject, called "Copernican letters," the other two being addressed to Piero Dini (February 16, 1615) and to Princess Marie-Christine de Lorraine, grand duchess (1615).

A misguided apologetic has reproached Galileo with having involved himself in questions not within his competence. This reproach was not leveled at him during his lifetime. The much-decried post-Tridentine mentality did not recognize a certain narrowness in exaggerated clericalism, a much more recent phenomenon. At that time it was admitted that the Bible is the patrimony of all Christians, even if its interpretation is determined by the ecclesiastical magisterium, ordinary or extraordinary.

More subtly, Galileo has been reproached with having put himself in the position of a buffoon, wanting to put the clergy under instruction, inasmuch as he had wished to use the Bible to prove the truth of Copernicanism. In my opinion, one should not be deceived by assuming even that Galileo took the position: "All things being considered, even I am able to have recourse to scripture to support what I propose, though basing myself on other reasons." A pugnacious polemicist by his gifts and by inclination, Galileo never gave up, and he hardly let pass occasions when he could argue by retort. But the basis of his thought is beyond doubt: God, in self-revelation to humankind through the words of human intermediaries, did not intend to give lessons in the natural sciences. Besides, even the planets known to the ancients are not mentioned in the books of the Bible.

The matter was brought before the Holy Office by a denunciation made by the Dominican Lorini, in February 1615. The theologian consulters delivered their expert conclusion in the session of February 23, 1616.

Two propositions attributed to Copernicus were censured. The proposition: "The sun is the center of the world [universe] and consequently is immobile" was judged "incongruous and formally heretical"; the second: "The earth is not the center of the world, and is not immobile, but is both wholly in motion, and also in diurnal rotation" was judged "meriting the same censure [as the first] in philosophy, and from the point of view of theological truth being also erroneous with regard to the faith."[49] Clumsy propositions and inadequate qualifications, emerging from a patched-up consultation, which had at no time been accompanied by serious debate. The censure was submitted to the General Congregation of the Inquisition, on February 25, and was ratified by Pope Paul V. At the session of the following week, on March 3, a decree was promulgated conferring executive validity on the censure; *De revolutionibus orbium caelestium* was inscribed in the Index of forbidden books "until corrected."[50]

Galileo had not been put into the role of a defendant, and one speaks improperly of a "first trial" that would have been held. It is nevertheless highly significant that on February 26, the day after the work of Copernicus had been put on the Index, Cardinal Robert Bellarmine of the Holy Office summoned Galileo to an audience in the presence of the commissioner general, the Dominican Michelangelo Seghizzi, to inform him of the condemnation of Copernicus's book and to invite him to cease teaching, publicly defending, and expounding Copernican astronomy. For the first time Galileo was officially recognized as the chief spokesman of Copernicanism.

How did the audience unfold? The answer to this question goes far behind anecdotal history, for it marks the beginning of a period of Galileo's career that we can truly call Copernican and it imparts a disastrous turn of events to what follows. Let us say that it was to act as a time bomb.

Cardinal Robert Bellarmine had received from Cardinal Millini, perfect of the Holy Office, instructions as to the procedure to follow. At this point I need to invite the reader to follow me into the mysteries of canon law. To reduce Galileo to obedience, three successive stages were foreseen in order to meet three different eventualities:

1. Cardinal Bellarmine would invite Galileo by a "warning (*monitum*) to submit to the consequences of the censure incurred by the works of Copernicus.

2. In the event that Galileo objected, Cardinal Bellarmine should then proceed to a formal injunction (*praeceptum*).

3. Finally, in the event that this did not suffice, Galileo should be formally indicted and arrested.

To the present day nobody knows exactly what transpired. Here I shall summarize one of the most likely scenarios, following the account of the facts proposed by Stillman Drake.[51] Cardinal Bellarmine, whose own "Controversies" had been placed on the Index by Sixtus V in 1590 "until corrected" (*donec corregetur*), and who, himself a Jesuit, had consulted his professor confreres of the Roman College, was rather benevolent toward Galileo. He seems to have been content with the "warning," at the same time advising Galileo to speak of Copernicum astronomy only *ex hypothesi*, by way of supposition, while awaiting the time when he would be able to furnish more decisive proofs, if this should ever be possible. Seghizzi, more suspicious, was convinced that Galileo would not give in so easily, and that being so deeply committed, he would certainly raise objections. Thus, before the audience took place, he prepared the draft of the formal injunction that figures in the dossier of instructions of the affair. It was placed there inopportunely, all the more so because, without the signatures of the relevant authorities, it had no validity as a trial record.

The situation became increasingly complicated. The recommendation to keep to the cautious attitude of one who does not in any way speak of a confirmed hypothesis came to Galileo at the very moment when he had put the finishing touches to the physical proof that he thought he had discovered in favor of Copernicanism. In effect, despite the remonstrations of the grand duke's ambassador not to go there, Galileo arrived in Rome at the end of 1615 to make a final effort to save the Copernican cause. In the gardens of the Medici villa, residence of the ambassador, as a first salvo he had written the "Discourse on the Ebb and Flow of the Sea," which, on January 8, 1616, he had addressed to Alexander Orsini, who had just been made a cardinal.[52] The three letters to Mark Welser, published in 1613 under the title "History and Demonstrations concerning Sunspots," had been reprinted in Rome. Now the third of these "Roman letters" contains the first apology for Copernican astronomy published by Galileo. The ecclesiastical authorities allowed the republishing of this work without reacting. In it for the first time Galileo expounded an astronomical proof that he always held to be one of the strongest, derived from the observation of seasonal variations of the trajectory followed by sunspots.

He returns to it again in the "Dialogue" where the argument derived from the rotation of the sunspots is developed on the third day. He linked it with the argument from ocean tides taken up on the fourth and last day:

> From the discourse of these four days we have thus drawn great attestations in favor of the Copernican system; among which three have shown themselves to be sufficiently conclusive:
>
> —the first, the taking of the stations and retrogradations of the planets by reason of their approaches and recessions relative to the earth:
>
> —the second, from the revolution of the sun on its own axis and that which is observed in the sunspots;
>
> —the third, from the ebb and flow of the sea.[53]

These three major proofs follow the Aristotelian schema of reasoning *ex suppositione*:[54] granted the twofold movement of the earth, annual and diurnal, the explanation of planetary appearances, sunspot trajectories, oceanic tides, and trade winds becomes particularly simple and clear. Galileo had observed that sunspots appear on the eastern edge of the solar disc and disappear two weeks later on the western edge after having described the arc of an ellipse, the projection of a circle as viewed from earth. He had deduced that the sun is impelled by a rotation from west to east, taking a little less than a month. And he perceived as a consequence that when the earth, in its revolution around the sun in the ecliptic, occupies a position such that the radius vector joining the earth's center to the sun's center is in the sun's equatorial plane, the sunspots then appear to follow rectilinear trajectories, instead of their usual elliptical trajectories. From this he concluded that the annual revolution of the earth associated with the semimonthly rotation of the sun sufficed to explain the annual cycle of variations of the monthly trajectories of the sunspots, even to the extent that, according to him, the annual rotation of the earth around the sun coupled with its daily rotation on its own axis (spin) explains the twice-daily period of the ocean tides:

> Such are the surprising mutations which, according to my host [Salviati is speaking of his friend the "Lincean Academician," Galileo], should appear periodically in the journeyings of the sunspots, if it is admitted as true that the earth has an annual movement, and that the sun, established at the center of the ecliptic, turns upon itself [spins] about an axis that is not perpendicular to but inclined to the plane of the ecliptic.[55]

The physical proof drawn from the tides was even more important for Galileo for two reasons. First, as an able polemicist he liked to have recourse to arguments *ad hominem* and by retort, for their argumentative value. Here he seems to be saying to his adversaries: "Ptolemaic astronomers and Copernican astronomers use the geometric construction of epicycles to explain the apparent irregularities of the planetary motions. The Ptolemaists place the earth at the center of deferent circles; the Copernicans, on the contrary, place the sun there. But the hypothesis of epicycles has never been able to settle matters between them and has never given judgment to one group rather than to the other. Well then, as for myself, I am going to use it to prove the truth of Copernican astronomy."

What is comprised in the hypothesis of epicycles? Interpreting the trajectory of a planet as the resultant of an epicyclic motion consists in making the given planet P orbit on the circumference of a circle (epicycle) that has a simple reference point C as its center. . . . This latter point in turn orbits on the circumference of a circle with its center at T (the earth, according to the geostatic or geocentric point of view). With the requisite geometric virtuosity, one will always succeed in finding a ratio of the radius CP of the epicycle to the radius TC of the deferent such that one can account for the periods of time in which the movement of P, as observed from T, seems to change direction (retro-gradations) and the periods of time during which P slows down its progression to the point of seeming motionless to an observer located at T (stations). Within the framework of epicycles it was more difficult but nevertheless not impossible to explain the variations in the luminosity of the planets as a function of their approaches and recessions with respect to the earth. Farthest recession or apogee is when the points P, C, T are aligned in the sequence TCP; close approach or perigee occurs when the points P, C, T are aligned in the order TPC.

Epicycles played the same role in the heliocentric system of Copernicus. In fact the *De revolutionibus* follows the Almagest of Ptolemy in strict parallelism, chapter by chapter and table by table. One can even regard the Copernican system as an astronomical simplification of the Ptolemaic system because the models chosen by Copernicus for the movement of each planet even more require circles. Moreover, Copernicus was too scrupulous an astronomer, rigorously attentive to the relevant data, to locate the sun at the exact center of the planetary system;[56] he placed it at some distance from the geometric center of the orbits of the planets. He also drew attention to the lunar theory of Ptolemy and its incompatability with the observable parallaxes.[57] But it was above all the discussion of the distinction between inferior (inner) and superior (outer) planets that brought about confrontation between the Ptolemic and Copernican astronomic systems.[58] In brief, the greater simplicity of the Copernican system is of a different order from that of astronomical description: it is conceptual and cosmological. It laid the foundations for conceiving the solar system. One intuition in particular convinced Copernicus of the truth of his astronomic system: by imagining a planetary system nearly centered on the sun, he was finally able to gain an idea of the distances effectively separating the celestial bodies, in terms of heliocentric distance—that is, distances relative to the sun, something that the geocentric picture of the world did not allow.

Now let us come to the second particular feature of the physical proof—namely, explanation of the tides. Galileo had understood the thought of Copernicus in depth, even if he does not seem to have been an assiduous reader of *De revolutionibus*: the physical truth of Copernicanism interested him much more than its astronomic truth. Or let us say, more accurately, that for him, as for Kepler, astronomy is celestial physics, and that astronomic truth appeared to him to be a physical truth concerning the constitution of the world—physical, and even mechanical.

Galileo felt triumphant because he had thought of keeping to a proof that simultaneously involved terrestrial and celestial physics. Now this proof is strictly mechanical: it explains the periodic movement of the oceans by another movement, that of the earth. And luckily, the epicycles, which had hitherto served only as an expedient in astronomical descriptions, for the first time fulfilled a new function: they became a kinematic model.

In effect, if . . . we consider a point P on the terrestrial surface that rotates daily about the center of the earth, T, and if T in turn orbits annually around the sun, S, then once a day at P the speed of diurnal rotation adds to the speed of annual revolution; once a day at P the rotational speed substracts from the speed of revolution. The speed resulting from the two motions of the earth varies continuously; from P2 to P4 part of the rotational speed is subtracted from the annual speed of revolution; from P to P2 part of the rotational speed is added to the speed of revolution.

If, instead of considering an isolated point, we think of an arc of a circle that represents an ocean surface, we see that different points of the same ocean arc move at different speeds. Galileo allowed himself to be guided by an analogy:

> We can illustrate these effects [the tides] more clearly and render them more manifest to the sense [of sight] by the example of one of those barges that come from Lizzafusina, filled with fresh water for use in the city of Venice. Imagine, then, one of these barges coming at medium speed across the lagoon, placidly bearing the water in its hold. But then the barge slows down markedly, either to avoid shallow water or because of some other obstacle that opposes it. The water contained [in the hold] will not lose, to the same extent and in the same time, the impulse (impetus) that had been imparted to it; on the contrary, conserving its impulse, the water will flow toward the bow where it will rise significantly, while falling at the stern. On the other hand, if the same barge, in the setting of its uniform course, should undergo a significant increase in speed, the water contained [in the hold], before adapting itself to the new speed, persevering in its slowness, will remain behind—that is, toward the stern, where it will consequently rise, while falling at the bow. This effect is clear and beyond doubt, and can be experimentally tested at any time.[59]

It would be too hasty to retain from the Galilean explanation of the tides only its main fault—that of being erroneous. Certainly it has been definitively supplanted by the Newtonian explanation, which attributes the principal cause of the tides to the conjoint attractive influence of the moon and sun upon the earth. Nevertheless, it was not entirely erroneous. On the one hand, the effect due to the composition of the two movements of the earth is real, but the rise and fall of ocean waters that can be attributed to it is of the order of several centimeters, and would be quite insufficient to account for the tides that we observe. On the other hand, Galileo set forth valuable considerations on the oscillations of a liquid mass, which anticipated the results of a chapter in the history of the mechanics of fluids.

Winning Cause or Losing Cause?

After the censure of 1616, Galileo did not whisper a word about the Copernican cause for seven years, even though he held in his hand all the proof that he was to expound in the "Dialogue." He found himself engaged in two astronomical debates that did not involve Copernicanism, at least not directly:

The first had as its aim the identification of the nature of sunspots. Galileo's opponent was the Jesuit Christopher Scheiner, who taught mathematics and astrono-

my at Ingolstadt from 1610 to 1616, at Innsbruck from 1616 to 1620, and at Freiburg from 1620 to 1624. A specialist in the study of atmospheric refraction, Scheiner held that sunspots are produced by swarms of asteroids orbiting the sun, whereas Galileo maintained that it was a question of phenomena properly solar and whose location was the very surface of the sun.

The Galilean thesis dealt a new blow to the supposed immutability of the celestial world. A particularly tough adversary, Scheiner returned to the attack in the *Rosa Ursini sive sol* ["The rose or the sun of the Orsinis"], published in 1630 in Bracciano, the fief of the Orsini family. Galileo's disciples jokingly called it the *Ursa Rosina* ("the rose-colored bear"). Unshakeable, Scheiner was to set to work furiously at the moment of the trial directed against Galileo by writing in Vienna the *Prodromus pro Sole Mobili* ("the forerunner of the mobile sun"), the publication of which was to be forbidden by Jesuit superiors until 1651.

The second debate had as its aim to define the nature of comets and brought Galileo into opposition with the Jesuit astronomer Orazio Grassi at the Roman College. The positions were to some extent the reverse of the previous debate. Grassi was no fool. He had been a "supporter" of Galileo's astronomical discoveries, and it only needed the appearance of three comets in 1618— an omen of disaster?—for friendship to be succeeded by animosity, followed by hatred. On this occassion, Grassi had given a public lecture, which he subsequently published anonymously under the title "Astronomical Disputation on the Subject of Three Comets."[60] In essence he was in the right: he upheld the celestial origin of the comets and their movement in a circular orbit. But he had a dull spirit: he reasoned in a manner that could be adopted only in Rome or Salamanca, deploying the entire arsenal of syllogistics, which could have been forgiven if he had not cluttered up his arsenal with a hodgepodge of classical erudition.

Galileo had inherited the very sure taste of the masters of the Renaissance, and in his eyes an esthetic fault was never found without an accompanying error of thought.[61] Furthermore he replied indirectly to the thesis defended by Grassi, through the mediation of Mario Giudicci, who published "The Discourse on the Comets" in Florence.[62] Riposte and counterriposte rapidly poisoned their relationship. In the form of an anagram, and under the pseudonym Lotario Sarsi, Grassi replied in 1619 with the *Libra astronomica ac philosophica* ([The Astronomical and Philosophical Balanced]).[63]

Stung to the quick by this invitation to "weigh his arguments better," Galileo replied four years later in a polemical and methodological masterpiece, *Il Saggiatore* ([The Assayer]—that is, the goldsmith's precision balance or scales).[64] The tale of lunges and counterlunges ends here. Grassi left the arena defeated, and the vanquished always cut a sorry figure, a thing he had in no way deserved. Galileo had administered to him an admirable lesson on how to reason scientifically, but had done so in the service of an erroneous thesis. Galileo continued in fact to think that comets were a meteorological phenomenon brought about by the action of the sun's rays in the higher regions of the earth's atmosphere.

Galileo had become an old man. Although painful arthritis, contracted during his years at Padua, periodically afflicted him, he had a robust constitution and a longevity exceptional for that time. Since the 1620s it is true that he found himself surrounded by young disciples, but many of those who had participated in his struggles for the Copernican cause had disappeared. The two friends to whom he had confided the discussion of his ideas in the "Dialogue" died before the definitive drawing up of the text, Filippo Salviati in 1614, and Gianfrancesco Sagredo in March 1620. Fra' Paolo Sarpi had departed this world in January 1623. The same fate had befallen the judges before whom Galileo had had to appear. Robert Bellarmine, worn out by his many duties carried out in the Roman Curia, died in Rome on September 17, 1621. Father Seghizzi, meanwhile nominated bishop of Lodi, carried with him to the grave the secret concerning the formal injuction. Had it been applied or not? It will probably never be made known.

A memorable day was to impart a new course to events: On August 16, 1623, the conclave of cardinals elected as successor to Pope Gregory XV (1621-1623) Cardinal Maffeo Barberini, who took the name Urban VIII. The unexpected but not entirely unpredictable choice was greeted with exultation at the Lincean Academy, and more generally by men of letters and intellectual pursuits. His nephew, a member of the academy and a cardinal of a year's standing, was then a legate in France. To replace him at the head of the Secretariat of State, the newly elected pope nominated his younger brother Antonio, whom he raised to the cardinalate with effect from October 1624.

In the course of his service as legate in France, Cardinal Francesco Barberini, who was a confrere of Galileo at the Roman Lincean Academy, spoke about him to a Provençal gentleman, a numismatist and bibliophile of great erudition, Nicolas Claude Fabri de Peiresc (1580-1637). He played an important role in the spread of Galilean thought in France. It was not long before it became known to Fermat, Descartes, and Roberval, as well as to all the friends and correspondents of the Minim friar, Marin Mersenne (1588-1648). On his return to Rome, Francesco Barberini directed the Vatican Library, where he established the precious Barberini collection.

In the month of April 1624, Galileo returned to Rome, this time to pay homage to a friend and patron, the new pope, and to offer him in person a copy of "The Assayer," which the Lincean Academy had published at its own expense at the end of the preceding year, and had dedicated to Pope Urban VIII. They had known and esteemed each other for a long time. When Pope Clement VIII (1592-1605) had charged Maffeo Barberini, not yet a cardinal, with the purification of the waters of Lake Trasimeno, he had found excellent expert hydrologists in Benedetto Castelli and Galileo. Later, in the dispute over floating bodies that took place in Florence during the summer of 1611, we find him on the side of Galileo.[65] Had the moment come to reopen the Copernican cause? Galileo thought so, without any presentiment of a dramatic outcome.

It is quite significant that in 1624 Galileo had taken up his pen to reply to an attack launched eight years previously by Francesco Ingoldi, an active and enterprising member of the Roman Curia, in his *De situ et quiete terrae contra Copernici systema disputatio* ([Disputed Question on the Site and Quiescence of the Earth against the System of Copernicus]). Galileo wrote him a long "Reply" when Ingoldi became secretary of Propaganda Fide, founded in 1622 by Pope Gregory XV and, as a man well versed in the knowledge of oriental languages, was working on the organization of the Vatican Polyglot Press and at the Urbanianum College for the training of missionaries. A man of vast designs, Urban VIII aimed at centering the administration of Catholic missions in Rome to distance them from colonial powers. It is in the remarkable "Reply to Francesco Ingoldi"[66] that there is to be found for the first time the thesis of the mechanical relativity of motions in the very terms that will be taken up again on the second day of the "Dialogue":

> SIMPLICIUS: According to the opinions of all groups of philosophers, sense and experience serve us as escorts when we philosophize; but in the position of Copernicus, it befalls the senses to deceive greatly, for they see close by and in the pure media very heavy bodies falling in a straight line by a hair's breadth. Now in all this, according to Copernicus, sight is deceived in this very clear perception, because the motion is not as straight as it seems, but is a mixture of rectilinear and circular.

> SALVIATI: This is the first objection raised by Aristotle and Ptolemy, and by all their disciples. This has been answered in full and has been shown to be a paralogism. It has been clearly illustrated how the movement that is common to us and to other mobiles is [for us] as if it had not been.[67]

It is a question of a mechanical relativity that adds something to the simple optical relativity of the displacement of a boat along a shore, a fact known and commented on since antiquity. Aristotle understood the optical relativity of displacements so well that he attributed the scintillation of the stars to a trembling of the eye, which has difficulty in keeping its sight fixed on such a remote object.[68] Galileo states precisely that in the cabin of a boat that traverses the sea at constant velocity, there results no mechanical effect that could help passengers to determine whether they are in motion or at rest. He gives this particularly striking example: A Venetian merchant, en route from Venice to Alexandria and writing a letter in his cabin, moves his hand to form the letters in the same way as he would on dry land. Let us imagine for a moment that his hand had not participated in the movement of the boat: in order to form a single letter of the alphabet, it would have had to move an arms's length![69]

After reflections on motions caused by gravity and reflections on telescopic images formed in conditions of immensity, the consideration of the relativity of motions in inertial frames of reference and the consequences for the perception of mobility is the third of the themes that have contributed most to the advance of the Copernican cause and to the progressive transformation of Copernican astronomy into a new cosmology.

Urged by his friends, and in particular by his friends in Rome, Federico Cesi and Giovanni Ciampoli, to write a definitive version of *De systemate mundi*, Galileo finally set to work. But his health, which was from now on unsettled, put his initial enthusiasm under severe trial and the work dragged on from 1628 to 1629.

Scipion Chiaramonte, praised by Galileo in "The Assayer" for his position in the dispute over the comets, taught philosophy at Padua from 1627 to 1636, and reopened the Copernican debate. In two works he strove to save the Aristotelian thesis of the unalterability of the heavens by using syllogisms and risky astronomical demonstrations.[70] He went pell-mell at Tycho Brahe, Kepler, and Galileo. A single example of his syllogisms will suffice:

> If one admits the Copernican hypothesis of the mobility of the earth, three movements will be needed to explain it; now the earth, which is a simple body, cannot be activated by a threefold movement; the hypothesis of Copernicus should therefore be rejected.[71]

More subtle but also fragile were the objections raised by Chiaramonte:

> If the earth does not occupy the center of the world [universe], the celestial vault should appear to us as dissymetric; and if the earth has an annual revolution about the sun, the stars should seem to suffer displacement relative to fixed bodies.

We have already seen how Galileo, basing himself on the Copernican premise of the immensity of the universe,

had demonstrated by a calculation of the parallaxes how the miniscule diameter of the earth's orbit around the sun relative to the earth's distance from the stars rendered imperceptible the consequences that one could properly draw from Copernican astronomy. Galileo expounds these results on the third day of the "Dialogue."

The intervention of Chiaramonte during the writing of the "Dialogue" was perhaps an inconvenience, burdening the composition of the work by several digressions, but it also had the advantage of renewing contacts between Galileo and Kepler. Kepler had sent Galileo a copy of his "Summary of Copernican Astronomy,"[72] but had found himself in disagreement with Galileo on the question of the comets. Always faithful in his friendships, Kepler defended the memory of his master Tycho Brahe against Chiaramonte in the *Hyperaspistes*,[73] in an appendix to which he dealt with the disputes that had set Galileo against Grassi. He anticipated that there would be no lack of occasions for Galileo to withdraw the praises he had bestowed on Chiaramonte. Mathias Bernegger, friend and correspondent of Kepler, who was to translate the "Dialogue" into Latin several years later, followed the progress being made in the writing of the work.

At Christmas 1629 Galileo informed Cesi that the "Dialogue" was practically complete. At that time he thought of giving it the title "Dialogue Concerning the Ebb and Flow of the Sea." A month previously, in a letter dated November 19, 1629, Galileo had consulted Giovanfrancesco Buonamici, a diplomat of the grand duke's on service in Spain, an expert in navigation, and moreover Galileo's distant relative by marriage:

> Because we are engaged in talking about marine matters, Monseigneur should know that I am on the point of concluding some dialogues in which I treat of the constitution of the universe, and among the principal themes I write about the ebb and flow of the sea, giving to understand that I have found the true cause of this effect—a cause far removed from that to which it has hitherto been attributed. I take it to be true, and so do all those with whom I have spoken about it. And because I do not have the leisure to set out on a voyage, and because an abundance of particular observations could confirm what I am expounding, I wish to beg Monseigneur to be kind enough to confer with someone who has done much navigation and who has had the curiosity to make some observations on the data of nature in the course of his navigations. In particular I wish to be assured of the truth of something that would very suitably confirm my thoughts—namely, whether it is true that while navigating on course to the West Indies between the tropics—that is, toward the equinoctial line, one finds a perpetual wind that blows from the levant and readily propels ships.[74]

From the evidence, Galileo was in the course of bringing complementary support to the physical proof that he drew from the tides, which he clung to because of the "geostrophic" explanation of the trade winds that he proposed. His theory of the trade winds is not entirely false, any more than is his theory of the tides; nevertheless the trade winds are only the secondary effect of a vast convection air current from the equator to the poles and from the poles to the equator. The question of the tides, moreover, imposed itself upon the attention of his contemporaries, and the Galilean explanation, as the letter to Buonamici shows, encountered rival explanations, that of Francis Bacon (1561-1626), for example, contained in the *Novum Organon* (1620), which incorporated the terminology of his own *De fluxu et refluxu maris* (of uncertain date), or that of the bishop of Spalato (Split), Marantonio de Dominis (1566-1624), in *Euripus sive sententia de fluxu et refluxu maris* (Rome, 1624).

Submitted to the Inquisitor of Florence, the manuscript of the "Dialogue" was sent to the Roman Inquisition, which entrusted its review to the master of the sacred palace, the Dominican Niccolò Riccardi, better known by his nickname Padre Mostro (Father Monster) bestowed upon him by the king of Spain, who was as impressed by his erudition as by his corpulence. Fr. Riccardi was not particularly prejudiced against Galileo. Benedetto Castelli, who kept Galileo informed as to all the transactions going on in Rome, wrote to him on February 26, 1628:

> In the presence of His Excellency Ascanio Piccolomini, I have spoken to Father Monster, endeavoring to get him to say what he thought about the opposition from Sarsi [the Jesuit Grassi]. He tells me that your opinions do not run directly counter to the faith, because they are simply philosophical, and that he would do all that you might have asked of him; but that he had not intended to make a public showing, in order to be able to help you on any occasion that might bring you irritations on the part of the Tribunal of the Holy Office, where he is a qualificator. In effect, if he spoke out prior to an official hearing, he would not be able to speak then. And he told me once more that on your account he had suffered some rough weather on the part of his colleagues.[75]

Things dragged on, which aroused mistrust on both sides. Galileo spent the months of May and June in Rome trying to obtain permission to have his work printed. At first he might well have believed that proceedings against him would come to nothing. Fr. Riccardi proposed revisions of matters of detail, which were nevertheless not insignificant, such as putting "the world" where Galileo had written "the universe"; modifying the title, which ought not to mention the tides, and above all, adding a preface in which he would recall the censure of the Copernican doctrine in 1616, and in which he would reaffirm his neutrality in expounding reasons for or against the Copernican sys-

tem. This was asking him to dance on a tightrope. But Galileo agreed. The proofs of the preface were submitted to Pope Urban VIII on July 31, 1630. The pope demanded that at the conclusion of the work there should figure argumentation as to the divine omnipotence, to which he attributed particular importance.

From then on, vicissitudes and setbacks followed each other in a headlong rush. Galileo passed through a difficult time. Physically depressed by persistent fever, he witnessed the sorrows of bereavement multiplying the gaps around him: on August 1, 1630, he lost his friend and protector, Federico Cesi; Kepler, his companion in the Copernican struggles, died in Regensburg on November 30 of the same year. Plague raged in Rome. At the Roman College, where all the Barberinis had studied, sentiments with regard to him had radically changed. The marked esteem of the times of Fathers Paolo Valla, Muzio Vitelleschi, and Christopher Clavius had given way to a tenacious animosity against the one who had attacked the honor of the Society of Jesus. Galileo did not conceal the mistrust in which he held Fathers Scheiner, Grassi, and Cabeo:

> I believe that we will not witness greater subtleties than those to which the Reverend Fathers have accustomed us, subtleties that, in my opinion, are great trivialities in the matter of philosophy. In connection with this I hear it said that (*Rosa Ursini*) is having a long treatise *de maculis solis* printed in Bracciano; its length makes me suspect that it is full of blunders, which, by their infinite number, can truly blemish pages in which truth occupies only a small place.[76]

Having once more returned to Rome in the spring of 1631, Galileo lost his patience. Barely in possession of the imprimatur that Fr. Riccardi sent to him on April 25, on condition that the corrections be made to the text as foreseen, and that the "Dialogue" be printed in Rome, Galileo made a pretext of the danger of infection by the plague and took the manuscript to Florence where he had it printed in the Landini printery. It was a fatal mistake.

In February 1632 the first printed copies arrived in Rome. Taking advantage of a journey of the archbishop of Florence to the Holy Sea, Galileo entrusted to him two copies to transmit in homage. One of them was destined for Cardinal Francesco Barberini. The title of the work was "Dialogue . . . in which in the meetings of four days a dissertation is given on the two principal world systems, the Ptolemaic and Copernican, proposing indiscriminately the philosophical and natural reasons as much in favor of the one as of the other."[77]

Urban VIII was seized by extreme rage. The imprimatur was overruled and annulled. In August the Inquisition notified the Landini printery to suspend dissemination of the "Dialogue," and on September 23 a summons was served at Galileo's residence, requiring him to present himself without delay before the commissioner-general of the Holy Office, the Dominican Vincenzo Maculano. Galileo's first reaction was one of bewilderment: he procrastinated and excused himself on the basis of three medical opinions to the effect that he was unable to face the fatigue of the journey. The pope threatened him with a warrant for forcible transportation.

On February 13 Galileo arrived in a pitiable state in Rome, where, restricted to the premises of the Palace of the Holy Office, he was subjected to judicial interrogation (on April 12 and 30 and June 21). What were the chief points in the accusation? Essentially he was reproached with having disobeyed the formal precept enjoined on him in 1616. Galileo protested that he had received a simple warning, but Maculano, who was nevertheless not at bottom unfavorable to him, showed him the fateful unsigned draft of the formal precept. Galileo found himself in the humiliating position of one who has given reasons for doubting his good faith; and no survivor of what is conveniently called the "first trial" of 1616 was present to give witness. On the other hand, a commission of three theologians, Oregio, Inchofer, and Pasqualigo, submitted the conclusions of their report on April 17: the "Dialogue" was declared to contravene in every respect the decree emanating from the Congregation of the Index in 1616.

On June 22, in the hall of sessions of the Inquisition adjoining the Dominican priory of St. Mary Minerva, Galileo was ordered to abjure the Copernican theory, and was condemned to imprisonment accompanied by penitential practices. All remaining copies of the "Dialogue" were ordered to be destroyed. On the same day Galileo read on his knees the official formula of renunciation and signed it. On the next day he was placed under guarded residence in the Medici villa, home of the ambassador of the grand duke of Tuscany at Trinità dei Monti. The curtain fell on the tragic denouement of the Copernican cause.

Was it the case that Urban VIII who, as late as May 1631 had received Galileo in audience with great marks of "esteem and affection," had thought himself mocked? It has often been claimed that he was offended at finding his own words put into the mouth of Simplicius:

> Always keeping before the eyes of the spirit the very solid doctine that I learned from a very informed and most eminent person, and in which one should rest, I know that both of you [Salviati and Sagredo], to whomsoever may ask you if God in His infinite power and wisdom could have conferred upon the aquatic element the alternating movement that we observed, in a way other than

moving the receiver that contains it, I know, I say that you will reply that God could bring about and knows how to bring about this same effect in many ways, and even in ways unthinkable for our intellect.[78]

But it is not true that Simplicius was the dull and simple-minded interlocutor of whom the Dominican Tommaso Campanella wrote to Galileo: "He supplies the amusement in your philosophical comedy by showing at the same time the stupidity of his clique, its verbosity, instability, obstinacy, and all the rest."[79] Galileo loved sarcasm, but he always retained a sense of proportion, which often made him suspicious and reticent with regard to Campanella's opinions.

Urban VIII had explicitly demanded the insertion of the argument contained in the passage quoted in the conclusion of the whole "Dialogue." He was upset not because Galileo had twisted his thought, but because he recoiled sharply from the context that Galileo did not concede him convincing value. Could he yield on a point of this importance? The game was too decisive for him to back out. It was a matter of the autonomy of scientific knowledge relative to theology. For Galileo the explanation of the tides followed from reasoning *ex suppositione*: if the astronomy of Copernicus is true, then the tides are given a mechanical explanation, an explanation that is not only possible, but simple and easy, the most "natural" there could be. In a word it was a question of a physical proof, "experimental" (before the term was in use), based on a verifiable hypothesis.

For Urban VIII, who reasoned as a theologian, reasoning ex suppositione could arrive only at a plausible explanation, a "proof" of convenientia, congruity. But such a conclusion will never amount to apodictic proof. In his eyes it was presumptuous and strictly impious to claim to penetrate the designs of God in the constitution of the world by means of observation and explanation of a terrestrial phenomenon as limited as the tides of the ocean. One fact can only be the more or less probable token of another fact; only premises of universal validity can lead to rational necessity at the conclusion of a chain of reasoning.

Curiously, Urban VIII conducted his defense in the name of a nominalist theology, which speaks of divine wisdom only in order to make the point that the sole limit to divine power is that God cannot contradict the laws of metaphysics. Rational necessity can only be logical and *a priori*: any human experience whatsoever can serve to manifest it, but no human experience can condition it. Rational knowledge cannot therefore emerge from experimental science.

The Copernican cause emerged from the scene defeated. Galileo paid a heavy price in order that the autonomy of scientific research with regard to theological and metaphysical thought might be won definitively.

Today, no theologian or philosopher would seriously seek to put the matter in doubt.

From Copernican Astronomy to the New Cosmology

The recounting of the relationships of Galileo with the thought of Copernicus, in circumstantial detail, has been necessary to help the reader understand the slow maturing of a study program that gradually became a research program. In the work of Galileo the justification of Copernican astronomy led to the first program of scientific research in modern times. But it should not be forgotten that at no time in his career, not even at the most crucial and dramatic moment of the condemnation, did Galileo occupy his whole spirit, a very vast spirit, with the Copernican cause alone. The summons to appear before the tribunal of the Holy Office surprised him at a time when, worried by the lengthening shadows, he was engaged in the geometry of indivisibles, in the methodology of microscopic observations, in research on the resistance of solid bodies, corpuscular atomism, the nature of heat, and finally, a too often neglected aspect of his work, analysis of the perception of sensible qualities, in particular acoustic perception.

The thought of Galileo and that of Copernicus converge in the "Dialogue Concerning the Two Principal World Systems," a work that took more than twenty years to compose, as much time as Kant's *Critique of Pure Reason*. The "Dialogue," in its four days, has the solidity and complexity of works having undergone a protracted maturation. The first day dismantles the Aristotelian cosmos and designs a new world in which the frontiers between celestial and sublunar regions have been demolished.

The constitution of this world in motion is described on the second and third days. The second day demolishes, one after another, the four traditional objections lodged against the diurnal rotation of the earth from Ptolemy up to Tycho-Brahe: the perpendicular fall of heavy bodies, the identical ranges of artillery pieces in all directions, the everyday experience of the courses followed by clouds and flocks of birds, and the absence of the centrifugal effect observed in a turning wheel that throws off splashes of mud. Galileo showed that the anti-Copernicans would conclude only what they had already presupposed: they could not conceive the motility of the earth, because they did not know how to distinguish between active and passive motion, between the persistence and acquisition of motion.

The third day investigates why it is that the annual revolution of the earth around the sun in the immense universe of stars is imperceptible under ordinary condi-

tions, and under what experimental conditions it would be possible to make it perceptible.

The fourth day dwells on the physical proof drawn from the tides and the trade winds. Mechanically reinterpreting the traditional division of the elements into earth, water, and air, which corresponds to the phenomenology of sensible perception, Galileo shows that these three elements have different inertial behaviors in the composition of the earth's rotational motion with its motion of annual revolution, and that these differences are at the origin both of the periodic movements observed in the oceans, and the perpetual current in the atmosphere in equatorial and tropical regions.

The "Dialogue" is a difficult, intricate, and surprising work. Alexandre Koyré sees in it above all "a war machine against the traditional science and philosophy," and he pronounces this judgment:

> "The Dialogue Concerning the Two Principal Systems of the World" claims to expound two vital astronomical systems. But in fact it is not a book of astronomy or even physics. It is above all a critical book; or a work of polemic and combat. It is at the same time a pedagogical work. And finally, it is a book about history: "The history of the spirit of Signor Galileo."[80]

Drawing the consequences of his interpretation, Koyré reserves no place for Galileo in his now classic study, *La révolution astronomique*.[81] It is divided into three parts: (1) Copernicus and the cosmic upheaval; (2) Kepler and the new astronomy; (3) Borelli and celestial mechanics. Such a drastic position arouses perplexity and indignation from the Italian side. But did not Stillman Drake, of whom it is no exaggeration to say that he knows the "Dialogue" by heart, and often finds himself in disagreement with Koyré's interpretations, "go one better" when he says:

> Galileo's concern with theoretical astronomy was never very great. Even his battle for Copernicanism was conducted mainly on physical grounds, centering as it did on a mechanical theory of the tides and on the removal of some fancied physical objections to the movement of the earth. So far as his Dialogue is concerned, the Copernican theory was presented in the absurdly simple form, with the sun at the exact center of concentric circular orbits— a scheme which Copernicus himself had recognized as untenable, and which could never have been reconciled with any astronomical tables ever compiled.[82]

Nevertheless, such as it is, the "Dialogue" remains one of the major works of scientific literature of all time. Recent rereadings witness to this.[83] The "Dialogue" will always be a marvelous treatise of argumentative logic. With an extraordinary dialectical agility, Galileo, who on many occasions placed himself under the patronage of Socrates, demonstrates how frequently it is difficult for discursive thought to escape a *petitio principii*, and why this is the case. He shows how we often ought to conclude the opposite of what we are in fact concluding, if we interpret more exactly and coherently the premises from which we are commencing. Finally Galileo applied himself methodically to make sensible experience (*esperienze sensate*) go hand in hand with geometrical demonstrations (*ragioni necessarie*). Thus he defined the ideal of a new knowledge that finds it expression in a discourse that is at the same time rational and experimental.

The "Dialogue" will also remain the manual of proofs in favor of Copernican astronomy. It is wrong to claim that Galileo did not prove what he put forward, just as it is erroneous to maintain that the decisive proof of Copernicanism came only with the first observation of the annual parallax of a star by the astronomer Friedrich Bessel in 1837, and in the invention of the pendulum experiment by the physicist Léon Foucault in 1851. It is not even necessary to await Newton's discovery of the law of universal gravitation for the Copernican truth to be confirmed by observation. Stillman Drake is right to affirm that "stellar parallax is hardly more conclusive proof of the earth's annual motion than was Jupiter's shadow as used by Galileo, which latter is merely harder to explain to lay readers."[84]

I shall continue to revere the "Dialogue" because in it I find the manifesto of a new philosophy of nature. As Galileo clearly announced from the first pages of the first day, the "Dialogue" was destined to replace the *De caelo* of Aristotle. The real greatness of Galileo consists in transforming the astronomy of Copernicus into a new cosmology. He explains himself, and it is suitable to leave the last word to him, a word that has become the first word for all science:

> May it be our lot, by the grace of the true Son, pure and immaculate, to learn from Him, with all other truths, that which we are now seeking, blinded and groping our way as it were, about the other sun, material and covered with spots. . . .

> But it does not seem to me that we should despair of coming to understand the properties of bodies very far from us, which are no less comprehensible than the properties of bodies nearer to us; it is possible, in fact, that we could grasp the former more exactly than the latter.[85]

Abbreviations

EN, *Edizione Nazionale delle Opere di Galileo Galilei*, 20 vols., by Antonio Favaro, Isidoro Del Lungo,
and Umberto Marchesini (Florence, Giunti Berbera, 1890-1909; reprinted, 1929-1939). Cited here by volume and page (e.g., EN, VI, 199).

LCL, "Lettre à Christine de Lorraine, grande-duchesse de Tosçane" (EN, V, 309-48), French translation by François Russo, in *Galilée, aspects de sa vie et de son oeuvre* (PUF, 1968), pp. 331-59.

LS, Libero Sosio, editor, manual edition of Galileo's *Dialogo sopra i Massimi Sistemi del Mondo* (Turin, Einaudi, 1982).

PUF, Presses Universitaires de France, Paris.

Notes

[1] EN, VII, 154-55; LS, 158-59.

[2] Deceived by his memory, otherwise exceptionally good, the man Galileo calls Christian Wursteisen, was really named Christopher Wursteisen. A certain Christopher Wursteisen is in fact enrolled on the registers of the Faculty of Law of the University of Padua, for the date of November 5, 1595, whereas Christian Wursteisen from Basel, who died in 1588, never seems to have set foot in Padua. Rostock was the first European university in which Copernicanism was taught. In Peking, Copernicanism was taught at a very early date by Jesuit astronomers.

[3] B. L. Van der Waarden, "The Earliest Form of Epicycle Theory," *Journal of the History of Astronomy*, 5 (1974) 175-78: on the formation of the quadrivium, see particularly pp. 179-82.

[4] John of Holywood (Johannes de Sacro Bosco, in the Latin form of his name), who died in Paris in 1256, was the first to give a systematic presentation of the Ptolemaic system concerning the movements of the planets. His *Traité de la sphère* very soon became the scholastic manual of elementary cosmography. J. L. E. Dreyer comments of this in *A History of Astronomy from Thales to Kepler* (Cambridge University Press, 1906; numerous reprintings): "After the long undisputed reign of Pliny and of Martianus Capella, Ptolemy finally reached the first rank" (p. 233).

[5] The Barberini collection in the Vatican Library includes a manuscript copy of the *Traité de la Sphère* by Galileo (call number, 4.371).

[6] Florence, Giunti Barbèra, 20 volumes, 1890-1909; reprinted, 1929-1939.

[7] "*Ptolemäus*" (art. by B. L. van der Waerden) in Pauly-Wissowa, *Realencyklopädie der classischen Altertumswissenschaft*. See also Derek J. Price, *The Equatorie of the Planetis* (Cambridge University Press, 1955), pp. 93-117.

8 Stations and retrogradations are the apparent movements of the superior planets—that is, the planets whose orbits lie outside the annual orbit of the earth around the sun, when these movements are observed from the earth. As viewed from the earth, when a planet has the same celestial longtitude as the sun it is said to be in conjunction with the sun, and it then moves on the celestial sphere from west to east, in the same direction as the sun. On the contrary, whenever the celestial longitude of a planet differs by 180° from that of the sun, it is said to be in opposition to the sun; it then appears to move in retrograde direction of the celestial sphere—that is, from east to west, in the opposite direction to the movement of the sun.

9 Copernicus died in Frauenburg on May 25, 1543. On the very day of his death he received a copy of his work *De revolutionibus orbium celestium* that Joachim Rheticus had arranged to have printed at Nuremberg. See *Des révolutions des orbes célestes*, introduction, translation of the first ten chapters, with notes, by Alexandre Koyré (Paris, A. Blanchard, 1934; new impression, 1970).

10 EN, II, 198.

11 EN, XX, 67-68.

12 Carlo Maccagni, *Riscontri platonici relative alla matematica* in Galileo e Torricelli (Pisa, Domus Gelileiana).

13 EN, VII, 53-54; LS, 37-38.

14 Galileo Galilei: *On Motion and On Mechanics*, English translation by E. I. Drabkin and Stillman Drake (University of Wisconsin Press, 1960). "The Mechanics" was not published in Italy until 1649, under the title *Della scienza mecanica e delle utilità che si traggono di quella.*

15 Galileo Galilei, *Discorsi e dimostrazioni matematiche intorno a due Nuove Scienza attenenti alla meccanica e moi vimenti locali*, work published by the Elseviers of Leyden in 1638. See the annotated edition by A. Carugo and L. Geymonat (Turin, Boringhieri, 1958).

16 Stillman Drake, *Galileo at Work*, chap. 3, 2, pp. 36-37; idem, *Galileo Studies: Personality, Tradition and Revolution* (University of Michigan Press, 1970). chap. 10, "Galileo's Theory of the Tides," pp. 200-213.

17 Fra' Paolo Sarpi (1552-1623), *Scritti folosofici e teologici, editi ed inediti*, Romano Amerio, ed. (Bari, Laterza, 1951), Pensieri 569-71, p. 115.

18 Basing himself on the relativity of local motion, Descartes attached little importance to the movement of the earth rather than that of the sun, while placing the sun at the center of the planetary system and counting the earth among the planets. See *Les principes de la philosophie*, 3e partie, "Du monde visible," in particular chapters 11, 13, 15, 16, and 19. See also Léon petit "L'affaire Galilée vue par Descartes et Pascal," VIIᵉ siecle, 28 (1955) 231-39.

19 Drake, *Galileo Studies*, chap. 6, "Galileo, Kepler and their intermediaries," pp. 123-39.

20 *De revolutionibus*, book 1, chap. 9 (in Koyré, Des révolutions, p. 101).

21 Johannes Kepler, *Astronomia Nova, Gesammelte Werke*, under the direction of Walther von Dyke and Max Caspar (Munich), vol. 3 (1937). There one finds: gravity is "the mutual material tendency of bodies of similar nature to unite and join together."

22 *Ibid*. Kepler annotated the writing of his youth, *Somnium, seu Opus Posthumum de Astronomia Lunari*, an imaginary account of a voyage on the moon, which was published posthumously in 1634. In note 66 we read: "I define 'gravity' as a force of mutual attraction, similar to magnetic attraction. But the power of this attraction is greater for bodies close together than for bodies far apart. It follows that they show a greater resistance to separation when they are in the proximity of each other." See Kepler's *Somnium, The Dream or Posthumous Work on Lunar Astronomy*, translated and annotated by Edward Rosen (University of Wisconsin Press, 1967), p. 71.

23 Kepler, *Astronomia Nova*, p. 25. He adds: "Supposing that the lunar matter had the same density as terrestrial matter, then the earth would climb toward the moon by a 54th part of their distance of separation, while the moon would descend toward the earth by the remaining 53 parts of the separation."

24 The first time we meet with the term "satellite," in print, is in the "Account of the Proper Observations of Four Satellites of Jupiter" written by Kepler and signed September 11, 1610. Some months previously, on May 3, Kepler had sent to Galileo his *Dissertatio cum Sidereo Nuntio* ("conversation with the celestial messenger"), in which he indifferently designated the Medici stars by the expressions "circumjovial planets" or "satellites of Jupiter." See "Kepler's Conversation with Galileo's Sidereal Messenger," first complete translation, with notes and introduction, by Edward Rosen, in *The Sources of Science* (New York and London, 1965), p. 76-77.

25 EN, VII, 486; LS, 545-46. The text of the *Somnium* alludes to oceanic tides on the moon. Kepler annotates this passage as follows: "It is matter of a probable conjecture that has not received a complete proof. Ex-

perienced mariners say that ocean tides are higher when the luminaries (the sun and moon) are in syzygy (conjunction or opposition) rather than in quadrature. The causes of the oceanic tides thus seem to be the attraction of the waters of the ocean by the sun and the moon. The earth, of course, similarly attracts its own waters, and we call this attraction 'gravity'. What then hinders us from saying that the earth equally attracts the lunar waters as the moon attracts the terrestrrial waters?" (note 22 to the *Somnium*, p. 123).

[26] Drake, *Galilean Studies*, chap. 11, "The Fall and Uniform Acceleration," pp. 214-40.

[27] EN, VII, 37; LS, 53-54: "Motion along a horizontal line, neither ascending nor descending, is circular motion about a center: circular motion will therefore not come about naturally without a preceding rectilinear motion, but once it is established it will continue perpetually with a uniform speed."

[28] Members of Fr. Mersenne's circle extensively discussed the axioms and conclusions expounded by Beaugrand in his *Géostatique* (1636). During a journey to Italy in 1635, he had met Bonaventura Cavalieri and Benedetto Castelli and had informed them of the work of Pierre Fermat. The "geostatic debate," forgotten today, had as its aim the confrontation of the purely geometric with the purely physical definition of verticality and horizontality. It was born from the rereading of the treatises by Archimedes, "On Floating Bodies" and "On the Equilibrium of Planes." The two principal questions debated were: (1) How to affirm that all vertical lines are parallel if they all converge to the center of the earth?, and (2) How to accommodate the horizontal plane to the terrestrial surface, if the latter is spherical?

Roberval and Descartes, disagreeing on everything else, were in agreement on rejecting Beaugrand's position, which returned to the view of or according precedence to the physical or "geostatic" definition over the geometric definition, to the point of distinguishing between the theory of balances of small dimensions and the theory of balances of large dimensions. Nevertheless Beaugrand at least had the merit of drawing attention to the problem of whether a body always had the same weight, no matter what its distance from the center of the earth, by asking if the same mass would act in an identical fashion if directly attached to a balance arm or if suspended at the end of a long string.

On the question of circular inertia in the thought of Galileo, one can consult Drake, *Galilean Studies*, chap. 13, "The Case against Circular Inertia," pp. 257-78.

[29] EN, VIII, 260-61; LS, 284-86.

[30] Vasco Ronchi, *Il cannochiale di Galilei e la scienza del Seicento* (Turin, Boringhieri, 1958) 2nd ed. Ed-

ward Rosen, *The Naming of the Telescope* (New York, 1947). First called perspicillium, the instrument was publicly named "telescope" on April 14, 1611, according to Rosen. Geronimo Sirturi reported several pieces of information connected with the invention of the telescope in his work entitled precisely *Telescopium* (Frankfurt, 1618).

[31] In 1655 Christian Huygens (1629-1695) was to discover Titan, a satellite of Saturn, together with a thin ring around the main planet (Nouvelles observations des satellites de Saturne, 1656). In addition, he explained the appearances of Saturn, observed by Galileo, by the phases of the ring inclined at 31 degrees to the plane of the ecliptic. In fact, the plane of the ring is inclined at 28 degrees to Saturn's orbital plane, which is in turn at an angle of 2 degrees 30 minutes to the ecliptic plane.

[32] Stillman Drake, "Galileo and Satellite Prediction," *Journal for the History of Astronomy*, 10/28 (June 1979); idem, in collaboration with Charles T. Kowal, "Galileo's Observations of Neptune," *Nature*, 287/5780 (Sept. 25 1980).

[33] Letter of Galileo to Giuliano de'Medici, ambassador to the grand duke of Tuscany in Prague, dated January 1, 1611; EN, XI, 11-12.

[34] EN, XI, 105.

[35] *Ibid.*

[36] Letter of April 27, 1611, to Kepler from Martin Horky, author of the *Brevissima Peregrinatio contra Nuncium Sidereum* (Modena, 1610).

[37] EN, VII, 363-67; LS, 401-5.

[38] EN, VII, 387; LS, 429.

[39] *Ad Vitellionem Paralipomena, quibus Astronomiae Pars Optica traditur*, Frankfurt, 1604.

[40] See the review by Prof. Giorgio Tabarroni in *Physis*, 9 (1967) 253, of the article by Edward Rosen, "Galileo and Kepler: Their First Two Contacts," *Isis*, 57 (1966).

[41] *Dioptrice, seu Demonstratio eorum quae visui et visibilibus propter Conspicilla non ita pridem inventa accidunt* (Augsburg, 1611).

[42] Copernicus, *De revolutionibus orbium caelestium*, I, 6, in fine (ed. Alexandre Koyré, p. 84). It was only in 1837 that the astronomer Bessel succeeded in determining by telescopic observation at the observatory of Königsberg the annual parallax of a star. The star was 61 Cygni and its parallax measured 0". 294. The near-

est star to the earth is Proxima Centauri and its annual parallax measures 0". 764.

[43] *Sidereus Nuncius, magna longeque admirabilia spectacula pandens, suspiciendaque proponens unicuique, praesertim vero philosophia atque astronomia, quae a Galileo Galilei . . . perspicilli nuper a se reperti beneficio sunt observata in Lunae facie, fixis innumeris, Lacteo Circulo, Stellis Nebulosis, apprime vero in quatuor Planetis circa Iovis Stellam . . . atque Medicea Sidera numcumpandos decrevit* (Venice, Tomaso Baglioni, 1610).

[44] *Dissertatio cum Nuncio Sidereo nuper ad mortales misso a Galileo Galilei* (Prague, 1610). The Latin *nuntius* can be translated either "message" or messenger." Whereas Galileo addresses his "starry message" to the House of Medici and to the world, Kepler replies to him by praising the "Starry Messenger."

[45] EN, X, 348-53.

[46] *Istoria e Dimostrazioni intorno alle Macchie Solari e loro accidenti comprese in tre lettere scritte all'Ill.mo Sig. Marco Velseri Linceo dal Sig. Galileo Galilei Linceo* (Rome, Giacomo Macardi, 1613).

[47] The fact is reported much later in the *Lettere inedite di Uomini Illustri of Angelo Fabroni (Florence*, 1773-1775), I, p. 47. The diatribes of Frs. Caccini and Lorini were probably inspired by the first refutation of Copernican astronomy, by the Dominican Giovanni M. Tolosoni. See I. S. Camporeale, O.P., "Umanesimo e Teologia tra' 400 e 500," *Memorie Domenicane*, new series, 8-9 (1977-1978), 414-16.

[48] The play on words in the exclamation cited in the previous reference, referring to the Acts of the Apostles 1:11, is perhaps again to be found in the poem composed by Thomas Seggeth, inserted in the *Narratio de observatis a se quatuor Jovis satellibus of Johannes Kepler* (Frankfurt, 1611; reprinted in Florence in the same year). In writing "O Galilean, you have conquered the heavens," Seggeth could also have been thinking about the exclamation of the Emperor Julian the Apostate: "Thou hast won, Galilean!" One finds an allusion of the same nature in the letter of Bartolomeo Imperiali to Galileo, March 21, 1626 (EN, XIII, 314).

[49] Giorgio de Santillana, *The Crime of Galileo* (University of Chicago Press, 1955), chap. 7, "The Decree of Interdiction"; idem; "Nuove ipotesi sul processo di Galileo," in *Saggi su Galileo Galilei raccolti e pubblicati a cura di Carlo Maccagni* (publication of the National Committee for the Celebrations of the Fourth Centenary of the Birth of Galileo (Florence, G. Berbèra, 1972) pp. 474-87.

[50] The decree of condemnation made a distinction between the astronomical hypothesis and its theological interpretation. Works such as those of the Carmelite Paul Foscarini, which proposed a reconciliation of Copernican astronomy with the biblical picture of the world, were proscribed and ordered to be destroyed. *The Commentaire du Livre de Job*, of the Augustinian Diego de Zuñiga, which gave favorable mention of the doctrines of Copernicus, had its dissemination suspended "until correction" of the incriminating passages. Copernicus's work fell under this latter kind of censure. The difference between the qualification of the correctors of the Holy Office and the decree of the censure of the Congregation of the Index of proscribed books is doubtless echoed in the report given by G. F. Buonamici in his *Journal*: "Paul V was of the opinion that it was necessary to declare the work of Copernicus to be contrary to the faith, whereas Cardinals Caetani and Maffeo Barberini openly opposed the pope, who ended by coming over to their good reasons" (EN, XV, 3).

[51] This interpretation is to be found in Appendix A of the English version of the book by Ludovico Geymonat, *Galileo Galilei* (Turin, Einaudi, 1957); transl. by Prof. S. Drake, New York, 1965). Appendix B gives the reply by Giorgio de Santillana (pp. 221-25).

[52] Fourteen manuscript copies, of which twelve date back to the 17th century, of the "Discourse" published in vol. 5 of the Edizione Nazionale, pp. 371-95, are preserved to this day. The Barberini collection in the Vatican Library contains one of them (MS 4271).

[53] EN, VII, 487, LS, 546.

[54] William A. Wallace, O. P., *Prelude to Galileo: Essays on Medieval and Sixteenth-Century Sources of Galileo's Thought* (Hingham, Mass., D. Reidel Publ. Co., 1981), part 3, chap. 8, "Galileo and Reasoning ex suppositione," pp. 129-60.

[55] EN, VII, 372-73; LS, 412-20. The passage cited is found EN, VII, 379; LS, 419.

[56] O. Neugebauer, *The Exact Sciences in Antiquity* (Providence, R. I., 2nd ed., 1957), 82. A remarkably clear and simple exposition of the theory of epicycles is to be found in 64.

[57] Ibid., 77.

[58] Ibid., 54.

[59] EN, VII, 450-51; LS, 503.

[60] Orazio Grassi, S. J., *De tribus cometis Disputatio astronomica publice habita in Collegio Romano Societatis Jesu ab uno ex patribus eiusdem Societatis* (Rome, Jacopo Mascardi, 1619).

[61] See the celebrated essay of Erwin Panofsky, "Galileo as a Critic of the Arts," *Isis*, 47 (1956) 3-15. The author points out "the Galilean presupposition, in conformity with classicism, in favor of simplicity, of order, and of separation of genres, and on the contrary his opposition to complication, disorder, and any form of fusion" (p. 9). It has often been noted that Galileo preferred Aristotle to Tasso.

[62] *Discorso delle Comete di Mario Guiducci, fatto de lui nell' Accademia fiorentina nel suo medesimo consolato* (Florence, 1619), reproduced in the Edizione Nazionale, vol 6.

[63] *Libra astronomica ac philosophica, qua Gallilaei Galilaei opiniones da cometis a Mario Giudiccio in Florentina Academia expositae, atque in lucem nuper editae, examinaretur a Lothario Sarsi Sigensano* (Perugia, Marco Naccarini, 1619). Lothario Sarsio Sigensano represents the anagram of Horatio Grassio Savonensi. The anagram is imperfect, because instead of a "v" there is an "l," which caused Fr. Grassi's adversaries to say that he did not come from "Savona" but from "Salona," known for its buxom women.

[64] *Il Saggiatore, nel quale con bilancia esquisita e giusta si ponderano le cose contenute nella libra astronomica e filosofica di Lotario Sarsi Sigensano, scritto in forma di lettere all' Ill.mo et Rever.mo Mons.re D. Virginio Cesarini, Acc.o Linceo . . .* (Rome, Giacomo Mascardi, 1623; EN, VI, 197-312). The saggiatore is the goldsmith's scales, which serve to weigh ounces of gold and carats of precious stones, and which is therefore much more precise than the cruder steelyard.

[65] *Discorso al Seren.mo don Cosimo II, Gran Duca di Tuscana, intorno alle cose che stanno in sù l'acqua, o che in quella si muovono* (Florence, Cosimo Giunti, 1612; EN, IV, 57-141).

[66] *Lettera a Franceso Ingoli in risposta alla Disputatio de situ et quiete Terra*, 1624 e (EN, VI, 509-61); the text of the *Disputatio of Ingoli* is to be found in EN, V, 397-412.

[67] EN VII, 273; LS, 301.

[68] Aristotle, De caelo, book 2, 8.

[69] EN, VII, 197-98; LS, 210-11.

[70] Scipion Chiaramonte (1565-1652), *Antitycho* (Cesena, 1621); *De tribus novis stellis quae annis 1572, 1600, 1604 comparuere . . .* (Cesena, 1628).

[71] Cited as a note by Libero Sosio, in his edition of the "Dialogue," LS, 300.

[72] Johannes Kepler, *Epitome Astronomiae Copernicanae, Libri I, II, III, de Doctrina Sphaerica* (Linz, 1618);

Liber IV, *Physica Coelestis* (Linz, 1620); Libri V, VI, VII, *Doctrina Theorica* (Frankfurt, 1621).

[73] *Tychonis Brahei Dani Hyperaspistes adversus Scipionis Claramontii Anti-Tychoneum* (Frankfurt, 1625). It was a Baroque title: aspistes is a soldier furnished with a buckler. It should thus be translated: The unconquerably armed defender of Tycho-Brahe against the Anti-Tycho of Scipion Chiaramonte."

[74] Letter of Galileo to Gianfrancesco Buonamici, dated from Florence, November 19, 1629 (EN, XIV, 54). Buonamici (1592-1669) in the course of 1629 had become an in-law of Galileo after Vincenzo, Galileo's son, had married his stepsister, Sestilia Bocchimeri. A diplomat in the service of the grand duke of Tuscany, he was at that time posted to Madrid. He should not be confused with Francesco Buonamici (1535-1613), Aristotelian professor at Pisa and author of a work *De motu* (Florence, 1591).

In his reply dated February 1, 1630, Buonamici directed Galileo to consult the observations of Lodovico Guicciardini and Antonio Herrera.

[75] Letter of Benedetto Castelli to Galileo, February 26, 1628 (EN, XIII, 393-94). On the personality of Fr. Riccardi, see A. K. Eszer, O. P., "Niccolò Riccardi, O. P., il Padre Mostro (1585-1639)," *Angelicum*, 60 (1983) 3, 428-61.

[76] Letter of Galileo to Cesare Marsili, April 21, 1629 (EN, XIV, 35-36).

[77] *Dialogo di Galileo Galilei Linceo, Matematico sopraordinario dello Studio di Pisa e Filosofo e Matematico primario del Serenissimo Gr. Duca di Toscana, dove ne i congressi di quattro giornate si discorre sopra i due Massimi Sistemi del Mondo, Tolemaico e Copernicano; proponendo indeterminatamente la ragioni folosofiche e naturali tanto per l'una, quanto per l'altra parte* (Florence, Gio. Battista Landini, 1632).

The Latin translation by Matthias Bernegger, in Augsburg in 1635, after the condemnation of 1633, carried on its frontispiece a quotation from Seneca: *Inter nullos magis quam inter Philosophos esse debet aequa libertas.*

[78] EN, VII, 488; LS, 548. It must be conceded that Maffeo Barberini (Pope Urban VIII) was quite logical in his thinking: he sought to uphold in theological argument, to which he so closely held, the distinction between astronomic hypotheses and theological interpretation, a distinction that he had defended in 1616 (see note 50, above). At the time of the condemnation, before Francesco Niccolini, ambassador of the grand duke in Rome and an in-law of Fr. Riccardi, he again

alluded to "these difficulties from which we have preserved him [Galileo], since the time we became a cardinal." But what would science have been if it had always to leave the last word to theology? There cannot be true science without the autonomy of science: this was the conviction that gave meaning and significance to the Galilean struggle.

79 Letter from Campanella to Galileo, August 5, 1632 (EN,XIV, 366-67). In the same letter there is to be found: "We certainly have nothing for which to envy Plato. Salviati is a great Socrates who reveals much more than he conceals. As to Sagredo, there is a free intelligence, one not spoiled by the schools and judging all things with much sagacity."

80 Alexandre Koyré, *Estudes Galiléennes* (Paris, Hermann, 1966), p. 212. In the same passage, Koyré explains his point of view: "As to the new physics, mathematical, Archimedean, Galileo well knew that its establishment necessitated a recasting and rebuilding of all its concepts; and that it was necessary to base it, as solidly as possible, on a *philosophy*. Hence the subtle admixture in the Galilean work of 'science' and 'philosophy', and the impossibility for the historian—short of giving up the attempt to understand—of separating the two unifying elements of his thought."

81 Alexandre Koyré, *La Révolution astronomique: Copernic, Kepler, Borelli (Paris, Hermann, 1961). Gianalfonso Borelli* (1608-1679) was one of the principal Galileans of the generation following the death of the master. He belonged to the famous Accademia del Cimento, founded and protected by the Grand Duke Ferdinand II and above all by his brother, Prince Leopold. Active in the years 1657 to 1667, he is mainly known for the *Saggi di Naturali Esperienze* (Florence, 1667), which recounts his works.

82 Stillman Drake. "Galileo's 'Platonic' Cosmology and Kepler's Prodromus," *Journal for the History of Astronomy*, 4/3 (1973) 173-91; the passage quoted is on p. 174. Galileo had no deep knowledge of Copernicus's texts. See Edward Rosen, "Galileo's Mis-Statements about Copernicus," *Isis*, 49 (1959) 319-30.

83 William Shea, *Galileo's Intellectual Revolution* (London, MacMillan, 1972); Maurice A. Finnochiaro, *Galileo and the Art of Reasoning* (Hingham, Mass., D. Reidel Publ. Co., 1980); Stillman Drake, "The Organizing Theme of the Dialogue," lecture delivered at a colloquium organized by the Lincean Academy, on the occasion of the 350th anniversary of the publication of the "Dialogue," May 6 and 7, 1982.

84 Stillman Drake, "Ptolemy, Galileo, and Scientific Method," *Studies in History and Philosophy of Science*, 9/2 (June 1978) 99-115; the passage quoted is on p. 115.

85 Galileo, *Istoria e Dimostrazioni intorno alle Macchie Solari*; the passage quoted is to be found in the third letter (EN, V, 187).

Hans Blumenberg (essay date 1987)

SOURCE: "The Theoretician as 'Perpetrator'" in *The Genesis of the Copernican World*, The MIT Press, 1987, pp. 264-89.

[*In the following essay, Blumenberg discusses the metaphors of revolution and violence that have characterized assessments of Copernican cosmology through the years.*]

On the base of the Copernicus monument in Torun stands this inscription: *Terrae Motor Solis Caelique Stator* [Mover of the Earth and Stayer of the Sun and the Heavens]. The kings of Prussia had owed the monument to Copernicus for a long time. On 12 August 1773—that is, in the year of the astronomer's 300th birthday—Frederick the Great had made this promise in a letter to Voltaire. The only small blemish in this for the king was that the year before, in the first partition of Poland, of all towns the town of Copernicus's birth had escaped him.[7] It was still more than half a century after the third partition of Poland before the monument could be erected in Torun. One of the bitter witnesses of political developments after 1848, Karl August Varnhagen von Ense, saw Friedrich Tieck's sculpture in Berlin, before it was shipped, in 1852, and noted in his diary, "Saw the colossal bronze statue of Copernicus, which is to go to Torun, in the Münzstrasse. Broad, ponderous, devoid of expression. . . ."[8]

The inscription on Tieck's monument has, one might think, precisely the "fine, grand ring to it" that Droysen, in the same century, considered characteristic of the linguistic formations of his time. But the formula does not belong to the lofty style of the nineteenth century. The metaphors of the 'perpetrator' can be followed back to close to Copernicus's time, and, with a characteristic interchange of subjects, right to Copernicus's own writing.

At first the image of Copernicus the 'perpetrator' who stops the heavens and puts the Earth in motion seems to be a rhetorical element in the polemics against Copernicanism, in connection with which the important thing is not so much the kind of changes made in the world construction as rather the act of overthrow and the forcibleness of its intervention. The Jesuit Melchior Inchofer, who participated as a consultant in the proceedings against Galileo, composed an accusation against the Copernicans—designated as "neo-Pythagoreans"—whom he characterizes as *terrae motores et solis statores* [movers of the Earth and stayers of the Sun].[9] The designation of Copernicus's adherents as Pythagoreans is meant to evoke the odium of a heretical sect and may indeed have succeeded in conveying that impression, whereas a century earlier, when Copernicus himself appealed to the Pythagoreans, as a Renaissance gesture, he could count instead on goodwill.

The formula of abjuration that was imposed on Galileo in 1633 contains not only the antithesis of rest and motion but also an emphasis on the central position: " . . . ut omnino desererem falsam opinionem, quae tenet Solem esse centrum mundi et immobilem, et terram non esse centrum ac moveri" [that I must altogether abandon the false opinion that the Sun is the center of the world and immovable, and that the Earth is not the center of the world, and moves]. In contrast to this double definition of Copernicanism's "false opinion," the demonizing description concentrates on making the exchange of the predicates of rest and motion appear not only as a transaction within theory but also as a criminal deed. The consequence of this prominent linguistic and metaphorical appearance is that the event is moralized.

In his satire *Ignatius His Conclave* of 1611, John Donne sketched a vision of hell in the course of which Copernicus, together with other audacious revolutionaries, appears before Lucifer and obstreperously beats on the doors of Hell. In an ironical lament he complains over the fact that these gates should remain shut against one to whom the mysteries of the heavens were open and who had been able to give the Earth motion, as though he were a soul to it. Should these gates—Copernicus complains—be open to small innovators but resist him, who had reversed the frame of the world and had thereby almost become its new Creator?[10]

Even if it is just as suitable for disparaging as for heroizing, the formula of the theoretician as the perpetrator who makes the Sun stand still and the Earth move could still be mere rhetoric. But even what one describes so contemptuously precisely as "mere rhetoric" speculates on the thoroughly real pregiven potential of its audience, which either is or can be filled with fears about the dependability of what it stands on, or with admiration for the daring of the performer. Perhaps the triumph of Copernicanism, as it was to be expressed on the nineteenth-century monument [in Torun], was only secure and unambiguous when, with the domestication of comets in the astronomical system, the connection between motion and uncertainty was dissolved. Until then one could also appeal to people's fears in order to make Copernicus's violation of the sanction of geocentrism appear not only dogmatic but also inhuman.

One is given grounds for wondering about the assumption that the formula represents mere rhetorical or poetical exaggeration by the fact that Galileo, when he sets out in the Second Day of his *Dialogue on the Two Chief World Systems* to deal with the emotional resistance to Copernicanism, sees its source in the fact that the more or less naive onlooker at the change in astronomy confuses the inversion that takes place in the assertions of theory with the real unrest of the ground under his feet, which he now imagines that he feels. Galileo is referring to the objection (already brought forward by Ptolemy) against the rotation of the Earth that rocks and animals would have to be flung toward the stars by the centrifugal force that would arise, and that no mortar could keep a building connected to its foundation while it was under this influence. Engaging in a certain amount of hairsplitting, in his dialogue Galileo makes Salviati point out that Ptolemy's argumentation already presupposes the existence of animals, people, and buildings on the Earth, so as to discuss the effects that the Earth's motion would have on them, whereas after all the preexisting motion of the Earth would not permit the existence of animals, people, and buildings in the first place if Ptolemy's assumption were correct. So the opposing argumentation would have to assume that the Earth at first stood still, so as to allow those things to be formed in reality and to colonize the Earth, and that a cosmological reformer (the talk is always of Pythagoras) then set it in motion.

More important in this context is what Salviati says about an observation that he has been able to make a thousand times, and not without amusement. Almost everyone, when they heard for the first time of the thesis that the Earth moves, had the impression, which they received with a shock, that the Earth's millenniums-long rest had been converted into motion for the first time by this assertion "of Pythagoras." As though reality itself obeyed the decree of the theoretician: " . . . quasi che, dopo averla egli tenuta immobile, scioccamente pensi, allora, e non prima, essersi ella messa in moto, quando Pitagora o chi altro si fusse il primo a dir che ella si muoveva" [as if such a person, after having held it to be motionless, foolishly imagined it to have been set in motion when Pythagoras (or whoever it was) first said that it moved, and not before].[11] And (so Salviati continues his report of his observations) not only uneducated and superficial people (uomini vulgari e di senso leggiero) had this silly idea that the Earth, from its creation up to the time of Pythagoras, had stood still and had only been put in motion by him—even Aristotle and Ptolemy had not escaped such childishness (incorsi in questa puerizia).

Even against the doubts of his partner in the dialogue, Sagredo, Salviati insists on his suggestion that the arguments against the motion of the Earth assumed as resulting phenomena things that could only occur if the Earth, having previously been at rest, were suddenly forced by a violent action to rotate. It should not be forgotten that Galileo held to the idea of circular motion as a "natural motion," and thus at bottom still availed himself of the argument, which was discovered by Copernicus himself, that what is natural cannot have destructive effects, and the motion of the Earth is, precisely, natural. It could be a "violent" motion only if at some time it had had a beginning. So Copernicus cannot be described as a perpetrator, precisely because that would have implied what the Copernicans had been charged with, as an objection to the motion of the Earth.

Apocalyptic fears—even those that are connected with the actions of the intraworldly agent of scientific innovation—are counteracted by means of the concept of nature and its unconditional reliability. As the appearance of what is essential, it is immutability. In relation to its object, knowledge of nature is subject to the condition that innovations put it in the wrong. Copernicus himself knew that the suspicion of a mania for innovation would burden his work more heavily than its difference in content from the traditional cosmology and its geocentric pattern, and also more than the difficulties with individual Bible texts. An appeal to the immutability of nature was one of the strongest means of argument in the Renaissance. It is even the assumption underlying the literary reaching back to the texts of antiquity. It ensured the possibility not only of reading and understanding the newly accessible writings of the ancients but also of assuring oneself of their validity, as though they had been written in the present.

Machiavelli had given expression to this ahistoricism during Copernicus's lifetime in the *Discorsi sopra la prima decade di Tito Livio* [*Discourses on the First Decade of Livy*] (1513), when he writes that imitation of the ancients in law as well as in medicine and in politics depends upon the immutability of nature. This holds, he says, in opposition to those who regarded such imitation as anachronistic—as though the heavens, the Sun, the elements, and men were different in their motion, their order, and their power from what they had been in antiquity.[12]

This language contains an elementary realism of metaphors—a constitutive confusion of reality with the way in which it is apprehended. There is no awareness of the fact that the immutability of nature does not of itself legitimize the immutability of our ideas of it. The screening off of this objection is one of the preconditions—which are difficult to get at—of the not merely rhetorical identification of making a change in theory with making a change in reality. Depriving the revolution that theory inflicts on the object, nature, of its plausibility and probability from the very beginning had the fundamental character of self-preservation. Theory is subjected to the criterion of the characteristics of its object, so that even a reformer with Coper-

nicus's genuinely conservative discretion lays himself open to the metaphor of violent action. The reproach that Copernicus overturned the whole order of nature in order to preserve his hypothesis[13] is serious enough, independently of the actual changes contained in his system. As long as people held to the dependence of all human ideas of order on nature, they could not admit that man could act and could succeed, theoretically and technically, 'against nature.'

Carried over to the dimension of time, this is the Stoics' idea of the *consensus omnium* [consensus of everyone] as the teleologically founded mark of truth—a mark that only the Enlightenment thinkers will come to regard as a mere appearance. Copernicus knew what he was saying when he wanted to make his daring undertaking plausible to Paul III: He had risked it, he says, both against the received opinion of the experts and also *propemodum contra communem sensum* [almost against common sense], after he had realized that the astronomers had no consistent tradition (*mathematicas sibi ipsis non constare*). The consensus of common sense could only be invalidated by the 'dissensus' of the professionals.[14] Undoubtedly Copernicus's strongest, even though highly indirect, effect was that he broke the natural guarantee of the consensus; but in order to be able to break it he could not escape the odium of one who forcibly violated what it vouched for.

In Galileo's dialogue—to return to it once more—he tries to find the root of the defensive reaction against Copernicus in a realism of metaphor. In the antique costume of the shock supposedly produced by Pythagoras, the contemporaries' emotional resistances are presented. More important than this costuming, however, is the argumentative advantage arising from the fact that the ancient philosopher's analogous role as 'perpetrator' makes it possible to present Aristotle and Ptolemy as theorists who already represent this emotional resistance. They are not systematizers of an authentic geocentrism founded on the common sense of the life-world; instead they are the prototypes of reactive shock. This trick makes hostile Scholasticism appear as a secondary formation of all-too-human fears in the face of the painfulness of an old truth. The tradition that Copernicus's opponents defend as though it were an original revelation is only, for its part, the result of the intolerability of Pythagoras for the authoritative figures of the system of cosmological dogma. On this assumption, the conflict appears not to be tied to biblical and Christian premises. It is reduced to a more general need for cosmic security. It is of course human to oppose Copernicus's demand, but for that very reason it is not specifically Christian.

We have before us here an excellent example of the basic pattern of modern 'paratheories' in which, for a given system of assertions, one is immediately provided also with the explanation of why this system is bound to attract the opposition of its contemporaries. Only from the perspective of Galileo does one perceive how dexterously and appropriately Copernicus had argued when he took the 'natural' character of the Earth's motion as his point of departure. Galileo's parrying of the assertions about the ruinous consequences of the Earth's motion is directed precisely at showing that this objection would only hold in relation to a *motus violentus* [violent motion]—that is, only if (expressed in Christian terms) the Earth's motion had not been set going immediately at the time of the Creation. The introduction of the concept of creation simplifies the argument once again, since everything that is posited with this divine act is eo ipso 'natural,' however 'violent' this act of God's may happen to be represented, linguistically, as being.

Without its being explicitly mentioned, Galileo's argument is also directed against the anti-Copernican objections that appeal, with Luther and others, to the standstill of the Sun in the book of Joshua. If Copernicus had only asserted something that was supposed to have proceeded naturally and regularly since the beginning of the world, this seems like the lesser demand on the human power of comprehension, in comparison to the violent deed of cosmic dimensions that had taken place when the Sun stood still over the battlefield of Gibeon.

This biblical passage, which was to achieve a certain melancholy fame in the course of the Inquisition's proceedings against Copernicanism, had never had any prominent importance before Luther referred to it against the fool, Copernicus. One will have to understand the slight pleasure taken by the exegetes in this great miracle as a result not least of all of the fact that this sort of divine display did not fit the alliance of biblical theology with antiquity's cosmos metaphysics very well.

After the disappointment of the earliest eschatological expectations, which were able to repress all secular conformism, the proclamation of the Christian gospel turned out to have an elementary interest in ridding itself of any suspicion of hostility toward the cosmos and its security. For a long time Christianity remained sensitive to the reproach that by its original eschatology it epitomized unreliability and irresponsibility in relation to the continued existence of the world, and that by its belief in miracles it was permeated by an inclination toward the catastrophic disordering of natural courses of events. And it is in fact in such a context—however surprising it may sound—that the formula of the standstill of the heavens and the motion of the Earth is used for the first time.

Without presenting a cosmological assertion, as such, Tertullian (around the turn from the second to the third

century A.D.) grimly formulates the animosity of the persecutors of Christianity as their supposed right of self-defense against the Christian promoters of chaos who are intent on the end or at least the confusion of the world: " . . . si caelum stetit, si terra movit, si fames, si lues, statim: Christianos ad leonem acclamatur!" [. . . if the heavens have stood still, if the Earth has moved, if there is famine or plague, the cry is immediately: To the lion with the Christians!][15] The alliance with a metaphysics that seemed to ensure the reliability of the world to such an extent that it made the Bible's catalogue of signs of the coming of the apocalypse into an enumeration of perceptual illusions more than of real possibilities was finally able to reverse the direction of confrontation in such a way that Copernicus and his followers are pushed, or are meant to be pushed, into the role of the early Christians who were suspected of wanting the world's downfall. The metaphors of the 'perpetrator' continue to imply the utmost irresponsibility with regard to the world's stability, for Copernicus's mark is none other than the one coined by Tertullian: that the heavens stand still and the Earth moves.

Seen in the perspective of the turning away from the early eschatological expectations and of the rationalization of their disappointment, the Joshua text becomes instructive even in the scanty instances where it is given exegetical attention prior to the Copernican turning. Once the command to the Sun to stand still is drawn into the arguments about Copernicanism, its interpreters differ above all in their decisions as to whether they will regard the Sun's standstill as real or as only apparent. When the test is economy in the attainment of the goal to be achieved in the biblical scene, mere appearance is regarded as sufficient. The pre-Copernican interest in the Old Testament text sees it from a different angle: It weighs the display of the biblical God's power over the immutability of antiquity's celestial spheres against the distinction conferred on Joshua, as the sole speaker in the battle scene, by having the divine ability delegated to him to exercise power by the word alone. Of course this choice between alternatives requires a resolute exegetical realism.

Neither the demonstration of divine power nor the demonstration of its having been conferred on man had to assume this reality and thus require literal faith if the production of a deception of the senses that was sufficient for the purpose (and thus for reason) could reduce intervention that was contrary to order to a superfluous exercise of force. With this consideration, which opposes voluntarism, Kepler tried to remove the text's awkwardness for the Copernicans. Joshua himself, he suggests, would have admitted that "the important thing to him was only that the day should be lengthened for him, irrespective of how this was accomplished. . . . Of course it seemed to him as though the Sun stood still, since the object of Joshua's prayer was that it should seem so to him, regardless of what actually happened."[16] How, though, would Kepler avoid docetism in relation to Christianity's central phenomenon, if in the peripheral zones of miraculous events he was ready to sacrifice realism, and with it literalism, in the interest of weakening the opposition to Copernicus?

Christianity's burden of proving that it did not, at least, *promote* the end of the world disappeared to the extent that the cosmos metaphysics that it received from antiquity itself appeared as a constituent part of the Christian system. Then theology's interest in the demonstrations of divine power against the background of the consolidated cosmos could return without embarrassment, without emphasizing, again, the world's constitutive decline toward its speedy end. What the pre-Copernican exegesis of the Joshua episode had made manifest was not the preference given to the geocentric cosmology but the way nature was at the disposition of the divine purpose of salvation, which suspended the apparent necessity of what indeed *could* have an end, but above all *had to* have a beginning. So interpretation of the passage stressed the disturbance of the cosmic lawfulness that was possible at any time: *Quod si ita est, diaphoniam passa est caelestis illa harmoniae suavitas. . . .* [But if it is so, then that sweetness of the celestial harmony suffered discord.][17] It is not the ordinary course of nature but its extraordinary interruptions that become, for the believer, the auguries of his salvation, just as for Joshua there had been no contradiction between his interest in his army's victory in battle and the intervention in the motion of the heavenly bodies for which he asked God.

Nature's serviceability to man relates to the salvation story rather than to physical teleology. It was not adapted to serving as a principle from which an expectation of theoretical understanding and reliability could be derived. If a thinker like Nicholas of Cusa could find a positive clue in this text, it was a clue to a Christian form of rhetoric. In a sermon, *Debitores sumus*, extracted from the collection made by Aldobrandinus de Tuscanella, the Cusan links to Joshua an idea about the power of the word, an idea that opposes philosophy's long tradition of denouncing rhetoric. In view of a God who exercises His power of creation through the word, and His will to salvation again through the word, the 'art' of mastery through words cannot be illegitimate. True, the celestial bodies are still moved by the old powers of the spheres' 'intelligences' (which have become angels), but speech proves to be more powerful. It is able to stand up to those secondary causes and bring the motions that they produce to a standstill: "Est enim oratio omnibus creaturis potentior: nam Angeli seu Intelligentiae movent orbem, Solem, stellas, sed oratio potentior, quia impedit motum; sicut oratio Josue fecit sistere Solem." [For speech is more powerful than any created thing; for instance, angels or intelligences move the spheres, the Sun, the stars, but speech, which checks their motion, is more powerful, as when Joshua's speech makes the Sun stand still.][18] The Cusan's metaphysics cannot refuse to man what it ascribes to God as His self-expression, if it is to stick to its intention of linking theology, cosmology, and anthropology. The world is not a contingent 'given' if it is supposed to have proceeded from the word, and nothing arbitrary or violent can be done to it through man's word. In this sense the action of the word, which is superior to all creatures, is still not a 'deed.' If the Cusan nevertheless speaks here in a language that presses toward man's being a 'perpetrator,' through the word, over against nature, then this is an autonomous tendency, one that evades his intention of preserving the medieval. It approaches the fundamental conception of Francis Bacon, who will present human domination over nature through the word as the essence of the Paradise that was lost and is to be regained. But Bacon will draw from the spirit of magic what the Cusan thought he could arrive at from the spirit of theology.

The fact that the Joshua episode contains a cosmological dogmatics could only emerge when the interchangeability of the real predicates of motion and rest between the heaven of the fixed stars and the Earth was at least considered, speculatively. Strict Scholastic Aristotelianism, which regarded the motion of the first sphere as the effect of the divine *causa finalis* [final cause] and thus as the principle of the world's preservation and its processes, could not allow even the thought experiment of the heavens' standing still to be accepted as meaningful. Nominalism, for the first time, is cautious about asserting 'necessities' in the relation between God and the world. If Nicole Oresme wants to play through his cosmological variations, he has to shield himself against the Aristotelian assumption that the motion of the heavens follows necessarily from God's existence. Here he makes use of the figure of thought, which was central for the Middle Ages, of the *gloria dei* [glory of God]: True, God is, as in Aristotle, the cause of the world's motion, as its *finis* [end, goal], but that makes Him the *causa finalis* [final cause] primarily, and necessarily, only for Himself. Only secondarily and only by His will does He become this also for the world: " . . . it does not follow that, if God is, the heavens are; consequently, it does not follow that the heavens move. For, in truth, all these things depend freely upon the will of God without any necessity. . . . ."[19] The ordinary course of the heavenly bodies is determined by the same volition as is its infringement; miracles are, by their nature, only 'phenomenal.' Consequently the Joshua episode can become, for Oresme, the license for precisely what was to be prohibited, on the strength of that episode, to Copernicanism. And with some reason, it must be said. Copernicus himself, by his rationalization of anthropocentric teleology, refused precisely the freedoms that medieval voluntarism had appropriated to itself after 1277.

Toward a typology of post-Copernican uses of the Joshua text, I would like to offer three characteristic examples. First of all Hermann Samuel Reimarus, with his *Apologie oder Schutzschrift für die vernünftigen Verehrer Gottes* [Apology for the Rational Worshippers of God], which after more than two centuries has finally been published in full. The scandal that was bound to be created, and was created, for the Enlightener by the fact that Joshua "in the pursuit of his victory told the Sun and the Moon to stand still," and still more that "God actually granted his wish," becomes evident in its full severity.[20] Miracles of this kind, which violate the essential tenor of nature as the completed and self-maintaining work of the Creation, are (he says) no longer even relished by the theologians. "Then gradually the theologians themselves begin to be ashamed of such monstrosities, which throw the whole of nature into disorder. No doubt they comprehend that the interruption of the motion of the great heavenly bodies has to mean more than if someone wanted to make the pendulum of his clock stand still for a day, and that if this *perpetuum mobile* [perpetual motion] stood still for even a moment it would cost the life of everything that breathes." The reproach that makes the perpetrator of the Sun's standstill into a monster has its rationality in the fact that this offense is no longer one of violating the sublimity of a sanctioned world-order so much as it is one that would have to endanger the sensitive mechanism of self-preservation that life represents.

The legend of the Sun's standstill gives the philologist Reimarus the occasion to distinguish sharply between its source, in an oriental work of poetic fiction, and its misuse. For the Old Testament author's having "taken the matter seriously and literally," there is no excuse. Such an excuse would always be available for the poet who described the following "natural experience": "If the Israelites at the battle of Gibeon had, from the rays of the declining Sun and the rising Moon, an evening and a night that were as clear and luminous as though the day continued beyond its time—then it was poetic to enliven the event as though Joshua had commanded the Sun and Moon to stand still and to remain above the horizon for another whole day." The historiographer, "out of a love for the miraculous," took literally what was not too audacious for the poet, and thus "made the poem into a history that we, as rational people, must liberate again from its theatrical dress."

Herder, too, distinguishes the poetic source from the momentous piece of supposed historiography. But with greater partiality for the poetic, even in its displacement, he sees the inexcusable abuse only in those who made the text from a remote time into an instrument of the Inquisition. In his essay "Über die verschiedene Schätzung der Wissenschaften nach Zeiten und Na-

tionen" ["On the Different Valuations of the Sciences in Different Periods and Nations"], Herder describes the effect of the legend of the Sun's standing still at Gibeon as one of the dangers to the progress of astronomy that, by good fortune, have been surmounted: "The Sun's standstill in the Book of Joshua would almost have imposed a standstill on genuine astronomy if Galileo and Kepler had not remained faithful, in spite of all persecutions, to Copernicus. . . . ."[21] Herder concludes his plea against any plan to assign a goal to "science's spirit of inquiry" by means of a dogma with the rhetorical question, "That you apprehend (and interpret) unpoetically an enthusiastic exclamation of Joshua's, of which a heroic song sang—is the world system supposed to accommodate itself to this obtuseness?"

Voltaire gave a witty culmination to the history of the effects of the Sun's standstill at Gibeon. In one of his invented anecdotes under the title "Jusqu'à quel point on doit tromper le peuple" ["Up to What Point Is One Permitted to Deceive the People?"] he has a Dominican and an English philosopher meet in the street in Rome. The monk abuses the philosopher for teaching that the Earth moves and forgetting, in doing so, that after all in Joshua the Sun was brought to a standstill. The philosopher answers that it was just that that he merely endorsed. For precisely since that moment the Sun has in fact stood still. Reconciled, they fall into each other's arms. Since that time even in Italy people dare to believe that the Earth moves.[22]

It had been Luther who first invoked Joshua as an authority against Copernicus. In his *Table Talk* we find on 4 June 1539—no doubt occasioned by the same reports that had decided Joachim Rheticus, a month earlier, to set out for Frauenburg—this laconic objection: *nam Josua iussit solem stare, non terram* [because Joshua commanded the Sun to stand still, not the Earth].[23] The position of one who carries out cosmic changes not only was stamped in advance by Joshua but was also occupied by him. The only way in which such a thing could be legitimated was firmly established. Laying claim to the language of the command to the Sun to stand still, as being descriptive of a theorist's action, seemed to be something reserved for the rhetoric of condemnation. Nevertheless, however surprising it may sound, Copernicus himself prepared the way for these metaphors. In doing so, he departed from his cautious efforts to soften the forcible demands that he was making on his contemporaries and colleagues and to wrap those demands in a protective raiment of humanistic citations and allusions.

Only in a late passage of his chief work, where he makes the reader look back at the most important part of his presentation, does Copernicus choose the language of metaphorical action. The actor is, admittedly, not himself, but the Earth. Although it had in fact only become the complex that conditions appearances, it is addressed as a factor that generates realities, as a subject in a network of forces and a relation of power—in other words, precisely in the language in which Copernicus was to become the demonized actor who changes the world. At the beginning of the sixth book of the **De revolutionibus** he speaks of the Earth as, by its motion (*revolutio terrae*), not only exercising force and efficacy (*vim effectumque*) on the apparent longitudinal motion of the planets and forcing their regularity upon them ("in quem ea omnia cogat ordinem") but imposing its command and its laws on the planets' paths ("exercet imperia legesque praescripsit illis") also in respect to their motion in latitude.

One must not overlook the fact that Copernicus could not use such a language in any but a metaphorical way. Ptolemy's epistemological license retains its linguistic equivalent at least where the talk is supposed to be of cause and effect in the connection between astronomical objects. The first conjectures about an active connection in reality between heavenly bodies were advanced by Kepler. So when Copernicus speaks of the Earth's force, efficacy, commands, and legislation in regard to the phenomena in the heavens, only the choice of metaphors is instructive, not the metaphorical manner of speaking itself. One could call this a classic case of "absolute metaphor." The speaker is simply not free to mean what he says realistically. The choice of metaphors of action violates above all Aristotelianism's dogma that the Earth consists of the most sluggish element and consequently, as a body in the universe, can only be motionless and passive, that is, without any action upon other bodies in the universe. When Copernicus metaphorically makes the Earth into the agent in an action, this is only in accordance with the theoretical change by which the Earth has become a star. The function of these metaphors has established itself in an intermediate realm; it makes it possible to experience something that is not sufficiently substantiated in the domain of objective experience: that the Earth has become a cosmic agent.

This language neutralizes the change in the Earth's position from the center of the universe to an eccentric location, by replacing the criterion of topography by the criterion of efficacy, of action in a story. If Copernicus had been intent on justifying his reform in the manner familiar to the Renaissance, by providing the Sun with the specially distinguished position in the center, then in view of his ignorance of the importance of the greatest mass in the system this proves to be a misjudgment of the criteria by which 'importance' was to be assigned in the future. Once again Kepler enables us to see how little the position in the center, as such, still meant, if it could not be equipped with the central function of the power that causes motion. As long as one did not have the concept of action at a distance, the criterion was satisfied by the complexity

of the proper motions of a heavenly body, because the multiplicity of the astronomical phenomena, and thus 'importance' in the theory of those phenomena, went with it. The Earth had not only become an object for astronomy but had immediately become its most important object.

Petrus Ramus expressed Copernicus's accomplishment in a single sentence: "Astrologiam non ex Astrorum sed ex Terrae motu demonstravit" [He demonstrated astrology (i.e., astronomy) not from the stars but from the motion of the Earth.] At the same time, in the place where he promises his professorial chair to the person who satisfies the requirement of an astronomy without hypotheses, he says that this would have had to be an easy matter for Copernicus, after he had accomplished the gigantic labor of putting the Earth in motion.[24] Whatever it may have been that the Paris professor of rhetoric understood by an "astronomy without hypotheses," it is evident from the formulation of his spectacular offer that he meant the metaphor of the theorist's gigantic labor, in regard to Copernicus, to be understood above all as describing the breaching of the epistemological barrier. Evidently for him Osiander's anonymous preface, with its proviso of the hypothetical nature of Copernicus's results, stood in the way of the perfection of astronomy. He believed, on the strength of it, that Copernicus—a perpetrator who lacked the utmost resolution—had not dared to take the step of laying claim to truth. The metaphor of the perpetrator is in the service of the break with astronomy's epistemological timidity—of promoting the astronomical realism of which Copernicus had supposedly fallen short and that still had to be demanded. The realistic use of the metaphor according to which Copernicus put the Earth in motion proves to be only a source of rhetorical support for the possibility of proceeding to unambiguous knowledge.

In the field of Copernicus's early influence, Petrus Ramus is one of the few who do not share the eschatological basic mood of the century. When he has Copernicus the 'perpetrator' still miss his goal by an amount reflecting the absence of a thoroughly consistent effort, he nevertheless takes Copernicus as the point of departure for his anticipating and soliciting the execution of what remains to be done. Almost at the same time, it is possible to perceive in the figure of the astronomical perpetrator what is already the lost grandeur of the past. This is the characteristic mood of the poem by Nikodemus Frischlin that takes as its subject the astronomical clock at the Strasbourg cathedral and the portrait of Copernicus, situated on the housing of the clock weights, which was painted—on the basis of a self-portrait that has disappeared—between 1571 and 1574 by Tobias Stimmer.[25]

The Tübingen Humanist's *Carmen* [Song] has a melancholy and culture-critical disposition. The astronomical clock appears to him as the 'Gesamt-Kunstwerk' ['total work of art' (R. Wagner)] of a late age, which once again pulled together, and displays, the powers and the potential in the world's old age.[26] The portrait of Copernicus shows him in his youth, with a lily of the valley in his hand as the symbol of the medical art. Not accidentally, the astronomer's portrait is mounted just where the clock's mechanism moves the circles of the heavens and the signs of the time. It may have been the preexisting symbolism of this spatial proximity between the portrait and the mechanism that decided the poet to find in the figure of Copernicus also the element of the power of causing motion, of which the restrained portrait itself wants to show so little. In the portrait that was copied here, the canon of Frauenburg wanted to draw himself as a medical helper of men; the Humanist poet, on the other hand, wants him to be imagined as the researcher and teacher, as he appeared at the moment when he commanded the stars and the heavens to stand still, represented the Earth as rotating, and placed the Sun in the center of the universe.[27] The poet, wearied by the spirit of the age, claims to know and wants us to know that the present no longer has the stature for such things.

A half a century, at the latest, after Nikodemus Frischlin's *Carmen*, the repertory of Copernicus the 'perpetrator' is gathered together in full mythical superrelief in Simon Starowolski's biography of him, which was published in 1627.[28] Jupiter sees how man, through Copernicus's spirit, creates the world for himself, halts the heavens, and puts the Earth in motion; and in watching this, Jupiter uneasily remembers the battle of the giants, and fears that such a god could have survived on Earth. More important than the employment of the mythical scenery is the formula that Copernicus did this *contra naturae iura* [against the law of nature]. This formula, in the wording *naturae iura mutare* [to change the law of nature] or *contra naturam facere* [to act against the law of nature], reaches back as far as early Scholasticism. In Peter Damian it is related to God himself, the Creator, for Whom the "philosophical" concept of nature, deriving from antiquity, is supposed to be proclaimed as "no longer" binding.[29] When Copernicus is elevated to the role of 'perpetrator' *contra naturae iura*, the possibility of reoccupying the position for whose occupant the concept of nature is not binding is announced.

The restraint that Copernicus himself had practiced in regard to the stirring gesture of the perpetrator—so as to accent still more sharply the enhanced status of the Earth—can be made clear from still another angle if one brings in the parallel that is provided by Celio Calcagnini's treatise on the motion of the Earth. This work was dated by Franz Hipler—on the admittedly untenable assumption that it was influenced by reports of Copernicus's early essay—to the period between 1518 and 1524.[30] If we disregard anxiety about pro-

tecting Copernicus's priority, the work could also have been written before 1518, or later, between 1524 and 1541, the year of Calcagnini's death. The public was first apprised of it in 1544, when it was printed in Basel. This posthumous printing could indeed have been a result of the interest in similar manuscripts that had been awakened by Copernicus.

The life paths of the later canons of Frauenburg and Ferrara had twice come very close to one another. After his studies in Bologna and Padua, Copernicus had gained the degree of a doctor of canon law in 1503 in Ferrara. He could very well have known Calcagnini, who had been born there in 1479 (so that he was only a few years younger), and could have acquainted him with the Hicetas quotation that he noted in his Pliny. If that could be verified, it would at least inform us regarding the point that Calcagnini was not to go beyond. But nothing in the contents of the little treatise on the motion of the Earth allows us to infer that Calcagnini could have turned to advantage the much later accident that in 1518 he came to Cracow, as an attendant of his duke, in order to take part in the festivities at the wedding of King Sigismund of Poland with a princess of the house of Sforza. If Calcagnini had received information, during this visit, of the way in which Copernicus's ideas had matured in the meantime, he would not in any case have benefited from it in any discernible way.

The sole motion of the Earth of which Calcagnini speaks is the diurnal motion, as an alternative explanation of the rotation of the heaven of the fixed stars. The system of the planets, on the other hand, is not discussed at all; indeed it is not even mentioned. Nor will one be able to say that Calcagnini went just halfway—in which case the imagined encounter of the young men in Ferrara could just as well have inspired Copernicus as Calcagnini. The solution of the problems of the system of the planets is the key to a cosmological reform of which the first partial accomplishment must, by its genetic logic, be the Earth's annual motion. If one has not found an access to this solution, the assumption of the Earth's diurnal motion is a dead end. Calcagnini would not only have made poor use of any information he might have gained, during his stay in Cracow, from the ***Commentariolus***—he would simply not have understood it if he had appropriated only the element of the diurnal motion.

Celio Calcagnini's treatise on the motion of the Earth has to be seen in the context of a process of disintegration that made theoretical assertions frequently take the form of mere paradoxes. That is still the case with Giordano Bruno at the end of the century. When one mentions this name, one must be struck by the ease with which Calcagnini expounds his paradox, an ease that is an index of the *leggierezza* [lightness] with which cosmological speculations could still be expounded at the beginning of the century. The demonization of Copernicus—and a fate like that of Giordano Bruno—already presuppose the altered conditions of institutionalized irritability that are associated with the advancing Counterreformation.

Calcagnini employs the formula of the theorist as perpetrator with the most charming ingenuousness. It only proves how little he has to shun the stirring gesture of the cosmological overthrow. In his dedicatory preface Calcagnini compares the effect of his thesis of the Earth's rotation to the accomplishments of the great artificers of antiquity, among these especially Archimedes, who were able to move very great weights with small mechanisms: " . . . *iure admirati sunt, quod parvis machinis ingentes moles agitarent*" [they are justly admired for moving huge masses by little devices].[31] The highest admiration (*summa admiratio*), which, according to the author's explicit declaration, the little work deserves, is supposed to refer to the act of force with which it brings the irresistible course of the Sun and the six planets, and especially the incredible impetus of the rotation of the sphere of the fixed stars, to a halt ("*incredibilem impetum sistit*"), while on the other hand it abolishes the inertia of the Earth and incites it to the most rapid motion: " . . . *ita impellit atque urgit, ut citatissimo cursu deferatur.*"

More amazing than *what* the little book (which, as the agent of the action, deputizes for the author) changes in the world-order is *how* this change is pictured. This action is carried out not with levers and screws, as the mention of Archimedes, who had promised to change the world if he were given one fixed point, seemed to announce, but only by the aid of the magical efficacy of the word: "Solo magicae orationis beneficio tantum nobis miraculum constat." [By the aid of magical speech alone, we achieve such a great marvel.] The addressee of the dedication could, its author writes, describe that, without fear of contradiction, as a paradox.

The execution of Calcagnini's deed of theoretical violence does not measure up to this preparatory rhetoric of the cosmic perpetrator. He introduces it with the skeptical observation that we cannot trust our eyes, which means initially only that the appearance of the heavens' rotation does not speak against the motion of the Earth. By assuming a hiatus between the senses and reason, between appearances and valid reality, Calcagnini at first presents himself as a Platonist. However, the heart of our ignorance is not, he says, that we do not know that which truly exists, but rather that we do not perceive our own human situation in the prodigious rotation of the heavenly body on which we live: "Tanta in mole constituti rapimur atque agimur . . . nostrae humanae conditionis ignari." The placement of the accent shows where the author's interest lies and what cannot be expected from him. Man's

ignorance about himself is more surprising to him than what could take place with the ground under his feet.

Platonism, for Calcagnini, means above all to make a metaphysically grounded decision as to how motion and rest are to be apportioned, in the hierarchical system of cosmic objects, as real predicates. What is supposed to be eternal, immortal, and immutable cannot be endowed with the most rapid of all motions, while the lowest sphere, the sphere of instability and mutability, is conceived as being at a standstill. If it should not be possible to adduce proofs (which was the situation sanctioned by the epistemological tradition of astronomy), then, in case of doubt, the motion must be awarded to the Earth: "Hoc vero multo iustius ac rationabilius terrae quam coelo irrogaveris." [You will in truth have imposed this much more properly and rationally on the Earth than on the heavens.]

The form of the terrestrial body at least offers no argument against assuming that it moves. Here Calcagnini is momentarily in accord with Copernicus's argumentation for the *mobilitas terrae* [mobility of the Earth]. Calcagnini, too, speaks of the Earth's *absoluta rotunditas* [absolute roundness] and extracts from it a principle guaranteeing the persistence of its revolving—precisely not, however, for the stationary rotation that he asserts: The perfect ball that rolls on a flat, smooth surface pauses in its course only when it encounters an obstacle or an unevenness.[32]

Not only are Calcagnini's and Copernicus's arguments from the Earth's globular shape and its equivalence to the spherical shape of the heaven of the fixed stars not sufficiently improbable, in their specific forms, to allow us to assume a dependence of one on the other—they are also employed too differently in their argumentative functions. Copernicus only shields his further considerations on the correction of the planetary system by introducing the idea, from natural philosophy, of the connection between form and motion, whereas when Calcagnini presents it he has already reached the center of his demonstration. Everything beyond this point is a search for a corroborating investment with meaning. The fact that the Earth turns around its axis is an expression of its heliotropism, which it shares with the whole of organic nature. Its turning toward the sunlight, by rotating, is only a special case of the most universal conservation drive of all things, "ut se suaque tueantur" [that they should preserve themselves and theirs]. So Archimedes's fixed point and lever are not really needed in order to make us (in Calcagnini's fine image) become our own antipodes every day ("nos ipsi nobis quotidie efficiamur antipodes").

The organic explanation, by means of heliotropism, is only one aspect of the Earth's motion; the other one is mechanical. The Earth does not change its position, which not only represents the center of the universe but also, according to the Aristotelian schema, the lowest position and the one subject to the most pressure. Calcagnini uses both views in one single formula: "Tellus in medio mundi constituta, loco scilicet omnium infimo ac pressissimo. . . . " [The Earth is fixed in the center of the universe, that is, in the lowest and most pressed upon place of all.] He derives the Earth's stationariness and its heliotropic mobility from the premise that, on the one hand, the center of the world is the point at which all material heaviness is directed, while, on the other hand, the Earth's matter cannot reach this point by means of its heaviness, but can only revolve around it. Just as in the relation between the first sphere and the unmoved mover in Aristotle's *Metaphysics*, earlier, here too the circular motion arises precisely from the fact that the absolute goal of accomplished rest cannot be arrived at. For the Earth's matter, the center of the world is just as transcendent as the immobility of the unmoved mover had been for the first sphere. The basic pattern of the argumentation corresponds to the *tonos* [tension, force] of Stoic cosmology, although the latter had not derived from the centripetal cycle of fire any circular motion of the terrestrial body, which represented only the stationary framework for the cycles of the other elements.

Just as Calcagnini underpins the Earth's axial rotation with a Stoicizing argumentation, he uses an Aristotelianizing reflection to strengthen still further the argument for the heavens' being at rest. It is precisely the fifth substance, of which Aristotle had said the heavenly bodies were composed and by virtue of which he was able to ascribe to them freedom from fatigue and resistance, that requires absolute immobility, Calcagnini says, on account of its simplicity and purity and its lack of any weight. This train of thought shows that cosmic motion arises, for Calcagnini, only from weight operating toward the center of the world, and that he lacks the idea of the metaphysical superiority of circular motion as the, in the strict sense, "natural" motion. As is so often the case, here too the mention of Plato on behalf of a theory that diverges from the Scholastic tradition is a self-deception.[33]

Calcagnini's universe remains geocentric if only because he sees no other possibility of saving it as anthropocentric—and it is so by his explicit statement. The Earth, he says, is placed in the center of the world so that by its motion it can stimulate the other elements to fertility and thus preserve the living creatures that the immortal God created to contemplate the divine objects.[34] If one thinks of the teleological world-formula in Copernicus's preface, it lacks precisely the connection that is set up here between man's being intended for contemplation and the Earth's being placed at the center. It is a connection, once again, that the Stoics had established. Calcagnini was not able to carry out the program, which he regarded as Platonic, of

relating cosmic anthropocentrism only to reason and not to sensual 'intuition.' It is true that he intensifies his assessment of the certainty of his argumentation up to the formulation—which he admits he would only venture when he had been provoked and his spleen aroused—that hardly anything more absurd had been invented by the philosophers than the proposition that the heavens move.[35] But this strong language is only justified by the long-familiar reflection about the dimensions of the eighth sphere and the resulting incredible speed of its rotation. The circumference of the sphere is "immense," and to determine it exceeds mortals' powers of comprehension.

Toward the end of his treatise Calcagnini takes account of the objection that the authorities and the great names are on the side opposed to his. His opinion too has its gods, he says, varying Heraclitus with a play on words: *numina* [gods], here, in place of *nomina* [names]. Here he takes up once again the figure of Archimedes, from the preface, and gives it an original twist. Could the Syracusan have made his famous remark that he would remove the Earth from its place with his mechanical arts (*architectonica arte*) if only he were given a fixed point on which he could station himself— could he have said this if he had not regarded the Earth as a movable body ("*nisi terram mobilem existimasset*")?[36]

It is remarkable that Calcagnini lays claim to Archimedes's remark on behalf of an idea of the motion of the Earth by which a change in its location in the cosmos was supposed to be excluded, and the fixity of its position in the center of the world was supposed to be ensured, in spite of the diurnal rotation. One would think that the figure of Archimedes would have to be more readily related to Copernicus's "deed."

That this had indeed occurred is something that, at any rate, we find already presupposed by John Wilkins, who deals with the appeal to Archimedes's remark in his *The Discovery of A World in the Moon*, which appeared in a German translation, under the title *Vertheidigter* Copernicus [Copernicus Defended], in 1713. This, no doubt, most widely read Copernican of the turn of the century writes, "To this purpose likewise is that Inference of Lansbergius, who from Archimedes his saying, that he could move the Earth, if he knew where to stand and fasten his Instrument; concludes, that the Earth is easily movable: whereas it was the intent of Archimedes, in that Speech, to shew the infinite power of Engines; there being no Weight so great but that an Instrument might be invented to move it."[37]

What could not be used as an argument remained as a rhetorical figure to use in remembering the one who, in two centuries, had changed more than the planetary system. By the anniversary of Copernicus's death, in

1743, the metaphor of theorist as perpetrator was so familiar that in his memorial address, Johann Christoph Gottsched was bound to make the most of it. "The news went out that the keen-eyed Copernicus had found, as it were, on the tower of his cathedral, where he was accustomed to observing the heavens, the fixed point outside the Earth that Archimedes had wanted—so as, from that position, to move the whole terrestrial globe from its place by means of his lever mechanism. With his daring hand he had shattered the crystal spheres of the heavens, so as to assign to all the planets a free path through the thin celestial atmosphere. He had released the Sun from the paths that it had traveled for so many thousands of years, and had as it were anchored it and brought it to a standstill. In short, he had transformed the terrestrial globe, also, into a runaway top, which was supposed to whirl once annually around the Sun, in the midst of the planets' courses. The entire learned Occident heard with horror of a cathedral canon who had made men's hitherto secure and firmly established residence insecure and unsteady."[38]

Finally Lichtenberg, the most thoroughgoing of the eighteenth-century Copernicans, gave the rhetorical figure of the Archimedean deed a very individual, unsurpassed turning. Raising the question—which, in view of the impossibility of seeing to the end of scientific progress, has obtruded itself from time to time, and will obtrude itself in the future—as to whether we do not already have enough knowledge of the universe, Lichtenberg communicates some of the latest information about the Sun. He contradicts the remonstrances of theoretical resignation, arguing that we cannot determine what is enough for the human spirit, because, for all the finite determinateness of its capacities, the extent of the objects that it can comprehend remains undeterminable. The disparity between man and the world is the fundamental post-Copernican experience whose continual intensification constitutes one of the main lines of the history of consciousness in the modern age. Lichtenberg points out that the oppressive disproportion is the result of a one-sided way of regarding the question. One must insist, he says, that man has been able continually to expand his sensorium by providing himself with, in the place of his body, a cosmic reference system of his experiences. "Man's body is a point, in comparison to the Earth, just as the Earth is a point in comparison to the planetary system and the planetary system is a point in comparison to the whole structure of the universe. Only that first point, the seemingly circumscribed apparatus of sense organs, is connected to the whole by relationships that, having been spied out and ordered by our spirit, give it a range that has no limits but nature. Thus the spirit, by studying nature, constructs a body for itself, and the Earth, with all the powers of the materials that make it up, becomes its organ; and the powers that previously seemed unimportant become of great importance, only on account of this machinery."[39] What is only a point in relation to the planet on which it exists, and still more in relation to the cosmic system in which this planet, as a particle, also disappears, nevertheless provides its 'punctuality' with the importance of the Archimedean self-consciousness.

This self-consciousness of course immediately involves Lichtenberg in the ambivalence of his view of man. Motion and annihilation turn out to have an unsuspected affinity. The magnification that man was able to give to his powers and his faculties has its apocalyptic dimension: "He who previously still had to doubt whether he could carry twice the weight of his body can now say, Give me a place to stand and I will move the Earth for you or, if you would rather, burst it in pieces for you." In a footnote Lichtenberg analyzes the boast, as he formulated it, as a combination of two elements, of which, for him, the first one stands at the beginning of a historical sequence and the other one at the end: "The first was said by an ancient Greek as early as two hundred years before the Christian time reckoning began, and the second by a Frenchman three years after this same time reckoning had ceased in his native country. The first speaker probably thought of mechanics, of levers and gears, while the other perhaps thought of chemistry and fulminating silver." The figure of the theoretician as perpetrator need not find its point of application outside the world that it removes from its state of rest, but can just as well have it inside a reality to which the theory that creates a disposition to active deeds refers. The remark that is ascribed to Archimedes had excluded just this possibility. The only one who could gain power over the Earth as a whole would be someone who was in a position to approach it from outside: "Archimedes, the Sicilian, demanded a site outside the Earth, in order to be able to turn the whole Earth upside down, because as long as he was in it, he had no power over it."[40]

One can see in the case of Lichtenberg that alongside the pride of the Copernican 'mover' there had also been growing, since the middle of the eighteenth century (especially after the earthquake at Lisbon), an uneasiness. The modern age's first 'perpetrator' in the realm of theory is joined by a second: the mover by the preserver. It was a reassurance in the grand manner when Laplace, with his celestial mechanics, which solved the "many-body" problem, had provided a theory ensuring the endurance of the solar system. Beginning in 1799, the five volumes of the *Mécanique céleste* [Celestial Mechanics] appeared. The first volume, with its general theory of the motions and shapes of the heavenly bodies—in particular, the periodicity of their perturbations of earch other's orbits—already made Laplace, in a new manner, into a 'perpetrator.' The work that he had already carried out in the years from 1773 to 1784 on the stability of the solar system was meant to show that the planets' mutual disturbances had no influence on their mean motions and distances and that the great orbital axes returned, in thousand-year-long rotations, to their old positions again. Thus the solar system was integrated into the great rational principle of self-preservation.

Herder, of whom Goethe said that his "existence was a perpetual blowing of bubbles," and whom Kant called a "great artist of illusions," described in his way the intermeshing, in the realm of theory, of the deed of violence and the need for security: "Just as Copernicus overthrew the heavens of the ancients, and Kepler did the same to Copernicus's epicycles, so Newton's simple law drove Descartes's vortices from the empty aether. . . . The whole century adorned itself, in astronomy, with Newton's name, and pursued its calculations according to his law, and at the end of it there arose a second Newton—de la Place—who perfected, by the most profound analysis, what Newton and his successors had left unfinished. He not only harmonized the heavenly bodies' disturbances of one another—their long-term inequalities, and so forth; he also calculated the effects of the universal law of gravitation on all the bodies, both fluid and solid, of our solar system, and thus secured our universe through eons. By showing that the mean motions and the great axes of the planets' orbits are constant, he as it were commanded the universe to endure."[41]

The astronomical reformer's role as 'perpetrator' can be measured by the opposition that he is said to have had to overcome, and also to have aroused. Feuerbach writes that Copernicus was the "first revolutionary of modern times," and that is said on the premise (which is taken for granted) that he "overturned the most universal, the oldest, the most sacred belief of mankind, the belief in the Earth's immobility, and with this blow shook the old world's whole system of faith." The metaphorical cosmic deed of violence in its turn becomes a metaphor for interference with a system of tradition shared by all mankind, as a model for all subsequent interferences of this kind. "As a genuine 'subversive,' he turned the lowest into the highest and the highest into the lowest . . . gave the Earth the initiative of motion and thus opened the door to all the Earth's subsequent and different revolutions. . . . With his audacious hand he burst open the celestial firmament, which before him was closed and impenetrable to even the great intellects of antiquity, with the exception of a few heretical thinkers, and served only as the breastwork of human narrowness, thoughtlessness, and credulity. . . . It is Copernicus who deprived mankind of its heaven."[42]

The history of metaphors of the 'perpetrator' in the reception of Copernicus is more than anything else the history of a great modern need to see concepts as guarantors of reality—to realize the idea, which was invested in the medieval conception of the Divinity,

that thought as such, and without delay, could determine (if not, in fact, produce) the world. Consequently the history of this Copernican metaphor is a history of the most welcome confusions between theory and practice: that theory, if indeed it cannot be practical, might at least be an assurance of the possible effects of thought on action too. Finally, the history of the metaphor is also the history of the disappointing discovery that the ease with which man 'makes' the history of his knowledge of the universe implies little or nothing in connection with the making of history in any other sense—to that extent, the history of science, precisely as the history that is most nearly 'made' by men, is the least specific history of human actions. The Scholastic axiom that "Praxis primo dicitur de actu voluntatis" [It is the act of the will, first of all, that is called action] hardly holds for one who knew and intended as little of his effects (indeed, even of the possibility of his effects) as Copernicus did.

Notes

[7] Voltaire, *Correspondence*, ed. Th. Besterman (Geneva: Institut et musée Voltaire, 1953-1965), vol. 85, p. 211 (no. 17417): "Thorn ne se trouve point dans la partie qui m'est échue de la Pologne . . . mais j'érigerai dans une petite ville de la Warmie un monument sur le tombeau du fameux Copernic, qui s'y trouve enterré."

[8] K. A. Varnhagen von Ense, *Tagebücher*, vol. 9 (Hamburg: 1868), p. 5: 3 January 1852.

[9] *Vindiciae sedis apostolicae adversus Neo-Pythagoreos terrae motores et solis statores* (1635), in D. Berti, *Il processo originali di Galileo Galilei pubblicato per la prima volta* (Rome: 1876), par. CXXXV. P. Duhem (*Le Système du monde* [Paris: Hermann, 1913-1954], vol. 1, p. 21) insists that Copernicus cited the Pythagorean Philolaus only for the proposition that the Earth is a star, while Gassendi, in a *Vita Copernici* of 1654, was the first to ascribe heliocentrism, also, to the Pythagoreans. After all, it was sufficient for the stellar quality that the Earth should have one motion, namely, its rotation around its axis, in its old place. G. Schiaparelli, in his *Precursori di Copernico nell' Antichità* (Milan: 1873; German trans. M. Kurtze, Leipzig: 1876), was the first to draw the ultimate conclusion that without the Pythagoreans, Copernicus and his successors would not have been possible at all. In his preliminary work (done before 1870) for an unfinished treatise on the question of the authenticity of the catalogue of titles of works of Democritus, Nietzsche, for whom Copernicus was later to take on an entirely different significance in relation to the specificity of the post-Christian idea of science, noted, "Copernicus relies on Pythagorean tradition; the Congregation of the Index calls his doctrine *a doctrina Pythagorica.*" (*Gesammelte Werke* [Munich: Musarion, 1920-], vol. 2, p. 139.)

[10] John Donne, *Complete Poetry and Selected Prose*, ed. J. Hayward (London: Nonesuch Press, 1955), p. 363: " . . . beat the dores, and cried: 'Are these shut against me, to whom all the Heavens were ever open, who was a soul to the Earth, and gave it motion?'" Copernicus has to refer to the most extreme misdeed that the author thinks he can formulate: He withdrew Lucifer from God's punishment by raising him, together with his prison, the Earth, from the center of the world into the heavens, and by thrusting the Sun, God's eye, into the lowest place instead of them. As in Dante, geocentrism here is not an indicator of anthropocentrism but of infernocentrism, and Copernicus has violated this. "Shall these gates be open to such as have innovated in small matters? and shall they be shut againt me, who have turned the whole frame of the world, and am thereby almost a new Creator?"

[11] Galileo, *Opere*, ed. S. Timpanaro (Milan and Rome: Rizzoli, 1936-), vol. 1, p. 258.

[12] Machiavelli, *Opere complete* (Milan, 1850), vol. 1, p. 327: " . . . come se il cielo, il sole, gli elementi, gli uomini fossero variati di moto, di ordine e di potenza da quello ch'egli erano anticamente."

[13] Christopher Heydon, *A Defence of Judiciall Astrologie* (1603): Copernicus "altered the whole of nature in order to rectifie his Hypothesis" (quoted in P. Meissner, *Die geistesgeschichtlichen Grundlagen des englischen Literaturbarocks* [Munich: Hueber, 1934], pp. 62-63: "What stands behind all the criticism of Copernicus is fear of the cultural revolution . . .").

[14] E. Rosen, "Copernicus' Attitude Toward the Common People," *Journal of the History of Ideas* 32 (1971): 281-289.

[15] Tertullian, *Apologeticum XL*, 2 (with the dreadfully magnificent apostrophe to the "Ad leonem!": "Tantos ad unum?")

[16] Kepler, Introduction to *Commentaria de motibus stellae Martis* (Werke, ed. Ch. Frisch [Frankfurt, 1858-1871], vol. 3, p. 154): "Facile autem Deus ex Josuae verbis quid is vellet intellexit praestitique inhibito motu Terrae; ut illi stare videretur Sol. Petitionis enim Josuae summa huc redibat, ut sic sibi videri posset, quicquid interim esset."

[17] Gunzo of Novara (*Patrologia latina*, ed. J. P. Migne [Paris, 1844-1864], vol. 136, col. 1299), cited after H. M. Klinkenberg, "Der Verfall des Quadriviums im frühen Mittelalter," in *Artes Liberales*, ed. J. Koch (Leiden: Brill, 1955), pp. 25-26.

[18] Nicholas of Cusa, *Excitationes VII* [Opera, ed. J. Lefèvre d'Étaples (Paris: 1514)].

[19] Nicole Oresme, *Le Livre du ciel et du monde*, fols. 91d-92b (trans. A. D. Menut [Madison: University of Wisconsin Press, 1968], p. 365): "Dieu est fin principal de Lui meisme. . . . Il ne s'ensuit pas se Dieu est que le ciel soit et, par consequent, il ne s'ensuit pas que le mouvement du ciel soit, car selon verité, tout ce depent de la volenté de Dieu franchement sanz ce que il soit aucune neccessité. . . . Et selon verité, ce monstra Il ou temps de Josué, quant le soleil se arresta." On the regularization of miracles: "Also, when God performs a miracle, we must assume and maintain that He does so without altering the common course of nature, inso far as possible" (Oresme, op. cit., fol. 144a; trans. A. D. Menut, p. 537.)

[20] H. S. Reimarus, *Apologie,* ed. G. Alexander (Frankfurt: Insel, 1972), vol. 1, pp. 494-495.

[21] Herder, *Adrastea* III, 6; *Sämtliche Werke*, ed. B. Suphan (Berlin: Weidmann, 1877-1913), vol. 23, p. 551.

[22] Voltaire, *Oeuvres complètes* (Basel, 1792), vol. 40, p. 190.

[23] Luther, *Tischreden,* vol. 4 (Weimar: Bohlau, 1916), No. 4638. Melanchthon is the first to apply the 'perpetrator' language, with a negative evaluation, to the "Sarmatian astronomer," who thinks he has to distinguish himself with his *res absurda*, and *qui movet terram et figit Solem* (to Burkard Mithobius, 16 October 1541; Opera, *Corpus Reformatorum* vols. 1-28 [Halle, 1834-1860], vol. 4, p. 679). Recently Z. Wardeska ("Copernicus und die deutschen Theologen des 16. Jahrhunderts," in *Nicolaus Copernicus zum 500. Geburtstag*, ed. F. Kaulbach, U. W. Bargenda, and J. Blühdorn [Cologne: Böhlau, 1973], pp. 165-169) has thought that the two versions of Luther's remark in the Tischreden exhibit contradictory evaluations—indeed that they differ in principle—and that "the fact that there exists a positive remark by Luther about Copernicus" is a "discovery that has not been taken advantage of in previous investigations of the reception of Copernicanism in Germany, and has been undervalued." This thesis must be based on a misunderstanding of the texts—on a failure to appreciate both the irony directed at the passion for innovation, and the connection of the formula "qui totam astrologiam invertere vult" with the following concessive *"Etiam illa confusa tamen ego credo . . . ,"* which by no means refers to a knowledge of the sad state of the old astronomy, but rather to the inversion carried out by the new one.

[24] Petrus Ramus, *Scholae mathematicorum* (Paris: 1565), quoted by Kepler, Astronomia nova (Gesammelte Werke, ed. W. von Dyck and M. Caspar [Munich: Beck, 1937-1982], vol. 3, p. 6): "Longe enim facilius ei fuisset, Astrologiam, astrorum suorum veritati respondentem describere, quam gigantei cuiusdam

laboris instar, Terram movere, ut ad Terrae motum quietas stellas specularemur."

[25] Nikodemus Frischlin (1547-1590), *Carmen de astronomico horologio Argentoratensi* (Strasbourg: 1575). On the portrait: E. Schwenk zu Schweinsberg, "Kopernikus-Bildnisse," in *Nikolaus Kopernikus*, ed. F. Kubach (Munich: 1943), pp. 278-279.

[26] N. Frischlin, op. cit., praefatio (1574): "Videmus enim hac extrema mundi senecta politiorem literaturam, et sublimiora artium ac disciplinarum studia paulatim vilescere; et hominum nostrorum animos aut ad luxum et volupates rapi, aut ad quaestuosas artes et splendida pecuniarum aucupia converti. . . . Artes autem humanitatis, et Mathematica studia minus ubique florere, nec nisi a paucissimis excoli videmus. Solet enim pueritia ea, quae a superiorum ordinum hominibus negligi et contemptim habere videt, ipsa etiam negligere atque contemnere. . . . "

[27] Loc. cit.: "Illum scrutanti similem, similemque docenti/ Aspiceres: qualis fuerat, cum sidera iussit / Et coelum constare loco: terramque rotari/ Finxit, et in medio mundi Titana locavit."

[28] Simon Starowolski, *Vita Copernici*, ed. F. Hipler in *Zeitschrift für die Geschichte und Altertumskunde Ermlands* 4 (1869): 539: "Juppiter ut vidit quod mente Copernicus orbem/ Contra naturae iura creasset homo,/ Ut vidit coelum firma statione teneri/ Currente et terra sydera stare bene. . . . "

[29] Peter Damian, *De divina omnipotentia*, chapters 10-12; *Patrologia latina*, ed. J. P. Migne, vol. 145, cols. 610-615.

[30] F. Hipler, "Die Vorläufer des Nikolaus Coppernicus insbesondere Celio Calcagnini," *Mitteilungen des Coppernicus-Vereins* 4 (Torun: 1882): 61.

[31] Calcagnini, *De perenni motu terrae*, ed. F. Hipler (in the paper cited in note 30), p. 70. On this see H. Blumenberg, "Der archimedische Punkt des Celio Calcagnini," in Studia Humanitatis. *Festschrift E. Grassi*, ed. E. Hora and E. Kessler (Munich: Fink, 1973), pp. 103-112.

[32] *De perenni motu terrae*, p. 72: "Nec enim tantisper rotari desinit, donec obiicem aut lacunam invenerit ubi sistat."

[33] Loc. cit.: "Hic ea sunt quae maximus ille philosophorum Plato nunquam fieri, semper esse praedicavit."

[34] *De perenni motu terrae*, p. 76: " . . . ita terra in medio collocata est mundo, que suo motu reliqua excitet ad generationem elementa, eaque animantia sustineat, quae ad rerum divinarum contemplationem deus immortalis procreavit."

[35] *De perenni motu terrae*, p. 74: "ausim dicere, uix aliud quicquam absurdius a philosophis commentatum esse, quam caelum moueri."

[36] Calcagnini's text contains, at this point, a misunderstanding of the ancient anecdote, when he speaks of a solid base onto which the Earth could be moved ("si modo basem in quam transferretur invenisset"), whereas the intended reference of Archimedes's remark is after all to the fixed point on which he would prop his lever. Even if Calcagnini did not understand the original sense of the anecdote, he nevertheless brings it under the premises of the cosmology that he accepts: Only in the center of of the universe, as its "natural place," does the Earth rest on its own and unsupported in space, while if it were moved (in accordance with the thought experiment) to another location, it would have to have a foundation underneath it if it were not to fall back to its original central position. The idea that the center of the world could also be a 'contingent' location for the Earth presupposes the abandonment of the Aristotelian premise that the center of the sphere is at the same time the 'lowest place of all' for weight. Calvin's perspective on geocentrism was that the Earth's resting in the center, "floating in the air," could only result from a special exertion of power on God's part. In a sermon on Job 26:7 (". . . et appendit terram super nihilum") he says, "Or il est vrai que les Philosophes disputent bien pourquoi c'est que la terre est ainsi demeuree, veu qu'elle est au plus profound du monde: et qu c'est merveille comme ellse n'est abysmee, veu qu'il n'y a rien qui la soustienne . . ." (*Corpus Reformatorum*, vol. 62, p. 430). And on psalm 104:5 ("Fundavit terram super bases suas . . .") Calvin explains, "Hic in terrae stabilitate praedicat Dei gloriam, quomodo enim locum suum tenet immobilis, quum in medio aere pendeat, et solis aquis fulciatur? Non caret hoc ratione fateor, quia terra infimum locum occupans, ut est centrum mundi, naturaliter illic subsidit, sed in hoc quoque artificio relucet admirabilis Dei potentia" (*Corpus Reformatorum*, vol. 32, p. 86). That what happens *naturaliter* can nevertheless be *artificium* is, for its part, highly artificial.

[37] John Wilkins, *A Discovery of a New World*, book 2, proposition 9; 5th ed. (London: 1684) p. 156. [The title given in the text is that of the first edition, published in 1638.]

[38] Gottsched, *Gesammelte Schriften*, ed. E. Reichel (Berlin: Gottsched-Verlag, 1903-), vol. 4 pp. 141-142.

[39] Lichtenberg, *Vermischte Schriften* (Göttingen: 1800-1806), vol. 7, pp. 155ff.

[40] Synesius of Cyrene, *De somniis* 133 A [following the German translation of W. Lang, *Des Traumbuch*

des Synesios von Kyrene. Übersetzung und Analyse der philosophischen Grundlagen (Tübinger Mohr, 1926), p. 6, which the author uses in the original].

[41] Herder, Adrastea III, 6; *Sämtliche Werke*, ed. B. Suphan (Berlin: Weidmann, 1877-1913), vol. 23, pp. 511-512.

[42] Feuerbach, *Die Naturwissenschaft und die Revolution* (1850); *Sämtliche Werke*, ed. W. Bolin and F. Jodl (Stuttgart: Frommann-Holzboog, 1960-1964), vol. 10, pp. 9-10.

Ann Blair (essay date 1990)

SOURCE: "Tycho Brahe's Critique of Copernicus and the Copernican System" in *Journal of the History of Ideas*, Vol. LI, No. 3, July-Sept., 1990, pp. 355-77.

[*Below, Blair discusses astronomer Tycho Brahe's ambivalence toward Copernican cosmology. Brahe admired Copernicus's desire for mathematical simplicity in his calculations of the motions of the heavenly bodies, but he could not accept Copernicus's theory of heliocentrism.*]

For Luther he was the "fool who wanted to turn the art of astronomy on its head"[1]; for François Viète he was the paraphraser of Ptolemy and "more a master of the dice than of the (mathematical) profession"[2]; for nearly every intellectual in the century following *De revolutionibus* Copernicus was a figure to be evaluated and criticized, if not always understood. Tycho Brahe's critique of Copernicus is not summed up in any pithy statement but rather spread throughout his life's work. Yet it reveals the constant importance of Copernicus and his shortcomings as the point of departure for Tycho's own model and observations.

Tycho Brahe (1546-1601) was not unusual in combining a certain admiration for Copernicus with a consistent rejection of heliocentrism. Beyond the rather commonplace criticisms of the Copernican system based on physical, scriptural, and cosmological arguments, Tycho's published works and astronomical correspondence reveal countless attempts to disprove or discredit the Copernican hypothesis on empirical grounds. This criticism of Copernicus's parameters and observational practice, although less well known,[3] is an integral part of, perhaps even a source for, Tycho's influential new agenda of "restoring" astronomy through greater observational accuracy and a more directly empirical derivation of planetary models.

I. The Development of Tycho's Agenda

In his first public reference to Copernicus, when lecturing on mathematics for a few months in 1574 at the University of Copenhagen, Tycho formulated what would remain his basic attitude toward the Copernican system. He hailed Copernicus as a second Ptolemy, praising him for avoiding the mathematical absurdity of the equant point and for "philosophizing more exactly than anyone before him" about the course of the stars. At the same time he criticized the heliocentric hypothesis for its features that were "opposed to physical principles," the motion of the earth and immobility of the sun and of the sphere of the fixed stars.[4] Tycho then promised that while abiding by the spirit and numbers (*mentem et numeros*) of Copernicus, he would reestablish the stability of the earth and show "how the appearances of the other planets could be adapted to the stability of the earth, while the Copernican numbers stayed the same, and how this could be done differently from Peucer and Dasypodius" (I, 173). Although Tycho clearly expressed praise for Copernicus's work and even a preference for the physical absurdities of heliocentrism over the "mathematical" absurdity of non-uniform circular motion in the Ptolemaic system,[5] he never doubted that Copernicus's hypothesis was flawed.

Throughout his writings Tycho would continue to display great admiration for Copernicus, whom he usually called *ingens* or *incomparabilis* (VI, 102; VII, 199, for example), citing above all his ingenuity and mathematical talent. Tycho devoted a prominent portion of his book of published astronomical letters to a fulsome description, complete with poetic elegies of his own composition, of the mementos of Copernicus and other great astronomers which surrounded him in his workplace at Uraniborg. On his wall Tycho kept portraits of Timocharis, Hipparchus, Ptolemy, al-Bitruji, Alphonso X, and Copernicus, alongside those of himself and his young son Tychonides, whom he included in the pantheon in anticipation of great work to come. Of Copernicus in particular Tycho cherished the parallactic instrument which an assistant had brought back from an observing expedition to Frauenburg and which was displayed at Uraniborg, accompanied by a special ode. Once included amid the great astronomers of all time, however, Copernicus was not only owed deep respect, but was also open to that reverent yet critical examination characteristic of Copernicus's own treatment of Ptolemy or of Vesalius's attitude toward Galen.

As early as 1574 Tycho expressed his enthusiasm for what Copernicus had "restored" in astronomy only alongside his own call for astronomy to be further "restored," first by reestablishing the stability of the earth and later by improving through better observation the hypotheses of planetary motion. It is precisely to this "restoration" (*redintegratio* or *restitutio*) that Tycho devoted the rest of his life and writings. The concept was not peculiar to Tycho but appeared in the writings of many contemporaries[6] and can be recognized for example in Copernicus's preface to *De rev-*

olutionibus, in which he deplores the jumbled and monstrous state of astronomy.[7] Rather than a return to any particular cosmological system or set of parameters, the term referred more loosely to an unspecified ideal astronomy from a mythical past, perfect in all respects. But while all sixteenth-century astronomers agreed that astronomy had to be restored, they differed on exactly which aspects of astronomy required most attention. Tycho expressed his personal goal in a letter to Rothmann in August 1588: "I will endeavor to adapt my restorations [*restitutiones*] in the course of all the planets to my own hypothesis, not one already invented, and to show the agreement of computation with them and with the heavens themselves, and I have decided therefore to set them out in a special work, God willing" (VI, 147).

Tycho's agenda at its maturity was thus two-fold, to find a new hypothesis, in particular one that avoided the absurdities of both the Ptolemaic and the Copernican systems, and to establish through observations its agreement with the heavens themselves rather than with any given parameters. While Tycho's lectures of 1574 already outlined the first part of this project, to reestablish the stability of the earth to the otherwise admirable Copernican system, they did not yet involve much criticism, like that implicit in the letter to Rothmann and explicit in so many other instances after 1578, of Copernicus's observations or parameters. As Tycho recounts in his work on the comet of 1577, *De mundi aetherei recentioribus phaenomenis liber secundus,*[8] it was only in attempting to trace the course of the comet that he first began to check Copernicus's parameters and to find them wanting.

Tycho found that the positions of the stars in relation to which he would chart the comet's path corresponded neither to Ptolemy's nor to Copernicus's computations. Both had relied, Tycho concluded, on the tables of latitudes and longitudes established by Hipparchus and Ptolemy which involved errors of one degree or more.[9] Tycho attributed these errors to "the carelessness (*incuria*) either of the observers or of the transcribers or rather of both" (IV, 20). Before he could calculate the successive positions of the comet, Tycho's first task was to "restore to pristine condition" (*in integrum restituere*), from his own observations, the positions of all the stars he would use as points of reference. Tycho devoted the second chapter of *De mundi recentioribus phenomenis* to his results, and thus initiated the second part of his "restoration" project which would before long grow to include new and more reliable observations for virtually all the celestial bodies.

Whereas in 1574 Tycho had been content to accept Copernicus's "numbers," by 1578 he realized that he could no longer rely on them. Spurred from then on by his dissatisfaction with both the parameters and the hypotheses of Copernicus, Tycho strove toward a model which would satisfy the requirements of mathematics, physics, and his own more accurate observations. By the mid-1580s Tycho had settled on his geoheliocentric model, first outlined in print in 1588.[10] He offered it as the perfect compromise between the Scylla of Ptolemy and the Charybdis of Copernicus (IV, 473-740, combining what he admired in both systems while avoiding the absurdities of each. Meanwhile Tycho continued his exacting restoration of the motions of the celestial bodies throughout his life, and would use his numerous corrections to claim, with rhetorical rather than logical force, that his system alone could account exactly for the phenomena.

Tycho never presented his system in final and fully argued form as he had hoped to some day in a *Theatrum astronomicum,*[11] but his massive astronomical correspondence, available in three volumes of the Opera omnia, offers a wealth of detail and debate from which to follow his argument. The letters are dated between 1571 and a few months before his death in 1601, but most were written after the mid-1580s, once he had developed his own cosmological system and was comfortably installed with his observatories and assistants on the island of Hveen.[12] In keeping with the habits of late humanist scholars, Tycho corresponded with serious astronomers throughout Europe employed in a variety of occupations.[13] These ranged from university professors of mathematics and/or medicine to the physicians and astronomers attached to imperial or princely courts, to officials and rulers in the Holy Roman Empire, who often cultivated a personal interest in astronomy and measurement.[14] Of the professors, some he had known while a student, like Caspar Peucer at Wittenberg and Henry Brucaeus at Rostock, others he knew only through letters and intermediaries, like Giovanni Antonio Magini at the University of Bologna or Joseph Justus Scaliger at Leiden. Tycho carried on lively exchanges from Hveen with Thaddeus Hagecius, physician to the emperor in Bohemia and, after leaving Denmark in 1597, with his assistant Johannes Kepler, and with Herwart von Hohenburg, chancellor of Bavaria, among others. Most importantly Brahe corresponded regularly between 1586 and 1591 with Wilhelm IV, Landgrave of Hesse, whose observatory at Kassel was a major center of astronomical activity, and with his court astronomer, Christoph Rothmann, a convinced Copernican. Tycho published these letters to Kassel in 1596 as his *Epistolarum astronomicarum liber primus*[15] but never carried out plans for publishing more of his correspondence.

II. Tycho's Assessment of Heliocentrism

In an important letter of 1588 to Caspar Peucer, Tycho presented most completely his perception of the shortcomings of Ptolemy which Copernicus had resolved:

> [In examining the Ptolemaic hypotheses] I
> noticed . . . that although they save to a great extent

the heavenly appearances, because however they allow that the motion of a circle be regular not around its own center, but around some other point, they sin against the first principles of the art, which Copernicus himself seems to have criticized in these hypotheses; furthermore the great number and great size of the epicycles that are assumed take up much space in the sky and are superfluous. I considered whether everything could be resolved by fewer [of them], and it gave me great concern that no necessary cause or natural combination explained why the superior planets are bound to the sun in such a way that at conjunction they always occupy the top of their epicycles, at opposition the lowest point of the same, and that the two planets that are called inferior always have the same mean position with the sun and are close to it at the apogee and perigee of their epicycles. (VII, 128)

Tycho admires the Copernican system because he finds it far more elegant than the Ptolemaic (*longe concinnior*, VII, 80). And, without considering for the moment the triple motion of the earth, Tycho finds that Copernicus "resolves well all the other aspects of the Ptolemaic arrangement which are confused and superfluous, and in no way sins against the principles of mathematics" (VII, 128).

This appraisal of the advantages of the Copernican system was fairly common in the sixteenth century even among those who, like Tycho, rejected heliocentrism because of the motion of the earth. Although widespread, it was not particularly accurate, however, as Copernicus's completed model used no fewer circles than Ptolemy's. But in the skeleton of the Copernican model at least, the epicycle that Ptolemy had attributed to each individual planet could be accounted for by the single annual rotation of the earth. It is no doubt this conceptual simplicity which appealed to Tycho and many contemporaries. Indeed Tycho probably rejected the Ptolemaic system in the first place and devised a system of his own precisely in order to preserve the explanatory power he found so attractive in Copernicus's heliocentrism. In the Tychonic system the motion of the planets around the sun, while the sun revolved around the earth, still accounted for the stations and retrogradations of the planets which had required the epicycles in the Ptolemaic model. But when Tycho actually adjusted his theory to fit the parameters derived from his observations, as he did in the case of the moon for example, he too in the end had only added further epicycles to the existing models.

In many instances, starting with his 1574 lecture, Tycho praised Copernicus for avoiding Ptolemy's "sin" against the "first" or the "mathematical" principles of the art. Like many before him, including Copernicus, Tycho objected here to Ptolemy's explicit use of non-uniform circular motion and what was later called the equant point—a point around which the epicycle of a planet maintains a constant angular velocity even while it follows a path centered on a different point. But Copernicus no less than Ptolemy needed the planets in his model to move in a non-uniform circular motion, in order to approximate, quite successfully in fact, Ptolemy's own model. He did so more subtly than Ptolemy, however, through a combination of eccentric circles and epicycles, which yielded almost the same result as the problematic circle revolving around a point other than its center.

The equivalence of Copernicus's eccentrepicyclic model to Ptolemy's equant point was not lost on some students of Copernicus, such as Michael Maestlin and Kepler, who corresponded on the subject.[16] Tycho, however, never alluded to the problem in Copernicus and on the contrary praised the latter precisely for avoiding the mathematical absurdities of the Ptolemaic system. He seemed satisfied with Copernicus's more discreet model for producing non-uniform circular motion and in any case had no alternative to offer. Tycho focused rather on those problems in the Copernican system which he felt he could resolve.

Tycho's main objection to the Copernican system, and one that geoheliocentrism avoided, concerned the motion of the earth. Tycho shows no sign of having speculated, as Copernicus did in *De Revolutionibus* book I, about alternatives to Aristotelian physics that could accommodate a moving earth. The annotations in Tycho's copy of the *De Revolutionibus,* once taken as evidence for such speculation, have now been identified as those of Paul Wittich.[17] Already in 1574 Tycho made it clear that the motion of the earth violated "physical principles" and could not be tolerated. In 1584, in a letter to his friend Henry Brucaeus, professor of medicine and mathematics at Rostock, Tycho expressed a rare moment of doubt. Of the three motions Copernicus had assigned to the earth, Tycho believed that he had disproved the annual motion by his measurement of the parallax of Mars at opposition and had dismissed Copernicus's libration of the earth, added to account for the precession of the equinoxes, as both unnecessary and in any case based on inaccurate observations. As for the third, daily rotation of the earth, Tycho briefly wondered:

> But whether this third motion, that accounts for the daily revolution, belongs to the earth and nearby elements, is hard to say. For with the same reason the appearance of so great a motion can be explained in the earth and in the *primum mobile* [the outermost sphere] and the sudden return from East to West of all the spheres in the second mover [beneath the fixed stars] can be saved with a much smaller revolution, and therefore a more convenient shortcut, as I see that the Pythagoreans and Platonists believed. (VII, 80)

This was the extent of Tycho's consideration, however, as he immediately concluded: "It is likely nonetheless that such a fast motion could not belong to the earth, a body very heavy and dense and opaque, but rather belongs to the sky itself whose form and subtle and constant matter are better suited to a perpetual motion, however fast" (VII, 80).[18] On other occasions Tycho dismissed the motion of the earth as useless (*irritus*, VI, 27) and an absurdity (VI, 177; VII, 199).

Tycho's rejection of the motion of the earth rested at times on Aristotelian physics and his conviction that the earth is a "lazy and ignoble" body (*piger et ignobilior*, VII, 128) whose nature does not lend itself to motion, unlike the ethereal substance of the heavenly bodies for whom motion, "however fast," is natural. At other times Tycho reasoned from common sense, adducing in his responses to Christoph Rothmann arguments made famous by Galileo's dialogues: that if the earth were turning, a canon-ball fired in the direction of the motion of the earth would travel farther than one fired in the opposite direction (VI, 219), or that a lead ball dropped from a tower would fall beyond the bottom of the tower (VI, 197). Neither was original with Tycho, who could have read them in the writings of Caspar Peucer, for example.[19]

In summarizing his reasoning for Peucer, Tycho also reveals the importance of "the unquestionable authority of the holy scriptures," which he cites as the second "obstacle to the regular and perpetual revolution of the earth" (VII, 129).[20] Although Tycho rarely used this argument in isolation, he did take it seriously, and contrasted the clear position of the Bible on the motion of the earth with its silence concerning the reality of celestial spheres. In the wake of the comet of 1577 Tycho had taken the novel position that the orbs carrying the planets had no real existence and was thus particularly interested in anticipating possible objections to his views based on the Bible. As Christine Schofield points out,[21] Tycho concluded in his *Astronomiae instauratae progymnasmata*,[22] that "neither scripture nor true philosophy will prove that the heavens have solid orbs" (III, 151). He based this conclusion not on the weakness of the authority of scripture, but rather on the ambiguity of the authoritative texts, for while some passages in the Bible seem to imply solid orbs, "there are many other places in the holy scripture to the contrary which show that the sky is something very liquid and very fine" (III, 151). Tycho even made the further claim that "the very liquid and permeable substance of the heavenly world can be proved from the sacred writings" (VI, 187).[23]

In his debate with Rothmann on the motion of the earth, however, Tycho found the Bible both literally authoritative and unambiguous. Rothmann argued, much as Galileo would later in his "Letter to the Grand Duchess Christina," that the biblical texts that seemed to deny the motion of the earth were written to accommodate the understanding of the common man and could not constitute an objection to the Copernican system, about which "we will know only as much as we find through mathematical demonstrations" (VI, 160). Far from being convinced, Tycho responded so forcefully that in his next letter he had to reassure Rothmann that he had not meant to accuse him of impiety, adding: "I do not take it upon myself to judge anyone's piety or impiety" (VI, 185).

Tycho refused to allow that the prophets, even while addressing the crowds, might have spoken untruths. "The authority and reverence of the divine scriptures is and must be greater than as if it were appropriate to treat them in the manner of a play script. Granted that in physics and some other fields they adjust themselves very well to the level of the crowd, nonetheless far be it from us to decide that they speak in so vulgar a way that they do not also seem to set out truths" (VI, 177). In using a theory of accommodation to dismiss certain of their statements, Rothmann "detracts too much from the prophets by saying that they did not understand more about the nature of things than other vulgar men. Although they did not treat of physics by profession, indeed this was not the nature of their gift, nonetheless they mixed many physical propositions in with their prophecies, which no one, however deeply imbued in natural philosophy, could deny" (VI, 177-78).

Instead of interpreting the Bible "more freely" as Rothmann proposes, citing Augustine as an example (VI, 181), Tycho praises contemporaries who study the physics contained in the scriptures. Francisco Valles, for example, "explained many things which must not be neglected among the matters of physics contained in the scriptures" and Lambert Daneau is hailed as "a very erudite man and one who has done excellent service in educating others" for his "theological physics" drawn from the old and new testaments.[24] Tycho concludes: "It is possible that many things lurk here that should be explained differently, to follow a better system of physics—which is itself, perhaps, to be found to a considerable extent in scripture" (VI, 185).

Tycho's parting challenge to Rothmann to "cite any text you have from the holy oracles or their commentators that supports the Copernican assertion" (VI, 186) is, on the one hand, a rhetorical ploy; indeed Tycho adds immediately: "I know this well enough that Augustine, the only one you name, never conceded the annual or diurnal motion of the earth; not being much of a mathematician, he questioned the very roundness of the earth by denying the antipodes" (VI, 186). But on the other hand it also grows out of his conviction that many truths of physics are contained in the holy scriptures. If Tycho left to others the practice of a scriptural physics, he remained deeply committed to the physical truth of those biblical statements which entailed the stability of the earth. After this heated exchange with Rothmann, however, Tycho rarely discussed the issue, but focused instead on astronomical arguments against Copernicus.

In the absence of any observed stellar parallax, Tycho scoffed for example at the absurdity of the distance and the sizes of the fixed stars that the Copernican system required:

> Then the stars of the third magnitude which are one minute in diameter will necessarily be equal to the entire annual orb [of the earth], that is, they would comprise in their diameter 2284 semidiameters of the earth. They will be distant by about 7850000 of the same semidiameters. What will we say of the stars of first magnitude, of which some reach two, some almost three minutes of visible diameter? and what if, in addition, the eighth sphere were removed higher, so that the annual motion of the earth vanished entirely [and was no longer perceptible] from there? Deduce these things geometrically if you like, and you will see how many absurdities (not to mention others) accompany this assumption [of the motion of the earth] by inference. (VI, 197)

Tycho also shared this misgiving with a number of contemporaries. He himself had searched repeatedly for any sign of a parallax in the sphere of the fixed stars, but to no avail (VIII, 209). The consequences, then, were simply too monstrous to be believable. Tycho stressed his conviction on this point in the *Progymnasmata*: "It is necessary to preserve in these matters some decent proportion, lest things reach out to infinity and the just symmetry of creatures and visible things concerning size and distance be abandoned: it is necessary to preserve this symmetry because God, the author of the universe, loves appropriate order, not confusion and disorder" (II, 435).

There is nothing particularly unusual in Tycho's use of these three arguments against the Copernican system. The physical absurdity of the motion of the earth, confirmed by the enormous distance to the fixed stars and evidence from the Bible, sealed Tycho's rejection of heliocentrism. Schofield also suggests that Tycho's dissatisfaction with Copernican parameters contributed to his "loss of confidence" in the new system;[25] but from the chronology of Tycho's development it is clear that Tycho rejected the motion of the earth already in 1574, well before he had begun seriously to investigate the accuracy of Copernicus's numbers. Once he had started his vast observational project, however, Tycho discovered a whole new range of arguments with which to undermine the Copernican system.

III. Two Empirical "Proofs"

The first of Tycho's empirical arguments, from the observation of the parallax of Mars, might have been quite convincing had he been able to sustain it. In his letter to Brucaeus of 1584 Tycho recounted how he

had devised a simple empirical test of the Copernican system. In the Ptolemaic system Mars is always further away from the earth than the sun. The Copernican model, however, places Mars at opposition closer to the earth than the sun is to the earth. Therefore a simple comparison of the parallaxes of the sun and of Mars at opposition should determine conclusively which of the two systems is true, a smaller parallax of Mars disproving the Copernican system. Tycho reported that at the end of 1582 and especially in 1583, "by most frequent and precise observations," he had found that the parallax of Mars was much smaller than that required by Copernicus; he concluded that "the whole sphere of Mars is further removed from us than the sun" and "the annual motion of the earth in a great circle around the sun does not exist" (VII, 80). Tycho had not redetermined the solar parallax for this test, but used throughout his writings the Ptolemaic value of approximately 2'50", while the solar parallax actually does not exceed 9 seconds.[26] Given the value he assumed for the solar parallax, his observation of a smaller parallax of Mars is perhaps not surprising.

What is startling, however, is the further development of Tycho's account of the parallax of Mars. In his letter of 1588 to Caspar Peucer, Tycho's description of the parallax test based on those same observations of 1582-83 and on the same value for the solar parallax, had changed drastically:

> And finally with great diligence and at no small cost using various astronomical instruments by which the movements of the heavenly bodies can be measured accurately not only to the minute, but even to the half or quarter of a minute of arc, and having taken many such accurate observations at the rising, setting and meridian transit of Mars, I found that Mars displays a *greater* parallax than the sun and is therefore closer to the earth than the sun when it is in opposition, which is in agreement with the Copernican numbers. (VII, 129; my emphasis)

This reversal has puzzled many commentators, starting with Kepler, who tried to justify it by attributing it to the error of Tycho's assistants, who had misunderstood their instructions.[27] As J. L. E. Dreyer points out, however, Tycho's notes on the observation and the parallax calculation were taken in his own hand (X, 196ff. and 283ff.).[28] Schofield suggests that Tycho's later version of the test was due to his faulty recollection of what had impressed him about Copernicus's model for Mars: when he found that the positions of Mars corresponded better to the Copernican than to the Ptolemaic model, Tycho erroneously assumed that the parallax he had observed earlier also supported Copernicus over Ptolemy.[29] On this interpretation Tycho would have rather surprisingly confused a weak argument from the agreement of parameters with a much stronger kind of empirical test.

Whatever the observational basis for the two versions of the story,[30] the shift cannot be understood without reference to the development of Tycho's cosmological commitments. In the early 1580s Tycho was simply opposed to heliocentrism and used his observation of the parallax of Mars as one of his strongest arguments against the Copernican system. But by 1588 Tycho had also settled on an alternative to heliocentrism in his geoheliocentric model, which, like the Copernican system, placed Mars closer to the earth than the sun at opposition. This arrangement, with its overlapping spheres of Mars and the sun, was possible only after Tycho had abandoned his belief in the solidity of the celestial spheres. Tycho was thus forced to abandon his first account of the parallax of Mars, as it would infirm not only the Copernican but also his own cosmological model, to which he was deeply attached.

So if Tycho's second and final account of his observation of the parallax of Mars[31] supported his own system, by the same token it involved abandoning one of his strongest arguments against Copernicus. In order to maintain the symmetry of his carefully constructed letter to Peucer, Tycho used his discussion of the parallax of Mars to refute the *Ptolemaic* system and offered another refutation of the Copernican system instead. Comets, Tycho pointed out, do not display retrograde motion. As he explained in the *De mundi aetherei phaenomenis* however, they behave like planets in many ways. Located in the ethereal region with the planets, comets travel around the sun just beyond the sphere of Venus. Their orbit is freer than the planets' but still roughly similar: "It is probable that comets, since they do not have perfect bodies designed to last forever . . . do not observe in their orbits such an absolute and constant continuity and equality, but only like mimes emulate in some way the uniform regularity of the planets, but do not attain it in all things" (IV, 162). Since, although planet-like, the comets do not display retrograde motion, Tycho argued that the stations and retrogradations that we see in the motion of the planets must really be theirs rather than due to the motion of the earth as Copernicus claims: "In addition the two comets which were carried near the opposition of the sun showed clearly enough that the earth does not in fact revolve annually, since the motion of the earth did not detract in any way from their regular and established motion, as happens to the planets which Copernicus believes move backward because of the motion of the earth" (VII, 130). In short, if the earth revolved annually around the sun, why would the comets not also display retrograde motion?

Tycho's argument is not entirely consistent: in his system no less than Copernicus's the stations and retrogradations of bodies revolving around the sun are due to the position of the observer on earth, which is either stationary while the sun is not (geoheliocentrism), or in motion while the sun is immobile (heliocentrism).

Therefore comets that revolved like the planets around the sun would be expected to display retrograde motion in both systems. Furthermore, even if Tycho did not see this fundamental flaw in his argument, he might have noticed that it affected only the annual, not the daily rotation of the earth. Nevertheless, Tycho clearly believed that his argument from the behavior of comets was forceful. In a letter to Magini, professor of mathematics at Bologna, dated 1590, Tycho described his arguments about comets. The Copernican system, he proclaimed, with its "triple motion of the earth will be unquestionably refuted, not simply theologically and physically, but even mathematically, even though Copernicus hoped that he had proposed to mathematicians sufficiently mathematical statements to which they could not object" (VII, 295). Tycho was especially proud to announce a refutation of Copernicus on his own ground, responding to the latter's remark in the preface to *De revolutionibus* that "mathematics is written for mathematicians."[32]

IV. The Evidence of Copernicus's Parameters

At a loss for other "mathematical" proofs, Tycho most often attacked Copernican parameters and observations. When taken individually, none of the discrepancies he catalogued actually disproved the Copernican system, which could have been modified in each detail as necessary to fit his new data; yet Tycho clearly hoped to discredit heliocentrism by pointing to the unreliability of Copernicus's numbers, as if it logically entailed that the Copernican system could not be sustained.

Tycho never advocated simple empiricism nor claimed a direct derivation of his geoheliocentric model from observations free of "hypotheses." This is clear from his position on the famous call by the contemporary French philosopher Peter Ramus for an "astronomy without hypotheses" modelled on the strict empiricism of the Egyptians. In a letter to Rothmann sixteen years later, Tycho reports that in 1571 Ramus had suggested to him over a meal one day in Augsburg that he attempt to constitute an astronomy "through logical reasons without hypotheses." But Tycho "resisted him, showing that without hypotheses the celestial phenomena cannot be reduced to a certain science nor dispensed with so as to be understood" (VI, 88). He concluded that Ramus, although "gifted with a perspicacious intelligence and a lover of truth if any there was, did not seem to have penetrated deeply into this art [of astronomy]" (VI, 88). Hypotheses are necessary because "they show the measure of apparent motion through a circle and other figures which arithmetic solves into numbers" (VI, 89). Although in principle both the Copernican and the Tychonic hypotheses could be modified to accommodate more precise observations, once he had settled on his geoheliocentric system for the reasons outlined above, Tycho used Copernicus's errors in describing the motions of the earth/

sun,[33] moon and planets, the positions of the stars and the precession of the equinoxes as evidence that Copernicus's inadequate standards of observation and derivation could not be trusted to yield a valid cosmological system.

After his first mention of errors in Copernicus's stellar positions in 1577, which he had meekly attributed to the errors of the ancient observations or of those who transcribed them, Tycho discovered more and more discrepancies between the Copernican parameters and his own observations, which he increasingly blamed on Copernicus himself and his poor observational practice. Copernicus's errors in predicting the course of the sun were the first that Tycho examined closely. In 1580 already, in a letter to the Bohemian physician-astronomer Thaddeus Hagecius, Tycho complained:

> The calculations of Alphonso and Copernicus sometimes differ from [my] observations [of the course of the sun] by half of one degree, or at times more. . . . The motion of the center of the sun's eccentric in its epicycle is very different than our predecessors and even Copernicus himself determined, so that the eccentricity of the sun is now 2°5', that is 13' greater than what Copernicus thought. The apogee of the sun is near 5° of Capricorn, much farther ahead of what the hypotheses of Copernicus say. (VII, 60)

In a letter to Rothmann in 1587, Tycho could provide an explanation for these errors. Indeed "the fact that the eccentricity of the sun, its apogee and entire course had come to disagree so enormously from Copernicus's hypotheses in a short number of years" (VI, 103) led him to suspect an error in Copernicus's measurement of the polar altitude of Frauenburg. Tycho sent one of his assistants to Copernicus's home in Prussia with a load of precision equipment to measure the elevation with his own instruments. The observations yielded a polar elevation of 54°22' and one-quarter for Frauenburg, a value in excess of Copernicus's by "about three minutes" (VI, 103). Tycho concluded from Copernicus's writings that the latter "had probably not avoided the effects of refraction at his inclined location and perhaps also had not taken parallax into account" (VI, 103). By Tycho's standards, Copernicus had failed to fulfill the responsibilities of the careful observer.

As a mitigating circumstance, Tycho did recognize that Copernicus's tools, such as the parallactic instrument which was brought back for him from Frauenburg, were primitive. Laying out new ground rules for the observational astronomer, Tycho wrote in his *Apologetica responsio ad Craigum Scotum* (1589):

> If you have made your rulers out of wood, you accomplish nothing because they are not well enough suited to fine divisions and are not free from

all change; if you have made them of metal, they will not suffice unless they are of the right length and size to allow for the divisions that yield minutes; but when they have the requisite size, their own bulk weighs them down so that when inclined however slightly away from the level of the straight line they cause a loss of the sought-after certainty, as daily experience has taught me. (IV, 464)

Tycho concluded therefore that the "rulers of wood" which Copernicus had made and that were given to him by the canon of Warmia were "totally useless because of the instability of the material" (IV, 464).[34]

In keeping with his aristocratic self-image,[35] Tycho was proud to point out that the construction of the huge metal instruments he owned required considerable patronage, and he willingly granted in his letter to Peucer that many of his colleagues were not as fortunate as he:

> The mathematicians of our age are nevertheless excusable because they do not own large enough and appropriate instruments with which to investigate the motions of the stars, since their salaries and all their yearly revenues would hardly suffice to pay for a single properly built instrument. Indeed I know that I own many instruments each one of which would far surpass in price of construction the annual salary, even the highest, of any university professor. (VII, 139)

Thus Tycho conceded to Rothmann that if Copernicus had had at his disposal the fine-tuned instruments available at Uraniborg, he would have reached far better results (VI, 102).

Nonetheless, good instruments alone could not guarantee the best results. Ptolemy, for example, had used instruments built at the expense of the "royal Egyptians" and still got results that Tycho sometimes found wanting in precision (VII, 259). A prerequisite for reaching good results even with good instruments was a commitment to observation itself which Copernicus seemed to lack. Tycho's discussion of the lunar model provides a good example of his combined admiration and disappointment. On the one hand Tycho believed that Copernicus was both "correct and ingenious to hypothesize that the revolutions of the moon around the earth happen in a concentric circle with two epicycles" and suggested to Peucer that the superior planets should be modelled in the same way (VII, 136). On the other hand Tycho expressed his misgivings to Hagecius in 1595. Although more elegant and probable than Ptolemy's model, Copernicus's theory was not sufficient to save the phenomena:

> At the new and full moons and both quadratures he obtains in any case a position such that he does not

even there explain all things with the requisite precision. But in the four places which are intermediate to these, he does not at all save the appearances, unless we count for nothing the loss of one half degree when the moon is near the mean elongations of the bigger epicycle and of almost one whole degree when it is near apogee or perigee. (VII, 370)

In order to account for his observations Tycho introduced the third inequality of the moon, or variation.[36] The problem, as Tycho explained in 1599 to Herwart von Hohenburg, was that Copernicus, following the practice of earlier astronomers, had used only three eclipse observations, "which do not suffice to explain the first inequality of the moon, to say nothing of the other more complicated one." Establishing new standards for derivation, Tycho insisted rather that it was "necessary to have more very accurate observations taken in different places of the eccentric or the major epicycle" (VIII, 161).

Although Tycho recognized that Copernicus had simply followed a long-standing practice in deriving the lunar inequalities from only three observations, he was especially critical of this tendency of his contemporaries, and of Copernicus in particular, to rely on the authority of received values rather than on their own observations. When determining the maximal lunar latitude for example, Tycho obtained a value of 5°15', rather than the 5° that Ptolemy and modern astronomers after him had thought to be correct. As Victor Thoren has argued, this reassessment played an important role in leading Tycho to his new theory of the lunar latitude and oscillation.[37] But when he first suggested the new parameter, his friend and correspondent Henry Brucaeus objected that the traditional value must be the more accurate. In his reply in 1588 Tycho lashed out against Brucaeus for his excessive deference to authority, but Copernicus once again bore the brunt of his criticism:

> The authority of Regiomontanus, Copernicus, Werner, and others (whoever they are) does not move me on this issue, since the restoration of astronomy must derive not from the authority of men, but from reliable observations and demonstrations based on them. . . . Copernicus accepted without change the maximal latitude of the moon from Ptolemy and did not try to see for himself in the sky whether it was the case or not; Copernicus used as an excuse the fact that fate had not given him the same opportunity to see for himself that Ptolemy had, because the obstacles of the lunar parallaxes at his greater polar elevation could not be easily avoided as they could in Alexandria, which Copernicus makes clear in his own words in *De revolutionibus* book 4, chapter 15. (VII, 152-53)[38]

In this instance Tycho agreed with Copernicus's assessment of Ptolemy's superior observational conditions and results. Tycho did not replace Ptolemy's value of the maximal lunar latitude with his own, but rather used it as "correct in his time" and concluded from the difference between his own observations and Ptolemy's values that there had been a secular shift in the maximal latitude of the moon similar to that in the angle of the obliquity of the ecliptic (VII, 153). Although Tycho later rejected this particular interpretation and concluded that the important difference between "his and Ptolemy's determinations was the phase of the moon rather than the era of observation,"[39] he maintained that the deviation of Ptolemy's value from his own "by a quarter of a degree was not the result of a fault of instrumentation or observation" (VII, 153). Copernicus's real mistake, then, was not so much that he trusted Ptolemy's value but rather that he did not even try to make his own observations. Tycho had little sympathy for Copernicus's argument that his northerly location created insurmountable obstacles for observing the moon. Despite his own far worse conditions, as Tycho reminded Kepler in a letter in 1599, he had obtained reliable results from even more difficult observations: "Though it [Mercury] rarely passes beyond the sun's rays [which make it invisible] and the sphere is more inclined in our Denmark than in Frauenburg in Prussia where Copernicus lived, and the sea around our island creates more fogs than the Vistula: nonetheless we have frequently made accurate observations even of Mercury, a most difficult planet to follow" (VIII, 208).[40]

Tycho's own attitude toward the observations of the ancients is interesting and complex. On the one hand he clearly appreciated Ptolemy's skill as an observational astronomer, as in the case of the lunar latitude. Tycho also expressed great respect for the observations of Hipparchus (VII, 373-74; VIII, 104). On the other hand, however, Tycho was also willing to consider ancient observations erroneous by a certain margin when they seemed unreasonable. For example, when Tycho planned an expedition to Alexandria to measure the polar elevation there, he told Magini in a letter dated 1590 that he wanted to show that the "elevation of the pole had not noticeably changed over the intervening centuries, unless perhaps Ptolemy erred by a very few minutes" (VII, 298). Intent on refuting the suggestion by Domenicus Maria of Novara that latitudes had changed over the centuries and that the pole had shifted toward the zenith since Ptolemy's time, Tycho would have concluded that any difference of "a very few minutes" between Ptolemy's and his own observations reflected an error on Ptolemy's part rather than a secular shift. In fact the expedition never took place.[41]

The estimation of the rate of the precession of the equinoxes offers another example of Tycho's attitudes toward ancient observations since it relies crucially on earlier results. Copernicus had proceeded with total confidence in the accuracy of all available observations and, when comparing them with his own, arrived at a figure for the rate of precession which was both faster than Ptolemy's and itself irregular. It was to account for this irregularity that Copernicus introduced the libration of the third motion of the earth, which, of all the motions that Copernicus had attributed to the earth, Tycho had always found particularly useless (*otiosus*, VIII, 45).

In 1595 in a discussion of the calendar with Isaac Pontanus, royal historian of Denmark, Tycho justified his determination of the length of the year over the past few centuries from its length in the last hundred years, on the grounds that the length of the year does not change with the precession of the equinoxes as quickly as Copernicus had claimed. Tycho reveals here how he established this fact to his satisfaction. Unlike the "lax and credulous" Copernicus, Tycho compared his results with only the most trustworthy of those of the ancients and as a consequence found precession to be smaller and more regular than Copernicus had:

> Although the quantity of the equinoctial or solar year that I use for these centuries was derived only from an epoch one hundred years ago, from the observations of Regiomontanus and his student Walther, deliberately, so that I avoided the labyrinths of inequality which Copernicus and others introduced (as I see it) because of their excessive credulity and laxity: nonetheless if a proper comparison is made with the observations of centuries earlier, especially with those which are deserving of our trust beyond a doubt (such as I judge those of Hipparchus above all others, who most diligently attended to the appearances of both the sun and the moon), the annual quantity defined by us falls short by very few, possibly 5 or 6, seconds and thus in no way affects the determination of the years. But my observations when applied to the best of the ancient ones show that the disparity in the quantity of the year and the motion of the fixed stars is not as great nor of such great moment as astronomers think. (VII, 373-74)

The key to Tycho's approach to the precession was a circumspect attitude toward ancient parameters rather than the excessively confident trust that Tycho attributed in Copernicus not only to credulity but also to a certain "laxity," a reluctance to make countless diligent observations as Tycho had.

Tycho was equally distressed by Copernicus's planetary positions. He found "no small deviation from the measure of the sky in the latitudes" of Mercury and the three superior planets (VIII, 161). As for Venus, Tycho told Kepler, its eccentricity was much smaller than Ptolemy or Copernicus had thought and its apogee was not fixed with respect to the stars as Coper-

nicus had believed, but now had already reached the beginning of Cancer (VIII, 45). Although more conciliatory in the early stages of his observational project, Tycho still reported errors by Copernicus for each of the superior planets in a 1590 letter to Hagecius:

> The hypothesis of Copernicus is nonetheless closer [than Ptolemy's] to the measure of the heavens, except that in Jupiter it deviates sometimes by more than one degree, and in Saturn up to one half of a degree. I have not found until now that Copernicus committed a greater discrepancy from the sky in the two slowest planets, though for Mars the discrepancy reaches sometimes three degrees, or even a little more. . . . Our observations, compared with the ancient ones will provide some day, God willing, a more exact correspondence with the celestial appearances of the planets. (VII, 269)

Five years later, writing to Hagecius again, Tycho sounded more exasperated:

> In constituting the apogees of the other planets (not to speak of the eccentricities, which he derived too confidently from Ptolemy) the great Copernicus, who is never enough praised, erred in no small way. . . . In the numbers of Copernicus the apogee of Mars is more than five degrees beyond where the measure of the heavens demands, and the eccentricity, which he made smaller than the Ptolemaic value (perhaps so that he could with more probability support his own speculation about the motion of the earth and the changed eccentricity of the sun) is so far from being smaller that it is necessary to make the same rather barely larger (by a very few minutes though) only to satisfy the phenomena of Mars in all respects. (VII, 370)

Tycho concluded the tirade with an explicit statement of the argument underlying most of his parametric complaints: "And on the basis of this *experimentum* alone, the position of Copernicus on the motion of the earth and the immobility of the sun is weakened" (VII, 370).[42] In a similar way Tycho argued with Rothmann that "the fact that the eccentricity of Mars by no means corresponds to what the Copernican theories require is a strong argument for their weakness" (VI, 336). Tycho concluded with the implication that it was Copernicus's faulty parameters which had led him to doubt the veracity of the heliocentric system: "the fact that his hypotheses are less correct [than Ptolemy's] causes me no small hesitation" (VI, 336).

Tycho's litany of criticisms of Copernicus's parameters and observations is in part a contribution to his ongoing argument against the Copernican system as a whole and especially its heliocentrism. Although Tycho would no doubt have recognized that each particular discrepancy could be resolved without affecting the hypothesis of the motion of the earth, to tarnish the Copernican system even if only by association by pointing to its numerous empirical flaws was, Tycho hoped, to make the Tychonic system more appealing. Given the otherwise wide acclaim of sixteenth-century astronomers for the Copernican parameters, to which Tycho himself had contributed as a young lecturer, these specifically parametric criticisms are unique and proved to have a more enduring impact than Tycho's system itself.[43]

V. Tycho's Legacy

In addition to undermining the Copernican system in a loose way, Tycho's critique of Copernicus's parameters served as the background against which Tycho defined his own, new standards of astronomical practice. Tycho would certainly not have attacked Copernicus's parameters had he not already been particularly sensitive, for whatever combination of factors, to numerical accuracy. Nonetheless it is probable that Tycho's constantly renewed awareness of Copernicus's shortcomings contributed to a more explicit realization and discussion of his own suggestions for "restoring" astronomy.

Thus, for example, Tycho called for a closer consideration of the effects of refraction. Refraction had probably distorted Copernicus's estimate of the polar elevation of Frauenburg, and, as Tycho commented in a number of places, refraction also caused Copernicus to underestimate the obliquity of the ecliptic by three or four minutes (VII, 280-81; VIII, 197-98). Although Tycho himself believed that refraction was caused by atmospheric vapors that disappeared above a certain altitude,[44] for all observations at an altitude of less than 45° at least Tycho insisted that refraction be taken into account. He drew up tables of refraction to that end which, albeit unpublished, circulated as an appendix to his catalogue of 1000 stars to Tycho's potential patrons.[45]

Tycho also laid down clear rules for the construction of accurate instruments—to be made only of metal and of sufficient size to bear graduations down to the minute. Tycho was proud to have devised a method for "subdividing degrees of arc through the use of transversal points and of tiny slit sights on alidades," so proud in fact that he accused Rothmann of stealing it from him without acknowledgment.[46] As well as a bid for patronage, Tycho's description of his instruments and installation at Uraniborg in his *Astronomiae instauratae mechanica* constituted a normative depiction of how astronomy should be practised, and included detailed specifications of his different instruments, complete with illustrations.

Tycho's criticisms of Copernicus especially emphasized what could be called his "astronomical method." Tycho's most common criticism of Copernicus's method was that he relied excessively and too confidently on received parameters, notably Ptolemy's. Tycho insisted rather that the sky was the only guide to be followed. Tycho himself, however, was guilty of the same offense, although he certainly would never have admitted it. Tycho accepted without recomputation the traditional value for the solar parallax for example. Although Tycho's final verdict on the relative positions of Mars and the sun favored the Copernican and Tychonic systems, it rested less on solid empirical ground—Tycho claimed to have found a greater parallax for Mars than for the sun while using an excessively large value for the latter—than on Tycho's own cosmological commitments. But Tycho's great reputation for observational accuracy, which in this case was hardly warranted, turned his "test" from the parallax of Mars into a powerful argument in favor of heliocentrism; long after his death his "observation" of the greater parallax of Mars was cited with unquestioning approval.[47]

Where Tycho really did differ from Copernicus was not so much in his rejection of authority, which was sometimes more pretense than reality, but rather in his insistence on the difficulty of observational astronomy. Tycho had attacked Copernicus for relying on too few observations for his derivations. Three eclipse observations alone could not establish the first lunar inequality; furthermore, as Tycho warned Magini in 1598, "neither do three observations suffice to explain the apogees and eccentricities [of the planets] as astronomers in imitation of Ptolemy and Copernicus have in vain believed until now" (VIII, 121). Tycho on the contrary expressed his dissatisfaction, in a letter to Kepler in 1598, with the number of observations that even he had accumulated by the end of his years in Hveen: "if truer measurements of the eccentricities of each planet were available, such as those that I have at my disposal gathered over many years, they could allow a more accurate judgment in these matters" (VIII, 44). He concluded to Maestlin later that year that too little was known of the motions of the planets to support a hypothesis: "the double inequalities of the planets, which [astronomers] explain by a double eccentric or epicycle, are not yet well enough unravelled" (VIII, 53).

Tycho was clearly willing to be patient. He had painstakingly observed Mercury whenever possible despite the difficult conditions at Uraniborg. He noted in his preface to his astronomical letters how slow his work had been: if Mercury was notoriously hard to see, "even observations of the three slow-moving planets, which [astronomers] call superior, sufficient to restore their motions appropriately, require no small amount of time" (VI, 20). As a consequence, Tycho recognized that some parts of astronomy would perhaps never be completed. The motion of the fixed stars due to the precession of the equinoxes was a particularly difficult topic since "it is not reasonable that the inequality be at all noticeable in the stars in the life of one man" and Tycho conceded to the Landgrave of Hesse in 1587: "I believe that an exact knowledge of the apparent motion of the eighth sphere is hardly attainable for any mortal" (VI, 73).

Finally, Tycho stressed the need to verify observations and derivations. Especially for observations of the fixed stars "Ptolemy did not use in verifying them the diligence and precision which were necessary, and still less did Copernicus" (VII, 268). Although Dreyer was "disappointed" with Tycho's own verifications and care in determining the positions of the stars outside the ecliptic in his star catalogues, Tycho is noted for his "practice of using redundant data and admitting scatter into his results."[48] Tycho also suspected that in determining the eccentricity and apogee of Mars, "since in both cases the error was perceptible enough, Copernicus had arranged his results to fit his assumptions rather than testing the latter sufficiently against indubitable observations" (VII, 292-93).

Tycho's novel appreciation of the arduous and slow process of collecting and then using good observations may have prevented him from ever presenting his own system in detail. As Thoren has noted, however, the models which Tycho did complete, for the motions of the moon and the sun for example, constitute examples of empirical derivation of the highest caliber.[49] No doubt Tycho's critique of Copernicus grew out of his commonplace rejection of heliocentrism on physical, scriptural, and cosmological grounds, and was fueled in part by his self-interest in promoting his own geoheliocentric system; nonetheless in his unique attack on Copernicus's observational practice and derivation of parameters, Tycho became aware of the shortcomings of his predecessors and formulated explicitly his own requirements for the restoration of astronomy. With a keen sense of the commitment and constant effort required of whomever would restore the discipline, Tycho called for better instruments, more careful and diligent observations and greater prudence and patience in a directly empirical derivation of models. Drawing on this refined program of astronomical practice, Kepler in turn would refine the notion of astronomical theory, its nature, development, and sources.[50]

Notes

[1] "Der Narr will die ganze Kunst Astronomiae umkehren." Martin Luther, *Tischreden* IV, no. 4630 (Weimar, 1916), as quoted in Noel Swerdlow and Otto Neugebauer, *Mathematical Astronomy in Copernicus' De Revolutionibus* (2 vols.; New York, 1984), I, 3.

[2] François Viète, "Apollonius Gallus" (Paris, 1600) in *Opera mathematica*, 343, as quoted in Otto Neugebauer, "On the Planetary Theory of Copernicus," *Astronomy and History: Selected Essays* (New York, 1983), 491-505.

[3] Reference is made to certain of these arguments in Christine Schofield, *Tychonic and Semi-Tychonic World Systems* (New York, 1981), 37-39, and in Kristian Peder Moesgaard, "Copernican Influence on Tycho Brahe," *Studia Copernicana*, V (Warsaw, 1973), 31-56.

[4] Tycho Brahe, "De disciplinis mathematicis oratio" (1574), J. L. E. Dreyer (ed.), *Opera omnia* (14 vols.; Copenhagen, 1913-29), I, 149. Further references to the *Opera omnia* will be made by volume and page number in parentheses; all translations are my own.

[5] Tycho would continue to perceive Copernicus's motion of the earth as a lesser evil than Ptolemy's use of the equant point, as he does for example in a letter to Christoph Rothmann dated 1587 (VI, 102).

[6] Charles Whitney suggests that Tycho's use of the related concept of an *"instaurata astronomia"* (renovated astronomy) was influential in Bacon's choice of title for his *Instauratio magna* ("Francis Bacon's instauratio: Dominion of and over Humanity," *JHI*, 50 [1989], 371).

[7] Nicolas Copernicus, *De revolutionibus orbium coelestium*, facsimile reprint of 1543 edition (New York and London, 1965), f. iij v.

[8] Brahe, *De mundi aetherei recentioribus phaenomenis liber secundus qui est de illustri stella caudata ab elapso fere triente Novembris Anni 1577, usque in finem Ianuarij sequentis conspecta* (Uraniborg, 1588), reprinted in *Opera omnia*, IV, also available in translation: *Sur des phénomènes plus récents du monde éthéré*, tr. Jean Peyroux (Paris, 1984). The work was already at least partially composed by 1578 (Schofield, 52).

[9] For Tycho's judgment of their relative merits, see below p. 18.

[10] *De mundi aetherei recentioribus phaenomenis liber secundus*, ch. 8.

[11] Moesgaard, 40.

[12] The main building of Tycho's estate, the Uraniborg proper, served as both dwelling and workplace and was completed in 1580. It included a large library containing major instruments like the mural quadrant in use from 1582, and two small observatories. A separate observatory, the Stjerneborg, was built, largely beneath ground for protection from the wind, in 1584. Tycho first set up his own printing press in the same year. Tycho's first assistant arrived in 1578, then Paul Wittich in 1580; Gellius, Olsen, and Longomontanus are the better known of the pupils who worked at Hveen during the 1580s and 1590s. J. L. E. Dreyer, *Tycho*

Brahe: A Picture of Scientific Life and Work in the Sixteenth Century (New York, 1963), 94-104, 115-27.

[13] On the emergence of a status of "scholar" see Erich Trunz, "Der deutsche Späthumanismus um 1600 als Standeskultur," Richard Alewyn (ed.), *Deutsche Barockforschung: Dokumentation einer Epoche* (Cologne, 1965), 147-81.

[14] See for example Bruce T. Moran, "Princes, Machines and the Valuation of Precision in the Sixteenth Century," *Sudhoffs Archiv*, 61 (1977), 209-28, and "German Prince-Practitioners: Aspects in the Development of Courtly Science, Technology, and Procedures in the Renaissance," *Technology and Culture*, 22 (1981), 253-74.

[15] Brahe, *Epistolarum astronomicarum liber primus* (Uraniborg, 1596), reprinted as vol. VI of Dreyer's Opera omnia.

[16] Anthony Grafton, "Michael Maestlin's Account of Copernican Planetary Theory," *Proceedings of the American Philosophical Society*, 117 (1973), 523-50.

[17] Owen Gingerich and Robert S. Westman, *The Wittich Connection: Conflict and Priority in Late Sixteenth-Century Cosmology: Transactions of the American Philosophical Society*, vol. 78, part 7 (Philadelphia, 1988), 23.

[18] For a similar discussion of the possibility of daily rotation see Tycho's letter to Kepler in 1598 (VIII, 45).

[19] Schofield, 92.

[20] See also III, 175; VII, 199.

[21] Schofield, 90.

[22] Brahe, *Astronomiae instauratae progymnasmata quorum haec prima pars de restitutione motuum solis et lunae stellarumque inerrantium tractat et praeterea de admiranda nova stella Anno 1572 exorta luculenter agit* (Prague, 1602), reprinted in *Opera omnia*, II and III. The printing was begun at Uraniborg in 1588.

[23] See also IV, 474.

[24] Tycho is referring here to their recent works: Franciscus Valles, *De iis quae scripta sunt physice in libris sacris, sive de Sacra Philosophia liber singularis* (Lyon, 1588), and Lambert Daneau, *Physica Christiana, sive de Rerum creatarum cognitione et usu, disputatio e Sacrae Scripturae fontibus hausta et decerpta* (Geneva, 1576).

[25] Schofield, 38.

[26] J. L. E. Dreyer, "Note on Tycho Brahe's Opinion About the Solar Parallax," *Monthly Notices of the Royal Astronomical Society*, 71 (1910), 74-76. As Schofield points out (p. 70), in the *Progymnasmata* Tycho endorsed the number mysticism of Johannes Francus Offusius who set the earth-sun distance at 576 earth diameters, the square of 24 (II, 421-22).

[27] Johannes Kepler, *Astronomia nova seu Physica coelestis, tradita commentariis de motibus stellae Martis* (Prague, 1609), *Gesammelte Werke*, Max Caspar (ed.) (18 vols.; Munich, 1937-59), III, 121, 461-62.

[28] Dreyer, *Tychonis Brahe opera omnia*, I, xxxix-xl. Dreyer had earlier accepted Kepler's account in Tycho Brahe, 179, but changed his opinion on the basis of Tycho's notebooks. Owen Gingerich, "Dreyer and Tycho's World System," *Sky and Telescope*, 64 (1982), 138-40.

[29] Schofield, 66-68.

[30] A close reading of the notebooks might elucidate this problem.

[31] Tycho repeats the argument to Rothmann (VI, 179) and Hagecius (VII, 199-200) in 1589.

[32] Copernicus, f. iiij v. In this passage a "mathematical" argument for Tycho seems to be one that depends on the internal consistency of a system.

[33] Given his commitment to the immobility of the earth Tycho discusses Copernicus's motion of the earth as the motion of the sun. The two are interchangeable in the geocentric and heliocentric models.

[34] See the similar discussion in his *Astronomiae instauratae mechanica* (Wandesburg, 1598), V, 45.

[35] See Owen Hannaway, "Laboratory Design and the Aim of Science: Andreas Libavius versus Tycho Brahe," *Isis*, 77 (1986), 585-610.

[36] See Victor E. Thoren, "Tycho Brahe's Discovery of the Variation," *Centaurus*, 12 (1967), 151-66.

[37] Victor E. Thoren, "An Early Instance of Deductive Discovery: Tycho Brahe's Lunar Theory," *Isis*, 58 (1967), 19-36.

[38] The reference is to *De revolutionibus*, book IV, chapter 15: "Because of the obstacle of the lunar parallaxes, fortune did not give us the opportunity to test, as it gave Ptolemy, that the greatest latitude of the moon, conforming to the angle of intersection of its orb and the ecliptic, is 5°." Copernicus, f. 117r.

[39] Victor E. Thoren, "Tycho and Kepler on the Lunar Theory," *Publications of the Astronomical Society of the Pacific*, 114 (1967), 484.

[40] Tycho is referring to Copernicus's complaints in *De revolutionibus*, book V, chapter 30, on Mercury: "Of course the ancients showed us this way of examining the path of this star [Mercury], but they enjoyed a more serene sky, where no doubt the Nile, as they say, does not exhale vapors like the Vistula where we are. Nature has denied us this advantage since we live in a more rigorous climate where calm weather is rarer and in addition it is more rarely possible to see Mercury because of the great inclination of the sphere." Copernicus, f. 369r.

[41] William Norlind, "Tycho Brahe et ses rapports avec l'Italie," *Scientia*, 49 (1955), 51.

[42] *Experimentum* here denotes a refined observation to be used as the basis for a choice between theories. For more on the use of the term in this period see Charles B. Schmitt, "Experience and Experiment: A Comparison of Zabarella's View with Galileo's in de Motu," *Studies in the Renaissance*, 16 (1969), 80-138.

[43] See C. Doris Hellman, "Was Tycho Brahe as Influential as He Thought?" *British Journal for the History of Science*, 1 (1963), 295-324.

[44] Dreyer, *Tycho Brahe*, 336.

[45] Ibid., 265.

[46] Bruce T. Moran, "Christoph Rothmann, the Copernican Theory and Institutional and Technical Influences on the Criticism of Aristotelian Cosmology," *Sixteenth-Century Journal*, 13 (1982), 90-97.

[47] Schofield, 69.

[48] J. L. E. Dreyer, "Tycho Brahe's Catalogue of Stars," *Observatory*, 40 (1917), 233. Victor E. Thoren, "The Comet of 1577 and Tycho Brahe's System of the World," *Archives Internationales d'Histoire des Sciences*, 29 (1979), 55.

[49] Victor E. Thoren, "Tycho and Kepler on the Lunar Theory," 483.

[50] See for example Judith V. Field, *Kepler's Geometrical Cosmology* (Chicago, 1988) and Bruce Stephenson, *Kepler's Physical Astronomy* (New York, 1987).

Irving A. Kelter (essay date 1995)

SOURCE: "The Refusal to Accommodate: Jesuit Exegetes and the Copernican System" in *Sixteenth Century Journal*, Vol. XXVI, No. 2, 1995, pp. 273-83.

[*In the following essay, Kelter traces the early response of the Catholic exegetical community to Copernican theory.*]

On March 5, 1616, the Roman Catholic Church's Sacred Congregation of the Index issued a decree concerning the new Copernican cosmology and current works defending it. The edict prohibited, until corrected, both Nicholas Copernicus' classic work, the ***Revolutions of the Heavenly Spheres*** (1543), and the commentary on Job (1584) by the Spanish theologian Didacus à Stunica (Diego de Zúñiga). The Carmelite Paolo Foscarini's *Letter . . . on the Opinion of the Pythagoreans and of Copernicus on the Mobility of the Earth and the Stability of the Sun* (1615) was prohibited absolutely for attempting to reconcile Copernicanism with the Bible and for attempting to prove Copernicanism to be consonant with the truth. All other books of this nature were similarly condemned. This condemnation, which rested on the judgment that the new heliocentric and geokinetic cosmology was formally heretical and contrary to the faith, also led to the later, far more famous personal condemnation of Galileo.[1]

In his study of the condemnation of Copernicanism, R. J. Blackwell properly directs our attention to the problem of biblical objections to the heliocentric cosmology and to the standards of biblical exegesis current in the Counter-Reformation Church.[2] To understand the condemnation of Copernicanism in 1616 and its role in that of Galileo in 1633, one must determine how the Copernican theory was received by the Catholic exegetical community at the time of condemnation.

To gauge this reception, one must go back to the sixteenth century and to the first figure in this tale, Didacus à Stunica (1536-1597), the Augustinian monk whose work on Job was included in the condemnation of March 5, 1616. Stunica was the first Catholic exegete to examine the Copernican theory in a printed biblical commentary. Stunica's earliest examination of Copernican theory, his 1584 *In Iob commentaria* (Toledo; reprint Rome, 1591), has become justly famous in the annals of Copernicanism. It is the only printed work of Catholic biblical exegesis between Copernicus' 1543 ***On the Revolutions*** and Foscarini's 1615 *Letter*, which attempts to reconcile scriptural passages with the new system of the universe. Strictly speaking, Foscarini's *Letter* is a short treatise couched in the form of a letter and not truly a work of biblical commentary at all, and Stunica's work on Job is the only pro-Copernican Catholic biblical commentary known from the early modern period.[3]

Medieval and early modern exegetes routinely incorporated philosophical and scientific material into their works. Stunica is no exception, so it is not surprising that in discussing Job 9:6, "Who shaketh the Earth out of her place, and the pillars thereof tremble," which seems to speak of the motion of the Earth, Stunica enter into a detailed astronomical discourse. He argues that the mystery of this passage can be wiped away by employing the Pythagorean opinion of the motion of the Earth, revived in early modern times by Copernicus. According to Stunica, Copernicus' theory enabled professional astronomers to resolve problems such as the determination of the year (the problem of calendar reform) and the rate of the precession of the equinoxes. Consequently, Copernicus' theory was the best scientific theory available.[4]

Stunica then turned to reconciling anti-Copernican biblical passages with the new astronomy. He resolved the problem of Eccl. 1:4, "One generation passeth away, and another generation cometh, but the Earth standeth for ever"—a classic anti-Copernican passage—by arguing that this passage does not deal with terrestrial immobility but only with the Earth's remaining unchanged in contrast to the vagaries of human existence. Stunica contended that no passage of scripture contradicts Copernicus if it is interpreted correctly, and any passage which speaks of the motion of the Sun, such as Eccl. 1:5-6, can be understood as speaking in the language of the people and not in the language of physical truth.[5] This theory of accommodation was standard for later Catholic Copernicans, notably Galileo and Foscarini.

As proof of his commitment to Copernicanism, Stunica argues that the biblical passages which assert the Earth's immobility are far outweighed by the assertion of the Earth's mobility in Job 9:6. Indeed, he concludes his exegesis by remarking that Job 9:6 demonstrates the miraculous power and wisdom of God, which can imbue the excessively heavy Earth with motion.[6] Such a declaration leads to the conclusion that Stunica, at least in 1584, was leaning towards accepting the physical truth of the Copernican theory of the motion of the Earth. It must be pointed out that in his later work of philosophy, the *Philosophiae prima pars* (Toledo, 1597), Stunica came to reject the mobility of the Earth, not on exegetical and theological grounds but on physical ones.[7]

In the last years of the sixteenth century and the early years of the seventeenth, Catholic exegetes paid more attention to the astronomy of Copernicus. This attention, however, was of a negative sort. Nicolaus Serarius (Niccolò Serario, 1555-1609), Johannes Lorinus (Jean Lorin, 1559-1634), and Johannes de Pineda (Juan de Pineda, 1557-1637), all members of the scientifically prestigious Jesuit Order and exegetes of distinction, knew something of Copernicus' theories and harshly rejected them.

For twenty years, Serarius occupied the chairs of theology and sacred scripture at Wurtzburg and Mainz,

and was called by Cardinal Baronius "the light of the Church of Germany." Lorinus taught philosophy, theology, and sacred scripture in Rome, Paris, and Milan; during one part of his life, he was also theologian to the Father General of the order. Pineda first taught on Aristotle in Seville and Cordova and then made a particular study of the Bible, which he taught for eighteen years in Cordova, Seville, and Madrid.[8] All three wrote numerous biblical commentaries and were Bible authorities to be reckoned with. Stunica's commentary and the response to it inaugurated what Zofia Wardeska calls a new stage in the religious reception of Copernicanism, one of a theological, semiofficial polemic.[9]

Lorinus, in his commentaries on the Acts of the Apostles and Ecclesiastes, attacks the theory of the motion of the Earth, defended by Copernicus and Stunica among others. Lorinus supports his arguments by citing the writings of "our Clavius," the famed Jesuit astronomer at the Collegio Romano, and the exegetical writings of the Spanish Jesuit Pineda. Before detailing Lorinus' objections to Copernicanism, the importance of the works of Clavius should be underscored. Edward Grant writes that Christopher Clavius' *In Sphaeram Ioannis de Sacro Bosco Commentarius* (Rome, 1570), a best-selling astronomical textbook, was an immediate source for at least three biblical passages used against heliocentrism and geokineticism, namely Eccl. 1:4-5, Ps. 18:6-7, and Ps. 103:5.[10] The use of biblical passages to support the idea of the Earth's immobility also appeared in the Coimbra Jesuits' influential *Commentarii . . . In quatuor libros De coelo Aristotelis Stagaritae* (1st ed., Coimbra, 1592).[11] According to Grant, these passages were of great import; for Catholic Aristotelians, they became "the most potent weapon in defense of the traditional geocentric cosmology."[12]

In his *In Acta Apostolorum commentarii* (Lyon, 1605), Lorinus denounces the supporters of the theory of the mobility of the Earth as supporting falsehood. The theory was proclaimed to be "dangerous and repugnant to the faith," as is shown in Eccl. 1:4. Although Lorinus admitted that Eccl. 1:4 could be interpreted correctly in the manner of Stunica and that the passage could very well be interpreted as referring to the Earth's ability to preserve its own nature in contrast to the changing generations of human beings, still Lorinus rejects such a reading. He argues for a fuller and deeper interpretation in which the Latin term stat, used in this passage, must also be taken to mean terrestrial immobility.[13] Such arguments reappeared in Lorinus' *Commentarii in Ecclesiasten* (Lyon, 1606).[14]

Nicolaus Serarius considers the Copernican theory at length in volume 1, part 2, question 14 ("Whether the Sun and Moon can be motionless by nature?") of his massive *Iosue, ab utero ad ipsum usque tumulum* (Paris, 1610). Whereas Serarius describes Copernicus as "the renowned astronomer of our age, called by some another Ptolemy," and notes that Copernicus had been praised by Catholic astronomers such as Clavius and Magini, still Serarius rejects Copernicus' revolutionary ideas. Distinguishing between "hypotheses" and "truths" in astronomy, Serarius contends that if one asserted seriously Copernicus' "hypotheses" to be "true," one could not possibly be immune from the charge of heresy. "Truly, Scripture always attributes quietude to the Earth and motion to the Sun and Moon and when the latter stars are said to be stationary this is signified as having been accomplished by a great miracle." Serarius concludes this denunciation of the new cosmology by arguing that "this opinion has been destroyed by all philosophers, save for Nicetas [read Hicetas] and a few Pythagoreans and their disciples, and all the Fathers [of the Church] and the theologians of every school have spoken out against it." Of course, Serarius buttresses his denunciation by citing the now standard anti-Copernican texts of Eccl. 1:4 and Ps. 103:5.[15] This particular biblical commentary was cited by the Dominican friar Tommaso Caccini in his inflammatory sermon delivered in Florence against Galileo and his followers on December 20, 1614.[16]

Johannes de Pineda, to whom Lorinus refers as an authority, was the first to take up the cudgels against Stunica and Copernicus. Pineda attacks both of them in his *Commentariorum in Iob libri tredecim tomis duobus distincti* (1597, 1600, 1612) and *In Ecclesiasten commentariorum liber unus* (1619, 1620).[17] His denunciation grew in force until, in the first edition of the work on Ecclesiastes (1619), Pineda criticizes Stunica, a fellow Spaniard, as "clearly deluded" ("*perspicue hallucinatus est*") when he had offered his pro-Copernican exegesis. Pineda admits, as a number of Catholic exegetes did, that the true intention and meaning of Eccl. 1:4 appeared to be satisfied if it was understood to refer to the Earth's withstanding destruction and change caused by generation and corruption. Nonetheless, he went on to affirm that the use of "*stat*" in this most crucial passage meant "not only incorruptible, but truly immobile and fixed" ("*sed stet non solum incorrupta, sed etiam immota et fixa*"). At the very end of his discussion of Eccl. 1:4, after attacking Stunica and citing the anti-Copernican Jesuit astronomer Christopher Scheiner, Pineda derides the Copernican system as "absurd and false." Such words echoed those used by Clavius in his astronomical textbook and possibly those of the Church theologians who had officially condemned the new cosmology in 1616.[18]

A denunciation of Stunica and Copernicus remained a commonplace of Jesuit exegesis. As examples of other rejections, one can cite the *Commentarius in Ecclesiasten* (Antwerp, 1638) by Cornelius à Lapide (Cornelius van den Steyn, 1567-1637), christened the "universal commentator of the Baroque age,"[19] and the *Iob*

elucidatus (Antwerp, 1646) of Balthasarus Corderus (Balthasar Cordier, 1592-1650). In his commentary on Ecclesiastes, Lapide again argues that the literal sense of "*stat*" must be that of terrestrial immobility and fixity, and goes on to cite explicitly the condemnation of Copernicanism under Paul V in 1616.[20]

In Corderus' elucidation of Job 9:6, one finds again the appeal to Clavius' text and to biblical passages such as Eccl. 1:4. Corderus roundly rejects the Copernican interpretation of Stunica and instead proposes that the motion of the pillars of the Earth referred to in the passage from Job could be understood either as the motion of the Earth's mountains or as motions in the Earth's subterranean depths.[21] This exegesis simply continued that of Thomas Aquinas in his own *Literal Exposition on Job*,[22] and Corderus acknowledges Aquinas' authority in this regard, as had Pineda in his earlier commentary of 1612. It must be remembered that the Jesuits had taken Aquinas to their hearts as a teacher in theology, although, according to Rivkha Feldhay, Jesuit Thomism, as distinct from Dominican Thomism, was neither uncritical nor all-encompassing.[23]

What conclusions can be drawn from this exploration of Catholic exegetes and the Copernican system around the time of the condemnation of 1616? It is certainly true that these Counter-Reformation Jesuit exegetes held tightly to what they conceived to be the readily apparent "literal" sense of the biblical passages being debated. This emphasis on the simple literal interpretation of the Bible was a growing tendency in the Catholic exegetical community at this time.

The literal sense was in fact the foundation of all scriptural exegesis. In his study of Genesis commentaries of the early modern era, Arnold Williams discerns not only a decrease in the spiritual exegesis common in the Middle Ages but also a shift in the treatment of it to that of an "application" rather than a true "interpretation."[24] Experts have noted the growth among Catholics of what is called the "Theory of Dictation," which taught that God dictated not only the ideas present in the Bible but also all of the words and verbal expressions.[25]

The distinguished Jesuit theologian and opponent of Copernicanism, Robert Cardinal Bellarmine, exhibited such an extreme devotion to the words of the Bible. As he wrote in one of his major theological works, "not the propositions alone [of the Bible], but each and every word pertains to the faith. We believe that no word in scripture is unnecessary, nor is it incorrectly placed." This statement, coupled with Bellarmine's belief that every biblical passage has a simple, literal interpretation but all do not have a "figurative" or "spiritual" interpretation, led him to conclude "at least some of the passages implying geocentrism had a simple ("*simplex*") literal sense and were, therefore, explicit divine teachings."[26] As Ugo Baldini and George Coyne show so well, this devotion to the words of the Bible and their "literal" interpretation led Bellarmine to deny such tenets of the traditional cosmology/astronomy as the perfect heavenly ether and the use of eccentrics and epicycles. Such devotion also led him to uphold, against the Copernicans, geocentrism and terrestrial immobility.[27]

The Jesuit critics of Copernicus, however, did not denounce the theory of accommodation and the explication of biblical passages according to appearances *in toto*, but only their specific applications in pro-Copernican works. Indeed, they themselves admitted that in certain cases the pro-Copernican exegesis of passages such as Eccl. 1:4 was quite acceptable.

One example of the Jesuit use of the principle of accommodation was the discussion of the heavenly spheres in yet another biblical commentary, the *Commentariorum et disputationum in Genesim, tomi quatuor* (1st ed., Rome, 1589-1598) by Benedictus Pererius (Benito Pereyra, 1535-1610). He was, at various times, professor of philosophy, theology, and sacred scripture at the Collegio Romano, and was the author of a number of important works on science and philosophy, as well as on the Bible. Alistair Crombie and William Wallace point to Pererius' lectures in Rome as influential in the formation of the young Galileo.[28] In the *Commentariorum et disputationum in Genesim*, which has been credited with being the most popular Christian commentary on Genesis of the early modern period,[29] Pererius analyzes the nature of the heavens and of the supposed heavenly spheres. He utilizes the theory of accommodation and exegesis *secundum apparentiam* to reconcile those biblical passages which seem to ascribe motion to the planets themselves with the Aristotelian idea of invisible spheres which move the planets.[30] Here accommodation was used to uphold Aristotle and not to destroy his authority.

How firmly wedded Pererius was to the Aristotelian worldview is revealed by his *Commentariorum et disputationum in Genesim*. Pererius never mentions the Copernican theory in his commentary and Copernicus' name appears only in a discussion of when the world would end.[31] However, in a discussion of Josh. 10:12, Pererius treats the traditional exegesis as unquestionable and speaks of Joshua as "ruling" ("*imperaret*") the Sun and the Moon.[32] In his analysis of the nature of the Sun, Pererius points to Eccl. 1:5 as proof that, according to Solomon, the Sun moves in a circle in the heavens.[33] In a rather lengthy "Section on the Position and Immobility of the Earth," Pererius includes citations to standard philosophical and biblical texts (Aristotle's *De coelo*, Ps. 103, Eccl. 1:4) which argue against the motion of the Earth, and he insists on the Earth's centrality and its lack of motion.[34]

Pererius' devotion to such scientific ideas as the Earth's centrality and immobility leads to another conclusion concerning these Jesuit exegetes and their relationship to Copernican cosmology. The Jesuits were indisputably the educators of Counter-Reformation Europe. In their ideas and methods they were not hide-bound traditionalists and they were receptive to new ideas in the humanities and the sciences.[35] Yet in the end, they saw themselves as the defenders of the old intellectual order. "The Jesuits," in the words of Richard Westfall, "sought to employ the new learning to bolster the old. In natural philosophy, they were wedded to Aristotle, whose philosophy they saw as the foundation of Scholastic theology, the intellectual rampart of the Catholic religion."[36]

Finally, more important than the details of the reception of the Copernican cosmology by these Jesuit exegetes and more important than their devotion to Aristotle was their conception of the proper relationship between science and religion. Their entire approach to the problem of Copernicanism was the reverse of that taken by Stunica, Foscarini, and Galileo. Whereas the latter tend to argue that biblical passages about the natural world should be judged against philosophical and scientific truths, a Jesuit exegete such as Pineda argues that physical truths must be judged against biblical passages.

What can be more revealing of this approach than the very beginning of Pineda's exegesis of Eccl. 1:4: "Physical truths have been very carefully revealed by this judgment from Solomon" ("*Physica dogmata subtiliter hac sententia a Salomone indicata*")? Pineda then lists seven fundamental propositions confirmed by biblical passages, all of which deal with the centrality and immobility of the Earth.[37] Such an attitude is also evident in Lapide's *Commentarium in Pentateuchum Mosis* (1st ed., 1617), in which it is asserted that "one must adapt philosophy and physics to sacred scripture and the word of God. . . . It is forbidden on the contrary to subordinate sacred scripture to the words of the philosophers or to the light of nature. . . ."[38]

What was at stake here was not only a matter of differing interpretations of the Bible or even of warring cosmologies. What was at stake was the proper relationship of the emerging natural sciences—among them astronomy—to theology. Were these sciences to be subordinate to theology, "queen of the sciences," as it was called in the Middle Ages, or were they to be independent of its control? Copernicus had already called for this independence when, in his preface to Pope Paul III, he asked for protection from "babblers" who would use biblical passages against his theory and who were ignorant of astronomy.[39] Such a call for independence must certainly have antagonized the professional theologians and exegetes of the Counter-Reformation Church.

Intertwined with this independence movement was the contemporary debate concerning the status of the mathematical sciences, including astronomy. Contrary to the claims of a number of contemporary Aristotelian philosophers, certain mathematicians and mathematical astronomers had made expanded claims for the nobility of their science and for the physical truth of its assertions. Such a debate between the philosophers and the mathematicians was raging within the Jesuit Order itself, Clavius being the most prominent defender of the dignity and worth of mathematics.[40]

Is the Jesuit struggle between the philosophers and the mathematicians in some way behind this rejection of Copernicus? It is certainly no accident that none of the Jesuit exegetes under examination had any close connection to the mathematical sciences, although several taught and wrote philosophy. Was the refusal to accept the new worldview based also on Clavius' inability to raise the status of the mathematical disciplines to that of "true sciences" which could claim certain knowledge? Was this defeat within the Jesuit Order itself a by-product of the Jesuits' return to "solid and uniform doctrine" as ordered by the general, Claudio Aquaviva, in the years immediately preceding the condemnation of 1616? Motivated by concerns of internal philosophical differences and external criticisms, notably by Dominican theologians, Aquaviva reaffirmed the stipulations that all Jesuits were to teach according to the authority of Aristotle in philosophy and Aquinas in theology. By creating "solid and uniform doctrine," Aquaviva intended to restore unity, strengthen the order, and authenticate its orthodoxy. Contemporary Aristotelianism and Thomism, however, did not allow the mathematical sciences to claim "methodological autonomy" and only allowed them to claim probable knowledge.[41]

This form of Aristotelian-Thomist criticism of the mathematical sciences was evident as early as 1544 in the *De veritate sacrae scripturae* by the Dominican friar Giovanni Maria Tolosani. Tolosani sharply rebuked Copernicus, an expert in mathematics and astronomy, for being deficient in physics and logic. The Dominican friar also rebuked Copernicus for being ignorant of the Bible and for misplacing the mathematical science of astronomy over physics and over theology.[42]

Is this not the key to understanding Serarius' statement that if one asserted Copernicus' "hypotheses" to be "true" then one could not be immune from the charge of heresy? Is this not behind the famous warning issued by Bellarmine to Foscarini in April 1615 to speak of Copernicanism solely in a hypothetical sense lest it conflict with philosophy and the Bible?[43] Are these not all important factors behind the Jesuits' response to Copernicus and their refusal to accommodate?

Notes

[1] For the text of the condemnation, see S. Pagano, ed., *I documenti del processo di Galileo Galilei* (Vatican City: Pontificia Academica Scientiarum, 1984), 102-3. For the final results of the papal investigation of the "Galileo Affair," see *Origins* 22 (November 12, 1992): 369, 371-75.

[2] R. J. Blackwell, *Galileo, Bellarmine, and the Bible* (Notre Dame: University of Notre Dame Press, 1991), which includes new translations of many valuable texts, including the work of Foscarini. For my review of this book, see *The Modern Schoolman* 69 (January 1992): 149-52.

[3] The case of Marin Mersenne's *Quaestiones celeberrimae in Genesim* (1623) must be mentioned here. In that work Mersenne treated extensively the arguments for and against Copernicanism, and seems to have been disposed favorably to some aspects of the new astronomy. Still, he argued that no proof was available to substantiate it. Therefore, those who propounded Copernicanism were judged correctly by the Church to have been guilty of temerity in supporting it. However, Mersenne left the door open for a change if and when proof was available. See the important study of W. L. Hine, "Mersenne and Copernicanism," *Isis* 64 (1973): 18-32. P. Dear, Mersenne and the Learning of the Schools (Ithaca: Cornell University Press, 1988), 32-34, argues that Mersenne's position on this issue was governed by his "probabilistic" understanding of the status of astronomical theories. When he wrote his *Quaestiones*, Mersenne viewed the Ptolemaic system as having the weight of probability behind it. Later, the "probabilities" shifted in favor of Copernicanism.

[4] See Z. Wardeska, *Teoria heliocentryczna w interpretacji teologów xvi wieku* (Wroclaw: Ossolineum, 1975), photoreproduction 47a, for a convenient reproduction of this section of Stunica's commentary. Also see G. McColley, ed., "A Facsimile of Salusbury's Translation of Didacus à Stunica's Commentary Upon Job," *Annals of Science* 2 (1937): 179-82; for a new translation, see *Blackwell, Galileo, Bellarmine, and the Bible*, 185-86; for Stunica, see also F. Barone, "Diego de Zúñiga e Galileo Galilei: Astronomia eliostatica ed esegesi biblica," *Critica storica* 19 (1982): 319-34.

All translations of biblical passages in this article are from the Rheims-Douay English translation.

[5] See Wardeska, *Teoria heliocentryczna*, photoreproduction 47b, for this portion of the commentary. Stunica's interpretation of Eccl. 1:4 goes back at least as far as the writings of Gregory the Great and Bede; for these references, see Thomas Aquinas, *Catena Aurea* as given in M. F. Toal, ed. and trans., *The Sunday Sermons of the Great Fathers* (Chicago: Henry Regnery Co., 1958), 1:8.

[6] Wardeska, *Teoria heliocentryczna*, photoreproduction 47b.

[7] *Didacus à Stunica, Philosophiae prima pars* (Toledo, 1597), book 4, chap. 5. Stunica's argument was against the diurnal rotation of the Earth; he contended that he could come to no conclusive statement concerning the annual revolution of the Earth.

[8] For basic bio-bibliographical information on these Jesuits see A. de Backer, *Bibliothèque des écrivains de la Compagnie de Jésus ou Notices Bibliographiques* (Liège, 1872), 2: 807-9, 1981-83; 3: 761-66. R. Westman, "The Copernicans and the Churches," in *God & Nature: Historical Essays on the Encounter between Christianity and Science,* ed. D. C. Lindberg and R. L. Numbers (Berkeley: University of California Press, 1986), 93-95, discusses briefly the reception of Copernicanism by some Jesuit thinkers.

[9] Wardeska, *Teoria heliocentryczna*, 137.

[10] E. Grant, "In Defense of the Earth's Centrality and Immobility: Scholastic Reaction to Copernicanism in the Seventeenth Century," *Transactions of the American Philosophical Society* 74 (1984): 61; see Wardeska, *Teoria heliocentryczna,* photoreproduction 6b, for this section of Clavius' text. The most detailed treatment of Clavius' response to Copernicus is J. M. Lattis, "Christopher Clavius and the Sphere of Sacrobosco: The Roots of Jesuit Astronomy on the Eve of the Copernican Revolution" (Ph.D. dissertation, University of Wisconsin, Madison, 1989), 184-228; at 193-94, Lattis observes that Clavius did not explicitly link Copernicus' name and theory with the citations of biblical passages against the motion of the Earth. Lattis' work appears revised as *Between Copernicus and Galileo: Christoph Clavius and the Collapse of Ptolemaic Cosmology* (Chicago: University of Chicago Press, 1994).

[11] Wardeska, *Teoria heliocentryczna*, photoreproduction 7.

[12] Grant, "In Defense of the Earth's Centrality," 63.

[13] Wardeska, *Teoria heliocentryczna*, photoreproduction 22.

[14] Ibid., photoreproduction 23.

[15] N. Serarius, S.J., *Iosue, ab utero ad ipsum usque tumulum . . . , Tomus prior gesta eius usque ad bella, tomus posterior bella omnia ab eo gesta . . .* (Paris, 1610), cols. 1004-6.

[16] J. Brodrick, S.J., *The Life and Work of Blessed Robert Francis Cardinal Bellarmine S.J. 1542-1621* (London: Burns Oates and Washbourne, 1928), 2: 352-53. On the use of Serarius, also see Caccini's deposition of March 20, 1615, to the Inquisition in: M.A. Finocchiaro, ed. and trans., *The Galileo Affair: A*

Documentary History (Berkeley: University of California Press, 1989), 137.

[17] H. Grisar, S.J., *Galileistudien* (Regensburg, 1882), 264, and Wardeska, *Teoria heliocentryczna*, photoreproduction 31, provide references to Pineda's 1597 and 1600 commentaries on Job. For the later commentaries on Job and Ecclesiastes see J. de Pineda, S.J., *Commentariorum in Iob libri tredecim tomis duobus distincti* (Antwerp, 1612), 415-17; *Commentarii in Ecclesiasten* (Antwerp, 1619), fols. 128-31; *Commentarii in Ecclesiasten* (Antwerp, 1620), fols. 111-14.

[18] Pineda, *Commentarii in Ecclesiasten*, (1619) fol. 131; (1620) fol. 114. In defense of his geocentric and geostatic cosmology, Pineda cited Clavius, *In Sphacram Ioannis de Sacro Bosco Commentarius*, and the work of Christopher Scheiner, S.J., whom Pineda took to be the author of the *Disquisitiones mathematicae* (Ingolstadt, 1614). For an excellent summary of Pineda's exegesis, sec C. Martini, "Gli esegeti del tempo di Galileo," in *Nel quarto centenario della nascita di Galileo Galilei* (Milan: Societa editrice Vita e pensiero, 1966), 119-21; a briefer notice is found in R. Fabris, *Galileo Galilei e gli orientamenti esegetici del suo tempo* (Vatican City: Pontificia Academica Scientiarum, 1986), 39.

Pineda's relationship to the condemnation of 1616 is difficult to determine. Although the first edition of his *In Ecclesiasten commentariorum liber unus* appeared in 1619, Pineda made no mention of the earlier condemnation. Martini argued that Pineda was probably unaware of the ruling; otherwise he would have cited it. This may not have been the case. It is important to note that Pineda was the author of the Spanish version of the *Index of Prohibited Books*, which should have contained the emended edition of Copernicus, *Revolutions*, as required by the condemnation of 1616. As shown by O. Gingerich, "The Censorship of Copernicus' De Revolutionibus," *Annali dell' Istituto e Musco di Storia della Scienza di Firenze* 6 (1981): 57-59, no changes were required in Copernicus' masterpiece according to the *Index* printed in Seville in 1632. Gingerich, "Censorship of Copernicus," contends that Pineda and other Spaniards took the condemnation of 1616 to have been purely an Italian affair seemingly not binding on Catholics in other countries. Consequently, the fact that Pineda made no mention of the condemnation in his work on Ecclesiastes does not mean that he was unaware of the ruling; however, J. Pardo Tomás in his *Ciencia y Censura: La Inquisición Española y los libros científicos en los siglos XVI y XVII* (Madrid: Consejo Superior de Investigaciones Científicas, 1991), 183-89, indicates that Copernicus' work was missing from the Seville Index because of a "mistake," and that the required corrections to it are included in later indexes under the heading of Rheticus, a disciple of Copernicus.

19 E. J. Creehan, S.J., "The Bible in the Roman Catholic Church from Trent to the Present Day," in *The Cambridge History of the Bible*, ed. S. L. Greenslade (Cambridge: Cambridge University Press, 1976), 3: 216.

20 Cornelius à Lapide, S.J., *Commentaria in Vetus et Novum Testamentum* (Venice, 1761), 5: 21-23; the New York Public Library's copy of this work has the volume marked as volume four.

21 J. P. Migne, ed., *Scripturae Sacrae cursus completus* (Paris: 1839), 13: 822-24. Such was the reading of Mersenne, as demonstrated by Hine, "Mersenne and Copernicanism," 25; Mersenne also was leery concerning the use of the principle of accommodation, as recommended by the Copernicans. It is worth observing that thirteen years after the condemnation of Galileo and thirty years after the condemnation of Copernicanism, the work of Corderus contains no mention of those crucial events in the history of the relationship between Catholicism and modern astronomy.

22 Thomas Aquinas, T*he Literal Exposition on Job: A Scriptural Commentary Concerning Providence*, trans. A. Damico (Atlanta: Scholars Press, 1989), 168.

23 R. Feldhay, "Knowledge and Salvation in Jesuit Culture," *Science in Context* 1 (1987): 198-201.

24 A. Williams, T*he Common Expositor: An Account of the Commentaries on Genesis 1527-1633* (Chapel Hill: University of North Carolina Press, 1948), 20-21.

25 On the theory of "dictation" among Catholic theologians and exegetes during this period, see R. F. Smith, S.J., "Inspiration and Inerrancy," in *The Jerome Biblical Commentary*, ed. R. E. Brown, S.S., J. A. Fitzmyer, S.J., and R. E. Murphy, O.Carm. (Englewood Cliffs: Prentice Hall, 1968), 2: 505; B. Vawter, *Biblical Inspiration* (Philadelphia: Westminster Press, 1972), 58-63.

26 The statement by Bellarmine is taken from his *Prima controversia generalis de concilis, et ecclesia militante;* the Latin text and its analysis is in U. Baldini and G. Coyne, S.J., eds. and trans., *The Louvain Lectures (Lectiones Lovanienses) of Bellarmine and the Autograph Copy of his 1616 Declaration to Galileo* (Vatican City: Specola Vaticana, 1984), 40, n. 92.

27 Ibid., 18-22, 38-43, nn. 83-94.

28 For basic bio-bibliographical information, see de Backer, *Bibliothèque des écrivains*, 2: 1861-66; for material on Pererius and the young Galileo see A. C. Crombie, "The Sources of Galileo's Early Natural Philosophy," in *Reason, Experiment, and Mysticism in the Scientific Revolution,* ed. M. L. Righini-Bonelli and W. R. Shea (New York: Science History Publications, 1975), 162-66; W. A. Wallace, ed. and trans. *Galileo's*

Early Notebooks: The Physical Questions (Notre Dame: University of Notre Dame Press, 1977), 13-15 and passim.

29 Williams, *The Common Expositor*, 8.

30 Ibid., 186; Pererius was aware of astronomical observations such as those of the nova of 1572 which cast doubt on the traditional system of the heavens. As Williams, *The Common Expositor*, 189, observes: "He [Pererius] offers three possible explanations [of the nova of 1572]: that it was generated and corrupted in the heavens, that it was another wandering planet in addition to the seven already known, and that the supposedly fixed stars are not fixed but also have their proper courses. Any one of these explanations tears a hole in the approved system. Pererius apparently did not see their bearing, for instance, on the theory of the solid spheres." On this matter, see also Baldini and Coyne, *The Louvain Lectures*, 34, n. 40.

31 Williams, *The Common Expositor*, 189.

32 B. Pererius, S.J., *Commentariorum et disputationum in Genesim*, 4 vols. (Cologne, 1601), 3: 962.

33 Ibid., 1: 92.

34 B. Pererius, S.J., *Prior tomus commentariorum et disputationum in Genesim* (Ingolstadt, 1590), 66-67; the relative length of Pererius' section on the centrality and immobility of the Earth may very well reflect his knowledge of, and opposition to, the Copernican theory; I thank Thomas Settle and Nancy Siraisi for this suggestion.

35 G. E. Ganss, S.J., *Saint Ignatius' Idea of a Jesuit University* (Milwaukee: Marquette University Press, 1956), is a good study of Jesuit education and how it related to medieval and Renaissance educational ideas and practices. J. W. O'Malley, *The First Jesuits* (Cambridge, MA: Harvard University Press, 1993), 243-64, has perceptive remarks on the Jesuit adoption of both scholasticism and humanism. On the scientific interests and activities of the Jesuits, see the introductory studies by J. L. Heilbron, "Science in the Church," and S. J. Harris, "Transposing the Merton Thesis: Apostolic Spirituality and the Establishment of the Jesuit Scientific Tradition," in *Science in Context* 3 (1989): 9-65. For more detail, see the study of S. J. Harris, "Jesuit Ideology and Jesuit Science: Scientific Activity in the Society of Jesus, 1540-1773" (Ph.D. dissertation, University of Wisconsin, Madison, 1988).

36 R. S. Westfall, "Galileo and the Jesuits," in *Metaphysics and Philosophy of Science in the Seventeenth and Eighteenth Centuries: Essays in honor of Gerd Buchdahl*, ed. R. S. Woolhouse (Dordrecht: Kluwer Academic Publishers, 1988), 58. This essay is reprint-

ed in R. S. Westfall, *Essays on the Trial of Galileo* (Notre Dame: University of Notre Dame Press, 1989), 31-57.

[37] Pineda, *Commentarii in Ecclesiasten*, (1619) fol. 128, (1620) fol. 111.

[38] F. Laplanche, "Herméneutique biblique et cosmologie mosaïque," in *Les Églises face aux sciences du Moyen Age au XXe siècle*, ed. O. Fatio (Geneva: Droz, 1991), 34, quotes and translates into French this passage from the Paris, 1621, edition of Lapide's commentary. The Latin passage is in Migne, ed., *Scripturae Sacrae cursus completus*, 5: 81.

[39] N. Copernicus, On the Revolutions, ed. J. Dobryzycki, trans. and comm. E. Rosen (Baltimore: Johns Hopkins University Press, 1978), 5.

[40] On this important issue, see U. Baldini, "Legem impone subactis: Teologia, filosofia e scienze matematiche nella didattica e nella dottrina della Compagnia di Gesù (1550-1630)," in his *Legem impone subactis: Studi su filosofia e scienza dei Gesuiti in Italia 1540-1632* (Rome: Bulzoni editore, 1992), 19-73; W. A. Wallace, *Galileo and His Sources: The Heritage of the Collegio Romano in Galileo's Science* (Princeton: Princeton University Press, 1984), 126-48, and Lattis, "Christopher Clavius," 41-52. For a recent analysis of this struggle in the context of Galileo's career, see M. Biagioli, *Galileo, Courtier: The Practice of Science in the Culture of Absolutism* (Chicago: University of Chicago Press, 1993), 211-44.

[41] The relationship between the adoption of Aristotelianism and Thomism and the critique of the mathematical sciences is developed by Feldhay, "Knowledge and Salvation," 195-213, and continued in R. Feldhay and M. Heyd, "The Discourse of Pious Science," *Science in Context* 3 (1989): 109-42, esp. 123-27. For details on the return to "solid and uniform doctrine" under Aquaviva, see U. Baldini, "Uniformitas et soliditas doctrinae. Le censure librorum e opinionum," in idem, *Legem impone subactis*, 75-119; Blackwell, *Galileo, Bellarmine, and the Bible*, 135-64, and Harris, "Jesuit Ideology and Jesuit Science," 114-19. Blackwell discerns a sharp conflict between obedience to traditional positions and anti-Aristotelian science, and presents evidence suggesting that certain "anti-Copernican" Jesuit scientists, such as Clavius and Scheiner, were more attracted to the new astronomy than has been thought. The spread of new cosmological ideas in the Jesuit Order is charted in three excellent studies: U. Baldini, "La nova del 1604," "Dal geocentrismo alfonsino al modello di Brahe: La discussione Grienberger-Biancani" and "Nuova astronomia e vecchia fisica: La reazione dei filosofi del Collegio Romano alla nuova cosmologia (1604-1618)" in idem, *Legem impone subactis.*, 155-82, 217-18.

[42] E. Rosen, *Copernicus and the Scientific Revolution* (Malabar, Fla.: Krieger Publishing, 1984), 188-91, and Westman, "The Copernicans and the Churches," 88-89. Another example of Dominican criticism of the Copernican theory is a work published in 1616 in which Paul Minerva, O.P., of Bari argued that the motion of the Earth contradicts reason, sense, and the Bible; on Minerva and Copernicanism, see L. Thorndike, *A History of Magic and Experimental Science* (New York: Columbia University Press, 1941), 6; 63-64.

[43] Blackwell, *Galileo, Bellarmine, and the Bible*, 103-6, 265-67. As Westman, "The Copernicans and the Churches," 95 and 109, nn. 62-63, states, it appears significant that Bellarmine knew Lorinus personally and had a copy of Pineda's *Commentariorum in Iob libri tredecim* in his library. It is also undeniable that Bellarmine was influenced by the unsigned letter to the reader in Copernicus' masterpiece, a letter authored by Andreas Osiander. This letter argues that astronomers' theories do not assert anything concerning physical reality but are only mathematical constructions designed to "save the phenomena." Most likely other Jesuit theologians and exegetes were influenced by this letter, if they examined Copernicus' work directly. On this letter, see E. Rosen, "The Exposure of the Fraudulent Address to the Reader in Copernicus' Revolutions," *Sixteenth Century Journal* 14 (1983): 283-91.

FURTHER READING

American Philosophical Society. *Proceedings of the American Philosophical Society Held at Philadelphia for Promoting Useful Knowledge: Symposium on Copernicus.* Philadelphia: American Philosophical Society, 1973, 550 p.

A collection of scholarly papers presented at the symposium by Owen Gingerich, Anthony Grafton, Willy Hartner, and Noel Swerdlow on the five hundredth centenary of Copernicus's birth.

Armitage, Angus. *Copernicus: The Founder of Modern Astronomy.* London: George Allen & Unwin Ltd, 1938, 183 p.

Presents an account of the research that led Copernicus to form his theories of planetary motion.

———. *The World of Copernicus.* 1947. Reprint. Wakefield, England: EP Publishing Ltd., 1972, 165 p.

Gives an account of the history of astronomy and the impact of Copernicus's thought. Armitage provides insight into the intellectual tradition from which Copernican thought developed.

Duncan, A. M. Introduction to *Copernicus: On the Revolution of the Heavenly Spheres*, by Nicolaus

Copernicus, translated by A. M. Duncan, pp. 7-27. Newton Abbot, Eng.: David & Charles, 1976.

> Provides a concise outline of prevalent cosmological and astronomical thought before the time of Copernicus and then discusses the revolution in thinking caused by Copernicus's work.

Grant, Edward. "Late Medieval Thought, Copernicus, and the Scientific Revolution." *Journal of the History of Ideas* XXIII, No. 2 (April-June 1962): 197-220.

> Offers an examination of the factors that shaped the medieval conception of a scientific hypothesis, and explores the dramatic ways that Copernicus's heliocentric theory departed from this accepted scholastic tradition.

————. "The Earth's Immobility." *Transactions of the American Philosophical Society* 74, No. 4 (1984): 33-64.

> Presents an overview of works written between 1616 and 1665 in refutation of Copernican theory .

Hoyle, Fred. *Nicolaus Copernicus: An Essay on His Life and Work*. London: Heinemann, 1973, 84 p.

> A concise biographical essay focusing on those points of Copernicus's life that bear on his astronomical achievements.

Kesten, Hermann. *Copernicus and His World*. New York: Roy Publishers, 1945, 408 p.

> A thorough and accessible account of Copernicus's life and achievement. A concluding five-chapter section deals with the reception of Copernicus's published theory after his death and his gradual vindication through the work of Giordano Bruno, Tycho Brahe, Johannes Kepler, and Galileo Galilei.

Kuhn, Thomas S. *The Copernican Revolution: Planetary Astronomy in the Development of Western Thought*. Cambridge: Harvard University Press, 1957, 297 p.

> Examines the long-ranging effects that Copernicus's theories had and continue to have on the fields of cosmology, physics, philosophy, and religion in addition to astronomy.

Price, Derek J. de S. "Contra-Copernicus: A Critical Re-Estimation of the Mathematical Planetary Theory of Ptolemy, Copernicus, and Kepler." In *Critical Problems in the History of Science*, edited by Marshall Clagett, pp. 197-218. Madison: University of Wisconsin Press, 1959.

> Suggests that Copernicus made significant advances in cosmology without employing any new or complex mathematical techniques.

Prosch, Harry. "The Copernican Revolution." In *The Genesis of Twentieth Century Philosophy: The Evolution of Thought from Copernicus to the Present*, pp. 9-21. Garden City, N.Y.: Doubleday & Co., 1964.

> Declares "the Copernican revolution" in astronomical thought to be the single great event that separates medieval and modern thought. Prosch suggests that an under-standing of Copernicus and his achievement is essential to a basic understanding of modern philosophy.

Rosen, Edward. "Copernicus' Attitude toward the Common People." *Journal of the History of Ideas* XXXII, No. 2 (April-June 1971): 281-89.

> Focuses on Copernicus's social attitudes and on the question of whether he valued the study of science in the abstract or for practical purposes.

Rybka, Eugeniusz. *Four Hundred Years of the Copernican Heritage*. Cracow, Poland: Jagelonian University of Cracow, 1964, 229 p.

> An approving overview of Copernicus's life and work, noting the wide-ranging impact of his thought

Stahlman, William D. "On Recent Copernicana." *Journal of the History of Ideas* XXXIV, No. 3 (July-September 1973): 483-89.

> Discusses the content of some new and revised publications dealing with Copernicus.

Swerdlow, N. M., and O. Neugebauer. *Mathematical Astronomy in Copernicus's "De Revolutionibus"*. New York: Springer-Verlag, 1984, 537 p.

> Evaluates the position of ancient science in the development of a system of mathematical astronomy.

Westman, Robert S., ed. *The Copernican Achievement*. Berkeley: University of California Press, 1975, 405 p.

> Presents revised versions of papers presented at a symposium during the five-hundredth anniversary year of Copernicus's birth.

————. "The Copernicans and the Churches." In *God and Nature: Historical Essays on the Encounter between Chris-tianity and Science*, edited by D. C. Lindberg and R. L. Numbers, pp. 76-113. Berkeley: University of California Press, 1986.

> Supplies information about Copernicus's life and the development of his astronomical theories. Westman discusses the condemnation of Galileo Galilei for teaching, holding, and defending Copernican theory. Westman finds these events illustrative of a long-standing conflict between science and Christianity.

Galileo Galilei

1564-1642

Italian astronomer, mathematician, physicist, and philosopher.

INTRODUCTION

Galileo is regarded as one of the greatest scientific thinkers of the Renaissance. His questioning of Aristotelian and Ptolemaic concepts of physics and astronomy, his studies of motion, his refinement of the telescope, and his subsequent discoveries about the universe were to have far-reaching, influential effects on the way people think about the earth and the heavens. Galileo's ideas also got him into trouble: condemned by the Inquisition for espousing a heliocentric world system, which violated Catholic Church teachings that the Earth was the center of the universe, he spent the last years of his life under house arrest.

Biographical Information

Galileo Galilei was born in Pisa in 1564 to a cloth merchant/musician and member of the minor nobility. In 1581 he enrolled at the University of Pisa as a medical student, but his interests soon turned to the field of mathematics, and he received a teaching position at the University in 1589. From the beginning, Galileo's strong disagreement with popular Aristotelian theories of motion and gravity led him into conflict with his academic peers, and he was eventually forced to resign as Chair of Mathematics at Pisa. In 1592, however, he was appointed Professor of Mathematics at Padua. On vacation from the University of Padua in 1605 he tutored Cosimo, the Prince of Tuscany. Cosimo was later to become the Grand Duke of Tuscany and Galileo's patron. And it was to the Grand Duke's mother, Christina, that Galileo wrote his fateful *Lettera a Madama Cristina de Lorena* (written 1615; published 1636; *Letter to Madame Christina of Lorraine, Grand Duchess of Tuscany*), in which he unsuccessfully attempted to reconcile the Church and Biblical exegesis with the Copernican heliocentric system. Well before this disastrous event, however, a supernova occurred in 1604; it was visible to the human eye and drew Galileo into a heated debate with those who believed in Aristotle's theory that the heavens were immutable. Galileo's life took a decisive turn in 1608 with the invention of the telescope in Holland. A year later, Galileo made refinements to the telescope which allowed him to view not only the stars in the Milky Way but also four moons around Jupiter, spots on the sun, and the rugged and uneven surface of the earth's

moon. Galileo published these findings in *Sidereus nuncius* (1610; *The Starry Messenger*) in which he began to think seriously about the likelihood of a Copernican universe. *The Starry Messenger* was well-received, but a later, more candid discussion of Copernicanism, published in 1613 as *Historia e dimonstrazioni intorno alle macchie solari* (*Sunspot Letters*) was condemned by the Church as an outspoken defense of heliocentrism. In 1625, Galileo began working on a discourse entitled *Dialogo dei due massimi sistemi del mondo—Tolemaico e Copernicano* (1632; *Dialogue Concerning the Two Chief World Systems*). This venture initially received Pope Urban VIII's blessing as a measured discussion of the compatibility of Church doctrine and the Copernican system. After it was written, however, the Pontiff criticized the *Dialogue* for two reasons: first, he felt that he himself had been portrayed as an object of ridicule in the discourse; and second, he was notified of the apparent existence of a document signed by Galileo in 1616 promising never again to advocate or even discuss Copernicanism. Events happened fairly quickly after that:

In February of 1632, the *Dialogue* was published; in October of that same year, Galileo was ordered to come to Rome to answer before the Inquisition. In June of 1633, Galileo was compelled to repudiate the *Dialogue* on his knees before his accusers. He was sentenced as a heretic and condemned to imprisonment for life—a sentence that was softened to house arrest with the understanding that Galileo would never again publish his writings. When he died in 1642, he was blind but still publishing—although outside Italy. To the end of his life, Galileo insisted that there was no conflict between Copernicanism and his own devotion to the Church.

Major Works

Galileo's major works include *The Starry Messenger,* which generated much positive excitement when it focused people's eyes for the first time on what was actually happening in the sky. His *Sunspot Letters,* on the other hand, are notorious. As Stillman Drake points out, Galileo wrote these *Letters* in Italian rather than in Latin (a scholarly and liturgical language that was universal only to those who were educated); by contrast, the colloquial *Letters* were accessible to "practically everyone in Italy who could read." Significantly, the arguments contained in them described a Copernican or heliocentric universe rather than the Ptolemaic or world-centered universe advocated by the Church. Galileo's most famous work, the *Dialogue Concerning the Two Chief World Systems,* is well-known not for its rigid defense of the Copernican against the Ptolemaic system (for it was meant to consider the two impartially); instead, it is infamous because Galileo wrote it after he had apparently been forbidden to write or teach anything at all about the Copernican system. Thus the *Dialogue* was the catalyst for Galileo's appearance and conviction before the Inquisition. Ironically, as Jean Dietz Moss points out, it is the *Letter to the Grand Duchess Christina* where Galileo unequivocally advocates the Copernican system. Yet he does so while trying to prove that heliocentrism and the interpretation of the Bible are not at odds. Thus, it has "become a classic in literature relating to the conflict between science and religion," and "passages [from it] are often quoted for the sheer power of their expression and the acuity of their observations."

Critical Reception

Today, experts on the life and works of Galileo are increasingly coming to believe that he was a victim not of his ideas, but of politics. Several scholars have called into question the very existence of the document of 1616 in which Galileo was supposed to have promised never to teach or write about the Copernican system. Instead, some specialists now argue that the sharp-tongued and not always diplomatic Galileo became a convenient pawn in a power struggle between members of the Church of Rome as a result of the Counter-Reformation—a time when the Catholic Church was trying to reform itself in response to the Protestant Reformation. As Maurice A. Finocchiaro observes, Galileo's trial occurred "during the so-called Thirty Years War between Catholics and Protestants. . . ." At that time "Pope Urban VIII, who had earlier been an admirer and supporter of Galileo, was in an especially vulnerable position; thus not only could he not continue to protect Galileo, but he had to use Galileo as a scapegoat to reassert . . . his authority and power."

PRINCIPAL WORKS

De motu [*On Motion*] (originally untitled treatise) 1589?

Sidereus nuncius [*The Starry Messenger;* also translated as *The Sidereal Messenger;* or as *Astronomical Announcement*] (essay) 1610

Discorso intorno alle cose che stanno su l'acqua [*Discourse on Floating Bodies;* also translated as *Discourse on Bodies in Water*] (essay) 1612

Historia e dimonstrazioni intorno alle macchie solari [*Sunspot Letters;* also translated as *Letters on Sunspots*] (letters) 1613

Lettera a Madama Cristina de Lorena [*Letter to Madame Christina of Lorraine, Grand Duchess of Tuscany;* also translated as *Letter to the Grand Duchess Christina;* or simply, *Letter to Christina*] (treatise) written 1615; published 1636

Il saggiatore [*The Assayer*] (essay) 1623

Dialogo dei due massimi sistemi del mondo—Tolemaico e Copernicano [*Dialogue on the Two Principal World Systems—Ptolemaic and Copernican;* also translated as *Dialogue Concerning the Two Chief World Systems;* also referred to as *Dialogue*] (dialogue) 1632

Discorsi e dimonstrazioni matematiche intorno a due nuove scienze . . . [*Mathematical Discourses and Demonstrations, Touching Two New Sciences . . .*] (essay) 1638

CRITICISM

Sir Robert S. Ball (essay date 1895)

SOURCE: "Galileo," in *Great Astronomers,* Isbister and Company, Ltd., 1895, pp. 67-95.

[*In the following excerpt, Ball gives a nineteenth-century perspective of Galileo's life and career, focusing in particular on letters from his daughter Sister Maria Celeste.*]

Among the ranks of the great astronomers it would be difficult to find one whose life presents more interesting features and remarkable vicissitudes than does that of Galileo. We may consider him as the patient investigator and brilliant discoverer. We may consider him in his private relations, especially to his daughter, Sister Maria Celeste, a woman of very remarkable character; and we have also the pathetic drama at the close of Galileo's life, when the philosopher drew down upon himself the thunders of the Inquisition.

The materials for the sketch of this astonishing man are sufficiently abundant. We make special use in this place of those charming letters which his daughter wrote to him from her convent home. More than a hundred of these have been preserved, and it may well be doubted whether any more beautiful and touching series of letters addressed to a parent by a dearly loved child have ever been written. An admirable account of this correspondence is contained in a little book entitled *The Private Life of Galileo,* published anonymously by Messrs. Macmillan in 1870, and I have been much indebted to the author of that volume for many of the facts contained in this chapter.

Galileo was born at Pisa, on 18th February, 1564. He was the eldest son of Vincenzo de' Bonajuti de' Galilei, a Florentine noble. Notwithstanding his illustrious birth and descent, it would seem that the home in which the great philosopher's childhood was spent was an impoverished one. It was obvious at least that the young Galileo would have to be provided with some profession by which he might earn a livelihood. From his father he derived both by inheritance and by precept a keen taste for music, and it appears that he became an excellent performer on the lute. He was also endowed with considerable artistic power, which he cultivated diligently. Indeed, it would seem that for some time the future astronomer entertained the idea of devoting himself to painting as a profession. His father, however, decided that he should study medicine. Accordingly, we find that when Galileo was seventeen years of age, and had added a knowledge of Greek and Latin to his acquaintance with the fine arts, he was duly entered at the University of Pisa.

Here the young philosopher obtained some inkling of mathematics, whereupon he became so much interested in this branch of science, that he begged to be allowed to study geometry. In compliance with his request, his father permitted a tutor to be engaged for this purpose; but he did so with reluctance, fearing that the attention of the young student might thus be withdrawn from that medical work which was regarded as his primary occupation. The event speedily proved that these anxieties were not without some justification. The propositions of Euclid proved so engrossing to Galileo that it was thought wise to avoid further distraction by terminating the mathematical tutor's engagement. But

it was too late for the desired end to be attained. Galileo had now made such progress that he was able to continue his geometrical studies by himself. Presently he advanced to that famous 47th proposition which won his lively admiration, and on he went until he had mastered the six books of Euclid, which was a considerable achievement for those days.

The diligence and brilliance of the young student at Pisa did not, however, bring him much credit with the University authorities. In those days the doctrines of Aristotle were regarded as the embodiment of all human wisdom in natural science as well as in everything else. It was regarded as the duty of every student to learn Aristotle off by heart, and any disposition to doubt or even to question the doctrines of the venerated teacher was regarded as intolerable presumption. But young Galileo had the audacity to think for himself about the laws of nature. He would not take any assertion of fact on the authority of Aristotle when he had the means of questioning nature directly as to its truth or falsehood. His teachers thus came to regard him as a somewhat misguided youth, though they could not but respect the unflagging industry with which he amassed all the knowledge he could acquire.

We are so accustomed to the use of pendulums in our clocks, that perhaps we do not often realise that the introduction of this method of regulating time-pieces was really a notable invention worthy the fame of the great astronomer to whom it was due. It appears that sitting one day in the Cathedral of Pisa, Galileo's attention became concentrated on the swinging of a chandelier which hung from the ceiling. It struck him as a significant point, that whether the arc through which the pendulum oscillated was a long one or a short one, the time occupied in each vibration was sensibly the same. This suggested to the thoughtful observer that a pendulum would afford the means by which a time-keeper might be controlled, and accordingly Galileo constructed for the first time a clock on this principle. The immediate object sought in this apparatus was to provide a means of aiding physicians in counting the pulses of their patients.

The talents of Galileo having at length extorted due recognition from the authorities, he was appointed, at the age of twenty-five, Professor of Mathematics at the University of Pisa. Then came the time when he felt himself strong enough to throw down the gauntlet to the adherents of the old philosophy. As a necessary part of his doctrine on the movement of bodies, Aristotle had asserted that the time occupied by a stone in falling depends upon its weight, so that the heavier the stone the less time would it require to fall from a certain height to the earth. It might have been thought that a statement so easily confuted by the simplest experiments could never have maintained its position in any accepted scheme of philosophy. But Aristotle had said it, and to any one who ventured to express a doubt the ready sneer was forthcoming, "Do you think yourself a cleverer man than Aristotle?" Galileo determined to demonstrate in the most emphatic manner the absurdity of a doctrine which had for centuries received the sanction of the learned. The summit of the Leaning Tower of Pisa offered a highly dramatic site for the great experiment. The youthful professor let fall from the overhanging top a large heavy body and a small light body simultaneously. According to Aristotle the large body ought to have reached the ground much sooner than the small one, but such was found not to be the case. In the sight of a large concourse of people the simple fact was demonstrated that the two bodies fell side by side, and reached the ground at the same time. Thus the first great step was taken in the overthrow of that preposterous system of unquestioning adhesion to dogma, which had impeded the development of the knowledge of nature for nearly two thousand years.

This revolutionary attitude towards the ancient beliefs was not calculated to render Galileo's relations with the University authorities harmonious. He had also the misfortune to make enemies in other quarters. Don Giovanni de Medici, who was then the Governor of the Port of Leghorn, had designed some contrivance by which he proposed to pump out a dock. But Galileo showed up the absurdity of this enterprise in such an aggressive manner that Don Giovanni took mortal offence, nor was he mollified when the truths of Galileo's criticisms were abundantly verified by the total failure of his ridiculous invention. In various ways Galileo was made to feel his position at Pisa so unpleasant that he was at length compelled to abandon his chair in the University. The active exertions of his friends, of whom Galileo was so fortunate as to have had throughout his life an abundant supply, then secured his election to the Professorship of Mathematics at Padua, whither he went in 1592.

It was in this new position that Galileo entered on that marvellous career of investigation which was destined to revolutionize science. The zeal with which he discharged his professorial duties was indeed of the most unremitting character. He speedily drew such crowds to listen to his discourses on Natural Philosophy that his lecture-room was filled to overflowing. He also received many private pupils in his house for special instruction. Every moment that could be spared from these labours was devoted to his private study and to his incessant experiments.

Like many another philosopher who has greatly extended our knowledge of nature, Galileo had a remarkable aptitude for the invention of instruments designed for philosophical research. To facilitate his practical work, we find that in 1599 he had engaged a skilled workman who was to live in his house, and thus be

constantly at hand to try the devices for ever springing from Galileo's fertile brain. Among the earliest of his inventions appears to have been the thermometer, which he constructed in 1602. No doubt this apparatus in its primitive form differed in some respects from the contrivance we call by the same name. Galileo at first employed water as the agent, by the expansion of which the temperature was to be measured. He afterwards saw the advantage of using spirits for the same purpose. It was not until about half a century later that mercury came to be recognised as the liquid most generally suitable for the thermometer.

The time was now approaching when Galileo was to make that mighty step in the advancement of human knowledge which followed on the application of the telescope to astronomy. As to how his idea of such an instrument originated, we had best let him tell us in his own words. The passage is given in a letter which he writes to his brother-in-law, Landucci.

> I write now because I have a piece of news for you, though whether you will be glad or sorry to hear it I cannot say; for I have now no hope of returning to my own country, though the occurrence which has destroyed that hope has had results both useful and honourable. You must know, then, that two months ago there was a report spread here that in Flanders some one had presented to Count Maurice of Nassau a glass manufactured in such a way as to make distant objects appear very near, so that a man at the distance of two miles could be clearly seen. This seemed to me so marvellous that I began to think about it. As it appeared to me to have a foundation in the Theory of Perspective, I set about contriving how to make it, and at length I found out, and have succeeded so well that the one I have made is far superior to the Dutch telescope. It was reported in Venice that I had made one, and a week since I was commanded to show it to his Serenity and to all the members of the senate, to their infinite amazement. Many gentlemen and senators, even the oldest, have ascended at various times the highest bell-towers in Venice to spy out ships at sea making sail for the mouth of the harbour, and have seen them clearly, though without my telescope they would have been invisible for more than two hours. The effect of this instrument is to show an object at a distance of say fifty miles, as if it were but five miles.

The remarkable properties of the telescope at once commanded universal attention among intellectual men. Galileo received applications from several quarters for his new instrument, of which it would seem that he manufactured a large number to be distributed as gifts to various illustrious personages.

But it was reserved for Galileo himself to make that application of the instrument to the celestial bodies by which its peculiar powers were to inaugurate the new era in astronomy. The first discovery that was made in this direction appears to have been connected with the number of the stars. Galileo saw to his amazement that through his little tube he could count ten times as many stars in the sky as his unaided eye could detect. Here was, indeed, a surprise. We are now so familiar with the elementary facts of astronomy that it is not always easy to realise how the heavens were interpreted by the observers in those ages prior to the invention of the telescope. We can hardly, indeed, suppose that Galileo, like the majority of those who ever thought of such matters, entertained the erroneous belief that the stars were on the surface of a sphere at equal distances from the observer. No one would be likely to have retained his belief in such a doctrine when he saw how the number of visible stars could be increased tenfold by means of Galileo's telescope. It would have been almost impossible to refuse to draw the inference that the stars thus brought into view were still more remote objects which the telescope was able to reveal, just in the same way as it showed certain ships to the astonished Venetians, when at the time these ships were beyond the reach of unaided vision.

Galileo's celestial discoveries now succeeded each other rapidly. That beautiful Milky Way, which has for ages been the object of admiration to all lovers of nature, never disclosed its true nature to the eye of man till the astronomer of Padua turned on it his magic tube. The splendid zone of silvery light was then displayed as star-dust scattered over the black background of the sky. It was observed that though the individual stars were too small to be seen severally without optical aid, yet such was their incredible number that the celestial radiance produced that luminosity with which every star-gazer was so familiar.

But the greatest discovery made by the telescope in these early days, perhaps, indeed, the greatest discovery that the telescope has ever accomplished, was the detection of the system of four satellites revolving around the great planet Jupiter. This phenomenon was so wholly unexpected by Galileo that, at first, he could hardly believe his eyes. However, the reality of the existence of a system of four moons attending the great planet was soon established beyond all question. Numbers of great personages crowded to Galileo to see for themselves this beautiful miniature representing the sun with its system of revolving planets.

Of course there were, as usual, a few incredulous people who refused to believe the assertion that four more moving bodies had to be added to the planetary system. They scoffed at the notion; they said the satellites may have been in the telescope, but that they were not in the sky. One sceptical philosopher is reported to have affirmed, that even if he saw the moons of Jupiter himself he would not believe in them, as their existence was contrary to the principles of common-sense!

There can be no doubt that a special significance attached to the new discovery at this particular epoch in the history of science. It must be remembered that in those days the doctrine of Copernicus, declaring that the sun, and not the earth, was the centre of the system, that the earth revolved on its axis once a day, and that it described a mighty circle round the sun once a year, had only recently been promulgated. This new view of the scheme of nature had been encountered with the most furious opposition. It may possibly have been that Galileo himself had not felt quite confident in the soundness of the Copernican theory, prior to the discovery of the satellites of Jupiter. But when a picture was there exhibited in which a number of relatively small globes were shown to be revolving around a single large globe in the centre, it seemed impossible not to feel that the beautiful spectacle so displayed was an emblem of the relations of the planets to the sun. It was thus made manifest to Galileo that the Copernican theory of the planetary system must be the true one. The momentous import of this opinion upon the future welfare of the great philosopher will presently appear.

It would seem that Galileo regarded his residence at Padua as a state of undesirable exile from his beloved Tuscany. He had always a yearning to go back to his own country, and at last the desired opportunity presented itself. For now that Galileo's fame had become so great, the Grand Duke of Tuscany desired to have the philosopher resident at Florence, in the belief that he would shed lustre on the Duke's dominions. Overtures were accordingly made to Galileo, and the consequence was that in 1616 we find him residing at Florence, bearing the title of Mathematician and Philosopher to the Grand Duke.

Two daughters, Polissena and Virginia, and one son, Vincenzo, had been born to Galileo in Padua. It was the custom in those days that as soon as the daughter of an Italian gentleman had grown up, her future career was somewhat summarily decided. Either a husband was to be forthwith sought out, or she was to enter the convent with the object of taking the veil as a professed nun. It was arranged that the two daughters of Galileo, while still scarcely more than children, should both enter the Franciscan convent of St. Matthew, at Arcetri. The elder daughter, Polissena, took the name of Sister Maria Celeste, while Virginia became Sister Arcangela. The latter seems to have been always delicate and subject to prolonged melancholy, and she is of but little account in the narrative of the life of Galileo. But Sister Maria Celeste, though never leaving the convent, managed to preserve a close intimacy with her beloved father. This was maintained only partly by Galileo's visits, which were very irregular and were, indeed, often suspended for long intervals. But his letters to this daughter were evidently frequent and affectionate, especially in the latter part of his life. Most unfortunately, however, all his letters have been lost. There are grounds for believing that they were deliberately destroyed when Galileo was seized by the Inquisition, lest they should have been used as evidence against him, or lest they should have compromised the convent where they were received. But Sister Maria Celeste's letters to her father have happily been preserved, and most touching these letters are. We can hardly read them without thinking how the sweet and gentle nun would have shrunk from the idea of their publication.

Her loving little notes to her "dearest lord and father," as she used affectionately to call Galileo, were almost invariably accompanied by some gift, trifling it may be, but always the best the poor nun had to bestow. The tender grace of these endearing communications was all the more precious to him from the fact that the rest of Galileo's relatives were of quite a worthless description. He always acknowledged the ties of his kindred in the most generous way, but their follies and their vices, their selfishness and their importunities, were an incessant source of annoyance to him, almost to the last day of his life.

On 19th December, 1625, Sister Maria Celeste writes:—

> I send two baked pears for these days of vigil. But as the greatest treat of all, I send you a rose, which ought to please you extremely, seeing what a rarity it is at this season; and with the rose you must accept its thorns, which represent the bitter passion of our Lord, whilst the green leaves represent the hope we may entertain that through the same sacred passion we, having passed through the darkness of the short winter of our mortal life, may attain to the brightness and felicity of an eternal spring in heaven.

When the wife and children of Galileo's shiftless brother came to take up their abode in the philosopher's home, Sister Maria Celeste feels glad to think that her father has now some one who, however imperfectly, may fulfil the duty of looking after him. A graceful note on Christmas Eve accompanies her little gifts. She hopes that—

> In these holy days the peace of God may rest on him and all the house. The largest collar and sleeves I mean for Albertino, the other two for the two younger boys, the little dog for baby, and the cakes for everybody, except the spice-cakes, which are for you. Accept the good-will which would readily do much more.

The extraordinary forbearance with which Galileo continually placed his time, his purse, and his influence at the service of those who had repeatedly proved themselves utterly unworthy of his countenance, is thus commented on by the good nun:—

> Now it seems to me, dearest lord and father, that your lordship is walking in the right path, since you take hold of every occasion that presents itself to shower continual benefits on those who only repay you with ingratitude. This is an action which is all the more virtuous and perfect as it is the more difficult.

When the plague was raging in the neighbourhood, the loving daughter's solicitude is thus shown:—

> I send you two pots of electuary as a preventive against the plague. The one without the label consists of dried figs, walnuts, rue, and salt, mixed together with honey. A piece of the size of a walnut to be taken in the morning, fasting, with a little Greek wine.

The plague increasing still more, Sister Maria Celeste obtained, with much difficulty, a small quantity of a renowned liqueur, made by Abbess Ursula, an exceptionally saintly nun. This she sends to her father with the words:—

> I pray your lordship to have faith in this remedy. For if you have so much faith in my poor miserable prayers, much more may you have in those of such a holy person; indeed, through her merits you may feel sure of escaping all danger from the plague.

Whether Galileo took the remedy we do not know, but at all events he escaped the plague.

From Galileo's new home in Florence the telescope was again directed to the skies, and again did astounding discoveries reward the astronomer's labours. The great success which he had met with in studying Jupiter naturally led Galileo to look at Saturn. Here he saw a spectacle which was sufficiently amazing, though he failed to interpret it accurately. It was quite manifest that Saturn did not exhibit a simple circular disc like Jupiter, or like Mars. It seemed to Galileo as if the planet consisted of three bodies, a large globe in the centre, and a smaller one on each side. The enigmatical nature of the discovery led Galileo to announce it in an enigmatical manner. He published a string of letters which, when duly transposed, made up a sentence which affirmed that the planet Saturn was three-fold. Of course we now know that this remarkable appearance of the planet was due to the two projecting portions of the ring. With the feeble power of Galileo's telescope, these seemed merely like small globes or appendages to the large central body.

The last of Galileo's great astronomical discoveries related to the libration of the moon. I think that the detection of this phenomenon shows his acuteness of observation more remarkably than does any one of his other achievements with the telescope. It is well known that the moon constantly keeps the same face turned towards the earth. When, however, careful measurements have been made with regard to the spots and marks on the lunar surface, it is found that there is a slight periodic variation which permits us to see now a little to the east or to the west, now a little to the north or to the south of the average lunar disc.

But the circumstances which make the career of Galileo so especially interesting from the biographer's point of view, are hardly so much the triumphs that he won as the sufferings that he endured. The sufferings and the triumphs were, however, closely connected, and it is fitting that we should give due consideration to what was perhaps the greatest drama in the history of science.

On the appearance of the immortal work of Copernicus, in which it was taught that the earth rotated on its axis, and that the earth, like the other planets, revolved round the sun, orthodoxy stood aghast. The Holy Roman Church submitted this treatise, which bore the name *De Revolutionibus Orbium Coelestium,* to the Congregation of the Index. After due examination it was condemned as heretical in 1615. Galileo was suspected, on no doubt excellent grounds, of entertaining the objectionable views of Copernicus. He was accordingly privately summoned before Cardinal Bellarmine on 26th February, 1616, and duly admonished that he was on no account to teach or to defend the obnoxious doctrines. Galileo was much distressed by this intimation. He felt it a serious matter to be deprived of the privilege of discoursing with his friends about the Copernican system, and of instructing his disciples in the principles of the great theory of whose truth he was perfectly convinced. It pained him, however, still more to think, devout Catholic as he was, that such suspicions of his fervent allegiance to his Church should ever have existed, as were implied by the words and monitions of Cardinal Bellarmine.

In 1616, Galileo had an interview with Pope Paul V., who received the great astronomer very graciously, and walked up and down with him in conversation for three-quarters of an hour. Galileo complained to his Holiness of the attempts made by his enemies to embarrass him with the authorities of the Church, but the Pope bade him be comforted. His Holiness had himself no doubts of Galileo's orthodoxy, and he assured him that the Congregation of the Index should give Galileo no further trouble so long as Paul V. was in the chair of St. Peter.

On the death of Paul V. in 1623, Maffeo Barberini was elected Pope, as Urban VIII. This new Pope, while a cardinal, had been an intimate friend of Galileo's, and had indeed written Latin verses in praise of the great astronomer and his discoveries. It was therefore not unnatural for Galileo to think that the time had arrived when, with the use of due circumspection, he might continue his studies and his writings, without fear of incurring the displeasure of the Church. Indeed, in 1624, one of Galileo's friends writing from Rome, urges Galileo to visit the city again, and added that—

> Under the auspices of this most excellent, learned, and benignant Pontiff, science must flourish. Your arrival will be welcome to his Holiness. He asked me if you were coming, and when, and in short, he seems to love and esteem you more than ever.

The visit was duly paid, and when Galileo returned to Florence, the Pope wrote a letter from which the following is an extract, commending the philosopher to the good offices of the young Ferdinand, who had shortly before succeeded his father in the Grand Duchy of Tuscany.

> We find in Galileo not only literary distinction, but also the love of piety, and he is also strong in those qualities by which the pontifical good-will is easily obtained. And now, when he has been brought to this city to congratulate us on our elevation, we have very lovingly embraced him; nor can we suffer him to return to the country whither your liberality calls him, without an ample provision of pontifical love. And that you may know how dear he is to us, we have willed to give him this honourable testimonial of virtue and piety. And we further signify that every benefit which you shall confer upon him, imitating or even surpassing your father's liberality, will conduce to our gratification.

The favourable reception which had been accorded to him by Pope Urban VIII. seems to have led Galileo to expect that there might be some corresponding change in the attitude of the Papal authorities on the great question of the stability of the earth. He accordingly proceeded with the preparation of the chief work of his life, *The Dialogue of the two Systems.* It was submitted for inspection by the constituted authorities. The Pope himself thought that, if a few conditions which he laid down were duly complied with, there could be no objection to the publication of the work. In the first place, the title of the book was to be so carefully worded as to show plainly that the Copernican doctrine was merely to be regarded as an hypothesis, and not as a scientific fact. Galileo was also instructed to conclude the book with special arguments which had been supplied by the Pope himself, and which appeared to his Holiness to be quite conclusive against the new doctrine of Copernicus.

Formal leave for the publication of the Dialogue was then given to Galileo by the Inquisitor General, and it was accordingly sent to the press. It might be thought that the anxieties of the astronomer about his book would then have terminated. As a matter of fact, they had not yet seriously begun. Riccardi, the Master of the Sacred Palace, having suddenly had some further misgivings, sent to Galileo for the manuscript while the work was at the printer's, in order that the doctrine it implied might be once again examined. Apparently, Riccardi had come to the conclusion that he had not given the matter sufficient attention, when the authority to go to press had been first and, perhaps, hastily given. Considerable delay in the issue of the book was the result of these further deliberations. At last, however, in June, 1632, Galileo's great work, *The Dialogue of the two Systems,* was produced for the instruction of the world, though the occasion was fraught with ruin to the immortal author.

The book, on its publication, was received and read with the greatest avidity. But presently the Master of the Sacred Palace found reason to regret that he had given his consent to its appearance. He accordingly issued a peremptory order to sequestrate every copy in Italy. This sudden change in the Papal attitude toward Galileo formed the subject of a strong remonstrance addressed to the Roman authorities by the Grand Duke of Tuscany. The Pope himself seemed to have become impressed all at once with the belief that the work contained matter of an heretical description. The general interpretation put upon the book seems to have shown the authorities that they had mistaken its true tendency, notwithstanding the fact that it had been examined again and again by theologians deputed for the duty. To the communication from the Grand Duke the Pope returned answer, that he had decided to submit the book to a congregation of "learned, grave, and saintly men," who would weigh every word in it. The views of his Holiness personally on the subject were expressed in his belief that the Dialogue contained the most perverse matter that could come into a reader's hands.

The Master of the Sacred Palace was greatly blamed by the authorities for having given his sanction to its issue. He pleaded that the book had not been printed in the precise terms of the original manuscript which had been submitted to him. It was also alleged that Galileo had not adhered to his promise of inserting properly the arguments which the Pope himself had given in support of the old and orthodox view. One of these had, no doubt, been introduced, but, so far from mending Galileo's case, it had made matters really look worse for the poor philosopher. The Pope's argument had been put into the mouth of one of the characters in the Dialogue named "Simplicio." Galileo's enemies maintained that by adopting such a method for the expression of his Holiness's opinion, Galileo had intended to hold the Pope himself up to ridicule. Galileo's friends maintained that nothing could have been farther from his intention. It seems, however, highly probable that the suspicions thus aroused had something to say to the sudden change of front on the part of the Papal authorities.

On 1st October, 1632, Galileo received an order to appear before the Inquisition at Rome on the grave charge of heresy. Galileo, of course, expressed his submission, but pleaded for a respite from compliance with the summons, on the ground of his advanced age and his failing health. The Pope was, however, inexorable; he said that he had warned Galileo of his danger while he was still his friend. The command could not be disobeyed. Galileo might perform the journey as slowly as he pleased, but it was imperatively necessary for him to set forth, and at once.

On 20th January, 1633, Galileo started on his weary journey to Rome, in compliance with this peremptory summons. On 13th February he was received as the guest of Niccolini, the Tuscan ambassador, who had acted as his wise and ever-kind friend throughout the whole affair. It seemed plain that the Holy Office were inclined to treat Galileo with as much clemency and consideration as was consistent with the determination that the case against him should be proceeded with to the end. The Pope intimated that in consequence of his respect for the Grand Duke of Tuscany he should permit Galileo to enjoy the privilege, quite unprecedented for a prisoner charged with heresy, of remaining as an inmate in the ambassador's house. He ought, strictly, to have been placed in the dungeons of the Inquisition. When the examination of the accused had actually commenced, Galileo was confined, not, indeed, in the dungeons, but in comfortable rooms at the Holy Office.

By the judicious and conciliatory language of submission which Niccolini had urged Galileo to use before the Inquisitors, they were so far satisfied that they interceded with the Pope for his release. During the remainder of the trial Galileo was accordingly permitted to go back to the ambassador's, where he was most heartily welcomed. Sister Maria Celeste, evidently thinking this meant that the whole case was at an end, thus expresses herself:—

> The joy that your last dear letter brought me, and the having to read it over and over to the nuns, who made quite a jubilee on hearing its contents, put me into such an excited state that at last I got a severe attack of headache.

In his defence Galileo urged that he had already been acquitted in 1616 by Cardinal Bellarmine, when a charge of heresy was brought against him, and he contended that anything he might now have done, was no more than he had done on the preceding occasion, when the orthodoxy of his doctrines received solemn confirmation. The Inquisition seemed certainly inclined to clemency, but the Pope was not satisfied. Galileo was accordingly summoned again on the 21st June. He was to be threatened with torture if he did not forthwith give satisfactory explanations as to the reasons which led him to write the Dialogue. In this proceeding the Pope assured the Tuscan ambassador that he was treating Galileo with the utmost consideration possible in consequence of his esteem and regard for the Grand Duke, whose servant Galileo was. It was, however, necessary that some exemplary punishment be meted out to the astronomer, inasmuch as by the publication of the Dialogue he had distinctly disobeyed the injunction of silence laid upon him by the decree of 1616. Nor was it admissible for Galileo to plead that his book had been sanctioned by the Master of the Sacred College, to whose inspection it had been again and again submitted. It was held, that if the Master of the Sacred College had been unaware of the solemn warning the philosopher had already received sixteen years previously, it was the duty of Galileo to have drawn his attention to that fact.

On the 22nd June, 1633, Galileo was led to the great hall of the Inquisition, and compelled to kneel before the cardinals there assembled and hear his sentence. In a long document, most elaborately drawn up, it is definitely charged against Galileo that, in publishing the Dialogue, he committed the essentially grave error of treating the doctrine of the earth's motion as open to discussion. Galileo knew, so the document affirmed, that the Church had emphatically pronounced this notion to be contrary to Holy Writ, and that for him to consider a doctrine so stigmatized as having any shadow of probability in its favour was an act of disrespect to the authority of the Church which could not be overlooked. It was also charged against Galileo that in his Dialogue he has put the strongest arguments into the mouth, not of those who supported the orthodox doctrine, but of those who held the theory as to the earth's motion which the Church had so deliberately condemned.

After due consideration of the defence made by the prisoner, it was thereupon decreed that he had rendered himself vehemently suspected of heresy by the Holy Office, and in consequence had incurred all the censures and penalties of the sacred canons, and other decrees promulgated against such persons. The graver portion of these punishments would be remitted, if Galileo would solemnly repudiate the heresies referred to by an abjuration to be pronounced by him in the terms laid down.

At the same time it was necessary to mark, in some emphatic manner, the serious offence which had been committed, so that it might serve both as a punishment to Galileo and as a warning to others. It was accordingly decreed that he should be condemned to imprisonment in the Holy Office during the pleasure of the Papal authorities, and that he should recite once a week for three years the seven Penitential Psalms.

Then followed that ever-memorable scene in the great hall of the Inquisition, in which the aged and infirm Galileo, the inventor of the telescope and the famous astronomer, knelt down to abjure before the most eminent and reverend Lords Cardinal, Inquisitors General throughout the Christian Republic against heretical depravity. With his hands on the Gospels, Galileo was made to curse and detest the false opinion that the sun was the centre of the universe and immovable, and that the earth was not the centre of the same, and that it moved. He swore that for the future he will never say nor write such things as may bring him under suspicion, and that if he does so he submits to all the pains and penalties of the sacred canons. This abjuration was subsequently read in Florence before Galileo's disciples, who had been specially summoned to attend.

It has been noted that neither on the first occasion, in 1616, nor on the second in 1633, did the reigning Pope sign the decrees concerning Galileo. The contention has accordingly been made that Paul V. and Urban VIII. are both alike vindicated from any technical responsibility for the attitude of the Romish Church towards the Copernican doctrines. The significance of this circumstance has been commented on in connection with the doctrine of the infallibility of the Pope.

We can judge of the anxiety felt by Sister Maria Celeste about her beloved father during these terrible trials. The wife of the ambassador Niccolini, Galileo's steadfast friend, most kindly wrote to give the nun whatever quieting assurances the case would permit. There is a renewed flow of these touching epistles from the daughter to her father. Thus she sends word—

> The news of your fresh trouble has pierced my soul with grief all the more that it came quite unexpectedly.

And again, on hearing that he had been permitted to leave Rome, she writes—

> I wish I could describe the rejoicing of all the mothers and sisters on hearing of your happy arrival at Siena. It was indeed most extraordinary. On hearing the news the Mother Abbess and many of the nuns ran to me, embracing me and weeping for joy and tenderness.

The sentence of imprisonment was at first interpreted leniently by the Pope. Galileo was allowed to reside in qualified durance in the archbishop's house at Siena. Evidently the greatest pain that he endured arose from the forced separation from that daughter, whom he had at last learned to love with an affection almost comparable with that she bore to him. She had often told him that she never had any pleasure equal to that with which she rendered any service to her father. To her joy, she discovers that she can relieve him from the task of reciting the seven Penitential Psalms which had been imposed as a penance:—

I began to do this a while ago . . . and it gives me much pleasure. First, because I am persuaded that prayer in obedience to Holy Church must be efficacious; secondly, in order to save you the trouble of remembering it. If I had been able to do more, most willingly would I have entered a straiter prison than the one I live in now, if by so doing I could have set you at liberty.

Sister Maria Celeste was gradually failing in health, but the great privilege was accorded to her of being able once again to embrace her beloved lord and master. Galileo had, in fact, been permitted to return to his old home; but on the very day when he heard of his daughter's death came the final decree directing him to remain in his own house in perpetual solitude.

Amid the advancing infirmities of age, the isolation from friends, and the loss of his daughter, Galileo once again sought consolation in hard work. He commenced his famous dialogue on Motion. Gradually, however, his sight began to fail, and blindness was at last added to his other troubles. On January 2nd, 1638, he writes to Diodati:—

Alas, your dear friend and servant, Galileo, has been for the last month perfectly blind, so that this heaven, this earth, this universe, which I by my marvellous discoveries and clear demonstrations have enlarged a hundred thousand times beyond the belief of the wise men of bygone ages, henceforward is for me shrunk into such a small space as is filled by my own bodily sensations.

But the end was approaching—the great philosopher, was attacked by low fever, from which he died on the 8th January, 1643.

Albert Einstein (essay date 1953)

SOURCE: Foreword to *Galileo Galilei: "Dialogue Concerning the Two Chief World Systems—Ptolemaic & Copernican,"* by Galileo Galilei, translated by Stillman Drake, with the foreward translated by Sonja Bargmann, University of California Press, 2nd ed., 1967, pp. vii-xix.

[*In the following essay, originally published in 1953 and reprinted in 1967, Einstein expresses his admiration for Galileo's creativity and remarks that the theme of "Galileo's work is the passionate fight against any kind of dogma based on authority."*]

Galileo's **Dialogue Concerning the Two Chief World Systems** is a mine of information for anyone interested in the cultural history of the Western world and its influence upon economic and political development.

A man is here revealed who possesses the passionate will, the intelligence, and the courage to stand up as the representative of rational thinking against the host of those who, relying on the ignorance of the people and the indolence of teachers in priest's and scholar's garb, maintain and defend their positions of authority. His unusual literary gift enables him to address the educated men of his age in such clear and impressive language as to overcome the anthropocentric and mythical thinking of his contemporaries and to lead them back to an objective and causal attitude toward the cosmos, an attitude which had become lost to humanity with the decline of Greek culture.

In speaking this way I notice that I, too, am falling in with the general weakness of those who, intoxicated with devotion, exaggerate the stature of their heroes. It may well be that during the seventeenth century the paralysis of mind brought about by the rigid authoritarian tradition of the Dark Ages had already so far abated that the fetters of an obsolete intellectual tradition could not have held much longer—with or without Galileo.

Yet these doubts concern only a particular case of the general problem concerning the extent to which the course of history can be decisively influenced by single individuals whose qualities impress us as accidental and unique. As is understandable, our age takes a more sceptical view of the role of the individual than did the eighteenth and the first half of the nineteenth century. For the extensive specialization of the professions and of knowledge lets the individual appear "replaceable," as it were, like a part of a mass-produced machine.

Fortunately, our appreciation of the **Dialogue** as a historical document does not depend upon our attitude toward such precarious questions. To begin with, the **Dialogue** gives an extremely lively and persuasive exposition of the then prevailing views on the structure of the cosmos in the large. The naïve picture of the earth as a flat disc, combined with obscure ideas about star-filled space and the motions of the celestial bodies, prevalent in the early Middle Ages, represented a deterioration of the much earlier conceptions of the Greeks, and in particular of Aristotle's ideas and of Ptolemy's consistent spatial concept of the celestial bodies and their motions. The conception of the world still prevailing at Galileo's time may be described as follows:

There is space, and within it there is a preferred point, the center of the universe. Matter—at least its denser portion—tends to approach this point as closely as possible. Consequently, matter has assumed approximately spherical shape (earth). Owing to this formation of the earth the center of the terrestrial sphere practically coincides with that of the universe. Sun, moon, and stars are prevented from falling toward the center of the universe by being fastened onto rigid (transparent) spherical shells whose centers are identical with that of the universe (or space). These spherical shells revolve around the immovable globe (or center of the universe) with slightly differing angular velocities. The lunar shell has the smallest radius; it encloses everything "terrestrial." The outer shells with their heavenly bodies represent the "celestial sphere" whose objects are envisaged as eternal, indestructible, and inalterable, in contrast to the "lower, terrestrial sphere" which is enclosed by the lunar shell and contains everything that is transitory, perishable, and "corruptible."

Naturally, this naïve picture cannot be blamed on the Greek astronomers who, in representing the motions of the celestial bodies, used abstract geometrical constructions which grew more and more complicated with the increasing precision of astronomical observations. Lacking a theory of mechanics they tried to reduce all complicated (apparent) motions to the simplest motions they could conceive, namely, uniform circular motions and superpositions thereof. Attachment to the idea of circular motion as the truly natural one is still clearly discernible in Galileo; probably it is responsible for the fact that he did not *fully* recognize the law of inertia and its fundamental significance.

Thus, briefly, had the ideas of later Greece been crudely adapted to the barbarian, primitive mentality of the Europeans of that time. Though not causal, those Hellenistic ideas had nevertheless been objective and free from animistic views—a merit which, however, can be only conditionally conceded to Aristotelian cosmology.

In advocating and fighting for the Copernican theory Galileo was not only motivated by a striving to simplify the representation of the celestial motions. His aim was to substitute for a petrified and barren system of ideas the unbiased and strenuous quest for a deeper and more consistent comprehension of the physical and astronomical facts.

The form of dialogue used in his work may be partly due to Plato's shining example; it enabled Galileo to apply his extraordinary literary talent to the sharp and vivid confrontation of opinions. To be sure, he wanted to avoid an open commitment in these controversial questions that would have delivered him to destruction by the Inquisition. Galileo had, in fact, been expressly forbidden to advocate the Copernican theory. Apart from its revolutionary factual content the **Dialogue** represents a downright roguish attempt to comply with this order in appearance and yet in fact to disregard it. Unfortunately, it turned out that the Holy Inquisition was unable to appreciate adequately such subtle humor.

The theory of the immovable earth was based on the hypothesis that an abstract center of the universe exists. Supposedly, this center causes the fall of heavy bodies at the earth's surface, since material bodies have the tendency to approach the center of the universe as far as the earth's impenetrability permits. This leads to the approximately spherical shape of the earth.

Galileo opposes the introduction of this "nothing" (center of the universe) that is yet supposed to act on material bodies; he considers this quite unsatisfactory.

But he also draws attention to the fact that this unsatisfactory hypothesis accomplishes too little. Although it accounts for the spherical shape of the earth it does not explain the spherical shape of the other heavenly bodies. However, the lunar phases and the phases of Venus, which latter he had discovered with the newly invented telescope, proved the spherical shape of these two celestial bodies; and the detailed observation of the sunspots proved the same for the sun. Actually, at Galileo's time there was hardly any doubt left as to the spherical shape of the planets and stars.

Therefore, the hypothesis of the "center of the universe" had to be replaced by one which would explain the spherical shape of the stars, and not only that of the earth. Galileo says quite clearly that there must exist some kind of interaction (tendency to mutual approach) of the matter constituting a star. The same cause has to be responsible (after relinquishing the "center of the universe") for the free fall of heavy bodies at the earth's surface.

Let me interpolate here that a close analogy exists between Galileo's rejection of the hypothesis of a center of the universe for the explanation of the fall of heavy bodies, and the rejection of the hypothesis of an inertial system for the explanation of the intertial behavior of matter. (The latter is the basis of the theory of general relativity.) Common to both hypotheses is the introduction of a conceptual object with the following properties:

(1). It is not assumed to be real, like ponderable matter (or a "field").

(2). It determines the behavior of real objects, but it is in no way affected by them.

The introduction of such conceptual elements, though not exactly inadmissible from a purely logical point of view, is repugnant to the scientific instinct.

Galileo also recognized that the effect of gravity on freely falling bodies manifests itself in a vertical acceleration of constant value; likewise that an unaccelerated horizontal motion can be superposed on this vertical accelerated motion.

These discoveries contain essentially—at least qualitatively—the basis of the theory later formulated by Newton. But first of all the general formulation of the principle of inertia is lacking, although this would have been easy to obtain from Galileo's law of falling bodies by a limiting process. (Transition to vanishing vertical acceleration.) Lacking also is the idea that the same matter which causes a vertical acceleration at the surface of a heavenly body can also accelerate another heavenly body; and that such accelerations together with inertia can produce revolving motions. There was achieved, however, the knowledge that the presence of matter (earth) causes an acceleration of free bodies (at the surface of the earth).

It is difficult for us today to appreciate the imaginative power made manifest in the precise formulation of the concept of acceleration and in the recognition of its physical significance.

Once the conception of the center of the universe had, with good reason, been rejected, the idea of the immovable earth, and, generally, of an exceptional role of the earth, was deprived of its justification. The question of what, in describing the motion of heavenly bodies, should be considered "at rest" became thus a question of convenience. Following Aristarchus and Copernicus, the advantages of assuming the sun to be at rest are set forth (according to Galileo not a pure convention but a hypothesis which is either "true" or "false"). Naturally, it is argued that it is simpler to assume a rotation of the earth around its axis than a common revolution of all fixed stars around the earth. Furthermore, the assumption of a revolution of the earth around the sun makes the motions of the inner and outer planets appear similar and does away with the troublesome retrograde motions of the outer planets, or rather explains them by the motion of the earth around the sun.

Convincing as these arguments may be—in particular coupled with the circumstance, detected by Galileo, that Jupiter with its moons represents so to speak a Copernican system in miniature—they still are only of a qualitative nature. For since we human beings are tied to the earth, our observations will never directly reveal to us the "true" planetary motions, but only the intersections of the lines of sight (earth-planet) with the "fixed-star sphere." A support of the Copernican system over and above qualitative arguments was possible only by determining the "true orbits" of the planets—a problem of almost insurmountable difficulty, which, however, was solved by Kepler (during Galileo's lifetime) in a truly ingenious fashion. But this decisive progress did not leave any traces in Galileo's life work—a grotesque illustration of the fact that creative individuals are often not receptive.

Galileo takes great pains to demonstrate that the hypothesis of the rotation and revolution of the earth is not refuted by the fact that we do not observe any mechanical effects of these motions. Strictly speaking, such a demonstration was impossible because a complete theory of mechanics was lacking. I think it is just in the struggle with this problem that Galileo's originality is demonstrated with particular force. Galileo is, of course, also concerned to show that the fixed stars are too remote for parallaxes produced by the yearly motion of the earth to be detectable with the measuring instruments of his time. This investigation also is ingenious, notwithstanding its primitiveness.

It was Galileo's longing for a mechanical proof of the motion of the earth which misled him into formulating a wrong theory of the tides. The fascinating arguments in the last conversation would hardly have been accepted as proofs by Galileo, had his temperament not got the better of him. It is hard for me to resist the temptation to deal with this subject more fully.

The *leitmotif* which I recognize in Galileo's work is the passionate fight against any kind of dogma based on authority. Only experience and careful reflection are accepted by him as criteria of truth. Nowadays it is hard for us to grasp how sinister and revolutionary such an attitude appeared at Galileo's time, when merely to doubt the truth of opinions which had no basis but authority was considered a capital crime and punished accordingly. Actually we are by no means so far removed from such a situation even today as many of us would like to flatter ourselves; but in theory, at least, the principle of unbiased thought has won out, and most people are willing to pay lip service to this principle.

It has often been maintained that Galileo became the father of modern science by replacing the speculative, deductive method with the empirical, experimental method. I believe, however, that this interpretation would not stand close scrutiny. There is no empirical method without speculative concepts and systems; and there is no speculative thinking whose concepts do not reveal, on closer investigation, the empirical material from which they stem. To put into sharp contrast the empirical and the deductive attitude is misleading, and was entirely foreign to Galileo. Actually it was not until the nineteenth century that logical (mathematical) systems whose structures were completely independent of any empirical content had been cleanly extracted. Moreover, the experimental methods at Galileo's disposal were so imperfect that only the boldest speculation could possibly bridge the gaps between the empirical data. (For example, there existed no means to measure times shorter than a second.) The antithesis Empiricism *vs.* Rationalism does not appear as a controversial point in Galileo's work. Galileo opposes the deductive methods of Aristotle and his adherents only when he considers their premises arbitrary or untenable, and he does not rebuke his opponents for the mere fact of using deductive methods. In the first dialogue, he emphasizes in several passages that according to Aristotle, too, even the most plausible deduction must be put aside if it is incompatible with empirical findings. And on the other hand, Galileo himself makes considerable use of logical deduction. His endeavors are not so much directed at "factual knowledge" as at "comprehension." But to comprehend is essentially to draw conclusions from an already accepted logical system.

Giorgio de Santillana (essay date 1964)

SOURCE: "Galileo in the Present," in *Homage to Galileo: Papers Presented at the Galileo Quadricentennial, University of Rochester, October 8 and 9, 1964,* edited by Morton F. Kaplon, The M.I.T. Press, 1965, pp. 1-25.

[*In the following essay, first presented as a paper in 1964 and published in 1965, de Santillana argues that Galileo was the first to combine the study of science with the usefulness of technology, or "technique," in order to find out the "how" of things in nature.*]

Galileo has by now moved out of history into myth. He is more than the creator of an era. He has become a hero of civilization, the symbol of a great adventure like Prometheus, or rather like the Ulysses of Dante and Tennyson.

There was in his earlier triumph the note of divine surprise, of an incredible world opening up. There also is, later, darkness closing in on the hero. Let me quote a famous letter of his to Diodati from 1638:

> Alas, honoured Sir, Galileo, your dear friend and servant, has become by now irremediably blind. Your Honour may understand in what affliction I find myself, as I consider how *that* heaven, that world, that universe, that by my observations and clear demonstrations I had amplified a hundred and a thousand times over what had been seen and known by the learned of all past centuries, has now shrunk for me to the space occupied by my person.

"That heaven, that world, that universe." This has the epic ring, the love for the discovery of creation, that would well have befitted the Argonauts' enterprise, where modesty would hardly have been fitting. At this point, already the prisoner of darkness, compelled to silence, Galileo goes on with the temper of a heroic heart, re-examining, reorganizing, reshaping without cease the vast array of his ideas in a creative impulse which leads him to his most powerful achievement, the *Discourses on Two New Sciences.*

He was establishing the foundations of dynamics, inflexibly bent on the same enterprise that his judges could not stop, short of killing him. Indeed, his judges, having humiliated him and debarred him from his main object, had no further concern, incapable as they were of realizing that all science is one and that it will break forth again at any point.

"In this way"—writes Galileo to his dear old friar friend, Fulgenzio Micanzio—"I carry on in my darkness, wondering and dreaming over this or that effect of nature, and I cannot quiet my restless brain which keeps me through the night in tormenting wakefulness." We cannot but be reminded here of the Ulysses of Dante, who carries on forever with his great dream even in the darkness of Hell.

It is not perchance that Galileo has always remained at the core of a great dramatic situation. What more dramatic event than the onset of the greatest revolution in history, than this opening up of thought to the idea of infinity—this soaring off on the powerful wings of mathematics, as Galileo once wrote? The magic circle of a closed world centered on man was broken, and it did not go without alarm and distress among many. In the words of a worthy bishop, there was at the time "an universal Exclamation of the world's Decline and approximation to its Period." But if such was a widespread feeling among the learned, all the more admirable to us is the reckless plunging ahead of the great creative minds. "Oh Nicholas Copernicus," Galileo once wrote, "what must have been thy joy in seeing thy thought confirmed despite so many contrary appearances in nature, and all the learning of past ages." It is this joy that we feel in Kepler announcing his new harmonies, in Galileo's light-hearted bantering and his cutting disregard of the powers leagued against him— even in Bruno's overreaching "heroic frenzies."

Those men felt no reason to be afraid for their souls. As Galileo said, why should we be called innovators and trouble-makers, if what we have been able to prove demonstratively belongs to God's eternal truths, that only the ignorance of men could have obscured? There was no fear in the souls of Galileo's own Church friends— those who were able to understand him—but a serene happiness worthy of old medieval Christianity, for they were sure that no discovery of God's works could threaten God's Word, but rather enhance it. The "new philosophy," far from putting all in doubt, was a vividly affirmative one and full of great hope. No one had experienced yet the raw reality of what we call progress. Much rather, science had come in to check that strange feeling of decline, of impending social chaos, that we see coexisting so strangely in John Donne together with a disturbed awareness of the new discoveries.

Even more—Galileo discarded the robed Latin of learning and went straight to the people, writing for them in the vernacular, trusting in all those, he said, who had eyes to see and minds to understand.

His thinking is as straight and limpid as his new style. He has concentrated on the problem of motion as providing an essential clue to the mystery of nature and the real decision between Aristotle and Copernicus—which Copernicus himself had not been able to provide. For cosmology always comes first in Galileo's mind. He has chosen the burning issue. The thought of a sphere turning on itself in a void with no reason to stop—a typical Gedanken experiment—gives him the idea of inertia. And why should this not be the earth itself? Then come twenty years of search leading to the laws of fall, which show motion to be subject to mathematics—the great issue is resolved in Galileo's mind. Not quality, but quantity, rules. Now if the moon can be thought of as moving by the same law which controls the projected stone—and the earth too—namely, inertia, then they are no different in nature from the earthly missile. The earth loses its privileged unique condition and is found to be "in heaven" too. The earth *is a star.* The great prophetic Pythagorean word has fallen. When the discovery of the telescope showed the moon to be made of ordinary rock, the circle of proof was concluded in his mind. The distinction between heavenly and earthly conditions is wiped out; the Aristotelian architecture of the universe has fallen. But this time he has proved his case—not only by the telescope but also by the laws of dynamics he has discovered, founded on the new concepts of Galilean *relativity, inertial mass, momentum, instant velocity, acceleration.* Or at least he feels he has, even without Newton—quite enough for a scientific imagination.

He is ready to face the dramatic issue.

It has now become a commonplace to consider Pope Urban VIII and his court as the oppressors of science who jailed and silenced its first representative. It would be perhaps more correct to see them as ordinary administrators surprised by events beyond their ken. They had come into collision with a new force which they could not evaluate. Both sides, the Pope and Galileo, were profoundly bewildered by their unexpected collision. Galileo could not understand that "they" should not grasp the new power of mathematical physics that he was offering them and walked into his trial still refusing to believe that his judges should prove, as he said, "immovable and unpersuadable." *They,* on the other hand, were utterly unaware of the mechanism of scientific discovery, which they could no more stop than issue a writ against an avalanche. In their minds, schooled in the humanistic tradition, they thought they were dealing with *this* particular **Dialogue**—an unique piece of paradoxical ingenuity brought forth by a great writer. They saw it—and Galileo would not have gainsaid it—as a new type of poem. Silence Dante or Virgil, and there would be no *Aeneid,* no *Divine Comedy;* literature would take another course. Excellence meant literary excellence. It could also be suppressed.

As for science and wisdom, why that was another thing. It was in gravity and ponderousness akin to the business of lawyers, which the doctors strove to imitate even in their solemn caps and gowns. It went on forever in the way of disputation and classification, coordinating all things in a vast verbiage without end. It was law and order itself. Confronted with Galileo's dangerous conclusions, the Aristotelian doctor would indeed lose his head and start clamoring, as he does in the **Dialogue:** "This manner of thinking tends to the subversion of all natural philosophy and to the disorder and subversion of heaven and earth and the whole universe!" If Galileo makes gentle fun of this way of identifying his interests with those of the universe as a whole, we still might have a heart for his predicament. Of the heavens, it was understood that man knew little, except their perfection and immutability, a moving image of eternity. They remained inaccessible, it seemed, even with this new gadget, the telescope, for too much had been said about tricky optical effects.

And should we now subvert the vast and documented discourse of the schools—which allows us to account in an orderly manner for nature and life and the soul itself and fits in so handsomely with revealed truth—to launch ourselves in a sea of paradoxes and unnatural conclusions simply because a man has come forward with two lenses in a length of pipe?

It was the professors, and not the clerics, who started the scandal which led to the prohibition of Copernicanism in 1616.

The crisis and the tragedy came later. They have been obscured by so much equivocation that we ought to set the record straight.

Galileo had been authorized by Pope Urban (who had been his friend and protector as Cardinal Barberini) to write a dialogue in which he should examine impartially all the reasons pro and contra the old and the new systems. This was meant by the Pope to be a literary exercise and a further public proof that the question had been maturely weighed before the Church took her decision. For that decision had already fallen twelve years before, in 1616, when it was decreed that the Copernican system ran against both philosophy and Scripture and should be dropped. Still, the Pope now yielded good-naturedly to Galileo's entreaties for a fresh discussion of the problem with the understanding that any system of the universe cannot but remain a pure hypothesis, a "mere" mathematical model. He assumed it was well understood that the actual truth was beyond our reach and that God could have produced the same observable effects in infinitely many ways, for we must not constrain omnipotence within the limits of our particular imagination. In fact, the Pope actually dictated this conclusion in advance and then left his friend Galileo free to display what he was pleased to call his admirable and delectable ingenuity. This has been understood by certain modern positivists as sound scientific prudence *avant la lettre*. It was, of course, nothing of the kind—it was old-fashioned wisdom making sure that nothing should be allowed to disturb it, nor to disturb the approved system of teaching. It was still to be Milton's position forty years later, when he said that God allowed men to conjecture without end,

> Perhaps to move
> his laughter at their quaint opinions wide
> hereafter.

This was the charm of divine philosophy, of God's secrets "to be scanned by them who ought rather admire."

Galileo had to concur respectfully, but, needless to say, his intention was vastly different. He hoped to provide under this proper cover such irresistible proofs of the truth of Copernicanism that the Church would quietly drop its veto and move over to new positions, as it had so often done in the past, in time to be spared an acutely embarrassing predicament. There was thus a deep miscomprehension from the start, what I called a collision course. The manuscript was submitted to the Church censors, examined word for word, and came out with official approval. The censors found it good and full of laudable reverence. The *Dialogue on the Great World Systems* came out in 1632; it was an instant enthusiastic success—and then all at once the authorities realized that they had made a frightful mistake. The usual advisors rushed to tell the Pope that, under pretence of following his instructions, the work was really a demolition charge planted by an expert, that it made a shambles of official teaching, and that it was apt to prove more dangerous to Catholic prestige than Luther and Calvin put together.

Actually, Galileo had deceived no one—except perhaps himself. He had followed instructions, but his persuasiveness had outrun his prudence. He had laid himself open to his enemies by speaking openly. In his work, style and thought go together. The *Dialogue* is and remains a masterpiece of Baroque style, which knows how to move effortlessly through tight passages of reasoning, unroll with a rustle of silk, sparkle with malice and restrained good humor, maintain its cadence through vast reaches of syntactic intricacy, and rise without break to the solemnity of prophetic invective. It was not only ruthless analysis, it was the magic of the Italian language handled by a master, which broke the monopoly of stuffy Latin learning, which took the people into camp and revealed to them the new unimagined power of mathematical physics. Copernicus had remained almost unnoticed, by now half-forgotten. Pascal himself was to state, "It will be a good idea not to go any deeper into the opinion of Copernicus." If that was the policy, it had already failed. Here at last heliocentrism had come into its own.

In his triumph, Galileo could afford to be generous. His scorn and ridicule are only for the silly pedants who had turned Aristotle into a vested interest and were afraid even of looking through the telescope. Aristotle himself, he insisted, would have been the first to come over to his side if he had learned about the new discoveries. And may I quote here something that I have come upon, which Galileo never knew, but which confirms him utterly. It is a passage from Averroes, surely the greatest of Aristotelians, who had lived 400 years before: "In my youth," he says, "I had hoped that the better scrutiny of the heavens that we need would be achieved by me. In my old age now I despair, but I still hope that my words will induce someone to carry on the search." Is it not a way of begging for the telescope, which Galileo was to offer him too late?

The *Dialogue* is thus a work, truly a poem, of reconciliation. Worldly-wise, it remained terribly dangerous.

If anybody was technically at fault, it was the censors who had been unable to understand. But now the Pope's anger flared high, for he realized that Galileo had only tagged on perfunctorily the profound philosophical ideas that *he,* the Pope, had dictated. There is no fury like a philosopher scorned. Urban wanted now to make a resounding example.

Still the law was on Galileo's side. All the Pope could do by rights was punish the censors and have the book prohibited administratively. It was frustrating and infuriating.

At this point the Inquisition "discovered" in the file a heaven-sent forgotten document. That document gave out that *when* Galileo was informed of the anti-Copernican decree in 1616, the Commissary-General of the Inquisition had been present and served a stringent personal injunction on the astronomer to cease and desist from ever discussing it verbally or in writing, in any way whatsoever, under the dire penalties of the Holy Office.

This changed the figure of Galileo from that of a harmless respected consultant to that of a man considered by the Inquisition a special and dangerous suspect and held under surveillance by the thought police. By disregarding the injunction, he had exposed himself to being considered an obdurate heretic, which meant death at the stake. The authorities could try him at last. They now had an airtight case. They could even afford to be lenient and to let Galileo off with a public abjuration and a life sentence, which was further commuted into house arrest.

The trouble is that the famous injunction seems to have been a forgery—a false record carefully planted by the Inquisitors in their secret file in case it might come in handy. It did. Galileo had never dreamed of it, and that explains why he did not ask the Pope for explicit clearance before he raised the dangerous subject again.

The forgery, or rather the plant, has been proved beyond doubt, to my mind, by historical research over a century. The best proof is that when I published the findings in systematic form in 1955, not one authorized voice was raised to contradict me, although a fascinating amount of evasive action has been taken since that time. (I have in my file some strange cases of dialectical teratology.) It might have provided a good occasion to annual at last the old sentence and rehabilitate Galileo, as was done in the case of Joan of Arc, the more so as I had made a good case for pinning down the guilt on a small group of minor officials who had plotted and acted on their own. Pope Urban stood now in the light of history as a chief badly deceived by his subordinates. He was entitled to rehabilitation himself. But the authorities preferred to stand by their ancient decision, as a distinguished cleric recently remarked out of turn, probably because, however faulty juridically, it represented a philosophical decision concerning the *spirit* of modern science from which the Catholic Church still remains unwilling to withdraw. Be that as it may—I would not dare to judge. The reasons on either side are of such majestic import and profound significance for the fate of mankind that we must expect the unresolved tension to last beyond our time. But as far as Galileo went, his personal position remained clear. His recantation, in the civilized language of his times, meant simply that he would not oppose his will to that of his Church and would not separate himself from the communion of the faithful. As for his scientific opinion, it was understood that he would keep it, and in fact he did not refrain from saying so, at considerable risk. What he thought of his judges, he wrote straight and clear:

> I do not hope for any relief, and that is because I have committed no crime. I might hope for and obtain pardon, if I had erred; for it is to faults that the prince can bring indulgence, whereas against one wrongfully sentenced while he was innocent, it is expedient, in order to put up a show of strict legality, to uphold rigor. . . .

The animosity, which has never abated, shows how much he remains alive and kicking among us to this day. The strangest misrepresentations have found their way even into unsuspecting Protestant sources; witness the writings of Mallet du Pan and Sir David Brewster in the last centuries.

Again, there have come up writers in our own time, acute and modern minds, mark, bound to no confessional obedience, who suddenly saw in Copernicus and Galileo the "sleepwalkers" who moved in to wreck inadvertently the great unity of science and metaphysics which had held our civilization together over many ages. Those writers were inspired, certainly, by a noble cause and by justifiable alarm, but that hardly justifies their attacking Galileo as a vainglorious "intellectual adventurer" who replaced the absence of proof with "effrontery and illusionism," with "an utter disregard for the intelligence of his readers." Still less does it justify their attempted whitewash of the Inquisition proceedings. Clearly the name of the old man is still potent at conjuring the spirit of hatred and confusion.

This appears more significantly in a work that revives the tragedy on the stage: Bertolt Brecht's famous play, where Galileo is made the hero of scientific civilization as a whole, with its awful contradictions, its revolutionary promises, its human weakness, and its sinister power overshadowed by the cloud of Hiroshima. There is no doubt that Brecht also had in mind the Moscow trials, the conflict of the modern intellectual with totalitarian authority, and that what he denounces is the modern alienation of man's conscience. But in the poetic liberties he takes with his subject, Brecht reveals all the more clearly the misunderstandings that so many of us harbor concerning science itself. Galileo is shown as the exponent of cold invincible scientific method, even a materialist, with a mind that could have led the people to emancipation; but he surrendered miserably once he realized where real power lay, and then wept useless tears of regret. There is a grave misconception here, which goes to the very foundations. No one would deny Galileo's down-to-earth capacities, his enjoyment of the sensuous side of life; but what is so terribly wrong with being a *bon vivant,* in favoring "the newer the idea, the older the wine"? There is no doubt, either, that he impatiently dispelled many dreamy, wonderful, and magic aspects of Renaissance imagination by discovering scientific method—the awful art of separation inexorably divides the true from the false. But his real greatness was not in experimenting with weights, it lay in the power of abstract thinking, in the Pythagorean metaphysical faith which throws a bridge across the chasm between the world of the senses and the realm of pure mathematical abstraction.

In his very language, the greatest Italian prose of the times, Galileo spans the centuries. He is not pushing for a novel philosophy, he is reminding his enemies of theirs, which had been the metaphysical Platonism of the Great Middle Ages. In him there lives the ancient ecumenic and conciliar spirit of Christendom with its rights and its freedoms; when he addresses the spiritual rulers, the clauses of submissiveness scarcely veil the power and authority of his speech, which accuses and exhorts with the dignity of the early Fathers. It is he who is going to save Scripture from the incompetence of its guardians. And he solemnly warns: "The greatest detriment for souls would be, if they were to see *proved* a proposition which it is then made a *sin* to *believe.*"

In fact, it was easy to see even in his own times that he stood for all that was sound in established law and custom, whereas the authorities were resorting to political expediency and juridical improvisation, as they had become the unwitting tools of the streamlined, the efficient, and the new. "These" he wrote bitterly, he who had been accused of introducing novelties, "these are the real novelties which have the power of ruining the State and subverting the Commonwealth."

So much should be said, I feel, to disengage the great struggle from the clichés of conventional history, from the "terrible simplifiers," who see in it only the conflict of free thought against obscurantism. It was, from the start, a conflict among the faithful themselves, who disagreed about the correct approach to natural philosophy. On one side were the professors, the administrators, the representatives of ancient tradition, supported by the massive authority of Aristotle, by Greek astronomy itself in its late phase. This was the house that had been built through the centuries, seemingly on rock. On the other were the new minds, who had grasped the possibility that mathematics and physics, hitherto disjoined, should effect an overwhelming conjunction to show us at last a true universe.

They were perforce a minority, but they had the holy fire. Wrote the good and pious friar, Micanzio, to Galileo during the trial: "But what manner of men are these, to whom any good effect, and well-founded in nature, should appear contrary and odious . . . if this were now to prevent you from further work, I shall send to the hundred thousand devils these hypocrites without nature and without God."

Here we have the call to insurrection, the true revolutionary cry—already in the name of "Nature and Nature's God"—which announces the social breakthrough. And indeed today, at four centuries' remove, we know that it *was* a revolution, that the split was never healed.

Some of us may wonder whether we are not reading dramatic upheavals into the past, while reality may have been a sequence of slow and unnoticed alluvial effects. Was not the whole Renaissance, in fact, were not the medieval schools of science, leading up to this? I suggest that it is best to be coldly phenomenological about it. Revolutionary is as revolutionarily does.

Uprisings, *jacqueries,* justified as they may be, are revolts of the slighted or the oppressed; they are not revolutions. It is only when a group of individuals arises in which the community recognizes in some way the right to think legitimately in universal terms that a revolution is on its way. "What is the Third Estate?" said Sieyès. "Nothing. What could it be? Everything. What is it asking to be? Something." This is fair and reasonable, but that "something" has not been granted or taught from above, it is dictated to them by an inner

reasoned certainty, and it is that no-longer-disputable certainty which makes all the difference. Here in the French Revolution are men whose philosophy has grown to impose itself, as it does in the calm utterances of the American Declaration of Independence, men who know they can assume responsibility for the whole body social, not only in the running of its affairs, but in its decisions about first and last things. When these decisions sweep even the entrenched opposition off its feet and move it to yield freely its privileges, as on the historic night of August 4th, then we know that a real revolution has taken place. It is the resolute assumption of responsibility which forms the criterion. It was *that,* and not, as is currently said, the empirical approach.

As if *that* had not existed before. Galileo was not alone in believing what we see by experience. In fact, the scholars of his own time had an exaggerated respect for the raw data of observation and the commonsense physics that goes with those. Let me say more. If there is any dealing with physical nature by trial and error in the Renaissance, it is rather on the side of the magic-mystic materialists and alchemists, of those of the Stoic descendance. It is they who tirelessly push, mix, drop, concoct, distill, extract, combine and separate, operate with fire, with acids, with solvents and coagulants—always in the effort to move qualities around experimentally. In their *furor empiricus* they ask Nature to speak to them through its many names, effects, and "signatures"; whereas Galileo insisted that the "book of nature is written only in mathematical characters"—by which he meant that, out of indubitable premises arising out of number, weight, and measure, we can set the deductive course of our reasoning as geometers do.

More than once Alistair Crombie, one of our most distinguished students of medieval science, has to speak of the strange "irresolution" which acutely characterizes the attitude of medieval scientists, even the most advanced, either in equipping themselves with the proper knowledge of mathematics or in their way of attempting experiment. Pierre Buridan himself does not really hope that nature will provide the conditions for mathematical laws to be fulfilled, "although it *could* happen that they should be realized through the omnipotence of God." In other words, wouldn't it be wonderful—but only a miracle of divine benevolence could free us from the Aristotelian bondage, which emphasizes commonsense. This is exactly the attitude of the submissive traditionalist versus the revolutionary. Yet Buridan is no timid spirit. His work shows him to be a true rationalist, but he has to defer to long-established authority, whose dictates become akin in his mind to the Deposit of the Faith or the divine rights of kings. For two centuries this kind of speculation has been going on without much happening. Even in the most daring nominalists, the world of the scholar is too well-knit, spiritually and conceptually, not to keep dangerous deviations in check. Nicole d'Autricourt is free to suggest atomism as a natural philosophy, but once the chips are down, he has to back out or become a heretic.

Here and there, the scholar can risk bold theorizing, he can intimate, adumbrate, and prophesy; but he must be prepared for an intervention of authority that tells him to drop his playthings and come back to a correct attitude. This intervention did come at last, brutally, with the anti-Copernican decree of 1616. But this time, however, even if alone and abandoned by the scholars in retreat, there was Galileo. He stated in no uncertain terms that in such grave matters of natural philosophy, his authority was fully equal to that of the Church Fathers themselves. This is what I call the assumption of responsibility. Galileo does not hesitate to denounce the authorities for playing irresponsibly with reactionary subversion. The freedoms granted by tradition, he insists, are his protection, the reason that God gave us to understand His laws is on his side. He makes it clear by his attitude that he will not compromise, that he will not retreat, and that he will be heard.

As we know, Galileo could have gone on establishing the formal science of dynamics without all this fuss. He actually did—by the time he was debarred from writing about cosmology. This would be enough to prove that he did not consider his thought the empiricistic outcome of industrial *division of labor* or *advanced technology* or *bookkeeping* or whatever *gadget* it is that amateur sociologists have devised for his rationale. He felt he had to face the central issue: To the well-worked-out cosmos of his predecessors he opposed another cosmology, another way of knowledge, whereby man has to go ahead forever in discovery, trusting Providence that it will not lead him to perdition. This Galileo maintained even when told by the Successor to Peter, the Vicar of Christ, that his doctrine was "pernicious in the most extreme degree." He alone, with very few men of his time, perhaps only Kepler and Castelli, could really know what he was doing. He saw himself not as the depositary of the truth, but as the initiator of an unending march of ever-growing cohorts, of the whole of mankind, towards an ever-vaster vision of truth, ever receding beyond man's horizon. Here is what I consider Galileo's assumption of responsibility for the whole body social in first and last things. It stands with us to this day.

As for the secularization of thought, it is surely a consequence; it is not the one that Galileo had wished. He still stood for a contemplative natural philosophy in the ancient spirit. He was, as Einstein said of himself, a "gläubiger Physiker." And after all the sound and the fury, there is now at last a glimmer of light on the horizon, a hint of peace. I understand a petition has been introduced in the present Ecumenical Council, by French Catholic scientists, suggesting an official rehabilitation of Galileo. The long refusal and the empty words are now at an end. There is some hope for a true reconciliation.

So much for the past.

There is one aspect of Galileo which is undeniably modern and ours. To use the words of Aubrey, "He was a very ingeniose man, and had a very Mechanicall head. He was much for Trying of Experiments. . . ." He was indeed, for he himself invented the idea of Experiment, as opposed to the old notion of Experience. He even had to invent a word for it: he called it "The *Ordeal* of Experience." This involved extracting a straight yes or no out of nature in answer to a clear theoretical question, and not the usual bewildering play of effect and wonders. It puts theory first, as it should, but it provides a way of testing it—to divide the true from the false. This is the ironclad aspect of Galileo's discoveries, which will go on through the aeons.

But, with this, a great revolution is running its course. It is not so much methodology—a much abused and rather empty word—as the close collaboration of science and technique. The very fact of being content with the *how* instead of the *why* implies the attitude of the man who is concerned with knowing *how;* in turn, he is going to deal with nature in order to obtain the desired result. The physicist operates as a technician. And, with Bacon, Galileo was the first who insisted on the role of the arts then called low, vile, sordid, and mechanical in obtaining knowledge. In his famous address to the Venetians, he pointed out that among the men handling machinery in their arsenal, there must come up experts of unparalleled experience and very subtle intelligence. When the scientist puts nature to the "ordeal of experience," he has to appeal to the technician to help him—as his equal. The experiment that *works is,* after all, the only way to check his deductions.

This is the way of modern science, and it implies changes that are no less impressive in the social outlook than in the strictly philosophical. For it is the new team of scientist and technician which, by opening up the cataracts of successful results, has freed science from the initial metaphysical mortgage. The scientist needs no longer the philosopher's guarantee about the soundness of his approach; nor will he underlie the philosopher's strictures. Nothing succeeds like success.

But freedom has its price. The magic catchword "research and development" has turned science in the public mind into a handmaiden of technology. Nor would the scientists make much of a stand, bewildered as they are about their own assumptions, caught again, as one of them said rather tauntingly, in embarrassing epicyclic expedients as they wait for a true theory.

If we still at least believed with a simple faith in mathematic—But do we really, caught as we are in conventions? A recent paper by Eugene Wigner left me wondering. Its title is "Of the unreasonable success of mathematics in dealing with nature." Such a title would have been unthinkable even fifty years ago.

So many basic ideas are gone that we cannot even put our house in order. The split between the two cultures is widening; the unity of culture, of which science was so large a part, is shattered. The theoretical freedom that we needed for dealing with quantum and particle phenomena has given us an arbitrariness in physical thinking which goes at the expense of metaphysical consistency, as Einstein ruefully pointed out. When the empiricist suggests that science is a set of operational rules for changing marks on paper, he is obviously overdoing it. Science cannot but remain the search for some kind of being, however elusive. But when we are willing to suppose anything that will "work," when nothing is too far-fetched to try, we have surrendered choice of thought and entered a phase which has some of the aspects of intellectual nihilism.

In that sense, we are moving at present out of the era that began with Galileo. We are in search of a new philosophy, for success is not enough. And we must hope that it will be found soon, for otherwise we have a grave crisis in civilization. Inevitably, if science were to insist on presenting itself as an assemblage of devices for pragmatic power and economy of thought, if it were to disguise its poetic objectivity under technological wizardry, then misunderstandings would be found to occur. Outsiders—the other culture—will ask whether such a program could not just as well have fitted Renaissance nigromancy, with its system of recipes.

The *vox populi* is hard to discern. But maybe some of it spoke to us through the unexpected voice of Salvador Dali, the other day: "For myself, I like it le best today nuclear microphysics because no understand, myself no understand *no-thing* of these. Is *tremendous* attraction for understand something in this way."

We have come a long way since Voltaire.

Those who believe intransigently in the right of science to lead may find those signs irrelevant. The researcher's business is simply to go ahead. But what is left of tradition has a way of turning against those who disregard it. Words such as epicycles and nigromancy coming up in the historical consciousness make one doubt and wonder. The scientist has ceased taking part in the great dialogue as a cultural being. The little gusts of revolt blowing through society are the kind that the statesman might find worthy of attention. *Forsitan et Priami fuerint quae fata requiras?*

If it be true that we are really moving out of the Galilean era, then perhaps you will bear with me if I have so insistently dwelt on Galileo's metaphysics; they are his mark and the mark of that era. I would even go farther, and say: it is not perchance that science was born in the epoch that first took metaphysical commitment seriously.

This may sound paradoxical, for the Middle Ages are supposed to be *the* age of metaphysics. But it was a very different thing, based on the inscrutable will of God, operating inductively from hints of that absolute will. What the Pope instructed Galileo to do was correctly medieval: "Surrender to the inscrutable, speculate as you like, but do not believe that we can really *know*." When the Pope rose in fury against him, it was not because of his experimental discoveries, surely not. Those discoveries he loved. It was because he spotted the pride of intellect which thinks it can establish a true order deductively.

Let me tell you the story. At one point before the trial, the Pope gave audience to the Florentine Ambassador who had come again to plead desperately for Galileo. "I made free to remark to His Beatitude," reports the Ambassador, "that since God could have made the world in infinitely many ways, it could not be denied that this might be one of those ways, as Il Signor Galileo thought he had discovered." At which the Pope, red in the face and pounding the padded armrest of his pontifical chair, shouted: "We must not impose necessity on God Almighty, do you understand?"

Necessity is indeed the fatal word that marks our science. Where there is mathematical deduction of reality, there is necessity itself, which could not be otherwise. This is what Galileo asserts, powerfully and dangerously, in his **Dialogue,** where he says that when the mind has deduced a necessary proposition, it perceives it as God himself perceives it. There is, he says, an identity at that point between man's mind and God's. The idea of a necessity that is freedom, of a freedom that is necessity, was present in Galileo's metaphysics and not in the Pope's. That is what Sir Thomas Browne had in mind when he spoke of "that exaltation of Truth, in which, against all passions of prescription and prejudice, this century now prevaileth."

The true rationalist instinct is to believe in the reality of what thought is constructing: the Platonist strain will reappear perpetually to breed new scandal. Even to believe in two and two makes four as an eternal verity is to project back archetypes on the mind of God to limit his absolute will. This is what Descartes realized, and dodged accordingly. But the sound Pythagorean canon of deduction has been re-established, and mathematical physics is on its way, however meagre the results that it can yet show to the public: it may be a shade heretical, or at least "offensive to pious ears," as they said, but it is what we are agreed to call science.

When the God of Job displays his heralding of prodigies, unicorns, and Leviathans brought forth according to his pleasure, he expects Job to break down in uncomprehending wonder. The modern physicist would take it another way. He would say that the arbitrary will of the Deity is a random noise in the system which prevents us from deriving any predictable statements. We cannot try for a science in those conditions.

But if, according to the pious but unhesitating Pythagorean, the holy Number, which is the fountainhead of all things, is an archetype connatural to the divine mind, then the random noise is cut out: our mind is present across the aeons at the stillness of Creation.

I have been using somewhat fanciful language to indicate what, in technical philosophy, would be the need for a prescriptive link between essence and existence. It becomes central, and clearly expressed, in Descartes and Leibniz. That is why it would be fair to call the seventeenth century not only the age of Victorious Analysis, but also that of metaphysical commitment.

But it would be unfair to think of Galileo as the man who, by setting mathematical physics on its way, taught us to see the world as sheer mechanism. He was providing only a mathematical framework for the cosmos, not a universal explanation. As far as the hidden forces of nature go, he was holding on to the good old Renaissance vitalism. His idea of nature is as different from the Aristotelian caricature taught in the schools as it is from the scant and angular mechanism that Descartes was to introduce a few years later and Newton reluctantly adopt as a basis for his theories. It is not quite biological, for Galileo is essentially a physicist; not mechanical, surely, for the underlying reality is imagined to be a flow of transforming and vivifying energy which should be, in essence, light itself. It is what he does not shy from calling by its proper name, the "Pythagorean philosophy."

As those ancients themselves had done, we see Galileo finding expressive symbols of the unifying power of reason in the creative force of life:

> It seems to me that, if the celestial bodies concur to the generation and alteration of the Earth, they themselves are also of necessity alterable; for otherwise I cannot understand how the application of the Sun and Moon to the Earth to effect production should be any other than to lay a marble statue in the chamber of the bride and from that conjunction to expect children.

He goes even further: he delves with fine sarcasm into the unconscious motives of conventional theories. Those modern demonologists of the psyche, who with true plebeian instinct undermine abstract science as a form of escape from reality, might do worse than consider this first inventor of the psychoanalytic approach as he relies on his physics to lead him toward a loving acceptance of life:

Dialogue on the Great World Systems, pp. 68-69:

> Sagredus: I cannot without great wonder, nay more, disbelief, hear it being attributed to natural bodies as a great honour and perfection that they are impassible, immutable, inalterable, etc.: as, conversely, I hear it esteemed a great imperfection to be alterable, generable, mutable, etc. It is my opinion that the Earth is very noble and admirable by reason of the many and different alterations, mutations, generations, etc., which incessantly occur in it. And if, without being subject to any alteration, it had been all one vast heap of sand, or a mass of jade, or if, since the time of the deluge, the waters freezing which covered it, it had continued an immense globe of crystal, wherein nothing had ever grown, altered, or changed, I should have esteemed it a wretched lump of no benefit to the Universe, a mass of idleness, and in a word superfluous, exactly as if it had never been in Nature. The difference for me would be the same as between a living and a dead creature. I say the same concerning the Moon, Jupiter, and all the other globes of the Universe. The more I delve into the consideration of the vanity of popular discourses, the more empty and simple I find them. What greater folly can be imagined than to call gems, silver, and gold noble and earth and dirt base? For do not these persons consider that, if there were as great a scarcity of earth as there is of jewels and precious metals, there would be no king who would not gladly give a heap of diamonds and rubies and many ingots of gold to purchase only so much earth as would suffice to plant a jessamine in a little pot or to set a tangerine in it, that he might see it sprout, grow up, and bring forth goodly leaves, fragrant flowers, and delicate fruit? It is scarcity and plenty that make things esteemed and despised by the vulgar, who will say that here is a most beautiful diamond, for it resembles a clear water, and yet would not part with it for ten tuns of water. These men who so extol incorruptibility, inalterability, etc., speak thus, I believe, out of the great desire they have to live long and for fear of death, not considering that, if men had been immortal, *they* would not have come into the world. These people deserve to meet with a Medusa's head that would transform them into statues of diamond and jade, that so they might become more perfect than they are.

Stillman Drake (essay date 1970)

SOURCE: "The Effectiveness of Galileo's Work," in *Galileo Studies: Personality, Tradition, and Revolution,* The University of Michigan Press, 1970, pp. 95-122.

[In the following excerpt, Drake asserts that Galileo was revolutionary for being the first to integrate the heretofore separate disciplines of mathematics, physics, and astronomy in scientific thought.]

Until the present century it was customary to call Galileo the founder of modern physical science. Ancient science was thought of as having ended with the decline of Greek civilization, and no real contribution to scientific thought was known to have been made during the long ensuing period to the late Renaissance. The seemingly abrupt emergence of many recognizably modern scientific concepts early in the seventeenth century thus appeared to have been a true revolution in human thought. In that scientific revolution, Galileo appeared as the prime mover. The persecution that he suffered as a result of his active propagation of new ideas lent color to the idea that his had been a totally new and revolutionary kind of science.

As historians of ideas gave more careful attention to the treatment of scientific questions in medieval and early Renaissance times, the traditional role that had rather romantically been assigned to Galileo was critically reexamined. Many early anticipations of modern science or its fundamental concepts were found in manuscript commentaries on the philosophy of Aristotle and in treatises on statics forming what is known as the medieval science of weights. Anti-Aristotelian traditions were shown to have existed perennially in the universities, particularly those of Oxford, Paris, and Padua—traditions which had long been obscured by an overwhelming ascendancy of the Peripatetic philosophy in the official curricula at most times. Study of works by such men as Philoponus, Jordanus Nemorarius, Thomas Bradwardine, Walter Burley, Robert Grosseteste, Nicole Oresme, and Jean Buridan, coupled with evidence that their writings had circulated widely among scholars, first in manuscript and later in printed form, suggested that modern science was not suddenly born with Galileo, but simply emerged about that time after a long period of incubation. Many scholars now question whether it is proper to speak of a scientific revolution as having occurred in the late Renaissance or at any other time, and believe that it would be more accurate to characterize the emergence of modern science as a gradual event in a continuous process of thought which has merely shown periods of slower and of more rapid development.

Though much may be said for this sophisticated modern viewpoint, it does tend to obscure a striking historical fact which the older, more naïve conception recognized and at least attempted to explain. The fact is that man's attitude toward the world about him and his control of natural phenomena have altered more in the four centuries that have elapsed since the birth of Galileo than in as many millennia before that time. No matter how many of the fundamental ideas underlying modern science were in some sense anticipated by his medieval predecessors, their insights had no marked effect on the pursuits of other men as did those of Galileo. Whether or not one wishes to call his undoubted effectiveness "revolutionary" is a matter of taste; but whatever one calls it, the manner in which it is to be explained is still deserving of serious study.

The principal sources of Galileo's effectiveness, as I see them, were intimately related to the temper of the time in which he lived. But in saying that, I do not mean that the emergence of a Galileo at that period was in any way inevitable. Such social-deterministic views are coming to be more and more widely held, but to me they seem too smug, implying as they do that we now know so much that we can retroactively predict the appearance of a genius, or perceive that the spirit of an age is bound to produce one.

Reflecting on what I know of Galileo's contemporaries, I find it hard to select one who could have filled his place. Those who took up his work did not hesitate to credit him with having placed them on the path to further achievement. Those who opposed his work rarely even understood what Galileo was telling them, despite his clarity of expression; hence I think it unlikely that they would have found out the same things for themselves. Two of his great contemporaries, Kepler and Descartes, each excelled him in one field—Kepler in astronomy and Descartes in mathematics—but they were both woefully deficient as physicists. And this leads me to the first point that I wish to make in explanation of Galileo's effectiveness.

Galileo was born into a world that already had a highly developed and technically advanced mathematical astronomy, but it had no coherent mathematical physics and no physical astronomy at all.[1] It was Galileo who, by consistently applying mathematics to physics and physics to astronomy, first brought mathematics, physics, and astronomy together in a truly significant and fruitful way. The three disciplines had always been looked upon as essentially separate; Galileo revealed their triply paired relationships and thereby opened new fields of investigation to men of widely divergent interests and abilities. Mathematical astronomy, mathematical physics, and physical astronomy have ever since constituted an inseparable triad of sciences at the very base of modern physical science. Therein, I think, lies the primary explanation of Galileo's effectiveness.

The inner unity of mathematics, astronomy, and physics is more often implied than overtly stated in the work of Galileo. It is to me doubtful whether a philosophical theory of that unity would have sufficed to produce the effects here under consideration. A contrary view may be taken by those historians who see in Galileo's work little more than a loyal carrying out of the philosophical program of Plato, through showing that geometry indeed governs the physical universe. But there are difficulties with that view. Galileo did not acknowledge any leadership but that of Archimedes; he spent most of his life trying to persuade people not to swear by the words of any master; his notion of the instrumental role of geometry in understanding nature is quite different from that of Plato; and eminent Platonists of the time were much better informed in that philosophy than Galileo, yet had no discernible influence on the study of physical science.

In any event Galileo, not content with a general statement from outside science concerning the relationship of mathematics, astronomy, and physics, set forth particulars within each pairing of those sciences which established their interconnections. And that suggests a second source of his effectiveness: he was an acknowledged expert in each of the three separate disciplines. In view of the recognized merit of his own contributions to each of them, it was evident that he knew what he was talking about, even when what he said appeared paradoxical or absurd. Astronomers were drawn to his physics by his eminence in astronomy; mathematicians took up his mechanics because he was a respected professor of mathematics.

One may contrast the case of Galileo with that of his contemporary Francis Bacon, who likewise formulated a program for the reform of knowledge. That program included three basic ideas which are also found in Galileo's works; namely, recognition of the inadequacy of traditional knowledge, an understanding of the obstacles standing in the way of any departure from it, and the suggestion of methods by which real advances in knowledge might be made. But Bacon, unlike Galileo, was no expert in mathematics or science; hence, though he could discern the goal and suggest a path, he did not actually lead others along that path to the goal. As he himself wrote in a letter to Dr. Playfere: "I have only taken upon me to ring a bell to call other wits together."[2] Bacon's program stressed the accumulation of observational data, a valuable antidote to authority and a most useful procedure in the natural sciences. But it did not clearly open a new path to physical science, as did the bringing together of mathematics, astronomy, and physics. Bacon's bell served its purpose; but—at least so far as physical science was concerned—when the wits assembled, it was in Galileo's study.

Of course, to be an expert in as many as three separate fields was not uncommon for men of the Renaissance. That is the way in which Galileo's effectiveness was closely related to the temper of his time. But to be an expert in each of the three disciplines now under discussion was not a likely combination at his time for reasons which will presently appear. It was not unusual in 1600 to be an expert in mathematics, astronomy, and music, for example, or in astronomy, physics, and

metaphysics. But Galileo's expertness in mathematics, astronomy, and physics was exceptional, and in certain curious ways was largely accidental. Indeed I believe that it was only gradually that Galileo himself fully discerned the essential interrelationships of his deepest interests. Eventually he did so, and as a result he became a critic and a reformer of, as well as a contributor to, science; that is, a man with a definitely formulated program for the study of natural phenomena, not just a versatile technical specialist. That, in my opinion, was the third source of his effectiveness.

Certain personal traits of Galileo's also contributed to his effectiveness. They have been discussed in a preceding essay; here it will be remarked only that his concern for precision was sufficient to protect him from indulging in rash conjectures, but not so great as to hinder him from declaring certain kinds of observed discrepancies or apparent contradictions to be irrelevant or negligible. This is essential in a discoverer of truly fundamental laws, just as an inflexible and uncompromising precision is necessary for their refinement and extension. It is interesting that most of Galileo's scientific contemporaries tended to fret over detail, which fitted them admirably for the next step in physical science, but made it hard for them to perceive and formulate its first mathematical laws. The exception is Kepler, and it is interesting that his contribution was essentially mathematical rather than physical in the modern sense.

Let us next examine the origin and development of Galileo's program for the reform of physical science, beginning with the period of his life immediately before his full comprehension of the magnitude of his task. In so doing we shall be better able to see how his work contrasted with that of his predecessors and what traditions and prejudices he was obliged to break down.

For a period of more than twenty years, from 1589 to 1610, Galileo was a professor of mathematics, first at the University of Pisa and then at Padua. No record remains of his lectures at Pisa. At Padua, however, records show his assigned subjects for various years.

1593—*leget Sphaeram et Euclidem.*

1594—*leget quintum librum Euclidis et theoricas planetarum.*

1598—*leget Euclidis Elementa et Mechanicas Aristotelis Quaestiones.*

1599—*Leget Sphaeram et Euclidem.*

1603—*leget librum De sphera et librum Elementorum Euclidis.*

1604—*leget theoricem planetarum.*

By *librum De sphera,* in the entry for 1603, we may assume that the text of Sacrobosco was meant and that the same text was explained in 1593 and 1599.[3] The syllabus of Galileo's public lectures on that subject is preserved in five closely corresponding copies in manuscript, one of which was published in 1656 by Urbano D'Aviso as the *Trattato della Sfera di Galileo Galilei.* Apart from its clarity of style, it differs little from dozens of similar treatises of the epoch.

Galileo's lectures on Euclid's *Elements* probably likewise represented merely the usual course in geometry; if he wrote a syllabus for them, it has been lost. The fifth book of Euclid, however, was of particular interest to Galileo, and we have what is probably an edited version of his course of 1594 in a book published by Vincenzio Viviani in 1674 under the title, "The fifth book of Euclid or the universal science of proportion explained by the teaching of Galileo, arranged in a new order." Galileo's special interest in the theory of proportion had an important bearing on his method of applying mathematics to physics, but it is unlikely that such applications were discussed in his public lectures at Padua.

There is strong reason to believe that Galileo also wrote a syllabus for his course on the treatise *Questions of Mechanics,* then attributed to Aristotle though now ascribed to one of his disciples.[4] That syllabus, now lost, must not be confused with Galileo's own treatise **On Mechanics,** drafted about 1593 and successively revised, which seems to have been used by Galileo in his private lessons to special pupils. At the end of that treatise and in a letter written in 1610, Galileo refers specifically to another work on questions of mechanics.

The basis of Galileo's lectures on planetary theory is conjectural, as again no syllabus has survived. Probably they constituted an exposition of Ptolemy's *Almagest,* for Galileo once mentioned that he had composed a commentary on Ptolemy about 1590, which he intended to publish. It is improbable that his public lectures included an exposition of the Copernican theory, though the heliocentric theory was probably mentioned in passing—as it was, contrary to the assertion of many modern historians, in his lectures on the sphere.[5]

In short, Galileo's public teaching had the general characteristics of most courses offered in mathematics at any leading university around 1600. Even at the enlightened University of Padua, Galileo appears to have departed only to a small degree from conventional routine instruction. In the six years for which we have a definite record, he lectured in only one term on anything that might today be considered as related to physics—and even that course was designed as a commentary on an ancient treatise.

Physics at that time belonged to philosophy rather than mathematics and was taught in universities by philosophers as an exposition of Aristotle's *Physica.* Such a course was probably taken by Galileo as a student at Pisa under Francesco Buonamico or Girolamo Borro. Since the chair of mathematics at Pisa was vacant during most of Galileo's student days, his only formal instruction in astronomy was probably associated with philosophy rather than with mathematics. From the so-called **Juvenilia** preserved among his papers, it appears that he heard the lectures of Buonamico on Aristotle's *De caelo,* a purely speculative treatment of astronomy devoid not only of what we should call physics, but even of the mathematical theory of astronomical calculation which had long since been brought to an impressive degree of accuracy.

It should be remembered that the entire tradition in professional astronomy up to that time was essentially technical rather than scientific. The task of astronomers was to improve the methods of describing and calculating the observed positions and motions of heavenly bodies, rather than to explain such motions physically. That tradition found strong support in the Aristotelian philosophy, which made a fundamental distinction between terrestrial and celestial matter and motions. Such a distinction had long been incorporated into Christian theology. Thus astronomy, like physics, had evolved along two distinct paths in formal education. The philosophical part of each science remained quite foreign to the mathematical part in the minds of even the best-educated men. Astronomical calculations, moreover, which fell to the mathematicians, remained strictly kinematic. The science of dynamics had not yet been born, and even if terrestrial dynamics had existed, it would not have been applied to astronomy so long as celestial objects were regarded as pure lights constituted of quintessential material. But not even terrestrial dynamics existed; such a science was effectively precluded in scholarly circles by Aristotle's dictum that every body moved must be in contact with a separate mover. With respect to physics, all that was traditionally open to mathematical treatment was a single branch of mechanics; namely, statics.

Even in his earliest studies, however, Galileo defied Aristotle and attempted to expand the applications of mathematics to physics. . . .

Galileo's assigned university courses gave him little or no scope for the communication of his researches in mathematical physics. He went on with them, but one might say that he did so almost despite his official position rather than in pursuance of it. From a letter written to him by Luca Valerio, a Roman mathematician best known for his work on centers of gravity, it is evident that by June 1609 Galileo had selected two fundamental propositions on which he was prepared to found the science of mechanics. But in that same month, his attention was diverted from that project by news of the telescope, and his energies were applied immediately to its improvement and to the astronomical discoveries which soon made him famous throughout Europe.

Galileo's sudden celebrity quickly suggested to him a way in which he might free himself from routine teaching and find time to write and publish the books which had been evolving in his mind. It was mainly for that purpose that, after twenty years of university teaching, he applied for a court position with the grand duke of Tuscany. In making his application he included a significant and unusual request: " . . . As to the title of my position," he wrote, "I desire that in addition to the title of 'mathematician,' his Highness will annex that of 'philosopher,' for I may claim to have studied for a greater number of years in philosophy than months in pure mathematics."[10]

To the historian, Galileo's request is striking in two respects: first, because he sought the unusual title of court philosopher, and second, because he *did not* seek the customary title of court astronomer. That title was not uncommon in Europe at that time. Johannes Kepler, for example, was imperial astronomer at the court of Rudolph II at Prague. That Galileo did not even mention, let alone demand, such a title is made still more striking by the fact that his chief claim to fame in 1610 lay in the astronomical discoveries he had just published in his *Sidereus Nuncius* and dedicated to his proposed employer, the grand duke of Tuscany.

Galileo's failure to seek the title of court astronomer, although curious at first glance, is not difficult to explain. In the first place, a court astronomer at that period was in fact an astrologer, or at least his primary value to his employer lay in that capacity. Any contributions he might make to theoretical or observational astronomy were the merest by-products, so far as the sovereign was concerned. As Kepler ruefully remarked, the wayward daughter astrology had to support the honest dame astronomy. Galileo was perfectly competent to cast horoscopes, but he did not enjoy doing so; on the contrary, he was openly critical of both astrology and alchemy. In the second place, he does not seem to have cared much about mathematical astronomy outside his routine public lectures, which in fact were offered by the university chiefly because of their astrological applications, deemed necessary for medical students especially.

As we have seen, the subject to which Galileo *had* devoted his principal researches during twenty years of teaching was the application of mathematics to problems of motion and mechanics. But in applying for employment by the grand duke, he could scarcely have described that specialty as physics, nor could he have asked for the title of "physicist" with any hope of being

understood. Physics was no more an independent subject than was metaphysics or ethics. It was merely a branch of philosophy—and that is what throws light on Galileo's otherwise odd request for the title of "philosopher." It was, in fact, the only appropriate word, when we consider that the term "mechanic" was entirely undignified and unthinkable as a court title. The historic appropriateness of Galileo's choice of title is shown by the fact that long after his time, the term "natural philosopher" served as the official name for a physicist in England, the word "physics" itself being no more than a synonym for "nature."

I am inclined to believe that the philosophy which Galileo had in mind when he asked for the title of philosopher was that which he later described in one of his most frequently cited passages, which begins: "Philosophy is written in that grand book of nature that stands forever open to our eyes. . . ."[11] I think it is not too far-fetched to say that what Galileo was seeking, when he asked to be made mathematician and philosopher to the Tuscan court, was the world's first post as a mathematical physicist.

Support for this viewpoint is afforded by a difficulty that arose in Galileo's securing of the title he had asked for. The grand duke, doubtless in the belief that he was granting the request, sent to Galileo a document naming him chief philosopher to the court and chief mathematician at the University of Pisa. But Galileo was not satisfied with this, which is puzzling unless it was because he wanted the two titles definitely combined. Eventually he had his way and was named chief mathematician and philosopher to the grand duke and chief mathematician at the University of Pisa without obligation to reside or teach there. It may seem that he had made a major issue of a minor point, but I believe that even before Galileo moved from Padua to Florence, he had in mind the conception that completes the famous quotation of which the opening words were previously cited. To paraphrase the rest of it: " . . . that grand book of nature . . . is written in the language of mathematics, without a knowledge of which one cannot understand a word of it, but must wander about forever as in a maze."[12] What Galileo wanted, and could get only from a powerful patron, was a position in which he could openly expound the unity of mathematics and physics—and probably astronomy also, but without any astrological connotations. The grand duke could grant him this, but the departments of philosophy were too strong and the departments of mathematics too weak to accommodate such a program in the universities. . . .

Aristotelian philosophy insisted on a complete dichotomy between terrestrial and celestial substances and motions. Astronomers were concerned not with the nature of heavenly bodies, but only with purely mathe-

Galileo with his telescope.

matical descriptions of the observed motions and predictions of positions. Christian theology had adopted the Aristotelian separation of base earth from noble heavens, making it dangerous as well as difficult to attack. Nevertheless, the opening sections of Galileo's *Dialogue* were devoted to a refutation of the Aristotelian assumption, as a point of departure for his pioneer attempt to unify astronomy and physics.

A complete chronological account of Galileo's efforts to bring physics and astronomy together would take us back to 1597, when he wrote to Kepler that he believed certain physical events on earth to be explicable only by its motions.[14] But his first public attempts to relate physics and astronomy are found in the *Starry Messenger* of 1610.

In announcing his first telescopic observations, Galileo declared the moon to be like another earth because of its rough, mountainous surface. Applying geometric methods familiar to land surveyors, he calculated the heights of the lunar mountains from their

shadows. Denying the Peripatetic contention that all heavenly bodies were perfect spheres, he accounted in later years for the moon's roughness by assuming its material to be similar to that of the earth and similarly drawn to its common center of gravity. The darker surfaces of the moon were taken, on terrestrial analogies, to be relatively smooth as compared to the brighter parts. Conversely, he deduced from the moon's rough surface and its bright reflection of sunlight that the earth, with similar surface, must reflect sunlight to the moon; and in that way he correctly explained the secondary light on the moon, seen when it is thinly crescent. At first he suggested also that the moon had an atmosphere, but he later withdrew that further analogy between the moon and the earth. However, he postulated an atmosphere for Jupiter in order to account for changes in the appearances of its satellites in their various positions. All Galileo's physical analogies between the earth and any heavenly body, even the lowly moon, aroused strong opposition from philosophers and some protest from theologians.

When Galileo wrote the *Starry Messenger,* he was rapidly approaching his ultimate firm conviction that astronomy must be completely integrated with physics. But his interest in astronomy was then still subsidiary to his absorption in the application of mathematics to physics on which he had labored for so many years. The telescope was for a time principally a means to him for gaining fame and improving his position. Thus he first observed sunspots not later than the spring of 1611, but paid little attention to them except as a curiosity to show his friends. He did not seize immediately on them as a ready basis for expansion of his analogies between terrestrial and celestial phenomena, as one would expect him to do had he already completely formulated his program to unify mathematics, physics, and astronomy. But the sunspots were destined to be decisive in that regard when a rival astronomer proposed a theory about the spots.

Galileo's treatise on bodies placed in water was about to go to press when he received from Mark Welser three printed letters on sunspots written by a German Jesuit, Christopher Scheiner. Scheiner argued that the spots were only apparently on the sun and were in reality varying clusters of small opaque bodies rotating about it at some distance. His opinion probably had its origin in a desire to maintain, for religious and philosophical reasons, the doctrine of incorruptibility of heavenly bodies, especially the sun. Welser wrote to ask for Galileo's opinion on the whole subject, and Galileo undertook a series of careful observations, after which he replied in refutation of the Jesuit's theory.

By precise mathematical reasoning, Galileo demonstrated that the sunspots must be located either on the surface of the sun or at a negligible distance from it. He went on to say that the only proper method available for assigning the causes of distant or unfamiliar events was to apply our experience of things near at hand, and he suggested that the sunspots might better be explained as vast clouds or smokes than as stars or planets. He noted that terrestrial clouds often cover a whole province and that when a terrestrial cloud happens to be near the sun and is compared with a sunspot, it generally appears much darker than the spot. Still more significant was his explanation of the rotation of the sunspots, which he attributed to an axial rotation of the sun itself, for that in turn led him to a first attempt in the direction of celestial dynamics. Following his first published reference to an inertial principle, cited elsewhere in this volume, he wrote:

> Now if this is true, as indeed it is, what would an inert body do if continually surrounded with an ambient that moved with a motion to which it was indifferent? I do not see how one can doubt that it would move with the motion of the ambient. And the sun, a body of spherical shape suspended and balanced on its own center, cannot fail to follow the motion of its ambient, having no intrinsic repugnance or external impediment

to rotation. It cannot have an internal repugnance because by such a rotation it is neither moved from its place, nor are its parts permuted among themselves. Their natural arrangement is not changed in any way, so that as far as the constitution of its parts is concerned, such movement is as if it did not exist. . . . This may be further confirmed, as it does not appear that any movable body can have a repugnance to a movement without having a natural propensity to the opposite motion, for in indifference no repugnance exists. . . .[15]

Here Galileo's knowledge of the conservation of angular momentum was brought to bear on a problem of celestial motion—a real step toward the unification of physics and astronomy. Mathematics having already been linked firmly to both the latter sciences, Galileo's program was now essentially complete. That program was presented successively in *The Assayer* (1623), Galileo's scientific manifesto (as it was called by Leonardo Olschki); in the *Dialogue* (1632), dealing primarily with astronomical arguments but heavily weighted with physics; and in the *Two New Sciences* (1638), dealing exclusively with physics (since Galileo was forbidden to deal with astronomy after writing the *Dialogue*) but extending beyond mechanics to include speculations on sound, light, and other physical topics. *The Assayer* and the *Dialogue* offer many illustrations of Galileo's program of linking physics with astronomy and of his simultaneous linkage of all three sciences. I shall consider a few of these here, neglecting the *Two New Sciences,* since examples have already been given of Galileo's methods of applying mathematics to physics.

In *The Assayer,* Galileo had occasion to discuss the so-called third motion attributed by Copernicus to the earth in order to maintain the earth's axis continually parallel throughout the year. Of this he says:

> This extra rotation, opposite in direction to all other celestial motions, appeared to many people to be a most improbable thing. . . . I used to remove the difficulty by showing that such a phenomenon was far from improbable, . . . for any body resting freely in a thin and fluid medium will, when transported along the circumference of a large circle, spontaneously acquire a rotation in the direction contrary to the larger movement. This is seen by taking in one's hand a bowl of water, and placing in it a floating ball. Then, turning about on one's toe with the hand holding the bowl extended, one sees the ball turn on its axis in the opposite direction, and completing its revolution in the same time as one's own. [Really] . . . this would not be a motion at all, but a kind of rest. It is certainly true that to the person holding the bowl, the ball appears to move with respect to himself and to the bowl, turning on its axis. But with respect to the wall . . . the ball does not turn, and any point on its surface will continue to point at the same distant object.[16]

Galileo's appeal to familiar terrestrial observations in explanation of heavenly events was designed to pave the way to physical astronomy, which would eliminate the clumsy hypothetical apparatus of crystalline spheres which earlier astronomers had introduced as a means of accounting for the motions of heavenly bodies. The idea of relative motion, introduced in the preceding passage, became pivotal in the later *Dialogue.* Astronomers, it is true, had long been aware of the importance of optical relativity, but even Tycho Brahe had been unable to conceive of a literal physical relativity of motion. Galileo, armed with that concept and with his principles of the composition of motions, inertia, and conservation of angular momentum, was able effectively to meet many commonsense objections against motion of the earth. Thus, replying to the claim that if the earth really moves, we should see a departure from straight motion in the free fall of a body from a tower, Galileo said:

> Rather, we never *see* anything but the simple downward motion, since this other circular one, common to the earth, the tower, and ourselves, remains imperceptible and as if nonexistent. Only that motion of the stone which we do not share is perceptible, and of this, our senses show us that it is along a straight line parallel to the tower. . . . With respect to the earth, the tower, and ourselves, all of which keep moving with the diurnal motion along with the stone, the diurnal motion is as if it did not exist; it remains insensible, imperceptible and without any effect whatever. All that remains observable is the motion which we lack, and that is the grazing drop to the base of the tower. You are not the first to feel a great repugnance toward recognizing this nonoperative quality of motion among things which share it in common.[17]

A good example of Galileo's effectiveness at persuasion through the use of terrestrial and celestial analogies occurs in the First Day of the *Dialogue.* His Aristotelian opponent cannot believe that the rough, dark earth could possibly shine in the sky as brightly as the moon. Galileo points out to him that the comparison must be drawn for the moon as seen in daytime, since that is the only time we can see the earth illuminated, and then proceeds:

> Now you yourself have already admitted having seen the moon by day among little whitish clouds, and similar in appearance to one of them. This amounts to your granting that clouds, though made of elemental matter, are just as fit to receive light as the moon is. More so, if you will recall having seen some very large clouds at times, white as snow. It cannot be doubted that if such a cloud could remain equally luminous at night, it would light up the surrounding regions more than a hundred moons.
>
> If we were sure, then, that the earth is as much lighted by the sun as one of these clouds, no question would remain that it is no less brilliant than the moon. Now all doubt on this point ceases when we see those clouds, in the absence of the sun, remaining

as dark as the earth all night long. And what is more, there is not one of us who has not seen such a cloud low and far off, and wondered whether it was a cloud or a mountain—a clear indication that mountains are no less luminous than clouds.[18]

Two arguments for a motion of the earth that were particularly dear to Galileo's heart, arguments which simultaneously link mathematics, astronomy, and physics, fell on deaf ears in Galileo's time. Those arguments related to the ocean tides and to cyclical changes in the paths of sunspots. Correctly understood, they were unanswerable at the time they were propounded. It may seem paradoxical, in explanation of Galileo's effectiveness, to mention two arguments of his that were (and still are) ineffective. But I think that the paradox is only apparent. The prime source of Galileo's effectiveness was his bringing together of mathematics, astronomy, and physics in an inseparable relationship. Hence even a questionable example of such a relationship given by him was still capable of revealing to others what *sort* of thing should be sought in a scientific explanation.

The tidal and sunspot arguments are the subjects of separate essays in this volume; here it suffices to outline their nature. Galileo's theory of the tides occupies the final section of the *Dialogue.* He says that, in his opinion, the ocean tides cannot be explained physically if we assume a perfectly stationary earth. So far he is quite right. He then asserts that the double motion of the earth, around its axis and around the sun, affords a purely mechanical means of explaining the tides. His argument is that the two circular motions are additive on one side of the earth and subtractive on the other, so that the extremities of any large east-west basin of water, such as an ocean, will be traveling with nonuniform velocity. Since direct experience teaches us that water in a basin is disturbed when its velocity is altered, Galileo thought that he had found a basic cause of periodic disturbances in the ocean waters.

The principal objection was that only one high tide a day would be expected from this model, whereas there are approximately two. This did not escape Galileo's attention, but neither did it bother him. So long as he had a primary mechanical cause for periodic disturbance, he was content. He pointed out that a wide variety of other factors would affect its progress, such as the length of the basin, its orientation, its depth, the shape of its coasts, the action of winds, and so on. Since Galileo had never observed tides except along the Adriatic and the Tyrrhenian seas, where they are not very impressive, it is not surprising that he thought such factors sufficient to account for the observed discrepancy of period.

On the other hand, Galileo did not neglect the fact of variations in tidal effects related to the seasons and to phases of the moon. These he accounted for in his theory by postulating cyclical changes in the earth's orbital speed, which would appear to us as related to the sun's position, and by drawing an analogy between the earth-moon system and a moving weight on a rotating rod driven by a constant force to account for monthly tidal changes.

This whole theory illustrates vividly Galileo's program of seeking mechanical explanations for all physical effects. Celestial appearances were accommodated to a tidal theory having a mechanical basis; for discrepancies with observed phenomena, he invoked further mechanical phenomena. All this was in keeping with his expressed principles; thus his admiration for Copernicus was only heightened by the latter's loyalty to heliocentrism in the face of unexplained discrepancies between the apparent and theoretical sizes of Venus at opposition and conjunction—discrepancies which were eventually reconciled by telescopic observations after the death of Copernicus.

The other argument in which Galileo combined mathematics, astronomy, and physics in support of the earth's motion concerns the annual variations in the paths of sunspots. Twice in the year, the paths are straight and tilted to the ecliptic; twice a year, they are at maximum curvature with the ends lying in the ecliptic; at all times, they change cyclically in tilt and degree of curvature. Galileo pointed out that those variations are easily explained if the earth has the two motions attributed to it by Copernicus. But for an absolutely stationary earth, they can be explained only by ascribing to the sun a highly complicated set of motions. First, the sun must have a rotation about an axis tilted to the ecliptic, having a period of about one month. Second, in its annual revolution about the earth, the sun's axis must rotate conically about another axis perpendicular to the ecliptic, in circles having a radius measured by the tilt of the first axis. The period of this conical rotation must be annual. A still further daily motion of the sun's axis would be necessary to keep the paths of the spots undisturbed on the face of the sun during each day.

The essential difference in the two cases lies in the fact that the sun presents almost exactly the same face to a terrestrial observer throughout a day. This was first known from the positions of sunspots. But the earth obviously cannot present the same face to an imaginary solar observer throughout any day. Hence the explanations required in the two systems are not simply interchangeable.

Galileo duly acknowledged that it would be theoretically possible, from a strictly geometric point of view, to endow the sun with the necessary motions to produce these appearances. But he saw that any such device led to grave difficulties from the standpoint of dynamics. Galileo was aware of the principle of conservation of angular momentum and of the inertial path of the axis of a rotating body, as mentioned earlier; thus, to him, the physical difficulties were very real. But to his contemporaries, who felt obliged only to link mathematics with astronomy and not astronomy with physics, his argument remained inconclusive.

Galileo's theory of the tides and his argument from the paths of sunspots are important in showing the manner in which he brought together simultaneously the fields of mathematics, astronomy, and physics. Whatever their defects, those two arguments for the earth's motion were founded on a fundamentally sound conception of the manner in which all physical phenomena, terrestrial and celestial, ought to be consistently explained. It was that conception which made Galileo's work more effective scientifically than the work of any one of his great contemporaries or recent predecessors. It was a conception which he himself thoroughly grasped and consciously applied to a definite program. It was a conception, moreover, which profoundly appealed to many of Galileo's contemporaries and exerted a recognizable influence upon them, suggesting a wide variety of further investigations once it had been broached. Since this particular unifying conception had been lacking in all previous science, the unsophisticated view that Galileo was the revolutionary founder of modern science is not to be rejected outright, no matter how many elements of his program may prove to have been anticipated by others before him.

Notes

[1] The work of Simon Stevin is an example of sound mathematical physics prior to the work of Galileo. Since Galileo was born in 1564, and Stevin's first book on physics appeared in 1586, the statement above remains literally true. Stevin first published in Dutch, and his work remained relatively unnoticed until 1605, when a Latin translation appeared. Galileo was by that time far along with his own mechanical investigations. Johannes Kepler contributed to physical astronomy, but his contributions were contemporary with Galileo's. The work of René Descartes began to appear only at the close of Galileo's life.

[2] Cited from R. F. Jones, *Ancients and Moderns* (Berkeley, 1965), p. 41.

[3] The evidence is given in "Galileo Gleanings VII"; *Physis* I, 4 (1957), 296.

[4] The *Questions of Mechanics,* unknown in the Middle Ages, played an important role in sixteenth-century physical speculations.

[5] *Le Opere di Galileo Galilei* (20 vols.), Florence, 1929-39; reprint of the Edizione Nationale; vol. II, p. 223.

"The present question [whether the earth is motionless] is worthy of consideration, there being no lack of very great philosophers and mathematicians who, deeming the earth a star, have made it movable." Probably no passage in Galileo's writings is more widely misrepresented than that in which he explained to his students at Padua the motions that might be attributed to the earth, and the objections to its rotation, before expounding to them the geostatic theory as required by the university. In the most recent instance I have noted, the writer not only states that Galileo "taught cosmography without making the slightest allusion to an alternative way of explaining the celestial phenomena," but misquotes one of the few biographers who had correctly appraised Galileo's comments; see W. Hartner, "Galileo's Contribution to Astronomy," *Galileo Man of Science*, ed. E. McMullin (New York, 1968), p. 184, and cf. E. Wohlwill, *Galilei und sein Kampf,* vol. I (Hamburg, 1909), p. 210. . . .

. . .[10] *Stillman Drake, Discoveries and Opinions of Galileo,* New York, 1957 p. 64.

[11] *Discoveries,* p. 237.

[12] *Discoveries,* p. 238. This passage is often cited as an argument that Galileo believed the "real" world to be mathematical. On that argument, the "real" Hamlet must have been English. . . .

. . .[14] See essay 6.

[15] *Discoveries,* pp. 113-14. Preceding passages are given in essay 12.

[16] *Discoveries,* pp. 264-65.

[17] *Dialogue,* pp. 163, 171.

[18] *Dialogue,* pp. 88-89.

Pope John Paul II (essay date 1979)

SOURCE: "Epilogue: 'The Greatness of Galileo Is Known to All,'" in *Galileo Galilei: Toward a Resolution of 350 Years of Debate—1633-1983,* edited by Paul Cardinal Poupard, with the "Epilogue" translated by Ian Campbell from a speech given in 1979, Duquesne University Press, 1987, pp. 195-200.

[*In the following essay, first presented as a speech in 1979 and reprinted in 1987, Pope John Paul II undertakes to reconcile the views of the Catholic Church with those of Galileo, arguing that Galileo was not in fact in opposition to the Church.*]

During the centenary commemoration of the birth of Albert Einstein,[1] celebrated by the Pontifical Academy of the Sciences on November 10, 1979, Pope John Paul II spoke on the profound harmony between the truth of faith and the truth of science in the following terms.

I feel myself to be fully one with my predecessor Pius XI, and with the two who followed him in the Chair of Peter, in inviting the members of the Academy of the Sciences and all scientists with them, to bring about "the ever more noble and intense progress of the sciences, without asking any more from them; and this is because in this excellent proposal and this noble work there consists that mission of serving truth with which we charge them."[2]

The search for truth is the fundamental task of science. The researcher who moves on this plane of science feels all the fascination of St. Augustine's words, *Intellectum valde ama,*[3] "love intelligence greatly," and its proper function, which is to know the truth. Pure science is a good in itself which deserves to be greatly loved, for it is knowledge, the perfection of human beings in their intelligence. Even before its technical applications, it should be loved for itself, as an integral part of human culture. Fundamental science is a universal boon, which every nation should cultivate in full freedom from all forms of international servitude or intellectual colonialism.

The freedom of fundamental research

Fundamental research should be free vis-à-vis political and economic powers, which should cooperate in its development, without fettering its creativity or enslaving it to their own ends. As with all other truth, scientific truth has, in fact, to render an account only to itself and to the supreme truth that is God, the creator of humankind and of all that is.

On its second plane, science turns toward practical applications, which find their full development in various technologies. In the phase of its concrete applications, science is necessary for humanity in order to satisfy the just requirements of life, and to conquer the various evils that threaten it. There is no doubt that applied science has rendered and will render humankind immense services, especially if it is inspired by love, regulated by wisdom, and accompanied by the courage that defends it against the undue interference of all tyrannical powers. Applied science should be allied with conscience, so that, in the triad, science-technology-conscience, it may be the cause of the true good of humankind, whom it should serve.

Unhappily, as I have had occasion to say in my encyclical *Redemptor hominis,* "Humankind today seems constantly to be menaced by what it constructs. . . . In this there seems to consist the principal chapter of the drama of human existence today" (§ 15). Humankind should emerge victorious from this drama, which threatens to degenerate into tragedy, and should once more find its authentic sovereignty over the world and its full mastery of the things it has made. At this present hour, as I wrote in the same encyclical, "the fundamental significance of this "sovereignty" and this 'mastery' of humankind over the visible world, assigned to it as a task by the Creator, consists in the priority of ethics over technology, in the primacy of person over things, and in the superiority of spirit over matter" (§ 16).

This threefold superiority is maintained to the extent that there is conserved the sense of human transcendence over the world and God's transcendence over humankind. Exercising its mission as guardian and defender of both these transcendences, the church desires to assist science to conserve its ideal purity on the plane of fundamental research, and to help it fulfill its service to humankind on the plane of practical applications.

The church freely recognizes, on the other hand, that it has benefited from science. It is to science, among other things, that there must be attributed that which Vatican II has said with regard to certain aspects of modern culture:

> New conditions in the end affect the religious life itself. . . . The soaring of the critical spirit purifies that life from a magical conception of the world and from superstitious survivals, and demands a more and more personal and active adhesion to faith; many are the souls who in this way have come to a more living sense of God.[4]

The advantage of collaboration

Collaboration between religion and modern science is to the advantage of both, and in no way violates the autonomy of either. Just as religion requires religious freedom, so science legitimately requires freedom of research. The Second Vatican Council, after having affirmed, together with Vatican I, the just freedom of the arts and human disciplines in the domain of their proper principles and method, solemnly recognized "the legitimate autonomy of culture and particularly that of the sciences."[5]

On this occasion of the solemn commemoration of Einstein, I wish to confirm anew the declarations of Vatican II on the autonomy of science in its function of research into the truth inscribed in nature by the hand of God. Filled with admiration for the genius of the great scientist, a genius in which there is revealed the imprint of the Creator Spirit, the Church, without in any way passing a judgment on the doctrine concerning the great systems of the universe, since that is not its area of competence, nevertheless proposes this doctrine to the reflection of theologians in order to discov-

er the harmony existing between scientific and revealed truth.

Mr. President, in your address you have rightly said that Galileo and Einstein have characterized an epoch. *The greatness of Galileo is known to all,* as is that of Einstein; but with this difference, that by comparison with the one whom we are today honoring before the College of Cardinals in the Apostolic Palace, the first had much to suffer—we cannot conceal it—at the hands of men and departments within the church. The Second Vatican Council has recognized and deplored certain undue interventions: "May we be permitted to deplore"—it is written in § 36 of the Conciliar Constitution *Gaudium et Spes*—"certain attitudes that have existed among Christians themselves, insufficiently informed as to the legitimate autonomy of science. Sources of tension and conflict, they have led many to consider that science and faith are opposed." The reference to Galileo is clearly expressed in the note appended to this text, which cites the volume *Vita e opere di Galileo Galilei* by Pio Paschini, published by the Pontifical Academy of Sciences.

In order to go beyond this position adopted by the Council, I desire that theologians, scientists, and historians, animated by a spirit of sincere collaboration, deepen their examination of the Galileo case, and, in a loyal recognition of errors, from whatever side they come. I also desire that they bring about the disappearance of the mistrust that, in many souls, this affair still arouses in opposition to a fruitful concord between science and faith, between the church and the world. I give my full support to this task, which can honor the truth of faith and of science, and open the door to future collaboration.

The case of the scientist Galileo Galilei

May I be permitted, gentlemen, to submit to your attention and your reflection, some points that seem to me important for placing the Galileo affair in its true light, in which agreements between religion and science are more important than those misunderstandings from which there has arisen the bitter and grievous conflict that has dragged itself out in the course of the following centuries.

He who is justly entitled the founder of modern physics, has explicitly declared that the truths of faith and of science can never contradict each other: "Holy Scripture and nature equally proceed from the divine Word, the first as dictated by the Holy Spirit, the second as the very faithful executor of God's commands," as he wrote in his letter to Fr. Benedetto Castelli on December 21, 1613.[6] The Second Vatican Council does not differ in its mode of expression; it even adopts similar expressions when it teaches: "Methodical research, in all domains of knowledge, if it follows moral norms, will never really be opposed to faith; both the realities of this world and of the faith find their origin in the same God."[7]

In scientific research Galileo perceived the presence of the Creator who stimulates it, anticipates and assists its intuitions, by acting in the very depths of its spirit. In connection with the telescope, he wrote at the commencement of the **Sidereus Nuntius,** (**"the starry messenger"**), recalling some of his astronomical discoveries: *Quae omnia ope perspicilli a me excogitavi divina prius illuminante gratia, paucis abhinc diebus reperta, atque observata fuerunt,*[8] "I worked all these things out with the help of the telescope and under the prior illumination of divine grace they were discovered and observed by me a few days ago."

The Galilean recognition of divine illumination in the spirit of the scientist finds an echo in the already quoted text of the Conciliar Constitution on the church in the modern world: "One who strives, with perseverance and humility, to penetrate the secret of things, is as if led by the hand of God, even if not aware of it."[9] The humility insisted on by the conciliar text is a spiritual virtue equally necessary for scientific research as for adhesion to the faith. Humility creates a climate favorable to dialogue between the believer and the scientist, it is a call for illumination by God, already known or still unknown but loved, in one case as in the other, on the part of the one who is searching for truth.

Galileo has formulated important norms of an epistemological character, which are confirmed as indispensable for placing Holy Scripture and science in agreement. In his letter to the grand duchess of Tuscany, Christine of Lorraine, he reaffirms the truth of Scripture:

> Holy Scripture can never propose an untruth, always on condition that one penetrates to its true meaning, which—I think nobody can deny—is often hidden and very different from that which the simple signification of the words seems to indicate.[10]

Galileo introduced the principle of an interpretation of the sacred books that goes beyond the literal meaning but is in conformity with the intention and type of exposition proper to each one of them. As he affirms, it is necessary that "the wise who expound it show its true meaning."

The ecclesiastical magisterium admits the plurality of rules of interpretation of Holy Scripture. It expressly teaches, in fact, with the encyclical *Divino Afflante Spiritu* of Pius XII, the presence of different genres in the sacred books and hence the necessity of interpretations conforming to the character of each of them.

An Honest and loyal solution of long-standing oppositions

The various agreements that I have recalled do not by themselves solve all the problems of the Galileo affair, but they help to create a point of departure favorable to their honorable solution, a frame of mind propitious for an honest and loyal resolving of long-standing oppositions.

The existence of this Pontifical Academy of Science, with which Galileo was to some extent associated through the venerable institution that preceded the academy of today, in which eminent scientists participate, is a visible sign that demonstrates to all, with no racial or religious discrimination, the profound harmony that can exist between the truths of science and the truths of faith.

Notes

[1] Albert Einstein, illustrious scientist of our time (1879-1955), was the discoverer of the theories of special and general relativity. According to special relativity, measurements of space and time depend on the speed of light which transmits signals. One of the most remarkable consequences of special relativity is the equivalence of mass and energy ($e = mc^2$, c being the velocity of light). Whereas special relativity introduces time as a coordinate of all measurements (four-dimensional space-time), general relativity geometrizes the distribution of material masses, by assigning to each point of space-time a curvature determined by the mass located there. In addition, general relativity predicts that a moving mass will emit gravitational waves, a prediction that seems to have been recently confirmed in radio astronomy by experimental means. The hypothesis of universal gravitation, proposed by Newton, must thus be revised, and the conceptual difference between inertial and gravitational mass disappears. Traditional concepts of mathematics and physics are thus radically transformed.

[2] Motu Proprio *In Multis Solaciis* of October 28, 1936, concerning the Pontifical Academy of Sciences: A.A.S., 28 (1936) 424.

[3] St. Augustine, *Epist.* 120, 3, 13; P.L. 33, 49.

[4] *Gaudium et Spes,* 7.

[5] Ibid., 59.

[6] Galileo Galilei, "Letter to Father Benedetto Castelli," December 21, 1613; EN, V, 282-85.

[7] *Gaudium et Spes,* 36.

[8] Galileo Galilei, *Sidereus Nuntius, Venetiis, apud Thomam Baglionum,* MDCX, fol. 4.

[9] Ibid.

[10] Galileo Galilei, "Letter to Christine of Lorraine"; EN, V, 315.

Jean Dietz Moss (essay date 1983)

SOURCE: "Galileo's *Letter to Christina:* Some Rhetorical Considerations," in *Renaissance Quarterly,* Vol. XXXVI, No. 4, Winter, 1983, pp. 547-76.

[*In the following essay, Moss argues that Galileo's letter to his patron's mother, the Grand Duchess of Tuscany, in which he defends his position on Copernicus would have been more likely to save him had it stayed within his own area of expertise—mathematics—rather than strayed into theology, the specialty of his accusers.*]

The year 1982 marked the 350th anniversary of the publication of Galileo's **Dialogue Concerning the Two Chief World Systems,** a work that was to have a tragic impact on the astronomer's life, and also on the relations between science and religion. It was the publication of the **Dialogue** that precipitated the trial of Galileo before the Inquisition on charges of teaching the Copernican system, which had been condemned in 1616. The book sets forth the inadequacies of the Ptolemaic system and the superiority of the Copernican for "saving the appearances" of celestial motion, but it does not press openly for acceptance of the theory. An earlier writing of Galileo, the **Letter to Madame Christina of Lorraine, Grand Duchess of Tuscany,** referred to in short as the **Letter to Christina,** does just that. It was written in 1615 before the opinion on Copernicanism was delivered, and written, moreover, to dissuade the Church from condemning Copernicus's *De revolutionibus* of 1543. The letter, which has since become a classic in literature relating to the conflict between science and religion, attempts to work out an acceptable solution that would preserve the autonomy of each. Passages are often quoted for the sheer power of their expression and the acuity of their observations.

A recent work, *Galileo and the Art of Reasoning* by Maurice A. Finocchiaro, has drawn attention to a neglected dimension of the much discussed **Dialogue.**[1] Finocchiaro suggests that the rhetoric Galileo uses in the **Dialogue** was a form of scientific proof; thus Finocchiaro's subtitle: *Rhetorical Foundations of Logic and Scientific Method.* By a careful analysis of the form and content of the **Dialogue** and its relation to the argumentation developed in the work, Finocchiaro has illuminated not only the multifaceted nature of Galileo's rhetoric, but made some provocative assertions regarding the complex nature of scientific reasoning itself.

While this essay takes its inspiration from Finocchiaro's approach, it has a more modest aim. It focuses mainly on the rhetorical aspects of the **Letter to Christina,** particularly on the audience and the appeals used by Galileo to move them. At the same time it sounds a theme similar to Finocchiaro's: that Galileo attempted to influence his audience by using an impressive array of rhetorical appeals. His attention was to induce his readers to see that a condemnation of Copernicus' book was inappropriate, even immoral. Since the letter did not succeed in this, an examination of the strategies employed by Galileo to move his readers might reveal some of the reasons for its failure. What follows is an analysis of these strategies within the context of *ars dictaminis,* continuously taking into account the audience Galileo addressed and the responses that might be conjectured for it.

It could be argued that the **Letter** should not be treated as part of the letter genre at all because of its length and subject matter, that it is really a treatise. In response to this objection one need only consider the fact that many Renaissance letters cross the narrow line between letter and treatise, as Paul Oskar Kristeller has pointed out.[2] But, as he suggests, another characteristic that distinguishes letters from treatises is whether they arise from particular occasions. Galileo's composition was certainly prompted by specific circumstances, and even more importantly, he addresses the Duchess several times in the text; sufficient reason, then, for maintaining that Galileo deliberately chose the letter format and for analyzing the text within that genre.

What precipitated the letter was actually a conversation at a dinner party given by the mother of Galileo's patron Cosimo II de Medici, the Grand Duchess of Tuscany, Christina of Lorraine.[3] She had voiced concern about the new Copernican system in view of the prevailing interpretations of the Scriptures, especially those texts that spoke of the earth as stationary. Father Benedetto Castelli, a Benedictine monk and a friend of Galileo, tried to allay her doubts and to counter the objections of Cosimo Boscaglia, a Pisan professor, who was also present. Castelli had succeeded Galileo in the chair of mathematics at the University of Pisa and was aware of the growing opposition to Galileo's views on astronomy and physics from Boscaglia and others, such as the Florentine philosopher Ludovico delle Colombe. Their antipathy had been growing since the publication of Galileo's **Sidereus nuncius** in 1610, describing his discoveries with the telescope and the inferences he drew from them. His critics thought he claimed too much in view of the Scriptures and the province of natural philosophy. Castelli reported by letter on the argument, outlining his own answers, which he felt effectively refuted the contentions of Professor Boscaglia.

Fearing perhaps a threat to his position as the Tuscan court philosopher and mathematician, Galileo gathered his observations on the problem and sent them to Castelli, and the monk seems to have widely circulated copies of the missive. During the year following the exchange, anti-Galileist sentiment grew in Florence among friends and supporters of Colombe. On December 14, 1614, the Dominican Tomasso Caccini preached a sermon in Santa Maria Novella attacking Galileo, reputedly by using a pun on the text of Acts 1:1, "ye men of Galilee [Galileo], why stand ye gazing up into heaven?"[4] About the same time another Dominican friar, Niccolò Lorini, sent to the Holy Office a replica of Galileo's letter to Castelli, which seems to have contained some alterations by an unknown hand that rendered the thought suspect of heresy.[5] Upon hearing of this Galileo retrieved the original and sent his own authenticated copy to his friend Bishop Piero Dini in Rome. He asked that it be shown to influential clerics, Cardinal Bellarmine among them, to aid in the defense of the Copernican system, rumored to be facing condemnation. At the same time, mid-February of 1615, he told Bishop Dini that he was at work on an amplified version of the letter that he would send to him soon. Galileo took much more time than he had anticipated, however, probably because he decided to consult theologians in order to buttress his views with references to the Scriptures and the Church Fathers. He evidently pressed Castelli and others into helping him in this. A letter from Castelli in January 1615 mentions that he will send on to Galileo some opinions of St. Augustine and other recognized authorities, which had been compiled by a Barnabite priest on the subject of the proper relationship of science to Scripture.[6]

The new version of the letter was completed sometime before Galileo made a visit to Rome at the end of 1615 to press his case for Copernicus. In its much expanded form the letter seems to have been widely circulated there, as the numerous extant manuscript copies and correspondence about it suggest.[7] Neither it nor the original version had the desired effect, unfortunately, for on February 26, 1616, Galileo was told in an interview in Rome with Cardinal Bellarmine that the Holy Office had decided to ban the teaching of the heliocentrism espoused by Copernicus. For this reason Galileo would be expected not to advocate the system. Under this stricture he could not afford to expose his **Letter to Christina** to a wider audience at that time. The letter was not actually published until 1636, when it was issued as an appendix to the Italian-Latin version of the **Dialogue Concerning the Two Chief World Systems,** a final apologia published despite his trial and abjuration of 1633.[8]

Paradoxically, the essence of the view of science vis-à-vis Scriptural interpretation that Galileo urges in the letter is one that the Church had entertained since the time of St. Augustine, as the astronomer points out. In addition, and just as paradoxically, Cardinal Bellarmine argues against the Copernican system on some of the same grounds that Galileo presses upon the Church as support for his own stand. In view of these remarkable congruities, one cannot help but wonder why Galileo was so unsuccessful in his determined and eloquent attempt to persuade at least part of his audience, indeed the most important part, the ecclesiastical hierarchy. The reasons become clearer when one examines the composition of the letter, its audience, and the techniques used to move them. Two other rhetorical reference points, author and occasion, also become clearer in the process.

The letter follows for the most part the conventions of the art of letter writing developed at Bologna centuries before. Galileo employs the traditional parts: *salutatio, captatio benevolentiae, narratio, petitio,* and *conclusio.*[9] Yet he occasionally departs from this form, incorporating into it other elements of classical oratory following the practice of his contemporaries. As will be seen, he introduces an elaborate argumentative strategy to support his *petitio.*

In the *salutatio* he addresses his patroness with appropriate deference, almost in the same breath reminding her of his own claim to renown:

> Galileo Galilei, To the Most Serene Grand Duchess Mother: Some years ago, as Your Serene Highness well knows, I discovered in the heavens many things that had not been seen before our age. (p. 175)[10]

The *captatio benevolentiae* he here begins, modeled as it was on the classical oration, allows him to recite his singular accomplishments and to appeal to his reader's sympathies by describing the unjustified attacks of skeptical rivals. The fact that he chooses to address the Grand Duchess instead of Dom Castelli or Bishop Dini in what became the preferred version of the letter is appropriate in a number of ways. The observations he refers to in the first sentence were those, after all, he reported in **Sidereus nuncius** (1610), which he dedicated to her son Cosimo II. The satellites of Jupiter there described he named the Medicean stars, and he explains in the preface to the work that he did so in hope that "this name will bring as much honor to them as the names of other heroes have bestowed on other stars."[11]

The discoveries earned him fame. But more importantly his elegant compliment was helpful in effecting his release from teaching at the University of Padua and in obtaining for him the post of chief mathematician and philosopher to the Grand Duke. Thus Castelli's earlier conversation with the Grand Duchess on the new astronomy served as a convenient pretext for Galileo's again addressing a member of the Medici family on the subject of the stars. It served too as another tribute to those illustrious patrons of learning, and at the same time reminded his readers of his association with them. At a point when Galileo's detractors seemed to be growing, the gesture also might have helped to consolidate his position with the family.

From a rhetorical standpoint the choice of audience must have seemed particularly apropos. The Grand Duchess had shown herself interested in the topic and desirous of enlightenment on subjects beyond her ken: philosophy, mathematics, and theology. She was also devout. In addressing such a personage Galileo would not have to be embarrassed at starting at ground level to build his argument. He need not suppose a reader more familiar with theology than himself, as he would were he to address Dini or Castelli. In this way too he might hope to reach a much wider audience than if he were to direct his discourse to either of them.

Writing to Christina gave Galileo the opportunity to address the lay public in general, a kind of secondary audience that contained the politically powerful, as well as mathematicians and philosophers like himself. That these considerations are important to him is evidenced by the thrust of his arguments, which seem to court a larger appreciative readership of friends. In this regard, of course, Galileo followed the general practice of humanists of his day, who almost always had more than the titular audience in mind for their elaborate letters. Interestingly enough, an even larger audience of modern readers find his letter quite convincing, as is shown by the reprinting of the letter in anthologies and by the enthusiastic response to it by Galileo scholars such as Stillman Drake and Giorgio de Santillana.[12]

Nevertheless, Galileo's underlying purpose, as noted earlier, was to dissuade the religious authorities, who he believed were planning to condemn Copernicus. They were actually his primary audience, and he appeals to them in the implicit *petitiones* he interjects at various points in his discourse. Part of the reason for the letter's failure to accomplish its purpose lies in Galileo's focus on Christina as the titular audience, and his appeal to the secondary audience of laymen instead of the primary shadow audience he really needed to move. In effect, he compounded an already difficult task by attempting to persuade a public so different in terms of familiarity with the subject matter he discusses, and so variously disposed in attitudes toward it.

Galileo's choice of the vernacular was also a decision of rhetorical importance. It was especially suitable for the circulation of his views on a theological matter, for he had been warned by both Cardinal Bellarmine and Cardinal Barberini against invading the province of theologians, a point discussed at greater length below. By writing to his patroness in the Italian he customarily used for friendly correspondence, and on a topic of

conversation she had raised, he might have hoped to circumvent the objections a more formal treatise in Latin on the subject would have aroused. Moreover, he seems to have arrived at his rhetorical strategy gradually. The earliest version of the letter shows that he originally planned to send it as before to Father Castelli: it is addressed simply to "Paternità," and modifications in Galileo's hand direct it instead to her most serene highness, "Sua Altezza Serenissima," the Grand Duchess Christina.[13] It too is written in Italian, further evidence that he hesitated to make a formal exposition of his opinions in these earliest stages. His decision to shift the focus from Castelli to Christina might be seen as underscoring his desire to keep the discussion on an informal plane, so that it could appear to be "overheard," as it were, by the primary shadow audience.

The letter itself is quite long, comprising thirty-nine pages of text in the National Edition, as compared with seven pages for the original letter to Castelli in the same work. Both the *captatio benevolentiae* and the *narratio* clearly display the *ethos* of the writer. The style is straightforward and logical, suiting the image of an earnest, devout, yet embattled philosopher. Galileo projects himself as a man of good will who seeks only to disclose the truth. Still, the tone of the emotional appeals he introduces seems to undercut on occasion the spirit of the ethical appeal, at least for his shadow audience. In the *captatio benevolentiae* he mentions that he has been unfairly treated by "no small number of professors" (p. 175). These men appear to be upset because what he has discovered in the heavens has contradicted traditional views. It is as if they believe "I had placed these things in the sky with my own hands in order to upset nature and overturn the sciences." He goes on to say that they choose to ignore the fact that "the increase of known truths stimulates the investigation, establishment, and growth of the arts; not their diminution or destruction" (p. 175). The edge of ridicule and impatience in his voice establishes at once the stance he is to maintain throughout. This tone might be expected to arouse a sympathetic response in the Duchess, who would not want to see her resident philosopher insulted, and also from philosophers with views similar to his, but he could not expect his opponents to be placed in a receptive mood for what was to follow. And what of the primary audience whose minds were not yet quite made up? Cardinal Bellarmine and many other theologians were conservative in the original sense of the term. They were primarily interested in conserving the teachings of the Church, and these new theories were indeed revolutionary. Moreover their implications threatened traditional wisdom regarding the cosmos and man's place in it.

By his deprecating tone Galileo effectively marks off a group of philosophers and theologians as adversaries whose faults he proceeds to define in the *narratio*. They are, he says, men determined in "hypocritical zeal" to preserve at all costs what they believe, rather than admit what is obvious to their eyes (p. 179). Instead they go about invoking the Bible to disprove arguments on physical matters "they do not understand." On the other hand, those who are well-versed in physical science and astronomy are quite able to see the truth of his discoveries (pp. 175-176).

Ethos and *pathos* commingle as he adds that his enemies prefer to "cast against me imputations of crimes, which must be and are more abhorrent to me than death itself" (p. 176). The reference undoubtedly is to the allegations of Colombe, Lorini, Caccini, and others that Galileo's views were opposed to the reigning theological opinions. Here he may well have been distracted by his titular audience and his own indignation from realizing that to achieve his purpose he needed to reach those who might sympathize with his opponents.

At this stage of Galileo's life, it must be remembered, his critics were scattered and did not present an organized or powerful opposition. In fact, following the publication of his **Sidereus nuncius** he had many admirers among clerics and the scholarly world in general. No battle between science and religion had yet begun. In retrospect, then, this was a crucial period. Whatever Gaileo wrote or said was to be extraordinarily magnified.

The author's castigation of his adversaries for their stupidity and hypocrisy is repeated often throughout the letter. In this, Galileo departs from advice offered by classical rhetoricians and the *dictatores* not to antagonize the audience or readers through arrogance. The astronomer's rivals were themselves vituperative, it is true, but one wonders why he responded in equally inflammatory fashion, astute rhetorician that he was. The answer seems not to lie in any innate maliciousness: rather it appears that Galileo was very sensitive to criticism. Evidence of this trait occurs in the memoranda for his **De motu,** written as a young man, long before his writing had become known and provoked controversy. He conjectures even then that many will on reading his writings "turn their minds not to reflecting whether what I have written is true, but solely to seeking how they can, justly or unjustly, undermine my arguments."[14] A similar defensiveness is evident in Galileo's references, just noted, to the professors opposed to his discoveries. He says that a few of these have been persuaded, but others "now take refuge in obstinate silence," but in their exasperation "divert their thoughts to other fancies and seek new ways to damage me" (p. 176). Two paragraphs later he maintains that they are "persisting in their original resolve to destroy me and everything mine by any means they can think of" (p. 177).

One of the reasons for the stubborn resistance to Galileo's assertions regarding his discoveries was that some academicians were very concerned about what they perceived as an erosion of their disciplinary kingdoms. This is what Galileo refers to in the quotation cited above that his critics fear he will "overturn the sciences." A recent essay by Robert Westman describes in detail the importance of the political dimension of this interdisciplinary dispute and the repercussions the discoveries in astronomy had upon what had been considered the superior discipline: natural philosophy.[15] Its province included speculations about the physical world, while astronomy was simply to be concerned with mathematical theory or "saving the appearances," not with analyzing the nature of the physical world.

Following his initial reference to the intentions of his enemies, Galileo interjects a quotation from St. Augustine, which actually becomes a theme of the letter:

> Now keeping always our respect for moderation in grave piety, we ought not to believe anything inadvisedly on a doubious point, lest in favor to our error we conceive a prejudice against something that truth hereafter may reveal to be not contrary in any way to the sacred books of either the Old or the New Testament. (pp. 175-176)

The quotation derives from Augustine's commentary on the book of Genesis, *De Genesi ad litteram* (Lib. 2, cap. 18), where he considers what can be said with certainty about the heavenly bodies. The next provides a perfect transition to Galileo's *narratio* and his description of the circumstances behind the current controversy over the Copernican system. He repeats the motif at several places in the letter, using it as the context from which to issue his *petitio* to the ecclesiastical authorities for freedom of thought. Throughout the letter, in fact, Galileo relies heavily upon the *De Genesi ad litteram,* citing it more frequently than any other source.

The elaborate argument Galileo develops in his letter rests initially upon the previously noted assumption that his opponents are seeking to discredit him, and it is against them that he directs his refutation. What might be termed the *divisio,* ordinarily not found in letters, follows the *narratio.* He says, "I shall therefore discourse of the particulars which these men produce to make this opinion detested and to have it condemned not merely as false but as heretical." Then he adds pointedly,

> I hope to show that I proceed with much greater piety than they do, when I argue not against condemning this book, but against condemning it in the way they suggest—that is, without understanding it, weighing it, or so much as reading it. (p. 179)

He says that his motive is "to justify myself in the eyes of men whose judgments in matters of religion and reputation I hold in great esteem" (p. 179). The defense he develops here he hopes might aid the Church, but if his effort is not viewed as constructive he vows to "renounce any errors" he might make concerning religious questions. He does not "desire in these matters to engage in disputes with anyone, even on points that are disputable." "And if not," he adds, "let my book be torn and burnt, as I neither intend nor pretend to gain any fruit that is not pious and Catholic" (pp. 180-181). These words are touchingly prophetic of the events of the trial that was to follow sixteen years later. The reference to "my book" is Drake's free translation of *"mia scrittura"* in the Favaro edition, that is, "my writing."[16] Galileo probably was referring to the letter itself, not, as one might be tempted to conjecture, to the *Dialogue* on which he was already at work.

In setting forth the *divisio* Galileo explains that in condemning the twofold claim that "the earth rotates on its axis and revolves around the sun," his detractors would also suppress any discussion of other related observations and physical statements. This view of the planetary system, he points out, was really not original with him but was that of Copernicus too, a fact that his enemies have attempted to hide from the "common people." The academic philosophers "pretend not to know" that Copernicus was "not only a Catholic, but a priest and a canon"; yet the work of this esteemed scholar, *De revolutionibus,* "has been read and studied by everyone without the faintest hint of any objection ever being conceived against its doctrines."[17] Galileo claims that only the campaign to discredit himself, moreover, has prompted this effort to have Copernicus' book condemned (pp. 178-179).

Galileo may not have known it, but he was in error in his appeal to precedent here. The Church had not previously received Copernicus' work with universal approval. In this regard, Westman cites the discovery of Eugenio Garin that *De revolutionibus* had been challenged by a Dominican theologian and astronomer named Tolosani as early as 1544. Tolosani mentions that in fact the Master of the Sacred Palace (the pope's theologian) intended to condemn the book, but was taken ill before he could do so. Although Tolosani expressed the hope that his writings would accomplish the same purpose, they had not done so by the time Galileo began his letter.[18] In *The Sleepwalkers* Arthur Koestler makes a similar point, drawing further inferences. Rather than seeing the growing opposition to Galileo's teachings as responsible for the disapproval of Copernicus, as Galileo himself does, Koestler sees the *Letter to Christina* as the precipitating factor in converting the Church's ambivalent stance to an antagonistic one. He terms the letter a "theological atom bomb" because it was "the principal cause of the prohibition of Copernicus and Galileo's downfall." And he adds that its "radioactive fallout is still being felt."[19]

In the development of the main points of his argument against his opponents, the author's tone is not as continuously querulous as in the introductory parts, although the text is still interlaced with incisive, scornful comments delivered at strategic places. Generally Galileo proceeds in the manner of a philosopher-scientist who is also skilled in rhetoric. Because of this it is especially important to note the precise terminology he uses when advancing an argument, and particularly when characterizing it as a "necessary demonstration"— a nuance generally overlooked by Finocchiaro in his analysis of the *Dialogue,* possibly because of the paucity of such arguments in that work. With regard to Galileo's knowledge of rhetorical techniques, one can presume that his training in classical rhetoric and poetics during his student days at Vallombrosa and the University of Pisa had equipped him well in these areas.[20] Surely he was acquainted with the dialectical and persuasive reasoning expounded by Aristotle in the *Topics* and *Rhetoric* respectively, and then carried on in the revived classical tradition of Cicero, the *Rhetorica ad Herennium,* and Quintilian.[21] The literary circles in which Galileo moved, and his own compositions previous to the *Letter to Christina,* amply confirm his acquaintance with artistic devices and polemical modes of argumentation.[22] Less appreciated is his understanding of the techniques of proof as explained in Aristotle's *Posterior Analytics,* the portion of the *Organon* that set the standards of scientific methodology generally accepted in the universities throughout the Middle Ages and the Renaissance. In fact Galileo wrote a commentary on this work, which unfortunately was misdated by Favaro and not included by him in the National Edition.[23] The manuscript has recently been transcribed in its entirety by William F. Edwards.[24] When one studies its contents, and notes Galileo's continued use of its terminology in his later writings, to be cited below, one can appreciate more fully the logical force of the claims advanced in the *Letter to Christina.*

The *refutatio* portion of Galileo's argument begins after the *divisio* and the declaration of his intent to aid the Church. He states the principal issue in a provocative and dramatic manner:

> The reason produced for condemning the opinion that the earth moves and the sun stands still is that in many places in the Bible one may read that the sun moves and the earth stands still. Since the Bible cannot err, it follows as a necessary consequent that anyone takes an erroneous and heretical position who maintains that the sun is inherently motionless and the earth movable. (p. 181)

That he presents the issue in this way after showing his own ideas to be identical with Copernicus' is a direct and unprecedented challenge for an avowedly believing Catholic to most of his primary audience. It shows

Galileo's enormous faith in his own powers of persuasion. It also signals his decision to pursue the issue on theological grounds. Even as empathic a commentator as Stillman Drake sees that decision as a daring move. He remarks that Galileo was proceeding against "advice from his friends at Rome [Prince] Cesi, [Monsignor] Ciampoli and [Cardinal] Barberini to keep the battle on general grounds."[25] They said that as long as Galileo spoke as a mathematician and regarded the Copernican system as an hypothesis there would be no problem. But to venture into theological arguments and to maintain that the theory was demonstrable would be foolhardy. Galileo recognized this much earlier and remarked to Bishop Dini that he had been advised not to discuss Scriptural matters and that "no astronomer or scientist who remained within the proper bounds had ever got into such things."[26] Why did he do so? Drake advances the most plausible reason. He thinks that reading a work by a provincial of the Carmelite Order, Paolo Antonio Foscarini, published just at the time Galileo was rewriting his letter, led to a hardening of his position. In that work Foscarini defends Galileo's discoveries and the Copernican system, arguing that the Scriptures could be interpreted differently.[27] The priest sent the book to Cardinal Bellarmine for his reactions and received a courteous reply in mid-April 1615 that outlined the Church's position. Galileo seems to have believed that he could successfully counter Bellarmine's opinion, for even though he knew of the prelate's views he attempted to contravene them.[28]

On his part the Cardinal must have meant his letter to apply to Galileo as well as Foscarini, for he begins by saying, "it appears to me that your Reverence and Sig. Galileo did prudently content yourselves with speaking hypothetically and not positively, as I always believed Copernicus did."[29] He goes on to warn them that to maintain "that the earth is situated in the third sphere and revolves very swiftly around the sun is a very dangerous thing" because it irritates "all the theologians and scholastic philosophers" and is inimical to faith since it makes "the sacred Scripture false." He agrees with Foscarini and Galileo that the Copernican system "saves the appearances better than [the Ptolemaic] eccentrics and epicycles," and thinks that this is what the mathematicians might well state.

His second point concerns the decree of the Council of Trent prohibiting statements that contradict the consensus of the holy Fathers. The case of the earth's being stationary in the center of the universe is one of these, he says, for all the "commentaries of modern writers" and "Greek and Latin expositors" agree that this is the sense of the Scripture.

The last point of Bellarmine's letter is crucial to our appraisal of the *logos* of Galileo's argument. The Cardinal says that the Scripture would be in need of a new interpretation in the event that there were "a true demonstration that the sun was the center of the universe . . . and that the sun did not go around the earth but the earth went around the sun." He adds:

> But I do not think there is any such demonstration, since none has been shown to me. To demonstrate that the appearances are saved by assuming the sun is at the center and the earth in the heavens is not the same thing as to demonstrate that in fact the sun is in the center and the earth in the heavens. I believe that the first demonstration may exist, but I have very grave doubts about the second; and in case of doubt one may not abandon the Holy Scriptures as expounded by the holy Fathers.[30]

For the Cardinal this is the crux of the matter, the point on which the argument turns. If astronomers can *demonstrate* the physical fact of the Copernican system, then Scripture will have to be reinterpreted.

Now the use of the term "demonstration," or, as Bellarmine's Italian gives it, *"vera demostratione"* [sic], meant that a rigorous argument could be supplied following the formal methodology of Aristotle's *Posterior Analytics*.[31] This mode of proof is not in the rhetorical sphere but belongs in the logic of scientific demonstration. Galileo also thought demonstration was important to the case, as is obvious from a letter he wrote to Bishop Dini in mid-May—probably after learning of Cardinal Bellarmine's response to Foscarini:

> To me the surest and swiftest way to prove that the position of Copernicus is not contrary to Scripture would be to give a host of proofs that it is true and that the contrary cannot be maintained at all; thus, since no two truths can contradict one another, this and the Bible must be perfectly harmonious.[32]

But he says that he does not intend to proceed in this way because the Peripatetics who must be convinced "show themselves incapable of following even the simplest and easiest of arguments."[33]

The magnitude of the task that Galileo has set for himself now becomes clearer. To argue for the Copernican system without offering demonstrative proof in view of its contradiction of Scripture would be to defy traditional procedures in the eyes of his principal audience.

The manner in which Galileo handles this critical dilemma, as we shall see, is simply to presume at the outset that such proofs exist. In the *divisio* where he remarks on the Church's supposed prior acceptance of Copernicus' book, Galileo says flatly that he finds it difficult to believe that people would see the statements therein as heretical, "now that manifest experiences and necessary demonstrations have shown them to be well grounded" (p. 179).[34]

In spite of the advice of his ecclesiastical friends, Galileo thus does not choose to press the case for the Copernican system on scientific grounds. Rather, and this is most surprising, throughout the letter he never presents a confirmation of inductive or deductive proofs for his position, but instead relies upon a refutation of deductive arguments from theology to counter his opponents' contentions. For the Grand Duchess, and other unsophisticated readers, he evidently assumes that he need only state that demonstrations exist and then in a rhetorical mode take up the theological difficulties. As for his opponents, he simply lumps them together as Peripatetics, those academicians who look only to the text of Aristotle for proof of a proposition. They would not be expected to listen to arguments, whatever the physical evidence offered or however cogently proofs were presented, if corroboration could not be found in Aristotle's works. In this characterization of his opponents, Galileo fails to consider that among his audience for the letter were others, opposed or unconvinced, who were progressive Aristotelians like himself, such as Bishop Dini, Cardinals Bellarmine and Barberini, and the Jesuit astronomers at the Collegio Romano.[35] They, unlike the conservative Peripatetics, would have been responsive to a scientific demonstration. But he does not give one or explain that one might in time be given; he prefers to attack the theological views of his opponents.

Following his bold recognition of the possibly heretical character of the Copernican position at the beginning of his *refutatio,* Galileo sets out to show why such a characterization is untenable. In summary, his argument runs as follows: first, it is true that the Bible cannot err, that is, if its true meaning is understood. However, its true meaning is not always clear, for sometimes it speaks ambiguously, and sometimes it adopts common parlance in order to accommodate itself to the untutored mind. Therefore, one cannot hold that its statements about physical things are meant to be taken literally.

Further, he says that two truths cannot contradict one another; Nature like Scripture cannot be false because they both have their origin in the Holy Spirit. Nature is what our senses and necessary demonstrations show her to be. Therefore, since Nature cannot be other than she is, while Scripture can be and sometimes is interpreted differently than the strict meaning of its words, Nature should not be called into question because of particular biblical passages.

Galileo concludes this line of reasoning by quoting Tertullian: "God is known first through Nature, and then again, more specifically by doctrine; by Nature in his works and by doctrine in his revealed word" (pp. 181-183).

As one of the main supports in his refutation Galileo adroitly uses a theological argument, often called the accommodation theory. The Holy Spirit "accommodates" its language to the "capacities of the common people who are rude and unlearned." He returns to the same argument later in the letter and there he seeks to add further dignity to it by attributing it to St. Jerome and to St. Thomas Aquinas (pp. 200-201). Nevertheless the effect that the argument would have on his primary audience, regardless of such appeals to authority, is predictable. In their eyes it would be acceptable to apply the accommodation principle to selected texts if one were a theologian, but it would be improper, even presumptuous, for a non-theologian to advance it. Actually Bishop Dini had raised the possibility of such a defense in a conversation with Cardinal Bellarmine, as he himself informed Galileo, but the prelate warned against it. No doubt Bellarmine feared that some theologians would be incensed at a mathematician deciding that particular texts do not say what they patently mean.

Having given the reason for textual contradictions of physical truths, Galileo next explains why the Scriptures do not reveal the nature of physical reality. This explanation supplies the other main pillar of his refutation and is often referred to as the irrelevance theory. He quotes St. Augustine: "Hence let it be said briefly, touching the form of heaven, that our authors knew the truth, but the Holy Spirit did not desire that men should learn things that are useful to no one for salvation" (p. 185). Galileo adds the inescapable conclusion that since the Holy Spirit did not give us knowledge about the heavens because it is "irrelevant to our salvation," then belief about celestial bodies should not be made obligatory to faith. He inquires, "Can an opinion be heretical and yet have no concern with the salvation of souls?" Lightening the tone he quotes the words of Cardinal Baronius, "the intention of the Holy Ghost is to teach us how one goes to heaven, not how heaven goes" (pp. 185-186).

In the matter that most troubled theologians, namely, the conflict of Scripture with the Copernican system, Galileo has offered two important counterarguments, both drawn from the most highly respected Fathers of the Church: Aquinas, Jerome, and Augustine. The two arguments are today acceptable to the Roman Catholic Church and are in accord with Pope Leo XIII's encyclical of 1893, *Providentissimus Deus,* which outlines how Scripture should be interpreted.[36] And yet most theologians and philosophers of the seventeenth century were not persuaded by them. When Galileo advanced them in his letter they were not convincing, and this for a number of reasons: many resented his arrogant tone, his presumption in speaking about theological matters, and his crossing over from the world of mathematical astronomy into natural philosophy. The most important reason, however, was that first mentioned by Cardinal Bellarmine. For the Church to relinquish an authoritative theological position about the nature of the universe that might have vast repercussions on the faith of the people, a necessary demonstration of the physical realities would have to be presented. Galileo speaks at the beginning of the letter as if such demonstrations are available. Then, leaving this matter undeveloped, he leads the reader through the argument just reviewed regarding the twin truths of the Holy Spirit: Nature and Scripture. Having made these points with admirable logic, one would expect him to return to the reason for offering them in the first place: the physical evidence that eliminates the Scriptural difficulties.

Unfortunately the path of Galileo's reasoning has led his readers to an insurmountable wall, but through rhetorical magic he almost succeeds in making the wall disappear. Following his opening statement, previously noted, about "manifest experience and necessary demonstration" having shown the validity of Copernicus' views, he goes on to mention the importance of demonstration some twenty-five times, speaking as if such proofs exist.[37] Generally the terminology is introduced in the context of the need for new Scriptural interpretations. Galileo also introduces some sense observations, which he says should accompany necessary demonstration: his sightings of the great variations in position of the orbits of Venus and Mars relative to earth and the changes he saw in the appearance of Venus. But he makes no attempt to incorporate these into a demonstration. He claims, however, that they and other observations "can never be reconciled with the Ptolemaic system in any way, but are very strong arguments for the Copernican" (p. 196).

In this connection Galileo certainly must have known that they could also be used as arguments for the Tychonian system.[38] As most historians of science are aware, no commonly accepted proof of the earth's diurnal rotation on its axis and its annual revolution around the sun was available until the early nineteenth century.[39]

In view of these facts, the best explanation for Galileo's argumentative strategy seems to be that he was convinced that the Polish astronomer was right and he so intensely desired to prove it that he must have believed that true demonstrations could soon be made.[40] Furthermore, as suggested earlier, since Christina was the nominal audience he must have decided that he could dispense with proofs and simply assure her that they existed.

Galileo does develop a lengthy defense of scientific demonstration in general. He establishes through references to the Church Fathers that scientific proofs have been highly regarded in the past and asks that they continue to be respected by theologians (pp. 186-187). Then he turns his attention to the delicate problem of the relations between theology and physical astronomy. Here again he does not establish common cause with the academic theologians. Instead, he depicts them

as obstinate in their desire to preserve their domain. They maintain that "theology is the queen of the sciences" and therefore she does not need to adjust herself to the findings of "less worthy sciences." He next considers in what sense theology should be presumed to be queen, whether for the reason that her study contains the fruits of all the other sciences or because her subject matter "excels in dignity" and is "divulged in more sublime ways?" He concludes that it is the latter explanation, and suggests that if theology does not deign to descend to the "humbler speculations of the subordinate sciences" it would behoove her professors not to make pronouncements on subjects they have "neither studied nor practiced" (pp. 191-193). The major problem with these professors lies in their demand that astronomers retract their proofs as fallacious. But, he says, "this would amount to commanding that they not see what they see and not understand what they know, and that in searching they find the opposite of what they actually discover" (p. 193). Although the passage is a stirring defense of intellectual freedom, it is actually a misinterpretation of the Church's position as Bellarmine presented it. His letter had asked only that until proof was at hand, astronomers refrain from making strong truth claims and present their results merely hypothetically.[41]

Following these assertions Galileo performs the most remarkable rhetorical feat of the letter. Almost imperceptibly he turns the tables on the theologians and ends by maintaining that *they* must offer proof that the astronomers are wrong. First he makes the distinction between truths that are merely stated and those that are demonstrated, echoing Bellarmine's words to Foscarini. He goes on to argue that if "truly demonstrated physical conclusions" do not have to be modified in light of the Bible but rather the Scripture must be reinterpreted, then before authorities condemn a physical proposition "it must be shown to be not rigorously demonstrated" (p. 194). Now he demands that a physical proposition be accepted even if it conflicts with Scripture unless it can be proved *false!* The most startling point follows: the proposition (not to say its demonstration) must be disproved "by those who judge it to be false" (p. 195). In support of this demand he reiterates the theme of his *captatio benevolentiae,* the words of St. Augustine mentioned above, which he now quotes at even greater length (p. 196). He returns to the same point a few pages later and adds a further crowning passage from *De Genesi ad litteram,* which he presents in the following way:

> And later it is added, to teach us that no proposition can be contrary to the faith unless it has first been proven to be false: "A thing is not forever contrary to the faith until disproved by most certain truth. When that happens, it was not holy Scripture that ever affirmed it, but human ignorance that imagined it." (p. 206)

Near the close of the letter, continuing in the same vein, Galileo says "these men are wasting their time clamoring for condemnation of the motion of the earth and stability of the sun, which they have not yet demonstrated to be impossible or false" (pp. 210-211). In this passage Galileo clearly extends the intention of St. Augustine to maintain, in effect, that scientists do not have to prove their claims; it is up to others to prove them false.

Having disposed magisterially of the pretensions of the theologians, Galileo turns to an objection that Cardinal Bellarmine raised against the new astronomy: the necessity of following the consensus of the Fathers, as mentioned by the Council of Trent. Galileo contends that the Fathers were not in agreement; in fact, they never even debated the issue because it had not been raised. On the other hand, he adds, some theologians have lately begun to consider that the mobility of the earth is compatible with the Scriptures. He mentions as evidence a passage from the *Commentaries on Job* by Diego de Zuñiga (1584), where the author cites a significant text from that book, "Who moveth the earth from its place" (p. 203).[42] Galileo next takes issue with the application of the ruling of the Council to the case of physical matters:

> Besides I question the truth of the statement that the Church commands us to hold as matters of faith all physical conclusions bearing the stamp of harmonious interpretations by all the Fathers. I think this may be an arbitrary simplification of various council decrees by certain people to favor their own opinion. So far as I can find, all that is really prohibited is the "perverting into senses contrary to that of the holy Church or that of the concurrent agreement of the Fathers those passages, and those alone, which pertain to faith or morals, or which concern the edification of Christian doctrine." (p. 203)

Today the words echo truly and bravely against the Vatican walls; we applaud the author's insight, and take satisfaction in the fact that the Church at last follows these principles. But for the prelates of the time too much ground seemed to be yielding under attack, without the opportunity for slow and sober deliberation over all the implications. Moreover, how arrogant to ears accustomed to graceful compliments his tone must have sounded in the passage quoted and in the hortatory sentence that followed: "Hence it remains the office of grave and wise theologians to interpret the passages according to their true meaning" (p. 203). And he adds, they should do so after first "hearing the experiences, observations, and proofs of philosophers and astronomers on both sides" (p. 205).

Galileo concludes his examination of the problem with an implicit *petitio* for liberty of thought directed to the ecclesiastical authorities. This is especially moving because of the ironic insight it offers in view of the trial and its creation of an adversary relationship between science and religion. People should not demand that the Church "flash her sword" just because it is within her power to do so, he says. "Such men fail to realize that it is not always profitable to do everything that lies within one's power" (p. 206).

Although the tone and content of the letter offer an unmistakable challenge to prevailing Church authority, Cardinal Bellarmine seems not to have allowed it to govern his treatment of its author. In his audience with Galileo concerning the ruling of the Holy Office with regard to Copernicus, he remained courteous and protective of the astronomer's reputation. According to the latter's testimony at the trial years later, Bellarmine furnished him with a letter after the audience that attested to his good standing in the Church. One might well wonder about the effect that Galileo's **Letter to Christina** may have had on more irascible men. Perhaps it is not going too far to suggest that much of the animosity exhibited during the trial may have been fired by its rhetoric.[43]

The fears that haunted academic theologians and the ecclesiastical hierarchy were raised in the same paragraph as the preceding plea to the Church for liberty of thought, even though the text was intended by Galileo to augment his theme. In attempting to show the negligible effect the Gospels would have upon infidels who knew more of astronomy than those who preach a naive and fallacious application of Scripture to the heavens, he asks:

> And why should the Bible be believed concerning the resurrection of the dead, the hope of eternal life, and the Kingdom of Heaven, when it is considered to be erroneously written as to points which admit of direct demonstration or unquestionable reasoning? (p. 208)

This is just what the Church feared would occur in the case of uneducated believers.

Ahead of his time as he was in his advocacy of a more reasonable interpretation of the Scriptures, Galileo also shows himself to be bound by his era in the last part of the letter. Following the *petitio* is an appendix-like section in which he examines a passage from Joshua that the Grand Duchess Christina first questioned Dom Castelli about at dinner. The text is the one in which Joshua commands the sun to stand still, and Galileo is concerned to prove that the Copernican system accords better with the sense of the passage than does the Ptolemaic. In the process not only does he use Scripture to hallow a physical conclusion, a practice he criticizes in his opponents, but he develops his support in a thoroughly medieval way: he appeals to the authority of Dionysius the Areopagite, a sixth-century Neoplatonist whose opinions on science he would not ordinarily entertain. He says that this author spoke of the "admirable power and energy of the sun," whose energy is in turn the cause of the planets' motion. Under the Copernican system if God willed the sun to stand still all the other motions of the planets would cease as well, since they are dependent upon it, whereas in the Ptolemaic system the text would make no sense at all (pp. 211-216). This somewhat contrived explanation would never have been convincing to his primary audience, though Christina may have been reassured.

In his *conclusio,* Galileo suggests that just as the passage from Joshua can be viewed as harmonious with what scientists have learned about the physical world, so other passages might be found by theologians that are also in accord with these discoveries. "Especially," he says, "if they would add some knowledge of astronomical science to their knowledge of divinity." He cites a text from Proverbs 8:26 suggesting that the theologians think of the earth's poles as they read, "He had not yet made the earth, the river and the hinges of the terrestrial orb." After all, the astronomer reminds them, "hinges would seem to be ascribed in vain to the earth unless it needed them to turn upon" (p. 216).

Rereading the ***Letter to Christina*** today is a poignant experience, poignant because we are gifted with hindsight; we know through the discoveries of modern science that Galileo was right. And it is poignant also because we know about the tragic sequel to the letter, the humiliation forced upon a brave yet imprudent spirit. But when we employ the device of rhetorical inquiry and examine the letter from the standpoint of the audience—its effect upon them, and their expectations of it—then we transport ourselves into a very different context. That context comprises a world-view very different from our own, where the effort is made to keep scientific and religious matters safely apart. Still the facts of human personalities and emotions are the same in both eras.

In concluding these rhetorical considerations, it would be well to look again briefly at the principal audience, to discern what we can about the attitudes of the men Galileo intended to address. We know of the goodwill his friends in Rome bore him: Bishop Dini, Monsignor Ciampoli, Prince Cesi. But what of the Cardinals Bellarmine and Barberini, to whom much of the correspondence preceding the letter refers, and of others who, like them, were part of the ecclesiastical power structure? Cardinal Bellarmine was a Jesuit who evidently respected Galileo and had a real interest in science, having lectured in his early years on astronomy. He did not believe that Copernicus' book would be condemned, and he urged Galileo not to exacerbate the situation which he judged to be quiescent. Some Jesuits even appeared to have favored Galileo's opinions, according to Dini.

Father Grassi, a Jesuit who was to become involved in a polemical exchange with Galileo some years later, might reflect the view of a number of his Order, and others as well, when he said:

> As for Mr. Galileo's displeasure, I tell you most sincerely that I, too, am displeased. I have always had more love for him than he has for me. And last year at Rome [during the trial] when I was requested to give my opinion on his book on the motion of the earth, I took the utmost care to allay minds harshly disposed toward him and to render them open to conviction of the strength of his arguments, so much so, indeed, that certain people who supposed me to have been offended by Galileo . . . marveled at my solicitude. But he has ruined himself by being so much in love with his own genius, and by having no respect for others. One should not wonder that everybody conspires to damn him.[44]

And when the letter was written what was the frame of mind of Cardinal Barberini who was to become Pope Urban VIII and an implacable enemy of the astronomer? It was he who warned Galileo through Bishop Dini to use "greater caution in not going beyond the arguments used by Ptolemy and Copernicus" and thus exceed the "limitations of physics and mathematics." He had reminded him that "the explanation of Scripture is claimed by the theologians as their field, and if new things are introduced, even by a capable mind, not everyone has the dispassionate faculty of taking them just as they are said."[45]

Not all those who made up the primary audience were, then *initially* ill-disposed: some expressed a genuine interest, others found his views too novel and as yet unproved. Those who were opposed saw his theological and astronomical positions as eroding, even threatening, conclusions generally accepted in their own disciplines. An examination of key rhetorical aspects shows graphically why the letter was ineffective in its day. The *ethos* the author wished to project is undercut by his decision not to offer proof on the terms that were expected. The *pathos* he introduced because of his temperament led him to use appeals that must have rankled precisely those he needed to convince. Finally, the ultimate test of the argument for his primary audience was in the *logos,* the scientific demonstrations he implied but did not present. Instead he carried his argument into the courts of his opponents the theologians, who, unfortunately, made the rules of the game.

Notes

1 Volume 61, Boston Studies in the Philosophy of Science (Dordrecht, 1980).

2 Edward P. Mahoney, ed. and tr., "The Scholar and his Public in the Late Middle Ages and the Renaissance," *Medieval Aspects of Renaissance Learning:*

Three Essays by Paul Oskar Kristeller (Durham, North Carolina, 1974), pp. 12-13. I have greatly benefited from Professor Kristeller's and Professor Mahoney's observations on a number of points in this essay.

[3] See the discussion of the background of the letter in Stillman Drake, *Discoveries and Opinions of Galileo* (New York, 1957), pp. 145-171, and in Jerome Langford, *Galileo, Science and the Church* (Ann Arbor, 1971), pp. 50-78. Another quite different view is that of Arthur Koestler, *The Sleepwalkers* (New York, 1968), pp. 415-463. An earlier and very careful recapitulation of the events leading up to the trial is in Karl von Gebler, *Galileo Galilei and the Roman Curia,* tr. Mrs. George Sturge (London, 1879).

[4] The sermon was deplored by Luigi Maraffi, a preacher general of the Dominican Order. See Maraffi to Galileo in the National Edition of Galileo's works, *Le Opere di Galileo Galilei* (henceforth referred to as *Opere*), ed. Antonio Favaro, 20 vols. in 21 (Florence, 1890-1909, rpt. 1968), XII, 127-128.

[5] Lorini to the Holy Office, *Opere* XII, 297ff.

[6] Castelli says that the Barnabite had promised passages from St. Augustine and other doctors who confirm Galileo's preferred interpretation of Joshua, developed in the earlier letter to Castelli, *Opere* XII, 126-127. François Russo conjectures that Galileo used St. Augustine's commentary on Genesis more frequently than the others because that was the source most sympathetic to his views, "Lettre à Christine de Lorraine Grande-Duchesse de Toscane (1615)," *Revue d'histoire des sciences,* 17 (1964), 337.

[7] Favaro examined 34 manuscript copies of the letter in preparing his edition; *Opere* V, 272-278, contains a discussion of these.

[8] See the communication of Mathias Bernegger to Elio Diodati, December 1634, referring to the letter's forthcoming publication, *Opere* XVI, 168. According to Bernegger the letter was furnished by his and Galileo's friend Diodati, who translated it into Latin. One might conjecture that this was with Galileo's knowledge, but Favaro points out there is no evidence in Galileo's correspondence that he was aware of these preparations, *Opere* V, 275.

[9] For discussions of the influence of *ars dictaminis* through the Renaissance see Kristeller, "The Scholar and his Public," pp. 10-14, and "Humanism and Scholasticism in the Italian Renaissance" in his collected essays, *Renaissance Thought and its Sources,* Michael Mooney, ed. (New York; 1979), pp. 85-105. Jerrold E. Seigel treats the topic in *Rhetoric and Philosophy in Renaissance Humanism* (Princeton, 1968), ch. 7. For the late Middle Ages see James J. Murphy, *Rhetoric in the Middle Ages* (Berkeley, 1974), ch. 5, and Ronald Witt, "Medieval 'Ars Dictaminis' and the Beginnings of Humanism: A New Construction of the Problem," *Renaissance Quarterly,* 35 (Spring 1982), 1-35. See also Helene Wieruszowski, "Ars dictaminis in the Time of Dante," *Politics and Culture in Medieval Spain and Italy* (Rome, 1971).

[10] Favaro's critical edition of the letter appears in *Opere* V, 309-348. For the convenience of the reader I have followed Drake's English translation in this essay, emending it occasionally for style and nuances in conformity with Favaro's version. (Drake's translation is in *Discoveries,* pp. 175-216). It was based on Thomas Salusbury's 1661 English translation and Favaro's edition.

[11] The National Edition includes facsimiles of the *Sidereus Nuncius* in autograph and in its first printed edition, *Opere* III. 1, 15-96. Drake translated the work in *Discoveries,* pp. 23-58.

[12] Drake's attitude is apparent in his introduction to the letter in *Discoveries* where he presents it as a valiant and uncompromising effort to describe the "proper relation of science to religion," p. 145 (cf. p. 165). De Santillana places the letter on a plane with Milton's *Areopagitica* in his well known work on the trial, *The Crime of Galileo* (Chicago, 1955), pp. 96-98.

[13] Favaro discusses the evidence for this, based on the draft of the *Letter* found in Codex Volpicelliano, *Opere, V,* 274-275.

[14] *Opere* I, 412 [m. 17], English translation by Drake in *Mechanics in Sixteenth Century Italy* (Madison, 1969), p. 382. The same sentiment is sounded in Galileo's *Dialogue on Motion* of c. 1586-87, *Opere* I, 398, also in *Mechanics,* pp. 364-365.

[15] Robert Westman, unpublished paper, "The Copernicans and the Churches: From *De Revolutionibus* to the Decree of 1616," for the Carner Foundation—University of Wisconsin Conference on "Christianity and Science: Two Thousand Years of Conflict and Compromise," Madison, 23-25 April 1981, pp. 8-10, 31. The thesis will be further developed in Professor Westman's forthcoming book, *The Copernicans: Universities, Courts and Interdisciplinary Conflict, 1543-1700.* In his Oberlin lecture on Aristotelianism, Kristeller makes the same point, emphasizing the fact that Galileo's new conception of a physics based on mathematics was thought to be an intrusion by a mathematician and astronomer upon the field of natural philosophy that had previously been separate from mathematics and astronomy (*Renaissance Thought and Its Sources,* pp. 48-49). See also the discussion of disciplinary rivalries among Florentine humanists and philosophers before Galileo's day in Seigel, pp. 68-98.

[16] *Opere* V, 315, lines 2-3.

[17] Here Galileo's enthusiasm carries him too far. Although, as is well known, Copernicus' uncle was archbishop of Frauenburg and he himself was a canon of the cathedral there, the Polish astronomer was never ordained to the priesthood. Moreover, Galileo's first reference to Copernicus occurs in his *Tractatio de caelo, Opere* I, 43, 47-48, an early work wherein he himself rejects outright the heliocentric teaching. Alistair Crombie provides a replica of the folio containing this reference in Galileo's own handwriting in his "Sources of Galileo's Early Natural Philosophy," in *Reason, Experiment, and Mysticism in the Scientific Revolution,* M. L. Righini Bonelli and W. R. Shea, eds. (New York, 1975), facing p. 162.

[18] Westman, pp. 14-16. Garin's account of Tolosani's work is in his *Rinascite e rivoluzioni. Movimenti culturali dal XIV al XVIII secolo* (Bari, 1976), pp. 255-281, giving Tolosani's text on pp. 283-295.

[19] Koestler, pp. 433-434. Koestler's treatment of Galileo's *Letter to Christina* and the character of the astronomer is too harsh, and his book has been countered in reviews by De Santillana, Drake, and others. Koestler does not distinguish carefully enough between the earlier version of the letter written to Castelli and the later one to Christina. On the other hand, De Santillana makes too much of the effect of the *Letter to Christina* on Cardinal Barberini, based on a conversation with Galileo recorded by Giovanfrancesco Buonamici in the latter's diary. A rereading of Buonamici's diary by a disinterested eye does not yield the interpretation that the Cardinal was persuaded by the letter to counsel the Holy Office against accusing Galileo of heresy in 1616; cf. De Santillana, pp. 203, 289, and *Opere* XV, 111.

[20] Fragments of classical selections, probably written by Galileo as scholastic exercises at Vallombrosa, have been assembled by Favaro in Vol. 9 of the National Edition. The extent of Galileo's training in rhetoric at the University of Pisa is difficult to ascertain, and more research is required in this area. Angelo Fabroni provides a survey of the professors and texts used in Galileo's time in his history of the university, *Historia Academiae Pisanae,* 3 vols. (Pisa, 1791-1795), Vol. II, cap. 15. The principal rhetoricians who taught there were Francesco Robortello, Ciriaco Strozzi, Pietro Angelio Bargeo, and Aldo Manucci. Especially noteworthy is the fact that the funeral oration for Bargeo was delivered in 1595 by Jacopo Mazzoni (II, 431, n. 1), the close friend of Galileo and his father, which could indicate that Bargeo was also part of their circle. See notes 22 and 35, *infra.*

[21] A translation of a passage from Isocrates, the Greek rhetorican, into Latin, probably done by Galileo during his student days, is in *Opere* IX, 283-284. Fabroni states that the translation of Isocrates into Latin was a part of the requirement introduced by Lorenzo Lippi at Pisa near the end of the fifteenth century (I, 373). The *Rhetorica ad Herennium,* Cicero's rhetorical works, and Quintilian's, were newly appreciated in the early Renaissance and commentaries on them again appeared; see the discussion in Kristeller, *Renaissance Thought,* pp. 239, 245-255, and George A. Kennedy, *Classical Rhetoric and Its Christian and Secular Tradition from Ancient to Modern Times* (Chapel Hill, 1980), pp. 195-217. Aristotle's *Rhetoric* was part of the curriculum for universities in Italy in the sixteenth century according to the researches of Lisa Jardine, *Studies in the Renaissance,* 11 (1974), 31-62. In his "Rhetoric in the Middle Ages," *Speculum,* 17 (1942), 1-32, Richard McKeon points out that close connections between rhetoric and logic lingered on into the Renaissance and beyond, 31-32. Kristeller also discusses this connection and notes that dialectical argument emerged in Italy about the same time as Humanism, *Renaissance Thought,* pp. 99-101.

[22] Galileo was reared in a family with extensive cultural and literary contacts. His father was a lutenist and musicologist, well acquainted with classical languages and mathematics, and their home was the frequent meeting place for the *litterati* of Pisa and Florence. Apart from his knowledge of Virgil, Ovid, and Seneca, Galileo was particularly interested in the essays of Berni, the comedies of Ruzzante, and the verse of Ariosto and Tasso. In 1588 he delivered two lectures at the Florentine Academy on the dimensions of hell as set out in Dante's *Inferno,* and while teaching at Pisa around 1590 he composed a satirical poem "Against wearing the toga." These are included in Vol. 9 of the National Edition (pp. 31-57 and 212-223 respectively), along with his other literary and poetic compositions. Ludovico Geymonat describes Galileo's literary interests in *Galileo Galilei: A Biography and Inquiry into his Philosophy of Science,* S. Drake, tr. (New York: 1965), pp. 9-15. Even more polemical and rhetorical in style are two pseudonymous dialogues written in Tuscan dialect in 1605 and 1606, which Drake has shown to be Galileo's and which he regards as the astronomer's first published work; see his *Galileo Against the Philosophers* (Los Angeles, 1976).

[23] The autograph is preserved in the collection of Galileiana at the Biblioteca Nazionale Centrale in Florence with the signature MS Gal. 27. Misled by a statement in Vincenzo Viviani's biography of Galileo, Favaro regarded it as a mere scholastic exercise composed while the young Pisan was studying at the Monastery of Vallombrosa, and published only a brief excerpt from it and a listing of the questions they contain, now generally referred to as the "Logical Questions," in *Opere* IX, 279-282, 291-292.

[24] Edwards' transcription, with an introduction and commentary by William A. Wallace, is forthcoming. Another transcription has been made independently by Adriano Carugo, and a brief summary of its contents appears in Crombie's essay, "Sources of Galileo's Early Natural Philosophy," pp. 171-175.

[25] Drake, *Galileo at Work: His Scientific Biography* (Chicago, 1978), p. 245, and *Discoveries,* p. 167.

[26] See *Opere* XII, 183-184; his letter is translated in Drake, *Discoveries,* p. 167.

[27] Foscarini's defense of Copernicanism also took the form of a published letter. Its long title is *Lettera del R.P.M. Paolo Antonio Foscarini Carmelitano Sopra l'Opinione de'Pittagorici e del Copernico, della Mobilità della Terre e Stabilità del Sole, e del Nuovo Pittagorico Sistema del Mondo* (Naples, 1615).

[28] Notes made by Galileo and containing rebuttals of the various points in Bellarmine's letter have been transcribed by Favaro and published under the title *Considerazioni circa l'opinione Copernicana, Opere V,* 349-370; excerpts from this material are translated by Drake in *Discoveries,* pp. 167-170. The notes were probably written before Galileo revised his epistle to Castelli, but in any event Ballarmine's observations are all taken into account in the *Letter to Christina.*

[29] *Opere* XII, 171; the letter is translated in *Discoveries,* pp. 162-164.

[30] *Opere* XII, 173, 3°.

[31] See *Opere* XII, 171, line 32. That Galileo understood the precise meaning of this expression is clear from his commentary on the *Posterior Analytics* contained in the Logical Questions. The second treatise in this work is in fact entitled *De demonstratione,* and it consists of three disputations, the first on the nature and importance of demonstration, the second on its properties, and the third on its kinds (*Opere* IX, 280-281). W. A. Wallace has given the more important readings from this treatise and has traced their recurrence in Galileo's later writings on his "The Problem of Causality in Galileo's Science," *The Review of Metaphysics,* 36 (1983), 607-632. Additional details are provided in his "Aristotle and Galileo: The Uses of ΥΠΟΘΕΣΙΣ (Suppositio) in Scientific Reasoning," in *Studies in Aristotle,* Dominic O'Meara, ed. (Washington, D.C., 1981), pp. 47-77. I am indebted to Professor Wallace for discussions of this and other points related to Galileo's science and scientific reasoning.

[32] *Opere* XII, 185; Drake, *Discoveries,* p. 166.

[33] Ibid.

[34] The Italian reads ". . . quanto ella sia ben fondata sopra manifeste esperienze e necessarie dimostrazioni . . ." (*Opere* V, 312, lines 27-28). In view of Galileo's understanding of the expression "necessarie dimostrazioni," there is an ambiguity in this statement that will be exploited throughout the remainder of the *Letter.* As Galileo states it, the Copernican system is "well grounded" (*ben fondata*) on manifest experiences and necessary demonstrations. Does this mean that the system is actually demonstrated on the basis of sense experience, or that it is merely a plausible hypothesis that can be supported in part by observation and strict mathematical reasoning? The first is the impression Galileo intends to convey, as can be seen throughout the remainder of the *Letter,* whereas the second would be consonant with Bellarmine's understanding of the proofs Galileo and Foscarini were alleging, which would not be sufficient to evoke a wholesale reinterpretation of the Scriptures, as Galileo states in the *Letter.* The authority of the Bible, he says there, "ought to be preferred over that of all human writings which are supported only by bare assertions and probable arguments, and not set forth in a demonstrative way" (*Opere* V, 317, lines 21-24; *Discoveries,* p. 183). See also my comparision of Galileo's argumentation in the *Letter* with that employed in his *Dialogue* of 1632, "Galileo's Rhetorical Strategies in Defense of Copernicanism," in *Novità Celesti, Crisi del Sapere,* Paolo Galluzzi, ed., forthcoming.

[35] Galileo describes himself as an Aristotelian in his scientific reasoning in his letter of September 14, 1640, to Fortunio Liceti, *Opere* XVIII, 248; see the passage translated into English in Wallace, "Aristotle and Galileo," p. 75. The "progressive Aristotelianism" of Galileo in matters methodological is delineated by Wallace in his "Aristotelian Influences on Galileo's Thought," in *Aristotelismo Veneto e Scienza Moderna,* Luigi Olivieri, ed., 2 vols. (Padua, 1983), I, 349-378. This is not to deny that Galileo was also influenced by Plato, as has been noted by Kristeller in his *Renaissance Thought,* p. 64 and notes 47 and 48 on pp. 269-270, and also urged by Alexandre Koyré in his *Metaphysics and Measurement: Essays in the Scientific Revolution* (Cambridge, Mass., 1968), pp. 16-43. During Galileo's days at Pisa the oppositions between Aristotelianism and Platonism were not as clearly noted as they are in our times; both Jacopo Mazzoni and Cosimo Boscaglia taught Aristotle and Plato at the university there, and Mazzoni even attempted a complete reconciliation of the two philosophers. Galileo studied with Mazzoni in 1590, as he records in his letter to his father on November 15th of that year (*Opere* X, 44-45), and seems to have been particularly impressed with the way in which his father's friend used mathematics to remove *impedimenti* to man's knowledge of the physical world. For more details, see Frederick Purnell, "Jacopo Mazzoni and Galileo," *Physis,* 3 (1972), 273-294.

[36] Augustin Cardinal Bea, S.J., in fact, speaks of *Providentissimus Deus* as "the Magna Carta of biblical studies" for the Catholic Church; see his Foreword to *The Jerome Biblical Commentary,* Raymond E. Brown et al., eds. (Englewood Cliffs, N.J., 1968), the standard text now in use in Catholic seminaries.

[37] So frequently does Galileo refer to "necessary demonstration" and "sensate experience" throughout the *Letter* that these expressions form almost a litany to mesmerize his readers. A partial list of their occurrence, or that of equivalent expressions, follows: ". . . trattate con astronomiche e geometriche dimostrazioni, fondata prima sopra sensate esperienze ed accuratissime osservazioni" (*Opere* V, 313, lines 23-25); ". . . cominciare . . . dalle sensate esperienze e dalle dimostrazioni necessarie" (p. 316, lines 24-25); ". . . effetti naturali che o la sensata esperienza ci pone dinanzi a gli occhi o le necessarie dimostrazioni ci concludono . . ." (p. 317, lines 1-2); ". . . venuti in certezza di alcune conclusioni naturali . . ." (p. 317, lines 12-13); ". . . in quelle conclusioni naturali, che o dalle sensate esperienze o dalle necessarie dimostrazioni ci vengono esposte innanci a gli occhi e all'intelletto . . ." (p. 317, lines 29-31); ". . . delle infinite conclusioni ammirande che in tale scienza si contengono e si dimostrano . . ." (p. 318, lines 9-10); ". . . quanto nelle conclusioni naturali si devono stimar le dimostrazioni necessarie e le sensate esperienze . . ." (p. 319, lines 29-31); ". . . che indubitabilmente saranno concordanti con quelle conclusioni naturali, delle quali il senso manifesto o le dimostrazioni necessarie ci avessero prima resi certi e sicuri" (p. 320, lines 13-16); ". . . quelle conclusioni naturali, delle quali una volta il senso e le ragioni dimostrative e necessarie ci potessero manifestare . . ." (p. 320, lines 23-25); ". . . con molte osservazioni e dimostrazioni confermata . . ." (p. 321, lines 14-15); ". . . che sarebbe necessaria prima a capire . . . le dimostrazioni con le quali le acutissime scienze procedono . . ." (p. 321, lines 26-28); ". . . le conclusioni dimostrate circa le cose della natura e del cielo . . ." (p. 326, lines 18-19); ". . . alcune cose della natura dimostrate veracemente . . ." (p. 327, lines 13-14); ". . . o si ha, o si può credere fermamente che aver si possa, con esperienze, con lunghe osservazioni e con necessarie dimostrazioni, indubitata certezza, quale è, se la Terra e 'l Sole si muovino o no . . ." (p. 330, lines 17-20); ". . . si deva considerar se elle sono indubitabilmente dimostrate o con esperienze sensate conosciute . . ." (p. 332, lines 5-6); ". . . esquisite osservazioni e sottili dimostrazioni . . ." (p. 332, lines 12-13); ". . . dopo aver prima dimostrato che i movimenti li quali a noi appariscono esser [sic] del Sole o del firmamento son veramente della Terra . . ." (p. 334, line 24-335, line 1); ". . . l'esperienze, l'osservazioni, le ragioni e la dimostrazioni de' filosofi ed astronomi . . ." (p. 338, lines 7-8); ". . . definire conclusioni naturali, delle quali, o con esperienze o con dimostrazioni necessarie, si potrebbe in qualche tempo dimostrare il contrario . . ." (p. 338, lines 33-35); ". . . negare l'esperienze e le dimostrazioni necessarie" (p. 339, line 19); ". . . aver molte esperienze sensate e molte dimostrazioni necessarie per la parte sua . . ." (p. 341, lines 32-33); ". . . oppugnar le manifeste esperienze o le necessarie dimostrazioni" (p. 342, lines 12-13). Only once in this long list does Galileo state that natural conclusions *might in time* (si potrebbe in qualche tempo, p. 338, line 35) be demonstrated to be contrary to the sense of Scripture; in all other cases he conveys the impression that demonstrations based on sense experience were or actually are available to determine the sense in which the Bible is to be understood.

[38] See the many references to the work of Tycho Brahe throughout the National Edition, *Opere* XX, 98-99. In the Tychonian system the earth is posited as stationary at the center of the universe, but the planetary spheres rotate around the sun, and the whole ensemble, together with the moon, around the earth. Many were attracted to the theory, which had the advantage of not contradicting Scripture; on this ground it was clearly favored by Jesuit astronomers.

[39] The usual evidence cited is Foucault's experiments with pendulums swinging freely on the earth's surface and Bessel's measurements of stellar parallax, both of which date from the nineteenth century; see, however, Giorgio Tabbaroni, "Giovanni Battista Guglielmini e la prima verifica sperimentale della rotazione terrestre (1790)," *Angelicum,* 60 (1983), 462-486. All are agreed that Galileo's argument from the tides, hinted at in the *Letter to Christina (Opere* V, 311, lines 6-8; *Discoveries,* p. 177) and explained in his discourse addressed to Cardinal Orsini on 8 January 1616, *Del flusso e reflusso del mare (Opere* V, 377-395), and again in the *Dialogue* of 1632, is defective. On this matter, see William R. Shea, *Galileo's Intellectual Revolution: The Middle Period, 1610-1632* (New York, 1972), pp. 172-189, and the more recent analysis of Mario G. Galli, "L'argomentazione di Galileo in favore del sistema copernicano dedotta dal fenomeno delle maree," *Angelicum,* 60 (1983), 386-427.

[40] This interpretation has been advanced by W. A. Wallace in two recent articles: "Galileo's Science and the Trial of 1633," *The Wilson Quarterly,* 7 (1983), 154-164; and "Galileo and Aristotle in the *Dialogo,*" *Angelicum,* 60 (1983), 311-332. Wallace's view differs from that of Finocchiaro, who argues on the basis of the *Dialogue* that Galileo never intended to produce demonstrative proofs but was content with plausible or rhetorical arguments from beginning to end. Wallace, on the other hand, notes a change in Galileo's aspirations after the decree of 1616 against Copernicus. Prior to the decree, as in the *Letter to Christina,* he spoke as if necessary demonstrations based on sense experience were already, or soon would be, available; after it, as in the *Dialogue,* he attenuated his claims consid-

erably. For additional details, see Wallace's review of Finocchiaro's book, *Journal of the History of Philosophy,* 20 (1982), 307-309.

[41] The expression Bellarmine uses, which Drake translates as "hypothetically," is the technical Latin phrase *ex suppositione (Opere* XII, 171, line 9[2]), which can take on a variety of meanings. In his examination of the various points made by Bellarmine in the letter to Foscarini, Galileo distinguishes two senses of *suppositio (supposizione,* in Italian), one of which would lead to a merely hypothetical conclusion, the other to a demonstrated result (*Opere* V, 357-359). Professor Wallace has shown in his *Prelude to Galileo* (Dordrecht, 1981) that Galileo was unable to authenticate the suppositions on which his proofs for the earth's motion were based, whereas he was eventually successful in doing so for the demonstration of the law of falling bodies in the *Two New Sciences* of 1638 (pp. 129-159). For fuller details and documentation, see Wallace's "Aristotle and Galileo" and his *Galileo and His Sources: The Heritage of the Collegio Romano in Galileo's Science,* forthcoming from Princeton University Press.

[42] This citation was unfortunate, for, unknown to Galileo, Zuñiga had been vigorously reprimanded by the Jesuit theologian Juan de Piñeda in his *Commentariorum in Iob libri tredecim* (Coloniae Agrippinae, 1600, p. 340). The latter's work was well known and Bellarmine himself possessed a copy. Since Zuñiga's *Commentaries on Job* was singled out for correction in the 1616 decree, Galileo's citation may have actually had the effect of increasing the oppostion to Copernicanism. Westman discusses this issue in his "The Copernicans and the Churches," pp. 23-24, 39, 48, n. 46.

[43] One of the consultants to the Inquisition, Melchior Inchofer, regarded the *Letter to Christina* as prime evidence at the trial for Galileo's heretical teachings, *Opere* XIX, 349.

[44] Quoted by Pasquale M. D'Elia, *Galileo in China.* Rufus Suter and Matthew Sciasa, eds. and trs. (Cambridge, Mass., 1960), pp. 57-58.

[45] Quoted in Langford, p. 58.

Richard S. Westfall (essay date 1985)

SOURCE: "Science and Patronage: Galileo and the Telescope," in *Isis,* Vol. 76, March, 1985, pp. 11-30.

[In the following essay, Westfall argues that the heavy reliance upon and competition for patronage in the seventeenth century might have affected the truthfulness of some of the scientific conclusions and discoveries made by scientists of that period, including Galileo.]

Sometime late in 1610, probably near 11 December, Galileo received a letter from his disciple Benedetto Castelli:

> If the position of Copernicus, that Venus revolves around the sun, is true (as I believe), [Castelli wrote], it is clear that it would necessarily sometimes be seen by us horned and sometimes not, even though the planet maintains the same position relative to the sun. . . . Now I want to know from you if you, with the help of your marvellous glasses, have observed such a phenomenon, which will be, beyond doubt, a sure means to convince even the most obstinate mind. I also suspect a similar thing with Mars near the quadrature with the sun; I don't mean a horned or non-horned shape, but only a semicircular and a more full one.[1]

How readily the passage summons up familiar images of Galileo, the Copernican polemicist, who turned the telescope on the heavens, if not first, surely first in an effective manner, and with his discoveries forever transformed the terms of the debate. Some twenty years after Castelli's letter, in the Fourth Day of the ***Dialogue Concerning the Two Chief World Systems*** (1632), Galileo summed up what he considered the most convincing arguments in favor of the Copernican system: first, the retrograde motions of the planets and their approaches toward and recessions from the earth (a reference primarily to Venus and Mars); second, the rotation of the sun on its own axis; third, the tides.[2] Half of the first argument and all of the second and third arguments were Galileo's own work. The theory of the tides did not depend on the telescope, of course, but the arguments from the rotation of the sun and the approaches of the planets could not have existed without it. For all that, we must not allow the ***Sidereus nuncius*** and Galileo's early discoveries with the telescope to dazzle us. Before the arrival of Castelli's letter, Galileo does not appear to have thought out a serious program of observation with his new instrument to settle, or to attempt to settle, the Copernican question. Quite the contrary, his attention appears to have focused almost exclusively on the telescope's capacity to insure his own future. The episode of the Castelli letter tells us something about Galileo's commitment to Copernicanism, but it tells us a great deal more about the system of patronage and the material circumstances under which Galileo pursued his career in science.

We can best understand the Castelli letter if we look first into its background. Let us start with Galileo's father, who was a distinguished musician but hardly an economic success. As a consequence, though Galileo was descended from an old Florentine patrician family, he found himself upon the death of his father, which came when Galileo himself was approaching thirty, heir to some sizable obligations but to no material means worth mentioning. To make matters worse, he would soon have no income; although he held a chair (with a miserable salary, to be sure) at the University of Pisa, he had offended powerful people and thus insured that the appointment would not be renewed in 1592. From that time his primary asset would be his wits, a formidable asset indeed, but not one directly negotiable in the marketplace. In the late sixteenth century, the system of patronage was one of the principal devices by which to convert wits (I refer of course to wits of Galileo's caliber) into the material necessities of life.

An appointment as professor of mathematics at the University of Padua in the autumn of 1592 provided an income. In the mind of a twentieth-century reader, such a position does not raise the suggestion of patronage. In the late sixteenth century, however, different considerations determined university appointments, and without the effective intervention of Guidobaldo del Monte, Galileo would never have occupied the Paduan chair.[3] Moreover, the university appointed him for a limited period of four years with guaranteed extension of two more. Although he continued in 1598 and in 1604 to teach and to be paid after two six-year appointments had expired, the university did in the end explicitly reappoint him both times. Not only was reappointment not guaranteed, but Galileo always wanted an increase in salary. That is, he had continuing need of patrons in Padua, and he took care that he did not lack them. The great majority of the friends he cultivated in Venice were members of the highest ranks of Venetian nobility.[4] The word *friend* carries special connotations within a context of patronage; authorities on patronage distinguish what they call instrumental friendship from emotional friendship. Galileo's "friends" in Venice appear to have understood that the "friendship" entailed the use of their connections and influence on his behalf; certainly Galileo expected as much. In the late summer of 1599, a year after his appointment had expired, the *riformati,* the highest authorities of the university, who were appointed by and responsible to the Venetian government, took his reappointment under consideration. Antonio Quirini, who had himself received commendations from three men of influence, visited Leonardo Donato, one of the *riformatori,* on Galileo's behalf. Giovanfrancesco Sagredo visited all three of the *riformatori,* one of them three times, and he indicated that the nephews of this man, Zaccaria Contarini, had also been working on him. The sticking point was the raise that Galileo wanted. Sagredo, who was clearly tiring of the exercise, wanted to be sure that Galileo understood he had fulfilled his duty as a patron. "Since I have already satisfied abundantly enough the friendship I hold for you, the obligations to you which I acknowledge, and the favor and help that true gentlemen try to extend to the qualified who deserve it," he wrote, he thought he might now honorably desist.[5] One would be hard pressed to find a better example of the language of patronage. The net result of this marshalling of influence was a raise from 180 to 320 florins *per annum,* effective in 1598, when the original appointment had expired. In the fall of 1605, when the second reappointment was taken up, Galileo was able to call on no one less than the grand duke of Tuscany, who did indeed intervene and was apparently instrumental in obtaining a further raise to 520 florins.[6]

By that time Galileo had already begun to cast his gaze beyond Padua, where he continually had to direct a choir of patrons to sing his praises, and where the officials frankly told him that he would need to supplement his salary by private lessons. This he had resorted to, in addition to using his home as a hostel and manufacturing instruments for sale. He could have been writing of his own situation when, soon afterwards, he described to Grand Duchess Cristina the plight of his friend Fabrizio, who, "finding himself . . . scarcely able to endure the continual labors he needs to undertake every day to serve his many friends and patrons, and hence wanting very much to find a little quiet, both to sustain his life and to bring some of his works to a conclusion," hoped to enter the service of the grand duke.[7] Galileo had similarly concluded that serving a single patron might be easier than serving many. In the spring of 1604, after instructing Vincenzo Gonzaga, the duke of Mantua, in the use of his geometric and military compass, he presented the duke with a compass and received in return gifts worth more than a year's salary at its current rate. This was suggestive indeed; without further ado he undertook negotiations to enter Gonzaga's service. The gift turned out to have been misleading, however. Gonzaga was only a duke, whereas Galileo had a princely stipend in mind. Galileo decided to stay on in Padua for the time.[8]

Almost at once Galileo earnestly began to woo the Medici rulers of his native Tuscany. He had prepared his instructions for the use of the geometric and military compass for publication as a pamphlet, and in the spring of 1605 he formally sought permission to dedicate it to the crown prince, Cosimo. Galileo parlayed acceptance of the dedication into an invitation to instruct the prince in mathematics during his summer vacation and did not thereafter relent in his quest. He wrote the prince the flattering letters that an absolute ruler expected of a client, declaring himself "one of his most faithful and devoted servants," and proclaiming his desire to demonstrate "by how much I prefer his yoke to that of any other Master, since it seems to me that the suavity of his manner and the humanity of his nature are able to make anyone desire to be his slave."[9] The terms of Galileo's address, jarring to twentieth-century ears, would not have seemed sycophantic to Galileo's contemporaries. Almost no one challenged the legitimacy of a hierarchically ordered society, the precondition of the patronage that supported Galileo in an economically unproductive occupation. Even if Cosimo was a dull student incapable of profiting from the instruction he received, Galileo's words spoke to his position, not to his person, and expressed the practical necessities that had to be faced.

Summer instruction became an annual affair. In the fall of 1607, when magnetism seized the fancy of the prince, the court consulted Galileo as its authority on such matters. He informed them that he owned a lodestone that weighed about half a pound and was quite strong but not well formed. Like everything he owned, he assured them, it was at the prince's command. However, he knew of another, far better, one that weighed about five pounds. It was owned by a friend of his—he referred to Sagredo—who was ready to part with it at a fair price. The friend had refused an offer of two hundred gold scudi from a representative of the emperor; Galileo suggested that four hundred scudi sounded about right. It quickly transpired that four hundred scudi was more than the Tuscan court intended to spend to pamper the ephemeral fancy of even the crown prince, and with some embarrassment Galileo ascertained that Sagredo would accept two hundred after all.[10] The negotiations and arrangements stretched out over a period of six months, during which Galileo experimented extensively with the lodestone's capacity. It was even better than he had originally determined. It would support over twice its own weight, but it would do so only in the hands of one who knew how to apply the weights properly to the poles. To insure that the prince not be disappointed, Galileo decided to send the lodestone with the weights in place. Not just any weights would please a crown prince of Tuscany, however, and seizing upon the fable of a lodestone strong enough to raise an anchor, he had two little anchors of the proper weight made of iron. Indeed he traveled to Venice more than once to supervise the artisans at work on them. Meanwhile, as he kept learning about the lodestone, his imagination embroidered his knowledge into ever more elaborate images. Because the lodestone, far from exhausting itself, appeared to gain strength as it held the weight, Galileo proposed that on the support for the whole device one could inscribe the motto, *Vim facit amor,* "love produces strength." This motto suggested, he added, "the dominion of God conferred upon the just and legitimate prince over his subjects, which should be such that with loving violence it draws to itself the devotion, loyalty, and obedience of the subjects."[11] Galileo, taken with the figure and doubtful that the secretary of state, to whom he had sent it, had passed it on to the ruling family, repeated the conceit to Grand Duchess Cristina in the fall on the occasion of Cosimo's marriage, when it became doubly suitable. By now his imagination had embroidered it still further. Obviously the lodestone represented the prince. The ancient symbol of the Medici embodied its shape. Moreover, the earth was known to be a great magnet, and the prince's name, Cosimo (or Cosmo) was a synonym for *Mondo,* or Earth. Hence it was possible, he concluded, "through the most noble metaphor of a globe of lodestone to indicate our great Cosimo."[12] Such evidence reveals how the subtle alchemy of patronage transmuted an object of science into an *objet d'art* to amuse and flatter a prince.

Meanwhile, well before the prince's marriage, Galileo had sent the lodestone to Florence on 3 May 1608. Florentine officials, concerned that it not be injured in transit, had instructed him to deliver it to the Tuscan resident in Venice for shipment via their own courier, but he had sent it instead by the common courier. Three weeks later, having received no word of acknowledgment, Galileo was almost beside himself with anxiety.[13] After another week had passed with still no word, convinced that his use of the common courier in defiance of explicit orders had given offense, he composed a long letter of explanation. The scene he painted is not one commonly associated with Galileo; we might search some time, however, to find a better description of the mores of patronage. Galileo had spent all of the first three days of May in Venice supervising the final completion of the device. (We ought to remember those three days when we hear Galileo complain about the demands that his life in Padua placed on his time.) On the third day, a Sunday, the festival of Santa Croce, he had forced two artisans to work on the anchors against their will. When night came with the work not yet completed, he sent a note to the resident asking the hour at which the Tuscan courier would leave. Word came back that he could deliver the package as late as the fourth hour of the night, and the artisans worked on until the deadline approached. Galileo called for a gondola, which he had trouble finding because of the hour and the rain. They set out, the gondolier grumbling every stroke of the way, and found the general area of the resident's home. Alas, it was so dark and rainy that they could not locate his house. They knocked on various doors, and received in reply either silence or words Galileo thought it better not to repeat in his letter. Finally, in desperation, determined that his offering not wait for the next official courier, he took his box to the master of the couriers.[14] By the time he wrote the explanation, it was no longer necessary; a letter had been sent from Florence informing him that the lodestone had arrived safely.

Soon it appeared that his diligent labor to provide an occasional amusement for the crown prince had been most prudently expended. Nine months later, Ferdinand I died, and Cosimo succeeded him as grand duke of Tuscany. Galileo wrote to him, of course, offering the customary mixture of condolences on his father's death and congratulations on his succession. "I supplicate Your Most Serene Highness," he concluded, "that as you have been established by God as the ruler of all your most devoted subjects, do not disdain now and then to turn the favorable eye of your grace toward me, one of your most faithful and devoted servants, for which grace I devotedly entreat while I bow before you in all humility and kiss your hand."[15] To an official of the court he wrote a much longer letter that frankly laid out his aspirations:

> Having labored now twenty years, the best ones of my life, in dispensing at retail, as the saying goes, at the demand of everyone, that little talent in my profession that God and my own efforts have given me, my desires would truly be to obtain enough leisure and quiet as would enable me before I die to complete three great works that I have in hand in order to be able to publish them, perhaps with some praise for me and for whoever has helped me in the business. . . . It is not possible to receive a salary from a Republic, however splendid and generous, without serving the public, because to get something from the public one must satisfy it and not just one particular person; and while I remain able to teach and to serve, no one can exempt me from the burden while leaving me the income; and in sum I cannot hope for such a benefit from anyone but an absolute prince.[16]

He specified his current income and assured the grand duke once more that the prince who patronized him could expect to receive more reflected glory than most clients delivered. A reply came back that Cosimo would write when he was able. It was the classic formula of evasion, the seventeenth-century equivalent of a promise to call for lunch, and indeed silence followed the letter. Galileo, who had spent his vacations in the summer with the ducal family, instructing Cosimo the crown prince in mathematics in 1605, 1606, and 1608 (with 1607 omitted at his own request), did not receive an invitation from Cosimo the grand duke for 1609. The weeks stretched into months. Though Galileo could not have known it in the summer of 1609, the months would stretch into a year, and who knows how long Galileo might have waited had nothing else intervened. Perhaps his efforts in wooing the prince had been in vain after all; perhaps he was destined to stay on in Padua wearing himself out peddling his wares at retail.

But something did intervene. Call it fate. In the spring of 1609 a man from Flanders appeared in Venice with a device that magnified the images of things and enabled one to see objects at a distance. Galileo may have seen the instrument firsthand; he certainly heard it described by some who had. Within a short time he was able to reproduce it and, what was far more important, to improve upon it.[17] Whereas the instrument from Flanders magnified three times, by late August Galileo had one that magnified eight or nine times. It caused a sensation in Venice. Aged senators struggled to the top of the campanile to see ships approaching the harbor two hours before they became visible to the naked eye. The Flemish adventurer had offered his eyeglass to the Senate for 1,000 *zecchini,* very nearly

four times Galileo's annual salary. With supreme insight, Galileo presented his to the Doge. He made the presentation before the College, a sort of council of ministers, which forthwith ordered the *riformatori* of the university to renew his contract for life at a salary of 1,000 florins. "Knowing how hope has wings that are very slow and fortune wings most swift," Galileo reported to his brother-in-law, "I said that I was content with how much it pleased His Highness."[18]

Since a great deal has been made of that 1,000 florins, it is useful to put it briefly into perspective. During his entire preceding career in Padua, Galileo had lived, in terms of salary, in the shadow of Cesare Cremonini, the Aristotelian philosopher who was at once his rival and his friend. Cremonini had gone to Padua in 1590 at a salary of 200 florins; Galileo's initial salary had been 180. In 1599, when Galileo's salary had increased to 320 florins, Cremonini's had risen to 400. In 1601, Cremonini's salary had increased again to 600 florins. Only in 1606 had Galileo's reached 520, and two years later Cremonini's had risen once more, this time to 1,000. What the college offered to Galileo in 1609 was, in fact, not an unprecedented salary but one merely equal with Cremonini's. Moreover, the lifetime contract would have effectively foreclosed any future negotiations for more. Cremonini's contract did not, and his salary did increase further, to 1,400 florins in 1616, then to 1,800 in 1623. Ultimately it reached 2,000 florins. As for the indignation in Venice when Galileo chose to leave, it is worth noting that the original action of the college, to make the new salary effective for the current year, was rescinded by the senate.[19] Since he left for Florence before the next year began, Galileo never received the salary of 1,000 florins.

Meanwhile, the Tuscan court was as interested in the new device as everyone else. Six days after the presentation of the instrument to the doge, exactly the time ordinarily required for communications between Venice and Florence, a Tuscan official wrote to tell Galileo how much the grand duke would like to have one of the eyeglasses, and three weeks later they sent him pieces of glass to work into lenses for it.[20] There is no evidence, however, that the grand duke received one at this time. The Venetian government had ordered its servant to make twelve more telescopes and not to reveal their secret. Galileo needed no encouragement on the latter score. Already in September others were offering for sale telescopes like the one that had appeared during the summer, and by November every ordinary maker of spectacles in Venice could produce them.[21] Galileo's prestige rested on the fact acknowledged by everyone who tried them that his telescopes were better than any others, and he kept them that way by making them himself in private. Early in 1610 he stated that he had already made over sixty telescopes.[22] Galileo was usually inclined to exaggerate to his own advantage, but there is no reason to doubt that he spent much of the autumn of 1609 making telescopes and further improving them. By late autumn, as a result of his own efforts, he had a twenty-power instrument.

Sometime during the autumn, probably near the end of November, Galileo found time to turn his telescope on the heavens.[23] He was not the first to do so. He was not even the second, though he had no knowledge of earlier observers at the time.[24] Having the best instrument, he discovered things no one before him had seen, and having a clear idea of what he might do with such discoveries, he succeeded in attaching his name to the new celestial world forever. No records of his observations before 7 January 1610 have survived. The *Sidereus nuncius,* which offers the principal account of them, seems to suggest that initially Galileo merely looked at the most obvious celestial objects—the moon and then the stars, including the Milky Way. From the first moment, however, he was aware that he was taking a historic step. As he wrote to Antonio de' Medici on 7 January 1610, after describing his discoveries, "None of the observations mentioned above are seen or can be seen without an exquisite instrument; hence I can believe that I am the first in the world to observe so close and so distinctly these features of the heavenly bodies." Since the letter is long and carefully composed and uses some phrases and comparisons that would make their way into the *Sidereus nuncius,* we can well believe that Galileo had already given thought to the advantages of a publication that would announce what had been observed and, of course, who the observer was. That he had not yet begun to compose the *Sidereus nuncius* appears from the reference in the first paragraph to discoveries made after 7 January: Galileo waited until he had a purpose associated with patronage.[25]

On the night he wrote the letter, Galileo had turned his telescope toward Jupiter, and he reported to Antonio that among the new stars he had seen in the heavens were three near Jupiter. Why had he chosen Jupiter as the first planet to observe? Like Saturn, it circles far outside the earth in both the Ptolemaic and the Copernican systems, and it seems one of the least likely candidates to reveal anything of decisive importance to an astronomer. Why look at Jupiter? For no better reason than the fact it was there. The records of Galileo's observations seem to reveal a man who, like many, preferred staying up in the evening to rising before dawn. On 7 January 1610, only Jupiter and Saturn appeared in the evening sky, and Saturn was so low that half an hour after sunset it stood only a few degrees above the horizon and was probably invisible. Jupiter was high in the eastern sky. When he pointed his telescope at Jupiter, Galileo did nothing more premeditated than to look at the only planet readily available for observation.

For the second time fate intervened, offering with Jupiter a prize there could have been no reason to expect. Galileo was even fortunate in the time when he happened to look at Jupiter. As he wrote Antonio de' Medici that night, he was just completing a new telescope that would magnify thirty times, nearly the ultimate level to which he brought his instrument, and he had it available for the observations that followed.[26] As before, he was not slow to seize the bounty that fate held out. The three new stars he saw near Jupiter must have sparked some premonition. Not only did he mention them to Antonio de' Medici; not only did he make a record of the observation, the first such one that survives; but he returned to observe the three objects on the following night. The ninth was cloudy, but he observed them again on the tenth, increasingly intrigued by their changing positions relative to Jupiter. By the eleventh he was certain about what he discovered: "there are around Jupiter three other wandering stars that have been invisible to everyone until this time."[27] Two days later his cup ran over; he identified a fourth. Four was a happy number; Cosimo was one of four brothers. Now Galileo was sure he had found what he wanted, a ticket to Florence.

By the end of the month he had prepared the *Sidereus nuncius,* a message from the stars to be sure, but a message composed with the grand duke always in mind. He wrote to Belisario Vinta, the Florentine secretary of state, from Venice, where he had gone to have it printed, about his observations: "as they are amazing without limit, so I render thanks without limit to God who has been pleased to make me alone the first observer of things worthy of admiration but kept secret through all the centuries." He ran through his discoveries—the surface of the moon, the new stars, the nature of the Milky Way. "But that which exceeds all the marvelous things, I have discovered four new planets."[28] Vinta answered in the least possible time. Immediately upon the arrival of Galileo's letter, he had taken it to the grand duke, who was rendered "stupified beyond measure by this new proof of your almost supernatural genius." Assured that the prey was taking the bait, Galileo sprang the trap. He was willing, he told Vinta, to publish his observations only under the auspices of the grand duke, in order that "his glorious name live on the same plane with the stars." As the discoverer of the new planets, it was his privilege to name them. "However, I find a point of ambiguity, whether I should consecrate all four to the Grand Duke alone, calling them with his name the *Cosmici,* or whether, since they are exactly four in number, I should dedicate them to the group of brothers with the name of *Medicean Stars.*"[29] In fact, Galileo did not entertain any large doubt as to which alternative would be preferable, and he proceeded to print the pamphlet using the name *Cosmica Sydera,* in the heading on the first page and elsewhere. Alas, someone in the court observed that since *Cosimo* derived from the Greek *kosmos,* people might mistake the name *Cosmici* for a reference, not to the grand duke, but to the nature of the bodies, and the *Sidereus nuncius* came out with the name *Medicean Stars* on a slip pasted over the original.[30]

The book, rushed into print, as Galileo explained to Vinta, lest someone forestall him both in the discoveries and in the right to name them, duly appeared in March.[31] The dedication to the grand duke explained how through the ages mankind had attempted to preserve the memory of distinguished men by erecting statues of them and by attaching their names to columns, pyramids, and even cities. In the end, however, every human invention perishes; the heavens alone are eternal. Hence men have given to the brightest stars the names of those "whose eminent and godlike deeds have caused them to be accounted worthy of eternity in the company of the stars."[32] He received for his pains a gold chain worth four hundred scudi plus a medal of the grand duke to hang on it.

Galileo's discoveries have not suffered from neglect, but in assessing them from the perspective of nearly four centuries, one should not underestimate the excitement they aroused in their own age. Italian dukes, German princes, the queen of France, the Holy Roman Emperor, half the cardinals in Rome wrote to Galileo asking for one of the instruments that made the celestial wonders visible.[33] Correspondents and commentators vied with each other in plundering mythology and history to find an appropriate symbol for the man who had uncovered such marvels. Giovanni Battista Manso of Naples likened him to Atlas in relation to the new heavenly spheres. Orazio del Monte, Guidobaldo's son, compared the discovery of new planets to the discovery of the new world and assured Galileo that he would "compete in glory with Columbus." In England, Sir William Lower opined that "my diligent Galileus hath done more in his threefold discoverie than Magellane in opening the streights to the South Sea."[34] More than the other revelations of the telescope, the new "planets" and Galileo's masterstroke of naming them for the Medicean ruler of Florence fired men's imaginations. Should he discover another planet, he heard from Paris, and name it for the French king, not only would he do a just thing but he would "make himself and his family rich forever."[35] During the following years, a French supporter of the proposition that sunspots were in reality planets near the sun named them for the Bourbons, while a Belgian proponent of the same position named them for the Hapsburgs.[36] Obviously both imitated what Galileo had done first.

In a word, Galileo had raised himself with one inspired blow from the level of an obscure professor of mathematics at the University of Padua to the status of the most desirable client in Italy. He had no intention of allowing his opportunity to slip by. With a copy of the *Sidereus nuncius,* he sent the grand duke the very telescope with which he had made the discoveries. Already he had indicated his concern that people unfamiliar with the telescope might not succeed in observing the Medicean stars, and he had resolved to follow his gift to Florence during the Holy Week vacation, which would last most of April, to insure that the grand duke not be disappointed. "Because of my having been able to demonstrate how much I am a very devoted servant of my Lord in so exotic a manner," he wrote to Vinta, himself a client who would understand, "and because I could never hope for another chance like it, this occasion is so important to me that I do not want to be disturbed by any difficulty or obstacle."[37] The upshot was that he did spend approximately two weeks with the court in Pisa, and correspondence makes it clear that they came to general agreement on his entering the grand duke's service. Almost immediately upon his return, he wrote a long letter that spelled out his current financial situation and stated his desires. He was able, he assured the Florentine court, to double his salary of one thousand florins by giving private lessons and taking students into his house, but they consumed his time. "Hence if I am to return to my native land, I desire that the primary intention of His Highness shall be to give me leave and leisure to draw my works to a conclusion without my being occupied in teaching." Arrangements were quickly made final. Galileo would return to Tuscany with the titles of professor of mathematics at the University of Pisa, without any obligation to teach or to reside in Pisa, and philosopher and mathematician to the grand duke. More than once the court explicitly acknowledged its primary intention of giving Galileo leisure to complete his works. The stipend was set at one thousand scudi in Florentine money. He departed from Padua on 7 September, after a final observation of the Medicean stars before dawn, and arriving in Florence on 12 September, entered the service of the grand duke. Henceforth, as Galileo himself put it, he would earn his bread from his books, "dedicated always to my lord."[38]

Two letters that Galileo received soon after the move to Florence suggest both the values and aspirations that animated the system of patronage and the status that Galileo had achieved within it. Cardinal del Monte was delighted that the grand duke had called Galileo back home with an honorable title and a noble provision, "which action is truly worthy of such a Prince, who has shown himself to be like Augustus in favoring the exceptional." For his part, Giuliano de' Medici expressed his pleasure that Galileo had received from the grand duke "that recognition which corresponds to his quality."[39] If the grand duke demonstrated his magnificence by favoring excellence, Galileo in his turn could not afford to assume that his excellence had been established once and for all. Here was a new dilemma, one that he could not avoid once he had gained the summit of the pyramid of patronage—to wit, those at the top must fight to stay there.

Galileo began to face the issue even before he arrived in Florence. His letter of 7 May had promised the grand duke "many discoveries and such as perhaps no other prince can match, for of these I have a great many and am certain I can find more as occasion presents itself."[40] But the opportunity was also a threat. Thus the thought occurred that other "planets" like the Medicean stars, which had made his fortune, might be waiting out there to be discovered. What if someone else beat him to them? What if someone else conferred another name on them so that Galileo's gift to the grand duke ceased to be unique and thereby lost its value? On 18 June 1610, in the letter that accepted the terms offered by the Grand Duke, Galileo assured Vinta that he had looked for satellites around Mars and Saturn many times as he observed them in the morning before dawn. Nearly a month before, in May, Jupiter had become invisible in the western sky at sunset as it approached conjunction. Mars and Saturn both stood high in the morning sky, though later evidence suggests that the observations Galileo alluded to were more perfunctory than his words implied. A week later, in a letter to Vincenzo Giugni, also a member of the court, he was more explicit about the object of central concern. After quoting the letter from Paris that urged him to name any further "planet" after the French king, he went on to assure the grand duke he had reserved that honor for him alone, for many observations and investigations had convinced him he would not find any more.[41]

Meanwhile, the Medicean stars did not yet prove to be his private possession. Discovering them was one thing; defining their periods would be something else. In the *Sidereus nuncius,* Galileo stated that he had not yet been able to determine the periods. Letters to Florence during the following months indicated that he was working hard on the problem, and the record of his observations confirms as much.[42] From the moment he discovered them, they became the primary object of his attention in the heavens. Almost no records of other observations survive, and there is no reason to think they ever existed. When he went to Rome in 1611, he set his telescope up every night as he traveled south, in order to measure the positions of the satellites, and he did the same every clear night in Rome. He even recorded observations for the nights of Cesi's banquet and the gathering at the Collegio Romano, at both of which he was the guest of honor.[43] He would continue to return to the satellites until 1619, always working to determine their periods more accurately, always concerned to maintain his priority. There was an issue of practical importance involved, to be sure: if he could define the periods with sufficient accuracy to permit tables of the satellites' positions to be calculated, he would have the crucial ingredient of a method to determine longitude at sea. Galileo made more than one effort to peddle this idea to the seafaring nations, and he would undoubtedly have reaped a bounteous harvest had he brought the method to perfection. More

was at stake than a practical device, however. His acknowledged position as the messenger from the heavens was threatened. His friend Cigoli reported that Magini had said that the discovery of the satellites was nothing and that all the praise would belong to the man who established their periods. Magini, the report continued, was bending every effort to be that man.[44] When Kepler pronounced the task to be almost impossible, and the Jesuits in Rome agreed with him, the glory to be won increased all the more.[45] Galileo did succeed in defining the periods in 1612. Quite unmindful of the possibility that he was giving away a lucrative advantage in regard to navigation, he rushed his discovery into print in a work to which they had no relation.[46]

Well before he had untangled the periods, his pursuit of the satellites had led him to another discovery. On 25 July 1610 Jupiter became visible to him again after its conjunction with the sun. Perforce he had to observe it before dawn, when Saturn was also visible high in the western sky. Whatever Galileo's fine words a month earlier about his many observations of Saturn, he cannot have looked at it closely before this time, for now he immediately saw, or thought he saw, exactly what he had solemnly assured the grand duke was not there. He had discovered, he wrote in excitement to Vinta, "another most fantastic marvel," which he wanted the ducal family to know about although he asked them to keep it secret until he could publish it. "I have wished to give an account of it to their Most Serene Highnesses," he continued, "so that if others chance upon it they [their Highnesses] will know that no one observed it before me."[47] Saturn, he had discovered, consists of three bodies, a central sphere plus two smaller ones immediately adjacent on either side, Galileo's interpretation of the rings as they appeared through his telescope. "Behold," he wrote elsewhere, "I have found the court of Jupiter and the two servants of this old man, who help him walk and never leave his side."[48] "I have found"—one cannot miss the significance of the personal pronoun. To protect his priority, he concealed the discovery in a cipher and sent it to Prague, where it thoroughly excited the emperor. When Galileo sent the solution to the cipher in the fall, without waiting for publication, he received word in return that it had given the emperor "no less pleasure than amazement" and that the emperor had immediately set Kepler the task of confirming it.[49] Although we do not have any explicit evidence, there is no reason to think the new observation aroused any less pleasure and amazement in Florence than it did in Prague. Thus scarcely a month before he formally entered the grand duke's service, he began to fulfill his promise of many more discoveries, the first installment against the never-ending demand to justify his status as a client likely to confer glory upon his patron.

Exactly three weeks and one day after Galileo sent the solution of the Saturn cipher to Prague, Benedetto Castelli sat down in Brescia to write the letter quoted at the opening of this article, asking about the appearances of Venus and Mars. Six days later, on 11 December 1610, Galileo sent a second cipher to Prague, "of another thing just observed by me which involves the outcome of the most important issue in astronomy and, in particular, contains in itself a strong argument for the Pythagorean and Copernican system."[50] The cipher concealed the sentence, "The mother of love emulates the figures of Cynthia," that is, Venus reveals phases like those of the moon. Galileo sent the cipher not only to Giuliano de' Medici in Prague but to at least three others.[51] At the end of December he wrote two long letters, one to Father Clavius in Rome and one to Castelli, describing in detail the observations of Venus that he had been making over the past three months— its appearance, round and very small, as it emerged in the western sky after its superior conjunction with the sun, its steady increase in size, its loss of roundness as it approached maximum elongation, and its assumption of a crescent shape as it passed maximum elongation, where it was standing at the date of his letter. He went on to predict its future changes of appearance as it went through inferior conjunction and proceeded through the rest of a complete cycle.[52] Towards Castelli he assumed an avuncular tone:

> O how many consequences and ones of such import have I deduced, my Master Benedetto, from these and from my other observations. You almost made me laugh when you said that with these manifest observations the obstinate could be convinced. Well then, don't you know that to convince those capable of reason and anxious to know the truth the other demonstrations already produced were enough, but to convince the obstinate who care only for the empty applause of the stupid and dull crowd, the testimony of the stars themselves, come down to earth to discuss themselves, would not suffice? Let us then endeavor to learn something for ourselves and rest satisfied with this alone, but as for advancing ourselves in popular opinion or gaining the assent of philosophers in books, let us give up the desire and the hope.

Castelli's letter and Galileo's activities during December raise several questions. Had Galileo received Castelli's letter from Brescia before he sent off the cipher on 11 December? We do not know, but it was easily possible. Brescia is about eighty kilometers east of Milan and about the same distance, via Bologna, from Florence as Venice is. Repeatedly, when he was in Padua, Galileo answered letters from Florence six days after they were written, and officials in Florence answered him after the same intervals. There are instances of letters making the trip in five days. Galileo himself, no longer a young man, spent six days on the journey when he moved from Padua to Florence in September. Castelli had indicated on another occasion that Brescia did not have regular mail service to Flo-

rence; that time he had sent his letter with a friend to Milan for posting.[53] In the silence surrounding the episode, we can readily imagine any number of possible scenarios, such as a friend's setting out for Bologna, or even Florence. This would have put the letter in Galileo's hands on 11 December. The coincidence of Galileo's cipher leaving on exactly the day that Castelli's letter would most likely have arrived makes it difficult to believe that Galileo wrote his cipher in ignorance of Castelli's communication.

A more important question concerns the truth of Galileo's assertions to Clavius and to Castelli at the end of December, as well as to others later, that he had been observing Venus for three months, that is, from the beginning of October, long before Castelli wrote. Again we cannot answer with assurance. Aside from Galileo's claims, there is no evidence whatever for such observations, but silence does not yield a definite answer. However, there is considerable evidence that casts doubt on Galileo's statements. At the beginning of October Galileo was still completing his transfer to Florence. He did not systematically resume his interrupted observations of the satellites of Jupiter until the middle of November, though he made three isolated observations on 25 October and 4 and 5 November. It is true that Jupiter presented a problem that he did not experience with Venus. Jupiter was then visible in the east in the morning, and the house in which he lived temporarily until the end of October did not, as he complained, have a view to the east.[54] In contrast, Venus stood well up in the western sky in the autumn of 1610, so there was not any obstacle, as far as we know, to seeing it. Not only is there no mention of such observations, however, but in the middle of November, together with his translation of the cipher about Saturn, Galileo informed Giuliano de' Medici that he did not have any new discoveries about the other planets to report.[55] If he was in fact observing Venus at that time, a time when its gibbous appearance would have been in flat contradiction to Ptolemaic expectations, it is hard to reconcile his words with the excitement of the new cipher composed less than a month later.

Possibly relevant here is another statement by Galileo. In his letter in late December to Castelli about the observations of Venus, he wrote that he had been observing Mars for four months. We might note in passing what this dating implies about the truthfulness of his assertion to the grand duke the previous June that he had observed Mars many times. Be that as it may, in the autumn of 1610 Mars stood high in the morning sky, observable when Jupiter and Saturn were observable, and therefore possibly subject as well to the same obstacles that interrupted observation of them through September and October. I say "possibly subject" because Mars was west of the meridian in the morning, and if Galileo was moved to get up before dawn to look at Mars, the lack of an eastern view would not have presented a problem. I should add that Galileo's exact words were "four months," which take us back to the end of August, when he did record observations of Jupiter made in Padua as late as 7 September, the morning he left. He could easily have looked at Mars at the same time. In assessing the truth of his claims, moreover, we must also bear in mind the ease with which he could set up his telescope for the sort of qualitative observations in question here. Recall that in order to observe the satellites of Jupiter, he set up his telescope every night as he journeyed south to Rome in March of 1611. The domestic upheaval of the move to Florence and the house that lacked a proper view may have posed obstacles to observations during the early fall of 1610, but they were not insuperable obstacles. Nevertheless, the preponderance of evidence, especially the statement to Giuliano de' Medici in mid November that he had not made any new discoveries about the other planets, decidedly inclines me to doubt the truth of Galileo's assertions.

The evidence thus suggests that at the time Galileo began his celestial observations, he had not formulated a program of systematic observations designed to settle the Copernican issue. Rather, as I have asserted, he saw the telescope more as an instrument of patronage than as an instrument of astronomy. When Galileo, having seized what the moon and stars could quickly offer, had turned his telescope on the next brightest object in the evening sky, Jupiter, early in January, Venus was visible in the predawn sky. For a Copernican, Venus was in a critical part of its orbit, past maximum elongation, approaching superior conjunction, and thus exhibiting a shape incompatible with the Ptolemaic system. As we have seen, however, Jupiter had offered something quite different, an incomparable present to the grand duke, and Galileo had not paused to look further. We have two accounts of his early telescopic discoveries, by informed friends, apparently written before publication of the **Sidereus nuncius** and thus independent of it.[56] They bring up all the major discoveries announced by the book; they do not, however, mention observations of Venus, thereby tending to confirm the reading of Galileo's own silence as due to his not having noticed the planet's phases. In fact, the **Sidereus nuncius** was not totally silent about Venus. Galileo mentions it once, in his discussion of irradiation, his theory of an optical phenomenon within the eye that makes stars appear larger than they are. He suggests that his readers observe how small stars look when they first emerge from the twilight at sunset. "Venus itself, when visible in broad daylight," he adds, "is so small as scarcely to appear equal to a star of the sixth magnitude."[57] If he paused to consider its apparent shape at that time, he made no mention of it. By the time he completed the **Sidereus nuncius,** Venus was too close to the sun to be visible.

When Venus reappeared in the western sky near the end of July (judging by the angular distance from the sun when Jupiter was visible to Galileo), a few days after Jupiter reappeared in the east before dawn, Galileo was intently observing the satellites of Jupiter so that he could define their periods. At this time he also made his discovery about Saturn. He never claimed that he observed Venus during the month it was visible to him before he left Padua. The move to Florence with its attendant upheaval accompanied the steady rise of Venus in the western sky. When Galileo was finally ready to resume regular observations, he riveted his attention once more on the satellites of Jupiter; his records show almost daily observations of them beginning in the middle of November, that is, predawn observations while Venus was visible in the evening sky. All during this period Galileo seems to have used his telescope to further his advancement rather than Copernicanism.

Galileo probably read Castelli's letter on 11 December 1610, against the background I have described of eighteen months dominated by the telescope and the new possibilities it had opened to him. He had been attacked by enemies and challenged by rivals. It was Benedetto Castelli, however, his devoted student and disciple, who unintentionally delivered the unkindest cut of all, by pointing out that in his pursuit of celestial novelties to dazzle the grand duke, Galileo had neglected a phenomenon of supreme importance, which had been there all the time, virtually asking to be observed. Galileo must have understood instantly the significance of Castelli's query, a significance not confined to astronomy. Less than a month later, as he deciphered the anagram for Giuliano de' Medici, he explained the significance as he saw it. "From this marvelous experience we have a sensible and sure proof of two major suppositions which have been doubted until now by the greatest minds in the world"—namely, that the planets are dark by nature, and that Venus and Mercury revolve around the sun as Copernicus believed.[58] The subordinate clause in the sentence is no less important than the main one. The premise on which Galileo's position in Florence rested was his status as the one who revealed things the greatest minds in the world had not known. Was he now to admit that someone else, indeed one of his students, had understood what he had not? It appears evident to me that he instantly decided no. With good fortune but also with much effort, he had won the position he desired. At that point he had held it exactly three months, and he could well have felt insecure. The cipher was his announcement that he did not intend to surrender it lightly.

As we know, his tactics were completely successful. The very existence of Castelli's letter was not known for another two centuries and has been generally ignored since it was published. Castelli, who was not only a devoted follower of Galileo but his client, who hoped to exploit Galileo's new prominence to move himself from the monastery in Brescia into a life in science, was not one to raise claims. When Galileo wrote his first letter on sunspots in May 1612, he described the phases of Venus "discovered by me about two years ago."[59] His addition of three more months to his priority was of no great import. No one came forward to dispute any aspect of his claim.

I have suggested that the episode casts light on Galileo's commitment to Copernicanism. It is frequently asserted—indeed I think it is the majority opinion—that Galileo remained unconvinced of the truth of the Copernican system until the telescope revealed new evidence to him.[60] I see good reason to doubt this proposition. The *Sidereus nuncius* was an explicitly Copernican work, but when he wrote it, Galileo was not yet aware of any of the telescopic observations that he would later point to as decisive evidence. Castelli's letter, written by a student who had left Padua in 1607, well before Galileo's involvement with the telescope, is the expression of one Copernican who understood that he was writing to another. If my analysis of the episode is correct, Galileo composed the cipher asserting that Venus displays phases on the sole basis of his prior commitment to the Copernican system, which allowed him to predict what he had not then seen. His letter to Castelli did, after all, insist that even without Venus there was plenty of evidence to convince those capable of reason.[61]

The cipher he sent on 11 December had a double advantage. It protected his priority, but it concealed the statement he was making in case he might need to withdraw it. Before Galileo wrote to Clavius and Castelli at the end of December, he had two and a half weeks in which to observe. Fate had returned to his side once more. During those two and a half weeks Venus was going through a critical portion of its orbit, in which at maximum elongation it gradually changed from a slightly gibbous shape to a thick crescent. At no point during December was its shape compatible with the Ptolemaic system. Galileo could also call upon the single observation of Venus mentioned in the *Sidereus nuncius,* when he had seen the planet small and fully round as it approached superior conjunction, and seizing its significance now, fit it into the Copernican pattern. By the end of December he was sure enough to send the full argument, not only to Castelli, but to Clavius in Rome. He had not earlier committed himself so far as to send Clavius the cipher. I should add, in partial support of the accepted position, that Galileo's sudden eagerness in January to carry the Copernican argument to Rome, the first serious step down the path that would lead him, two decades later, into the dungeon of the Inquisition, may very well have stemmed from his observation of Venus's phases.[62]

My primary interest in the episode focuses, however, on the light it casts on the system of patronage. As I realize all too well, even to bring the matter up is to court hostility. So well have we defended the pantheon of science from any suggestion of stain that only after I had pursued this question nearly to its conclusion did I discover it had been raised once before, nearly a century ago, by an Italian scholar, Raffaello Caverni. Caverni, who wrote during the springtime of Italian unity, was summarily drummed right out of the Italian learned community for casting a shadow on the name of a national hero.[63] Since I have no desire to suffer a similar fate, I trust that I am far enough removed from the seat of such emotions. I do wish to emphasize that it is not my purpose in any way to call Galileo's position in the history of science into question. If my analysis is correct, it does take away one small part of his reputation, though nothing that pertains to his major accomplishment. I reject, however, any implication that similar detailed analyses will dissolve away the whole. It appears to me that some degree of disillusionment is likely to accompany most examinations of the social setting of science. By their nature, they lead us out of the context of justification and into the context of discovery, where we see the play of human motives instead of the finished products of reason. To show that Galileo was no plaster saint does not discredit him. The *Dialogue* remains the *Dialogue,* the *Discourses* remain the *Discourses,* and nothing in the episode of Venus even begins to undermine the validity of his enormous achievement.

Nevertheless, we do face the question of why Galileo acted as he appears to have done. Why did a man of so many accomplishments and achievements strive compulsively to monopolize all discoveries with the telescope? In different circumstances with different details and more justice, he would before long repeat his performance in regard to the discovery of sunspots. Why did Galileo feel that he had to take all the credit? I suspect no single explanation suffices to answer these questions. Surely Galileo's aggressive personality must enter into consideration. I do want to argue, however, that part of the answer has to do with patronage. The ultimate truth about what I have been calling the system of patronage is that it was not a system at all. It was a set of dyadic relations between patrons and clients, each of them unique. Patronage had no institutions and little if any formal structure. It embodied no guarantees. The relation between patron and client was voluntary on both sides and subject always to disintegration. Past performance counted only to the extent that it promised more in the future. A client's only claim on a patron was his capacity to illuminate further the magnificence of the man who recognized his value and encouraged him. From our perspective, Galileo was secure beyond possible challenge, and without loss to himself could have acknowledged Castelli's critical role in the discovery of the phases of Venus. Thus, in his second letter on sunspots, Galileo did credit Castelli with the method of drawing the spots that he described, and he did not suffer any consequent loss of reputation.[64] No doubt Galileo's perspective differed from ours, and living in early seventeenth-century Italian society, he may have understood its imperatives better than we do. In 1610 the **Dialogue** and the **Discourses** existed only as aspirations. His one serious accomplishment was the telescope plus the **Sidereus nuncius** it had produced. How far could he ride that horse? Consider the reply Galileo received from Antonio Santini, one of the men to whom he sent the cipher about Venus. Accepting the promise of the cipher without question, Santini assured Galileo that he "was born to honor our century with new discoveries and with the perfection of your industry to enrich the world of knowledge with so many noble and hidden objects that I am persuaded you walk out there among those lights."[65] Such a perception, spread abroad through the world of culture, was the very rock on which Galileo's position as a client stood, and Santini's letter is by itself evidence that the phases of Venus contributed to sustaining that perception. As John North has said of Galileo, "He gave glory to senates and princes, in the expectation of rewards, and it was important that he not only reveal new truths, but also master the art of establishing priority in his discoveries."[66] Such an argument does not excuse Galileo's apparent dishonesty in the matter of Venus. It may help us to understand what drove him to it.

Patronage cannot provide the universal key to an understanding of the social history of the Scientific Revolution. Some figures in the movement were not sustained by patronage, and it is not yet clear how many were so supported. Nevertheless, patronage was perhaps the most pervasive institution of preindustrial society; it animated the worlds of art, music, and literature.[67] Only now are scholars beginning to chart its course in the science of the age, and we have every reason to expect that it will prove to be very important there as well. I would like to suggest, that patronage, together with other practices that the age itself reveals to us, may be the avenue most likely to lead us into a fruitful social history of the Scientific Revolution, a movement to which the present generation of scholars has devoted itself extensively. In our investigations, it appears to me, we have allowed ourselves to be dominated excessively by concepts derived in the nineteenth century which are more applicable to that century and our own than to Galileo's age. Efforts to impose them on the seventeenth century have appeared forced and largely barren, and I want to propose, not as a new dogmatism, but as a topic for discussion, the possibility that we need to come at the problem from a different angle, using seventeenth-century categories instead of nineteenth-century ones. Patronage was certainly a seventeenth-century category. I hope that the episode of Galileo and the phases of Venus reveals to others as it has to me the promise that patronage offers as one device by which we can probe the social dimension of the Scientific Revolution.

Notes

[1] Castelli to Galileo, 5 Dec. 1610; *Opere di Galileo Galilei,* ed. Antonio Favaro, 20 vols. (Florence: G. Barbera, 1890-1909), Vol. X, pp. 480-483. (Unless otherwise specified, all translations are mine.) Two versions of this letter exist among Galileo's papers, both apparently in Castelli's hand, one labeled (by Castelli) "copy," though its wording differs modestly from the other's. Castelli first dated the original 5 Nov. 1610 but altered it at some time to 5 Dec. I am strongly inclined to treat the November date as a slip and to believe that Castelli made his correction at the time rather than later, which might call the December date into question. For other interpretations, which I find unconvincing, see Raffaello Caverni, *Storia del metodo sperimentale in Italia,* 6 vols. (Florence, 1891-1900), Vol. II, pp. 359-360; Antonio Favaro, "Galileo Galilei, Benedetto Castelli e la scoperta delle fasi di Venere," *Archeion,* 1919, *1:*283-296.

[2] Galileo, *Dialogue Concerning the Two Chief World Systems,* trans. Stillman Drake, (2nd ed., Berkeley: Univ. California Press, 1967), p. 462; cf. pp. 349-355. The argument from the approaches and recessions of Venus embodied its phases (see p. 321), which furnish the only rigorous part of the argument.

[3] Guidobaldo was a recognized authority in mathematics whose friendship with Galileo rested almost entirely on their shared interest in mathematics. Their correspondence concerning Galileo's appointment in Padua (*Opere,* Vol. X, pp. 26-54), however, convinces me that his being the Marchese del Monte, brother of the Cardinal del Monte, was the significant factor there.

[4] For Galileo's correspondents during the Paduan years see *Opere,* Vol. X, pp. 55-256; for his private students see Antonio Favaro, *Galileo e lo studio di Padova* (Florence: Le Monnier, 1883), Vol. II, pp. 184-192. Galileo's initial salary at Padua was 180 florins, which according to my calculations somewhat more than doubled his previous salary at Pisa. For the Paduan salary, actually calculated in lire, at the rate of five lire per florin, see *ibid.,* p. 142. For the silver in these lire, see Nicolò Papadopoli, *Le monete di Venezia,* 4 vols. (Venice/Bologna: Ongania, 1893-1907), Vol. II, pp. 393-422. For the silver equivalent of the Pisan salary, see Giuseppe Parenti, *Prime ricerche sulla rivoluzione dei prezzi in Firenze* (Florence: C. Cya, 1939), p. 58. My calculations from the exchange rates as found in José-Gentil da Silva, *Banque et crédit en Italie aux XVIIe siecle,* 2 vols. (Paris: Klincksieck, 1969), Vol. I, pp. 296, 320, gave a similar result (1:2.13, as against 1:2.4). Experts advise that such calculations involve many pitfalls.

[5] Quirini to Galileo, 24 Aug. 1599; Sagredo to Galileo, 1 Sept. 1699; *Opere,* Vol. X, pp. 76, 77.

[6] Barbolani to Ferdinand I, 29 Oct. 1605, 10 June 1606; Saracinelli to Galileo, 26 May 1606; unsigned to Vinta, 12 Aug. 1606; *ibid.,* pp. 147-161.

[7] Galileo to Cristina, 8 Dec. 1606; *ibid.,* pp. 164-166.

[8] See Galileo's accounts, *ibid.,* Vol. XIX, p. 155, line 194; Galileo to Gonzaga, 22 May 1604; *ibid.,* Vol. X, pp. 106-107.

[9] Giugni to Galileo, 4 June 1605; Galileo to Cosimo, 29 Dec. 1605; *ibid.,* pp. 144, 153-154.

[10] Galileo to Picchena, 6 Nov. 1607; *ibid.,* pp. 185-186. Correspondence about the lodestone occupies most of pp. 185-213.

[11] Galileo to Vinta, 3 May 1608; *ibid.,* pp. 205-209.

[12] Galileo to Cristina, Sept. 1608; *ibid.,* p. 222.

[13] Galileo to Vinta, 23 May 1608; *ibid.,* p. 209.

[14] Galileo to Vinta, 30 May 1608; *ibid.,* p. 212.

[15] Galileo to Cosimo, 26 Feb. 1609; *ibid.,* pp. 230-231.

[16] Galileo to "S. Vesp." (Geraldini?), Feb. 1609; *ibid.,* pp. 231-234.

[17] See Albert Van Helden, *The Invention of the Telescope* (Transactions of the American Philosophical Society, 67. 4) (Philadelphia: APS, 1977); and Van Helden, "The Telescope in the Seventeenth Century," *Isis,* 1974, *65:*38-58.

[18] Galileo to Landucci, 29 Aug. 1609; *Opere,* Vol. X, pp. 253-254. Cf. the independent account in Priuli's chronicle, cited in Edward Rosen, "The Authenticity of Galileo's Letter to Landucci," *Modern Language Quarterly,* 1951, *12:*482.

[19] Rosen, "Authenticity," p. 481; on Cremoni see Favaro, *Galileo e Padova,* Vol. II, pp. 424-425.

[20] Piccolomini to Galileo, 29 Aug., 19 Sept. 1609; *Opere,* Vol. X, 255, 258-259.

[21] Bartoli to Vinta, 26 Sept., 7 Nov. 1609; *ibid.,* pp. 259-260, 267. In strict usage, the word *telescope* is an anachronism before April 1611, when it was put into currency at the banquet in Rome that Federigo Cesi gave in honor of Galileo; see Edward Rosen, *The Naming of the Telescope* (New York: Schuman, 1947).

[22] Galileo to Vinta, 7 May, 19 Mar. 1610; *Opere,* Vol. X, pp. 350, 301. In the first draft of the second letter, the number was more than 100 (*ibid.,* p. 298).

[23] In the *Sidereus nuncius,* composed in early February 1610, Galileo spoke of observations made over the past two months; see Galileo, *The Starry Messenger,* in *Discoveries and Opinions of Galileo,* trans. Stillman Drake (Garden City, N.Y.: Doubleday, 1957), p. 31. Guglielmo Righini, in *Contributo alla interpretazione scientifica dell'opera astronomica di Galileo* (Istituto e Museo di Storia della Scienze, monografia 2) (Florence: Istituto e Museo di Storia della Scienza, 1978 [1980]), concludes that Galileo probably began observing early in October. His argument, also set forth in Righini, "New Light on Galileo's Lunar Observations," in *Reason, Experiment, and Mysticism in the Scientific Revolution,* ed. M. L. Righini Bonelli and William R. Shea (New York: Science History, 1975), pp. 59-76, is challenged by Owen Gingerich, "Dissertatio cum Professore Righini et Sidereo nuncio," pp. 77-88. More recently, Ewan A. Whitaker, by comparing modern photographs of the moon with Galileo's drawings, convincingly places the date at the end of November, in agreement with Galileo's assertion; see Whitaker, "Galileo's Lunar Observations and the Dating of the Composition of *Sidereus nuncius,*" *Journal for the History of Astronomy,* 1978, *9:*155-169.

[24] On a report published in 1608 mentioning that the new eyeglass revealed stars invisible to the naked eye, see Edward Rosen, "Stillman Drake's *Discoveries and Opinions of Galileo,*" *Journal of the History of Ideas,* 1957, *18:*446. On Thomas Harriot's observations of the moon in England by August 1609, see Van Helden, *Invention of the Telescope,* p. 27.

[25] Galileo to Antonio de' Medici, 7 Jan. 1610; *Opere,* Vol. X, p. 277; cf. Galileo, *Sidereus nuncius,* in *Opere,* Vol. III, Pt. 1, p. 17. Favaro guessed that the letter's recipient, not named, was Antonio de' Medici. In an article filled with information, Stillman Drake opines that the recipient was instead Enea Piccolomini; see Drake, "Galileo's First Telescopic Observations," *Journal for the History of Astronomy,* 1976, *7:*153-168; cf. Drake, "Galileo and Satellite Prediction," *ibid.,* 1979, *10:*75-95.

[26] Galileo to Antonio de' Medici, 7 Jan. 1610, p. 277. In the *Sidereus nuncius,* Galileo stated that he was already using the new instrument on 7 Jan.; Galileo, *Starry Messenger,* trans. Drake, p. 51. Drake argues instead that Galileo used his twenty-power instrument; Drake, "Galileo's First Observations," pp. 158-159.

[27] Galileo, *Osservazioni,* in *Opere,* Vol. III, Pt. 2, p. 427.

[28] Galileo to Vinta, 30 Jan. 1610; *ibid.,* Vol. X, p. 280.

[29] Vinta to Galileo, 6 Feb. 1610; Galileo to Vinta, 13 Feb. 1610; *ibid.,* pp. 281, 282-284.

[30] Galileo, *Sidereus nuncius ibid.,* Vol. III, Pt. 1, p. 9, cf. p. 46; Vinta to Galileo, 20 Feb. 1610; *ibid.,* Vol. X, pp. 284-285.

[31] Galileo to Vinta, 19 March 1610; *ibid.,* p. 298.

[32] Galileo, *Starry Messenger,* trans. Drake, p. 23.

[33] See among the letters in *Opere,* Vol. X, p. 318, to Vol. XI, p. 208.

[34] Manso to Galileo, 18 Mar. 1610; Del Monte to Galileo, 16 June 1610; *ibid.,* Vol. X, pp. 296, 372; and Lower to Harriot, 21 June 1610; quoted in John Roche, "Harriot, Galileo, and Jupiter's Satellites," *Archives internationales d'histoire des sciences,* 1982, *32*:16.

[35] Galileo to Giugni, 25 June 1610; *Opere,* Vol. X, p. 381.

[36] John North, "Thomas Harriot and the First Telescopic Observations of Sunspots," in *Thomas Harriot: Renaissance Scientist,* ed. John W. Shirley (Oxford: Clarendon Press, 1974), p. 134.

[37] Galileo to Vinta, 13 March 1610; *Opere,* Vol. X, p. 389.

[38] Galileo to Vinta, 7 May 1610; *Opere,* Vol. X, pp. 350-351; as trans. by Drake in *Discoveries and Opinions,* p. 62. If calculations are made like those in note 4 above, the stipend from the grand duke appears a bit less than 50% higher than Galileo's final promised salary at the University of Padua. Galileo gave up the additional income earned from private lessons and taking in students, an income he probably exaggerated in the letter to Vinta. To insure his economic security, he abandoned his common-law wife in Padua, and he protected himself from the threat of dowries by placing his two daughters in a convent.

[39] Del Monte to Galileo, 9 Oct. 1610; Giuliano to Galileo, 6 Sept. 1610; *Opere,* Vol. X, pp. 444, 427.

[40] Galileo to Vinta, 7 May 1610; *ibid.,* p. 351; as trans. by Drake in *Discoveries and Opinions,* p. 62, modified slightly (esp. in rendering *invenzioni* as *discoveries*).

[41] Galileo to Vinta, 18 June 1610; Galileo to Giugni, 25 June 1610; *Opere,* Vol. X, pp. 374, 382.

[42] Galileo, *Starry Messenger,* trans. Drake, p. 56; Galileo to Vinta, 19 Mar, 7 May 1610; *Opere,* Vol. X, pp. 299, 352.

[43] Galileo, *Osservazioni,* in *Opere,* Vol. III, Pt. 2, pp. 442-444.

[44] Cigoli to Galileo, 23 Aug. 1611; *ibid.,* Vol. XI, p. 175.

[45] Galileo to Vinta, 1 Apr. 1611; *ibid.,* p. 80.

[46] Galileo, *Discourse on Bodies in Water,* trans. Thomas Salusbury, ed. Stillman Drake (Urbana: Univ. Illinois Press, 1960), pp. 1-2. See also the excellent account of this considerable achievement in Drake, "Galileo and Satellite Prediction," (cit. n. 25). Measured by our present figures, Galileo's periods, published in 1612, were accurate for each of the four satellites to well less than one part in a thousand; see Righini, *Interpretazione scientifica* (cit. n. 23), p. 56.

[47] Galileo to Vinta, 30 July 1610; *Opere,* Vol. X, p. 410.

[48] Galileo to Giuliano de' Medici, 13 Nov. 1610; *ibid.,* p. 474.

[49] Hasdale to Galileo, 19 Dec. 1610; *ibid.,* p. 491.

[50] Galileo to Giuliano de' Medici, 11 Dec. 1610; *ibid.,* p. 483.

[51] See the references to the cipher in Santini to Galileo, 25 Dec. 1610; Magini to Galileo, 28 Dec. 1610; and Gualdo to Galileo, 29 Dec. 1610; *ibid.,* pp. 495, 496, 498.

[52] Galileo to Clavius, 30 Dec. 1610; Galileo to Castelli, 30 Dec. 1610; *ibid.,* pp. 499-500, 502-504.

[53] Castelli to Galileo, 27 Sept. 1610; *ibid.,* p. 436.

[54] Galileo to Giuliano de' Medici, 1 Oct. 1610; *ibid.,* p. 441.

[55] Galileo to Giuliano de' Medici, 13 Nov. 1610; *ibid.,* p. 474.

[56] Sarpi to Leschassier, 16 Mar. 1610; Manso to Beni, Mar. 1610; *ibid.,* pp. 272, 291-296. Paolo Beni lived in Padua; Manso's letter replied to his account of the observations and discussed them in great detail.

[57] Galileo, *Starry Messenger,* trans. Drake, p. 46. An astronomer friend assures me that such an observation in broad daylight is entirely possible.

[58] Galileo to Giuliano de' Medici, 1 Jan. 1611; *Opere,* Vol. XI, p. 12.

[59] Galileo, *Letters on Sunspots,* in *Discoveries and Opinions,* trans. Drake, p. 93; on Castelli's attitude see, e.g., Castelli to Galileo, 24 Dec. 1610; *Opere,* Vol. X, pp. 493-494.

[60] See, e.g., Willy Hartner, "Galileo's Contribution to Astronomy," in *Galileo: Man of Science,* ed. Ernan McMullin (New York: Basic Books, 1968), pp. 178-194.

[61] Cf. Galileo to Giuliano de' Medici, 1 Jan. 1611; *Opere,* Vol. XI, p. 11.

[62] See Galileo to Vinta, 15 Jan. 1611; *ibid.,* p. 27.

[63] Caverni, *Storia* (cit. n. 1), Vol. II, pp. 357-361. See also Favaro's passionate repudiation of Caverni, "Galileo e la scoperta delle fasi"; and Giorgio Tabarroni's appreciative introduction to Caverni (New York: Johnson Reprints, 1971), Vol. I, pp. vii-xxii. Even a sympathetic observer such as Tabarroni regards Caverni's passage on the phases of Venus as a "malicious and unfounded accusation" (p. xviii).

[64] Galileo, *Letters on Sunspots,* trans. Drake, p. 115.

[65] Santini to Galileo, 25 Dec. 1610; *Opere,* Vol. X, p. 495.

[66] John North, "Thomas Harriot and the First Telescopic Observations of Sunspots," p. 130.

[67] See Werner L. Gundesheimer, "Patronage in the Renaissance: An Exploratory Approach," in *Patronage in the Renaissance,* ed. Guy F. Lytle and Stephen Orgel (Princeton: Princeton Univ. Press, 1981), pp. 3-23.

Charles E. Hummel (essay date 1986)

SOURCE: "Galileo: Physics and Astronomy," in *The Galileo Connection: Resolving Conflicts between Science and the Bible,* Intervarsity Press, 1986, pp. 81-102.

[*In the following excerpt, Hummel outlines Galileo's early years, and describes the steps in Galileo's own particular scientific method.*]

> *Philosophy is written in this grand*
> *book of the universe,*
> *which stands continually open to our gaze. . . .*
> *It is written in the language of mathematics.*
> GALILEO GALILEI

Renaissance Italy was a collection of states with a wide variety of governmental structures. In one the people might hold power; another would have a hereditary ruler. Such diversity fostered the idea that there could be more than one way to govern. Differences of opinion on economic and social issues flourished. In that relatively open society, ready in many areas to consider new ideas, Galileo Galilei began his education.

In two arenas, however, the strong hand of authority maintained a firm grip. The Roman Catholic Church had a monopoly on religious life, and Aristotelian philosophy dominated science in the universities. Yet in Galileo's time both institutions found themselves on the defensive against swirling currents of Reformation and Renaissance. Those currents converged in the life and work of this controversial figure sometimes called the father of modern science. Few episodes in the history of science have generated more intense debate than the ecclesiastical condemnation of Copernicus's astronomy in 1616 and the trial of Galileo in 1633. In one form or another that controversy continues unabated almost four centuries later.

Galileo was of average height, a heavyset man quick both to anger and to return to good humor. He was a passionate, powerful character who could dominate any room or discussion. His talent and wit won a variety of illustrious friends in university, court and church circles, and among artists, musicians and craftsmen. At the same time his biting sarcasm against those whose arguments were vulnerable to his scientific discoveries made him some formidable enemies. Galileo thrived on debate, the clash of minds and words. He knew that although theories have to be proved, people have to be persuaded. His professional life was spent not only in observing and calculating but also in arguing and convincing. His goal was to promote as well as develop a new scientific world view.

Galileo's career divides easily into three main periods. The first (1564-1610) includes his life as a student and professor at Pisa and then Padua. The middle years (1610-1632) extend from his return to Florence to the publication of his *Dialogue.* The final period (1633-1643), beginning with his trial, covers the decade of his house arrest. . . .

Early Years

Galileo came from an old noble Florentine family that had seen better times. His father, Vincenzio, was a musician who performed well on the lute and was also interested in music theory. He studied the new music, especially problems of instrumental music with a single voice. Conducting experiments with a specially constructed single-stringed instrument, he discovered a mathematical law contradicting the fundamental assumption of traditional music theory.

Vincenzio engaged in sharp controversy with Gioseffo Zarlino, an acknowledged musical authority with whom he had studied for two years in Venice.[1] Following an acrimonious correspondence, Vincenzio wrote a *Dialogue on Ancient and Modern Music.* When Zarlino prevented its publication in Venice, the volume was published in Florence. For Vincenzio, even an ingenious and authoritative theory could not replace a trained musician's ear. His experimental approach and polemic writing must have made an impression on his son, who dealt with issues and opponents in the same way some years later.

In 1562 Vincenzio married Giulia Ammannati, a woman of intelligence and education, in Pisa, where he settled. The first of seven children, Galileo was born on February 15, 1564, the year of Shakespeare's birth. He grew up in an artistic home, sharing many interests with his father, from whom he derived a love of music and a keen interest in mathematics. Young Galileo became a fine lute player and competent organist; his musical background may have been useful in his scientific work. He was fond of poetry and loved to draw and paint. He picked up his father's confidence in experiments and enjoyed making mechanical devices, just as Newton did a century later. Galileo's mechanical bent persisted. As a scientist he constructed instruments both to test his theories and to make practical use of his discoveries.

In 1574 the family moved to Florence. Galileo attended school at a famous Benedictine monastery, Santa Maria at Vallombrosa, where he received the usual Renaissance education and religious training. When Galileo considered entering monastic life, his father wasted no time in diverting him from that course. Nevertheless, the boy continued his studies with the monks until 1581.

At the age of seventeen Galileo entered the school of medicine at the University of Pisa. At that time Italy was rich in centers of learning, with thirteen universities (in contrast to the three in England and Scotland). Yet for all the discoveries and innovations of the Renaissance, academic instruction was largely authoritarian. Like most established powers, it discouraged creative thinking and viewed new outlooks with disfavor. With Aristotelianism reigning supreme in philosophy and science, the golden age of Greece might be recaptured but never surpassed. All teaching took place in Latin, which students were expected to speak outside class as well. The academic establishment looked back to tradition, as yet unaware of the new world on its doorstep.

As long as the only books were manuscripts, universities could maintain a monopoly on science.[2] After about 1500 that situation changed rapidly. Printers in many cities made their investments in equipment pay off by keeping their new presses running. They issued inexpensive books appealing to wider audiences, soliciting works of public interest from new authors. With new opportunities to communicate practical information, the domain of useful science spread far from the centers of learning, often independently of them.

The outpouring of cheap books benefited the universities least. Having flourished for centuries without multiple copies of texts, they continued to base their instruction on lectures and debates. Handbooks and compendiums comprised the main texts. The task of the natural philosophers (that is, the scientists) was to trans-mit that tradition to students, not to experiment or innovate. Except for medicine, the important scientific advances in sixteenth-century Italy occurred outside the universities. The new astronomies of Copernicus and Tycho Brahe and developments in mechanics and physics rarely made their way into the curriculum. In some respects university science was less advanced than it had been two centuries earlier because it failed to keep up with these changes.

In such an academic climate, young Galileo encountered both the tradition of the first-century Roman physician Galen and the more ancient authority of Aristotle. Even as a student he developed an independence of thought and an argumentative style that earned him the nickname "The Wrangler." His running controversy with Aristotelian professors lasted almost half a century.

Meanwhile Galileo's interest in medicine wanted. When his funds ran out in 1584 he left Pisa without a degree. Wanting to concentrate on mathematics and physics, Galileo pursued the study of Euclid and Archimedes under the tutelage of his father's friend Ostilio Ricci. Within a year Galileo constructed an improved hydro-static balance which brought him to the attention of the nobles of Florence. His new theorems concerning the center of gravity of certain solids earned Galileo his first recognition abroad. Both the problem and his method of solving it showed the influence of Archimedes, to whom Galileo frequently turned for inspiration and guidance.[5] Although not unknown during the Middle Ages, Archimedes' works had received little attention before the sixteenth century. During his stay at home Galileo also developed a love for the classics and an interest in popular literature.

Professor at Pisa and Padua

After several years of scientific successes, Galileo returned to Pisa in 1589 with a three-year appointment as professor of mathematics. As he studied natural phenomena, he recognized the crucial importance of mechanics, the science of motion which was the simplest kind of change so important in Aristotle's natural philosophy. But for Galileo an exact understanding of movement would play a much larger role: the first and indispensable kind of knowledge of the physical universe. The mathematicians, guided by Euclid and Archimedes, viewed the world in terms of geometrical shapes and mathematical laws to account for observations. But their status was inferior to that of the natural philosophers, whose province was explanation of the physical world. These Aristotelians were not prepared to have a mere mathematician invade their field of physics and argue for new concepts of motion.

Galileo soon began writing an untitled treatise, now referred to as *De motu* (*On Motion*), which was not published but circulated privately.[4] He attacked Aristotle's concept of two classes of motion: *natural,* as in the fall of an object to earth, and *violent,* as in the flight of a projectile. Galileo introduced imaginary rotations of massive spheres and defined "neutral" motions, an idea that eventually led to his concept of inertia in terrestrial physics. His genius enabled him to devise "thought experiments" by imagining idealized situations—for example, a motion without friction.

On Motion sought to negate Aristotle's two rules on the speed of a falling body: (1) that it is proportional to the body's weight, and (2) that it is inversely proportional to the density of the medium. Although he demonstrated conditions of equilibrium on inclined planes, Galileo failed at that time to recognize the importance of gravitational acceleration. As a result he was unable to reconcile his conclusions about motion with the observed facts. (The story of Galileo's experiment of dropping large and small cannonballs from the top of the tower of Pisa, told by a later biographer, is probably unfounded. Yet subsequent writers filled in the details to embellish that account, which until recently was called "the most famous of all experiments.")

Unfortunately, Galileo had a knack for antagonizing people. His outspoken criticism of the academic establishment made him many enemies. He even wrote a satire in verse on a university ordinance requiring professors to wear their academic gowns *at all times* (including the bedroom?). That bit of poetic ridicule appeared not in Latin but in everyday Italian—a medium that proved effective for Galileo in later controversies. By his last year at Pisa, his faculty colleagues had suffered so much at Galileo's hands that in revenge they attended his lectures and hissed at comments with which they disagreed.

When his appointment ended in 1592, Galileo knew it would be useless to apply for renewal. So he enlisted the support of several influential friends to secure an appointment as professor of mathematics at the University of Padua near Venice. The chair was given to him rather than an Aristotelian, Giovanni Magini, whose term at Bologna was about to end. From then on, Magini bore Galileo a grudge. Padua's freedom of thought attracted the ablest students from all over Europe, many of whom came to study with Galileo during his eighteen years at that university.

Galileo continued his work as a mathematician, experimental physicist and practical inventor.[5] In 1595 he devised a mechanical explanation for the tides that required the two circular motions of the earth assumed by Copernicus. Even though his theory turned out to be wrong, evidently it marked the beginning of Galileo's interest in astronomy. Two years later a German visitor gave him Kepler's first book, the *Cosmographic Secret.* In thanking him, Galileo affirmed that he had long accepted the new astronomy.

Investigating a way to measure temperature by constructing an air thermometer, Galileo set up a workshop and designed some of the equipment himself. To augment his salary, he offered private instruction to young foreign noblemen in military architecture, surveying, fortification and mechanics. Galileo invented a "geometric and military compass" that could be used for calculations in surveying, navigation, gunnery and sundial construction. In 1599 he hired a craftsman to make those instruments for sale.

When his father Vincenzio had died a decade earlier, Galileo had shouldered the financial responsibility for his mother, brothers and sisters. The outside income from consulting and manufacture of instruments supplemented his meager professorial salary and enabled Galileo to provide a generous dowry when his sister married in 1601. During his Paduan years Galileo had a Venetian mistress named Marina Gamba, who bore him two daughters and a son. The elder daughter, Virginia, entered a convent with her sister Livia, took the name Maria Celeste and later became her father's chief solace. The son, Vincenzio, assisted his father during the last years of his life. When Galileo went to Florence in 1610, Marina Gamba returned to Venice, and eventually married.

The Paduan years were particularly fruitful for Galileo's study of mechanics. In 1602 he investigated pendulums and the descent of bodies along arcs and chords of circles, with special interest in acceleration. His initial calculations were made under an (incorrect) assumption that the speed of a falling body is proportional to the distance traversed. His later studies of pendulums and inclined planes were integrated under his (correct) law of acceleration: the speed is proportional to the square of the elapsed time. In that research Galileo's application of mathematics to dynamics went beyond his mentor Archimedes, who had worked only with statics.

In 1604, as Galileo was writing about his law of falling bodies, a supernova appeared in the evening sky.[6] Comparing observations in other cities with his own and finding no evidence of parallax, Galileo concluded that the supernova was at a great distance among the fixed stars. Yet according to Aristotle no change could take place in the heavens. To capitalize on the general excitement over the unusual event, Galileo gave three public lectures explaining how observations and careful measurements proved that the object was indeed a new star, not just a motionless comet near the moon. It was clear that Aristotle must be wrong.

That event led to the *first* of *five crucial controversies* with university philosophers in which Galileo continued to attack the scientific establishment. Cesare Cremonini, the ranking professor of philosophy at Padua, rose to Aristotle's defense. He could hardly let a mere mathematician prove actual change in the heavens, even though the mathematician was a long-time personal friend. To engage in a public feud the two professors went into print under assumed names.

Galileo adopted a literary technique that in his hands became a sharp polemic weapon. He countered Cremonini's arguments in a dialog between two peasants written in rustic Paduan dialect. One of the peasants reasoned more effectively than the prestigious professor. To the professor's argument that measurements on earth do not apply to vast distances in the heavens, the peasant asked sarcastically, "What do philosophers know about measuring anything?"

Although the Aristotelian tradition valued observations, its concern was primarily *qualitative*. Galileo's interest, on the other hand, was *quantitative;* wherever possible, he made accurate measurements. As a pioneer of the new science, he also showed how much ingenuity and how many precautions are required to obtain useful results.[7]

Cremonini opposed that idea and stood against Galileo on the scientific issues discussed during their time together at Padua. Five years later, when Galileo reported his telescopic observations, Cremonini refused even to look at the sky through the newfangled instrument. No wonder he eventually became the model Aristotelian philosopher in Galileo's famous **Dialogue.**

Telescopic Discoveries

Although Galileo had become convinced that the earth moves around the sun, he remained a closet Copernican—much to the discomfiture of Kepler, who urged him to come out publicly with his belief.[8] Galileo continued to wait until he could make a convincing case for the public, whose ridicule he feared. Then a dramatic discovery altered his scientific interest for many years.

In mid-1609 Galileo heard that a Dutch instrument maker had put lenses together in order to make distant objects look closer.[9] Realizing the importance of such an instrument to Venice as a maritime power, Galileo quickly obtained two lenses and assembled his own telescope. After much experimentation, he built an effective instrument that magnified nine times, a little more than most ordinary modern binoculars. By late August he demonstrated to the Venetian senate a telescope that could identify approaching ships two hours before they could be spotted by trained naked-eye observers. In gratitude the doge (ruler) of Venice granted Galileo the chair at Padua for life at double the salary, a level unprecedented for mathematicians.

Galileo immediately converted his workshop facilities to telescope production, refining his techniques to meet a sudden spate of orders. No one could match the quality he achieved through painstaking efforts. He experimented with dozens of instruments and made hundreds of observations over the years. Responding to criticism of his discoveries, Galileo asserted that people had no reason to believe he had deceived them with his reported observations.

With a twenty-power telescope he scanned the heavens and discovered countless new worlds. The Milky Way became a gigantic collection of stars. The vast expanse of the universe taught by Copernicus suddenly appeared plausible. More startling were several discoveries closer to earth that flatly contradicted Aristotle's teaching. Galileo could see that the moon is not a perfect sphere shining with its own light. Rather it has imperfections, mountains and valleys, much like the earth. Galileo was able to calculate the depth of those valleys from the length of their shadows and the position of the moon. He also discovered that the planet Venus has phases like those of the moon. To make matters worse, the sun has dark spots that appear and disappear; even the sun is not the perfect, unchangeable sphere of Aristotle's astronomy. Galileo concluded that either the sun turns on its own axis or the earth must move around the sun.

Equally disturbing, and of greater importance for the Copernican theory, was the discovery of four smaller bodies moving near Jupiter. As Galileo viewed them at different times and calculated their movements, it became clear that the four bodies are moons revolving around Jupiter. Yet according to Aristotle and the scientists of the day, only the earth as the center of the universe could have a moon. Now Jupiter and its four moons could be seen as a model for Copernicus's conception of the solar system: the planets (including the earth) moving around the sun.

Although Copernicus's theory had seemed to contradict common sense, the new evidence for the Copernican system was plainly visible to anyone who could peer through a telescope. Gazing at the heavens became a favorite after-dinner activity for guests of princes and prelates. After 1609 people without mathematical training could see for themselves that Aristotle could be wrong: "The telescope did not prove the validity of Copernicus's conceptual scheme. But it did provide an immensely effective weapon for the battle. It was not proof, but it was propaganda. . . . That is the greatest importance of Galileo's astronomical work; it popularized astronomy, and the astronomy it popularized was Copernican."[10]

Galileo soon recognized the importance of his discoveries. By March 1610 he published a slim volume entitled **Sidereus nuncius (The Starry Messenger)** with a promise of "unfolding great and marvellous sights."[11] The results were presented in a clear and compelling

Reconstruction of Galileo's telescope.

style. That simple metal tube with two lenses constituted a bludgeon for beating the Aristotelians and demolishing their universe. Yet the best-selling **Starry Messenger** gave no unambiguous evidence that Galileo accepted the Copernican system.

A second edition was published in Frankfurt within months. At the age of forty-five, Galileo suddenly became famous throughout Europe. In Prague the Tuscan ambassador gave Kepler a copy with a request from Galileo for comments. Kepler's pamphlet, *A Discussion with the Starry Messenger,* extolled Galileo's work. The two publications spurred a frenzy of telescope building and star watching.

Galileo soon made another remarkable discovery while observing Venus. That planet had been too close to the sun to observe when he made his first telescopic discoveries. During the last half of 1610, though, Galileo observed the entire range of phases (from a dark disk through crescent and gibbous forms to a bright disk) expected of the planet in the Copernican model. At one blow the phases of Venus falsified the Ptolemaic system.

In Galileo's *second* public controversy, his opponent was the same Giovanni Magini who had lost the chair of mathematics at Padua to Galileo eighteen years ear-

lier. Magini, who had become professor of astronomy at Bologna, said after publication of the **Starry Messenger** that he would see Galileo's Jovian satellites "extirpated from the sky." A Magini protégé, Martin Horky, published a book denouncing Galileo's claims. Indeed, for the most part, astronomers ridiculed Galileo or accused him of fraud.

Magini became the first academic to draw the clergy into such scientific controversies. He prompted a young religious zealot, Francesco Sizi, to publish an incredible book advancing semireligious arguments that there should be only seven planets, and claiming the supposed moons orbiting Jupiter to be an illusion. Although only a popgun, Sizi's book showed the lengths to which Galileo's opponents would go. Galileo did not consider that kind of attack worthy of reply, but one of his students did answer it on his behalf.

The Gathering Storm

In June 1610 Galileo took a fateful step whose consequences were unforeseen. He resigned the life appointment and generous salary at Padua granted by the doge of Venice to whom he had presented his first telescope. Leaving the political safety of the Republic of Venice, Galileo returned to Florence to become "Philosopher and Mathematician to the Grand Duke."

Galileo's new post gave him official recognition as a philosopher and a strong base for challenging the universities. Free from the demands of academic life, he could continue his experiments and proceed with his two books, "an immense design, full of philosophy, astronomy, and geometry."[12] After two decades of thought, he intended those works to establish the Copernican system on the basis of new discoveries in astronomy and physics.

Galileo moved to Florence in September, but hardly to the "perfect state of quiet of mind" he needed. For a while he thought his continuing discoveries, especially the phases of Venus he observed in October, would convince the most stubborn Aristotelian professors. But some refused to peer through his slight "optical reed"; others looked but professed to see nothing; a few argued that his "discoveries" were really due to flaws in the lenses, or were optical illusions.

Galileo perceived danger in the hardening attitude of the scientific establishment as he saw the lengths to which they would go to preserve their tradition and writings. Envious of Galileo's large salary and the favors bestowed on him by the grand duke, his opponents were out to safeguard their own professional status and properties. Galileo could feel a solid front building against him, from his alma mater of Pisa, from Padua and from Bologna.

At that point Galileo decided he needed independent confirmation of his observations. So in April 1611 he traveled to Rome, where he contacted Father Clavius and other Jesuit astronomers at the Roman College. He took along one of his telescopes, demonstrated it and then left it with them so they could check his discoveries night by night. Seeing the phenomena for themselves, those astronomers became convinced and enthusiastically honored Galileo. Old Father Clavius was shaken in his strict Ptolemaic faith. It was difficult for the undisputed leader of Jesuit astronomy to yield to new appearances in the skies, but he gave in gracefully. In a later report to a church commission chaired by Cardinal Robert Bellarmine, however, Clavius pointed out (correctly) that the observations themselves did not unequivocally support the Copernican theory.

While in Rome Galileo was elected to the Lincean Academy, a "scientific society" founded by Prince Federico Cesi.[13] At a banquet given for the visiting scientist, the word *telescope* was coined. Galileo's subsequent correspondence with other members kept him well informed of scientific developments in Rome.

On the same visit Galileo obtained an audience with Pope Paul V, whom he favorably impressed. The scientist also visited Cardinal Maffeo Barberini, a mathematician and member of a rich Florentine family who later became Pope Urban VIII. Barberini seemed to appreciate the new discoveries, and in the years to come Galileo kept hoping he might openly accept the new theory.

Overjoyed at the reception of his discoveries, Galileo returned home confident that his trip had been an unqualified success. Had not his observations been confirmed by the highest astronomical authority in the land? Further, he now had the friendship of Cardinal Bellarmine and Prince Cesi. With church and society both on his side, what was there to fear? The answer was not long in coming.

Disgruntled professors at Pisa now allied themselves with a set of courtiers at Florence in a secret and loosely organized resistance movement known as the *Liga*.[14] The leading figure was the Florentine philosopher Ludovico delle Colombe. Later in 1611 he published in Italian a treatise that began with traditional arguments against the earth's motion but ended with quotations to show that such motion was incompatible with Holy Scripture. If Galileo could not be beaten by purely scientific arguments, the *Liga* resolved to take the battle into theological terrain. Nicknamed the "pigeons" (*colombi*) after their leader, that academic group comprised the "conspiracy" of which Galileo often spoke.

With his astronomy becoming so popular, the *Liga* decided to tackle Galileo in the arena of physics, and in Florence, where he had the fewest allies. He would be engaged in open discussion where he could be defeated. They chose the villa of Galileo's friend Filippo Salviati, a frequent meeting place for courtiers and professors on leave from Pisa. The dinner-party controversies over floating bodies and their shapes soon became notorious. Colombe offered to show experimentally that his opponent was wrong. He already bore a grudge because of Galileo's attack on Colombe's book about the new star of 1604. The two exchanged letters and public experiments to support their arguments. The grand duke invited Galileo to debate the issue with a professor of philosophy at Pisa during a court dinner for two visiting cardinals. Galileo's position, which was supported by Cardinal Maffeo Barberini, was completely vindicated.

This *third* public dispute led to a book, ***Discorso intorno alle cose che stanno su l'acqua*** (***Discourse on Floating Bodies***), which became another best seller and went through two editions in 1612. Public interest was stimulated by the variety and appeal of experiments that required no special equipment and were amusing to perform. Galileo had again tweaked the scientific establishment. He remarked that the *authority* of Archimedes (his favorite Greek natural philosopher) was worth no more than that of Aristotle; Archimedes was right only because his propositions agreed with experiments. In the debates Galileo accused Colombe of "word spinning" in problems he didn't understand. The professor's rancor increased until he eventually sought revenge in a more serious way than scientific dispute.

Meanwhile Galileo became enmeshed in a *fourth* public controversy, one with dire consequences. Below the surface of what appeared to be simply an astronomical disagreement lurked much larger implications. Father Christopher Scheiner, a Jesuit astronomer at the University of Ingolstadt in Bavaria, constructed telescopes based on Kepler's design and in April 1611 began using them to observe the sun. Seven months later he discovered spots on the solar surface. Scheiner reasoned that the spots either lay on the sun's surface as blemishes or were caused by small orbiting planets. He favored the second possibility since dark spots on such a bright surface seemed unlikely. More important to Scheiner was their contradiction of Aristotle's teaching that celestial bodies are perfect, not subject to change or decay.

When Galileo read the printed reports in 1612 he strongly disagreed. To Galileo it was important for the spots to be on the sun; he was glad to have evidence that, like the earth, the sun was an ordinary, imperfect body. He was able to demonstrate from Scheiner's drawings as well as his own observations that the spots changed shape. They were immense clouds on the solar surface.

In 1613 Galileo's *Historia e dimonstrazioni intorno alle macchie solari* (*Letters on Sunspots*) was published by the Lincean Academy. For the first time Galileo openly advocated the new astronomy. An appendix presented convincing evidence for the Copernican view: the eclipses of Jupiter's moons and a simple method to predict them.

Aristotle had taught that celestial phenomena were essentially different from the terrestrial; their explanations had entirely different bases. Against that view, Galileo interpreted heavenly phenomena by means of earthly analogies. The *Letters* made it clear that Galileo was not only anti-Aristotelian but also a thoroughgoing Copernican. Only the new theory could make sense of the telescopic discoveries. Galileo's preface, claiming priority of discovery of sunspots, angered Scheiner. Many other Jesuits were offended and supported Scheiner in a long, bitter feud.

That same year Galileo's former pupil Benedetto Castelli was appointed to the chair of mathematics at Pisa. The professors at Pisa were hostile to Castelli from the start. When warned by the university's overseer not to teach Copernicanism, Castelli replied that he had already been given that advice by Galileo.

A Flank Attack

Disappointed by their failure to break through Galileo's lines on the fronts of physics and astronomy, the *Liga* adopted a new strategy. Carrying the attack into court circles, they would make his scientific discoveries a religious issue. Late in 1613, at a formal dinner given by Grand Duke Cosimo II (Galileo's employer), the new astronomy became a subject of discussion. Since Galileo was not present, Benedetto Castelli defended his former mentor's views. During the informal debate Cosimo Bostaglia declared that any motion of the earth was impossible since it would contradict Holy Scripture. After dinner Grand Duchess Christina persistently questioned Castelli on that issue.[15] During their discussion Professor Bostaglia made no comments.

Castelli wrote Galileo a full account of the discussion. It had been customary to debate issues of natural philosophy on their own merits. Concerned that his enemies were now dragging scientific questions into the perilous waters of theology, Galileo decided the time had come to meet such a challenge head-on. In a *Letter to Castelli* just before Christmas 1613, Galileo carefully spelled out his position as a scientist and a Catholic. He reaffirmed his commitment to the truth and authority of the Bible, then raised the question of its proper interpretation. Obviously it speaks at times in figurative terms and language understandable to the average person. Galileo expressed concern about "the carrying of Holy Scripture into disputes about physical [that is, scientific] conclusions." God has given us two books, one of nature, the other of Scripture. "Both the Holy Scriptures and Nature proceed from the Divine Word, the former as the saying of the Holy Spirit and the latter as the most observant executrix of God's orders."[16] He affirmed that the "two truths can never contradict each other," even though they are expressed in different languages for different disciplines: religion and ethics in Scripture; physics in nature. Why, then, should the Bible be used to support the opinion of fallible philosophers against others, to the jeopardy of its authority?

As copies of that letter circulated freely, battle lines were drawn, with both theologians and courtiers taking sides. Although Galileo had intended to silence illogical objections to Copernicus, his enemies turned his arguments into an occasion for innuendo, misrepresentation and rumor. Throughout 1614 the scientist was accused of undermining Scripture and meddling in theology.

Galileo's *fifth* major conflict suddenly became very public. On December 20, 1614, Father Tommaso Caccini, a Dominican friar with connections to the Aristotelian professors, preached a sermon from the pulpit of a principal church in Florence. In his sermon on Joshua's miracle of making the sun stand still, Caccini strongly condemned the idea of a moving earth as being very close to heresy. He branded all "mathematicians" as agents of the devil who ought to be banned from Christendom. That was a serious charge; in the public mind "mathematicians" were identical with astrologers, who at that time were viewed with growing suspicion.

To friends in Rome Galileo wrote that he was concerned to have been the subject of a Sunday sermon. The fact that the leader of the Dominicans wrote a formal apology did little to placate him. Even though it was known that the authorities were keeping an open mind about the new discoveries, Caccini's sermon strengthened the opposition against Galileo.

Shortly after Caccini's attack, a priest named Niccolo Lorini read a copy of the *Letter to Castelli.* It was one thing for a scientist to speculate about nature; it was quite another for a layman to write a thesis interpreting Scripture to fit those speculations. Lorini may have been haunted by the specter of Protestant exegesis and private interpretation of the Bible. So on February 7, 1615, he sent a copy of the *Letter* to one of the Inquisitors-General in Rome with his concern that the followers of Galileo "were taking upon themselves to expound the Holy Scriptures according to their private lights, . . . that they were trampling underfoot all of Aristotle's philosophy. . . . I believe that the Galileans are orderly men and all good Christians, but a little wise and cocky in their opinions."[17]

When Galileo heard that his *Letter* had been submitted to the Holy Office, he immediately sent an authentic copy to his friend Archbishop Piero Dini in Rome, asking him to show it to Cardinal Bellarmine. Galileo pointed out that he had written that letter in haste and was now expanding his exposition. In June 1615 he en-titled a new treatise, *Letter to the Grand Duchess Christina.* That work was copied and widely circulated (though not published until 1636 in Strasbourg).

. . . [We] should summarize the main elements of Galileo's scientific activity.

Galileo's Science

The most vexing problem in assessing Galileo's contribution to Western thought is the extent to which he introduced a new "scientific method." Our answer must distinguish between Galileo the scientist and Galileo the symbol. He became a legend almost in his own lifetime. For many he has become the symbol of a revolt of reason against prejudice and authority, of the clear certainties of science against murky opinions of medieval theology.

The first historians of science, the French Encyclopedists of the late eighteenth century, saw his work as a watershed between old and new ways of doing science, a sharp creative break with the past. For them the scientist was a symbol. They presented Galileo as protomartyr and patron of the cause of intellectual freedom from benighted religious authoritarianism. Not until the early twentieth

century was the natural philosophy of the late medieval and Renaissance periods fully appreciated. Scholars then became aware of non-Aristotelian mathematical mechanics dating back to the fourteenth century. The pendulum swung to the opposite extreme: some saw Galileo as simply rescuing that discovery from neglect and carrying through its first general formulation.

Granting that the truth probably lies somewhere between those extremes, certain questions remain. How original was Galileo's science? What was his method? How did the results of his work contribute to the "new science" he attempted to construct?

We have already sketched the climate of Aristotelian natural philosophy within which Galileo began his work in mathematics and mechanics. We have seen some of the subjects on which he challenged the scientific establishment of his time as his steps began to diverge from the traditional path. Since Galileo's work did not take place in a vacuum, we may inquire about the sources of his inspiration. Four main influences have been suggested: (1) reading, (2) experiment, (3) conceptual formulation and (4) Copernicanism.[18]

As to the first, Galileo's early efforts at Pisa to explain motion show that he had certainly read earlier writings, especially those of the "impetus" school. As a teacher at Padua he would have been familiar with the major variations of Aristotle's dynamics worked out by earlier theorists, as well as the complicated mathematics derived from the Merton school. As to experiment, Galileo was clearly able to perform experiments, though he did not do them often. He stressed their importance. "Where mathematical demonstrations are applied to natural phenomena, . . . the principles once established by well-chosen experiments become the foundation of the entire superstructure."[19]

With respect to the third influence, Galileo frequently devised "thought experiments" to explore the implications of a hypothesis and demonstrate its logical consistency. His conceptual ability is evident in the way he reinterpreted facts already available. In the *Dialogue,* for example, he persuaded readers by helping them see familiar facts in a new light, not new facts never before discovered. As to the fourth element, Galileo's early commitment to the Copernican system as the "true" view of the universe (not just the most convenient mathematical way to describe planetary motions) provided a framework and motivation for his lifelong work in mechanics. In fact, Galileo's mechanics and astronomy were remarkably interdependent as he tackled the age-old problem of motion.

Although some scholars attribute the major role in the drama of Galileo's creative achievement to one or another of those factors, each of them played its part in the complex thought and activity of the great scientist.

The tendency to oversimplify must also be resisted in explaining Galileo's scientific method. Unlike Kepler, he did not provide a systematic treatment of his views on this subject. He wrote almost nothing for publication during the crucial Paduan period (1597-1610) when a new and different mechanics gradually took shape in his mind. Galileo's ideas on procedure and epistemology at times were confused and inconsistent in the tentative fitting and trying that went on throughout his life. Like most practicing scientists, he phrased his insights according to the exigencies of the moment rather than a defined philosophy. Since Galileo could see green grass on both sides of the fence, he has been claimed by a variety of philosophical schools. Here we avoid such debate in the interest of briefly noting the main elements in Galileo's practice of science.

For Galileo mathematics was the key to unlocking the secrets of the universe.

> This grand book . . . cannot be understood unless one first learns to comprehend the language and to read the alphabet in which it is composed. It is written in the language of mathematics, and its characters are triangles, circles, and other geometric figures, without which it is humanly impossible to understand a single word of it; without these, one wanders about in a dark labyrinth.[20]

As a mathematician turned physicist, Galileo equated understanding the physical world with knowing its geometrical structure. He believed that nature could be interrogated in the language of mathematics, but he was also convinced that it should be allowed to answer for itself. In other words, mathematical analysis and theory must have empirical confirmation. For Galileo scientific facts had to do with observations and measurements of "primary" characteristics such as quantity, shape, size and motion, and not "secondary" qualities such as color, sound and smell so important in Aristotelian natural philosophy. Nature replies to mathematical questions because nature is the domain of measure and order.

The role of experiment in Galileo's work has long been debated. Many of the experiments attributed to him, and some which he himself describes, were not actually carried out. He was a great interpreter, not a gatherer of facts. Some of these were "thought experiments" in which he imagined a specific situation and thought through the consequences of a given idea or hypothesis. Galileo was a true "experimenter" in this basic respect: he constantly aimed to confirm features of his theories by specially designed experiments. His clear lesson was that assumptions made in setting up a hypothesis must be verified; good scientific theories must return naturally to reality.[21] Galileo's approach is not purely mathematical; it is *physico-mathematical*. Reality is the incarnation of mathematics.

How, then, should experiments be conducted? Experimentation must be more than the simple accumulation of data. For Galileo the laboratory is not the breeding ground but the testing ground of theories. Whether real or mental, experiments are productive only if they are arranged in accordance with a hypothesis that determines the data to be obtained for mathematical analysis. Facts do not speak unless interrogated, and the kind of question one asks determines the range of meaningful answers. Experiments by themselves do not provide theoretical statements; they illustrate, confirm or falsify an existing hypothesis. Yet a well-designed critical experiment may call for a change in current theory. It may even suggest the direction such a change should take to fit the new experimental results.

One of Galileo's most important contributions to scientific methodology was his knack of *idealizing* a problem. He was able to reduce each problem to its basic, essential form; to eliminate factors not immediately relevant; to reach "laws" that did not describe the motion of any actual body, but rather stated what its behavior would be if the influence of environment were eliminated or standardized. For example, idealization treats the earth's surface as a plane, and perpendiculars to it as parallel. It ignores friction and resistance in the study of falling bodies. It conceives the idea of the mass-point. Galileo was able to distinguish between the primary and secondary qualities of Aristotle and concentrate on measuring the former. He by-passed the complex problem of *causes* in order to discover a mathematical *description*. This knack of idealizing enabled Galileo to go right to the heart of a problem and develop a simple mathematical theory.[22]

The three major elements in Galileo's scientific method are intuition, demonstration and experiment. First, he idealized a problem to identify its essential form, isolate the basic elements to be analyzed and formulate a hypothesis or model. Second, he deductively worked out a mathematical demonstration of several conclusions and devised well-chosen experiments to test them. Third, he carried out his experiments—real or mental—and evaluated the results. Galileo observed that, although such a method begins with the data of sense perception, it sometimes leads to conclusions that seem to contradict the senses. For example, in the Copernican astronomy mathematical reason (the earth moves around the sun) overrides our senses (we see the sun moving).

A New Science?

In a reaction against the sterility of sixteenth-century Aristotelian science, pioneers like Bacon and Descartes claimed to have an entirely new method. But is that what Galileo meant when in the ***Discourses*** he proposed a "brand-new science concerning a very old subject"? In what sense did he consider it "brand-new"?

What he presented there was not a new method or conception of science but aspects of motion that "had not hitherto been remarked, let alone demonstrated."[23]

Galileo inherited and confirmed Aristotle's general conception of science as knowledge that can be "shown" or "demonstrated," that is, proved, explained and taught.[24] To qualify as fully "scientific," knowledge must fulfill all three goals, but especially be proved (established) and explained. Aristotle distinguished between two kinds of scientific knowledge, the "what" and the "why," effects and causes. One establishes the facts (that is, the behavior of a ball rolling down an inclined plane); the other "gives the why of" the facts (a mathematical explanation). Although Galileo set out to dismantle Aristotle's physics, in the **Dialogue** he was careful not to criticize the latter's conception of science. Galileo disagreed with the Greek philosopher on the consequences of "new events and observations," but he stated that if Aristotle were alive, "I have no doubt he would change his opinion."

Galileo also shared Aristotle's "scientific realism," the view that there is a uniquely true physical theory, discoverable by human reason and observation, and that alternative theories are consequently false. Galileo believed that the distinguishing features of the natural sciences are conclusions that are "true and necessary." True knowledge of causes is obtained by "certain demonstration." The **Discourses** is dotted with terms like *rigorous proof* and *demonstration.*

He disagreed with Aristotle, however, on the nature of physical reality, claiming that it is mathematical in form and that mathematical theory should determine the structure of experimental research. Only in mathematics do we find certainty. The full demonstrative ideal of science can be achieved only to the extent that a physical science can simulate mathematics. Here Galileo was guided by his mentor, Archimedes.

Unfortunately, the telescope opened up a new and puzzling realm where this "true and necessary" demonstration was not possible. The heavenly bodies demanded a different kind of science, a new and less direct mode of proof, since they were remote and unfamiliar. Causal reasoning was difficult to test since direct experiments were not possible. Galileo realized that demonstrative science could not handle questions like the nature of comets. (Nor could it operate in the realm of the "very small," with the problem of atoms.) As a result, Galileo's conclusions about features of the moon were based on analogy, inference and retroduction, which goes from effect to proximate cause and back to effect, relying on confirmation through testing predictions. . . .

In Copernican astronomy Galileo's problems with demonstrative science came to a head. He used Kepler's recommended method of getting "true knowledge" by excluding all hypotheses except one. To that end he argued against the physics of Aristotle and the astronomy of Ptolemy. He gave seven arguments to show how much simpler it is to postulate the earth's rotation rather than that of the stars. But Galileo admitted that he was not "drawing a necessary proof from them, merely a greater probability." In order to *demonstrate* the movement of the earth he would have to use a causal argument. For this proof he turned his attention to the tides, an argument with farreaching consequences. . . .

So two different conceptions of science animated Galileo's work. The demonstrative ideal, which he inherited from the Greek tradition, was the one he formally held and never abandoned, despite the difficulties it created in the realm of cosmology. The other conception was the principle of retroduction exemplified in his discussions of phenomena whose causes are remote (comets, sunspots), enigmatic (motions of the earth) or invisible (atoms). Although he used retroductive inference with great skill, Galileo refused to consider anything less than rigorous demonstration as genuine "science."[25]

While others talked about the need for new methods of science, Galileo endeavored to discover a demonstrative science of motion. He was not a philosopher but a scientist; he did not propose a new theory of science but a new science as he laid the foundations for modern mathematical physics. Yet in doing so he pioneered a path that ultimately led to a new conception of the scientific enterprise.

Notes

[1] Stillman Drake, *Galileo Studies: Personality, Tradition, and Revolution* (Ann Arbor: University of Michigan Press, 1970), pp. 55-59.

[2] Drake, *Galileo,* p. 15.

[3] William R. Shea, *Galileo's Intellectual Revolution* (London: Macmillan, 1972), p. 2.

[4] Stillman Drake, "Galileo Galilei," in Gillispie, *Dictionary of Scientific Biography,* vol. 5, p. 238.

[5] Stillman Drake, *Galileo at Work: His Scientific Biography* (Chicago: University of Chicago Press, 1978), chap. 3.

[6] Ibid., pp. 104-10.

[7] Paul Tannery, "Galileo and the Principles of Dynamics," in *Galileo: Man of Science,* ed. Ernan McMullin (New York: Basic Books, 1967), p. 170.

[8] Drake, *Galileo Studies,* chap. 6, "Galileo, Kepler and Their Intermediaries."

[9] Ibid., "Galileo and the Telescope," chap. 7.

[10] [Thomas S. Kuhn, *The Copernican Revolution* (Cambridge, Mass.: Harvard University Press, 1957)] pp. 224-25.

[11] Galileo, *The Sidereal Messenger,* trans. E. Carlos (London: Dawson's, 1959), p. 11.

[12] [Giorgio de Santillana, *The Crime of Galileo* (Chicago: Chicago University Press, 1955)] p. 6.

[13] Drake, *Galileo Studies,* chap. 4, "The Accademia dei Lincei."

[14] Olaf Pedersen, "Galileo and the Council of Trent: The Galileo Affair Revisited," *Journal for the History of Astronomy* 14 (1983), pp. 6-7.

[15] Jerome J. Langford, *Galileo, Science and the Church* (Ann Arbor: University of Michigan Press, 1971), pp. 54-58.

[16] Quoted in Drake, *Galileo at Work,* pp. 224-25. See A. R. Peacocke, *Creation and the World of Science* (Oxford: Clarendon Press, 1979), pp. 3-7.

[17] Quoted in Langford, *Galileo, Science and the Church,* p. 57.

[18] McMullin, *Galileo,* pp. 11-13.

[19] Galileo, *Discourses Concerning Two New Sciences,* quoted in McMullin, *Galileo,* p. 11.

[20] Galileo, *The Assayer,* quoted in Drake, *Galileo,* p. 70.

[21] Dominique Dubarle, "Galileo's Methodology of Natural Science," in McMullin, *Galileo,* pp. 308-10.

[22] A. Rupert Hall, "The Significance of Galileo's Thought for the History of Science," in McMullin, *Galileo,* pp. 73-74.

[23] Galileo, *Opere* 8, quoted in Ernan McMullin, "The Conception of Science in Galileo's Work," in Robert E. Butts and Joseph C. Pitt, eds., *New Perspectives on Galileo* (Dordrecht: D. Reidel Pub., 1978), p. 217.

[24] Ibid., pp. 213-17.

[25] Ibid., pp. 251-52.

William R. Shea (essay date 1986)

SOURCE: "Galileo and the Church," in *God and Nature: Historical Essays on the Encounter between Christianity and Science,* edited by David C. Lindberg and Ronald L. Numbers, University of California Press, 1986, pp. 114-35.

[In the following essay, Shea details the theological, political, and scientific temper of the era and country in which Galileo lived, and argues that Galileo was more a victim of politics than of inflexible beliefs.]

The condemnation of Galileo (1564-1642) is perhaps the most dramatic incident in the long and varied history of the relations between science and religious faith. Honest seekers after truth have been shocked by the attempt to suppress the claim that the earth moves and have seen in the trial of Galileo decisive evidence that religion is dangerous, not only when willfully perverted to secular ends but also, and perhaps more especially, when pursued by sincere men who consider themselves the stewards of God's revealed truth.[1] But Galileo's condemnation must be seen in historical perspective. We must remember that he was born in 1564, the year after the close of the Council of Trent, which may be considered as setting the tone of Roman Catholicism until a new spirit came to prevail with John XXIII in our own century. The opposition he encountered can only be understood if it is related to a period in which modern liberal values were far from commanding the assent that we have come to take for granted.

An Age of Restrictive Orthodoxies

For the cultural historian and the student of the development of dogma, sixteenth-century Italy is notorious for its return to the rigor of an earlier age. This has conventionally been blamed on the Counter-Reformation, but to see it in this light is to take the symptom for the cause. The Counter-Reformation must not be viewed as an external and reactionary movement or wave of obscurantism that suddenly banished all intellectual creativity. It was rather a crisis of confidence that took place within the Italian mind.[2] The sack of Rome in 1527 and the collapse of the Florentine Republic in 1530, followed by Spanish domination over most of the peninsula, left Italians sorely disillusioned. Many lost faith in reforms aimed solely at the improvement of political institutions and became not only willing but anxious to exchange the burden of freedom for the security of regulated order. One notices this in the greater emphasis on the authority of princes and the new accent on the importance of titles, even if those who bore them had to be fixed up with spurious genealogies and endowed with the nobility somehow inherent in the cities of their birth.

The writings of Aristotle that had earlier stimulated lively discussion were increasingly turned into rigid dogma and a mechanical criterion of truth. Other philosophical systems were viewed with suspicion. When the Platonic chair of Francesco Patrizi (1529-1597) at the University of the Sapienza in Rome fell vacant at his death, Pope Clement VIII consulted Cardinal Robert Bellarmine (1542-1621), who had recently been called from Naples as papal theologian and counselor to the Holy Office. Bellarmine judged that Platonism contained more insidious subtleties than Aristotelianism—not because it was more erroneous but on account of its deceptive affinity with Christianity. Platonism was therefore more dangerous than paganism, and Bellarmine recommended suppression of the chair.[3] The widely accepted authority of Aristotle helped to make his disciple Thomas Aquinas (1224-1274) the most popular guide to the meaning of the faith in the late sixteenth century. Named a doctor of the church in 1567, Aquinas was considered the supreme authority in theology by Cardinal Bellarmine. The Jesuit *Ratio Studiorum,* although permitting deviation from Aquinas's theology on particulars, prescribed dismissal for any professor who showed himself hostile to the system as a whole. The task of theology under these circumstances was chiefly to systematize and to clarify the faith, conceived as a body of coherent intellectual propositions, in such a way as to maximize its certainty and finality. The articulation of Catholic belief almost became an administrative problem, and Bellarmine an administrator of doctrines. He organized them into systems so that they might be directed, in their most unequivocal and effective form, against doubt and heresy. Indeed, to make confrontation easier he even systematized the views of his opponents.[4]

The cultural authoritarianism of the papacy was greatly assisted by the Italianization of the papal court and the growth of a centralized bureaucracy within the church. At the beginning of the sixteenth century the Sacred College of Cardinals numbered thirty-five, of whom twenty-one (60 percent) were Italians. By 1598, when the number had risen to fifty-seven, forty-six (more than 80 percent) were from Italy.[5] A similar reduction in the proportion of foreigners was occurring at the lower levels of the papal bureaucracy. The Italian influence had already been decisive at the Council of Trent (1545-1563), called to formulate a response to the Protestant challenge; there, of 270 bishops attending at one time or another, 187 were Italian, 31 Spanish, 26 French, and 2 German. Moreover, by the procedural rules adopted in 1545, only bishops and the generals of a few religious orders could vote in the full sessions. This decision strengthened the Italian contingent, many of whom were financially dependent on the papacy and therefore under its influence. The sharp increase in the number of cardinals reduced the importance of individual figures, as, in an aristocratic age, did the elevation of clergy of low social origins. The sudden appointment, in 1583, of nineteen new cardinals by Gregory XIII, without consultation or advance notice, ruffled the feathers of those already belonging to the Sacred College but led to little open resistance.

Sixtus V (1585-1590) took the further step of dividing the papal bureaucracy into fifteen smaller bodies that functioned separately and henceforth rarely assembled as a whole. This effectively converted the Curia from a quasi-constitutional agency into an appointive and specialized bureaucracy. In his justification of papal claims, the *Controversia Generalis de Summo Pontifice,* Cardinal Bellarmine argued that a monarchical form of government was preferable to a democratic one because it was more natural.[6] And Bellarmine did not hesitate to tell Catholic princes that they had a moral obligation to enforce true belief among their subjects.[7]

This reassertion of pontifical authority is likely to appear anachronistic. European life had been too thoroughly secularized to give any hope of success to the effort to impose an ecclesiastical tutelage. But none of this was obvious in Italy during the latter half of the sixteenth century: the sufferings, the fragmentation, and the weakness of Italy made the new secular accomplishments appear singularly vulnerable. Ecclesiastical authority appeared to triumph and thus to fulfill the values of the Counter-Reformation.[8] But the aspirations of Rome were also based on faith in the ultimate course of history arising not from a scrutiny of actual conditions but from divine promise. For Rome, what ought to be must eventually be. Meanwhile she would do everything in her power to hasten the event.

At the end of the sixteenth century her efforts intensified. Heartened by signs that the Turks could be beaten, and supported by powerful new religious orders, such as the Jesuits, and a reorganized and efficient bureaucracy, the papacy mounted a systematic campaign against the dangerous political and philosophical ideas of the Renaissance and the Reformation. The chronology of the papal counteroffensive is significant. In 1559 Paul IV issued the first official Roman Index of Prohibited Books, an undiscriminating list, which included all the works of Erasmus, all the production of sixty-one printers, and all translations of the Bible into vernacular languages.[9] Its harshness was mitigated by the Council of Trent in 1562, but shortly thereafter, under the pontificate of Pius V (1566-1572), it became implacably severe. Pius changed the nature of the Index, intending it no longer as a fixed list of condemned writings but as a continuous action of vigilance and censorship; in 1571 he set up a special Congregation of the Index to oversee this enterprise.

Thus by the end of the sixteenth century, the Catholic church appeared to have emerged from the struggle against Protestantism with renewed strength. It continued to keep an eye on theologians, such as Michel Baius and Bartolomé de Carranza, but it now extended its vigilance to all manifestations of social and spiritual life; that is, it reached beyond the religious realm to ethics, politics, philosophy, art, and even manners and customs.

The last decade of the sixteenth century and the early years of the seventeenth produced a wave of ideological assaults and condemnations. Although Niccolò Machiavelli had been on the Index since 1559, he was systematically refuted only after 1589; in that year Giovanni Botero's *Della ragion di stato* appeared, closely followed by the conservative works of Antonio Possevino and Tommaso Bozio and by Pedro de Ribadeneira's *Princeps Christianus*. The works of Jean Bodin were condemned in 1592; two years later his political doctrines were refuted by Fabio Albergati. It was also at this time that the Platonism of Patrizi was denounced and the old philosopher forced to profess his total submission. The work of Bernardino Telesio was proscribed as subversive in 1596, and nine years later his views were sweepingly condemned. During the same period Pietro Pomponazzi's condemnation was renewed, and Tommaso Campanella, Francesco Pucci, and Giordano Bruno were imprisoned for their ideas. Pucci perished at the stake in 1597, Bruno in 1600.[10]

During the pontificates of Gregory XIII (1572-1585) and Sixtus V (1585-1590) the radical papism of Augustinus Triumphus (fourteenth century) was revived in the form of his *Summa de Potestate Ecclesiastica*. This work, printed four times between 1582 and 1585, encouraged the view that all particular kingdoms and republics are subordinate to a world state under papal leadership. Gregory and Sixtus were convinced that Christendom must become an effective political reality. Any fragmentation of the social order was judged intrinsically evil, the expression and consequence of sin. Individuals and governments were considered subject to a single eternal system of justice based ultimately on eternal and divine law, of which the Catholic church was sole guardian and interpreter. In this climate of opinion a revolution in science or any other field of human endeavor could easily be perceived as a threat unless shown to agree with the teachings of the church.

Galileo's Exegetical Challenge

The heliocentric theory had been given scientific status by Nicolaus Copernicus in his *De Revolutionibus Orbium Caelestium* of 1543, but it was not until the invention of the telescope in the first decade of the seventeenth century that it received sufficient confirmation to pose a problem to the traditional imagery embedded in the Christian worldview. When Galileo turned his looking glass to the heavens in 1609, he discovered fresh arguments for the centrality of the sun in the phases of Venus and the satellites of Jupiter. Although the new observations were suggestive, they were by no means conclusive, and the debate over Copernicanism, which had flagged, received new impetus. Galileo's *Sidereal Messenger,* published in 1610, was an instant success, as was his trip to Rome the next year, when the Jesuits publicly confirmed his tele-

scopic discoveries and Prince Federico Cesi (1585-1630) made him a member of the Accademia dei Lincei. So great was the applause that Cardinal Francesco Maria del Monte wrote to the grand duke Cosimo II: "Were we living in the ancient Roman Republic, I have no doubt that a statue would be erected in the Campidoglio in honor of his [Galileo's] outstanding merit."[11]

Galileo was elated by his warm reception in Rome, but an editorial incident that occurred when Prince Cesi offered to publish his *Letters on Sunspots* in 1612 should have made him wary of theologians. The cavils of the censors forced successive revisions upon him, and it is perhaps in an editorial incident of this kind that we can appreciate the day-to-day workings of the Counter-Reformation.

The book was to have opened with a letter from Marc Welser in which he quoted from Matthew 11:12: "The kingdom of heaven suffers violence, and men of violence take it by force." The censors objected to the quotation as likely to give the impression that astronomers hoped to conquer a domain that was the prerogative of theologians. To allay these fears, the passage was paraphrased to read: "Already the minds of men assail the heavens, and the more valiant conquer it."[12] Although there was no significant change in content, the biblical passage had disappeared! In a second passage Galileo had written that "divine goodness" had directed him to display the Copernican system publicly. The censors had him substitute "favorable winds."[13] A third amendment reveals the censors' desire to save the incorruptibility of the heavens, a doctrine to which they still subscribed.[14] In his original version Galileo had described the immutability of the heavens as "not only false, but erroneous and repugnant to the indubitable truths of the Scriptures," and had attributed the new astronomy to divine inspiration. When the censors demurred, he produced a new draft in which he called his own theory "most agreeable to the indubitable truths of Holy Writ" and praised his predecessors for their subtlety in finding ways of reconciling biblical passages on the mutability of the heavens with the conflicting evidence in favor of their immutability.[15] The tacit implication was that, since theologians had long interpreted the texts to show their agreement with Aristotelian doctrine, there already existed in the church a nonliteral way of reading biblical passages on astronomy. The censors deemed the revision inadequate and demanded a third version, in which Galileo reluctantly excised all mention of Scripture.

The attitudes of both the censors and Galileo are instructive. On the one hand, the censors adamantly refused a layman the right to meddle with Scripture. On the other, Galileo was inclined to describe his own point of view as "divinely inspired" and to brand that of his opponents "contrary to Scripture." The popular conception of Galileo as a martyr for freedom of thought is an oversimplification. That his views were different from those of the majority of the academic establishment did not make him a liberal. In philosophy he replaced the dogmatism of Aristotle with an equally dogmatic faith in the validity of a mathematical interpretation of nature. In politics he was weary of the time-consuming demands of democracy and longed for the haven of a princely court. In 1610 he pointed out in no uncertain terms that he had left the Venetian Republic for the grand duchy of Tuscany because freedom from teaching duties could only be granted by an absolute ruler.[16]

Galileo no doubt cherished the hope that the church would endorse his opinions. Along with many of his contemporaries he looked to an enlightened papacy as an effective instrument of scientific progress. But what Galileo does not seem to have understood is that the Catholic church, attacked by Protestants for neglecting the Bible, found itself compelled, in self-defense, to harden its ground. Whatever appeared to contradict Holy Writ had to be treated with the utmost caution.

Galileo's favorite pupil, the Benedictine priest Benedetto Castelli (1578-1643), was appointed to the chair of mathematics at the University of Pisa in November 1613. In December of that year he was invited to dine with the grand duke Cosimo II, his mother the grand duchess Christina of Lorraine, and several dignitaries. The conversation turned to Galileo's celestial discoveries. Everyone praised them except the grand duchess, who, prompted by a professor of philosophy, began to raise objections from Scripture against the motion of the earth. Castelli replied as best he could and later reported the conversation to Galileo, who sent him a letter in which he outlined his views on Scripture. This was to form the basis of his **Letter to the Grand Duchess Christina** of 1615, the fullest statement of his views on the relations between science and religion.[17]

A Florentine layman, Lodovico delle Colombe, had criticized Galileo as early as 1610 for contradicting Scripture, but it was not until the fourth Sunday of Advent, 1614, that the matter became serious when Tommaso Caccini, a Dominican friar, preached against the motion of the earth and blasted mathematicians for promoting it. Galileo, incensed, complained to a distinguished preacher-general of the order, Fr. Luigi Maraffi, who apologized most courteously for the misdemeanor of a member of his order known for his intemperate and ill-advised rhetoric.[18] Galileo also wrote to Federico Cesi, asking how he could obtain redress. The advice of the religious, yet worldly-wise, prince could have taught him much about the Roman milieu he was so sorely to misjudge:

> Concerning the opinion of Copernicus, Bellarmine himself, who is one of the heads of the Congregation that deals with these matters, told me that he considers it heretical, and that the motion of the earth is

undoubtedly against Scripture; so you can see for yourself. I have always feared that if Copernicus were discussed in the Congregation of the Index, they would proscribe him.[19]

Matters were brought to a head by the arrival in Rome, at the beginning of 1615, of a Carmelite priest, Paolo Antonio Foscarini (ca. 1580-1616), who had just published a letter on the *Opinion of the Pythagoreans and Copernicus Regarding the Motion of the Earth*. Foscarini made a forceful but serene plea for the compatibility of the Copernican hypothesis with Scripture. He did not assert that the new theory was true, but argued that the Bible was written to be understood by all men and hence employed popular rather than scientific language. God chose to reveal only what could not be discovered by the light of reason; the rest he left to human disputation.[20] Foscarini was anxious to make his views known and therefore wrote to Bellarmine himself, enclosing a copy of his book. The cardinal tactfully replied that, to the best of his knowledge, the motion of the earth had not yet been proved and that it was best treated as a convenient device rather than a physical truth since it ran counter to clear biblical assertions about the rising and setting of the sun. Bellarmine then added:

> It cannot be answered that this is not a matter of faith, for if it is not a matter of faith *ex parte objecti* [with respect to the subject matter], it is a matter of faith *ex parte dicentis* [with respect to the one who asserts it]. Hence a man who denied that Abraham had two sons and Jacob twelve would be as much a heretic as one who denied the Virgin Birth of Christ, since both are declared by the Holy Ghost through the mouths of the prophets and the apostles.

The cardinal, however, was far from taking an intolerant and inflexible stance:

> If there were a true demonstration that the sun is at the center of the world and the earth in the third sphere, and that the sun does not revolve around the earth but the earth around the sun, then we would have to use great care in explaining those passage of Scripture that seem contrary. . . . But I cannot believe that there is such a demonstration until someone shows it to me.

Bellarmine proceeded to point out that using a theory to compute the position of the planets is not tantamount to affirming its physical reality. He was unmoved by the analogy, already invoked by Copernicus, of the beach that appears to recede when we leave the harbor aboard ship. No one, he pointed out, ever argued that the shore and not the ship was in motion.[21]

The cardinal's letter was sent to Galileo, who wrestled with the theological arguments. Replying to the objection that the motion of the sun is a matter of faith *ex parte dicentis* if not *ex parte objecti,* Galileo claimed that the Council of Trent upheld the authority of Scripture only in matters of faith and morals:

> Having said therefore *in rebus fidei* [in matters of the faith], we see that the Council meant *in rebus fidei ratione objecti* [in matters of the faith by reason of the object]. It is much more a matter of faith that Abraham had sons and that Tobit had a dog, because it is stated in Scripture, than that the earth moves . . ., for since there have always been men who have had two, four, six, or no sons . . . there does not appear any reason or cause why the Holy Spirit should state in such matters anything but the truth, since the affirmative and the negative are equally credible for all men. But this is not so with the motion of the earth and the immobility of the sun. These propositions are far removed from the comprehension of the common people.[22]

Galileo's Conception of Science

Galileo seems to have been oblivious to the danger of trying to enlighten the foremost Catholic theologian of the day on the interpretation of the decrees of the Council of Trent. He also jeopardized his case by overstating the degree of proof that he could provide:

> It is prudent to believe that there is no proof that the earth moves until it has been produced, and we do not ask that anyone believe such a thing without proof. On the contrary, for the good of the church, we have no other wish than that what is adduced by the followers of this doctrine be strictly examined and that nothing be granted unless it greatly outweighs the rival arguments. If they are only 90 percent right, we shall consider them refuted. . . . We can afford to be so generous because it is clear that those who are of the wrong position cannot have any valid reason or experiment, whereas for those on the right side everything necessarily fits.

Commenting on the relative motion of the boat and the shore, he wrote:

> The error of regarding the apparent motion of the shore and the immobility of the boat is clear to us once we have observed several times the motion of the boat from the shore, and the shore from the boat. Thus if we could stand on the earth and then go to the sun or some other planet, perhaps we would gain certain and sensory knowledge as to which moves.[23]

But would such sensory evidence in fact yield certainty? A lunar inhabitant would see the earth and the sun revolve around *his* planet, and he would *feel himself* to be at rest.

Why did Galileo thus overstate his case? To make sense of his claims, we must understand his conception of science. We can hardly overestimate the importance of the ideas that a scientist brings to his scientific work, especially those that concern what he looks for and how he goes about finding it. Before a scientist can even begin to work, he must have some idea about what it means to know—that is, to know scientifically—and at least a general plan for advancing toward his knowledge. These ideas we may call the scientist's heuristic structure.

Galileo never vouchsafed a definition of science or a systematic account of scientific procedure. Yet his practice is eloquent. There is no doubt that he considered himself a disciple of Archimedes and that he believed mathematics to be the key to the interpretation of nature:

> Philosophy is written in this great book—I mean the universe—which stands continually open to our gaze, but it cannot be understood unless one first studies the language and the characters in which it is written. It is written in the language of mathematics, and its characters are triangles, circles, and other geometrical figures, without which is it humanly impossible to understand a single word of it.[24]

This view of nature is the hidden root of natural science in the Renaissance. Galileo loathed people who reiterated "trumpetlike" everything that was old, but he adhered dogmatically to the notion that the world was written in mathematical symbols. His instinct for theoretical elegance told him that Copernicus was right, and although the actual observations were only partially in his favor, he was certain that he would be vindicated in the end. He displayed a scornful impatience with the complexity of data, a kind of self-righteousness characteristic of minds whose goals, when they address themselves to nature, are order and simplicity.

How did this outlook agree with early-seventeenth-century attitudes? Despite considerable opposition, Aristotle's view that true theories are discoverable still held sway in physics, while astronomy was dominated by the Ptolemaic reliance on geometrical arguments to "save the phenomena" without necessarily claiming that these arguments were true in nature. Hence, the orthodoxy of the day called for naive realism in physics and instrumentalism in astronomy.

Aristotle's position is particularly important because, however much his latter-day opponents attacked him, they usually retained more of his philosophy than they would have been fond of admitting. Galileo attacked several of Aristotle's ideas, but he never queried Aristotle's scientific realism—namely, the view that there is a uniquely true physical theory, discoverable by human powers of reason and observation, and that alternative theories are consequently false. Where Galileo differed from Aristotle was in his conception of the nature of this physical reality. To speak very broadly, Aristotle looked at nature as a process by which things fulfill their potential, and this turned speculation away from questions of structure and mechanism toward questions of function and development. This concern with teleology was allied with the belief that natural philosophy could be built directly on perception and that mathematics could not explain the colorful and qualitatively determined facts of common experience. Galileo considered such an approach naive and misleading, and he sought to transcend the limitations of Aristotelian empiricism by claiming that reality is mathematical in form and that mathematical theory should determine the very structure of experimental research. In this he was following the ancient mathematician Archimedes, who was commonly regarded by Galileo's contemporaries as a Platonist. Galileo's mathematical essentialism (the view that nature is basically mathematical) must, in fact, be seen against the background of the Platonic revival of the period, especially in Florence, despite the fact that Galileo differed from Plato in the character of his essentialism. Plato had held that the physical world was a copy or likeness of a transcendent, ideal world of mathematical forms; it was an inexact copy, and therefore physics could never yield absolute truth but only likely stories. Galileo, by contrast, held that the world actually consisted of the mathematical primary and secondary qualities and their laws and that these laws were discoverable in detail and with absolute certainty.

Conflict and Condemnation

It was in this frame of mind that Galileo, encouraged by his admirers, expanded the letter to Castelli into a brilliant treatise on hermeneutics, which he dedicated to Cosimo's mother, the grand duchess Christina. His friends, however, warned him "to keep out of the sacristy" and urged him to reiterate frequently his willingness to submit to the proper authorities.[25] The specific shoals Galileo had to avoid were issues that are little dwelt on now but that were of paramount importance to men of his time. The four main ones were the possible existence of rational creatures on other planets, the location of hell, Christ's ascension, and the anthropocentric purpose of creation.

Giovanni Ciampoli (ca. 1590-1643), who was later to be involved in the publication of Galileo's *Dialogue,* wrote from Rome on 28 February 1615, warning Galileo of the dangerous speculations to which his astronomical discoveries gave rise:

> Your opinion of the phenomena of light and shade on the clear and spotted surfaces of the moon assumes some analogy between the earth and the moon. Someone adds to this and says that you assume that the moon is inhabited by men. Then another starts discussing how they could be descended from Adam

or how they could have gotten out of Noah's ark, and many other extravagant ideas that you never even dreamed of. It is indispensable, therefore, to remove the possibility of malignant rumors by repeatedly protesting of one's willingness to defer to the authority of those who have jurisdiction over the human intellect in matters of the interpretation of the Scriptures.[26]

That people should have been exercised over the location of hell will come as a surprise to the modern reader, be he Christian or agnostic. Yet the belief that hell was a real place situated in the center of the earth was widely held among Christians well into the seventeenth century. Francesco Ingoli, the first secretary of the *Sacra Congregatio de Propaganda Fide,* one of the most successful ventures of the new bureaucracy of the Counter-Reformation, objected to Galileo on precisely this point.[27] Characteristically, he appealed for support to the Roman authority of the day, Cardinal Bellarmine. The cardinal's influential views are worth rehearsing. In a chapter of his *Controversia Generalis de Christo* entitled "Hell is a subterranean place distinct from the tombs," he gives several arguments, and concludes:

> The last is natural reason. There is no doubt that it is indeed reasonable that the place of devils and wicked damned men should be as far as possible from the place where angels and blessed men will be forever. The abode of the blessed (as our adversaries agree) is heaven, and no place is further removed from heaven than the center of the earth.[28]

Phrases such as "natural reason" and "it is indeed reasonable" illustrate how "reason," like its yokefellow "nature," could be made equivalent, in less guarded moments, to the usual assumptions of contemporary good sense, where "good sense" was implicitly defined by the Council of Trent.

Centuries of theological insight had purged the Christian supernatural order of cruder elements, and by the seventeenth century the spatial location of hell was no longer held by all Christians to be an article of faith. But side by side with this rational religion, or concealed beneath it, there still persisted mental habits more deep-rooted and more ancient, which expressed themselves in the pictorial beliefs Bellarmine was defending. It is, of course, easier to think pictorially than abstractly; hence the vitality, for instance, of popular demonology. The factual basis of Christ's ascension seemed also to be imperiled by the motion of the earth. Here again the diagrammatic representation of theory that placed the sun at the center of the universe and the earth above or below it added to the difficulty of visualizing Christ ascending into the uppermost region of the heavens.[29] Finally, the notion that the world had been created for mankind set up psychological barriers to accepting the earth as merely another planet revolving about the sun. After his interview with the archbishop of Pisa in 1615, Benedetto Castelli wrote to Galileo: "He took but a single reason from his stock, omitting all others, and the gist of it was that since all things are created for man, it is clearly a necessary consequence that the earth cannot move like the stars."[30]

It was with these difficulties in mind that Galileo set out to reconcile the Scriptures with the Copernican theory by reinterpreting contentious passages in the Bible and confuting current "misinterpretations." Galileo's solution was to affirm that the "Word of God" can be read not only in Scripture, where it is often to be understood metaphorically (as when God is said to have hands and feet, or that he is angry and repents) or according to the common parlance (as when it is stated that the sun rises and sets), but also in nature, where it is to be interpreted with all the rigor of mathematical language. Nature, which is the undoubted word of God, we are never to renounce. What, then, are we to do when Scripture, which we acknowledge to be supernaturally inspired, appears to conflict with nature? In his ***Letter to the Grand Duchess Christina,*** Galileo offered two quite different views of the relation between the Bible and natural science. One series of arguments was to become the characteristic reply of the latter part of the seventeenth century. According to this line of argument, there can be nothing in Scripture contrary to reason, but there are many things that are above reason. Moreover, where Scripture appears to contradict reason it requires reinterpretation, since God, the author of the two inspired books, cannot contradict himself. No one prior to Galileo spoke with such clarity of the relationship between science and Scripture:

> I think that in discussing natural problems we should not begin from the authority of scriptural passages, but from sensory experiences and necessary demonstrations; for Holy Scripture and nature proceed alike from the divine Word, the former as the dictate of the Holy Spirit and the latter as the faithful executrix of God's commands. Furthermore, Scripture, adapting itself to the understanding of the common man, is wont to say many things that appear to differ from absolute truth as far as the bare meaning of the words is concerned. Nature, on the contrary, is inexorable and immutable; she never transcends the limits of the laws imposed upon her, and she is indifferent whether her secret reasons and ways of operating are understood by men. It would seem, therefore, that nothing physical that sense experience sets before our eyes, or that necessary demonstrations prove to us, should be called in question, not to say condemned, because of biblical passages that have an apparently different meaning. Scriptural statements are not bound by rules as strict as natural events, and God is not less excellently revealed in these events than in the sacred propositions of the Bible.[31]

Quoting the *bon mot* of Cardinal Baronius—"The intention of the Holy Ghost is to teach us how one goes to heaven, not how heaven goes" Galileo added that the aim of Scripture is not to disclose what we can know by our senses and intellect (for then why would God have endowed us with these faculties?) but what surpasses human understanding.[32] In his view, therefore, incidental references to physical phenomena in the Scriptures are simply irrelevant to problems of natural science: the conveyance of scientific truth is not the Bible's purpose.

But Galileo also made use of another line of argument that leads to a different conclusion. It was inspired by the traditional hermeneutics of Saint Augustine, who made clear that the literal interpretation of any given biblical passage that is not clearly allegorical or metaphorical is to be preferred at all times. Only when a *demonstrated* scientific truth conflicts with a passage as literally interpreted can that passage be reinterpreted. Galileo quotes Saint Augustine with approval on this point and then proceeds to observe:

> In the books of the sages of this world, some natural things are truly demonstrated while others are merely stated. As to the former, it is the office of wise theologians to show that they are not contrary to the Holy Scriptures; as to the latter, which are asserted but not rigorously demonstrated, if they contain anything contrary to Holy Writ, they are to be considered undoubtedly false and proved so by every possible means.[33]

The question, of course is: into which category does the heliocentric theory fall? Galileo was convinced that he had found a compelling physical proof of the motion of the earth. This is his celebrated, but unfortunately mistaken, argument from the tides. Galileo believed that the ebb and flow of the sea was caused by a combination of the earth's daily rotation on its axis and its annual revolution around the sun.[34] Confident that his new proof would take Rome by storm, Galileo journeyed to the Eternal City at the end of 1615. When the Tuscan ambassador, Pietro Guicciardini, heard that Galileo was coming, he quickly dispatched a letter to the secretary of state in Florence reminding him that Rome was hardly "a place to discuss things on the moon." Pope Paul V (1605-1621), apprised of Galileo's theory by the young Cardinal Alessandro Orsini, immediately replied: "You would do well to dissuade him from holding such a view."[35] The matter was referred to the Holy Office. The result was that Copernicus's *De Revolutionibus* and Foscarini's *Letter* were placed on the Index of Prohibited Books. Galileo, however, was spared any unpleasantness and even given a certificate by Cardinal Bellarmine to the effect that he had not been asked to recant any of his theories.

Galileo had practically resigned himself to silence when Cardinal Maffeo Barberini, a native Florentine, was elected pope in 1623 under the name Urban VIII (1623-1644). In the following spring Galileo journeyed to Rome where Urban VIII granted him no less than six audiences; gave him a painting, two medals, several *Agni Dei,* and the promise of a pension for his son; and, last but not least, agreed that he could write about the motion of the earth provided he represented it not as reality but as a scientific hypothesis. During his stay in Rome, Galileo made the acquaintaince of Cardinal Frederic Eutel Zollern, who offered to discuss the Copernican question with the pope before his return to Germany. Zollern represented to the pope that the German Protestants were all in favor of the new system and hence that it was necessary to proceed with the utmost caution before the church attempted to settle the Copernican question. The pope replied that the church had never declared the view of Copernicus to be heretical and would not do so, but that there was no reason to suppose that a proof of the Copernican system would ever be forthcoming.[36] Galileo returned to Florence with this encouraging news and set to work on his **Dialogue on the Two Chief World Systems.** Unfortunately, Cardinal Zollern died in 1625, and Galileo lost a friend who could have been a key witness at his trial eight years later. Misfortune also struck in the form of ill health; between 1626 and 1629 Galileo was unable to work with any regularity, and it was only in January 1630 that he managed to finish his long-awaited masterpiece. He hoped that it would be steered through the shoals of Roman censorship by his friends Cesare Ciampoli and the Dominican Niccolò Riccardi, who had become Master of the Apostolic Palace and whose duty it was to authorize the publication of books.

When Riccardi received the manuscript of the **Dialogue** from Galileo's hands in the spring of 1630, he passed it on to a fellow Dominican, Raffaello Visconti. Visconti was sympathetic to astronomy, but his interests extended to astrology and the occult sciences as well. He was a personal friend of Orazio Morandi, the abbot of S. Prassede in Rome, who was known to have spent a considerable time in the company of Antonio and Giovanni de' Medici, mastering the secrets of the Hermetic tradition. In the spring of 1630, probably in the first fortnight of May, Morandi published certain prophecies based on astrological computations, among them one that predicted the early death of the pope. Galileo, who had arrived in Rome on 3 May, was almost certainly unaware of this incident when he received, on the 24th of May, an invitation to dine with Morandi in the company of Visconti; but Roman gossip had already linked his name with theirs. Galileo left Rome on 26 June, and shortly thereafter Morandi was imprisoned in the Tor di Nona. Galileo requested information from a mutual friend, who replied on 17 August that the trial was so secret that there was no way of knowing what was happening. At the trial an "Astrological Discourse on the Life of Urban VIII" bearing Visconti's name was brought forward. Viscon-

ti must have been at least partly successful in his plea of innocence, since he was only banished from Rome, while several others received heavy sentences. Morandi himself died in prison on 9 October 1630, before the completion of his trial.

In the spring of 1631 Urban VIII issued a bull (renewing the prescriptions of Sixtus V's bull *Coeli et Terrae Creator* of 5 January 1586) against astrologers who claimed the power of knowing the future and of setting in motion secret forces for the good or harm of the living. Urban commanded that an eye should be kept on such magical arts as were directed against the life of the pope and that of his relatives down to the third degree. Guilty parties were to be punished not only with excommunication but also with death and confiscation of property. That Galileo's name should have been associated with those of Morandi and Visconti was unfortunate, to say the least. Little did he suspect that his intimacy with Ciampoli would prove even more damaging.

Urban VIII was a poet in his leisure hours and enjoyed the company of literary men, one of whom was Giovanni Ciampoli, his secretary of briefs. Ciampoli's relations with the pope were quite intimate, and he became confident that he could read his master's mind. He was also impatient to secure the cardinal's hat that Urban VIII distributed to men whom Ciampoli considered his inferiors. In his frustration he became reckless and allowed himself to be befriended by acquaintances of the Spanish cardinal Gaspare Borgia, the spokesman of Philip IV and a thorn in Urban's flesh. When Cardinal Borgia publicly protested against the pope's position in the struggle between France and the House of Hapsburg in a stormy consistory on 8 March 1632, Urban decided to purge his entourage of pro-Spanish elements. He was particularly incensed upon hearing of Ciampoli's relations with the Spaniards. He stripped Ciampoli of his considerable powers and in August 1632 exiled him to the governorship of the small town of Montalto; Ciampoli was never allowed to return to Rome.

Ciampoli's downfall was to have important consequences for Galileo. In 1630 and 1631 Ciampoli had played a vital role in securing permission for the printing of Galileo's **Dialogue.** Visconti had informed Riccardi that he approved of the book and that it needed only a few minor corrections. Riccardi, after considerable anguish and delay, granted the *imprimatur,* first for Rome, later for Florence where it was to be censored by the local consultor of the Inquisition. He insisted, however, that the preface and the conclusion be forwarded to him. When the Florentine censor gave permission to go to press in September 1630, Riccardi began to raise difficulties and to claim that Galileo had agreed to return to Rome to discuss the final draft. Meanwhile, an outbreak of plague had rendered travel between Florence and Rome difficult, and Riccardi proposed that a copy of the work be sent to Rome "to be revised by Monsignor Ciampoli and myself."[37] Even this requirement was eventually waived, and thereafter Riccardi heard no more of the book until a printed copy reached him in Rome; above the Florentine *imprimatur* he discovered, to his horror, his own approbation. As Urban VIII remarked to the Tuscan ambassador, "the name of the Master of the Holy Palace has nothing to do with books printed elsewhere."[38] Summoned to account for his behavior, Riccardi excused himself by saying that he had received orders to license the book from Ciampoli himself.[39]

The *Dialogue* had gone to press in June 1631. The publisher had decided to print a thousand copies, a large edition for the time, and the work was not completed until 21 February 1632. Copies did not reach Rome until the end of March or early April, thus bursting onto the Roman scene only a few weeks after the consistory in which Cardinal Borgia attacked Urban VIII. Any "Ciampolata," as Urban put it,[40] was bound to be looked at closely. Moreover, the Roman *imprimatur* on a Florentine publication was bound to arouse suspicion. Riccardi was instructed to write to the Florentine inquisitor and have a ban placed on the sale of Galileo's book pending further notice. In the climate of deep suspicion that followed the Borgia incident, even the emblem of three dolphins (which could be associated with Hermetism) on the frontispiece caused concern. It was with relief that Riccardi learned that the device was not Galileo's but the printer's and appeared on all of his publications.

In the summer of 1632 Urban VIII ordered a Preliminary Commission to investigate the licensing of the *Dialogue.* In the file on Galileo in the Holy Office the Commission found an unsigned memorandum of an injunction, allegedly received by Galileo in 1616, "not to hold, teach or defend *in any way whatsoever*" that the earth moves.[41] The authenticity of the document is now contested, but the commissioners considered it genuine and concluded that Galileo had contravened a formal order of the Holy Office.[42] In the light of this discovery Galileo was summoned to Rome, arriving, after much delay, on 13 February 1633; he remained in Rome as guest of the Tuscan ambassador while three theologians read his *Dialogue* to ascertain whether he had presented the Copernican doctrine as a proved fact rather than a hypothesis. The closing paragraph of the *Dialogue* contained a statement, proposed by Urban himself, to the effect that the Copernican view was "neither true nor conclusive" and that "it would be excessive boldness for anyone to limit and restrict the divine power and wisdom to one particular fancy of his own."[43] Unfortunately, Galileo had put these words into the mouth of Simplicio, the Aristotelian pedant, who cuts such a poor intellectual figure throughout the *Dialogue.* The theologians were quick to spot this; and

A representation of Galileo's Dialogue.

the pope, when it was called to his attention, was personally affronted.

On 12 April Galileo was summoned to the Holy Office; there he was kept in custody and twice interrogated, before being allowed to return to the residence of the Tuscan ambassador. He appeared again before the tribunal on 10 May and 21 June, but at no time was he physically tortured or molested. In the end, despite a vigorous denial that he had intended to argue in favor of the truth of the heliocentric system, Galileo was judged to have contravened the orders of the church. On the morning of 22 June 1633 he was taken to a hall in the convent of Santa Maria sopra Minerva in Rome, where he was made to kneel while the sentence condemning him to imprisonment was read. Still kneeling, Galileo was ordered to abjure his error. He recanted in the following words:

> I, Galileo Galilei, son of the late Vincenzio Galilei of Florence, aged seventy years, tried personally by this court, and kneeling before you, most Eminent and Reverend Lord Cardinals, Inquisitors-General throughout the Christian Republic against heretical depravity, having before my eyes the most Holy

Gospels, and laying my own hands on them, do swear that I have always believed, do now believe, and with God's help will in the future believe all that the Holy Catholic and Apostolic Church does hold, preach, and teach. But since I, after having been admonished by this Holy Office entirely to abandon the false opinion that the sun is the center of the universe and immovable, and that the earth is not the center of the same and that I was neither to hold, defend, nor teach in any manner whatsoever, either orally or in writing, the said false doctrine, . . . did write and cause to be printed a book in which I treat of the said already condemned doctrine, and bring forward arguments of much efficacy in its favor, without arriving at any solution; I have been judged vehemently suspected of heresy, that is, of having held and believed that the sun is the center of the universe and immovable and that the earth is not the center of the same nor immovable.

Nevertheless, wishing to remove from the minds of your Eminences and all faithful Christians this vehement suspicion reasonably conceived against me, I abjure with a sincere heart and unfeigned faith, I curse and detest the aforesaid errors and heresies. . . . And I swear that for the future I will neither say nor assert in speaking or writing such things as may bring upon me similar suspicion. . . .[44]

Galileo was not formally incarcerated but was allowed to leave for Siena and later Florence, where he was confined to his country estate.

Galileo sought comfort in work, and within two years he completed the ***Two New Sciences,*** the book to which his lasting fame as a scientist is attached. When he cast about for a publisher, he came up against a new problem: the church had issued a general prohibition against printing or reprinting any of his books. Through a friend in Venice, Galileo's manuscript reached the famous publisher Louis Elzevir in Holland, a Protestant country over which the Roman church had no power. At once Elzevir undertook the printing; Galileo feigned surprise and pretended not to know how the manuscript had left Italy. Although it is unlikely that anyone believed his story, the church let the publication of the ***Two New Sciences*** in 1638 go unchallenged. Galileo, however, was never successful in obtaining the pardon he longed for and was still under house arrest when he received the visit of the young English poet John Milton. Of this visit little is known, but the context in which Milton mentions it is highly significant. It occurs in the *Areopagita,* a speech addressed to Parliament against an ordinance requiring the licensing of all books:

I could recount what I have seen and heard in other countries where this kind of Inquisition tyrannizes . . . that this was it which had damped the glory of Italian wits; that nothing had been there

written now these many years but flattery and fustian. There it was that I found and visited the famous Galileo, grown old, a prisoner of the Inquisition, for thinking in astronomy otherwise than the Franciscan and Dominican licensers thought.[45]

In fact, Galileo's condemnation was the result of the complex interplay of untoward political circumstances, personal ambitions, and wounded prides. Nevertheless, Milton was right in believing that the whole episode had the effect of inhibiting scientific speculation in Catholic countries. He was also right in sensing the underlying conflict between the authoritarian ideal of the Counter-Reformation and the nascent desire and need for freedom in the pursuit of scientific knowledge. Had Galileo been less devout, he could have refused to go to Rome; Venice offered him asylum. Had he been less convinced of the truth of his theory, he could have treated it as mere conjecture and remained at peace with the church. But Galileo could not resign himself to either course. He pressed for a prompt acceptance of his theories, and Urban VIII responded with a stern reaffirmation of the authority of the pope. Science and religion were both to suffer from the clash, and what could have been a fruitful dialogue proved to be a bitter feud. It was not until 1832 that Galileo's ***Dialogue*** was dropped from the Index of Prohibited Books and Catholics allowed to teach Copernicanism with complete freedom.

Notes

[1] For an introductory account of Galileo's difficulties with the church see Jerome L. Langford, *Galileo, Science, and the Church,* rev. ed. (Ann Arbor: Univ. of Michigan Press, 1971); also Giorgio de Santillana, *The Crime of Galileo* (Chicago: Univ. of Chicago Press, 1955). Pietro Redondi has recently argued, in *Galileo eretico* (Turin: Einaudi, 1983), that the trial for teaching that the earth moves was a cover-up for the more serious charge that Galileo's atomism imperiled the Catholic dogma of transubstantiation. Redondi's case rests on the highly conjectural attribution of an anonymous letter to the Jesuit Orazio Grassi.

[2] For a general account of the Counter-Reformation see Arthur G. Dickens, *The Counter Reformation* (London: Thomas & Hudson, 1968); Marvin R. O'Connell, *The Counter Reformation* (New York: Harper & Row, 1974).

[3] Luigi Firpo, "Filosofia italiana e contriforma," *Rivista di filosofia* 41 (1950): 166, relying on I. Fuligatti, *Vita Roberti Bellarmini Politiani S.J.* (Antwerp, 1631), pp. 189-190.

[4] Another great systematizer was the Dominican Melchior Cano, whose *De Locis Theologicis Libri Duodecim* was published in 1563 and reprinted six times

before 1605; see P. Mandonnet, "Melchior Cano," *Dictionnaire de théologie catholique* 2:1538.

[5] Jean Delumeau, *Vie économique et sociale de Rome dans la seconde moitié du XVIe siècle,* 2 vols. (Paris: E. de Boccard, 1957-1959), 1:219.

[6] Robert Bellarmine, *Controversia Generalis de Summo Pontifice* 1.2, in *Opera Omnia,* 12 vols. (Paris: L. Vivès, 1870-1874), 1:464-465.

[7] Bellarmine, *De Officio Principis Christiani Libri Tres* 1.11, in *Opera Omnia* 8:109-110.

[8] See H. Outram Evennett, *The Spirit of the Counter-Reformation* (Cambridge: Cambridge Univ. Press, 1968), pp. 109-110.

[9] Heinrich Reusch, *Die "Indices Librorum Prohibitorum" des sechzehnten Jahrhunderts* (Nieuwkoop: B. de Graaf, 1961), pp. 176-208.

[10] Luigi Firpo, "Il processo di Giordano Bruno," *Rivista storica italiana* 60 (1948): 542-597; 61 (1949): 5-59; Luigi Firpo, "Processo e morte di Francesco Pucci," *Rivista di filosofia* 40 (1949): 371-405.

[11] *Le opere di Galileo Galilei,* ed. Antonio Favaro, 20 vols. (Florence: G. Barbèra, 1899-1909), 11:119 (letter of 31 May 1611). On Galileo and Copernicanism see William R. Shea, *Galileo's Intellectual Revolution,* 2d ed. (New York: Science History Publications, 1977); Maurice Clavelin, *The Natural Philosophy of Galileo,* trans. A. J. Pomerans (Cambridge, Mass.: Harvard Univ. Press, 1978); Ernan McMullin, ed., *Galileo: Man of Science* (New York: Basic Books, 1967); *Discoveries and Opinions of Galileo,* trans. Stillman Drake (Garden City, N.Y.: Anchor, 1957); and Alexandre Koyré, *Galileo Studies,* trans. John Mepham (Atlantic Highlands, N.J.: Humanities Press, 1978).

[12] Galileo Galilei, *Istoria e dimostrazioni intorno alle macchie solari,* in *Opere* 5:93.

[13] Ibid., p. 238, and critical apparatus for lines 29-30.

[14] As late as 1618 Federico Cesi found it necessary to argue that the heavens are not crystalline spheres. See his letter of 14 Aug. 1618 to Cardinal Bellarmine, "De caeli unitate, tenuitate fusaque et pervia stellarum motibus natura ex sacris litteris," and Bellarmine's reply, in Christoph Scheiner, *Rosa Ursina* (Bracciano, 1630), pp. 777-783.

[15] Galileo, *Istoria e dimostrazioni,* in *Opere* 5:138-139, and critical apparatus for line 24.

[16] Galileo's letter to a Florentine correspondent, Feb. 1610, *Opere* 10:233.

[17] An incomplete translation of this work is given in Drake's *Discoveries and Opinions of Galileo,* pp. 175-216.

[18] Letter from Luigi Maraffi to Galileo, 10 Jan. 1615, *Opere* 12:127.

[19] Letter from Cesi to Galileo, 12 Jan. 1615, *Opere* 12:129.

[20] Paolo Antonio Foscarini, *Lettera sopra l'opinione de Pittagorici e del Copernico della mobilità della terra* (Naples, 1615).

[21] Letter from Bellarmine to Foscarini, 12 Apr. 1615, in Galileo, *Opere* 12:171-172.

[22] "Considerazioni sopra l'opinione Copernicana," *Opere* 5:367-368.

[23] Ibid., pp. 368-370.

[24] Galileo, *The Assayer,* in *Discoveries and Opinions,* trans. Drake, pp. 237-238. Here and in what follows I have made substantial alterations to Drake's translations. See *Opere* 6:232.

[25] Letter from Piero Dini to Galileo, 2 May 1615, *Opere* 12:175.

[26] Letter from Ciampoli to Galileo, 28 Feb. 1615, *Opere* 12:146. As early as 1611 Campanella had used Galileo's discovery of similarities between the earth and the moon as a peg on which to hang some of his most daring speculations: "There is much to be discussed about the shape of the stars and the planets and the kind of government to be found among the inhabitants of celestial bodies. . . . If the moon is more contemptible than the earth . . . its inhabitants are less happy than we are" (letter to Galileo, 12 Jan. 1610, in Galileo, *Opere* 11:22). As such ideas became widespread, Galileo felt it necessary to write to Cardinal Giacomo Muti in 1616 to deny that he assumed the existence of rational creatures on the moon (letter to Muti, 28 Feb. 1616, *Opere* 12:240-241).

[27] Ingoli, *De Situ et Quiete Terrae contra Copernicum Disputatio,* in Galileo, *Opere* 5:408.

[28] Robert Bellarmine, *Controversia Generalis de Christo* 5.10, in *Opera Omnia* 1:418. Bellarmine also located purgatory and limbo at the center of the earth, near hell (*Controversia Generalis de Purgatorio,* 2.6, in *Opere Omnia* 3:109-112).

[29] This was felt to be a serious difficulty by J. G. Locher, *Disquisitiones Mathematicae de Controversiis et Novitatibus Astronomicis* (Ingolstadt, 1614), p. 23; Paolo Foscarini, *Lettera sopra l'opinione de Pittagorici,* pp. 15-16; Marin Mersenne, *Quaestiones Celeber-*

rimae in Genesim (Paris, 1624), col. 897. Galileo sought to allay such fears in his *Dialogue Concerning the Two Chief World Systems,* trans. Stillman Drake, 2d ed. (Berkeley and Los Angeles: Univ. of California Press, 1967), p. 357.

[30] Castelli to Galileo, 12 Mar. 1615, in Galileo, *Opere* 12:154.

[31] *Discoveries and Opinions,* trans. Drake, pp. 182-183; *Opere* 5:316-317. This letter was first published by Matthias Bernegger in Strassburg in 1636, but it had already enjoyed a wide manuscript circulation; for example, in the "Fondo Corsiano" of the Roman Accademia dei Lincei alone, Ada Alessandrini found four manuscript copies (*Galileo Galilei: Celebrazioni del IV centenario della nascita* [Rome: Accademia dei Lincei, 1965], p. 174).

[32] *Discoveries and Opinions,* trans. Drake, p. 186; *Opere* 5:319.

[33] *Discoveries and Opinions,* trans. Drake, p. 194; *Opere* 5:327.

[34] For Galileo's argument see Shea, *Galileo's Intellectual Revolution,* pp. 172-189.

[35] Guicciardini to Curzio Picchena, 5 Dec. 1615, in Galileo, *Opere* 12:242.

[36] Letter from Galileo to Federico Cesi, 8 June 1624, *Opere* 13:182.

[37] Letter from Castelli to Galileo, 21 Sept. 1630, *Opere* 14:150.

[38] Letter from Niccolini to Andrea Cioli, 5 Sept. 1632, *Opere* 14:384.

[39] From an account of Galileo's trial written by Giovanfrancesco Buonamici, in Galileo, *Opere* 19:410.

[40] Letter from Niccolini to Cioli, 26 Feb. 1633, *Opere* 15:56. Ciampoli was not the only dignitary to incur the wrath of the pope. In July 1633 Cardinal Roberto Ubaldini, suspected of sympathizing with the Spaniards, was deprived of "the share of the poor cardinals," namely the emolument paid by the Holy See to prelates who had no independent means of subsistence. Ubaldini was one of the cardinals to have received a telescope from Galileo, and in his letter of acknowledgment had professed himself eager to help Galileo (letter of 29 July 1618, *Opere* 12:401).

[41] *Opere* 19:322.

[42] On this document see de Santillana, *Crime of Galileo,* pp. 261-274. Langford, *Galileo, Science, and the Church,* pp. 93-97; Stillman Drake and Giorgio de Santillana, in appendices to Ludovico Geymonat, *Galileo Galilei: A Biography and Inquiry into His Philosophy of Science,* trans. Stillman Drake (New York: McGraw-Hill, 1965), pp. 205-225.

[43] *Opere* 7:489. The pope's argument had already appeared in print in Agostino Oregio, *De Deo Uno* (Rome, 1629), pp. 193-195; quoted in Antonio Favaro, *Gli oppositori di Galileo VI: Maffeo Barberini* (Venice: Antonelli, 1921), pp. 26-27.

[44] *Opere* 19:406-407; see also Langford, *Galileo, Science, and the Church,* pp. 153-154.

[45] *The Essential Milton,* ed. Douglas Bush (London: Chatto & Windus, 1949), p. 183.

Richard S. Westfall (essay date 1989)

SOURCE: "Bellarmino, Galileo, and the Clash of Two World Views," in *Essays on the Trial of Galileo,* Vatican Observatory Publications, 1989, pp. 1-30.

[*In the following essay, Westfall summarizes the backgrounds of Galileo and his adversary, Cardinal Bellarmino (also known as Bellarmine), and argues that their conflict regarding Galileo's officially heretical belief in a Copernican or heliocentric universe began as early as 1610 with the publication of* Sidereus nuncius (The Starry Messenger).]

> And because it has also come to the attention of the aforementioned Sacred Congregation [the final paragraph of a decree of 5 March 1616 by the Congregation of the Index stated] that the Pythagorean doctrine concerning the mobility of the earth and the immobility of the sun, which Nicholas Copernicus, *De revolutionibus orbium coelestium,* and Diego de Zùñiga [in his commentary] on Job also taught, and which is false and altogether incompatible with divine Scripture, is now spread abroad and accepted by many, as appears from a certain printed Epistle of a certain Carmelite Father [Foscarini] . . . ; therefore, in order that an opinion ruinous to Catholic truth not creep [*serpat*] further in this manner, the Sacred Congregation decrees that the said Nicholas Copernicus, *De revolutionibus orbium,* and Diego de Zùñiga on Job be suspended until corrected; that the book of the Carmelite Father Paolo Antonio Foscarini be indeed altogether prohibited and damned; and that all other books similarly teaching the same thing be prohibited: as accordingly it prohibits, damns, and suspends them all by the present Decree.[1]

Although Galileo was not mentioned in the decree of the Congregation of the Index, which made Copernican astronomy a forbidden topic among faithful Catholics for the following two centuries, the decree was the direct outcome of events of the previous two years that had centered on him. The decree was equally the direct outcome of the resolution Cardinal Roberto Bellarmino had begun to form almost as soon as Galileo had published his *Sidereus nuncius* early in 1610. The trial of Galileo in 1633, one of the climactic events of the Scientific Revolution, and indeed of all European history, would have been unthinkable without the prior decree of 1616, the culmination of what is sometimes called the first trial of Galileo. Central to both trials was the confrontation between two antithetical world views, embodied of course in Galileo and Bellarmino.

Galileo

In the case of Galileo as well as Bellarmino it is perhaps more valid to look back, not just to the previous two years, but beyond them to the *Sidereus nuncius.* Although there is evidence that Galileo may have considered himself a Copernican by 1597,[2] it took the telescopic discoveries to turn him into Copernicus' ardent champion. For other reasons as well, the *Sidereus nuncius,* the small book that announced the first discoveries, had made Galileo a figure of controversy. By naming the satellites of Jupiter after the ruling family in his native Tuscany and dedicating the book to Cosimo II, Galileo had used his discoveries to win appointment as Mathematician and Philosopher to the Grand Duke, and the handsome stipend that accompanied the appointment focused envy on him from the day he arrived home in Florence. Galileo was supremely self-assured and abrasively self-assertive in any case; the favor shown him by the Grand Duke did nothing to dull the cutting edge of his personality. Already in 1611, his friend Cigoli reported a rumor that Galileo's enemies around the Tuscan court were plotting to attack him through the Church on the issue of the motion of the earth,[3] and a year later Galileo confronted one of the leaders in the circle of his opponents, Niccolo Lorini, about statements he was reported to have made against Galileo.[4] It was not until 12 December 1613, however, that the rumors took on solid substance. On that day, Benedetto Castelli, Galileo's student, follower, and devoted friend, whom the master's influence had recently installed as Professor of Mathematics at the University of Pisa, was honored to dine with the court, then in residence in Pisa. Talk at dinner had centered on Galileo's discoveries, and one Cosimo Boscaglia, the Professor of Philosophy, had whispered in the ear of the dowager Grand Duchess, Christina of Lorraine, that passages in Scripture opposed the concept of a moving earth. As Castelli was leaving after dinner, he found himself called back to a further discussion, which lasted two hours, of Copernicanism and the Scriptures, in which everyone present understood that Castelli was substituting for Galileo, while the Grand Duchess actively attacked his position.[5]

In response to Castelli's report of this occasion, Galileo composed a long letter on the authority of Scripture in science.[6] For a year nothing further happened, at least overtly, though copies of Galileo's letter circulated in Florence. Then in December of 1614 a young Dominican anxious to make a name for himself, Tommaso Caccini, was preaching in Santa Maria Novella on the book of Joshua. When he came to the famous verse in which Joshua, needing more time to smite the Amorites, prayed that the sun should stand still, a passage which Galileo had explicated at length in his letter, Caccini suddenly launched into a vigorous attack on Galileo, Copernican astronomers, and mathematicians in general.[7] Caccini later testified before the Inquisition that Niccolo Lorini had shown him Galileo's letter to Castelli after the sermon.[8] In view of the prominence of the passage in Joshua in Galileo's letter, this order of events is scarcely credible; on the contrary, one perceives the figure of Lorini lurking in the background from the beginning, busily stirring up the entire imbroglio. In any case, Caccini proceeded to lay a copy of Galileo's letter before the Inquisition in Florence, and when nothing happened, Lorini summoned up enough courage to make one move for himself and to send a copy of Galileo's letter to the Inquisition in Rome early in February 1615.

The Roman Inquisition was more vigorous than its Florentine office; it immediately initiated an investigation of Galileo, with the interrogation of witnesses and later the examination of one of his publications, which continued through the rest of 1615.[9] In December Galileo, who understood that the charges against him were nearing their resolution, came to Rome to defend himself. At this point the record becomes confusing; one of my purposes in this paper is to offer a possible resolution, necessarily speculative in view of the evidence available, of the confusion. On the one hand, early in February, 1616, Galileo was writing home that he had cleared himself and convinced the authorities of his integrity.[10] The silence of the Congregation of the Index on Galileo, together with absence of a condemnation by the Holy Office, certainly seems to indicate that he was not mistaken. The confusion arises from the fact that, on the other hand, scarcely two weeks after Galileo said he had cleared himself, the Holy Office asked its consultors to consider two propositions, that the sun is motionless in the center of the world, and that the earth moves in an orbit around the center and rotates on its axis.[11] Identified as "the propositions of the Mathematician Galileo," the two assertions were found to be heretical because opposed to passages in Scripture. That decision was the foundation of a private warning by the Holy Office to Galileo that he should abandon Copernicanism and of the decree by the Congregation of the Index that I have quoted. Why then was Galileo left untouched in public? Integrity in upholding opinions deemed heretical was not usually considered a virtue.

Bellarmino

Cardinal Bellarmino was undoubtedly an important factor, and probably the determinative agent, in the decision of the Church against the heliocentric system in 1616. Elevated to the dignity of cardinal by Clement VIII because, as the Pope said, "he has not his equal for learning in the Church of God,"[12] Bellarmino exercised a spiritual hegemony in Rome, because of his personal qualities, similar to his intellectual one. Nothing illustrates his position in the Church better than the scenes, incredible to the 20th century, at his death and funeral. Everyone recognized his saintliness; everyone was convinced that sainthood, in the Catholic definition of the term, would crown his life, as indeed it did finally, three centuries later. While Bellarmino lay dying, interminably it must have seemed, and in fact for two and a half weeks, cardinals and other prelates of the Church, worldly men who had not hesitated to exploit their positions to enrich themselves, testified by their actions that they nevertheless still acknowledged the medieval ideal of sainthood. Crowding into his chamber, touching and kissing his body, catching his blood in their handkerchiefs when leeches were applied to him, they refused to let the poor man die in peace. When death finally delivered him, they plundered his spartan quarters for relics, even ripping the clothes off his body—indeed more than once. As he lay in state in the church of the Gesu, the mob—not cardinals in this case, though one doubts that they would have held back at the end—nearly tore the body apart for the same purpose, and only with difficulty did the authorities preserve his remains intact for burial.[13] Alive, he had been a member of every congregation of the cardinals in Rome. Cardinal del Monte left testimony that the Congregation of Rites, which included some thirteen other cardinals, often altered decisions reached by common consent of the others, because Bellarmino alone took the opposing side.[14] During the final years of his life, the Cardinal was prefect of both the Holy Office and the Congregation of the Index. This was after the events of 1615-16, to be sure, but he was very much a member of both at the time of those events and therefore, almost by definition, the most important voice in their decisions.[15]

Roberto Bellarmino's whole existence had been shaped by the struggle against heresy. Born in 1542, he entered the world almost simultaneously with the outbreak of the initial war of religion (1546) and the founding of the Jesuit order (1540), the weapon of the Catholic Church against the Protestant heresy, in the service of which Bellarmino would spend his life. His years of childhood and education almost coincided with the Council of Trent (1545-63). Having entered the Society of Jesus in 1560, Bellarmino received his first important assignment at Louvain, in what is now Belgium, in 1569. The low countries were at that time the focal point of the struggle between Catholicism and Protestantism. Bellarmino's seven years in Louvain did much to determine the rest of his career. There he began the study of Protestant theology, his knowledge of which, unrivalled in the Catholic world, was the necessary foundation for his work of refutation.[16] There he met a band of English Catholics led by Nicholas Sanders, whose series of answers to the Protestant enemies appealed to Bellarmino's soul as precisely the sort of militant theology, girded for battle and facing the foe, that the age demanded.[17] Called back to the Society's *Collegio Romano* in 1576, he became the Professor of Controversial Theology in the most important university of the Jesuit order and indeed of the whole Catholic world. By their power, his great *Disputationes de controveriis christianae fidei, adversus nostri temporis haereticos,* in effect, the texts of his lectures delivered during the following twelve years in Rome, made Bellarmino the Catholic theologian most hated in Protestant Europe; they have demonstrated the solidity of their content by remaining the definitive statement of the principles of Catholic faith against the challenge of Protestantism down to our own age. Bellarmino experienced the battle not only as the clash of ideas but also as the clash of swords, and not merely from the safe distance of Rome. In 1590 he accompanied Cardinal Cajetan on his mission to France and was penned up with the Cardinal in Paris during the terrible blockade.[18]

Nor was Protestantism the only heresy the champion of the Catholic Church confronted as the entire edifice of the medieval world was beginning to crumble in the late years of the 16th century. New philosophies also challenged Catholic truth. In 1592, the Inquisition in Venice arrested Giordano Bruno after he had been incautious enough to venture back across the Alps, and a year later Venice had handed Bruno over to Rome. It does not appear to be true that Bellarmino was the principal factor in the ultimate condemnation and execution of Bruno, but there is no doubt that he participated prominently in the process. In 1599, after the Roman Inquisition had shown itself uncertain what to do with its prisoner and had merely left him to languish in prison, Bellarmino, with his years of confronting and defining error and his scholastic habit of reducing every issue to a numbered series of points, boiled the case against Bruno down to eight specific charges.[19] The horrific climax did not then wait much longer. At much the same time, quite another issue also associated with the collapse of the unified order of medieval Europe arose. Like other states of Europe, the Republic of Venice was determined to control the Church within its borders. In 1606 the Pope excommunicated the Doge and the Senate and laid the entire city under interdict until the republic repealed certain laws concerning ecclesiastical affairs and handed over to the Church two priests imprisoned in Venice. It was Bellarmino to whom the Catholic Church entrusted the task of replying to the pamphlets of Paolo Sarpi, the defender of Venetian claims.[20] Soon thereafter James I of England raised much the same question, with all of the details altered, in his theory of the divine right of kings. Again it was Bellarmino who replied to James in the name of the Church.[21]

Not surprisingly, Roberto Bellarmino held definite views about truth and falsehood, and whatever the issue under discussion, he tended to express himself in those terms, usually unqualified by modifiers suggesting uncertainty or doubt.[22] Late in 1591 the Hungarian Jesuit, Stephen Arator, raised objections to passages in Bellarmino's *Controversies.* Replying with spirit, Bellarmino informed Aquaviva, the General of the order, about Arator, whose opinions he found "dangerous and in some cases embarrassing to the Company," "unacceptable and scandalous." Nor was that all; besides Arator's mistakes about the *Controversies,* Bellarmino found, he informed Aquaviva, more than ten erroneous doctrines in his statement; "and if I were not certain that you will remedy this by making him retract, and that he is prone to obey, I would feel obliged in conscience to denounce him to the Holy Office as a man who is dangerous in this time and in those places."[23] Some might think that heresy is a minor problem, he asserted in the preface of his *Controversies.*

> Let me say this one thing; the perversity of heretics is as much worse than all other evils and afflictions as the dreadful and fearful plague is worse than the more common diseases.[24]

Using the same figure years later, he congratulated Maximilian of Bavaria for keeping his lands free from "the dreadful contagion of false doctrine . . ."[25] On the whole, however, Bellarmino found military metaphors more expressive. He was, after all, a Jesuit. In his view of human history, the never ending struggle against heresy was the central theme. The "enemy of the human race" had not assaulted the truth of the Catholic Church without a plan, he argued, in a passage that sounds almost Manichean. During the first two centuries of the Christian era, he had concentrated on the first article of the creed, the conception of one God. When those heresies had failed, he turned during the third and fourth centuries against the second article, the nature of Christ, and then to the mystery of the incarnation and to the doctrine of the Holy Spirit. Failing also in all these attempts, he began about the year 1000 to attack the articles of the creed that concern the Church and the sacraments, and that battle still raged. Bellarmino referred to "the most crafty enemy" who continually schemes against us, and no one is likely to object when I assert that he saw himself called upon to lead the Church in the ongoing war against the foe of humanity itself.[26]

Of necessity, from the nature of the controversies in which he engaged, Bellarmino had a carefully elaborated conception of divine revelation and its authority. Against the Catholic Church, Protestantism had raised the standard of Scripture as the sole authority in matters of faith. Bellarmino replied to the Protestants by insisting that Catholics revered the word of God every bit as much as they did. He devoted the first "Controversy" in his great work to "The Word of God," and he began his exposition with a demonstration that "the Prophetic & Apostolic books . . . are the true word of God, & the certain and fixed rule of faith."[27] However, Bellarmino continued, distinguishing himself from Protestant bibliolators with precision, Scripture is not so open in itself that without explication it is sufficient to settle all controversies about the faith. The manifold differences of interpretation among Protestants seemed to demonstrate this proposition without further argument. Frequently passages in Scripture have two senses, a literal one and a spiritual or mystical one. Thus the flight from Egypt, the crossing of the Red Sea, and the manna that fed Israel all have, in addition to their literal meaning, a spiritual meaning for Christians. Moreover, the literal meaning can be twofold—simple (which is the direct meaning of the words) and figurative (by which the words take on a different meaning). When Christ says, in John x, that he has other sheep which are not of this fold, he means, in a literal but figurative sense, other men beyond the Jews. A literal sense is found in every sentence in both the Old and the New Testaments, and occasionally there are several literal meanings in the same sentence. Although spiritual meanings are common, every sentence does not have one of them. The command to love the Lord with all your heart has only the one, literal meaning. Nothing in Bellarmino's analysis corresponded precisely to the problem Galileo would raise about passages expressed in the language of the common people. However, the notion was not original with Galileo by any means, and Bellarmino would certainly have agreed that one cannot accept the simple literal meaning of anthropomorphic statements attributing human limbs and human passions to God. His doctrine of interpretation seems so readily adaptable to this small extension that there is no need to pause with it. "This in general we say:" Bellarmino concluded, "the judge of the true sense of Scripture and of all controversies is the Church, that is, the Pope with a Council in which all Catholics come together."[28]

Since Bellarmino's insistence, that is, the orthodox Catholic insistence, on the Church would later bear directly on Galileo, let us pause with it for a moment. His concept of the word of God included an unwritten word of God. This did not refer, as it would for Galileo and numerous other scientists of the 17th century, to nature as the creation of God. It referred rather to the tradition of the Church. The Scriptures without tradition are neither necessary nor sufficient. They are not necessary because tradition alone preserved the Church before the time of Moses, though Bellarmino

conceded that in this latter corrupted age the Scriptures are necessary. They are not sufficient, however. Some authority must establish what is the true revelation of God. Moreover, the Scriptures are often ambiguous and perplexed and cannot be understood unless interpreted by an authority which cannot err. That authority, of course, is the Church that embodies the authentic tradition. "For the universal Church not only cannot err in believing," Bellarmino asserted, "but also not in acting and especially in rites and divine worship . . ." When all of the learned teachers [*doctores*] agree on something, then it must be true. "The reason . . . is that if all the learned Teachers of the Church can err when they agree on some opinion, then the whole Church errs . . ."[29] Why can the whole Church not err? Because it is not an institution of men but an institution of God, an institution founded by God, an institution ruled by God. When Bellarmino wrote the words above about the inability of all the learned teachers of the Church to err, he was defending the Catholic tradition against Protestant attack. As Galileo would find out on a wholly different issue, Bellarmino did not limit the scope of that judgment to traditions challenged by Protestantism.

In Bellarmino's view, the role of the Church as the ordained interpreter did not derogate from the authority of Scripture but rather enhanced it. "Scripture," he insisted, "is the word of God immediately revealed & written in a certain way as God speaks. . . . The sacred writers are said to have had an immediate revelation, & to have written the words of God himself, because either certain new & hitherto unknown things were revealed to them by God . . . Or God immediately inspired, & moved the writers to write what they saw or heard, & guided them so that they did not err in any way." He went on to add that "in Scripture there can be no error whether it is concerned with faith or with morals, & whether something general & common to the whole Church is asserted, or something particular, & pertaining only to one man. . . . in Scripture not only the sentences but also each & every word pertains to faith. Indeed we believe that no word has been used in Scripture at random or incorrectly."[30]

Although Bellarmino, who found in the defense of Catholicism in those strenuous times work enough to fill a hundred lives, never devoted himself primarily to natural philosophy, he did have occasion to touch on topics of astronomy when first he lectured at Louvain in the period 1570-72. Already at that time, on matters not directly concerned with Copernicanism and forty years before Galileo would prompt a confrontation with the heliocentric system, Bellarmino was projecting the literal word of the Bible into questions of astronomy in a way that sounds surprisingly like Protestant fundamentalism in a later age on a different issue. One must resist any temptation to apply the word "arrogant" to Bellarmino. A prince of the Church who was ready to

take his turn in the scullery at the *Collegio Romano,* he made his whole life an implicit protest against the arrogance all too common among contemporary members of the hierarchy of the Church he served. Nevertheless, Bellarmino never doubted that he had recognized that one thing of great value, and he never doubted that everything else was to be measured by its standard. A sense, which one might mistakenly confuse with arrogance, that he represented the spiritual elite pervades his autobiography. Technical astronomy was not one of the primary concerns of the spiritual elite; with all eternity stretching before him, Bellarmino could not understand why some men thought that the physical structure of the universe was so important. Baldini and Coyne have emphasized how Bellarmino's biblicism freed him to recognize the hypothetical nature of much contemporary astronomy and thus to question it. One should add to this that the basis on which he questioned contemporary astronomy was not astronomical evidence but Scripture.

How many heavens are there? Bellarmino answered three, while noting that some "stupid astrologers [read astronomers]" claimed there are as many heavens as there are heavenly bodies. Because the Hebrew word *shamayim* has only the plural form, its use in Scripture does not allow us to settle whether there is a single heaven or more than one. However, the Scriptures definitely refer in other language to two heavens and apparently to a third, and almost all of the Church fathers can be brought into conformity with the latter number.[31] Are the sun and the stars fixed in the sky so that they move with its motion? Scripture does not say they are; its implication is quite the opposite, that they move independently in the sky like birds in the air and fish in the sea. Bellarmino went on to note that philosophers were not in agreement about the motions of the heavenly bodies and that it was not the business of theologians to consider the technical arguments of different hypotheses. "Thus it is possible for us to select among them the one which best corresponds to the Sacred Scriptures."[32] As Bellarmino understood this statement, he was not selecting the hypothesis most congenial to theologians, but, without reference to astronomical evidence, the one which was true. Was the moon, next to the sun, the largest body in the heavens? Despite the fact that astronomers, as he knew, made the moon the smallest celestial body except for Mercury, Bellarmino was convinced that it ranked with the sun because the Scriptures referred to those two as "luminaria magna."[33]

Years later, indeed exactly one year after the Church's judgment against Copernicanism, Bellarmino returned to the question of the size of the moon. Do not object to me that astronomers disagree, he said. They cannot demonstrate their opinion, and the Scriptures speak of the two great luminaries. "Besides did not St. Augustine (*De Genesi ad litteram* xxi, 16) say that it is much

better to believe the scriptures than the astrologers with respect to the size of the moon . . . ?"[34] Bellarmino concluded the latter passage with the statement that he had never wanted to enter into hostilities with astronomers. But one must understand that, for all the intended charity of his gesture, it assumed that astronomers would recognize their place, as theologians such as Bellarmino defined it, and that they would stay there.

This was the man who witnessed, along with everyone else in Europe and especially in Italy, the display of celestial fireworks that Galileo orchestrated in 1610. It is worth recalling that only a decade earlier he had been involved deeply in the traumatic trial of Giordano Bruno. Although it is often asserted that the Church pursued Bruno and burned him at the stake because he held Copernican beliefs, this is flatly untrue. The principal charges against Bruno were theological by any reasonable definition of the word—related to issues such as transubstantiation, the Trinity, and the substantiality of the individual soul. However, matters concerned with natural philosophy had been involved in the proceedings against Bruno from the beginning, and they also appeared in Bellarmino's list of eight charges. Prominent among them was the doctrine of the plurality of worlds, which is not explicitly Copernican but which had a historical affinity with Copernicanism.[35] Although the motion of the earth was not listed as a charge against Bruno, interrogations did raise the question and treat it as repugnant to the faith.[36] It would not be surprising, against this background, if the *Sidereus nuncius,* an explicitly Copernican book, aroused the suspicions of a man accustomed to believe that eternal truth was eternally under attack.

The Developing Conflict

Although the *Sidereus nuncius* was unmistakable in its adhesion to heliocentric astronomy, it apparently took the later observation of the phases of Venus, in December 1610, to turn Galileo into Copernicus' crusading champion. No sooner did he discover the phases of Venus than Galileo arranged a trip to Rome, where he began openly to assume the role of advocate. He arrived in the Papal city on 29 March 1611 and found himself immediately an object of attention. Federico Cesi gave a magnificent banquet in his honor and inducted him into his *Accademia dei Lincei.* In May the *Collegio Romano* arranged a convocation in his honor. Well before the convocation he had met Cardinal Bellarmino and helped him to observe the new celestial phenomena that the telescope revealed.[37] The Cardinal cannot have failed to note the confidence with which Galileo proclaimed the demise of the geocentric system. I assume it was after this encounter when Bellarmino wrote to Father Clavius and his mathematical colleagues in the *Collegio Romano* on 19 April, asking whether Galileo's five major observations—the multitude of stars invisible to the naked eye,

Saturn's strange shape, the phases of Venus, the roughness of the lunar surface, and the satellites of Jupiter—were "well-founded" or whether they might not be "a mere illusion." While offering minor differences of interpretation in two cases, the Jesuit astronomers assured Bellarmino that the observations were indeed well founded.[38] Nevertheless, a month later, on 17 May, shortly after the convocation in the *Collegio Romano,* the Holy Office entered the first reference to Galileo into its minutes.

> Let it be seen whether Galileo, a Professor of Philosophy and Mathematics, is named in the case of Doct. Cesare Cremonini.[39]

Cremonini, a prominent Aristotelian philosopher at Padua, where he had been at once the friend and opponent of Galileo, was under almost continual investigation by the Inquisition from 1604 until his death because of the naturalism of his philosophy. Needless to say, the record does not specify who raised the query. Nevertheless, Bellarmino was one of seven cardinals of the congregation present that day, and when all things are considered—his role in combatting heresy, his familiarity with Venetian developments, his ascendancy in the Holy Office, his enquiry to the *Collegio Romano* about Galileo's discoveries, and later events yet to be mentioned—it is difficult to believe that he was not the source of the question.

A year later Galileo was preparing his letters on sunspots, which insisted against Scheiner, who strove to preserve the immutability of the heavens, on the evidence the sunspots offered of corruption and change. Near the beginning of July, 1612, along with a copy of his recently published *Discourse on Bodies in Water,* Galileo addressed a letter to Cardinal Conti, prefect of the Congregation of the Index, asking about the extent to which Scripture seemed to dictate certain aspects of Aristotelian philosophy. Conti replied that Scripture says nothing about the incorruptibility of the heavens and the orbital motion of the earth; it does state unequivocally that heavenly bodies rise and set, though it could be speaking the language of the common people in these passages. Apparently still not satisfied, Galileo wrote again and received another answer to the same effect.[40] The second letter on sunspots, which Galileo dated 14 August, after Conti's initial letter though before his following one, proceeded then to conclude its extended argument for the mutability of the heavens with the assertion that this opinion was also conformable "to the indubitable truths of the Holy Scriptures which in many places that are very clear and obvious assert the unstable and fallen nature of the heavenly matter."[41] Toward the end of the year, however, when Prince Cesi sought to gain a license for the *Letters* which his *Accademia dei Lincei* was publishing, the censors suddenly began to find problems with the reference to Scripture, and the book could not

appear until Galileo had removed it.[42] Again no specific name appeared, only "the censors." Nevertheless one begins to get the impression of a watchful presence monitoring a potential source of dangerous ideas.

Galileo's **Letters on Sunspots,** a more blatantly Copernican book than the **Sidereus nuncius,** appeared in the spring of 1613. There followed that December the dinner with the Grand Ducal family in Pisa and a year later Caccini's sermon in Florence and the denunciation to the Inquisition, as I have already related. It is perhaps relevant to the argument to note that Lorini and his friends, in sending Galileo's letter to Castelli to Rome, were explicit in their desire that Cardinal Bellarmino see it.[43] Even before the denunciation, however, a Galileo greatly agitated by Caccini's sermon wrote to Cesi at the end of December. It seems to me that the import of Cesi's reply in January has not been sufficiently noted. Cesi wrote from his country seat in Acquasparta, some eighty kilometers (to use a later unit of measure) north of Rome. He had left the papal city early in October, long before Caccini's sermon.[44] What he had to say about opinion in Rome was so phrased that it clearly implied oral communication rather than correspondence, and it appears to me that it must have reflected information he had received prior to and independent of the event in Florence. Cesi assured Galileo that he understood his feelings, but "with things as they are at the [Papal] Court," he urged him in the strongest terms to contain his resentment and to conduct himself "with great caution."

> As for the theory of Copernicus [Cesi continued], Bellarmino himself, who is among the principal figures in the congregations concerned with these things, has told me that he considers it heretical, and that the motion of the earth is, beyond any doubt, contrary to Scripture: so that you can see how things stand. I have always wondered whether he would not, when he finds it convenient, bring Copernicus up in the Congregation of the Index and have him prohibited, nor is there need to say more.

Cesi went on to counsel Galileo to stand out of sight while others manned the defense, which should concentrate on Caccini's attack on mathematics and remain entirely silent about astronomy, and again he warned Galileo to "proceed cautiously."[45] It has been the almost universal opinion that Galileo's troubles with the Church began in Florence, with Lorini, Boscaglia, Caccini, and others of that circle. The implication of Cesi's letter, which I find unavoidable, however, is that prior to Caccini's sermon and independently of events in Florence Cardinal Bellarmino had decided that Copernican astronomy was opposed to Scriptural truth and would have to be suppressed. With its repeated warnings to Galileo, the letter also implies that Bellarmino had expressed some reservations about him as well. This puts the whole of the trial in a new per-

spective. As for the exchange between Galileo and Bellarmino during 1615, it is best understood if we realize that both men came to it with their minds made up.

The Exchange of 1615

Obviously, Galileo did not initially address the long letter about science and Scripture, written to Castelli in the wake of his report on the dinner in Pisa, to Bellarmino. When he heard that a copy of the letter had been sent to the Inquisition, however, he feared that it might have been altered in a way that would injure him, and he hastened to send a correct copy of the original to Rome. He was anxious that the Cardinal see it.[46] Galileo's enemies, in their desire to lay the matter before Bellarmino, appear to have understood the Cardinal better than he did. Meanwhile, we can legitimately treat the letter to Castelli as the first item in their exchange.

The Bible is the word of God, Galileo agreed; "the Holy Scriptures can never speak untruth or err . . ."[47] Interpreters of the Bible are human, however, and they can err. Nature, as the creation of God, is also His revelation; both the Bible and nature "proceed alike from the divine Word, the former as the dictate of the Holy Ghost and the latter as the observant executrix of God's commands."[48] The Bible speaks in the language of the common people, and in many places its literal meaning cannot be accepted. Thus the literal words of Scripture attribute feet, hands, and eyes to God and ascribe to him emotions such as anger, repentance, and hatred, passages which would, if accepted literally, lead one into "grave heresies and follies."[49] In contrast to the Bible in this respect, nature is "inexorable and immutable; she never transgresses the laws imposed upon her, or cares one whit whether her abstruse reasons and methods of operation are understandable to men."[50] Galileo insisted further, and this was the crux of his argument, "that two truths cannot contradict one another . . ."[51] It is then the function of expositors of the Bible to find the correct interpretation of Scripture, which must agree with the well-established conclusions of natural philosophy.

The purpose of Scripture is to persuade men to those doctrines necessary to their salvation. Galileo was adamant that science had nothing to say about doctrines of faith, and he acknowledged the inerrancy of Scripture on such matters. On the other hand, the Bible does not attempt to treat natural philosophy. For example, it hardly addresses astronomy, and does not so much as mention any of the planets.[52] If it was the intention of God to employ Revelation to instruct mankind in astronomy, surely He would have devoted more attention to it. Galileo could not believe, he continued, "that the same God who has endowed us with senses, reason, and intellect has intended to forego their use and by some other means to give us knowledge which we can attain by them."[53] Thus he concluded that "it would be the part of prudence not to permit anyone to usurp scriptural texts and force them in some way to maintain any physical conclusion to be true, when at some future time the senses and demonstrative or necessary reasons may show the contrary."[54]

His opponents were proceeding in an irregular manner. If they really believed that they had the correct sense of Scripture, it followed inevitably that they had "the absolute truth" on the issue under debate. Hence they had a great advantage. Because they advocated the truth, they had to have "many sense-experiences and rigorous proofs" on their side, while Galileo could have only illusory appearances, quibbles, and fallacies. Why then, with this advantage, did they seize instead "the dreadful weapon which cannot be turned aside . . . ?"[55] To conclude the letter Galileo offered a brilliant exposition of the famous passage from Joshua which Caccini would make the occasion of his attack. Caccini cannot have read very carefully, for Galileo demonstrated conclusively that if the literal meaning of Scripture is the criterion, the passage in Joshua is incompatible with the Ptolemaic system.[56]

The letter to Castelli presented a powerful argument for the independence of science from theological domination. Bellarmino's insistence that Scripture is unable to err expressed one of Christianity's central affirmations, which animated the ideal for which he spoke—that God has revealed himself to mankind. To Bellarmino and the Church this meant that truth in everything that matters is known, and that activities such as natural philosophy, which are subordinate to the ultimate end of mankind, must be carried on within the boundaries defined by revealed truth. The power of Galileo's letter to Castelli lay in his appeal to other equally central affirmations of the faith and in his ability to weave from them the fabric of the new ideal he represented—that the world also proceeds from the word of God, and that God has created man in His own image. Bellarmino would have served his Church well had he been capable of imagining, after a lifetime spent defending the faith, that he was not the sole custodian of the ark.

Early in 1615 the Carmelite theologian, Paolo Foscarini, published a *Letter . . . on the Opinion of the Pythagoreans and of Copernicus concerning the Mobility of the Earth and the Stability of the Sun,* addressed to Sebastiano Fantoni, General of the Order of Carmelites.[57] Foscarini wrote as a Copernican, convinced that only the Copernican system was consistent with the new observations of the telescope, and concerned to refute the objection that heliocentric astronomy is impossible because it is repugnant to Scripture. Dated 6 January 1615, the letter appeared too early to have been a reply to Caccini's sermon; it thus offers

further testimony that a number of people perceived independently that the Copernican issue was coming to a head about 1615 and that it was not solely the circle of Galileo's enemies in Florence who precipitated the crisis.

Foscarini's argument, that the Scriptures speak in the language of the common people, was very similar to Galileo's. For my purposes, the importance of the letter lies in the facts that its author requested Cardinal Bellarmino's opinion on it and that Bellarmino, by lumping Galileo together with Foscarini and by insuring that Galileo immediately saw a copy of his reply, effectively made it a commentary on the letter to Castelli.[58] First, Foscarini and Galileo would act prudently, Bellarmino began in his typically numbered sequence of points, by speaking only hypothetically and not absolutely. To say that celestial appearances are explained better on the Copernican supposition is to speak well, but to affirm that the sun is the center of the universe and that the earth moves "is a very dangerous attitude and one calculated not only to annoy all scholastic philosophers and theologians but also to injure our holy faith by contradicting the Scriptures." One might observe two points in passing: that the later actions of both the Holy Office and the Congregation of the Index condemned Copernicanism in terms of exactly these two propositions about the sun and the earth, and that Ballarmino, if not a scholastic philosopher, was most assuredly a scholastic theologian, and was thus proclaiming his own annoyance. He continued, second, that the Council of Trent had forbidden the interpretation of Scripture in a way contrary to the common opinion of the Fathers, but all of the Fathers agreed in interpreting the critical passages as saying that the sun is in the heavens and revolves around the earth which is at rest. "Consider then, in your prudence," he added, in what Galileo should have read as a warning couched in the gravest terms, "whether the Church can tolerate that the Scriptures should be interpreted in a manner contrary to that of the holy Fathers and of all modern commentators . . ." It would not do to say that this is not a matter of faith. He who denies that Abraham had two sons and Jacob twelve is as much a heretic as he who denies the virgin birth of Christ, "because it is the Holy Spirit who makes known both truths by the mouth of the Prophets and Apostles." Third, if there were a real proof of the Copernican system, we should have to proceed cautiously with the Scriptures and acknowledge that we do not comprehend them. But there is no such proof, and hence we should be very careful in abandoning the established interpretation. Solomon, who wrote that the sun rises and sets, was a man learned beyond all others in the knowledge of created things; he would not have spoken in contradiction to the truth.

Near the beginning of the twentieth century, Pierre Duhem pointed to Bellarmino's letter as a clearer expression of the scientific attitude than Galileo's. Naively overconfident in science, Galileo spoke as though the conclusions he defended were demonstrated truths, while Bellarmino, who had digested the medieval tradition of "saving the phenomena," understood correctly the hypothetical nature of Copernicanism.[59] This may all be well and good when we restrict ourselves only to parts of Bellarmino's letter, but if we are discussing science, we need to recall other parts of it, which were also essential aspects of Bellarmino's position—to wit, that the word of Scripture, which speaks the truth of God, outweighs the hypothetical conclusions of science, not just in questions of theology, but also in questions of science.

We need also to recall the conclusion of the letter, which Duhem neglected to mention. Restricting himself there to scientific considerations, Bellarmino forgot what he had just said about hypotheses. In the final sentences he brought up the comparison with a man watching the shore from a moving ship, used by Copernicans to justify the assertion that celestial appearances will be the same whether the heavens turn from east to west once a day or the earth turns on its axis from west to east. The comparison is not valid, Bellarmino told Foscarini and Galileo, because a man on a ship knows very well that the shore is at rest, and he can correct the illusion. "But as to the sun and the earth a wise man has no need to correct his judgment, for his experience tells him plainly that the earth is standing still and that his eyes are not deceived when they report that the sun, moon, and stars are in motion." Less than a year later, when the consultors of the Holy Office were called upon to consider the two propositions about the stability of the sun and the motion of the earth, they did not confine themselves to a theological opinion. Both propositions they concluded, in words that might be mistaken for a summary of Bellarmino's letter, as they probably were, are not only heretical but absurd in philosophy.[60]

Galileo received Bellarmino's letter well before the end of April. As we know from his correspondence with Msgr. Dini, he was at that time expanding the letter to Castelli into the considerably longer *Letter to the Grand Duchess Christina.* An extended section of the new treatise addressed itself to "some theologians whom I consider men of profound learning and devout behavior" whom he held in great esteem.[61] Who can doubt that he had Bellarmino in mind? Indeed it appears to me that the entire revision of the letter to Castelli was addressed to Bellarmino. There is no evidence that Bellarmino saw it, but I find it difficult to believe that he did not. If Galileo had not succeeded in having the *Letter* delivered to the Cardinal before December, he would have brought a copy with him when he came to Rome. His letters from Rome to the court in Florence mentioned his efforts to present his case directly to the men who counted; There was no one in Rome who fitted that

description better than Bellarmino.[62] It appears to me that we are unlikely to miss the mark in considering the *Letter to the Grand Duchess Christina* as part of the dialogue between the two men.

Since the *Letter to the Grand Duchess* embodied the letter to Castelli, much of it verbatim, there is no need to repeat its central argument. In the newly added address to some theologians of profound learning, Galileo confessed with candor that they [that is, Bellarmino] made him uncomfortable when they pretended, on scriptural authority, to constrain others, in physical matters, to follow opinions the theologians found in agreement with the Bible, but then believed themselves not bound to answer the opposing evidence and arguments. Theologians asserted that theology is queen of all the sciences. Galileo found an equivocation in the concept. If they meant that theology excels the others in dignity, he agreed, but theology is not queen in the sense that it contains the subordinate sciences and can therefore dictate their conclusions. To censure Copernicanism at that time, just as evidence that confirmed it was appearing, would give men an occasion "to see a proposition proved that it was heresy to believe." And to censure the whole science of astronomy would be to censure a hundred passages in the Bible that teach how the glory of God can be read in the book of the heavens.

> For let no one believe [Galileo spoke to Bellarmino here as one professional to another, insisting with the voice of the new world view on the dignity of scientific disciplines, almost pleading with Bellarmino to perceive that something had come to exist beyond the boundaries of his closed medieval universe] that reading the lofty concepts written in that book leads to nothing further than the mere seeing of the splendor of the sun and the stars and their rising and setting, which is as far as the eyes of brutes and of the vulgar can penetrate. Within its pages are couched mysteries so profound and concepts so sublime that the vigils, labors, and studies of hundreds upon hundreds of the most acute minds have still not pierced them even after continual investigations for thousands of years. . . . that which presents itself to mere sight is as nothing in comparison to the high marvels that the ingenuity of learned men discovers in the heavens by long and accurate observation.[63]

To Bellarmino's statement that there was no demonstration of the truth of the heliocentric system, Galileo replied in effect that the story of natural philosophy was only beginning to be told and that, whatever the conclusiveness of present demonstrations, theology would be wise if it refused to commit itself to the literal word of the Bible on questions subject in principle to confirmation by evidence of the senses or by necessary demonstrations. The man who only recently had discovered a host of new bodies and new truths in the sky, and who before that had elaborated the structure of what he would later publish as a "new science" of motion, was convinced that human knowledge, and especially knowledge of nature, increases over time. Already in the letter to Castelli, in a passage I have quoted, he referred to what the sciences might prove "at some future time." References to the possibility of further proofs at some later time pervade the *Letter to the Grand Duchess.* Duhem must have failed to notice them; in my opinion they seriously modify what he had to say about Galileo's scientific attitude. The Fathers of the Church, Galileo said, knew how prejudicial it would be to use Scripture to decide physical conclusions when experience and reason "might in time" show the contrary.[64] Insisting on the literal text in questions of philosophy could prejudice the dignity of the Bible in the event that "later truth" showed the contrary.[65] To Bellarmino, in contrast, truth was known; the problem was not to expand it but to defend it against error. No more pronounced difference separated the two men. Especially here Galileo expressed the world view of the new age, calling in vain across the chasm that divided it from the one now passing away.

If he called here in vain, in other respects Galileo failed even more. He opened the *Letter* with an account of the envy his astronomical discoveries had created and the assertion that personal animosities against him were the source of the whole issue. This theme continued throughout the treatise. Bellarmino could examine himself, however, for evidence that more than personal motives were in play. With the assistance of Castelli, Galileo, who had probably never read a book by Augustine from beginning to end, filled the *Letter* with quotations from his works and from other Fathers of the Church. Bellarmino, a profound student of patristic literature, was bound to have recognized the shallowness of Galileo's knowledge in this respect, and one can readily imagine how gladly he received instruction on the Fathers from such a master. And Galileo could hardly have found a theme more likely to antagonize the man he addressed than his treatment of interpreters and interpretations of the Bible. To Bellarmino, the learned teachers of the Church, speaking in unanimity, expressed the truth of God. Galileo treated them as mere fallible human beings. He suggested to Bellarmino that the universal agreement of the Fathers should count only on those propositions which they had discussed carefully. The motion of the earth was not such a proposition; Galileo wondered if the question had ever entered their minds.[66] Thus he proceeded again to explain away the passage in Joshua as he had done before.

> As to other scriptural passages which seem to be contrary to this opinion [he continued], I have no doubt that if the opinion itself were known to be true and proven, those very theologians who, so long as they deem it false, hold these passages to be incapable of harmonious exposition with it,

would find interpretations for them which would agree very well, and especially if they would add some knowledge of astronomical science to their knowledge of divinity.[67]

Galileo never ceased to be enamored of the brilliance of his own wit. In this case he was seeking to convince one of the very theologians he was choosing to lampoon, a man who saw himself as part of a tradition inspired by God. Whatever hair was left on Bellarmino's seventy year old head must have stood straight up when he read those words. As it happened, and as Galileo knew very well, the man thus satirized was also the dominant voice in the Holy Office.

As I said above, I find it impossible to believe that Bellarmino did not receive and read the *Letter to the Grand Duchess.* His reply to it was twofold, an equally eloquent composition of his own and a decisive official act. The composition was his great devotional tract, *De ascensione mentis in Deum, The Mind's Ascent to God.* In the literal sense, it is improper to treat *De ascensione* as a reply to the *Letter.* Although Bellarmino published it in 1615, the year of their exchange, he had composed it the previous autumn.[68] Nevertheless the tract, beyond its devotional purpose, which transcends its age, spoke so directly to the issues that Galileo had already injected into the age that one can legitimately consider *De ascensione* as the supreme expression of the medieval world view replying to the new age Galileo represented. We mortal men, Bellarmino asserted in his introduction, "find no other ladder whereby to ascend unto God, than the works of God." All creatures are the works of God; "man and the angels are not only his works, but also his images, as the Scriptures teach us."[69] If the words sound at first like those of Galileo, Bellarmino followed them down a path that diverged completely. Where for Galileo nature as the work of God demanded that we study its structure with faculties which are also divinely created, Bellarmino strove to raise his soul to God by learning from the world to despise it. The seventh step in the mind's ascent is the consideration of the heavens.

> But, my soul, rise thou up a little higher, if thou canst, and as thou observest the great splendour of the sun, the beauty of the moon, the number and variety of other luminaries, the wonderful harmony of the heavens and the delightful movement of the stars, consider: what it will be to see God above the heavens, as it were a sun, 'dwelling in the light which no man can approach unto' [1 Tim. vi, 16] . . . Thus it will come to pass that the beauty of the heavens will not appear so very great, and the things that are beneath the sky will seem altogether insignificant, indeed almost nothing, and to be considered despicable and worthy of contempt.[70]

If Galileo's *Letter* called in vain across the chasm dividing two worlds, so did Bellarmino's *Ascent* call just as vainly from the farther side. Like the passage above, it is filled with quotations from Scripture, which Bellarmino must have known by heart. That testimony in the language of the common people, which Galileo had to interpret away lest it impede the progress of science, was to Bellarmino, in its every word, a priceless guide to those things which alone matter in life. He had observed Galileo's self-esteem at first hand, and at times he seemed to speak directly to him, as a priest.

> Wherefore, my soul, if thou are wise, pursue the knowledge of salvation and the wisdom of the saints which lies in this, that thou fear God and keep his commandments: that prayer delight thee more than disputations, and the charity which buildeth up more than the knowledge which puffeth up; for this is the way that leadeth unto life and the kingdom of heaven . . .[71]

But Galileo was no more capable of comprehending Bellarmino's call than Bellarmino his. I have spoken of the clash of two world views. The clash occurs in our 20th century minds. Instead of clashing in the early 17th century, they passed by each other wholly without contact.

The Condemnation of 1616

On another plane, however, there was contact enough, for Bellarmino commanded the repressive machinery of the Church. The charge lodged against Galileo in February 1615 focused on the letter to Castelli, and the Inquisition's investigation concentrated initially on it. In fact they found there nothing of substance at all. Nevertheless someone kept the investigation alive. On 25 November, 1615, the Holy Office resolved to examine Galileo's **Letters on Sunspots,**[72] and in February 1616 it found two "propositions of the Mathematician Galileo" heretical and absurd in philosophy—the same two propositions that Cardinal Bellarmino had found heretical and absurd in philosophy in his letter to Foscarini. As we have seen, however, the Holy Office did not condemn the author of the two propositions. We have good evidence that Galileo had his defenders in Rome. Maffeo Barberini would later claim that he had preserved him in 1616,[73] and there were in addition Galileo's other two patrons, the Grand Duke Cosimo de' Medici and Prince Federico Cesi of the *Accademia dei Lincei*. The general context, with Galileo's prominence on the intellectual scene, suggests that they were not the only defenders.

Can one explain the contradictions in the record of 1616 by assuming that a compromise was struck? Bellarmino had no personal vendetta to wage against Galileo. He was not a member of the Florentine League of Pigeons, who were apparently moved by envy as Galileo always claimed.[74] On the contrary, his concern

was solely to preserve Catholic truth in his age from the unending assault of heresy. Can we assume then that he accepted a compromise? There would be no need to condemn Galileo if, on the one hand, the Congregation of the Index would move unambiguously against Copernicanism and if, on the other hand, the principal agent in the promotion of Copernicanism were solemnly ordered to desist. Let me be frank in labelling the assumption as speculation, which every interpretation of the trial inevitably becomes, given the evidence available. The speculative assumption appears to me to explain the known facts, however, and it does not completely lack supportive evidence. There is at least one indication in the wording of the decree by the Congregation of the Index that Bellarmino himself composed it.[75] There is more than an indication of his participation in the order to Galileo. Of the various other prelates available for the task, it was nevertheless busy Cardinal Bellarmino whom, at the meeting of the Holy Office, His Holiness instructed—at Bellarmino's own insistence, I am suggesting—to call Galileo in and warn him to abandon the condemned opinion. Busy Cardinal Bellarmino found time to carry out the commission the very next day.[76]

The record of the interview in which Bellarmino issued the warning has been the subject of controversy since it became known about a hundred years ago. The document is not properly signed, and what it registers is not in agreement with the instructions given by the Holy Office. Bellarmino was to warn Galileo to give up the condemned opinion, and if Galileo refused to obey, the Commissary General of the Holy Office was to order him before witnesses and a notary to abstain altogether from teaching and defending a doctrine of this sort and from treating it. The document states that Galileo acquiesced and promised to obey, but it nevertheless indicates that (in what was supposed to follow if he refused to obey) Galileo was ordered to relinquish the opinion altogether and not to hold, teach, or defend it in any way, orally or in writing. Commentary has frequently assumed that gentle compassionate Saint Roberto would not have done anything harsh.[77] But gentle compassionate Saint Roberto had a backbone of steel. He held stern notions about the "divine wrath of God" and "how great must be his hatred of crimes and evil deeds . . ."[78] He would not have understood a concept of gentleness and compassion that lacked a backbone of steel. The welfare of the Church and indeed of all mankind was at stake. To me, at least, the evidence I have presented indicates clearly that Bellarmino was greatly concerned that Galileo stop helping error to creep among the flock to the ruin of Catholic truth, and that he stop forthwith. Without denying the irregularities of the disputed document and the difficulties they create, I am nevertheless convinced that on 26 February 1616 Cardinal Bellarmino did in fact do what His Holiness—at Bellarmino's own insistence, in my understanding—instructed him to do; that is, he warned Galileo in unmistakable terms to abandon the condemned opinion.

We must not allow ourselves to formulate the events of 1615-16 in misleading terms. It was not ignorance and narrow-mindedness that condemned Copernicanism. Cardinal Bellarmino represented the finest flower of Catholic learning. I myself have come to appreciate his various qualities to a degree quite scandalous in a Presbyterian elder. Far from being ignorant, Bellarmino was the captive, as all of us are captives, of his lifetime's experience, in his case the defense of his Church and of the world view his experience fostered. The tragedy of his Church lay in the fact that he saw the rise of modern science on the analogy of Protestantism and failed to recognize that it was instead a fundamental reshaping of the intellectual landscape within which Christianity, Catholic and Protestant alike, would have henceforth to proceed. In the 13th century, the recovery of Aristotle had presented Christianity with a similar challenge, and Christianity had been able to continue fashioning medieval culture because it learned to state its message in Aristotle's idiom. Beside the earthquake that was the rise of modern science, however, the recovery of Aristotle in the 13th century had been a mere tremor. Bellarmino was of course not by himself the Catholic Church. Institutions cannot make decisions, however, only the individuals who lead them, and I have been arguing, as I am convinced, that Bellarmino was the determinative voice on this issue at that time, though obviously within a context prepared to accept his views. To the misfortune of the Catholic Church Bellarmino failed to recognize what was happening. Locked within his world view, he met the challenge of the rise of modern science with a response that served only, in the end, greatly to injure the institution he wanted above all to defend.

As for Galileo, it is equally mistaken to see in him an enemy of that Church, or in any of the leaders of the new science an enemy of Christianity. It is true that Galileo was not given to spiritual exaltation, but one must not believe that spiritual exaltation is essential to sincere belief. Recall the scene on 23 June 1633, when Galileo stood before the assembled cardinals of the Church and learned to his surprise that he was being forced publicly to abjure Copernicanism. It is probably not true that Galileo had been shown the instruments of torture. He knew what they were without seeing them, and his correspondence makes it clear he was terrified that they might be used on him. He was an old man, almost seventy, who had been seriously ill without much respite for the past twenty years. He knew very well that he did not have the strength to resist those terrible engines and that they could reduce him to jelly in a matter of minutes. He nevertheless told the assembled cardinals that though he would do what they were going to force him to do, he would not say he was not a Catholic because he was one and intended to die one despite his enemies.[79]

Galileo had entered, however, willy-nilly, into the new world shaped by the earthquake then in progress, and everything that Bellarmino saw from his world view looked different from Galileo's. The issue has nothing to do with the relative merits of the two world views. To me they appear incommensurable. The issue rather is the compulsion exercised by historical reality. As the Church had remained a central factor in European life for more than fifteen hundred years by refusing ever to put itself in opposition to prevailing learning, so it would remain a factor in the new age then being formed if it refused to be at odds with modern science. The net result of Cardinal Bellarmino's devoted effort to defend his Church was to place an incubus to its back that it struggles still to shake off.

Thus Galileo, who spoke from the perspective of the new world view, had the final word in the exchange. It was 1633 when he uttered it, in a letter to Elia Diodati composed shortly before he travelled to Rome to face his second trial by the Inquisition. Cardinal Bellarmino had been in his grave for more than a decade, and Galileo's words overtly concerned the recent book of Libert Froidmont against Copernicus. I do not find it fanciful to imagine that he had Bellarmino in mind as well.

> When Froidmont or others have established that to say the earth moves is heresy, while demonstrations, observations, and necessary conclusions show that it does move, in what a swamp will he have lost himself and the Holy Church?[80]

Notes

[1] *Le Opere di Galileo Galilei,* ed. naz., ed. Antonio Favaro, 20 vols. (Firenze: Barbéra, 1890-1909), *19,* 323.

[2] Galileo to Mazzoni, 30 May 1597, Galileo to Kepler, 4 Aug. 1597; *ibid., 2,* 197-202 and *10,* 67-8. A letter of Castelli to Galileo, 5 December 1610, (*ibid., 10,* 480-2) was explicitly Copernican and appears to have assumed that it was addressing another acknowledged Copernican. Castelli had been Galileo's student in Padua, and there is every reason to refer the apparently shared conviction to his student years, well before the discoveries with the telescope.

[3] Cigoli to Galileo, 16 December 1611; *ibid., 11,* 241-2.

[4] Galileo's letter to Lorini has been lost, but see Lorini's reply on 5 Nov. 1612; *ibid., 11,* 427.

[5] Castelli to Galileo, 14 Dec. 1613; *ibid., 11,* 606.

[6] Galileo to Castelli, 20 Dec. 1613; *ibid., 5,* 281-8.

[7] See the record of the Inquisition on which I primarily rely for the following narrative; *ibid., 19,* 275-324.

[8] See his deposition in the records of the Inquisition; *ibid., 19,* 307-11.

[9] See the record of the Inquisition; *ibid., 19,* 275-9, 295-324.

[10] Galileo to Picchena, 6 Feb. 1616; *ibid., 12,* 230.

[11] *Ibid., 19,* 320-1. The wording of the second proposition was not as I have given it, but I take this to have been its meaning.

[12] Quoted in James Brodrick, *Robert Bellarmine, Saint and Scholar,* (Westminster: Newman Press, 1961), p. 156.

[13] Brodrick quotes at length the contemporary account, by an English priest, Father Edward Coffin, *A True Relation of the last Sickness and Death of Cardinal Bellarmine,* (Saint-Omer, 1622); *ibid.,* pp. 413-21.

[14] *Ibid.,* pp. 303-4.

[15] Without specific reference to the years 1615-16, Bellarmino listed the two among the Congregations on which he served. *Die Selbstbiographie des Cardinals Bellarmin,* ed. Joh. Jos. Ign. Döllinger and Fr. Heinrich Reusch, (Bonn: Neusser, 1887), p. 44.

[16] See Bellarmino to Mercurian (General of the Company of Jesus), 1 Aug. 1573, and Bellarmino to Card. Sirlet, 1 April 1575; Xavier-Marie Le Bachelet, *Bellarmin avant son cardinalat, 1542-1598. Correspondence et documents,* (Paris: Beauchesne, 1911), pp. 84-5 and 90-4. A fragment of the dedication of the *Controveries* to Pope Sixtus V, dated 1586, stated that he had devoted the previous fifteen years to controversies explicating the faith; *ibid.,* pp. 145-6. This chronology extends back nearly to the beginning of the years in Louvain.

[17] Chapter II. Seven Years in Louvain; Brodrick, *Bellarmine,* pp. 25-50.

[18] See the relevant letters in Le Bachelet, *Bellarmin,* pp. 245-77.

[19] Galla Galli, *La Vita e il pensiero di Giordano Bruno,* (Milano: Marzorati, 1973), pp. 44-5.

[20] Chapter IX. Trouble with the Republic of Venice; Brodrick, *Bellarmine,* pp. 249-63.

[21] *Ibid.,* pp. 279, 294-8.

[22] See for example Bellarmino's judgment on the propositions of Jan Jansen, his report on the controversy in Louvain, and his letter to Deckers, 5 Oct. 1591; Le Bachelet, *Bellarmin,* pp. 162-3, 211-13, and 311-13. All of these documents concern the controversy in Louvain, the forerunner of the Jansenist controversy, over free will and efficacious grace. Although Bellarmino supported the Jesuit Leonard Leys (Lessius) in this struggle, he did not hesitate to say, in typical fashion, that Leys's proposition on election seemed "false" to him; *ibid.,* p. 199.

[23] Bellarmino to Aquaviva, 27 Dec. 1591 and 28 Jan. 1592; *ibid.,* pp. 317-21 and 326-7.

[24] Roberto Bellarmino, *Disputationes Roberti Bellarmini Politiani, S.J., S.R.E. Cardinalis, de controversiis christianae fidei, adversus nostri termporis haereticos,* 4 vols. (Venezia: Malachino, 1721), *1,* Praefatio, n.p. See also the fragment of the dedication of volume one to Pope Sixtus V: With St. Jerome he holds that "there is no one so impious whom a heretic does not exceed in impiety. For because faith is the foundation and source of the whole spiritual structure and of all heavenly benefits, those who labor to take away the faith of the Church, which heretics do, corrupt the entire welfare of the Church at the same time, and strive completely to overthrow the Church itself." (Le Bachelet, *Bellarmin,* p. 145.)

[25] Quoted in Brodrick, *Bellarmine,* p. 318.

[26] *De controversiis, 1,* Praefatio, n.p.

[27] *De verbo dei. Liber primus,* Chap. 1; *ibid..1,* 1.

[28] *De verbi dei interpretatione. Liber tertius* (despite the additional word in the title, book three of the first Controversy, *De verbo dei*), especially Chapter 3; *ibid., 1,* 69. Those familiar with Ugo Baldini and George V. Coyne, "The Louvain Lectures (Lectiones Lovanienses) of Bellarmine and the Autograph Copy of his 1616 Declaration to Galileo," *Vatican Observatory Publications: Studi Galileiani, 1.2* (1984), will recognize that I have received and accepted great assistance from the authors in finding relevant sections in Bellarmino's voluminous writings.

[29] *De verbo dei non scripto. Liber quartus* (again, despite the two additional words, book four of the first Controversy, *De verbo dei*); I quote here from Chapter 9; *ibid., 1,* 80-94. See also the Fourth Controversy, *De conciliis, et ecclesia militante,* Chapter 14, *2,* 73-4. "The Church is not able to err in any way, not even in forsaking God." He brings up Calvin's restriction of the Church's inerrancy to doctrines explicitly in Scripture and to the church universal as opposed to the present Catholic Church. "However our opinion is that the Church absolutely cannot err, neither in things absolutely necessary nor in other things which it proposes to us to believe or to do, whether they are explicitly

set down in the Scriptures or not." The Church (which is of course the present Catholic Church) is governed by Christ as by its head and spouse and by the Holy Spirit as by its soul. They guard it against every error.

[30] *Prima (i.e., the first in vol. 2, but really the fourth) controversia generalis. De conciliis, et ecclesia militante,* Chapter 12; *ibid., 2,* 43. To amplify the understanding of the last passage, let me quote the slightly different but not contradictory translation of Baldini and Coyne: "in Scripture not only the meaning but all the words and individual words pertain to faith. For we believe that no word has been inserted in Scripture uselessly or imprecisely." Baldini and Coyne, "Louvain Lectures," p. 40.

[31] *Ibid.,* p. 16.

[32] *Ibid.,* pp. 18-20.

[33] *Ibid.,* p. 22.

[34] Quoted in *ibid.,* p. 45.

[35] Angelo Mercati, *Il sommario del processo di Giordano Bruno,* (Vatican City: Biblioteca Apostolica Vaticana, 1942), pp. 5-9, 55-119 (especially 79-83). Galli, *Bruno,* p. 45.

[36] Mercati, *Sommario,* pp. 7 and 117.

[37] Bellarmino's letter to the mathematicians at the *Collegio Romano* on 19 April stated that he had observed the new phenomena through the telescope, though he did not say that Galileo had assisted him; *Opere, 12,* pp. 87-8. In a letter to Galileo four years later, Piero Dini repeated Bellarmino's recollection of a discussion with Galileo about the discoveries; Dini to Galileo, 15 May 1615; *ibid., 12,* 151.

[38] *Opere, 11,* 87-8, 92-3. English translation in Brodrick, *Bellarmine,* pp. 343-5.

[39] *Ibid., 19,* 275.

[40] Galileo's two letters to Conti do not survive; I infer their content from Conti's replies. Conti to Galileo, 7 July and 18 Aug. 1612; *ibid., 11,* 354-5 and 376.

[41] *Ibid., 5,* 138-9. Galileo had become familiar with the Scriptural passages in question some twenty years earlier in the course of digesting the lecture notes of professors of natural philosophy at the *Collegio Romano.* William A. Wallace, *Galileo's Early Notebooks: the Physical Questions,* (Notre Dame: Univ. of Notre Dame Press, 1977), pp. 94, 101-2.

[42] Cesi to Galileo between 24 Nov. 1612 and 26 Jan. 1613; *ibid., 11,* 437-72 passim.

[43] This is what Galileo stated in his letter to Msgr. Piero Dini, 16 Feb. 1615; *Opere, 5,* 292.

[44] In a letter to Galileo on 4 October 1614, Cesi said that he was about to leave for Acquasparta. His correspondence shows that he was there from that time until the beginning of the following March, restricted in his movements by his concern over the illness of his wife, who would die without recovering on 1 November 1615. Giuseppe Gabrieli, "Il carteggio linceo della vecchia accademia di Federico Cesi," *Memorie della R. Accademia Nazionale dei Lincei, Classe di scienze morali, storiche e filologiche, ser. VI, 7.1,* (1938), 462-87.

[45] Cesi to Galileo, 12 Jan. 1615; *ibid., 12,* 128-31.

[46] Galileo to Dini, 16 Feb. 1615; *ibid., 5,* 292.

[47] Galileo to Castelli, 21 Dec. 1613; *Opere, 5,* 282. The letter to Castelli became the first draft of the well known *Letter to Madame Christina of Lorraine, Grand Duchess of Tuscany,* which Stillman Drake has translated, *Discoveries and Opinions of Galileo,* (Garden City, N.Y.: Doubleday, 1957), pp. 175-216. Galileo copied much of the letter to Castelli verbatim into the *Letter to the Grand Duchess Christina,* and I will use Drake's translations, modified where differences in the original Italian texts make it necessary, as in this case. The modestly different form of this passage appears in *Discoveries and Opinions,* p. 181.

[48] *Opere, 5,* 282. *Discoveries and Opinions,* p. 182.

[49] *Opere, 5,* 282. *Discoveries and Opinions,* p. 181.

[50] *Opere, 5,* 282. *Discoveries and Opinions,* p. 182.

[51] *Opere, 5,* 283. *Discoveries and Opinions,* p. 186.

[52] *Opere, 5,* 284. Castelli corrected Galileo's imperfect knowledge of Scripture on this point; the *Letter to the Grand Duchess* said that the Bible mentioned only Venus; *Discoveries and Opinions,* p. 184.

[53] *Opere, 5,* 284. *Discoveries and Opinions,* p. 183.

[54] *Opere, 5,* 284. *Discoveries and Opinions,* p. 187.

[55] *Opere, 5,* 285. *Discoveries and Opinions,* p. 209.

[56] *Opere, 5,* 286-7. *Discoveries and Opinions,* pp. 211-15.

[57] A translation of the letter into English appears in Thomas Salusbury, *Mathematical Collections and Translations,* a reissue of vol. 1 of the original publication, (London: Leybourn, 1667), Pt. 1, pp. 473-503.

[58] Bellarmino to Foscarini, 12 April 1615; *Opere, 12,* 171-2. It is translated in full in Brodrick, *Bellarmine,*

pp 362-3, from which I quote. Msgr. Dini sent a copy to Galileo on 18 April; *Opere, 12,* 173.

59 Pierre Duhem, *To Save the Phenomena: an Essay on the Idea of Physical Theory from Plato to Galileo,* tr. Edmund Doland and Chaninah Maschler, (Chicago: Univ. of Chicago Press, 1969), pp. 104-12. The original was published in France in 1908. See also Duhem, *The Aim and Structure of Physical Theory,* tr. Philip P. Wiener, (Princeton: Princeton Univ. Press, 1954), p. 43. The original French edition of this work appeared in 1906.

60 *Opere, 19,* 320-1.

61 *Discoveries and Opinions,* p. 191.

62 Galileo to Picchena, 23 Jan. 1616; *Opere, 12,* 227-8.

63 *Discoveries and Opinions.* pp. 191-7.

64 *Ibid.,* p. 206.

65 *Ibid.,* p. 209. See also analogous texts on pp. 175, 176, 196, 197, 199, 200.

66 *Ibid.,* pp. 202-3.

67 *Ibid.,* p. 215.

68 Brodrick, *Bellarmine,* p. 382.

69 *The Mind's Ascent to God by a Ladder of Created Things,* tr. Monialis, (London: Mowbray, 1925), p. 4.

70 *Ibid.,* p. 106.

71 *Ibid.,* p. 124.

72 *Opere, 19,* 278.

73 The Tuscan ambassador to Rome, Niccolini, repeated the claim in a letter to the court in Florence, 13 Nov. 1632; *ibid., 14,* 428.

74 References to the "League of Pigeons," Galileo's derisory title for the group led by Ludoviso delle Colombe, appear in his correspondence in connection with the controversy over his *Discourse on Bodies in Water.* See Galileo to Cesi, 5 Jan. 1613, and Cigoli to Galileo, 1 Feb. 1613; *ibid., 11,* 461 and 476.

75 I refer to its use of the verb "serpere." The verb is not a very common one. I can recall only one other place where I have seen it, the preface to Bellarmino's *Controversies,* in which he speaks of how the venom of heresy, infecting a hundred others for every one it kills, "creeps [serpit]" far and wide. (*De controversiis,*

Praefatio, n.p.) The context was identical in the two places, and the verb, with its evocation of the scene in the Garden of Eden, was peculiarly appropriate to Bellarmino's purpose in both.

76 *Opere, 19,* 321-2.

77 I take such an assumption to be implicit, for example, in the treatments of Giorgio di Santillana, *The Crime of Galileo,* (Chicago: Univ. of Chicago Press, 1955), pp. 242-3, and Stillman Drake, *Galileo at Work,* (Chicago: Univ. of Chicago Press, 1978), pp. 252-5.

78 *The Mind's Ascent,* pp. 76-7.

79 The account of the trial by Giovanfrancesco Buonamici, July 1633; *Opere, 19,* 411. See Giorgio Spini, "The Rationale of Galileo's Religiousness," in *Galileo Reappraised,* ed. Carlo L. Golino, (Berkeley and Los Angeles: Univ. of California Press, 1966), pp. 44-66; and the same article in its original Italian, "La religiosità di Galileo," in *Saggi su Galileo Galilei,* ed. Carlo Maccagni, (Firenze: Barbera, 1972), *2,* 416-40.

80 Galileo to Diodati, 15 Jan. 1633; *Opere, 15,* 25.

Maurice A. Finocchiaro (essay date 1989)

SOURCE: Introduction to *The Galileo Affair: A Documentary History,* edited and translated by Maurice A. Finocchiaro, University of California Press, 1989, pp. 1-46.

[*In the following excerpt, Finocchiaro describes Galileo's personality as it clashed with the tenor of the times, and explains Copernicus's heliocentric theory as well as its limitations, showing how, thanks to his improvements on the recently invented telescope, Galileo was able to eliminate most of those limitations.*]

Nonintellectual Factors

Beginning with personal or psychological factors, it is easy to see that Galileo had a penchant for controversy, was a master of wit and sarcasm, and wrote with unsurpassable eloquence. Interacting with each other and with his scientific and philosophical virtues, these qualities resulted in his making many enemies and getting involved in many other bitter disputes besides the main one that concerns us here. Typically these disputes involved questions of priority of invention or discovery and fundamental disagreements about the occurrence and interpretation of various natural phenomena. It may be of some interest to give a brief list of the other major controversies: a successful lawsuit against another inventor for plagiarism in regard to Galileo's invention of a calculating device and in regard to its accompanying instructions; a dispute with his philosophy colleagues at the University of Padua, where he taught mathematics, about the exact location of the novas that became visible in the heavens in October 1604; a dispute with other philosophers in Florence in 1612 about the reason why bodies float in water; a dispute with an astronomer named Christopher Scheiner about priority in the discovery of sunspots and about their proper interpretation; and a dispute with an astronomer named Orazio Grassi about the nature of comets, occasioned by the appearance of some of these phenomena in 1618. If we remember all this, and what it indicates about Galileo's personality, we may wonder how he managed to acquire and keep the many friends and admirers he did.

In regard to social and economic factors, it should be noted that Galileo was not wealthy. He had to earn his living, first as a university professor and then under the patronage of the grand duke of Tuscany.[13] During his university career in the first half of his life, his economic condition was always precarious. His university salary was very modest, and this was especially so given that he taught mathematics and thus received only a fraction of the remuneration given to a professor of philosophy.[14] This only compounded other unlucky family circumstances, such as having to provide dowries for his sisters. Galileo was forced to supplement his salary by giving private lessons, by taking on boarders at his house, and by working in and managing a profitable workshop which built various devices, some of his own invention. These financial difficulties eased in the second half of his life when he attained the position of "philosopher and chief mathematician" to the grand duke of Tuscany. In this position he was constantly facing a different problem, however, stemming from the nature of patronage and his relationship to his patron: since the fame and accomplishments of an artist or scientist were meant to reflect on the magnificence of his patron, Galileo was in constant need to prove himself scientifically and philosophically, either by surpassing the original accomplishments that had earned him the position or by giving new evidence for that original worth.[15]

Let us now go on to the politics of the Galileo affair. Here we have first the political background of the Catholic Counter-Reformation. Martin Luther had started the Protestant Reformation in 1517, and the Catholic church had convened the Council of Trent in 1545-1563. So Galileo's troubles developed and climaxed during a time of violent struggle between Catholics and Protestants. Since he was a Catholic living in a Catholic country, it was also a period when the decisions of that council were being taken seriously and implemented and thus affected him directly. Aside from the question of papal authority, one main issue dividing the two camps was the interpretation of the Bible—both how specific points were to be interpreted and who was entitled to do the interpreting. The Prot-

cstants, of course, were inclined toward relatively novel and individualistic or pluralistic interpretations, whereas the Catholics were committed to relatively traditional interpretations by the appropriate authorities. In this regard, it is instructive to see exactly what the most relevant decrees of the Council of Trent stated. At its Fourth Session (8 April 1546), the council had issued two decrees about Holy Scripture, one of which contains the following paragraph:

> Furthermore, to check unbridled spirits, it decrees that no one relying on his own judgment shall, in matters of faith and morals pertaining to the edification of Christian doctrine, distorting the Holy Scriptures in accordance with his own conceptions, presume to interpret them contrary to that sense which holy mother Church, to whom it belongs to judge of their true sense and interpretation, has held and holds, or even contrary to the unanimous teaching of the Fathers, even though such interpretations should never at any time be published. Those who act contrary to this shall be made known to ordinaries and punished in accordance with the penalties prescribed by the law.[16]

And the Fifth Session (17 June 1546) issued a decree regulating the teaching of Holy Scripture, stating in part: "[so] that under the semblance of piety impiety may not be disseminated, the same holy council has decreed that no one be admitted to this office of instructor, whether such instruction be public or private, who has not been previously examined and approved by the bishop of the locality as to his life, morals and knowledge."[17]

A more specific element of religious politics concerns the fact that the final climax of the affair in 1632-1633 was taking place during the so-called Thirty Years War between Catholics and Protestants (1618-1648). At that particular juncture Pope Urban VIII, who had earlier been an admirer and supporter of Galileo, was in an especially vulnerable position; thus not only could he not continue to protect Galileo, but he had to use Galileo as a scapegoat to reassert, exhibit, and test his authority and power. The problem stemmed from the fact that in 1632 the Catholic side led by the king of Spain and by the Bohemian Holy Roman Emperor was disastrously losing the war to the Protestant side led by the king of Sweden Gustavus Adolphus. Religion was not the only issue in the war, however, which was being fought also over dynastic rights and territorial disputes. In fact, ever since his election in 1623, the pope's policy had been motivated primarily by political considerations, such as his wish to limit and balance the power of the Hapsburg dynasty which ruled Spain and the Holy Roman Empire. And it had also been motivated by personal interest—that is, by cooperation with the French, whose support had been instrumental in his election, and who for nationalistic reasons also opposed the Hapsburg hegemony. However, in the wake of Gustavus Adolphus's spectacular victories, the Spanish and imperial ambassadors were accusing Urban of having in effect favored and helped the Protestant cause. They mentioned such matters as his failure to send the kind of military and financial support that popes had usually provided on such occasions and his refusal to declare the war a holy war. There were even suspicions of a more direct understanding with the Protestants. Thus the pope's own religious credentials were being questioned, and there were rumors of convening a council to depose him.[18]

Then there was what may be called the Tuscan factor, which had at least two aspects. One was that the Grand Duchy of Tuscany whose ruler Galileo served was closely allied with Spain, and so the pope's intransigence with him was in part a way of getting back at Spain. The other was related to the fact that almost all the leading protagonists and many of the secondary figures in the Galileo affair were Tuscan. Pope Urban VIII himself was a Florentine of the House of Barberini; Tuscan also was Cardinal Robert Bellarmine, the key figure in the earlier phase of the affair; and so was the commissary general of the Inquisition during the later phase. Thus the entire episode has some of the flavor of a family squabble.

Finally, another political element involved the internal power struggle within the Church, on the part of various religious orders, such as the Jesuits and the Dominicans. Although such details are beyond the scope of this Introduction, it is interesting to note that in the earlier phase of the affair climaxing in 1616, Galileo seems to have been attacked by Dominicans and defended by Jesuits, whereas in the later phase, in 1632-1633, it seems that the two religious orders had exchanged roles.

Just as the political background of the affair involved primarily matters of religious politics, so the legal background involved essentially questions of ecclesiastical, or "canon," law. In Catholic countries, the activities of intellectuals like Galileo were subject to the jurisdiction of the Congregation of the Index and the Congregation of the Holy Office, or Inquisition. In the administration of the Catholic church a "congregation" is a committee of cardinals charged with some department of Church business. The Congregation of the Index was instituted by Pope Pius V in 1571 with the purpose of book censorship; one of its main responsibilities was the compilation of a list of forbidden books (called *Index librorum prohibitorum*); this congregation was abolished by Pope Benedict XV in 1917, and book censorship was then handled once again by the Congregation of the Holy Office, which had been in charge of the matter before 1571. The Congregation of the Holy Office, in turn, had been instituted in 1542 by Pope Paul III with the purpose of defending and upholding Catholic faith and morals; one of its specific

duties was to take over the suppression of heresies and heretics which had been handled by the Medieval Inquisition; hence, from that time onward, the Holy Office and the Inquisition became practically synonymous. In 1965 at the Second Vatican Council, its name was officially changed to Congregation for the Doctrine of the Faith. The Holy Office or Inquisition was, therefore, more important and authoritative than the Index. By the time Galileo got into religious trouble, the notion of heresy had been given something of a legal definition, and inquisitorial procedures had been more or less codified. Let us examine some of the most relevant details.[19]

Although the Inquisition dealt with other offenses such as witchcraft, it was primarily interested in two main categories of crimes: formal heresy and suspicion of heresy. Here, the term *suspicion* did not have the modern legal connotation pertaining to allegation and contrasting it to proof. One difference between formal heresy and suspicion of heresy was the seriousness of the offense. For example, a standard Inquisition manual of the time stated that "heretics are those who say, teach, preach, or write things against Holy Scripture; against the articles of the Holy Faith; . . . against the decrees of the Sacred Councils and the determinations made by the Supreme Pontiffs; . . . those who reject the Holy Faith and become Moslems, Jews, or members of other sects, and who praise their practices and live in accordance with them. . . ."[20] The same manual stated that "suspects of heresy are those who occasionally utter propositions that offend the listeners . . . those who keep, write, read, or give others to read books forbidden in the Index and in other particular Decrees; . . . those who receive the holy orders even though they have a wife, or who take another wife even though they are already married; . . . those who listen, even once, to sermons by heretics. . . ."[21] Another difference between formal heresy and suspicion of heresy was whether or not the culprit, having confessed the incriminating facts, admitted having an evil intention.[22] Furthermore, within the major category of suspicion of heresy, two main subcategories were distinguished: vehement suspicion of heresy and slight suspicion of heresy;[23] their difference depended on the seriousness of the crime. Thus, in effect there were three main types of religious crimes, in descending order of seriousness: formal heresy, vehement suspicion of heresy, and slight suspicion of heresy.

In regard to procedure, there were two ways in which legal proceedings could begin: either by the initiative of an inquisitor, responding to publicly available knowledge or publicly expressed opinion; or in response to a complaint filed by some third party, who was required to make a declaration of the purity of his motivation and to give a deposition. Then there were specific rules about the interrogation of defendants and witnesses; how injunctions and decrees were to be worded; how, when, and why interrogation by torture was to be used; and the various judicial sentences and defendant's abjurations with which to conclude the proceedings.

However important all this psychological, social, economic, political, and legal background is, the intellectual background is even more important. To this we now turn.

Copernicus's Challenge to Traditional Ideas

In 1543 Copernicus published his epoch-making book *On the Revolutions of the Heavenly Spheres*. In it he updated an idea which had been advanced as early as Pythagoras in ancient Greece but had been almost universally rejected—that is, the idea that the earth moves by rotating on its own axis daily and by revolving around the sun once a year. This means that the earth is not standing still at the center of the universe, with all the heavenly bodies revolving around it. In its essentials this geokinetic idea turned out to be true, as we know today beyond any reasonable doubt, after five centuries of accumulating evidence. At the time, however, the situation was very different. In fact, Copernicus's accomplishment was really to give a *new* argument in support of the *old* idea that had been considered and rejected earlier: he was able to demonstrate that the *known* details about the motions of the heavenly bodies could be explained *more simply* and *more coherently* if the sun rather than the earth is assumed to be at the center and the earth is taken to be the third planet circling the sun.

In regard to simplicity, for example, there are thousands fewer moving parts in the geokinetic system since the apparent daily motion of all heavenly bodies around the earth is explained by the earth's axial rotation, and thus there is only one thing moving daily (the earth), rather than thousands of stars. Moreover, in the geostatic system there are *two* opposite directions of motion, whereas in the geokinetic system all bodies rotate or revolve in the same direction. That is, in the geostatic system, while all the heavenly bodies revolve around the earth with the diurnal motion from *east to west,* the seven planets (moon, Mercury, Venus, sun, Mars, Jupiter, and Saturn) also simultaneously revolve around it from *west to east,* each in a different period of time (ranging from one month for the moon, to one year for the sun, to many years for Saturn). On the other hand, in the geokinetic system there is only one direction of motion since, for example, if the apparent diurnal motion from *east to west* is explained by attributing to the earth an axial rotation, then the direction of the latter has to be reversed (*west to east*), whereas if the apparent annual motion of the sun from *west to east* is explained by attributing to the earth an orbital revolution around the sun then the same direction has to be retained.[24]

In regard to explanatory coherence, without giving examples, I mean that Copernicus was able to explain many phenomena in detail by means of his basic assumption of a moving earth, without having to add artificial and ad hoc assumptions; the phenomena in question were primarily the various known facts about the motions and orbits of the planets. On the other hand, in the previous geostatic system, the thesis of a motionless earth had to be combined with a whole series of unrelated assumptions in order to explain what is observed to happen.[25]

Despite these geokinetic advantages, however, as a proof of the earth's motion Copernicus's argument was far from conclusive. Notice first that his argument is hypothetical. That is, it is based on the claim that *if* the earth were in motion *then* the observed phenomena would result. But from this it does not follow with logical necessity that the earth is in motion; all we would be entitled to infer is that the earth's motion offers an explanation of observed facts. Now, given the greater simplicity and coherence just mentioned, we could add that the earth's motion offered a simpler and more coherent explanation of heavenly phenomena. This does indeed provide a reason for preferring the geokinetic idea, but it is not a *decisive* reason. It would be decisive only in the absence of reasons for rejecting the idea or for preferring the opposite. In short, one has to look at counterarguments, and there were plenty of them.

The arguments against the earth's motion can be classified into various groups, depending on the branch of learning or type of principle from which they stemmed. In fact, these objections reflected the various traditional beliefs which contradicted or seemed to contradict the Copernican system. Thus, there were epistemological, philosophical, theological, religious, physical, mechanical, astronomical, and empirical objections. It is instructive to begin with the last type to underscore the fact that the opposition to Copernicanism was neither all mindless nor simply religious; however, to set the stage for the empirical details, it is best to begin with an argument which is empirical in the sense of involving observation and sensory experience, but which does so in such a way that it amounts to an epistemological objection.

The argument was aptly called the *objection from the deception of the senses.* To understand the deception involved, note that Copernicus did not claim that he could feel, see, or otherwise perceive the earth's motion by means of the senses. Like everyone else, Copernicus's senses told him that the earth is at rest. Therefore, if his theory were true, then the human senses would not be reporting the truth, or would be lying to us. But it was regarded as absurd that the senses should deceive us about such a basic phenomenon as the state of rest or motion of the terrestrial globe on which we live. In other words, the geokinetic theory seemed to be in flat contradiction with direct sense experience and appeared to violate the fundamental epistemological principle that under normal conditions the senses are reliable and provide us with one of the best instruments to learn the truth about reality.[26]

One could begin trying to answer this difficulty by saying that deceptions of the senses are neither unknown nor uncommon, as shown, for example, by the straight stick half immersed in water which appears bent or by the shore appearing to move away from a ship to an observer standing on the ship and looking at the shore.[27] However, the difference was that these perceptual illusions involve relatively minor and secondary experiences, whereas to live all one's life on a moving globe without noticing it would be a gigantic and radical deception. Moreover, it was added, the former illusions are corrigible, since we have other ways of discovering what really happens, whereas there is no way of correcting the perception of the earth being at rest.

This general empirical difficulty is in a sense the reverse side of the coin of the fundamental advantage of the geostatic system, which was that it corresponds to direct observation and sensory experience. (The same applies, of course, to all the other anti-geokinetic objections, which may thus be easily turned into pro-geostatic arguments.) This difficulty may be labeled an epistemological objection because the real issues are whether the earth's motion ought to be observable and whether the human senses ought to be capable of revealing the fundamental features of physical reality. The other empirical difficulties are more specific. They are based primarily on effects in the heavens which ought to be observed in a Copernican universe, but which in fact were not; these *specific empirical difficulties* may therefore be called the *astronomical objections*.

The *objection from the earth-heaven dichotomy*[28] argued that if Copernicus were right then the earth would share many physical properties with the other heavenly bodies, especially the planets, since the earth would itself be a planet, the third one circling the sun. However, it was widely believed that whereas the heavenly bodies are made of the element aether which is weightless, luminous, and changeless, the earth is made of rocks, water, and air which have (positive or negative) weight, are dark, and subject to constant changes. Before the telescope this belief had considerable empirical support.

The *appearance of the planet Venus*[29] was the basis of another objection. For if the Copernican system were correct, then this planet should exhibit phases similar to those of the moon but with a different period; however, none were visible (before the telescope). The

reason why Venus would have to show such phases stems from the fact that in the Copernican system it is the second planet circling the sun, the earth is the third, and these two planets have different periods of revolution. Therefore, the relative positions of the sun, Venus, and the earth would be changing periodically and so would the amount of Venus's surface visible from the earth: when Venus is on the far side of the sun from the earth, its entire hemisphere lit by the sun is visible from the earth, and the planet should appear as a disk full of light (like a full moon, though much smaller); when Venus comes between the sun and the earth, none of its hemisphere lit by the sun is visible from the earth, and the planet would be invisible (as in the case of a new moon); and at intermediate locations, when the three bodies are so positioned that the line connecting them forms a noticeable angle, then different amounts would be visible, giving Venus an appearance ranging from nearly fully lit, to half lit, to a crescent shape.

The *apparent brightness and size of the planet Mars* involved another problematic issue. In the Copernican system this planet is the next outer one after the earth, and, since they also revolve at different rates, they are relatively close to each other when their orbital revolutions align both on the same side of the sun and relatively far when they are on opposite sides of the sun. Because the variation in distance is considerable, this would cause a corresponding variation in apparent size and an ever greater change in brightness, since the intensity of light varies as the square of the distance. Now, the difficulty was that although Mars did indeed exhibit a noticeable change in brightness with periodic regularity, this change was not nearly as much as it should be; further, there was practically no variation in apparent size.[30]

The last of the empirical arguments to be discussed here was based on the fact that observation revealed no change in the *apparent position of the fixed stars;*[31] this is commonly known as the objection from stellar *parallax,* a term that denotes a change in the apparent position of an observed object due to a change in the observer's location. At its simplest level, the apparent position of a star may be thought of as its location on the (imaginary) celestial sphere, which in a sense is its position relative to all the other stars (also located on that sphere); or, from the viewpoint of the Copernican system, it may be conceived as measured by the angular position of the star above the plane of the earth's orbit. Now, if the earth were revolving around the sun, then in the course of a year its position in space would change by a considerable amount defined by the size of the earth's orbit. Therefore, a terrestrial observer looking at the same star at six-month intervals would be observing it from different positions, the difference being a distance equal to the diameter of the earth's orbit. Consequently, the same star should appear as having shifted its position either on the celestial sphere or in terms of its angular distance above the plane of the earth's orbit. It follows that if Copernicanism were correct, we should be able to see stellar parallaxes with a periodic regularity of one year; but none were observed.

It should be noted that the first three of these empirical-astronomical objections were not answered until Galileo's telescopic discoveries and that the stellar parallax was not detected until much later (1838). In fact, the magnitude of parallax varies inversely as the distance of the observed object; the stars are so far away that their parallax is exceedingly small; and for about two centuries telescopes were not sufficiently powerful to make the fine discriminations required. One may then begin to sympathize with Copernicus's contemporaries, who found his idea very hard to accept. However, as mentioned earlier, there were many other reasons for their opposition. The next group may be labeled *mechanical* or *physical,* in the sense that they are based directly or indirectly on a number of principles of the branch of physics which today we call mechanics, the study of how bodies move. We shall first mention four objections which hinge indirectly (though crucially) on the laws of motion and may therefore initially appear as empirical objections; later we shall present two others where the appeal to such physical principles is direct and explicit.

The *objection from vertical fall* began with the fact that bodies fall vertically. This is something that everyone can easily observe by looking at rainfall when there is no disturbing wind; or one can take a small rock into one's hand, throw it directly upward, and notice that it then falls back to the place from which it was thrown; or one can drop a rock from the top of a building or tower and notice that it moves perpendicularly downward, landing directly below. Then it was argued that this could not happen if the earth were rotating; for, while the body is falling through the air, the ground below would move a considerable distance to the east (due to the earth's axial rotation), and although the building and person would be carried along, the unattached falling body would be left behind; so that on a rotating earth the body would land to the west of where it was dropped and would appear to be falling along a slanted path. Since this is not seen, but rather bodies fall vertically, it was concluded that the earth does not rotate.[32]

An analogous argument was advanced by the *objection from the motion of projectiles.* The relevant observation here was that, when ejected with equal force, projectiles range an equal distance to the east and to the west. This can be most easily observed by throwing a rock with the same exertion in opposite directions in turn and then measuring the two distances; one could also use bow and arrow to have a slightly better mea-sure of the propulsive force; or one could use a gun, and shoot it first to the east and then to the west with the same amount of charge. Now, the argument claimed that on a rotating earth such projectiles should instead range further toward the west than toward the east. The reason given was that in its westward flight the projectile would be moving against the earth's rotation, which would carry the place of ejection and the ejector some extra distance to the east; whereas, in its eastward flight, the projectile would be traveling in the same direction as the ejector, due to the latter being carried eastward by the earth's rotation. Therefore, on a rotating earth the westward projectiles would range further by a distance equal to the amount of the earth's motion, while the eastward ones would fall short by the same amount. Again, since observation reveals that this is not so, it supposedly follows that the earth does not rotate.[33]

Of course, today these arguments can be refuted. However, their refutation requires knowledge of at least two fundamental principles of mechanics. One is the law of conservation of momentum, or more simply the principle of conservation of motion, according to which the motion acquired by a body is conserved unless an external force interferes with it; the other is the principle of superposition, which specifies how motions in different directions are to be added to each other to yield a resultant motion. The details of these mechanical principles and their application are beyond the scope of this Introduction. The point that needs to be stressed here is that since the phenomena appealed to are indeed true, the two objections just presented raised issues about how bodies would move on a rotating earth, and the resolution of these issues depended on the possession of more accurate mechanical principles. The next objection raised these same issues, but also the question of the true facts of the case; however, to establish these facts was not so easy as it might seem.

The *ship analogy objection*[34] referred to an experiment to be made on a ship, and it then drew an analogy between the earth and the ship. The experiment was that of dropping a rock from the top of a ship's mast, both when the ship is motionless and when it is advancing, and then checking the place where the rock hits the deck. It was asserted that the experiment yielded different results in the two cases—that when the ship is standing still the rock falls at the foot of the mast, but when the ship is moving forward the rock hits the deck some distance to the back. Then the moving ship was compared to a portion of land on a rotating earth, and a tower on the earth was regarded as the analogue of the ship's mast. From this it was inferred that if the earth were rotating, then a rock dropped from a tower would land to the west of the foot of the tower, just as it happens on a ship moving forward; since the rock can be observed to land at the foot of the tower, however, they concluded that the earth must be standing still.

This objection partly involves the empirical issue of exactly what happens when the experiment is made on a moving ship. If the experiment is properly made, the rock still falls at the foot of the mast. However, it is easy to get the wrong result due to extraneous causes, such as wind and any rocking motion the boat may have in addition to its forward motion. Therefore, it is not surprising that there were common reports of the experiment having been made and yielding anti-Copernican results.[35] Nor is it surprising that when Galileo tried to refute the objection, although he disputed the results of the actual experiment, he emphasized a more theoretical answer in terms of the principles of conservation and superposition of motion.[36] The principles are needed to determine what will happen to the horizontal motion the rock had before it was dropped from the mast of the moving ship, and how it is to be combined with the new vertical motion of fall it acquires.

The last of the indirectly mechanical objections to be discussed here is the *argument from the extruding power of whirling,*[37] or, as we might say today, the *centrifugal force argument*. The basis of this objection was the fact that in a rotating system, or in motion along a curve, bodies have a tendency to move away from the center of rotation or the center of the curve. For example, if one is in a vehicle traveling at a high rate of speed, whenever the vehicle makes a turn one experiences a force pushing one away from the center of the curve defined by the turn: if the vehicle turns right, one experiences a push to the left and vice versa. Or one could make the simple experiment of tying a small pail of water at the end of a string and whirling the pail in a vertical circle by the motion of one's hand. Now suppose a small hole is made in the bottom of the pail; as the pail is whirled one will see water rushing out of the hole always in a direction away from one's hand. Then the argument called attention to the fact that, if the earth rotates, bodies on its surface are traveling in circles around its axis at different speeds depending on the latitude, the greatest being about 1000 miles per hour at the equator. This sounds like a very high rate of speed, which would generate such a strong extruding power that all bodies would fly off the earth's surface and the earth itself might disintegrate. Since this obviously does not happen, it was concluded that the earth must not be rotating.

This objection raised issues whose resolution involves the correct laws of centrifugal force. At the time, therefore, it was felt to be a very strong objection. Next, we come to the objections according to which the conflict with physical principles was so explicit that the earth's motion seemed a straightforward physical impossibility.

The *natural motion argument*[38] claimed that the earth's motion (whether of axial rotation or orbital revolution) is physically impossible because the natural motion of earthly bodies (rocks and water) is to move in a *straight* line toward the center of the *universe*. The context of this argument was a science of physics which contrasted natural motion to forced or violent motion, which postulated three basic types of natural motion, and which attributed each type to one or more of the basic elements: circular motion around the center of the universe was attributed to aether, the element of the heavenly bodies; straight motion away from the center of the universe was ascribed to the elements air and fire; and straight motion toward the center of the universe was given to the elements earth and water. Thus, unlike natural circular motion which can last forever, straight natural motion, especially straight downward, cannot: once the center (of the universe) is reached, the body will no longer have any natural tendency to move. Now, the terrestrial globe on which we live is essentially the collection of all things made of the elements earth and water, which have collected at the center (of the universe) or as close to it as possible. Therefore, this whole collection cannot move around the center (in an orbital revolution as Copernicus would have it), because such a motion would be unnatural, could not last forever, and would in any case be overcome by the tendency to move naturally in a straight line toward the center; further, for the same reasons, once at the center the whole collection could not even acquire any axial rotation.

The Copernican system was also deemed physically impossible because it was in direct violation of the principle according to which *every simple body can have one and only one natural motion*.[39] This principle was another aspect of the laws of motion of Aristotelian physics just sketched, whereas Copernicanism seemed to attribute to the earth at least three natural motions: the revolution of the whole earth in an orbit around the sun, the rotation of the earth around its own axis, and the downward motion of parts of the earth in free fall.

Just as the last two objections are essentially unanswerable as long as one accepts the two principles of traditional physics just mentioned, they are easily answerable by rejecting these two principles. However, rejecting them is easier said than done since, to be effective, the rejection should be accompanied by the formulation of some alternatives. In short, what was really required was the construction of a new science of motion, a new physics. In fact, the alternatives were such cornerstones of modern physics as the law of inertia, the law of gravitational force, and the law of conservation of (linear and angular) momentum. For example, according to the law of inertia, the natural motion of *all* bodies is uniform and rectilinear; and according to the law of gravitation, all bodies attract each other with a force that makes them accelerate toward each other or diverge from their natural inertial motion in a measurable way. Thus, the earth's orbital motion becomes a forced motion under the influence of the sun's gravitational attraction; the axial rotation of the whole earth becomes a type of natural motion in accordance with conservation laws; and the downward fall of heavy bodies near the earth's surface becomes a forced motion under the influence of the earth's gravitational attraction.

Finally, there were theological and religious objections. One of these appealed to the *authority of the Bible*.[40] It claimed that the idea of the earth moving is heretical because it conflicts with many biblical passages which state or imply that the earth stands still. For example, Psalm 104:5 says that the Lord "laid the foundations of the earth, that it should not be removed for ever"; and this seems to say rather explicitly that the earth is motionless. Other passages were less explicit, but they seemed to attribute motion to the sun and thus to presuppose the geostatic system. For example, Ecclesiastes 1:5 states that "the sun also riseth, and the sun goeth down, and hasteth to the place where he ariseth"; and Joshua 10:12-13 asserts: "Then spake Joshua to the Lord in the day when the Lord delivered up the Amorites before the children of Israel, and he said in the sight of Israel, 'Sun, stand thou still upon Gibeon; and thou, Moon, in the valley of Ajalon.' And the sun stood still, and the moon stayed, until the people had avenged themselves upon their enemies."

The biblical objection had greater appeal to those (such as Protestants) who took a literal interpretation of the Bible more seriously. However, for those (such as Catholics) less inclined in this direction, the same conclusion could be reinforced by appeal to the *consensus of Church Fathers*;[41] these were the saints, theologians, and churchmen who had played an influential and formative role in the establishment and development of Christianity. The argument claimed that all Church Fathers were unanimous in interpreting relevant biblical passages (such as those just mentioned) in accordance with the geostatic view; therefore, the geostatic system is binding on all believers, and to claim otherwise (as Copernicans did) is heretical.

In summary, the idea updated by Copernicus was vulnerable to a host of counterarguments and counterevidence. The earth's motion seemed epistemologically absurd because it flatly contradicted direct sensory experience and thus undermined the normal procedure in the search for truth; it seemed empirically untrue because it had astronomical consequences that were not seen to happen; it seemed a physical impossibility because it seemed to have consequences that contradicted the most incontrovertible mechanical phenomena, and because it directly violated many of the most basic principles of the available physics; and it seemed a religious heresy because it conflicted with the words of the Bible and the biblical interpretations of the Church Fathers.

Copernicus was aware of these difficulties.[42] He realized that his novel argument did not conclusively prove the earth's motion and that there were many counterarguments of apparently greater strength. I believe that these were the main reasons why he delayed publication of his book until he was almost on his deathbed.

Galileo's Reassessment of Copernicanism

Galileo's attitude was at first similar to that of Copernicus. The main difference was that Galileo's central interest was physics, mechanics, and mathematics, rather than astronomy. He began university teaching in 1589, almost fifty years after Copernicus's death. In his official position as professor of mathematics, his duties included the teaching of astronomy and physics, as well as mathematics. Although acquainted with the Copernican theory, Galileo did not regard it as sufficiently well established to teach it in his courses; instead he covered traditional geostatic astronomy. Nor was he directly pursuing the geokinetic theory in his research. Rather his research consisted of investigations into the nature of motion and the laws in accordance with which bodies move. Here his work was original and revolutionary, for he was critical of the traditional physics of motion and was attempting to construct a new mechanics and physics. It did not take him long to realize that the physics he was building was very much in line with the geokinetic theory: what he was discovering about the motion of bodies in general made it possible for the earth to move and rendered unlikely its rest at the center of the universe. In short, Galileo soon realized that his physical research had important consequences in the astronomical field—namely, to strengthen the Copernican theory by removing the physical and mechanical objections against it and providing new arguments in its favor.

We have evidence that he was aware of this reinforcement but still was dissatisfied with the Copernican theory. After all, the other objections were still there, especially the all-important empirical-astronomical difficulties. It was only the invention of the telescope, and the astronomical discoveries it made possible, which removed most of them and paved the way for removing the others.

The invention of the telescope and Galileo's role in it is a fascinating story in its own right, but too long and complex to be told here.[43] Suffice it to say the following. This instrument was first invented by others in 1608, but in 1609 Galileo was able to improve its quality and magnification sufficiently to produce an astronomically useful instrument that could not be duplicated by others for quite some time. With this instrument, in the next few years he made a number of startling discoveries: that, like the earth, the moon has a rough surface covered with mountains and valleys and appears to be made of the same rocky, opaque, and nonluminous substance; that the planet Jupiter has at least four satellites and thus constitutes a miniature planetary system; that the planet Venus does show phases similar to those of the moon; that the planet Mars does show changes in brightness and apparent size of about sixtyfold; and that there are dark spots on the surface of the sun which appear and disappear at irregular intervals but move in such a way as to indicate that the sun rotates on its own axis once a month.

Some of these discoveries were published in 1610 in a book entitled *The Starry Messenger;* others were published in 1613 in a book entitled *Sunspot Letters.* His 1610 book allowed Galileo to leave the position of professor of mathematics at the University of Padua which he had held for some twenty years. He went back to his native Tuscany to be under the patronage of its ruling grand duke and to devote full time to research and writing. Galileo requested that his official title should include the word philosopher as well as mathematician, and so for the rest of his life he held the position of philosopher and chief mathematician to the grand duke of Tuscany.[44]

The new telescopic evidence led Galileo to reassess the status of Copernicanism, for it removed most of the empirical-astronomical objections against the earth's motion and added new arguments in its favor. Thus, Galileo now believed not only that the geokinetic theory was simpler and more coherent than the geostatic theory (as Copernicus had shown), not only that it was more physically and mechanically adequate (as himself had been discovering in his twenty years of university research), but also that it was empirically superior in astronomy (as the telescope now revealed). However, he had not yet published anything of his new physics, and the epistemological and especially theological objections had not yet been dealt with; so the case in favor of the earth's motion was still not conclusive.

Thus, Galileo's new attitude toward the geokinetic theory could be described as one of direct pursuit and tentative acceptance, by contrast with the indirect pursuit and contextually divided loyalty of the pretelescopic situation.[45] However, in Galileo's publications of this period we find yet no explicit acceptance of or committed belief in the earth's motion. We do find a more favorable attitude expressed in his private correspondence, as well as a stronger endorsement in the *Sunspot Letters* of 1613 than in *The Starry Messenger* of 1610. But that is as one would expect.

Besides realizing that the pro-Copernican arguments were still not absolutely conclusive, Galileo must have also perceived the potentially explosive character of the biblical and religious objections. In fact, for a number of years he did not get involved even though his book of 1610 had been attacked by several authors on biblical grounds, among others. Eventually, however, he was dragged into the theological discussion. . . .

Notes

[13] One is tempted to say that in 1610 Galileo went back to his native Tuscany to be the "scientific advisor" of the grand duke, but this description would be too modern and ultimately anachronistic; for a discussion of the nature of patronage and its importance, see Westfall (1984, 1985).

[14] He began with a salary of 180 florins, and after about twenty years, as a result of his telescope, his salary of 500 was doubled to 1000 florins; even so, the senior professor of philosophy was earning 2000 florins. See Drake (1978, p. 160); Koestler (1959, p. 364); and Santillana (1955, p. 3).

[15] See Westfall (1984, 1985).

[16] Schroeder (1978, pp. 18-19).

[17] Ibid., p. 25.

[18] Ranke (1841, vol. II: 98-125, especially pp. 116-19).

[19] The following account is based on Masini (1621).

[20] Masini (1621, pp. 16-17).

[21] Ibid., pp. 17-18.

[22] Ibid., pp. 166-67.

[23] In principle there was also a third subcategory, namely, "violent suspicion of heresy"; however, the manual clarified that in practice this was equated to "vehement" suspicion of heresy (Masini 1621, p. 188).

[24] For more details on this last point, see, for example, Kuhn (1957, pp. 160-65); this work may also be consulted for other details since Kuhn's classic remains the best account of the Copernican revolution.

[25] For more details on what I am here calling explanatory coherence, see Lakatos and Zahar (1975, pp. 368-81), and Millman (1976); note, however, that their terminology is different.

[26] An allusion to this objection is found in the letter by "Cardinal Bellarmine to Foscarini" in Chapter I; for more details, see Galilei (1967, pp. 32-38, and 247-56).

[27] See section III, paragraphs 9 and 10, of "Galileo's Considerations on the Copernican Opinion" in Chapter II.

[28] See Galilei (1967, pp. 38-105); see also section 18 of "Galileo's Reply to Ingoli" in Chapter VI.

[29] See section 3 of "Galileo's Letter to the Grand Duchess Christina" in Chapter III (corresponding to Favaro 1890-1909, vol. 5, p. 328, hereafter cited as Favaro 5:328); see also Galilei (1967, pp. 318-40).

[30] In many places—for example, in the "Letter to the Grand Duchess Christina" (Chapter III; see Favaro 5:328)—Galileo states that the expected variation in apparent size and brightness is of the order of 60; his discussion of this point in the *Dialogue* (Favaro 7:349-50; Galilei 1967, p. 321) indicates that this is meant to be approximately the square of 8, which he gives as the ratio of the maximum to the minimum distance between Mars and the earth. I am not sure how he arrives at this figure, given that the Copernican estimate of the mean distance between Mars and the sun is 1.52 times the mean distance between the earth and the sun (Dreyer 1953, p. 339), which would yield a ratio of about 4.85 to 1. Even if we add the eccentricity of Mars's orbit, which I estimate at about 0.1 (Dreyer 1953, p. 336), we would still have a ratio of 5.9. Adding the eccentricity of the earth's orbit would further increase this factor, but not by the required amount to make it correspond to 8. The reason why the observed variation in apparent brightness of Mars presented a serious difficulty for the Copernican system but not for the Ptolemaic system was that in the latter the relevant quantities (distance, epicycle, etc.) could be adjusted to correspond to the actual observations, whereas in the former the variation could be derived from other elements of the system, because of its greater coherence mentioned above.

[31] See especially sections 2 and 11, but also section 3, of "Galileo's Reply to Ingoli," in Chapter VI; see also Galilei (1967, pp. 377-89).

[32] For more details, including an answer, see sections 8 and 9 of "Galileo's Reply to Ingoli" in Chapter VI; for an even more extended analysis, see Galilei (1967, pp. 138-67).

[33] For more details, see section 10 of "Galileo's Reply to Ingoli" in Chapter VI; for a full answer, see Galilei (1967, pp. 167-71).

[34] See section 9 of "Galileo's Reply to Ingoli" in Chapter VI; see also Galilei (1967, pp. 143-49).

[35] Chiaramonti (1633, p. 339).

[36] See section 9 of "Galileo's Reply to Ingoli" in Chapter VI; see also Galilei (1967, pp. 143-49).

[37] See Galilei (1967, pp. 132 and 188-218); see also section 7 of "Galileo's Reply to Ingoli" in Chapter VI.

[38] See sections 6 and 17 of "Galileo's Reply to Ingoli" in Chapter VI; see also Galilei (1967, pp. 14-38 and 133-36).

[39] See section 17 of "Galileo's Reply to Ingoli" in Chapter VI; see also Galilei (1967, pp. 256-64).

[40] See the letters by "Galileo to Castelli" and by "Cardinal Bellarmine to Foscarini" in Chapter I; and especially "Galileo's Letter to the Grand Duchess Christina" in Chapter III, which is devoted to a detailed refutation of this objection.

[41] See the letter by "Cardinal Bellarmine to Foscarini" in Chapter I and the criticism in section 4 of "Galileo's Letter to the Grand Duchess Christina" in Chapter III.

[42] For example, he discussed some of these objections in Book One of his great work; see, for example, Copernicus (1976).

[43] For a general account, see Drake (1957, pp. 1-88; 1978, pp. 134-76); for an account that stresses the scientific and epistemological issues, see Ronchi (1958).

[44] Favaro (10:369).

[45] This also contrasts with the attitude of a true believer and that of zealous commitment, which one finds attributed to Galileo in such works as Feyerabend (1978), Koestler (1959), and Langford (1966). However, see Finocchiaro (1988b) for more details and documentation of my interpretation, which also corresponds in large measure to Drake (1978). . . .

Works Cited

Chiaramonti, Scipione. 1633. *Difesa . . . al suo Anticone e Libro delle tre nuove Stelle*. Florence: Landini. . . .

Drake, Stillman, editor, 1957. *Discoveries and Opinions of Galileo*. Garden City: Doubleday. . . .

Drake, Stillman. 1978. *Galileo at Work: His Scientific Biography*. Chicago: University 0f Chicago Press. . . .

Dreyer, J. L. E. 1953. *A History of Astronomy from Thales to Kepler*. revised by W. H. Stahl. New York: Dover. . . .

Favaro, Antonio, editor. 1890-1909. *Le Opere di Galileo Galilei*. 20 vols. National Edition of Galile"s collected works. Florence: Barbèra. . . .

Feyerabend, Paul K. 1978. *Against Method*. New York: Schocken Books. . . .

Finocchiaro, Maurice A. 1988b. "Galileo's Coperni-canism and the Acceptability of Guiding Assump-tions." In *Scrutinizing Science: Empirical Studies of Scientific Change*, edited by Arthur Donovan, Larry Laudan, and rachel Laudan, pp. 49-67. Dordrecht: Reidel. . . .

Galilei, Galileo. 1967. *Dialogue Concerning the Two Chief World Systems*. Translated by Stillman Drake. 2nd ed. Berkeley: University of California Press. . . .

Galluzzi, Paolo, editor. 1984. *Novità celesti e crisi del sapere: Atti del Convegno Internazionale di Studi Galileiani*. Florence: Antenore. . . .

Koestler, Arhtur. 1959. *The Sleepwalkers: A History of Man's Changing Vision of the Universe*. New York: Macmillan. . . .

Kuhn, Thomas S. 1957. *The Copernican Revolution*. Cambridge: Harvard University Press.

Lakatos, Imre, and E. Zahar. 1975. "Why Did Coper-nicus' Research Program Supersede Ptolemy's." In *The Copernican Achievement*, edited by Robert S. West-man, pp. 354-83. Berkeley: University of California Press.

Langford, Jerome J. 1966. *Galileo, Science and the Church*. Ann Arbor: University of Michigan Press. . . .

Masini, Eliseo. 1621. *Sacro arsenale overo Prattica dell'officio della Santa Inquisitione*. Genoa: Appresso Giuseppe Pavoni. . . .

Millman Arhtur B. 1976. "The Plausibility of Research programs." In *PSA 1976: Proceedings of the 1976 Biennial Meeting of the Philosophy of Science Associ-ation*, edited by Frederick Suppe and P. D. Asquith, vol. 1, pp. 140-48. East Lansing, Mich.: Philosophy of Science Association. . . .

Ranke, Leopold. 1841. *The Ecclesiastical and Politi-cal History of the Popes of Rome*. 2 vols. Translated by S. Austin. Philadelphia: Lea & Blanchard. . . .

Santillana, Giorgio de. 1955. *The Crime of Galileo*. Chicago: University of chicago Press. . . .

Schroeder, H. J., translator and editor. 1978. *Canons and Decrees of the Council of Trent*. St. Louis: Herd-er, 1941. Reprint. Rockford, Ill.: Tan Books and pub-lishers. . . .

Westfall, Richard S. 1984. "Galileo and the *Accademia dei Lincei*." in Galluzzi (1984), pp. 189-200.

Westfall, Richard S. "Science and Patronage: Galileo and the Telescope." *Isis* 76: 11-30. . . .

Eileen Reeves (essay date 1991)

SOURCE: "Daniel 5 and the *Assayer*: Galileo Reads the Handwriting on the Wall," in *The Journal of Me-dieval and Renaissance Studies,* Vol. 21, No. 1, Spring, 1991, pp. 1-27.

[*In the following essay, Reeves portrays Galileo's* Assayer *as a witty and rigorous linguistic attack against scientific ignorance and vanity.*]

I

In that great catalog of wit and invective which Galileo Galilei published in 1623 as the *Assayer,* the rather unlikely issue of Babylonian cookery is singled out as particularly deserving of ridicule. The matter arose in the course of the debate over the comets of 1618—the ostensible subject of the *Assayer*—between Galileo and his opponent Orazio Grassi, S.J., when the latter main-tained that motion, not friction, was the cause of heat. Grassi offered as proof several verses from Ovid, Lu-can, Lucretius, and Virgil in which arrows were ignit-ed or even melted as they flew through the air; not content with mere poetry, he enhanced his argument with the testimony of the tenth-century lexicographer Suidas, a man "of great authority and trustworthiness,"[1] who had written that "the Babylonians, whirling eggs in slings, were no strangers to the simple diet of the hunter, but rather accustomed to the demands of the wilderness, such that they were able to cook even raw eggs by this motion."[2]

It is reasonable to assume that neither Grassi nor Ga-lileo actually prepared this Babylonian delicacy. The Pisan scientist, however, was quick to express both his scepticism of Suidas and his scorn for his credulous opponent:

> If [Grassi] wants me to believe from Suidas that the Babylonians cooked eggs by whirling them rapidly in slings, I shall do so; but I must say that the cause of this effect is very far from that which he attributes to it. To discover truth I shall reason thus: "If we do not achieve an effect which others formerly achieved, it must be that in our operations we lack something which was the cause of this effect succeeding, and if we lack but one single thing, then this alone will be the cause. Now we do not lack eggs, or slings, or sturdy fellows to whirl them; and still they do not cook, but rather they cool down faster if hot. And since nothing is lacking to us except being Babylonian, then being Babylonian is the cause of the eggs hardening."[3]

Though he went on to dispute Grassi's other authori-ties, Galileo returned to the antique recipe, arguing that if, as Grassi had conceded, scorched arrows, melt-ed cannonballs, and eggs cooked in slings were rari-ties, they ought to be treated as miracles, not as limpid illustrations of natural laws, and still less as evidence that comets might be ignited by the motion of the air. To be perfectly fair—an undertaking that had not the least appeal for either Galileo or Grassi—the Jesuit mathematician had written that the air did not *normally* heat eggs or arrows or cannonballs to such an extent, and that the events which he had described were considered *paene miraculo,* "almost as miracles." The conditions required, Grassi suggested, prevailed only infrequently, and yet they in no way violated the laws of nature, for they confirmed the precepts established by Aristotle.

Galileo's modification of Grassi's *paene miraculo* was a sound rhetorical tactic, for in calling eggs cooked in slings "miracles" he hoped to end discussion of their frequency and to disqualify them as proof of aerial friction. Yet the question which he posed his exasperating rival is a curious and dangerous one, and it signals the issue to which this essay is devoted, the Biblical backdrop of certain passages in the *Assayer.* "Can [you] prefer to believe things which happened two thousand years ago in Babylon, as related by others, rather than present things which [you yourself] experience?" Galileo asked Grassi, as if there were somehow a difference between the natural laws prevailing in antiquity and those of the seventeenth century, and as if some vanished quality, such as being Babylonian, might serve to explain these discrepancies.[4] Suidas's obscure story aside, the question would not have occurred to many of those who followed the debate over the comets of 1618, for much of what Galileo and Grassi and all Christians were meant to believe consisted in fact of incidents that had taken place two thousand years before in Babylon, and that had been related by men hallowed as chroniclers and prophets. Galileo's objection is therefore a problematic one, for within the context of seventeenth-century science the storehouse of arguments offered by Scripture could not be dismissed in such summary fashion.

The implied choice between belief in Biblical events or in present-day experiences, the sharp divide on which our sense of modernity rests, is all the more puzzling when Galileo and Grassi debate the relative transparence of a flame, and by implication of a comet. Among their arguments is a second Babylonian story, that of the miraculous survival of the young Israelites Shadrach, Meshach, and Abednego in the furance of King Nebuchadnezzar. In the last pages of his *Astronomical and Philosophical Balance* (1619), Grassi introduced the events of the third chapter of the Book of Daniel as evidence that neither flames nor comets were opaque. Drawing on Nebuchadnezzar's words, "Lo, I see four men loose, walking in the midst of the fire, and they have no hurt; and the form of the fourth is like the son of God" (Daniel 3:25), he argued that the astonished king would not have been able to see the three young men and an angel walking unharmed in the midst of

the fire if the blaze were not transparent. The miracle, Grassi stated, lay in the fact that Daniel's companions were protected from the fire, and not in the king's ability to witness their survival.[5]

In responding to the challenge posed by Grassi, Galileo had no choice but to treat the Biblical story as a pertinent bit of data which might be reinterpreted but not wholly discredited. In the *Assayer* he insisted, therefore, upon a curious distinction between "flame" and "fire," and he noted that the angel of the Lord had removed the former from the furnace. What was miraculous, in Galileo's view, was the advent of the angel, and not this messenger's entirely reasonable effort to put out the blaze surrounding the three young men.[6] Grassi, tiring less quickly than Galileo of the long debate, countered this interpretation of Daniel 3 in his *Reckoning of Measures for the Balance and the Small Scale* (1626); he objected that while the middle of the furance had been cleared by the angel, the fire was roaring everywhere else, and that Nebuchadnezzar had not looked through thin air, but through a wall of flames. He ended the pages devoted to this rather sinister argument with a humble comparison, as if the naturalness of his analogy could somehow mask the horror of Daniel 3, and as if readers unfamiliar with Babylonian furnaces need only extrapolate from other fireside experiences.[7] "But why [did Galileo say that] it was necessary to remove the flames, in order that the young boys be seen walking freely amidst the fire? We ourselves can see both live coals and charred wood even through the greatest of blazes."[8]

Such speculation—whether it is Galileo's cautious and awkward exegesis or Grassi's aggressive and overly elaborate analysis—seems no more appropriate to cometary theory than does Suidas's tale of the swinging eggs. Discussion of Daniel 3 is clearly an issue which Galileo would have preferred to avoid, and his interpretation, based on the alleged difference between flames and fire, has none of the vigor or intellectual daring of his exposition of Joshua 10 in the disastrous *Letter to the Grand Duchess Christina.* Yet he could not ignore the argument once it was introduced, and he was compelled to delimit the miraculous element in the story of the Babylonian furnace in order that those more natural aspects—the opacity of a flame, for instance—confirm, or at the very least, not contradict his notions about comets. For his rival Grassi, and for some of his audience, particularly those well versed in scriptural exegesis, the references to the Book of Daniel would have seemed, however, a collection of respected arguments which any scientist might invoke. As I will show, it was in order to accommodate and overcome those expectations that Galileo himself drew upon the commentary tradition surrounding the prophetic book, such that early modern exegesis served as the very backdrop of the great controversy over the comets, and an arena from which such exchanges could not be displaced. Galileo derived certain of his most celebrated statements from seventeenth-century discussions of a third Babylonian story, for he made the exegetical comments on Belshazzar's legendary feast—the banquet where the prophet Daniel read the handwriting on the wall to the mystified Chaldeans—the subtext of several points central to the *Assayer.* He did so in order that present-day experience not be opposed to those events which had happened some two thousand years before in Babylon, but rather complemented by them, and so that his rivals' theories might take on the antique, outmoded flavor of the knowledge possessed by those men who were Babylonian.

II

As Galileo finished his brief discussion of Daniel 3, he criticized his opponent for a certain lack of procedural rigor.

> You must show us [he wrote] that counter to our assertion, the interposed flame was insufficient to expose the stars, and in order to convince us by experiments you say that if we try to look at people, firebrands, coals, writings, and candles placed behind flames we shall see them quite clearly. Did it not enter your head to tell us that we might try looking at stars?[9]

There was no point in arguing, as Grassi had, that the printed page of a book would be legible through a flame, because the issues at hand were the nature of the comet, and the visibility of the stars beyond it. Galileo thus disagreed with Grassi's analogy for two reasons. He was not convinced that the comet was composed of a fiery substance—indeed, he believed that it more closely resembled a vaporous mass illuminated by sunlight—and he also implied that printed texts ought not to be so readily substituted for the starry sphere: "Instead of saying that letters may be perceived through a candle's flame, you might have asserted that a *star* is thus perceived."[10]

Galileo's dissociation of writing and the firmament appears at first glance unusual, for his own work consistently features explicit comparisons of textual and astronomical phenomena. From the *Sidereus Nuncius,* where he first noted that illustrious men inscribed their names on the brightest heavenly bodies, to the *Letters on the Sunspots,* where he described shadowy patches on the moon as if they were "as dark as is the ink on this paper," to the ill-fated *Letter to the Grand Duchess Christina,* where he favored the Book of the Heavens over that of Scripture, Galileo exploited and improved upon the traditional association of reading and celestial observation.[11] What differentiates Galileo's analogy from that of Grassi is, however, that in the latter's argument the printed page on the other side of the candle does not involve intelligibility but rather

sheer visibility. There is, in other words, no interpretive act that accompanies Grassi's little experiment: seeing the text, not understanding it, is the objective, and the words lying beyond the flame differ not at all from the people, wood, candle snuffs, and coals similarly enveloped in fire.

Aside, then, from its scientific import, Galileo's objection serves two related purposes. It is first of all a way of distinguishing between his own frequent substitution of words for astronomical phenomena and Grassi's wanton association of writing and stars. The point is crucial for the *Assayer,* for it is in this work that Galileo's most celebrated uses of the analogy occur; as I will show, they derive from commentaries on Daniel 5, where King Belshazzar's feast was interrupted by the mysterious handwriting on the wall. More importantly, Galileo's criticism of Grassi's experiment is a way of casting his chief rivals—Grassi and his mentor, the Danish astronomer Tycho Brahe—in the role of the Chaldeans present at the banquet, or making them play at "being Babylonian."

There were several reasons for such an association: it was, after all, the Chaldeans, the ruling class in Babylon, who were the foremost astronomers of the ancient world.[12] Like Tycho Brahe, they were also renowned for their skill in astrology,[13] and like the Jesuit Grassi, they were members of a priestly elite. And though Galileo would not have voiced such a parallel himself, he would have known that his analogy was enriched by the fact that Grassi's adopted city, Rome, was at times associated with the fallen kingdom of Babylon.[14] Finally—and this is the basis of the whole comparison—Tycho, Grassi, and their followers most strongly resembled the Chaldeans in that they could see, but not interpret, the phenomena that lay before them.

The subject to which early modern commentaries on the fifth chapter of Daniel were devoted was the reason that the prophet was able to read the handwriting on the wall. It is easy to see the relevance which such speculation would have had for contemporary astronomers, who wondered why the same phenomena came to be understood in such different fashions. I am arguing, therefore, not only that there is great similarity between the explanations offered by exegetes and those expounded in a less tactful way by Galileo himself, but also that here the scientist was influenced by the commentary tradition. As the summary of arguments presented by the Jesuit Cornelius a Lapide (1567-1637) in his *Commentaria in Danielem Prophetam* (1621) most closely resembles Galileo's repeated association of the starry firmament and writing in the *Assayer,* my discussion will focus largely on the work of the Belgian exegete.

I will be comparing, in particular, Galileo's recourse to the metaphor of reading and misreading, a *topos* which he uses several times in a twenty-page section of the *Assayer,* and Cornelius a Lapide's explanation of the Chaldeans' inability to interpret the message on the wall. The other authorities on whom I draw—mainly other Jesuit commentators of the era—are anterior to Cornelius, and their arguments are subsumed by him; I include their interpretations in order to elaborate Cornelius' summary, but there is no reason to suppose that Galileo would have been familiar with the work of these individuals.[15] Because Cornelius, like Galileo's rival Grassi, was at the Collegio Romano, and because his authoritative commentary on the Book of Daniel was published in 1621,[16] it seems most likely that Galileo, anxious to anticipate the kinds of arguments Grassi would use in his further discussion of Daniel 3, would have consulted this work while writing the *Assayer,* which he completed in October 1622.[17] As I noted above, Galileo's remarks on the story of Shadrach, Meshach, and Abednego in the furnace of King Neb-uchadnezzar were singularly circumspect, as if the Pisan were eager to keep the interpretation of Scriptural events separate from his understanding of astronomical mat-ters. On the other hand, the gratuitous question that came after his evaluation of Suidas's tale, "Can [you] prefer to believe things which happened two thousand years ago in Babylon, as related by others, rather than present things which [you yourself] experience?" is a way of integrating the problem of "being Babylonian" into an early modern scientific text. I will argue, there-fore, that Galileo's use of the metaphor of misreading forms an oblique but persistent allusion to the most celebrated of Babylonian stories, that of Daniel 5, a tale with unflattering implications for his rivals.

III

Galileo's references to contemporary assessments of Daniel 5 are part of a larger pattern in the *Assayer,* and I shall focus on two of these more general arguments before examining the issue of misreading the heavens. The greatest threat posed by Grassi's first and second works, the modest *Disputation on the Three Comets of 1618* (1618), and the vituperative *Astronomical and Philosophical Balance on which the Opinions of Galileo Galilei regarding the Comets are Weighed* (1619), was the credence that they gave to Tycho Brahe's no-tion of the comets and, more pertinently, of the cosmos itself. Tycho had stated that the comets were some-where above the moon, and he assumed that their or-bits circled the sun. He believed that if the earth were mobile, the comets, like the revolving planets, would appear to move in retrograde fashion against the back-ground of the starry sphere, and the fact that they dis-played no such movement encouraged him to assert that the earth was stationary.[18]

The cosmological system that Tycho then established, something of a compromise between the Ptolemaic and Copernican models, found particular favor with the sev-enteenth-century Jesuits, whose Society included some of the greatest astronomers of the age.[19] The appeal of the Tychonic universe was its double center. At the heart of the cosmos was the motionless earth, surround-ed by the concentric orbits of the moon, sun, and starry sphere, and in this the Tychonic system resembled the traditional one attributed to Ptolemy. The disposition of the other planets about the sun, however, was more like the scheme devised by Copernicus, for Mercury, Venus, Mars, Jupiter, and Saturn revolved about the sun. Mercury and Venus moved so close to the sun that they were always between that body and the earth, while the orbits of the superior planets Mars, Jupiter, and Saturn enclosed both centers. In this way the order suggested by Copernicus and his followers—the sun, Mercury, Venus, the earth, Mars, Jupiter, Saturn, and finally the fixed stars—was preserved in appearance but the heretical notion of a mobile earth was avoided.

Since the strongest of arguments against the Coperni-can system were posed not by followers of Ptolemy but rather those of Tycho, it was Galileo's objective to discredit Grassi's analysis of the comet, and by impli-cation, of the cosmos said to lie beyond it. He did so by maintaining that the comet itself was a type of illu-sion not unlike a rainbow, and a body whose apparent orbit could not be used as an index of the structure of the heavens. He also criticized the methodology, pre-mises, and conclusions drawn by both Tycho and his Jesuit disciple, repeatedly exploiting the analogy be-tween celestial observation and writing to rectify his rivals' errors. The shortcomings that he detected in their work are rather heterogeneous, as my subsequent discussion will show, but their common denominator lies in the corrective metaphor of misreading that Galileo consistently applied to them. In brief, the por-trait that Galileo offered of Grassi and Tycho in a central section of the *Assayer* is not unlike that of the confused Chaldeans of Daniel 5.

The other issue associated with Galileo's discussion of the comet is the unacceptability of the Copernican world system. Galileo's several references to the recently con-demned hypothesis stress the fact that it is not reason but Scripture, or rather contemporary interpretation of Scripture, that obliged him and all true Catholics to reject the notion of a mobile earth and stable sun.[20] The authenticity of these pious conjectures is not a question that concerns us here, but the context in which they occur is worthy of note. Since the backdrop of these discussions is, as I argue, the fifth chapter of the Book of Daniel—the archetypal story of Scriptural in-terpretation—and since Galileo's role is, not surpris-ingly, that of Daniel, his suggestion is that those Bib-lical passages that seem to preclude a Copernican read-ing might also bear reexamination, presumably by a modern-day version of the prophet. It was just such an immodest proposal that animated the disastrous *Letter to the Grand Duchess Christina* (1615), where Galileo attempted to read Joshua 10: 12-14 as evidence of Copernicanism;[21] here, of course, Galileo's suggestion is both more oblique and more audacious. The point of the Danielic echoes present in the *Assayer* is not, however, so much the favorable light in which Galileo's work is cast—for this happens more or less by default—but rather the way in which the challenge of the Tychonic system is met.

IV

Aside from its peculiar presence in Galileo's discussion of the comets of 1618, the story of the handwriting on the wall is a curious anecdote in its own right. It has little importance as prophecy, given that Daniel does no more than warn a decadent king whose city is under siege that it will in fact be taken and divided among his enemies, and that the ruler himself will die; the same events could have been foreseen by a statesman or a court fool. The prediction, moreover, cost Belshazzar a gold necklace and a purple robe, but it benefitted him not at all, since he had no time to react, nor power to alter what had been divinely ordained. As modern Biblical scholarship has recognized, the message itself—*Mane, tekel, phares*—probably involved a kind of pun about the relative decline of the regal lineage, for if the words are properly punctuated they name three weights or coins, a *mina,* a *shekel,* and a half *mina,* and they suggest that Belshazzar, the alleged "half *mina,*" was the "worthless son of a great father."[22] Though Daniel offered a different reading of the three words, the outcome was of course the same: *Mina,* he said, meant "God has numbered your kingdom and brought it to an end;" *tekel,* "you have been weighed in the balances and have been found wanting;" *phares,* "your kingdom will be divided between the Medes and the Persians" (Daniel 5: 26-28). The importance of the episode does not, obviously, lie in what Daniel saw, but in the way in which he rendered the handwriting on the wall intelligible to the thousand guests at the feast, and especially to the Chaldeans, who, though they were the most learned men of the Babylonian world, could not read the message.

It was to some extent inevitable that the message on the wall be associated with the comet, because the significance of the words *Mane, tekel, phares* was the fall and impending division of the Babylonian kingdom, while the natural sign for a *mutatio regni* was the comet. As the following example will suggest, the similarity between the two kinds of signs was strong enough that some men felt that they might be compared, while others saw the need to contrast them. In his thirteenth-century treatise on comets, for instance, Gilles de Lessines (1230-1304) drew on the story of Belshazzar's feast in order to oppose the legitimate task of the prophet to the fraudulent practices of astrologers:

Furthermore we read in holy Scripture that signs given by God as indices of the future only appeared to him who had the gift of the Holy Spirit for seeing things that were to come, as in the Book of Daniel, in the chapter where the hand wrote *Mane tekel phares* on the wall. Thus if these signs are divinely manifested and are indicative of what God wills with respect to man's future, they will be clear only to those who have the gift of prophecy. Therefore the books of the astrologers are useless and full of superstitions.[23]

If treatises on astronomical topics evoked the story of Daniel 5, commentaries on that prophetic book turned even more often to celestial subjects. Two questions were most frequently entertained by exegetical discussions of the story of Belshazzar's banquet: first, the nature of the hand that inscribed the three words, and secondly, the reason that Daniel alone could interpret them. As it is within the context of these debates that certain of Galileo's remarks—those involving the relationship of reading to celestial observation—have the most resonance, the commentary tradition of Daniel 5 merits careful elaboration.

The celebrated medieval exegete Nicholas of Lyra (1270-1340) distinguished himself by offering a reading of Belshazzar's feast that, because it appealed to no one, was attacked and expounded by all. In interpreting the fifth verse of the fifth chapter,

Suddenly there appeared fingers like those of a human hand (*digiti quasi manus hominis*) writing on the plaster of the palace wall opposite the lamp, and the king saw the palm of the hand as it wrote,

Nicholas suggested that the king was alone in seeing the hand, though his thousand guests were able to perceive the message that it inscribed on the wall.[24] While he did not attribute the unique vision to any particular characteristic of the king, certain commentators understood Nicholas's remark to be a reference to Belshazzar's drunkenness, as if this condition would have somehow distinguished the ruler from his guests. Exegetes generally began their discussion of the passage with an unfavorable reference to Nicholas of Lyra and the Hebrew scholars believed to have influenced him,[25] and they argued against the possibility of regal hallucination.

The greatest of early modern commentators, Cornelius a Lapide, offered a particularly interesting analysis of whatever it was that Belshazzar saw on the eve of his death. Cornelius affirmed that the hand was not a product of the king's imagination, and that it could be seen by everyone in the Babylonian palace. He went so far as to divulge its actual substance:

Nicholas of Lyra on the basis of the word *quasi* (like) supposed that this hand did not truly exist, but that it was in the king's imagination, and that it was not seen by the others. Indeed this is wrong on two counts. For Scripture said that the hand wrote on the wall *Mane, tekel, phares,* and that the words there were read by Daniel, since the other people [in the palace] could see the letters but were unable to read and interpret them. Scripture says therefore *quasi manus hominis* [like the hand of a man], because it was not in truth the hand of a man, but *a shape like it made of condensed air* and borne by an angel, who used it to write on the wall.[26]

It is difficult, even impossible, to imagine the angelic prosthesis with which Cornelius believed the message was written, but the commentator's intention is clear: while the hand belonged to neither man nor spirit, it did indeed exist outside of the king's imagination. As it was formed of "condensed air," it was not the particular and private vision of the drunken Belshazzar, but rather a phenomenon to be witnessed by all the guests at the banquet.

What is most interesting about Cornelius's description is its resemblance to Galileo's explanation of the comets of 1618. I will not argue, of course, that either Grassi or Galileo based their initial depictions of the comet on the exegetical tradition; I will, however, show that Galileo's later discussions of what lay beyond the comet—the analogies between letters and stars introduced in the *Assayer*—were informed by commentaries on the writing behind the hand itself. At present I will demonstrate what was similar about Cornelius's notion of the hand-like effigy and Galileo's characterization of the comet, and I will then suggest that the scientist's discovery of this entirely fortuitous resemblance—presumably detected while he looked over Cornelius's commentary on Daniel 3—led him to elaborate other and more ironic Danielic echoes in the *Assayer.*

A crucial point in Orazio Grassi's *Disputation* (1619), and the issue that most interested Galileo, was the Jesuit scientist's insistence on the negligible parallax shown by the comets. Because parallax and distance are inversely proportional, the fact that the comet appeared to be in more or less the same place in the firmament even when it was observed by astronomers far from each other allowed the Tychonians to place the apparition beyond the sphere of the moon, to argue that it had a planet-like orbit, and to make serious claims about the structure of the heavens. In his earliest essay on comets, the *Discourse* of 1619, Galileo countered Grassi's theories by challenging the value of his parallactic measurements; he stated that this means of determining distances, while useful to astronomers, was not always applicable, and that it could lead to error unless an important distinction was made:

> There exist two sorts of objects; some are real, actual, individual, and immovable, while others are

mere appearances, reflections of light, images, and wandering simulacra which are so dependent for their existence upon the vision of the observer that not only do they change position when he does, but I believe they would vanish entirely if his vision were taken away. Parallax operates reliably in real and permanent things whose essence is not affected by anyone's vision; these do not change place when the eye is moved. But parallax does not function in mere appearances.[27]

Parallax was, in other words, no index of distance if the object in question was not real. Galileo went on to offer his own notion of the comet, and though he described an apparition far more lovely than Grassi's celestial flare, he made it clear that what he portrayed was mere illusion. After discussing simulacra as familiar as haloes, rainbows, and parhelia, he began the analogy which he would sustain throughout the long conflict:

> But let us speak of things which more resemble comets. Some of you, Academicians, have often seen in the evening, when the sky is cloudy, long rays of sunlight coming through holes in the clouds and descending to the earth. These look brighter and narrower at the apertures where they originate than where, continually widening, they extend a long distance if they do not actually meet the earth. Though the whole horizon may be dotted with similar spotty clouds, these rays appear to our eyes only in the place corresponding to the position of the sun; they appear to be confined within a definite angle, and beyond this nothing particularly bright is to be seen. . . . In sum, every eye sees a different rainbow, a different halo, or a particular set of mock suns; those which are seen from the different places are not derived from the same rays, the same apertures in clouds, nor the same parts of the water, but from diverse ones.[28]

Galileo's patient comparison of the comets of 1618 to the illuminated vapors that on occasion streak the evening sky implies that his rival was taken in by the beautiful sight, and that he was misled more than most observers, for not only had he believed the comet to be real, he had even assigned it to the highest heavens. Galileo's point is, of course, that Grassi's parallactic measurements are in no way valid because the apparent position of the comet will vary with the eye of each spectator, and that the sunlit patches in the earthly atmosphere tell us rather little about the structure of the starry sphere behind them.

> In order to have the comet appear as without parallax to all observers and still originate in the elemental sphere, it would suffice for vapors (or other material of whatever sort) to be diffused on high and to be capable of reflecting the sun's light through distances and spaces equal to, or somewhat less than, those from which the comet is perceived.[29]

In the context of the present discussion, what is most striking about this argument is its relationship to Cornelius a Lapide's commentary on Daniel 5. The Jesuit exegete believed that the hand was seen by all observers, and that while it was neither human nor angelic, it did have some substance, that of "condensed air." If illusion was involved, it consisted in the fact that the thing the angel carried was not actually a hand, but what was evidently a rather convincing effigy of one. Galileo's discussion of the comet, presented before he ever looked at the work of Cornelius, involved some of these same elements, but the interpretation was different: the phenomenon was composed of vapor, and it was visible to all, but not so real that it could be said to exist independently of its viewers. What made it illusory was its apparent place, because it shifted, like a rainbow, with the eye of each observer. Thus while Cornelius believed that the fact that the hand could be seen by all meant that it was real, Galileo argued that the same great visibility was an index of its want of reality. To the extent that the apparitions described by Cornelius and Galileo can both be said to exist, they offer illusions that are not the privilege of one person, but a state shared, albeit individually, by all onlookers.

V

The comet, whether it occupied the lofty place assigned it by Grassi or the marginal area portrayed by Galileo, was merely the pretext for other and more involved discussions about the starry sphere beyond it. What was really at stake was not the three bright flares that the world witnessed in the fall of 1618, but the vastly different notions of the heavens in which these comets appeared. The telescope, far from resolving these conflicts, had in fact multiplied them, because early versions of that instrument varied greatly in quality, and—more crucially—because theoretical understanding of optics lagged somewhat behind its practical applications. Much of Galileo's conflict with Grassi, therefore, concerned their strongly divergent interpretations of identical phenomena, and these discussions, like those of the comet itself, parallel the arguments rehearsed within the commentary tradition of the Book of Daniel. Here, however, the question of authorial intent is pertinent: while the similarity between the simulacra of "condensed air" and sunlit vapor is an amusing coincidence, the resemblance between the arguments about the Chaldeans' inability to read and the criticisms offered in the *Assayer* is, I suggest, a matter of deliberate choice on the part of Galileo, and a ploy to discredit his rivals.

Cornelius a Lapide, reviewing the conflict over Daniel 5, stated that there were usually six reasons offered to explain why the Chaldeans were unable to read, or perhaps interpret, the words inscribed on the wall at Belshazzar's feast. The first and most rapidly dismissed explanation, and the only one that appeared historical-ly naive from an early modern perspective, was that the mysterious writing was in Hebrew, which the Chaldean court astrologers were unable to read. Well before the seventeenth century, however, all commentators agreed that the difference between Chaldean and Hebrew was no greater than that between related dialects of other languages such as Attic and Doric Greek, and that these linguistic divergences should have posed no problem for the wisemen.[30] The other five possibilities were more seriously entertained by late Renaissance scholars, and they find analogues in Galileo's criticisms of Grassi and Tycho.

The first theory to which scholars devoted attention was generally attributed to the great Jewish thinker Saadias (Joseph ben Sa'adjah, *Gaon*) (841-942), whose work was by then well known in the Latin West.[31] He had suggested in his commentary on the Book of Daniel that the words *Mane, tekel, phares* were actually written on the wall in front of the king, but that they could not be read by the Chaldeans, much less by the monarch or his guests, because the letters were "transposed."[32] It is likely that what Saadias meant was that either the order of the letters was altered, or that certain characters were exchanged for others, just as one might substitute Z for *A, Y* for *B, X* for *C,* and so forth. Commentators in the Latin West, sometimes unfamiliar with this system of alphabetic equivalences,[33] tended to fuse the two suggestions, saying that the letters were *mutatae aut transpositae,* as if the various characters had simply been shifted about with respect to each other. They did not explain why Saadias believed that it was Daniel, and not any clever literate, who was able to read the encoded words. Moreover, they associated the alleged lucky guess with the Cabalistic practices of the Jewish priesthood, and they condemned those mystical readings as irrational and lacking in rigor.

Though he had a more sophisticated understanding of Saadias' theories than did most of his peers, Jean Calvin found such Rabbinical exercises "presumptuous unless they were performed with a certain measure of reason."[34] Juan Maldonado, S.J. (1538-1583), still less tolerant of Cabalism, dismissed the conjecture in more summary fashion: "This is just guessing without the use of reason."[35] Cornelius a Lapide was similarly unimpressed with Saadias' notion, and equally hurried in his criticism: "But as this [solution] is contrived, it is to be rejected."[36]

When he attacked Grassi's, and more crucially, Tycho's pronouncements on parallax in the course of his *Assayer,* the error that Galileo condemned in his rivals' astronomical interpretation was that mentioned in a favorable way by Saadias. Tycho had written that the same fixed star observed from two points as distant as Prague and Uraniborg would be seen in the same place in the eighth sphere, and the reason that he offered to explain the absence of parallax was the insignificance of the earth's size relative to the vast dimensions of the eighth sphere. Galileo, recognizing a flawed argument in a host of other more imposing ones, challenged it with his usual enthusiasm for polemics, noting that

> the largeness or the smallness of the earth has nothing to do with the case. Seeing the same star in the same place from all parts of the earth depends upon the star's truly being in the eighth sphere, and upon nothing else, in exactly the same way as the letters on this page will never change their apparent positions with respect to this page no matter how much you change the position of the eye with which you look at it.[37]

Galileo's analogy is interesting for several reasons: it is undoubtedly one in series of references to Grassi's name[38] and to the transparent maneuver whereby Horatio Grassi Savonensi wrote under the pseudonym of Lothario Sarsi Sigensani. (The anagram's imperfection failed to prevent the gentleman from Siguenza from being recognized as the Jesuit mathematician.) If the letters of Grassi's name could change their respective positions whenever he desired anonymity, the stars of the eighth sphere could not be so rearranged. They were at the outermost reaches of the heavens, and beyond them there was nothing if not darkness, and they suffered no change, least of all alterations caused by the universe beneath them. The same sense of the immutable guided the commentators in their unanimous rejection of Saadias' suggestion: no matter how cryptic the message had appeared, it had not undergone any giddy transposition of letters, and its ultimate legibility did not depend upon the eye of the beholder.

Those who did not attribute Daniel's reading to a miracle alone generally sustained either of the two following conjectures: the words *Mane, tekel, phares* could not be understood by the Chaldeans because they were written without the diacritical marks that signified the proper vowel sounds,[39] or because only the first letter of each word was inscribed on the wall. Antonio Fernandez and the Jesuits Juan Maldonado (1538-1583) and Gaspar Sanchez (1554-1628), all of whose work was published between the years 1609 and 1619, favored the second thesis. Though the possibilities are mutually exclusive—either all consonantal letters appeared, or only the initial ones did—Cornelius a Lapide found them similar enough to present them together, and he showed his preference for the one over the other only by calling the hypothesis involving initial letters "likely" and the other "genuine."[40]

The Belgian exegete elaborated what was a somewhat unusual choice by explaining the potential for confusion in words written without vowel sounds:

> The Chaldeans and the Israelites wrote only consonants; there were no diacritical marks, no vowels. The Chaldeans did not know, therefore, which vowel sounds were to be substituted here, whether they were to read *mane* or *mina* or *meno;* whether *tekel* or *tokel* or *takal.*[41]

Though Cornelius's interpretation diverges in this particular from that of Maldonado, Fernandez, and Sanchez, their conclusions are identical, for in all cases the commentators must then explain how Daniel made sense of the words *Mane, tekel, phares* once he had supplied either the missing vowels or the appropriate final letters. In discussing this second part of his vision, this necessary complement to whatever ability allowed him to see letters that were invisible to all other onlookers, the commentators agree that Daniel was divinely inspired.

This is the same ground that Galileo and Grassi cover in their discussions of telescopic magnification, and the way in which Galileo frames their dispute mirrors both the similarity and the mutual exclusivity of the two solutions. The issue in question was telescopic magnification. Grassi, determined to prove that the comet was not a dull sublunary flare but rather a celestial apparition, argued its great distance on the grounds of the scant enlargement it suffered when observed through the telescope. His appeal to "the law that the enlargement appears less and less the farther away [phenomena] are from the eye"[42] made little sense to Galileo, and still less his conclusion that "the fixed stars, the most remote of all from us, receive no perceptible magnification from the telescope."[43] The fact that the problem of magnification had been addressed as early as 1610 in the **Sidereus Nuncius** and that those explanations had evidently gone unnoticed was perhaps irritating to Galileo, and he rejected Grassi's hypotheses with his usual candor. The ratio of telescopic magnification, he declared, was constant: it did not diminish with distance. The effect observed by Grassi, where faraway stars appeared to be enlarged scarcely at all by the telescope, or even slightly diminished in size by it, occurred because that instrument allowed the observer to see the object as it really was, and not surrounded by rays due to the refraction of light in the eye.

Galileo was especially critical of the Jesuit mathematician's assertion that the most remote stars underwent only an "insensible" magnification, and he answered,

> If by enlarging their images . . . [the telescope] changes them from invisible to visible—that is, if from insensibility to us it renders them quite perceptible—then I do not know why such enlargement ought to be called "insensible" rather than "infinite"; for the ratio of something to nothing is infinite.[44]

This argument, more intriguing than rigorous, was countered by Grassi in the *Astronomical and Philosophical Balance;* he objected that if the ratio of enlargement were indeed constant, then it would hardly do to call it "infinite" when describing the magnification of the most remote stars. Moreover, the ratio of nothing to something was not infinite, it was nonexistent.[45] Galileo responded by saying that he had used "infinite" in its everyday sense, and that it was understood by all men, save perhaps the obtuse Sarsi of Siguenza, to mean "very large." After asking Grassi rather pointedly what he understood by the verse from Ecclesiastes, "The number of fools is infinite," Galileo returned to the issue of magnification, making elaborate and ironic use of his rival's suggestion that "the passage from nonexistence into existence" be substituted for the word "enlargement."

> Hence, for example, when the telescope enables us to read from a great distance some writing of which we should see only the capital letters without it, to speak logically one should not say that the telescope enlarges the capitals, but causes the small letters to pass from nonexistence into existence.[46]

This is, of course, exactly what some of the commentators believed happened when Daniel beheld the writing on the wall, for in that vision, the small letters—either the diacritical points for vowel sounds, or all characters following the capitalized initial ones—did indeed pass from nonexistence to existence. It would appear, moreover, that the various exchanges over the ratio of enlargement—whether it be insensible or infinite—reflect the difference in the interpretations of Cornelius a Lapide and his contemporaries. The Belgian Jesuit would have maintained that there was an infinite interval between *tekel* and *tkl,* and that it was the immensity of this gap that rendered the writing impenetrable to the Chaldeans. Juan Maldonado, Antonio Fernandez, and Gaspar Sanchez, on the other hand, because they believed that words would be legible only when the letters following the initial ones passed from "nonexistence to existence," would have found the difference described by Cornelius imperceptible, or "insensible," and far too insignificant to explain the apparent illegibility of the message.

Those commentators who believed neither that the handwriting on the wall was scrambled, nor that only the initial letters of each word were written, nor that the absence of their diacritical marks made them unrecognizable, often favored the fourth hypothesis mentioned by Cornelius. In their opinion, the mysterious message could not be understood by the Chaldeans because the wisemen were in some way temporarily disabled. Those who supported this line of reasoning, far from minimizing Daniel's accomplishment, sought to represent him not as a clever literate, but as a man hallowed by God and glorified by Him. As Cornelius said, "The Chaldeans were handicapped by God in order that this honor be reserved for Daniel alone."[47] It comes as no particular surprise that this notion of the elect was vigorously supported by Jean Calvin; after dismissing the Cabalis-

tic interpretation of the Rabbis as "presumptuous," he outlined the two arguments which most appealed to him: "It is probable that either the writing was exposed to the King and hidden from all the Chaldeans, or that they were blinded in such a way that in seeing they saw not."[48] Juan Maldonado, wavering between the prosaic and the miraculous, appears not to have decided if Daniel alone could read the message because only the initial letters of each word appeared, or because the Chaldeans were "divinely handicapped."[49] The Jesuit Benito Pereyra (1535-1610) was less free with the possible explanations, and he cautioned his audience against ascribing the uniqueness of Daniel's vision to anything other than divine inspiration, for he who believed that the Chaldeans were suddenly stricken with blindness or illiteracy would have to introduce a new miracle in the sacred text to explain their short-lived condition and its cure.[50] This rational and rather economical approach to the miraculous is typical of the Aristotelianism that Pereyra practiced in his scientific works;[51] his attitude stands in contrast, however, to the fullblown marvels imagined by most commentators of his age.

It was precisely this kind of solution, where the vision of one individual is explained in terms of the blindness and impediments of others around him, that Galileo offered as a sarcastic response to Grassi's hair-splitting logic. The Jesuit mathematician had stated that it was incorrect to maintain, as Galileo had, that the disclosure of the invisible fixed stars resulted from the use of the telescope, and he had based his objection on the grounds that one effect—enlargement—might have been derived from several causes. "Why yes," agreed the exasperated Galileo,

> in order to escape Sarsi's imputations, [I] would have to show that first, bringing the telescope to the eye would not in itself and by itself increase visual power (for this, indeed, is a cause that might make something visible that was not seen previously); second, [I] would have to show that this act would not be a removing of clouds, trees, roofs, or other intervening obstacles; third, that it was not a mere use of ordinary spectacles; fourth, that it was not an improved illumination of the object; fifth, that it was not a bringing down of the star to earth or a venturing forth on our part into the sky, by which the interval between would be diminished; sixth, that it did not make the stars swell up so as to enlarge and become more easily visible; seventh and last, that it was not an opening of closed eyes. Each of these—and especially the last—is sufficient to make us see what we did not see before.[52]

Though it seems fairly unlikely that Galileo knew more of Calvin's work than the succinct restatement offered by Cornelius, two of the hypotheses mentioned here are the analogues of those raised by the reformer to explain Daniel's vision. Just as Calvin had argued that it was probable either that the message was hidden from the Chaldeans' view, or that the host of wisemen had been temporarily blinded, so Galileo—in a less sincere vein—suggested that one could not, in fact, attribute the magnification normally associated with telescopic vision to that instrument until other possible causes, such as inconveniently placed architectural features or the observer's own shut eyes, had been eliminated. There is a curious admixture of the mysterious and the banal in what Calvin took to be similar possibilities: the secrecy of the message might have depended upon either divinely imposed blindness or upon some undisclosed obstruction—one imagines a low wall or cornice—but not, in any case, upon Daniel's perspicacity.[53] The fact that he alone could interpret the handwriting on the wall distinguished him as a member of the elect, but it in no way implied that his intellectual ability was out of the ordinary. The vision would have been accessible to all, if only the Chaldeans had been able to remove the "clouds, trees, roofs, or other intervening obstacles," or if their Creator had chosen to open their eyes.

The last reason offered by Cornelius in explanation of the Chaldeans' inability to read the handwriting on the wall was that *Mane, tekel, phares* was written in "strange and foreign letters."[54] This hypothesis would imply either than Daniel, in addition to his other gifts, was something of a linguist, or that he was divinely inspired for the occasion. Antonio Fernandez was nearly alone[55] among early modern commentators in supporting the possibility of a foreign script, and he did so only as an alternative to the solution he most preferred, that involving the initial letters of each word. Daniel's linguistic knowledge, moreover, was a function of his status as prophet, and so various practical questions— what that mysterious language might have been, among which peoples it might have been used, how Daniel alone came by such knowledge—do not come into play. In this sense, then, the fact that the words were composed of incomprehensible characters of some language is much less important than the divine inspiration that it took to decipher them: the hand that inscribed them might as well have written them in invisible ink, or represented them by musical notation, or displayed them in a series of emblems.

> There are those who say that the handwriting was inscribed in foreign characters, letters of which the Chaldean wisemen had no knowledge. In fact Daniel was divinely inspired with such knowledge, and his mind illuminated from above by God, in order that he make plain to the king not only the words themselves, but also their deepest meaning, along with the design of the Divine Will.[56]

When Galileo invoked a language understood only by the happy few, he associated it with a rare veracity, and he implied that the idiom employed by most men was at best a kind of accommodation, and at worst a lie.

> Philosophy is written in this grand book—I mean the universe—which stands continually open to our gaze, but it cannot be understood unless one first learns to comprehend the language and interpret the characters in which it is written. It is written in the language of mathematics, and its characters are triangles, circles, and other geometrical figures, without which it is humanly impossible to understand a word of it; without these, one is wandering about in a dark labyrinth.[57]

It is as if Galileo had chosen to elaborate the very linguistic issues which Fernandez swept aside, for he describes the only language by which mortals can know the universe, warning that he who cannot read those characters and interpret those words must wander forever in the maze of his own ignorance. The proviso he offers is worth noting: "without which it is *humanly* impossible" acknowledges the remote prospect of divine inspiration, whereby Daniel, without knowing the language which he read, was able to tell Belshazzar that he would soon die, and that his kingdom would fall to the Medes and Persians.

Galileo's notion of the labyrinth of ignorance, moreover, was anticipated by another writer who sought to revolutionize the world's image of the heavens, and while there can be no question of influence, the similarity, based perhaps on a common topos, is one worth noting by way of conclusion.[58] Jean Calvin was fond enough of the metaphor of the labyrinth to use it to describe the confused king Belshazzar; he noted that the monarch had to be reminded by his wife of the very existence of Daniel, despite the important position which the prophet had occupied in the days of Nebuchadnezzar, and he affirmed that Belshazzar had indeed long been "walking in darkness" and "wandering as if through a maze."[59] As Calvin stated towards the end of his commentary, that condition was not the king's alone, but was shared by all who were not divinely inspired, by all, that is, who could not read the writing on the wall. "Indeed," he warned his readers, "even the faithful who are reflecting on this prophecy are to some extent like people lost in a labyrinth."[60] The crucial difference in the positions of Galileo and Calvin is, of course, that the astronomer believed that some men might learn the language which even the Chaldeans could not understand, and that they might thus escape the maze of their own ignorance, and discover something of the heavens while yet on earth. To do as Grassi and Tycho had done, to see without reading, to observe without understanding, meant abandoning this goal, and "being Babylonian."

Notes

[1] Orazio Grassi, *The Astronomical and Philosophical Balance on which the Opinions of Galileo Galilei regarding the Comets are Weighed,* in *The Controversy*

on the Comets of 1618, trans. Stillman Drake and C. D. O'Malley (Philadelphia: University of Pennsylvania Press, 1960), 119. Grassi's faith in his source notwithstanding, "Suidas" had already been denounced by Jean Bodin in the *Colloquium Heptaplomeres de Rerum Sublimium Abditis:* "Suidas' *History* is not even approved by any Christian except Suidas, since it clearly contradicts all the writers of the gospels." See *Colloquium of the Seven about the Secrets of the Sublime,* trans. with an introduction by Marion Leathers Daniels (Princeton: Princeton University Press, 1975), 287.

2 Grassi, *Balance,* 119.

3 Galileo Galilei, *The Assayer in which with a Delicate and Precise Scale will be Weighed the Things Contained in The Astronomical and Philosophical Balance of Lothario Sarsi of Siguenza,* in *The Controversy on the Comets of 1618,* 301.

4 Ibid.

5 Grassi, *Balance,* 128.

6 Galileo, *Assayer,* 329-30.

7 The references to men in the midst of flames seem particularly malevolent in light of the hypothesis recently advanced by Pietro Redondi, who suggests that Father Grassi was the person who denounced Galileo for eucharistic heresy. Individuals convicted of such charges risked death by fire. See *Galileo Heretic,* trans. Raymond Rosenthal (Princeton: Princeton University Press, 1987).

8 "Sed quid erat necesse flammas abigere, ut ambulantes inter ignes pueri libere spectarentur? Quando et prunas et ambusta ligna ingentes etiam inter flammas spectamus." Orazio Grassi, *Ratio ponderum librae et simbellae* in Galileo Galilei, *Opere,* ed. A. Favaro, vol. 6 (Florence: G. Barbèra, 1968²) 497. Translation mine.

9 Galileo, *Assayer,* 330.

10 Ibid., 330-31.

11 *Sidereus Nuncius,* in *Discoveries and Opinions of Galileo,* trans. Stillman Drake (Garden City, New York: Doubleday, 1957), 23-24; *Letters on the Sunspots,* in *Discoveries and Opinions,* 93; *Letter to the Grand Duchess Christina,* in *Discoveries and Opinions,* 196.

12 The word "Chaldean" indicated both a people originally from a territory south-east of Babylon who had become by 600 B.C. the ruling class of that country, and a priestly elite skilled in divination and astrology. This latter connotation was the more familiar one in the Latin West: see the list of sources in Juvenal, *Thirteen Satires,* ed. and comm. John E. B. Mayor

(London: Macmillan, 1877), 2:104-5, 329-31. See also R. H. Charles, *A Critical and Exegetical Commentary on the Book of Daniel* (Oxford: Clarendon Press, 1929), 14-15. For a general survey of the activities of the Babylonian kings' advisors, see Leo Oppenheim, "Divination and Celestial Observation," *Centaurus* 14 (1969): 97-135, esp. 102-5, 114, 121-26.

13 Galileo makes several gratuitous references to Tycho's interest in astrology, though it was quite common for seventeenth-century astronomers to practice this art. See, for example, *The Assayer,* 183, where Galileo asserts that he himself need not employ either Tycho's splendid instruments or his astrological knowledge to solve a geometrical problem.

14 The kinship of the two cities was exploited by writers from St. Peter, who offered "Greetings from your sister church in Babylon" (1 Peter 5:13), to Thomas Beverley, who published *The Command of God to His People to Come Out of Babylon: Revel. 18.4 Demonstrated to Mean the Coming Out of the Present Papal Rome* ([London]: n.p., 1688). The latter was just one in a long series of Reformation tracts directed against the Papacy.

15 I list the first editions of the works with which I supplement Cornelius a Lapide's *Commentaria:* Juan Maldonado, S.J., *Commentarii in Jeremiam, Baruch, Ezechielem, et Danielem* (Lyon: Horatius Cardon, 1609); Benito Pereyra, S.J., *Commentariorum in Danielem Prophetam Libri sexdecim* (Rome: Georgius Ferrarius, 1587); Gaspar Sanchez, S.J., *In Ezechielem et Danielem Prophetas Commentarii cum Paraphrasi* (Lyon: Horatius Cardon, 1619). In citing the *Commentarii in visiones Veteris Testamenti* by the rather more obscure Antonio Fernandez, I have used the Lyon 1617 edition printed by J. Cardon and P. Cavellat, though this may not be the first edition of the work. Another extremely interesting commentary on *The Book of Daniel* is the Portuguese mystic Heitor Pinto's *In Danielem, Lamentationes Heremiae, et Nahum Divinos Vates Commentarii* (Cologne: Birckmann, 1582), the most striking feature of which is its obsessive return to astronomical imagery. Though praised in Guglielmo Franchi's *Sole della lingua santa* (Bergamo: C. Ventura, 1599) for his knowledge of Hebrew and Aramaic, Pinto does not seem to have greatly influenced other Biblical scholars of the period.

16 On Cornelius a Lapide's career and publications, see Carlos Sommervogel, *Bibliothèque de la Compagnie de Jésus* (Brussels: O. Schepens; Paris: A. Picard, 1890-1932) vol. 4, cols. 1511-26.

17 Drake and O'Malley, *Controversy on the Comets of 1618,* xviii.

18 For a background discussion of the comet, see Doris C. Hellman, *The Comet of 1577: Its Place in the History*

of Astronomy (New York: AMS Press, 1971), especially 118-37. For two somewhat opposed interpretations of the conflict over the comets of 1618—the first rather more favorable to Galileo's position than the second— see the introduction in Drake and O'Malley's *Controversy on the Comets,* and William Shea, *Galileo's Intellectual Revolution* (New York: Science History Publications, 1977), 75-108.

[19] For a summary of the positions adopted by Jesuit astronomers and mathematicians, see Christine Jones Schofield, *Tychonic and Semi-Tychonic World Systems* (New York: Arno Press, 1981), 172-79, 277-89.

[20] See for example Galileo, *Assayer,* 192.

[21] "On that day when the Lord delivered up the Amorites into the hands of Israel, Joshua spoke with the Lord, and in the presence of Israel said: Stand still, you sun, at Gibeon; you moon, at the vale of Ajalon. The sun stood still and the moon halted until the nation had taken vengeance on its enemies, as indeed is written in the Book of Jashar. The sun stayed in mid-heaven and made no haste to set for almost a whole day."

[22] Charles, *Commentary,* 137, summarizing the findings of Charles Clermont-Ganneau, "Mane, Thecal, Phares, et le festin de Balthasar," *Journal Asiatique,* 8th ser., 8 (1886): 36-37.

It is worth nothing that the sequence established by the three coins named in the message is suggested by the titles which Grassi and Galileo gave to their works. Grassi named his second treatise the *Libra astronomica ac philosophica* or *The Astronomical and Philosophical Balance* because he said the comet was first seen in the sign of Libra, and because he wanted to subject Galileo's arguments to a "careful weighing." Galileo responded with the *Saggiatore* or *Assayer,* a finer type of scale, and he noted that Grassi's balance seemed a crude and inaccurate instrument. Grassi's last work on the comet exploits the same metaphor, for the title *Ratio ponderum librae et simbellae,* scarcely less obscure when translated into English, means the *Reckoning of Measures for the Balance and the Small Scale,* a *simbella* being a small coin and the device for weighing the same. While the point of the (largely unknown) Biblical pun was that the coins decreased in value as the regal family became more and more decadent, the intention underlying the metaphorical titles used by Grassi and Galileo was that each weighing was more accurate than the last, and thus the scales and weights associated with them became smaller and smaller, while gaining in figurative value. The rough equivalency of the two series is at most a coincidence, but an interesting one; the *mina,* like the *libra,* corresponds to 100 denarii; the *shekel,* like the *exagium* at the root of the *Saggiatore,* is a much smaller coin; *phares,* like the

simbella, suggests a divided weight, these two insignificant coins being a half-*mina* and a *semi-libella.* In the Horatian closing of the *Ratio* Grassi includes one last reference to the *libella,* as if it were interchangeable with the *libellus,* his little book: "nunc demum, quamdiu licuerit, conticescam, atque interim mecum ipse libro meo submurmurem: ohe iam satis est, ohe libelle. Dicerem etiam libella, si versus permitteret." Grassi, *Ratio,* 500.

[23] "Praeterea in scriptura sancta legimus quod signa divinitus data in signal futurorum tantummodo illi apparuerunt qui spiritum sanctum singulariter ad cognoscendum futura habuit, ut in *libro Danielis,* capitulo de manu scribente in pariete, Mane Thecel Phares. Igitur si haec sunt signa divinitus ostensa et indicitiva voluntatis divinae respectu futurorum contingentium, illis solum patebunt qui spiritum prophetiae accipiunt. Frustra ergo sunt et superstitione plena libri iudicorum astronomicorum." Cited in Lynn Thorndike, *Latin Treatises on Comets between 1238-1368 A.D.* (Chicago: University of Chicago Press, 1950), 141. Translation mine.

[24] "Hic non dicitur, quod alii viderunt, ex quo videtur, quod non erat ibi manus scribens secundam existentiam, quia talia communiter videntur ab omnibus assistentibus, sed solem erat talis apparitio in oculis regis & sententia in pariete scribebatur divinitus, ministerio tamen angelico, quia eorum ministerio talia fiunt." *Biblia Sacra cum Glossa Ordinaria Primum Quidem à Strabo Fuldensi Monacho . . . Et Postillae Nicolai Lirani,* vol. 4 (Douai: B. Bellerus, 1617), 1558.

[25] Nicholas of Lyra, unlike most exegetes of his day, was familiar with the commentaries of Saadias (892-941) and Abraham Ibn Ezra (m. 1167).

[26] "Lyranus ex voce *quasi* autumat manum hanc vere non extitisse sed tantum in phantasia regis, unde ab aliis non esse visam. Verum utrumque falsum est. Nam Scriptura ait hanc manum scripsisse in pariete *mane, tekel, phares;* ibique haec scripta legisse Danielem; cum caeteri literas viderent, sed eas legere & interpretari nequirent. Dicit ergo quasi manus hominis, quia vere non erat manus hominis, sed ei similis *formata ex aere condensato,* & assumpta ab angelo, qui per eam scribebat in pariete." Cornelius a Lapide, *Commentaria in quattuor Prophetas Maiores* (Antwerp: I. Meursius, 1664), 1390. Emphasis mine. This translation and all succeeding ones drawn from Latin commentaries on Daniel 5 are mine.

[27] Galileo Galilei, *Discourse on the Comets,* in *Controversy on the Comets of 1618,* 36-37.

[28] Ibid., 37-38; 39.

[29] Ibid., 40.

[30] The name "Chaldean" for the language supposedly spoken by the Chaldeans is the result of an exegetical error. The Chaldean astrologers spoke Akkadian, a language that had died out by the time of the first commentaries on the Book of Daniel. Because they knew that the Jews spoke Aramaic after the Babylonian Captivity, early commentators assumed that they had learned this language, which they also called "Chaldean," from the priestly astrologers. See Giorgio Raimondo Cardona, *Storia universale della scrittura* (Milan: Arnaldo Mondadori, 1986), 156.

[31] For background on Saadias, see Henry Malter, *Saadia Gaon, His Life and His Works* (Philadelphia: Jewish Publication Society, 1942).

[32] For a very brief summary of Saadias' commentary, see A. F. Gallé, *Daniel: avec commentaires de R. Saadia, Aben-Ezra, Raschi, etc., et variantes des versions arabe et syriaque* (Paris: E. Leroux, 1900), 52-61. The references made to the interpretations of Saadias and Abraham Ibn Ezra (Aben-Ezra) in the works of seventeenth-century writers who knew them only indirectly are nonetheless much more informative than the study provided by Gallé.

[33] The system was called *athbasch,* and those who mentioned it usually offered Jeremiah 25:26, where the word *Sheshak* was written for *Babel,* as the most obvious example of the cipher. See for instance Gaspar Sanchez, *In Ezechielem & Danielem,* 233, who does not, however, favor this particular explanation of the Chaldeans' inability to read the message on the wall.

[34] "Sed alibi diximus Iudaeos audaces esse in suis divinitationibus, quoties non occurrit illis certa ratio." *Praelectiones Ioannis Calvini in librum prophetiarum Danielis* ([Lyon]: Bartholomaeus Vincentius, 1571), 64.

[35] "At hoc est velle sine ratione divinare." *Commentarii in praecipvos sacrae Scriptvrae libros Veteris Testamenti* (Paris: Sebastian Cramoisy, 1643), 718.

[36] "Sed hoc uti fingitur, ita rejicitur." *Commentaria,* 1309.

[37] *Assayer,* 181-82.

[38] The unfortunate connotation of "Grassi" probably underlies some of Galileo's several references to the greasy and viscous materials of which some supposed the comet to be formed. More curious still is Galileo's bizarre illustration of the visual aspects of the comet: he states that a clean carafe, if streaked with oil and held up to a lighted candle, will appear to have a miniature comet move across its surface. Galileo finished this experiment with the following admonition: "I do not mean to imply by this that there is a huge carafe in the sky, and someone oiling it with his finger, and

that thus a comet is formed" (*Assayer,* 246-47). Whatever the demonstration suggests in the way of astronomical knowledge, it is difficult not to see in *una gran caraffa e chi col dito la* [*va*] *ungendo* a reference to an alliance which Grassi may have wished to establish with the powerful Caraffa family.

[39] This hypothesis was anachronistic, as diacritical marks were not used to indicate vocalization in Hebrew until the fifth or sixth century A.D. See Cardona, *Storia Universale,* 156, and Albertine Gaur, *The Story of Writing* (London: The British Library, 1984), 93.

[40] *Commentaria,* 1309-10.

[41] "Chaldaei & Hebraei scribebant solas literas consonantes sine punctis, sine vocalibus. Unde Chaldaei nesciebant quae puncta hic essent substituenda, scilicet an legendum esset *mane,* an *mina,* an *meno;* an *tekel,* an *tokel,* an *takal.*" *Ibid.,* 1310.

[42] Grassi, *An Astronomical Disputation on the Three Comets of 1618,* in *The Controversy on the Comets of 1618,* 17.

[43] Ibid., 17.

[44] Galileo, *Discourse,* 41-42.

[45] Grassi, *Balance,* 76-77.

[46] *Assayer,* 2000.

[47] "A Deo fuisse impeditos Chaldaeos, ut Danieli haec gloria servaretur." *Commentaria,* 1309.

[48] "Quia probabile est, vel scripturam fuisse Regi propositam, & latuisse omnes Chaldaeos: vel ita excaecatos fuisse, ut videndo non viderent." Calvin, *Praelectiones,* 64.

[49] "Mihi vero similius videtur, aut divinitus impeditos Chaldaeos, ne scripturam minime obscuram possent legere." Maldonado, *Commentaria,* 718.

[50] Benito Pereyra, S.J., *Commentaria in Danielem Prophetam* (Lyon: Horatius Cardon, 1588), 311.

[51] Pereyra wrote commentaries on Aristotle's *Physics* and *On the Heavens.* For a brief discussion of his scientific activity and of his place within the Collegio Romano, see Riccardo Garcia Villoslada, S.J., *Storia del Collegio Romano* (Rome: Gregoriana, 1954), 51-52.

[52] *Assayer,* 202.

[53] As David Bjelajac mentions in *Millennial Desire* (Washington, D.C.: Smithsonian Institution Press,

1988), 25-26, in Renaissance paintings of Belshazzar's feast the handwriting on the wall was sometimes relegated to a dim background, and may have been hidden by the architectural features around it. In the tableau by Viviano Codazzi (1603-1672), for instance, the words are all but lost in the massive banquet hall and would certainly not have been visible to all who were present at the feast. See *L'Arte* 16 (1913):113.

[54] "Alii respondent, peregrinas hasce fuisse literas, extraordinarias & insole [n]tes." Cornelius, *Commentaria,* 1309.

[55] The Jesuit Juan de Pineda also offered this explanation among others in the thirteenth chapter of the fifth book of his *De Rebus Salomonis Regis* (Lyon: H. Cardon, 1609).

[56] "Sunt ergo qui asserant Scripturam hanc fuisse exaratam literis peregrinis, quarum sapientes illi notitiam non habebant. Danieli autem divinitus infusam talem notitiam, ac mentem desuper illuminatam a Deo, ut non solum verba ipsa, sed & reconditum verborum sensum, iuxta divinae voluntatis propositum, Regi manifestaret." Fernandez, *Commentarii in visiones Veteris Testamenti,* 605.

[57] *Assayer,* 183-84.

[58] In this same period Francis Bacon also used the metaphor of the maze, writing that "the universe to the eye of the human understanding is framed like a labyrinth," and that men "have gone altogether astray, either leaving and abandoning experience entirely, or losing their way in it and wandering round and round as in a labyrinth." See *The New Organon and Related Writings,* edited, with an introduction, by Fulton H. Anderson (New York: The Liberal Arts Press, 1960), 12, 80.

[59] Calvin uses the phrases *errare in tenebris* and *vagatur per ambages* to describe the king's distress and confusion. See *Praelectiones,* 64.

[60] "Deinde alii etiam fideles versati sunt in hoc vaticinio quasi in labyrintho aliqua ex parte." Ibid., 170.

Annibale Fantoli (essay date 1994)

SOURCE: "The Storm Breaks Loose: The Trial and Condemnation of Galileo," in *Galileo: For Copernicanism and for the Church,* translated by George V. Coyne, S. J., Vatican Observatory Publications, 1994, pp. 369-462.

[In the following excerpt, Fantoli provides transcripts of Galileo's questioning by the Inquisition and his testimony concerning the publication of his Dialogue.*]*

6. *The Trial of 1633 and Galileo's Defense*

Finally the two-month long uncertainty came to an end. [Francesco Niccolini, Ambassador of the grand Duke of Tuscany to Rome's Holy See and spokesperson on behalf of Galileo,] was summoned by Cardinal Francesco Barberini, who informed him that by order of the Pope and of the Congregation of the Holy Office Galileo should be summoned to that same Holy Office. He also let him know that, as a special gesture of respect to the Grand Duke, since a few hours of interrogation would not be enough, it would perhaps be necessary to retain him at the Holy Office. Once more Niccolini tried to make clear the state of health of Galileo, who, as he wrote three days later to Cioli, "for two nights running here had groaned and complained continuously of his arthritic pains, of his age and of the suffering he would experience from all of this" (XV, 85) and he asked the cardinal if it would not be possible to allow him to return each evening to the embassy. But the cardinal did not want to make any promises, even though he gave assurances that Galileo "would be kept there not as if in a prison nor in secret, as was usually done with others, but that he would be provided with good rooms which would perhaps even be left open" (XV, 85).

On 9 April Niccolini went to thank the Pope for the special respect shown towards the Grand Duke, but he found him more than ever fixed in the positions taken: "His Holiness complained that he [Galileo] has entered into that matter which for him [the Pope] it is still a most serious matter and one that has great consequences for religion" (XV, 85).

Niccolini was worried about such rigidity on Urban VIII's part and, as he informed Galileo of the imminent summons to the Holy Office, he recommended that he not try to defend his positions but "that he submit to what he might see they would want him to believe and hold in that particular about the mobility of the earth". And Niccolini added: "He is extremely afflicted by this; and judging by how much I have seen him go down since yesterday, I have very serious worries about his life" (XV, 85).

On 12 April Galileo appeared before the Commissary of the Holy Office who, as Niccolini wrote to Cioli four days later,

> . . . received him in a friendly manner and had him lodged in the chambers of the prosecutor of that Tribunal, rather than in the cells usually given to criminals; thus, not only does he reside among the officials, but he is free to go out into the courtyard of that house. (XV, 94; trans. by Finocchiaro, 250).

Niccolini added that they allowed his domestic to serve him and stay with him and that the servants of the embassy would bring him his food in the morning and the evening.[57] "These unusual and pleasing ways" made Niccolini hope for a quick and benign solution to the matter. The ambassador again promised to continue to work towards such an end, even though they were dealing with a very delicate task because, as he wrote, "in that Tribunal one deals with men who do not speak, nor do they answer, either vocally or by letter, thus it is even more difficult to deal with them or to penetrate what they are thinking" (XV, 95).

Through the acts of Galileo's trial we are able to know the details of the first interrogation which was held on the same day.[58]

After some preliminary questions, the Commissary began to interrogate Galileo about the events of 1616. Obviously they wanted to clarify his responsibility in transgressing the orders received from Bellarmine, for this constituted, as we know, the principal charge against him.

After having stated that he had come on his own to Rome on that occasion because he had heard that doubts were being raised about the Copernican opinion and in order to make sure that "he hold only holy and catholic opinions", Galileo admitted that he had treated of the Copernican doctrines with some cardinals of the Holy Office who were desirous of having explanations of Copernicus' book, because it was so difficult to understand for those who were not mathematicians or astronomers.

At this point Father Maculano asked Galileo to tell him what had been decided on that occasion about the problem of Copernicanism. Galileo answered:

> Respecting the controversy which had arisen on the aforesaid opinion that the Sun is stationary and that the Earth moves, it was decided by the Holy Congregation of the Index that such an opinion, considered as an established fact, contradicted Holy Scripture and was only admissible as a conjecture [*ex suppositione*], as it was held by Copernicus [*sic*]. (XIX, 338; trans. by de Santillana 1955, 238).

The Commissary insisted: "Were you notified of the aforesaid decision of the Congregation of the Index, and by whom?" Galileo answered: "I was notified of the aforesaid decision of the Congregation of the Index, and I was notified by the Lord Cardinal Bellarmine". And immediately afterwards, upon being further questioned by Maculano, he specified:

> The Lord Cardinal Bellarmine signified to me that the aforesaid opinion of Copernicus might be held as a conjecture, as it had been held by Copernicus, and His Eminence was aware that, like Copernicus, I only held that opinion as a conjecture, which is

evident from an answer of the same Lord Cardinal to a letter of Father Paolo Antonio Foscarini, provincial of the Carmelites, of which I have a copy, and in which these words occur: "It appears to me that Your Reverence and Signor Galileo act wisely in contenting yourselves with speaking *ex suppositione* and not with certainty." This letter of the Cardinal is dated April 12, 1615. It means, in other words, that that opinion, taken absolutely, must not be either held or defended. (XIX, 339; trans. by de Santillana 1955, 238-239).

Indubitably this answer of Galileo must have appeared to be completely insufficient to the Commissary who knew of the document found in the archives of the Holy Office. So he made the question more specific: "What would he say had been decided and notified to him at that time, that is in the month of February 1616"? And Galileo answered:

> In the month of February, 1616, the Lord Cardinal Bellarmine told me that, as the opinion of Copernicus, if adopted absolutely, was contrary to Holy Scripture, it must neither be held nor defended but that it could be taken and used hypothetically. In accordance with this I possess a certificate of Cardinal Bellarmine, given on May 26, 1616, in which he says that the Copernican opinion may neither be held nor defended, as it is opposed to Holy Scripture, of which certificate I herewith submit a copy. (XIX, 339; trans. by de Santillana 1955, 239).[59]

The difference between the content of the document signed by Bellarmine, presently before his eyes, and the one from the archives could not escape the Commissary. The latter document, as we know, spoke of the intervention of Maculano's predecessor right after the communication given by Bellarmine to Galileo. The Commissary, therefore, put another question to Galileo: "When the above communication was made to him, were any other persons present, and who?" Galileo admitted that: "When the Lord Cardinal made known to me what I have reported about the Copernican views, some Dominican Fathers were present, but I did not know them and have never seen them since." Finally Maculano could put to him the most important question: "Was any other command [*praeceptum*] communicated to him on this subject, in the presence of those Fathers, by them or anyone else, and what?" Galileo answered:

> I remember that the transaction took place as follows: The Lord Cardinal Bellarmine sent for me one morning and told me certain particulars which I had rather reserve for the ear of His Holiness before I communicate them to others.[60] But the end of it was that he told me that the Copernican opinion, being contradictory to Holy Scripture, must not be held or defended. It has escaped my memory whether those Dominican Fathers were present before or whether they came afterward; neither do I remember whether they were present when the Lord Cardinal told me the said

opinion was not to be held. It may be that a command [*precetto*] was issued to me that I should not hold or defend the opinion in question, but I do not remember it, for it is several years ago. (XIX, 339-340, trans. by de Santillana 1955, 239-240).

So as to recall to Galileo's memory a fact which he had forgotten, Maculano said that that command given to him in the presence of witnesses contained the words: " . . . that he must neither hold, defend, nor teach [*nec docere*] that opinion in any way whatsoever [*quovis modo*]" and he asked Galileo whether he now remembered how and from whom that command had been enjoined on him. Galileo repeated what he had already declared:

> I do not remember that the command was intimated to me by anybody but by Cardinal Bellarmine verbally; and I remember that the command was "not to hold or defend." It may be that "and not to teach" was also there. I do not remember it, neither the clause "in any way whatsoever" [*quovis modo*], but it may be that it was; for I thought no more about it or took any pains to impress the words on my memory, as a few months later I received the certificate now produced, of the said Lord Cardinal Bellarmine, of May 26, in which the order [*ordine*] given me, *not to hold or defend* that opinion, is expressly found. The two other clauses of the said command which have just been made known to me, namely, *not to teach* and *in any way,* I have not retained in my memory, I suppose because they are not mentioned in the said certificate, on which I have relied, and which I have kept as a reminder. (XIX, 340; trans. by de Santillana 1955, 240-241).

Galileo's response was clever. He knew he held a precious document, that of Bellarmine, and he had made use of it to his own advantage. But the fact still stood that Galileo had admitted having received a command from Bellarmine not to hold or to defend the Copernican opinion. And this was enough for Maculano, even leaving aside the document of the Holy Office archives which was even more precise and stronger.[61] And so the Commissary insisted: "How in the world, therefore, despite that command, had Galileo written and published the ***Dialogue?*** Had he received a special permission allowing him to do it?".

Therein stood the crux of the question and Galileo knew it. But by now he had decided upon his line of defense. And so he responded:

> After the command mentioned above I have received no permission to write the aforementioned book . . . because I do not claim by writing said book, to have at all gone against the command given to me not to hold nor defend nor teach the opinion in question, but to refute it. (XIX, 340).

To refute it! This statement of Galileo must have caused the Commissary to give a start since he knew well what the commission had thought of this "refutation", the commission to whom the previous September there had been passed along the examination of the ***Dialogue.*** At any rate, the affair would have been examined by a new commission and so it was of no use to start arguing now with Galileo.[62]

There remained the more delicate question, the one to do with the permission to print. Maculano put the question to Galileo in these terms:

> When asking permission to print the book, did he tell the Master of the Palace about the *precetto* which had been issued to him? (XIX, 341; trans. by de Santillana 1955, 241).

Galileo's reply was in line with the previous one:

> I did not happen to discuss that command with the Master of the Palace when I asked for the imprimatur, for I did not think it necessary to say anything, because I had no doubts about it; for I have neither maintained nor defended in that book the opinion that the Earth moves and that the Sun is stationary but have rather demonstrated the opposite of the Copernican opinion and shown that the arguments of Copernicus are weak and not conclusive. (XIX, 341; trans. by de Santillana 1955, 241).[63]

And so the first interrogation was completed. Galileo signed the minutes[64] and he took the oath to observe secrecy. He was then told to stop in at the Holy Office, at the Prosecutor's apartment. Galileo had undoubtedly hoped to be able to return to Villa Medici that same day. But the courteous attitude of the Commissary and the special respect shown to him must have made his disillusionment less bitter. And he perhaps had some consolation in the fact that it would only be a matter of a few days.

In fact, that is not the way it was. On 23 April he was still at the Holy Office. He wrote on that same day to Geri Bocchineri from his bed where he was suffering from a leg pain and among other matters he said:

> A little while ago the Commissary and the Prosecutor, who are the ones who examine me, came to pay a visit; and they gave me their word and the firm intention to dispatch matters for me as soon as I had gotten out of bed, answering me many times that I be of happy and of good spirit. I give more importance to this promise than to any of the hopes that have been given me in the past, hopes which experience has shown to have been founded more on conjectures than on real knowledge. I have always hoped that my innocence and my sincerity would come to be known, and now my hope is greater than ever. (XV, 101).

Even Niccolini seemed fundamentally optimistic. When he wrote that same day to Cioli, among other things he told him:

> As to Mr. Galileo, he is still in the same place, with the same comfortable arrangements. He writes to me every day, and I answer him and I freely tell him my intentions, without giving a second thought to it, and I go on wondering whether this matter [*questa festa*] is not destined to finish on some one else's shoulders. He has been examined once only, and I think that they will free him as soon as His Holiness returns from Castel Gandolfo, which will be for the Ascension.[65] Up to now there is no talk of the material of the book and the only pressure is to find out why the Father Master of the Sacred Palace has given permission for it, while His Holiness says that he never knew anything and that he had not ordered that permission be granted. (XV, 103-104).

In fact during the rest of the trial the permission to print will not be dealt with anymore. Indubitably it was concluded that the permission had been given on the initiative of [Monsignor Giovanni] Ciampoli, who had probably adduced an order of the Pope which, in fact, had never been given.[66] . . .

Notes

[57] Even Galileo, writing on that same day to Geri Bocchineri, after having informed him of his "business", added: " . . . for the continuation of which it has been arranged for me to remain in retreat, but with unusual largesse and comfort, in 3 rooms which are a part of those where the Lord Prosecutor of the Holy Office lives, and with free and ample permission to take walks in wide spaces. As to my health I am well, thanks to God and to the exquisite government of the most courteous house of the Lord Ambassador and of Her Ladyship, who are most careful about providing all comforts even beyond the most abundant for me". (XV, 88).

[58] XIX, 336-342. In addition to Father Maculano, his assistant, Father Carlo Sincero, Prosecutor of the Holy Office, and a secretary, who transcribed the minutes, were also present.

[59] The original declaration will be delivered by Galileo on 10 May.

[60] D'Addio writes in this regard:

> The Commissary was very careful not to insist. To what are we to attribute that "particular"? Was it to the fact that Maffeo Barberini had intervened on behalf of Galileo in 1616 by maintaining that the Copernican opinion should not be declared heretical, not even formally so, and that this was the understanding to

which the majority of the Cardinals of the Congregation of the Inquisition had arrived, and that, with reference to this precedent, the Pope had agreed to the publication of the *Dialogue?* Galileo kept this particular to himself and he did not speak of it any more in the following depositions, nor was he asked to clarify it, to specify why he had to speak of it first directly to the Pope and why he could not speak of it to the Commissary and the members of the Congregation: in this case the true intentions of the accused were not sought out, it was agreed that he should keep his "secret", most probably with appreciation for Galileo's reserve. (D'Addio 1985, 99).

While I consider D'Addio's interpretation to be plausible, I would like to note that "formally heretical" is not an attenuation of the qualification "heretical" (as the expression "not even formally heretical" used by him seems to suggest) but, on the contrary, it gives it a more explicit and stronger meaning. Furthermore, in 1616 Maffeo Barberini was not a member of the Holy Office but of the Congregation of the Index. Given the extreme secrecy which bound the deliberations of the Holy Office, he was not at all, therefore, in a position to know anything about "an understanding to which the majority of the Cardinals of the Congregation of the Inquisition had arrived". Rather, as we know . . . , it is most probable that it was within the Congregation of the Index that he successfully opposed the qualification of the Copernican thesis as "heretical".

[61] On the other hand, even if we limit ourselves to the content of Bellarmine's testimony, it spoke of the communication given to Galileo that the Copernican theory could not "be either held or defended". Even though this was not a personal command in Galileo's regard, it was the communication of a command which bound every Catholic and, therefore, Galileo himself. It is precisely that which Maculano himself will later on make Galileo notice (and it will be emphasized in the final sentence of the condemnation). Galileo was surely aware of the problem. Indubitably it was for that reason that he will claim immediately thereafter that he had not wanted to defend Copernicanism but that, on the contrary, he had wished to prove that it was false.

[62] On the other hand, during this interrogation, as well as following it, the Commissary did not show hostility towards Galileo. He interrogated him because of the obligations of his office but without showing a grudge or an argumentative punctiliousness.

[63] Geymonat (1965, 149) comments: "This absurd pretense [i.e. to have wanted to show that Copernicus' reasons were invalid and not conclusive] was in fact the downfall of Galileo's position; it impaired the value of all his subsequent replies". D'Addio 1985, 101 also speaks of "an excessive defense" on Galileo's part and he adds:

Surely Maculano thought to make Galileo remember this statement of his which he could no longer deny: if this had been his intention, he must recognize that the arguments developed in the *Dialogue* did not correspond to it, because they always concluded in favor of the Copernican thesis.

It appears to me, nevertheless, that terms like "absurd pretense" and "excessive defense" are a projection of our reaction (correct as it might be) upon the scene which unfolded more than 350 years ago in that chamber of the Holy Office, and they do not take into account that Maculano did not necessarily have to have had the same type of reaction. Far from showing himself "scandalized" by Galileo's statements, the Commissary (undoubtedly acting on instructions received from Cardinal Francesco Barberini, with the assent of Urban VIII) will try in fact, in the phase immediately following this first interrogation, to save Galileo with an extra-judiciary procedure, about which I will speak immediately. This is a further proof of the good dispositions of the Commissary towards Galileo, even after the first interrogation. Still it remains true that this claim of Galileo will not be forgiven by the rigorist current within the Holy Office with the result that they will be brought to the final decision of an abjuration.

[64] In XIX, 342 the confirmation in Galileo's hand placed on the minutes is reproduced: "I Galileo Galilei have born witness as above". Comparing this attestation with that of the second interrogation held on 30 April, the writing on the former appears to be much more nervous, a sign of the tension with which Galileo had presented himself at the first interrogation. We will find a similar, even greater, tension in Galileo's writing after the interrogation of 21 June.

[65] That year the feast of the Ascension fell on Thursday, 5 May.

[66] The last words of Niccolini seem to confirm, as we have already seen, the version of the facts given by Buonamici (XIX, 410). . . .

FURTHER READING

Biography

Broderick, James. *Galileo: The Man, His Work, His Misfortunes.* New York: Harper and Row, 1964, 152 p.
    Traces the life of Galileo as a man of "genius" forced to struggle against the outmoded ideas of Aristotle and of Ptolemy, as well as with the implacability of the Inquisition.

Drake, Stillman. *Galileo at Work: His Scientific Biography.* Chicago: The University of Chicago Press, 1978, 536 p.

Looks at Galileo's life from the point of view of his publications, with a particular focus on his lesser known writings.

——. *Galileo.* New York: Hill and Wang, 1980, 100 p.
    Brief but comprehensive biography of the life, work, and trial of Galileo.

Fermi, Laura, and Bernardini, Gilberto. *Galileo and the Scientific Revolution.* New York: Basic Books, Inc., 1961, 150 p.
    Looks at the personal as well as the scientific side of Galileo's life.

Geymonat, Ludovico. *Galileo Galilei: A Biography and Inquiry into His Philosophy of Science.* Translated by Stillman Drake. New York: McGraw-Hill, 1965, 260 p.
    Examines Galileo's life from his childhood to his death, and includes a debate between Stillman Drake and Giorgio de Santillana on the Bellarmine-Galileo confrontation.

Reston, James, Jr. *Galileo: A Life.* New York: Harper Perennial, 1995, 319 p.
    Places the life and inventiveness of Galileo within the context of the Renaissance.

Santillana, Giorgio de. *The Crime of Galileo.* New York: Time, Inc., Book Division, 1955, 371 p.
    Offers a scientific history of Galileo's life and work, with an emphasis on Renaissance culture.

Seeger, Raymond J. *Men of Physics: Galileo Galilei, His Life and His Works.* Oxford: Pergamon Press, 1966, 286 p.
    Overview of Galileo's life, with a bibliography; followed by a detailed discussion of his scientific work.

Criticism

Berry, Arthur. *A Short History of Astronomy.* London: John Murray, 1898, 435 p.
    Examines the development of astronomy from early Chinese and Egyptians, through Galileo, and finally to the nineteenth century.

Brophy, James and Paolucci, Henry (eds.). *The Achievement of Galileo.* New York: Twayne Publishers, 1962, 256 p.
    A collection of essays by Galileo, as well as other writers' articles about Galileo's work and the controversy surrounding it.

Campanella, Thomas. *Apologiae Pro Galileo: A Defense of Galileo, the Mathematician from Florence.* Translated by Richard J. Blackwell. Notre Dame, IN: University of Notre Dame Press, 1994, 157 p.
    Translation of a theological defense of the theories of Galileo from one of his Renaissance contemporaries.

Drake, Stillman (trans.). *Discoveries and Opinions of Galileo.* Garden City, NY: Doubleday Anchor Books, 1957, 302 p.

Provides translations of along with an introduction and notes to Galileo's major writings.

Fantoli, Annibale. *Galileo: For Copernicanism and for the Church.* Translated by George V. Coyne. Vatican City State, Rome: Vatican Observatory Publications, 1994, 540 p.

Under the auspices of Pope John Paul II, tries to reexamine in detail the events that resulted in Galileo's conviction by the Inquisition, considering along the way the theories of Ptolemy, Tycho Brahe, and Copernicus.

Golino, Carlo L. (ed.). *Galileo Reappraised.* Berkeley: University of California Press, 1966, 110 p.

A collection of papers presented at a conference in Los Angeles in honor of the four-hundredth anniversary of Galileo's birth.

Hummel, Charles E. "Galileo: Science and Theology." In *The Galileo Connection: Resolving Conflicts between Science and the Bible,* pp. 103-25. Downers Grove, IL: Intervarsity Press, 1986.

Examines Galileo's condemnation by the Inquisition and his insistence to the end of his life of his faithfulness to the Church.

Koyré, Alexandre. "*The Dialogue Concerning the Two Chief World Systems* and the Anti-Aristotelian Polemic." In *Galileo Studies,* pp. 154-75. Translated by John Mepham. Atlantic Highlands, NJ: Humanities Press, 1978.

Looks closely at Galileo's views on the theories of Ptolemy, Aristotle, and Copernicus, and his conclusion that the most important differences between these views was the concept of motion.

Naylor, Ronald H. "Galileo's Method of Analysis and Synthesis." *Isis* 81, No. 309 (December 1990): 695-707.

Attempts to shed new light on Galileo's methods of experimentation, and discusses the debate between

"pre-" and "post-" 1973 scholarly assessments of Galileo's experiments.

Noyes, Alfred. "Galileo." In *The Torch-Bearers: Watchers of the Sky,* pp. 131-83. New York: Frederick A. Stokes Company, 1922.

Galileo's loves and life presented as a long poem.

Redondi, Pietro. *Galileo: Heretic.* Translated by Raymond Rosenthal. Princeton, NJ: Princeton University Press, 1987, 356 p.

Attempts, from a twentieth-century perspective, to "reconstruct" the motives of the principal people involved in the Galileo affair.

Segre, Michael. "Light on the Galileo Case?" *Isis* 88, No. 3 (September 1997): 484-504.

Argues that in two separate speeches, Pope John Paul II contradicts himself in his assessment of Galileo's relationship to the Catholic Church.

Van Helden, Albert. "Galileo, Telescopic Astronomy, and the Copernican System." In *The General History of Astronomy, Vol. 2: Planetary Astronomy from the Renaissance to the Rise of Astrophysics, Part A: Tycho Brahe to Newton,* pp. 81-105. Edited by René Taton and Curtis Wilson. Cambridge: Cambridge University Press, 1989.

Discusses in detail Galileo's experiments with the telescope; accompanied by copies of sketches and manuscripts.

Wallace, William A. *Prelude to Galileo: Essays on Medieval and Sixteenth-Century Sources of Galileo's Thought.* Edited by Robert S. Cohen and Marx W. Wartofsky. Dordrecht, Holland: D. Reidel Publishing Company, 1981, 369 p.

A collection of essays on Galileo by Wallace published over fifteen years and attempting to see Galileo within the context of his era.

Johannes Kepler

1571-1630

German astronomer, essayist, and nonfiction writer.

INTRODUCTION

Kepler is regarded as a towering figure of the scientific renaissance and a seminal catalyst in bridging the medieval cosmology and the modern world-view. Building on the heliocentric theory of the Polish astronomer Nicolaus Copernicus, Kepler established the three laws of planetary motion and corrected the central fault of Copernican astronomy, which had wrongly determined the orbital paths of the planets to be circular. Kepler described a universe in which planets spinning on their axis rotate around the sun in elliptical orbits and provided the mathematical equations to verify his premise. The new astronomy replaced the earth-centered Ptolemaic system that had prevailed since the second century. Utilizing the skillful observations of the Danish astronomer Tycho Brahe, Kepler was the first to demand irrefutable mathematical proof to validate his scientific theories. He is also considered the father of modern optics for first correctly describing both the physics and physiology of vision. He further utilized his optical knowledge in making important contributions to the design of the refracting telescope. His extensive work in mathematics led to the development of infinitesimal calculus. A deeply religious man, Kepler viewed the universe as the perfect creation of God, the prime mover and perfect geometrician. It was up to the scientist to unravel the natural laws of providential design. But Kepler's insistence that all theories must be confirmed by precise, verifiable data made him a seminal figure in the development of empiricism and the scientific method. His groundbreaking theories and rigorous methodologies laid the path for Newtonian physics and the laws of universal gravity, which clearly marked the arrival of the modern era.

Biographical Information

Kepler was born at Weil der Stadt, Swabia in southwest Germany on December 27, 1571. His father, Heinrich, was a ne'er-do-well mercenary who often left his family for long periods before permanently abandoning them during Kepler's teen-age years. His mother Katharina was a meddlesome, disagreeable woman who was charged with being a witch in her later years. Kepler's childhood was unhappy and marked by recurring sickness, and it was apparent early on that he was ill suited for manual labor. His keen intelligence was noted, however, and he was the fortuitous benefi-

ciary of a practice of the dukes of Württemberg that provided educational scholarships for intellectually gifted but impoverished students. Kepler attended several elementary and secondary schools where part of his early schooling stressed learning a very formal and ornate Latin writing style that would be reflected in Kepler's later writings. He attended the Protestant University of Tübingen on scholarship, graduating in 1587. He continued his studies there and received his master's degree in 1591. Intending to enter the Lutheran ministry, Kepler pursed a curriculum in the arts. While at Tübingen he studied astronomy with Michael Maestlin who introduced him to both the Ptolemaic and Copernican systems. They began a friendship that would be of lasting importance throughout Kepler's life. Upon graduation Kepler began theological studies. But shortly before completing his course, Lutheran officials decided that Kepler's religious heterodoxy and refusal to sign the Formula of Concord made him an unsuitable candidate for the clergy. They recommended instead that he take a mathematics teaching post at a Protestant school at Graz in Austria. It was while giving a lecture one day that Kepler experienced a brilliant insight that explained the architectural order of the solar system. Kepler based his vision on what he believed to be an integral relationship between the six known planets and the five regular solids of Pythagorean mathematics. Kepler published his theory in the *Mysterium Cosmographicum* (1596; *Mystery of the Universe*) when he was twenty-six and sent copies of his work to both Tycho Brahe and Galileo. Even though he rejected the thesis of Kepler's work, Tycho immediately recognized Kepler's brilliance and was especially impressed by his mathematical skills. When religious turmoil forced Kepler to leave Graz in 1600, he traveled to Prague to meet with Tycho who had just been appointed as the Imperial Mathematician by Emperor Rudolph II. Tycho had been working on his own theory of the universe which was a hybrid of the Ptolemaic and Copernican systems; the sun revolved around the Earth while all the other planets revolved around then sun. He invited Kepler to join him in his work in his observatory and to work particularly on determining the orbit of Mars. Expecting to be considered more as a colleague, the relationship was a bit strained when Tycho treated Kepler as a subordinate. The alliance had also been tested by the revelation of some old correspondence between Kepler and Nicolaus Raymarus Ursus who had also once served as Imperial Mathematician. Their exchanges had begun in 1595 with a letter Kepler sent to Ursus praising him for his work. Tycho and Ursus were nemeses and rivals, the former having accused the latter of plagiarism. Brahe assigned Kepler the uncomfortable task of writing a major defense of his work against Ursus in which Kepler had to explain away his early correspondence as the fawning of a novice. Kepler and Tycho worked together, if a bit tenuously, for ten months before Tycho's unexpected death in 1601. Within two months Rudolph II named Kepler to the position of Imperial Mathematician. Besides formal scientific work Kepler's duties included providing astrological forecasts for the royal family. Kepler assumed numerous posts during his lifetime and the moves were generally precipitated by his having to leave an area due to reoccurring religious turmoil. A man of great faith, Kepler was nonetheless very tolerant of dissident views and his heterodoxy often placed him in disfavor with the authorities. The peaks and valleys that marked Kepler's professional life touched his personal life as well. In 1597 he married Barbara von Müller, a prosperous heiress, who at age twenty-three had already been widowed twice. Though Kepler had initially been much in love with her, it soon became an unhappy marriage as Kepler found his wife to be undereducated and ill mannered, unable to comprehend or appreciate the importance of his work. Still the marriage endured for fourteen years until her death in 1611. Together they had five children of whom only two survived. She did not leave a will and Kepler was left virtually penniless. In 1612 Rudolph II was deposed and Kepler lost his post as Imperial Mathematician while increas-ing religious strife made it impossible for Lutherans to remain in Prague. Kepler moved to Linz and took the assignment of district mathematician. In 1613 Kepler wed Susanna Reutlinger, age twenty-four, who had been an orphan. It proved to be a much happier marriage and together they had seven children, but once again only two survived childhood. Beginning in 1615 Kepler's mother, still living in Württemberg, had become the subject of rumors involving sorcery. Kepler, living in Linz, became aware in 1617 of the seriousness of his mother's plight and became actively involved in her defense. Although formally charged as a witch in 1621, she was eventually freed but died within several months of her release. Kepler's efforts on her behalf were partly motivated by filial duty and partly by self-defense. If his mother had been convicted both his mathematics career and personal safety would be imperiled. Still Kepler suffered more religious persecution during the Counter-Reformation and was forced once again to relinquish a job and leave his home. Beginning in 1628 Kepler spent the last years of his life studying and publishing at Zagao in Silesia under the patronage of Albrecht von Wallenstein, a duke and prosperous soldier of fortune. While traveling to Austria to collect a debt Kepler became ill and succumbed to fever at age fifty-nine at Regensburg, Germany on November 15, 1630.

Major Works

Kepler published The *Mysterium Cosmographicum* when he was twenty-six and the work reveals both the mystical and empirical elements in Kepler's intellectual orientation. Kepler posited that the five polyhedral shapes of Pythagorean mathematics were essential elements in the design of the universe. In Kepler's Platonic vision, each of the five shapes fit nearly into the spaces between the orbits of the six known planets. Neptune, Uranus, and Pluto had yet to be discovered. While the first part of the book reveals Kepler's mystical orientation in suggesting that the geometrical perfection of the universe is the manifestation of a divinely inspired plan, the second half reflects Kepler's commitment to empiricism. He simply states that if observable and verifiable data cannot prove his theory, the thesis must be jettisoned. *Astronomiae Pars Optica* (1604; *The Optical Part of Astronomy*) contains Kepler's theories on how vision occurs through the process of refraction within the eye, discusses the development of glasses for both near sightedness and far sightedness, and explains how both eyes work together for depth perception. In the treatise Kepler also examines why the sun appears to vary in size at different times and discusses the creation of images using the pinhole camera. *Astronomia Nova* (1609; *The New Astronomy*) is Kepler's most important work and contains his first two laws on planetary motion. Tycho's observational data on Mars played a seminal role in Kepler's calculations. Copernican cosmology was a highly complicated system that resembled clockwork architecture with complex orbits and epicycles that were not precise or provable. This work established Kepler's first two laws of planetary motion. The first law states that all planets travel on an elliptical orbit that has the sun as one point of its focus. The sun is off-center in the ellipse and a planet's distance from the sun varies according to where the planet is during its rotation. The second law postulates that the line connecting the sun and a planet will sweep through equal area in equal time regardless of where the planet is in its orbit. At the points when the planet is closer to the sun it travels faster; conversely, when a planet is farther from the sun the speed of its rotation is slower. But the area transversed in any period by a planet remains the same regardless of the speed at which the planet is traveling. *Somnium Seu Astronomia* (1634; *A Dream of the Moon*), Kepler's early experiment in writing science fiction, is the tale of an imaginary voyage to the moon. Although the story began circulating in manuscript form shortly after its completion in 1609, it was not published until after Kepler's death. In *Dioptrice* (1611) Kepler discussed the refraction of the lens in human eyesight leading to the concept of the inverted telescope indispensable to astronomical observation. The *Harmonice Mundi* (1619; *Harmony of the World*) actually had its genesis as early as 1599 as Kepler sought to reconcile the natural harmony of the universe with the objectivity of scientific proof. This work contains Kepler's third law, which describes the relationship between planetary movements and their distances from the sun. His third law states that the cube of the average distance of each individual planet from the sun is proportional to the square of the time required for the planet to complete one full orbit. The treatise also contains elaborate musical equations and scales correlated with Pythagorean theory and to suggest the natural order, symmetry, and harmony of the universe. As a Platonist, Kepler sought to correlate musical forms with heavenly bodies as part of God's design for a flawless universe. In *Epitome Astronomiae Copernicanae* (1621; *The Epitomy of Copernican Astronomy*) Kepler established the true orbits of all the planets as well the satellites of Jupiter. In the *Tabulae Rudolphinae* (1629; *Rudolphine Tables*), Kepler's last major work, he expanded on Tycho's observation and established in a comprehensive catalog of known celestial bodies the positions of the planets and of over 1000 stars. Besides major treatises Kepler's work also includes over 800 existing astrology forecasts done for himself, as part of his duties as Imperial Mathematician, and for wealthy patrons when financial need required him to do so.

Critical Reception

Kepler's scientific contemporaries immediately regarded his work as serious and important contributions to astronomy and cosmology, yet his writings were not widely disseminated for forty or fifty years after his death. But by the time Isaac Newton was building on Kepler's work, however, Kepler's theories were becoming increasingly known even in the popular culture. Critics have suggested that Kepler's highly formal Latin writing style made his work difficult to read in its original. He also had a habit of interjecting into his work all of his self-doubts suggesting where he may be in error—a practice that led to a very digressive writing style that many readers found tedious. Kepler explained that these frequent sidebars were merely intended to provide guidance to future students and readers of his work, something he wished his scientific predecessors would have done. While newer data and observations have supplanted some of Kepler's theories and calculations, the bulk of his work remains accurate and applicable to modern physics, astronomy, optics, and mathematics. Much recent Kepler criticism focuses on the unique blend of mysticism and empiricism that is the hallmark of Kepler's vision.

PRINCIPAL WORKS

Prodromus Dissertationum Mathematicarum Continens Mysterium Cosmographicum [*The Forerunner of Dissertations on the Universe, containing the Mystery of the Universe*] (non-fiction) 1596

De Fundamentis Astrologiae Certioribus [*The More Reliable Bases of Astrology*] (non-fiction) 1601

Ad Vitellionem Paralipomena, Quibus Astronomiae Pars Optica Traditur [*Supplement to Witelo, Expounding the Optical Part of Astronomy*] (non-fiction) 1604

De Stella Nova in Pede Serpentarii [*The New Star in the Foot of the Serpent Bearer*] (non-fiction) 1606

Astronomia Nova [*The New Astronomy*] (non-fiction) 1609

Phaenomenon Singulare [*Singular Phenomena*] (non-fiction) 1609

Dissertatio cum Nuncio Sidereo Nuper ad Mortales Misso a Galilaeo Galilaeo [*Conversation with the Sidereal Messenger*] (letter) 1610

Tertius Interveniens [*Third Man in the Middle*] (non-fiction) 1610

Strena [*A New Year's Gift, or On the Six-Cornered Snowflake*] (letter) 1611

Dioptrice [*Optical Tubes*] (non-fiction) 1611

Narratio de Observatis Quatuor Jovis satellitibus [*Narration about Four satellites of Jupiter Observed*] (non-fiction) 1611

Bericht vom Geburtsjahr Christi (non-fiction) 1613

De Vero Anno quo Aeternus Dei Filius Humanan Naturam in Utero Benedictae Virginis Mariae Assumpsit [*Concerning the True Year in which the Son of God assumed a Human Nature in the Uterus of the Blessed Virgin Mary*] (non-fiction) 1614

Eclogae Chronicae (non-fiction) 1615

Nova Stereometria Doliorum Vinariorum (non-fiction) 1615

Messekunst Archimedis (non-fiction) 1616

Epitome Astronomiae Copernicanae [*Epitome of Copernican Astronomy*] 7 vols. (non-fiction) 1618-21

De Cometis Libelli Tre (non-fiction) 1619

Harmonice Mundi [*Harmonics of the World*] (non-fiction) 1619

Pro suo Opere Harmonice Mundi Apologia (non-fiction) 1622

Chilias Logarithmorum (non-fiction) 1624

Hyperaspistes (non-fiction) 1625

De Raris Mirisque Anni 1631 Phenomenis (non-fiction) 1629

Tabulae Rudolphinae [*Rudolphine Tables*] (non-fiction) 1629

*Somnium, Sive Astronomia Lunaris [*Somnium—A Dream of the Moon*] (fiction) 1634

**First circulated as an unpublished manuscript in 1609.

Gerald Holton (essay date 1956)

SOURCE: "Johannes Kepler's Universe: Its Physics and Metaphysics," in *Thematic Origins of Scientific Thought: Kepler to Einstein,* Harvard University Press, 1973, pp. 69-90.

[*In the following essay, originally published in 1956 and reprinted in 1976, Holton discusses why Kepler is often difficult to read and how his digressive style primarily reflects the difficulties seventeenth-century scientists encountered in making the transition from medieval to modern explanations of the cosmos. He further asserts that Kepler's juxtaposition of mathematical, astronomical, and metaphysical ideas are really a manifestation of his simultaneously seeing "the universe as physical machine, the universe as mathematical harmony, and the universe as central theological order."*]

The important publications of Johannes Kepler (1571-1630) preceded those of Galileo, Descartes, and Newton in time, and in some respects they are even more revealing. And yet, Kepler has been strangely neglected and misunderstood. Very few of his voluminous writings have been translated into English.[1] In this language there has been neither a full biography[2] nor even a major essay on his work in over twenty years. Part of the reason lies in the apparent confusion of incongruous elements—physics and metaphysics, astronomy and astrology, geometry and theology—which characterizes Kepler's work. Even in comparison with Galileo and Newton, Kepler's writings are strikingly different in the *quality* of preoccupation. He is more evidently rooted in a time when animism, alchemy, astrology, numerology, and witchcraft presented problems to be seriously argued. His mode of presentation is equally uninviting to modern readers, so often does he seem to wander from the path leading to the important questions of physical science. Nor is this impression merely the result of the inevitable astigmatism of our historical hindsight. We are trained on the ascetic standards of presentation originating in Euclid, as reestablished, for example, in Books I and II of Newton's *Principia,*[3] and are taught to hide behind a rigorous structure the actual steps of discovery—those guesses, errors, and occasional strokes of good luck without which creative scientific work does not usually occur. But Kepler's embarrassing candor and intense emotional involvement force him to give us a detailed account of his tortuous progress. He still allows himself to be so overwhelmed by the beauty and variety of the world as a whole that he cannot yet persistently limit his attention to the main problems which can in fact be solved. He gives us lengthy accounts of his failures, though sometimes they are tinged with ill-concealed pride in the difficulty of his task. With rich imagination he frequently finds analogies from every phase of life, exalted or commonplace. He is apt to interrupt his scientific thoughts, either with exhortations to the reader to follow a little longer through the almost unreadable account, or with trivial side issues and textual quibbling, or with personal anecdotes or delighted exclamations about some new geometrical relation, a numerological or musical analogy. And sometimes he breaks into poetry or a prayer—indulging, as he puts it, in his "sacred ecstasy." We see him on his pioneering trek, probing for the firm ground on which our science could later build, and often led into regions which we now know to be unsuitable marshland.

These characteristics of Kepler's style are not merely idiosyncrasies. They mirror the many-sided struggle attending the rise of modern science in the early seventeenth century. Conceptions which we might now regard as mutually exclusive are found to operate side-by-side in his intellectual make-up. A primary aim of this essay is to identify those disparate elements and to show that in fact much of Kepler's strength stems from their juxtaposition. We shall see that when his physics fails, his metaphysics comes to the rescue; when a mechanical model breaks down as a tool of explanation, a mathematical model takes over; and at its boundary in turn there stands a theological axiom. Kepler set out to unify the classical picture of the world, one which was split into celestial and terrestrial regions, through the concept of a universal physical *force;* but when this problem did not yield to physical analysis, he readily returned to the devices of a unifying *image,* namely, the central sun ruling the world, and of a unifying *principle,* that of all-pervading mathematical harmonies. In the end he failed in his initial project of providing the mechanical explanation for the observed motions of the planets, but he succeeded at least in throwing a bridge from the old view of the world as unchangeable *cosmos* to the new view of the world as the playground of dynamic and mathematical laws. And in the process he turned up, as if it were by accident, those clues which Newton needed for the eventual establishment of the new view.

Toward a Celestial Machine

A sound instinct for physics and a commitment to neo-Platonic metaphysics—these are Kepler's two main guides which are now to be examined separately and at their point of merger. As to the first, Kepler's genius in physics has often been overlooked by critics who were taken aback by his frequent excursions beyond the bounds of science as they came to be understood later, although his *Dioptrice* (1611) and his mathematical work on infinitesimals (in *Nova Stereometria*, 1615) and on logarithms (*Chilias Logarithmorum*, 1624) have direct appeal for the modern mind. But even Kepler's casually delivered opinions often prove his insight beyond the general state of knowledge of his day. One example is his creditable treatment of the motion of projectiles on the rotating earth, equivalent to the formulation of the superposition principle of velocities.[4] Another is his opinion of the *perpetuum mobile*:

> As to this matter, I believe one can prove with very good reasons that neither any never-ending motion nor the quadrature of the circle—two problems which have tortured great minds for ages—will ever be encountered or offered by nature.[5]

But, of course, on a large scale, Kepler's genius lies in his early search for a physics of the solar system. He is the first to look for *a universal physical law based on terrestrial mechanics* to comprehend the whole universe in its quantitative details. In the Aristotelian and Ptolemaic world schemes, and indeed in Copernicus's own, the planets moved in their respective orbits by laws which were either purely mathematical or mechanical in a nonterrestrial sense. As [Ernst] Goldbeck reminds us, Copernicus himself still warned to keep a clear distinction between celestial and merely terrestrial phenomena, so as not to "attribute to the celestial bodies what belongs to the earth."[6] This crucial distinction disappears in Kepler from the beginning. In his youthful work of 1596, the *Mysterium Cosmographicum,* a single geometrical device is used to show the necessity of the observed orbital arrangement of all planets. In this respect, the earth is treated as being an equal of the other planets.[7] In the words of Otto Bryk,

> The central and permanent contribution lies in this, that for the first time the whole world structure was subjected to a single law of construction—though not a force law such as revealed by Newton, and only a non-causative relationship between spaces, but nevertheless one single law.[8]

Four years later Kepler meets Tycho Brahe and from him learns to respect the power of precise observation. The merely approximate agreement between the observed astronomical facts and the scheme laid out in the *Mysterium Cosmographicum* is no longer satisfying. To be sure, Kepler always remained fond of this work, and in the *Dissertatio Cum Nuncio Sidereo* (1610) even hoped that Galileo's newly-found moons of Jupiter would help to fill in one of the gaps left in his geometrical model. But with another part of his being Kepler knows that an entirely different approach is wanted. And here Kepler turns to the new conception of the universe. While working on the *Astronomia Nova* in 1605, Kepler lays out his program:

> I am much occupied with the investigation of the physical causes. My aim in this is to show that the celestial machine is to be likened not to a divine organism but rather to a clockwork . . . , insofar as nearly all the manifold movements are carried out by means of a single, quite simple magnetic force, as in the case of a clockwork all motions [are caused] by a simple weight. Moreover I show how this physical conception is to be presented through calculation and geometry.[9]

The celestial machine, driven by a single terrestrial force, in the image of a clockwork! This is indeed a prophetic goal. Published in 1609, the *Astronomia Nova* significantly bears the subtitle *Physica Coelestis.* The book is best known for containing Kepler's First and Second Laws of planetary motion, but it represents primarily a search for one universal force law to explain the motions of planets—Mars in particular—as well as gravity and the tides. This breathtaking conception of unity is perhaps even more striking than Newton's, for the simple reason that Kepler had no predecessor.

The Physics of the Celestial Machine

Kepler's first recognition is that forces between bodies are caused not by their relative positions or their geometrical arrangements, as was accepted by Aristotle, Ptolemy, and Copernicus, but by mechanical interactions between the material objects. Already in the *Mysterium Cosmographicum* (Chapter 17) he announced *"Nullum punctum, nullum centrum grave est,"* and he gave the example of the attraction between a magnet and a piece of iron. In William Gilbert's De Magnete (1600), published four years later, Kepler finds a careful explanation that the action of magnets seems to come from pole points, but must be attributed to the parts of the body, not the points.

In the spirited *Objections* which Kepler appended to his own translation of Aristotle's [*Peri ouranou*], he states epigrammatically *"Das Mittele is nur ein Düpffin,"* and he elaborates as follows:

How can the earth, or its nature, notice, recognize and seek after the center of the world which is only a little point [*Düpffin*]—and then go toward it? The earth is not a hawk, and the center of the world not a little bird; it [the center] is also not a magnet which could attract the earth, for it has no substance and therefore cannot exert a force.

In the Introduction to the **Astronomia Nova,** which we shall now consider in some detail, Kepler is quite explicit:

> A mathematical point, whether it be the center of the world or not, cannot move and attract a heavy object. . . . Let the [Aristotelian] physicists prove that such a force is to be associated with a point, one which is neither corporeal nor recognisable as anything but a pure reference [mark].

Thus what is needed is a "true doctrine concerning gravity"; the axioms leading to it include the following:

> Gravitation consists in the mutual bodily striving among related bodies toward union or connection; (of this order is also the magnetic force).

This premonition of universal gravitation is by no means an isolated example of lucky intuition. Kepler's feeling for the physical situation is admirably sound, as shown in additional axioms:

> If the earth were not round, a heavy body would be driven not everywhere straight toward the middle of the earth, but toward different points from different places.

> If one were to transport two stones to any arbitrary place in the world, closely together but outside the field of force [*extra orbe virtutis*] of a third related body, then those stones would come together at some intermediate place similar to two magnetic bodies, the first approaching the second through a distance which is proportional to the mass [*moles*] of the second.

And after this precursor of the principle of conservation of momentum, there follows the first attempt at a good explanation for the tides in terms of a force of attraction exerted by the moon.

But the Achilles' heel of Kepler's celestial physics is found in the very first "axiom," in his Aristotelian conception of the law of inertia, where inertia is identified with a tendency to come to rest—*causa privativa motus:*

> Outside the field of force of another related body, every bodily substance, insofar as it is corporeal, by

nature tends to remain at the same place at which it finds itself.[10]

This axiom deprives him of the concepts of mass and force in useful form—the crucial tools needed for shaping the celestial metaphysics of the ancients into the celestial physics of the moderns. Without these concepts, Kepler's world machine is doomed. He has to provide separate forces for the propulsion of planets tangentially along their paths and for the radial component of motion.

Moreover, he assumed that the force which reaches out from the sun to keep the planets in tangential motion falls inversely with the increasing distance. The origin and the consequences of this assumption are very interesting. In Chapter 20 of the MYSTERIUM COSMOGRAPHICUM he speculated casually why the sidereal periods of revolution on the Copernican hypothesis should be larger for the more distant planets, and what force law might account for this:

> We must make one of two assumptions: either the forces of motion [*animae motrices*] [are inherent in the planets] and are feebler the more remote they are from the sun, or there is only one *anima motrix* at the center of the orbits, that is, in the sun. It drives the more vehemently the closer the [moved] body lies; its effect on the more distant bodies is reduced because of the distance [and the corresponding] decrease of the impulse. Just as the sun contains the source of light and the center of the orbits, even so can one trace back to this same sun life, motion and the soul of the world. . . . Now let us note how this decrease occurs. To this end we will assume, as is very probable, that the moving effect is weakened through spreading from the sun in the same manner as light.

This suggestive image—with its important overtones which we shall discuss below—does, however, not lead Kepler to the inverse-square law of force, for he is thinking of the spreading of light *in a plane,* corresponding to the plane of planetary orbits. The decrease of light intensity is therefore associated with the linear increase in circumference for more distant orbits! In his pre-Newtonian physics, where force is proportional not to acceleration but to velocity, Kepler finds a ready use for the inverse first-power law of gravitation. It is exactly what he needs to explain his observation that the speed of a planet in its elliptical orbit decreases linearly with the increase of the planet's distance from the sun. Thus Kepler's Second Law of Planetary Motion—which he actually discovered *before* the so-called First and Third laws—finds a partial physical explanation in joining several erroneous postulates.

In fact, it is clear from the context that these postulates originally suggested the Second Law to Kepler.[11] But not always is the final outcome so happy. Indeed, the hypothesis concerning the physical forces acting on the planet seriously delays Kepler's progress toward the law of elliptical orbits (First Law). Having shown that "the path of the planet [Mars] is not a circle but an oval figure," he attempts (Chapter 45, *Astronomia Nova*) to find the details of a physical force law which would explain the "oval" path in a quantitative manner. But after ten chapters of tedious work he has to confess that "the physical causes in the forty-fifth chapter thus go up in smoke." Then in the remarkable fifty-seventh chapter, a final and rather desperate attempt is made to formulate a force law. Kepler even dares to entertain the notion of combined magnetic influences and animal forces [*vis animalia*] in the planetary system. Of course, the attempt fails. The accurate clock-work-like celestial machine cannot be constructed.

To be sure, Kepler does not give up his conviction that a universal force exists in the universe, akin to magnetism. For example, in Book 4 of the *Epitome of Copernican Astronomy* (1620), we encounter the picture of a sun as a spherical magnet with one pole at the center and the other distributed over its surface. Thus a planet, itself magnetized li ke a bar magnet with a fixed axis, is alternately attracted to and repelled from the sun in its elliptical orbit. This is to explain the radial component of planetary motion. The tangential motion has been previously explained (in Chapter 34, *Astronomia Nova*) as resulting from the drag or torque which magnetic lines of force from the rotating sun are supposed to exert on the planet as they sweep over it. But the picture remains qualitative and incomplete, and Kepler does not return to his original plan to "show how this physical conception is to be presented through calculation and geometry."[9] Nor does his long labor bring him even a fair amount of recognition. Galileo introduces Kepler's work into his discussion on the world systems only to scoff at Kepler's notion that the moon affects the tides,[12] even though Tycho Brahe's data and Kepler's work based on them had shown that the Copernican scheme which Galileo was so ardently upholding did not correspond to the experimental facts of planetary motion. And Newton manages to remain strangely silent about Kepler throughout Books I and II of the Principia, by introducing the Third Law anonymously as "the phenomenon of the 3/2th power" and the First and Second Laws as "the *Copernican* hypothesis."[13] Kepler's three laws have come to be treated as essentially empirical rules. How far removed this achievement was from his original ambition!

Kepler's First Criterion of Reality: The Physical Operations of Nature

Let us now set aside for a moment the fact that Kepler failed to build a mechanical model of the universe, and ask why he undertook the task at all. The answer is that Kepler (rather like Galileo) was trying to establish a new philosophical interpretation for "reality." More-

over, he was quite aware of the novelty and difficulty of the task.

In his own words, Kepler wanted to "provide a philosophy or physics of celestial phenomena in place of the theology or metaphysics of Aristotle."[14] Kepler's contemporaries generally regarded his intention of putting laws of physics into astronomy as a new and probably pointless idea. Even Michael Mästlin, Kepler's own beloved teacher, who had introduced Kepler to the Copernican theory, wrote him on October 1, 1616:

> Concerning the motion of the moon you write you have traced all the inequalities to physical causes; I do not quite understand this. I think rather that here one should leave physical causes out of account, and should explain astronomical matters only according to astronomical method with the aid of astronomical, not physical, causes and hypotheses. That is, the calculation demands astronomical bases in the field of geometry and arithmetic. . . .

The difference between Kepler's conception of the "physical" problems of astronomy and the methodology of his contemporaries reveals itself clearly in the juxtaposition of representative letters by the two greatest astronomers of the time—Tycho Brahe and Kepler himself. Tycho, writing to Kepler on December 9, 1599, repeats the preoccupation of two millennia of astronomical speculations:

> I do not deny that the celestial motions achieve a certain symmetry [through the Copernican hypothesis], and that there are reasons why the planets carry through their revolutions around this or that center at different distances from the earth or the sun. However, the harmony or regularity of the scheme is to be discovered only a posteriori. . . . And even if it should appear to some puzzled and rash fellow that the superposed circular movements on the heavens yield sometimes angular or other figures, mostly elongated ones, then it happens accidentally, and reason recoils in horror from this assumption. For one must compose the revolutions of celestial objects definitely from circular motions; otherwise they could not come back on the same path eternally in equal manner, and an eternal duration would be impossible, not to mention that the orbits would be less simple, and irregular, and unsuitable for scientific treatment.

This manifesto of ancient astronomy might indeed have been subscribed to by Pythagoras, Plato, Aristotle, and Copernicus himself. Against it, Kepler maintains a new stand. Writing to D. Fabricius on August 1, 1607, he sounds the great new *leitmotif* of astronomy: *"The difference consists only in this, that you use circles, I use bodily forces."* And in the same letter, he defends his use of the ellipse in place of the superposition of circles to represent the orbit of Mars:

When you say it is not to be doubted that all motions occur on a perfect circle, then this is false for the composite, i.e., the real motions. According to Copernicus, as explained, they occur on an orbit distended at the sides, whereas according to Ptolemy and Brahe on spirals. But if you speak of components of motion, then you speak of something existing in thought; i.e., something that is not there in reality. For nothing courses on the heavens except the planetary bodies themselves—no orbs, no epicycles. . . .

This straightforward and modern-sounding statement implies that behind the word "real" stands "mechanical," that for Kepler the real world is the world of objects and of their mechanical interactions in the sense which Newton used; e.g., in the preface to the *Principia*:

Then from these [gravitational] forces, by other propositions which are also mathematical, I deduce the motions of the planets, the comets, the moon, and the sea. I wish we could derive the rest of the phenomena of nature by the same kind of reasoning from mechanical principles. . . .[15]

Thus we are tempted to see Kepler as a natural philosopher of the mechanistic-type later identified with the Newtonian disciples. But this is deceptive. Particularly after the failure of the program of the **Astronomia Nova,** another aspect of Kepler asserted itself. Though he does not appear to have been conscious of it, he never resolved finally whether the criteria of reality are to be sought on the *physical* or the *metaphysical* level. The words "real" or "physical" themselves, as used by Kepler, carry two interpenetrating complexes of meaning. Thus on receiving Mästlin's letter of October 1, 1616, Kepler jots down in the margin his own definition of "physical":

I call my hypotheses physical for two reasons. . . . My aim is to assume only those things of which I do not doubt they are real and consequently physical, where one must refer to the nature of the heavens, not the elements. When I dismiss the perfect eccentric and the epicycle, I do so because they are purely geometrical assumptions, for which a corresponding body in the heavens does not exist. The second reason for my calling my hypotheses physical is this . . . I prove that the irregularity of the motion [of planets] corresponds to the nature of the planetary sphere; i.e., is physical.

This throws the burden on the *nature* of heavens, the *nature* of bodies. How, then, is one to recognize whether a postulate or conception is in accord with the nature of things?

This is the main question, and to it Kepler has at the same time two very different answers, emerging, as it were, from the two parts of his soul. We may phrase one of the two answers as follows: *the physically real world, which defines the nature of things, is the world of phenomena explainable by mechanical principles.* This can be called Kepler's first criterion of reality, and assumes the possibility of formulating a sweeping and consistent dynamics which Kepler only sensed but which was not to be given until Newton's *Principia*. Kepler's other answer, to which he keeps returning again and again as he finds himself rebuffed by the deficiencies of his dynamics, and which we shall now examine in detail, is this: *the physically real world is the world of mathematically expressed harmonies which man can discover in the chaos of events.*

Kepler's Second Criterion of Reality: The Mathematical Harmonies of Nature

Kepler's failure to construct a *Physica Coelestis* did not damage his conception of the astronomical world. This would be strange indeed in a man of his stamp if he did not have a ready alternative to the mechanistic point of view. Only rarely does he seem to have been really uncomfortable about the poor success of the latter, as when he is forced to speculate how a soul or an inherent intelligence would help to keep a planet on its path. Or again, when the period of rotation of the sun which Kepler had postulated in his physical model proved to be very different from the actual rotation as first observed through the motion of sunspots, Kepler was characteristically not unduly disturbed. The truth is that despite his protestations, Kepler was not as committed to mechanical explanations of celestial phenomena as was, say, Newton. He had another route open to him.

His other criterion, his second answer to the problem of physical reality, stemmed from the same source as his original interest in astronomy and his fascination with a universe describable in mathematical terms, namely from a frequently acknowledged metaphysics rooted in Plato and neo-Platonists such as Proclus Diadochus. It is the criterion of *harmonious regularity in the descriptive laws of science.* One must be careful not to dismiss it either as just a reappearance of an old doctrine or as an aesthetic requirement which is still recognized in modern scientific work; Kepler's conception of what is "harmonious" was far more sweeping and important than either.

A concrete example is again afforded by the Second Law, the "Law of Equal Areas." To Tycho, Copernicus, and the great Greek astronomers, the harmonious regularity of planetary behavior was to be found in the uniform motion in component circles. But Kepler recognized the orbits—after a long struggle—as ellipsi on which planets move in a nonuniform manner. The figure is lopsided. The speed varies from point to point. And yet, nestled within this double complexity is hidden a harmonious regularity which transports its ecstatic discoverer—namely, the fact that a constant area is swept out in equal intervals by a line from the focus of the ellipse, where the sun is, to the planet on the ellipse. For Kepler, the law is harmonious in three separate senses.

First, *it is in accord with experience.* Whereas Kepler, despite long and hard labors, had been unable to fit Tycho's accurate observations on the motion of Mars into a classical scheme of superposed circles, the postulate of an elliptical path fitted the observations at once. Kepler's dictum was: "harmonies must accommodate experience."[16] How difficult it must have been for Kepler, a Pythagorean to the marrow of his bones, to forsake circles for ellipsi! For a mature scientist to find in his own work the need for abandoning his cherished and ingrained preconceptions, the very basis of his previous scientific work, in order to fulfill the dictates of quantitative experience—this was perhaps one of the great sacrificial acts of modern science, equivalent in recent scientific history to the agony of Max Planck. Kepler clearly drew the strength for this act from the belief that it would help him to gain an even deeper insight into the harmony of the world.

The second reason for regarding the law as harmonious is its reference to, or discovery of, a *constancy,* although no longer a constancy simply of angular velocity but of areal velocity. The typical law of ancient physical science had been Archimedes' law of the lever: a relation of direct observables in static configuration. Even the world systems of Copernicus and of Kepler's **Mysterium Cosmographicum** still had lent themselves to visualization in terms of a set of fixed concentric spheres. And we recall that Galileo never made use of Kepler's ellipsi, but remained to the end a true follower of Copernicus who had said "the mind shudders" at the supposition of noncircular nonuniform celestial motion, and "it would be unworthy to suppose such a thing in a Creation constituted in the best possible way."

With Kepler's First Law and the postulation of elliptical orbits, the old simplicity was destroyed. The Second and Third Laws established the physical law of constancy as an ordering principle in a changing situation. Like the concepts of momentum and caloric in later laws of constancy, areal velocity itself is a concept far removed from the immediate observables. It was therefore a bold step to search for harmonies beyond both perception and preconception.

Thirdly, the law is harmonious also in a grandiose sense: the fixed point of reference in the Law of Equal Areas, the "center" of planetary motion, is the center of the *sun itself,* whereas even in the Copernican scheme the sun was a little off the center of planetary orbits. With this discovery Kepler makes the planetary system at last truly heliocentric, and thereby satisfies his instinctive and sound demand for some material object as the "center" to which ultimately the physical effects that keep the system in orderly motion must be traced.

A Heliocentric and Theocentric Universe

For Kepler, the last of these three points is particularly exciting. The sun at its fixed and commanding position at the center of the planetary system matches the picture which always rises behind Kepler's tables of tedious data—the picture of a centripetal universe, directed toward and guided by the *sun* in its manifold roles: as the *mathematical* center in the description of celestial motions; as the central *physical* agency for assuring continued motion; and above all as the *metaphysical* center, the temple of the Deity. The three roles are in fact inseparable. For granting the special simplicity achieved in the description of planetary motions in the heliocentric system, as even Tycho was willing to grant, and assuming also that each planet must experience a force to drag it along its own constant and eternal orbit, as Kepler no less than the Scholastics thought to be the case, then it follows that the common need is supplied from what is common to all orbits; i.e., their common center, and this source of eternal constancy itself must be constant and eternal. Those, however, are precisely the unique attributes of the Deity.

Using his characteristic method of reasoning on the basis of archetypes, Kepler piles further consequences and analogies on this argument. The most famous is the comparison of the world-sphere with the Trinity: the sun, being at the center of the sphere and thereby antecedent to its two other attributes, surface and volume, is compared to God the Father. With variations the analogy occurs many times throughout Kepler's writings, including many of his letters. The image haunts him from the very beginning (e.g., Chapter 2, **Mysterium Cosmographicum**) and to the very end. Clearly, it is not sufficient to dismiss it with the usual phrase "sunworship."[17] At the very least, one would have to allow that the exuberant Kepler is a worshipper of the whole solar system in all its parts.

The power of the sun-image can be traced to the acknowledged influence on Kepler by neo-Platonists such as Proclus (fifth century) and Witelo (thirteenth century). At the time it was current neo-Platonic doctrine to identify light with "the source of all existence" and to hold that "space and light are one."[18] Indeed, one of the main preoccupations of the sixteenth-century neo-Platonists had been, to use a modern term, the transformation properties of space, light, and soul. Kepler's discovery of a truly heliocentric system is not only in perfect accord with the conception of the sun as a ruling entity, but allows him, for the first time, to focus attention on the sun's position through argument from physics.

In the medieval period the "place" for God, both in Aristotelian and in neo-Platonic astronomical metaphysics, had commonly been either beyond the last celestial sphere or else all of space; for only those alternatives provided for the Deity a "place" from which all celestial motions were equivalent. But Kepler can adopt a third possibility: in a truly heliocentric system God can be brought back into the solar system itself, so to speak, enthroned at the fixed and common reference object which coincides with the source of light and with the origin of the physical forces holding the system together. In the *De Revolutionibus* Copernicus had glimpsed part of this image when he wrote, after describing the planetary arrangement:

> In the midst of all, the sun reposes, unmoving. Who, indeed, in this most beautiful temple would place the light-giver in any other part than that whence it can illumine all other parts.

But Copernicus and Kepler were quite aware that the Copernican sun was not quite "in the midst of all"; hence Kepler's delight when, as one of his earliest discoveries, he found that orbital planes of all planets intersect at the sun.

The threefold implication of the heliocentric image as mathematical, physical, and metaphysical center helps to explain the spell it casts on Kepler. As Wolfgang Pauli has pointed out in a highly interesting discussion of Kepler's work as a case study in "the origin and development of scientific concepts and theories," here lies the motivating clue: "It is because he sees the sun and planets against the background of this fundamental image [*archetypische Bild*] that he believes in the heliocentric system with religious fervor"; it is this belief "which causes him to search for the true laws concerning the proportion in planetary motion. . . ."[19]

To make the point succinctly, we may say that in its final version *Kepler's physics of the heavens is heliocentric in its kinematics, but theocentric in its dynamics,* where harmonies based in part on the properties of the Deity serve to supplement physical laws based on the concept of specific quantitative forces. This brand of physics is most prominent in Kepler's last great work, the **Harmonice Mundi** (1619). There the so-called Third Law of planetary motion is announced without any attempt to deduce it from mechanical principles, whereas in the **Astronomia Nova** magnetic forces had driven—no, obsessed—the planets. As in his earliest work, he shows that the phenomena of nature exhibit underlying mathematical harmonies. Having not quite found the mechanical gears of the world machine, he can at least give its equations of motion.

The Source of Kepler's Harmonies

Unable to identify Kepler's work in astronomy with physical science in the modern sense, many have been tempted to place him on the other side of the imaginary dividing line between classical and modern science. Is it, after all, such a large step from the harmonies which the ancients found in circular motion and rational numbers to the harmonies which Kepler found in elliptical motions and exponential proportions? Is it not merely a generalization of an established point of view? Both answers are in the negative. For the ancients and for most of Kepler's contemporaries, the hand of the Deity was revealed in nature through laws which, if not qualitative, were harmonious in an essentially self-evident way; the axiomatic simplicity of circles and spheres and integers itself proved their deistic connection. But Kepler's harmonies reside in the very fact that the relations *are quantitative,* not in some specific simple *form* of the quantitative relations.

It is exactly this shift which we can now recognize as one point of breakthrough toward the later, modern conception of mathematical law in science. Where in classical thought the quantitative actions of nature were limited by a few necessities, the new attitude, whatever its metaphysical motivation, opens the imagination to an infinity of possibilities. As a direct consequence, where in classical thought the quantitative results of experience were used largely to fill out a specific pattern by a priori necessity, the new attitude permits the results of experience to reveal in themselves whatever pattern nature has in fact chosen from the infinite set of possibilities. Thus the seed is planted for the general view of most modern scientists, who find the world harmonious in a vague aesthetic sense because the mind can find, inherent in the chaos of events, order framed in mathematical laws—of whatever form they may be. As has been aptly said about Kepler's work:

> Harmony resides no longer in numbers which can be gained from arithmetic without observation. Harmony is also no longer the property of the circle in higher measure than the ellipse. Harmony is present when a multitude of phenomena is regulated by the unity of a mathematical law which expresses a cosmic idea.[20]

Perhaps it was inevitable in the progress of modern science that the harmony of mathematical law should now be sought in aesthetics rather than in metaphysics. But Kepler himself would have been the last to propose or accept such a generalization. The ground on which he postulated that harmonies reside in the quantitative properties of nature lies in the same metaphysics which helped him over the failure of his physical dynamics of the solar system. Indeed, the source is as old as natural philosophy itself: *the association of quantity per se with Deity.* Moreover, as we can now show, Kepler held that man's ability to discover harmonies, and therefore reality, in the chaos of events is due to a direct connection between ultimate reality; namely, God, and the mind of man.

In an early letter, Kepler opens to our view this mainspring of his life's work:

> May God make it come to pass that my delightful speculation [the **Mysterium Cosmographicum**] have everywhere among reasonable men fully the effect which I strove to obtain in the publication; namely, that the belief in the creation of the world be fortified through this external support, that thought of the creator be recognized in its nature, and that His inexhaustible wisdom shine forth daily more brightly. Then man will at last measure the power of his mind on the true scale, and will realize that *God, who founded everything in the world according to the norm of quantity, also has endowed man with a mind which can comprehend these norms.* For as the eye for color, the ear for musical sounds, so is the mind of man created for the perception not of any arbitrary entities, but rather of quantities; the mind comprehends a thing the more correctly the closer the thing approaches toward pure quantity as its origin.[21]

On a superficial level, one may read this as another repetition of the old Platonic principle [*hò theos aei geōmetei*] and of course Kepler does believe in "the creator, the true first cause of geometry, who, as Plato says, always geometrizes."[22] Kepler is indeed a Platonist, and even one who is related at the same time to both neo-Platonic traditions—which one might perhaps better identify as the neo-Platonic and the neo-Pythagorean—that of the mathematical physicists like Galileo and that of the mathematical mysticism of the Florentine Academy. But Kepler's God has done more than build the world on a mathematical model; he also specifically created man with a mind which "carries in it concepts built on the category of quantity," *in order that man may directly communicate with the Deity:*

> Those laws [which govern the material world] lie within the power of understanding of the human mind; God wanted us to perceive them when he created us in His image in order that we may take part in His own thoughts. . . . Our knowledge [of numbers and quantities] is of the same kind as God's, at least insofar as we can understand something of it in this mortal life.[23]

The procedure by which one apprehends harmonies is described quite explicitly in Book 4, Chapter 1, of **Harmonice Mundi.** There are two kinds of harmonies; namely, those in sense phenomena, as in music, and in "pure" harmonies such as are "constructed of mathematical concepts." The feeling of harmony arises when there occurs a matching of the perceived order with the corresponding innate archetype [*archetypus, Urbild*]. The archetype itself is part of the mind of God and was impressed on the human soul by the Deity when He created man in His image. The kinship with Plato's doctrine of ideal forms is clear. But whereas the latter, in the usual interpretation, are to be sought outside the human soul, Kepler's archetypes are within the soul. As he summarizes at the end of the discussion, the soul carries "not an image of the true pattern [*paradigma*], but the true pattern itself. . . . Thus finally the harmony itself becomes entirely soul, nay even God."[24]

This, then, is the final justification of Kepler's search for mathematical harmonies. The investigation of nature becomes an investigation into the thought of God, Whom we can apprehend through the language of mathematics. *Mundus est imago Dei corporea,* just as, on the other hand, *animus est imago Dei incorporea.* In the end, Kepler's unifying principle for the world of phenomena is not merely the concept of mechanical forces, but God, expressing Himself in mathematical laws.

Kepler's Two Deities

A final brief word may be in order concerning the psychological orientation of Kepler. Science, it must be remembered, was not Kepler's original destination. He was first a student of philosophy and theology at the University of Tübingen; only a few months before reaching the goal of church position, he suddenly—and reluctantly—found himself transferred by the University authorities to a teaching position in mathematics and astronomy at Graz. A year later, while already working on the **Mysterium Cosmographicum,** Kepler wrote: "I wanted to become a theologian; for a long time I was restless: Now, however, observe how through my effort God is being celebrated in astronomy."[25] And more than a few times in his later writings he referred to astronomers as priests of the Deity in the book of nature.

From his earliest writing to his last, Kepler maintained the direction and intensity of his religio-philosophical interest. His whole life was one of uncompromising piety; he was incessantly struggling to uphold his strong and often nonconformist convictions in religion as in science. Caught in the turmoil of the Counter-Reformation and the beginning of the Thirty Years' War, in the face of bitter difficulties and hardships, he never compromised on issues of belief. Expelled from communion in the Lutheran Church for his unyielding individualism in religious matters, expelled from home and position at Graz for refusing to embrace Roman Catholicism, he could truly be believed when he wrote, "I take religion seriously, I do not play with it,"[26] or "In all science there is nothing which could prevent me from holding an opinion, nothing which could deter me from acknowledging openly an opinion of mine, except solely the authority of the Holy Bible, which is being twisted badly by many."[27]

But as his work shows us again and again, Kepler's soul bears a dual image on this subject too. For next to the Lutheran God, revealed to him directly in the words of the Bible, there stands the Pythagorean God, embodied in the immediacy of observable nature and in the mathematical harmonies of the solar system whose design Kepler himself had traced—a God "whom in the contemplation of the universe I can grasp, as it were, with my very hands."[28]

The expression is wonderfully apt: so intense was Kepler's vision that the abstract and concrete merged. Here we find the key to the enigma of Kepler, the explanation for the apparent complexity and disorder in his writings and commitments. In one brilliant image, Kepler saw the three basic themes or cosmological models superposed: *the universe as physical machine, the universe as mathematical harmony, and the universe as central theological order.* And this was the setting in which harmonies were interchangeable with forces, in which a theocentric conception of the universe led to specific results of crucial importance for the rise of modern physics.

Notes

[1] Books 4 and 5 of the *Epitome of Copernican Astronomy*, and Book 5 of the *Harmonies of the World*, in *Great Books of the Western World* (Chicago: Encyclopedia Britannica, 1952), Volume 16.

[2] The definitive biography is by the great Kepler scholar Max Caspar, *Johannes Kepler*, Stuttgart: W. Kohlhammer, 1950; the English translation is *Kepler*, trans. and ed. C. Doris Hellman, New York: Abelard-Schuman, 1959. Some useful short essays are in *Johann Kepler 1571-1630* (A series of papers prepared under the auspices of the History of Science Society in collaboration with the American Association for the Advancement of Science), Baltimore: Williams & Wilkins Co., 1931. [Since this article was written, a number of useful publications on Kepler have appeared—Ed.]

[3] But Newton's *Opticks*, particularly in the later portions, is rather reminiscent of Kepler's style. In Book II, Part IV, Observation 5, there is, for example, an attempt to associate the parts of the light spectrum with the "differences of the lengths of a monochord which sounds the tones in an eight."

[4] Letter to David Fabricius, October 11, 1605.

[5] Letter to Herwart von Hohenburg, March 26, 1598, i.e., seven years before Stevinus implied the absurdity of perpetual motion in the *Hypomnemata Mathematica* (Leyden, 1605). Some of Kepler's most important letters are collected in Max Caspar and Walther von Dyck, *Johannes Kepler in seinen Briefen*, Munich and Berlin: R. Oldenbourg, 1930. A more complete collection in the original languages is to be found in Vols. 13-15 of the modern edition of Kepler's collected works, *Jo-*

hannes Keplers gesammelte Werke, ed. von Dyck and Caspar, Munich: C. H. Beck, 1937 and later. In the past, these letters appear to have received insufficient attention in the study of Kepler's work and position. (The present English translations of all quotations from them are the writer's.) Excerpts from some letters were also translated in Carola Baumgardt, *Johannes Kepler*, New York: Philosophical Library, 1951.

[6] Ernst Goldbeck, *Abhandlungen zur Philosophie und ihrer Geschichte, Keplers Lehre von der Gravitation* (Halle: Max Niemeyer, 1896), Volume VI—a useful monograph demonstrating Kepler's role as a herald of mechanical astronomy. The reference is to *De Revolutionibus*, first edition, p. 3. [The main point, which it would be foolhardy to challenge, is that in the description of phenomena Copernicus still on occasion treated the earth differently from other planets.]

[7] In Kepler's Preface to his *Dioptrice* (1611) he calls his early *Mysterium Cosmographicum* "a sort of combination of astronomy and Euclid's Geometry," and describes the main features as follows: "I took the dimensions of the planetary orbits according to the astronomy of Copernicus, who makes the sun immobile in the center, and the earth movable both round the sun and upon its own axis; and I showed that the differences of their orbits corresponded to the five regular Pythagorean figures, which had been already distributed by their author among the elements of the world, though the attempt was admirable rather than happy or legitimate. . . ." The scheme of the five circumscribed regular bodies originally represented to Kepler the *cause* of the observed number (and orbits) of the planets: *"Habes rationem numeri planetarium."*

[8] Johannes Kepler, *Die Zusammenklänge der Welten*, Otto J. Bryk, trans. and ed. (Jena: Diederichs, 1918), p. xxiii.

[9] Letter to Herwart von Hohenburg, February 10, 1605. At about the same time he writes in a similar vein to Christian Severin Longomontanus concerning the relation of astronomy and physics: "I believe that both sciences are so closely interlinked that the one cannot attain completion without the other."

[10] Previously, Kepler discussed the attraction of the moon in a letter to Herwart, January 2, 1607. The relative motion of two isolated objects and the concept of inertia are treated in a letter to D. Fabricius, October 11, 1605. On the last subject see Alexandre Koyré, *Galileo and the Scientific Revolution of the Seventeenth Century, The Philosophical Review*, 52, No. 4: 344-345, 1943.

[11] Not only the postulates but also some of the details of their use in the argument were erroneous. For a short discussion of this concrete illustration of Kepler's

use of physics in astronomy, see John L. E. Dreyer, *History of the Planetary System from Thales to Kepler* (New York: Dover Publications, 1953), second edition, pp. 387-399. A longer discussion is in Max Caspar, *Johannes Kepler, neue Astronomie* (Munich and Berlin: R Oldenbourg, 1929), pp. 3*-66*.

[12] Giorgio de Santillana, ed., *Dialogue on the Great World Systems* (Chicago: University of Chicago Press, 1953), p. 469. However, an oblique compliment to Kepler's Third Law may be intended in a passage on p. 286.

[13] Florian Cajori, ed., *Newton's Principia: Motte's Translation Revised* (Berkeley: University of California Press, 1946), pp. 394-395. In Book III, Newton remarks concerning the fact that the Third Law applies to the moons of Jupiter: "This we know from astronomical observations." At last, on page 404, Kepler is credited with having "first observed" that the 3/2th power law applies to the "five primary planets" and the earth. Newton's real debt to Kepler was best summarized in his own letter to Halley, July 14, 1686: "But for the duplicate proportion [the inverse-square law of gravitation] I can affirm that I gathered it from Kepler's theorem about twenty years ago."

[14] Letter to Johann Brengger, October 4, 1607. This picture of a man struggling to emerge from the largely Aristotelian tradition is perhaps as significant as the usual one of Kepler as Copernican in a Ptolemaic world. Nor was Kepler's opposition, strictly speaking, Ptolemaic any longer. For this we have Kepler's own opinion (*Harmonice Mundi*, Book 3): "First of all, readers should take it for granted that among astronomers it is nowadays agreed that all planets circulate around the sun . . . ," meaning of course the system not of Copernicus but of Tycho Brahe, in which the earth was fixed and the moving sun served as center of motion for the other planets.

[15] Cajori, *op. cit.,* p. xviii.

[16] Quoted in Kepler, *Weltharmonik*, ed. Max Caspar (Munich and Berlin: R. Oldenbourg, 1939), p. 55*.

[17] E.g., Edwin Arthur Burtt, *The Metaphysical Foundations of Modern Science* (London: Routledge & Kegan Paul, 1924 and 1932), p. 47 ff.

[18] For a recent analysis of neo-Platonic doctrine, which regrettably omits a detailed study of Kepler, see Max Jammer, *Concepts of Space* (Cambridge: Harvard University Press, 1954), p. 37 ff. Neo-Platonism in relation to Kepler is discussed by Thomas S. Kuhn, *The Copernican Revolution*, Cambridge: Harvard University Press, 1957.

[19] Wolfgang Pauli, *Der Einfluss archetypischer Vorstellungen auf die Bildung naturwissenschaftlicher The-* *orien bei Kepler*, in *Naturerklärung und Psyche* (Zurich: Rascher Verlag, 1952), p. 129.

An English translation of Jung and Pauli is *The Interpretation of Nature and the Psyche*, trans. R. F. C. Hull and Priscilla Silz, New York: Pantheon Books, 1955.

[20] Hedwig Zaiser, *Kepler als Philosoph* (Stuttgart: E. Suhrkamp, 1932), p. 47.

[21] Letter to Mästlin, April 19, 1597. (Italics supplied.) The "numerological" component of modern physical theory is in fact a respectable offspring from this respectable antecedent. For example, see Niels Bohr, *Atomic Theory and the Description of Nature* (New York: Macmillan Co., 1934), pp. 103-104: "This interpretation of the atomic number [as the number of orbital electrons] may be said to signify an important step toward the solution of one of the boldest dreams of natural science, namely, to build up an understanding of the regularities of nature upon the consideration of pure number."

[22] *Harmonice Mundi*, Book 3.

[23] Letter to Herwart, April 9/10, 1599. Galileo later expressed the same principle: "That the Pythagoreans had the science of numbers in high esteem, and that Plato himself admired human understanding and thought that it partook of divinity, in that it understood the nature of numbers, I know very well, nor should I be far from being of the same opinion." de Santillana, *op. cit.*, p. 14. Descartes's remark, "You can substitute the mathematical order of nature for 'God' whenever I use the latter term" stems from the same source.

[24] For a discussion of Kepler's mathematical epistemology and its relation to neo-Platonism, see Max Steck, *Über das Wesen des Mathematischen und die mathematische Erkenntnis bei Kepler, Die Gestalt* (Halle: Max Niemeyer, 1941), Volume V. The useful material is partly buried under nationalistic oratory. Another interesting source is Andreas Speiser, *Mathematische Denkweise*, Basel: Birkhäuser, 1945.

[25] Letter to Mästlin, October 3, 1595.

[26] Letter to Herwart, December 16, 1598.

[27] Letter to Herwart, March 28, 1605. If one wonders how Kepler resolved the topical conflict concerning the authority of the scriptures *versus* the authority of scientific results, the same letter contains the answer: "I hold that we must look into the intentions of the men who were inspired by the Divine Spirit. Except in the first chapter of Genesis concerning the supernatural origin of all things, they never intended to inform men concerning natural things." This view, later asso-

ciated with Galileo, is further developed in Kepler's eloquent introduction to the *Astronomia Nova*. The relevant excerpts were first translated by Thomas Salusbury, *Mathematical Collections* (London: 1661), Part I, pp. 461-467.

[28] Letter to Baron Strahlendorf, October 23, 1613.

Max Caspar (essay date 1959)

SOURCE: *Kepler,* translated and edited by C. Doris Hellman, Abelard-Schuman, 1959, pp. 376-88.

[*Below, Caspar argues that religious zeal and a desire to explore the universe as a manifestation of God's plan were the prime motivations for Kepler's scientific ventures.*]

2. Kepler's View of the World and His Doctrine of Knowledge

Now what, more exactly, was it which invested Kepler with such great rapture and let him hope for such a great moral effect among people? It was, as we have seen throughout this biography, the passionate experience of order which he encountered in the universe, an experience which even in his youth had seized him most vehemently and which influenced him throughout his whole life so that, as his son-in-law Bartsch said after his death, his devotion to the contemplation of heavenly things was almost like a miracle. *Forma mundi,* the shape of the world, formed the great theme of his life's work. In it the idea, form, does not have the pale meaning of today's usage. It concerns the principles of order and configuration, that which makes the chaotic material into a cosmos, and also the epitome of the idea of the lovely, made real in the world. Copernicus, in the dedication of his work to Pope Paul III, had already advanced, as that which especially strengthened him in his conviction of the truth of his world picture and consequently as the goal of his investigation, the "form of the world and the symmetry of its parts" resulting from his concept. And Rheticus, who by talking with him had best come to know the thinking of the Frauenburg Magister, had uttered the thought that God had so arranged the world that a heavenly harmony in which each planet would have a particular place would be perfected by the six movable spheres. This thought had ignited in Kepler's head a half century after it had been uttered. It fashioned his life's program. What Copernicus had expressed only in one single sentence, Kepler wanted to develop unto the last conclusion and exhibit—the *forma mundi* as harmony. His enthusiasm had blazed up at this idea. It was to form the subject of his announcement to the world.

What supported and gave wings to Kepler in the execution of his program was a refreshing optimism about cognition. "Man, stretch thy reason hither, so that thou mayest comprehend these things"; that was the call which rang out for him from the material world. While he accepted this call with open ear, with the complete and unreserved readiness of a young mind, he believed in the reality of the things outside us and in the possibility of being able to comprehend them in their essence, order and meaning. What the eye brought him was that which he saw, and was in reality as he saw it; and the mind repeated the thoughts which God had materialized in His Creation. He did not start with doubt, as another[1] soon did, but with an unquestioned faith in *ratio*. He did not limit himself to the framework of immanent thought, but became intoxicated with the contemplation of a transcendental truth. He had not yet fallen into the abyss of relativity, but was deeply convinced that there is an absolute truth. Admittedly our mind never can completely grasp this truth, but it is the noble task of scientific and philosophical research to draw nearer to it. Thus to our searcher after truth that call signifies a moral obligation imposed on mankind in the observation of nature giving research its direction and goal.

In his youth Kepler had expressed the basic thoughts of his outlook on the world in two memorable sentences: "Mundus est imago Dei corporea" and "Animus est imago Dei incorporea." "The world is the corporeal image of God" and "The soul is the incorporeal image of God." God, World, Human—prototype, copy, likeness: the circle of his thoughts is shut in this trinity. These ideas hold together and fasten tightly everything which presents itself to him, when he looks inward and reflects about his own soul or glances outward and inspects the world of phenomena or when, in veneration, he speculates on the original cause of all existence, out of which everything has come. Prototype, copy, image: these ideas give to his picture of the world that completeness and inspiration in which he found his happiness, his satisfaction, his peace and his delight.

"The world is the corporeal image of God." How can the corporeal be a copy of the absolute soul? According to Kepler this contradiction is reconciled by the idea of quantity which has its origin in the divine being. Quantities can be compared with each other; they form relationships. Now God, by certain selection in creating the world has, so to speak, taken such relationships out of Himself; He has made order out of chaos, given form to matter, in accordance with the word of the Bible that everything is regulated by number, size and weight. So to Kepler's contemplating eye the cosmos seems constructed like an ancient temple, a pyramid, a gothic cathedral, in the building of which the architect measured off the size according to aesthetic norms. And just as God himself proceeded in this work of creation, so he endowed everything to which he gave life with a power of creation which moves and works by the same laws. "As God the Creator played / so He also taught nature, as His image, to play / the very game / which He had played before her."[2]

Our mathematical mystic goes into still further detail in his view of the world as reflecting the divine image. The sphere is the most excellent of all geometrical images, the bearers of quantities. Therefore the sphere had to provide the prototype of the universe. The spherical shape of the real world was constructed for Kepler just as, indeed, our sensual-intellectual nature is so created in order that, in contemplating the whole, the rays of sight reach out from the eye equally in all directions into space. Kepler has the sphere formed so that an equal flowing out (*effluxus*) takes place in all directions from one point. Therefore, aroused by similar speculations in the works of Nicholas of Cusa and others, he sees in it a symbolic copy of the Holy Trinity, a thought which he expresses in various ways in many places in his works and which even furnishes him with an argument for the correctness of the Copernican doctrine. The center point denotes God the Father, the surface God the Son, the space between, the Holy Ghost. From the center point of the sphere, as the origin, the surface emerges by means of radiation, whereby the surrounding equal intervening space is produced of its own accord. "The little dot in the middle gives birth to and forms the circumference, as soon as the point moves around in circles." The mere point would be invisible without spherical expansion; it can only make itself evident in the shape of the outflowing surface of the sphere. All three—centerpoint, surface, intervening space—stand in most intimate relationship, in loveliest accord, in the best proportioned ratio to each other. Together they form a unity so that not once can one of them be thought of as missing without the whole being annihilated. So the secret, unfathomable existence of the divine Trinity mirrors itself for Kepler in the visible world. The world is a sphere, the sphere a picture of the Holy Trinity; consequently the world is the corporeal image of God. This is not the ultimate thought on whose account he embraced the universe with such great fervor. For he loves the world of phenomena, because it is God's and wears God's features. God, playing, created in the sphere a picture of His Trinity, so worthy of adoration (*lusit imaginem*). And when Kepler sees children amusing themselves with soap bubbles he thinks of them as playing the role of the Creator because they blow up the drops into a sphere. In this he is only disturbed by the fact that a droplet continues to hang beneath the soap bubble instead of marking the center.

"The soul is the incorporeal image of God." This thought, confirmed by the Bible, which says that God created man in His own image, had been developed by Christian philosophers and theologians in profound speculations. Kepler took it up and embraced it with the complete accord of heart and soul. He expressed it in numerous places in his works in ever new words and established it as the foundation stone of his doctrine of cognition. Yet in doing so he follows different paths from those of the theologians, such as Augustine, who in contemplating his own soul sought therein a mirror image of the triune God and found the similarity to God based on the trinity, memory, will and cognition. Kepler does not speak of the trinitarian nature of God, as he had done with the picture of the universe. His speculation circles about the ideas of quantity and harmony. Just as God had fashioned these ideas out of himself at the creation of the world, so he also communicated them to man as his image when he breathed life into him and caused his countenance to shine down upon him. It is the reflection of divinity which becomes known to us in the quantities, their relationships and connections, in the structure of geometric figures, in the laws to which these are subject. "God wanted to have us recognize these laws when He created us in His image, so that we should share in His own thoughts. For what remains in the minds of humans other than numbers and sizes? These alone do we grasp in the proper manner and, what is more, if piety permits one to say so, in doing so our knowledge is of the same kind as the divine, as far as we, at least in this mortal life, are able to comprehend something about these." These thoughts are completely expressed in the sentence: "Geometry is unique and eternal, a reflection from the mind of God. That mankind shares in it is because man is an image of God."

In the variety of quantities Kepler beholds "a wonderful and positively divine state." They express the divine and the human symbolically in the same manner. It is they which establish the structure of order in the visible world. It is the deepest desire of the human mind to comprehend this order, to agree with it, to become assimilated with it. "Even if an order should once be produced by chance, still the minds fly together there; therein lies their pleasure, their life." If an order appears anywhere, there always arises in the mind a great trust, a strong confidence. He even seeks the reason for this "in the deepest original cause of geometry." The part which he assigns to this science at the same time illustrates his interpretation of the existence of mathematical things. These have their foundation in the divine being himself, and man meets them in his mind by virtue of his being in the image of God. What from outside meets him by means of the senses merely arouses him to become clearly cognizant of that which is already contained in them and belongs to his nature. That there are only five regular solids, that the diagonal of a square is in irrational proportion to the side, that the seven-sided figure cannot be constructed with ruler and compass—these statements Kepler, anointed with Pythagorean oil, considers metaphysically given. Therefore he also rejects Aristotle most positively when the latter compares the soul with a *tabula rasa,* a blank slate, which is first written upon by sense experiences.

He follows Plato's doctrine of ideas and the views of Proclus, the Neo-Platonist, whom he highly esteems. "Geometry, being part of the divine mind from time immemorial, from before the origin of things, being God Himself, has supplied God with the models for the creation of the world and has been transferred to man together with the image of God. Geometry was not received inside through the eyes."[3] This conception also makes the close connection which Kepler establishes between mathematics and philosophy comprehensible. He is convinced "that the whole of philosophy arose out of mathematical things, exists therein mixed among them and so closely related that whoever proceeds without it in studies merely beats the air and fights with a shadow: nor may he in eternity be called a philosopher with honor."

So, for Kepler, understanding nature signifies nothing else than to think in accordance with the thoughts of God, who always pursues geometry. The fact that the world and man's mind are images of God in their manner, makes knowledge possible, a knowledge which not only is certain but also carries sense and value in itself.

The path he followed in his research as well as the ethos of his work is expressed by Kepler in the loveliest manner in a place in the *Epitome,* where he suddenly interrupts his scientific research and writes: "With a pure mind I pray that we may be able to speak about the secrets of His plans according to the gracious will of the omniscient Creator, with the consent and according to the bidding of His intellect. I consider it a right, yes a duty, to search in cautious manner for the numbers, sizes and weights, the norms for everything He has created. For He Himself has let man take part in the knowledge of these things and thus not in a small measure has set up His image in man. Since He recognized as very good this image which He made, He will so much more readily recognize our efforts with the light of this image also to push into the light of knowledge the utilization of the numbers, weights and sizes which He marked out at creation. For these secrets are not of the kind whose research should be forbidden; rather they are set before our eyes like a mirror so that by examining them we observe to some extent the goodness and wisdom of the Creator."

That Kepler here accounts to himself on the question of the admissibility of his questions of nature and thereby announces, as he also does elsewhere in various places, that he has questions which have not been permitted, is a fine thought. He knows that there is a limit between that which is accessible to our knowledge and that which is impenetrable, and that man must be prepared to accept this limit reverently. He is completely free of the sovereignty which seeks the measure of all things in mankind, and of the promethean stubbornness which, in reliance on its own knowledge and ability, challenges the Divinity.

First of all we broke down the mathematical-metaphysical side of Kepler's world of thought. That was necessary because, in the conventional expositions of his lifework, that part consistently is treated too briefly. In our expositions of his activity, however, we met in the discussion of his works an entirely different Kepler, the exact astronomer, the dispassionate mathematician, the tireless computor, the realistic physicist, the rigorous logician, the clear methodician, the experienced empiricist. We have come to know him as the discoverer of the planet laws and in doing so we followed him on the very tortuous path which he broke for himself through the denseness of his numbers until he reached the magnificent summit, rich in prospects. We recall his tireless effort in this, the mastery with which he handled the task, the ingenious strategy with which he laid his plans, the tactical skill with which he inserted the observations, and the unerring instinct for facts which excluded their ever being shrouded. And what incredible application, solicitude and patience did he spend in working out the tables until they reached the final point which he had set as his goal! We have evaluated his inestimable service to optics, which he could only attain by a strong scholarly (in the modern sense) combination of theory and practice. It was he who first successfully introduced physical contemplation of the heavenly motions into astronomy and thereby laid the foundation for celestial mechanics. He set entirely new tasks for mathematics and by his accomplishments in a significant manner paved the way for the infinitesimal calculus. Besides, in his chronological researches, by the critical examination and elaboration of extensive basic material he also proved himself a first rate philologist and historian.

The gap between his metaphysical speculations and his exact research shows the striking polarity in Kepler's intellectual giftedness. His innermost nature drives him to an aesthetic-artistic consideration of the universe, whose geometrical structure he wants to ascertain. Everywhere he looks for symmetry, for analogies, for a well-proportioned equalizing of the parts in accordance with a static order, in the contemplation of which he goes into the most extreme rapture. And yet it was he who established the dynamic explanation of the heavenly motions, who tracked the tensions between the sun and the planets and could not do enough in investigating the processes of motion. "The bodies would not be beautiful if they did not move," we hear him say. Motivated by metaphysical expectations he tried to interpret the meaning of the phenomena in all aspects, large and small. At every number which he established, at every connection which he ferreted out, the question always immediately flew in his head: why is that so? And still is there any scholar who would have followed up the given facts more diligently and more open-mindedly? However hard he was driven to encompass the whole, just so true and patient was he in inquiring into the parts. We see him now floating in the highest heights into which his faculty for enthusiasm carries him, now standing with both feet on the ground, indefatigably turning clod after clod. In contrast to his ever wakeful fantasy, which continually brought new ideas to him, was his strong ability to concentrate, which the solution of his difficult problems demanded. His exuberance hindered him no more than his rare nimbleness of mind from following a logical line of thought. The more one becomes absorbed in his main works, so much higher mounts one's admiration for the powerful logic disclosed in the planning and detailed carrying out. Yes, in all the bubbling delight in speculation, which inspired him, the mathematical-logical stamp of his thinking stood out so much the more conspicuously. He is equally familiar with deductive and inductive trains of thought. Even though he felt it his duty to explain the world by *a priori* principles, he was, nevertheless, the first who, making use of the inductive method, today self-evident to everyone, directed questions to nature and immediately applied this method with remarkable skill in the discovery of his two first planet laws.

Even if Kepler with his aesthetic world view was imprisoned by the Renaissance, still on the other hand his unusual genius opened up entirely new paths for scientific research. On the one hand he supplied his astounding intellectual capacity with special preference for morphological and teleological conceptions and deductions, but on the other hand he cleared the path for the causal explanation of nature. Alongside of the prototype, he helped the cause to obtain its right. He was suspended between an animistic and a mechanistic view of nature. The enthusiastic thinker, which he was, so easily talked and tunneled himself into an idea as to make his way to its root and to track down its last consequence. He penetrated deeply into the province of the psychic. He felt or divined psychic powers back of all visible and tangible things. For him the world is not an aggregate of dead bodies. Everywhere he finds life as an expression of a psychic principle; everywhere he suspects psychic influences. We know his view about the earth soul and its geometric instinct. In eloquent words he repeatedly expresses his belief in spontaneous generation; he lets the little souls of the plants be ignited at the earth soul. His astrology is supported entirely on conceptions from the domain of the psychic. And yet it was he who founded the mechanistic explanation of the heavenly motions. He disposed of the medieval concept which, referring to Aristotle, had the rotation of the planet spheres taken care of by spirit beings or angels and showed that in this there is in operation only a force similar to that which draws the stone down from above to the earth. It is very fascinating to follow in him the transition from the animistic to the mechanistic explanation of the models of the motions. How can a planet find its path around the sun when this is in no way indicated by marks? How far is it possible to explain the individual phenomena in the

planetary motions by a material compulsion (*necessitas materiae*)? On the other hand, to what extent is the acceptance of a psychic principle necessary for this? Those are questions which he investigates and decides with the greatest care. A later era has raised the completely mechanistic explanation of the models of nature to a principle and, with a remarkable shyness of everything which is called soul, required, in the name of science, the weeding out of every psychic power. Certainly, such a point of view would have been an abomination for Kepler. He would never have been able to conceive the universe, the animal, the human as machine. With all the dualism of his being, his view was more open, freer, deeper.

3. Kepler's Cosmography

Now, what is the appearance of the astronomical world picture which Kepler, following the various tendencies of his thinking, developed on the foundation of the Copernican conception? Indeed, at the beginning of Kepler's research stood Copernicus; he was an inspirer. Kepler made serving him his life's task. "I deem it my duty and task," so he explains at an early age, "to advocate outwardly also with all the powers of my intellect the Copernican theory, which I in my innermost have recognized as true and whose loveliness fills me with unbelievable rapture when I contemplate it."

When speaking of Copernicus' world picture it is necessary to guard against introducing conceptions and knowledge which only arose in the course of the development for which he laid the foundation. It is customary to think of the countless number of stars swimming in an infinite space.[4] Our sun moving in this swarm is a fixed star like others and our earth a diminutive companion of it so that, in the immense party of dancers of milliards of fire balls which unite into systems and systems of systems, it appears as a completely insignificant member of the universe. Such concepts were wholly foreign to the Frauenburg astronomer. He put the sun at rest in the absolute center of the world. If there is a center, there can be no infinite space. So he assumed the fixed stars as lights on a very large sphere. He had the earth with the five other planets circle the sun. Since this motion showed no displacement of the fixed stars, he had to assume that the diameter of the sphere of the fixed stars is so great that in comparison with it the diameter of the earth's orbit is of no account. He does not express himself about how the orbits of the planets will be formed. There is basis for the assumption that for each of them he assumed a solid sphere to which it is fastened. We know from our previous arguments that in his theoretical presentation of the planet orbits he saw his triumph in reducing them to superimposed similar circular motions. Kepler did not alter much in the over-all picture of this world concept. For him, too, the sun stands in the absolute center of the world. To be sure, he lets it rotate on an axis, but to assume a motion in space lies completely outside his range of conception. Correspondingly he expressly and decisively rejects the assumption of a real infinite space. Assuredly, he already knew that meanwhile, in bold speculation, Giordano Bruno had advanced the theory that the fixed stars are nothing else but suns, like ours, and distributed in infinite numbers in infinite space. Yet Kepler argued against these revolutionary theories with sharp words. He shuddered, so he says, at these concepts. He reproaches the Italian philosopher for misusing Copernicus' view and consequently all astronomy. Indeed, the thesis of Giordano Bruno, who understood nothing about astronomy and did not want to understand anything, did not grow in the soil of astronomical research but originated from theological speculations and a pantheistic interpretation of nature. The idea of an infinite space is not rooted in experience but in metaphysics. Indeed, several decades ago science again gave it up.

With the Greeks Kepler seeks the perfect in the moderate regulated finite. For him as for Copernicus the world is a real sphere. He assumes that the fixed stars, about the nature of which he does not express himself further, are distributed in a shell-like finite space, spherical inside and out. As a whole they form, according to his conception, a kind of wall or a vault and create the space in whose center stands the immovable sun which lights the whole space, the sun which is the heart of the world, the source of light. Thus, for him, the whole world is comparable to a great lantern or a concave mirror. On the inside of this ball lies the system of the six wandering stars. In composition and motion, this is exceedingly artistic. These planets or wandering stars—Mercury, Venus, Earth, Mars, Jupiter and Saturn—form the brilliant princely household of the queen, the sun. The measurements for the distances are furnished by the five regular solids which, after the sphere, are the most perfect and loveliest geometrical creations. These measurements are not entirely exact but in close approximation. Between these static sizes and the sizes of the motions there is a remarkable relationship governed by law: the squares of the periods of revolution are to each other as the cubes of the mean distances from the sun. And in relation to these distances, how great is the radius of the sphere of fixed stars? Since Kepler cannot ascertain it empirically, an analogy must help him. He fancies that his analogy fits extremely well if he assumes that the radius of the sphere of the fixed stars is to the distance from the sun of the outermost planet, Saturn, as this distance is to the radius of the sun's sphere. And how do the motions of the wandering stars take place? In the sun there is a moving force, which emits its rays as does light. The sun is the source of the motion. Since it rotates, it pulls the planets around with these rays of force. Since the effect of this force is so much the greater, the closer the planet is to the sun, the motion is rapid at perihelion, slow at aphelion. The radius vector describes equal areas in equal times. The circular form of the orbits is given up. The old axiom of similar shaped circular motion is annulled. By the operation of the solar power on the planet bodies, which are thought of as polarized, orbits arise. They have the form of ellipses with the sun in one focus. But the eccentricities of these ellipses are no more arbitrary and without rule than any other measures. No, in this fine construction the highly artistic formative hand of the Creator is shown in a very special way. Since the eccentricities determine the rates of the planets at aphelion and perihelion, they have been so measured by the Creator that between them appear the harmonic proportions which are to be presented by geometry and which are the foundation of music. So a divine sound fills the whole world. To be sure, sensual hearing is unable to perceive the wonderful harmony. But the spiritual ear perceives it, just as it is also the spiritual eye with which we see the loveliness of the sizes.

And the earth? Was it humiliated by being pushed out of the center of the world? By no means. "Our little hut" has retained a favored position between the planets. Two are inside, three outside its orbit. By its motion around the sun its inhabitants will be enabled to ascertain the size of the world. The unchanging inclination of the earth's axis takes care of the change of seasons and brings about an equitable distribution of the sunshine on the inhabitants of the various zones. By the earth's position midway between the other planets the spectacle, which her five sisters with their dance produce on the world stage for her, acquires a lovely variety. On this trip around the stationary sun, man can observe with understanding the wonder of the world in its diversity of phenomena. For everything is there because of man. That was the spectacle which stood before Kepler's eyes in his astronomical researches. His earnest endeavor was to paint this picture in all its details. The contemplation of this picture lifted him above all earthly misery and provided him peace, solace and happiness. Here there were no storms, no persecutions, no disputes, no wars. Here he found his never barred refuge, his home. He rejoiced because he knew himself to be inside of the sphere. For it is the image of God, of the Father, of the Son and of the Holy Ghost. And everything which happens in this sphere bears witness to the wisdom and kindness of the Creator. That gave the restless pilgrim on earth the feeling of blissful security. With curiosity he looked on the trip around the sun. Enraptured, he listened to the harmonies which resounded in his direction. This judgment flowed over him: everything is good which has been created here.

That was and is Johannes Kepler. For he continues to live among us through the work he created and the example he set us. As long as men reach for the stars in yearning and desire for knowledge, as long as they preserve the respect for spiritual and material greatness and their strength to draw themselves up before examples remains, his name will not perish. Besides, in the three hundred years since his death many have shown the highest admiration for him and extolled him in words full of appreciation and veneration. The loudest voices were raised abroad. Immediately after Kepler's death Horrox, the young English astronomer, enthusiastically called upon the poets to sing his praises and on the philosophers to make him known; for, so he says, "he who has Kepler, has everything." Bailly, the French astronomer and historian of astronomy in the second half of the eighteenth century, enrolls him among the greatest men who have lived on earth. Leibniz bows in appreciation before the greatness of the "incomparable man." Goethe, Hölderlin, Mörike considered themselves fortunate and exalted in their contact with the great genius. Since Kepler, science has built further on the foundation which he laid and has erected an amazing structure. It was Leibniz who used the same words about him which Kepler once had uttered about Copernicus: he did not know how rich he was. Certainly, with the progress of knowledge, some of Kepler's views have proved erroneous. His view of nature was conditioned by the time. But the ethos by which he performed his work has also changed and this is a pity. This change went so far that in a time which looked upon the task of science purely as the collection of facts all understanding for his aesthetic-metaphysical view of nature was lost and it was branded as "chimeric speculation." Laplace who pronounced this judgment even viewed it as "distressing for the human spirit" to have to see how ecstatically Kepler pursued the idea of his world harmony. The number of those who accepted the opinion of the great French astronomer is not small. Novalis, a great contemporary of that Frenchman, gave the right answer to all of them when he said: "To you I return, noble Kepler. Your noble mind created a spiritual moral universe. Instead of that, in our times it is considered wisdom to kill everything, to lower the high instead of raising the low and even to bend the mind of man under mechanistic laws." Novalis, too, has many followers. I hope the reader of this book will be among them.

Notes

[1] ED. NOTE. Doubtless, reference here is to Descartes (1596-1650).

[2] ED. NOTE. This is from section 126 of *Tertius Interveniens* and can be found in *Johannes Kepler Gesammelte Werke,* IV, 246, and is translated into English, p. 172, in *The Influence of Archetypal Ideas on the Scientific Theories of Kepler. . . .*

[3] ED. NOTE. *Harmonice Mundi,* Book IV, chapter I. . . .

[4] ED. NOTE. There are many scientists in the twentieth century who question this view.

Owen Gingerich (essay date 1972)

SOURCE: "Johannes Kepler and the New Astronomy," in *The Eye of Heaven: Ptolemy, Copernicus, Kepler,* American Institute of Physics, 1993, pp. 305-22.

[*In the essay below, originally published in 1973 and reprinted in 1993, Gingerich provides a concise, lucid sketch of several of Kepler's complex astrological and mathematical principles, calling him the "first astrophysicist."*]

Johannes Kepler was conceived on 16 May 1571 at 4:37 A.M. and born on 27 December at 2:30 P.M. We therefore see that 1971 was the four-hundredth anniversary not only of Kepler's birth but also of his conception. The existence of such accurate dates reminds us that Kepler lived in an age when astronomer still meant astrologer and when the word "scientist" had not yet been invented. Kepler wrote down these dates when he was 25 years old and much fascinated by astrology. Like many of the world's greatest scientists, he had a profound feeling for the harmony of the heavens; Kepler believed in a powerful concord between the cosmos and the individual, although he rejected many of the traditional details of astrology.

From our own scientific and philosophical vantage point far removed from the turn of the seventeenth century, any assessment of this man's genius must be incomplete and imperfect. Nevertheless, our twentieth-century perspective can offer insights overlooked by the interpreters of previous generations. If Kepler could have chosen from our twentieth-century words, I suppose that he would have called himself a cosmologist. I should like to argue that we can accurately call Kepler the first astrophysicist.

Kepler stands at a junction in the history of astronomy when the old Earth-centered universe was giving way to the new Sun-centered system. Yet the heliocentric system as presented by Copernicus contained many vestiges of the old astronomy. Kepler's greatest book was the ***Astronomia nova.*** Published in 1609, it broke the two-millennium spell of perfect circles and uniform angular momentum—it was truly the New Astronomy. It is this work, which Kepler called his "warfare on Mars," that will form the focus of my remarks.

There was little in Kepler's youth to indicate that he would become one of the foremost astronomers of all time. Although Tycho's supernova of 1572 burst forth when Kepler was a mere infant, the Great Comet of 1577 made a lasting impression. Kepler was a weak and sickly child, but intelligent, and after the elementary Latin school he easily won a scholarship to the nearby Tübingen University so that he could study to become a Lutheran clergyman. There he produced a straight-A record—but the grade records preserved at

Tübingen show that nearly everyone was an A student in 1589. In recommending him for a scholarship renewal, the University Senate noted that Kepler had "such a superior and magnificent mind that something special may be expected of him."

Yet Kepler himself wrote that, although he had done well in the prescribed mathematical studies, nothing indicated to him a special talent for astronomy. Hence, he was surprised and distressed when, midway through his third and last year as a theology student at Tübingen, he was summoned to Graz, far away in southern Austria, to become an astronomy teacher and the provincial mathematician.

At the Protestant high school in Graz, Kepler turned out not to be a very good teacher. In the first year he had only a few students, in the second none at all. Needless to say, this gave him more time to pursue his own research! Nevertheless, it was in one of his class lectures that Kepler hit upon what he believed to be the secret key to the construction of the universe.

This key hung upon a crucial thread: at Tübingen, Kepler had become a Copernican. The astronomy teacher at the University, Michael Maestlin, was remarkably knowledgeable about Copernicus's *De revolutionibus.* Yet, strangely enough, his popular and often reprinted textbook, *Epitome astronomiae,* never even hinted at the heliocentric cosmology. Nevertheless, in his lectures at Tübingen, Maestlin included a discussion of the new Copernican system. He explained how this system accounted for the retrogradations in a most natural way, and how the planets were laid out in a very harmonic fashion, both with respect to their spacing from the Sun and with respect to their periods.

It was undoubtedly the beautiful harmonic regularities "so pleasing to the mind" that appealed strongly to Kepler's sense of the aesthetic and induced him to become such an enthusiastic Copernican—as opposed to Maestlin, the timid Copernican. To Kepler the theologian, such regularities revealed the glory of God. When he finally hit upon that secret key to the universe, he attributed it to Divine Providence. "I believe this," he wrote, "because I have constantly prayed to God that I might succeed in what Copernicus had said was true."[1] Later, in writing to his teacher Maestlin, he said, "For a long time I wanted to become a theologian; for a long time I was restless. Now, however, behold how through my effort God is being celebrated in astronomy."[2]

Because of his preoccupation with the Copernican system, Kepler began to ask himself three unusual questions: Why are the planets spaced this way? Why do they move with these regularities? Why are there just six planets? All these questions are very Copernican, the last one particularly so because a traditional geo-

centrist would have counted both the Sun and the Moon, but not the Earth, thereby listing seven planets.

. . . Kepler hit upon his secret key to the universe. In a lecture to his class, he had drawn the ecliptic circle and he was illustrating how the great conjunctions of Jupiter and Saturn, which take place every 20 years, fall almost one-third of the way around the sky in successive approaches. As he connected the successive conjunctions by quasi-triangles, the envelope of lines outlined a circle with a radius half as large as that of the outer ecliptic circle. The proportion between the circles struck Kepler's eye as almost identical with the proportions between the orbits of Saturn and Jupiter. Immediately, he began a search for a similar geometrical relation to account for the spacing of Mars and the other planets, but his quest was in vain.

"And then again it struck me," he wrote. "Why have plane figures among three-dimensional orbits? Behold, reader, the invention and the whole substance of this little book!"[3] He knew that there were five regular polyhedra—that is, solid figures each with faces all the same kind of regular polygon. By inscribing and circumscribing these figures with spheres (all nested in the proper order), he found that the positions of the spheres closely approximated the spacings of the planets. . . . Since there are five and only five of these regular or Platonic polyhedra, Kepler thought that he had explained the reason why there were precisely six planets in the solar system.

Kepler published this scheme in 1596 in his **Mysterium cosmographicum,** the "Cosmographic Secret." It was the first new and enthusiastic Copernican treatise in over 50 years, since *De revolutionibus* itself. Without a Sun-centered universe, the entire rationale of the book would have collapsed.

Kepler also realized that the center of the Copernican system was the center of the Earth's orbit, not the Sun. Although the Sun was nearby, it played no physical role. But Kepler argued that the Sun's centrality was essential and that the Sun itself must supply the driving force to keep the planets in motion. Not only did he propose this very significant physical idea, but he attempted to describe mathematically how the Sun's driving force diminished with distance. Again, his result was only approximate, but at least the important physical-mathematical step had been taken. This idea, which was to be much further developed in the **Astronomia nova,** establishes Kepler as the first scientist to demand physical explanations for celestial phenomena. Although the principal idea of the **Mysterium cosmographicum** was erroneous, never in history has a book so wrong been so seminal in directing the future course of science.

Kepler sent a copy of his remarkable book to the most famous astronomer of the day, Tycho Brahe. Unknown

Illustration of a model of the orbits of the planets by Johannes Kepler.

to Kepler, the renowned Danish astronomer was in the process of leaving his homeland. He had boasted that his magnificent Uraniborg Observatory had cost the king more than a ton of gold. Now, however, fearing the loss of royal support, Tycho had decided to join the court of Rudolf II in Prague. Emperor Rudolf was a moody, eccentric man whose love of the occult made him more than willing to support a distinguished astronomer-astrologer.

Kepler describes this sequence of events in the *Astronomia nova* itself. The Danish astronomer had been impressed by the *Mysterium cosmographicum,* though he was unwilling to accept all its strange arguments; then, Kepler writes,[4]

> Tycho Brahe, himself an important part in my destiny, continually urged me to come to visit him. But since the distance of the two places would have deterred me, I ascribe it to Divine Providence that he came to Bohemia. I arrived there just before the beginning of the year 1600 with the hope of obtaining the correct eccentricities of the planetary orbits. Now at that time Longomontanus had taken up the theory of Mars, which was placed in his hands so that he might study the Martian opposition with the Sun in 9° of Leo [that is, Mars near perihelion]. Had he been occupied with another planet, I would have started with that same

one. That is why I again consider it an effect of Divine Providence that I arrived in Prague at the time when he was studying Mars; because for us to arrive at the secret knowledge of astronomy, it is absolutely necessary to use the motion of Mars; otherwise that knowledge would remain eternally hidden.

Kepler's *Astronomia nova* was not to be published until nine years later. Never had there been a book like it. Both Ptolemy in the *Almagest* and Copernicus in *De revolutionibus* had carefully dismantled the scaffolding by which they had erected their mathematical models. Although Kepler's book is well organized, it is nearly an order of magnitude more complete and complex than anything that had gone before; our astronomer himself admits that he might have been too prolix.

In the first great battle in his warfare on Mars, Kepler describes the so-called vicarious hypothesis. This was an attempt to represent the motions of Mars on an eccentric circle driven by uniform angular motion about a point called an equant—essentially a traditional model cast into the new heliocentric pattern. Kepler achieved the great accuracy in the longitudes by allowing the equant to fall at an arbitrary position. . . . In this scheme, which he was to call the "vicarious hypothesis," the true anomaly is (neglecting terms in e^3):

$$v = T - (f + g)\sin T + g\frac{(f + g)}{2}\sin 2T + ...,$$

where g is the eccentricity from the Sun to the center of the circle, and f is the eccentricity from the equant to the center. For comparison, the motion in an ellipse with the law of areas is

$$v = T - 2e\sin T + \tfrac{5}{4}e^2 \sin 2T + ...,$$

Hence, if $g = \tfrac{5}{4}e$ and $f = \tfrac{3}{4}e$, the vicarious hypothesis satisfies the equations to second order and we can show that the remaining error is approximately $\tfrac{1}{4}e$, which, in the case of Mars with its eccentricity of nearly 0.1, amounts to about 1'. Thus, in predicting the longitudes, Kepler succeeded brilliantly, with an accuracy almost two orders of magnitude better than that of either Ptolemy or Copernicus.

There exists among Kepler's manuscript pages still preserved in Leningrad a remarkable sheet showing a diagram of the vicarious orbit. . . .[5] It is very carefully laid out in a publishable form as one of the first few pages of a book on Mars, and it includes the opening lines of the poetic tribute to Tycho that ultimately appeared in the *Astronomia nova.* The diagram, with its unequally spaced equant in the ratio 5:3, can be seen at the bottom of the page. Kepler was always very eager to publish, and elsewhere in the manuscript material we see the titles for chapters in a book that he was organizing before he even knew that Mars had a noncircular orbit. Apparently, this page comes from about the same period—evidently at one point he was prepared to publish his vicarious orbit as the solution of the riddle of Mars. Fortunately, Divine Fate prevented him from publishing his commentary on Mars until it indeed was truly the New Astronomy.

Although Kepler's scheme had achieved a great triumph with respect to the longitudes, it failed with respect to distances. In observational astronomy, longitudes can be determined directly with great precision, but in general the distances must be deduced by other methods. Here Kepler very cleverly used the latitudes of Mars to deduce the distances—but alas, this led to an absurdity and showed that his orbit could not, in fact, be the real one. Hence, he named it the vicarious orbit in contradistinction to the real or "physical" hypothesis that he was seeking.

Ptolemy, in his orbit for Mars, had constrained the equant to fall directly opposite the center of the orbit from the Earth and equally distant from it. Kepler now realized that such an equal-and-opposite equant more closely approximated the real orbit than did his vicarious orbit, which satisfied the longitude so well. This case is represented by equation (1) when $e = f = g$, or

$$v = T - 2e \sin T + e^2 \sin 2T + ...,$$

so that the error in heliocentric longitude is $\frac{1}{4} e^2 \sin 2T$; in the case of Mars, this gives 8' in the octants, an error easily detectable with Tycho's data, which Kepler believed were generally accurate to about 2'. In a celebrated passage, Kepler wrote: "God's goodness has granted us such a diligent observer in Tycho Brahe that his observations convicted the Ptolemaic calculation of an error of 8' of arc. It is therefore right that we should with a grateful mind make use of this gift to find the true celestial motions."[6]

. . . Because the angular motion is uniform about the equant, the opposite angles are equal, and the orbital motion at the aphelion is much less than at the perihelion. this was precisely the kind of motion that Kepler the astrophysicist desired: the planet's speed is inversely proportional to its distance from the Sun, a quite reasonable hypothesis if we assume that some physical emanation from the Sun is responsible for propelling the planet in its orbit. For Kepler this was a very fundamental idea; we can call it his distance law.

Although the outer planets had an equal-and-opposite equant in the Ptolemaic system, Kepler knew that the Sun-Earth orbit did not. In order for the Copernican system to be a real physical one, Kepler recognized that the same mechanism must apply for the orbit of the Earth as for that of Mars. The varying speed in longitude of the apparent Sun throughout the year required a certain definite spacing between the Sun and the point of uniform angular motion (traditionally taken as the center of the orbital circle). The same spac-

ing can be preserved, however, if we retain an equant but recenter the circle midway between the old center and the position of the Sun. Such a model will predict virtually the same longitudinal motion, but with different Earth-Sun distances, and would, of course, provide a physical mechanism similar to that for Mars.

But how to find the varying distance of the Sun? One way would be to measure the apparent diameter of the Sun at different times throughout the year. And so let me digress here, just as Kepler did.

When Kepler arrived in Prague, he bet Longomontanus that he could solve the theory of Mars within a week. He lost the bet, of course—it actually took five years, but, as he apologized in the *Astronomia nova,* he took one year out for optics. His resultant work, the *Astronomiae pars optica,* lays the foundation for modern geometrical optics. In it he explains, for the first time, how an inverted image is formed on the retina of the eye, and he clearly defines the light ray. Also, he investigates the effects of apertures of various sizes and shapes on the formation of an image.[7] Such considerations were of fundamental importance in observing the solar diameter, because the variations were rather small, but unfortunately the results were not conclusive.

Thus, Kepler turned his attention to another exceedingly ingenious way to locate the position of the Earth's orbit. He knew that Mars returned to the same point in space every 687 days, but that the Earth would be at two different points in its orbit since in that time it would not yet have completed its second full revolution. Kepler's manuscripts for the first two years of his work on Mars are apparently almost completely intact. . . . [In about 1600] Kepler tried such a triangulation. These results were ultimately very important, for they showed that his physical intuition was correct and that the Earth's orbit had to be moved to a new center. Hence, it could have a physical mechanism and a distance law, just as did the other planets.

Kepler, in fact, already had rather definite ideas about the physical mechanism involved. Through Johannes Taisner's book on the magnet (1562) and, later, William Gilbert's, he convinced himself that the planetary driving force emanating from the Sun must be magnetic. He believed that both the Sun and the magnetic emanation were necessarily rotating in order to impart a continuous motion to the planets. From the distance law, he deduced that the strength of the emanation decreased in inverse proportion to distance, and he therefore concluded that the emanation spread out in a thin plane—unlike light, which filled space and decreased as $1/r^2$.

When he applied the distance law to the Earth's orbit, a difficult quadrature resulted that he could handle only by laborious numerical calculations. Then Kepler had the fortunate inspiration to replace the sums of the radius vectors required by the distance law with the areas within the orbit. Thus, the radius vector swept out equal areas in equal times. Kepler recognized that this was mathematically objectionable, but, like a miracle, it provided an accurate approximation to the orbital motion predicted by the distance law. . . . [The] equant theory represents the law of areas only if the equant is placed directly opposite the Sun and at an equal distance from the center; the distance law and the law of areas are then rigorously equivalent at aphelion and perihelion.

At this point, Kepler had (1) an accurate but physically inadmissible scheme for calculating longitudes (the vicarious hypothesis) and (2) an intuitively satisfactory physical principle (the distance law) that was applicable to the Earth as well as to the other planets but which left an unacceptable 8' error in predicting the heliocentric longitudes of Mars. In order to preserve simultaneously both his accurate longitude predictions and the properly centered circular orbit, Kepler next added a small epicycle to his circle. This was a time-honored device, used not only by Ptolemy but by Copernicus and Brahe as well. The earliest pages of Kepler's Mars notebook from the first few weeks with Tycho Brahe in Prague show numerous experiments with epicycles. It is fascinating to see that, although Kepler is here exploring very new ground, he can still adapt his tools from traditional astronomy. Nevertheless, he was distressed by having to introduce such an absurd device. He argued that, just as sailors cannot know from the sea alone how much water they have traversed, since their route is not distinguished by any markers, so the mind of the planet will have no control over its motion in an imaginary epicycle except possibly by watching the apparent diameter of the Sun.

Kepler had difficulty in preserving the circular motion when he adopted an epicycle; it is therefore not surprising to find that our astronomer next turned to a closer examination of the shape of Mars's path. Having established the proper position of the Earth's orbit by triangulation of Mars, he was able to turn the procedure around and to investigate a few points in the orbit of Mars itself. . . . Kepler recognized that observational errors prevented him from getting precise distance to the orbit. Because of this scatter, he had to use, as he picturesquely described it, a method of "votes and ballots."

Armed with these results, Kepler found in the epicycle the convenient means for generating a simple noncircular path. . . . On this scale, it differs imperceptibly from an ellipse, although actually the curve is slightly egg-shaped, with the fat end toward the Sun.

Kepler required that the motion with the generating epicycle should satisfy his law of distances, which

could be approximated by the law of areas . . . [In the caption to an unreproduced diagram, the critic writes in regard to the epicyclic construction of Kepler's ovoid: "*The epicycle has radius* e. *Angle* α *moves uniformly with time, whereas* φ *moves nonuniformly in order to satisfy the area law, so that* $\int_0^\phi r^2 d\phi = c\alpha$.

If this construction had an equant, it would fall 2e *from the Sun at* E, *and Mars would reach* Q *in a quarter period; hence,* α_1 *in the epicycle must be very close to* 90°. *As the epicycle center moves through angle* δ, *the epicycle vector will also advance by* δ *since* dφ *is very near its mean rate in this part of the orbit (so* dα≈dφ). *Thus,* $\alpha_2 = \alpha_1 + \delta$, *and the angle at* T *is a right angle. Then the line* SUN-T = $\sqrt{1-e^2}$ *and* TC = $\sqrt{1-2e^2}$. *Since the semiminor axis of an ellipse is* a $\sqrt{1-e^2}$, *the approximating ellipse to Kepler's ovoid has eccentricity* $\sqrt{2}e$. *Kepler called angle* δ *the 'optical equation.' He finally realized that an ellipse of eccentricity of* e *gave the required path when he noticed that* sec δ $(= 1/\sqrt{1-e^2} = 1 + \frac{1}{2}e^2)$ *exceeded unity by precisely the width of the lunula between the circle and the noncircular orbit. 'It was as if I had awakened from a sleep,' wrote Kepler.*"] If Kepler had had access to the integral calculus, he would have found that the egg-shaped or ovoid curve has a very elementary equation, but this he did not know. We must remember that even the equals sign had been invented only in the preceding generation, and Descartes' analytic geometry was still in the coming generation.

In working with the ovoid, Kepler got himself into a very messy quadrature problem that could best be tackled with the help of an approximating ellipse. Most popular accounts of his warfare on Mars leave the reader puzzled as to why Kepler did not immediately abandon the ovoid and adopt the ellipse. . . . [The] approximating ellipse has an effective eccentricity of $\sqrt{2}e$, where e is the distance from the center of the circle to the Sun. The diagrams show how inaccurately the triangulation method determined the points on the orbit of Mars. If these points had been well determined, Kepler would have seen immediately that the ovoid departed from the circular orbit by twice as much as it should have. His real hold on the problem came through the predicted longitudes, not the distances, and here again he found the 8' discrepancy in the longitudes at the octants. Kepler wrote the previously quoted celebrated passage about the 8' in connection with the errors of a circle, but it is quite possible that he first discovered it in examining the ovoid. The symmetry of the situation shows that, if there is an 8' error in a circular Ptolemaic orbit, there ought also to be about an 8' error in the ovoid, which deviates equally on the other side of the correct ellipse.

Luckily, in the end Kepler abandoned the epicycle and adopted the ellipse that lay halfway between his ovoid and the circle. But the process was not simply the method of "cut and try" so often imputed to Kepler by popular accounts. He was still seeking a single physical mechanism to explain not merely the varying speed of Mars in its orbit but also the varying distances. His answer came in an extension of the magnetic effects that propel the planets in their orbits. Kepler drew a very charming analogy to a boatman in an amusement park. Apparently, a cable was stretched across a stream and the small boat attached to the cable. The oarsman, by directing the rudder, could use the flow of the stream to propel the craft back and forth from one side to another.

From Gilbert's book, Kepler knew about the magnetic axis of the Earth. Such a magnetic axis, he proposed, could act as the rudder in the Sun's magnetic emanation, guiding the planet first near and then far from the Sun. If the magnetic axis is fixed in space, then its projection as seen from the Sun will be cos θ. Such a cosine term appears in the polar equation for the ellipse:

$$r = \alpha\left(1 - e^2\right)/\left(1 + e\cos\theta\right).$$

To the first order in eccentricity, the ellipse satisfies this physical picture of the magnetic axis governing the advance and retreat of the planet. For Kepler, who did not work with the polar equation, the real hurdle was to find the geometrical equivalents between the librating magnetic axis and the ellipse. "I was almost driven to madness in considering and calculating this matter," he wrote. "I could not find out why the planet would rather go on an elliptical orbit. Oh, ridiculous me! As if the libration on the diameter could not also be the way to the ellipse. So this notion brought me up short, that the ellipse exists because of the libration. With reasoning derived from physical principles agreeing with experience, there is no figure left for the orbit of the planet except a perfect ellipse."[8]

Indeed, Kepler was luckier than he knew. Just as there is an approximating ellipse to the oval he originally tried, so there is an approximating oval indistinguishable (with Tycho's data) from this final ellipse, the so-called *via buccosa*. But when Kepler found that the ellipse satisfied the observations, he must have hastily assumed that no other curve would do; thus, driven by his persistent physical intuition, he had continued until he almost accidentally hit upon the right curve.

With justifiable pride he could call his book *The New Astronomy;* its subtitle emphasizes its repeated theme: "Based on Causes, or Celestial Physics, Brought Out by a Commentary on the Motion of the Planet Mars." Today, Kepler is primarily remembered for his laws of planetary motion. Although his magnetic forces have fallen by the wayside, his requirement for a celestial physics based on causes has deeply molded science as we know it today. It was, in effect, the mechanization and the cleansing of the Copernican system, setting it into motion like clockwork and sweeping away the vestiges of Ptolemaic astronomy. The results can very appropriately be called the Keplerian system. In the preface to Kepler's long-awaited *Rudolphine Tables,* finally published in 1627, he felt compelled to excuse the extended delay. He says that "the novelty of my discoveries and the unexpected transfer of the whole of astronomy from fictitious circles to natural causes were most profound to investigate, difficult to explain, and difficult to calculate, since mine was the first attempt."[9] Kepler's *Astronomia nova* might have been forgotten had it not been for the brilliant success of the *Rudolphine Tables,* whose predictions were nearly two orders of magnitude more accurate than previous methods. Today, with the clarity of hindsight, we see not only that the *Astronomia nova* was truly "the new astronomy" but that Johannes Kepler himself deserves to be remembered as the first astrophysicist.

Notes

[1] J. Kepler, *Mysterium cosmographicum* (1596). Reprinted in the standard Kepler edition *Johannes Kepler Gesammelte Werke* (*JKGW,* Munich, 1937-), vol. 1, p. 11.

[2] Kepler to Maestlin, 3 October 1595; *JKGW,* vol. 13, p. 40.

[3] J. Kepler, *Mysterium cosmographicum* (1596); *JKGW,* vol. 1, p. 13.

[4] J. Kepler, *Astronomia nova* (1609); *JKGW,* vol. 3, p. 109. It is scandalous that this work has never been published in English; the passage quoted has been prepared by Ann W. Brinkley and myself.

[5] After Kepler's death in 1630, his manuscripts changed hands repeatedly—they were once owned by Hevelius and a list of them appears in the *Philosophical Transactions,* vol. 9 (1674), 29-31, but they were finally bought by Catherine the Great for the Academy of Sciences in St. Petersburg, and to this day they are preserved there. I wish to thank Dr. P. G. Kulikovsky and Dr. V. L. Chenakal for providing me with an excellent microfilm of Volume XIV, which contains the principal papers relating to the analysis of Mars. The greater part of this volume comprises a notebook of nearly 600 pages, which represents virtually all the work for 1600 and 1601. There are several draft chapters for the *Astronomia nova* and material for an ephemeris. It was not until 1605 that he found the ellipse, and unfortunately virtually no manuscripts remain from that part of the work.

[6] J. Kepler (1609), *op. cit.*, p. 178.

[7] 1971 was not only the four-hundredth anniversary of Kepler, but also the five hundredth anniversary of Albrecht Dürer. It is interesting to note that Kepler knew Dürer's great book on art theory, the *Underweysung der Messung* (1525), which illustrates not only the Platonic solids and a construction for an erroneously egg-shaped ellipse but also a device that uses threads to assist in drawing an object in perspective. Kepler employed a rather similar procedure of threads to investigate the formation of an image, and Stephen Straker, in a doctoral dissertation written at the University of Indiana, suggests that Kepler may have gotten the ideas from Dürer.

[8] J. Kepler (1609), *op. cit.*, p. 366.

[9] J. Kepler, *Tabulae Rudolphinae* (1627); *JKGW*, vol. 10, pp. 42-43.

Bruno Morando (essay date 1975)

SOURCE: "Kepler's Scientific and Astronomical Achievements," in *Kepler: Four Hundred Years: Proceedings of Conferences Held in Honour of Johannes Kepler,* edited by Arthur Beer and Peter Beer, in *Vistas in Astronomy*, Vol. 18, Pergamon Press, 1975, pp. 109-17.

[*In the essay below, Morando provides a concise overview of Kepler's career that includes a brief discussion of his upbringing and early years.*]

Johannes Kepler lived in a Germany still shaken by religious warfare and soon to be plunged into the Thirty Years War. His genius, which today seems so profound and so naïve, his personality, by turns self-doubting and aggressive, his work, full of mysticism and rigour—all these are very much in the image of the European society of his time. Kepler was mid-way between the Aristotelianism and superstition of the Middle Ages and the proud confidence in reason of the Enlightenment, and we see him picking his way among sorcerers, astrologers, plaques and massacres, working out confused and closely argued theories in the intolerant atmosphere of drab provincial universities, and in the end, without realizing their true importance, formulating eternal laws of Physics.

Johannes Kepler was born on 27 December 1571 at Weil der Stadt. His family, which was Protestant, considered itself noble, but although Johannes' grandfather Sebaldus, a furrier by trade, was Mayor of Weil, we cannot pretend that the Kepler family was any longer particularly distinguished. Johannes' father, mercenary and something of a drunkard, disappeared without trace during a military campaign from which he had hoped to make money; his mother, Katherine, an orphan brought up by an aunt, who was eventually burnt as a witch, was the daughter of an innkeeper. As a child Kepler was sickly, and as a man he was always in poor health. Furthermore, he was myopic, and even sometimes saw double, so that he was never to be a good observer.

In 1575 the Kepler family moved to Leonberg, where young Johannes went to school, and then worked as a waiter at the inn until he was 12. Then he went to the little Seminary of Adelberg. Kepler later remembered his first contact with astronomy. He tells us he saw the comet of 1577, and also an eclipse of the Moon, probably that of 31 January 1580.

He obtained a scholarship to the University of Tübingen, and intelligence and hard work at last allowed him to follow an intellectual career, for the moment in preparation for becoming a Lutheran pastor. It was in fact with the purpose of training future leaders of the reformed religion that the Dukes of Württemberg, recently converted to Protestantism, had founded the famous Universities of Tübingen and Wittenberg. The curriculum was heavy and very varied. It included theology, music and mathematics, meaning mainly geometry and astronomy. For this last subject Kepler had the good fortune to have as his teacher one of the most distinguished astronomers of his time, Michael Mästlin. Born in 1550, Mästlin spent his life teaching astronomy at Tübingen. In 1572 he showed that the nova which appeared that year was fixed with respect to the stars and was thus a very distant object, not an atmospheric phenomenon. This idea, which ran counter to the Aristotelian belief that the heavens were immutable, was accepted only with a great deal of difficulty. Mästlin's chief merit, however, was certainly that he taught the Copernican system and defended it unequivocally.

In the scholarly atmosphere of Tübingen Kepler's character revealed itself in all its complexity. He was hypersensitive, sometimes servile and sometimes arrogant, and later in his letters and books he was to describe his methods, his hesitations, his errors and his victories.

In 1593 Kepler renounced an ecclesiastical career: he accepted a post as professor of mathematics at the Protestant school of Graz, a city which at the time was tolerant enough to allow a Protestant school to flourish alongside a Catholic university. Kepler, indeed, turned Calvinist while he was there and was of course censured for having done so. His refusal to commit himself to any particular religious faction caused him trouble throughout his life.

Appointed "Mathematicus" at Graz in 1594, Kepler taught the Copernican system to a number of pupils so small that in the end he was asked to give courses on Virgil and on rhetoric as well. He also worked on the

publication of an annual calendar which included astrological predictions. Kepler, like other astronomers of his time, drew up horoscopes on request. It has also been said that he profoundly despised this activity and thought its only merit was that it brought in money. His description of astrology has become famous: he called it the "shameless daughter who keeps her poor mother astronomy". In fact, it is very difficult for us to imagine the attitude of astronomers to astrology in Kepler's time. Scientific rationalism was only just emerging from a whole system of thought very foreign to it, and we may indeed consider it a piece of intellectual courage to reject some astrological predictions as absurd while at the same time trying to make the principles of astrology more "scientific". Be that as it may, Kepler had to make a living, and he rapidly made himself a reputation by predictions of a Turkish invasion and of a cold spell, both of which took place.

The Five Regular Polyhedra

It was while he was drawing a figure on the blackboard for his pupils in July 1595 that Kepler was seized by an idea which today seems completely vain but to which he attached considerable importance throughout his life: Why, he asked himself, has the solar system six planets—Mercury, Venus, the Earth, Mars, Jupiter, and Saturn, and what relations are there between the dimensions of their orbits? He had tried unsuccessfully to inscribe these orbits in regular polygons when he suddenly thought of the regular polyhedra—the solids formed by a certain number of faces which are all regular polygons, each of equal size. Euclid had given a simple proof that there can only exist five convex regular polyhedra, and this gave Kepler the idea of fitting these polyhedra between the orbits. Long and complicated calculations led him to the following system: A dodecahedron is circumscribed round the sphere which contains the orbit of the Earth and this dodecahedron is then inscribed in a sphere on which is drawn the orbit of Mars. Round this sphere of Mars one circumscribes a tetrahedron which is inscribed in the sphere of Jupiter. In the same way we move to the orbit of Saturn by using a cube. Also, if one draws an icosahedron inside the sphere of the Earth one gets to the orbit of Venus and then to that of Mercury by means of an octahedron. In fact, to make all this work it was necessary to cheat a little. Also, since the orbits of the planets are not circles, the spheres on which they are drawn have a certain thickness so that they can contain both the perihelion and the aphelion.

Delighted by his discovery, Kepler published it in 1596 in his **Mysterium Cosmographicum.** The work contains much more than the description of the theory of the polyhedra, and is completely typical of Kepler's later scientific works. It is full of ideas, some right, some wrong. Heavy and boring calculations are broken by brilliant flashes of imagination, and we find an empirical attitude and Kepler's valuable description of his intellectual steps, and how he felt his way and what methods he used. The work was well received, and Kepler began to establish a reputation in Europe. With pride he tried to persuade the Duke of Württemberg to have a cup made of precious metal to represent the system of polyhedra, and from which one could pour out various delightful beverages, symbolizing the various planets. Kepler tried to perfect his system, and to unify all the sciences in some way by associating the musical intervals of the diatonic scale with the orbits of the planets. For this he needed good observations, spread out over a sufficiently large interval of time. Such observations were in existence: they were the work of Tycho Brahe, who had recently come to Bohemia. Life in Graz had become rather uncertain in other respects so Kepler made his decision, and on the first of January 1600 he set out for Prague.

Kepler and Tycho Brahe

Born in 1546, Tycho Brahe came from a noble Danish family. The sight of an eclipse of the Sun so struck him that he became deeply interested in a science which could make accurate predictions of such phenomena. He studied at Copenhagen, then at Leipzig, and built up a collection of instruments. He tried to determine parallaxes of stars, but naturally, since the largest of these parallaxes is less than 1", he found nothing. In November 1572 the famous nova, which we have already mentioned in connection with Mästlin, attracted his interest and led him to publish a work on this subject, *De Stella Nova*.

As we have remarked the fact that this nova was fixed shook belief in the fundamentals of the physics of Aristotle. Also Tycho Brahe himself showed that comets are at least six times further away than the Moon, which was another blow against the belief that the heavens were immutable.

In 1576 Frederick II of Denmark offered Tycho, who had an immense reputation as an astronomer, the island of Hven as a site for an observatory. There he built the famous observatory of Uranienburg, an extravagant Baroque Palace full of costly instruments. For 21 years Tycho Brahe was to live there, devoting himself to the luxurious pursuits of a rich and authoritarian feudal overlord and to the meticulous observations of a dedicated and methodical astronomer. He established a catalogue of 777 stars, of unequalled precision; 223 other stars are also mentioned, but their coordinates are less good. In 1597 Tycho Brahe, who had made himself unbearable at Uranienborg by his extravagances and his harsh treatment of his vassals, left the island of Hven and set off across Europe, accompanied by a retinue of wagons containing weapons, baggage, astronomical instruments and printing presses. He visited Hamburg, Dresden and Wittenberg.

In June 1599 he arrived in Prague, residence of the Emperor Rudolf II, who appointed him Imperial Mathematician at the fabulous salary of 3000 florins. (Kepler at Graz only earned 200.) Tycho took up residence at the Castle of Benatek, near Prague.

Tycho Brahe and Kepler had already been corresponding for 2 years, but soon nearly quarrelled over a certain Ursus, Tycho Brahe's predecessor in the post of Imperial Mathematician, who had published as his own a "system" completely identical with Tycho Brahe's system. This system was not new, and strongly resembled those of Heraclides and Aristarchus of Samos: the Sun moved round the Earth, taking with it the planets orbiting around it. Kepler made the blunder of congratulating Ursus on this ingenious work, while Tycho was accusing Ursus of having stolen his system.

On 4 February 1600 Kepler arrived at the Castle of Benatek. As Arthur Koestler has written: "Kepler, who had dreamed of Benatek as a serene temple of Urania, arrived in a madhouse". The Palace was still in the hands of the tapestry-hangers, the huge instruments had not arrived; Tycho, in the midst of this tumult, had reopened his quarrel with Ursus, and the crowd of courtiers was excited over the love affair between his daughter Elizabeth and his assistant Tengnagel.

A decision of capital importance for Kepler's future was taken as soon as he arrived. He was told to study the orbit of Mars, a particularly difficult orbit on which Longomontanus, an assistant of Tycho, had been working in vain for a long time. Inspired with enthusiasm by the difficult problem given him, Kepler boasted he would solve it in 8 days. He was to work at it for 8 years, but he found the solution.

However, 2 months after Kepler's arrival there was a dispute over a contract, which Kepler wanted Tycho Brahe to sign. Kepler left after a scene, then came back 3 weeks later after having written a letter of apology.

Tycho Brahe died on 13 October 1601, and on 6 November 1601 Kepler was made Imperial Mathematician in his place. He was to stay in Prague until the death of Rudolf II in 1612.

The Two First Laws

From then on he was occupied with the difficult problem of the orbit of Mars. He began to attack the problem by referring the positions to the Sun as centre, and proved that the orbit is fixed and that its plane is at an angle of 1° 50' to the ecliptic. (The modern value for the inclination is 1° 51'.) He quickly realized that he had to abandon the old theory of uniform circular movement, and tried to revive the equant point invented by Ptolemy. This point is a point symmetrical to the Sun with respect to the centre of the orbit, which Kepler continued to believe to be circular. With respect to this equant point the movement of the radius vector is uniform. He chose four positions of Mars from amongst those left by Tycho Brahe, and by heavy calculations, containing errors which by an extraordinary coincidence compensated each other, he managed to find a circle and a satisfactory equant point. Then an important thing happened. Kepler wanted to include in the newly found orbit some other positions observed by Tycho Brahe, and he succeeded satisfactorily except for two of them, whose observed positions were 8' from the theoretical ones. A new era then opened in the history of science. Far from rejecting these two observations, Kepler bowed to the facts and gave up his first hypothesis. The orbit cannot be a circle. The exact form must be sought without any preconceived idea and must be such as to include *all* the positions observed by Tycho Brahe.

Before attacking this new problem he decided to make a careful revision of the Earth's orbit, and in the course of these calculations two serious errors of principle, which compensated each other, led him to the truth. We know in fact that at aphelion and at perihelion the velocity of a planet, which at these moments is perpendicular to the radius vector, has a magnitude inversely proportional to the distance. Kepler generalized this and believed that the same is true at every point of the orbit; in fact, it is the projection of the velocity on the normal to the radius vector which is inversely proportional to the distance. But here he made a second error; when a planet moves from one point to a nearby one with the velocity V, the element of area swept out by the radius vector is equal to half the product of V (but in fact it is the projection of V, as mentioned above), and the length of the radius vector. Bringing these two facts together he deduced the result: "the radius vector sweeps out equal areas in equal times". Thus Kepler's first law enters the history of science. Later, he was to notice his mistake and the incredible luck he had had in nevertheless stumbling on the correct law.

He then continued his study of the orbit of Mars and realized that he was dealing with an oval, which he tried to construct. At first he found a sort of egg, pointed at perihelion, which did not satisfy him. Then he tried to use the ellipse, a curve which had been well studied for a long time, as an intermediary in calculation. He finally succeeded in relating the radius vector r to the angle v which this radius makes with the direction of perihelion, by the following formula:

$$r = a\,(1 - e\cos v),$$

where e is a number smaller than unity, and the quantity a is half the distance from aphelion to perihelion. We know that if e is sufficiently small the above formula is a good approximation to the equation of the

ellipse. Kepler, however, knew no analytic geometry, and set out to construct point by point the curve corresponding to the equation he had found. He made so many mistakes in his calculations that he arrived at a sort of bulbous curve which did not go through his positions of Mars. Discouraged, he gave up his equation, went back to the ellipse, and succeeded in making it go through the positions of Mars, while noticing that the curve $r = a (1 - e \cos v)$ is indeed an ellipse (to first order in the eccentricity). Hence he stated his Second Law: the planets describe ellipses having the centre of the Sun as one focus.

He published these results in the *Astronomia Nova* which appeared in Prague in 1609, after an important work on Optics: *Ad Vitellionem, etc.* (Frankfurt, 1604) containing tables of refraction (that could be used accurately up to 80° from the zenith), a means of calculating the differences in longitude between two places by means of eclipses, results concerning transits of the inferior planets across the Sun, and the law that the intensity of illumination decreases as the inverse square of the distance.

The *Astronomia Nova* was not published without great difficulties. In particular, Tycho's former assistant, Tengnagel, who had become his son-in-law, had appropriated his father-in-law's observations when he died, and had only allowed Kepler to use them on condition that he was allowed to sign his works with him. Tengnagel luckily gave up this pretension when he realized that he would have to pay for the printing.

Kepler's new work was received without enthusiasm, and the two laws were only accepted slowly. Nevertheless his fame increased and he was made a member of the Academia dei Lincei.

In March 1600 he was visited by a certain Wackher von Wackenfels who told him that Galileo, with the help of a telescope he had invented, had discovered new planets. Kepler speculated on the subject and did not understand how the theory of regular polyhedra, which he still clung to, could explain the existence of new planets. He was led to think that the discovery was in fact of satellites to the planets, and when he at last received the *Sidereus Nuncius* of Galileo he saw his intuition confirmed. Galileo, born in 1564, had obtained a chair of mathematics at Padua in 1592. He had already corresponded with Kepler at the time of the publication of the *Mysterium Cosmographicum,* but he had later been annoyed by Kepler's having reproached him for not definitely committing himself to the Copernican system.

The discovery of the four so-called Galilean satellites of Jupiter (Io, Europa, Ganymede, Callisto) caused a great stir throughout Europe, but it was immediately challenged. Interested scholars had considerable difficulty in confirming the discovery; Galileo's telescope was so rudimentary and its field was so small that as was pertinently said "the most surprising thing was not to have discovered the satellites, but to have succeeded in getting Jupiter in the field of view".

Galileo asked Kepler's opinion through the Tuscan Ambassador in Prague. Without having seen the satellites himself, Kepler enthusiastically defended the discovery in his famous pamphlet **"Dissertatio cum Sidereo Nuncio"**, where he uses it to explain certain ideas on astronomy, and repeats his theory of regular polyhedra. When he at last had a telescope at his disposal, Kepler saw the famous moons of Jupiter, during observations he made from 3 August to 9 September 1610. He wrote a description where the word "satellite" appears, for the first time in astronomy.

The "Harmonice Mundi" and the Third Law

In 1610 Kepler published his **Dioptrice,** a first essay in geometrical optics, in which he explained the principle of the telescope.

The year 1611 was gloomy. There were wars and epidemics, Kepler lost his wife and one of his children, and his patron, the Emperor Rudolf II, abdicated. Kepler left Prague for Linz, where he was appointed Provincial Mathematician. He was to remain there 14 years, divided between the work involved in publishing the **Harmonice Mundi** and **Rudolphine Tables** and the religious persecutions of all kinds which led to his excommunication. A serious accusation of witchcraft, brought against his mother, led him to make long visits to Leonberg during her trial. He finally succeeded in getting his mother released; she died 6 months later at the age of nearly 80. In 1613 he married again, his new wife being Susanna Reuttinger.

During this time Kepler was interested in finding other harmonies among the planetary orbits, still without giving up his cherished polyhedra. He tried to associate musical intervals with the diameters of the orbits. It was in the course of this work that he was led to state his "Third Law": "The cubes of the major axes are proportional to the squares of the periods". We now know that this law is not completely correct, unless we neglect the masses of the planets compared with that of the Sun. As the largest mass in the solar system is that of Jupiter, which is about one-thousandth of that of the Sun, Kepler's Third Law is an excellent approximation, and it was to contribute much to the confirmation of Newton's later work.

Such a relation between period and distance from the Sun had long preoccupied Kepler. His first fruitless attempt, made many years before, had given him the incorrect law that:

$$\frac{r_1}{r_2} = \frac{2P_1}{P_1 + P_2}, \quad \text{instead of} \quad \frac{r_1^3}{r_2^3} = \frac{P_1^2}{P_2^2}$$

r_1 and r_2 being the distances from the Sun of the planets M_1 and M_2, and P_1 and P_2 their periods.

The **Harmonice Mundi** appeared in 1619. The **Rudolphine Tables,** which Kepler had with great pains extracted from Tycho Brahe's observations, were at last ready in 1627. He had them printed in Ulm just in time for the book-fair in Frankfurt. They contained 1005 stars.

Kepler's last years were stamped with melancholy. Appointed mathematician to the famous warrior Wallenstein, Duke of Sagan, he left Linz and became very bored. It was while publishing Ephemerides for 1629 and 1630 that he went back to an old project for a strange work which he left unfinished and which was published after his death. This was a forerunner of our science-fiction novels in which he imagines a journey to the Moon.

In his attempt to find a more interesting post he travelled widely. On 2 November 1630 he arrived ill in Regensburg (Ratisbon) and on 15 November he died.

Such was the life of that genius who opened to Newton the doors of modern astronomy. A dedicated and enthusiastic worker, although he hardly realized what he was doing he nevertheless revolutionized the habits of thought of the learned men of his time. His intuition, which so often led him astray, brought him to the edge of even Newton's discoveries. In the introduction to the **Astronomia Nova** one comes upon the following passage: "If one puts two stones somewhere in space, far from any other body, they will be attracted to each other like magnets—each covering a distance proportionate to the mass of the other", and again: "if the Earth ceased to attract the waters of the seas, the seas would rise as far as the Moon."

On the other hand, he tried for a long time to discover what force might emanate from the Sun to pull the planets round in their orbits, but he did not know the law of inertia in its correct form. He thought that a body subject to no force should be at rest, whereas in fact it can also be in uniform motion in a straight line. Thus, for Kepler, the force, although it came from the Sun, was tangential to the orbit, and this led him into insurmountable difficulties.

We have seen that in other matters he persisted with fruitless ideas, presenting his conclusions with just as much enthusiasm as he showed for the laws which have made him immortal. It is Kepler himself to whom we turn for our concluding remark, when he wrote in the **Astronomia Nova**: "The ways by which men arrive at truth seem to me as worthy of admiration as this truth itself."

Edward Rosen (essay date 1985)

SOURCE: "Kepler's Early Writings," in *Journal of the History of Ideas,* Vol. XLVI, No. 3, July-September, 1985, 449-54.

[*Below, Rosen discusses both the background and publication history of two of Kepler's important early writings:* Mysterium Cosmographicum, *his initial description of the universe, and* Apologia, *an unfinished manuscript defending Tycho Brahe that was circulated in incomplete form in his day, but was not printed until the nineteenth century.*]

While teaching school in Graz, Austria, Johannes Kepler (1571-1630) wrote **Mysterium cosmographicum,** his first major work (Tübingen, 1596). Its printing and publication were supervised by Michael Maestlin (1550-1631), Kepler's former mentor at the University of Tübingen. Having introduced Kepler to Copernicus' astronomy, Maestlin rejoiced that his ex-pupil advocated it openly. But he was somewhat disappointed that in the **Mysterium cosmographicum** the treatment of some topics was too brief. To remedy this defect, Maestlin, as the editor, might have turned to Copernicus' *De revolutionibus orbium caelestium,* but preferred to invoke the *Narratio prima (First Report on Copernicus' Revolutions)* by George Joachim Rheticus (1514-74), the only disciple attracted by Copernicus' astronomical theory during Copernicus' lifetime. Rheticus' *Narratio prima* was regarded by Maestlin as a better exposition than "many rather obscure passages in Copernicus' work." Hence Maestlin in Tübingen decided to add Rheticus' *Narratio prima* to Kepler's **Mysterium cosmographicum,** "even though Kepler himself did not know [about the addition] and was not consulted on account of his absence"[1] in Graz.

"At the time he wrote the **Mysterium cosmographicum,**" according to a frequent contributor to the *Journal for the History of Astronomy* (hereafter *JHA*), "Kepler knew the *Narratio prima* far better than Copernicus' *Revolutions.* Perhaps reflecting his own experience, he writes in the first chapter of the **Mysterium cosmographicum,** on the evidence for the Copernican theory,

> Nunquam id facilius docuero Lectorem, quam si ad Narrationem Rhetici legendam illi author et persuasor existam. Nam ipsos Copernici libros Revolutionum legere non omnibus vacat.[2]

This passage[3] was quoted in *JHA* in the original Latin without being translated. This untranslated passage strikingly demonstrates the value of a translation of Kepler in correcting distortions of history by anyone who quotes Latin uncomprehendingly. Kepler judged that "only Copernicus magnificently gives the explanation, and removes the cause of wonder, which is not knowing causes." This judgment immediately precedes the passage left untranslated in *JHA*, but translated by Alistair M. Duncan as follows (75 / 21-23):

> The easiest way for me to show the reader that [the *Revolutions* is magnificent] would be for me to incite and persuade him to read Rheticus' *Narratio,* for not everyone has the leisure to read Copernicus' *Revolutions* itself.[4]

As E. J. Aiton says (17 / 25-31) in his introduction to Duncan's translation: "On the basis of Maestlin's lectures and his own reflections, he [Kepler] gradually compiled a list of superiorities of Copernicus over Ptolemy from the mathematical point of view. At the time of these early studies, Kepler had evidently not read the *Narratio prima,* for he remarked later that Rheticus, who had made the comparison briefly and clearly in his *Narratio prima,* could have saved him the trouble of compiling the list himself."

Not having Rheticus' *Narratio prima* while he was compiling his list of Copernican superiorities over Ptolemy, Kepler worked exclusively with Copernicus' *Revolutions.* This was a struggle comparable to "rolling that stone,"[5] i.e., Sisyphus' stone which, as it neared the top of the incline, always slipped down again to the bottom. This was Kepler's experience in grappling with Copernicus' *Revolutions* in the absence of Rheticus' *Narratio prima.* In the passage left untranslated in *JHA*, Kepler says nothing about "reflecting his own experience." Instead, to those lacking the leisure to master Copernicus' *Revolutions,* he recommends the reading of Rheticus' *Narratio prima.* The untranslated passage does not deal with "the evidence for the Copernican theory." Nor does it support the contention that "at the time he wrote the *Mysterium cosmographicum* Kepler knew the *Narratio prima* far better than Copernicus' *Revolutions.*" The historical record says exactly the opposite to those who can understand Kepler's Latin.

The Duncan-Aiton volume forms part of Abaris' Janus Library, a bilingual series of outstanding works in translation. The original language is printed on the left-hand, even-numbered pages, facing the English translation on the right-hand, odd-numbered pages. Duncan-Aiton adheres to this pattern for both editions of the *Mysterium cosmographicum,* which was unique among Kepler's numerous publications as the only work that enlisted his active participation in producing a second edition during his lifetime.

In February 1613 Kepler's assistant informed Maestlin that "a Basel printer . . . was about to publish Copernicus' *De revolutionibus* in a new edition. He wants to be advised about correcting the errors in the previous editions [Nuremberg, 1543; Basel, 1566]. In this understanding my cooperation is also sought,"[6] as Maestlin told Kepler. Maestlin also wrote to the printer, asking whether he planned to append Rheticus' *Narratio prima* to Copernicus' *De revolutionibus,* as had been done in the Basel 1566 edition. In his letter of 28 April 1613 to Kepler, Maestlin reported:

> Furthermore, I added that in my opinion the scholarly world and students of astronomy would be highly pleased if your **Mysterium cosmographicum** were likewise included, provided this could be done with your approval and permission. This I ask, in the name of all students of astronomy, and I beseech you eagerly and most earnestly. Of course, in that edition you could correct some passages, delete or add, as you wished. But I leave that to your judgment.[7]

Kepler's response was to reject Maestlin's proposal on the ground that with the addition of his **Mysterium cosmographicum** to Copernicus' *De revolutionibus* "the volume would become too long and too diffuse."[8] Some eight years later, however, Kepler made his own somewhat different arrangements. He republished the **Mysterium cosmographicum,** followed by Rheticus' relatively brief *Narratio prima,* without Copernicus' lengthy *De revolutionibus.* In the new dedication to the second edition of his **Mysterium cosmographicum** (Frankfurt, 1621), Kepler referred to "so many readers, who . . . have now for very many years been demanding copies of this, my first little book, long out of print."[9]

> Then since my friends, not only booksellers, but also those versed in philosophy, were pressing me to prepare a second edition, I did indeed think it my duty not to object any longer; yet I disagreed with them a little over the character of the edition. For there were some who advised me to emend, enlarge, and complete the book; that is to say, I should myself adopt the custom of other authors, which they observe in refining their own books. It seemed to me on the contrary that I could not complete the book, except by transcribing into it several of my works, which I have published during these twenty-five years [1596-1621], almost in their entirety; that this was no longer the time for putting out a book with this title, after I had published others, as if it were new; and lastly that the little book itself, on account of its remarkable success, should not be thought of as my own, to alter or enlarge at will, but that it was rather of interest for the reader to understand from what beginnings, and to what point my studies of the universe have been brought. This reasoning won, then, and I chose the form of edition which is usually adopted in reprinting other people's books, in which we change nothing. Those places which need emendation, or explanation, or completion, we reinforce with commentaries, set in different type.[10]

Kepler's plan called for keeping the text of the first edition of the **Mysterium cosmographicum** intact, while setting the second edition's commentary in contrasting type. "This form assisted both religion and brevity, so that I could frankly refute and expunge the errors which had sprung indeed from the darkness of my mind," as Duncan translates (41 / 33-35). True, Kepler used the word *religioni*. But he was talking, not about religion as Duncan supposes, but about scrupulous adherence to the original text. Just as historical inferences are drawn from a translation of Kepler more accurately than from none, two translations serve better than one. For Alain Segonds (6/4↑-3↑) writes: *un scrupuleux respect du texte*. Segonds' scrupulous respect for historical truth is absolutely admirable. So is his amazing capacity for absorbing his subject's vast multilingual literature.

Yet even he stumbles. Thus, Maestlin's effort to assist in the preparation of a third edition of Copernicus' *De revolutionibus* began in 1613 (not 1612, as in *Secret,* x1 / 9↑); he desisted after the third edition was published in Amsterdam (not Leiden, as in *Secret,* xlii / 10↑, lvii, n. 12) in 1617. Two years later Kepler published a work which Segonds calls *Harmonia*. This was the tentative title used by Kepler in a letter to Maestlin on 29 August 1599 (GW, *14:* 46 / 140). But a few months later, on 14 December 1599 he switched to **Harmonice** (GW, *14:* 100 / 12-13). "Harmony" is an agreeable blending of musical tones produced at the same time in the form of a chord; as a musical discipline, "harmony" studies such chords in sequence. "Harmonics," on the other hand, asks how musical harmonies and dissonances are produced. When Kepler dropped *Harmonia* from his title to replace it by **Harmonice,** he kept that Greek word in its original form. Aristotle, for example (*Metaphysica,* III, 2: 997b21), used the feminine adjectival form of the word as a noun, leaving unexpressed some term translatable as "study" or "knowledge." In this way *harmonice* became a designation of a discipline. Kepler's 1619 title page announced "Five Books about the Harmonics of the Universe." As the key word, **Harmonice** was placed first. Its genitive form in Greek *(Harmonices)* was necessary on account of its syntactical dependence on "Books." (*Harmonices,* being a dependent genitive, cannot stand by itself as a short title. If this is desired, *Harmonice,* without the final *s,* is suitable in Greek or Latin (which was Kepler's language here), and in English *Harmonics* (French *Harmoniques*) matches optics, acoustics, dioptrics, and the like.

Segonds' reader cannot do what Duncan's can: glance from left to right and right to left while comparing Kepler's Latin with a modern translation. But by way of recompense, in four appendices Segonds offers historically significant relevant texts in French translation. First comes Maestlin's essay[11] (on the dimensions of the Copernican celestial spheres) which he inserted after Rheticus' *Narratio prima* in the first edition of Kepler's **Mysterium cosmo graphicum.** From Kepler's preface to his **Astronomia nova,** Appendix II extracts

the section dealing with biblical objections to the Copernican—Keplerian system.[12] In response to the Sacred Congregation's decree condemning Copernican books in 1616, the answer Maestlin intended to include in the projected Basel third edition of *De revolutionibus* that failed to materialize is presented in Appendix III. The last appendix extracts the response to Kepler, particularly to his **Mysterium cosmographicum** on the part of Giovanni Battista Riccioli (1598-1671), the famous Jesuit anti-Copernican, in his *Almagestum novum* (Bologna, 1671).

"Almagestum" is a bilingual Arabo-Greek hybrid misnomer of Ptolemy's *Syntaxis*. This Greek treatise in thirteen Books was later condensed in an untitled influential Latin manuscript, in some copies called *Almagesti minoris libri VI* (Abbreviated Almagest in Six Books). To obtain a convenient short title, the number of Books may be dropped, leaving "Almagesti minoris." This is unacceptable as an independent title, however, because (like *Harmonices*) it is in the genitive case. It must therefore be shifted to the corresponding nominative case, beginning with *Almagestum*. This belongs to the neuter gender, as in Riccioli's widely consulted *Almagestum novum*. The *Dictionary of Scientific Biography* (hereafter DSB), however, couples "Almagestum minor,"[13] thereby violating an elementary rule of Latin grammar by combining a neuter noun with a masculine / feminine adjective. The *DSB* article is a joint product, finished by a younger contemporary after the death of an older colleague. Which one was responsible for this gross solecism? Not the older partner, in whose own writings it cannot be found. But the younger contributor has printed it three times.[14] Being unfamiliar with beginners' Latin, he offered no translation of the lines he quoted from Kepler's **Mysterium cosmographicum** (at note 2, above), and drew unwarranted inferences from the passage he left untranslated.

While Kepler was living in Graz, it began to be recatholicized. He could not remain without turning Catholic. He would rather die than do that. But the talent exhibited in his **Mysterium cosmographicum** saved him. For Tycho Brache (1546-1601) arranged to have Kepler join his staff. Imposed on the new assistant was the task of drafting **A Defence of Tycho against Ursus.** Both combatants died before Kepler quite completed this **Apologia,** which he left as an unfinished manuscript in deplorable condition. So it remained for two and a half centuries until it was printed for the first time in the great nineteenth-century edition of his complete works. From the manuscript preserved in the U.S.S.R. Academy of Sciences, Leningrad, and from a microfilm in the Württembergische Staatsbibliothek, Stuttgart, West Germany, Nicholas Jardine has published a much better text than was printed in 1858, together with the first translation of the *Apologia* into any modern language (85-207).

Before Kepler completed the *Mysterium cosmographicum,* he wrote a letter about it to Nicholas Reimers Ursus (1551-1600), the Imperial Mathematician of the Holy Roman Empire. Ursus ignored Kepler's letter until he noticed in a book catalog that the *Mysterium cosmographicum* was in print. Then he promptly wrote to Kepler, asking for a copy. Kepler sent two, one for Ursus, whom he asked in all innocence to forward the other copy to Brahe. At that time (15 November 1595) Kepler had not yet heard about their deadly feud, with Brahe accusing Ursus of plagiarizing his cosmic system. In replying to Brahe, Ursus printed the letter Kepler had written to him, full of (insincere) praise, and exclaiming "I love your hypotheses." Ursus did not ask Kepler's permission to print the letter; he did not inform Kepler that he had printed it; and he did not send Kepler a copy of his response to Brahe.

Outraged by Ursus' conduct, Kepler nevertheless tried to be fair in the *Apologia.* His construction of it along the lines recommended by the current handbooks of rhetoric is skillfully analyzed by Jardine. To carry out this scheme, Kepler had to parry Ursus' counterattack on Brahe. According to Ursus, since Brahe had proposed nothing original, there was nothing to be plagiarized. To sustain his position, Ursus concocted a weird misrepresentation of the history of astronomy. In rebuttal, Kepler had to delve into a tangled mass of historical sources. Moreover, he had to refute Ursus' misconception of the logical structure of cosmological thought. In so doing, Kepler created in the *Apologia* the earliest systematic treatment of the history of science and the philosophy of science.

Before writing the *Apologia,* Kepler composed three earlier assessments of Ursus' argumentation. These are translated by Jardine (59-71), who also makes available (41-57) the key section in Ursus' counterattack on Brahe. This was published in 1597, pointing to 1600 as the year in which Kepler began the preface to the *Apologia*: "Three years ago . . . Ursus . . . published a little book" (134 / 1-2). Kepler then goes on to say that his *Mysterium cosmographicum* (Tübingen, 1596) belongs to the previous year, *anno priore* (85 / 8). This is mistranslated by Jardine as "last year" (134 / 9), which would be 1599.

Peter Ramus (Pierre de la Ramée, 1515-72) plays a prominent part in Jardine's masterful survey of Kepler's predecessors. Ramus was assailed by Jacques Charpentier (Carpentarius; 1521-74), *Admonitio ad Thessalum Academiae Parisiensis Methodicum* (Paris, 1567). Throughout the 102 folios of this book Charpentier's target is always named "Thessalus," recalling Thessalus of Tralles in Lydia, a member of the ancient medical sect of 'Methodiste,' who proclaimed himself "victor over the physicians" (Pliny, *Natural History,* 29.5.9). In like manner the *Admonitio* (fol.

97r / 15) sneers at its Thessalus as "Triumphator." However, the inclusion (fol. 8r-v) of the decree of King Francis I, 19 March 1544, forbidding philosophical teaching or writing by Ramus, conclusively identifies him with Charpentier's Thessalus. Jardine (44 / 4↑-3↑) has Ursus say: "there was once a Thessalian medicine more perfect than Galenic medicine," and then Jardine adds (45, n. 43): "By Thessalian medicine Ursus presumably means the medicine of Asklepios, god of healing, whose birthplace was, on some accounts, Thessaly." Jardine (156 / 5↑-3↑) has Kepler retort: "There are indeed those who imagine Thessalian medicine *(medicina Thessalica)* to have been something more excellent than is apparent from the surviving records." Thessalus' writings survive only in fragments. Even these have not yet been collected, edited, and published. Hence, modern historians of medicine are in no better position than Kepler to evaluate Thessalus' claims, which have no connection whatever with the region Thessaly or any divinity.

It is startling to notice the Lecturer in the History and Philosophy of Science, and Fellow of Darwin College, University of Cambridge, misusing the adjective "due" (44 / 3↑, 181 / 13, 276 / 3↑), and writing: " . . . learned men, whom I knew did not think very highly of him" (18 / 20-21). Such blemishes are regrettably permitted to stain this praiseworthy presentation of "The Birth of History and Philosophy of Science." Unfortunately for mankind, the three and a half centuries during which the *Apologia* languished in oblivion, followed by the additional century and a third waiting for Jardine, made it a stillbirth.

Notes

[1] Johannes Kepler, *Gesammelte Werke* (hereafter *GW;* Munich, 1937-), I, 85 / 23, 26-27; unless indicated otherwise, translations are mine (E.R.).

[2] Noel M. Swerdlow, "On Establishing the Text of *De revolutionibus," Journal for the History of Astronomy,* 12 (1981), 45.

[3] *GW,* I, 15 / 1-4.

[4] If Swerdlow did not have access to Duncan, he might have consulted Johannes Kepler, *Mysterium cosmographicum, Das Weltgeheimnis,* trans. Max Caspar (Augsburg, 1923; Berlin and Munich, 1936), 29 / 13↑-10↑.

[5] *GW,* I, 9 / 23-24.

[6] *GW,* XVII, 53 / 10-14.

[7] *GW,* 54 / 39-45.

[8] *GW,* XVII, 67 / 32-33.

[9] *GW,* VIII, 10 / 2-4.

[10] Duncan-Aiton, 41 / 15-33.

[11] English translation by Anthony Grafton, *Proceedings of the American Philosophical Society* (hereafter PAPS), 117 (1973), 523-50.

[12] Segonds' translation differs markedly from the version in Jean Kepler, *Astronomie nouvelle,* trans. J. Peyroux (Paris, Blanchard, 1979).

[13] XV (New York, 1978), 477.

[14] *PAPS,* 117 (1973), 425-26, n. 4, 512.

Richard S. Westfall (essay date 1986)

SOURCE: "The Rise of Science and the Decline of Orthodox Christianity: A Study of Kepler, Descartes, and Newton," in *God and Nature: Historical Essays on the Encounter between Christianity and Science,* edited by David C. Lindberg and Ronald L. Numbers, University of California Press, 1986, pp. 218-37.

[*Below, Westfall discusses the theological underpinnings of Kepler's scientific thought.*]

Johannes Kepler: Christian Cosmologist

After his skill in astronomy, religious devotion is probably the best-known characteristic of Johannes Kepler (1571-1630). One is tempted to use him as the example of traditional orthodoxy on the eve of Europe's plunge into the cold bath of skeptical inquiry. Such a use would do scant justice to the intensity of Kepler's religious pilgrimage. Differences on essential doctrines separated him from each of the major denominations and greatly complicated his life in an age of confessional conflict. "Yet it is not my way to become a hypocrite in matters of conscience," he insisted to his former teacher, Michael Maestlin, as he explained his unwillingness to compromise.[1] Whatever we say about Kepler, we shall not dare to present him as an unquestioning supporter of inherited tradition.

Nevertheless, in Kepler's religious thought Christianity remained intact, harmoniously interwoven with his science and scarcely altered by it. His personal piety furnished the background to his work, forcing itself as it were onto the printed page, as though he were unable to contain it. He called book 5 of the *Harmonies of the World* "a sacred sermon, a veritable hymn to God the Creator" in which he would worship, not by offering sacrifices to God, not by burning incense, "but first in learning and then in teaching others how great are His wisdom, power, and goodness."[2] When he came to chapter 9, the climax both of book 5 and of the entire work, where he revealed the ultimate harmonies of the world, he introduced it with a prayer that wove Christian and cosmological themes together in one continuous fabric:

> Holy Father, preserve us in the harmony of mutual love so that we may be one even as you with your Son, our Lord, and the Holy Spirit are one, and as you have through the gentle bonds of harmony made all your works one; and from the renewed concord of your people let the body of your church on earth be built from harmonies as you have constructed the heavens themselves.[3]

He concluded the chapter with a second prayer that his work contain nothing unworthy of God, and he closed the *Harmonies* as a whole with a hymn to the glory of the Creator.

It is true that we can distinguish tendencies in Kepler that point toward a different relation of science with Christianity. Jürgen Hübner has examined these tendencies in considerable detail in his recent study of Kepler's religious thought.[4] The basic change, in Hübner's analysis, was a shift of attention away from the central concerns of medieval Christian theology. These concerns had focused on the redemptive relationship of God to man. God had revealed Himself by coming into the world to restore fallen humanity and had codified that revelation in a written record, the Bible, the source to which mankind must turn for knowledge unto life eternal. In contrast, Kepler fastened his gaze on God the creator. His God also had revealed Himself. He had revealed his wisdom in the act of creation, and Kepler's primary theological interest centered on the wisdom of God. Without denying the concept of redemption, he paid it scant attention, while with rapt devotion he explored the details of the creation. Thus Kepler not only redirected the focus of Christian thought but also elevated nature as a revelation of God to a status equal to that of the Bible. "For you, God entered the world," he wrote to David Fabricius; "for me, nature strives toward God."[5]

Even if we grant Hübner's argument, it does not seriously compromise the original assertion that in Kepler traditional Christianity remained virtually unaltered by the impact of science. To be sure, his Pythagorean God, who eternally manifested arcane geometrical and harmonic relations in the physical creation, differed clearly enough from the traditional God of Christian theology, but this has to do with another level of thought. Kepler's reverence for the written revelation was so intense that we might well overlook his subtle shift of attention if we were not aware of the future direction of Western thought. Whatever his concern with God the creator, the concept of redemption also played a central role in Kepler's life. Exclusion from the sacrament—that is, in his terms, exclusion from the presence of the spirit of Christ—was a personal tragedy, which he refused to accept but struggled against for the rest of his life. We shall not be wise in pressing his departure from received tradition too far.

When we turn to Kepler's natural philosophy, we find a conception of nature that directly supported his religious position. Of foremost importance is the fact that the universe remained for him a cosmos. It is well known that much of Kepler's significance in the history of science stems from the impulse he gave to causal analyses of phenomena and to the concept of mathematical laws. Kepler's laws were never impersonal laws, however, and the universe in which they worked was not for him the chance product of their blind operation. It was an ordered cosmos consciously contrived. Giordano Bruno's speculative system, "that dreadful philosophy," represented to him the blind operation of impersonal causes.[6] He feared the very idea and fled from it. Where means are adapted to definite purposes, Kepler insisted, "there order exists, not chance; there is pure mind and pure Reason."[7] "The Creator," he informed Maestlin, "does nothing by chance."[8]

It was, of course, Kepler's further conviction that the Creator had used the principles of geometry in constructing his universe. The five regular solids, which define the ratios between six spheres that can be inscribed within and circumscribed around them, and hence (because there are only five regular solids) establish the necessity of the six planets in the Copernican system, were the supreme manifestation of Kepler's geometrically ordered cosmos. They were by no means the sole example. Essentially the same mode of thought presented itself with nearly every question in natural philosophy. Consider the number of days in the year, 365¼. It is close to one of the archetypal numbers, 360, and Kepler readily convinced himself that God created the earth's motive force to turn it 360 times a year, not 365¼, a "disjointed and ignoble fraction." The presence of the sun, which stimulates the earth's faculty, upsets the pristine purity of the ratio, which the discerning cosmologist can nevertheless preceive.[9] Similarly, on a completely different topic, Galileo's discovery of four satellites around Jupiter immediately led Kepler to inquire into the pattern that would establish the number of satellites around each planet.[10] For God does nothing by chance, and He orders his works according to the mathematical principles that are coeternal with Him.

I need not insist on the ready, and indeed necessary, harmony between such principles and a theistic conception of reality. Theism is not identical with Christianity, of course. Kepler drew heavily on the Platonic concept of a mathematically ordered reality in elaborating his philosophy, not on the Bible. When he used the Christian concept that man is the image of God to explicate human knowledge of the geometric cosmos, he went beyond mere theism, and so also when he

insisted on the uniqueness of the solar system in the universe.

The ultimate union of Christianity and science in Kepler's mind, however, lay in a further feature of his conception of nature, a feature possible only because his universe remained an ordered cosmos. Wherever he looked, and he looked everywhere, Kepler saw a universe organized in triads, and not just ordinary triads, but triads that are at the same time unities. It was not by accident that Kepler's universe remained finite, finite and spherical, because to him the sphere represented an embodiment of the Trinity.

> For in the sphere, which is the image of God the Creator and the Archetype of the world . . . there are three regions, symbols of the three persons of the Holy Trinity—the center, a symbol of the Father; the surface, of the Son; and the intermediate space, of the Holy Ghost. So, too, just as many principal parts of the world have been made—the different parts in the different regions of the sphere: the sun in the center, the sphere of the fixed stars on the surface, and lastly the planetary system in the region intermediate between the sun and the fixed stars.[11]

He was prepared to inject the Trinity into purely scientific questions. Thus he was able to calculate the densities of the sun, the sphere of the fixed stars, and the intermediate aether by reasoning that the equality of the three persons of the Trinity demanded an equal division of the matter in the universe among its three principal parts.[12] Likewise, the image contributed to his criticism of Ptolemy (second century A.D.), a pagan, who had considered the stars as visible gods. Such reasoning, he declared, "cannot be tolerated in a Christian discipline."[13]

Kepler did not stop with the mere image of the Trinity. He pursued its implications to the farthest detail, carving from it an extraordinary jewel of many facets, each of which reflected the splendor of Christian doctrine. In the creation, he explained, God expressed the difference between the straight and the curved, the images of the created and the divine. All rectilinear figures are inherently imperfect. Participating in three dimensions, they participate equally in materiality. Described by the motions of points, lines, and planes, they are by nature posterior to points and the space in which points move.[14] The curved is otherwise. A sphere is not generated by the rotation of a circle, because the sphere is prior to the circle. In respect to other figures, the sphere can be called ungenerated in that it is not produced from them but stands before them, the result of a wholly different process, whereby the central point communicates itself equally in all directions. Thus the sphere, the outpouring of a point, constitutes the space that other figures, generated by the finite motions of points, assume. A sphere has, as well, the form of immateriality because it is free of internal solidity. A sphere differs from a globe, which is a sphere filled with solid body.[15]

The sphere was thus to Kepler more than the shape of the universe. As the image of the divine, it was the form that every being that aspires to perfection assumes, as far as it is able to do so. Bodies, which are confined by the limits of their surfaces, nevertheless expand spherically in a vicarious manner through the powers with which they are endowed. The soul, and to Kepler everything was ensouled, pours itself forth from its punctiform abode, both in perceiving external things that surround it in a spherical fashion, and in governing its body, which also lies around it.[16] Inevitably he applied the same analogy to light as one of the foremost powers inherent in bodies.

> Is it any wonder, then, if that principle of all beauty in the world, which the divine Moses introduces into scarcely created matter, even on the first day of creation, as (so to speak) the Creator's instrument, by which to give visible shape and life to all things— is it any wonder, I say, if this primary principle and this most beautiful being in the whole corporeal world, the matrix of all animal faculties and the bond between the physical and the intellectual world, submitted to those very laws by which the world was to be formed? Hence the sun is a certain body in which resides that faculty, which we call light, of communicating itself to all things. For this reason alone its rightful place is the middle point and centre of the whole world, so that it may diffuse itself perpetually and uniformly throughout the universe. All other beings that share in light imitate the sun.[17]

He could heighten the trinitarian image still further. A point, the center of a sphere, is invisible; it reveals itself by flowing outward in all directions. The surface is its image, the way to the center. Who sees the surface also sees the center, and in no other way.[18] No doubt the image explains why Kepler insisted that light is not the rays that spread out from luminous and illuminated points. The rays are only the lines of motion. Light itself is the spherical surface that their equal motions constitute, the surface that represents the Son in the trinitarian sphere. Hence in optics as in most of his science, Kepler's contemplation of nature brought him back, not just to theism, but to the very heart of the Gospels. Jesus said, "I am the light of the world.". . .

Notes

[1] Kepler to Maestlin, 22 Dec. 1616, *Gesammelte Werke*, ed. Walther von Dyck and Max Caspar, 22 vols. (Munich: Beck, 1937-), 17:203. I quote the translation from Carola Baumgardt, *Johannes Kepler: Life and Letters* (New York: Philosophical Library, 1951), p. 107.

[2] *Werke* 6:287.

[3] Ibid., pp. 330-331.

[4] Jürgen Hübner, *Die Theologie Johannes Keplers zwischen Orthodoxie und Naturwissenschaft* (Tübingen: Mohr, 1975); Hübner, "Johannes Kepler als theologischer Denker," in *Kepler Festschrift 1971,* ed. Ekkehard Preuss (Regensburg: Naturwissenschaftlicher Verein Regensburg, 1971), pp. 21-44.

[5] Kepler to Fabricius, 4 July 1603, *Werke* 14:421.

[6] *Kepler's Conversation with Galileo's Sidereal Messenger,* trans. Edward Rosen (New York: Johnson Reprint, 1965), p. 37.

[7] *The Six-Cornered Snowflake,* trans. Colin Hardie (Oxford: Clarendon Press, 1966), p. 33.

[8] Kepler to Maestlin, 2 Aug. 1595, *Werke* 13:27.

[9] *Epitome of Copernican Astronomy,* in *Great Books of the Western World,* ed. Robert M. Hutchins, vol. 16 (Chicago: Encyclopaedia Britannica, 1952), pp. 916-917.

[10] *Conversation,* p. 14.

[11] *Epitome, Great Books* 16:853-854.

[12] Ibid., p. 885.

[13] Ibid., p. 889.

[14] *Epitome, Werke* 7:50.

[15] Ibid., pp. 50-51.

[16] *Harmonice mundi, Werke* 6:275.

[17] *Paralipomena, Werke* 2:19. I quote the translation in W. Pauli, "The Influence of Archetypal Ideas on the Scientific Theories of Kepler," in C. G. Jung and W. Pauli, *The Interpretation of Nature and the Psyche* (New York: Pantheon, 1955), pp. 169-170.

[18] *Epitome, Werke* 7:51.

Anthony Grafton (essay date 1992)

SOURCE: "Kepler as a Reader," in *Journal of the History of Ideas,* Vol. 53, No. 4, October-December, 1992, pp. 561-72.

[In the following essay, Grafton discusses how Kepler, like other scientists of his day, referred heavily upon older texts to give authority to his work, and how his reading of the mistakes of others influenced him to include much self-criticism in his own writings so that future readers would be better able to identify its

weaknesses, and thus be more readily able to build upon his work.]

Kepler, like Galileo, often rebelled against the cultural authority of old books. In 1599 his teacher of astronomy, Michael Maestlin, asked him to collaborate in preparing an encyclopedic commentary on Homer. Maestlin wanted him to interpret the encounters of the gods in the *Iliad* and *Odyssey* as conjunctions of the planets named after them and to compute their exact dates. Kepler clearly rejected the notion that one could find precise astronomical data in the ancient epics. Diplomatically, he did not say so. Instead, he suggested that Maestlin compute the dates; then he, Kepler, would supply astrological interpretations. He thus neatly ensured that the project came to nothing.[1]

Kepler's refusal to collaborate in weaving a Homeric allegory seems natural, even inevitable. He had already broken with basic elements of traditional cosmology in his ***Mysterium cosmographicum.*** And he would soon set out to create a new astronomy—one that broke, as Copernican astronomy had not, with the classical tradition that stretched from Ptolemy to his own time. He did this, as is well known, by using Tycho's unique new stores of empirical data, far more precise than the data available to the ancients, and by sticking to his own conviction that he could create a physically as well as a mathematically rigorous astronomy.[2] Kepler himself insisted again and again that even though he was only one little German working at what he expected to be the end of history, he had the right to introduce new ideas into cosmology. He warned traditional philosophers not to try to repress those who sought to change and improve natural philosophy "by the prescription of antiquity." Aristotle's opinions could not and should not be maintained against the "new discoveries that are being made every day."[3] It seems altogether reasonable that Kepler, unlike his more old-fashioned teachers in Tübingen, could see Homer as a poet, not a master of the sciences and could draw the conclusion that mathematical and astronomical analysis of his work would only waste time, paper, and spirit.

In fact, however, relations between the book of nature and the books of men were tangled in these transitional years. In the telescope wars of 1609 and after, Galileo artfully deployed an anti-scholarly rhetoric. He contrasted fertile reality to sterile books, the practical work of engineers and craftsmen to the tedious squabbling of pedants.[4] But in other texts, as Paolo Rossi and Eileen Reeves have shown, he took the books of men (and the written book of God) quite seriously. By the time he wrote the *Assayer,* he had steeped himself in Jesuit commentaries on the book of Daniel. More surprisingly, he cast his own view of his enterprise in the language not of the practical man of vision but of the learned commentator on texts. He compared nature to a book written in the language of mathematics—a

language, he insisted, that only experts could read. This second set of metaphors represented nature not as a user-friendly, unrolled scroll accessible to anyone with open eyes but as an encrypted text which only virtuous mathematicians—the prophets of Galileo's time—could decipher.[5]

Kepler's ideas about reading and its traditions were even deeper and more complex than Galileo's. In the specific case of Homer, he did not need his mastery of modern science to reject the notion that his poems encoded astrological messages. Ancient Greek Homeric scholars had already rejected the effort to read the conversations, battles and sexual activities of the Homeric gods as literary horoscopes. More recently, Erasmus and Rabelais had debunked Homeric allegoresis in famous books. Kepler, acting as a sensible humanist, simply revived the healthy scepticism of his predecessors. He did not reject the humanist tradition but recovered a critical element within it.[6] Even when he attacked Aristotle on comets, he described himself in ambivalent terms, as "creating new doctrines, or rather recovering the old ones of Anaxagoras and Democritus."[7]

More generally, Kepler devoted himself throughout his life to traditional forms of scholarship as well as modern forms of science. Like a good northern Protestant, he grew up listening to sermons and disputations. Long hours of practice gave him a discriminating ear for exegesis. At the age of twelve he already found it shocking when a preacher distorted the text of Paul's Epistles to make it support a sermon that bashed the Calvinists.[8] The six stately volumes of Kepler's correspondence, those macaronic monuments, half Latin and half German, half mathematical and half unintelligible, to the folly and grandeur of the German baroque mind, contain dozens of discussions of passages from the Bible and the classics. Several of his scientific works include detailed digressions about problems in the early history of the exact sciences. His ***Apologia*** for Tycho against Ursus, which has received two substantial editions and commentaries in the last decade, offers one of the earliest full-scale efforts to trace the history of ancient astronomy.[9]

Comments scattered throughout Kepler's work show how much the act of reading meant to him. He described his encounters with books with articulate interest, dating the most important ones—like his reading, at the age of seventeen, of Julius Caesar Scaliger's *Exercitationes* against Cardano, which had inspired him to study natural philosophy.[10] Kepler's accounts of reading show meticulous attention to nuances and differences and are couched in a crisply precise terminology. He evoked at different times the horror with which he read the paranoid, weirdly argued pamphlet by Nicolas Ursus against Tycho, with its apparently deliberate misreadings of ancient and modern texts; the delight with which he savored Erasmus Reinhold's ruminations, "purissimo et suavissimo sermonis genere," on the general effects of the stars on the sublunary world; the microscopic attention with which he scrutinized Girolamo Cardano's detailed descriptions of comets, word by word. Kepler used Cardano's crisp, well-chosen adjectives to compensate for the weakness of his own eyesight. The Italian magus's vivid prose made clear to Kepler what a comet's tail actually looked like.[11]

Kepler, moreover, did not always read literally or resist the temptation to find hidden meanings in the classics. Annotating his **Somnium,** a rich, if strange account of a voyage to the moon, he dated with exquisite care his first encounters with the relevant ancient texts by Plutarch and Lucian. He also stated, curiously, that Lucian had hinted that he meant his satirical *True History* as a profound account of the physical world.[12] Evidently Kepler saw reading as a range of possible responses to an equally wide range of forms of writing. One might compare his sense of discrimination to the trained attention he presciently brought to bear on astronomical data and conditions of observation.

Sustained interest in older texts was only natural in someone of Kepler's time and place. Style interested him deeply—strange though that statement may seem to those who have enjoyed a bracing dip in the chill waters of Kepler's Latin syntax. He had a humanist education, which gave him the normal sense that the ancients had said most things better than moderns could[13] and he wrote for courtly patrons, who were also expert humanists and had a sharp and appreciative eye for striking turns of Latin phrase. Like most products of this system of training and patronage, he never lost his desire to adorn his own style with gems and gewgaws filched from the best ancient writers. In pursuit of these he read and reread the classics. As a mature astronomer reprinting his **Mysterium cosmographicum,** he lamented the fact that he had not yet read Seneca's *Natural Questions* when he first wrote the book. Accordingly he had failed to quote Seneca in the preface, where he argued that nature retained plenty of secrets not yet explored. Kepler now provided the relevant sentence, "adorned," he said, "with the little flowers of Latin eloquence," in a footnote.[14]

Kepler's interest in the substance of ancient texts was just as natural as his concern for their style and even more sustained. Most sixteenth- and early seventeenth-century scientists, as the late Charles Schmitt, Ian Maclean, and others have shown, resorted to books not only when explicating the natural world in university courses but also when writing about it for a mature public. Commentators by vocation, they saw their duty not as discovering facts never before seen and drawing inferences from them but as assembling facts from reliable sources in a new and revealing order. Most sci-

entific research took the form of a search for *experientia litterata,* the written records of scientific facts, ancient or modern. Most scientific writing resulted not in reports on controlled situations but in commentary or *bricolage*—the discussion of canonical texts, line by line, in marginal notes or the rearrangement of fragments from them into new treatises. The normal early modern scientist resembled a bookworm dragging its endless length down endless bookstacks rather than Cesi's lynx fiercely scrutinizing the secrets of nature.[15]

The young Kepler frequently mounted this sort of scientific expedition around the shelves of a library. Discussing magnetism and the compass with the learned madman Herwart von Hohenburg, Chancellor of Bavaria, he quoted lavishly. His sources included Cardano's rich compendium of anecdotes about seals and symbols, candles made from the fat of corpses and the curative powers of saliva, the *On Subtlety;* Scaliger's *Exercitationes* on that work, at five hundred pages perhaps the longest as well as the most venomous book review in literary history; and Theodor Zwinger's genuinely weighty *Theatrum humanae vitae,* with its 3000 pages of carefully indexed anecdotes and examples from the ancients.[16] Every German university student and teacher knew these useful handbooks. Kepler's colleagues ransacked them for ideas and evidence when producing doctoral theses for debate. Such short treatises, normally written by professors for their students, for a fee, made no pretense to intellectual innovation. Rather, they reaffirmed the solvency of individual accounts in the vast savings bank of bookish knowledge.[17] When Kepler produced comparable Mannerist assemblages of quotation and argument, he engaged in normal science of the bookish kind. And his results could be as unsurprising as his reading matter.

But Kepler read in many ways, some of them highly complex. Reading, as he knew well, was a learned art *par excellence,* one governed by complex, explicit rules. German Protestants in Kepler's time wrote the first full-scale manuals that framed these rules and even devised the name of the art they defined: hermeneutics. Like the dancing of the time, reading had an etiquette. Machiavelli never seems more conventional than when he describes himself, in a famous letter, brushing off the mud and debris he has accumulated in a day spent fishing, gambling, and drinking, and putting on royal garments before he ventures to address the ancients, in their splendid courts. Like dancing, reading followed complex, preprogrammed steps but allowed for a certain amount of individual innovation. But unlike dancing in the Renaissance or reading now, however, reading in Kepler's time remained western culture's central, normal way of obtaining important information. Indeed, it offered the model, as Galileo's case shows, for all complex forms of learning. Two brief studies will suggest some of the distinctive features of Kepler's practice as a reader and a few of the ways in which these interacted with his practice as a scientist.

First, the reader as courtier. No author found more readers in early modern courts than Tacitus, the grimly analytical historian of the Roman empire. His mordant dissections of character and conflict revealed a world startlingly like that of the late sixteenth century, a chiaroscuro panorama of corruption in high places, its foreground crowded by the bodies of honorable dissenters foully murdered, its center dominated by scowling tyrants. Translations of his difficult text, commentaries on his political lessons, and rearrangements of his stories and lessons into more systematic order filled the shelves of the specialists called "politicians" (*politici, politiques*).[18] These men advised rulers and aristocrats, often disastrously, and taught university courses on the arts of empire and diplomacy. They read, as Lisa Jardine and I have argued elsewhere, less for private enlightenment than for public consumption, basing their authority and influence on their claim to make ancient texts teach modern lessons.[19]

Like the *politici,* Kepler read Tacitus in a public context—at the imperial court in Prague, where he collated the original text with translations into French, Italian, and German and made his own version of *Histories* I. Like the *politici,* he took an almost obsessive interest in the text. The brilliant Flemish humanist Justus Lipsius offered to recite all of Tacitus, word by word, with a dagger held to his throat, to be plunged in if he made one mistake. Kepler made his fifth child, Ludwig, learn Latin partly from his German Tacitus. Starting at the advanced age of six, the boy spent three years translating Kepler's German back into Latin and comparing his results with the original. Like the *politici,* Kepler commented at length on the problems and lessons of his text in parenthetical remarks he inserted into the body of his translation rather than in a separate commentary.[20]

Normal interpreters—the most influential of whom was Lipsius—treated the text less as an organic whole than as a set of lessons to be memorized. Lipsius's own most famous book, the *Politica,* simply rearranged tags from Tacitus and others to fit the topics of a systematic treatment of politics. Arnold Clapmarius, the Helmstedt prodigy whose posthumous *De arcanis rerumpublicarum* made a great splash on its appearance in 1605, went even further in the same direction. He insisted that Tacitus offered his readers all the *arcana* of government, the secret principles that Roman emperors had employed to retain their power; and he diced the text into pill-sized axioms, topic by topic.[21]

Kepler clearly shared the belief that Tacitus could provide instruction in prudence for modern *politici.* He also clearly shared the hope that his scholarship could help courtly readers to extract this. When Ludwig published Kepler's translation, he described it as "Voller trefflicher Regiments- und Kriegsdiscursen, Diser Zeit nit weniger nutzlich/ als von vergleichung wegen der alten und newen Welt annemblich zu lesen"—a sharply practical work on government and warfare. Ludwig dedicated it to Maria Salome, Gräfin von Hebersdorff, who had asked him for a copy of the text for her son, later an officer in Wallenstein's army.[22] Kepler's version, with its general introductions and helpful, sometimes elementary glosses, was clearly intended to serve a public of rulers, not one of scholars.[23] It provided material for the collective discussions of politics, in which modern cases were referred to ancient examples, that made up so much of court life in the Latin-drenched courts of central Europe. Kepler's reading of Tacitus thus had a public and collective as well as a private dimension, amounting as much to performance as to meditation.

All of this was conventional, but Kepler's actual analysis of his text contrasted sharply with the fashionable ones. He insisted on treating Tacitus's work as an organic whole, in both its content and its expression. He urged his reader to find in it not simple, ready-to-serve lessons but a complex, supple portrait of a moving target. Tacitus, he explained, had represented the Roman state at a time of strain, in a situation of civil war which had forced it to use all its sinews and muscles—a situation like that of the modern Holy Roman Empire. He had thus revealed its strengths and weaknesses in vivid detail—but in a way that the reader could capture only by working through his text as a whole, not by snipping it into bits and reassembling them like the parts of a jigsaw puzzle.[24]

Kepler warned the reader not to look for simple, schoolboy lessons about political prudence. Tacitus wrote that Nero's death and Galba's rise to empire had revealed an *arcanum imperii*—that one could become an emperor without being at Rome. Clapmarius inferred that Tacitus was stating a formal, secret law of the Roman empire, a principle consciously (if covertly) applied by Augustus and Tiberius. He dutifully wrote a chapter about the need for emperors to be crowned only in their capitals.[25] Kepler, by contrast, insisted that one should take the passage in a much more general way. Tacitus meant only that 'the secret was out'; one could become emperor in the provinces if one had sufficient military and political support. He meant not to state a formal rule of empire but to describe a single political situation.[26] In this case the scientist clearly read the text with more penetration than the humanist. Kepler responded to the same needs and interests that the humanist commentators on Tacitus confronted; but he framed his response in a characteristically individual way. In his version of Tacitism as in his aversion to allegoresis, Kepler showed the density and intricacy of his involvement with textual knowledge. He also showed that though he aimed his work at a court audience, he did not feel he had to cut his cloth exactly as courtly fashion dictated.

Second, the scientist. Kepler's astronomical work constantly refers and responds to earlier texts. In his first major book, the **Mysterium cosmographicum,** he argued at length that his thesis about the five regular solids both drew on and improved on Pythagoras and Plato. He also discussed Ptolemy's astronomy at length, comparing his models for planetary motion to the Copernican ones—though he owed the substance of his discussion not to mother wit but to his helpful teacher, Maestlin.[27] In later books, notably the **Tabulae Rudolphinae,** he sketched a full-scale history of astronomy from its ancient origins to his own day.

Kepler gradually developed a new story about the development of his science. It had come into being— here he agreed with such contemporaries as Henry Savile—in the ancient Near East in the land of the Chaldeans, whose eclipse observations Ptolemy cited. But the Chaldean astronomers had not begun work at the fabulously early dates claimed by some of the "Chaldeans" mentioned in classical texts (Cicero recorded a boast of 470,000 years of observation). The earliest observations referred to with any precision were those that Callisthenes, Aristotle's disciple, had supposedly turned up in Babylon. These began only 1903 years before Babylon fell to Alexander the Great. As to the observations actually used by ancient astronomers, the earliest were the Babylonian eclipse records used by Ptolemy. These began only with the era of Nabonassar in 747 BC. Astronomy, in short, was not as venerable as history or poetry.

The best of ancient astronomy was in fact quite recent. Kepler thought that Dionysius, an astronomer of the third century BC mentioned in the *Almagest,* had begun the systematic observation of planetary motions, with some help from the Chaldeans. Hipparchus produced the first rough tables in the second century BC, and ancient planetary theory reached completion in the double form of precise geometrical models and accurate predictive tables, only in the work of Ptolemy in the second century AD.[28]

Astronomy, moreover, was no pure science even as Ptolemy practised it. Its ancient students had been inspired less by the austere task of predicting the motions of the planets than by the profitable one of predicting events on earth, which they saw as controlled by the stars. Ptolemy himself wrote the standard manual of astrology, the *Tetrabiblos,* and all classical astronomy, before and after his time, retained the clear signs of its origin in superstition. As a tree could be tracked unequivocally to its roots, so astronomy could be tracked back to the divinatory beliefs that had spawned it. Its technical substance, like the tree's rings, bore the ineradicable evidence of its history.[29]

Classical astrology Kepler treated in an especially insightful way—not as a bundle of implausible superstitions but as a discipline with all the apparent order, rigor, and elaboration of a valid ancient science. Originally, to be sure, celestial divination had been nothing more than the normal superstition of the Chaldeans, a bundle of obvious *nugae*. But Ptolemy and other Greek astronomers had used the tools of logic and computation to make the *nugae* seem precise and coherent. They had thus made superstition look as rigorous as science—and ensured that their predecessors would continue to take both studies very seriously.[30]

Kepler's sketches of the history of astronomy differ sharply, as Nicholas Jardine has shown, from the ones that frequently provided a starting point for sixteenth-century university lecture courses on classical astronomy. These usually took the form of set pieces, like modern introductory lectures; they were designed to enhance the lecturer's prestige and bolster his enrollments. To make the genealogy of his discipline as noble as possible, the lecturer would push its beginning to the earliest possible date and identify as its inventors the most famous possible individuals. He could attain both ends, and often did, by making Adam and Noah the inventor and the transmitter of real astronomy. The teacher wanted his field to be glamorous as well as ancient. So he usually insisted that astronomy had been cultivated above all in the mysterious Near East, by sage Chaldeans, Magi, and Egyptians. Zoroaster and Hermes might receive as much space, attention and praise as Hipparchus and Ptolemy. Miraculous feats—like Thales's famous eclipse prediction— bulked larger than humble accumulation of data and drawing up of tables. The whole enterprise, finally, was not analysed in technical detail but apotheosized in the fluffy adjectival clouds of epideictic rhetoric. Astronomy's past, so evoked, gave it legitimacy and prestige. The real details of parentage and the like—as so often—were prudently left unexamined.[31]

Kepler's history, by contrast, rested on close examination of primary sources. He portrayed astronomy as the result of human effort, carried out by boring Greeks, rather than that of divine revelation, freely offered to exciting Orientals; and he insisted on the flawed and contingent nature even of the science of Ptolemy, Copernicus, and Kepler himself.

This history had a genealogy of its own, as Kepler scrupulously stated. Giovanni Pico della Mirandola analyzed the claims of classical astronomy and astrology to an ancient Near Eastern pedigree a hundred years before Kepler, in the brilliant *Disputationes* against astrology that he had almost finished when he died (on the day the astrologers had predicted). He dismantled the Chaldeans' claims as dextrously as Kepler would, using the same evidence. And Kepler repeatedly said that he took Pico's work very seriously, even if he did not accept all of its conclusions.[32]

But Kepler did not simply copy his predecessor. Pico strictly distinguished between astronomy, which he praised as rigorous science, and astrology, which he dismissed as worthless superstition. Moreover, he inserted astrology into a single, constricted position in his family tree of the mathematical sciences. He described it not as the wicked stepmother but only as the worthless daughter of the other art. Ancient astronomers, he argued, echoing Aristotle's account of the school of Pythagoras, were overcome by the elegance and predictive power of their art. They made the natural but deadly mistake of overestimating its powers; hence their assumption that the movements of the heavens could be used to predict individual fates and historical events. Superstition arose from the abuse of science.[33]

Kepler, by contrast, insisted that science had sprung from superstition in the first place. In its final form astrology embodied the sophisticated mathematics of Ptolemy, but in its origins the belief in divination from the stars had preceded and inspired the growth of astronomy. The desire to know the human future gave rise to the science of planetary motions, and the two were intertwined throughout history. Kepler's attack on myth was even more radical than Pico's; he extended it to the mythical autonomy of science.

Kepler addressed his history, like his German Tacitus, to patrons at court. But it too was unfashionable. Kepler's dismissal of horoscopic astrology, his downgrading of Near Eastern sages and his diminuendo treatment of the rigor of astronomy all contradicted positions that the alchemists and astrologers of the Habsburg court loved to maintain.[34] His reading of early astronomy produced critical history, not fluffy genealogy.

Kepler's interests and practices as a reader reveal a great deal. In the first place, they show that not all humanistic scholarship was the same. Like the most original scholars of his time, Scaliger and Casaubon, Kepler chose his methods and questions with discrimination and independence. He rightly dismissed some humanistic methods as arbitrary. But he accepted others as rigorous and valid, and fused them in his own readings of the sources. Kepler distinguished between mathematics and philology and strongly preferred the former to the latter.[35] But he insisted that astronomers had to use history and philology as well as computation and observation. Otherwise they could not assess their oldest data—those preserved by ancient writers. Problems of interpretation were not confined to the early history of astronomy. Copernicus suggested that Ptolemy and other ancients had deliberately altered certain observations to make them fit their theories.[36] Herwart and other contemporaries of Kepler revived this thesis, which had some *prima facie* support in the *Almagest* itself. Only close scrutiny of the surviving sources, rigorously conducted, enabled Kepler to reject

their critique.[37] Direct study of classical texts thus formed an integral part of Kepler's astronomy, as it had formed part of Copernicus's before him.

Similarly, Kepler's case shows that not all the bookish science of the years around 1600 led into dead ends or labyrinths with no centers. The work of readers was as varied as it was profuse, and some of it had organic connections to the most powerful empirical and mathematical science of the time. Advanced natural philosophy and advanced textual scholarship were first brought together by Regiomontanus, Poliziano and others in late fifteenth-century Italy. More than a century later, science and scholarship were still tightly connected in many sectors. The nature of their bonds awaits, and will certainly reward, exploration.

In Kepler's own case, finally, awareness of his ways of reading and his meticulous attention to the grain and texture of past astronomy help to explain a crucial feature of his scientific writing. Historians have long wondered why Kepler included so much information in his works about his own trials and failures. It seems likely that he did so precisely because he had a humanist's sense of his own position in history. After spending a lifetime reading Virgil and Ovid, Petrarch wrote a formal letter *To Posterity* to answer his future readers' questions. After devoting much of his life to Ptolemy and Copernicus, Kepler provided a rich set of historical glosses for his own texts, which would enable his readers to answer some of the questions that he could not ask his predecessors. He identified the sources and weaknesses of his data, explained his assumptions, and corrected his own slips and errors. Kepler knew that earlier astronomers had made bad assumptions and come to wrong conclusions. But the austere, finished literary form adopted by Ptolemy and imitated by Copernicus made it impossible to see exactly where and how they had gone wrong. By adopting an open, even labyrinthine, form of exposition, by making his texts into open-ended dialogues with his earlier selves, Kepler provided his future readers with exactly the information that his own sources denied him.[38]

Kepler had learned the humanists' crucial lesson. His texts, like all others, should be understood as the product of a specific time, place, and experience. Exposure to and participation in textual scholarship taught Kepler to treat his own work as contingent, not absolute. He learned from the humanists to present himself as the object, as well as the subject, of the history of science. Like Galileo's brilliant, polished rhetoric, Kepler's devoted self-scrutiny belongs to a period style of intellectual inquiry. The contrast between the two reveals the complexity and richness of the marriage between humanism and science which took place in the fifteenth century and did not dissolve until almost two hundred years later.

Notes

[1] Johannes Kepler, *Gesammelte Werke,* ed. M. Caspar et al. (Munich, 1937—), XIII, 330; XIV, 45.

[2] See B. Stephenson, *Kepler's Physical Astronomy* (New York, 1987).

[3] Kepler, *Gesammelte Werke,* VIII, 225.

[4] See e.g. Kepler, *Gesammelte Werke,* XVI, 329.

[5] P. Possi, *La scienza e la filosofia dei moderni* (Turin, 1989), chs. 3-4; E. Reeves, "Daniel 5 and the *Assayer:* Galileo reads the Handwriting on the Wall," *Journal of Medieval and Renaissance Studies,* 21 (1991), 1-27; "Augustine and Galileo on Reading the Heavens," *JHI,* 52 (1991), 563-79; cf. B. Goldstein, "Galileo's Account of Astronomical Miracles in the Bible: A Confusion of Sources," *Nuncius,* 5 (1990), 3-16. See more generally H. Blumenberg, *Die Lesbarkeit der Welt,* 2d ed. (Frankfurt, 1983).

[6] See in general J. Seznec, *The Survival of the Pagan Gods,* tr. B. F. Sessions (New York, 1953); T. Bleicher, *Homer in der deutschen Literatur (1450-1740)* (Stuttgart, 1972). For classical attacks on astronomical readings of Homer see Heraclitus, *Problemata Homerica* 53 and Plutarch, *De audiendis poetis* 19E.

[7] Kepler, *Gesammelte Werke,* VIII, 225: "Ignoscant igitur Philosophi, antiqua dogmata tuentes, nova fabricanti dogmata, seu potius vetera illa ANAXAGORAE et DEMOCRITI revocanti. . . . "

[8] Kepler, *Gesammelte Werke,* XII, 49.

[9] Jardine, *The Birth of History and Philosophy of Science* (Cambridge, 1984; repr. with corrections, 1988); V. Bialas in Kepler, *Gesammelte Werke,* XX, 1.

[10] Kepler, *Gesammelte Werke,* VIII, 15.

[11] Kepler, *Gesammelte Werke,* XIII, 344-45; X, 40 (Kepler describes Reinhold's text colorfully: "in ea namque flores halant ex hortis Philosophiae penitissimis, admirabilis fragrantiae, quae lectori veluti mentem ipsam eripit"); VIII, 227-28 (on Cardano he says: "Propemodum ad vivum depinxit nostros Cometas, excepto colore").

[12] Kepler, *Opera omnia,* ed. C. Frisch (Frankfurt and Erlangen, 1858-71), VIII, pt. 1, 40: "quae [sc. Lucian's *fabula*] tamen aliquid de totius universi natura innuebat, ut quidem ipse Lucianus monet in exordio." See the excellent analysis by J. S. Romm, "Lucian and Plutarch as Sources for Kepler's *Somnium,*" *Classical and Modern Literature,* 9 (1989), 97-107.

[13] See F. Seck's edition of and commentary on Kepler's Latin poems, in Kepler, *Gesammelte Werke,* XII; also Seck's article "Johannes Kepler als Dichter," in *Internationales Kepler-Symposium: Weil der Stadt 1971. Referate und Diskussionen,* ed. F. Krafft (Hildesheim, 1973), 427-51.

[14] Kepler, *Gesammelte Werke,* VIII, 22: "Non legeram SENECAM, qui pene eandem sententiam Eloquentiae Romanae flosculis sic exornavit. . . ."

[15] See C. Schmitt, *Studies in Renaissance Philosophy and Science* (London, 1981); I. Maclean, "The interpretation of natural signs: Cardano's *De subtilitate* versus Scaliger's *Exercitationes,"* *Occult and Scientific Mentalities in the Renaissance,* ed. B. Vickers (Cambridge, 1984), 231-52.

[16] Kepler, *Gesammelte Werke,* XIII, 188-97.

[17] See A. Grafton, "The World of the Polyhistors: Humanism and Encyclopedism," *Central European History,* 18 (1985), 31-47.

[18] See A. Momigliano, "The First Political Commentary on Tacitus," *Essays in Ancient and Modern Historiography* (Oxford, 1977), 205-29; P. Burke, "Tacitism," in *Tacitus,* ed. T. A. Dorey (London, 1979); G. Oestreich, *Neostoicism and the Early Modern State,* tr. D. McClintock (Cambridge, 1982); M. Morford, *Stoics and Neostoics* (Princeton, 1991).

[19] L. Jardine and A. Grafton, "'Studied for Action': How Gabriel Harvey read his Livy," *Past & Present,* 129 (1990), 30-78.

[20] See the excellent presentation of the text by F. Boockmann in Kepler, *Gesammelte Werke,* XII, 367-75.

[21] See in general M. Stolleis, *Arcana imperii und Ratio status* (Göttingen, 1980); P. S. Donaldson, *Machiavelli and Mystery of State* (Cambridge, 1988), ch. 4.

[22] Kepler, *Gesammelte Werke,* XII, 103, 371-2.

[23] Kepler, *Gesammelte Werke,* XII, 377.

[24] Kepler, *Gesammelte Werke,* XII, 112.

[25] A. Clapmarius, *De arcanis rerumpublicarum* (Amsterdam, 1644), II.xx, 98-100.

[26] Kepler, *Gesammelte Werke,* XII, 126: "Nicht / dass es ein lang verschwiegener / unnd etlichen wenigen bekandter Griff gewest wäre: sondern weil sie jetzo an Käyser Galba ein Exempel hatten: da gedacht ein jeder Obrister unnd Röm: Rathsherr: halt still / wil es nun hinfort also zugehn / wil ich mir selber das beste gönnen."

[27] For the first edition of the *Mysterium* see Kepler, *Gesammelte Werke,* I; for the second, with his commentary, see *Gesammelte Werke* VIII. See also the reprint of the second edition with a translation by A. M. Duncan, ed. E. J. Aiton (New York, 1981).

[28] Kepler, *Gesammelte Werke,* X, 37-8.

[29] Kepler, *Gesammelte Werke,* X, 36: "ut in arborum fibris anni, sic in tota divinissimae artis compositione lineamenta quaedam apparent ortus hujus: ut Matrem et Nutricem Astrologiam abnegare non possit Astronomia filia et alumna."

[30] Kepler, *Gesammelte Werke,* X, 38.

[31] See Jardine, *The Birth of History and Philosophy of Science.* For a more critical assessment of Kepler's philological attainments, see B. Eastwood, "Kepler as Historian of Science: Precursors of Copernican Heliocentrism according to *De revolutionibus* I, 10," *Proceedings of the American Philosophical Society,* 126 (1982), 367-94. W. N. Stevenson has undertaken a detailed study of Kepler's work on Lucan, which promises to offer the fullest and most precise assessment yet of Kepler's Latin scholarship.

[32] See e.g. Kepler, *Gesammelte Werke,* VI, 266; XIV, 285.

[33] G. Pico della Mirandola, *Disputationes contra astrologiam divinatricem,* ed. E. Garin (Florence, 1946-52).

[34] See O. Hannaway, *The Chemists and the Word* (Baltimore, 1975); and, more generally, R. Evans, *Rudolf II and his World* (Oxford, 1973); H. Trevor-Roper, *Princes and Artists* (London, 1976), ch. 3. True, some artists and intellectuals at Rudolf's court nourished a real appreciation for technological and artistic progress; see T. D. Kaufmann, *The School of Prague* (Chicago and London, 1988), 96-99. Courts, like other early modern institutions, were highly complex organizations—as Kepler's case itself clearly shows.

[35] Kepler, *Gesammelte Werke,* XIV, 165; see Jardine, *Birth of History and Philosophy of Science,* 27, for the circumstances.

[36] Kepler, *Gesammelte Werke,* VIII, 102-3 (from Rheticus' report). Copernicus supposedly remarked that "plerasque observationes veterum synceras non esse, sed accommodatas ad eam doctrinam motuum, quam sibiipsi vnusquisque peculiariter constituisset"; he also lamented, showing his own high degree of philological insight, that "Non habere nos tales auctores, quales PTOLEMAEUS habuisset post Babylonios et Chaldaeos, illa lumina artis, HIPPARCHUM, TIMOCHAREM, MENELAUM, et caeteros, quorum et nos observationibus ac praeceptis niti ac confidere possemus."

[37] See e.g. Kepler, *Gesammelte Werke,* XIV, 285.

[38] A recent study makes insightful use of Kepler's comments on his own work, and sheds a new light on his debt to a number of ancient works (notably Plato's *Timaeus* and Proclus' commentary on book 1 of Euclid): J. V. Field, *Kepler's Geometrical Cosmology* (Chicago, 1988).

Job Kozhamthadam, S. J. (essay date 1994)

SOURCE: "Kepler's Scientific Ideas," in *The Discovery of Kepler's Laws: The Interaction of Science, Philosophy, and Religion,* University of Notre Dame Press, 1994, pp. 84-109.

[*In the following essay, Kozhamthadam examines the lasting contribution of Kepler's scientific principles and discusses his methodology.*]

Among the founders of modern science Kepler occupies an immortal place. But he would not have earned this privileged position for himself had he stopped at his religious and philosophical views, insightful and creative though they were. He could go beyond most of his contemporaries and rise above their world infested with mysterious and occult forces, precisely because he demanded that his system should include empirical or scientific thought as well. He enjoyed speculating, he could soar to the heights of speculative ideas, yet he never lost contact with the ground. Time and again he insisted that no idea, however startling and attractive, was any good if it could not agree with experience. This requirement was strikingly evident in his view on astronomy. He declared to [Carteggio] Brengger that he was giving "a physics of the heavens in place of a theology of the heavens or a metaphysics of Aristotle."[1] For many Aristotelians, cosmology or study of the universe, especially of the heavenly bodies, was a part of metaphysics. Kepler wanted to give a new direction and scope to the study of the heavens. His was a new science, a new physics in which "I teach a new mathematics of computing not from circles but from natural faculties and from the magnetic properties."[2] As [Robert] Small and [Alexandre] Koyré point out, the emphasis on physical explanation distinguished Kepler from practically all his predecessors and contemporaries (except Galileo). Emphasis on physical interpretation was perhaps the most crucial part of his scientific view. Since demand for physical explanation has become commonplace for us, indeed it has become part of our common-sense wisdom, we shall never be able to appreciate fully how novel and revolutionary were Kepler's contributions to science. Apart from stressing realism, his scientific outlook took in several other vistas as well. For instance, he wrote in the *Epitome:* "I build my whole astronomy on Copernicus's hypothesis concerning the world, upon the observations of T. Brahe, and lastly upon the Englishman, W. Gilbert's philosophy of magnetism."[3]

Observation

Kepler considered observations uniquely important in his system. Galileo, to a great extent, and Newton, to some extent,[4] failed to give due recognition to this fact. On the other hand, Small and [J. L. E.] Dreyer seem to have overemphasized this dimension of Kepler's investigations. In this context [Max] Caspar has the following to say: "As daring and rich in fantasy as he was in his speculations about the universe, just as thoroughly did he now proceed, taking no step without gathering authorization and confirmation from the observations. Indeed, while following his Mars researches, one almost gets the impression that sometimes he deals with individual tasks and proofs out of pure delight and pleasure in the observations."[5] In this emphasis on observation Kepler departed decisively from his predecessors and contemporaries alike (except for Galileo). Indeed, others considered observation important, but neither in the way nor to the extent that Kepler did.

Plato's position on the importance of observation in the acquisition of scientific knowledge is very controversial. Most of his writings, especially the earlier ones, leave little doubt that observations played no major role in his science. For instance, in the *Republic* he had the following to say:

> Thus we must pursue astronomy in the same way as geometry, dealing with its fundamental questions. But what is seen in the heavens must be ignored if we truly want to have our share in astronomy. . . . Although celestial phenomena must be regarded as the most beautiful and perfect of that which exists in the visible world (since they are formed of something visible), we must, nevertheless, consider them as far inferior to the true, that is, to the motions . . . really existing behind them. This can be seen by reason and thought, but not perceived with the eyes.[6]

According to this passage, astronomy or science should engage in the study of the fundamental questions and that is to be done not so much by investigating the fleeting and inferior observed phenomena as by discovering the real motion behind the observed ones. Such fundamental questions can be tackled only by the eyes of reason, not of vision. Just as in geometry the power of reason is decisive, so in astronomy the same power should predominate. According to the second sentence of the passage above, we must reject what is seen externally, which, according to the third, must be considered inferior. Plato himself seemed to be hesitating between ruling out and undervaluing the role of observation in empirical science. In his later writings he seemed to attach some importance to observations. In the *Timaeus* he wrote: "Sight, then, in my judgment is the cause of the highest benefits to us in that no

word of our present discourse about the universe could ever have been spoken, had we never seen stars, sun, and sky. But as it is, the sight of day and night . . . has caused the invention of number and bestowed on us the notion of time and the study of the nature of the world. . . ."[7] These statements and others like them show that observations did have a place in Plato's study of nature; his exact position on the role of observation remains unclear. But whatever be the final interpretation, Plato did not consider observation crucial for science. The same point of view was upheld by the later Platonists as well.

Aristotle, on the other hand, stressed sense observation for the acquisition of knowledge, as is evident from his idea that nothing can be in the intellect unless it enters through the senses first. Consequently, sense observation is a necessary condition for cognition. Aristotle's insistence on observation can be seen from the fact that he is often considered the founder of zoology because of his book *The Natural History of Animals*, where he classified more than five hundred different species. In the study of cosmology, too, he gave evidence from everyday experience. For instance, he argued from experience to establish that the earth has a spherical shape. Even though reliance or insistence on observation was not absent in the writings of Aristotle and his later followers, the experimental probing of nature certainly was not a crucial factor. Furthermore, where experiments were performed (e.g., Jordanus and the opticians), attention to quantitative precision was minimal. The concern remained very much on the qualitative.

Although like Plato, Kepler emphasized the importance of geometry and geometrical method, and although like Aristotle, Kepler made constant use of philosophical principles in his scientific work, he considered precise and quantitative observations crucial for scientific work. He affirmed: "Without appropriate experiments I conclude nothing."[8] Again, he told Fabricius: "Hypothesis must be built upon and confirmed by observations. . . ."[9] In *AN* [*Astronamia nova*] he called them *fidissimi duces,* "most reliable guides."[10] Indeed, they were the most reliable guides in his adventurous and challenging search for the secrets of nature. He could trust the verdict of observation, and, once his theory had been attested to by observation, he could rest assured that he had either reached his goal or was on the right track. When his theory was attacked by others, his major defense consisted in referring his opponent to observational data. He asked: "Is there anything in astronomy more certain than the observations either of the sun or Mars? I make judgments from these."[11]

He himself made many observations,[12] despite his own visual problems[13] and the lack of accurate and advanced instruments. He refused to believe the Copernican explanation for the failure to observe stellar parallax.

According to Kepler, the universe is not infinite and the stars are not at an infinite distance from us. To verify this claim, he looked for stellar parallax, but with no success. This failure led him to conclude that the parallax of the Polestar must be smaller than eight minutes "because my instrument cannot measure angles smaller than this."[14] In his letters to various people he talked about the many observations he made. For instance, he had observed Halley's comet. Again, in his letter to Galileo he requested the Italian to make some specific observations.[15] Kepler wanted to make observations as accurate as possible; if experimental conditions did not permit accurate results, he wanted to take several observations because "all doubts are to be excluded by many observations."[16]

It seems that he sensed a kind of divine aura surrounding observations. The expressions he used, the respect he showed to them, evoked the presence of something holy and divine. His words about Tycho's observations illustrate this point: "Let all be silent, and give heed to Tycho Brahe, the Dane, who now for the thirty-fifth year is devoting himself to observation, who sees more with his eyes than many others with mental vision, a single instrument of whom cannot be counterbalanced by my whole thought and being. . . ."[17] Obviously this statement involves a lot of exaggeration. At the same time we notice a deep feeling of reverence as though for something divine. He expressed this idea once again in his letter to Maestlin on March 5, 1605: "I consider as an honor only one thing that by divine disposition I have been permitted to be in close contact with Tycho's observations."[18] His association of observational data with divinity was made clear also when he refused to accept an error of 8 minutes because he believed that Tycho's observations were a gift from God and hence deserved to be given utmost importance. Observations overwhelmed him. He wrote to Herwart: "I would have concluded my research on the harmonies of the world long ago, if Tycho's astronomy had not won me over so strongly that I almost went out of my mind."[19]

How much he valued accurate observations is again manifested by his willingness to make exceptions to many other principles he otherwise so zealously cherished in life. He was deeply attached to the principle of circularity according to which heavenly bodies always move in circular orbits. He gave it up, however, when observations convinced him that the Martian orbit deviated from the circle. Similarly, he was convinced of the supreme power of geometry to reveal the structure of the universe, yet when Tycho's observations disclosed that geometrical considerations alone were inadequate to reveal the structure of the universe, Kepler was willing to accept the verdict of empirical data and look for additional laws required to give a complete picture of the universe. He had insisted on individual freedom, he publicly professed selflessness in his scientific work, and he always loved peace and shunned occasions of petty fights and quarrels. But when Tycho's observations were at stake he seemed to have forgotten all these other fine rules that he had striven so much to cultivate. Kepler, the great advocate of personal freedom and selflessness in scientific work, asserted: "This is my opinion about Tycho: although he abounds in riches, like very many rich persons, he does not know how to make proper use of them. Therefore . . . let us take measures to wring [*extorqueamus*] his treasures from him so that we can improve on them. . . ."[20] Kepler did not hesitate to advocate the use of some force to get the Dane's observations from him!

Why did Kepler insist on observation so much? He was too original to be overwhelmingly influenced by other individuals. Nevertheless, Copernicus and Tycho exerted major influence on him. And of course, his beloved teacher Maestlin also was another important authority, yet in a different way. The success of the Copernican theory, which had a strong observational basis, further reinforced Kepler's belief that a true theory should be based on observations.

In addition, the ideas and works of Tycho convinced Kepler of the unique importance of observations in scientific investigation. He had sent a copy of his *MC* [*Mysterium Cosmographicum*] to Tycho who promptly expressed his deep and personal appreciation for the ingenious book. The Dane agreed with our astronomer's idea that in the universe existed a certain symmetry and harmony, but Tycho made the following point: "However, the harmony and proportion of this arrangement must be [sought for] a posteriori, where the motions and the circumstances of the motions have been definitely established, and must not be determined a priori as you and Maestlin would do; even there they are difficult to find."[21] In his letter to Maestlin on April 21, 1598, Tycho was less inhibited by any constraints of tactfulness: "If improvement in astronomy must be made a priori, by means of these regular solids, rather than a posteriori, we shall assuredly have to wait too long, if not forever and in vain, until someone does it."[22] He did not believe that an a priori method would lead astronomy very far. Such a program was doomed to failure.

However, we must not conclude that Kepler would not have emphasized observation had he not come under the influence of Tycho. Some scholars seem to imply that interest in empirical inquiry in general, and observational data in particular, was a temporary phase for Kepler and was confined to the *AN*. In their view, his interest was just a temporary deviation from his lifelong career of speculation and "mystical" contemplation. Nothing can be further from the truth. Even in his *MC*, his highly speculative book, he took observational evidence into consideration. In fact, after proposing his polyhedral hypothesis, he subjected it to empirical verification, checking it with Copernican data. Although there was fairly satisfactory agreement between theory and observation, there were discrepancies; he took special pains to account for these discrepancies.[23]

Kepler stressed the need for observation all through his career because he was a firm believer of the principle of realism. His realism looked for tangible and observable evidence for scientific theories.

Inference to Generalization

Kepler's emphasis on observation in no way made him a positivist who refuses to go beyond the observable. He believed that many things, though unobservable, could be known by inference. In fact, many significant results in his science he arrived at by inference, rather than by direct observation. For instance, in his research on the planetary motion he studied in detail only the planet Mars. However, he generalized his finding to all the planets. Thus already in the *AN* in the beginning of part 4 he wrote: "Whatever I have demonstrated in the third part are applicable to all the planets. Hence without hesitation they can be considered the key to the genuine astronomy. . . ."[24] In the *Epitome* he made this generalization absolutely explicit.[25] Obviously, this generalization in the *AN* was not based on direct observations, but he had to rely on inference. One may object to this position by saying that in the *Epitome* Kepler gave the eccentricity and position of the aphelion for Mercury and Venus; for Mercury the eccentricity was 0.210 and aphelion at 255 degrees, for Venus 0.00604 and 302 degrees respectively. The objection is not serious. And these determinations came much later than *AN*. Again, being able to determine the eccentricities and positions of two or three planets does not entitle one to claim that the planetary laws are applicable to all planets. To make such a general claim, one needs to know all the relevant aspects—not just one or two—to which the laws are applied.

Another remarkable instance in which Kepler made an inference to generalization was in his study of star-globes. He argued that the globes of the stars were similar to the earth although "experience is silent about it, since nobody has been there. Therefore experience neither denies nor confirms [the claim]."[26] He stated that he arrived at this general conclusion by inference on the basis of the similarity between the earth and the heavenly bodies.

He refused to believe that something did not exist just because it had not been observed. For instance, he argued that just because a particular comet could not be seen, we should not deny its existence. "You believe that one should see them [comets] if they exist. I deny this. For if they traverse a path far away from the earth, it is not necessary, if they are small, that one be able to see them."[27] In such cases, however, he cautioned that we should only talk of probable existence.

Kepler could make many generalizations because he believed in the principle of generalizability. Obviously, this philosophical principle enabled him to make extremely important generalizations that were crucial for his scientific work.

Inference to the Unobservable

In the previous section we have been discussing instances of inference to unobserved, but in principle observable, entities. Kepler believed that such inference was applicable to unobservable entities as well. These directly unobservable entities in present-day philosophy of science we call "theoretical entities." His stressing observation in no way ruled out the possibility and reality of his considering theoretical entities.[28] True, he never called them "theoretical entities," but he talked about "forces," "solar emanation," "magnetism," "animal forces," etc., entities that admittedly were unobservable and yet real for him. Unobservable themselves, their effects could be observed and experienced.

Kepler's belief that inference to the unobserved is legitimate was firmly rooted in the principles of causality, realism, and unity. The principle of causality stipulates that for every effect there must be a cause; invisibility or unobservability of the cause cannot mean impossibility of the cause. Along with causality, adherence to realism makes possible the attribution of reality to the unobserved or unobservable world because the effects observed are real and hence the source responsible for them must also be real. Further, the principle of unity holds that the observable and the unobservable realms are interrelated and constitute one unified whole.

Kepler's religious beliefs made him readily willing to make inference to the unobserved and the unobservable and to affirm them as real and existing. In religion, many fundamental claims he accepted as true and existing though unobservable, for instance, the Holy Trinity—what is real need not in every case be observable and such instances must have encouraged him to infer to the unobservable without undue hesitation.

Force

One of Kepler's major contributions was that he emphasized the need for moving away from explanation in terms of abstract principles like "substantial forms" and "natural places" to explanation using real, physical forces. He made this point clear when he contrasted his method with Fabricius's. Kepler wrote on August 1, 1607: "The difference is to be found in the fact that you [Fabricius] use circles and I use corporeal forces."[29] This statement implies that in order to explain certain natural phenomena, his friend took recourse to certain metaphysical presuppositions, whereas Kepler relied on real and corporeal forces. For instance, according to Fabricius and other traditional astronomers, heavenly bodies have to move with uniform circular motion because the sky is spherical and its sphericity demands that the motion be uniform and circular. In contrast to this metaphysical explanation, Kepler wanted to consider the forces involved in the motion and their interaction with the planetary body. We shall see that Keplerian force operated midway between the Newtonian force and the traditional Aristotelian contact force without being either one of them.

Kepler's idea of force underwent a gradual but remarkable change during the course of his career: a transition from the souls to real, physical forces as the cause of planetary motion. That the varying and unpredictable souls of the early days gave way to invariant and predictable forces implied a shift from explaining planetary motion in terms of forms to accounting for it in terms of forces. In turn, the explanatory factor shifted from *a definite way of acting* to *something that acts in a definite way*. This major development in his idea of force is most conspicuously brought out in the two editions of *MC.* In the first edition he believed that the cause of planetary motion was a soul indwelling in the sun, the effect of the power of which diminished with distance. In the *AN* he discarded the idea of a soul and postulated an immaterial *species* emanating from the body of the sun.

This immaterial *species* had a number of particular characteristics that prevented it from being cast into any known traditional category. Though immaterial, it was not purely spiritual. It was, in a sense, corporeal because it resided in the material body. Kepler clearly stated that the emanation or *species* "flowed from its [the sun's] body out to its distance without the passing of any time. . . ."[30] The *species* was therefore independent of time in the sense that it moved without the passage of time. It lacked any weight.[31] He insisted that, although it was immaterial and weightless, it did not have infinite velocity.[32] Again, it was quantifiable and hence amenable to mathematical treatment. As he put it, "For we see these motions taking place in space and time and this virtue emanating from its source and diffusing through the spaces of the universe, which are all mathematical [geometrical] realities. From this it follows that this virtue is subject also to other mathematical laws [*necessitatibus*]."[33] It follows, therefore, that the Keplerian force described in the *AN* is an immaterial but corporeal *species* that is seated within a material body and is quantifiable. Thus he had taken a giant step away from the soul of the *MC* of 1596. Kepler made sure that his readers captured this evolution of his idea when he wrote the important note in the second edition of the *MC:*

> If for the word "soul" you substitute the word "force," you have the very same principle on which the celestial

physics is established in the *Commentaries on Mars,* and elaborated in Book IV of the *Epitome of Astronomy.* For once I believed that the cause which moves the planets was precisely a soul, as I was of course imbued with the doctrine of J. C. Scaliger on moving intelligences. But when I pondered that this moving cause grows weaker with distance, and that the sun's light grows thinner with distance from the sun, from that I concluded, that this force is something corporeal, that is, an emanation which a body emits, but an immaterial one.[34]

According to Max Jammer, this move from soul to Keplerian force "announces the birth of the Newtonian concept of force."[35] Koestler believes that Kepler's was "the first serious attempt to explain the mechanism of the solar system in terms of physical forces."[36]

Kepler's idea of force was midway between the Newtonian and the Aristotelian concepts. With its corporeal and quantifiable nature Kepler's force certainly was non-Aristotelian. It also differed from the Newtonian notion of force in several respects. First, it was a tangential, pushing force propagated from the body of the sun in straight lines producing velocity, whereas the Newtonian idea was of central force producing acceleration; he believed that the body of the sun along with the immaterial *species* rotated continuously, thereby whirling the planets around the sun. Furthermore, the Newtonian force could act on bodies at a distance without material contact, whereas Kepler still subscribed to the Aristotelian idea of contact forces.

This idea involved serious philosophical problems. For instance, if the emanation was immaterial, how could it interact with material bodies, causing them to move? To this question Kepler replied that though immaterial, the force was directed to matter and exerted no influence in the space between the sun and the planets. The force was not like odor that gets spent up in the intervening space. "It is propagated through the universe . . . but it is nowhere received except where there is a moveable body. . . . [Like light] it has no present existence in the space between the source and the object which it lights up, although it has passed through that space in the past; it 'is' not, it 'was,' so to speak."[37] Again, Kepler said that the immaterial emanation could affect material bodies, which seems to bring up the problem of the interaction between body and soul. His only answer to the challenge was to point his critic to the analogy of light, in which, he argued, such an interaction took place. However, we know that this is only an analogy because there are marked differences between the action of light and of the immaterial emanation. For instance, in an eclipse, light is blocked off and the action of light stops, whereas the action of the immaterial emanation continues to be effective, since planets continue to move at the time of eclipse. The argument from analogy, even if it is valid, cannot solve the philosophical problem but only minimize the strangeness of the case. After all, one can ask how immaterial light can affect material bodies; the basic problem remains unaccounted for.

Kepler indeed seemed to be quite uneasy about the ontology of this emanation. He seemed to have great difficulty explaining exactly what the nature of this force was, although he had hardly any difficulty describing what it did. Comparing the emanation with magnetism also could not get him out of difficulties because with magnetism also the force had serious differences. Magnetic force is attractive or repulsive, whereas this one is tangential. Such a magnetic force would change the orbit of planets considerably. On the other hand, the planets would have to continue moving unaltered in their orbits.

The Keplerian idea of force had its roots in his philosophical and religious ideas.[38] The principle of dynamism, based on a dynamic God, states that our universe is dynamic. The presence of forces is an external manifestation of this dynamism because force is the cause of motion and other activities. The principle of causality requires that the activities in the universe should have an active cause: planetary motion should have an active cause, and Kepler postulated force as the efficient cause of planetary motion.

His all-important concept of dynamic force had its firm basis in his religious view, especially his idea of the trinitarian God. In fact, force was the reflection of the Holy Spirit. He argued that just as God the Father acts through the Holy Spirit, the sun diffused and bestowed motive power across the *intermedium*. Then he affirmed that his description was not a mere heuristic analogy but the true picture of how the universe existed and operated.[39]

Mass

The development of the concept of mass was another important contribution of Kepler. The concepts of mass and force are closely related, complementary concepts, as Max Jammer points out. This complementarity becomes obvious when we realize that force refers to the cause of motion, whereas (inertial) mass to what resists motion. Jammer presents another insight: the idea of force had its origin in the Aristotelian concept of form (the soul being the form of the living being), whereas mass took its origin from the Aristotelian concept of prime matter. Since substantial form and prime matter are complementary facets of the same reality, force and mass should also have a similar relation.

Kepler proposed his idea of mass in *AN* in connection with planetary motion under the influence of the force from the sun. He said that when the sun's force tried to take the planet along with it, the planet resisted such

a motion, since as a material body it had an inherent property "to rest or to privation of motion."[40] A clearer description he gave in the *Epitome* when he attributed to the planets "a natural and material resistance or inertia to leaving a place, once occupied."[41] In his note to the second edition of *MC* he made the point more openly still: "Clearly the bodies of the planets in motion, or in the process of being carried round the sun, are not to be considered as mathematical points, but definitely as material bodies, and with something in the nature of weight (as I have written in my book *On the New Star*), that is, to the extent to which they possess the ability to resist a motion applied externally, in proportion to the bulk of the body and the density of its matter."[42] From this statement can be inferred: (1) (inertial) mass has the nature of weight; (2) it resists a force which is externally applied; (3) this resistance is proportional to the quantity of matter in the body. The Keplerian concept of mass fell short of the Newtonian in certain significant respects. For instance, although Kepler rejected the doctrine of natural places, he adhered to Aristotelian inertia; he still lacked the modern concept of inertia. Again, the resistance offered by the material body was to motion, not, as in Newton's second law, to acceleration.

Despite these drawbacks, Kepler's idea of mass had original features. For example, as in the case of force, mass is quantifiable. Describing the property of mass or *moles,* as he called it, he wrote: "If two stones were placed in any part of the world, near each other yet beyond the sphere of influence [*orbem virtutis*] of a third cognate body, these two stones, like two magnetic bodies, would come together at some intermediate place, each approaching the other through a distance in proportion to the mass of the other."[43] The distance each stone will move depends on the ratio of their respective masses, and, just like the distances, the masses can also be quantified.

Furthermore, like force, mass is something dynamic and active. It actively fights with the force emanating from the sun: "The transporting power of the sun and the impotence of the planet or its material inertia fight with each other [*pugnant inter se*]."[44] A closely related idea is that the time period of the revolution of the planet is dependent on the mass, just as it is on the force from the sun. This idea, too, departed from the past; according to the traditional view, the celestial bodies offered no resistance to motion and so the matter in them had no role in determining their period of revolution. True, Kepler did not arrive at the Newtonian concept of mass, but he definitely moved away from traditional ideas and contributed to the development of the modern concept.

How did he come up with these new ideas? Reflection on the observed phenomena certainly had a crucial role to play in this context. He wrote in the *Epitome:* "If the matter of celestial bodies were not endowed with inertia, something similar to weight, no force would be needed for their movement from their place; the smallest motive force would suffice to impart to them an infinite velocity. Since, however, the periods of planetary revolutions take up definite times, some longer and others shorter, it is clear that matter must have inertia which accounts for these differences."[45] As in the concept of force, the philosophical principles of dynamism of nature and of causality also must have played an important role in the development of Kepler's concept of mass.

Physical Explanation

The emphasis on physical explanation in the study of nature was another one of Kepler's original contributions. [Owen] Gingerich points out that "Kepler was the first and until Descartes the only scientist to demand a physical explanation for celestial phenomena."[46] Kepler insisted on the physical as a necessary condition for any interpretation of natural phenomena. Despite its extreme importance in physical science, no fully satisfactory definition of a physical explanation has emerged, nor is it my purpose to develop a formal definition. An explanation can be looked upon as an attempt to unfold (*explico*) or to elucidate how a phenomenon has come about the way it is. An explanation of spectral lines, for instance, consists in pointing out that they are formed by electron jumps from one energy level to another. Notice that such an elucidation involves theoretical terms like "electron," "stationary orbits," "electronic states," "energy levels," and "electron jumps." Whatever one may say about physical explanation, for Kepler, at least, it was an unfolding where the cause of the phenomenon is given in terms of physical, real factors. Such an explanation, he argued, must remove the "cause of wonder" by specifying the real causes.

Kepler's idea of physical explanation is intimately connected to, and a direct application of, the philosophical principles discussed in chapter 2. These philosophical principles provide the rational basis for a physical explanation. For instance, one of the chief requirements of a rationally acceptable explanation is that it should not violate the philosophical principles of simplicity, economy, causality, etc. Undoubtedly, this scientific view of Kepler had its basis in his philosophical view.

What is "physical"? Although Kepler gave no formal definition of "physical," he did present a good idea of what he meant when he discussed his hypothesis of the oval orbit of Mars in a letter to Maestlin on December 22, 1616: "The hypothesis is physical because it uses the physical example of a magnet. It is physical, i.e. natural, because it is true and is derived from the very internal nature of planetary and solar bodies. It is physical because it pertains to all modes of natural motion."[47] This is the most detailed and least unclear description of his idea of the physical that I have been able to find in his voluminous writings. The passage gives three different reasons or criteria for considering a hypothesis H physical: (1) H is physical if it involves real forces (since for Kepler magnetism was a paradigm of a real physical force, this interpretation seems to be correct). (2) H is physical (i.e., natural) if it is deduced from the very internal nature of bodies like the sun and the planets; H is physical if it is real and derived from the internal, as opposed to the accidental or transitory, characteristics of material bodies. (3) H is physical if it accounts for all modes of natural motions of planets: H is physical if it can account for all real observable phenomena under consideration. This interpretation (3) seems to me to be correct because Kepler is talking of H in the context of explaining the different observed motions of Mars. So, Kepler himself set down three conditions that specify the meaning of "physical."

As we have already noted, for a physical explanation he stipulated one more condition: all explanations in science must be consistent with philosophical principles. This point he brought out very clearly when he talked about his aim to mechanize the heavens. He sought not only a mechanical explanation, but an explication where the causes involved were characterized by the principles of simplicity, unity, etc.[48]

The question now is whether these different requirements individually or collectively constitute the sufficient condition for a physical explanation. Kepler, as usual, was not clear about this question. If they collectively constitute the sufficient condition, what is the status of each individually? Is each principle a necessary condition for physical explanation? I think that together they are collectively sufficient and individually each is a necessary condition to unfold a satisfactory physical account of phenomena. For just the presence of physical force alone cannot render an explanation physical; it should be able to account for observed phenomena. Conversely, just being able to account for observed phenomena will not make research findings physical because a metaphysical working-out for such phenomena could suffice, as the Aristotelians always held. The Ptolemaic method could account for the phenomena, but Kepler never accepted that path as physical. Furthermore, just because an explanation is derived from the internal nature of material bodies need not mean it is physical. This condition can guarantee that the explanatory factor has a basis in reality, but not that it can account for the phenomena itself. Again, consistency and coherence are necessary for any acceptable explanation, but having these two qualities need not entitle the presentation of the findings to be a physical explanation—purely mathematical or logical explanation can be both consistent and coherent without being physical. I think that a variety of different factors collectively constitute a physical explanation for Kepler.

Thus a physical explanation, according to Kepler, accounts for or gives reasons for the true working of a phenomenon in terms of matter, known or knowable forces, and other theoretical entities that have a real basis in the internal, as opposed to the transitory or superficial, characteristics of matter, and that does so in a way consistent with certain philosophical principles.

A prime example was his treatment of planetary motion. The explanation was in terms of the effluvia emanating from the whole body of the sun. This emanation was like a magnetic force whose effects could be explained, although its cause remained unknown. The effects of the force could account for the observed motion of the planets around the sun. Finally, this example harmonized with the principles of simplicity, generalizability, and so forth.

The discussion above can reveal the shortcomings of some earlier attempts by Kepler scholars to describe his idea of "physical" and hence of "physical explanation." Holton thinks that mechanical explainability was the heart of Kepler's idea of physical explanation: "The physically real world, which defines the nature of things, is the world of phenomena explainable by mechanical principles."[49] This obviously raises questions about the meaning of "mechanical principles." Holton says that "mechanical" refers to "the world of objects and of their mechanical interactions in the sense which Newton used."[50] In other words, the physically real must be explainable in terms of matter and forces or interaction. However, the Newtonian forces could act at a distance. Kepler, on the other hand, still adhered to the notion of contact forces. He certainly wanted a scientific explanation to be mechanical in the sense that it involved matter and (contact) forces.[51] But he wanted much more. An explanation may be mechanical, but not real. Galileo's explanation of the tides was certainly mechanical but failed to correspond to reality;[52] Kepler did not go along with the Italian's position.[53] Thus explainability in terms of mechanical principles was only a necessary condition for a physical explanation. For Kepler another condition must be met: consistency with his philosophical principles. He was no Baconian empiricist or Laplacian mechanist. Indeed, he believed in empiricism and mechanism, but both his empiricism and mechanism were grounded deeply in his philosophy.

This insistence on physical explanation as a necessary condition for scientific inquiry was one of Kepler's new and original contributions. This originality can be seen from the fact that Aristotle and the Aristotelians in general did not emphasize the physical as a necessary element in their explanation of natural phenomena. Being guided by the principles of the *Posterior Analytics,* very often their interpretations consisted in logical deductions from certain presuppositions assumed to be true of the universe on the basis of logical rather than physical entities. For instance, consider Aristotle's explanation for the observed fact that heavy objects fall to the ground. He explained the phenomenon in terms of "natural places." The "natural place" of an earthy object was the center of the universe and so it would always tend to move towards that point even if no physical object were there. On the other hand, Newton explained the same phenomenon in terms of an attractive force between the earth and the object. Newton introduced a definite physical factor into his explanation. Of course, there were philosophical problems with Newton's forces, which Leibniz and Berkeley were not slow to point out. And even several thirteenth-century scientists did indeed introduce physical factors into their explanation of natural phenomena like the rainbow (I have already pointed out several marked differences between Kepler and them); nevertheless, their physics still remained Aristotelian. Our astronomer, on the other hand, emphasized both physical explanation and a new physics.

Another consideration also can bring out the originality of Kepler's contribution. Often opposition from others, especially from one's own peers in the field, is a reliable gauge to assess the degree of originality of a new view. An original idea often goes against, or at least challenges, the established set of ideas and norms and thus becomes a threat to the status quo. Hence opposition. If such opposition be regarded as a criterion, then Kepler's view was highly original indeed. His emphasis on physical explanation drew opposition from friends and foes alike.

Perhaps the most vehement opposition came from the clergyman Fabricius, Kepler's persistent and tireless correspondent. Fabricius's strong voluntaristic tendencies surfaced in his reaction to Kepler's emphasis on the explanation of natural phenomena in terms of physical causes. According to voluntarism, God's will is responsible for the different events and phenomena in the universe and so their explanation is to be sought in God's will rather than in any physical causes, which are responsible only indirectly (*mediate*), if at all. Fabricius echoed the same sentiment in his reply to Kepler in a letter on February 7, 1603,[54] asserting that causes of sickness and other natural phenomena were to be found in the will of God (*ordinationem divinam*). Taking place in the universe were so many events, none of which depended on physical causes. He illustrated his case with an example. A stone can be a boundary marker, a road sign, or the cornerstone of a house. The stone's function depends, not on its internal nature, but on the desire and will of humans.[55] Looking for the cause in the stone itself for its being sometimes a milestone, sometimes a cornerstone, etc., would be stupid. Fabricius pointed out that even Holy Scripture attested to his position, for according to the Bible, the stars are endowed with light in order that they may be signs—not causal agents to explain physical phenomena. They are just a passive medium through which God's will is manifested. He concluded his attack: "Therefore it is exceedingly gross [*crassus*] and worthless [*carnale*] to wish to refer all the works of God to physical causes or to philosophical standards. We have seen how invalid the physical and philosophical explanations are from many works of God. . . . By just one single little word of God . . . a multitude of arguments can be brought forth [for the solution of an issue] that cannot be solved sufficiently satisfactorily by all philosophical secrets [wisdom]."[56] According to Fabricius, Kepler's search for physical causes was simply wasted effort, totally unworthy of a believer like his friend.

Kepler was far from being impressed with Fabricius's arguments. Being a firm believer in God, Kepler recognized the efficaciousness of God's will and power. But he refused to go along with his friend's naive interpretation of that will. According to Kepler, God may permit certain events. This would imply that the events follow the laws of nature set by God at the time of creation. God does not interfere with them. God permits certain events to take place at certain times, but God does not will them to existence. Fabricius's position would make God a continuous creator, since every event has to come to existence by God's will. For Kepler, God is the continuous conserver of the universe. Furthermore, he pointed out that his friend's position had to resort to explanations purely in terms of occult divine relations. Regarding the will of God, Kepler argued that Fabricius's position, which relegated the events and operations in the universe to the arbitrary will of God, would render rational science impossible.[57]

Kepler pointed out further that in his eagerness to attribute everything to God, Fabricius was making God a part of nature. Our astronomer then characterized his and his friend's positions: "For you God turns to the constellation to give rise to the different temperaments and inclinations. For me the sublunar souls look after the same function."[58] According to Fabricius, to account for many natural phenomena, one had to resort to God's direct intervention, whereas according to Kepler, such an account could be given by means of the sublunar souls created by God. Later on Kepler would exorcise these souls and bring in forces in their place. What he wanted to say was that he could explain many workings of nature in terms of natural forces rather than by God's direct intervention.

Not even Maestlin appreciated this emphasis on physical explanation. Kepler informed Peter Crüger, professor of mathematics in Danzig, that "Maestlin used to laugh about my endeavors to reduce everything, also

in regard to the Moon, to physical origin. In fact, this is my delight, the main consolation and pride of my work, that I succeeded in that. . . ."[59] Writing in this context, Maestlin took his disciple to task:

> When you write about the moon, you say that you would like to adduce physical causes for all its inequalities. I simply do not understand this. On the contrary, I believe that physical causes can be dismissed altogether, and that it is fitting to explain astronomical phenomena only through astronomical methods, by means of astronomical, not physical, causes and hypotheses. For calculations demand astronomical bases from geometry and arithmetic, which, so to speak, represent their wings, rather than physical hypothesis, which would more likely confuse than instruct the reader.[60]

This remarkable letter, written in 1616, long after the *AN* had been published, makes clear how deep rooted the Ptolemaic conception of astronomy was even in the mind of a moderate like Maestlin. Kepler replied that his teacher's objection arose from an ambiguity concerning the concept "physical." He believed that once this notion was clarified, Maestlin's objection would be taken care of; the objection came, not because the physical method was false, but because the concept had not been clarified.

In the marginal notes of *AN* he tried to clarify the concept "physical." A physical hypothesis must correspond to something real, it cannot be just a geometrical hypothesis based purely on geometrical assumptions. "I shall accept only that which cannot be doubted as truly real and therefore physical. . . ."[61] Secondly, "physical" refers to something proper to the very nature of the body under consideration, as opposed to something accidental. Thus nonuniform motion of planets he considered physical because it is "appropriate for the nature of the planets, and is therefore physical."[62] (These ideas agree with the passages from Kepler that I quoted earlier.) He went on to say that his ideas were in accord with the true nature of things and since Maestlin was a seeker after this true nature, his clarifications should put his teacher's objections to rest.

The Scientific Method

Kepler made outstanding contributions also in the development of the method of modern science. However, since he never gave any systematic or detailed discussion of his method, we have to depend mainly on his actual practice and occasional statements on the subject. He often called his approach to science an "a priori method." Maestlin commended his devoted student for espousing this method, which for him was a "frontal" approach, while the a posteriori method was a "backdoor" approach. Recommending the *Mysterium Cosmographicum* to Hafenreffer, the prorector of Tübingen, Maestlin asked in 1596: "For whoever conceived the idea or made such a daring attempt as to demonstrate a priori the number, the order, the magnitude, and the movements of the celestial spheres . . . and to elicit all this from the secret, unfathomable decrees of heaven!"[63] Like his teacher, Kepler also preferred this method, finding it was superior to all other methods. In *MC* he wrote:

> For what could be said or imagined which would be more remarkable, or more convincing, than that what Copernicus established by observation, from the effects, a posteriori, by a lucky rather than a confident guess, like a blind man, leaning on a stick as he walks (as Rheticus himself used to say) and believed to be the case, all that, I say, is discovered to have been quite correctly established by reasoning derived a priori, from the causes, from the idea of creation?[64]

He was convinced in his early days that this method was the best: "For God knows, this a priori method serves to improve the study of the movements of the celestial bodies."[65]

What is the a priori method? It is a deductive method as opposed to the inductive, a posteriori method advocated by Tycho. Certain hypotheses concerning the explanation of natural phenomena are presupposed.[66] These hypotheses are expressed in mathematical formulations, and particular mathematical deductions are drawn from them. The mathematical formulations and deductions make the approach a priori, since they are considered strictly valid in contrast to the merely empirical observations and generalizations that are involved in induction. The propositions need not always be given a mathematical formulation; however, in his work, Kepler usually did so.

This a priori method seemed to fit well with Kepler's understanding of what astronomy should be.[67] According to him, astronomers should give *causas probabiles* (causes worthy of approval) for the phenomena under consideration. To achieve this he stipulated that the principles of astronomy must be anchored in a higher science, namely physics or metaphysics. The a priori method could provide the *causas probabiles* by way of deduction from higher principles.

I believe that the name "a priori" is misleading and that Kepler's method in essence was the hypothetico-deductive method (H-D method) as understood by several modern philosophers of science. The name "a priori" implies that observation has no real role in the method, which is far from the truth; for despite all the emphasis Kepler placed on metaphysical and mathematical reasoning, despite all the criticism he raised against the a posteriori method of Tycho and others, he also recognized the importance of observation. Thus already in 1595, in the prime of the *MC,* he wrote to Maestlin: "We can put all our hopes into it [the a priori method] if others cooperate who have observations at their disposal. . . ."[68] To Herwart on July 12, 1600, he affirmed that the a priori speculations must not contradict manifest experience but, rather, agree with it.[69] Therefore the a priori method was not purely mathematical, and still less was it purely speculative. Experience played a significant role. This was quite evident from Kepler's extreme eagerness to see Tycho's observational data in order to verify the findings of his polyhedral theory.

Kepler's a priori method was not purely a priori, rather combined a priori and a posteriori principles. In this regard Kepler's method is very similar to the *argumentatio ex suppositione* that Galileo was to employ years later;[70] this form of argument also has two distinct parts: the a priori and the empirical. The a priori part provides conceptual aids such as axioms and definitions and also specifies that the reasoning involved is to be based on logical dependencies. On the other hand, the empirical dimension relates the propositions obtained by means of a priori arguments to empirical existential statements. Tycho seemed to have overlooked this point when he criticized Kepler and Maestlin for attempting to build up an astronomy without using accurate empirical data. Kepler insisted on agreement with observed data, and when there was an appreciable discrepancy he looked for an explanation. For instance, he noticed that the polyhedral theory had a great discrepancy: his value for the distance of Mercury was 577 whereas the Copernican data gave 723. He tried to get around this problem by arguing that Mercury was an exception. This planet, he maintained, should not be inscribed within the sphere of the octahedron, as would be expected according to the original model, but within the circle of the octahedron square. This gave a value of 707, much closer to the Copernican value of 723. He tried to give some justification for this special treatment of the innermost planet. The key point of his argument was that the exceptional character of Mercury demanded that it be treated differently.[71] His explanation turned out to be false. But the point is that he took the disagreement with observation seriously and attempted to provide an explanation by using tools available to him.[72]

Kepler's so-called a priori method has one major difference from the H-D method: the hypothesis is not a product of some irrational or purely psychological process.[73] According to him, a scientific hypothesis has a rational basis. This point is very clear from his response to Fabricius: "But you think that I can just invent some elegant hypothesis and pat myself on the back for embellishing it and then finally examine it with respect to observations. But you are far off."[74] Hypothesis is not the figment of one's imagination, as he illustrated by a concrete example: "I demonstrated the oval figure from the observations. . . ."[75]

No doubt he used hypotheses in this sense in the *AN*. But one may object that in *MC* and *HM [Harmonices Mundi]* such was not the case. For instance, the opponent may say that the polyhedral theory came to him by chance. In his own words, "Eventually by a certain mere accident I chanced to come closer to the actual state of affairs."[76] First of all, Kepler did not use the word "chance" in the sense of "at random" or "irrationally." For him a chance event was simply an unforeseen event, an event that he did not anticipate. Here, for instance, after making the statement above he went on to give the different steps he used to arrive at the hypothesis.[77] Moreover, Kepler truly believed that this hypothesis came to him as a gift from God, the gift of Divine Providence. He continued: "I thought it was by divine intervention that I gained fortuitously what I was never able to obtain by any amount of toil; and I believed that all the more because I had always prayed to God that if Copernicus had told the truth, things should proceed in this way."[78] Here Kepler says that God gave him this hypothesis as a gift. However, this belief did not render the hypothesis any the less rationally founded, because he was convinced that the supremely rational God must have had a good reason for it. Hence even here the hypothesis was not the product of irrationality.

From the hypothesis thus rationally arrived at he made certain rational deductions that he subjected to observational tests. This point also he explained in no uncertain terms: "I put forward [or presuppose] a few things as a groundwork and from there I follow observations."[79] The same idea he expressed in another letter to Fabricius: "It is true that when a hypothesis is constructed from observations and then confirmed by them, I am wonderfully excited afterwards, if I can discover in it something consonant with [*concinnitatem*] nature."[80] This statement specifies that the item derived from the hypothesis is not just anything, but something consonant or in agreement with accepted principles of nature.[81]

Hypothesis formation has at least two constraints. First of all, it must be consonant with his principles. Secondly, it has to have a basis in observation. It is not created in a vacuum, it is not a product of pure imagination. A hypothesis is hypothetical, not because it does not have any basis in principles and observation, but because these bases are not adequate or sufficient.

Kepler's method basically consisted in deriving certain testable deductions from such a hypothesis and subjecting them to observational scrutiny. That this was his general method not only in the *AN* but even in his highly speculative *MC* can be seen from a brief examination of his polyhedral theory. This hypothesis had a strong basis in his religious belief in a geometer God. It also took root in his philosophical view that the universe is geometrical, rational, and intelligible to us

humans. In a way it had an observational basis too, because, as he narrated, the idea came to him when he inscribed "many triangles, or quasi-triangles, in the same circle, so that the end of one was the beginning of another."[82] He observed that the points at which the sides of the triangles intersected traced out a smaller circle. "The ratio of the circles to each other appeared to the eye almost the same as that between Saturn and Jupiter."[83] Consequently, this hypothesis was not the product of a random process. Once the hypothesis was formed, he deduced from it the relative distances of the planets from the sun. Then he checked the values obtained from the theory against those given by Copernicus.

It can be shown that in all his three major works (i.e., *MC*, *AN*, and *HM*) the method used is basically the same.[84] In all of them the principal goal is the same: scientifically, to discover the structure and operation of the universe; religiously, to give praise and honor to the supreme creator; and philosophically, to establish the universe as rational, intelligible, and accessible to human inquiry. All three use the same kind of tools of inquiry. Sometimes a particular tool may be used more than at another time. For instance, reliance on observational data is more conspicuous in *AN* than in *HM* and *MC*, harmonic considerations are more pronounced in *HM* than in the other two works, geometrical inquiry is more conspicuous in MC. In all the three works, however, he basically employs the H-D method in the sense we have discussed above—in *AN* as has been discussed by many Kepler scholars, and in *MC* and *HM* as we are about to see. In *MC* the basic contention is the polyhedral hypothesis that the solar system has been created as a series of spheres in which are nested the five regular solids according to a certain pattern. In *HM* the basic hypothesis is that the whole universe is governed by the rules of harmony, especially those of musical harmony, and that the creator made use of these rules in the creation of the universe. Both hypotheses have empirical backing. From both hypotheses particular observable consequences have been deduced. We have already seen what the empirical deductions were in the polyhedral theory. For the harmonic theory he also looked for empirical verification.[85] He found that it can quite well account for the eccentricities of the planetary orbits. Another remarkable point that once more bears eloquent testimony to the fact that Kepler, even in his most speculative moments, remained a scientist at heart is seen in one of the suggestions he made while discussing the harmonic theory: this theory could yield the age of the universe, or at least of the solar system.[86] He deduced from this theory by calculation the number of years needed for two planets to come into consonance. Then he noted that a consonance between three planets could be calculated. Similarly, the number of years required for a consonance among all the planets of the solar system could be obtained from the theory. He identified the beginning of the universe, or at least of the solar system, with the instant of consonance among all the planets. Thus he argued that his theory could give the age of the universe. Although here he did not carry out the actual calculation, he gave directions for it.[87]

I do not deny that there are differences in the methods of *AN, MC,* and *HM,* but I think that the differences are only a matter of degree of emphasis, rather than of basic nature. If we are inclined to think that *AN* is very scientific in method and that *MC* and *HM* are unscientific, then perhaps we are prejudiced in favor of the theory that turned out to be correct. Thanks to hindsight. There is, in fact, no radical difference of method. This is quite understandable because Kepler always modified his method to suit the goal he had in mind. Thus in *MC* and *HM* he was dealing with wider, cosmological questions such as Why did the creator make the universe as we see and experience it? He wanted to discover cosmic secrets, laws governing the whole cosmos. On the other hand, in *AN* he was investigating a specific problem: the laws governing the motion of planets, more exactly of just one planet. In all three works he was investigating laws of nature, but I notice a progressive widening of the goal or scope envisaged as we move from *AN* to *MC* and *HM.* Obviously, here I am not considering the chronological ordering of these books but the progression in the domain explored by the theories. In *AN* the goal is restricted since it confines itself to the motion of a single planet. In *MC* it is wider since it envisages the whole solar system. Finally in *HM* it is the widest, embracing the whole cosmos. At the same time I see a progressive deemphasis on the reliance on observations as we move from *AN* to *HM.* I suggest that the difference between *AN* and *HM* is a difference between science of specific things (e.g., study of nuclear fusion reaction in the laboratory) and science of cosmic and general phenomena (e.g., study of the origin of the universe). They may differ in the accurate, reliable results they can provide but not in their basic methodology.

Our study shows that Kepler made significant contributions in the development of the methodology of modern science. He can be rightly considered the first among the moderns to use the H-D method effectively in science. His other contributions to the development of modern science include his emphasis on the need for observation and for physical explanation in scientific inquiry. All were crucial for the transition of science from the medieval to the modern.

Notes

[1] Kepler's letter to Brengger on October 4, 1607, GW XVI, nr. 448: ll. 4-6.

[2] Ibid., nr. 448: ll. 8-10. I have translated the term *arithmeticam* as "mathematics." Although literally it should be "arithmetic," I think my translation is more faithful to what Kepler is conveying.

[3] GW VII, p. 254: ll. 40-42, tr. GB, p. 850.

[4] Newton said that Kepler got the laws by guesswork, rather than from observational study.

[5] Max Caspar, *Johannes Kepler,* p. 130.

[6] Plato, *Republic,* 529D and 530C, tr. Olaf Pederson, *Early Physics and Astronomy* (London: MacDonald and James, 1974), p. 27.

[7] Plato, *Timaeus* 47A, tr. F. M. Cornford, *Plato's Cosmology* (London: Routledge and Kegan Paul, 1956), p. 157.

[8] Kepler, GW VI, p. 226: ll. 21-22. Also in *Opera Omnia,* vol. 5, p. 224.

[9] Kepler's letter to Fabricius on July 4, 1603, in GW XIV, nr. 262: ll. 129-130.

[10] GW III, p. 191: l. 11.

[11] Kepler's letter to Fabricius on October 1, 1602, in GW XIV, nr. 226: ll. 394-395.

[12] For instance, see GW III, p. 124: l. 17-129: l. 35.

[13] Kepler suffered from myopia and multiple vision.

[14] Kepler's letter to Herwart on December 16, 1598, in GW XIII, nr. 107: ll. 135-136.

[15] See Kepler's letter to Galileo on October 13, 1597, in GW XIII, nr. 76: ll. 55-70.

[16] Kepler's letter to Herwart on March 26, 1598, in GW XIII, nr. 91: ll. 150-151.

[17] Kepler's letter to Herwart on April 10, 1599, in GW XIII, nr. 117: ll. 19-22, tr. SM, p. 110.

[18] GW XV, nr. 335: ll. 10-12.

[19] Kepler's letter to Herwart on July 12, 1600, in GW XIV, nr. 168: ll. 102-104.

[20] Kepler's letter to Maestlin on February 26, 1599, in GW XIII, nr. 113: ll. 89-92.

[21] Tycho's letter to Kepler on December 9, 1599, in GW XIV, nr. 145: ll. 197-200.

[22] GW XIII, nr. 94: ll. 18-22, tr. KY, p. 161.

[23] In fact, he confessed to Herwart: "One of the most important reasons for my visit to Tycho was my desire

to learn from him more correct figures for the eccentricities, by which I could check my *Mysterium* and the just mentioned *Harmony*. For these speculations a priori must not conflict with clear experimental evidence. Indeed they must be in conformity with it" (letter to Herwart on July 12, 1600, in GW XIV, nr. 168: ll. 105-109).

[24] GW III, p. 272: ll. 1-2.

[25] See GW VII, p. 318: ll. 20ff.

[26] Kepler's letter to Brengger on November 30, 1607, in GW XVI, nr. 463: ll. 88-89.

[27] Kepler's letter to Brengger on April 5, 1608, in GW XVI, nr. 488: ll. 348-349.

[28] Examples of such terms are "force," "field," "atom," "gene," "subconscious," "drive," etc. They refer to certain entities which are introduced into scientific theories to explain phenomena under consideration. What is their ontological status? How are they related to observable factors? How are they verified? These are much talked-about issues in twentieth-century philosophy of science. My own concern is to discuss what place such entities had in Kepler's system.

[29] GW XVI, nr. 438: ll. 18-19, tr. KY, p. 263.

[30] GW III, p. 242: ll. 29-30, tr. *Great Ideas Today,* p. 326.

[31] See ibid., p. 244: ll. 12-13.

[32] See ibid., p. 243: ll. 30-31.

[33] GW III, p. 241: ll. 10-13. See also Max Jammer, *Concepts of Force* (New York: Harper Torch Books, 1962), p. 87.

[34] MC, p. 203.

[35] Jammer, *Concepts of Force,* p. 90.

[36] Arthur Koestler, "Kepler, Johannes," *The Encyclopedia of Philosophy,* vol. 4 (New York: Macmillan, 1972), p. 333.

[37] GW III, p. 241: ll. 5-23, tr. Koestler, *Watershed,* p. 157.

[38] Concerning the Neoplatonic roots of this idea of force, see Fritz Krafft, "The New Celestial Physics of Johannes Kepler," p. 195.

[39] Kepler's argument goes as follows: Just as in the trinitarian sphere the Holy Spirit fills the space between the center and the surface, so also in the sphere of the universe the *species* or emanation fills the space between the fixed stars and the sun. Just as the Holy Spirit is ever active and dynamic, so too the emanation in the intervening space is active and dynamic. Just as the Holy Spirit can affect the universe and bring about changes, so too the emanation in the intervening space can exert an influence on bodies and cause changes in them.

[40] GW III, p. 244: ll. 20-21, tr. *Great Ideas Today,* p. 327.

[41] GW VII, p. 333: ll. 2-4. See also GW III, p. 244: ll. 20-21.

[42] MC, p. 171.

[43] GW III, p. 25: ll. 32-36. See Jammer, *Concepts of Mass* (Cambridge, Mass.: Harvard University Press, 1961), p. 54.

[44] GW VII, p. 301: ll. 22-25. Also *Opera Omnia* vol. 6, p. 346.

[45] Literally the last part of the quotation reads as follows: "with respect to the motive force, the inertia of matter is not like nothing to something" (GW VII, pp. 296: l. 42-297: l. 2). For the translation, see Jammer, *Concepts of Mass,* p. 55.

[46] Owen Gingerich, "Kepler, Johannes," *Dictionary of Scientific Biography,* vol. 7 (New York: Charles Scribner's, 1973), p. 292.

[47] GW XVII, nr. 750: ll. 194-197.

[48] See Kepler's letter to Herwart on February 10, 1605, in GW XV, nr. 325: ll. 60-61.

[49] Gerald Holton, "Johannes Kepler's Universe," p. 346.

[50] Ibid., p. 347.

[51] Also it may be noted that because of the problem of "action at a distance," Newton and others did not regard the Newtonian forces as giving a fully satisfactory explanation.

[52] Galileo's theory of the tide was incorrect. For one thing, unlike Kepler, he refused to attribute any definite role to the moon. Also, his theory could predict only one high tide daily. See Stillman Drake, *Galileo Studies* (Ann Arbor: University of Michigan Press, 1970), p. 205.

[53] For Kepler's explanation of the tide, see GW III, p. 26: ll. 1-23.

[54] See GW XIV, nr. 248: ll. 240ff.

[55] See ibid., nr. 248: ll. 350-359.

[56] Ibid., nr. 248: ll. 379-384.

[57] This point we have discussed in chapter 1. See Kepler's comment in Fabricius's letter, dated February 7, 1603, in GW XIV, nr. 248: ll. 375-377.

[58] Kepler's letter to Fabricius on July 4, 1603, in GW XIV, nr. 262: ll. 421-422. Here Kepler refers to the astrological beliefs of Fabricius, who was also a professional astrologer.

[59] Letter written on February 28, 1624, in GW XVIII, nr. 974: ll. 211-213, tr. CB, p. 149.

[60] Letter on September 21, 1616, in GW XVII, nr. 744: ll. 24-30.

[61] Ibid., nr. 744: ll. 77-78.

[62] Ibid., nr. 744: ll. 92-93.

[63] GW XIII, nr. 43: ll. 6-10, tr. CB, p. 37.

[64] MC, pp. 96-99.

[65] Kepler's letter to Maestlin on October 3, 1595, in GW XIII, nr. 23: ll. 203-204, tr. CB, p. 31.

[66] See CB, p. 30.

[67] See Jardine, *Birth of History and Philosophy of Science,* p. 250.

[68] Kepler's letter to Maestlin on October 3, 1595, in GW XIII, nr. 23: ll. 204-205, tr. CB, p. 31.

[69] See GW XIV, nr. 168: ll. 108-109.

[70] See Jürgen Mittelstrass, "Methodological Elements of Keplerian Astronomy," *Studies in History and Philosophy of Science* 3 (1972), 222.

[71] See MC, p. 173.

[72] It may be objected that Kepler's investigation of Mercury was a counterexample to my claim that he was using the H-D method, since if he really adhered to that method, he should have discarded the whole hypothesis because it failed to account for Mercury. However, this kind of problem is not peculiar to Kepler alone. In fact, this objection points to a general criticism of the H-D method, namely, in actual practice scientists do not discard a hypothesis simply because it fails to account for a particular result. They usually propose auxiliary hypotheses to modify the original one. Just because they employ auxiliary hypotheses, we do not say that they have given up the H-D method. It shows only that the H-D method has to be modified, and that this modified form of the method is more satisfactory. Kepler's study of Mercury in this context shows that he already had discovered this modified form of the H-D method.

[73] It is true that not all philosophers of science believe that the hypothesis in the H-D method is obtained from irrational (or nonrational) or psychological sources. However, the rational basis of such a hypothesis is still a matter of controversy.

[74] Kepler's letter to Fabricius on July 4, 1603, in GW XIV, nr. 262: ll. 127-129.

[75] Ibid., nr. 262: ll. 158-159.

[76] MC, p. 65.

[77] This Keplerian use of chance will appear again in part 2, in connection with an important step in the discovery of the ellipse.

[78] Idem.

[79] Letter to Fabricius on February 7, 1603, in GW XIV, nr. 248: ll. 487-489.

[80] Letter to Fabricius on July 4, 1603, in GW XIV, nr. 262: ll. 129-131.

[81] These are mainly the principles discussed in chapters 1 and 2.

[82] MC, p. 65.

[83] Ibid., pp. 65-67.

[84] The *Epitome,* although important, is not discussed here, because it is basically a systematic summary of all his major works.

[85] In the case of this theory he seems to be less particular about observational testing.

[86] See GW VI, pp. 323: l. 14-324: l. 15.

[87] However in his letter to Matthias Bernegger on June 30, 1625, he reported that he had arrived at the moment of creation by calculation (see GW XVIII, nr. 1010: ll. 30-38).

FURTHER READING

Ball, Sir Robert S. "Kepler." In his *Great Astronomers,* pp. 96-115. London: Isbister and Company, 1895.
    Brief biographical sketch of Kepler's life and career.

Bell, Arthur E. "The Example of Johann Kepler." In his *Newtonian Science*, pp. 18-38. London: Edward Arnold, 1961.

> Discusses the intellectual influences on scientists during the sixteenth and seventeenth century and of the importance of mathematics for grounding the theories of Kepler, Newton, and others in breaking away from the formalism of Greek science.

Berstein, Jeremy. "Heaven's Net." *The American Scholar*, (Spring 1997): 175-95.

> Exploration of the chance meetings and possible influences of Kepler and Donne on each other's work that includes biographical sketches highlighting their divergent personalities and differences in how each man responded to the religious turmoil of the day.

Dreyer, J.L.E. "Kepler." In his *A History of Astronomy from Thales to Kepler*, pp. 372-412. 2d edition. Dover Publications: U.S.A., 1953,.

> Examines how Kepler's work rid Copernican astronomy of the vestiges of the Ptolemaic system and prepared the way for Isaac Newton to build upon Kepler's theories.

Koestler, Arthur. *The Watershed: A Biography of Johannes Kepler*. Garden City, N. Y.: Anchor Books, 1960, 280 p.

> Seminal biography of Kepler by a noted novelist and essayist that explores the compelling, multi-faceted personality of Kepler as well as providing lucid explications of his theories.

Noyes, Alfred. "Kepler." In his *The Torch-Bearers: Watchers of the Sky*, pp.102-30. New York: Frederick A. Stokes, 1922.

> Noted poet's lyrical interpretation of Kepler's life and scientific quests in a volume celebrating scientific discovery.

Rosen, Edward. *Three Imperial Mathematicians: Kepler Trapped Between Tycho Brahe and Ursus*. New York: Abaris Books, 1986, 384 p.

> Detailed study of Kepler's role in a controversial rivalry between Tycho and Ursus, all three having held the post of Imperial Mathematician in the service of the Emperor Rudolph II.

Small, Robert. *An Account of the Astronomical Discoveries of Kepler*. 1804. Reprint. Madison: The University of Wisconsin Press, 1963, 386 p.

> Reprint of important early book-length study of Kepler's work that discusses both where he rejected and built upon the theories of his predecessors.

Thiel, Rudolph. "Kepler the God-Seeker." In his *And There Was Light: The Discovery of the Universe*, pp. 114-37. Translated by Richard and Clara Winston. New York: Alfred A. Knopf, 1957.

> Discusses how Kepler's faith influenced his work as a quest for harmony and order in the cosmos and his belief the geometry was a means to deciphering and appreciating the perfection of a divinely created universe.

Literature Criticism from 1400 to 1800

Cumulative Indexes

How to Use This Index

The main references

Calvino, Italo
1923–1985 .... CLC 5, 8, 11, 22, 33, 39,
73; SSC 3

list all author entries in the following Gale Literary Criticism series:

BLC = *Black Literature Criticism*
CLC = *Contemporary Literary Criticism*
CLR = *Children's Literature Review*
CMLC = *Classical and Medieval Literature Criticism*
DA = *DISCovering Authors*
DAB = *DISCovering Authors: British*
DAC = *DISCovering Authors: Canadian*
DAM = *DISCovering Authors: Modules*
    DRAM: *Dramatists Module;* *MST*: *Most-Studied Authors Module;*
    MULT: *Multicultural Authors Module;* *NOV*: *Novelists Module;*
    POET: *Poets Module;* *POP*: *Popular Fiction and Genre Authors Module*
DC = *Drama Criticism*
HLC = *Hispanic Literature Criticism*
LC = *Literature Criticism from 1400 to 1800*
NCLC = *Nineteenth-Century Literature Criticism*
PC = *Poetry Criticism*
SSC = *Short Story Criticism*
TCLC = *Twentieth-Century Literary Criticism*
WLC = *World Literature Criticism, 1500 to the Present*

The cross-references

See also CANR 23; CA 85-88;
   obituary CA116

list all author entries in the following Gale biographical and literary sources:

AAYA = *Authors & Artists for Young Adults*
AITN = *Authors in the News*
BEST = *Bestsellers*
BW = *Black Writers*
CA = *Contemporary Authors*
CAAS = *Contemporary Authors Autobiography Series*
CABS = *Contemporary Authors Bibliographical Series*
CANR = *Contemporary Authors New Revision Series*
CAP = *Contemporary Authors Permanent Series*
CDALB = *Concise Dictionary of American Literary Biography*
CDBLB = *Concise Dictionary of British Literary Biography*
DLB = *Dictionary of Literary Biography*
DLBD = *Dictionary of Literary Biography Documentary Series*
DLBY = *Dictionary of Literary Biography Yearbook*
HW = *Hispanic Writers*
JRDA = *Junior DISCovering Authors*
MAICYA = *Major Authors and Illustrators for Children and Young Adults*
MTCW = *Major 20th-Century Writers*
NNAL = *Native North American Literature*
SAAS = *Something about the Author Autobiography Series*
SATA = *Something about the Author*
YABC = *Yesterday's Authors of Books for Children*

Literary Criticism Series
Cumulative Author Index

Abasiyanik, Sait Faik 1906-1954
See Sait Faik
See also CA 123

Abbey, Edward 1927-1989 **CLC 36, 59**
See also CA 45-48; 128; CANR 2, 41

Abbott, Lee K(ittredge) 1947- **CLC 48**
See also CA 124; CANR 51; DLB 130

Abe, Kobo 1924-1993**CLC 8, 22, 53, 81; DAM NOV**
See also CA 65-68; 140; CANR 24, 60; DLB 182; MTCW

Abelard, Peter c. 1079-c. 1142 **CMLC 11**
See also DLB 115

Abell, Kjeld 1901-1961 **CLC 15**
See also CA 111

Abish, Walter 1931- **CLC 22**
See also CA 101; CANR 37; DLB 130

Abrahams, Peter (Henry) 1919- **CLC 4**
See also BW 1; CA 57-60; CANR 26; DLB 117; MTCW

Abrams, M(eyer) H(oward) 1912- **CLC 24**
See also CA 57-60; CANR 13, 33; DLB 67

Abse, Dannie 1923- **CLC 7, 29; DAB; DAM POET**
See also CA 53-56; CAAS 1; CANR 4, 46; DLB 27

Achebe, (Albert) Chinua(lumogu) 1930- **CLC 1, 3, 5, 7, 11, 26, 51, 75; BLC 1; DA; DAB; DAC; DAM MST, MULT, NOV; WLC**
See also AAYA 15; BW 2; CA 1-4R; CANR 6, 26, 47; CLR 20; DLB 117; MAICYA; MTCW; SATA 40; SATA-Brief 38

Acker, Kathy 1948-1997 **CLC 45, 111**
See also CA 117; 122; 162; CANR 55

Ackroyd, Peter 1949- **CLC 34, 52**
See also CA 123; 127; CANR 51; DLB 155; INT 127

Acorn, Milton 1923- **CLC 15; DAC**
See also CA 103; DLB 53; INT 103

Adamov, Arthur 1908-1970 **CLC 4, 25; DAM DRAM**
See also CA 17-18; 25-28R; CAP 2; MTCW

Adams, Alice (Boyd) 1926-**CLC 6, 13, 46; SSC 24**
See also CA 81-84; CANR 26, 53; DLBY 86; INT CANR-26; MTCW

Adams, Andy 1859-1935 **TCLC 56**
See also YABC 1

Adams, Brooks 1848-1927 **TCLC 80**
See also CA 123; DLB 47

Adams, Douglas (Noel) 1952- **CLC 27, 60; DAM POP**
See also AAYA 4; BEST 89:3; CA 106; CANR 34, 64; DLBY 83; JRDA

Adams, Francis 1862-1893 **NCLC 33**

Adams, Henry (Brooks) 1838-1918 **TCLC 4, 52; DA; DAB; DAC; DAM MST**
See also CA 104; 133; DLB 12, 47, 189

Adams, Richard (George) 1920-**CLC 4, 5, 18; DAM NOV**
See also AAYA 16; AITN 1, 2; CA 49-52; CANR 3, 35; CLR 20; JRDA; MAICYA;

MTCW; SATA 7, 69

Adamson, Joy(-Friederike Victoria) 1910-1980 **CLC 17**
See also CA 69-72; 93-96; CANR 22; MTCW; SATA 11; SATA-Obit 22

Adcock, Fleur 1934- **CLC 41**
See also CA 25-28R; CAAS 23; CANR 11, 34, 69; DLB 40

Addams, Charles (Samuel) 1912-1988**CLC 30**
See also CA 61-64; 126; CANR 12

Addams, Jane 1860-1945 **TCLC 76**

Addison, Joseph 1672-1719 **LC 18**
See also CDBLB 1660-1789; DLB 101

Adler, Alfred (F.) 1870-1937 **TCLC 61**
See also CA 119; 159

Adler, C(arole) S(chwerdtfeger) 1932-**CLC 35**
See also AAYA 4; CA 89-92; CANR 19, 40; JRDA; MAICYA; SAAS 15; SATA 26, 63

Adler, Renata 1938- **CLC 8, 31**
See also CA 49-52; CANR 5, 22, 52; MTCW

Ady, Endre 1877-1919 **TCLC 11**
See also CA 107

A.E. 1867-1935 **TCLC 3, 10**
See also Russell, George William

Aeschylus 525B.C.-456B.C. **CMLC 11; DA; DAB; DAC; DAM DRAM, MST; DC 8; WLCS**
See also DLB 176

Aesop 620(?)B.C.-564(?)B.C. **CMLC 24**
See also CLR 14; MAICYA; SATA 64

Africa, Ben
See Bosman, Herman Charles

Afton, Effie
See Harper, Frances Ellen Watkins

Agapida, Fray Antonio
See Irving, Washington

Agee, James (Rufus) 1909-1955 **TCLC 1, 19; DAM NOV**
See also AITN 1; CA 108; 148; CDALB 1941-1968; DLB 2, 26, 152

Aghill, Gordon
See Silverberg, Robert

Agnon, S(hmuel) Y(osef Halevi) 1888-1970
CLC 4, 8, 14; SSC 30
See also CA 17-18; 25-28R; CANR 60; CAP 2; MTCW

Agrippa von Nettesheim, Henry Cornelius 1486-1535 **LC 27**

Aherne, Owen
See Cassill, R(onald) V(erlin)

Ai 1947- **CLC 4, 14, 69**
See also CA 85-88; CAAS 13; DLB 120

Aickman, Robert (Fordyce) 1914-1981 **CLC 57**
See also CA 5-8R; CANR 3

Aiken, Conrad (Potter) 1889-1973**CLC 1, 3, 5, 10, 52; DAM NOV, POET; SSC 9**
See also CA 5-8R; 45-48; CANR 4, 60; CDALB 1929-1941; DLB 9, 45, 102; MTCW; SATA 3, 30

Aiken, Joan (Delano) 1924- **CLC 35**
See also AAYA 1, 25; CA 9-12R; CANR 4, 23,

34, 64; CLR 1, 19; DLB 161; JRDA; MAICYA; MTCW; SAAS 1; SATA 2, 30, 73

Ainsworth, William Harrison 1805-1882 **NCLC 13**
See also DLB 21; SATA 24

Aitmatov, Chingiz (Torekulovich) 1928- **CLC 71**
See also CA 103; CANR 38; MTCW; SATA 56

Akers, Floyd
See Baum, L(yman) Frank

Akhmadulina, Bella Akhatovna 1937- **CLC 53; DAM POET**
See also CA 65-68

Akhmatova, Anna 1888-1966 **CLC 11, 25, 64; DAM POET; PC 2**
See also CA 19-20; 25-28R; CANR 35; CAP 1; MTCW

Aksakov, Sergei Timofeyvich 1791-1859 **NCLC 2**
See also DLB 198

Aksenov, Vassily
See Aksyonov, Vassily (Pavlovich)

Akst, Daniel 1956- **CLC 109**
See also CA 161

Aksyonov, Vassily (Pavlovich) 1932- **CLC 22, 37, 101**
See also CA 53-56; CANR 12, 48

Akutagawa, Ryunosuke 1892-1927 **TCLC 16**
See also CA 117; 154

Alain 1868-1951 **TCLC 41**
See also CA 163

Alain-Fournier **TCLC 6**
See also Fournier, Henri Alban
See also DLB 65

Alarcon, Pedro Antonio de 1833-1891**NCLC 1**

Alas (y Urena), Leopoldo (Enrique Garcia) 1852-1901**TCLC 29**
See also CA 113; 131; HW

Albee, Edward (Franklin III) 1928-**CLC 1, 2, 3, 5, 9, 11, 13, 25, 53, 86, 113; DA; DAB; DAC; DAM DRAM, MST; WLC**
See also AITN 1; CA 5-8R; CABS 3; CANR 8, 54; CDALB 1941-1968; DLB 7; INT CANR-8; MTCW

Alberti, Rafael 1902- **CLC 7**
See also CA 85-88; DLB 108

Albert the Great 1200(?)-1280 **CMLC 16**
See also DLB 115

Alcala-Galiano, Juan Valera y
See Valera y Alcala-Galiano, Juan

Alcott, Amos Bronson 1799-1888 **NCLC 1**
See also DLB 1

Alcott, Louisa May 1832-1888 **NCLC 6, 58; DA; DAB; DAC; DAM MST, NOV; SSC 27; WLC**
See also AAYA 20; CDALB 1865-1917; CLR 1, 38; DLB 1, 42, 79; DLBD 14; JRDA; MAICYA; YABC 1

Aldanov, M. A.
See Aldanov, Mark (Alexandrovich)

Aldanov, Mark (Alexandrovich) 1886(?)-1957 **TCLC 23**

See also CA 118
Aldington, Richard 1892-1962 **CLC 49**
See also CA 85-88; CANR 45; DLB 20, 36, 100,
149
Aldiss, Brian W(ilson) 1925- **CLC 5, 14, 40;**
DAM NOV
See also CA 5-8R; CAAS 2; CANR 5, 28, 64;
DLB 14; MTCW; SATA 34
Alegria, Claribel 1924- **CLC 75; DAM MULT**
See also CA 131; CAAS 15; CANR 66; DLB
145; HW
Alegria, Fernando 1918- **CLC 57**
See also CA 9-12R; CANR 5, 32; HW
Aleichem, Sholom **TCLC 1, 35**
See also Rabinovitch, Sholem
Aleixandre, Vicente 1898-1984 **CLC 9, 36;**
DAM POET; PC 15
See also CA 85-88; 114; CANR 26; DLB 108;
HW; MTCW
Alepoudelis, Odysseus
See Elytis, Odysseus
Aleshkovsky, Joseph 1929-
See Aleshkovsky, Yuz
See also CA 121; 128
Aleshkovsky, Yuz **CLC 44**
See also Aleshkovsky, Joseph
Alexander, Lloyd (Chudley) 1924- **CLC 35**
See also AAYA 1; CA 1-4R; CANR 1, 24, 38,
55; CLR 1, 5, 48; DLB 52; JRDA; MAICYA;
MTCW; SAAS 19; SATA 3, 49, 81
Alexander, Samuel 1859-1938 **TCLC 77**
Alexie, Sherman (Joseph, Jr.) 1966- **CLC 96;**
DAM MULT
See also CA 138; CANR 65; DLB 175; NNAL
Alfau, Felipe 1902- **CLC 66**
See also CA 137
Alger, Horatio, Jr. 1832-1899 **NCLC 8**
See also DLB 42; SATA 16
Algren, Nelson 1909-1981 **CLC 4, 10, 33**
See also CA 13-16R; 103; CANR 20, 61;
CDALB 1941-1968; DLB 9; DLBY 81, 82;
MTCW
Ali, Ahmed 1910- **CLC 69**
See also CA 25-28R; CANR 15, 34
Alighieri, Dante
See Dante
Allan, John B.
See Westlake, Donald E(dwin)
Allan, Sidney
See Hartmann, Sadakichi
Allan, Sydney
See Hartmann, Sadakichi
Allen, Edward 1948- **CLC 59**
Allen, Paula Gunn 1939- **CLC 84; DAM**
MULT
See also CA 112; 143; CANR 63; DLB 175;
NNAL
Allen, Roland
See Ayckbourn, Alan
Allen, Sarah A.
See Hopkins, Pauline Elizabeth
Allen, Sidney H.
See Hartmann, Sadakichi
Allen, Woody 1935- **CLC 16, 52; DAM POP**
See also AAYA 10; CA 33-36R; CANR 27, 38,
63; DLB 44; MTCW
Allende, Isabel 1942- **CLC 39, 57, 97; DAM**
MULT, NOV; HLC; WLCS
See also AAYA 18; CA 125; 130; CANR 51;
DLB 145; HW; INT 130; MTCW
Alleyn, Ellen
See Rossetti, Christina (Georgina)
Allingham, Margery (Louise) 1904-1966 **CLC**

19
See also CA 5-8R; 25-28R; CANR 4, 58; DLB
77; MTCW
Allingham, William 1824-1889 **NCLC 25**
See also DLB 35
Allison, Dorothy E. 1949- **CLC 78**
See also CA 140; CANR 66
Allston, Washington 1779-1843 **NCLC 2**
See also DLB 1
Almedingen, E. M. **CLC 12**
See also Almedingen, Martha Edith von
See also SATA 3
Almedingen, Martha Edith von 1898-1971
See Almedingen, E. M.
See also CA 1-4R; CANR 1
Almqvist, Carl Jonas Love 1793-1866 **NCLC**
42
Alonso, Damaso 1898-1990 **CLC 14**
See also CA 110; 131; 130; DLB 108; HW
Alov
See Gogol, Nikolai (Vasilyevich)
Alta 1942- **CLC 19**
See also CA 57-60
Alter, Robert B(ernard) 1935- **CLC 34**
See also CA 49-52; CANR 1, 47
Alther, Lisa 1944- **CLC 7, 41**
See also CA 65-68; CANR 12, 30, 51; MTCW
Althusser, L.
See Althusser, Louis
Althusser, Louis 1918-1990 **CLC 106**
See also CA 131; 132
Altman, Robert 1925- **CLC 16**
See also CA 73-76; CANR 43
Alvarez, A(lfred) 1929- **CLC 5, 13**
See also CA 1-4R; CANR 3, 33, 63; DLB 14,
40
Alvarez, Alejandro Rodriguez 1903-1965
See Casona, Alejandro
See also CA 131; 93-96; HW
Alvarez, Julia 1950- **CLC 93**
See also AAYA 25; CA 147; CANR 69
Alvaro, Corrado 1896-1956 **TCLC 60**
See also CA 163
Amado, Jorge 1912- **CLC 13, 40, 106; DAM**
MULT, NOV; HLC
See also CA 77-80; CANR 35; DLB 113;
MTCW
Ambler, Eric 1909- **CLC 4, 6, 9**
See also CA 9-12R; CANR 7, 38; DLB 77;
MTCW
Amichai, Yehuda 1924- **CLC 9, 22, 57**
See also CA 85-88; CANR 46, 60; MTCW
Amichai, Yehudah
See Amichai, Yehuda
Amiel, Henri Frederic 1821-1881 **NCLC 4**
Amis, Kingsley (William) 1922-1995 **CLC 1, 2,**
3, 5, 8, 13, 40, 44; DA; DAB; DAC; DAM
MST, NOV
See also AITN 2; CA 9-12R; 150; CANR 8, 28,
54; CDBLB 1945-1960; DLB 15, 27, 100,
139; DLBY 96; INT CANR-8; MTCW
Amis, Martin (Louis) 1949- **CLC 4, 9, 38, 62,**
101
See also BEST 90:3; CA 65-68; CANR 8, 27,
54; DLB 14, 194; INT CANR-27
Ammons, A(rchie) R(andolph) 1926- **CLC 2, 3,**
5, 8, 9, 25, 57, 108; DAM POET; PC 16
See also AITN 1; CA 9-12R; CANR 6, 36, 51;
DLB 5, 165; MTCW
Amo, Tauraatua i
See Adams, Henry (Brooks)
Anand, Mulk Raj 1905- **CLC 23, 93; DAM**
NOV

See also CA 65-68; CANR 32, 64; MTCW
Anatol
See Schnitzler, Arthur
Anaximander c. 610B.C.-c. 546B.C. **CMLC 22**
Anaya, Rudolfo A(lfonso) 1937- **CLC 23;**
DAM MULT, NOV; HLC
See also AAYA 20; CA 45-48; CAAS 4; CANR
1, 32, 51; DLB 82; HW 1; MTCW
Andersen, Hans Christian 1805-1875 **NCLC 7;**
DA; DAB; DAC; DAM MST, POP; SSC
6; WLC
See also CLR 6; MAICYA; YABC 1
Anderson, C. Farley
See Mencken, H(enry) L(ouis); Nathan, George
Jean
Anderson, Jessica (Margaret) Queale 1916-
CLC 37
See also CA 9-12R; CANR 4, 62
Anderson, Jon (Victor) 1940- **CLC 9; DAM**
POET
See also CA 25-28R; CANR 20
Anderson, Lindsay (Gordon) 1923-1994 **CLC**
20
See also CA 125; 128; 146
Anderson, Maxwell 1888-1959 **TCLC 2; DAM**
DRAM
See also CA 105; 152; DLB 7
Anderson, Poul (William) 1926- **CLC 15**
See also AAYA 5; CA 1-4R; CAAS 2; CANR
2, 15, 34, 64; DLB 8; INT CANR-15;
MTCW; SATA 90; SATA-Brief 39
Anderson, Robert (Woodruff) 1917- **CLC 23;**
DAM DRAM
See also AITN 1; CA 21-24R; CANR 32; DLB
7
Anderson, Sherwood 1876-1941 **TCLC 1, 10,**
24; DA; DAB; DAC; DAM MST, NOV;
SSC 1; WLC
See also CA 104; 121; CANR 61; CDALB
1917-1929; DLB 4, 9, 86; DLBD 1; MTCW
Andier, Pierre
See Desnos, Robert
Andouard
See Giraudoux, (Hippolyte) Jean
Andrade, Carlos Drummond de **CLC 18**
See also Drummond de Andrade, Carlos
Andrade, Mario de 1893-1945 **TCLC 43**
Andreae, Johann V(alentin) 1586-1654 **LC 32**
See also DLB 164
Andreas-Salome, Lou 1861-1937 **TCLC 56**
See also DLB 66
Andress, Lesley
See Sanders, Lawrence
Andrewes, Lancelot 1555-1626 **LC 5**
See also DLB 151, 172
Andrews, Cicily Fairfield
See West, Rebecca
Andrews, Elton V.
See Pohl, Frederik
Andreyev, Leonid (Nikolaevich) 1871-1919
TCLC 3
See also CA 104
Andric, Ivo 1892-1975 **CLC 8**
See also CA 81-84; 57-60; CANR 43, 60; DLB
147; MTCW
Androvar
See Prado (Calvo), Pedro
Angelique, Pierre
See Bataille, Georges
Angell, Roger 1920- **CLC 26**
See also CA 57-60; CANR 13, 44; DLB 171,
185
Angelou, Maya 1928- **CLC 12, 35, 64, 77; BLC**

Bell, Gertrude (Margaret Lowthian) 1868-1926
TCLC 67
See also DLB 174

Bell, James Madison 1826-1902   TCLC 43;
BLC 1; DAM MULT
See also BW 1; CA 122; 124; DLB 50

Bell, Madison Smartt 1957-   CLC 41, 102
See also CA 111; CANR 28, 54

Bell, Marvin (Hartley) 1937-CLC 8, 31; DAM
POET
See also CA 21-24R; CAAS 14; CANR 59; DLB
5; MTCW

Bell, W. L. D.
See Mencken, H(enry) L(ouis)

Bellamy, Atwood C.
See Mencken, H(enry) L(ouis)

Bellamy, Edward 1850-1898   NCLC 4
See also DLB 12

Bellin, Edward J.
See Kuttner, Henry

Belloc, (Joseph) Hilaire (Pierre Sebastien Rene
Swanton) 1870-1953 TCLC 7, 18; DAM
POET
See also CA 106; 152; DLB 19, 100, 141, 174;
YABC 1

Belloc, Joseph Peter Rene Hilaire
See Belloc, (Joseph) Hilaire (Pierre Sebastien
Rene Swanton)

Belloc, Joseph Pierre Hilaire
See Belloc, (Joseph) Hilaire (Pierre Sebastien
Rene Swanton)

Belloc, M. A.
See Lowndes, Marie Adelaide (Belloc)

Bellow, Saul 1915-CLC 1, 2, 3, 6, 8, 10, 13, 15,
25, 33, 34, 63, 79; DA; DAB; DAC; DAM
MST, NOV, POP; SSC 14; WLC
See also AITN 2; BEST 89:3; CA 5-8R; CABS
1; CANR 29, 53; CDALB 1941-1968; DLB
2, 28; DLBD 3; DLBY 82; MTCW

Belser, Reimond Karel Maria de 1929-
See Ruyslinck, Ward
See also CA 152

Bely, Andrey   TCLC 7; PC 11
See also Bugayev, Boris Nikolayevich

Belyi, Andrei
See Bugayev, Boris Nikolayevich

Benary, Margot
See Benary-Isbert, Margot

Benary-Isbert, Margot 1889-1979   CLC 12
See also CA 5-8R; 89-92; CANR 4; CLR 12;
MAICYA; SATA 2; SATA-Obit 21

Benavente (y Martinez), Jacinto 1866-1954
TCLC 3; DAM DRAM, MULT
See also CA 106; 131; HW; MTCW

Benchley, Peter (Bradford) 1940-   CLC 4, 8;
DAM NOV, POP
See also AAYA 14; AITN 2; CA 17-20R; CANR
12, 35, 66; MTCW; SATA 3, 89

Benchley, Robert (Charles) 1889-1945 TCLC
1, 55
See also CA 105; 153; DLB 11

Benda, Julien 1867-1956   TCLC 60
See also CA 120; 154

Benedict, Ruth (Fulton) 1887-1948 TCLC 60
See also CA 158

Benedict, Saint c. 480-c. 547   CMLC 29

Benedikt, Michael 1935-   CLC 4, 14
See also CA 13-16R; CANR 7; DLB 5

Benet, Juan 1927-   CLC 28
See also CA 143

Benet, Stephen Vincent 1898-1943 TCLC 7;
DAM POET; SSC 10
See also CA 104; 152; DLB 4, 48, 102; DLBY

97; YABC 1

Benet, William Rose 1886-1950   TCLC 28;
DAM POET
See also CA 118; 152; DLB 45

Benford, Gregory (Albert) 1941-   CLC 52
See also CA 69-72; CAAS 27; CANR 12, 24,
49; DLBY 82

Bengtsson, Frans (Gunnar) 1894-1954 TCLC
48

Benjamin, David
See Slavitt, David R(ytman)

Benjamin, Lois
See Gould, Lois

Benjamin, Walter 1892-1940   TCLC 39
See also CA 164

Benn, Gottfried 1886-1956   TCLC 3
See also CA 106; 153; DLB 56

Bennett, Alan 1934- CLC 45, 77; DAB; DAM
MST
See also CA 103; CANR 35, 55; MTCW

Bennett, (Enoch) Arnold 1867-1931 TCLC 5,
20
See also CA 106; 155; CDBLB 1890-1914;
DLB 10, 34, 98, 135

Bennett, Elizabeth
See Mitchell, Margaret (Munnerlyn)

Bennett, George Harold 1930-
See Bennett, Hal
See also BW 1; CA 97-100

Bennett, Hal   CLC 5
See also Bennett, George Harold
See also DLB 33

Bennett, Jay 1912-   CLC 35
See also AAYA 10; CA 69-72; CANR 11, 42;
JRDA; SAAS 4; SATA 41, 87; SATA-Brief
27

Bennett, Louise (Simone) 1919-CLC 28; BLC
1; DAM MULT
See also BW 2; CA 151; DLB 117

Benson, E(dward) F(rederic) 1867-1940
TCLC 27
See also CA 114; 157; DLB 135, 153

Benson, Jackson J. 1930-   CLC 34
See also CA 25-28R; DLB 111

Benson, Sally 1900-1972   CLC 17
See also CA 19-20; 37-40R; CAP 1; SATA 1,
35; SATA-Obit 27

Benson, Stella 1892-1933   TCLC 17
See also CA 117; 155; DLB 36, 162

Bentham, Jeremy 1748-1832   NCLC 38
See also DLB 107, 158

Bentley, E(dmund) C(lerihew) 1875-1956
TCLC 12
See also CA 108; DLB 70

Bentley, Eric (Russell) 1916-   CLC 24
See also CA 5-8R; CANR 6, 67; INT CANR-6

Beranger, Pierre Jean de 1780-1857NCLC 34

Berdyaev, Nicolas
See Berdyaev, Nikolai (Aleksandrovich)

Berdyaev, Nikolai (Aleksandrovich) 1874-1948
TCLC 67
See also CA 120; 157

Berdyayev, Nikolai (Aleksandrovich)
See Berdyaev, Nikolai (Aleksandrovich)

Berendt, John (Lawrence) 1939-   CLC 86
See also CA 146

Beresford, J(ohn) D(avys) 1873-1947 TCLC
81
See also CA 112; 155; DLB 162, 178, 197

Bergelson, David 1884-1952   TCLC 81

Berger, Colonel
See Malraux, (Georges-)Andre

Berger, John (Peter) 1926-   CLC 2, 19

See also CA 81-84; CANR 51; DLB 14

Berger, Melvin H. 1927-   CLC 12
See also CA 5-8R; CANR 4; CLR 32; SAAS 2;
SATA 5, 88

Berger, Thomas (Louis) 1924-CLC 3, 5, 8, 11,
18, 38; DAM NOV
See also CA 1-4R; CANR 5, 28, 51; DLB 2;
DLBY 80; INT CANR-28; MTCW

Bergman, (Ernst) Ingmar 1918-   CLC 16, 72
See also CA 81-84; CANR 33

Bergson, Henri(-Louis) 1859-1941   TCLC 32
See also CA 164

Bergstein, Eleanor 1938-   CLC 4
See also CA 53-56; CANR 5

Berkoff, Steven 1937-   CLC 56
See also CA 104

Bermant, Chaim (Icyk) 1929-   CLC 40
See also CA 57-60; CANR 6, 31, 57

Bern, Victoria
See Fisher, M(ary) F(rances) K(ennedy)

Bernanos, (Paul Louis) Georges 1888-1948
TCLC 3
See also CA 104; 130; DLB 72

Bernard, April 1956-   CLC 59
See also CA 131

Berne, Victoria
See Fisher, M(ary) F(rances) K(ennedy)

Bernhard, Thomas 1931-1989 CLC 3, 32, 61
See also CA 85-88; 127; CANR 32, 57; DLB
85, 124; MTCW

Bernhardt, Sarah (Henriette Rosine) 1844-1923
TCLC 75
See also CA 157

Berriault, Gina 1926-   CLC 54, 109; SSC 30
See also CA 116; 129; CANR 66; DLB 130

Berrigan, Daniel 1921-   CLC 4
See also CA 33-36R; CAAS 1; CANR 11, 43;
DLB 5

Berrigan, Edmund Joseph Michael, Jr. 1934-
1983
See Berrigan, Ted
See also CA 61-64; 110; CANR 14

Berrigan, Ted   CLC 37
See also Berrigan, Edmund Joseph Michael, Jr.
See also DLB 5, 169

Berry, Charles Edward Anderson 1931-
See Berry, Chuck
See also CA 115

Berry, Chuck   CLC 17
See also Berry, Charles Edward Anderson

Berry, Jonas
See Ashbery, John (Lawrence)

Berry, Wendell (Erdman) 1934-   CLC 4, 6, 8,
27, 46; DAM POET
See also AITN 1; CA 73-76; CANR 50; DLB 5,
6

Berryman, John 1914-1972CLC 1, 2, 3, 4, 6, 8,
10, 13, 25, 62; DAM POET
See also CA 13-16; 33-36R; CABS 2; CANR
35; CAP 1; CDALB 1941-1968; DLB 48;
MTCW

Bertolucci, Bernardo 1940-   CLC 16
See also CA 106

Berton, Pierre (Francis De Marigny) 1920-
CLC 104
See also CA 1-4R; CANR 2, 56; DLB 68

Bertrand, Aloysius 1807-1841   NCLC 31

Bertran de Born c. 1140-1215   CMLC 5

Beruni, al 973-1048(?)   CMLC 28

Besant, Annie (Wood) 1847-1933   TCLC 9
See also CA 105

Bessie, Alvah 1904-1985   CLC 23
See also CA 5-8R; 116; CANR 2; DLB 26

Bethlen, T. D.
See Silverberg, Robert

Beti, Mongo   **CLC 27; BLC 1; DAM MULT**
See also Biyidi, Alexandre

Betjeman, John 1906-1984 **CLC 2, 6, 10, 34, 43; DAB; DAM MST, POET**
See also CA 9-12R; 112; CANR 33, 56; CDBLB 1945-1960; DLB 20; DLBY 84; MTCW

Bettelheim, Bruno 1903-1990   **CLC 79**
See also CA 81-84; 131; CANR 23, 61; MTCW

Betti, Ugo 1892-1953   **TCLC 5**
See also CA 104; 155

Betts, Doris (Waugh) 1932-   **CLC 3, 6, 28**
See also CA 13-16R; CANR 9, 66; DLBY 82; INT CANR-9

Bevan, Alistair
See Roberts, Keith (John Kingston)

Bey, Pilaff
See Douglas, (George) Norman

Bialik, Chaim Nachman 1873-1934 **TCLC 25**

Bickerstaff, Isaac
See Swift, Jonathan

Bidart, Frank 1939-   **CLC 33**
See also CA 140

Bienek, Horst 1930-   **CLC 7, 11**
See also CA 73-76; DLB 75

Bierce, Ambrose (Gwinett) 1842-1914(?)
TCLC 1, 7, 44; DA; DAC; DAM MST; SSC 9; WLC
See also CA 104; 139; CDALB 1865-1917; DLB 11, 12, 23, 71, 74, 186

Biggers, Earl Derr 1884-1933   **TCLC 65**
See also CA 108; 153

Billings, Josh
See Shaw, Henry Wheeler

Billington, (Lady) Rachel (Mary) 1942- **CLC 43**
See also AITN 2; CA 33-36R; CANR 44

Binyon, T(imothy) J(ohn) 1936-   **CLC 34**
See also CA 111; CANR 28

Bioy Casares, Adolfo 1914-1984**CLC 4, 8, 13, 88; DAM MULT; HLC; SSC 17**
See also CA 29-32R; CANR 19, 43, 66; DLB 113; HW; MTCW

Bird, Cordwainer
See Ellison, Harlan (Jay)

Bird, Robert Montgomery 1806-1854**NCLC 1**

Birney, (Alfred) Earle 1904-1995 **CLC 1, 4, 6, 11; DAC; DAM MST, POET**
See also CA 1-4R; CANR 5, 20; DLB 88; MTCW

Bishop, Elizabeth 1911-1979 **CLC 1, 4, 9, 13, 15, 32; DA; DAC; DAM MST, POET; PC 3**
See also CA 5-8R; 89-92; CABS 2; CANR 26, 61; CDALB 1968-1988; DLB 5, 169; MTCW; SATA-Obit 24

Bishop, John 1935-   **CLC 10**
See also CA 105

Bissett, Bill 1939-   **CLC 18; PC 14**
See also CA 69-72; CAAS 19; CANR 15; DLB 53; MTCW

Bitov, Andrei (Georgievich) 1937-   **CLC 57**
See also CA 142

Biyidi, Alexandre 1932-
See Beti, Mongo
See also BW 1; CA 114; 124; MTCW

Bjarme, Brynjolf
See Ibsen, Henrik (Johan)

Bjoernson, Bjoernstjerne (Martinius) 1832-1910   **TCLC 7, 37**
See also CA 104

Black, Robert

See Holdstock, Robert P.

Blackburn, Paul 1926-1971   **CLC 9, 43**
See also CA 81-84; 33-36R; CANR 34; DLB 16; DLBY 81

Black Elk 1863-1950 **TCLC 33; DAM MULT**
See also CA 144; NNAL

Black Hobart
See Sanders, (James) Ed(ward)

Blacklin, Malcolm
See Chambers, Aidan

Blackmore, R(ichard) D(oddridge) 1825-1900
TCLC 27
See also CA 120; DLB 18

Blackmur, R(ichard) P(almer) 1904-1965
CLC 2, 24
See also CA 11-12; 25-28R; CAP 1; DLB 63

Black Tarantula
See Acker, Kathy

Blackwood, Algernon (Henry) 1869-1951
TCLC 5
See also CA 105; 150; DLB 153, 156, 178

Blackwood, Caroline 1931-1996**CLC 6, 9, 100**
See also CA 85-88; 151; CANR 32, 61, 65; DLB 14; MTCW

Blade, Alexander
See Hamilton, Edmond; Silverberg, Robert

Blaga, Lucian 1895-1961   **CLC 75**
See also CA 157

Blair, Eric (Arthur) 1903-1950
See Orwell, George
See also CA 104; 132; DA; DAB; DAC; DAM MST, NOV; MTCW; SATA 29

Blais, Marie-Claire 1939- **CLC 2, 4, 6, 13, 22; DAC; DAM MST**
See also CA 21-24R; CAAS 4; CANR 38; DLB 53; MTCW

Blaise, Clark 1940-   **CLC 29**
See also AITN 2; CA 53-56; CAAS 3; CANR 5, 66; DLB 53

Blake, Fairley
See De Voto, Bernard (Augustine)

Blake, Nicholas
See Day Lewis, C(ecil)
See also DLB 77

Blake, William 1757-1827 **NCLC 13, 37, 57; DA; DAB; DAC; DAM MST, POET; PC 12; WLC**
See also CDBLB 1789-1832; CLR 52; DLB 93, 163; MAICYA; SATA 30

Blasco Ibanez, Vicente 1867-1928   **TCLC 12; DAM NOV**
See also CA 110; 131; HW; MTCW

Blatty, William Peter 1928-**CLC 2; DAM POP**
See also CA 5-8R; CANR 9

Bleeck, Oliver
See Thomas, Ross (Elmore)

Blessing, Lee 1949-   **CLC 54**

Blish, James (Benjamin) 1921-1975 **CLC 14**
See also CA 1-4R; 57-60; CANR 3; DLB 8; MTCW; SATA 66

Bliss, Reginald
See Wells, H(erbert) G(eorge)

Blixen, Karen (Christentze Dinesen) 1885-1962
See Dinesen, Isak
See also CA 25-28; CANR 22, 50; CAP 2; MTCW; SATA 44

Bloch, Robert (Albert) 1917-1994   **CLC 33**
See also CA 5-8R; 146; CAAS 20; CANR 5; DLB 44; INT CANR-5; SATA 12; SATA-Obit 82

Blok, Alexander (Alexandrovich) 1880-1921
TCLC 5; PC 21
See also CA 104

Blom, Jan
See Breytenbach, Breyten

Bloom, Harold 1930-   **CLC 24, 103**
See also CA 13-16R; CANR 39; DLB 67

Bloomfield, Aurelius
See Bourne, Randolph S(illiman)

Blount, Roy (Alton), Jr. 1941-   **CLC 38**
See also CA 53-56; CANR 10, 28, 61; INT CANR-28; MTCW

Bloy, Leon 1846-1917   **TCLC 22**
See also CA 121; DLB 123

Blume, Judy (Sussman) 1938-   **CLC 12, 30; DAM NOV, POP**
See also AAYA 3; CA 29-32R; CANR 13, 37, 66; CLR 2, 15; DLB 52; JRDA; MAICYA; MTCW; SATA 2, 31, 79

Blunden, Edmund (Charles) 1896-1974 **CLC 2, 56**
See also CA 17-18; 45-48; CANR 54; CAP 2; DLB 20, 100, 155; MTCW

Bly, Robert (Elwood) 1926-**CLC 1, 2, 5, 10, 15, 38; DAM POET**
See also CA 5-8R; CANR 41; DLB 5; MTCW

Boas, Franz 1858-1942   **TCLC 56**
See also CA 115

Bobette
See Simenon, Georges (Jacques Christian)

Boccaccio, Giovanni 1313-1375   **CMLC 13; SSC 10**

Bochco, Steven 1943-   **CLC 35**
See also AAYA 11; CA 124; 138

Bodel, Jean 1167(?)-1210   **CMLC 28**

Bodenheim, Maxwell 1892-1954   **TCLC 44**
See also CA 110; DLB 9, 45

Bodker, Cecil 1927-   **CLC 21**
See also CA 73-76; CANR 13, 44; CLR 23; MAICYA; SATA 14

Boell, Heinrich (Theodor) 1917-1985 **CLC 2, 3, 6, 9, 11, 15, 27, 32, 72; DA; DAB; DAC; DAM MST, NOV; SSC 23; WLC**
See also CA 21-24R; 116; CANR 24; DLB 69; DLBY 85; MTCW

Boerne, Alfred
See Doeblin, Alfred

Boethius 480(?)-524(?)   **CMLC 15**
See also DLB 115

Bogan, Louise 1897-1970 **CLC 4, 39, 46, 93; DAM POET; PC 12**
See also CA 73-76; 25-28R; CANR 33; DLB 45, 169; MTCW

Bogarde, Dirk   **CLC 19**
See also Van Den Bogarde, Derek Jules Gaspard Ulric Niven
See also DLB 14

Bogosian, Eric 1953-   **CLC 45**
See also CA 138

Bograd, Larry 1953-   **CLC 35**
See also CA 93-96; CANR 57; SAAS 21; SATA 33, 89

Boiardo, Matteo Maria 1441-1494   **LC 6**

Boileau-Despreaux, Nicolas 1636-1711 **LC 3**

Bojer, Johan 1872-1959   **TCLC 64**

Boland, Eavan (Aisling) 1944-   **CLC 40, 67, 113; DAM POET**
See also CA 143; CANR 61; DLB 40

Boll, Heinrich
See Boell, Heinrich (Theodor)

Bolt, Lee
See Faust, Frederick (Schiller)

Bolt, Robert (Oxton) 1924-1995**CLC 14; DAM DRAM**
See also CA 17-20R; 147; CANR 35, 67; DLB 13; MTCW

15
See also CA 19-20; 25-28R; CANR 40, 60; CAP 2; DLB 65; MTCW

Breytenbach, Breyten 1939(?)- **CLC 23, 37; DAM POET**
See also CA 113; 129; CANR 61

Bridgers, Sue Ellen 1942- **CLC 26**
See also AAYA 8; CA 65-68; CANR 11, 36; CLR 18; DLB 52; JRDA; MAICYA; SAAS 1; SATA 22, 90

Bridges, Robert (Seymour) 1844-1930 **TCLC 1; DAM POET**
See also CA 104; 152; CDBLB 1890-1914; DLB 19, 98

Bridie, James **TCLC 3**
See also Mavor, Osborne Henry
See also DLB 10

Brin, David 1950- **CLC 34**
See also AAYA 21; CA 102; CANR 24; INT CANR-24; SATA 65

Brink, Andre (Philippus) 1935- **CLC 18, 36, 106**
See also CA 104; CANR 39, 62; INT 103; MTCW

Brinsmead, H(esba) F(ay) 1922- **CLC 21**
See also CA 21-24R; CANR 10; CLR 47; MAICYA; SAAS 5; SATA 18, 78

Brittain, Vera (Mary) 1893(?)-1970 **CLC 23**
See also CA 13-16; 25-28R; CANR 58; CAP 1; DLB 191; MTCW

Broch, Hermann 1886-1951 **TCLC 20**
See also CA 117; DLB 85, 124

Brock, Rose
See Hansen, Joseph

Brodkey, Harold (Roy) 1930-1996 **CLC 56**
See also CA 111; 151; DLB 130

Brodsky, Iosif Alexandrovich 1940-1996
See Brodsky, Joseph
See also AITN 1; CA 41-44R; 151; CANR 37; DAM POET; MTCW

Brodsky, Joseph 1940-1996 **CLC 4, 6, 13, 36, 100; PC 9**
See also Brodsky, Iosif Alexandrovich

Brodsky, Michael (Mark) 1948- **CLC 19**
See also CA 102; CANR 18, 41, 58

Bromell, Henry 1947- **CLC 5**
See also CA 53-56; CANR 9

Bromfield, Louis (Brucker) 1896-1956 **TCLC 11**
See also CA 107; 155; DLB 4, 9, 86

Broner, E(sther) M(asserman) 1930- **CLC 19**
See also CA 17-20R; CANR 8, 25; DLB 28

Bronk, William 1918- **CLC 10**
See also CA 89-92; CANR 23; DLB 165

Bronstein, Lev Davidovich
See Trotsky, Leon

Bronte, Anne 1820-1849 **NCLC 71**
See also DLB 21, 199

Bronte, Charlotte 1816-1855 **NCLC 3, 8, 33, 58; DA; DAB; DAC; DAM MST, NOV; WLC**
See also AAYA 17; CDBLB 1832-1890; DLB 21, 159, 199

Bronte, Emily (Jane) 1818-1848 **NCLC 16, 35; DA; DAB; DAC; DAM MST, NOV, POET; PC 8; WLC**
See also AAYA 17; CDBLB 1832-1890; DLB 21, 32, 199

Brooke, Frances 1724-1789 **LC 6**
See also DLB 39, 99

Brooke, Henry 1703(?)-1783 **LC 1**
See also DLB 39

Brooke, Rupert (Chawner) 1887-1915 **TCLC 2, 7; DA; DAB; DAC; DAM MST, POET; WLC**
See also CA 104; 132; CANR 61; CDBLB 1914-1945; DLB 19; MTCW

Brooke-Haven, P.
See Wodehouse, P(elham) G(renville)

Brooke-Rose, Christine 1926(?)- **CLC 40**
See also CA 13-16R; CANR 58; DLB 14

Brookner, Anita 1928- **CLC 32, 34, 51; DAB; DAM POP**
See also CA 114; 120; CANR 37, 56; DLB 194; DLBY 87; MTCW

Brooks, Cleanth 1906-1994 **CLC 24, 86, 110**
See also CA 17-20R; 145; CANR 33, 35; DLB 63; DLBY 94; INT CANR-35; MTCW

Brooks, George
See Baum, L(yman) Frank

Brooks, Gwendolyn 1917- **CLC 1, 2, 4, 5, 15, 49; BLC 1; DA; DAC; DAM MST, MULT, POET; PC 7; WLC**
See also AAYA 20; AITN 1; BW 2; CA 1-4R; CANR 1, 27, 52; CDALB 1941-1968; CLR 27; DLB 5, 76, 165; MTCW; SATA 6

Brooks, Mel **CLC 12**
See also Kaminsky, Melvin
See also AAYA 13; DLB 26

Brooks, Peter 1938- **CLC 34**
See also CA 45-48; CANR 1

Brooks, Van Wyck 1886-1963 **CLC 29**
See also CA 1-4R; CANR 6; DLB 45, 63, 103

Brophy, Brigid (Antonia) 1929-1995 **CLC 6, 11, 29, 105**
See also CA 5-8R; 149; CAAS 4; CANR 25, 53; DLB 14; MTCW

Brosman, Catharine Savage 1934- **CLC 9**
See also CA 61-64; CANR 21, 46

Brother Antoninus
See Everson, William (Oliver)

The Brothers Quay
See Quay, Stephen; Quay, Timothy

Broughton, T(homas) Alan 1936- **CLC 19**
See also CA 45-48; CANR 2, 23, 48

Broumas, Olga 1949- **CLC 10, 73**
See also CA 85-88; CANR 20, 69

Brown, Alan 1950- **CLC 99**
See also CA 156

Brown, Charles Brockden 1771-1810 **NCLC 22**
See also CDALB 1640-1865; DLB 37, 59, 73

Brown, Christy 1932-1981 **CLC 63**
See also CA 105; 104; DLB 14

Brown, Claude 1937- **CLC 30; BLC 1; DAM MULT**
See also AAYA 7; BW 1; CA 73-76

Brown, Dee (Alexander) 1908- **CLC 18, 47; DAM POP**
See also CA 13-16R; CAAS 6; CANR 11, 45, 60; DLBY 80; MTCW; SATA 5

Brown, George
See Wertmueller, Lina

Brown, George Douglas 1869-1902 **TCLC 28**
See also CA 162

Brown, George Mackay 1921-1996 **CLC 5, 48, 100**
See also CA 21-24R; 151; CAAS 6; CANR 12, 37, 67; DLB 14, 27, 139; MTCW; SATA 35

Brown, (William) Larry 1951- **CLC 73**
See also CA 130; 134; INT 133

Brown, Moses
See Barrett, William (Christopher)

Brown, Rita Mae 1944- **CLC 18, 43, 79; DAM NOV, POP**
See also CA 45-48; CANR 2, 11, 35, 62; INT

CANR-11; MTCW

Brown, Roderick (Langmere) Haig-
See Haig-Brown, Roderick (Langmere)

Brown, Rosellen 1939- **CLC 32**
See also CA 77-80; CAAS 10; CANR 14, 44

Brown, Sterling Allen 1901-1989 **CLC 1, 23, 59; BLC 1; DAM MULT, POET**
See also BW 1; CA 85-88; 127; CANR 26; DLB 48, 51, 63; MTCW

Brown, Will
See Ainsworth, William Harrison

Brown, William Wells 1813-1884 **NCLC 2; BLC 1; DAM MULT; DC 1**
See also DLB 3, 50

Browne, (Clyde) Jackson 1948(?)- **CLC 21**
See also CA 120

Browning, Elizabeth Barrett 1806-1861 **NCLC 1, 16, 61, 66; DA; DAB; DAC; DAM MST, POET; PC 6; WLC**
See also CDBLB 1832-1890; DLB 32, 199

Browning, Robert 1812-1889 **NCLC 19; DA; DAB; DAC; DAM MST, POET; PC 2; WLCS**
See also CDBLB 1832-1890; DLB 32, 163; YABC 1

Browning, Tod 1882-1962 **CLC 16**
See also CA 141; 117

Brownson, Orestes (Augustus) 1803-1876 **NCLC 50**

Brownson, Orestes Augustus 1803-1876 **NCLC 50**
See also DLB 1, 59, 73

Bruccoli, Matthew J(oseph) 1931- **CLC 34**
See also CA 9-12R; CANR 7; DLB 103

Bruce, Lenny **CLC 21**
See also Schneider, Leonard Alfred

Bruin, John
See Brutus, Dennis

Brulard, Henri
See Stendhal

Brulls, Christian
See Simenon, Georges (Jacques Christian)

Brunner, John (Kilian Houston) 1934-1995 **CLC 8, 10; DAM POP**
See also CA 1-4R; 149; CAAS 8; CANR 2, 37; MTCW

Bruno, Giordano 1548-1600 **LC 27**

Brutus, Dennis 1924- **CLC 43; BLC 1; DAM MULT, POET**
See also BW 2; CA 49-52; CAAS 14; CANR 2, 27, 42; DLB 117

Bryan, C(ourtlandt) D(ixon) B(arnes) 1936- **CLC 29**
See also CA 73-76; CANR 13, 68; DLB 185; INT CANR-13

Bryan, Michael
See Moore, Brian

Bryant, William Cullen 1794-1878 **NCLC 6, 46; DA; DAB; DAC; DAM MST, POET; PC 20**
See also CDALB 1640-1865; DLB 3, 43, 59, 189

Bryusov, Valery Yakovlevich 1873-1924 **TCLC 10**
See also CA 107; 155

Buchan, John 1875-1940 **TCLC 41; DAB; DAM POP**
See also CA 108; 145; DLB 34, 70, 156; YABC 2

Buchanan, George 1506-1582 **LC 4**
See also DLB 152

Buchheim, Lothar-Guenther 1918- **CLC 6**
See also CA 85-88

Buchner, (Karl) Georg 1813-1837 **NCLC 26**
Buchwald, Art(hur) 1925- **CLC 33**
See also AITN 1; CA 5-8R; CANR 21, 67; MTCW; SATA 10
Buck, Pearl S(ydenstricker) 1892-1973 **CLC 7, 11, 18; DA; DAB; DAC; DAM MST, NOV**
See also AITN 1; CA 1-4R; 41-44R; CANR 1, 34; DLB 9, 102; MTCW; SATA 1, 25
Buckler, Ernest 1908-1984 **CLC 13; DAC; DAM MST**
See also CA 11-12; 114; CAP 1; DLB 68; SATA 47
Buckley, Vincent (Thomas) 1925-1988 **CLC 57**
See also CA 101
Buckley, William F(rank), Jr. 1925- **CLC 7, 18, 37; DAM POP**
See also AITN 1; CA 1-4R; CANR 1, 24, 53; DLB 137; DLBY 80; INT CANR-24; MTCW
Buechner, (Carl) Frederick 1926- **CLC 2, 4, 6, 9; DAM NOV**
See also CA 13-16R; CANR 11, 39, 64; DLBY 80; INT CANR-11; MTCW
Buell, John (Edward) 1927- **CLC 10**
See also CA 1-4R; DLB 53
Buero Vallejo, Antonio 1916- **CLC 15, 46**
See also CA 106; CANR 24, 49; HW; MTCW
Bufalino, Gesualdo 1920(?)- **CLC 74**
See also DLB 196
Bugayev, Boris Nikolayevich 1880-1934 **TCLC 7; PC 11**
See also Bely, Andrey
See also CA 104; 165
Bukowski, Charles 1920-1994 **CLC 2, 5, 9, 41, 82, 108; DAM NOV, POET; PC 18**
See also CA 17-20R; 144; CANR 40, 62; DLB 5, 130, 169; MTCW
Bulgakov, Mikhail (Afanas'evich) 1891-1940 **TCLC 2, 16; DAM DRAM, NOV; SSC 18**
See also CA 105; 152
Bulgya, Alexander Alexandrovich 1901-1956 **TCLC 53**
See also Fadeyev, Alexander
See also CA 117
Bullins, Ed 1935- **CLC 1, 5, 7; BLC 1; DAM DRAM, MULT; DC 6**
See also BW 2; CA 49-52; CAAS 16; CANR 24, 46; DLB 7, 38; MTCW
Bulwer-Lytton, Edward (George Earle Lytton) 1803-1873 **NCLC 1, 45**
See also DLB 21
Bunin, Ivan Alexeyevich 1870-1953 **TCLC 6; SSC 5**
See also CA 104
Bunting, Basil 1900-1985 **CLC 10, 39, 47; DAM POET**
See also CA 53-56; 115; CANR 7; DLB 20
Bunuel, Luis 1900-1983 **CLC 16, 80; DAM MULT; HLC**
See also CA 101; 110; CANR 32; HW
Bunyan, John 1628-1688 **LC 4; DA; DAB; DAC; DAM MST; WLC**
See also CDBLB 1660-1789; DLB 39
Burckhardt, Jacob (Christoph) 1818-1897 **NCLC 49**
Burford, Eleanor
See Hibbert, Eleanor Alice Burford
Burgess, Anthony **CLC 1, 2, 4, 5, 8, 10, 13, 15, 22, 40, 62, 81, 94; DAB**
See also Wilson, John (Anthony) Burgess
See also AAYA 25; AITN 1; CDBLB 1960 to Present; DLB 14, 194
Burke, Edmund 1729(?)-1797 **LC 7, 36; DA; DAB; DAC; DAM MST; WLC**

See also DLB 104
Burke, Kenneth (Duva) 1897-1993 **CLC 2, 24**
See also CA 5-8R; 143; CANR 39; DLB 45, 63; MTCW
Burke, Leda
See Garnett, David
Burke, Ralph
See Silverberg, Robert
Burke, Thomas 1886-1945 **TCLC 63**
See also CA 113; 155; DLB 197
Burney, Fanny 1752-1840 **NCLC 12, 54**
See also DLB 39
Burns, Robert 1759-1796 **PC 6**
See also CDBLB 1789-1832; DA; DAB; DAC; DAM MST, POET; DLB 109; WLC
Burns, Tex
See L'Amour, Louis (Dearborn)
Burnshaw, Stanley 1906- **CLC 3, 13, 44**
See also CA 9-12R; DLB 48; DLBY 97
Burr, Anne 1937- **CLC 6**
See also CA 25-28R
Burroughs, Edgar Rice 1875-1950 **TCLC 2, 32; DAM NOV**
See also AAYA 11; CA 104; 132; DLB 8; MTCW; SATA 41
Burroughs, William S(eward) 1914-1997 **CLC 1, 2, 5, 15, 22, 42, 75, 109; DA; DAB; DAC; DAM MST, NOV, POP; WLC**
See also AITN 2; CA 9-12R; 160; CANR 20, 52; DLB 2, 8, 16, 152; DLBY 81, 97; MTCW
Burton, Richard F. 1821-1890 **NCLC 42**
See also DLB 55, 184
Busch, Frederick 1941- **CLC 7, 10, 18, 47**
See also CA 33-36R; CAAS 1; CANR 45; DLB 6
Bush, Ronald 1946- **CLC 34**
See also CA 136
Bustos, F(rancisco)
See Borges, Jorge Luis
Bustos Domecq, H(onorio)
See Bioy Casares, Adolfo; Borges, Jorge Luis
Butler, Octavia E(stelle) 1947- **CLC 38; BLCS; DAM MULT, POP**
See also AAYA 18; BW 2; CA 73-76; CANR 12, 24, 38; DLB 33; MTCW; SATA 84
Butler, Robert Olen (Jr.) 1945- **CLC 81; DAM POP**
See also CA 112; CANR 66; DLB 173; INT 112
Butler, Samuel 1612-1680 **LC 16, 43**
See also DLB 101, 126
Butler, Samuel 1835-1902 **TCLC 1, 33; DA; DAB; DAC; DAM MST, NOV; WLC**
See also CA 143; CDBLB 1890-1914; DLB 18, 57, 174
Butler, Walter C.
See Faust, Frederick (Schiller)
Butor, Michel (Marie Francois) 1926- **CLC 1, 3, 8, 11, 15**
See also CA 9-12R; CANR 33, 66; DLB 83; MTCW
Butts, Mary 1892(?)-1937 **TCLC 77**
See also CA 148
Buzo, Alexander (John) 1944- **CLC 61**
See also CA 97-100; CANR 17, 39, 69
Buzzati, Dino 1906-1972 **CLC 36**
See also CA 160; 33-36R; DLB 177
Byars, Betsy (Cromer) 1928- **CLC 35**
See also AAYA 19; CA 33-36R; CANR 18, 36, 57; CLR 1, 16; DLB 52; INT CANR-18; JRDA; MAICYA; MTCW; SAAS 1; SATA 4, 46, 80
Byatt, A(ntonia) S(usan Drabble) 1936- **CLC 19, 65; DAM NOV, POP**

See also CA 13-16R; CANR 13, 33, 50; DLB 14, 194; MTCW
Byrne, David 1952- **CLC 26**
See also CA 127
Byrne, John Keyes 1926-
See Leonard, Hugh
See also CA 102; INT 102
Byron, George Gordon (Noel) 1788-1824 **NCLC 2, 12; DA; DAB; DAC; DAM MST, POET; PC 16; WLC**
See also CDBLB 1789-1832; DLB 96, 110
Byron, Robert 1905-1941 **TCLC 67**
See also CA 160; DLB 195
C. 3. 3.
See Wilde, Oscar (Fingal O'Flahertie Wills)
Caballero, Fernan 1796-1877 **NCLC 10**
Cabell, Branch
See Cabell, James Branch
Cabell, James Branch 1879-1958 **TCLC 6**
See also CA 105; 152; DLB 9, 78
Cable, George Washington 1844-1925 **TCLC 4; SSC 4**
See also CA 104; 155; DLB 12, 74; DLBD 13
Cabral de Melo Neto, Joao 1920- **CLC 76; DAM MULT**
See also CA 151
Cabrera Infante, G(uillermo) 1929- **CLC 5, 25, 45; DAM MULT; HLC**
See also CA 85-88; CANR 29, 65; DLB 113; HW; MTCW
Cade, Toni
See Bambara, Toni Cade
Cadmus and Harmonia
See Buchan, John
Caedmon fl. 658-680 **CMLC 7**
See also DLB 146
Caeiro, Alberto
See Pessoa, Fernando (Antonio Nogueira)
Cage, John (Milton, Jr.) 1912- **CLC 41**
See also CA 13-16R; CANR 9; DLB 193; INT CANR-9
Cahan, Abraham 1860-1951 **TCLC 71**
See also CA 108; 154; DLB 9, 25, 28
Cain, G.
See Cabrera Infante, G(uillermo)
Cain, Guillermo
See Cabrera Infante, G(uillermo)
Cain, James M(allahan) 1892-1977 **CLC 3, 11, 28**
See also AITN 1; CA 17-20R; 73-76; CANR 8, 34, 61; MTCW
Caine, Mark
See Raphael, Frederic (Michael)
Calasso, Roberto 1941- **CLC 81**
See also CA 143
Calderon de la Barca, Pedro 1600-1681 **LC 23; DC 3**
Caldwell, Erskine (Preston) 1903-1987 **CLC 1, 8, 14, 50, 60; DAM NOV; SSC 19**
See also AITN 1; CA 1-4R; 121; CAAS 1; CANR 2, 33; DLB 9, 86; MTCW
Caldwell, (Janet Miriam) Taylor (Holland) 1900-1985 **CLC 2, 28, 39; DAM NOV, POP**
See also CA 5-8R; 116; CANR 5
Calhoun, John Caldwell 1782-1850 **NCLC 15**
See also DLB 3
Calisher, Hortense 1911- **CLC 2, 4, 8, 38; DAM NOV; SSC 15**
See also CA 1-4R; CANR 1, 22, 67; DLB 2; INT CANR-22; MTCW
Callaghan, Morley Edward 1903-1990 **CLC 3, 14, 41, 65; DAC; DAM MST**
See also CA 9-12R; 132; CANR 33; DLB 68;

Cohen-Solal, Annie 19(?)-   **CLC 50**
Colegate, Isabel 1931-   **CLC 36**
  See also CA 17-20R; CANR 8, 22; DLB 14;
  INT CANR-22; MTCW
Coleman, Emmett
  See Reed, Ishmael
Coleridge, M. E.
  See Coleridge, Mary E(lizabeth)
Coleridge, Mary E(lizabeth) 1861-1907 **TCLC
73**
  See also CA 116; 166; DLB 19, 98
Coleridge, Samuel Taylor 1772-1834 **NCLC 9,
54; DA; DAB; DAC; DAM MST, POET;
PC 11; WLC**
  See also CDBLB 1789-1832, DLB 93, 107
Coleridge, Sara 1802-1852   **NCLC 31**
  See also DLB 199
Coles, Don 1928-   **CLC 46**
  See also CA 115; CANR 38
Coles, Robert (Martin) 1929-   **CLC 108**
  See also CA 45-48; CANR 3, 32, 66; INT
  CANR-32; SATA 23
Colette, (Sidonie-Gabrielle) 1873-1954 **TCLC
1, 5, 16; DAM NOV; SSC 10**
  See also CA 104; 131; DLB 65; MTCW
Collett, (Jacobine) Camilla (Wergeland) 1813-
1895 **NCLC 22**
Collier, Christopher 1930-   **CLC 30**
  See also AAYA 13; CA 33-36R; CANR 13, 33;
  JRDA; MAICYA; SATA 16, 70
Collier, James L(incoln) 1928- **CLC 30; DAM
POP**
  See also AAYA 13; CA 9-12R; CANR 4, 33,
  60; CLR 3; JRDA; MAICYA; SAAS 21;
  SATA 8, 70
Collier, Jeremy 1650-1726   **LC 6**
Collier, John 1901-1980   **SSC 19**
  See also CA 65-68; 97-100; CANR 10; DLB
  77
Collingwood, R(obin) G(eorge) 1889(?)-1943
TCLC 67
  See also CA 117; 155
Collins, Hunt
  See Hunter, Evan
Collins, Linda 1931-   **CLC 44**
  See also CA 125
Collins, (William) Wilkie 1824-1889 **NCLC 1,
18**
  See also CDBLB 1832-1890; DLB 18, 70, 159
Collins, William 1721-1759   **LC 4, 40; DAM
POET**
  See also DLB 109
Collodi, Carlo 1826-1890   **NCLC 54**
  See also Lorenzini, Carlo
  See also CLR 5
Colman, George 1732-1794
  See Glassco, John
Colt, Winchester Remington
  See Hubbard, L(afayette) Ron(ald)
Colter, Cyrus 1910-   **CLC 58**
  See also BW 1; CA 65-68; CANR 10, 66; DLB
  33
Colton, James
  See Hansen, Joseph
Colum, Padraic 1881-1972   **CLC 28**
  See also CA 73-76; 33-36R; CANR 35; CLR
  36; MAICYA; MTCW; SATA 15
Colvin, James
  See Moorcock, Michael (John)
Colwin, Laurie (E.) 1944-1992 **CLC 5, 13, 23,
84**
  See also CA 89-92; 139; CANR 20, 46; DLBY
  80; MTCW

Comfort, Alex(ander) 1920- **CLC 7; DAM POP**
  See also CA 1-4R; CANR 1, 45
Comfort, Montgomery
  See Campbell, (John) Ramsey
Compton-Burnett, I(vy) 1884(?)-1969 **CLC 1,
3, 10, 15, 34; DAM NOV**
  See also CA 1-4R; 25-28R; CANR 4; DLB 36;
  MTCW
Comstock, Anthony 1844-1915   **TCLC 13**
  See also CA 110
Comte, Auguste 1798-1857   **NCLC 54**
Conan Doyle, Arthur
  See Doyle, Arthur Conan
Conde, Maryse 1937-   **CLC 52, 92; BLCS;
DAM MULT**
  See also Boucolon, Maryse
  See also BW 2
Condillac, Etienne Bonnot de 1714-1780 **L C
26**
Condon, Richard (Thomas) 1915-1996 **CLC 4,
6, 8, 10, 45, 100; DAM NOV**
  See also BEST 90:3; CA 1-4R; 151; CAAS 1;
  CANR 2, 23; INT CANR-23; MTCW
Confucius 551B.C.-479B.C.   **CMLC 19; DA;
DAB; DAC; DAM MST; WLCS**
Congreve, William 1670-1729   **LC 5, 21; DA;
DAB; DAC; DAM DRAM, MST, POET;
DC 2; WLC**
  See also CDBLB 1660-1789; DLB 39, 84
Connell, Evan S(helby), Jr. 1924- **CLC 4, 6, 45;
DAM NOV**
  See also AAYA 7; CA 1-4R; CAAS 2; CANR
  2, 39; DLB 2; DLBY 81; MTCW
Connelly, Marc(us Cook) 1890-1980   **CLC 7**
  See also CA 85-88; 102; CANR 30; DLB 7;
  DLBY 80; SATA-Obit 25
Connor, Ralph   **TCLC 31**
  See Gordon, Charles William
  See also DLB 92
Conrad, Joseph 1857-1924 **TCLC 1, 6, 13, 25,
43, 57; DA; DAB; DAC; DAM MST, NOV;
SSC 9; WLC**
  See also CA 104; 131; CANR 60; CDBLB
  1890-1914; DLB 10, 34, 98, 156; MTCW;
  SATA 27
Conrad, Robert Arnold
  See Hart, Moss
Conroy, Donald Pat(rick) 1945-   **CLC 30, 74;
DAM NOV, POP**
  See also AAYA 8; AITN 1; CA 85-88; CANR
  24, 53; DLB 6; MTCW
Conroy, Pat
  See Conroy, Donald Pat(rick)
Constant (de Rebecque), (Henri) Benjamin
1767-1830 **NCLC 6**
  See also DLB 119
Conybeare, Charles Augustus
  See Eliot, T(homas) S(tearns)
Cook, Michael 1933-   **CLC 58**
  See also CA 93-96; CANR 68; DLB 53
Cook, Robin 1940-   **CLC 14; DAM POP**
  See also BEST 90:2; CA 108; 111; CANR 41;
  INT 111
Cook, Roy
  See Silverberg, Robert
Cooke, Elizabeth 1948-   **CLC 55**
  See also CA 129
Cooke, John Esten 1830-1886   **NCLC 5**
  See also DLB 3
Cooke, John Estes
  See Baum, L(yman) Frank
Cooke, M. E.
  See Creasey, John

Cooke, Margaret
  See Creasey, John
Cook-Lynn, Elizabeth 1930-   **CLC 93; DAM
MULT**
  See also CA 133; DLB 175; NNAL
Cooney, Ray   **CLC 62**
Cooper, Douglas 1960-   **CLC 86**
Cooper, Henry St. John
  See Creasey, John
Cooper, J(oan) California   **CLC 56; DAM
MULT**
  See also AAYA 12; BW 1; CA 125; CANR 55
Cooper, James Fenimore 1789-1851 **NCLC 1,
27, 54**
  See also AAYA 22; CDALB 1640-1865; DLB
  3; SATA 19
Coover, Robert (Lowell) 1932- **CLC 3, 7, 15,
32, 46, 87; DAM NOV; SSC 15**
  See also CA 45-48; CANR 3, 37, 58; DLB 2;
  DLBY 81; MTCW
Copeland, Stewart (Armstrong) 1952- **CLC 26**
Copernicus, Nicolaus 1473-1543   **LC 45**
Coppard, A(lfred) E(dgar) 1878-1957 **TCLC
5; SSC 21**
  See also CA 114; DLB 162; YABC 1
Coppee, Francois 1842-1908   **TCLC 25**
Coppola, Francis Ford 1939-   **CLC 16**
  See also CA 77-80; CANR 40; DLB 44
Corbiere, Tristan 1845-1875   **NCLC 43**
Corcoran, Barbara 1911-   **CLC 17**
  See also AAYA 14; CA 21-24R; CAAS 2;
  CANR 11, 28, 48; CLR 50; DLB 52; JRDA;
  SAAS 20; SATA 3, 77
Cordelier, Maurice
  See Giraudoux, (Hippolyte) Jean
Corelli, Marie 1855-1924   **TCLC 51**
  See also Mackay, Mary
  See also DLB 34, 156
Corman, Cid 1924-   **CLC 9**
  See also Corman, Sidney
  See also CAAS 2; DLB 5, 193
Corman, Sidney 1924-
  See Corman, Cid
  See also CA 85-88; CANR 44; DAM POET
Cormier, Robert (Edmund) 1925- **CLC 12, 30;
DA; DAB; DAC; DAM MST, NOV**
  See also AAYA 3, 19; CA 1-4R; CANR 5, 23;
  CDALB 1968-1988; CLR 12; DLB 52; INT
  CANR-23; JRDA; MAICYA; MTCW; SATA
  10, 45, 83
Corn, Alfred (DeWitt III) 1943-   **CLC 33**
  See also CA 104; CAAS 25; CANR 44; DLB
  120; DLBY 80
Corneille, Pierre 1606-1684   **LC 28; DAB;
DAM MST**
Cornwell, David (John Moore) 1931- **CLC 9,
15; DAM POP**
  See also le Carre, John
  See also CA 5-8R; CANR 13, 33, 59; MTCW
Corso, (Nunzio) Gregory 1930-   **CLC 1, 11**
  See also CA 5-8R; CANR 41; DLB 5, 16;
  MTCW
Cortazar, Julio 1914-1984 **CLC 2, 3, 5, 10, 13,
15, 33, 34, 92; DAM MULT, NOV; HLC;
SSC 7**
  See also CA 21-24R; CANR 12, 32; DLB 113;
  HW; MTCW
CORTES, HERNAN 1484-1547   **LC 31**
Corwin, Cecil
  See Kornbluth, C(yril) M.
Cosic, Dobrica 1921-   **CLC 14**
  See also CA 122; 138; DLB 181
Costain, Thomas B(ertram) 1885-1965   **CLC**

See Agnon, S(hmuel) Y(osef Halevi)

Dabrowska, Maria (Szumska) 1889-1965 **CLC 15**
See also CA 106

Dabydeen, David 1955- **CLC 34**
See also BW 1; CA 125; CANR 56

Dacey, Philip 1939- **CLC 51**
See also CA 37-40R; CAAS 17; CANR 14, 32, 64; DLB 105

Dagerman, Stig (Halvard) 1923-1954 **TCLC 17**
See also CA 117; 155

Dahl, Roald 1916-1990 **CLC 1, 6, 18, 79; DAB; DAC; DAM MST, NOV, POP**
See also AAYA 15; CA 1-4R; 133; CANR 6, 32, 37, 62; CLR 1, 7, 41; DLB 139; JRDA; MAICYA; MTCW; SATA 1, 26, 73; SATA-Obit 65

Dahlberg, Edward 1900-1977 **CLC 1, 7, 14**
See also CA 9-12R; 69-72; CANR 31, 62; DLB 48; MTCW

Daitch, Susan 1954- **CLC 103**
See also CA 161

Dale, Colin **TCLC 18**
See also Lawrence, T(homas) E(dward)

Dale, George E.
See Asimov, Isaac

Daly, Elizabeth 1878-1967 **CLC 52**
See also CA 23-24; 25-28R; CANR 60; CAP 2

Daly, Maureen 1921- **CLC 17**
See also AAYA 5; CANR 37; JRDA; MAICYA; SAAS 1; SATA 2

Damas, Leon-Gontran 1912-1978 **CLC 84**
See also BW 1; CA 125; 73-76

Dana, Richard Henry Sr. 1787-1879 **NCLC 53**

Daniel, Samuel 1562(?)-1619 **LC 24**
See also DLB 62

Daniels, Brett
See Adler, Renata

Dannay, Frederic 1905-1982 **CLC 11; DAM POP**
See also Queen, Ellery
See also CA 1-4R; 107; CANR 1, 39; DLB 137; MTCW

D'Annunzio, Gabriele 1863-1938 **TCLC 6, 40**
See also CA 104; 155

Danois, N. le
See Gourmont, Remy (-Marie-Charles) de

Dante 1265-1321 **CMLC 3, 18; DA; DAB; DAC; DAM MST, POET; PC 21; WLCS**

d'Antibes, Germain
See Simenon, Georges (Jacques Christian)

Danticat, Edwidge 1969- **CLC 94**
See also CA 152

Danvers, Dennis 1947- **CLC 70**

Danziger, Paula 1944- **CLC 21**
See also AAYA 4; CA 112; 115; CANR 37; CLR 20; JRDA; MAICYA; SATA 36, 63; SATA-Brief 30

Dario, Ruben 1867-1916 **TCLC 4; DAM MULT; HLC; PC 15**
See also CA 131; HW; MTCW

Darley, George 1795-1846 **NCLC 2**
See also DLB 96

Darrow, Clarence (Seward) 1857-1938 **TCLC 81**
See also CA 164

Darwin, Charles 1809-1882 **NCLC 57**
See also DLB 57, 166

Daryush, Elizabeth 1887-1977 **CLC 6, 19**
See also CA 49-52; CANR 3; DLB 20

Dasgupta, Surendranath 1887-1952 **TCLC 81**
See also CA 157

Dashwood, Edmee Elizabeth Monica de la Pasture 1890-1943
See Delafield, E. M.
See also CA 119; 154

Daudet, (Louis Marie) Alphonse 1840-1897 **NCLC 1**
See also DLB 123

Daumal, Rene 1908-1944 **TCLC 14**
See also CA 114

Davenport, Guy (Mattison, Jr.) 1927- **CLC 6, 14, 38; SSC 16**
See also CA 33-36R; CANR 23; DLB 130

Davidson, Avram 1923-
See Queen, Ellery
See also CA 101; CANR 26; DLB 8

Davidson, Donald (Grady) 1893-1968 **CLC 2, 13, 19**
See also CA 5-8R; 25-28R; CANR 4; DLB 45

Davidson, Hugh
See Hamilton, Edmond

Davidson, John 1857-1909 **TCLC 24**
See also CA 118; DLB 19

Davidson, Sara 1943- **CLC 9**
See also CA 81-84; CANR 44, 68; DLB 185

Davie, Donald (Alfred) 1922-1995 **CLC 5, 8, 10, 31**
See also CA 1-4R; 149; CAAS 3; CANR 1, 44; DLB 27; MTCW

Davies, Ray(mond Douglas) 1944- **CLC 21**
See also CA 116; 146

Davies, Rhys 1901-1978 **CLC 23**
See also CA 9-12R; 81-84; CANR 4; DLB 139, 191

Davies, (William) Robertson 1913-1995 **CLC 2, 7, 13, 25, 42, 75, 91; DA; DAB; DAC; DAM MST, NOV, POP; WLC**
See also BEST 89:2; CA 33-36R; 150; CANR 17, 42; DLB 68; INT CANR-17; MTCW

Davies, W(illiam) H(enry) 1871-1940 **TCLC 5**
See also CA 104; DLB 19, 174

Davies, Walter C.
See Kornbluth, C(yril) M.

Davis, Angela (Yvonne) 1944- **CLC 77; DAM MULT**
See also BW 2; CA 57-60; CANR 10

Davis, B. Lynch
See Bioy Casares, Adolfo; Borges, Jorge Luis

Davis, Harold Lenoir 1896-1960 **CLC 49**
See also CA 89-92; DLB 9

Davis, Rebecca (Blaine) Harding 1831-1910 **TCLC 6**
See also CA 104; DLB 74

Davis, Richard Harding 1864-1916 **TCLC 24**
See also CA 114; DLB 12, 23, 78, 79, 189; DLBD 13

Davison, Frank Dalby 1893-1970 **CLC 15**
See also CA 116

Davison, Lawrence H.
See Lawrence, D(avid) H(erbert Richards)

Davison, Peter (Hubert) 1928- **CLC 28**
See also CA 9-12R; CAAS 4; CANR 3, 43; DLB 5

Davys, Mary 1674-1732 **LC 1**
See also DLB 39

Dawson, Fielding 1930- **CLC 6**
See also CA 85-88; DLB 130

Dawson, Peter
See Faust, Frederick (Schiller)

Day, Clarence (Shepard, Jr.) 1874-1935 **TCLC 25**
See also CA 108; DLB 11

Day, Thomas 1748-1789 **LC 1**
See also DLB 39; YABC 1

Day Lewis, C(ecil) 1904-1972 **CLC 1, 6, 10; DAM POET; PC 11**
See also Blake, Nicholas
See also CA 13-16; 33-36R; CANR 34; CAP 1; DLB 15, 20; MTCW

Dazai Osamu 1909-1948 **TCLC 11**
See also Tsushima, Shuji
See also CA 164; DLB 182

de Andrade, Carlos Drummond
See Drummond de Andrade, Carlos

Deane, Norman
See Creasey, John

de Beauvoir, Simone (Lucie Ernestine Marie Bertrand)
See Beauvoir, Simone (Lucie Ernestine Marie Bertrand) de

de Beer, P.
See Bosman, Herman Charles

de Brissac, Malcolm
See Dickinson, Peter (Malcolm)

de Chardin, Pierre Teilhard
See Teilhard de Chardin, (Marie Joseph) Pierre

Dee, John 1527-1608 **LC 20**

Deer, Sandra 1940- **CLC 45**

De Ferrari, Gabriella 1941- **CLC 65**
See also CA 146

Defoe, Daniel 1660(?)-1731 **LC 1; DA; DAB; DAC; DAM MST, NOV; WLC**
See also CDBLB 1660-1789; DLB 39, 95, 101; JRDA; MAICYA; SATA 22

de Gourmont, Remy(-Marie-Charles)
See Gourmont, Remy (-Marie-Charles) de

de Hartog, Jan 1914- **CLC 19**
See also CA 1-4R; CANR 1

de Hostos, E. M.
See Hostos (y Bonilla), Eugenio Maria de

de Hostos, Eugenio M.
See Hostos (y Bonilla), Eugenio Maria de

Deighton, Len **CLC 4, 7, 22, 46**
See also Deighton, Leonard Cyril
See also AAYA 6; BEST 89:2; CDBLB 1960 to Present; DLB 87

Deighton, Leonard Cyril 1929-
See Deighton, Len
See also CA 9-12R; CANR 19, 33, 68; DAM NOV, POP; MTCW

Dekker, Thomas 1572(?)-1632 **LC 22; DAM DRAM**
See also CDBLB Before 1660; DLB 62, 172

Delafield, E. M. 1890-1943 **TCLC 61**
See also Dashwood, Edmee Elizabeth Monica de la Pasture
See also DLB 34

de la Mare, Walter (John) 1873-1956 **TCLC 4, 53; DAB; DAC; DAM MST, POET; SSC 14; WLC**
See also CA 163; CDBLB 1914-1945; CLR 23; DLB 162; SATA 16

Delaney, Franey
See O'Hara, John (Henry)

Delaney, Shelagh 1939- **CLC 29; DAM DRAM**
See also CA 17-20R; CANR 30, 67; CDBLB 1960 to Present; DLB 13; MTCW

Delany, Mary (Granville Pendarves) 1700-1788 **LC 12**

Delany, Samuel R(ay, Jr.) 1942- **CLC 8, 14, 38; BLC 1; DAM MULT**
See also AAYA 24; BW 2; CA 81-84; CANR 27, 43; DLB 8, 33; MTCW

De La Ramee, (Marie) Louise 1839-1908
See Ouida
See also SATA 20

de la Roche, Mazo 1879-1961 **CLC 14**

Duclos, Charles Pinot 1704-1772   **LC 1**

Dudek, Louis 1918-   **CLC 11, 19**
    See also CA 45-48; CAAS 14; CANR 1; DLB 88

Duerrenmatt, Friedrich 1921-1990 **CLC 1, 4, 8, 11, 15, 43, 102; DAM DRAM**
    See also CA 17-20R; CANR 33; DLB 69, 124; MTCW

Duffy, Bruce (?)-   **CLC 50**

Duffy, Maureen 1933-   **CLC 37**
    See also CA 25-28R; CANR 33, 68; DLB 14; MTCW

Dugan, Alan 1923-   **CLC 2, 6**
    See also CA 81-84; DLB 5

du Gard, Roger Martin
    See Martin du Gard, Roger

Duhamel, Georges 1884-1966   **CLC 8**
    See also CA 81-84; 25-28R; CANR 35; DLB 65; MTCW

Dujardin, Edouard (Emile Louis) 1861-1949 **TCLC 13**
    See also CA 109; DLB 123

Dulles, John Foster 1888-1959   **TCLC 72**
    See also CA 115; 149

Dumas, Alexandre (Davy de la Pailleterie) 1802-1870 **NCLC 11; DA; DAB; DAC; DAM MST, NOV; WLC**
    See also DLB 119, 192; SATA 18

Dumas (fils), Alexandre 1824-1895 **NCLC 71; DC 1**
    See also AAYA 22; DLB 192

Dumas, Claudine
    See Malzberg, Barry N(athaniel)

Dumas, Henry L. 1934-1968   **CLC 6, 62**
    See also BW 1; CA 85-88; DLB 41

du Maurier, Daphne 1907-1989 **CLC 6, 11, 59; DAB; DAC; DAM MST, POP; SSC 18**
    See also CA 5-8R; 128; CANR 6, 55; DLB 191; MTCW; SATA 27; SATA-Obit 60

Dunbar, Paul Laurence 1872-1906 **TCLC 2, 12; BLC 1; DA; DAC; DAM MST, MULT, POET; PC 5; SSC 8; WLC**
    See also BW 1; CA 104; 124; CDALB 1865-1917; DLB 50, 54, 78; SATA 34

Dunbar, William 1460(?)-1530(?)   **LC 20**
    See also DLB 132, 146

Duncan, Dora Angela
    See Duncan, Isadora

Duncan, Isadora 1877(?)-1927   **TCLC 68**
    See also CA 118; 149

Duncan, Lois 1934-   **CLC 26**
    See also AAYA 4; CA 1-4R; CANR 2, 23, 36; CLR 29; JRDA; MAICYA; SAAS 2; SATA 1, 36, 75

Duncan, Robert (Edward) 1919-1988 **CLC 1, 2, 4, 7, 15, 41, 55; DAM POET; PC 2**
    See also CA 9-12R; 124; CANR 28, 62; DLB 5, 16, 193; MTCW

Duncan, Sara Jeannette 1861-1922 **TCLC 60**
    See also CA 157; DLB 92

Dunlap, William 1766-1839   **NCLC 2**
    See also DLB 30, 37, 59

Dunn, Douglas (Eaglesham) 1942- **CLC 6, 40**
    See also CA 45-48; CANR 2, 33; DLB 40; MTCW

Dunn, Katherine (Karen) 1945-   **CLC 71**
    See also CA 33-36R

Dunn, Stephen 1939-   **CLC 36**
    See also CA 33-36R; CANR 12, 48, 53; DLB 105

Dunne, Finley Peter 1867-1936   **TCLC 28**
    See also CA 108; DLB 11, 23

Dunne, John Gregory 1932-   **CLC 28**
    See also CA 25-28R; CANR 14, 50; DLBY 80

Dunsany, Edward John Moreton Drax Plunkett 1878-1957
    See Dunsany, Lord
    See also CA 104; 148; DLB 10

Dunsany, Lord   **TCLC 2, 59**
    See also Dunsany, Edward John Moreton Drax Plunkett
    See also DLB 77, 153, 156

du Perry, Jean
    See Simenon, Georges (Jacques Christian)

Durang, Christopher (Ferdinand) 1949- **CLC 27, 38**
    See also CA 105; CANR 50

Duras, Marguerite 1914-1996 **CLC 3, 6, 11, 20, 34, 40, 68, 100**
    See also CA 25-28R; 151; CANR 50; DLB 83; MTCW

Durban, (Rosa) Pam 1947-   **CLC 39**
    See also CA 123

Durcan, Paul 1944- **CLC 43, 70; DAM POET**
    See also CA 134

Durkheim, Emile 1858-1917   **TCLC 55**

Durrell, Lawrence (George) 1912-1990 **CLC 1, 4, 6, 8, 13, 27, 41; DAM NOV**
    See also CA 9-12R; 132; CANR 40; CDBLB 1945-1960; DLB 15, 27; DLBY 90; MTCW

Durrenmatt, Friedrich
    See Duerrenmatt, Friedrich

Dutt, Toru 1856-1877   **NCLC 29**

Dwight, Timothy 1752-1817   **NCLC 13**
    See also DLB 37

Dworkin, Andrea 1946-   **CLC 43**
    See also CA 77-80; CAAS 21; CANR 16, 39; INT CANR-16; MTCW

Dwyer, Deanna
    See Koontz, Dean R(ay)

Dwyer, K. R.
    See Koontz, Dean R(ay)

Dye, Richard
    See De Voto, Bernard (Augustine)

Dylan, Bob 1941-   **CLC 3, 4, 6, 12, 77**
    See also CA 41-44R; DLB 16

Eagleton, Terence (Francis) 1943-
    See Eagleton, Terry
    See also CA 57-60; CANR 7, 23, 68; MTCW

Eagleton, Terry   **CLC 63**
    See also Eagleton, Terence (Francis)

Early, Jack
    See Scoppettone, Sandra

East, Michael
    See West, Morris L(anglo)

Eastaway, Edward
    See Thomas, (Philip) Edward

Eastlake, William (Derry) 1917-1997 **CLC 8**
    See also CA 5-8R; 158; CAAS 1; CANR 5, 63; DLB 6; INT CANR-5

Eastman, Charles A(lexander) 1858-1939 **TCLC 55; DAM MULT**
    See also DLB 175; NNAL; YABC 1

Eberhart, Richard (Ghormley) 1904- **CLC 3, 11, 19, 56; DAM POET**
    See also CA 1-4R; CANR 2; CDALB 1941-1968; DLB 48; MTCW

Eberstadt, Fernanda 1960-   **CLC 39**
    See also CA 136; CANR 69

Echegaray (y Eizaguirre), Jose (Maria Waldo) 1832-1916   **TCLC 4**
    See also CA 104; CANR 32; HW; MTCW

Echeverria, (Jose) Esteban (Antonino) 1805-1851   **NCLC 18**

Echo
    See Proust, (Valentin-Louis-George-Eugene-) Marcel

Eckert, Allan W. 1931-   **CLC 17**
    See also AAYA 18; CA 13-16R; CANR 14, 45; INT CANR-14; SAAS 21; SATA 29, 91; SATA-Brief 27

Eckhart, Meister 1260(?)-1328(?)   **CMLC 9**
    See also DLB 115

Eckmar, F. R.
    See de Hartog, Jan

Eco, Umberto 1932- **CLC 28, 60; DAM NOV, POP**
    See also BEST 90:1; CA 77-80; CANR 12, 33, 55; DLB 196; MTCW

Eddison, E(ric) R(ucker) 1882-1945 **TCLC 15**
    See also CA 109; 156

Eddy, Mary (Morse) Baker 1821-1910 **TCLC 71**
    See also CA 113

Edel, (Joseph) Leon 1907-1997   **CLC 29, 34**
    See also CA 1-4R; 161; CANR 1, 22; DLB 103; INT CANR-22

Eden, Emily 1797-1869   **NCLC 10**

Edgar, David 1948-   **CLC 42; DAM DRAM**
    See also CA 57-60; CANR 12, 61; DLB 13; MTCW

Edgerton, Clyde (Carlyle) 1944-   **CLC 39**
    See also AAYA 17; CA 118; 134; CANR 64; INT 134

Edgeworth, Maria 1768-1849   **NCLC 1, 51**
    See also DLB 116, 159, 163; SATA 21

Edmonds, Paul
    See Kuttner, Henry

Edmonds, Walter D(umaux) 1903-   **CLC 35**
    See also CA 5-8R; CANR 2; DLB 9; MAICYA; SAAS 4; SATA 1, 27

Edmondson, Wallace
    See Ellison, Harlan (Jay)

Edson, Russell   **CLC 13**
    See also CA 33-36R

Edwards, Bronwen Elizabeth
    See Rose, Wendy

Edwards, G(erald) B(asil) 1899-1976 **CLC 25**
    See also CA 110

Edwards, Gus 1939-   **CLC 43**
    See also CA 108; INT 108

Edwards, Jonathan 1703-1758 **LC 7; DA; DAC; DAM MST**
    See also DLB 24

Efron, Marina Ivanovna Tsvetaeva
    See Tsvetaeva (Efron), Marina (Ivanovna)

Ehle, John (Marsden, Jr.) 1925-   **CLC 27**
    See also CA 9-12R

Ehrenbourg, Ilya (Grigoryevich)
    See Ehrenburg, Ilya (Grigoryevich)

Ehrenburg, Ilya (Grigoryevich) 1891-1967 **CLC 18, 34, 62**
    See also CA 102; 25-28R

Ehrenburg, Ilyo (Grigoryevich)
    See Ehrenburg, Ilya (Grigoryevich)

Ehrenreich, Barbara 1941-   **CLC 110**
    See also BEST 90:4; CA 73-76; CANR 16, 37, 62; MTCW

Eich, Guenter 1907-1972   **CLC 15**
    See also CA 111; 93-96; DLB 69, 124

Eichendorff, Joseph Freiherr von 1788-1857 **NCLC 8**
    See also DLB 90

Eigner, Larry   **CLC 9**
    See also Eigner, Laurence (Joel)
    See also CAAS 23; DLB 5

Eigner, Laurence (Joel) 1927-1996
    See Eigner, Larry
    See also CA 9-12R; 151; CANR 6; DLB 193

Einstein, Albert 1879-1955 **TCLC 65**
See also CA 121; 133; MTCW
Eiseley, Loren Corey 1907-1977 **CLC 7**
See also AAYA 5; CA 1-4R; 73-76; CANR 6
Eisenstadt, Jill 1963- **CLC 50**
See also CA 140
Eisenstein, Sergei (Mikhailovich) 1898-1948
TCLC 57
See also CA 114; 149
Eisner, Simon
See Kornbluth, C(yril) M.
Ekeloef, (Bengt) Gunnar 1907-1968 **CLC 27;**
DAM POET; PC 23
See also CA 123; 25-28R
Ekelof, (Bengt) Gunnar
See Ekeloef, (Bengt) Gunnar
Ekelund, Vilhelm 1880-1949 **TCLC 75**
Ekwensi, C. O. D.
See Ekwensi, Cyprian (Odiatu Duaka)
Ekwensi, Cyprian (Odiatu Duaka) 1921-**CLC**
4; BLC 1; DAM MULT
See also BW 2; CA 29-32R; CANR 18, 42; DLB
117; MTCW; SATA 66
Elaine **TCLC 18**
See also Leverson, Ada
El Crummo
See Crumb, R(obert)
Elder, Lonne III 1931-1996 **DC 8**
See also BLC 1; BW 1; CA 81-84; 152; CANR
25; DAM MULT; DLB 7, 38, 44
Elia
See Lamb, Charles
Eliade, Mircea 1907-1986 **CLC 19**
See also CA 65-68; 119; CANR 30, 62; MTCW
Eliot, A. D.
See Jewett, (Theodora) Sarah Orne
Eliot, Alice
See Jewett, (Theodora) Sarah Orne
Eliot, Dan
See Silverberg, Robert
Eliot, George 1819-1880 **NCLC 4, 13, 23, 41,**
49; DA; DAB; DAC; DAM MST, NOV; PC
20; WLC
See also CDBLB 1832-1890; DLB 21, 35, 55
Eliot, John 1604-1690 **LC 5**
See also DLB 24
Eliot, T(homas) S(tearns) 1888-1965**CLC 1, 2,**
3, 6, 9, 10, 13, 15, 24, 34, 41, 55, 57, 113;
DA; DAB; DAC; DAM DRAM, MST,
POET; PC 5; WLC
See also CA 5-8R; 25-28R; CANR 41; CDALB
1929-1941; DLB 7, 10, 45, 63; DLBY 88;
MTCW
Elizabeth 1866-1941 **TCLC 41**
Elkin, Stanley L(awrence) 1930-1995 **CLC 4,**
6, 9, 14, 27, 51, 91; DAM NOV, POP; SSC
12
See also CA 9-12R; 148; CANR 8, 46; DLB 2,
28; DLBY 80; INT CANR-8; MTCW
Elledge, Scott **CLC 34**
Elliot, Don
See Silverberg, Robert
Elliott, Don
See Silverberg, Robert
Elliott, George P(aul) 1918-1980 **CLC 2**
See also CA 1-4R; 97-100; CANR 2
Elliott, Janice 1931- **CLC 47**
See also CA 13-16R; CANR 8, 29; DLB 14
Elliott, Sumner Locke 1917-1991 **CLC 38**
See also CA 5-8R; 134; CANR 2, 21
Elliott, William
See Bradbury, Ray (Douglas)
Ellis, A. E. **CLC 7**

Ellis, Alice Thomas **CLC 40**
See also Haycraft, Anna
See also DLB 194
Ellis, Bret Easton 1964- **CLC 39, 71; DAM**
POP
See also AAYA 2; CA 118; 123; CANR 51; INT
123
Ellis, (Henry) Havelock 1859-1939 **TCLC 14**
See also CA 109; DLB 190
Ellis, Landon
See Ellison, Harlan (Jay)
Ellis, Trey 1962- **CLC 55**
See also CA 146
Ellison, Harlan (Jay) 1934- **CLC 1, 13, 42;**
DAM POP; SSC 14
See also CA 5-8R; CANR 5, 46; DLB 8; INT
CANR-5; MTCW
Ellison, Ralph (Waldo) 1914-1994 **CLC 1, 3,**
11, 54, 86; BLC 1; DA; DAB; DAC; DAM
MST, MULT, NOV; SSC 26; WLC
See also AAYA 19; BW 1; CA 9-12R; 145;
CANR 24, 53; CDALB 1941-1968; DLB 2,
76; DLBY 94; MTCW
Ellmann, Lucy (Elizabeth) 1956- **CLC 61**
See also CA 128
Ellmann, Richard (David) 1918-1987 **CLC 50**
See also BEST 89:2; CA 1-4R; 122; CANR 2,
28, 61; DLB 103; DLBY 87; MTCW
Elman, Richard (Martin) 1934-1997 **CLC 19**
See also CA 17-20R; 163; CAAS 3; CANR 47
Elron
See Hubbard, L(afayette) Ron(ald)
Eluard, Paul **TCLC 7, 41**
See also Grindel, Eugene
Elyot, Sir Thomas 1490(?)-1546 **LC 11**
Elytis, Odysseus 1911-1996 **CLC 15, 49, 100;**
DAM POET; PC 21
See also CA 102; 151; MTCW
Emecheta, (Florence Onye) Buchi 1944- **CLC**
14, 48; BLC 2; DAM MULT
See also BW 2; CA 81-84; CANR 27; DLB 117;
MTCW; SATA 66
Emerson, Mary Moody 1774-1863 **NCLC 66**
Emerson, Ralph Waldo 1803-1882 **NCLC 1,**
38; DA; DAB; DAC; DAM MST, POET;
PC 18; WLC
See also CDALB 1640-1865; DLB 1, 59, 73
Eminescu, Mihail 1850-1889 **NCLC 33**
Empson, William 1906-1984 **CLC 3, 8, 19, 33,**
34
See also CA 17-20R; 112; CANR 31, 61; DLB
20; MTCW
Enchi, Fumiko (Ueda) 1905-1986 **CLC 31**
See also CA 129; 121
Ende, Michael (Andreas Helmuth) 1929-1995
CLC 31
See also CA 118; 124; 149; CANR 36; CLR
14; DLB 75; MAICYA; SATA 61; SATA-
Brief 42; SATA-Obit 86
Endo, Shusaku 1923-1996 **CLC 7, 14, 19, 54,**
99; DAM NOV
See also CA 29-32R; 153; CANR 21, 54; DLB
182; MTCW
Engel, Marian 1933-1985 **CLC 36**
See also CA 25-28R; CANR 12; DLB 53; INT
CANR-12
Engelhardt, Frederick
See Hubbard, L(afayette) Ron(ald)
Enright, D(ennis) J(oseph) 1920-**CLC 4, 8, 31**
See also CA 1-4R; CANR 1, 42; DLB 27; SATA
25
Enzensberger, Hans Magnus 1929- **CLC 43**
See also CA 116; 119

Ephron, Nora 1941- **CLC 17, 31**
See also AITN 2; CA 65-68; CANR 12, 39
Epicurus 341B.C.-270B.C. **CMLC 21**
See also DLB 176
Epsilon
See Betjeman, John
Epstein, Daniel Mark 1948- **CLC 7**
See also CA 49-52; CANR 2, 53
Epstein, Jacob 1956- **CLC 19**
See also CA 114
Epstein, Joseph 1937- **CLC 39**
See also CA 112; 119; CANR 50, 65
Epstein, Leslie 1938- **CLC 27**
See also CA 73-76; CAAS 12, CANR 23, 69
Equiano, Olaudah 1745(?)-1797 **LC 16; BLC**
2; DAM MULT
See also DLB 37, 50
ER **TCLC 33**
See also CA 160; DLB 85
Erasmus, Desiderius 1469(?)-1536 **LC 16**
Erdman, Paul E(mil) 1932- **CLC 25**
See also AITN 1; CA 61-64; CANR 13, 43
Erdrich, Louise 1954- **CLC 39, 54; DAM**
MULT, NOV, POP
See also AAYA 10; BEST 89:1; CA 114; CANR
41, 62; DLB 152, 175; MTCW; NNAL;
SATA 94
Erenburg, Ilya (Grigoryevich)
See Ehrenburg, Ilya (Grigoryevich)
Erickson, Stephen Michael 1950-
See Erickson, Steve
See also CA 129
Erickson, Steve 1950- **CLC 64**
See also Erickson, Stephen Michael
See also CANR 60, 68
Ericson, Walter
See Fast, Howard (Melvin)
Eriksson, Buntel
See Bergman, (Ernst) Ingmar
Ernaux, Annie 1940- **CLC 88**
See also CA 147
Eschenbach, Wolfram von
See Wolfram von Eschenbach
Eseki, Bruno
See Mphahlele, Ezekiel
Esenin, Sergei (Alexandrovich) 1895-1925
TCLC 4
See also CA 104
Eshleman, Clayton 1935- **CLC 7**
See also CA 33-36R; CAAS 6; DLB 5
Espriella, Don Manuel Alvarez
See Southey, Robert
Espriu, Salvador 1913-1985 **CLC 9**
See also CA 154; 115; DLB 134
Espronceda, Jose de 1808-1842 **NCLC 39**
Esse, James
See Stephens, James
Esterbrook, Tom
See Hubbard, L(afayette) Ron(ald)
Estleman, Loren D. 1952-**CLC 48; DAM NOV,**
POP
See also CA 85-88; CANR 27; INT CANR-27;
MTCW
Euclid 306B.C.-283B.C. **CMLC 25**
Eugenides, Jeffrey 1960(?)- **CLC 81**
See also CA 144
Euripides c. 485B.C.-406B.C. **CMLC 23; DA;**
DAB; DAC; DAM DRAM, MST; DC 4;
WLCS
See also DLB 176
Evan, Evin
See Faust, Frederick (Schiller)
Evans, Evan

Figes, Eva 1932- **CLC 31**
See also CA 53-56; CANR 4, 44; DLB 14
Finch, Anne 1661-1720 **LC 3; PC 21**
See also DLB 95
Finch, Robert (Duer Claydon) 1900- **CLC 18**
See also CA 57-60; CANR 9, 24, 49; DLB 88
Findley, Timothy 1930- **CLC 27, 102; DAC; DAM MST**
See also CA 25-28R; CANR 12, 42, 69; DLB 53
Fink, William
See Mencken, H(enry) L(ouis)
Firbank, Louis 1942-
See Reed, Lou
See also CA 117
Firbank, (Arthur Annesley) Ronald 1886-1926 **TCLC 1**
See also CA 104; DLB 36
Fisher, M(ary) F(rances) K(ennedy) 1908-1992 **CLC 76, 87**
See also CA 77-80; 138; CANR 44
Fisher, Roy 1930- **CLC 25**
See also CA 81-84; CAAS 10; CANR 16; DLB 40
Fisher, Rudolph 1897-1934 **TCLC 11; BLC 2; DAM MULT; SSC 25**
See also BW 1; CA 107; 124; DLB 51, 102
Fisher, Vardis (Alvero) 1895-1968 **CLC 7**
See also CA 5-8R; 25-28R; CANR 68; DLB 9
Fiske, Tarleton
See Bloch, Robert (Albert)
Fitch, Clarke
See Sinclair, Upton (Beall)
Fitch, John IV
See Cormier, Robert (Edmund)
Fitzgerald, Captain Hugh
See Baum, L(yman) Frank
FitzGerald, Edward 1809-1883 **NCLC 9**
See also DLB 32
Fitzgerald, F(rancis) Scott (Key) 1896-1940 **TCLC 1, 6, 14, 28, 55; DA; DAB; DAC; DAM MST, NOV; SSC 6, 31; WLC**
See also AAYA 24; AITN 1; CA 110; 123; CDALB 1917-1929; DLB 4, 9, 86; DLBD 1, 15, 16; DLBY 81, 96; MTCW
Fitzgerald, Penelope 1916- **CLC 19, 51, 61**
See also CA 85-88; CAAS 10; CANR 56; DLB 14, 194
Fitzgerald, Robert (Stuart) 1910-1985 **CLC 39**
See also CA 1-4R; 114; CANR 1; DLBY 80
FitzGerald, Robert D(avid) 1902-1987 **CLC 19**
See also CA 17-20R
Fitzgerald, Zelda (Sayre) 1900-1948 **TCLC 52**
See also CA 117; 126; DLBY 84
Flanagan, Thomas (James Bonner) 1923- **CLC 25, 52**
See also CA 108; CANR 55; DLBY 80; INT 108; MTCW
Flaubert, Gustave 1821-1880 **NCLC 2, 10, 19, 62, 66; DA; DAB; DAC; DAM MST, NOV; SSC 11; WLC**
See also DLB 119
Flecker, Herman Elroy
See Flecker, (Herman) James Elroy
Flecker, (Herman) James Elroy 1884-1915 **TCLC 43**
See also CA 109; 150; DLB 10, 19
Fleming, Ian (Lancaster) 1908-1964 **CLC 3, 30; DAM POP**
See also CA 5-8R; CANR 59; CDBLB 1945-1960; DLB 87; MTCW; SATA 9
Fleming, Thomas (James) 1927- **CLC 37**
See also CA 5-8R; CANR 10; INT CANR-10;

SATA 8
Fletcher, John 1579-1625 **LC 33; DC 6**
See also CDBLB Before 1660; DLB 58
Fletcher, John Gould 1886-1950 **TCLC 35**
See also CA 107; DLB 4, 45
Fleur, Paul
See Pohl, Frederik
Flooglebuckle, Al
See Spiegelman, Art
Flying Officer X
See Bates, H(erbert) E(rnest)
Fo, Dario 1926- **CLC 32, 109; DAM DRAM**
See also CA 116; 128; CANR 68; DLBY 97; MTCW
Fogarty, Jonathan Titulescu Esq.
See Farrell, James T(homas)
Folke, Will
See Bloch, Robert (Albert)
Follett, Ken(neth Martin) 1949- **CLC 18; DAM NOV, POP**
See also AAYA 6; BEST 89:4; CA 81-84; CANR 13, 33, 54; DLB 87; DLBY 81; INT CANR-33; MTCW
Fontane, Theodor 1819-1898 **NCLC 26**
See also DLB 129
Foote, Horton 1916- **CLC 51, 91; DAM DRAM**
See also CA 73-76; CANR 34, 51; DLB 26; INT CANR-34
Foote, Shelby 1916- **CLC 75; DAM NOV, POP**
See also CA 5-8R; CANR 3, 45; DLB 2, 17
Forbes, Esther 1891-1967 **CLC 12**
See also AAYA 17; CA 13-14; 25-28R; CAP 1; CLR 27; DLB 22; JRDA; MAICYA; SATA 2
Forche, Carolyn (Louise) 1950- **CLC 25, 83, 86; DAM POET; PC 10**
See also CA 109; 117; CANR 50; DLB 5, 193; INT 117
Ford, Elbur
See Hibbert, Eleanor Alice Burford
Ford, Ford Madox 1873-1939 **TCLC 1, 15, 39, 57; DAM NOV**
See also CA 104; 132; CDBLB 1914-1945; DLB 162; MTCW
Ford, Henry 1863-1947 **TCLC 73**
See also CA 115; 148
Ford, John 1586-(?) **DC 8**
See also CDBLB Before 1660; DAM DRAM; DLB 58
Ford, John 1895-1973 **CLC 16**
See also CA 45-48
Ford, Richard 1944- **CLC 46, 99**
See also CA 69-72; CANR 11, 47
Ford, Webster
See Masters, Edgar Lee
Foreman, Richard 1937- **CLC 50**
See also CA 65-68; CANR 32, 63
Forester, C(ecil) S(cott) 1899-1966 **CLC 35**
See also CA 73-76; 25-28R; DLB 191; SATA 13
Forez
See Mauriac, Francois (Charles)
Forman, James Douglas 1932- **CLC 21**
See also AAYA 17; CA 9-12R; CANR 4, 19, 42; JRDA; MAICYA; SATA 8, 70
Fornes, Maria Irene 1930- **CLC 39, 61**
See also CA 25-28R; CANR 28; DLB 7, HW; INT CANR-28; MTCW
Forrest, Leon (Richard) 1937-1997 **CLC 4; BLCS**
See also BW 2; CA 89-92; 162; CAAS 7; CANR 25, 52; DLB 33
Forster, E(dward) M(organ) 1879-1970 **CLC 1, 2, 3, 4, 9, 10, 13, 15, 22, 45, 77; DA; DAB;**

DAC; DAM MST, NOV; SSC 27; WLC
See also AAYA 2; CA 13-14; 25-28R; CANR 45; CAP 1; CDBLB 1914-1945; DLB 34, 98, 162, 178, 195; MTCW; SATA 57
Forster, John 1812-1876 **NCLC 11**
See also DLB 144, 184
Forsyth, Frederick 1938- **CLC 2, 5, 36; DAM NOV, POP**
See also BEST 89:4; CA 85-88; CANR 38, 62; DLB 87; MTCW
Forten, Charlotte L. **TCLC 16; BLC 2**
See also Grimke, Charlotte L(ottie) Forten
See also DLB 50
Foscolo, Ugo 1778-1827 **NCLC 8**
Fosse, Bob **CLC 20**
See also Fosse, Robert Louis
Fosse, Robert Louis 1927-1987
See Fosse, Bob
See also CA 110; 123
Foster, Stephen Collins 1826-1864 **NCLC 26**
Foucault, Michel 1926-1984 **CLC 31, 34, 69**
See also CA 105; 113; CANR 34; MTCW
Fouque, Friedrich (Heinrich Karl) de la Motte 1777-1843 **NCLC 2**
See also DLB 90
Fourier, Charles 1772-1837 **NCLC 51**
Fournier, Henri Alban 1886-1914
See Alain-Fournier
See also CA 104
Fournier, Pierre 1916- **CLC 11**
See Gascar, Pierre
See also CA 89-92; CANR 16, 40
Fowles, John 1926- **CLC 1, 2, 3, 4, 6, 9, 10, 15, 33, 87; DAB; DAC; DAM MST**
See also CA 5-8R; CANR 25; CDBLB 1960 to Present; DLB 14, 139; MTCW; SATA 22
Fox, Paula 1923- **CLC 2, 8**
See also AAYA 3; CA 73-76; CANR 20, 36, 62; CLR 1, 44; DLB 52; JRDA; MAICYA; MTCW; SATA 17, 60
Fox, William Price (Jr.) 1926- **CLC 22**
See also CA 17-20R; CAAS 19; CANR 11; DLB 2; DLBY 81
Foxe, John 1516(?)-1587 **LC 14**
See also DLB 132
Frame, Janet 1924- **CLC 2, 3, 6, 22, 66, 96; SSC 29**
See also Clutha, Janet Paterson Frame
France, Anatole **TCLC 9**
See also Thibault, Jacques Anatole Francois
See also DLB 123
Francis, Claude 19(?)- **CLC 50**
Francis, Dick 1920- **CLC 2, 22, 42, 102; DAM POP**
See also AAYA 5, 21; BEST 89:3; CA 5-8R; CANR 9, 42, 68; CDBLB 1960 to Present; DLB 87; INT CANR-9; MTCW
Francis, Robert (Churchill) 1901-1987 **CLC 15**
See also CA 1-4R; 123; CANR 1
Frank, Anne(lies Marie) 1929-1945 **TCLC 17; DA; DAB; DAC; DAM MST; WLC**
See also AAYA 12; CA 113; 133; CANR 68; MTCW; SATA 87; SATA-Brief 42
Frank, Bruno 1887-1945 **TCLC 81**
See also DLB 118
Frank, Elizabeth 1945- **CLC 39**
See also CA 121; 126; INT 126
Frankl, Viktor E(mil) 1905-1997 **CLC 93**
See also CA 65-68; 161
Franklin, Benjamin
See Hasek, Jaroslav (Matej Frantisek)
Franklin, Benjamin 1706-1790 **LC 25; DA;**

See also CA 45-48; 29-32R; CANR 2, 35; DLB 72; MTCW

Giovanni, Nikki 1943- **CLC 2, 4, 19, 64; BLC 2; DA; DAB; DAC; DAM MST, MULT, POET; PC 19; WLCS**
See also AAYA 22; AITN 1; BW 2; CA 29-32R; CAAS 6; CANR 18, 41, 60; CLR 6; DLB 5, 41; INT CANR-18; MAICYA; MTCW; SATA 24

Giovene, Andrea 1904- **CLC 7**
See also CA 85-88

Gippius, Zinaida (Nikolayevna) 1869-1945
See Hippius, Zinaida
See also CA 106

Giraudoux, (Hippolyte) Jean 1882-1944 **TCLC 2, 7; DAM DRAM**
See also CA 104; DLB 65

Gironella, Jose Maria 1917- **CLC 11**
See also CA 101

Gissing, George (Robert) 1857-1903 **TCLC 3, 24, 47**
See also CA 105; DLB 18, 135, 184

Giurlani, Aldo
See Palazzeschi, Aldo

Gladkov, Fyodor (Vasilyevich) 1883-1958 **TCLC 27**

Glanville, Brian (Lester) 1931- **CLC 6**
See also CA 5-8R; CAAS 9; CANR 3; DLB 15, 139; SATA 42

Glasgow, Ellen (Anderson Gholson) 1873-1945 **TCLC 2, 7**
See also CA 104; 164; DLB 9, 12

Glaspell, Susan 1882(?)-1948 **TCLC 55**
See also CA 110; 154; DLB 7, 9, 78; YABC 2

Glassco, John 1909-1981 **CLC 9**
See also CA 13-16R; 102; CANR 15; DLB 68

Glasscock, Amnesia
See Steinbeck, John (Ernst)

Glasser, Ronald J. 1940(?)- **CLC 37**

Glassman, Joyce
See Johnson, Joyce

Glendinning, Victoria 1937- **CLC 50**
See also CA 120; 127; CANR 59; DLB 155

Glissant, Edouard 1928- **CLC 10, 68; DAM MULT**
See also CA 153

Gloag, Julian 1930- **CLC 40**
See also AITN 1; CA 65-68; CANR 10

Glowacki, Aleksander
See Prus, Boleslaw

Gluck, Louise (Elisabeth) 1943- **CLC 7, 22, 44, 81; DAM POET; PC 16**
See also CA 33-36R; CANR 40, 69; DLB 5

Glyn, Elinor 1864-1943 **TCLC 72**
See also DLB 153

Gobineau, Joseph Arthur (Comte) de 1816-1882 **NCLC 17**
See also DLB 123

Godard, Jean-Luc 1930- **CLC 20**
See also CA 93-96

Godden, (Margaret) Rumer 1907- **CLC 53**
See also AAYA 6; CA 5-8R; CANR 4, 27, 36, 55; CLR 20; DLB 161; MAICYA; SAAS 12; SATA 3, 36

Godoy Alcayaga, Lucila 1889-1957
See Mistral, Gabriela
See also BW 2; CA 104; 131; DAM MULT; HW; MTCW

Godwin, Gail (Kathleen) 1937- **CLC 5, 8, 22, 31, 69; DAM POP**
See also CA 29-32R; CANR 15, 43, 69; DLB 6; INT CANR-15; MTCW

Godwin, William 1756-1836 **NCLC 14**

See also CDBLB 1789-1832; DLB 39, 104, 142, 158, 163

Goebbels, Josef
See Goebbels, (Paul) Joseph

Goebbels, (Paul) Joseph 1897-1945 **TCLC 68**
See also CA 115; 148

Goebbels, Joseph Paul
See Goebbels, (Paul) Joseph

Goethe, Johann Wolfgang von 1749-1832 **NCLC 4, 22, 34; DA; DAB; DAC; DAM DRAM, MST, POET; PC 5; WLC 3**
See also DLB 94

Gogarty, Oliver St. John 1878-1957 **TCLC 15**
See also CA 109; 150; DLB 15, 19

Gogol, Nikolai (Vasilyevich) 1809-1852 **NCLC 5, 15, 31; DA; DAB; DAC; DAM DRAM, MST; DC 1; SSC 4, 29; WLC**
See also DLB 198

Goines, Donald 1937(?)-1974 **CLC 80; BLC 2; DAM MULT, POP**
See also AITN 1; BW 1; CA 124; 114; DLB 33

Gold, Herbert 1924- **CLC 4, 7, 14, 42**
See also CA 9-12R; CANR 17, 45; DLB 2; DLBY 81

Goldbarth, Albert 1948- **CLC 5, 38**
See also CA 53-56; CANR 6, 40; DLB 120

Goldberg, Anatol 1910-1982 **CLC 34**
See also CA 131; 117

Goldemberg, Isaac 1945- **CLC 52**
See also CA 69-72; CAAS 12; CANR 11, 32; HW

Golding, William (Gerald) 1911-1993 **CLC 1, 2, 3, 8, 10, 17, 27, 58, 81; DA; DAB; DAC; DAM MST, NOV; WLC**
See also AAYA 5; CA 5-8R; 141; CANR 13, 33, 54; CDBLB 1945-1960; DLB 15, 100; MTCW

Goldman, Emma 1869-1940 **TCLC 13**
See also CA 110; 150

Goldman, Francisco 1954- **CLC 76**
See also CA 162

Goldman, William (W.) 1931- **CLC 1, 48**
See also CA 9-12R; CANR 29, 69; DLB 44

Goldmann, Lucien 1913-1970 **CLC 24**
See also CA 25-28; CAP 2

Goldoni, Carlo 1707-1793 **LC 4; DAM DRAM**

Goldsberry, Steven 1949- **CLC 34**
See also CA 131

Goldsmith, Oliver 1728-1774 **LC 2; DA; DAB; DAC; DAM DRAM, MST, NOV, POET; DC 8; WLC**
See also CDBLB 1660-1789; DLB 39, 89, 104, 109, 142; SATA 26

Goldsmith, Peter
See Priestley, J(ohn) B(oynton)

Gombrowicz, Witold 1904-1969 **CLC 4, 7, 11, 49; DAM DRAM**
See also CA 19-20; 25-28R; CAP 2

Gomez de la Serna, Ramon 1888-1963 **CLC 9**
See also CA 153; 116; HW

Goncharov, Ivan Alexandrovich 1812-1891 **NCLC 1, 63**

Goncourt, Edmond (Louis Antoine Huot) de 1822-189 **NCLC 7**
See also DLB 123

Goncourt, Jules (Alfred Huot) de 1830-1870 **NCLC 7**
See also DLB 123

Gontier, Fernande 19(?)- **CLC 50**

Gonzalez Martinez, Enrique 1871-1952 **TCLC 72**
See also CA 166; HW

Goodman, Paul 1911-1972 **CLC 1, 2, 4, 7**

See also CA 19-20; 37-40R; CANR 34; CAP 2; DLB 130; MTCW

Gordimer, Nadine 1923- **CLC 3, 5, 7, 10, 18, 33, 51, 70; DA; DAB; DAC; DAM MST, NOV; SSC 17; WLCS**
See also CA 5-8R; CANR 3, 28, 56; INT CANR-28; MTCW

Gordon, Adam Lindsay 1833-1870 **NCLC 21**

Gordon, Caroline 1895-1981 **CLC 6, 13, 29, 83; SSC 15**
See also CA 11-12; 103; CANR 36; CAP 1; DLB 4, 9, 102; DLBY 81; MTCW

Gordon, Charles William 1860-1937
See Connor, Ralph
See also CA 109

Gordon, Mary (Catherine) 1949- **CLC 13, 22**
See also CA 102; CANR 44; DLB 6; DLBY 81; INT 102; MTCW

Gordon, N. J.
See Bosman, Herman Charles

Gordon, Sol 1923- **CLC 26**
See also CA 53-56; CANR 4; SATA 11

Gordone, Charles 1925-1995 **CLC 1, 4; DAM DRAM; DC 8**
See also BW 1; CA 93-96; 150; CANR 55; DLB 7; INT 93-96; MTCW

Gore, Catherine 1800-1861 **NCLC 65**
See also DLB 116

Gorenko, Anna Andreevna
See Akhmatova, Anna

Gorky, Maxim 1868-1936 **TCLC 8; DAB; SSC 28; WLC**
See also Peshkov, Alexei Maximovich

Goryan, Sirak
See Saroyan, William

Gosse, Edmund (William) 1849-1928 **TCLC 28**
See also CA 117; DLB 57, 144, 184

Gotlieb, Phyllis Fay (Bloom) 1926- **CLC 18**
See also CA 13-16R; CANR 7; DLB 88

Gottesman, S. D.
See Kornbluth, C(yril) M.; Pohl, Frederik

Gottfried von Strassburg fl. c. 1210- **CMLC 10**
See also DLB 138

Gould, Lois **CLC 4, 10**
See also CA 77-80; CANR 29; MTCW

Gourmont, Remy (-Marie-Charles) de 1858-1915 **TCLC 17**
See also CA 109; 150

Govier, Katherine 1948- **CLC 51**
See also CA 101; CANR 18, 40

Goyen, (Charles) William 1915-1983 **CLC 5, 8, 14, 40**
See also AITN 2; CA 5-8R; 110; CANR 6; DLB 2; DLBY 83; INT CANR-6

Goytisolo, Juan 1931- **CLC 5, 10, 23; DAM MULT; HLC**
See also CA 85-88; CANR 32, 61; HW; MTCW

Gozzano, Guido 1883-1916 **PC 10**
See also CA 154; DLB 114

Gozzi, (Conte) Carlo 1720-1806 **NCLC 23**

Grabbe, Christian Dietrich 1801-1836 **NCLC 2**
See also DLB 133

Grace, Patricia 1937- **CLC 56**

Gracian y Morales, Baltasar 1601-1658 **LC 15**

Gracq, Julien **CLC 11, 48**
See also Poirier, Louis
See also DLB 83

Grade, Chaim 1910-1982 **CLC 10**
See also CA 93-96; 107

Graduate of Oxford, A
See Ruskin, John

Grafton, Garth
  See Duncan, Sara Jeannette
Graham, John
  See Phillips, David Graham
Graham, Jorie 1951-   **CLC 48**
  See also CA 111; CANR 63; DLB 120
Graham, R(obert) B(ontine) Cunninghame
  See Cunninghame Graham, R(obert) B(ontine)
  See also DLB 98, 135, 174
Graham, Robert
  See Haldeman, Joe (William)
Graham, Tom
  See Lewis, (Harry) Sinclair
Graham, W(illiam) S(ydney) 1918-1986 **CLC 29**
  See also CA 73-76; 118; DLB 20
Graham, Winston (Mawdsley) 1910- **CLC 23**
  See also CA 49-52; CANR 2, 22, 45, 66; DLB 77
Grahame, Kenneth 1859-1932 **TCLC 64; DAB**
  See also CA 108; 136; CLR 5; DLB 34, 141, 178; MAICYA; YABC 1
Grant, Skeeter
  See Spiegelman, Art
Granville-Barker, Harley 1877-1946 **TCLC 2; DAM DRAM**
  See also Barker, Harley Granville
  See also CA 104
Grass, Guenter (Wilhelm) 1927- **CLC 1, 2, 4, 6, 11, 15, 22, 32, 49, 88; DA; DAB; DAC; DAM MST, NOV; WLC**
  See also CA 13-16R; CANR 20; DLB 75, 124; MTCW
Gratton, Thomas
  See Hulme, T(homas) E(rnest)
Grau, Shirley Ann 1929-   **CLC 4, 9; SSC 15**
  See also CA 89-92; CANR 22, 69; DLB 2; INT CANR-22; MTCW
Gravel, Fern
  See Hall, James Norman
Graver, Elizabeth 1964-   **CLC 70**
  See also CA 135
Graves, Richard Perceval 1945-   **CLC 44**
  See also CA 65-68; CANR 9, 26, 51
Graves, Robert (von Ranke) 1895-1985 **CLC 1, 2, 6, 11, 39, 44, 45; DAB; DAC; DAM MST, POET; PC 6**
  See also CA 5-8R; 117; CANR 5, 36; CDBLB 1914-1945; DLB 20, 100, 191; DLBY 85; MTCW; SATA 45
Graves, Valerie
  See Bradley, Marion Zimmer
Gray, Alasdair (James) 1934-   **CLC 41**
  See also CA 126; CANR 47, 69; DLB 194; INT 126; MTCW
Gray, Amlin 1946-   **CLC 29**
  See also CA 138
Gray, Francine du Plessix 1930-   **CLC 22; DAM NOV**
  See also BEST 90:3; CA 61-64; CAAS 2; CANR 11, 33; INT CANR-11; MTCW
Gray, John (Henry) 1866-1934   **TCLC 19**
  See also CA 119; 162
Gray, Simon (James Holliday) 1936- **CLC 9, 14, 36**
  See also AITN 1; CA 21-24R; CAAS 3; CANR 32, 69; DLB 13; MTCW
Gray, Spalding 1941- **CLC 49, 112; DAM POP; DC 7**
  See also CA 128
Gray, Thomas 1716-1771 **LC 4, 40; DA; DAB; DAC; DAM MST; PC 2; WLC**
  See also CDBLB 1660-1789; DLB 109

Grayson, David
  See Baker, Ray Stannard
Grayson, Richard (A.) 1951-   **CLC 38**
  See also CA 85-88; CANR 14, 31, 57
Greeley, Andrew M(oran) 1928-   **CLC 28; DAM POP**
  See also CA 5-8R; CAAS 7; CANR 7, 43, 69; MTCW
Green, Anna Katharine 1846-1935 **TCLC 63**
  See also CA 112; 159
Green, Brian
  See Card, Orson Scott
Green, Hannah
  See Greenberg, Joanne (Goldenberg)
Green, Hannah 1927(?)-1996   **CLC 3**
  See also CA 73-76; CANR 59
Green, Henry 1905-1973   **CLC 2, 13, 97**
  See also Yorke, Henry Vincent
  See also DLB 15
Green, Julian (Hartridge) 1900-
  See Green, Julien
  See also CA 21-24R; CANR 33; DLB 4, 72; MTCW
Green, Julien   **CLC 3, 11, 77**
  See also Green, Julian (Hartridge)
Green, Paul (Eliot) 1894-1981 **CLC 25; DAM DRAM**
  See also AITN 1; CA 5-8R; 103; CANR 3; DLB 7, 9; DLBY 81
Greenberg, Ivan 1908-1973
  See Rahv, Philip
  See also CA 85-88
Greenberg, Joanne (Goldenberg) 1932- **CLC 7, 30**
  See also AAYA 12; CA 5-8R; CANR 14, 32, 69; SATA 25
Greenberg, Richard 1959(?)-   **CLC 57**
  See also CA 138
Greene, Bette 1934-   **CLC 30**
  See also AAYA 7; CA 53-56; CANR 4; CLR 2; JRDA; MAICYA; SAAS 16; SATA 8
Greene, Gael   **CLC 8**
  See also CA 13-16R; CANR 10
Greene, Graham (Henry) 1904-1991 **CLC 1, 3, 6, 9, 14, 18, 27, 37, 70, 72; DA; DAB; DAC; DAM MST, NOV; SSC 29; WLC**
  See also AITN 2; CA 13-16R; 133; CANR 35, 61; CDBLB 1945-1960; DLB 13, 15, 77, 100, 162; DLBY 91; MTCW; SATA 20
Greene, Robert 1558-1592   **LC 41**
  See also DLB 62, 167
Greer, Richard
  See Silverberg, Robert
Gregor, Arthur 1923-   **CLC 9**
  See also CA 25-28R; CAAS 10; CANR 11; SATA 36
Gregor, Lee
  See Pohl, Frederik
Gregory, Isabella Augusta (Persse) 1852-1932 **TCLC 1**
  See also CA 104; DLB 10
Gregory, J. Dennis
  See Williams, John A(lfred)
Grendon, Stephen
  See Derleth, August (William)
Grenville, Kate 1950-   **CLC 61**
  See also CA 118; CANR 53
Grenville, Pelham
  See Wodehouse, P(elham) G(renville)
Greve, Felix Paul (Berthold Friedrich) 1879-1948
  See Grove, Frederick Philip
  See also CA 104; 141; DAC; DAM MST

Grey, Zane 1872-1939   **TCLC 6; DAM POP**
  See also CA 104; 132; DLB 9; MTCW
Grieg, (Johan) Nordahl (Brun) 1902-1943 **TCLC 10**
  See also CA 107
Grieve, C(hristopher) M(urray) 1892-1978 **CLC 11, 19; DAM POET**
  See also MacDiarmid, Hugh; Pteleon
  See also CA 5-8R; 85-88; CANR 33; MTCW
Griffin, Gerald 1803-1840   **NCLC 7**
  See also DLB 159
Griffin, John Howard 1920-1980   **CLC 68**
  See also AITN 1; CA 1-4R; 101; CANR 2
Griffin, Peter 1942-   **CLC 39**
  See also CA 136
Griffith, D(avid Lewelyn) W(ark) 1875(?)-1948 **TCLC 68**
  See also CA 119; 150
Griffith, Lawrence
  See Griffith, D(avid Lewelyn) W(ark)
Griffiths, Trevor 1935-   **CLC 13, 52**
  See also CA 97-100; CANR 45; DLB 13
Griggs, Sutton Elbert 1872-1930(?) **TCLC 77**
  See also CA 123; DLB 50
Grigson, Geoffrey (Edward Harvey) 1905-1985 **CLC 7, 39**
  See also CA 25-28R; 118; CANR 20, 33; DLB 27; MTCW
Grillparzer, Franz 1791-1872   **NCLC 1**
  See also DLB 133
Grimble, Reverend Charles James
  See Eliot, T(homas) S(tearns)
Grimke, Charlotte L(ottie) Forten 1837(?)-1914
  See Forten, Charlotte L.
  See also BW 1; CA 117; 124; DAM MULT, POET
Grimm, Jacob Ludwig Karl 1785-1863 **NCLC 3**
  See also DLB 90; MAICYA; SATA 22
Grimm, Wilhelm Karl 1786-1859   **NCLC 3**
  See also DLB 90; MAICYA; SATA 22
Grimmelshausen, Johann Jakob Christoffel von 1621-1676   **LC 6**
  See also DLB 168
Grindel, Eugene 1895-1952
  See Eluard, Paul
  See also CA 104
Grisham, John 1955-   **CLC 84; DAM POP**
  See also AAYA 14; CA 138; CANR 47, 69
Grossman, David 1954-   **CLC 67**
  See also CA 138
Grossman, Vasily (Semenovich) 1905-1964 **CLC 41**
  See also CA 124; 130; MTCW
Grove, Frederick Philip   **TCLC 4**
  See also Greve, Felix Paul (Berthold Friedrich)
  See also DLB 92
Grubb
  See Crumb, R(obert)
Grumbach, Doris (Isaac) 1918- **CLC 13, 22, 64**
  See also CA 5-8R; CAAS 2; CANR 9, 42; INT CANR-9
Grundtvig, Nicolai Frederik Severin 1783-1872 **NCLC 1**
Grunge
  See Crumb, R(obert)
Grunwald, Lisa 1959-   **CLC 44**
  See also CA 120
Guare, John 1938- **CLC 8, 14, 29, 67; DAM DRAM**
  See also CA 73-76; CANR 21, 69; DLB 7; MTCW
Gudjonsson, Halldor Kiljan 1902-1998

See Laxness, Halldor
See also CA 103; 164
Guenter, Erich
See Eich, Guenter
Guest, Barbara 1920- **CLC 34**
See also CA 25-28R; CANR 11, 44; DLB 5, 193
Guest, Judith (Ann) 1936- **CLC 8, 30; DAM NOV, POP**
See also AAYA 7; CA 77-80; CANR 15; INT CANR-15; MTCW
Guevara, Che **CLC 87; HLC**
See also Guevara (Serna), Ernesto
Guevara (Serna), Ernesto 1928-1967
See Guevara, Che
See also CA 127; 111; CANR 56; DAM MULT; HW
Guild, Nicholas M. 1944- **CLC 33**
See also CA 93-96
Guillemin, Jacques
See Sartre, Jean-Paul
Guillen, Jorge 1893-1984 **CLC 11; DAM MULT, POET**
See also CA 89-92; 112; DLB 108; HW
Guillen, Nicolas (Cristobal) 1902-1989 **CLC 48, 79; BLC 2; DAM MST, MULT, POET; HLC; PC 23**
See also BW 2; CA 116; 125; 129; HW
Guillevic, (Eugene) 1907- **CLC 33**
See also CA 93-96
Guillois
See Desnos, Robert
Guillois, Valentin
See Desnos, Robert
Guiney, Louise Imogen 1861-1920 **TCLC 41**
See also CA 160; DLB 54
Guiraldes, Ricardo (Guillermo) 1886-1927 **TCLC 39**
See also CA 131; HW; MTCW
Gumilev, Nikolai (Stepanovich) 1886-1921 **TCLC 60**
See also CA 165
Gunesekera, Romesh 1954- **CLC 91**
See also CA 159
Gunn, Bill **CLC 5**
See also Gunn, William Harrison
See also DLB 38
Gunn, Thom(son William) 1929-**CLC 3, 6, 18, 32, 81; DAM POET**
See also CA 17-20R; CANR 9, 33; CDBLB 1960 to Present; DLB 27; INT CANR-33; MTCW
Gunn, William Harrison 1934(?)-1989
See Gunn, Bill
See also AITN 1; BW 1; CA 13-16R; 128; CANR 12, 25
Gunnars, Kristjana 1948- **CLC 69**
See also CA 113; DLB 60
Gurdjieff, G(eorgei) I(vanovich) 1877(?)-1949 **TCLC 71**
See also CA 157
Gurganus, Allan 1947- **CLC 70; DAM POP**
See also BEST 90:1; CA 135
Gurney, A(lbert) R(amsdell), Jr. 1930- **CLC 32, 50, 54; DAM DRAM**
See also CA 77-80; CANR 32, 64
Gurney, Ivor (Bertie) 1890-1937 **TCLC 33**
Gurney, Peter
See Gurney, A(lbert) R(amsdell), Jr.
Guro, Elena 1877-1913 **TCLC 56**
Gustafson, James M(oody) 1925- **CLC 100**
See also CA 25-28R; CANR 37
Gustafson, Ralph (Barker) 1909- **CLC 36**

See also CA 21-24R; CANR 8, 45; DLB 88
Gut, Gom
See Simenon, Georges (Jacques Christian)
Guterson, David 1956- **CLC 91**
See also CA 132
Guthrie, A(lfred) B(ertram), Jr. 1901-1991 **CLC 23**
See also CA 57-60; 134; CANR 24; DLB 6; SATA 62; SATA-Obit 67
Guthrie, Isobel
See Grieve, C(hristopher) M(urray)
Guthrie, Woodrow Wilson 1912-1967
See Guthrie, Woody
See also CA 113; 93-96
Guthrie, Woody **CLC 35**
See also Guthrie, Woodrow Wilson
Guy, Rosa (Cuthbert) 1928- **CLC 26**
See also AAYA 4; BW 2; CA 17-20R; CANR 14, 34; CLR 13; DLB 33; JRDA; MAICYA; SATA 14, 62
Gwendolyn
See Bennett, (Enoch) Arnold
H. D. **CLC 3, 8, 14, 31, 34, 73; PC 5**
See also Doolittle, Hilda
H. de V.
See Buchan, John
Haavikko, Paavo Juhani 1931- **CLC 18, 34**
See also CA 106
Habbema, Koos
See Heijermans, Herman
Habermas, Juergen 1929- **CLC 104**
See also CA 109
Habermas, Jurgen
See Habermas, Juergen
Hacker, Marilyn 1942- **CLC 5, 9, 23, 72, 91; DAM POET**
See also CA 77-80; CANR 68; DLB 120
Haeckel, Ernst Heinrich (Philipp August) 1834-1919 **TCLC 83**
See also CA 157
Haggard, H(enry) Rider 1856-1925 **TCLC 11**
See also CA 108; 148; DLB 70, 156, 174, 178; SATA 16
Hagiosy, L.
See Larbaud, Valery (Nicolas)
Hagiwara Sakutaro 1886-1942 **TCLC 60; PC 18**
Haig, Fenil
See Ford, Ford Madox
Haig-Brown, Roderick (Langmere) 1908-1976 **CLC 21**
See also CA 5-8R; 69-72; CANR 4, 38; CLR 31; DLB 88; MAICYA; SATA 12
Hailey, Arthur 1920-**CLC 5; DAM NOV, POP**
See also AITN 2; BEST 90:3; CA 1-4R; CANR 2, 36; DLB 88; DLBY 82; MTCW
Hailey, Elizabeth Forsythe 1938- **CLC 40**
See also CA 93-96; CAAS 1; CANR 15, 48; INT CANR-15
Haines, John (Meade) 1924- **CLC 58**
See also CA 17-20R; CANR 13, 34; DLB 5
Hakluyt, Richard 1552-1616 **LC 31**
Haldeman, Joe (William) 1943- **CLC 61**
See also CA 53-56; CAAS 25; CANR 6; DLB 8; INT CANR-6
Haley, Alex(ander Murray Palmer) 1921-1992 **CLC 8, 12, 76; BLC 2; DA; DAB; DAC; DAM MST, MULT, POP**
See also BW 2; CA 77-80; 136; CANR 61; DLB 38; MTCW
Haliburton, Thomas Chandler 1796-1865 **NCLC 15**
See also DLB 11, 99

Hall, Donald (Andrew, Jr.) 1928- **CLC 1, 13, 37, 59; DAM POET**
See also CA 5-8R; CAAS 7; CANR 2, 44, 64; DLB 5; SATA 23, 97
Hall, Frederic Sauser
See Sauser-Hall, Frederic
Hall, James
See Kuttner, Henry
Hall, James Norman 1887-1951 **TCLC 23**
See also CA 123; SATA 21
Hall, (Marguerite) Radclyffe 1886-1943 **TCLC 12**
See also CA 110; 150
Hall, Rodney 1935- **CLC 51**
See also CA 109; CANR 69
Halleck, Fitz-Greene 1790-1867 **NCLC 47**
See also DLB 3
Halliday, Michael
See Creasey, John
Halpern, Daniel 1945- **CLC 14**
See also CA 33-36R
Hamburger, Michael (Peter Leopold) 1924- **CLC 5, 14**
See also CA 5-8R; CAAS 4; CANR 2, 47; DLB 27
Hamill, Pete 1935- **CLC 10**
See also CA 25-28R; CANR 18
Hamilton, Alexander 1755(?)-1804 **NCLC 49**
See also DLB 37
Hamilton, Clive
See Lewis, C(live) S(taples)
Hamilton, Edmond 1904-1977 **CLC 1**
See also CA 1-4R; CANR 3; DLB 8
Hamilton, Eugene (Jacob) Lee
See Lee-Hamilton, Eugene (Jacob)
Hamilton, Franklin
See Silverberg, Robert
Hamilton, Gail
See Corcoran, Barbara
Hamilton, Mollie
See Kaye, M(ary) M(argaret)
Hamilton, (Anthony Walter) Patrick 1904-1962 **CLC 51**
See also CA 113; DLB 10
Hamilton, Virginia 1936- **CLC 26; DAM MULT**
See also AAYA 2, 21; BW 2; CA 25-28R; CANR 20, 37; CLR 1, 11, 40; DLB 33, 52; INT CANR-20; JRDA; MAICYA; MTCW; SATA 4, 56, 79
Hammett, (Samuel) Dashiell 1894-1961 **CLC 3, 5, 10, 19, 47; SSC 17**
See also AITN 1; CA 81-84; CANR 42; CDALB 1929-1941; DLBD 6; DLBY 96; MTCW
Hammon, Jupiter 1711(?)-1800(?) **NCLC 5; BLC 2; DAM MULT, POET; PC 16**
See also DLB 31, 50
Hammond, Keith
See Kuttner, Henry
Hamner, Earl (Henry), Jr. 1923- **CLC 12**
See also AITN 2; CA 73-76; DLB 6
Hampton, Christopher (James) 1946- **CLC 4**
See also CA 25-28R; DLB 13; MTCW
Hamsun, Knut **TCLC 2, 14, 49**
See also Pedersen, Knut
Handke, Peter 1942-**CLC 5, 8, 10, 15, 38; DAM DRAM, NOV**
See also CA 77-80; CANR 33; DLB 85, 124; MTCW
Hanley, James 1901-1985 **CLC 3, 5, 8, 13**
See also CA 73-76; 117; CANR 36; DLB 191; MTCW
Hannah, Barry 1942- **CLC 23, 38, 90**

See also CA 108; 110; CANR 43, 68; DLB 6;
    INT 110; MTCW
Hannon, Ezra
    See Hunter, Evan
Hansberry, Lorraine (Vivian) 1930-1965**CLC
    17, 62; BLC 2; DA; DAB; DAC; DAM
    DRAM, MST, MULT; DC 2**
    See also AAYA 25; BW 1; CA 109; 25-28R;
    CABS 3; CANR 58; CDALB 1941-1968;
    DLB 7, 38; MTCW
Hansen, Joseph 1923-   **CLC 38**
    See also CA 29-32R; CAAS 17; CANR 16, 44,
    66; INT CANR-16
Hansen, Martin A. 1909-1955   **TCLC 32**
Hanson, Kenneth O(stlin) 1922-   **CLC 13**
    See also CA 53-56; CANR 7
Hardwick, Elizabeth 1916-   **CLC 13; DAM
    NOV**
    See also CA 5-8R; CANR 3, 32; DLB 6; MTCW
Hardy, Thomas 1840-1928**TCLC 4, 10, 18, 32,
    48, 53, 72; DA; DAB; DAC; DAM MST,
    NOV, POET; PC 8; SSC 2; WLC**
    See also CA 104; 123; CDBLB 1890-1914;
    DLB 18, 19, 135; MTCW
Hare, David 1947-   **CLC 29, 58**
    See also CA 97-100; CANR 39; DLB 13;
    MTCW
Harewood, John
    See Van Druten, John (William)
Harford, Henry
    See Hudson, W(illiam) H(enry)
Hargrave, Leonie
    See Disch, Thomas M(ichael)
Harjo, Joy 1951-   **CLC 83; DAM MULT**
    See also CA 114; CANR 35, 67; DLB 120, 175;
    NNAL
Harlan, Louis R(udolph) 1922-   **CLC 34**
    See also CA 21-24R; CANR 25, 55
Harling, Robert 1951(?)-   **CLC 53**
    See also CA 147
Harmon, William (Ruth) 1938-   **CLC 38**
    See also CA 33-36R; CANR 14, 32, 35; SATA
    65
Harper, F. E. W.
    See Harper, Frances Ellen Watkins
Harper, Frances E. W.
    See Harper, Frances Ellen Watkins
Harper, Frances E. Watkins
    See Harper, Frances Ellen Watkins
Harper, Frances Ellen
    See Harper, Frances Ellen Watkins
Harper, Frances Ellen Watkins 1825-1911
    **TCLC 14; BLC 2; DAM MULT, POET;
    PC 21**
    See also BW 1; CA 111; 125; DLB 50
Harper, Michael S(teven) 1938-   **CLC 7, 22**
    See also BW 1; CA 33-36R; CANR 24; DLB
    41
Harper, Mrs. F. E. W.
    See Harper, Frances Ellen Watkins
Harris, Christie (Lucy) Irwin 1907- **CLC 12**
    See also CA 5-8R; CANR 6; CLR 47; DLB 88;
    JRDA; MAICYA; SAAS 10; SATA 6, 74
Harris, Frank 1856-1931   **TCLC 24**
    See also CA 109; 150; DLB 156, 197
Harris, George Washington 1814-1869**NCLC
    23**
    See also DLB 3, 11
Harris, Joel Chandler 1848-1908   **TCLC 2;
    SSC 19**
    See also CA 104; 137; CLR 49; DLB 11, 23,
    42, 78, 91; MAICYA; YABC 1
Harris, John (Wyndham Parkes Lucas) Beynon

1903-1969
    See Wyndham, John
    See also CA 102; 89-92
Harris, MacDonald   **CLC 9**
    See also Heiney, Donald (William)
Harris, Mark 1922-   **CLC 19**
    See also CA 5-8R; CAAS 3; CANR 2, 55; DLB
    2; DLBY 80
Harris, (Theodore) Wilson 1921-   **CLC 25**
    See also BW 2; CA 65-68; CAAS 16; CANR
    11, 27, 69; DLB 117; MTCW
Harrison, Elizabeth Cavanna 1909-
    See Cavanna, Betty
    See also CA 9-12R; CANR 6, 27
Harrison, Harry (Max) 1925-   **CLC 42**
    See also CA 1-4R; CANR 5, 21; DLB 8; SATA
    4
Harrison, James (Thomas) 1937- **CLC 6, 14,
    33, 66; SSC 19**
    See also CA 13-16R; CANR 8, 51; DLBY 82;
    INT CANR-8
Harrison, Jim
    See Harrison, James (Thomas)
Harrison, Kathryn 1961-   **CLC 70**
    See also CA 144; CANR 68
Harrison, Tony 1937-   **CLC 43**
    See also CA 65-68; CANR 44; DLB 40; MTCW
Harriss, Will(ard Irvin) 1922-   **CLC 34**
    See also CA 111
Harson, Sley
    See Ellison, Harlan (Jay)
Hart, Ellis
    See Ellison, Harlan (Jay)
Hart, Josephine 1942(?)- **CLC 70; DAM POP**
    See also CA 138
Hart, Moss 1904-1961 **CLC 66; DAM DRAM**
    See also CA 109; 89-92; DLB 7
Harte, (Francis) Bret(t) 1836(?)-1902**TCLC 1,
    25; DA; DAC; DAM MST; SSC 8; WLC**
    See also CA 104; 140; CDALB 1865-1917;
    DLB 12, 64, 74, 79, 186; SATA 26
Hartley, L(eslie) P(oles) 1895-1972 **CLC 2, 22**
    See also CA 45-48; 37-40R; CANR 33; DLB
    15, 139; MTCW
Hartman, Geoffrey H. 1929-   **CLC 27**
    See also CA 117; 125; DLB 67
Hartmann, Sadakichi 1867-1944   **TCLC 73**
    See also CA 157; DLB 54
Hartmann von Aue c. 1160-c. 1205 **CMLC 15**
    See also DLB 138
Hartmann von Aue 1170-1210   **CMLC 15**
Haruf, Kent 1943-   **CLC 34**
    See also CA 149
Harwood, Ronald 1934-   **CLC 32; DAM
    DRAM, MST**
    See also CA 1-4R; CANR 4, 55; DLB 13
Hasegawa Tatsunosuke
    See Futabatei, Shimei
Hasek, Jaroslav (Matej Frantisek) 1883-1923
    TCLC 4
    See also CA 104; 129; MTCW
Hass, Robert 1941-   **CLC 18, 39, 99; PC 16**
    See also CA 111; CANR 30, 50; DLB 105;
    SATA 94
Hastings, Hudson
    See Kuttner, Henry
Hastings, Selina   **CLC 44**
Hathorne, John 1641-1717   **LC 38**
Hatteras, Amelia
    See Mencken, H(enry) L(ouis)
Hatteras, Owen   **TCLC 18**
    See also Mencken, H(enry) L(ouis); Nathan,
    George Jean

Hauptmann, Gerhart (Johann Robert) 1862-
    1946   **TCLC 4; DAM DRAM**
    See also CA 104; 153; DLB 66, 118
Havel, Vaclav 1936-   **CLC 25, 58, 65; DAM
    DRAM; DC 6**
    See also CA 104; CANR 36, 63; MTCW
Haviaras, Stratis   **CLC 33**
    See also Chaviaras, Strates
Hawes, Stephen 1475(?)-1523(?)   **LC 17**
    See also DLB 132
Hawkes, John (Clendennin Burne, Jr.) 1925-
    CLC 1, 2, 3, 4, 7, 9, 14, 15, 27, 49
    See also CA 1-4R; CANR 2, 47, 64; DLB 2, 7;
    DLBY 80; MTCW
Hawking, S. W.
    See Hawking, Stephen W(illiam)
Hawking, Stephen W(illiam) 1942- **CLC 63,
    105**
    See also AAYA 13; BEST 89:1; CA 126; 129;
    CANR 48
Hawkins, Anthony Hope
    See Hope, Anthony
Hawthorne, Julian 1846-1934   **TCLC 25**
    See also CA 165
Hawthorne, Nathaniel 1804-1864   **NCLC 39;
    DA; DAB; DAC; DAM MST, NOV; SSC
    3, 29; WLC**
    See also AAYA 18; CDALB 1640-1865; DLB
    1, 74; YABC 2
Haxton, Josephine Ayres 1921-
    See Douglas, Ellen
    See also CA 115; CANR 41
Hayaseca y Eizaguirre, Jorge
    See Echegaray (y Eizaguirre), Jose (Maria
    Waldo)
Hayashi, Fumiko 1904-1951   **TCLC 27**
    See also CA 161; DLB 180
Haycraft, Anna
    See Ellis, Alice Thomas
    See also CA 122
Hayden, Robert E(arl) 1913-1980 **CLC 5, 9,
    14, 37; BLC 2; DA; DAC; DAM MST,
    MULT, POET; PC 6**
    See also BW 1; CA 69-72; 97-100; CABS 2;
    CANR 24; CDALB 1941-1968; DLB 5, 76;
    MTCW; SATA 19; SATA-Obit 26
Hayford, J(oseph) E(phraim) Casely
    See Casely-Hayford, J(oseph) E(phraim)
Hayman, Ronald 1932-   **CLC 44**
    See also CA 25-28R; CANR 18, 50; DLB 155
Haywood, Eliza 1693(?)-1756   **LC 44**
    See also DLB 39
Haywood, Eliza (Fowler) 1693(?)-1756 **LC 1,
    44**
Hazlitt, William 1778-1830   **NCLC 29**
    See also DLB 110, 158
Hazzard, Shirley 1931-   **CLC 18**
    See also CA 9-12R; CANR 4; DLBY 82;
    MTCW
Head, Bessie 1937-1986 **CLC 25, 67; BLC 2;
    DAM MULT**
    See also BW 2; CA 29-32R; 119; CANR 25;
    DLB 117; MTCW
Headon, (Nicky) Topper 1956(?)-   **CLC 30**
Heaney, Seamus (Justin) 1939- **CLC 5, 7, 14,
    25, 37, 74, 91; DAB; DAM POET; PC 18;
    WLCS**
    See also CA 85-88; CANR 25, 48; CDBLB
    1960 to Present; DLB 40; DLBY 95; MTCW
Hearn, (Patricio) Lafcadio (Tessima Carlos)
    1850-1904   **TCLC 9**
    See also CA 105; 166; DLB 12, 78
Hearne, Vicki 1946-   **CLC 56**

See Jen, Gish
See also CA 135

Jenkins, (John) Robin 1912-   **CLC 52**
See also CA 1-4R; CANR 1; DLB 14

Jennings, Elizabeth (Joan) 1926-   **CLC 5, 14**
See also CA 61-64; CAAS 5; CANR 8, 39, 66;
DLB 27; MTCW; SATA 66

Jennings, Waylon 1937-   **CLC 21**

Jensen, Johannes V. 1873-1950   **TCLC 41**

Jensen, Laura (Linnea) 1948-   **CLC 37**
See also CA 103

Jerome, Jerome K(lapka) 1859-1927**TCLC 23**
See also CA 119; DLB 10, 34, 135

Jerrold, Douglas William 1803-1857 **NCLC 2**
See also DLB 158, 159

Jewett, (Theodora) Sarah Orne 1849-1909
TCLC 1, 22; SSC 6
See also CA 108; 127; DLB 12, 74; SATA 15

Jewsbury, Geraldine (Endsor) 1812-1880
NCLC 22
See also DLB 21

Jhabvala, Ruth Prawer 1927-**CLC 4, 8, 29, 94;
DAB; DAM NOV**
See also CA 1-4R; CANR 2, 29, 51; DLB 139,
194; INT CANR-29; MTCW

Jibran, Kahlil
See Gibran, Kahlil

Jibran, Khalil
See Gibran, Kahlil

Jiles, Paulette 1943-   **CLC 13, 58**
See also CA 101

Jimenez (Mantecon), Juan Ramon 1881-1958
**TCLC 4; DAM MULT, POET; HLC; PC
7**
See also CA 104; 131; DLB 134; HW; MTCW

Jimenez, Ramon
See Jimenez (Mantecon), Juan Ramon

Jimenez Mantecon, Juan
See Jimenez (Mantecon), Juan Ramon

Jin, Ha 1956-   **CLC 109**
See also CA 152

Joel, Billy   **CLC 26**
See also Joel, William Martin

Joel, William Martin 1949-
See Joel, Billy
See also CA 108

John, Saint 7th cent. -   **CMLC 27**

John of the Cross, St. 1542-1591   **LC 18**

Johnson, B(ryan) S(tanley William) 1933-1973
CLC 6, 9
See also CA 9-12R; 53-56; CANR 9; DLB 14,
40

Johnson, Benj. F. of Boo
See Riley, James Whitcomb

Johnson, Benjamin F. of Boo
See Riley, James Whitcomb

Johnson, Charles (Richard) 1948- **CLC 7, 51,
65; BLC 2; DAM MULT**
See also BW 2; CA 116; CAAS 18; CANR 42,
66; DLB 33

Johnson, Denis 1949-   **CLC 52**
See also CA 117; 121; DLB 120

Johnson, Diane 1934-   **CLC 5, 13, 48**
See also CA 41-44R; CANR 17, 40, 62; DLBY
80; INT CANR-17; MTCW

Johnson, Eyvind (Olof Verner) 1900-1976
CLC 14
See also CA 73-76; 69-72; CANR 34

Johnson, J. R.
See James, C(yril) L(ionel) R(obert)

Johnson, James Weldon 1871-1938 **TCLC 3,
19; BLC 2; DAM MULT, POET**
See also BW 1; CA 104; 125; CDALB 1917-

1929; CLR 32; DLB 51; MTCW; SATA 31

Johnson, Joyce 1935-   **CLC 58**
See also CA 125; 129

Johnson, Lionel (Pigot) 1867-1902 **TCLC 19**
See also CA 117; DLB 19

Johnson, Mel
See Malzberg, Barry N(athaniel)

Johnson, Pamela Hansford 1912-1981 **CLC 1,
7, 27**
See also CA 1-4R; 104; CANR 2, 28; DLB 15;
MTCW

Johnson, Robert 1911(?)-1938   **TCLC 69**

Johnson, Samuel 1709-1784**LC 15; DA; DAB;
DAC; DAM MST; WLC**
See also CDBLB 1660-1789; DLB 39, 95, 104,
142

Johnson, Uwe 1934-1984   **CLC 5, 10, 15, 40**
See also CA 1-4R; 112; CANR 1, 39; DLB 75;
MTCW

Johnston, George (Benson) 1913-   **CLC 51**
See also CA 1-4R; CANR 5, 20; DLB 88

Johnston, Jennifer 1930-   **CLC 7**
See also CA 85-88; DLB 14

Jolley, (Monica) Elizabeth 1923-**CLC 46; SSC
19**
See also CA 127; CAAS 13; CANR 59

Jones, Arthur Llewellyn 1863-1947
See Machen, Arthur
See also CA 104

Jones, D(ouglas) G(ordon) 1929-   **CLC 10**
See also CA 29-32R; CANR 13; DLB 53

Jones, David (Michael) 1895-1974**CLC 2, 4, 7,
13, 42**
See also CA 9-12R; 53-56; CANR 28; CDBLB
1945-1960; DLB 20, 100; MTCW

Jones, David Robert 1947-
See Bowie, David
See also CA 103

Jones, Diana Wynne 1934-   **CLC 26**
See also AAYA 12; CA 49-52; CANR 4, 26,
56; CLR 23; DLB 161; JRDA; MAICYA;
SAAS 7; SATA 9, 70

Jones, Edward P. 1950-   **CLC 76**
See also BW 2; CA 142

Jones, Gayl 1949-   **CLC 6, 9; BLC 2; DAM
MULT**
See also BW 2; CA 77-80; CANR 27, 66; DLB
33; MTCW

Jones, James 1921-1977   **CLC 1, 3, 10, 39**
See also AITN 1, 2; CA 1-4R; 69-72; CANR 6;
DLB 2, 143; MTCW

Jones, John J.
See Lovecraft, H(oward) P(hillips)

Jones, LeRoi   **CLC 1, 2, 3, 5, 10, 14**
See also Baraka, Amiri

Jones, Louis B.   **CLC 65**
See also CA 141

Jones, Madison (Percy, Jr.) 1925-   **CLC 4**
See also CA 13-16R; CAAS 11; CANR 7, 54;
DLB 152

Jones, Mervyn 1922-   **CLC 10, 52**
See also CA 45-48; CAAS 5; CANR 1; MTCW

Jones, Mick 1956(?)-   **CLC 30**

Jones, Nettie (Pearl) 1941-   **CLC 34**
See also BW 2; CA 137; CAAS 20

Jones, Preston 1936-1979   **CLC 10**
See also CA 73-76; 89-92; DLB 7

Jones, Robert F(rancis) 1934-   **CLC 7**
See also CA 49-52; CANR 2, 61

Jones, Rod 1953-   **CLC 50**
See also CA 128

Jones, Terence Graham Parry 1942- **CLC 21**
See also Jones, Terry; Monty Python

See also CA 112; 116; CANR 35; INT 116

Jones, Terry
See Jones, Terence Graham Parry
See also SATA 67; SATA-Brief 51

Jones, Thom 1945(?)-   **CLC 81**
See also CA 157

Jong, Erica 1942-   **CLC 4, 6, 8, 18, 83; DAM
NOV, POP**
See also AITN 1; BEST 90:2; CA 73-76; CANR
26, 52; DLB 2, 5, 28, 152; INT CANR-26;
MTCW

Jonson, Ben(jamin) 1572(?)-1637   **LC 6, 33;
DA; DAB; DAC; DAM DRAM, MST,
POET; DC 4; PC 17; WLC**
See also CDBLB Before 1660; DLB 62, 121

Jordan, June 1936-   **CLC 5, 11, 23; BLCS;
DAM MULT, POET**
See also AAYA 2; BW 2; CA 33-36R; CANR
25; CLR 10; DLB 38; MAICYA; MTCW;
SATA 4

Jordan, Neil (Patrick) 1950-   **CLC 110**
See also CA 124; 130; CANR 54; INT 130

Jordan, Pat(rick M.) 1941-   **CLC 37**
See also CA 33-36R

Jorgensen, Ivar
See Ellison, Harlan (Jay)

Jorgenson, Ivar
See Silverberg, Robert

Josephus, Flavius c. 37-100   **CMLC 13**

Josipovici, Gabriel 1940-   **CLC 6, 43**
See also CA 37-40R; CAAS 8; CANR 47; DLB
14

Joubert, Joseph 1754-1824   **NCLC 9**

Jouve, Pierre Jean 1887-1976   **CLC 47**
See also CA 65-68

Jovine, Francesco 1902-1950   **TCLC 79**

Joyce, James (Augustine Aloysius) 1882-1941
**TCLC 3, 8, 16, 35, 52; DA; DAB; DAC;
DAM MST, NOV, POET; PC 22; SSC 3,
26; WLC**
See also CA 104; 126; CDBLB 1914-1945;
DLB 10, 19, 36, 162; MTCW

Jozsef, Attila 1905-1937   **TCLC 22**
See also CA 116

Juana Ines de la Cruz 1651(?)-1695   **LC 5**

Judd, Cyril
See Kornbluth, C(yril) M.; Pohl, Frederik

Julian of Norwich 1342(?)-1416(?)   **LC 6**
See also DLB 146

Junger, Sebastian 1962-   **CLC 109**
See also CA 165

Juniper, Alex
See Hospital, Janette Turner

Junius
See Luxemburg, Rosa

Just, Ward (Swift) 1935-   **CLC 4, 27**
See also CA 25-28R; CANR 32; INT CANR-
32

Justice, Donald (Rodney) 1925-   **CLC 6, 19,
102; DAM POET**
See also CA 5-8R; CANR 26, 54; DLBY 83;
INT CANR-26

Juvenal c. 55-c. 127   **CMLC 8**

Juvenis
See Bourne, Randolph S(illiman)

Kacew, Romain 1914-1980
See Gary, Romain
See also CA 108; 102

Kadare, Ismail 1936-   **CLC 52**
See also CA 161

Kadohata, Cynthia   **CLC 59**
See also CA 140

Kafka, Franz 1883-1924**TCLC 2, 6, 13, 29, 47,**

53; DA; DAB; DAC; DAM MST, NOV;
SSC 5, 29; WLC
See also CA 105; 126; DLB 81; MTCW

Kahanovitsch, Pinkhes
See Der Nister

Kahn, Roger 1927-   **CLC 30**
See also CA 25-28R; CANR 44, 69; DLB 171;
SATA 37

Kain, Saul
See Sassoon, Siegfried (Lorraine)

Kaiser, Georg 1878-1945   **TCLC 9**
See also CA 106; DLB 124

Kaletski, Alexander 1946-   **CLC 39**
See also CA 118; 143

Kalidasa fl. c. 400-   **CMLC 9; PC 22**

Kallman, Chester (Simon) 1921-1975 **CLC 2**
See also CA 45-48; 53-56; CANR 3

Kaminsky, Melvin 1926-
See Brooks, Mel
See also CA 65-68; CANR 16

Kaminsky, Stuart M(elvin) 1934-   **CLC 59**
See also CA 73-76; CANR 29, 53

Kane, Francis
See Robbins, Harold

Kane, Paul
See Simon, Paul (Frederick)

Kane, Wilson
See Bloch, Robert (Albert)

Kanin, Garson 1912-   **CLC 22**
See also AITN 1; CA 5-8R; CANR 7; DLB 7

Kaniuk, Yoram 1930-   **CLC 19**
See also CA 134

Kant, Immanuel 1724-1804   **NCLC 27, 67**
See also DLB 94

Kantor, MacKinlay 1904-1977   **CLC 7**
See also CA 61-64; 73-76; CANR 60, 63; DLB
9, 102

Kaplan, David Michael 1946-   **CLC 50**

Kaplan, James 1951-   **CLC 59**
See also CA 135

Karageorge, Michael
See Anderson, Poul (William)

Karamzin, Nikolai Mikhailovich 1766-1826
NCLC 3
See also DLB 150

Karapanou, Margarita 1946-   **CLC 13**
See also CA 101

Karinthy, Frigyes 1887-1938   **TCLC 47**

Karl, Frederick R(obert) 1927-   **CLC 34**
See also CA 5-8R; CANR 3, 44

Kastel, Warren
See Silverberg, Robert

Kataev, Evgeny Petrovich 1903-1942
See Petrov, Evgeny
See also CA 120

Kataphusin
See Ruskin, John

Katz, Steve 1935-   **CLC 47**
See also CA 25-28R; CAAS 14, 64; CANR 12;
DLBY 83

Kauffman, Janet 1945-   **CLC 42**
See also CA 117; CANR 43; DLBY 86

Kaufman, Bob (Garnell) 1925-1986 **CLC 49**
See also BW 1; CA 41-44R; 118; CANR 22;
DLB 16, 41

Kaufman, George S. 1889-1961 **CLC 38; DAM
DRAM**
See also CA 108; 93-96; DLB 7; INT 108

Kaufman, Sue   **CLC 3, 8**
See also Barondess, Sue K(aufman)

Kavafis, Konstantinos Petrou 1863-1933
See Cavafy, C(onstantine) P(eter)
See also CA 104

Kavan, Anna 1901-1968   **CLC 5, 13, 82**
See also CA 5-8R; CANR 6, 57; MTCW

Kavanagh, Dan
See Barnes, Julian (Patrick)

Kavanagh, Patrick (Joseph) 1904-1967 **CLC
22**
See also CA 123; 25-28R; DLB 15, 20; MTCW

Kawabata, Yasunari 1899-1972 **CLC 2, 5, 9,
18, 107; DAM MULT; SSC 17**
See also CA 93-96; 33-36R; DLB 180

Kaye, M(ary) M(argaret) 1909-   **CLC 28**
See also CA 89-92; CANR 24, 60; MTCW;
SATA 62

Kaye, Mollie
See Kaye, M(ary) M(argaret)

Kaye-Smith, Sheila 1887-1956   **TCLC 20**
See also CA 118; DLB 36

Kaymor, Patrice Maguilene
See Senghor, Leopold Sedar

Kazan, Elia 1909-   **CLC 6, 16, 63**
See also CA 21-24R; CANR 32

Kazantzakis, Nikos 1883(?)-1957 **TCLC 2, 5,
33**
See also CA 105; 132; MTCW

Kazin, Alfred 1915-   **CLC 34, 38**
See also CA 1-4R; CAAS 7; CANR 1, 45; DLB
67

Keane, Mary Nesta (Skrine) 1904-1996
See Keane, Molly
See also CA 108; 114; 151

Keane, Molly   **CLC 31**
See also Keane, Mary Nesta (Skrine)
See also INT 114

Keates, Jonathan 1946(?)-   **CLC 34**
See also CA 163

Keaton, Buster 1895-1966   **CLC 20**

Keats, John 1795-1821   **NCLC 8; DA; DAB;
DAC; DAM MST, POET; PC 1; WLC**
See also CDBLB 1789-1832; DLB 96, 110

Keene, Donald 1922-   **CLC 34**
See also CA 1-4R; CANR 5

Keillor, Garrison   **CLC 40**
See also Keillor, Gary (Edward)
See also AAYA 2; BEST 89:3; DLBY 87; SATA
58

Keillor, Gary (Edward) 1942-
See Keillor, Garrison
See also CA 111; 117; CANR 36, 59; DAM
POP; MTCW

Keith, Michael
See Hubbard, L(afayette) Ron(ald)

Keller, Gottfried 1819-1890 **NCLC 2; SSC 26**
See also DLB 129

Keller, Nora Okja   **CLC 109**

Kellerman, Jonathan 1949-   **CLC 44; DAM
POP**
See also BEST 90:1; CA 106; CANR 29, 51;
INT CANR-29

Kelley, William Melvin 1937-   **CLC 22**
See also BW 1; CA 77-80; CANR 27; DLB 33

Kellogg, Marjorie 1922-   **CLC 2**
See also CA 81-84

Kellow, Kathleen
See Hibbert, Eleanor Alice Burford

Kelly, M(ilton) T(erry) 1947-   **CLC 55**
See also CA 97-100; CAAS 22; CANR 19, 43

Kelman, James 1946-   **CLC 58, 86**
See also CA 148; DLB 194

Kemal, Yashar 1923-   **CLC 14, 29**
See also CA 89-92; CANR 44

Kemble, Fanny 1809-1893   **NCLC 18**
See also DLB 32

Kemelman, Harry 1908-1996   **CLC 2**

See also AITN 1; CA 9-12R; 155; CANR 6;
DLB 28

Kempe, Margery 1373(?)-1440(?)   **LC 6**
See also DLB 146

Kempis, Thomas a 1380-1471   **LC 11**

Kendall, Henry 1839-1882   **NCLC 12**

Keneally, Thomas (Michael) 1935- **CLC 5, 8,
10, 14, 19, 27, 43; DAM NOV**
See also CA 85-88; CANR 10, 50; MTCW

Kennedy, Adrienne (Lita) 1931-**CLC 66; BLC
2; DAM MULT; DC 5**
See also BW 2; CA 103; CAAS 20; CABS 3;
CANR 26, 53; DLB 38

Kennedy, John Pendleton 1795-1870 **NCLC 2**
See also DLB 3

Kennedy, Joseph Charles 1929-
See Kennedy, X. J.
See also CA 1-4R; CANR 4, 30, 40; SATA 14,
86

Kennedy, William 1928- **CLC 6, 28, 34, 53;
DAM NOV**
See also AAYA 1; CA 85-88; CANR 14, 31;
DLB 143; DLBY 85; INT CANR-31;
MTCW; SATA 57

Kennedy, X. J.   **CLC 8, 42**
See also Kennedy, Joseph Charles
See also CAAS 9; CLR 27; DLB 5; SAAS 22

Kenny, Maurice (Francis) 1929-   **CLC 87;
DAM MULT**
See also CA 144; CAAS 22; DLB 175; NNAL

Kent, Kelvin
See Kuttner, Henry

Kenton, Maxwell
See Southern, Terry

Kenyon, Robert O.
See Kuttner, Henry

Kepler, Johannes 1571-1630   **LC 45**

Kerouac, Jack   **CLC 1, 2, 3, 5, 14, 29, 61**
See also Kerouac, Jean-Louis Lebris de
See also AAYA 25; CDALB 1941-1968; DLB
2, 16; DLBD 3; DLBY 95

Kerouac, Jean-Louis Lebris de 1922-1969
See Kerouac, Jack
See also AITN 1; CA 5-8R; 25-28R; CANR 26,
54; DA; DAB; DAC; DAM MST, NOV,
POET, POP; MTCW; WLC

Kerr, Jean 1923-   **CLC 22**
See also CA 5-8R; CANR 7; INT CANR-7

Kerr, M. E.   **CLC 12, 35**
See also Meaker, Marijane (Agnes)
See also AAYA 2, 23; CLR 29; SAAS 1

Kerr, Robert   **CLC 55**

Kerrigan, (Thomas) Anthony 1918- **CLC 4, 6**
See also CA 49-52; CAAS 11; CANR 4

Kerry, Lois
See Duncan, Lois

Kesey, Ken (Elton) 1935- **CLC 1, 3, 6, 11, 46,
64; DA; DAB; DAC; DAM MST, NOV,
POP; WLC**
See also AAYA 25; CA 1-4R; CANR 22, 38,
66; CDALB 1968-1988; DLB 2, 16; MTCW;
SATA 66

Kesselring, Joseph (Otto) 1902-1967 **CLC 45;
DAM DRAM, MST**
See also CA 150

Kessler, Jascha (Frederick) 1929-   **CLC 4**
See also CA 17-20R; CANR 8, 48

Kettelkamp, Larry (Dale) 1933-   **CLC 12**
See also CA 29-32R; CANR 16; SAAS 3; SATA
2

Key, Ellen 1849-1926   **TCLC 65**

Keyber, Conny
See Fielding, Henry

See also DLB 21, 70, 159, 178
Leffland, Ella 1931-   **CLC 19**
   See also CA 29-32R; CANR 35; DLBY 84; INT
      CANR-35; SATA 65
Leger, Alexis
   See Leger, (Marie-Rene Auguste) Alexis Saint-
      Leger
**Leger, (Marie-Rene Auguste) Alexis Saint-
   Leger** 1887-1975   **CLC 4, 11, 46; DAM
   POET; PC 23**
   See also CA 13-16R; 61-64; CANR 43; MTCW
Leger, Saintleger
   See Leger, (Marie-Rene Auguste) Alexis Saint-
      Leger
Le Guin, Ursula K(roeber) 1929- **CLC 8, 13,
   22, 45, 71; DAB; DAC; DAM MST, POP;
   SSC 12**
   See also AAYA 9; AITN 1; CA 21-24R; CANR
      9, 32, 52; CDALB 1968-1988; CLR 3, 28;
      DLB 8, 52; INT CANR-32; JRDA; MAICYA;
      MTCW; SATA 4, 52
Lehmann, Rosamond (Nina) 1901-1990**CLC 5**
   See also CA 77-80; 131; CANR 8; DLB 15
Leiber, Fritz (Reuter, Jr.) 1910-1992 **CLC 25**
   See also CA 45-48; 139; CANR 2, 40; DLB 8;
      MTCW; SATA 45; SATA-Obit 73
Leibniz, Gottfried Wilhelm von 1646-1716**LC
   35**
   See also DLB 168
Leimbach, Martha 1963-
   See Leimbach, Marti
   See also CA 130
Leimbach, Marti   **CLC 65**
   See also Leimbach, Martha
Leino, Eino   **TCLC 24**
   See also Loennbohm, Armas Eino Leopold
Leiris, Michel (Julien) 1901-1990   **CLC 61**
   See also CA 119; 128; 132
Leithauser, Brad 1953-   **CLC 27**
   See also CA 107; CANR 27; DLB 120
Lelchuk, Alan 1938-   **CLC 5**
   See also CA 45-48; CAAS 20; CANR 1
Lem, Stanislaw 1921-   **CLC 8, 15, 40**
   See also CA 105; CAAS 1; CANR 32; MTCW
Lemann, Nancy 1956-   **CLC 39**
   See also CA 118; 136
Lemonnier, (Antoine Louis) Camille 1844-1913
   TCLC 22
   See also CA 121
Lenau, Nikolaus 1802-1850   **NCLC 16**
L'Engle, Madeleine (Camp Franklin) 1918-
   CLC 12; DAM POP
   See also AAYA 1; AITN 2; CA 1-4R; CANR 3,
      21, 39, 66; CLR 1, 14; DLB 52; JRDA;
      MAICYA; MTCW; SAAS 15; SATA 1, 27,
      75
Lengyel, Jozsef 1896-1975   **CLC 7**
   See also CA 85-88; 57-60
Lenin 1870-1924
   See Lenin, V. I.
   See also CA 121
Lenin, V. I.   **TCLC 67**
   See also Lenin
Lennon, John (Ono) 1940-1980   **CLC 12, 35**
   See also CA 102
Lennox, Charlotte Ramsay 1729(?)-1804
   NCLC 23
   See also DLB 39
Lentricchia, Frank (Jr.) 1940-   **CLC 34**
   See also CA 25-28R; CANR 19
Lenz, Siegfried 1926-   **CLC 27**
   See also CA 89-92; DLB 75
Leonard, Elmore (John, Jr.) 1925-**CLC 28, 34,**

71; **DAM POP**
   See also AAYA 22; AITN 1; BEST 89:1, 90:4;
      CA 81-84; CANR 12, 28, 53; DLB 173; INT
      CANR-28; MTCW
Leonard, Hugh   **CLC 19**
   See also Byrne, John Keyes
   See also DLB 13
Leonov, Leonid (Maximovich) 1899-1994
   CLC 92; DAM NOV
   See also CA 129; MTCW
Leopardi, (Conte) Giacomo 1798-1837 **NCLC
   22**
Le Reveler
   See Artaud, Antonin (Marie Joseph)
Lerman, Eleanor 1952-   **CLC 9**
   See also CA 85-88; CANR 69
Lerman, Rhoda 1936-   **CLC 56**
   See also CA 49-52
Lermontov, Mikhail Yuryevich 1814-1841
   NCLC 47; PC 18
Leroux, Gaston 1868-1927   **TCLC 25**
   See also CA 108; 136; CANR 69; SATA 65
Lesage, Alain-Rene 1668-1747   **LC 28**
Leskov, Nikolai (Semyonovich) 1831-1895
   NCLC 25
Lessing, Doris (May) 1919-**CLC 1, 2, 3, 6, 10,
   15, 22, 40, 94; DA; DAB; DAC; DAM MST,
   NOV; SSC 6; WLCS**
   See also CA 9-12R; CAAS 14; CANR 33, 54;
      CDBLB 1960 to Present; DLB 15, 139;
      DLBY 85; MTCW
Lessing, Gotthold Ephraim 1729-1781   **LC 8**
   See also DLB 97
Lester, Richard 1932-   **CLC 20**
Lever, Charles (James) 1806-1872   **NCLC 23**
   See also DLB 21
Leverson, Ada 1865(?)-1936(?)   **TCLC 18**
   See also Elaine
   See also CA 117; DLB 153
Levertov, Denise 1923-1997 **CLC 1, 2, 3, 5, 8,
   15, 28, 66; DAM POET; PC 11**
   See also CA 1-4R; 163; CAAS 19; CANR 3,
      29, 50; DLB 5, 165; INT CANR-29; MTCW
Levi, Jonathan   **CLC 76**
Levi, Peter (Chad Tigar) 1931-   **CLC 41**
   See also CA 5-8R; CANR 34; DLB 40
Levi, Primo 1919-1987   **CLC 37, 50; SSC 12**
   See also CA 13-16R; 122; CANR 12, 33, 61;
      DLB 177; MTCW
Levin, Ira 1929-   **CLC 3, 6; DAM POP**
   See also CA 21-24R; CANR 17, 44; MTCW;
      SATA 66
Levin, Meyer 1905-1981   **CLC 7; DAM POP**
   See also AITN 1; CA 9-12R; 104; CANR 15;
      DLB 9, 28; DLBY 81; SATA 21; SATA-Obit
      27
Levine, Norman 1924-   **CLC 54**
   See also CA 73-76; CAAS 23; CANR 14; DLB
      88
Levine, Philip 1928-   **CLC 2, 4, 5, 9, 14, 33;
   DAM POET; PC 22**
   See also CA 9-12R; CANR 9, 37, 52; DLB 5
Levinson, Deirdre 1931-   **CLC 49**
   See also CA 73-76
Levi-Strauss, Claude 1908-   **CLC 38**
   See also CA 1-4R; CANR 6, 32, 57; MTCW
Levitin, Sonia (Wolff) 1934-   **CLC 17**
   See also AAYA 13; CA 29-32R; CANR 14, 32;
      JRDA; MAICYA; SAAS 2; SATA 4, 68
Levon, O. U.
   See Kesey, Ken (Elton)
Levy, Amy 1861-1889   **NCLC 59**
   See also DLB 156

Lewes, George Henry 1817-1878   **NCLC 25**
   See also DLB 55, 144
Lewis, Alun 1915-1944   **TCLC 3**
   See also CA 104; DLB 20, 162
Lewis, C. Day
   See Day Lewis, C(ecil)
Lewis, C(live) S(taples) 1898-1963**CLC 1, 3, 6,
   14, 27; DA; DAB; DAC; DAM MST, NOV,
   POP; WLC**
   See also AAYA 3; CA 81-84; CANR 33;
      CDBLB 1945-1960; CLR 3, 27; DLB 15,
      100, 160; JRDA; MAICYA; MTCW; SATA
      13
Lewis, Janet 1899-   **CLC 41**
   See also Winters, Janet Lewis
   See also CA 9-12R; CANR 29, 63; CAP 1;
      DLBY 87
Lewis, Matthew Gregory 1775-1818**NCLC 11,
   62**
   See also DLB 39, 158, 178
Lewis, (Harry) Sinclair 1885-1951   **TCLC 4,
   13, 23, 39; DA; DAB; DAC; DAM MST,
   NOV; WLC**
   See also CA 104; 133; CDALB 1917-1929;
      DLB 9, 102; DLBD 1; MTCW
Lewis, (Percy) Wyndham 1882(?)-1957 **TCLC
   2, 9**
   See also CA 104; 157; DLB 15
Lewisohn, Ludwig 1883-1955   **TCLC 19**
   See also CA 107; DLB 4, 9, 28, 102
Lewton, Val 1904-1951   **TCLC 76**
Leyner, Mark 1956-   **CLC 92**
   See also CA 110; CANR 28, 53
Lezama Lima, Jose 1910-1976**CLC 4, 10, 101;
   DAM MULT**
   See also CA 77-80; DLB 113; HW
L'Heureux, John (Clarke) 1934-   **CLC 52**
   See also CA 13-16R; CANR 23, 45
Liddell, C. H.
   See Kuttner, Henry
Lie, Jonas (Lauritz Idemil) 1833-1908(?)
   TCLC 5
   See also CA 115
Lieber, Joel 1937-1971   **CLC 6**
   See also CA 73-76; 29-32R
Lieber, Stanley Martin
   See Lee, Stan
Lieberman, Laurence (James) 1935- **CLC 4,
   36**
   See also CA 17-20R; CANR 8, 36
Lieh Tzu fl. 7th cent. B.C.-5th cent. B.C.
   CMLC 27
Lieksman, Anders
   See Haavikko, Paavo Juhani
Li Fei-kan 1904-
   See Pa Chin
   See also CA 105
Lifton, Robert Jay 1926-   **CLC 67**
   See also CA 17-20R; CANR 27; INT CANR-
      27; SATA 66
Lightfoot, Gordon 1938-   **CLC 26**
   See also CA 109
Lightman, Alan P(aige) 1948-   **CLC 81**
   See also CA 141; CANR 63
Ligotti, Thomas (Robert) 1953- **CLC 44; SSC
   16**
   See also CA 123; CANR 49
Li Ho 791-817   **PC 13**
Liliencron, (Friedrich Adolf Axel) Detlev von
   1844-1909   **TCLC 18**
   See also CA 117
Lilly, William 1602-1681   **LC 27**
Lima, Jose Lezama

See Lezama Lima, Jose

Lima Barreto, Afonso Henrique de 1881-1922
TCLC 23
See also CA 117

Limonov, Edward 1944-   **CLC 67**
See also CA 137

Lin, Frank
See Atherton, Gertrude (Franklin Horn)

Lincoln, Abraham 1809-1865   **NCLC 18**

Lind, Jakov   **CLC 1, 2, 4, 27, 82**
See also Landwirth, Heinz
See also CAAS 4

Lindbergh, Anne (Spencer) Morrow 1906-
CLC 82; DAM NOV
See also CA 17-20R; CANR 16; MTCW; SATA
33

Lindsay, David 1878-1945   **TCLC 15**
See also CA 113

Lindsay, (Nicholas) Vachel 1879-1931 **TCLC**
17; DA; DAC; DAM MST, POET; PC 23;
WLC
See also CA 114; 135; CDALB 1865-1917;
DLB 54; SATA 40

Linke-Poot
See Doeblin, Alfred

Linney, Romulus 1930-   **CLC 51**
See also CA 1-4R; CANR 40, 44

Linton, Eliza Lynn 1822-1898   **NCLC 41**
See also DLB 18

Li Po 701-763   **CMLC 2**

Lipsius, Justus 1547-1606   **LC 16**

Lipsyte, Robert (Michael) 1938-**CLC 21; DA;**
DAC; DAM MST, NOV
See also AAYA 7; CA 17-20R; CANR 8, 57;
CLR 23; JRDA; MAICYA; SATA 5, 68

Lish, Gordon (Jay) 1934-   **CLC 45; SSC 18**
See also CA 113; 117; DLB 130; INT 117

Lispector, Clarice 1925-1977   **CLC 43**
See also CA 139; 116; DLB 113

Littell, Robert 1935(?)-   **CLC 42**
See also CA 109; 112; CANR 64

Little, Malcolm 1925-1965
See Malcolm X
See also BW 1; CA 125; 111; DA; DAB; DAC;
DAM MST, MULT; MTCW

Littlewit, Humphrey Gent.
See Lovecraft, H(oward) P(hillips)

Litwos
See Sienkiewicz, Henryk (Adam Alexander
Pius)

Liu, E 1857-1909   **TCLC 15**
See also CA 115

Lively, Penelope (Margaret) 1933-   **CLC 32,**
50; DAM NOV
See also CA 41-44R; CANR 29, 67; CLR 7;
DLB 14, 161; JRDA; MAICYA; MTCW;
SATA 7, 60

Livesay, Dorothy (Kathleen) 1909-**CLC 4, 15,**
79; DAC; DAM MST, POET
See also AITN 2; CA 25-28R; CAAS 8; CANR
36, 67; DLB 68; MTCW

Livy c. 59B.C.-c. 17   **CMLC 11**

Lizardi, Jose Joaquin Fernandez de 1776-1827
NCLC 30

Llewellyn, Richard
See Llewellyn Lloyd, Richard Dafydd Vivian
See also DLB 15

Llewellyn Lloyd, Richard Dafydd Vivian 1906-
1983 **CLC 7, 80**
See also Llewellyn, Richard
See also CA 53-56; 111; CANR 7; SATA 11;
SATA-Obit 37

Llosa, (Jorge) Mario (Pedro) Vargas

See Vargas Llosa, (Jorge) Mario (Pedro)

Lloyd, Manda
See Mander, (Mary) Jane

Lloyd Webber, Andrew 1948-
See Webber, Andrew Lloyd
See also AAYA 1; CA 116; 149; DAM DRAM;
SATA 56

Llull, Ramon c. 1235-c. 1316   **CMLC 12**

Locke, Alain (Le Roy) 1886-1954   **TCLC 43;**
BLCS
See also BW 1; CA 106; 124; DLB 51

Locke, John 1632-1704   **LC 7, 35**
See also DLB 101

Locke-Elliott, Sumner
See Elliott, Sumner Locke

Lockhart, John Gibson 1794-1854   **NCLC 6**
See also DLB 110, 116, 144

Lodge, David (John) 1935-**CLC 36; DAM POP**
See also BEST 90:1; CA 17-20R; CANR 19,
53; DLB 14, 194; INT CANR-19; MTCW

Lodge, Thomas 1558-1625   **LC 41**
See also DLB 172

Lodge, Thomas 1558-1625   **LC 41**

Loennbohm, Armas Eino Leopold 1878-1926
See Leino, Eino
See also CA 123

Loewinsohn, Ron(ald William) 1937- **CLC 52**
See also CA 25-28R

Logan, Jake
See Smith, Martin Cruz

Logan, John (Burton) 1923-1987   **CLC 5**
See also CA 77-80; 124; CANR 45; DLB 5

Lo Kuan-chung 1330(?)-1400(?)   **LC 12**

Lombard, Nap
See Johnson, Pamela Hansford

London, Jack **TCLC 9, 15, 39; SSC 4; WLC**
See also London, John Griffith
See also AAYA 13; AITN 2; CDALB 1865-
1917; DLB 8, 12, 78; SATA 18

London, John Griffith 1876-1916
See London, Jack
See also CA 110; 119; DA; DAB; DAC; DAM
MST, NOV; JRDA; MAICYA; MTCW

Long, Emmett
See Leonard, Elmore (John, Jr.)

Longbaugh, Harry
See Goldman, William (W.)

Longfellow, Henry Wadsworth 1807-1882
NCLC 2, 45; DA; DAB; DAC; DAM MST,
POET; WLCS
See also CDALB 1640-1865; DLB 1, 59; SATA
19

Longinus c. 1st cent. -   **CMLC 27**
See also DLB 176

Longley, Michael 1939-   **CLC 29**
See also CA 102; DLB 40

Longus fl. c. 2nd cent. -   **CMLC 7**

Longway, A. Hugh
See Lang, Andrew

Lonnrot, Elias 1802-1884   **NCLC 53**

Lopate, Phillip 1943-   **CLC 29**
See also CA 97-100; DLBY 80; INT 97-100

Lopez Portillo (y Pacheco), Jose 1920-**CLC 46**
See also CA 129; HW

Lopez y Fuentes, Gregorio 1897(?)-1966 **CLC**
32
See also CA 131; HW

Lorca, Federico Garcia
See Garcia Lorca, Federico

Lord, Bette Bao 1938-   **CLC 23**
See also BEST 90:3; CA 107; CANR 41; INT
107; SATA 58

Lord Auch

See Bataille, Georges

Lord Byron
See Byron, George Gordon (Noel)

Lorde, Audre (Geraldine) 1934-1992 **CLC 18,**
71; BLC 2; DAM MULT, POET; PC 12
See also BW 1; CA 25-28R; 142; CANR 16,
26, 46; DLB 41; MTCW

Lord Houghton
See Milnes, Richard Monckton

Lord Jeffrey
See Jeffrey, Francis

Lorenzini, Carlo 1826-1890
See Collodi, Carlo
See also MAICYA; SATA 29

Lorenzo, Heberto Padilla
See Padilla (Lorenzo), Heberto

Loris
See Hofmannsthal, Hugo von

Loti, Pierre   **TCLC 11**
See also Viaud, (Louis Marie) Julien
See also DLB 123

Louie, David Wong 1954-   **CLC 70**
See also CA 139

Louis, Father M.
See Merton, Thomas

Lovecraft, H(oward) P(hillips) 1890-1937
TCLC 4, 22; DAM POP; SSC 3
See also AAYA 14; CA 104; 133; MTCW

Lovelace, Earl 1935-   **CLC 51**
See also BW 2; CA 77-80; CANR 41; DLB 125;
MTCW

Lovelace, Richard 1618-1657   **LC 24**
See also DLB 131

Lowell, Amy 1874-1925   **TCLC 1, 8; DAM**
POET; PC 13
See also CA 104; 151; DLB 54, 140

Lowell, James Russell 1819-1891   **NCLC 2**
See also CDALB 1640-1865; DLB 1, 11, 64,
79, 189

Lowell, Robert (Traill Spence, Jr.) 1917-1977
CLC 1, 2, 3, 4, 5, 8, 9, 11, 15, 37; DA; DAB;
DAC; DAM MST, NOV; PC 3; WLC
See also CA 9-12R; 73-76; CABS 2; CANR 26,
60; DLB 5, 169; MTCW

Lowndes, Marie Adelaide (Belloc) 1868-1947
TCLC 12
See also CA 107; DLB 70

Lowry, (Clarence) Malcolm 1909-1957 **TCLC**
6, 40; SSC 31
See also CA 105; 131; CANR 62; CDBLB
1945-1960; DLB 15; MTCW

Lowry, Mina Gertrude 1882-1966
See Loy, Mina
See also CA 113

Loxsmith, John
See Brunner, John (Kilian Houston)

Loy, Mina   **CLC 28; DAM POET; PC 16**
See also Lowry, Mina Gertrude
See also DLB 4, 54

Loyson-Bridet
See Schwob, (Mayer Andre) Marcel

Lucas, Craig 1951-   **CLC 64**
See also CA 137

Lucas, E(dward) V(errall) 1868-1938 **TCLC**
73
See also DLB 98, 149, 153; SATA 20

Lucas, George 1944-   **CLC 16**
See also AAYA 1, 23; CA 77-80; CANR 30;
SATA 56

Lucas, Hans
See Godard, Jean-Luc

Lucas, Victoria
See Plath, Sylvia

Maitland, Frederic 1850-1906   **TCLC 65**

Maitland, Sara (Louise) 1950-   **CLC 49**
See also CA 69-72; CANR 13, 59

Major, Clarence 1936- CLC 3, 19, 48; BLC 2;
DAM MULT
See also BW 2; CA 21-24R; CAAS 6; CANR
13, 25, 53; DLB 33

Major, Kevin (Gerald) 1949-   **CLC 26; DAC**
See also AAYA 16; CA 97-100; CANR 21, 38;
CLR 11; DLB 60; INT CANR-21; JRDA;
MAICYA; SATA 32, 82

Maki, James
See Ozu, Yasujiro

Malabaila, Damiano
See Levi, Primo

Malamud, Bernard 1914-1986 CLC 1, 2, 3, 5,
8, 9, 11, 18, 27, 44, 78, 85; DA; DAB; DAC;
DAM MST, NOV, POP; SSC 15; WLC
See also AAYA 16; CA 5-8R; 118; CABS 1;
CANR 28, 62; CDALB 1941-1968; DLB 2,
28, 152; DLBY 80, 86; MTCW

Malan, Herman
See Bosman, Herman Charles; Bosman, Herman
Charles

Malaparte, Curzio 1898-1957   **TCLC 52**

Malcolm, Dan
See Silverberg, Robert

Malcolm X   **CLC 82; BLC 2; WLCS**
See also Little, Malcolm

Malherbe, Francois de 1555-1628   **LC 5**

Mallarme, Stephane 1842-1898   **NCLC 4, 41;
DAM POET; PC 4**

Mallet-Joris, Francoise 1930-   **CLC 11**
See also CA 65-68; CANR 17; DLB 83

Malley, Ern
See McAuley, James Phillip

Mallowan, Agatha Christie
See Christie, Agatha (Mary Clarissa)

Maloff, Saul 1922-   **CLC 5**
See also CA 33-36R

Malone, Louis
See MacNeice, (Frederick) Louis

Malone, Michael (Christopher) 1942-CLC 43
See also CA 77-80; CANR 14, 32, 57

Malory, (Sir) Thomas 1410(?)-1471(?) LC 11;
DA; DAB; DAC; DAM MST; WLCS
See also CDBLB Before 1660; DLB 146; SATA
59; SATA-Brief 33

Malouf, (George Joseph) David 1934-CLC 28,
86
See also CA 124; CANR 50

Malraux, (Georges-)Andre 1901-1976 CLC 1,
4, 9, 13, 15, 57; DAM NOV
See also CA 21-22; 69-72; CANR 34, 58; CAP
2; DLB 72; MTCW

Malzberg, Barry N(athaniel) 1939-   **CLC 7**
See also CA 61-64; CAAS 4; CANR 16; DLB 8

Mamet, David (Alan) 1947-CLC 9, 15, 34, 46,
91; DAM DRAM; DC 4
See also AAYA 3; CA 81-84; CABS 3; CANR
15, 41, 67; DLB 7; MTCW

Mamoulian, Rouben (Zachary) 1897-1987
CLC 16
See also CA 25-28R; 124

Mandelstam, Osip (Emilievich) 1891(?)-1938(?)
TCLC 2, 6; PC 14
See also CA 104; 150

Mander, (Mary) Jane 1877-1949   **TCLC 31**
See also CA 162

Mandeville, John fl. 1350-   **CMLC 19**
See also DLB 146

Mandiargues, Andre Pieyre de   **CLC 41**
See also Pieyre de Mandiargues, Andre

See also DLB 83

Mandrake, Ethel Belle
See Thurman, Wallace (Henry)

Mangan, James Clarence 1803-1849NCLC 27

Maniere, J.-E.
See Giraudoux, (Hippolyte) Jean

Manley, (Mary) Delariviere 1672(?)-1724 L C
1
See also DLB 39, 80

Mann, Abel
See Creasey, John

Mann, Emily 1952-   **DC 7**
See also CA 130; CANR 55

Mann, (Luiz) Heinrich 1871-1950   **TCLC 9**
See also CA 106; 164; DLB 66

Mann, (Paul) Thomas 1875-1955 TCLC 2, 8,
14, 21, 35, 44, 60; DA; DAB; DAC; DAM
MST, NOV; SSC 5; WLC
See also CA 104; 128; DLB 66; MTCW

Mannheim, Karl 1893-1947   **TCLC 65**

Manning, David
See Faust, Frederick (Schiller)

Manning, Frederic 1887(?)-1935   **TCLC 25**
See also CA 124

Manning, Olivia 1915-1980   **CLC 5, 19**
See also CA 5-8R; 101; CANR 29; MTCW

Mano, D. Keith 1942-   **CLC 2, 10**
See also CA 25-28R; CAAS 6; CANR 26, 57;
DLB 6

Mansfield, KatherineTCLC 2, 8, 39; DAB; SSC
9, 23; WLC
See also Beauchamp, Kathleen Mansfield
See also DLB 162

Manso, Peter 1940-   **CLC 39**
See also CA 29-32R; CANR 44

Mantecon, Juan Jimenez
See Jimenez (Mantecon), Juan Ramon

Manton, Peter
See Creasey, John

Man Without a Spleen, A
See Chekhov, Anton (Pavlovich)

Manzoni, Alessandro 1785-1873   **NCLC 29**

Mapu, Abraham (ben Jekutiel) 1808-1867
NCLC 18

Mara, Sally
See Queneau, Raymond

Marat, Jean Paul 1743-1793   **LC 10**

Marcel, Gabriel Honore 1889-1973   **CLC 15**
See also CA 102; 45-48; MTCW

Marchbanks, Samuel
See Davies, (William) Robertson

Marchi, Giacomo
See Bassani, Giorgio

Margulies, Donald   **CLC 76**

Marie de France c. 12th cent. -   **CMLC 8; PC
22**

Marie de l'Incarnation 1599-1672   **LC 10**

Marier, Captain Victor
See Griffith, D(avid Lewelyn) W(ark)

Mariner, Scott
See Pohl, Frederik

Marinetti, Filippo Tommaso 1876-1944TCLC
10
See also CA 107; DLB 114

Marivaux, Pierre Carlet de Chamblain de 1688-
1763   **LC 4; DC 7**

Markandaya, Kamala   **CLC 8, 38**
See also Taylor, Kamala (Purnaiya)

Markfield, Wallace 1926-   **CLC 8**
See also CA 69-72; CAAS 3; DLB 2, 28

Markham, Edwin 1852-1940   **TCLC 47**
See also CA 160; DLB 54, 186

Markham, Robert

See Amis, Kingsley (William)

Marks, J
See Highwater, Jamake (Mamake)

Marks-Highwater, J
See Highwater, Jamake (Mamake)

Markson, David M(errill) 1927-   **CLC 67**
See also CA 49-52; CANR 1

Marley, Bob   **CLC 17**
See also Marley, Robert Nesta

Marley, Robert Nesta 1945-1981
See Marley, Bob
See also CA 107; 103

Marlowe, Christopher 1564-1593 LC 22; DA;
DAB; DAC; DAM DRAM, MST; DC 1;
WLC
See also CDBLB Before 1660; DLB 62

Marlowe, Stephen 1928-
See Queen, Ellery
See also CA 13-16R; CANR 6, 55

Marmontel, Jean-Francois 1723-1799   **LC 2**

Marquand, John P(hillips) 1893-1960 CLC 2,
10
See also CA 85-88; DLB 9, 102

Marques, Rene 1919-1979   **CLC 96; DAM
MULT; HLC**
See also CA 97-100; 85-88; DLB 113; HW

Marquez, Gabriel (Jose) Garcia
See Garcia Marquez, Gabriel (Jose)

Marquis, Don(ald Robert Perry) 1878-1937
TCLC 7
See also CA 104; 166; DLB 11, 25

Marric, J. J.
See Creasey, John

Marryat, Frederick 1792-1848   **NCLC 3**
See also DLB 21, 163

Marsden, James
See Creasey, John

Marsh, (Edith) Ngaio 1899-1982   **CLC 7, 53;
DAM POP**
See also CA 9-12R; CANR 6, 58; DLB 77;
MTCW

Marshall, Garry 1934-   **CLC 17**
See also AAYA 3; CA 111; SATA 60

Marshall, Paule 1929-   **CLC 27, 72; BLC 3;
DAM MULT; SSC 3**
See also BW 2; CA 77-80; CANR 25; DLB 157;
MTCW

Marsten, Richard
See Hunter, Evan

Marston, John 1576-1634LC 33; DAM DRAM
See also DLB 58, 172

Martha, Henry
See Harris, Mark

Marti, Jose 1853-1895NCLC 63; DAM MULT;
HLC

Martial c. 40-c. 104   **PC 10**

Martin, Ken
See Hubbard, L(afayette) Ron(ald)

Martin, Richard
See Creasey, John

Martin, Steve 1945-   **CLC 30**
See also CA 97-100; CANR 30; MTCW

Martin, Valerie 1948-   **CLC 89**
See also BEST 90:2; CA 85-88; CANR 49

Martin, Violet Florence 1862-1915   **TCLC 51**

Martin, Webber
See Silverberg, Robert

Martindale, Patrick Victor
See White, Patrick (Victor Martindale)

Martin du Gard, Roger 1881-1958 TCLC 24
See also CA 118; DLB 65

Martineau, Harriet 1802-1876   **NCLC 26**
See also DLB 21, 55, 159, 163, 166, 190; YABC

2

Martines, Julia
See O'Faolain, Julia
Martinez, Enrique Gonzalez
See Gonzalez Martinez, Enrique
Martinez, Jacinto Benavente y
See Benavente (y Martinez), Jacinto
Martinez Ruiz, Jose 1873-1967
See Azorin; Ruiz, Jose Martinez
See also CA 93-96; HW
Martinez Sierra, Gregorio 1881-1947 **TCLC 6**
See also CA 115
Martinez Sierra, Maria (de la O'LeJarraga)
1874-1974 **TCLC 6**
See also CA 115
Martinsen, Martin
See Follett, Ken(neth Martin)
Martinson, Harry (Edmund) 1904-1978 **CLC 14**
See also CA 77-80; CANR 34
Marut, Ret
See Traven, B.
Marut, Robert
See Traven, B.
Marvell, Andrew 1621-1678 **LC 4, 43; DA; DAB; DAC; DAM MST, POET; PC 10; WLC**
See also CDBLB 1660-1789; DLB 131
Marx, Karl (Heinrich) 1818-1883 **NCLC 17**
See also DLB 129
Masaoka Shiki **TCLC 18**
See also Masaoka Tsunenori
Masaoka Tsunenori 1867-1902
See Masaoka Shiki
See also CA 117
Masefield, John (Edward) 1878-1967 **CLC 11, 47; DAM POET**
See also CA 19-20; 25-28R; CANR 33; CAP 2; CDBLB 1890-1914; DLB 10, 19, 153, 160; MTCW; SATA 19
Maso, Carole 19(?)- **CLC 44**
Mason, Bobbie Ann 1940- **CLC 28, 43, 82; SSC 4**
See also AAYA 5; CA 53-56; CANR 11, 31, 58; DLB 173; DLBY 87; INT CANR-31; MTCW
Mason, Ernst
See Pohl, Frederik
Mason, Lee W.
See Malzberg, Barry N(athaniel)
Mason, Nick 1945- **CLC 35**
Mason, Tally
See Derleth, August (William)
Mass, William
See Gibson, William
Masters, Edgar Lee 1868-1950 **TCLC 2, 25; DA; DAC; DAM MST, POET; PC 1; WLCS**
See also CA 104; 133; CDALB 1865-1917; DLB 54; MTCW
Masters, Hilary 1928- **CLC 48**
See also CA 25-28R; CANR 13, 47
Mastrosimone, William 19(?)- **CLC 36**
Mathe, Albert
See Camus, Albert
Mather, Cotton 1663-1728 **LC 38**
See also CDALB 1640-1865; DLB 24, 30, 140
Mather, Increase 1639-1723 **LC 38**
See also DLB 24
Matheson, Richard Burton 1926- **CLC 37**
See also CA 97-100; DLB 8, 44; INT 97-100
Mathews, Harry 1930- **CLC 6, 52**
See also CA 21-24R; CAAS 6; CANR 18, 40

Mathews, John Joseph 1894-1979 **CLC 84; DAM MULT**
See also CA 19-20; 142; CANR 45; CAP 2; DLB 175; NNAL
Mathias, Roland (Glyn) 1915- **CLC 45**
See also CA 97-100; CANR 19, 41; DLB 27
Matsuo Basho 1644-1694 **PC 3**
See also DAM POET
Mattheson, Rodney
See Creasey, John
Matthews, Greg 1949- **CLC 45**
See also CA 135
Matthews, William (Procter, III) 1942-1997 **CLC 40**
See also CA 29-32R; 162; CAAS 18; CANR 12, 57; DLB 5
Matthias, John (Edward) 1941- **CLC 9**
See also CA 33-36R; CANR 56
Matthiessen, Peter 1927- **CLC 5, 7, 11, 32, 64; DAM NOV**
See also AAYA 6; BEST 90:4; CA 9-12R; CANR 21, 50; DLB 6, 173; MTCW; SATA 27
Maturin, Charles Robert 1780(?)-1824 **NCLC 6**
See also DLB 178
Matute (Ausejo), Ana Maria 1925- **CLC 11**
See also CA 89-92; MTCW
Maugham, W. S.
See Maugham, W(illiam) Somerset
Maugham, W(illiam) Somerset 1874-1965 **CLC 1, 11, 15, 67, 93; DA; DAB; DAC; DAM DRAM, MST, NOV; SSC 8; WLC**
See also CA 5-8R; 25-28R; CANR 40; CDBLB 1914-1945; DLB 10, 36, 77, 100, 162, 195; MTCW; SATA 54
Maugham, William Somerset
See Maugham, W(illiam) Somerset
Maupassant, (Henri Rene Albert) Guy de 1850-1893 **NCLC 1, 42; DA; DAB; DAC; DAM MST; SSC 1; WLC**
See also DLB 123
Maupin, Armistead 1944- **CLC 95; DAM POP**
See also CA 125; 130; CANR 58; INT 130
Maurhut, Richard
See Traven, B.
Mauriac, Claude 1914-1996 **CLC 9**
See also CA 89-92; 152; DLB 83
Mauriac, Francois (Charles) 1885-1970 **CLC 4, 9, 56; SSC 24**
See also CA 25-28; CAP 2; DLB 65; MTCW
Mavor, Osborne Henry 1888-1951
See Bridie, James
See also CA 104
Maxwell, William (Keepers, Jr.) 1908- **CLC 19**
See also CA 93-96; CANR 54; DLBY 80; INT 93-96
May, Elaine 1932- **CLC 16**
See also CA 124; 142; DLB 44
Mayakovski, Vladimir (Vladimirovich) 1893-1930 **TCLC 4, 18**
See also CA 104; 158
Mayhew, Henry 1812-1887 **NCLC 31**
See also DLB 18, 55, 190
Mayle, Peter 1939(?)- **CLC 89**
See also CA 139; CANR 64
Maynard, Joyce 1953- **CLC 23**
See also CA 111; 129; CANR 64
Mayne, William (James Carter) 1928- **CLC 12**
See also AAYA 20; CA 9-12R; CANR 37; CLR 25; JRDA; MAICYA; SAAS 11; SATA 6, 68
Mayo, Jim
See L'Amour, Louis (Dearborn)

Maysles, Albert 1926- **CLC 16**
See also CA 29-32R
Maysles, David 1932- **CLC 16**
Mazer, Norma Fox 1931- **CLC 26**
See also AAYA 5; CA 69-72; CANR 12, 32, 66; CLR 23; JRDA; MAICYA; SAAS 1; SATA 24, 67
Mazzini, Guiseppe 1805-1872 **NCLC 34**
McAuley, James Phillip 1917-1976 **CLC 45**
See also CA 97-100
McBain, Ed
See Hunter, Evan
McBrien, William Augustine 1930- **CLC 44**
See also CA 107
McCaffrey, Anne (Inez) 1926- **CLC 17; DAM NOV, POP**
See also AAYA 6; AITN 2; BEST 89:2; CA 25-28R; CANR 15, 35, 55; CLR 49; DLB 8; JRDA; MAICYA; MTCW; SAAS 11; SATA 8, 70
McCall, Nathan 1955(?)- **CLC 86**
See also CA 146
McCann, Arthur
See Campbell, John W(ood, Jr.)
McCann, Edson
See Pohl, Frederik
McCarthy, Charles, Jr. 1933-
See McCarthy, Cormac
See also CANR 42, 69; DAM POP
McCarthy, Cormac 1933- **CLC 4, 57, 59, 101**
See also McCarthy, Charles, Jr.
See also DLB 6, 143
McCarthy, Mary (Therese) 1912-1989 **CLC 1, 3, 5, 14, 24, 39, 59; SSC 24**
See also CA 5-8R; 129; CANR 16, 50, 64; DLB 2; DLBY 81; INT CANR-16; MTCW
McCartney, (James) Paul 1942- **CLC 12, 35**
See also CA 146
McCauley, Stephen (D.) 1955- **CLC 50**
See also CA 141
McClure, Michael (Thomas) 1932- **CLC 6, 10**
See also CA 21-24R; CANR 17, 46; DLB 16
McCorkle, Jill (Collins) 1958- **CLC 51**
See also CA 121; DLBY 87
McCourt, Frank 1930- **CLC 109**
See also CA 157
McCourt, James 1941- **CLC 5**
See also CA 57-60
McCoy, Horace (Stanley) 1897-1955 **TCLC 28**
See also CA 108; 155; DLB 9
McCrae, John 1872-1918 **TCLC 12**
See also CA 109; DLB 92
McCreigh, James
See Pohl, Frederik
McCullers, (Lula) Carson (Smith) 1917-1967 **CLC 1, 4, 10, 12, 48, 100; DA; DAB; DAC; DAM MST, NOV; SSC 9, 24; WLC**
See also AAYA 21; CA 5-8R; 25-28R; CABS 1, 3; CANR 18; CDALB 1941-1968; DLB 2, 7, 173; MTCW; SATA 27
McCulloch, John Tyler
See Burroughs, Edgar Rice
McCullough, Colleen 1938(?)- **CLC 27, 107; DAM NOV, POP**
See also CA 81-84; CANR 17, 46, 67; MTCW
McDermott, Alice 1953- **CLC 90**
See also CA 109; CANR 40
McElroy, Joseph 1930- **CLC 5, 47**
See also CA 17-20R
McEwan, Ian (Russell) 1948- **CLC 13, 66; DAM NOV**
See also BEST 90:4; CA 61-64; CANR 14, 41, 69; DLB 14, 194; MTCW

McFadden, David 1940-   **CLC 48**
See also CA 104; DLB 60; INT 104

McFarland, Dennis 1950-   **CLC 65**
See also CA 165

McGahern, John 1934- **CLC 5, 9, 48; SSC 17**
See also CA 17-20R; CANR 29, 68; DLB 14;
MTCW

McGinley, Patrick (Anthony) 1937- **CLC 41**
See also CA 120; 127; CANR 56; INT 127

McGinley, Phyllis 1905-1978   **CLC 14**
See also CA 9-12R; 77-80; CANR 19; DLB 11,
48; SATA 2, 44; SATA-Obit 24

McGinniss, Joe 1942-   **CLC 32**
See also AITN 2; BEST 89:2; CA 25-28R;
CANR 26; DLB 185; INT CANR-26

McGivern, Maureen Daly
See Daly, Maureen

McGrath, Patrick 1950-   **CLC 55**
See also CA 136; CANR 65

McGrath, Thomas (Matthew) 1916-1990**CLC
28, 59; DAM POET**
See also CA 9-12R; 132; CANR 6, 33; MTCW;
SATA 41; SATA-Obit 66

McGuane, Thomas (Francis III) 1939-**CLC 3,
7, 18, 45**
See also AITN 2; CA 49-52; CANR 5, 24, 49;
DLB 2; DLBY 80; INT CANR-24; MTCW

McGuckian, Medbh 1950-   **CLC 48; DAM
POET**
See also CA 143; DLB 40

McHale, Tom 1942(?)-1982   **CLC 3, 5**
See also AITN 1; CA 77-80; 106

McIlvanney, William 1936-   **CLC 42**
See also CA 25-28R; CANR 61; DLB 14

McIlwraith, Maureen Mollie Hunter
See Hunter, Mollie
See also SATA 2

McInerney, Jay 1955-**CLC 34, 112; DAM POP**
See also AAYA 18; CA 116; 123; CANR 45,
68; INT 123

McIntyre, Vonda N(eel) 1948-   **CLC 18**
See also CA 81-84; CANR 17, 34, 69; MTCW

McKay, ClaudeTCLC **7, 41; BLC 3; DAB; PC
2**
See also McKay, Festus Claudius
See also DLB 4, 45, 51, 117

McKay, Festus Claudius 1889-1948
See McKay, Claude
See also BW 1; CA 104; 124; DA; DAC; DAM
MST, MULT, NOV, POET; MTCW; WLC

McKuen, Rod 1933-   **CLC 1, 3**
See also AITN 1; CA 41-44R; CANR 40

McLoughlin, R. B.
See Mencken, H(enry) L(ouis)

McLuhan, (Herbert) Marshall 1911-1980
CLC 37, 83
See also CA 9-12R; 102; CANR 12, 34, 61;
DLB 88; INT CANR-12; MTCW

McMillan, Terry (L.) 1951- **CLC 50, 61, 112;
BLCS; DAM MULT, NOV, POP**
See also AAYA 21; BW 2; CA 140; CANR 60

McMurtry, Larry (Jeff) 1936-**CLC 2, 3, 7, 11,
27, 44; DAM NOV, POP**
See also AAYA 15; AITN 2; BEST 89:2; CA 5-
8R; CANR 19, 43, 64; CDALB 1968-1988;
DLB 2, 143; DLBY 80, 87; MTCW

McNally, T. M. 1961-   **CLC 82**

McNally, Terrence 1939-   **CLC 4, 7, 41, 91;
DAM DRAM**
See also CA 45-48; CANR 2, 56; DLB 7

McNamer, Deirdre 1950-   **CLC 70**

McNeile, Herman Cyril 1888-1937
See Sapper

See also DLB 77

McNickle, (William) D'Arcy 1904-1977 **CLC
89; DAM MULT**
See also CA 9-12R; 85-88; CANR 5, 45; DLB
175; NNAL; SATA-Obit 22

McPhee, John (Angus) 1931-   **CLC 36**
See also BEST 90:1; CA 65-68; CANR 20, 46,
64, 69; DLB 185; MTCW

McPherson, James Alan 1943-   **CLC 19, 77;
BLCS**
See also BW 1; CA 25-28R; CAAS 17; CANR
24; DLB 38; MTCW

McPherson, William (Alexander) 1933- **CLC
34**
See also CA 69-72; CANR 28; INT CANR-28

Mead, Margaret 1901-1978   **CLC 37**
See also AITN 1; CA 1-4R; 81-84; CANR 4;
MTCW; SATA-Obit 20

Meaker, Marijane (Agnes) 1927-
See Kerr, M. E.
See also CA 107; CANR 37, 63; INT 107;
JRDA; MAICYA; MTCW; SATA 20, 61

Medoff, Mark (Howard) 1940-   **CLC 6, 23;
DAM DRAM**
See also AITN 1; CA 53-56; CANR 5; DLB 7;
INT CANR-5

Medvedev, P. N.
See Bakhtin, Mikhail Mikhailovich

Meged, Aharon
See Megged, Aharon

Meged, Aron
See Megged, Aharon

Megged, Aharon 1920-   **CLC 9**
See also CA 49-52; CAAS 13; CANR 1

Mehta, Ved (Parkash) 1934-   **CLC 37**
See also CA 1-4R; CANR 2, 23, 69; MTCW

Melanter
See Blackmore, R(ichard) D(oddridge)

Melies, Georges 1861-1938   **TCLC 81**

Melikow, Loris
See Hofmannsthal, Hugo von

Melmoth, Sebastian
See Wilde, Oscar (Fingal O'Flahertie Wills)

Meltzer, Milton 1915-   **CLC 26**
See also AAYA 8; CA 13-16R; CANR 38; CLR
13; DLB 61; JRDA; MAICYA; SAAS 1;
SATA 1, 50, 80

Melville, Herman 1819-1891 **NCLC 3, 12, 29,
45, 49; DA; DAB; DAC; DAM MST, NOV;
SSC 1, 17; WLC**
See also AAYA 25; CDALB 1640-1865; DLB
3, 74; SATA 59

Menander c. 342B.C.-c. 292B.C.   **CMLC 9;
DAM DRAM; DC 3**
See also DLB 176

Mencken, H(enry) L(ouis) 1880-1956   **TCLC
13**
See also CA 105; 125; CDALB 1917-1929;
DLB 11, 29, 63, 137; MTCW

Mendelsohn, Jane 1965(?)-   **CLC 99**
See also CA 154

Mercer, David 1928-1980**CLC 5; DAM DRAM**
See also CA 9-12R; 102; CANR 23; DLB 13;
MTCW

Merchant, Paul
See Ellison, Harlan (Jay)

Meredith, George 1828-1909   **TCLC 17, 43;
DAM POET**
See also CA 117; 153; CDBLB 1832-1890;
DLB 18, 35, 57, 159

Meredith, William (Morris) 1919- **CLC 4, 13,
22, 55; DAM POET**
See also CA 9-12R; CAAS 14; CANR 6, 40;

DLB 5

Merezhkovsky, Dmitry Sergeyevich 1865-1941
TCLC 29

Merimee, Prosper 1803-1870**NCLC 6, 65; SSC
7**
See also DLB 119, 192

Merkin, Daphne 1954-   **CLC 44**
See also CA 123

Merlin, Arthur
See Blish, James (Benjamin)

Merrill, James (Ingram) 1926-1995 **CLC 2, 3,
6, 8, 13, 18, 34, 91; DAM POET**
See also CA 13-16R; 147; CANR 10, 49, 63;
DLB 5, 165; DLBY 85; INT CANR-10;
MTCW

Merriman, Alex
See Silverberg, Robert

Merriman, Brian 1747-1805   **NCLC 70**

Merritt, E. B.
See Waddington, Miriam

Merton, Thomas 1915-1968 **CLC 1, 3, 11, 34,
83; PC 10**
See also CA 5-8R; 25-28R; CANR 22, 53; DLB
48; DLBY 81; MTCW

Merwin, W(illiam) S(tanley) 1927- **CLC 1, 2,
3, 5, 8, 13, 18, 45, 88; DAM POET**
See also CA 13-16R; CANR 15, 51; DLB 5,
169; INT CANR-15; MTCW

Metcalf, John 1938-   **CLC 37**
See also CA 113; DLB 60

Metcalf, Suzanne
See Baum, L(yman) Frank

Mew, Charlotte (Mary) 1870-1928   **TCLC 8**
See also CA 105; DLB 19, 135

Mewshaw, Michael 1943-   **CLC 9**
See also CA 53-56; CANR 7, 47; DLBY 80

Meyer, June
See Jordan, June

Meyer, Lynn
See Slavitt, David R(ytman)

Meyer-Meyrink, Gustav 1868-1932
See Meyrink, Gustav
See also CA 117

Meyers, Jeffrey 1939-   **CLC 39**
See also CA 73-76; CANR 54; DLB 111

Meynell, Alice (Christina Gertrude Thompson)
1847-1922   **TCLC 6**
See also CA 104; DLB 19, 98

Meyrink, Gustav   **TCLC 21**
See also Meyer-Meyrink, Gustav
See also DLB 81

Michaels, Leonard 1933- **CLC 6, 25; SSC 16**
See also CA 61-64; CANR 21, 62; DLB 130;
MTCW

Michaux, Henri 1899-1984   **CLC 8, 19**
See also CA 85-88; 114

Micheaux, Oscar 1884-1951   **TCLC 76**
See also DLB 50

Michelangelo 1475-1564   **LC 12**

Michelet, Jules 1798-1874   **NCLC 31**

Michener, James A(lbert) 1907(?)-1997 **CLC
1, 5, 11, 29, 60, 109; DAM NOV, POP**
See also AITN 1; BEST 90:1; CA 5-8R; 161;
CANR 21, 45, 68; DLB 6; MTCW

Mickiewicz, Adam 1798-1855   **NCLC 3**

Middleton, Christopher 1926-   **CLC 13**
See also CA 13-16R; CANR 29, 54; DLB 40

Middleton, Richard (Barham) 1882-1911
TCLC 56
See also DLB 156

Middleton, Stanley 1919-   **CLC 7, 38**
See also CA 25-28R; CAAS 23; CANR 21, 46;
DLB 14

Middleton, Thomas 1580-1627 **LC 33; DAM DRAM, MST; DC 5**
See also DLB 58
Migueis, Jose Rodrigues 1901- **CLC 10**
Mikszath, Kalman 1847-1910 **TCLC 31**
Miles, Jack **CLC 100**
Miles, Josephine (Louise) 1911-1985 **CLC 1, 2, 14, 34, 39; DAM POET**
See also CA 1-4R; 116; CANR 2, 55; DLB 48
Militant
See Sandburg, Carl (August)
Mill, John Stuart 1806-1873 **NCLC 11, 58**
See also CDBLB 1832-1890; DLB 55, 190
Millar, Kenneth 1915-1983 **CLC 14; DAM POP**
See Macdonald, Ross
See also CA 9-12R; 110; CANR 16, 63; DLB 2; DLBD 6; DLBY 83; MTCW
Millay, E. Vincent
See Millay, Edna St. Vincent
Millay, Edna St. Vincent 1892-1950 **TCLC 4, 49; DA; DAB; DAC; DAM MST, POET; PC 6; WLCS**
See also CA 104; 130; CDALB 1917-1929; DLB 45; MTCW
Miller, Arthur 1915- **CLC 1, 2, 6, 10, 15, 26, 47, 78; DA; DAB; DAC; DAM DRAM, MST; DC 1; WLC**
See also AAYA 15; AITN 1; CA 1-4R; CABS 3; CANR 2, 30, 54; CDALB 1941-1968; DLB 7; MTCW
Miller, Henry (Valentine) 1891-1980 **CLC 1, 2, 4, 9, 14, 43, 84; DA; DAB; DAC; DAM MST, NOV; WLC**
See also CA 9-12R; 97-100; CANR 33, 64; CDALB 1929-1941; DLB 4, 9; DLBY 80; MTCW
Miller, Jason 1939(?)- **CLC 2**
See also AITN 1; CA 73-76; DLB 7
Miller, Sue 1943- **CLC 44; DAM POP**
See also BEST 90:3; CA 139; CANR 59; DLB 143
Miller, Walter M(ichael, Jr.) 1923- **CLC 4, 30**
See also CA 85-88; DLB 8
Millett, Kate 1934- **CLC 67**
See also AITN 1; CA 73-76; CANR 32, 53; MTCW
Millhauser, Steven (Lewis) 1943- **CLC 21, 54, 109**
See also CA 110; 111; CANR 63; DLB 2; INT 111
Millin, Sarah Gertrude 1889-1968 **CLC 49**
See also CA 102; 93-96
Milne, A(lan) A(lexander) 1882-1956 **TCLC 6; DAB; DAC; DAM MST**
See also CA 104; 133; CLR 1, 26; DLB 10, 77, 100, 160; MAICYA; MTCW; YABC 1
Milner, Ron(ald) 1938- **CLC 56; BLC 3; DAM MULT**
See also AITN 1; BW 1; CA 73-76; CANR 24; DLB 38; MTCW
Milnes, Richard Monckton 1809-1885 **NCLC 61**
See also DLB 32, 184
Milosz, Czeslaw 1911- **CLC 5, 11, 22, 31, 56, 82; DAM MST, POET; PC 8; WLCS**
See also CA 81-84; CANR 23, 51; MTCW
Milton, John 1608-1674 **LC 9, 43; DA; DAB; DAC; DAM MST, POET; PC 19; WLC**
See also CDBLB 1660-1789; DLB 131, 151
Min, Anchee 1957- **CLC 86**
See also CA 146
Minehaha, Cornelius

See Wedekind, (Benjamin) Frank(lin)
Miner, Valerie 1947- **CLC 40**
See also CA 97-100; CANR 59
Minimo, Duca
See D'Annunzio, Gabriele
Minot, Susan 1956- **CLC 44**
See also CA 134
Minus, Ed 1938- **CLC 39**
Miranda, Javier
See Bioy Casares, Adolfo
Mirbeau, Octave 1848-1917 **TCLC 55**
See also DLB 123, 192
Miro (Ferrer), Gabriel (Francisco Victor) 1879-1930 **TCLC 5**
See also CA 104
Mishima, Yukio 1925-1970 **CLC 2, 4, 6, 9, 27; DC 1; SSC 4**
See also Hiraoka, Kimitake
See also DLB 182
Mistral, Frederic 1830-1914 **TCLC 51**
See also CA 122
Mistral, Gabriela **TCLC 2; HLC**
See also Godoy Alcayaga, Lucila
Mistry, Rohinton 1952- **CLC 71; DAC**
See also CA 141
Mitchell, Clyde
See Ellison, Harlan (Jay); Silverberg, Robert
Mitchell, James Leslie 1901-1935
See Gibbon, Lewis Grassic
See also CA 104; DLB 15
Mitchell, Joni 1943- **CLC 12**
See also CA 112
Mitchell, Joseph (Quincy) 1908-1996 **CLC 98**
See also CA 77-80; 152; CANR 69; DLB 185; DLBY 96
Mitchell, Margaret (Munnerlyn) 1900-1949 **TCLC 11; DAM NOV, POP**
See also AAYA 23; CA 109; 125; CANR 55; DLB 9; MTCW
Mitchell, Peggy
See Mitchell, Margaret (Munnerlyn)
Mitchell, S(ilas) Weir 1829-1914 **TCLC 36**
See also CA 165
Mitchell, W(illiam) O(rmond) 1914-1998 **CLC 25; DAC; DAM MST**
See also CA 77-80; 165; CANR 15, 43; DLB 88
Mitchell, William 1879-1936 **TCLC 81**
Mitford, Mary Russell 1787-1855 **NCLC 4**
See also DLB 110, 116
Mitford, Nancy 1904-1973 **CLC 44**
See also CA 9-12R; DLB 191
Miyamoto, Yuriko 1899-1951 **TCLC 37**
See also DLB 180
Miyazawa, Kenji 1896-1933 **TCLC 76**
See also CA 157
Mizoguchi, Kenji 1898-1956 **TCLC 72**
Mo, Timothy (Peter) 1950(?)- **CLC 46**
See also CA 117; DLB 194; MTCW
Modarressi, Taghi (M.) 1931- **CLC 44**
See also CA 121; 134; INT 134
Modiano, Patrick (Jean) 1945- **CLC 18**
See also CA 85-88; CANR 17, 40; DLB 83
Moerck, Paal
See Roelvaag, O(le) E(dvart)
Mofolo, Thomas (Mokopu) 1875(?)-1948 **TCLC 22; BLC 3; DAM MULT**
See also CA 121; 153
Mohr, Nicholasa 1938- **CLC 12; DAM MULT; HLC**
See also AAYA 8; CA 49-52; CANR 1, 32, 64; CLR 22; DLB 145; HW; JRDA; SAAS 8; SATA 8, 97

Mojtabai, A(nn) G(race) 1938- **CLC 5, 9, 15, 29**
See also CA 85-88
Moliere 1622-1673 **LC 28; DA; DAB; DAC; DAM DRAM, MST; WLC**
Molin, Charles
See Mayne, William (James Carter)
Molnar, Ferenc 1878-1952 **TCLC 20; DAM DRAM**
See also CA 109; 153
Momaday, N(avarre) Scott 1934- **CLC 2, 19, 85, 95; DA; DAB; DAC; DAM MST, MULT, NOV, POP; WLCS**
See also AAYA 11; CA 25-28R; CANR 14, 34, 68; DLB 143, 175; INT CANR-14; MTCW; NNAL; SATA 48; SATA-Brief 30
Monette, Paul 1945-1995 **CLC 82**
See also CA 139; 147
Monroe, Harriet 1860-1936 **TCLC 12**
See also CA 109; DLB 54, 91
Monroe, Lyle
See Heinlein, Robert A(nson)
Montagu, Elizabeth 1917- **NCLC 7**
See also CA 9-12R
Montagu, Mary (Pierrepont) Wortley 1689-1762 **LC 9; PC 16**
See also DLB 95, 101
Montagu, W. H.
See Coleridge, Samuel Taylor
Montague, John (Patrick) 1929- **CLC 13, 46**
See also CA 9-12R; CANR 9, 69; DLB 40; MTCW
Montaigne, Michel (Eyquem) de 1533-1592 **LC 8; DA; DAB; DAC; DAM MST; WLC**
Montale, Eugenio 1896-1981 **CLC 7, 9, 18; PC 13**
See also CA 17-20R; 104; CANR 30; DLB 114; MTCW
Montesquieu, Charles-Louis de Secondat 1689-1755 **LC 7**
Montgomery, (Robert) Bruce 1921-1978
See Crispin, Edmund
See also CA 104
Montgomery, L(ucy) M(aud) 1874-1942 **TCLC 51; DAC; DAM MST**
See also AAYA 12; CA 108; 137; CLR 8; DLB 92; DLBD 14; JRDA; MAICYA; YABC 1
Montgomery, Marion H., Jr. 1925- **CLC 7**
See also AITN 1; CA 1-4R; CANR 3, 48; DLB 6
Montgomery, Max
See Davenport, Guy (Mattison, Jr.)
Montherlant, Henry (Milon) de 1896-1972 **CLC 8, 19; DAM DRAM**
See also CA 85-88; 37-40R; DLB 72; MTCW
Monty Python
See Chapman, Graham; Cleese, John (Marwood); Gilliam, Terry (Vance); Idle, Eric; Jones, Terence Graham Parry; Palin, Michael (Edward)
See also AAYA 7
Moodie, Susanna (Strickland) 1803-1885 **NCLC 14**
See also DLB 99
Mooney, Edward 1951-
See Mooney, Ted
See also CA 130
Mooney, Ted **CLC 25**
See also Mooney, Edward
Moorcock, Michael (John) 1939- **CLC 5, 27, 58**
See also CA 45-48; CAAS 5; CANR 2, 17, 38, 64; DLB 14; MTCW; SATA 93
Moore, Brian 1921- **CLC 1, 3, 5, 7, 8, 19, 32,**

90; DAB; DAC; DAM MST
See also CA 1-4R; CANR 1, 25, 42, 63; MTCW

Moore, Edward
See Muir, Edwin

Moore, George Augustus 1852-1933 **TCLC 7; SSC 19**
See also CA 104; DLB 10, 18, 57, 135

Moore, Lorrie　　　　　　　　**CLC 39, 45, 68**
See also Moore, Marie Lorena

Moore, Marianne (Craig) 1887-1972 **CLC 1, 2, 4, 8, 10, 13, 19, 47; DA; DAB; DAC; DAM MST, POET; PC 4; WLCS**
See also CA 1-4R; 33-36R; CANR 3, 61; CDALB 1929-1941; DLB 45; DLBD 7; MTCW; SATA 20

Moore, Marie Lorena 1957-
See Moore, Lorrie
See also CA 116; CANR 39

Moore, Thomas 1779-1852　　　　　　**NCLC 6**
See also DLB 96, 144

Morand, Paul 1888-1976　　**CLC 41; SSC 22**
See also CA 69-72; DLB 65

Morante, Elsa 1918-1985　　　　　**CLC 8, 47**
See also CA 85-88; 117; CANR 35; DLB 177; MTCW

Moravia, Alberto 1907-1990 **CLC 2, 7, 11, 27, 46; SSC 26**
See also Pincherle, Alberto
See also DLB 177

More, Hannah 1745-1833　　　　　**NCLC 27**
See also DLB 107, 109, 116, 158

More, Henry 1614-1687　　　　　　　　**LC 9**
See also DLB 126

More, Sir Thomas 1478-1535　　**LC 10, 32**

Moreas, Jean　　　　　　　　　　　**TCLC 18**
See also Papadiamantopoulos, Johannes

Morgan, Berry 1919-　　　　　　　　**CLC 6**
See also CA 49-52; DLB 6

Morgan, Claire
See Highsmith, (Mary) Patricia

Morgan, Edwin (George) 1920-　　　**CLC 31**
See also CA 5-8R; CANR 3, 43; DLB 27

Morgan, (George) Frederick 1922-　**CLC 23**
See also CA 17-20R; CANR 21

Morgan, Harriet
See Mencken, H(enry) L(ouis)

Morgan, Jane
See Cooper, James Fenimore

Morgan, Janet 1945-　　　　　　　**CLC 39**
See also CA 65-68

Morgan, Lady 1776(?)-1859　　　　**NCLC 29**
See also DLB 116, 158

Morgan, Robin (Evonne) 1941-　　　　**CLC 2**
See also CA 69-72; CANR 29, 68; MTCW; SATA 80

Morgan, Scott
See Kuttner, Henry

Morgan, Seth 1949(?)-1990　　　　　**CLC 65**
See also CA 132

Morgenstern, Christian 1871-1914　**TCLC 8**
See also CA 105

Morgenstern, S.
See Goldman, William (W.)

Moricz, Zsigmond 1879-1942　　　**TCLC 33**
See also CA 165

Morike, Eduard (Friedrich) 1804-1875 **NCLC 10**
See also DLB 133

Moritz, Karl Philipp 1756-1793　　　**LC 2**
See also DLB 94

Morland, Peter Henry
See Faust, Frederick (Schiller)

Morren, Theophil

See Hofmannsthal, Hugo von

Morris, Bill 1952-　　　　　　　　**CLC 76**

Morris, Julian
See West, Morris L(anglo)

Morris, Steveland Judkins 1950(?)-
See Wonder, Stevie
See also CA 111

Morris, William 1834-1896　　　　　**NCLC 4**
See also CDBLB 1832-1890; DLB 18, 35, 57, 156, 178, 184

Morris, Wright 1910-　　　**CLC 1, 3, 7, 18, 37**
See also CA 9-12R; CANR 21; DLB 2; DLBY 81; MTCW

Morrison, Arthur 1863-1945　　　　**TCLC 72**
See also CA 120; 157; DLB 70, 135, 197

Morrison, Chloe Anthony Wofford
See Morrison, Toni

Morrison, James Douglas 1943-1971
See Morrison, Jim
See also CA 73-76; CANR 40

Morrison, Jim　　　　　　　　　　　**CLC 17**
See also Morrison, James Douglas

Morrison, Toni 1931- **CLC 4, 10, 22, 55, 81, 87; BLC 3; DA; DAB; DAC; DAM MST, MULT, NOV, POP**
See also AAYA 1, 22; BW 2; CA 29-32R; CANR 27, 42, 67; CDALB 1968-1988; DLB 6, 33, 143; DLBY 81; MTCW; SATA 57

Morrison, Van 1945-　　　　　　　**CLC 21**
See also CA 116

Morrissy, Mary 1958-　　　　　　　**CLC 99**

Mortimer, John (Clifford) 1923- **CLC 28, 43; DAM DRAM, POP**
See also CA 13-16R; CANR 21, 69; CDBLB 1960 to Present; DLB 13; INT CANR-21; MTCW

Mortimer, Penelope (Ruth) 1918-　　　**CLC 5**
See also CA 57-60; CANR 45

Morton, Anthony
See Creasey, John

Mosca, Gaetano 1858-1941　　　　**TCLC 75**

Mosher, Howard Frank 1943-　　　　**CLC 62**
See also CA 139; CANR 65

Mosley, Nicholas 1923-　　　　　**CLC 43, 70**
See also CA 69-72; CANR 41, 60; DLB 14

Mosley, Walter 1952- **CLC 97; BLCS; DAM MULT, POP**
See also AAYA 17; BW 2; CA 142; CANR 57

Moss, Howard 1922-1987　**CLC 7, 14, 45, 50; DAM POET**
See also CA 1-4R; 123; CANR 1, 44; DLB 5

Mossgiel, Rab
See Burns, Robert

Motion, Andrew (Peter) 1952-　　　　**CLC 47**
See also CA 146; DLB 40

Motley, Willard (Francis) 1909-1965 **CLC 18**
See also BW 1; CA 117; 106; DLB 76, 143

Motoori, Norinaga 1730-1801　　　**NCLC 45**

Mott, Michael (Charles Alston) 1930- **CLC 15, 34**
See also CA 5-8R; CAAS 7; CANR 7, 29

Mountain Wolf Woman 1884-1960　　**CLC 92**
See also CA 144; NNAL

Moure, Erin 1955-　　　　　　　　**CLC 88**
See also CA 113; DLB 60

Mowat, Farley (McGill) 1921- **CLC 26; DAC; DAM MST**
See also AAYA 1; CA 1-4R; CANR 4, 24, 42, 68; CLR 20; DLB 68; INT CANAR-24; JRDA; MAICYA; MTCW; SATA 3, 55

Moyers, Bill 1934-　　　　　　　　**CLC 74**
See also AITN 2; CA 61-64; CANR 31, 52

Mphahlele, Es'kia

See Mphahlele, Ezekiel
See also DLB 125

Mphahlele, Ezekiel 1919-1983 **CLC 25; BLC 3; DAM MULT**
See also Mphahlele, Es'kia
See also BW 2; CA 81-84; CANR 26

Mqhayi, S(amuel) E(dward) K(rune Loliwe) 1875-1945 **TCLC 25; BLC 3; DAM MULT**
See also CA 153

Mrozek, Slawomir 1930-　　　　　**CLC 3, 13**
See also CA 13-16R; CAAS 10; CANR 29; MTCW

Mrs. Belloc-Lowndes
See Lowndes, Marie Adelaide (Belloc)

Mtwa, Percy (?)-　　　　　　　　　**CLC 47**

Mueller, Lisel 1924-　　　　　　　**CLC 13, 51**
See also CA 93-96; DLB 105

Muir, Edwin 1887-1959　　　　　　　**TCLC 2**
See also CA 104; DLB 20, 100, 191

Muir, John 1838-1914　　　　　　　**TCLC 28**
See also CA 165; DLB 186

Mujica Lainez, Manuel 1910-1984　　**CLC 31**
See also Lainez, Manuel Mujica
See also CA 81-84; 112; CANR 32; HW

Mukherjee, Bharati 1940- **CLC 53; DAM NOV**
See also BEST 89:2; CA 107; CANR 45; DLB 60; MTCW

Muldoon, Paul 1951- **CLC 32, 72; DAM POET**
See also CA 113; 129; CANR 52; DLB 40; INT 129

Mulisch, Harry 1927-　　　　　　　**CLC 42**
See also CA 9-12R; CANR 6, 26, 56

Mull, Martin 1943-　　　　　　　　**CLC 17**
See also CA 105

Mulock, Dinah Maria
See Craik, Dinah Maria (Mulock)

Munford, Robert 1737(?)-1783　　　　**LC 5**
See also DLB 31

Mungo, Raymond 1946-　　　　　　**CLC 72**
See also CA 49-52; CANR 2

Munro, Alice 1931-　　**CLC 6, 10, 19, 50, 95; DAC; DAM MST, NOV; SSC 3; WLCS**
See also AITN 2; CA 33-36R; CANR 33, 53; DLB 53; MTCW; SATA 29

Munro, H(ector) H(ugh) 1870-1916
See Saki
See also CA 104; 130; CDBLB 1890-1914; DA; DAB; DAC; DAM MST, NOV; DLB 34, 162; MTCW; WLC

Murasaki, Lady　　　　　　　　　　**CMLC 1**

Murdoch, (Jean) Iris 1919- **CLC 1, 2, 3, 4, 6, 8, 11, 15, 22, 31, 51; DAB; DAC; DAM MST, NOV**
See also CA 13-16R; CANR 8, 43, 68; CDBLB 1960 to Present; DLB 14, 194; INT CANR-8; MTCW

Murfree, Mary Noailles 1850-1922　　**SSC 22**
See also CA 122; DLB 12, 74

Murnau, Friedrich Wilhelm
See Plumpe, Friedrich Wilhelm

Murphy, Richard 1927-　　　　　　　**CLC 41**
See also CA 29-32R; DLB 40

Murphy, Sylvia 1937-　　　　　　　**CLC 34**
See also CA 121

Murphy, Thomas (Bernard) 1935-　　**CLC 51**
See also CA 101

Murray, Albert L. 1916-　　　　　　**CLC 73**
See also BW 2; CA 49-52; CANR 26, 52; DLB 38

Murray, Judith Sargent 1751-1820 **NCLC 63**
See also DLB 37, 200

Murray, Les(lie) A(llan) 1938- **CLC 40; DAM POET**

See also CA 21-24R; CANR 11, 27, 56
Murry, J. Middleton
See Murry, John Middleton
Murry, John Middleton 1889-1957 **TCLC 16**
See also CA 118; DLB 149
Musgrave, Susan 1951- **CLC 13, 54**
See also CA 69-72; CANR 45
Musil, Robert (Edler von) 1880-1942 **TCLC 12, 68; SSC 18**
See also CA 109; CANR 55; DLB 81, 124
Muske, Carol 1945- **CLC 90**
See also Muske-Dukes, Carol (Anne)
Muske-Dukes, Carol (Anne) 1945-
See Muske, Carol
See also CA 65-68; CANR 32
Musset, (Louis Charles) Alfred de 1810-1857 **NCLC 7**
See also DLB 192
My Brother's Brother
See Chekhov, Anton (Pavlovich)
Myers, L(eopold) H(amilton) 1881-1944 **TCLC 59**
See also CA 157; DLB 15
Myers, Walter Dean 1937- **CLC 35; BLC 3; DAM MULT, NOV**
See also AAYA 4, 23; BW 2; CA 33-36R; CANR 20, 42, 67; CLR 4, 16, 35; DLB 33; INT CANR-20; JRDA; MAICYA; SAAS 2; SATA 41, 71; SATA-Brief 27
Myers, Walter M.
See Myers, Walter Dean
Myles, Symon
See Follett, Ken(neth Martin)
Nabokov, Vladimir (Vladimirovich) 1899-1977 **CLC 1, 2, 3, 6, 8, 11, 15, 23, 44, 46, 64; DA; DAB; DAC; DAM MST, NOV; SSC 11; WLC**
See also CA 5-8R; 69-72; CANR 20; CDALB 1941-1968; DLB 2; DLBD 3; DLBY 80, 91; MTCW
Nagai Kafu 1879-1959 **TCLC 51**
See also Nagai Sokichi
See also DLB 180
Nagai Sokichi 1879-1959
See Nagai Kafu
See also CA 117
Nagy, Laszlo 1925-1978 **CLC 7**
See also CA 129; 112
Naidu, Sarojini 1879-1943 **TCLC 80**
Naipaul, Shiva(dhar Srinivasa) 1945-1985 **CLC 32, 39; DAM NOV**
See also CA 110; 112; 116; CANR 33; DLB 157; DLBY 85; MTCW
Naipaul, V(idiadhar) S(urajprasad) 1932- **CLC 4, 7, 9, 13, 18, 37, 105; DAB; DAC; DAM MST, NOV**
See also CA 1-4R; CANR 1, 33, 51; CDBLB 1960 to Present; DLB 125; DLBY 85; MTCW
Nakos, Lilika 1899(?)- **CLC 29**
Narayan, R(asipuram) K(rishnaswami) 1906- **CLC 7, 28, 47; DAM NOV; SSC 25**
See also CA 81-84; CANR 33, 61; MTCW; SATA 62
Nash, (Fredric) Ogden 1902-1971 **CLC 23; DAM POET; PC 21**
See also CA 13-14; 29-32R; CANR 34, 61; CAP 1; DLB 11; MAICYA; MTCW; SATA 2, 46
Nashe, Thomas 1567-1601(?) **LC 41**
See also DLB 167
Nashe, Thomas 1567-1601 **LC 41**
Nathan, Daniel
See Dannay, Frederic

Nathan, George Jean 1882-1958 **TCLC 18**
See also Hatteras, Owen
See also CA 114; DLB 137
Natsume, Kinnosuke 1867-1916
See Natsume, Soseki
See also CA 104
Natsume, Soseki 1867-1916 **TCLC 2, 10**
See also Natsume, Kinnosuke
See also DLB 180
Natti, (Mary) Lee 1919-
See Kingman, Lee
See also CA 5-8R; CANR 2
Naylor, Gloria 1950- **CLC 28, 52; BLC 3; DA; DAC; DAM MST, MULT, NOV, POP; WLCS**
See also AAYA 6; BW 2; CA 107; CANR 27, 51; DLB 173; MTCW
Neihardt, John Gneisenau 1881-1973 **CLC 32**
See also CA 13-14; CANR 65; CAP 1; DLB 9, 54
Nekrasov, Nikolai Alekseevich 1821-1878 **NCLC 11**
Nelligan, Emile 1879-1941 **TCLC 14**
See also CA 114; DLB 92
Nelson, Willie 1933- **CLC 17**
See also CA 107
Nemerov, Howard (Stanley) 1920-1991 **CLC 2, 6, 9, 36; DAM POET**
See also CA 1-4R; 134; CABS 2; CANR 1, 27, 53; DLB 5, 6; DLBY 83; INT CANR-27; MTCW
Neruda, Pablo 1904-1973 **CLC 1, 2, 5, 7, 9, 28, 62; DA; DAB; DAC; DAM MST, MULT, POET; HLC; PC 4; WLC**
See also CA 19-20; 45-48; CAP 2; HW; MTCW
Nerval, Gerard de 1808-1855 **NCLC 1, 67; PC 13; SSC 18**
Nervo, (Jose) Amado (Ruiz de) 1870-1919 **TCLC 11**
See also CA 109; 131; HW
Nessi, Pio Baroja y
See Baroja (y Nessi), Pio
Nestroy, Johann 1801-1862 **NCLC 42**
See also DLB 133
Netterville, Luke
See O'Grady, Standish (James)
Neufeld, John (Arthur) 1938- **CLC 17**
See also AAYA 11; CA 25-28R; CANR 11, 37, 56; CLR 52; MAICYA; SAAS 3; SATA 6, 81
Neville, Emily Cheney 1919- **CLC 12**
See also CA 5-8R; CANR 3, 37; JRDA; MAICYA; SAAS 2; SATA 1
Newbound, Bernard Slade 1930-
See Slade, Bernard
See also CA 81-84; CANR 49; DAM DRAM
Newby, P(ercy) H(oward) 1918-1997 **CLC 2, 13; DAM NOV**
See also CA 5-8R; 161; CANR 32, 67; DLB 15; MTCW
Newlove, Donald 1928- **CLC 6**
See also CA 29-32R; CANR 25
Newlove, John (Herbert) 1938- **CLC 14**
See also CA 21-24R; CANR 9, 25
Newman, Charles 1938- **CLC 2, 8**
See also CA 21-24R
Newman, Edwin (Harold) 1919- **CLC 14**
See also AITN 1; CA 69-72; CANR 5
Newman, John Henry 1801-1890 **NCLC 38**
See also DLB 18, 32, 55
Newton, Suzanne 1936- **CLC 35**
See also CA 41-44R; CANR 14; JRDA; SATA 5, 77

Nexo, Martin Andersen 1869-1954 **TCLC 43**
Nezval, Vitezslav 1900-1958 **TCLC 44**
See also CA 123
Ng, Fae Myenne 1957(?)- **CLC 81**
See also CA 146
Ngema, Mbongeni 1955- **CLC 57**
See also BW 2; CA 143
Ngugi, James T(hiong'o) **CLC 3, 7, 13**
See also Ngugi wa Thiong'o
Ngugi wa Thiong'o 1938- **CLC 36; BLC 3; DAM MULT, NOV**
See also Ngugi, James T(hiong'o)
See also BW 2; CA 81-84; CANR 27, 58; DLB 125; MTCW
Nichol, B(arrie) P(hillip) 1944-1988 **CLC 18**
See also CA 53-56; DLB 53; SATA 66
Nichols, John (Treadwell) 1940- **CLC 38**
See also CA 9-12R; CAAS 2; CANR 6; DLBY 82
Nichols, Leigh
See Koontz, Dean R(ay)
Nichols, Peter (Richard) 1927- **CLC 5, 36, 65**
See also CA 104; CANR 33; DLB 13; MTCW
Nicolas, F. R. E.
See Freeling, Nicolas
Niedecker, Lorine 1903-1970 **CLC 10, 42; DAM POET**
See also CA 25-28; CAP 2; DLB 48
Nietzsche, Friedrich (Wilhelm) 1844-1900 **TCLC 10, 18, 55**
See also CA 107; 121; DLB 129
Nievo, Ippolito 1831-1861 **NCLC 22**
Nightingale, Anne Redmon 1943-
See Redmon, Anne
See also CA 103
Nik. T. O.
See Annensky, Innokenty (Fyodorovich)
Nin, Anais 1903-1977 **CLC 1, 4, 8, 11, 14, 60; DAM NOV, POP; SSC 10**
See also AITN 2; CA 13-16R; 69-72; CANR 22, 53; DLB 2, 4, 152; MTCW
Nishida, Kitaro 1870-1945 **TCLC 83**
Nishiwaki, Junzaburo 1894-1982 **PC 15**
See also CA 107
Nissenson, Hugh 1933- **CLC 4, 9**
See also CA 17-20R; CANR 27; DLB 28
Niven, Larry **CLC 8**
See also Niven, Laurence Van Cott
See also DLB 8
Niven, Laurence Van Cott 1938-
See Niven, Larry
See also CA 21-24R; CAAS 12; CANR 14, 44, 66; DAM POP; MTCW; SATA 95
Nixon, Agnes Eckhardt 1927- **CLC 21**
See also CA 110
Nizan, Paul 1905-1940 **TCLC 40**
See also CA 161; DLB 72
Nkosi, Lewis 1936- **CLC 45; BLC 3; DAM MULT**
See also BW 1; CA 65-68; CANR 27; DLB 157
Nodier, (Jean) Charles (Emmanuel) 1780-1844 **NCLC 19**
See also DLB 119
Noguchi, Yone 1875-1947 **TCLC 80**
Nolan, Christopher 1965- **CLC 58**
See also CA 111
Noon, Jeff 1957- **CLC 91**
See also CA 148
Norden, Charles
See Durrell, Lawrence (George)
Nordhoff, Charles (Bernard) 1887-1947 **TCLC 23**
See also CA 108; DLB 9; SATA 23

DAM POET
See also CA 1-4R; 33-36R; CANR 3, 35; DLB
16, 48; MTCW

Pater, Walter (Horatio) 1839-1894 **NCLC 7**
See also CDBLB 1832-1890; DLB 57, 156

Paterson, A(ndrew) B(arton) 1864-1941
TCLC 32
See also CA 155; SATA 97

Paterson, Katherine (Womeldorf) 1932- **CLC
12, 30**
See also AAYA 1; CA 21-24R; CANR 28, 59;
CLR 7, 50; DLB 52; JRDA; MAICYA;
MTCW; SATA 13, 53, 92

Patmore, Coventry Kersey Dighton 1823-1896
NCLC 9
See also DLB 35, 98

Paton, Alan (Stewart) 1903-1988 **CLC 4, 10,
25, 55, 106; DA; DAB; DAC; DAM MST,
NOV; WLC**
See also CA 13-16; 125; CANR 22; CAP 1;
MTCW; SATA 11; SATA-Obit 56

Paton Walsh, Gillian 1937-
See Walsh, Jill Paton
See also CANR 38; JRDA; MAICYA; SAAS 3;
SATA 4, 72

Patton, George S. 1885-1945 **TCLC 79**

Paulding, James Kirke 1778-1860 **NCLC 2**
See also DLB 3, 59, 74

Paulin, Thomas Neilson 1949-
See Paulin, Tom
See also CA 123; 128

Paulin, Tom **CLC 37**
See also Paulin, Thomas Neilson
See also DLB 40

Paustovsky, Konstantin (Georgievich) 1892-
1968 **CLC 40**
See also CA 93-96; 25-28R

Pavese, Cesare 1908-1950 **TCLC 3; PC 13;
SSC 19**
See also CA 104; DLB 128, 177

Pavic, Milorad 1929- **CLC 60**
See also CA 136; DLB 181

Payne, Alan
See Jakes, John (William)

Paz, Gil
See Lugones, Leopoldo

Paz, Octavio 1914-1998 **CLC 3, 4, 6, 10, 19, 51,
65; DA; DAB; DAC; DAM MST, MULT,
POET; HLC; PC 1; WLC**
See also CA 73-76; 165; CANR 32, 65; DLBY
90; HW; MTCW

p'Bitek, Okot 1931-1982 **CLC 96; BLC 3;
DAM MULT**
See also BW 2; CA 124; 107; DLB 125; MTCW

Peacock, Molly 1947- **CLC 60**
See also CA 103; CAAS 21; CANR 52; DLB
120

Peacock, Thomas Love 1785-1866 **NCLC 22**
See also DLB 96, 116

Peake, Mervyn 1911-1968 **CLC 7, 54**
See also CA 5-8R; 25-28R; CANR 3; DLB 15,
160; MTCW; SATA 23

Pearce, Philippa **CLC 21**
See also Christie, (Ann) Philippa
See also CLR 9; DLB 161; MAICYA; SATA 1,
67

Pearl, Eric
See Elman, Richard (Martin)

Pearson, T(homas) R(eid) 1956- **CLC 39**
See also CA 120; 130; INT 130

Peck, Dale 1967- **CLC 81**
See also CA 146

Peck, John 1941- **CLC 3**

See also CA 49-52; CANR 3

Peck, Richard (Wayne) 1934- **CLC 21**
See also AAYA 1, 24; CA 85-88; CANR 19,
38; CLR 15; INT CANR-19; JRDA;
MAICYA; SAAS 2; SATA 18, 55, 97

Peck, Robert Newton 1928- **CLC 17; DA;
DAC; DAM MST**
See also AAYA 3; CA 81-84; CANR 31, 63;
CLR 45; JRDA; MAICYA; SAAS 1; SATA
21, 62

Peckinpah, (David) Sam(uel) 1925-1984 **CLC
20**
See also CA 109; 114

Pedersen, Knut 1859-1952
See Hamsun, Knut
See also CA 104; 119; CANR 63; MTCW

Peeslake, Gaffer
See Durrell, Lawrence (George)

Peguy, Charles Pierre 1873-1914 **TCLC 10**
See also CA 107

Peirce, Charles Sanders 1839-1914 **TCLC 81**

Pena, Ramon del Valle y
See Valle-Inclan, Ramon (Maria) del

Pendennis, Arthur Esquir
See Thackeray, William Makepeace

Penn, William 1644-1718 **LC 25**
See also DLB 24

PEPECE
See Prado (Calvo), Pedro

Pepys, Samuel 1633-1703 **LC 11; DA; DAB;
DAC; DAM MST; WLC**
See also CDBLB 1660-1789; DLB 101

Percy, Walker 1916-1990 **CLC 2, 3, 6, 8, 14, 18,
47, 65; DAM NOV, POP**
See also CA 1-4R; 131; CANR 1, 23, 64; DLB
2; DLBY 80, 90; MTCW

Perec, Georges 1936-1982 **CLC 56**
See also CA 141; DLB 83

Pereda (y Sanchez de Porrua), Jose Maria de
1833-1906 **TCLC 16**
See also CA 117

Pereda y Porrua, Jose Maria de
See Pereda (y Sanchez de Porrua), Jose Maria
de

Peregoy, George Weems
See Mencken, H(enry) L(ouis)

Perelman, S(idney) J(oseph) 1904-1979 **CLC
3, 5, 9, 15, 23, 44, 49; DAM DRAM**
See also AITN 1, 2; CA 73-76; 89-92; CANR
18; DLB 11, 44; MTCW

Peret, Benjamin 1899-1959 **TCLC 20**
See also CA 117

Peretz, Isaac Loeb 1851(?)-1915 **TCLC 16;
SSC 26**
See also CA 109

Peretz, Yitzkhok Leibush
See Peretz, Isaac Loeb

Perez Galdos, Benito 1843-1920 **TCLC 27**
See also CA 125; 153; HW

Perrault, Charles 1628-1703 **LC 2**
See also MAICYA; SATA 25

Perry, Brighton
See Sherwood, Robert E(mmet)

Perse, St.-John
See Leger, (Marie-Rene Auguste) Alexis Saint-
Leger

Perutz, Leo 1882-1957 **TCLC 60**
See also DLB 81

Peseenz, Tulio F.
See Lopez y Fuentes, Gregorio

Pesetsky, Bette 1932- **CLC 28**
See also CA 133; DLB 130

Peshkov, Alexei Maximovich 1868-1936

See Gorky, Maxim
See also CA 105; 141; DA; DAC; DAM DRAM,
MST, NOV

Pessoa, Fernando (Antonio Nogueira) 1898-
1935 **TCLC 27; HLC; PC 20**
See also CA 125

Peterkin, Julia Mood 1880-1961 **CLC 31**
See also CA 102; DLB 9

Peters, Joan K(aren) 1945- **CLC 39**
See also CA 158

Peters, Robert L(ouis) 1924- **CLC 7**
See also CA 13-16R; CAAS 8; DLB 105

Petofi, Sandor 1823-1849 **NCLC 21**

Petrakis, Harry Mark 1923- **CLC 3**
See also CA 9-12R; CANR 4, 30

Petrarch 1304-1374 **CMLC 20; DAM POET;
PC 8**

Petrov, Evgeny **TCLC 21**
See also Kataev, Evgeny Petrovich

Petry, Ann (Lane) 1908-1997 **CLC 1, 7, 18**
See also BW 1; CA 5-8R; 157; CAAS 6; CANR
4, 46; CLR 12; DLB 76; JRDA; MAICYA;
MTCW; SATA 5; SATA-Obit 94

Petursson, Halligrimur 1614-1674 **LC 8**

Phaedrus 18(?)B.C.-55(?) **CMLC 25**

Philips, Katherine 1632-1664 **LC 30**
See also DLB 131

Philipson, Morris H. 1926- **CLC 53**
See also CA 1-4R; CANR 4

Phillips, Caryl 1958- **CLC 96; BLCS; DAM
MULT**
See also BW 2; CA 141; CANR 63; DLB 157

Phillips, David Graham 1867-1911 **TCLC 44**
See also CA 108; DLB 9, 12

Phillips, Jack
See Sandburg, Carl (August)

Phillips, Jayne Anne 1952- **CLC 15, 33; SSC 16**
See also CA 101; CANR 24, 50; DLBY 80; INT
CANR-24; MTCW

Phillips, Richard
See Dick, Philip K(indred)

Phillips, Robert (Schaeffer) 1938- **CLC 28**
See also CA 17-20R; CAAS 13; CANR 8; DLB
105

Phillips, Ward
See Lovecraft, H(oward) P(hillips)

Piccolo, Lucio 1901-1969 **CLC 13**
See also CA 97-100; DLB 114

Pickthall, Marjorie L(owry) C(hristie) 1883-
1922 **TCLC 21**
See also CA 107; DLB 92

Pico della Mirandola, Giovanni 1463-1494 **LC
15**

Piercy, Marge 1936- **CLC 3, 6, 14, 18, 27, 62**
See also CA 21-24R; CAAS 1; CANR 13, 43,
66; DLB 120; MTCW

Piers, Robert
See Anthony, Piers

Pieyre de Mandiargues, Andre 1909-1991
See Mandiargues, Andre Pieyre de
See also CA 103; 136; CANR 22

Pilnyak, Boris **TCLC 23**
See also Vogau, Boris Andreyevich

Pincherle, Alberto 1907-1990 **CLC 11, 18;
DAM NOV**
See also Moravia, Alberto
See also CA 25-28R; 132; CANR 33, 63;
MTCW

Pinckney, Darryl 1953- **CLC 76**
See also BW 2; CA 143

Pindar 518B.C.-446B.C. **CMLC 12; PC 19**
See also DLB 176

Pineda, Cecile 1942- **CLC 39**

See also CA 118
Pinero, Arthur Wing 1855-1934   **TCLC 32;
DAM DRAM**
See also CA 110; 153; DLB 10
Pinero, Miguel (Antonio Gomez) 1946-1988
CLC 4, 55
See also CA 61-64; 125; CANR 29; HW
Pinget, Robert 1919-1997   **CLC 7, 13, 37**
See also CA 85-88; 160; DLB 83
Pink Floyd
See Barrett, (Roger) Syd; Gilmour, David; Mason, Nick; Waters, Roger; Wright, Rick
Pinkney, Edward 1802-1828   **NCLC 31**
Pinkwater, Daniel Manus 1941-   **CLC 35**
See also Pinkwater, Manus
See also AAYA 1; CA 29-32R; CANR 12, 38;
CLR 4; JRDA; MAICYA; SAAS 3; SATA 46,
76
Pinkwater, Manus
See Pinkwater, Daniel Manus
See also SATA 8
Pinsky, Robert 1940-**CLC 9, 19, 38, 94; DAM
POET**
See also CA 29-32R; CAAS 4; CANR 58;
DLBY 82
Pinta, Harold
See Pinter, Harold
Pinter, Harold 1930-**CLC 1, 3, 6, 9, 11, 15, 27,
58, 73; DA; DAB; DAC; DAM DRAM,
MST; WLC**
See also CA 5-8R; CANR 33, 65; CDBLB 1960
to Present; DLB 13; MTCW
Piozzi, Hester Lynch (Thrale) 1741-1821
NCLC 57
See also DLB 104, 142
Pirandello, Luigi 1867-1936**TCLC 4, 29; DA;
DAB; DAC; DAM DRAM, MST; DC 5;
SSC 22; WLC**
See also CA 104; 153
Pirsig, Robert M(aynard) 1928-**CLC 4, 6, 73;
DAM POP**
See also CA 53-56; CANR 42; MTCW; SATA
39
Pisarev, Dmitry Ivanovich 1840-1868   **NCLC
25**
Pix, Mary (Griffith) 1666-1709   **LC 8**
See also DLB 80
Pixerecourt, (Rene Charles) Guilbert de 1773-
1844 **NCLC 39**
See also DLB 192
Plaatje, Sol(omon) T(shekisho) 1876-1932
TCLC 73; BLCS
See also BW 2; CA 141
Plaidy, Jean
See Hibbert, Eleanor Alice Burford
Planche, James Robinson 1796-1880**NCLC 42**
Plant, Robert 1948-   **CLC 12**
Plante, David (Robert) 1940-   **CLC 7, 23, 38;
DAM NOV**
See also CA 37-40R; CANR 12, 36, 58; DLBY
83; INT CANR-12; MTCW
Plath, Sylvia 1932-1963   **CLC 1, 2, 3, 5, 9, 11,
14, 17, 50, 51, 62, 111; DA; DAB; DAC;
DAM MST, POET; PC 1; WLC**
See also AAYA 13; CA 19-20; CANR 34; CAP
2; CDALB 1941-1968; DLB 5, 6, 152;
MTCW; SATA 96
Plato 428(?)B.C.-348(?)B.C.   **CMLC 8; DA;
DAB; DAC; DAM MST; WLCS**
See also DLB 176
Platonov, Andrei   **TCLC 14**
See also Klimentov, Andrei Platonovich
Platt, Kin 1911-   **CLC 26**

See also AAYA 11; CA 17-20R; CANR 11;
JRDA; SAAS 17; SATA 21, 86
Plautus c. 251B.C.-184B.C.   **CMLC 24; DC 6**
Plick et Plock
See Simenon, Georges (Jacques Christian)
Plimpton, George (Ames) 1927-   **CLC 36**
See also AITN 1; CA 21-24R; CANR 32; DLB
185; MTCW; SATA 10
Pliny the Elder c. 23-79   **CMLC 23**
Plomer, William Charles Franklin 1903-1973
CLC 4, 8
See also CA 21-22; CANR 34; CAP 2; DLB
20, 162, 191; MTCW; SATA 24
Plowman, Piers
See Kavanagh, Patrick (Joseph)
Plum, J.
See Wodehouse, P(elham) G(renville)
Plumly, Stanley (Ross) 1939-   **CLC 33**
See also CA 108; 110; DLB 5, 193; INT 110
Plumpe, Friedrich Wilhelm 1888-1931 **TCLC
53**
See also CA 112
Po Chu-i 772-846   **CMLC 24**
Poe, Edgar Allan 1809-1849 **NCLC 1, 16, 55;
DA; DAB; DAC; DAM MST, POET; PC
1; SSC 1, 22; WLC**
See also AAYA 14; CDALB 1640-1865; DLB
3, 59, 73, 74; SATA 23
Poet of Titchfield Street, The
See Pound, Ezra (Weston Loomis)
Pohl, Frederik 1919-   **CLC 18; SSC 25**
See also AAYA 24; CA 61-64; CAAS 1; CANR
11, 37; DLB 8; INT CANR-11; MTCW;
SATA 24
Poirier, Louis 1910-
See Gracq, Julien
See also CA 122; 126
Poitier, Sidney 1927-   **CLC 26**
See also BW 1; CA 117
Polanski, Roman 1933-   **CLC 16**
See also CA 77-80
Poliakoff, Stephen 1952-   **CLC 38**
See also CA 106; DLB 13
Police, The
See Copeland, Stewart (Armstrong); Summers,
Andrew James; Sumner, Gordon Matthew
Polidori, John William 1795-1821   **NCLC 51**
See also DLB 116
Pollitt, Katha 1949-   **CLC 28**
See also CA 120; 122; CANR 66; MTCW
Pollock, (Mary) Sharon 1936- **CLC 50; DAC;
DAM DRAM, MST**
See also CA 141; DLB 60
Polo, Marco 1254-1324   **CMLC 15**
Polonsky, Abraham (Lincoln) 1910-   **CLC 92**
See also CA 104; DLB 26; INT 104
Polybius c. 200B.C.-c. 118B.C.   **CMLC 17**
See also DLB 176
Pomerance, Bernard 1940-   **CLC 13; DAM
DRAM**
See also CA 101; CANR 49
Ponge, Francis (Jean Gaston Alfred) 1899-1988
CLC 6, 18; DAM POET
See also CA 85-88; 126; CANR 40
Pontoppidan, Henrik 1857-1943   **TCLC 29**
Poole, Josephine   **CLC 17**
See also Helyar, Jane Penelope Josephine
See also SAAS 2; SATA 5
Popa, Vasko 1922-1991   **CLC 19**
See also CA 112; 148; DLB 181
Pope, Alexander 1688-1744   **LC 3; DA; DAB;
DAC; DAM MST, POET; WLC**
See also CDBLB 1660-1789; DLB 95, 101

Porter, Connie (Rose) 1959(?)-   **CLC 70**
See also BW 2; CA 142; SATA 81
Porter, Gene(va Grace) Stratton 1863(?)-1924
TCLC 21
See also CA 112
Porter, Katherine Anne 1890-1980**CLC 1, 3, 7,
10, 13, 15, 27, 101; DA; DAB; DAC; DAM
MST, NOV; SSC 4, 31**
See also AITN 2; CA 1-4R; 101; CANR 1, 65;
DLB 4, 9, 102; DLBD 12; DLBY 80;
MTCW; SATA 39; SATA-Obit 23
Porter, Peter (Neville Frederick) 1929-**CLC 5,
13, 33**
See also CA 85-88; DLB 40
Porter, William Sydney 1862-1910
See Henry, O.
See also CA 104; 131; CDALB 1865-1917; DA;
DAB; DAC; DAM MST; DLB 12, 78, 79;
MTCW; YABC 2
Portillo (y Pacheco), Jose Lopez
See Lopez Portillo (y Pacheco), Jose
Post, Melville Davisson 1869-1930   **TCLC 39**
See also CA 110
Potok, Chaim 1929-   **CLC 2, 7, 14, 26, 112;
DAM NOV**
See also AAYA 15; AITN 1, 2; CA 17-20R;
CANR 19, 35, 64; DLB 28, 152; INT CANR-
19; MTCW; SATA 33
Potter, (Helen) Beatrix 1866-1943
See Webb, (Martha) Beatrice (Potter)
See also MAICYA
Potter, Dennis (Christopher George) 1935-1994
CLC 58, 86
See also CA 107; 145; CANR 33, 61; MTCW
Pound, Ezra (Weston Loomis) 1885-1972**CLC
1, 2, 3, 4, 5, 7, 10, 13, 18, 34, 48, 50, 112;
DA; DAB; DAC; DAM MST, POET; PC
4; WLC**
See also CA 5-8R; 37-40R; CANR 40; CDALB
1917-1929; DLB 4, 45, 63; DLBD 15;
MTCW
Povod, Reinaldo 1959-1994   **CLC 44**
See also CA 136; 146
Powell, Adam Clayton, Jr. 1908-1972**CLC 89;
BLC 3; DAM MULT**
See also BW 1; CA 102; 33-36R
Powell, Anthony (Dymoke) 1905-**CLC 1, 3, 7,
9, 10, 31**
See also CA 1-4R; CANR 1, 32, 62; CDBLB
1945-1960; DLB 15; MTCW
Powell, Dawn 1897-1965   **CLC 66**
See also CA 5-8R; DLBY 97
Powell, Padgett 1952-   **CLC 34**
See also CA 126; CANR 63
Power, Susan 1961-   **CLC 91**
Powers, J(ames) F(arl) 1917- **CLC 1, 4, 8, 57;
SSC 4**
See also CA 1-4R; CANR 2, 61; DLB 130;
MTCW
Powers, John J(ames) 1945-
See Powers, John R.
See also CA 69-72
Powers, John R.   **CLC 66**
See also Powers, John J(ames)
Powers, Richard (S.) 1957-   **CLC 93**
See also CA 148
Pownall, David 1938-   **CLC 10**
See also CA 89-92; CAAS 18; CANR 49; DLB
14
Powys, John Cowper 1872-1963**CLC 7, 9, 15,
46**
See also CA 85-88; DLB 15; MTCW
Powys, T(heodore) F(rancis) 1875-1953

TCLC 9
See also CA 106; DLB 36, 162

Prado (Calvo), Pedro 1886-1952　　**TCLC 75**
See also CA 131; HW

Prager, Emily 1952-　　**CLC 56**

Pratt, E(dwin) J(ohn) 1883(?)-1964　**CLC 19; DAC; DAM POET**
See also CA 141; 93-96; DLB 92

Premchand　　**TCLC 21**
See also Srivastava, Dhanpat Rai

Preussler, Otfried 1923-　　**CLC 17**
See also CA 77-80; SATA 24

Prevert, Jacques (Henri Marie) 1900-1977
CLC 15
See also CA 77-80; 69-72; CANR 29, 61; MTCW; SATA-Obit 30

Prevost, Abbe (Antoine Francois) 1697-1763
LC 1

Price, (Edward) Reynolds 1933-**CLC 3, 6, 13, 43, 50, 63; DAM NOV; SSC 22**
See also CA 1-4R; CANR 1, 37, 57; DLB 2; INT CANR-37

Price, Richard 1949-　　**CLC 6, 12**
See also CA 49-52; CANR 3; DLBY 81

Prichard, Katharine Susannah 1883-1969
CLC 46
See also CA 11-12; CANR 33; CAP 1; MTCW; SATA 66

Priestley, J(ohn) B(oynton) 1894-1984 **CLC 2, 5, 9, 34; DAM DRAM, NOV**
See also CA 9-12R; 113; CANR 33; CDBLB 1914-1945; DLB 10, 34, 77, 100, 139; DLBY 84; MTCW

Prince 1958(?)-　　**CLC 35**

Prince, F(rank) T(empleton) 1912-　**CLC 22**
See also CA 101; CANR 43; DLB 20

Prince Kropotkin
See Kropotkin, Peter (Alekseievich)

Prior, Matthew 1664-1721　　**LC 4**
See also DLB 95

Prishvin, Mikhail 1873-1954　　**TCLC 75**

Pritchard, William H(arrison) 1932- **CLC 34**
See also CA 65-68; CANR 23; DLB 111

Pritchett, V(ictor) S(awdon) 1900-1997 **CLC 5, 13, 15, 41; DAM NOV; SSC 14**
See also CA 61-64; 157; CANR 31, 63; DLB 15, 139; MTCW

Private 19022
See Manning, Frederic

Probst, Mark 1925-　　**CLC 59**
See also CA 130

Prokosch, Frederic 1908-1989　　**CLC 4, 48**
See also CA 73-76; 128; DLB 48

Prophet, The
See Dreiser, Theodore (Herman Albert)

Prose, Francine 1947-　　**CLC 45**
See also CA 109; 112; CANR 46

Proudhon
See Cunha, Euclides (Rodrigues Pimenta) da

Proulx, Annie
See Proulx, E(dna) Annie

Proulx, E(dna) Annie 1935-　　**CLC 81; DAM POP**
See also CA 145; CANR 65

Proust, (Valentin-Louis-George-Eugene-) Marcel 1871-1922 **TCLC 7, 13, 33; DA; DAB; DAC; DAM MST, NOV; WLC**
See also CA 104; 120; DLB 65; MTCW

Prowler, Harley
See Masters, Edgar Lee

Prus, Boleslaw 1845-1912　　**TCLC 48**

Pryor, Richard (Franklin Lenox Thomas) 1940-
CLC 26

See also CA 122

Przybyszewski, Stanislaw 1868-1927**TCLC 36**
See also CA 160; DLB 66

Pteleon
See Grieve, C(hristopher) M(urray)
See also DAM POET

Puckett, Lute
See Masters, Edgar Lee

Puig, Manuel 1932-1990 **CLC 3, 5, 10, 28, 65; DAM MULT; HLC**
See also CA 45-48; CANR 2, 32, 63; DLB 113; HW; MTCW

Pulitzer, Joseph 1847-1911　　**TCLC 76**
See also CA 114; DLB 23

Purdy, A(lfred) W(ellington) 1918- **CLC 3, 6, 14, 50; DAC; DAM MST, POET**
See also CA 81-84; CAAS 17; CANR 42, 66; DLB 88

Purdy, James (Amos) 1923- **CLC 2, 4, 10, 28, 52**
See also CA 33-36R; CAAS 1; CANR 19, 51; DLB 2; INT CANR-19; MTCW

Pure, Simon
See Swinnerton, Frank Arthur

Pushkin, Alexander (Sergeyevich) 1799-1837
NCLC 3, 27; DA; DAB; DAC; DAM DRAM, MST, POET; PC 10; SSC 27; WLC
See also SATA 61

P'u Sung-ling 1640-1715　　**LC 3; SSC 31**

Putnam, Arthur Lee
See Alger, Horatio, Jr.

Puzo, Mario 1920-**CLC 1, 2, 6, 36, 107; DAM NOV, POP**
See also CA 65-68; CANR 4, 42, 65; DLB 6; MTCW

Pygge, Edward
See Barnes, Julian (Patrick)

Pyle, Ernest Taylor 1900-1945
See Pyle, Ernie
See also CA 115; 160

Pyle, Ernie 1900-1945　　**TCLC 75**
See also Pyle, Ernest Taylor
See also DLB 29

Pyle, Howard 1853-1911　　**TCLC 81**
See also CA 109; 137; CLR 22; DLB 42, 188; DLBD 13; MAICYA; SATA 16

Pym, Barbara (Mary Crampton) 1913-1980
CLC 13, 19, 37, 111
See also CA 13-14; 97-100; CANR 13, 34; CAP 1; DLB 14; DLBY 87; MTCW

Pynchon, Thomas (Ruggles, Jr.) 1937-**CLC 2, 3, 6, 9, 11, 18, 33, 62, 72; DA; DAB; DAC; DAM MST, NOV, POP; SSC 14; WLC**
See also BEST 90:2; CA 17-20R; CANR 22, 46; DLB 2, 173; MTCW

Pythagoras c. 570B.C.-c. 500B.C.　　**CMLC 22**
See also DLB 176

Q
See Quiller-Couch, SirArthur (Thomas)

Qian Zhongshu
See Ch'ien Chung-shu

Qroll
See Dagerman, Stig (Halvard)

Quarrington, Paul (Lewis) 1953-　　**CLC 65**
See also CA 129; CANR 62

Quasimodo, Salvatore 1901-1968　　**CLC 10**
See also CA 13-16; 25-28R; CAP 1; DLB 114; MTCW

Quay, Stephen 1947-　　**CLC 95**

Quay, Timothy 1947-　　**CLC 95**

Queen, Ellery　　**CLC 3, 11**
See also Dannay, Frederic; Davidson, Avram; Lee, Manfred B(ennington); Marlowe, Stephen; Sturgeon, Theodore (Hamilton); Vance, John Holbrook

Queen, Ellery, Jr.
See Dannay, Frederic; Lee, Manfred B(ennington)

Queneau, Raymond 1903-1976　　**CLC 2, 5, 10, 42**
See also CA 77-80; 69-72; CANR 32; DLB 72; MTCW

Quevedo, Francisco de 1580-1645　　**LC 23**

Quiller-Couch, SirArthur (Thomas) 1863-1944
TCLC 53
See also CA 118; 166; DLB 135, 153, 190

Quin, Ann (Marie) 1936-1973　　**CLC 6**
See also CA 9-12R; 45-48; DLB 14

Quinn, Martin
See Smith, Martin Cruz

Quinn, Peter 1947-　　**CLC 91**

Quinn, Simon
See Smith, Martin Cruz

Quiroga, Horacio (Sylvestre) 1878-1937
TCLC 20; DAM MULT; HLC
See also CA 117; 131; HW; MTCW

Quoirez, Francoise 1935-　　**CLC 9**
See also Sagan, Francoise
See also CA 49-52; CANR 6, 39; MTCW

Raabe, Wilhelm 1831-1910　　**TCLC 45**
See also DLB 129

Rabe, David (William) 1940-　　**CLC 4, 8, 33; DAM DRAM**
See also CA 85-88; CABS 3; CANR 59; DLB 7

Rabelais, Francois 1483-1553**LC 5; DA; DAB; DAC; DAM MST; WLC**

Rabinovitch, Sholem 1859-1916
See Aleichem, Sholom
See also CA 104

Rachilde 1860-1953　　**TCLC 67**
See also DLB 123, 192

Racine, Jean 1639-1699　　**LC 28; DAB; DAM MST**

Radcliffe, Ann (Ward) 1764-1823**NCLC 6, 55**
See also DLB 39, 178

Radiguet, Raymond 1903-1923　　**TCLC 29**
See also CA 162; DLB 65

Radnoti, Miklos 1909-1944　　**TCLC 16**
See also CA 118

Rado, James 1939-　　**CLC 17**
See also CA 105

Radvanyi, Netty 1900-1983
See Seghers, Anna
See also CA 85-88; 110

Rae, Ben
See Griffiths, Trevor

Raeburn, John (Hay) 1941-　　**CLC 34**
See also CA 57-60

Ragni, Gerome 1942-1991　　**CLC 17**
See also CA 105; 134

Rahv, Philip 1908-1973　　**CLC 24**
See also Greenberg, Ivan
See also DLB 137

Raimund, Ferdinand Jakob 1790-1836 **NCLC 69**
See also DLB 90

Raine, Craig 1944-　　**CLC 32, 103**
See also CA 108; CANR 29, 51; DLB 40

Raine, Kathleen (Jessie) 1908-　　**CLC 7, 45**
See also CA 85-88; CANR 46; DLB 20; MTCW

Rainis, Janis 1865-1929　　**TCLC 29**

Rakosi, Carl 1903-　　**CLC 47**
See also Rawley, Callman
See also CAAS 5; DLB 193

Raleigh, Richard

See Lovecraft, H(oward) P(hillips)
Raleigh, Sir Walter 1554(?)-1618 **LC 31, 39**
See also CDBLB Before 1660; DLB 172
Rallentando, H. P.
See Sayers, Dorothy L(eigh)
Ramal, Walter
See de la Mare, Walter (John)
Ramon, Juan
See Jimenez (Mantecon), Juan Ramon
Ramos, Graciliano 1892-1953 **TCLC 32**
Rampersad, Arnold 1941- **CLC 44**
See also BW 2; CA 127; 133; DLB 111; INT 133
Rampling, Anne
See Rice, Anne
Ramsay, Allan 1684(?)-1758 **LC 29**
See also DLB 95
Ramuz, Charles-Ferdinand 1878-1947 **TCLC 33**
See also CA 165
Rand, Ayn 1905-1982 **CLC 3, 30, 44, 79; DA; DAC; DAM MST, NOV, POP; WLC**
See also AAYA 10; CA 13-16R; 105; CANR 27; MTCW
Randall, Dudley (Felker) 1914-**CLC 1; BLC 3; DAM MULT**
See also BW 1; CA 25-28R; CANR 23; DLB 41
Randall, Robert
See Silverberg, Robert
Ranger, Ken
See Creasey, John
Ransom, John Crowe 1888-1974 **CLC 2, 4, 5, 11, 24; DAM POET**
See also CA 5-8R; 49-52; CANR 6, 34; DLB 45, 63; MTCW
Rao, Raja 1909- **CLC 25, 56; DAM NOV**
See also CA 73-76; CANR 51; MTCW
Raphael, Frederic (Michael) 1931- **CLC 2, 14**
See also CA 1-4R; CANR 1; DLB 14
Ratcliffe, James P.
See Mencken, H(enry) L(ouis)
Rathbone, Julian 1935- **CLC 41**
See also CA 101; CANR 34
Rattigan, Terence (Mervyn) 1911-1977**CLC 7; DAM DRAM**
See also CA 85-88; 73-76; CDBLB 1945-1960; DLB 13; MTCW
Ratushinskaya, Irina 1954- **CLC 54**
See also CA 129; CANR 68
Raven, Simon (Arthur Noel) 1927- **CLC 14**
See also CA 81-84
Ravenna, Michael
See Welty, Eudora
Rawley, Callman 1903-
See Rakosi, Carl
See also CA 21-24R; CANR 12, 32
Rawlings, Marjorie Kinnan 1896-1953 **TCLC 4**
See also AAYA 20; CA 104; 137; DLB 9, 22, 102; JRDA; MAICYA; YABC 1
Ray, Satyajit 1921-1992 **CLC 16, 76; DAM MULT**
See also CA 114; 137
Read, Herbert Edward 1893-1968 **CLC 4**
See also CA 85-88; 25-28R; DLB 20, 149
Read, Piers Paul 1941- **CLC 4, 10, 25**
See also CA 21-24R; CANR 38; DLB 14; SATA 21
Reade, Charles 1814-1884 **NCLC 2**
See also DLB 21
Reade, Hamish
See Gray, Simon (James Holliday)

Reading, Peter 1946- **CLC 47**
See also CA 103; CANR 46; DLB 40
Reaney, James 1926- **CLC 13; DAC; DAM MST**
See also CA 41-44R; CAAS 15; CANR 42; DLB 68; SATA 43
Rebreanu, Liviu 1885-1944 **TCLC 28**
See also CA 165
Rechy, John (Francisco) 1934- **CLC 1, 7, 14, 18, 107; DAM MULT; HLC**
See also CA 5-8R; CAAS 4; CANR 6, 32, 64; DLB 122; DLBY 82; HW; INT CANR-6
Redcam, Tom 1870-1933 **TCLC 25**
Reddin, Keith **CLC 67**
Redgrove, Peter (William) 1932- **CLC 6, 41**
See also CA 1-4R; CANR 3, 39; DLB 40
Redmon, Anne **CLC 22**
See Nightingale, Anne Redmon
See also DLBY 86
Reed, Eliot
See Ambler, Eric
Reed, Ishmael 1938-**CLC 2, 3, 5, 6, 13, 32, 60; BLC 3; DAM MULT**
See also BW 2; CA 21-24R; CANR 25, 48; DLB 2, 5, 33, 169; DLBD 8; MTCW
Reed, John (Silas) 1887-1920 **TCLC 9**
See also CA 106
Reed, Lou **CLC 21**
See also Firbank, Louis
Reeve, Clara 1729-1807 **NCLC 19**
See also DLB 39
Reich, Wilhelm 1897-1957 **TCLC 57**
Reid, Christopher (John) 1949- **CLC 33**
See also CA 140; DLB 40
Reid, Desmond
See Moorcock, Michael (John)
Reid Banks, Lynne 1929-
See Banks, Lynne Reid
See also CA 1-4R; CANR 6, 22, 38; CLR 24; JRDA; MAICYA; SATA 22, 75
Reilly, William K.
See Creasey, John
Reiner, Max
See Caldwell, (Janet Miriam) Taylor (Holland)
Reis, Ricardo
See Pessoa, Fernando (Antonio Nogueira)
Remarque, Erich Maria 1898-1970 **CLC 21; DA; DAB; DAC; DAM MST, NOV**
See also CA 77-80; 29-32R; DLB 56; MTCW
Remizov, A.
See Remizov, Aleksei (Mikhailovich)
Remizov, A. M.
See Remizov, Aleksei (Mikhailovich)
Remizov, Aleksei (Mikhailovich) 1877-1957 **TCLC 27**
See also CA 125; 133
Renan, Joseph Ernest 1823-1892 **NCLC 26**
Renard, Jules 1864-1910 **TCLC 17**
See also CA 117
Renault, Mary **CLC 3, 11, 17**
See also Challans, Mary
See also DLBY 83
Rendell, Ruth (Barbara) 1930- **CLC 28, 48; DAM POP**
See also Vine, Barbara
See also CA 109; CANR 32, 52; DLB 87; INT CANR-32; MTCW
Renoir, Jean 1894-1979 **CLC 20**
See also CA 129; 85-88
Resnais, Alain 1922- **CLC 16**
Reverdy, Pierre 1889-1960 **CLC 53**
See also CA 97-100; 89-92
Rexroth, Kenneth 1905-1982 **CLC 1, 2, 6, 11,**

22, 49, 112; **DAM POET; PC 20**
See also CA 5-8R; 107; CANR 14, 34, 63; CDALB 1941-1968; DLB 16, 48, 165; DLBY 82; INT CANR-14; MTCW
Reyes, Alfonso 1889-1959 **TCLC 33**
See also CA 131; HW
Reyes y Basoalto, Ricardo Eliecer Neftali
See Neruda, Pablo
Reymont, Wladyslaw (Stanislaw) 1868(?)-1925 **TCLC 5**
See also CA 104
Reynolds, Jonathan 1942- **CLC 6, 38**
See also CA 65-68; CANR 28
Reynolds, Joshua 1723-1792 **LC 15**
See also DLB 104
Reynolds, Michael Shane 1937- **CLC 44**
See also CA 65-68; CANR 9
Reznikoff, Charles 1894-1976 **CLC 9**
See also CA 33-36; 61-64; CAP 2; DLB 28, 45
Rezzori (d'Arezzo), Gregor von 1914-**CLC 25**
See also CA 122; 136
Rhine, Richard
See Silverstein, Alvin
Rhodes, Eugene Manlove 1869-1934**TCLC 53**
Rhodius, Apollonius c. 3rd cent. B.C.- **CMLC 28**
See also DLB 176
R'hoone
See Balzac, Honore de
Rhys, Jean 1890(?)-1979 **CLC 2, 4, 6, 14, 19, 51; DAM NOV; SSC 21**
See also CA 25-28R; 85-88; CANR 35, 62; CDBLB 1945-1960; DLB 36, 117, 162; MTCW
Ribeiro, Darcy 1922-1997 **CLC 34**
See also CA 33-36R; 156
Ribeiro, Joao Ubaldo (Osorio Pimentel) 1941- **CLC 10, 67**
See also CA 81-84
Ribman, Ronald (Burt) 1932- **CLC 7**
See also CA 21-24R; CANR 46
Ricci, Nino 1959- **CLC 70**
See also CA 137
Rice, Anne 1941- **CLC 41; DAM POP**
See also AAYA 9; BEST 89:2; CA 65-68; CANR 12, 36, 53
Rice, Elmer (Leopold) 1892-1967 **CLC 7, 49; DAM DRAM**
See also CA 21-22; 25-28R; CAP 2; DLB 4, 7; MTCW
Rice, Tim(othy Miles Bindon) 1944- **CLC 21**
See also CA 103; CANR 46
Rich, Adrienne (Cecile) 1929-**CLC 3, 6, 7, 11, 18, 36, 73, 76; DAM POET; PC 5**
See also CA 9-12R; CANR 20, 53; DLB 5, 67; MTCW
Rich, Barbara
See Graves, Robert (von Ranke)
Rich, Robert
See Trumbo, Dalton
Richard, Keith **CLC 17**
See also Richards, Keith
Richards, David Adams 1950- **CLC 59; DAC**
See also CA 93-96; CANR 60; DLB 53
Richards, I(vor) A(rmstrong) 1893-1979 **CLC 14, 24**
See also CA 41-44R; 89-92; CANR 34; DLB 27
Richards, Keith 1943-
See Richard, Keith
See also CA 107
Richardson, Anne
See Roiphe, Anne (Richardson)

Richardson, Dorothy Miller 1873-1957 **TCLC 3**
See also CA 104; DLB 36

Richardson, Ethel Florence (Lindesay) 1870-1946
See Richardson, Henry Handel
See also CA 105

Richardson, Henry Handel **TCLC 4**
See also Richardson, Ethel Florence (Lindesay)
See also DLB 197

Richardson, John 1796-1852 **NCLC 55; DAC**
See also DLB 99

Richardson, Samuel 1689-1761 **LC 1, 44; DA; DAB; DAC; DAM MST, NOV; WLC**
See also CDBLB 1660-1789; DLB 39

Richler, Mordecai 1931- **CLC 3, 5, 9, 13, 18, 46, 70; DAC; DAM MST, NOV**
See also AITN 1; CA 65-68; CANR 31, 62; CLR 17; DLB 53; MAICYA; MTCW; SATA 44, 98; SATA-Brief 27

Richter, Conrad (Michael) 1890-1968 **CLC 30**
See also AAYA 21; CA 5-8R; 25-28R; CANR 23; DLB 9; MTCW; SATA 3

Ricostranza, Tom
See Ellis, Trey

Riddell, Charlotte 1832-1906 **TCLC 40**
See also CA 165; DLB 156

Riding, Laura **CLC 3, 7**
See also Jackson, Laura (Riding)

Riefenstahl, Berta Helene Amalia 1902-
See Riefenstahl, Leni
See also CA 108

Riefenstahl, Leni **CLC 16**
See also Riefenstahl, Berta Helene Amalia

Riffe, Ernest
See Bergman, (Ernst) Ingmar

Riggs, (Rolla) Lynn 1899-1954 **TCLC 56; DAM MULT**
See also CA 144; DLB 175; NNAL

Riis, Jacob A(ugust) 1849-1914 **TCLC 80**
See also CA 113; DLB 23

Riley, James Whitcomb 1849-1916 **TCLC 51; DAM POET**
See also CA 118; 137; MAICYA; SATA 17

Riley, Tex
See Creasey, John

Rilke, Rainer Maria 1875-1926 **TCLC 1, 6, 19; DAM POET; PC 2**
See also CA 104; 132; CANR 62; DLB 81; MTCW

Rimbaud, (Jean Nicolas) Arthur 1854-1891 **NCLC 4, 35; DA; DAB; DAC; DAM MST, POET; PC 3; WLC**

Rinehart, Mary Roberts 1876-1958 **TCLC 52**
See also CA 108; 166

Ringmaster, The
See Mencken, H(enry) L(ouis)

Ringwood, Gwen(dolyn Margaret) Pharis 1910-1984 **CLC 48**
See also CA 148; 112; DLB 88

Rio, Michel 19(?)- **CLC 43**

Ritsos, Giannes
See Ritsos, Yannis

Ritsos, Yannis 1909-1990 **CLC 6, 13, 31**
See also CA 77-80; 133; CANR 39, 61; MTCW

Ritter, Erika 1948(?)- **CLC 52**

Rivera, Jose Eustasio 1889-1928 **TCLC 35**
See also CA 162; HW

Rivers, Conrad Kent 1933-1968 **CLC 1**
See also BW 1; CA 85-88; DLB 41

Rivers, Elfrida
See Bradley, Marion Zimmer

Riverside, John

See Heinlein, Robert A(nson)

Rizal, Jose 1861-1896 **NCLC 27**

Roa Bastos, Augusto (Antonio) 1917- **CLC 45; DAM MULT; HLC**
See also CA 131; DLB 113; HW

Robbe-Grillet, Alain 1922- **CLC 1, 2, 4, 6, 8, 10, 14, 43**
See also CA 9-12R; CANR 33, 65; DLB 83; MTCW

Robbins, Harold 1916-1997 **CLC 5; DAM NOV**
See also CA 73-76; 162; CANR 26, 54; MTCW

Robbins, Thomas Eugene 1936-
See Robbins, Tom
See also CA 81-84; CANR 29, 59; DAM NOV, POP; MTCW

Robbins, Tom **CLC 9, 32, 64**
See also Robbins, Thomas Eugene
See also BEST 90:3; DLBY 80

Robbins, Trina 1938- **CLC 21**
See also CA 128

Roberts, Charles G(eorge) D(ouglas) 1860-1943 **TCLC 8**
See also CA 105; CLR 33; DLB 92; SATA 88; SATA-Brief 29

Roberts, Elizabeth Madox 1886-1941 **TCLC 68**
See also CA 111; 166; DLB 9, 54, 102; SATA 33; SATA-Brief 27

Roberts, Kate 1891-1985 **CLC 15**
See also CA 107; 116

Roberts, Keith (John Kingston) 1935- **CLC 14**
See also CA 25-28R; CANR 46

Roberts, Kenneth (Lewis) 1885-1957 **TCLC 23**
See also CA 109; DLB 9

Roberts, Michele (B.) 1949- **CLC 48**
See also CA 115; CANR 58

Robertson, Ellis
See Ellison, Harlan (Jay); Silverberg, Robert

Robertson, Thomas William 1829-1871 **NCLC 35; DAM DRAM**

Robeson, Kenneth
See Dent, Lester

Robinson, Edwin Arlington 1869-1935 **TCLC 5; DA; DAC; DAM MST, POET; PC 1**
See also CA 104; 133; CDALB 1865-1917; DLB 54; MTCW

Robinson, Henry Crabb 1775-1867 **NCLC 15**
See also DLB 107

Robinson, Jill 1936- **CLC 10**
See also CA 102; INT 102

Robinson, Kim Stanley 1952- **CLC 34**
See also CA 126

Robinson, Lloyd
See Silverberg, Robert

Robinson, Marilynne 1944- **CLC 25**
See also CA 116

Robinson, Smokey **CLC 21**
See also Robinson, William, Jr.

Robinson, William, Jr. 1940-
See Robinson, Smokey
See also CA 116

Robison, Mary 1949- **CLC 42, 98**
See also CA 113; 116; DLB 130; INT 116

Rod, Edouard 1857-1910 **TCLC 52**

Roddenberry, Eugene Wesley 1921-1991
See Roddenberry, Gene
See also CA 110; 135; CANR 37; SATA 45; SATA-Obit 69

Roddenberry, Gene **CLC 17**
See also Roddenberry, Eugene Wesley
See also AAYA 5; SATA-Obit 69

Rodgers, Mary 1931- **CLC 12**

See also CA 49-52; CANR 8, 55; CLR 20; INT CANR-8; JRDA; MAICYA; SATA 8

Rodgers, W(illiam) R(obert) 1909-1969 **CLC 7**
See also CA 85-88; DLB 20

Rodman, Eric
See Silverberg, Robert

Rodman, Howard 1920(?)-1985 **CLC 65**
See also CA 118

Rodman, Maia
See Wojciechowska, Maia (Teresa)

Rodriguez, Claudio 1934- **CLC 10**
See also DLB 134

Roelvaag, O(le) E(dvart) 1876-1931 **TCLC 17**
See also CA 117; DLB 9

Roethke, Theodore (Huebner) 1908-1963 **CLC 1, 3, 8, 11, 19, 46, 101; DAM POET; PC 15**
See also CA 81-84; CABS 2; CDALB 1941-1968; DLB 5; MTCW

Rogers, Samuel 1763-1855 **NCLC 69**
See also DLB 93

Rogers, Thomas Hunton 1927- **CLC 57**
See also CA 89-92; INT 89-92

Rogers, Will(iam Penn Adair) 1879-1935 **TCLC 8, 71; DAM MULT**
See also CA 105; 144; DLB 11; NNAL

Rogin, Gilbert 1929- **CLC 18**
See also CA 65-68; CANR 15

Rohan, Koda **TCLC 22**
See also Koda Shigeyuki

Rohlfs, Anna Katharine Green
See Green, Anna Katharine

Rohmer, Eric **CLC 16**
See also Scherer, Jean-Marie Maurice

Rohmer, Sax **TCLC 28**
See also Ward, Arthur Henry Sarsfield
See also DLB 70

Roiphe, Anne (Richardson) 1935- **CLC 3, 9**
See also CA 89-92; CANR 45; DLBY 80; INT 89-92

Rojas, Fernando de 1465-1541 **LC 23**

Rolfe, Frederick (William Serafino Austin Lewis Mary) 1860-1913 **TCLC 12**
See also CA 107; DLB 34, 156

Rolland, Romain 1866-1944 **TCLC 23**
See also CA 118; DLB 65

Rolle, Richard c. 1300-c. 1349 **CMLC 21**
See also DLB 146

Rolvaag, O(le) E(dvart)
See Roelvaag, O(le) E(dvart)

Romain Arnaud, Saint
See Aragon, Louis

Romains, Jules 1885-1972 **CLC 7**
See also CA 85-88; CANR 34; DLB 65; MTCW

Romero, Jose Ruben 1890-1952 **TCLC 14**
See also CA 114; 131; HW

Ronsard, Pierre de 1524-1585 **LC 6; PC 11**

Rooke, Leon 1934- **CLC 25, 34; DAM POP**
See also CA 25-28R; CANR 23, 53

Roosevelt, Theodore 1858-1919 **TCLC 69**
See also CA 115; DLB 47, 186

Roper, William 1498-1578 **LC 10**

Roquelaure, A. N.
See Rice, Anne

Rosa, Joao Guimaraes 1908-1967 **CLC 23**
See also CA 89-92; DLB 113

Rose, Wendy 1948- **CLC 85; DAM MULT; PC 13**
See also CA 53-56; CANR 5, 51; DLB 175; NNAL; SATA 12

Rosen, R. D.
See Rosen, Richard (Dean)

Rosen, Richard (Dean) 1949- **CLC 39**
See also CA 77-80; CANR 62; INT CANR-30

NOV; WLC
See also CA 108; 132; CLR 10; DLB 72;
MAICYA; MTCW; SATA 20

St. John, David
See Hunt, E(verette) Howard, (Jr.)

Saint-John Perse
See Leger, (Marie-Rene Auguste) Alexis Saint-Leger

Saintsbury, George (Edward Bateman) 1845-1933   **TCLC 31**
See also CA 160; DLB 57, 149

Sait Faik   **TCLC 23**
See also Abasiyanik, Sait Faik

Saki   **TCLC 3; SSC 12**
See also Munro, H(ector) H(ugh)

Sala, George Augustus   **NCLC 46**

Salama, Hannu 1936-   **CLC 18**

Salamanca, J(ack) R(ichard) 1922- **CLC 4, 15**
See also CA 25-28R

Sale, J. Kirkpatrick
See Sale, Kirkpatrick

Sale, Kirkpatrick 1937-   **CLC 68**
See also CA 13-16R; CANR 10

Salinas, Luis Omar 1937-   **CLC 90; DAM MULT; HLC**
See also CA 131; DLB 82; HW

Salinas (y Serrano), Pedro 1891(?)-1951
TCLC 17
See also CA 117; DLB 134

Salinger, J(erome) D(avid) 1919- **CLC 1, 3, 8, 12, 55, 56; DA; DAB; DAC; DAM MST, NOV, POP; SSC 2, 28; WLC**
See also AAYA 2; CA 5-8R; CANR 39; CDALB 1941-1968; CLR 18; DLB 2, 102, 173; MAICYA; MTCW; SATA 67

Salisbury, John
See Caute, (John) David

Salter, James 1925-   **CLC 7, 52, 59**
See also CA 73-76; DLB 130

Saltus, Edgar (Everton) 1855-1921   **TCLC 8**
See also CA 105

Saltykov, Mikhail Evgrafovich 1826-1889
NCLC 16

Samarakis, Antonis 1919-   **CLC 5**
See also CA 25-28R; CAAS 16; CANR 36

Sanchez, Florencio 1875-1910   **TCLC 37**
See also CA 153; HW

Sanchez, Luis Rafael 1936-   **CLC 23**
See also CA 128; DLB 145; HW

Sanchez, Sonia 1934-   **CLC 5; BLC 3; DAM MULT; PC 9**
See also BW 2; CA 33-36R; CANR 24, 49; CLR 18; DLB 41; DLBD 8; MAICYA; MTCW; SATA 22

Sand, George 1804-1876 **NCLC 2, 42, 57; DA; DAB; DAC; DAM MST, NOV; WLC**
See also DLB 119, 192

Sandburg, Carl (August) 1878-1967 **CLC 1, 4, 10, 15, 35; DA; DAB; DAC; DAM MST, POET; PC 2; WLC**
See also AAYA 24; CA 5-8R; 25-28R; CANR 35; CDALB 1865-1917; DLB 17, 54; MAICYA; MTCW; SATA 8

Sandburg, Charles
See Sandburg, Carl (August)

Sandburg, Charles A.
See Sandburg, Carl (August)

Sanders, (James) Ed(ward) 1939-   **CLC 53**
See also CA 13-16R; CAAS 21; CANR 13, 44; DLB 16

Sanders, Lawrence 1920-1998 **CLC 41; DAM POP**
See also BEST 89:4; CA 81-84; 165; CANR

33, 62; MTCW

Sanders, Noah
See Blount, Roy (Alton), Jr.

Sanders, Winston P.
See Anderson, Poul (William)

Sandoz, Mari(e Susette) 1896-1966   **CLC 28**
See also CA 1-4R; 25-28R; CANR 17, 64; DLB 9; MTCW; SATA 5

Saner, Reg(inald Anthony) 1931-   **CLC 9**
See also CA 65-68

Sannazaro, Jacopo 1456(?)-1530   **LC 8**

Sansom, William 1912-1976 **CLC 2, 6; DAM NOV; SSC 21**
See also CA 5-8R; 65-68; CANR 42; DLB 139; MTCW

Santayana, George 1863-1952   **TCLC 40**
See also CA 115; DLB 54, 71; DLBD 13

Santiago, Danny   **CLC 33**
See also James, Daniel (Lewis)
See also DLB 122

Santmyer, Helen Hoover 1895-1986   **CLC 33**
See also CA 1-4R; 118; CANR 15, 33; DLBY 84; MTCW

Santoka, Taneda 1882-1940   **TCLC 72**

Santos, Bienvenido N(uqui) 1911-1996 **CLC 22; DAM MULT**
See also CA 101; 151; CANR 19, 46

Sapper   **TCLC 44**
See also McNeile, Herman Cyril

Sapphire 1950-   **CLC 99**

Sappho fl. 6th cent. B.C.-   **CMLC 3; DAM POET; PC 5**
See also DLB 176

Sarduy, Severo 1937-1993   **CLC 6, 97**
See also CA 89-92; 142; CANR 58; DLB 113; HW

Sargeson, Frank 1903-1982   **CLC 31**
See also CA 25-28R; 106; CANR 38

Sarmiento, Felix Ruben Garcia
See Dario, Ruben

Saroyan, William 1908-1981 **CLC 1, 8, 10, 29, 34, 56; DA; DAB; DAC; DAM DRAM, MST, NOV; SSC 21; WLC**
See also CA 5-8R; 103; CANR 30; DLB 7, 9, 86; DLBY 81; MTCW; SATA 23; SATA-Obit 24

Sarraute, Nathalie 1900- **CLC 1, 2, 4, 8, 10, 31, 80**
See also CA 9-12R; CANR 23, 66; DLB 83; MTCW

Sarton, (Eleanor) May 1912-1995 **CLC 4, 14, 49, 91; DAM POET**
See also CA 1-4R; 149; CANR 1, 34, 55; DLB 48; DLBY 81; INT CANR-34; MTCW; SATA 36; SATA-Obit 86

Sartre, Jean-Paul 1905-1980 **CLC 1, 4, 7, 9, 13, 18, 24, 44, 50, 52; DA; DAB; DAC; DAM DRAM, MST, NOV; DC 3; WLC**
See also CA 9-12R; 97-100; CANR 21; DLB 72; MTCW

Sassoon, Siegfried (Lorraine) 1886-1967 **CLC 36; DAB; DAM MST, NOV, POET; PC 12**
See also CA 104; 25-28R; CANR 36; DLB 20, 191; MTCW

Satterfield, Charles
See Pohl, Frederik

Saul, John (W. III) 1942- **CLC 46; DAM NOV, POP**
See also AAYA 10; BEST 90:4; CA 81-84; CANR 16, 40; SATA 98

Saunders, Caleb
See Heinlein, Robert A(nson)

Saura (Atares), Carlos 1932-   **CLC 20**

See also CA 114; 131; HW

Sauser-Hall, Frederic 1887-1961   **CLC 18**
See also Cendrars, Blaise
See also CA 102; 93-96; CANR 36, 62; MTCW

Saussure, Ferdinand de 1857-1913 **TCLC 49**

Savage, Catharine
See Brosman, Catharine Savage

Savage, Thomas 1915-   **CLC 40**
See also CA 126; 132; CAAS 15; INT 132

Savan, Glenn 19(?)-   **CLC 50**

Sayers, Dorothy L(eigh) 1893-1957 **TCLC 2, 15; DAM POP**
See also CA 104; 119; CANR 60; CDBLB 1914-1945; DLB 10, 36, 77, 100; MTCW

Sayers, Valerie 1952-   **CLC 50**
See also CA 134; CANR 61

Sayles, John (Thomas) 1950- **CLC 7, 10, 14**
See also CA 57-60; CANR 41; DLB 44

Scammell, Michael 1935-   **CLC 34**
See also CA 156

Scannell, Vernon 1922-   **CLC 49**
See also CA 5-8R; CANR 8, 24, 57; DLB 27; SATA 59

Scarlett, Susan
See Streatfeild, (Mary) Noel

Schaeffer, Susan Fromberg 1941- **CLC 6, 11, 22**
See also CA 49-52; CANR 18, 65; DLB 28; MTCW; SATA 22

Schary, Jill
See Robinson, Jill

Schell, Jonathan 1943-   **CLC 35**
See also CA 73-76; CANR 12

Schelling, Friedrich Wilhelm Joseph von 1775-1854   **CLC 30**
See also DLB 90

Schendel, Arthur van 1874-1946   **TCLC 56**

Scherer, Jean-Marie Maurice 1920-
See Rohmer, Eric
See also CA 110

Schevill, James (Erwin) 1920-   **CLC 7**
See also CA 5-8R; CAAS 12

Schiller, Friedrich 1759-1805 **NCLC 39, 69; DAM DRAM**
See also DLB 94

Schisgal, Murray (Joseph) 1926-   **CLC 6**
See also CA 21-24R; CANR 48

Schlee, Ann 1934-   **CLC 35**
See also CA 101; CANR 29; SATA 44; SATA-Brief 36

Schlegel, August Wilhelm von 1767-1845
NCLC 15
See also DLB 94

Schlegel, Friedrich 1772-1829   **NCLC 45**
See also DLB 90

Schlegel, Johann Elias (von) 1719(?)-1749 **LC 5**

Schlesinger, Arthur M(eier), Jr. 1917- **CLC 84**
See also AITN 1; CA 1-4R; CANR 1, 28, 58; DLB 17; INT CANR-28; MTCW; SATA 61

Schmidt, Arno (Otto) 1914-1979   **CLC 56**
See also CA 128; 109; DLB 69

Schmitz, Aron Hector 1861-1928
See Svevo, Italo
See also CA 104; 122; MTCW

Schnackenberg, Gjertrud 1953-   **CLC 40**
See also CA 116; DLB 120

Schneider, Leonard Alfred 1925-1966
See Bruce, Lenny
See also CA 89-92

Schnitzler, Arthur 1862-1931 **TCLC 4; SSC 15**
See also CA 104; DLB 81, 118

Schoenberg, Arnold 1874-1951   **TCLC 75**

Somers, Jane
See Lessing, Doris (May)
Somerville, Edith 1858-1949 **TCLC 51**
See also DLB 135
Somerville & Ross
See Martin, Violet Florence; Somerville, Edith
Sommer, Scott 1951- **CLC 25**
See also CA 106
Sondheim, Stephen (Joshua) 1930- **CLC 30, 39; DAM DRAM**
See also AAYA 11; CA 103; CANR 47, 68
Song, Cathy 1955- **PC 21**
See also CA 154; DLB 169
Sontag, Susan 1933-**CLC 1, 2, 10, 13, 31, 105; DAM POP**
See also CA 17-20R; CANR 25, 51; DLB 2, 67; MTCW
Sophocles 496(?)B.C.-406(?)B.C. **CMLC 2; DA; DAB; DAC; DAM DRAM, MST; DC 1; WLCS**
See also DLB 176
Sordello 1189-1269 **CMLC 15**
Sorel, Julia
See Drexler, Rosalyn
Sorrentino, Gilbert 1929-**CLC 3, 7, 14, 22, 40**
See also CA 77-80; CANR 14, 33; DLB 5, 173; DLBY 80; INT CANR-14
Soto, Gary 1952- **CLC 32, 80; DAM MULT; HLC**
See also AAYA 10; CA 119; 125; CANR 50; CLR 38; DLB 82; HW; INT 125; JRDA; SATA 80
Soupault, Philippe 1897-1990 **CLC 68**
See also CA 116; 147; 131
Souster, (Holmes) Raymond 1921- **CLC 5, 14; DAC; DAM POET**
See also CA 13-16R; CAAS 14; CANR 13, 29, 53; DLB 88; SATA 63
Southern, Terry 1924(?)-1995 **CLC 7**
See also CA 1-4R; 150; CANR 1, 55; DLB 2
Southey, Robert 1774-1843 **NCLC 8**
See also DLB 93, 107, 142; SATA 54
Southworth, Emma Dorothy Eliza Nevitte 1819-1899 **NCLC 26**
Souza, Ernest
See Scott, Evelyn
Soyinka, Wole 1934-**CLC 3, 5, 14, 36, 44; BLC 3; DA; DAB; DAC; DAM DRAM, MST, MULT; DC 2; WLC**
See also BW 2; CA 13-16R; CANR 27, 39; DLB 125; MTCW
Spackman, W(illiam) M(ode) 1905-1990 **CLC 46**
See also CA 81-84; 132
Spacks, Barry (Bernard) 1931- **CLC 14**
See also CA 154; CANR 33; DLB 105
Spanidou, Irini 1946- **CLC 44**
Spark, Muriel (Sarah) 1918-**CLC 2, 3, 5, 8, 13, 18, 40, 94; DAB; DAC; DAM MST, NOV; SSC 10**
See also CA 5-8R; CANR 12, 36; CDBLB 1945-1960; DLB 15, 139; INT CANR-12; MTCW
Spaulding, Douglas
See Bradbury, Ray (Douglas)
Spaulding, Leonard
See Bradbury, Ray (Douglas)
Spence, J. A. D.
See Eliot, T(homas) S(tearns)
Spencer, Elizabeth 1921- **CLC 22**
See also CA 13-16R; CANR 32, 65; DLB 6; MTCW; SATA 14
Spencer, Leonard G.
See Silverberg, Robert

Spencer, Scott 1945- **CLC 30**
See also CA 113; CANR 51; DLBY 86
Spender, Stephen (Harold) 1909-1995 **CLC 1, 2, 5, 10, 41, 91; DAM POET**
See also CA 9-12R; 149; CANR 31, 54; CDBLB 1945-1960; DLB 20; MTCW
Spengler, Oswald (Arnold Gottfried) 1880-1936 **TCLC 25**
See also CA 118
Spenser, Edmund 1552(?)-1599 **LC 5, 39; DA; DAB; DAC; DAM MST, POET; PC 8; WLC**
See also CDBLB Before 1660; DLB 167
Spicer, Jack 1925-1965 **CLC 8, 18, 72; DAM POET**
See also CA 85-88; DLB 5, 16, 193
Spiegelman, Art 1948- **CLC 76**
See also AAYA 10; CA 125; CANR 41, 55
Spielberg, Peter 1929- **CLC 6**
See also CA 5-8R; CANR 4, 48; DLBY 81
Spielberg, Steven 1947- **CLC 20**
See also AAYA 8, 24; CA 77-80; CANR 32; SATA 32
Spillane, Frank Morrison 1918-
See Spillane, Mickey
See also CA 25-28R; CANR 28, 63; MTCW; SATA 66
Spillane, Mickey **CLC 3, 13**
See also Spillane, Frank Morrison
Spinoza, Benedictus de 1632-1677 **LC 9**
Spinrad, Norman (Richard) 1940- **CLC 46**
See also CA 37-40R; CAAS 19; CANR 20; DLB 8; INT CANR-20
Spitteler, Carl (Friedrich Georg) 1845-1924 **TCLC 12**
See also CA 109; DLB 129
Spivack, Kathleen (Romola Drucker) 1938- **CLC 6**
See also CA 49-52
Spoto, Donald 1941- **CLC 39**
See also CA 65-68; CANR 11, 57
Springsteen, Bruce (F.) 1949- **CLC 17**
See also CA 111
Spurling, Hilary 1940- **CLC 34**
See also CA 104; CANR 25, 52
Spyker, John Howland
See Elman, Richard (Martin)
Squires, (James) Radcliffe 1917-1993 **CLC 51**
See also CA 1-4R; 140; CANR 6, 21
Srivastava, Dhanpat Rai 1880(?)-1936
See Premchand
See also CA 118
Stacy, Donald
See Pohl, Frederik
Stael, Germaine de 1766-1817
See Stael-Holstein, Anne Louise Germaine Necker Baronn
See also DLB 119
Stael-Holstein, Anne Louise Germaine Necker Baronn 1766-1817 **NCLC 3**
See also Stael, Germaine de
See also DLB 192
Stafford, Jean 1915-1979**CLC 4, 7, 19, 68; SSC 26**
See also CA 1-4R; 85-88; CANR 3, 65; DLB 2, 173; MTCW; SATA-Obit 22
Stafford, William (Edgar) 1914-1993 **CLC 4, 7, 29; DAM POET**
See also CA 5-8R; 142; CAAS 3; CANR 5, 22; DLB 5; INT CANR-22
Stagnelius, Eric Johan 1793-1823 **NCLC 61**
Staines, Trevor
See Brunner, John (Kilian Houston)

Stairs, Gordon
See Austin, Mary (Hunter)
Stannard, Martin 1947- **CLC 44**
See also CA 142; DLB 155
Stanton, Elizabeth Cady 1815-1902 **TCLC 73**
See also DLB 79
Stanton, Maura 1946- **CLC 9**
See also CA 89-92; CANR 15; DLB 120
Stanton, Schuyler
See Baum, L(yman) Frank
Stapledon, (William) Olaf 1886-1950 **TCLC 22**
See also CA 111; 162; DLB 15
Starbuck, George (Edwin) 1931-1996**CLC 53; DAM POET**
See also CA 21-24R; 153; CANR 23
Stark, Richard
See Westlake, Donald E(dwin)
Staunton, Schuyler
See Baum, L(yman) Frank
Stead, Christina (Ellen) 1902-1983 **CLC 2, 5, 8, 32, 80**
See also CA 13-16R; 109; CANR 33, 40; MTCW
Stead, William Thomas 1849-1912 **TCLC 48**
Steele, Richard 1672-1729 **LC 18**
See also CDBLB 1660-1789; DLB 84, 101
Steele, Timothy (Reid) 1948- **CLC 45**
See also CA 93-96; CANR 16, 50; DLB 120
Steffens, (Joseph) Lincoln 1866-1936 **TCLC 20**
See also CA 117
Stegner, Wallace (Earle) 1909-1993**CLC 9, 49, 81; DAM NOV; SSC 27**
See also AITN 1; BEST 90:3; CA 1-4R; 141; CAAS 9; CANR 1, 21, 46; DLB 9; DLBY 93; MTCW
Stein, Gertrude 1874-1946**TCLC 1, 6, 28, 48; DA; DAB; DAC; DAM MST, NOV, POET; PC 18; WLC**
See also CA 104; 132; CDALB 1917-1929; DLB 4, 54, 86; DLBD 15; MTCW
Steinbeck, John (Ernst) 1902-1968**CLC 1, 5, 9, 13, 21, 34, 45, 75; DA; DAB; DAC; DAM DRAM, MST, NOV; SSC 11; WLC**
See also AAYA 12; CA 1-4R; 25-28R; CANR 1, 35; CDALB 1929-1941; DLB 7, 9; DLBD 2; MTCW; SATA 9
Steinem, Gloria 1934- **CLC 63**
See also CA 53-56; CANR 28, 51; MTCW
Steiner, George 1929- **CLC 24; DAM NOV**
See also CA 73-76; CANR 31, 67; DLB 67; MTCW; SATA 62
Steiner, K. Leslie
See Delany, Samuel R(ay, Jr.)
Steiner, Rudolf 1861-1925 **TCLC 13**
See also CA 107
Stendhal 1783-1842 **NCLC 23, 46; DA; DAB; DAC; DAM MST, NOV; SSC 27; WLC**
See also DLB 119
Stephen, Adeline Virginia
See Woolf, (Adeline) Virginia
Stephen, SirLeslie 1832-1904 **TCLC 23**
See also CA 123; DLB 57, 144, 190
Stephen, Sir Leslie
See Stephen, SirLeslie
Stephen, Virginia
See Woolf, (Adeline) Virginia
Stephens, James 1882(?)-1950 **TCLC 4**
See also CA 104; DLB 19, 153, 162
Stephens, Reed
See Donaldson, Stephen R.
Steptoe, Lydia

See Barnes, Djuna
Sterchi, Beat 1949-   **CLC 65**
Sterling, Brett
  See Bradbury, Ray (Douglas); Hamilton,
    Edmond
Sterling, Bruce 1954-   **CLC 72**
  See also CA 119; CANR 44
Sterling, George 1869-1926   **TCLC 20**
  See also CA 117; 165; DLB 54
Stern, Gerald 1925-   **CLC 40, 100**
  See also CA 81-84; CANR 28; DLB 105
Stern, Richard (Gustave) 1928-   **CLC 4, 39**
  See also CA 1-4R; CANR 1, 25, 52; DLBY 87;
    INT CANR-25
Sternberg, Josef von 1894-1969   **CLC 20**
  See also CA 81-84
Sterne, Laurence 1713-1768 **LC 2; DA; DAB;**
    DAC; DAM MST, NOV; WLC
  See also CDBLB 1660-1789; DLB 39
Sternheim, (William Adolf) Carl 1878-1942
    TCLC 8
  See also CA 105; DLB 56, 118
Stevens, Mark 1951-   **CLC 34**
  See also CA 122
Stevens, Wallace 1879-1955 **TCLC 3, 12, 45;**
    DA; DAB; DAC; DAM MST, POET; PC
    6; WLC
  See also CA 104; 124; CDALB 1929-1941;
    DLB 54; MTCW
Stevenson, Anne (Katharine) 1933-**CLC 7, 33**
  See also CA 17-20R; CAAS 9; CANR 9, 33;
    DLB 40; MTCW
Stevenson, Robert Louis (Balfour) 1850-1894
    NCLC 5, 14, 63; DA; DAB; DAC; DAM
    MST, NOV; SSC 11; WLC
  See also AAYA 24; CDBLB 1890-1914; CLR
    10, 11; DLB 18, 57, 141, 156, 174; DLBD
    13; JRDA; MAICYA; YABC 2
Stewart, J(ohn) I(nnes) M(ackintosh) 1906-
    1994   **CLC 7, 14, 32**
  See also CA 85-88; 147; CAAS 3; CANR 47;
    MTCW
Stewart, Mary (Florence Elinor) 1916-**CLC 7,**
    35; DAB
  See also CA 1-4R; CANR 1, 59; SATA 12
Stewart, Mary Rainbow
  See Stewart, Mary (Florence Elinor)
Stifle, June
  See Campbell, Maria
Stifter, Adalbert 1805-1868**NCLC 41; SSC 28**
  See also DLB 133
Still, James 1906-   **CLC 49**
  See also CA 65-68; CAAS 17; CANR 10, 26;
    DLB 9; SATA 29
Sting
  See Sumner, Gordon Matthew
Stirling, Arthur
  See Sinclair, Upton (Beall)
Stitt, Milan 1941-   **CLC 29**
  See also CA 69-72
Stockton, Francis Richard 1834-1902
  See Stockton, Frank R.
  See also CA 108; 137; MAICYA; SATA 44
Stockton, Frank R.   **TCLC 47**
  See also Stockton, Francis Richard
  See also DLB 42, 74; DLBD 13; SATA-Brief
    32
Stoddard, Charles
  See Kuttner, Henry
Stoker, Abraham 1847-1912
  See Stoker, Bram
  See also CA 105; 150; DA; DAC; DAM MST,
    NOV; SATA 29

Stoker, Bram 1847-1912**TCLC 8; DAB; WLC**
  See also Stoker, Abraham
  See also AAYA 23; CDBLB 1890-1914; DLB
    36, 70, 178
Stolz, Mary (Slattery) 1920-   **CLC 12**
  See also AAYA 8; AITN 1; CA 5-8R; CANR
    13, 41; JRDA; MAICYA; SAAS 3; SATA 10,
    71
Stone, Irving 1903-1989   **CLC 7; DAM POP**
  See also AITN 1; CA 1-4R; 129; CAAS 3;
    CANR 1, 23; INT CANR-23; MTCW; SATA
    3; SATA-Obit 64
Stone, Oliver (William) 1946-   **CLC 73**
  See also AAYA 15; CA 110; CANR 55
Stone, Robert (Anthony) 1937- **CLC 5, 23, 42**
  See also CA 85-88; CANR 23, 66; DLB 152;
    INT CANR-23; MTCW
Stone, Zachary
  See Follett, Ken(neth Martin)
Stoppard, Tom 1937-**CLC 1, 3, 4, 5, 8, 15, 29,**
    34, 63, 91; DA; DAB; DAC; DAM DRAM,
    MST; DC 6; WLC
  See also CA 81-84; CANR 39, 67; CDBLB
    1960 to Present; DLB 13; DLBY 85; MTCW
Storey, David (Malcolm) 1933-**CLC 2, 4, 5, 8;**
    DAM DRAM
  See also CA 81-84; CANR 36; DLB 13, 14;
    MTCW
Storm, Hyemeyohsts 1935-   **CLC 3; DAM**
    MULT
  See also CA 81-84; CANR 45; NNAL
Storm, (Hans) Theodor (Woldsen) 1817-1888
    NCLC 1; SSC 27
  See also DLB 129
Storni, Alfonsina 1892-1938   **TCLC 5; DAM**
    MULT; HLC
  See also CA 104; 131; HW
Stoughton, William 1631-1701   **LC 38**
  See also DLB 24
Stout, Rex (Todhunter) 1886-1975   **CLC 3**
  See also AITN 2; CA 61-64
Stow, (Julian) Randolph 1935-   **CLC 23, 48**
  See also CA 13-16R; CANR 33; MTCW
Stowe, Harriet (Elizabeth) Beecher 1811-1896
    NCLC 3, 50; DA; DAB; DAC; DAM MST,
    NOV; WLC
  See also CDALB 1865-1917; DLB 1, 12, 42,
    74, 189; JRDA; MAICYA; YABC 1
Strachey, (Giles) Lytton 1880-1932 **TCLC 12**
  See also CA 110; DLB 149; DLBD 10
Strand, Mark 1934- **CLC 6, 18, 41, 71; DAM**
    POET
  See also CA 21-24R; CANR 40, 65; DLB 5;
    SATA 41
Straub, Peter (Francis) 1943-   **CLC 28, 107;**
    DAM POP
  See also BEST 89:1; CA 85-88; CANR 28, 65;
    DLBY 84; MTCW
Strauss, Botho 1944-   **CLC 22**
  See also CA 157; DLB 124
Streatfeild, (Mary) Noel 1895(?)-1986**CLC 21**
  See also CA 81-84; 120; CANR 31; CLR 17;
    DLB 160; MAICYA; SATA 20; SATA-Obit
    48
Stribling, T(homas) S(igismund) 1881-1965
    CLC 23
  See also CA 107; DLB 9
Strindberg, (Johan) August 1849-1912 **TCLC**
    1, 8, 21, 47; DA; DAB; DAC; DAM DRAM,
    MST; WLC
  See also CA 104; 135
Stringer, Arthur 1874-1950   **TCLC 37**
  See also CA 161; DLB 92

Stringer, David
  See Roberts, Keith (John Kingston)
Stroheim, Erich von 1885-1957   **TCLC 71**
Strugatskii, Arkadii (Natanovich) 1925-1991
    CLC 27
  See also CA 106; 135
Strugatskii, Boris (Natanovich) 1933-**CLC 27**
  See also CA 106
Strummer, Joe 1953(?)-   **CLC 30**
Stuart, Don A.
  See Campbell, John W(ood, Jr.)
Stuart, Ian
  See MacLean, Alistair (Stuart)
Stuart, Jesse (Hilton) 1906-1984**CLC 1, 8, 11,**
    14, 34; SSC 31
  See also CA 5-8R; 112; CANR 31; DLB 9, 48,
    102; DLBY 84; SATA 2; SATA-Obit 36
Sturgeon, Theodore (Hamilton) 1918-1985
    CLC 22, 39
  See also Queen, Ellery
  See also CA 81-84; 116; CANR 32; DLB 8;
    DLBY 85; MTCW
Sturges, Preston 1898-1959   **TCLC 48**
  See also CA 114; 149; DLB 26
Styron, William 1925- **CLC 1, 3, 5, 11, 15, 60;**
    DAM NOV, POP; SSC 25
  See also BEST 90:4; CA 5-8R; CANR 6, 33;
    CDALB 1968-1988; DLB 2, 143; DLBY 80;
    INT CANR-6; MTCW
Su, Chien 1884-1918
  See Su Man-shu
  See also CA 123
Suarez Lynch, B.
  See Bioy Casares, Adolfo; Borges, Jorge Luis
Suckow, Ruth 1892-1960   **SSC 18**
  See also CA 113; DLB 9, 102
Sudermann, Hermann 1857-1928   **TCLC 15**
  See also CA 107; DLB 118
Sue, Eugene 1804-1857   **NCLC 1**
  See also DLB 119
Sueskind, Patrick 1949-   **CLC 44**
  See also Suskind, Patrick
Sukenick, Ronald 1932-   **CLC 3, 4, 6, 48**
  See also CA 25-28R; CAAS 8; CANR 32; DLB
    173; DLBY 81
Suknaski, Andrew 1942-   **CLC 19**
  See also CA 101; DLB 53
Sullivan, Vernon
  See Vian, Boris
Sully Prudhomme 1839-1907   **TCLC 31**
Su Man-shu   **TCLC 24**
  See also Su, Chien
Summerforest, Ivy B.
  See Kirkup, James
Summers, Andrew James 1942-   **CLC 26**
Summers, Andy
  See Summers, Andrew James
Summers, Hollis (Spurgeon, Jr.) 1916-**CLC 10**
  See also CA 5-8R; CANR 3; DLB 6
Summers, (Alphonsus Joseph-Mary Augustus)
    Montague 1880-1948   **TCLC 16**
  See also CA 118; 163
Sumner, Gordon Matthew 1951-   **CLC 26**
Surtees, Robert Smith 1803-1864   **NCLC 14**
  See also DLB 21
Susann, Jacqueline 1921-1974   **CLC 3**
  See also AITN 1; CA 65-68; 53-56; MTCW
Su Shih 1036-1101   **CMLC 15**
Suskind, Patrick
  See Sueskind, Patrick
  See also CA 145
Sutcliff, Rosemary 1920-1992 **CLC 26; DAB;**
    DAC; DAM MST, POP

See also AAYA 10; CA 5-8R; 139; CANR 37; CLR 1, 37; JRDA; MAICYA; SATA 6, 44, 78; SATA-Obit 73

Sutro, Alfred 1863-1933   **TCLC 6**
See also CA 105; DLB 10

Sutton, Henry
See Slavitt, David R(ytman)

Svevo, Italo 1861-1928   **TCLC 2, 35; SSC 25**
See also Schmitz, Aron Hector

Swados, Elizabeth (A.) 1951-   **CLC 12**
See also CA 97-100; CANR 49; INT 97-100

Swados, Harvey 1920-1972   **CLC 5**
See also CA 5-8R; 37-40R; CANR 6; DLB 2

Swan, Gladys 1934-   **CLC 69**
See also CA 101; CANR 17, 39

Swarthout, Glendon (Fred) 1918-1992**CLC 35**
See also CA 1-4R; 139; CANR 1, 47; SATA 26

Sweet, Sarah C.
See Jewett, (Theodora) Sarah Orne

Swenson, May 1919-1989 **CLC 4, 14, 61, 106; DA; DAB; DAC; DAM MST, POET; PC 14**
See also CA 5-8R; 130; CANR 36, 61; DLB 5; MTCW; SATA 15

Swift, Augustus
See Lovecraft, H(oward) P(hillips)

Swift, Graham (Colin) 1949-   **CLC 41, 88**
See also CA 117; 122; CANR 46; DLB 194

Swift, Jonathan 1667-1745 **LC 1; DA; DAB; DAC; DAM MST, NOV, POET; PC 9; WLC**
See also CDBLB 1660-1789; DLB 39, 95, 101; SATA 19

Swinburne, Algernon Charles 1837-1909
   TCLC 8, 36; DA; DAB; DAC; DAM MST, POET; WLC
See also CA 105; 140; CDBLB 1832-1890; DLB 35, 57

Swinfen, Ann   **CLC 34**

Swinnerton, Frank Arthur 1884-1982**CLC 31**
See also CA 108; DLB 34

Swithen, John
See King, Stephen (Edwin)

Sylvia
See Ashton-Warner, Sylvia (Constance)

Symmes, Robert Edward
See Duncan, Robert (Edward)

Symonds, John Addington 1840-1893 **NCLC 34**
See also DLB 57, 144

Symons, Arthur 1865-1945   **TCLC 11**
See also CA 107; DLB 19, 57, 149

Symons, Julian (Gustave) 1912-1994 **CLC 2, 14, 32**
See also CA 49-52; 147; CAAS 3; CANR 3, 33, 59; DLB 87, 155; DLBY 92; MTCW

Synge, (Edmund) J(ohn) M(illington) 1871-1909   **TCLC 6, 37; DAM DRAM; DC 2**
See also CA 104; 141; CDBLB 1890-1914; DLB 10, 19

Syruc, J.
See Milosz, Czeslaw

Szirtes, George 1948-   **CLC 46**
See also CA 109; CANR 27, 61

Szymborska, Wislawa 1923-   **CLC 99**
See also CA 154; DLBY 96

T. O., Nik
See Annensky, Innokenty (Fyodorovich)

Tabori, George 1914-   **CLC 19**
See also CA 49-52; CANR 4, 69

Tagore, Rabindranath 1861-1941**TCLC 3, 53; DAM DRAM, POET; PC 8**
See also CA 104; 120; MTCW

Taine, Hippolyte Adolphe 1828-1893 **NCLC 15**

Talese, Gay 1932-   **CLC 37**
See also AITN 1; CA 1-4R; CANR 9, 58; DLB 185; INT CANR-9; MTCW

Tallent, Elizabeth (Ann) 1954-   **CLC 45**
See also CA 117; DLB 130

Tally, Ted 1952-   **CLC 42**
See also CA 120; 124; INT 124

Tamayo y Baus, Manuel 1829-1898 **NCLC 1**

Tammsaare, A(nton) H(ansen) 1878-1940
   TCLC 27
See also CA 164

Tam'si, Tchicaya U
See Tchicaya, Gerald Felix

Tan, Amy (Ruth) 1952-**CLC 59; DAM MULT, NOV, POP**
See also AAYA 9; BEST 89:3; CA 136; CANR 54; DLB 173; SATA 75

Tandem, Felix
See Spitteler, Carl (Friedrich Georg)

Tanizaki, Jun'ichiro 1886-1965**CLC 8, 14, 28; SSC 21**
See also CA 93-96; 25-28R; DLB 180

Tanner, William
See Amis, Kingsley (William)

Tao Lao
See Storni, Alfonsina

Tarassoff, Lev
See Troyat, Henri

Tarbell, Ida M(inerva) 1857-1944   **TCLC 40**
See also CA 122; DLB 47

Tarkington, (Newton) Booth 1869-1946**TCLC 9**
See also CA 110; 143; DLB 9, 102; SATA 17

Tarkovsky, Andrei (Arsenyevich) 1932-1986
   CLC 75
See also CA 127

Tartt, Donna 1964(?)-   **CLC 76**
See also CA 142

Tasso, Torquato 1544-1595   **LC 5**

Tate, (John Orley) Allen 1899-1979 **CLC 2, 4, 6, 9, 11, 14, 24**
See also CA 5-8R; 85-88; CANR 32; DLB 4, 45, 63; MTCW

Tate, Ellalice
See Hibbert, Eleanor Alice Burford

Tate, James (Vincent) 1943-   **CLC 2, 6, 25**
See also CA 21-24R; CANR 29, 57; DLB 5, 169

Tavel, Ronald 1940-   **CLC 6**
See also CA 21-24R; CANR 33

Taylor, C(ecil) P(hilip) 1929-1981   **CLC 27**
See also CA 25-28R; 105; CANR 47

Taylor, Edward 1642(?)-1729   **LC 11; DA; DAB; DAC; DAM MST, POET**
See also DLB 24

Taylor, Eleanor Ross 1920-   **CLC 5**
See also CA 81-84

Taylor, Elizabeth 1912-1975   **CLC 2, 4, 29**
See also CA 13-16R; CANR 9; DLB 139; MTCW; SATA 13

Taylor, Frederick Winslow 1856-1915 **TCLC 76**

Taylor, Henry (Splawn) 1942-   **CLC 44**
See also CA 33-36R; CAAS 7; CANR 31; DLB 5

Taylor, Kamala (Purnaiya) 1924-
See Markandaya, Kamala
See also CA 77-80

Taylor, Mildred D.   **CLC 21**
See also AAYA 10; BW 1; CA 85-88; CANR 25; CLR 9; DLB 52; JRDA; MAICYA; SAAS 5; SATA 15, 70

Taylor, Peter (Hillsman) 1917-1994 **CLC 1, 4, 18, 37, 44, 50, 71; SSC 10**
See also CA 13-16R; 147; CANR 9, 50; DLBY 81, 94; INT CANR-9; MTCW

Taylor, Robert Lewis 1912-   **CLC 14**
See also CA 1-4R; CANR 3, 64; SATA 10

Tchekhov, Anton
See Chekhov, Anton (Pavlovich)

Tchicaya, Gerald Felix 1931-1988   **CLC 101**
See also CA 129; 125

Tchicaya U Tam'si
See Tchicaya, Gerald Felix

Teasdale, Sara 1884-1933   **TCLC 4**
See also CA 104; 163; DLB 45; SATA 32

Tegner, Esaias 1782-1846   **NCLC 2**

Teilhard de Chardin, (Marie Joseph) Pierre 1881-1955 **TCLC 9**
See also CA 105

Temple, Ann
See Mortimer, Penelope (Ruth)

Tennant, Emma (Christina) 1937- **CLC 13, 52**
See also CA 65-68; CAAS 9; CANR 10, 38, 59; DLB 14

Tenneshaw, S. M.
See Silverberg, Robert

Tennyson, Alfred 1809-1892   **NCLC 30, 65; DA; DAB; DAC; DAM MST, POET; PC 6; WLC**
See also CDBLB 1832-1890; DLB 32

Teran, Lisa St. Aubin de   **CLC 36**
See also St. Aubin de Teran, Lisa

Terence 195(?)B.C.-159B.C. **CMLC 14; DC 7**

Teresa de Jesus, St. 1515-1582   **LC 18**

Terkel, Louis 1912-
See Terkel, Studs
See also CA 57-60; CANR 18, 45, 67; MTCW

Terkel, Studs   **CLC 38**
See also Terkel, Louis
See also AITN 1

Terry, C. V.
See Slaughter, Frank G(ill)

Terry, Megan 1932-   **CLC 19**
See also CA 77-80; CABS 3; CANR 43; DLB 7

Tertullian c. 155-c. 245   **CMLC 29**

Tertz, Abram
See Sinyavsky, Andrei (Donatevich)

Tesich, Steve 1943(?)-1996   **CLC 40, 69**
See also CA 105; 152; DLBY 83

Teternikov, Fyodor Kuzmich 1863-1927
See Sologub, Fyodor
See also CA 104

Tevis, Walter 1928-1984   **CLC 42**
See also CA 113

Tey, Josephine   **TCLC 14**
See also Mackintosh, Elizabeth
See also DLB 77

Thackeray, William Makepeace 1811-1863
   NCLC 5, 14, 22, 43; DA; DAB; DAC; DAM MST, NOV; WLC
See also CDBLB 1832-1890; DLB 21, 55, 159, 163; SATA 23

Thakura, Ravindranatha
See Tagore, Rabindranath

Tharoor, Shashi 1956-   **CLC 70**
See also CA 141

Thelwell, Michael Miles 1939-   **CLC 22**
See also BW 2; CA 101

Theobald, Lewis, Jr.
See Lovecraft, H(oward) P(hillips)

Theodorescu, Ion N. 1880-1967
See Arghezi, Tudor
See also CA 116

Theriault, Yves 1915-1983 **CLC 79; DAC; DAM MST**
See also CA 102; DLB 88

Theroux, Alexander (Louis) 1939- **CLC 2, 25**
See also CA 85-88; CANR 20, 63

Theroux, Paul (Edward) 1941- **CLC 5, 8, 11, 15, 28, 46; DAM POP**
See also BEST 89:4; CA 33-36R; CANR 20, 45; DLB 2; MTCW; SATA 44

Thesen, Sharon 1946-   **CLC 56**
See also CA 163

Thevenin, Denis
See Duhamel, Georges

Thibault, Jacques Anatole Francois 1844-1924
See France, Anatole
See also CA 106; 127; DAM NOV; MTCW

Thiele, Colin (Milton) 1920-   **CLC 17**
See also CA 29-32R; CANR 12, 28, 53; CLR 27; MAICYA; SAAS 2; SATA 14, 72

Thomas, Audrey (Callahan) 1935- **CLC 7, 13, 37, 107; SSC 20**
See also AITN 2; CA 21-24R; CAAS 19; CANR 36, 58; DLB 60; MTCW

Thomas, D(onald) M(ichael) 1935- **CLC 13, 22, 31**
See also CA 61-64; CAAS 11; CANR 17, 45; CDBLB 1960 to Present; DLB 40; INT CANR-17; MTCW

Thomas, Dylan (Marlais) 1914-1953 **TCLC 1, 8, 45; DA; DAB; DAC; DAM DRAM, MST, POET; PC 2; SSC 3; WLC**
See also CA 104; 120; CANR 65; CDBLB 1945-1960; DLB 13, 20, 139; MTCW; SATA 60

Thomas, (Philip) Edward 1878-1917 **TCLC 10; DAM POET**
See also CA 106; 153; DLB 19

Thomas, Joyce Carol 1938-   **CLC 35**
See also AAYA 12; BW 2; CA 113; 116; CANR 48; CLR 19; DLB 33; INT 116; JRDA; MAICYA; MTCW; SAAS 7; SATA 40, 78

Thomas, Lewis 1913-1993   **CLC 35**
See also CA 85-88; 143; CANR 38, 60; MTCW

Thomas, Paul
See Mann, (Paul) Thomas

Thomas, Piri 1928-   **CLC 17**
See also CA 73-76; HW

Thomas, R(onald) S(tuart) 1913- **CLC 6, 13, 48; DAB; DAM POET**
See also CA 89-92; CAAS 4; CANR 30; CDBLB 1960 to Present; DLB 27; MTCW

Thomas, Ross (Elmore) 1926-1995 **CLC 39**
See also CA 33-36R; 150; CANR 22, 63

Thompson, Francis Clegg
See Mencken, H(enry) L(ouis)

Thompson, Francis Joseph 1859-1907 **TCLC 4**
See also CA 104; CDBLB 1890-1914; DLB 19

Thompson, Hunter S(tockton) 1939- **CLC 9, 17, 40, 104; DAM POP**
See also BEST 89:1; CA 17-20R; CANR 23, 46; DLB 185; MTCW

Thompson, James Myers
See Thompson, Jim (Myers)

Thompson, Jim (Myers) 1906-1977(?) **CLC 69**
See also CA 140

Thompson, Judith   **CLC 39**

Thomson, James 1700-1748 **LC 16, 29, 40; DAM POET**
See also DLB 95

Thomson, James 1834-1882 **NCLC 18; DAM POET**
See also DLB 35

Thoreau, Henry David 1817-1862 **NCLC 7, 21,** 61; **DA; DAB; DAC; DAM MST; WLC**
See also CDALB 1640-1865; DLB 1

Thornton, Hall
See Silverberg, Robert

Thucydides c. 455B.C.-399B.C.   **CMLC 17**
See also DLB 176

Thurber, James (Grover) 1894-1961 **CLC 5, 11, 25; DA; DAB; DAC; DAM DRAM, MST, NOV; SSC 1**
See also CA 73-76; CANR 17, 39; CDALB 1929-1941; DLB 4, 11, 22, 102; MAICYA; MTCW; SATA 13

Thurman, Wallace (Henry) 1902-1934 **TCLC 6; BLC 3; DAM MULT**
See also BW 1; CA 104; 124; DLB 51

Ticheburn, Cheviot
See Ainsworth, William Harrison

Tieck, (Johann) Ludwig 1773-1853 **NCLC 5, 46; SSC 31**
See also DLB 90

Tiger, Derry
See Ellison, Harlan (Jay)

Tilghman, Christopher 1948(?)-   **CLC 65**
See also CA 159

Tillinghast, Richard (Williford) 1940- **CLC 29**
See also CA 29-32R; CAAS 23; CANR 26, 51

Timrod, Henry 1828-1867   **NCLC 25**
See also DLB 3

Tindall, Gillian (Elizabeth) 1938-   **CLC 7**
See also CA 21-24R; CANR 11, 65

Tiptree, James, Jr.   **CLC 48, 50**
See also Sheldon, Alice Hastings Bradley
See also DLB 8

Titmarsh, Michael Angelo
See Thackeray, William Makepeace

Tocqueville, Alexis (Charles Henri Maurice Clerel Comte) 1805-1859 **NCLC 7, 63**

Tolkien, J(ohn) R(onald) R(euel) 1892-1973 **CLC 1, 2, 3, 8, 12, 38; DA; DAB; DAC; DAM MST, NOV, POP; WLC**
See also AAYA 10; AITN 1; CA 17-18; 45-48; CANR 36; CAP 2; CDBLB 1914-1945; DLB 15, 160; JRDA; MAICYA; MTCW; SATA 2, 32; SATA-Obit 24

Toller, Ernst 1893-1939   **TCLC 10**
See also CA 107; DLB 124

Tolson, M. B.
See Tolson, Melvin B(eaunorus)

Tolson, Melvin B(eaunorus) 1898(?)-1966 **CLC 36, 105; BLC 3; DAM MULT, POET**
See also BW 1; CA 124; 89-92; DLB 48, 76

Tolstoi, Aleksei Nikolaevich
See Tolstoy, Alexey Nikolaevich

Tolstoy, Alexey Nikolaevich 1882-1945 **TCLC 18**
See also CA 107; 158

Tolstoy, Count Leo
See Tolstoy, Leo (Nikolaevich)

Tolstoy, Leo (Nikolaevich) 1828-1910 **TCLC 4, 11, 17, 28, 44, 79; DA; DAB; DAC; DAM MST, NOV; SSC 9, 30; WLC**
See also CA 104; 123; SATA 26

Tomasi di Lampedusa, Giuseppe 1896-1957
See Lampedusa, Giuseppe (Tomasi di)
See also CA 111

Tomlin, Lily   **CLC 17**
See also Tomlin, Mary Jean

Tomlin, Mary Jean 1939(?)-
See Tomlin, Lily
See also CA 117

Tomlinson, (Alfred) Charles 1927- **CLC 2, 4, 6, 13, 45; DAM POET; PC 17**
See also CA 5-8R; CANR 33; DLB 40

Tomlinson, H(enry) M(ajor) 1873-1958 **TCLC 71**
See also CA 118; 161; DLB 36, 100, 195

Tonson, Jacob
See Bennett, (Enoch) Arnold

Toole, John Kennedy 1937-1969 **CLC 19, 64**
See also CA 104; DLBY 81

Toomer, Jean 1894-1967 **CLC 1, 4, 13, 22; BLC 3; DAM MULT; PC 7; SSC 1; WLCS**
See also BW 1; CA 85-88; CDALB 1917-1929; DLB 45, 51; MTCW

Torley, Luke
See Blish, James (Benjamin)

Tornimparte, Alessandra
See Ginzburg, Natalia

Torre, Raoul della
See Mencken, H(enry) L(ouis)

Torrey, E(dwin) Fuller 1937-   **CLC 34**
See also CA 119

Torsvan, Ben Traven
See Traven, B.

Torsvan, Benno Traven
See Traven, B.

Torsvan, Berick Traven
See Traven, B.

Torsvan, Berwick Traven
See Traven, B.

Torsvan, Bruno Traven
See Traven, B.

Torsvan, Traven
See Traven, B.

Tournier, Michel (Edouard) 1924- **CLC 6, 23, 36, 95**
See also CA 49-52; CANR 3, 36; DLB 83; MTCW; SATA 23

Tournimparte, Alessandra
See Ginzburg, Natalia

Towers, Ivar
See Kornbluth, C(yril) M.

Towne, Robert (Burton) 1936(?)-   **CLC 87**
See also CA 108; DLB 44

Townsend, Sue   **CLC 61**
See also Townsend, Susan Elaine
See also SATA 55, 93; SATA-Brief 48

Townsend, Susan Elaine 1946-
See Townsend, Sue
See also CA 119; 127; CANR 65; DAB; DAC; DAM MST

Townshend, Peter (Dennis Blandford) 1945- **CLC 17, 42**
See also CA 107

Tozzi, Federigo 1883-1920   **TCLC 31**
See also CA 160

Traill, Catharine Parr 1802-1899 **NCLC 31**
See also DLB 99

Trakl, Georg 1887-1914   **TCLC 5; PC 20**
See also CA 104; 165

Transtroemer, Tomas (Goesta) 1931- **CLC 52, 65; DAM POET**
See also CA 117; 129; CAAS 17

Transtromer, Tomas Gosta
See Transtroemer, Tomas (Goesta)

Traven, B. (?)-1969   **CLC 8, 11**
See also CA 19-20; 25-28R; CAP 2; DLB 9, 56; MTCW

Treitel, Jonathan 1959-   **CLC 70**

Tremain, Rose 1943-   **CLC 42**
See also CA 97-100; CANR 44; DLB 14

Tremblay, Michel 1942- **CLC 29, 102; DAC; DAM MST**
See also CA 116; 128; DLB 60; MTCW

Trevanian   **CLC 29**
See also Whitaker, Rod(ney)

Niven 1921-
See Bogarde, Dirk
See also CA 77-80

Vandenburgh, Jane   **CLC 59**

Vanderhaeghe, Guy 1951-   **CLC 41**
See also CA 113

van der Post, Laurens (Jan) 1906-1996**CLC 5**
See also CA 5-8R; 155; CANR 35

van de Wetering, Janwillem 1931-   **CLC 47**
See also CA 49-52; CANR 4, 62

Van Dine, S. S.   **TCLC 23**
See also Wright, Willard Huntington

Van Doren, Carl (Clinton) 1885-1950 **TCLC 18**
See also CA 111

Van Doren, Mark 1894-1972   **CLC 6, 10**
See also CA 1-4R; 37-40R; CANR 3; DLB 45;
MTCW

Van Druten, John (William) 1901-1957**TCLC 2**
See also CA 104; 161; DLB 10

Van Duyn, Mona (Jane) 1921- **CLC 3, 7, 63; DAM POET**
See also CA 9-12R; CANR 7, 38, 60; DLB 5

Van Dyne, Edith
See Baum, L(yman) Frank

van Itallie, Jean-Claude 1936-   **CLC 3**
See also CA 45-48; CAAS 2; CANR 1, 48; DLB 7

van Ostaijen, Paul 1896-1928   **TCLC 33**
See also CA 163

Van Peebles, Melvin 1932- **CLC 2, 20; DAM MULT**
See also BW 2; CA 85-88; CANR 27, 67

Vansittart, Peter 1920-   **CLC 42**
See also CA 1-4R; CANR 3, 49

Van Vechten, Carl 1880-1964   **CLC 33**
See also CA 89-92; DLB 4, 9, 51

Van Vogt, A(lfred) E(lton) 1912-   **CLC 1**
See also CA 21-24R; CANR 28; DLB 8; SATA 14

Varda, Agnes 1928-   **CLC 16**
See also CA 116; 122

Vargas Llosa, (Jorge) Mario (Pedro) 1936-
CLC 3, 6, 9, 10, 15, 31, 42, 85; DA; DAB; DAC; DAM MST, MULT, NOV; HLC
See also CA 73-76; CANR 18, 32, 42, 67; DLB 145; HW; MTCW

Vasiliu, Gheorghe 1881-1957
See Bacovia, George
See also CA 123

Vassa, Gustavus
See Equiano, Olaudah

Vassilikos, Vassilis 1933-   **CLC 4, 8**
See also CA 81-84

Vaughan, Henry 1621-1695   **LC 27**
See also DLB 131

Vaughn, Stephanie   **CLC 62**

Vazov, Ivan (Minchov) 1850-1921   **TCLC 25**
See also CA 121; DLB 147

Veblen, Thorstein B(unde) 1857-1929   **TCLC 31**
See also CA 115; 165

Vega, Lope de 1562-1635   **LC 23**

Venison, Alfred
See Pound, Ezra (Weston Loomis)

Verdi, Marie de
See Mencken, H(enry) L(ouis)

Verdu, Matilde
See Cela, Camilo Jose

Verga, Giovanni (Carmelo) 1840-1922 **TCLC 3; SSC 21**
See also CA 104; 123

Vergil 70B.C.-19B.C.   **CMLC 9; DA; DAB; DAC; DAM MST, POET; PC 12; WLCS**

Verhaeren, Emile (Adolphe Gustave) 1855-1916
TCLC 12
See also CA 109

Verlaine, Paul (Marie) 1844-1896**NCLC 2, 51; DAM POET; PC 2**

Verne, Jules (Gabriel) 1828-1905 **TCLC 6, 52**
See also AAYA 16; CA 110; 131; DLB 123;
JRDA; MAICYA; SATA 21

Very, Jones 1813-1880   **NCLC 9**
See also DLB 1

Vesaas, Tarjei 1897-1970   **CLC 48**
See also CA 29-32R

Vialis, Gaston
See Simenon, Georges (Jacques Christian)

Vian, Boris 1920-1959   **TCLC 9**
See also CA 106; 164; DLB 72

Viaud, (Louis Marie) Julien 1850-1923
See Loti, Pierre
See also CA 107

Vicar, Henry
See Felsen, Henry Gregor

Vicker, Angus
See Felsen, Henry Gregor

Vidal, Gore 1925-**CLC 2, 4, 6, 8, 10, 22, 33, 72; DAM NOV, POP**
See also AITN 1; BEST 90:2; CA 5-8R; CANR 13, 45, 65; DLB 6, 152; INT CANR-13;
MTCW

Viereck, Peter (Robert Edwin) 1916- **CLC 4**
See also CA 1-4R; CANR 1, 47; DLB 5

Vigny, Alfred (Victor) de 1797-1863 **NCLC 7; DAM POET**
See also DLB 119, 192

Vilakazi, Benedict Wallet 1906-1947**TCLC 37**

Villa, Jose Garcia 1904-1997   **PC 22**
See also CA 25-28R; CANR 12

Villaurrutia, Xavier 1903-1950   **TCLC 80**
See also HW

Villiers de l'Isle Adam, Jean Marie Mathias Philippe Auguste, Comte de 1838-1889
NCLC 3; SSC 14
See also DLB 123

Villon, Francois 1431-1463(?)   **PC 13**

Vinci, Leonardo da 1452-1519   **LC 12**

Vine, Barbara   **CLC 50**
See also Rendell, Ruth (Barbara)
See also BEST 90:4

Vinge, Joan D(ennison) 1948-**CLC 30; SSC 24**
See also CA 93-96; SATA 36

Violis, G.
See Simenon, Georges (Jacques Christian)

Virgil
See Vergil

Visconti, Luchino 1906-1976   **CLC 16**
See also CA 81-84; 65-68; CANR 39

Vittorini, Elio 1908-1966   **CLC 6, 9, 14**
See also CA 133; 25-28R

Vizenor, Gerald Robert 1934-**CLC 103; DAM MULT**
See also CA 13-16R; CAAS 22; CANR 5, 21, 44, 67; DLB 175; NNAL

Vizinczey, Stephen 1933-   **CLC 40**
See also CA 128; INT 128

Vliet, R(ussell) G(ordon) 1929-1984   **CLC 22**
See also CA 37-40R; 112; CANR 18

Vogau, Boris Andreyevich 1894-1937(?)
See Pilnyak, Boris
See also CA 123

Vogel, Paula A(nne) 1951-   **CLC 76**
See also CA 108

Voigt, Cynthia 1942-   **CLC 30**
See also AAYA 3; CA 106; CANR 18, 37, 40;
CLR 13,48; INT CANR-18; JRDA;
MAICYA; SATA 48, 79; SATA-Brief 33

Voigt, Ellen Bryant 1943-   **CLC 54**
See also CA 69-72; CANR 11, 29, 55; DLB 120

Voinovich, Vladimir (Nikolaevich) 1932-**CLC 10, 49**
See also CA 81-84; CAAS 12; CANR 33, 67;
MTCW

Vollmann, William T. 1959-   **CLC 89; DAM NOV, POP**
See also CA 134; CANR 67

Voloshinov, V. N.
See Bakhtin, Mikhail Mikhailovich

Voltaire 1694-1778   **LC 14; DA; DAB; DAC; DAM DRAM, MST; SSC 12; WLC**

von Daeniken, Erich 1935-   **CLC 30**
See also AITN 1; CA 37-40R; CANR 17, 44

von Daniken, Erich
See von Daeniken, Erich

von Heidenstam, (Carl Gustaf) Verner
See Heidenstam, (Carl Gustaf) Verner von

von Heyse, Paul (Johann Ludwig)
See Heyse, Paul (Johann Ludwig von)

von Hofmannsthal, Hugo
See Hofmannsthal, Hugo von

von Horvath, Odon
See Horvath, Oedoen von

von Horvath, Oedoen
See Horvath, Oedoen von

von Liliencron, (Friedrich Adolf Axel) Detlev
See Liliencron, (Friedrich Adolf Axel) Detlev von

Vonnegut, Kurt, Jr. 1922- **CLC 1, 2, 3, 4, 5, 8, 12, 22, 40, 60, 111; DA; DAB; DAC; DAM MST, NOV, POP; SSC 8; WLC**
See also AAYA 6; AITN 1; BEST 90:4; CA 1-4R; CANR 1, 25, 49; CDALB 1968-1988;
DLB 2, 8, 152; DLBD 3; DLBY 80; MTCW

Von Rachen, Kurt
See Hubbard, L(afayette) Ron(ald)

von Rezzori (d'Arezzo), Gregor
See Rezzori (d'Arezzo), Gregor von

von Sternberg, Josef
See Sternberg, Josef von

Vorster, Gordon 1924-   **CLC 34**
See also CA 133

Vosce, Trudie
See Ozick, Cynthia

Voznesensky, Andrei (Andreievich) 1933-
CLC 1, 15, 57; DAM POET
See also CA 89-92; CANR 37; MTCW

Waddington, Miriam 1917-   **CLC 28**
See also CA 21-24R; CANR 12, 30; DLB 68

Wagman, Fredrica 1937-   **CLC 7**
See also CA 97-100; INT 97-100

Wagner, Linda W.
See Wagner-Martin, Linda (C.)

Wagner, Linda Welshimer
See Wagner-Martin, Linda (C.)

Wagner, Richard 1813-1883   **NCLC 9**
See also DLB 129

Wagner-Martin, Linda (C.) 1936-   **CLC 50**
See also CA 159

Wagoner, David (Russell) 1926- **CLC 3, 5, 15**
See also CA 1-4R; CAAS 3; CANR 2; DLB 5;
SATA 14

Wah, Fred(erick James) 1939-   **CLC 44**
See also CA 107; 141; DLB 60

Wahloo, Per 1926-1975   **CLC 7**
See also CA 61-64

Wahloo, Peter
See Wahloo, Per

Wain, John (Barrington) 1925-1994 **CLC 2, 11, 15, 46**
See also CA 5-8R; 145; CAAS 4; CANR 23, 54; CDBLB 1960 to Present; DLB 15, 27, 139, 155; MTCW

Wajda, Andrzej 1926- **CLC 16**
See also CA 102

Wakefield, Dan 1932- **CLC 7**
See also CA 21-24R; CAAS 7

Wakoski, Diane 1937- **CLC 2, 4, 7, 9, 11, 40; DAM POET; PC 15**
See also CA 13-16R; CAAS 1; CANR 9, 60; DLB 5; INT CANR-9

Wakoski-Sherbell, Diane
See Wakoski, Diane

Walcott, Derek (Alton) 1930- **CLC 2, 4, 9, 14, 25, 42, 67, 76; BLC 3; DAB; DAC; DAM MST, MULT, POET; DC 7**
See also BW 2; CA 89-92; CANR 26, 47; DLB 117; DLBY 81; MTCW

Waldman, Anne (Lesley) 1945- **CLC 7**
See also CA 37-40R; CAAS 17; CANR 34, 69; DLB 16

Waldo, E. Hunter
See Sturgeon, Theodore (Hamilton)

Waldo, Edward Hamilton
See Sturgeon, Theodore (Hamilton)

Walker, Alice (Malsenior) 1944- **CLC 5, 6, 9, 19, 27, 46, 58, 103; BLC 3; DA; DAB; DAC; DAM MST, MULT, NOV, POET, POP; SSC 5; WLCS**
See also AAYA 3; BEST 89:4; BW 2; CA 37-40R; CANR 9, 27, 49, 66; CDALB 1968-1988; DLB 6, 33, 143; INT CANR-27; MTCW; SATA 31

Walker, David Harry 1911-1992 **CLC 14**
See also CA 1-4R; 137; CANR 1; SATA 8; SATA-Obit 71

Walker, Edward Joseph 1934-
See Walker, Ted
See also CA 21-24R; CANR 12, 28, 53

Walker, George F. 1947- **CLC 44, 61; DAB; DAC; DAM MST**
See also CA 103; CANR 21, 43, 59; DLB 60

Walker, Joseph A. 1935- **CLC 19; DAM DRAM, MST**
See also BW 1; CA 89-92; CANR 26; DLB 38

Walker, Margaret (Abigail) 1915- **CLC 1, 6; BLC; DAM MULT; PC 20**
See also BW 2; CA 73-76; CANR 26, 54; DLB 76, 152; MTCW

Walker, Ted **CLC 13**
See also Walker, Edward Joseph
See also DLB 40

Wallace, David Foster 1962- **CLC 50**
See also CA 132; CANR 59

Wallace, Dexter
See Masters, Edgar Lee

Wallace, (Richard Horatio) Edgar 1875-1932 **TCLC 57**
See also CA 115; DLB 70

Wallace, Irving 1916-1990 **CLC 7, 13; DAM NOV, POP**
See also AITN 1; CA 1-4R; 132; CAAS 1; CANR 1, 27; INT CANR-27; MTCW

Wallant, Edward Lewis 1926-1962 **CLC 5, 10**
See also CA 1-4R; CANR 22; DLB 2, 28, 143; MTCW

Walley, Byron
See Card, Orson Scott

Walpole, Horace 1717-1797 **LC 2**
See also DLB 39, 104

Walpole, Hugh (Seymour) 1884-1941 **TCLC 5**

See also CA 104; 165; DLB 34

Walser, Martin 1927- **CLC 27**
See also CA 57-60; CANR 8, 46; DLB 75, 124

Walser, Robert 1878-1956 **TCLC 18; SSC 20**
See also CA 118; 165; DLB 66

Walsh, Jill Paton **CLC 35**
See also Paton Walsh, Gillian
See also AAYA 11; CLR 2; DLB 161; SAAS 3

Walter, Villiam Christian
See Andersen, Hans Christian

Wambaugh, Joseph (Aloysius, Jr.) 1937- **CLC 3, 18; DAM NOV, POP**
See also AITN 1; BEST 89:3; CA 33-36R; CANR 42, 65; DLB 6; DLBY 83; MTCW

Wang Wei 699(?)-761(?) **PC 18**

Ward, Arthur Henry Sarsfield 1883-1959
See Rohmer, Sax
See also CA 108

Ward, Douglas Turner 1930- **CLC 19**
See also BW 1; CA 81-84; CANR 27; DLB 7, 38

Ward, Mary Augusta
See Ward, Mrs. Humphry

Ward, Mrs. Humphry 1851-1920 **TCLC 55**
See also DLB 18

Ward, Peter
See Faust, Frederick (Schiller)

Warhol, Andy 1928(?)-1987 **CLC 20**
See also AAYA 12; BEST 89:4; CA 89-92; 121; CANR 34

Warner, Francis (Robert le Plastrier) 1937- **CLC 14**
See also CA 53-56; CANR 11

Warner, Marina 1946- **CLC 59**
See also CA 65-68; CANR 21, 55; DLB 194

Warner, Rex (Ernest) 1905-1986 **CLC 45**
See also CA 89-92; 119; DLB 15

Warner, Susan (Bogert) 1819-1885 **NCLC 31**
See also DLB 3, 42

Warner, Sylvia (Constance) Ashton
See Ashton-Warner, Sylvia (Constance)

Warner, Sylvia Townsend 1893-1978 **CLC 7, 19; SSC 23**
See also CA 61-64; 77-80; CANR 16, 60; DLB 34, 139; MTCW

Warren, Mercy Otis 1728-1814 **NCLC 13**
See also DLB 31, 200

Warren, Robert Penn 1905-1989 **CLC 1, 4, 6, 8, 10, 13, 18, 39, 53, 59; DA; DAB; DAC; DAM MST, NOV, POET; SSC 4; WLC**
See also AITN 1; CA 13-16R; 129; CANR 10, 47; CDALB 1968-1988; DLB 2, 48, 152; DLBY 80, 89; INT CANR-10; MTCW; SATA 46; SATA-Obit 63

Warshofsky, Isaac
See Singer, Isaac Bashevis

Warton, Thomas 1728-1790 **LC 15; DAM POET**
See also DLB 104, 109

Waruk, Kona
See Harris, (Theodore) Wilson

Warung, Price 1855-1911 **TCLC 45**

Warwick, Jarvis
See Garner, Hugh

Washington, Alex
See Harris, Mark

Washington, Booker T(aliaferro) 1856-1915 **TCLC 10; BLC 3; DAM MULT**
See also BW 1; CA 114; 125; SATA 28

Washington, George 1732-1799 **LC 25**
See also DLB 31

Wassermann, (Karl) Jakob 1873-1934 **TCLC 6**

See also CA 104; DLB 66

Wasserstein, Wendy 1950- **CLC 32, 59, 90; DAM DRAM; DC 4**
See also CA 121; 129; CABS 3; CANR 53; INT 129; SATA 94

Waterhouse, Keith (Spencer) 1929- **CLC 47**
See also CA 5-8R; CANR 38, 67; DLB 13, 15; MTCW

Waters, Frank (Joseph) 1902-1995 **CLC 88**
See also CA 5-8R; 149; CAAS 13; CANR 3, 18, 63; DLBY 86

Waters, Roger 1944- **CLC 35**

Watkins, Frances Ellen
See Harper, Frances Ellen Watkins

Watkins, Gerrold
See Malzberg, Barry N(athaniel)

Watkins, Gloria 1955(?)-
See hooks, bell
See also BW 2; CA 143

Watkins, Paul 1964- **CLC 55**
See also CA 132; CANR 62

Watkins, Vernon Phillips 1906-1967 **CLC 43**
See also CA 9-10; 25-28R; CAP 1; DLB 20

Watson, Irving S.
See Mencken, H(enry) L(ouis)

Watson, John H.
See Farmer, Philip Jose

Watson, Richard F.
See Silverberg, Robert

Waugh, Auberon (Alexander) 1939- **CLC 7**
See also CA 45-48; CANR 6, 22; DLB 14, 194

Waugh, Evelyn (Arthur St. John) 1903-1966 **CLC 1, 3, 8, 13, 19, 27, 44, 107; DA; DAB; DAC; DAM MST, NOV, POP; WLC**
See also CA 85-88; 25-28R; CANR 22; CDBLB 1914-1945; DLB 15, 162, 195; MTCW

Waugh, Harriet 1944- **CLC 6**
See also CA 85-88; CANR 22

Ways, C. R.
See Blount, Roy (Alton), Jr.

Waystaff, Simon
See Swift, Jonathan

Webb, (Martha) Beatrice (Potter) 1858-1943 **TCLC 22**
See also Potter, (Helen) Beatrix
See also CA 117

Webb, Charles (Richard) 1939- **CLC 7**
See also CA 25-28R

Webb, James H(enry), Jr. 1946- **CLC 22**
See also CA 81-84

Webb, Mary (Gladys Meredith) 1881-1927 **TCLC 24**
See also CA 123; DLB 34

Webb, Mrs. Sidney
See Webb, (Martha) Beatrice (Potter)

Webb, Phyllis 1927- **CLC 18**
See also CA 104; CANR 23; DLB 53

Webb, Sidney (James) 1859-1947 **TCLC 22**
See also CA 117; 163; DLB 190

Webber, Andrew Lloyd **CLC 21**
See also Lloyd Webber, Andrew

Weber, Lenora Mattingly 1895-1971 **CLC 12**
See also CA 19-20; 29-32R; CAP 1; SATA 2; SATA-Obit 26

Weber, Max 1864-1920 **TCLC 69**
See also CA 109

Webster, John 1579(?)-1634(?) **LC 33; DA; DAB; DAC; DAM DRAM, MST; DC 2; WLC**
See also CDBLB Before 1660; DLB 58

Webster, Noah 1758-1843 **NCLC 30**

Wedekind, (Benjamin) Frank(lin) 1864-1918 **TCLC 7; DAM DRAM**

DAB; DAC; DAM MST, NOV; WLCS 2
See also AAYA 7; AITN 1; CA 5-8R; CAAS 4;
CANR 8, 40, 65; DLB 83; DLBY 87; INT
CANR-8; MTCW; SATA 56

Wiggins, Marianne 1947- **CLC 57**
See also BEST 89:3; CA 130; CANR 60

Wight, James Alfred 1916-1995
See Herriot, James
See also CA 77-80; SATA 55; SATA-Brief 44

Wilbur, Richard (Purdy) 1921-**CLC 3, 6, 9, 14,
53, 110; DA; DAB; DAC; DAM MST,
POET**
See also CA 1-4R; CABS 2; CANR 2, 29; DLB
5, 169; INT CANR-29; MTCW; SATA 9

Wild, Peter 1940- **CLC 14**
See also CA 37-40R; DLB 5

Wilde, Oscar (Fingal O'Flahertie Wills)
1854(?)-1900 **TCLC 1, 8, 23, 41; DA; DAB;
DAC; DAM DRAM, MST, NOV; SSC 11;
WLC**
See also CA 104; 119; CDBLB 1890-1914;
DLB 10, 19, 34, 57, 141, 156, 190; SATA 24

Wilder, Billy **CLC 20**
See also Wilder, Samuel
See also DLB 26

Wilder, Samuel 1906-
See Wilder, Billy
See also CA 89-92

Wilder, Thornton (Niven) 1897-1975**CLC 1, 5,
6, 10, 15, 35, 82; DA; DAB; DAC; DAM
DRAM, MST, NOV; DC 1; WLC**
See also AITN 2; CA 13-16R; 61-64; CANR
40; DLB 4, 7, 9; DLBY 97; MTCW

Wilding, Michael 1942- **CLC 73**
See also CA 104; CANR 24, 49

Wiley, Richard 1944- **CLC 44**
See also CA 121; 129

Wilhelm, Kate **CLC 7**
See also Wilhelm, Katie Gertrude
See also AAYA 20; CAAS 5; DLB 8; INT
CANR-17

Wilhelm, Katie Gertrude 1928-
See Wilhelm, Kate
See also CA 37-40R; CANR 17, 36, 60; MTCW

Wilkins, Mary
See Freeman, Mary Eleanor Wilkins

Willard, Nancy 1936- **CLC 7, 37**
See also CA 89-92; CANR 10, 39, 68; CLR 5;
DLB 5, 52; MAICYA; MTCW; SATA 37, 71;
SATA-Brief 30

Williams, C(harles) K(enneth) 1936- **CLC 33,
56; DAM POET**
See also CA 37-40R; CAAS 26; CANR 57; DLB
5

Williams, Charles
See Collier, James L(incoln)

Williams, Charles (Walter Stansby) 1886-1945
TCLC 1, 11
See also CA 104; 163; DLB 100, 153

Williams, (George) Emlyn 1905-1987**CLC 15;
DAM DRAM**
See also CA 104; 123; CANR 36; DLB 10, 77;
MTCW

Williams, Hank 1923-1953 **TCLC 81**

Williams, Hugo 1942- **CLC 42**
See also CA 17-20R; CANR 45; DLB 40

Williams, J. Walker
See Wodehouse, P(elham) G(renville)

Williams, John A(lfred) 1925-**CLC 5, 13; BLC
3; DAM MULT**
See also BW 2; CA 53-56; CAAS 3; CANR 6,
26, 51; DLB 2, 33; INT CANR-6

Williams, Jonathan (Chamberlain) 1929-

CLC 13
See also CA 9-12R; CAAS 12; CANR 8; DLB
5

Williams, Joy 1944- **CLC 31**
See also CA 41-44R; CANR 22, 48

Williams, Norman 1952- **CLC 39**
See also CA 118

Williams, Sherley Anne 1944-**CLC 89; BLC 3;
DAM MULT, POET**
See also BW 2; CA 73-76; CANR 25; DLB 41;
INT CANR-25; SATA 78

Williams, Shirley
See Williams, Sherley Anne

Williams, Tennessee 1911-1983**CLC 1, 2, 5, 7,
8, 11, 15, 19, 30, 39, 45, 71, 111; DA; DAB;
DAC; DAM DRAM, MST; DC 4; WLC**
See also AITN 1, 2; CA 5-8R; 108; CABS 3;
CANR 31; CDALB 1941-1968; DLB 7;
DLBD 4; DLBY 83; MTCW

Williams, Thomas (Alonzo) 1926-1990**CLC 14**
See also CA 1-4R; 132; CANR 2

Williams, William C.
See Williams, William Carlos

Williams, William Carlos 1883-1963**CLC 1, 2,
5, 9, 13, 22, 42, 67; DA; DAB; DAC; DAM
MST, POET; PC 7; SSC 31**
See also CA 89-92; CANR 34; CDALB 1917-
1929; DLB 4, 16, 54, 86; MTCW

Williamson, David (Keith) 1942- **CLC 56**
See also CA 103; CANR 41

Williamson, Ellen Douglas 1905-1984
See Douglas, Ellen
See also CA 17-20R; 114; CANR 39

Williamson, Jack **CLC 29**
See also Williamson, John Stewart
See also CAAS 8; DLB 8

Williamson, John Stewart 1908-
See Williamson, Jack
See also CA 17-20R; CANR 23

Willie, Frederick
See Lovecraft, H(oward) P(hillips)

Willingham, Calder (Baynard, Jr.) 1922-1995
CLC 5, 51
See also CA 5-8R; 147; CANR 3; DLB 2, 44;
MTCW

Willis, Charles
See Clarke, Arthur C(harles)

Willy
See Colette, (Sidonie-Gabrielle)

Willy, Colette
See Colette, (Sidonie-Gabrielle)

Wilson, A(ndrew) N(orman) 1950- **CLC 33**
See also CA 112; 122; DLB 14, 155, 194

Wilson, Angus (Frank Johnstone) 1913-1991
CLC 2, 3, 5, 25, 34; SSC 21
See also CA 5-8R; 134; CANR 21; DLB 15,
139, 155; MTCW

Wilson, August 1945-**CLC 39, 50, 63; BLC 3;
DA; DAB; DAC; DAM DRAM, MST,
MULT; DC 2; WLCS**
See also AAYA 16; BW 2; CA 115; 122; CANR
42, 54; MTCW

Wilson, Brian 1942- **CLC 12**

Wilson, Colin 1931- **CLC 3, 14**
See also CA 1-4R; CAAS 5; CANR 1, 22, 33;
DLB 14, 194; MTCW

Wilson, Dirk
See Pohl, Frederik

Wilson, Edmund 1895-1972 **CLC 1, 2, 3, 8, 24**
See also CA 1-4R; 37-40R; CANR 1, 46; DLB
63; MTCW

Wilson, Ethel Davis (Bryant) 1888(?)-1980
CLC 13; DAC; DAM POET

See also CA 102; DLB 68; MTCW

Wilson, John 1785-1854 **NCLC 5**

Wilson, John (Anthony) Burgess 1917-1993
See Burgess, Anthony
See also CA 1-4R; 143; CANR 2, 46; DAC;
DAM NOV; MTCW

Wilson, Lanford 1937- **CLC 7, 14, 36; DAM
DRAM**
See also CA 17-20R; CABS 3; CANR 45; DLB
7

Wilson, Robert M. 1944- **CLC 7, 9**
See also CA 49-52; CANR 2, 41; MTCW

Wilson, Robert McLiam 1964- **CLC 59**
See also CA 132

Wilson, Sloan 1920- **CLC 32**
See also CA 1-4R; CANR 1, 44

Wilson, Snoo 1948- **CLC 33**
See also CA 69-72

Wilson, William S(mith) 1932- **CLC 49**
See also CA 81-84

Wilson, (Thomas) Woodrow 1856-1924**TCLC
79**
See also CA 166; DLB 47

Winchilsea, Anne (Kingsmill) Finch Counte
1661-1720
See Finch, Anne

Windham, Basil
See Wodehouse, P(elham) G(renville)

Wingrove, David (John) 1954- **CLC 68**
See also CA 133

Wintergreen, Jane
See Duncan, Sara Jeannette

Winters, Janet Lewis **CLC 41**
See also Lewis, Janet
See also DLBY 87

Winters, (Arthur) Yvor 1900-1968 **CLC 4, 8,
32**
See also CA 11-12; 25-28R; CAP 1; DLB 48;
MTCW

Winterson, Jeanette 1959-**CLC 64; DAM POP**
See also CA 136; CANR 58

Winthrop, John 1588-1649 **LC 31**
See also DLB 24, 30

Wiseman, Frederick 1930- **CLC 20**
See also CA 159

Wister, Owen 1860-1938 **TCLC 21**
See also CA 108; 162; DLB 9, 78, 186; SATA
62

Witkacy
See Witkiewicz, Stanislaw Ignacy

Witkiewicz, Stanislaw Ignacy 1885-1939
TCLC 8
See also CA 105; 162

Wittgenstein, Ludwig (Josef Johann) 1889-1951
TCLC 59
See also CA 113; 164

Wittig, Monique 1935(?)- **CLC 22**
See also CA 116; 135; DLB 83

Wittlin, Jozef 1896-1976 **CLC 25**
See also CA 49-52; 65-68; CANR 3

Wodehouse, P(elham) G(renville) 1881-1975
**CLC 1, 2, 5, 10, 22; DAB; DAC; DAM
NOV; SSC 2**
See also AITN 2; CA 45-48; 57-60; CANR 3,
33; CDBLB 1914-1945; DLB 34, 162;
MTCW; SATA 22

Woiwode, L.
See Woiwode, Larry (Alfred)

Woiwode, Larry (Alfred) 1941- **CLC 6, 10**
See also CA 73-76; CANR 16; DLB 6; INT
CANR-16

Wojciechowska, Maia (Teresa) 1927- **CLC 26**
See also AAYA 8; CA 9-12R; CANR 4, 41; CLR

1; JRDA; MAICYA; SAAS 1; SATA 1, 28, 83

Wolf, Christa 1929- **CLC 14, 29, 58**
See also CA 85-88; CANR 45; DLB 75; MTCW

Wolfe, Gene (Rodman) 1931- **CLC 25; DAM POP**
See also CA 57-60; CAAS 9; CANR 6, 32, 60; DLB 8

Wolfe, George C. 1954- **CLC 49; BLCS**
See also CA 149

Wolfe, Thomas (Clayton) 1900-1938 **TCLC 4, 13, 29, 61; DA; DAB; DAC; DAM MST, NOV; WLC**
See also CA 104; 132; CDALB 1929-1941; DLB 9, 102; DLBD 2, 16; DLBY 85, 97; MTCW

Wolfe, Thomas Kennerly, Jr. 1931-
See Wolfe, Tom
See also CA 13-16R; CANR 9, 33; DAM POP; DLB 185; INT CANR-9; MTCW

Wolfe, Tom **CLC 1, 2, 9, 15, 35, 51**
See also Wolfe, Thomas Kennerly, Jr.
See also AAYA 8; AITN 2; BEST 89:1; DLB 152

Wolff, Geoffrey (Ansell) 1937- **CLC 41**
See also CA 29-32R; CANR 29, 43

Wolff, Sonia
See Levitin, Sonia (Wolff)

Wolff, Tobias (Jonathan Ansell) 1945- **CLC 39, 64**
See also AAYA 16; BEST 90:2; CA 114; 117; CAAS 22; CANR 54; DLB 130; INT 117

Wolfram von Eschenbach c. 1170-c. 1220 **CMLC 5**
See also DLB 138

Wolitzer, Hilma 1930- **CLC 17**
See also CA 65-68; CANR 18, 40; INT CANR-18; SATA 31

Wollstonecraft, Mary 1759-1797 **LC 5**
See also CDBLB 1789-1832; DLB 39, 104, 158

Wonder, Stevie **CLC 12**
See also Morris, Steveland Judkins

Wong, Jade Snow 1922- **CLC 17**
See also CA 109

Woodberry, George Edward 1855-1930 **TCLC 73**
See also CA 165; DLB 71, 103

Woodcott, Keith
See Brunner, John (Kilian Houston)

Woodruff, Robert W.
See Mencken, H(enry) L(ouis)

Woolf, (Adeline) Virginia 1882-1941 **TCLC 1, 5, 20, 43, 56; DA; DAB; DAC; DAM MST, NOV; SSC 7; WLC**
See also CA 104; 130; CANR 64; CDBLB 1914-1945; DLB 36, 100, 162; DLBD 10; MTCW

Woolf, Virginia Adeline
See Woolf, (Adeline) Virginia

Woollcott, Alexander (Humphreys) 1887-1943 **TCLC 5**
See also CA 105; 161; DLB 29

Woolrich, Cornell 1903-1968 **CLC 77**
See also Hopley-Woolrich, Cornell George

Wordsworth, Dorothy 1771-1855 **NCLC 25**
See also DLB 107

Wordsworth, William 1770-1850 **NCLC 12, 38; DA; DAB; DAC; DAM MST, POET; PC 4; WLC**
See also CDBLB 1789-1832; DLB 93, 107

Wouk, Herman 1915- **CLC 1, 9, 38; DAM NOV, POP**
See also CA 5-8R; CANR 6, 33, 67; DLBY 82;

INT CANR-6; MTCW

Wright, Charles (Penzel, Jr.) 1935- **CLC 6, 13, 28**
See also CA 29-32R; CAAS 7; CANR 23, 36, 62; DLB 165; DLBY 82; MTCW

Wright, Charles Stevenson 1932- **CLC 49; BLC 3; DAM MULT, POET**
See also BW 1; CA 9-12R; CANR 26; DLB 33

Wright, Jack R.
See Harris, Mark

Wright, James (Arlington) 1927-1980 **CLC 3, 5, 10, 28; DAM POET**
See also AITN 2; CA 49-52; 97-100; CANR 4, 34, 64; DLB 5, 169; MTCW

Wright, Judith (Arandell) 1915- **CLC 11, 53; PC 14**
See also CA 13-16R; CANR 31; MTCW; SATA 14

Wright, L(aurali) R. 1939- **CLC 44**
See also CA 138

Wright, Richard (Nathaniel) 1908-1960 **CLC 1, 3, 4, 9, 14, 21, 48, 74; BLC 3; DA; DAB; DAC; DAM MST, MULT, NOV; SSC 2; WLC**
See also AAYA 5; BW 1; CA 108; CANR 64; CDALB 1929-1941; DLB 76, 102; DLBD 2; MTCW

Wright, Richard B(ruce) 1937- **CLC 6**
See also CA 85-88; DLB 53

Wright, Rick 1945- **CLC 35**

Wright, Rowland
See Wells, Carolyn

Wright, Stephen 1946- **CLC 33**

Wright, Willard Huntington 1888-1939
See Van Dine, S. S.
See also CA 115; DLBD 16

Wright, William 1930- **CLC 44**
See also CA 53-56; CANR 7, 23

Wroth, LadyMary 1587-1653(?) **LC 30**
See also DLB 121

Wu Ch'eng-en 1500(?)-1582(?) **LC 7**

Wu Ching-tzu 1701-1754 **LC 2**

Wurlitzer, Rudolph 1938(?)- **CLC 2, 4, 15**
See also CA 85-88; DLB 173

Wycherley, William 1641-1715 **LC 8, 21; DAM DRAM**
See also CDBLB 1660-1789; DLB 80

Wylie, Elinor (Morton Hoyt) 1885-1928 **TCLC 8; PC 23**
See also CA 105; 162; DLB 9, 45

Wylie, Philip (Gordon) 1902-1971 **CLC 43**
See also CA 21-22; 33-36R; CAP 2; DLB 9

Wyndham, John **CLC 19**
See also Harris, John (Wyndham Parkes Lucas) Beynon

Wyss, Johann David Von 1743-1818 **NCLC 10**
See also JRDA; MAICYA; SATA 29; SATA-Brief 27

Xenophon c. 430B.C.-c. 354B.C. **CMLC 17**
See also DLB 176

Yakumo Koizumi
See Hearn, (Patricio) Lafcadio (Tessima Carlos)

Yanez, Jose Donoso
See Donoso (Yanez), Jose

Yanovsky, Basile S.
See Yanovsky, V(assily) S(emenovich)

Yanovsky, V(assily) S(emenovich) 1906-1989 **CLC 2, 18**
See also CA 97-100; 129

Yates, Richard 1926-1992 **CLC 7, 8, 23**
See also CA 5-8R; 139; CANR 10, 43; DLB 2; DLBY 81, 92; INT CANR-10

Yeats, W. B.

See Yeats, William Butler

Yeats, William Butler 1865-1939 **TCLC 1, 11, 18, 31; DA; DAB; DAC; DAM DRAM, MST, POET; PC 20; WLC**
See also CA 104; 127; CANR 45; CDBLB 1890-1914; DLB 10, 19, 98, 156; MTCW

Yehoshua, A(braham) B. 1936- **CLC 13, 31**
See also CA 33-36R; CANR 43

Yep, Laurence Michael 1948- **CLC 35**
See also AAYA 5; CA 49-52; CANR 1, 46; CLR 3, 17; DLB 52; JRDA; MAICYA; SATA 7, 69

Yerby, Frank G(arvin) 1916-1991 **CLC 1, 7, 22; BLC 3; DAM MULT**
See also BW 1; CA 9-12R; 136; CANR 16, 52; DLB 76; INT CANR-16; MTCW

Yesenin, Sergei Alexandrovich
See Esenin, Sergei (Alexandrovich)

Yevtushenko, Yevgeny (Alexandrovich) 1933- **CLC 1, 3, 13, 26, 51; DAM POET**
See also CA 81-84; CANR 33, 54; MTCW

Yezierska, Anzia 1885(?)-1970 **CLC 46**
See also CA 126; 89-92; DLB 28; MTCW

Yglesias, Helen 1915- **CLC 7, 22**
See also CA 37-40R; CAAS 20; CANR 15, 65; INT CANR-15; MTCW

Yokomitsu Riichi 1898-1947 **TCLC 47**

Yonge, Charlotte (Mary) 1823-1901 **TCLC 48**
See also CA 109; 163; DLB 18, 163; SATA 17

York, Jeremy
See Creasey, John

York, Simon
See Heinlein, Robert A(nson)

Yorke, Henry Vincent 1905-1974 **CLC 13**
See also Green, Henry
See also CA 85-88; 49-52

Yosano Akiko 1878-1942 **TCLC 59; PC 11**
See also CA 161

Yoshimoto, Banana **CLC 84**
See also Yoshimoto, Mahoko

Yoshimoto, Mahoko 1964-
See Yoshimoto, Banana
See also CA 144

Young, Al(bert James) 1939- **CLC 19; BLC 3; DAM MULT**
See also BW 2; CA 29-32R; CANR 26, 65; DLB 33

Young, Andrew (John) 1885-1971 **CLC 5**
See also CA 5-8R; CANR 7, 29

Young, Collier
See Bloch, Robert (Albert)

Young, Edward 1683-1765 **LC 3, 40**
See also DLB 95

Young, Marguerite (Vivian) 1909-1995 **CLC 82**
See also CA 13-16; 150; CAP 1

Young, Neil 1945- **CLC 17**
See also CA 110

Young Bear, Ray A. 1950- **CLC 94; DAM MULT**
See also CA 146; DLB 175; NNAL

Yourcenar, Marguerite 1903-1987 **CLC 19, 38, 50, 87; DAM NOV**
See also CA 69-72; CANR 23, 60; DLB 72; DLBY 88; MTCW

Yurick, Sol 1925- **CLC 6**
See also CA 13-16R; CANR 25

Zabolotsky, Nikolai Alekseevich 1903-1958 **TCLC 52**
See also CA 116; 164

Zamiatin, Yevgenii
See Zamyatin, Evgeny Ivanovich

Zamora, Bernice (B. Ortiz) 1938- **CLC 89;**

Author Index

Literary Criticism Series
Cumulative Topic Index

This index lists all topic entries in Gale's *Classical and Medieval Literature Criticism, Contemporary Literary Criticism, Literature Criticism from 1400 to 1800, Nineteenth-Century Literature Criticism,* and *Twentieth-Century Literary Criticism.*

Topic Index

LC Cumulative Nationality Index

AFGHAN

Babur **18**

AMERICAN

Bradstreet, Anne **4, 30**
Edwards, Jonathan **7**
Eliot, John **5**
Franklin, Benjamin **25**
Hathorne, John **38**
Hopkinson, Francis **25**
Knight, Sarah Kemble **7**
Mather, Cotton **38**
Mather, Increase **38**
Munford, Robert **5**
Penn, William **25**
Sewall, Samuel **38**
Stoughton, William **38**
Taylor, Edward **11**
Washington, George **25**
Wheatley (Peters), Phillis **3**
Winthrop, John **31**

BENINESE

Equiano, Olaudah **16**

CANADIAN

Marie de l'Incarnation **10**

CHINESE

Lo Kuan-chung **12**
P'u Sung-ling **3**
Ts'ao Hsueh-ch'in **1**
Wu Ch'eng-en **7**
Wu Ching-tzu **2**

DANISH

Brahe, Tycho **45**
Holberg, Ludvig **6**

Wessel, Johan Herman **7**

DUTCH

Erasmus, Desiderius **16**
Lipsius, Justus **16**
Spinoza, Benedictus de **9**

ENGLISH

Addison, Joseph **18**
Andrewes, Lancelot **5**
Arbuthnot, John **1**
Aubin, Penelope **9**
Bacon, Francis **18, 32**
Barker, Jane **42**
Beaumont, Francis **33**
Behn, Aphra **1, 30, 42**
Boswell, James **4**
Bradstreet, Anne **4, 30**
Brooke, Frances **6**
Bunyan, John **4**
Burke, Edmund **7, 36**
Butler, Samuel **16, 43**
Carew, Thomas **13**
Cary, Elizabeth, Lady Falkland **30**
Cavendish, Margaret Lucas **30**
Caxton, William , **17**
Chapman, George **22**
Charles I **13**
Chatterton, Thomas **3**
Chaucer, Geoffrey **17**
Churchill, Charles **3**
Cleland, John **2**
Collier, Jeremy **6**
Collins, William **4, 40**
Congreve, William **5, 21**
Cowley, Abraham **43**
Crashaw, Richard **24**
Cromwell, Oliver **43**

Daniel, Samuel **24**
Davys, Mary **1**
Day, Thomas **1**
Dee, John **20**
Defoe, Daniel **1, 42**
Dekker, Thomas **22**
Delany, Mary (Granville Pendarves) **12**
Deloney, Thomas **41**
Dennis, John **11**
Devenant, William **13**
Donne, John **10, 24**
Drayton, Michael **8**
Dryden, John **3, 21**
Elyot, Sir Thomas **11**
Equiano, Olaudah **16**
Fanshawe, Ann **11**
Farquhar, George **21**
Fielding, Henry **1**
Fielding, Sarah **1, 44**
Fletcher, John **33**
Foxe, John **14**
Garrick, David **15**
Gray, Thomas **4, 40**
Greene, Robert **41**
Hakluyt, Richard **31**
Hawes, Stephen **17**
Haywood, Eliza (Fowler) **1, 44**
Henry VIII **10**
Herbert, George **24**
Herrick, Robert **13**
Hobbes, Thomas **36**
Howell, James **13**
Hunter, Robert **7**
Johnson, Samuel **15**
Jonson, Ben(jamin) **6, 33**
Julian of Norwich **6**
Kempe, Margery **6**
Killigrew, Anne **4**

455

LC Cumulative Title Index

Title Index

Title Index

Title Index

Title Index

Title Index

Title Index

ISBN 0-7876-2414-4

9 780787 624149

90000